Lecture Notes in Artificial Intelligence   4259

Edited by J. G. Carbonell and J. Siekmann

Subseries of Lecture Notes in Computer Science

Salvatore Greco   Yutaka Hata
Shoji Hirano   Masahiro Inuiguchi
Sadaaki Miyamoto   Hung Son Nguyen
Roman Słowiński (Eds.)

Rough Sets and Current Trends in Computing

5th International Conference, RSCTC 2006
Kobe, Japan, November 6-8, 2006
Proceedings

 Springer

Series Editors

Jaime G. Carbonell, Carnegie Mellon University, Pittsburgh, PA, USA
Jörg Siekmann, University of Saarland, Saarbrücken, Germany

Volume Editors

Salvatore Greco
University of Catania, Faculty of Economics, Italy
E-mail: salgreco@unict.it

Yutaka Hata
University of Hyogo, Graduate School of Engineering, Japan
E-mail: hata@ieee.org

Shoji Hirano
Shimane University, School of Medicine, Japan
E-mail: hirano@ieee.org

Masahiro Inuiguchi
Osaka University, Graduate School of Engineering Science, Japan
E-mail: inuiguti@sys.es.osaka-u.ac.jp

Sadaaki Miyamoto
University of Tsukuba, Faculty of Systems and Information Engineering, Japan
E-mail: miyamoto@risk.tsukuba.ac.jp

Hung Son Nguyen
Warsaw University, Institute of Mathematics, Poland
E-mail: son@mimuw.edu.pl

Roman Słowiński
Poznan University of Technology, Institute of Computing Science, Poland
E-mail: roman.slowinski@cs.put.poznan.pl

Library of Congress Control Number: 2006935019

CR Subject Classification (1998): I.2, F.4.1, F.1, I.5.1, I.4, H.2.8, H.3, H.4

LNCS Sublibrary: SL 7 – Artificial Intelligence

ISSN   0302-9743
ISBN-10   3-540-47693-8 Springer Berlin Heidelberg New York
ISBN-13   978-3-540-47693-1 Springer Berlin Heidelberg New York

Springer is a part of Springer Science+Business Media

springer.com

© Springer-Verlag Berlin Heidelberg 2006
Printed in Germany

Typesetting: Camera-ready by author, data conversion by Scientific Publishing Services, Chennai, India
Printed on acid-free paper   SPIN: 11908029   06/3142   5 4 3 2 1 0

In Memoriam

This volume is dedicated to Professor Zdzisław Pawlak, a father of rough sets, who passed away on April 7, 2006.

Preface

This volume contains the papers selected for presentation at the 5th International Conference on Rough Sets and Current Trends in Computing (RSCTC 2006) held in Kobe, Japan, November 6–8, 2006. There were 332 online submissions to RSCTC 2006 as well as two keynote papers, three plenary papers and two commemorative papers. Each submitted paper was reviewed by two or three referees. After a rigorous review process, the three PC chairs checked all the referees' comments and reviewed the papers again. As a result, 91 papers were selected for publication in this volume. The acceptance rate was only 27.4%.

RSCTC is an outgrowth of a series of annual International Workshops devoted to the subject of rough sets, started in Poznan, Poland in 1992, and then held in Canada, the USA, Japan and China (RSKD, RSSC, RSFDGrC, RSGrC series). The first RSCTC conference was held in Warsaw, Poland in 1998. It was followed by successful RSCTC conferences in Banff, Canada (2000), in Malvern, USA (2002) and in Uppsala, Sweden (2004).

Rough set theory, proposed by Zdzisław Pawlak in 1982, has been attracting researchers and practitioners in various fields of science and technology. The interest in rough set theory and applications has been remarkable since the beginning, and it is still growing. The ingenious concepts of rough sets have been a base for original developments in both theoretical research, including logics, algebra and topology, and applied research, including knowledge discovery, data mining, decision theory, artificial intelligence and approximate reasoning. The latter led to many real life applications in diversified areas such as medicine, bioinformatics, economy, finance, political analysis, chemistry, engineering, environment, and even art and culture. Since the rough set concept handles a specific type of data "imperfection" related to granularity of information, it is complementary to other concepts used for handling data "imperfection" such as fuzzy sets, Bayesian reasoning, neural networks, evolutionary algorithms, statistics and logical analysis of data. This complementarity is exploited in hybrid approaches improving the performance of data analysis tools.

In accordance with its motto "toward new paradigms in reasoning about data", the aim of RSCTC 2006 was to provide researchers and practitioners interested in new information technologies an opportunity to highlight innovative research directions, novel applications, and a growing number of relationships between rough sets and such areas as computational intelligence, knowledge discovery and data mining, intelligent information systems, web mining, synthesis and analysis of complex objects and non-conventional models of computation. Relevant topics included, but were not limited to:

-Rough set theory and applications
-Fuzzy set theory and applications
-Fuzzy-rough, rough-fuzzy and beyond

-Knowledge discovery and data mining
-Machine learning
-Hybrid and integrated intelligent systems
-Intelligent information systems
-Kansei engineering
-Logical aspects of soft computing
-Multi-agent systems
-Approximate and uncertain reasoning
-Bioinformatics
-Case-based reasoning
-Complexity aspects of soft computing
-Computational intelligence
-Computing with words
-Decision support systems
-Evolutionary computing
-Granular computing
-Multi-criteria decision support
-Neural networks
-Non-classical logic
-Pattern recognition and image processing
-Petri nets and concurrency
-Soft computing
-Spatial reasoning
-Statistical inference
-Web intelligence

It is our great pleasure to dedicate this volume to the father of rough set theory, Zdzisław Pawlak who passed away in April 2006. One of the last papers written by him is included in this volume. We would also like to dedicate this volume to the father of fuzzy set theory, Lotfi A. Zadeh, who proposed many new methods and paradigms related to rough sets including granular computing, which is strongly related to rough sets.

We would like to express our gratitude to Zdzisław Pawlak and Lotfi A. Zadeh, who kindly accepted our invitation to serve as honorary chairs and to deliver keynote speeches for the conference. We also wish to thank Didier Dubois, Mitsuo Nagamachi and Wojciech Ziarko for accepting our invitation to be plenary speakers at RSCTC 2006. Moreover, we would like to express our thanks to Andrzej Skowron and Shusaku Tsumoto for presenting speeches in the memorial session of Zdzisław Pawlak.

We wish to express our appreciation to all Advisory Board members and Program Committee members, who reviewed many papers, as well as to non-committee reviewers. Without their contributions, we could not have selected high-quality papers.

We also want to thank all the authors who submitted valuable papers and all conference participants.

This conference was partially supported by the Kayamori Foundation of Informational Science Advancement, by the "MEET IN KOBE 21st Century" Program of Kobe Convention & Visitors Association, by the Tsutomu Nakauchi Foundation, and by MDAI 2005. Shimane University Faculty of Medicine provided conference Web hosting support. All the submissions and reviews were made through the Cyberchair system (URL: http://www.cyberchair.org). We express our thanks to those organizations and the Cyberchair system development team.

Our special thanks go to Tsuneo Okura, Mika Kuroda, Daisuke Toyama, Namiko Sugimoto, and Masahiro Kagawa for their help in organizing the conference and registrations.

Finally, we wish to express our thanks to Alfred Hofmann at Springer for his support and cooperation.

November 2006

Salvatore Greco   Yutaka Hata
Shoji Hirano   Masahiro Inuiguchi
Sadaaki Miyamoto   Hung Son Nguyen
Roman Słowiński

RSCTC 2006 Conference Committee

Honorary Chairs:	Zdzisław Pawlak	Lotfi A. Zadeh
General Conference Chairs:	Roman Słowiński	Sadaaki Miyamoto
Program Committee Chairs:	Masahiro Inuiguchi	Salvatore Greco
	Hung Son Nguyen	
Local Committee Chairs:	Yutaka Hata	Shoji Hirano
Publication Chair:	Shoji Hirano	
Accounting Secretary:	Masayo Tsurumi	

Advisory Board

Malcolm Beynon	Sestuo Ohsuga	Hideo Tanaka
Gianpiero Cattaneo	Ewa Orłowska	Shusaku Tsumoto
Nick Cercone	James F. Peters	Guoyin Wang
Jerzy W. Grzymala-Busse	Lech Polkowski	Yiyu Yao
Jan Komorowski	Zbigniew W. Ras	Ning Zhong
T.Y. Lin	Andrzej Skowron	Wojciech Ziarko
Benedetto Matarazzo	Dominik Ślęzak	

Program Committee

Peter Apostoli	Bozena Kostek	Vijay V. Raghavan
Hans Dieter Burkhard	Vladik Kreinovich	Sheela Ramanna
Cory Butz	Marzena Kryszkiewicz	Kenneth Revett
Chien-Chung Chan	Mineichi Kudo	Hiroshi Sakai
Davide Ciucci	Yasuo Kudo	Roman Słowiński
Chris Cornelis	Churn-Jung Liau	Jerzy Stefanowski
Andrzej Czyzewski	Pawan Lingras	Jaroslav Stepaniuk
Jitender S. Deogun	Qing Liu	Zbigniew Suraj
Didier Dubois	Eric Louie	Robert Susmaga
Ivo Duentsch	Lawrence J. Mazlack	Roman Świniarski
Philippe Fortemps	Ernestina Menasalvas	Piotr Synak
Yutaka Hata	Wojtek Michalowski	Andrzej Szalas
Shoji Hirano	Sadaaki Miyamoto	Marcin Szczuka
Katsuhiro Honda	Mikhail Ju. Moshkov	Noboru Takagi
Xiaohua (Tony) Hu	Tetsuya Murai	Vicenç Torra
Van Nam Huynh	Michinori Nakata	Gwo-Hshiung Tzeng
Hidetomo Ichihashi	Sinh Hoa Nguyen	Julio Valdes
Jouni Jarvinen	Tuan Trung Nguyen	Anita Wasilewska
Janusz Kacprzyk	Koji Okuhara	Arkadiusz Wojna

Daijin Kim

Michiro Kondo

Jacek Koronacki

Sankar K. Pal

Krzysztof Pancerz

Witold Pedrycz

Jakub Wroblewski

Jing Tao Yao

Zhi-Hua Zhou

Non-committee Reviewers

Aijun An

Xiangdong An

Jan Bazan

Ryan Benton

Jerzy Błaszczyński

Silvia Calegari

Piotr Dalka

Arijit De

Krzysztof Dembczyński

Elizabeth Diaz

Anca Doloc-Mihu

Tomoe Entani

Peijun Guo

Shan Hua

Andrzej Kaczmarek

Akira Kanda

Vlado Keselj

Pavel Klinov

Syoji Kobashi

Wojciech Kotłowski

Krzysztof Krawiec

Pavani Kuntala

Rafał Latkowski

Rory Lewis

Jiye Li

Lalita Narupiyakul

Tatsushi Nishi

Tatsuo Nishino

Puntip Pattaraintakorn

Yuji Sakamoto

Biren Shah

Raj Singh

Piotr Szczuko

Masayo Tsurumi

Steven Wang

Piotr Wasilewski

Marcin Wolski

David Zhang

Pawel Zwan

Table of Contents

Invited Papers

Commemorative Papers for Professor Pawlak

Logics in Rough Sets

Incomplete/Nondeterministic Information Systems

Decision Support

Granular Computing

Grey Systems

Ontology and Mereology

Statistical Mathods

Machine Learning

Clustering

Data Mining

Evolutionary Computing

Intelligent Information Systems

Pattern Recognition and Image Processing

Data Clustering: Algorithms and Applications (Organized Session)

Decision Trees and Flow Graphs

Zdzisław Pawlak

Institute for Theoretical and Applied Informatics
Polish Academy of Sciences
ul. Bałtycka 5, 44-100 Gliwice, Poland
and
Warsaw School of Information Technology
ul. Newelska 6, 01-447 Warsaw, Poland
zpw@ii.pw.edu.pl

Abstract. We consider association of decision trees and flow graphs, resulting in a new method of decision rule generation from data, and giving a better insight in data structure. The introduced flow graphs can also give a new look at the conception of probability. We show that in some cases the conception of probability can be eliminated and replaced by a study of deterministic flows in a flow network.

1   Introduction

Decision tree is a very useful concept in computer science [7,9], decision science [2], probability [11] and others.

In this paper, we propose to associate with a decision tree another kind of graph, called flow graph, which gives better insight in data structure than the corresponding decision tree and reveals very interesting novel properties of decision trees, not visible directly from the tree. They can be used in many ways and, particularly, enable an efficient generation of decision rules from data.

Besides, the introduced flow graphs can also be used as a new look at the conception of probability. Łukasiewicz [6] claimed that probability defined by Laplace [5] and used today, is not a well defined concept and he proposed to base probability calculus on logical ground, which gives to probability sound mathematical foundations. Similar ideas have been proposed independently many years after Łukasiewicz by Carnap [3], Adams [1], Reichebach [10] and others.

We go a little bit farther and intend to show that in some cases the conception of probability can be eliminated and replaced by a study of deterministic flows in a flow network. The proposed approach gives a new method of decision rule generation from data, and permits to study data structure in a new way.

The paper is a continuation of some author's ideas presented in [8].

2   An Example

First, we explain our basic ideas by means of a simple example. Consider the set U of play blocks having various shapes (e.g., square, round), sizes (e.g., large,

S. Greco et al. (Eds.): RSCTC 2006, LNAI 4259, pp. 1–11, 2006.

small) and colors (e.g., black, white). Assume that the relation between different play blocks is given by a decision tree as shown in Fig.1. We will use standard terminology concerning decision trees, like root, branches, paths, etc.

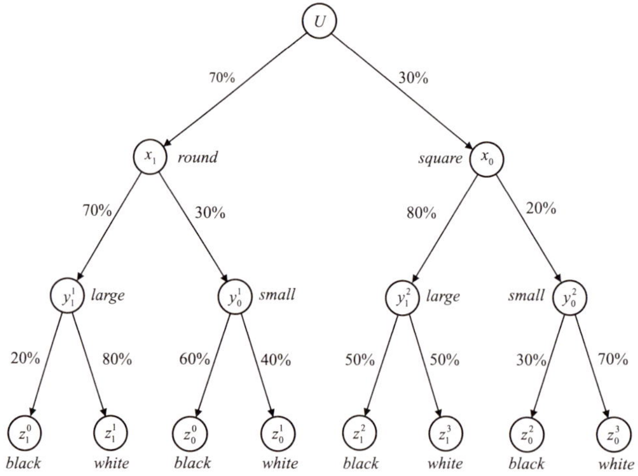

Fig. 1. Decision tree showing relations between different play blocks

The decision tree reveals statistical relationship between various types of play blocks. For example, the decision tree shows that there are 70% round and 30% square blocks in the set and among round blocks there are 70% large and 30% small blocks, whereas square blocks consist of 80% large and 20% small blocks. Moreover, the set of round and large blocks consists of 20% white and 80% black blocks, etc. In other words, the decision tree can be understood as a statistical data structure representation of the set U.

With every decision tree we can associate uniquely another graph, called a flow graph. The flow graph is an oriented graph obtained from a decision tree by removing the root and merging nodes labeled by the same "attribute", e.g. *small, large*, etc., as shown in Fig. 2.

The resulting flow graph is given in Fig. 3.

The flow graph reveals the relational structure among objects of the universe. For example, if the branch (*square, small*) is labeled by the number 0.06 it means that there are 6% objects in the universe which are square and small - the number 0.06 is computed from the data given in the decision tree.

Each path in the flow graph determines an "*if ..., then...*" decision rule. E.g., the path (*square, large, white*) determines a decision rule "*if square and large, then white*". In our approach, the number (percentage) associated with every branch can be interpreted as a flow intensity through the branch and used to study properties of decision rules. We can also interpret the flow graph in terms of probability, but we will refrain from this interpretation here and we claim that deterministic interpretation is more natural than the probabilistic one.

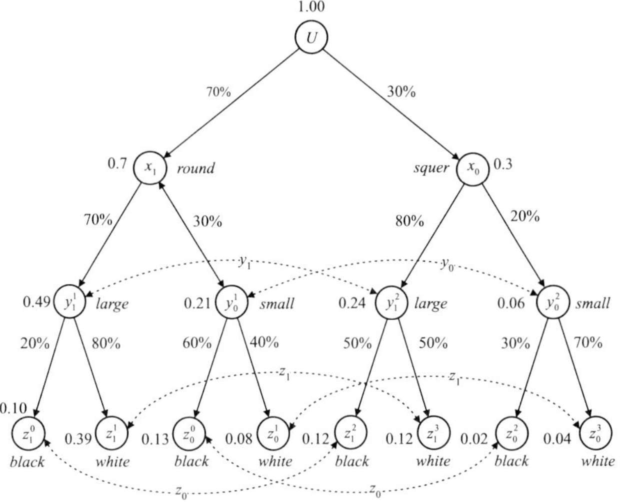

Fig. 2. Merging nodes labeled by the same "attribute"

In order to solve our problem we will analyze the structure of the flow graph in detail in the next section.

3   Flow Graphs – Basic Concepts

3.1   Flow Graphs

In this section we recall after [8] the fundamental concept of the proposed approach – a flow graph.

Flow graph is a *directed, acyclic, finite* graph $G = (N, \mathcal{B}, \sigma)$, where N is a set of *nodes*, $\mathcal{B} \subseteq N \times N$ is a set of *directed branches* and $\sigma : \mathcal{B} \to \langle 0, 1 \rangle$ is *a flow function* of (x, y) such that $\sigma(x, y)$ is a *strength* of (x, y). The strength of the branch expresses simply the percentage of a total flow through the branch.

Input of a node $x \in N$ *is the set* $I(x) = \{y \in N : (y, x) \in \mathcal{B}\}$; *output* of a node $x \in N$ is defined as $O(x) = \{y \in N : (x, y) \in \mathcal{B}\}$.

We will also need the concept of *input* and *output* of a graph G, defined, respectively, as: $I(G) = \{x \in N : I(x) = \emptyset\}$, $O(G) = \{x \in N : O(x) = \emptyset\}$.

Inputs and outputs of G are *external nodes* of G; other nodes are *internal nodes* of G.

If a flow graph G has only one input and every internal node of G has one input then such a flow graph with be called a *decision tree*.

Input of the decision tree will be referred to as *root*, whereas outputs - as *leaves* of the decision tree.

With every node x of a flow graph G we associate its *inflow* and *outflow* defined as

$$\sigma_+(x) = \sum_{y \in I(x)} \sigma(y, x) \tag{1}$$

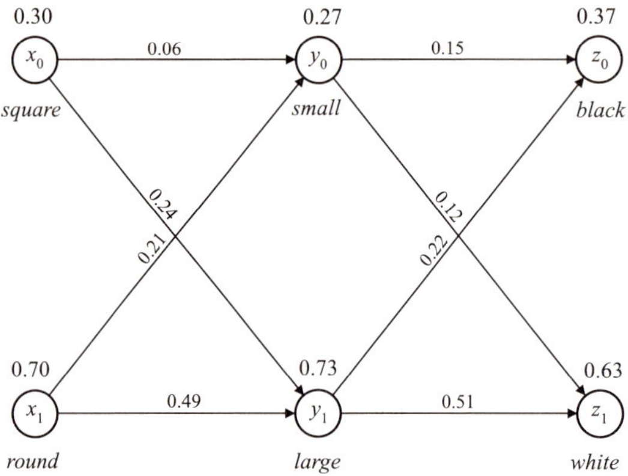

Fig. 3. Flow graph resulting from the decision tree

and

$$\sigma_-(x) = \sum_{y \in O(x)} \sigma(y, x). \tag{2}$$

For any internal node x, we have $\sigma_+(x) = \sigma_-(x) = \sigma(x)$, where $\sigma(x)$ is a *throughflow* of x. Moreover, let

$$\sigma_+(G) = \sum_{x \in I(G)} \sigma_-(x) \tag{3}$$

and

$$\sigma_-(G) = \sum_{x \in O(G)} \sigma_+(x). \tag{4}$$

Let us assume that $\sigma_+(G) = 1$, then $\sigma_+(G) = \sigma_-(G) = \sigma(G)$.

If we invert direction of all branches in G, then the resulting graph $G = (N, \mathcal{B}', \sigma')$ will be called an *inverted* graph of G. Of course, the inverted graph G' is also a flow graph and all inputs and outputs of G become inputs and outputs of G', respectively.

3.2 Certainty and Coverage Factors

With every branch (x, y) of a flow graph G we associate the *certainty* and the *coverage factors*.

The *certainty* and the *coverage* of (x, y) are defined as

$$cer(x, y) = \frac{\sigma(x, y)}{\sigma(x)}, \tag{5}$$

and

$$cer(x,y) = \frac{\sigma(x,y)}{\sigma(y)}. \tag{6}$$

respectively.

Evidently, $cer(x,y) = cov(y,x)$, where $(x,y) \in \mathcal{B}$ and $(y,x) \in \mathcal{B}'$.

Certainty and coverage factors for the flow graph shown in Fig. 3 are presented in Fig. 4.

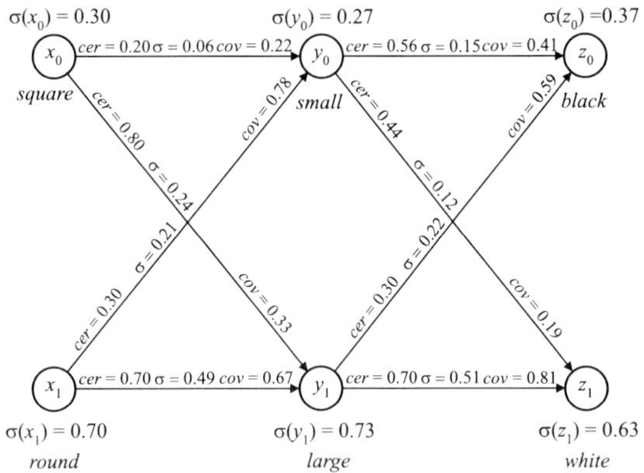

Fig. 4. Certainty and coverage factors

For every branch (x,y) of a decision tree $cov(x,y) = 1$.

Below, some properties, which are immediate consequences of definitions given above, are presented:

$$\sum_{y \in O(x)} cer(x,y) = 1, \tag{7}$$

$$\sum_{x \in I(y)} cov(x,y) - 1, \tag{8}$$

$$\sigma(x) = \sum_{y \in O(x)} cer(x,y)\sigma(x) = \sum_{y \in O(x)} \sigma(x,y), \tag{9}$$

$$\sigma(y) = \sum_{x \in I(y)} cov(x,y)\sigma(y) = \sum_{x \in I(y)} \sigma(x,y), \tag{10}$$

$$cer(x,y) = \frac{cov(x,y)\sigma(y)}{\sigma(x)}, \tag{11}$$

$$cov(x,y) = \frac{cer(x,y)\sigma(x)}{\sigma(y)}. \tag{12}$$

Obviously, the above properties have a probabilistic flavor, e.g., equations (9) and (10) have a form of total probability theorem, whereas formulas (11) and (12) are Bayes' rules. However, these properties in our approach are interpreted in a deterministic way and they describe flow distribution among branches in the network.

3.3   Paths, Connections and Fusion

A (*directed*) *path* from x to y, $x \neq y$ in G is a sequence of nodes $x_1, \ldots, x_n$ such that $x_1 = x$, $x_n = y$ and $(x_i, x_{i_1}) \in \mathcal{B}$ for every i, $1 \leq i \leq n - 1$. A path from x to y is denoted by $[x \ldots y]$ and $n - 1$ is called *length* of the path.

A flow graph is *linear* if all paths from node x to node y have the same length, for every pair of nodes x, y.

A set of nodes of a linear flow graph is called a *k-layer* if it consists of the set of all nodes of this graph linked by a path of the length k with some input node.

The set of all inputs of a flow graph will be called the *input layer* of the flow graph, whereas the set of all outputs of the flow graph is the *output layer* of the flow graph. For any input node x and output node y of a linear graph the length of the path $[x \ldots y]$ is the same. The layers different from the input layer and the output layer will be referred to as *hidden layers*.

In what follows we will interpret layers as attributes in an information system; input and hidden layers are interpreted as condition attributes, whereas output layer is interpreted as decision attribute.

The *certainty* of the path $[x_1 \ldots x_n]$ is defined as

$$cer[x_1 \ldots x_n] = \prod_{i=1}^{n-1} cer(x_i, x_{i+1}), \tag{13}$$

the *coverage* of the path $[x_1 \ldots x_n]$ is

$$cov[x_1 \ldots x_n] = \prod_{i=1}^{n-1} cov(x_i, x_{i+1}), \tag{14}$$

and the *strength* of the path $[x \ldots y]$ is

$$\sigma[x \ldots y] = \sigma(x) cer[x \ldots y] = \sigma(y) cov[x \ldots y]. \tag{15}$$

The set of all paths from x to $y(x \neq y)$ in G, denoted by $\langle x, y \rangle$, will be called a *connection* from x to y in G. In other words, connection $\langle x, y \rangle$ is a sub-graph of G determined by nodes x and y (see Fig. 5).

The *certainty* of the connection $\langle x, y \rangle$ is

$$cer\langle x, y \rangle = \sum_{[x \ldots y] \in \langle x, y \rangle} cer[x \ldots y], \tag{16}$$

the *coverage* of the connection $\langle x, y \rangle$ is

$$cov\langle x, y \rangle = \sum_{[x \ldots y] \in \langle x, y \rangle} cov[x \ldots y], \tag{17}$$

and the *strength* of the connection $\langle x, y \rangle$ is

$$\sigma\langle x, y \rangle = \sum_{[x\ldots y] \in \langle x,y \rangle} \sigma[x \ldots y] = \sigma(x)cer\langle x, y \rangle = \sigma(y)cov\langle x, y \rangle. \qquad (18)$$

If we substitute simultaneously for every sub-graph $\langle x, y \rangle$ of a given flow graph G, where x is an input node and y an output node of G, a single branch (x, y) such that $\sigma(x, y) = \sigma\langle x, y \rangle$, then in the resulting graph G', called the *fusion* of G, we have $cer(x, y) = cer\langle x, y \rangle$, $cov(x, y) = cov\langle x, y \rangle$ and $\sigma(G) = \sigma(G')$.

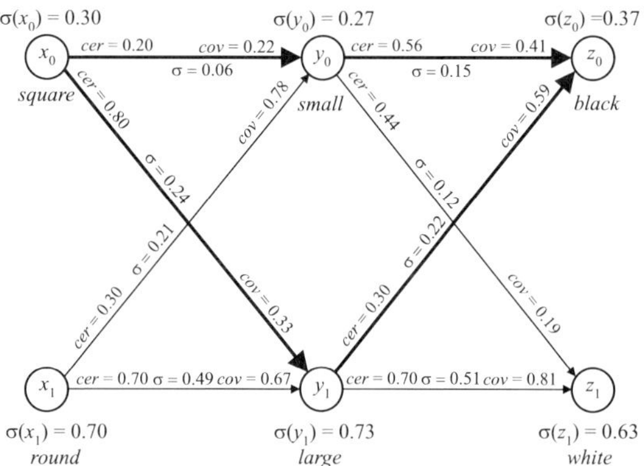

Fig. 5. Connection between x_0 and z_0

Thus fusion of a flow graph can be understood as a simplification of the graph and can be used to get a general picture of relationships in the flow graph (see Fig. 6).

3.4   Dependencies in Flow Graphs

Let x and y be nodes in a flow graph $G - (N, \mathcal{B}, \sigma)$, such that $(x, y) \in \mathcal{B}$.

Nodes x and y are *independent* in G if

$$\sigma(x, y) = \sigma(x)\sigma(y). \qquad (19)$$

From (19) we get

$$\frac{\sigma(x, y)}{\sigma(x)} = cer(x, y) = \sigma(y), \qquad (20)$$

and

$$\frac{\sigma(x, y)}{\sigma(y)} = cov(x, y) = \sigma(x). \qquad (21)$$

If

$$cer(x, y) > \sigma(y), \qquad (22)$$

or

$$cov(x, y) > \sigma(x), \tag{23}$$

x and y are *positively dependent* in G.

Similarly, if

$$cer(x, y) < \sigma(y), \tag{24}$$

or

$$cov(x, y) < \sigma(x), \tag{25}$$

then x and y are *negatively dependent* in G.

Relations of independency and dependencies are symmetric ones, and are analogous to those used in statistics.

For every branch $(x, y) \in \mathcal{B}$ we define a *dependency (correlation) factor* $\eta(x, y)$ defined as

$$\eta(x, y) = \frac{cer(x, y) - \sigma(y)}{cer(x, y) + \sigma(y)} = \frac{cov(x, y) - \sigma(x)}{cov(x, y) + \sigma(x)}. \tag{26}$$

Obviously, $-1 \leq \eta(x, y) \leq 1$; $\eta(x, y) = 0$ if and only if $cer(x, y) = \sigma(y)$ and $cov(x, y) = \sigma(x)$; $\eta(x, y) = -1$ if and only if $cer(x, y) = cov(x, y) = 0$; $\eta(x, y) = 1$ if and only if $\sigma(y) = \sigma(x) = 0$. Evidently, if $\eta(x, y) = 0$, then x and y are

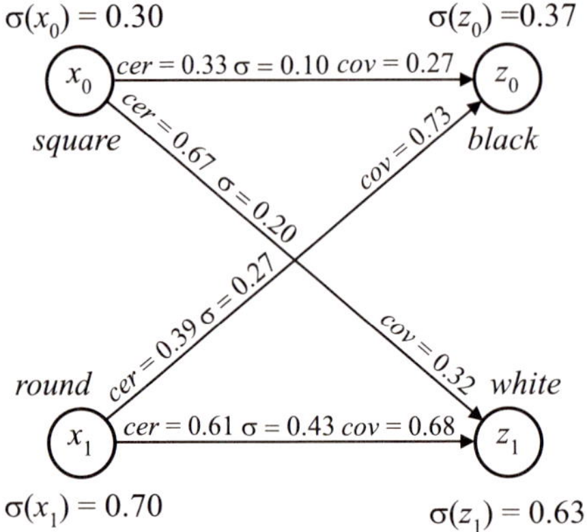

Fig. 6. Fusion of the flow graph

independent, if $-1 \leq \eta(x, y) < 0$, then x and y are negatively dependent, and if $0 < \eta(x, y) \leq 1$, then x and y are positively dependent (see Fig. 7). Thus, the dependency factor expresses a degree of dependency, and can be seen as a counterpart of correlation coefficient used in statistics.

4 Flow Graphs and Decision Algorithms

Flow graphs can be interpreted as decision algorithms. The most general case of this correspondence has been considered in [4].

Let us assume that the set of nodes of a flow graph is interpreted as a set of logical formulas. The formulas are understood as propositional functions and if x is a formula, then $\sigma(x)$ is to be interpreted as a truth value of the formula. Let us observe that the truth values are numbers from the closed interval $< 0, 1 >$, i.e., $0 \leq \sigma(x) \leq 1$.

These truth values can be also interpreted as probabilities. Thus $\sigma(x)$ can be understood as flow distribution ratio (percentage), truth value, or probability. We will stick to the first interpretation.

With every branch (x, y) we associate a decision rule $x \rightarrow y$, read as "*if x, then y*"; x will be referred to as *condition*, whereas y – *decision* of the rule. Such a rule is characterized by three numbers, $\sigma(x, y)$, $cer(x, y)$ and $cov(x, y)$.

Thus, every path $[x_1 \ldots x_n]$ determines a sequence of decision rules $x_1 \rightarrow x_2$, $x_2 \rightarrow x_3, \ldots, x_{n-1} \rightarrow x_n$.

From previous considerations it follows that this sequence of decision rules can be interpreted as a single decision rule $x_1 x_2 \ldots x_{n-1} \rightarrow x_n$, in short $x^* \rightarrow x_n$, where $x^* = x_1 x_2 \ldots x_{n-1}$, characterized by

$$cer(x^*, x_n) = \frac{\sigma(x^*, x_n)}{\sigma(x^*)}, \tag{27}$$

$$cov(x^*, x_n) = \frac{\sigma(x^*, x_n)}{\sigma(x_n)}, \tag{28}$$

and

$$\sigma(x^*, x_n) = \sigma(x^*)cer(x_{n-1}, x_n), \quad \sigma(x^*) = \sigma[x_1, \ldots, x_{n-1}]. \tag{29}$$

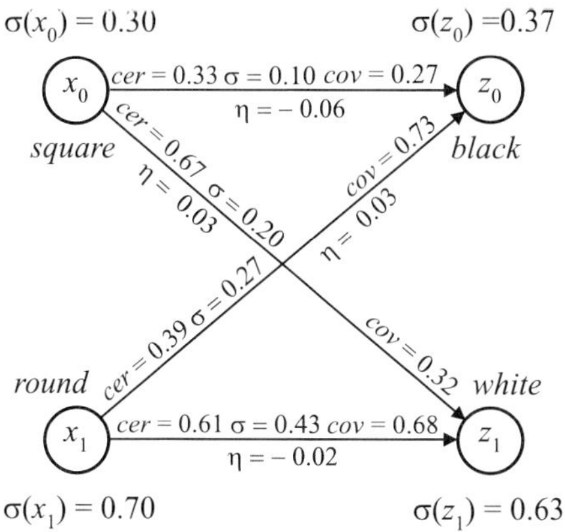

Fig. 7. Dependencies in the flow graph

The set of all decision rules $x_{i_1} x_{i_2} \ldots x_{i_{n-1}} \rightarrow x_{i_n}$ associated with all paths $[x_{i_n} \ldots x_{i_n}]$, such that x_{i_1} and x_{i_n} are input and output of the flow graph, respectively, will be called a *decision algorithm* induced by the flow graph.

The decision algorithm induced by the flow graph shown in Fig. 4 is shown in Table 1. The corresponding flow graph, and the dependency between conditions

Table 1. The decision algorithm induced by the flow graph

	certainty	coverage	strength
if square and small, then black	0.50	0.08	0.03
if square and small, then white	0.50	0.05	0.03
if square and large, then black	0.29	0.19	0.07
if square and large, then white	0.71	0.27	0.17
if round and small, then black	0.57	0.32	0.12
if round and small, then white	0.43	0.14	0.09
if round and large, then black	0.31	0.41	0.15
if round and large, then white	0.69	0.54	0.34

and decision in each decision rule are shown in Fig. 8.

It is interesting to compare diagrams shown in Fig. 1 and Fig. 8. Both diagrams show internal structure (relations) between various groups of play blocks. The decision tree reveals simple statistical structure of the relationship, whereas the flow graph gives much deeper insight into the relationship, and enables simple decision rule generation.

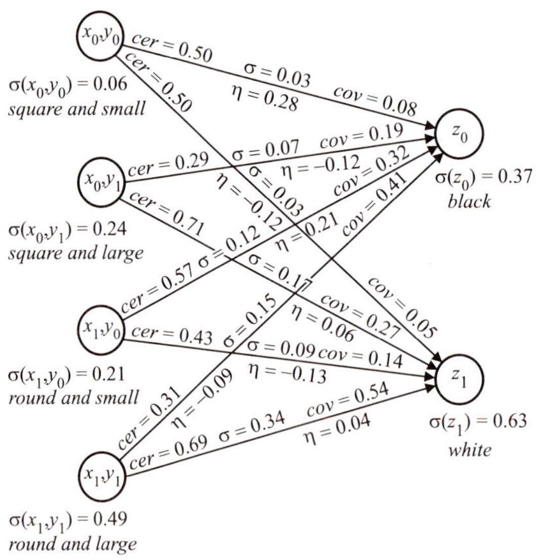

Fig. 8. Flow graph for the decision algorithm

5   Conclusions

Decision tree is an important concept, widely used in computer science, knowledge discovery from data, decision analysis, probability and others. In this paper, with every decision tree we associate another kind of graph, called a flow graph, which reveals deeper insight in data structure associated with a decision tree. This leads to novel methods of decision rule generation from data, and gives better look into decision process analysis. Besides, the proposed approach throws new light on the conception of probability.

References

1. Adams, E. A.: The Logic of Conditionals, an Application of Probability to Deductive Logic, D. Reidel Publishing Company, Dordrecht, Boston, 1975
2. Bernardo, J. M., M. Smith, A. F.: Bayesian Theory. Wiley series in probability and mathematical statistics. John Wiley & Sons, Chichester, New York, Brisbane, Toronto, Singapore, 1994
3. Carnap, R.: Logical Foundation of Probability, Routlege and Kegan Paul, London, 1950
4. Greco, S., Pawlak, Z., Słowiński, R.: Generalized decision algorithms, rough inference rules and flow graphs. In: J. J. Alpigini, J. F. Peters, A. Skowron, N. Zhong (eds.), Rough Sets and Current Trends in Computing. Lecture Notes in Artificial Intelligence 2475, Springer-Verlag, Berlin, 2002, pp. 93-104
5. Laplace, P. S.: Théorie Analytique des Probabilités, Paris, 1812
6. Łukasiewicz, J.: Die logischen Grundlagen der Wahrscheinilchkeitsrechnung. Kraków, 1913. In: L. Borkowski (ed.), Jan Lukasiewicz Selected Works, North Holland Publishing Company, Amsterdam, London, Polish Scientific Publishers, Warsaw, 1970, pp. 16-63
7. Moshkov, M.: On time complexity of decision trees. In: L. Polkowski, A, Skowron (eds.), Rough Sets in Knowledge Discovery 1, Physica-Verlag, Heidelberg, 1998, pp. 160-191
8. Pawlak, Z.: Flow graphs and data mining. In: J. F. Peters and A. Skowron (eds.), Transaction on Rough Sets III, LNCS 3400, Springer-Verlag, Berlin, 2005, pp. 1-36
9. Quinlan, J. R.: C4.5: Programs for machine learning. Morgan Kaufmann, San Mateo, CA, 1993
10. Reichenbach, H.: Wahrscheinlichkeitslehre: eine Untersuchung ber die logischen und mathematischen Grundlagen der Wahrscheinlichkeitsrechnung, 1935; (English translation: The theory of probability, an inquiry into the logical and mathematical foundations of the calculus of probability), University of California Press, Berkeley, 1948
11. Shafer, G.: The Art of Causal Conjecture, The MIT Press, Cambridge, Massachusetts, London, England, 1996

Granular Computing – The Concept of Generalized Constraint-Based Computation

Lotfi A. Zadeh

Department of EECS, University of California
Berkeley, CA 94720-1776, U.S.A.
Tel.: 510-642-4959; Fax: 510-642-1712
zadeh@eecs.berkeley.edu

Basically, granular computing is a mode of computing in which the objects of computation are granular variables. Let X be a variable which takes values in a universe of discourse, U. Informally, a granule is a clump of elements of U which are drawn together by indistinguishability, similarity or proximity. For example, an interval is a granule; so is a fuzzy interval; so is a gaussian distribution; and so is a cluster of elements of U. A granular variable is a variable which takes granules as values. If G is value of X, then G is referred to as a granular value of X. If G is a singleton, then G is a singular value of X. A linguistic variable is a granular variable whose values are labeled with words drawn from a natural language. For example, if X is temperature, then 101.3 is a singular value of temperature, while "high" is a granular (linguistic) value of temperature.

A granular value of X may be interpreted as a representation of one's state of imprecise knowledge about the true value of X. In this sense, granular computing may be viewed as a system of concepts and techniques for computing with variables whose values are not known precisely.

A concept which serves to precisiate the concept of a granule is that of a generalized constraint. The concept of a generalized constraint is the centerpiece of granular computing.

A generalized constraint is an expression of the form X isr R, where X is the constrained variable, R is the constraining relation, and r is an indexical variable whose values define the modalities of constraints. The principal modalities are: possibilistic ($r = blank$); veristic ($r = v$); probabilistic ($r = p$); usuality ($r = u$); random set ($r = rs$); fuzzy graph ($r = fg$); bimodal ($r = bm$); and group ($r = g$). The primary constraints are possibilistic, veristic and probabilistic. The standard constraints are bivalent possibilistic, bivalent veristic and probabilistic. Standard constraints have a position of centrality in existing scientific theories.

A generalized constraint, $GC(X)$, is open if X is a free variable, and is closed (grounded) if X is instantiated. A proposition is a closed generalized constraint. For example, "Lily is young," is a closed possibilistic constraint in which $X = Age(Lily)$; $r = blank$; and $R = young$ is a fuzzy set. Unless indicated to the contrary, a generalized constraint is assumed to be closed.

A generalized constraint may be generated by combining, projecting, qualifying, propagating and counterpropagating other generalized constraints. The set of all generalized constraints together with the rules governing combination,

S. Greco et al. (Eds.): RSCTC 2006, LNAI 4259, pp. 12–14, 2006.

projection, qualification, propagation and counterpropagation constitute the Generalized Constraint Language (GCL).

In granular computing, computation or equivalently deduction, is viewed as a sequence of operations involving combination, projection, qualification, propagation and counterpropagation of generalized constraints. An instance of projection is deduction of $GC(X)$ from $GC(X,Y)$; an instance of propagation is deduction of $GC(f(X))$ from $GC(X)$, where f is a function or a functional; an instance of counterpropagation is deduction of $GC(X)$ from $GC(f(X))$; an instance of combination is deduction of $GC(f(X,Y))$ from $GC(X)$ and $GC(Y)$; and an instance of qualification is computation of X isr R when X is a generalized constraint. An example of probability qualification is (X is small) is likely. An example of veristic (truth) qualification is (X is small) is not very true.

The principal deduction rule in granular computing is the possibilistic extension principle: $f(X)$ is $A \longrightarrow g(X)$ is B, where A and B are fuzzy sets, and B is given by $\mu_B(v) = \sup_u(\mu_A(f(u)))$, subject to $v = g(u)$. μ_A and μ_B are the membership functions of A and B, respectively.

A key idea in granular computing may be expressed as the fundamental thesis: information is expressible as a generalized constraint. The traditional view that information is statistical in nature may be viewed as a special, albeit important, case of the fundamental thesis.

A proposition is a carrier of information. As a consequence of the fundamental thesis, the meaning of a proposition is expressible as a generalized constraint. This meaning postulate serves as a bridge between granular computing and NL-Computation, that is, computation with information described in a natural language. The point of departure in NL-Computation is (a) an input dataset which consists of a collection of propositions described in a natural language; and (b) a query, q, described in a natural language. To compute an answer to the query, the given propositions are precisiated through translation into the Generalized Constraint Language (GCL). The translates which express the meanings of given propositions are generalized constraints. Once the input dataset is expressed as a system of generalized constraints, granular computing is employed to compute the answer to the query.

As a simple illustration assume that the input dataset consists of the proposition "Most Swedes are tall," and the query is "What is the average height of Swedes?" Let h be the height density function, meaning that $h(u)du$ is the fraction of Swedes whose height lies in the interval $[u, u + du]$. The given proposition "Most Swedes are tall," translates into a generalized constraint on h, and so does the translate of the query "What is the average height of Swedes?" Employing the extension principle, the generalized constraint on h propagates to a generalized constraint on the answer to q. Computation of the answer to q reduces to solution of a variational problem. A concomitant of the close relationship between granular computing and NL-Computation is a close relationship between granular computing and the computational theory of perceptions. More specifically, a natural language may be viewed as a system for describing perceptions. This observation suggests a way of computing with perceptions by reducing the problem of computation with perceptions to that of computation with their natural language descriptions, that is, to NL-Computation. In turn, NL-Computation is reduced to granular computing through translation/precisiation into the Generalized Constraint Language (GCL).

An interesting application of the relationship between granular computing and the computational theory of perceptions involves what may be called perception-based arithmetic. In this arithmetic, the objects of arithmetic operations are perceptions of numbers rather than numbers themselves. More specifically, a perception of a number, a, is expressed as usually $(*a)$, where $*a$ denotes "approximately a." For concreteness, $*a$ is defined as a fuzzy interval centering on a, and usually is defined as a fuzzy probability. In this setting, a basic question is: What is the sum of usually $(*a)$ and usually $(*b)$? Granular computing and, more particularly, granular arithmetic, provide a machinery for dealing with questions of this type.

Imprecision, uncertainty and partiality of truth are pervasive characteristics of the real world. As we move further into the age of machine intelligence and automated reasoning, the need for an enhancement of our ability to deal with imprecision, uncertainty and partiality of truth is certain to grow in visibility and importance. It is this need that motivated the genesis of granular computing and is driving its progress. In coming years, granular computing and NL-Computation are likely to become a part of the mainstream of computation and machine intelligence.

Acknowledgement

This Research is supported in part by ONR N00014-02-1-0294, BT Grant CT1080028046, Omron Grant, Tekes Grant, Chevron Texaco Grant and the BISC Program of UC Berkeley.

Bipolar Representations in Reasoning, Knowledge Extraction and Decision Processes

Didier Dubois and Henri Prade

IRIT, 118 route de Narbonne
31062 Toulouse Cedex, France
{dubois, prade}@irit.fr

Abstract. This paper surveys various areas in information engineering where an explicit handling of positive and negative sides of information is appropriate. Three forms of bipolarity are laid bare. They can be instrumental in logical representations of incompleteness, rule representation and extraction, argumentation, and decision analysis.

1 Introduction

Bipolarity refers to the propensity of the human mind to reason and make decisions on the basis of positive and negative affects. It expresses the fact that beyond ranking pieces of information or acts in terms of plausibility, utility and so on, the human mind also relies on absolute landmarks with positive and negative flavor, plus a third landmark expressing neutrality or indifference, corresponding to the boundary between positive and negative zones. For instance people make choices by checking the good sides and the bad sides of alternatives separately. Then they choose according to whether the good or the bad sides are stronger. Results in cognitive psychology have pointed out the importance of bipolar reasoning in human cognitive activities [19] [6] [22]. It even seems that positive and negative affects are not processed in the same area of the brain.

The presence of absolute landmarks in the way humans apprehend information creates limitations in some well-established theories of knowledge representation and reasoning. For instance, probability theory handles certainty and impossibility in a very rigid manner, leaving no room for the state of ignorance. Classical (Von-Neumann-Savage) utility theory builds interval scales for utilities regardless of positive and negative values, since a utility function is invariant with respect to increasing affine transformations. More generally ranking alternatives in a purely ordinal way cannot account for bipolarity in a straightforward manner. In decision theory, the first formal account of bipolarity is Cumulative Prospect Theory [23]. In quite a different matter, the fact that material implication does not provide a good model of if-then rules can be explained in terms of neglecting the bipolar nature of such rules, which have both examples and counter-examples.

The aim of this paper is to briefly survey some areas where bipolarity seems to be present and play a major role. The first section lays bare three forms

S. Greco et al. (Eds.): RSCTC 2006, LNAI 4259, pp. 15–26, 2006.

of bipolarity. The subsequent sections are devoted to various cognitive tasks that naturally involve bipolar ingredients: uncertainty representations, conjointly exploiting knowledge and data, learning, expressing conditional information, and finally decision-making.

2   A Typology of Bipolarity

There are several forms of bipolarity according to the strength of the link between the positive and the negative aspects; in the most constrained form, the positive is just the mirror image of the negative and they are mutually exclusive. A looser form of bipolarity considers a possible coexistence between positive and negative evaluations, while a duality relation between them is maintained. In the loosest form, the positive and the negative sides express pieces of information of a different nature.

2.1   Bipolar Scales

A bipolar scale $(L, >)$ is a totally ordered set with a prescribed interior element $\mathbf{0}$ called *neutral*, separating the positive evaluations $\lambda > \mathbf{0}$ from the negative ones $\lambda < \mathbf{0}$. Mathematically, if the scale is equipped with a binary operation $\star$ (an aggregation operator), $\mathbf{0}$ is an idempotent element for $\star$, possibly acting as an identity.

Examples:

- The most obvious quantitative bipolar scale is the (completed) real line equipped with the standard addition, where 0 is the neutral level. Isomorphic to it is the unit interval equipped with an associative uninorm like $\frac{xy}{xy+(1-x)(1-y)}$. Then the neutral point is 0.5, 0 plays the same role as $-\infty$ and 1 as $+\infty$ in the real line. Also the interval $[-1, 1]$ is often used as a bipolar scale;
- The simplest qualitative bipolar scale contains three elements: $\{-, \mathbf{0}, +\}$.

In such a bipolar scale, the negative side of the scale is the inverse mirror of the positive one. An object is evaluated on such a bipolar scale as being either positive or negative or neutral. It cannot be positive and negative at the same time. This is called a *univariate bipolar* framework.

Another type of bipolar framework uses two distinct totally ordered scales L^+ and L^- for separately evaluating the positive and the negative information. This is the *bivariate unipolar* framework. Here each scale is unipolar in the sense that the neutral level is at one end of the scale. In a *positive* scale the bottom element is neutral. In a *negative* scale the top element is neutral. A bipolar scale can be viewed as the union of a positive and a negative scale $L^+ \cup L^-$ extending the ordering relations on each scale so $\forall \lambda^+ \in L^+, \lambda^- \in L^-, \lambda^+ > \lambda^-$. The symmetrisation of finite unipolar scales is incompatible with associative operations [14] : only infinite bipolar scales seem to support such operations!

2.2 Symmetric, Dual and Loose Variants of Bipolarity

Three forms of bipolarity can be found at work in the literature, we call types I, II, III for simplicity.

- **Type I: Symmetric bipolarity**. It relies on the use of bipolar scales. Generally, positive and negative evaluations are comparable and sometimes can even add. Of course, the two truth-values *true* and *false* of classical logic offer a basic view of bipolarity. However, the neutral value only appears in three-valued logics. Note that the neutral truth value must be interpreted as *half-true*, and not as modalities such as *unknown* or *possible*. Probability theory exhibits a type I bipolarity as the probability of an event is clearly living on a bipolar scale $[0, 1]$ whose top means *totally sure* and bottom *impossible* (not to be confused with *true* and *false*). The neutral value is 0.5 and refers to the total uncertainty about whether an event or its contrary occurs (not to be confused with *half-true*). In decision theory, utility theory does not exhibit bipolarity as utility functions only encode an ordering relation between decisions. On the contrary, Tverski-Kahneman's Cumulative Prospect Theory uses the real line as a bipolar scale. It is numerical, additive, and bipolar. It measures the importance of positive affects and negative affects *separately*, by two monotonic set functions σ^+, σ^- and finally computes a net predisposition $N = \sigma^+ - \sigma^-$.

- **Type II: Homogeneous bivariate bipolarity.** It works with two separate positive and negative scales related via a duality relation. Here, an item is judged according to two independent evaluations : a positive one (in favor of the item), a negative one (in disfavor of the item). However positive and negative strengths are computed similarly on the basis of the same data. The point is here that the positive and the negative sides do not exhaust all possibilities. Part of the data may neither favor nor disfavor the evaluated item. Well-known examples of such a bipolarity can be found in formal frameworks for argumentation where reasons for asserting a proposition and reasons for refuting it are collected. In decision theory, one may compare decisions using pairs of positive and negative evaluations according to several criteria.

  Apart from the positive evaluation, a weak positive evaluation, gathering data not in disfavor of the item can be used. For instance, working with intervals on a (type I) bipolar univariate scale (in the case of an ill-known evaluation) comes down to a type II bipolarity. There is a duality relation relating the weak evaluation and the strong positive evaluation, if each item has a "contrary" : the weak evaluation of an item is the complement of the positive evaluation of the "contrary" item when the latter makes sense. This is typical of uncertainty theories leaving room for incomplete information. Namely, the confidence in some event A is evaluated by two set functions $C(A)$ and $\Pi(A)$ reflecting their certainty and plausibility respectively. They are related by the inequality $C(A) \leq \Pi(A)$, so that the certainty of A is expressed by $C(A) = \Pi(A) = 1$, the impossibility of A by $C(A) = \Pi(A) = 0$ while the neutral state of ignorance is when $C(A) = 0; \Pi(A) = 1$. Clearly, $C(A)$ lives on a positive scale, while $\Pi(A)$ lives on a negative one. The duality relation expresses that $C(A) = 1 - \Pi(A^c)$ where A^c is the complement of A. A good example of certainty/plausibility pairs displaying this kind of bipolarity are belief and plausibility functions of Shafer. In the case of possibility/necessity measures, type II bipolarity is also present in the sense that necessity degrees live on a positive scale while possibility degrees live on a negative scale. However, the two scales are tightly related by the constraint stating that positive necessity degree implies a maximal possibility degree for a given event. So in this case the bivariate setting is degenerated and the pair $(C(A), \Pi(A))$ can be mapped in a one-to-one way to a symmetric type I bipolar scale.

- **Type III: Heterogeneous bipolarity.** In this form of bipolarity, the negative part of the information does not refer to the same kind of source as as the positive part. So positive and negative information are of a different nature, while in type II bipolarity only the polarity is different. Especially, in the case of information merging, negative and positive pieces of information will not be aggregated using the same principles. The positive side is not a mirror image of the negative side either. Nevertheless, positive and negative information cannot be completely unrelated. They must obey minimal consistency requirements. In uncertainty modeling or knowledge representation heterogeneous bipolarity corresponds to the pair (knowledge, data). Knowledge is negative information in the sense that it expresses constraints on how the world behaves, by ruling out impossible or unlikely relations: laws of physics, common sense background knowledge (claims like "birds fly"). On the contrary, data represent positive information because it represents examples, actual observations on the world. A not yet observed event is not judged impossible; observing it is a positive token of support. Accumulating negative information leads to ruling out more possible states of the world (the more constraints, the less possible worlds). Accumulating positive information enlarges the set of possibilities as being guaranteed by empirical observation. In decision making, heterogeneous bipolarity concerns the opposition between constraints (possibly flexible ones) that state which solutions to a problem are unfeasible, and goals or criteria, that state which solutions are preferred.

3 Bipolarity in Logical Representations of Belief

As said above, bipolarity appears in logic in two forms, one pertaining to the truth or the falsity of propositions, and the other pertaining to a (sincere) agent's capability to assert a proposition or its contrary. It is important to notice the existence of two scales: one that measures truth, one that measures belief. A truth- scale is type I bipolar and, when many-valued, it enables propositional variables and propositions whose truth is a matter of degree to be modelled. The neutral point in the scale is *half-true*. Working with Boolean or non-Boolean propositions is a matter of modelling convention, not a matter of how much knowledge is available. So $[0, 1]$-valued membership functions of fuzzy sets are type I bipolar (non-membership 0 being negative, 0.5 being neutral). In the Boolean case, the truth-scale is reduced to the pair $\{0, 1\}$.

Another issue is the belief scale. It is positive unipolar in the sense that while believing p is a positive piece of information, not believing p is non-committal, because it differs from believing $\neg p$, the negation of p. There is a companion negative unipolar plausibility scale whose bottom expresses impossibility and whose top has a neutral value for expressing non-committal statements of the form p is possible. In classical logic, beliefs are represented by propositions assumed true and forming a belief base K. Belief is Boolean : either p is believed (when $K \vdash p$) or not. Moreover p is believed if and only if $\neg p$ is impossible, indicating that this is type II bipolarity. Clearly in the case of incomplete belief bases, the epistemic state of a proposition is ternary in classical logic even if truth is 2-valued: one may either believe p, believe $\neg p$, or believe neither due to ignorance.

There are temptations to use belief states or belief values as truth values (a set of the form $\{$*True, Unknown, False*$\}$) and build a 3-valued logic on it. This is basically what the so-called "partial logic" [5] does. Its truth-tables use an implicit order whereby *Unknown* is less true than *True*, more true than *False*. But this approach runs into paradoxes related to the excluded-middle law [11]. Adopting truth-tables for conjunction and disjunction, one must assign a truth-value to $p \vee q$ when p and q are both unknown, which clearly depends on whether p and q are logically independent or not. The point is that ultimately, in the Boolean framework p is true or false, so that $p \vee \neg p$ must be a tautology, even if the truth-value of p is not known. So *Unknown* is not a truth-value in the usual sense: it does not prevent 0 and 1 from being exhaustive and mutually exclusive as truth-values. *Unknown* lives on the belief /plausibility bivariate scale. Just like *Unknown*, *True* and *False*, understood as above, are not truth-values, they are epistemic states because they stand for *certainly* 1, and *certainly* 0, respectively. They can be modelled as disjunctive subsets of the truth scale: *Unknown* = $\{0, 1\}$, *True* = $\{1\}$, *False* = $\{0\}$. Belnap so-called "4-valued logic" [3] supposedly adds a fourth "truth-value" expressing the contradiction to $\{$*True, Unknown, False*$\}$. However it is subject to the same criticism as above, as to what this 4-valued logic means, regardless of the fact that a multivalued logic based on such a kind of truth-set (a bilattice) can be devised and enjoys nice properties.

One reason for this confusion between truth and certainty of truth is that the language of classical logic does not support the expression of unknown propositions: only believed propositions can be written in the knowledge base. It becomes clearer when prefixing each believed proposition in K with a necessity-like belief modality C. Then a possibility-like modality Π, such that Πp may stand for $\neg C \neg p$. It can be shown that the proper logic here is the KD45 modal logic. Then *True* can be interpreted, in some sense, as a truth-value of Cp, not of p. *Unknown* is encoded as $\Pi p \wedge \Pi \neg p$. It applies when $Cp \vee C \neg p$ is false, as clearly Cp is not the negation of $C \neg p$. So, the presence of the epistemic state *Unknown* does not question the excluded middle law at all. Casting propositional logic into an epistemic modal logic lays bare the type II bipolarity of reasoning in classical logic. In fact it can be proved [8] that, denoting $CK = \{Cp, p \in K\}$,

$K \vdash p$ in classical logic if and only if $CK \vdash Cp$ in KD45. Note that this kind of embedding is not the usual one of propositional logic into modal logic: it says that the fragment of KD45 made of classical propositions prefixed by C behaves like classical logic, which justifies the name "belief base" for a set of classical propositions.

Rough set theory [20] also displays a form of type II (symbolic) homogeneous bipolarity, since a set is approximated by a pair of subsets, respectively containing elements surely belonging to it (lower approximation), and elements surely not belonging to it. The so-called upper approximation of the set is again the complement of the lower approximation of its complement. This can be represented using ordered pairs of truth-values from $\{0, 1\}$, viewed as an elementary unipolar scale, assigning $(1, 1)$ to elements surely belonging to A, $(0, 0)$ to elements surely belonging to A^c, and $(0, 1)$ to elements whose membership is unknown. However, it does not lead to a truth-functional three-valued logic on a (type I) bipolar scale, since the lower (resp. upper) approximation of a union (resp. intersection) of sets is not the union (resp. intersection) of their lower (resp. upper) approximations. Yet, links between three-valued logics and rough sets have been explored in the literature (e.g. Banerjee [2]).

4 Heterogeneous Bipolar Information: Knowledge vs. Data, and Learning

In the previous section, bipolarity in knowledge representation was due to incomplete information. There is a very different kind of bipolarity, this time heterogeneous, opposing background knowledge and empirical data. Background knowledge takes the form of generic statements, integrity constraints, laws, necessary conditions, and point out what cannot be possibly observed. On the contrary, data is made of observed cases that are positive pieces of information. Beware that positive knowledge may not just mirror what is not impossible. Indeed what is not impossible, not forbidden, does not coincide with what is explicitly possible or permitted. So, a situation that is not impossible (i.e., possible) is not necessarily guaranteed possible (i.e., positive) if it is not explicitly permitted, observed or given as an example.

Possibility theory is a suitable framework for modelling and reasoning about this kind of bipolar information[12][8]. Negative and positive information is represented by two separate possibility distributions, denoted by π and δ, yielding possibility and guaranteed possibility measures respectively. A possibility distribution π encodes a total pre-order on a set S of interpretations or possible states. It associates to each interpretation s a real number $\pi(s) \in [0, 1]$, which represents the compatibility of the interpretation s with the available knowledge on the real world (in case of uncertain knowledge), or equivalently to what extent s is not impossible. The less $\pi(s)$, the more impossible s is. The second possibility distribution δ should be understood differently. The degree $\delta(s) \in [0, 1]$ estimates to what extent the presence of s is supported by evidence, and $\delta(s) = 0$ just means that s has not been observed yet. In the crisp case, the set I of impossible situations is $I = \{s \in S, \pi(s) = 0\}$, and the set GP of guaranteed possible situations is $GP = \{s \in S, \delta(s) = 1\}$.

A characteristic property of heterogeneous bipolarity is the fact that the sets of guaranteed possible (the support GP of δ) and impossible (I) situations should be disjoint and generally do not cover all the referential. This is expressed by the coherence condition $GP \subseteq I^c$. This condition means that what is guaranteed possible should be not impossible. When uncertainty is graded, this coherence condition now reads: $\delta \leq \pi$.

Example: Assume for instance one has some information about the opening hours and prices of a museum M. We may know that museum M is open from 2 pm to 4 pm, and certainly closed at night (from 9 pm to 9 am). Note that nothing forbids museum M to be open in the morning although there is no positive evidence supporting it. Its ticket fare is neither less than 2 euros nor more than 8 euros (following legal regulations), prices between 4 and 5 euros are guaranteed to be possible (they are prices actually proposed by the museum).

Since observations accumulate, while increasing background knowledge eliminate new possible worlds, positive information aggregate disjunctively, and negative information aggregate conjunctively. This can be understood in our setting in the following way. A constraint like *the value of X is restricted by A_i* is encoded by a possibility distribution π s. t. $\pi \leq \mu_{A_i}$. Several such constraints are thus equivalent to $\pi \leq \min_i \mu_{A_i}$. By the principle of minimal commitment (anything not declared impossible is possible), it leads to choose the greatest possibility distribution $\pi = \min_i \mu_{A_i}$ compatible with the constraints. Hence a conjunctive combination. In the case of positive information X *is A_i* is equivalent to $\delta \geq \mu_{A_i}$, since it reflects empirical support. Then several such observations are equivalent to $\delta \geq \max_i \mu_{A_i}$. By closed world assumption (anything not observed as actually possible is not considered), one gets $\delta = \max_i \mu_{A_i}$. Hence a disjunctive combination.

Given a pair of possibility distributions (π, δ), we can define. the possibility degree of an event A, $\Pi(A) = \max\{\pi(s) : s \in A\}$, the dual necessity degree $N(A) = 1 - \Pi(A^c)$ and the guaranteed possibility degree $\Delta(A) = \min\{\delta(s) : s \in A\}$ (let alone the dual degree of potential necessity $1 - \Delta(A^c)$). Note that set function Π underlies an existential quantifier since $\Pi(A)$ is high as soon as some $s \in A$ is plausible enough. It agrees with the negative nature of information, since A is impossible, i. e. $\Pi(A) = 0 \iff N(A^c) = 1$, corresponds to the non-existence of an interpretation $s \in A$ having a non-zero degree of possibility $\pi(s)$. In contrast, Δ underlies a universal quantifier since $\Delta(A)$ is high as soon as all $s \in A$ be supported by evidence. It agrees with the positive nature of information encoded by δ, since $\Delta(A) = 1$ requires that all states where A occurs be maximally supported by evidence. The duality between N and Δ ($\Delta(A) = N^c(A^c)$ where N^c is the necessity measure based on $\pi^c = 1 - \delta$) is different from the one (characteristic of type II bipolarity) between N and Π.

Merging bipolar information [12], by disjunctive (resp. conjunctive) combination of positive (resp. negative) information, may create inconsistency when the upper and lower possibility distributions, which represent the negative part and the positive part of the information respectively, fail to satisfy the consistency condition $\pi \geq \delta$. Then, since empirical observations are generally regarded as more solid information than prior knowledge, the latter must be revised for instance as $\pi' = \max(\pi, \delta)$, so as to account for unexpected evidence.

Learning processes turn data into knowledge, hence positive into negative information in the sense of type III bipolarity: situations that are often observed are eventually considered as normal and those never observed are considered as impossible. Recently [21], it has been shown that Mitchell's version space concept learning, based on an explicit set of examples and counterexamples, can be reformulated in the language of possibility theory under heterogeneous bipolarity. Distributions π (induced by counterexamples) and δ (induced by examples) respectively become the most general and the most specific hypotheses explaining the data. The theory also explains how these hypotheses are progressed as new data come in.

5   Bipolarity and If-Then Rules

An if-then rule is not a two-valued entity, it is a three valued one. To see it, consider a database containing descriptions of items in a set S. If a rule *if A then B* is to be evaluated in the face of this database, it clearly creates a 3-partition of S, namely:

1. the set of examples of the rule: $A \cap B$,
2. its set of counter-examples: $A \cap B^c$,
3. the set of irrelevant items for the rule: A^c.

Each situation should be encoded by means of a different truth-value. This view of a rule is at odds with the logical tradition, for which it is a material implication. The two first situations corresponding to the usual truth-values 1 (true) and 0 (false) respectively. The third case corresponds to a third truth-value that must be be interpreted as *irrelevant* as the rule does not apply. This idea of a rule as a *tri-event* actually goes back to De Finetti in the 1930's. This framework for modelling a rule produces a precise bipolar mathematical model: a rule is modeled as a pair of disjoint sets representing the examples and the counter-examples of a rule, namely $(A \cap B, A \cap B^c)$.

This definition has several consequences. First, it justifies the claim made by De Finetti that a conditional probability $P(B \mid A)$ is the probability of a particular entity denoted by $B \mid A$ that can be called *a conditional event*. Indeed it is obvious to see that the probability $P(B \mid A)$ is entirely defined by $P(A \cap B)$ and $P(A \cap B^c)$. Moreover it precisely shows that material implication only partially captures the intended meaning of an if-then rule. It is obvious that the set of items where the material implication $A^c \cup B$ is true is the complement of the set of counter-examples of a rule. Hence the usual logical view only emphasizes the negative side of the rule. It does not single out its examples. This is clearly in agreement with the fact that propositions in classical logic represent negative information. On the other hand, the set of examples of a rule is $A \cap B$ and clearly represents positive information. Thus, the three-valued representation of an if-then rule also strongly suggests that a rule contains both positive and negative information. Note that in data mining, the merit of an association rule $A \Rightarrow B$ extracted from a database is evaluated by two indices: the support and the confidence degrees, respectively corresponding to the probability $P(A \cap B)$ and the conditional probability $P(B \mid A) = \frac{P(A \cap B)}{P(A \cap B) + P(A \cap B^c)}$. This proposal may sound ad hoc. However the deep reason why two indices are necessary to evaluate the quality of a rule is because the rule generates a 3-partition of the database, and two evaluations are needed to picture their relative importance. In fact the primitive quality indices of an association rule are the proportion of its examples and the proportion of its counter-examples. All other indices derive from these basic evaluations.

It is intuitively satisfying to consider that a rule R1 = "if A then B" entails a rule R2 = "if C then D", if R2 has more examples and less counterexamples than R1 (in the sense of inclusion). R2 is safer than R1. This entailment relation (denoted $\models$) can be formally written as

$$B \mid A \models D \mid C \text{ if and only if } A \cap B \subseteq C \cap D \text{ and } C \cap D^c \subseteq A \cap B^c.$$

It is non-monotonic. Indeed, it has been shown [10] that the three-valued semantics of rules provide a representation for the calculus of conditional assertions of Kraus, Lehmann and Magidor [17], which is the main principled approach to nonmonotonic reasoning.

Lastly, the bipolar view has been also applied to fuzzy rules "if A then B" (when A and/or B are fuzzy sets). It is clear that the usual modeling of fuzzy rules in fuzzy control, based on the fuzzy conjunction of A and B corresponds to the positive information contained in rules, while the less usual approach based on many-valued implications views rules as constraints and better fits classical logic. The bipolar view can be exploited for building a typology of fuzzy if-then rules, based on multivalued implications or conjunctions, where each type of fuzzy rules serves a specific purpose [13]. It emphasizes the advantages of using conjointly implicative rules (encoding negative information) and conjunctive rules (encoding positive information) in the same rule-based system. Finally the bipolar view is instrumental in rigourously extending the support and the confidence degrees to fuzzy association rules [9].

6   Bipolarity and Decision

Decision processes are pervaded with bipolar notions. All types of bipolarity are involved. Type I bipolar decision-making stems from evaluating decision on a bipolar scale, thus providing an explicit account of whether a decision is good or bad. An automatic procedure ranking decisions from the best to the worst does not prevent the best ranked decision from being bad (the other ones being worse), nor, for another case, the worst decision from still being reasonably good. It is useful to propose absolute evaluations, at least a qualitative advice about what is good and what is bad. Using a bipolar scale is clearly instrumental, due to the presence of the neutral point separating good grades from bad ones. This type of bipolarity is especially used in Cumulative Prospect Theory and more recently by Grabisch and Labreuche [18].

Type II bipolarity occurs when faced with several criteria, and evaluating separately the criteria where the ratings of a decision are good and the criteria where the ratings are bad. Each criterion can be evaluated on a type I bipolar scale and the global evaluation on a bivariate unipolar scale, hence pairs (how good, how bad) of evaluations are compared. Or, in a more complex and more expressive setting, each criterion can be itself rated on a bivariate unipolar scale, as done by Greco et al. [16].

In the bipolar setting the importance of criteria cannot be assessed as usual using set functions g like capacities, $g(C)$ evaluating the importance of the group C of criteria. So-called bicapacities [15] are of the form $g(C^+, C^-)$ where C^+ (resp. C^-) is a set of criteria where the decision performance is good (resp. bad). If criteria are rated individually on a bipolar scale, $C^+ \cap C^- = \emptyset$. The overall evaluation is performed using a variant of Choquet integral adapted to bicapacities. In the more expressive model, criteria importance is evaluated by so-called bipolar capacities[16]. The idea is to use two measures, a measure of positiveness (that increases with the addition of positive arguments and the deletion of negative arguments) and a measure of negativeness (that increases with the addition of negative arguments and the deletion of positive arguments), without combining them.

A purely ordinal setting for bipolar decision-making was recently proposed by Dubois and Fargier [7]. Each criterion is rated on the basic qualitative bipolar scale $\{-, \mathbf{0}, +\}$. The set $\mathcal{C}$ of criteria is mapped on a unipolar positive scale, for instance $[0, 1]$, where 0 indicates no importance. Let $\pi(c)$ be the importance of criterion c. The weight of a subset C of criteria is supposed to be $\Pi(A)$, using a possibility measure; the idea is to focus on the most important affect when making a choice. For a decision a, the evaluation of criterion c is either positive or negative or zero. Let $A^+ = \{c, c(a) = +\}$, and $A^- = \{c, c(a) = -\}$ be the positive reasons for a and the negative reasons against a, respectively. Comparing decisions a and b in the type II bipolar framework is based on evaluations $\Pi(A^-)$, $\Pi(A^+)$, $\Pi(B^-)$, and $\Pi(B^+)$. Several decision rules can be proposed. The first one is a Pareto-based comparison of pairs $(N((A^-)^c), \Pi(A^+))$ and $(N((B^-)^c), \Pi(B^+))$. It is a transitive partial ordering. It is perhaps too partial: for instance, when $\Pi(A^-) > \Pi(A^+)$, it concludes that a is incomparable with b where $B^+ = B^- = \emptyset$. In this case, one would rather say that a is worse than an indifferent b. Another drawback is observed when $\Pi(A^+) > \Pi(B^+)$ and $\Pi(A^-) = \Pi(B^-)$: this enforces preference of a over b, even if $\Pi(A^+)$ is very weak w.r.t the order of magnitude of the negative arguments — in the latter case, a rational decider would examine the negative arguments in details before concluding.

The other decision rule is a complete preorder that assumes commensurability between positive and negative evaluations, counting a reason against b as a reason for a:

$$a \succeq^{Biposs} b \Leftrightarrow \max(\Pi(A^+), \Pi(B^-)) \geq \max(\Pi(B^+), \Pi(A^-))$$

Only the strict part of the generated ordering is transitive. This rule focuses on the most salient affects pertaining to a and b. $a \succeq^{Pareto} b$ implies $a \succeq^{Biposs} b$. It is also clear that $\succeq^{Biposs}$ is a bipolar generalisation of a possibility measure. However, $\succeq^{Biposs}$ and Pareto are very rough rules that may be not decisive enough. Lexicographic refinements of $\succeq^{Biposs}$ offer more decisive and actually realistic decision rules. One such rule checks how many reasons for a and for b there are at each importance level and decides on the basis of the most important such discriminating level. It can be simulated by Cumulative Prospect Theory. This kind of qualitative bipolar setting can be useful in formal argumentation for the evaluation and comparison of arguments[1].

Quite another form of bipolarity in decision refers to the (in some sense more classical) opposition between constraints and goals. It is a form of heterogeneous bipolarity. A decision problem on a solution space is then modelled by two possibility-like distributions π and δ [4]. However, now $\pi(s)$ evaluates to what extent a solution s is feasible, not rejected. It is a matter of degree in the face of soft constraints. On the contrary δ is an objective function and $\delta(s)$ evaluates the extent to which s is fully satisfactory. All formal considerations pertaining to type III bipolarity apply here, especially the consistency condition between π and δ. Distribution π is generally the conjunctive aggregation of local soft constraints. Distribution δ is generally the disjunctive or additive aggregation of several objective functions. This approach can be expressed in possibilistic logic using a constraint base (containing negative information as in classical logic) and a goal base (containing positive information and behaving like in a data-driven logic [8]). Several strategies for defining best solutions can be devised. The most natural scheme is to first check consistency between constraints and goals, possibly modifying goals if necessary, then define a set of feasible solutions that achieves a compromise between soft constraints, and finally finding the best feasible solutions according to δ inside this set.

7   Conclusion

This paper suggests that bipolarity is naturally present in cognitive and decision processes. Bipolarity lays bare the presence of absolute landmarks in evaluation scales, having positive or negative flavor, thus revealing a cognitive limitation of purely ordinal representations. Modelling bipolarity in an explicit manner is useful in many areas of information engineering such as knowledge representation, learning, decision analysis, inconsistency handling, argumentation, question-answering systems.

References

1. L. Amgoud and H. Prade. Comparing decisions on the basis of a bipolar typology of arguments . In A. Hunter J. Dix, editor, *Proc. 11th Workshop on Nonmonotonic Reasoning*, pages 426–432, Windermere U.K., 2006.

2. M. Banerjee. Rough sets and 3-valued Lukasiewicz logic. *Fundamenta Informaticae*, 32:213–220, 1997.

3. N. D. Belnap. A useful four-valued logic. In J.M. Dunn and G. Epstein, editors, *Modern Uses of Multiple-Valued Logic*, pages 8–37. D.Reidel, Dordrecht, The Netherlands, 1977.

4. S. Benferhat, D. Dubois, S. Kaci, and H. Prade. Bipolar possibility theory in preference modeling: Representation, fusion and optimal solutions. *Information Fusion*, 7:135–150, 2006.

5. S. Blamey. Partial logic. In D. Gabbay and F. Guentner, editors, *Handbook of Philosophical Logic, 2d Ed.*, volume 5, pages 261–353. Kluwer Academic Publ., Dordrecht, The Netherlands, 1998.

6. J. T. Cacioppo, W. L. Gardner, and G. G. Berntson. Beyond bipolar conceptualizations and measures: The case of attitudes and evaluative space. *Personality and Social Psychology Review*, 1:3– 25, 1997.

7. D. Dubois and H. Fargier. Qualitative decision making with bipolar information. In *Proc. of Int. Conf. on Principles of Knowledge Representation and Reasoning KR'06, Windermere, UK*, pages 175–186, Menlo Park, Ca., 2006. AAAI Press.

8. D. Dubois, P. Hajek, and H. Prade. Knowledge-driven versus data-driven logics. *J. of Logic, Language, and Information*, 9:65–89, 2000.

9. D. Dubois, E. Huellermeier, and H. Prade. A systematic approach to the assessment of fuzzy association rules. *Data Mining and Knowledge Discovery, to appear*, 2006.

10. D. Dubois and H. Prade. Conditional objects as non-monotonic consequence relationships. *IEEE Trans. on Systems, Man and Cybernetics*, 24:1724–1739, 1994.

11. D. Dubois and H. Prade. Possibility theory, probability theory and multiple-valued logics: A clarification. *Ann. Math. and Artificial Intelligence*, 32:35–66, 2001.

12. D. Dubois, H. Prade, and P. Smets. "Not impossible" vs. "guaranteed possible" in fusion and revision. In S. Benferhat and Besnard P., editors, *Proceedings of ECSQARU'01 - LNAI 2143*, pages 522–531, 2001.

13. D. Dubois, H. Prade, and L. Ughetto. A new perspective on reasoning with fuzzy rules. *Int. J. of Intelligent Systems*, 18:541–567, 2003.

14. M. Grabisch. The Moebius transform on symmetric ordered structures and its application to capacities on finite sets. *Discrete Math.*, 28(1-3):17–34, 2004.

15. M. Grabisch and Ch. Labreuche. Bi-capacities — parts I and II. *Fuzzy Sets and Systems*, 151(2):211–260, 2005.

16. S. Greco, B. Matarazzo, and R. Slowinski. Bipolar Sugeno and Choquet integrals. In *EUROFUSE Workshop on Information Systems*, pages 191–196, Varenna, 2002.

17. S. Kraus, D. Lehmann, and M. Magidor. Nonmonotonic reasoning, preferential models and cumulative logics. *Artificial Intelligence*, 44(1-2):167–207, 1990.

18. Ch. Labreuche and M. Grabisch. Generalized Choquet-like aggregation functions for handling bipolar scales. *Eur. J. of Operational Research*, 172(3):931–955, 2006.

19. C. E. Osgood, G.J. Suci, and P. H. Tannenbaum. *The Measurement of Meaning*. Univ. of Illinois Press, Chicago, 1957.

20. Z. Pawlak. *Rough Sets - Theoretical Aspects of Reasoning about Data*. Kluwer Academic Publ., Dordrecht, The Netherlands, 1991.

21. H. Prade and M. Serrurier. Version space learning for possibilistic hypotheses. In *Proc. of 17th Europ. Conf. on Art. Intel., ECAI'06*, Riva del Garda, Italy, 2006.

22. P. Slovic, M. Finucane, E. Peters, and D.G. MacGregor. Rational actors or rational fools? implications of the affect heuristic for behavioral economics. *The Journal of Socio-Economics*, 31:329–342, 2002.

23. A. Tversky and D. Kahneman. Advances in prospect theory: Cumulative representation of uncertainty. *Journal of Risk and Uncertainty*, 5:297–323, 1992.

Kansei Engineering and Rough Sets Model

Mitsuo Nagamachi

User Science Institute, Kyushu University
Fukuoka 815-8540, Japan

Abstract. M. Nagamachi founded Kansei Engineering at Hiroshima University about 30 years ago and it has spread out in the world as an ergonomic consumer-oriented product development. The aim of the kansei engineering is to develop a new product by translating a customer's psychological needs and feeling (kansei) concerning it into design specifications. The kansei data are analyzed by a multivariate statistical analysis to create the new products so far, but the kansei data not always have linear features assumed under the normal distribution. Rough sets theory is able to deal with any kind of data, irrespective of linear or non-linear characteristics of the data. We compare the results based on statistical analysis and on Rough Sets Theory.

1   Introduction

The trend of product development is becoming toward the consumer-oriented, namely the consumer's feeling and needs are recognized as invaluable in product development for manufacturers.

The kansei engineering was founded by M. Nagamachi at Hiroshima University about 30 years ago [1,2,3,4] and the kansei engineering aims at the implementation of the customer's feeling and demands in the product function and design. When a customer wants to purchase some thing, for instance to buy a passenger car, TV cumcorder or a costume etc., he/she will have a kind of feeling such as "graceful and looks intelligent, but not so expensivec" This feeling is called as "kansei" in Japanese. The kansei means the customer's psychological feeling as well as the physiological issues. For instance, if the developmental target will be a sophisticated room air-conditioner which is able to control room temperature automatically comfortable to person(s) working in the room, the mechanical function of the air-conditioner should be developed based on psychological feeling as well as dependent on physiological basis using control engineering. The kansei engineering is defined as "translating the customer's kansei into the product design domain". If the user's target would be an passenger car, all kansei concerning exterior, interior, engine, etc. are implemented in those designs. In this case, the surveyed kansei are transferred to physical traits first and these are transformed to the design domain. If it is concerned with urban planning and if what people want to design in terms of the kansei engineering is the community, the kansei included in the district culture and history as well as people's demands of kansei should be implemented in the urban redesign.

S. Greco et al. (Eds.): RSCTC 2006, LNAI 4259, pp. 27–37, 2006.

Kansei Engineering is powerful to develop new products in any design domain fit to customer's needs and feeling, and then it has spread out over the world. Especially, all countries in EU have much interested recently in the kansei engineering or the affective engineering, and a lot of researchers engage in kansei research under the EU research fund.

Manufacturers introduced successfully the kansei engineering are Mazda (Sports-car, *Miata*), Wacaol (Brassiere, *Good-Up Bra*), Sharp (TV camcorder, *Licked Crystal Viewcam*), Matsusita (Sitting shower, *The Shower*), Milbon (Shampoo and treatment, *Deesse's*), Mizuno (Golf club, *IntageX3*) and others. All kansei products have sold very well in the market so far, because they are well fit to the customer's feeling.

2   Methodology of Kansei Engineering

2.1   Category Classification

We survey a customer's behavior when using a product and name his/her feeling to write down on a keyword on a card one by one. Then we construct a tree structure from a top event (a top category) to the bottoms (subconcepts) with expressing all keywords. From subconcepts we choose the most important subconcepts concerning the coming new product and the selected subconcepts are examined in ergonomic experiments in order to specify the design specifications. Miata, a sports-car made by Mazda was made followed by the category classification.

First, Mazda researchers took many pictures of young drivers when driving a car and collected about 600 keywords expressing the young driver's observation. Then a tree structure was constructed of a top category to subconcepts using these keywords. The most related and important subconcepts were selected to lead to the final design specifications, which included an engine reformation, interior and exterior design as well.

2.2   Kansei Engineering Type I

Kansei words related the ongoing product domain are chosen in reference to magazines, customer conversation, and salesmen's words in the number of 30-40 words and then these words are in the scale of 5-point or 7point SD method. On the other side, many products are collected from the same design domain of the ongoing product and these selected products are evaluated using the kansei SD scaling. The evaluated data are analyzed by the multivariate analysis such as Factor Analysis, Regression Analysis or Quantification Theory Type I, Type II and Type III.

These kansei engineering methods are very effective and efficient to find out the relationship between customer's kansei and product design specifications. Good-Up Bra made by Wacoal and Deesse's (Figure 1) made by Milbon are successful followed this technique.

Fig. 1. Shampoo and treatment named "Deesse's"

2.3   Kansei Engineering System and Hybrid Kansei Engineering System

The system means a computerized assisting system to assist the designer activity or to help a customer's product choice fit to his/her feeling. The Kansei Systems consists of kansei word database, knowledge base, an inference engine, product parts database and system control. In Kansei Engineering System a kansei word is inputted into the computer and it recognizes the kansei which is transferred to design segmentation. Finally a selected candidate of products is displayed on the screen.

Hybrid Kansei Engineering System has the kansei engineering system which is called "forward kansei engineering", from kansei inputting to a candidate display. The system has so called "backward kansei engineering", which starts from a candidate. A designer watches a candidate and changes it with his/her idea based on inferred kansei result and the hybrid kansei system is able to assess the designer's decision with the kansei database. Nissan's steering wheel was designed using the hybrid kansei system.

2.4   Virtual Kansei Engineering System

Nagamachi collaborated with Matsusita Electric Works to create a new computerized design system which is able to design a kitchen in a virtual space. It is called ViVA system, which is able to display a kitchen design according to a house wife's kansei. The system consists of two subsystems, one of design decision system based on the kansei engineering system with 10,000 house wives database, and another of virtual reality system which displays on the screen kansei kitchen design based on her kansei. A house wife inputs her image of kitchen life such as "I want to invite my friends on Saturday to cook and chatter with them". And then the system can show the kitchen image on the screen decided by the kansei system (see Figure 2 and 3).

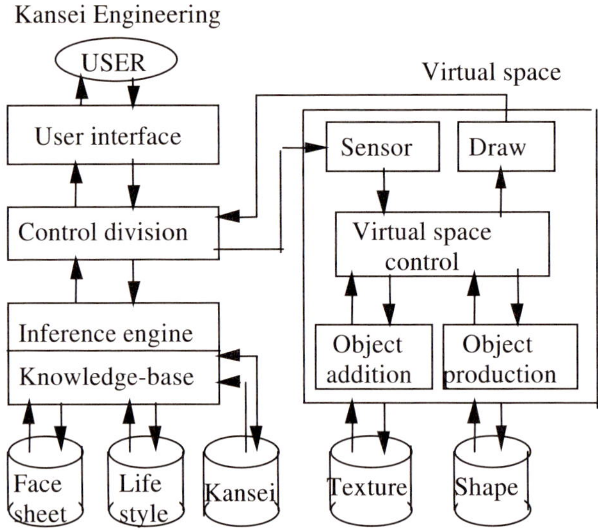

Fig. 2. ViVA System for kitchen design

Fig. 3. An example of kitchen design decided by ViVA system

The shell of ViVA system was extended to whole house design system, "Hous-Mall", which is able to deal with the designs of the exterior house, the front door, the western room, the Japanese room, the kitchen, the bath room, and the bed room as well. A customer inputs his/her kansei on each part, and the system displays each candidate image on the screen decided by the kansei engineering system. All customs participated in the system were surprised when watching the screen, since they were feel much fit to their image in mind.

2.5   Collaborate Kansei Design System

We attempted to construct "groupware designing system" using the Web which
has an intelligent design system and kansei databases. The system is very useful to do a joint work for designing a new product by several designers in the
separated position, for instance working in separate countries. The system has
a server implemented an intelligent software which supports collaborate designing, since the designers can use voice and see the other colleagues' work on the
screen with each other. Talking with other persons, a designer can make the design or correct it instantly using the kansei databases and the kansei engineering
systems. Figure 4 illustrates a scene of collaborative kansei designing.

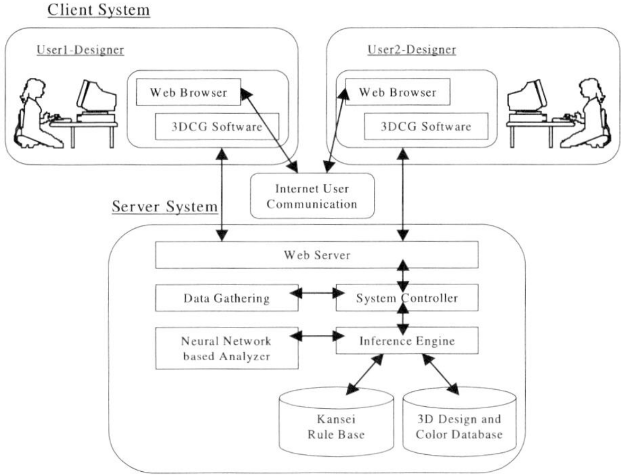

Fig. 4. A schema of Collaborative Kansei Designing System

2.6   Rough Sets Theory

We have produced many kansei products so far using the kansei engineering.
However, some of kansei have the linear characteristics, but others have non-
linear features. For instance, the length on design side increases linearly with
"small-large" kansei, but the evaluated kansei score for "beautiful-not beautiful"
shows non-linear feature compared with the horizontal numerical change. If the
kansei has in general non-linear characteristics, it is not correct to apply the
statistical analysis, since it has hypothesis of normal distribution on the basis.

However, Rough Sets Theory extended by Pawlak [8] can treat rough and
ambiguous data like kansei, irrespective of linear or non-linear data characteristics. The theory consists of seeking lower and upper approximation based on
the decision rules of rough kansei data, the former approximation to get the
crisp solution about kansei design, but the latter of getting more ambiguous and
uncertain solution including quite a new design idea [6,7].

3   Comparison Between Kansei Engineering and Rough Sets Model

In this section, we attempt to compare the calculated results of kansei designs by the kansei engineering and by Rough Sets Model. First, we describe the standard kansei engineering procedure and then Rough Sets Model procedure.

3.1   Principal Component Analysis of Toddler Shoes Design

Our kansei research is related to Kansei Engineering Type I technique [1], which aims at finding the relationship between the kansei and design specifications

In this case, we attempted to create very good kid shoes (toddler shoes) design in terms of Kansei Engineering. The experimental procedure of Kansei Engineering is as follows;

(1) Collection of toddler shoes from several different makers – We collected 29 different shoes from 5 manufacturers.
(2) Shoes design attributes – We defined design attributes concerning each shoes design, namely size, weight, surface design, sole, color and so on. We call these design elements as Item/Category.
(3) Collection of Kansei words – We collected 31 kansei words, mostly adjectives, from young mothers. For instance, they talk with their friends when purchasing shoes, cute, light, easy to wear, soft sole and so on. These kansei words are illustrated on 5-point SD scale for easy evaluation.
(4) Execution of kansei evaluation experiments. Twenty-six young mothers who have kindergarten's children were asked to evaluate their feeling on each shoes design with the 5-point kansei SD scale.
(5) After the experiments, all mother subjects discussed together about what attributes were good design for easy-to wear, safe running, comfortable usage, easy wash, and inexpensive as well.
(6) Calculation of evaluated data by Principal Component Analysis and Quantification Theory Type I

3.2   Data Analysis Using Principal Component Analysis

The evaluated data on 29 toddler shoes design were analyzed first by Principal Component Analysis. The cumulative contribution is shown in Table 1.As illustrated in Table 1, Component 1 and 2 explain 50%.

We are able to show the PCA charts which illustrate each factor graphic. Figure 7 illustrates the kansei word chart which shows the region surrounded by Component 1 and Component 2. In the chart, the horizontal axis implies Component 1 and the vertical one Component 2. The resulted three components lead to a new shoes product and accordingly the designer is able to develop a new product applying these design points.

Component 1 is grouped by the kansei "easy to move", "easy to put on", "easy to make put on" and others. Accordingly Component 1 is named "easy

Fig. 5. A scene of kansei experiment

Fig. 6. A sample of 29 toddler shoes

to use" component. Component 2 is grouped by the kansei "attractive", "good design" and other, and then this is named "good design" component. Figure 8 illustrates the positions of shoes sample on the kansei component map. It shows which samples are closer to what kansei. If we have a company strategy of the kansei about the next development project, we may choose the specific kansei. We constructed the new product of company strategy about a kansei product development.

3.3 Quantification Theory Type 1 Analysis of Toddler Shoes Design

Quantification Theory Type 1(QT1) was founded by DR. Mikio Hayashi for treating with qualitative data, which is similar with multiple regression analysis. It seeks a relation between kansei and design attributes. We can obtain using

Table 1. Cumulative Contribution of Principal Component Analysis

Principal Component	Eigen Value	Contribution	Cumulative Contribution
No.1	4.771	30.48%	30.48%
No.2	3.189	20.38%	50.85%
No.3	1.923	12.29%	63.14%
No.4	1.749	11.17%	74.31%
No.5	1.107	7.08%	81.39%

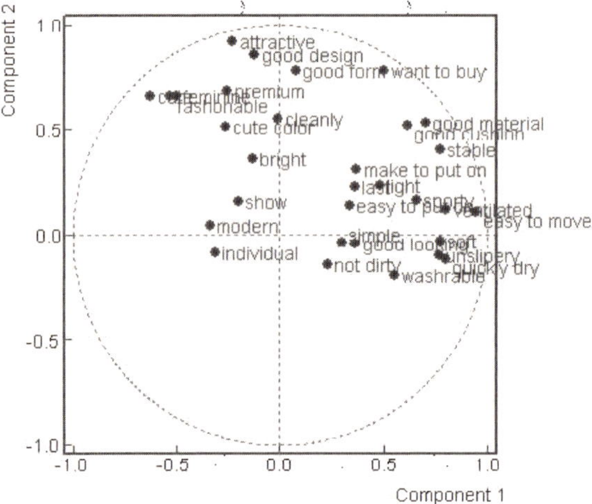

Fig. 7. A chart of Component 1 and 2

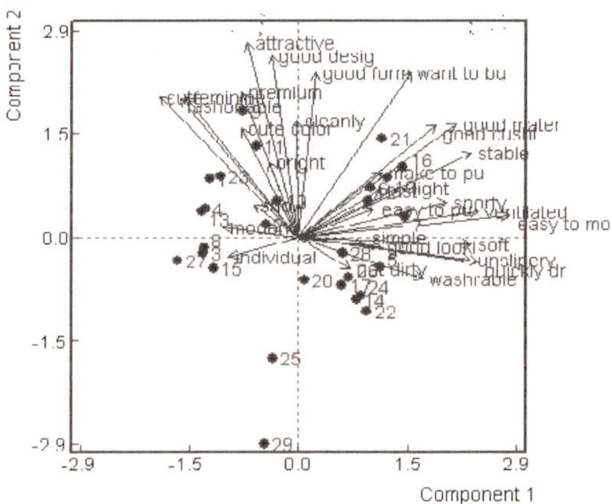

Fig. 8. PCA vector chart of Component 1 and 2

QT1 the relational function of design elements like size, width, color, and other categories fit to the specific kansei.

Since Component 2 was named "a good design", we try to get the design attributes concerning the kansei "a good design". Applying QT1 to the kansei, we obtained the following results. The analyzed results tell that the design of "a good design" should consist of red and blue or soft rubber or lower heel. Each design element is independent with the mathematical meaning of Quantification Theory.

3.4 Comparison with Rough Sets Model

One of problems in kansei is that people's kansei does not always have linear characteristics in statistical meaning. For instance, the kansei [big–small] has linearity in continuity axis, but the kansei [beautiful–not beautiful] has curved feature in physiological axis. In general we have used statistical analysis like cluster analysis and multiple regression analysis. If these kansei have non-linear characteristics, it is not appropriate to apply a multiple variate analysis. Therefore, we have used to Neural Networks, Genetic Algorithm and others so far.

Rough Sets Theory was founded by Pawlak [8] and it consists of Lower and Upper Approximation. We used three equations for deriving Lower and Upper approximation decision rules in terms of Rough sets model based on Nishino's model [7].

$$POS^{\beta}(D_j) = \bigcup \{E_i \mid g_{pos}(i,j) \geq \beta\}$$

$$= \bigcup \left\{ E_i \;\middle|\; P(D_j|E_i) \geq \frac{P(D_j)}{1-\beta} \right\},$$

$$NEG^{\beta}(D_j) = = \bigcup \left\{ E_i \;\middle|\; P(D_j|E_i) \leq \frac{P(D_j)-\beta}{1-\beta} \right\},$$

$$BND^{\beta}(D_j) = \bigcup \left\{ E_i \;\middle|\; P(D_j|E_i) \in \left(\frac{P(D_j)-\beta}{1-\beta}, \frac{P(D_j)}{1-\beta} \right) \right\}.$$

The following table is one of derived comparison by QT 1 (right) and by Rough sets model (left). In terms of QT1, each design element was derived independently. To the contrary, Rough Sets Model can derive the design speculations as a group. Lower approximation means a crisp solution which almost the same as the solution by QT1, but upper approximation means rough and ambiguous features which leads sometime inventive hints.

Table 2. The comparison of Rough sets model and QT1

Rough sets model	QT1
· sneaker type	red or blue
· a magic tape	solt rubber
· weak solt	;ower heel

Remarks

Kansei Engineering is a translating technology of kansei, namely customer's psychological feeling into design elements. The kansei is related to words, attitude, behavior or physiological measurement of EEG, EMG, Heart rate, GSR and other ergonomic measurement. Accordingly, it is very important and successful from the beginning to choose how to measure the kansei.

Secondly, the measured kansei is analyzed by statistical methods of multivariate analysis. We always use factor analysis, multiple regression analysis, cluster analysis and others. Quantification Theory I, II, III, IV are very well known as the excellent method for treating with qualitative data, especially like kansei data. Computer-assisted kansei systems with artificial intelligent system are also very effective for customers to select the appropriate goods and for designers to develop new products due to his/her own idea. In Japan, Nagamachi has developed a lot of new kansei products, automobile, construction machine, costume, cosmetics, lamp, golf club, toilet, bath and so many other products. All kansei products developed in terms of Kansei Engineering have been sold very well in the market and the manufacturers requested to support my effort have got a lot of profit through the kansei products.

Some of kansei have linear characteristics, but others don't. For instance, the kansei "large–small" has decrease feature according to data characteristics. But the kansei "beautiful–not beautiful" does not always linear characteristics, on the other hand it has curved function. In the latter cases, an application of statistical method to the kansei data is not correct. However, Pawlak's Rough Sets Theory does not have matter of linearity or non-linearity. Rather, it has very analytical power for rough, uncertain and ambiguous data. Therefore, it is very powerful analysis to the kansei data. We tried here to apply Rough Sets Model [5] for comparison with Quantification Theory Type 1. As our expectation, Rough Sets Model derived group wise solution to lead "the good design" toddler shoes. Our next research matter will find more useful and easy technique to lead solution in terms of sophisticated Rough Sets Model.

References

1. Nagamachi, M., Kansei Engineering, Kaibundo Publisher, Tokyo, 1989.
2. Nagamachi, M., Introduction of Kansei Engineering, Japan Standard Association, Tokyo, 1995
3. Nagamachi, M., Kansei engineering in consumer product development, Ergonomics in Design, 10 (2), 5–9, 2002
4. Nagamachi, M. (Ed.), Product Development and Kansei, Kaibundo Publishing, Tokyo, 2005.
5. Nishino, T., Rough sets and acquisition of kansei rules, in M. Nagamachi (Ed.), Production Development and Kansei, Chap.8, 177–219, Kaibundo Publishing, Tokyo, 2005

6. Nishino, T. and Nagamachi M., Rough set analysis on kansei evaluation of color and kansei structure, In; M. P. Dahlgaad, J. J. Dahlgaad (Eds.), Proc. of the 4th International QMOD Conference, 543–550 2001.
7. Nishino, T., Nagamachi, M. and Tanaka H., Variable precision bayesian rough set model and its application to human evaluation data, LNAI 3641, Springer, 294–303, 2005.
8. Pawlak, Z., Rough set elements, In: L.Polkowski, L. and Skowron, A. (Eds.), Rough Sets in Knowledge Discovery 1, Physica-Verlag, 10–30, 1998.

Stochastic Approach to Rough Set Theory

Wojciech Ziarko

Department of Computer Science, University of Regina
Regina, Saskatchewan, Canada S4S 0A2
ziarko@cs.uregina.ca

Abstract. The presentation introduces the basic ideas and investigates the stochastic approach to rough set theory. The major aspects of the stochastic approach to rough set theory to be explored during the presentation are: the probabilistic view of the approximation space, the probabilistic approximations of sets, as expressed via variable precision and Bayesian rough set models, and probabilistic dependencies between sets and multi-valued attributes, as expressed by the absolute certainty gain and expected certainty gain measures, respectively. The measures allow for more comprehensive evaluation of rules computed from data and for computation of attribute reduct, core and significance factors in probabilistic decision tables.

1   Introduction

The original rough set theory [1-2] was developed within the framework of set theory, algebra and logic. It was restricted to finite universes, which allowed the use of the set cardinality as a basis for the measures of quality of approximation, inter-attribute dependency etc. The natural extension of the cardinality measure, in the context of rough set theory applications to data analysis and modelling from data drawn from infinite or very high cardinality universes, is the adoption of the probability function. The probability function can be used to estimate the relative "sizes" of subsets of an infinite universe by properly designed sampling procedure. It turns out that the extended theory of rough sets can be developed around the notion of the probability function while preserving the basic properties of the original approach proposed by Zdzislaw Pawlak [1-2]. In addition, connections can be established with some of the well-known results of probability theory, such as Bayes theorem and the notion of event independence.

The attempts to generalize rough set theory based on probabilistic ideas were initiated soon after the introduction of rough sets [3-6]. In this article, the summary of basic results of the probabilistic approach to rough sets is presented. Due to space restrictions, the proofs of theorems are omitted. In brief, the results are the effect of the evolution of the early variable precision rough set model [3] and its merge with probability theory and Bayesian reasoning. The central notions of the probabilistic approach to rough sets are the prior and the conditional probabilities of an event (set)[4,13-14]. The probabilities are used to define information gain function, which in turn serves as a basis to define set

S. Greco et al. (Eds.): RSCTC 2006, LNAI 4259, pp. 38–48, 2006.

Table 1. Multivalued Classification Table

P	a	b	c	d
0.10	1	1	2	**1**
0.05	1	1	2	**1**
0.20	1	0	1	**1**
0.13	1	0	1	**2**
0.02	2	2	1	**2**
0.01	2	2	1	**2**
0.01	2	0	2	**1**
0.08	1	1	2	**1**
0.30	0	2	1	**3**
0.07	2	2	1	**2**
0.01	2	2	1	**2**
0.02	0	2	1	**1**

approximations in the style of the variable precision model of rough sets. It is also used to generalize the Pawlak's notion of attribute dependency (functional or partial functional dependency) by linking it with the idea of probabilistic dependence (independence). The generalized gain function-based dependency measure is able to capture subtle probabilistic dependencies, which are not visible to other measures. The measure has been demonstrated to exhibit the important monotonicity property [12], which allows for the extension of the notion of the *relative reduct* of attributes [2] to the probabilistic domain and for the application of existing algorithms for reduct computation. It also allows for the analysis of importance of individual attributes through computation of probabilistic significance factors. The comprehensive review of related probabilistic measures in the context of rough set theory is presented in [7].

2 Attribute-Based Classifications

In this section, we briefly review the essential assumptions and definitions of the rough set theory in the context of probability theory.

One of the prime notions is the universe of interest U, a set of objects $e \in U$ about which observations are acquired. The existence of *probabilistic measure* P over *σ-algebra* of *measurable subsets* of U is also assumed. We will assume here that the universe is infinite in general, but that we have access to a finite sample $S \subseteq U$, as represented by the available data. It is assumed that all subsets $X \subseteq U$ under consideration are measurable with $0 < P(X) < 1$. That is, from the probabilistic perspective, they are likely to occur but their occurrence is not certain. The probability of a set X, $P(X)$ can be estimated from data by calculating its frequency in the sample S. That is, $P(X) \simeq \frac{card(X \cap S)}{card(S)}$, where *card* denotes set cardinality. However, to simplify the notation in the rest of the paper, we will not be making any notational distinction between available sample $S \subseteq U$ and the universe U.

We also assume that observations about objects are expressed through values of functions, referred to as *attributes*, belonging to a finite set $C \cup D$, such that $C \cap D = \emptyset$. The functions belonging to the set C are called *condition attributes*, whereas functions in D are referred to as *decision attributes*. We can assume, without loss of generality, that there is only one decision attribute, that is $D = \{d\}$. Each attribute a belonging to $C \cup D$ is a mapping $a : U \to V_a$, where V_a is a finite set of values called the *domain* of the attribute a. In many applications, attributes are functions obtained by discretizing values of real-valued variables representing measurements taken on objects $e \in U$.

Each subset of attributes $B \subseteq C \cup D$ defines a mapping denoted as $\mathbf{B} : U \to \mathbf{B}(U) \subseteq \otimes_{a \in B} V_a$, where $\otimes$ denotes Cartesian product operator of all domains of attributes in B. The elements of the set $\mathbf{B}(U) \subseteq \otimes_{a \in B} V_a$ will be referred to as *tuples*.

For a tuple $z \in \mathbf{C} \cup \mathbf{D}(U)$ and a subset of attributes $B \subseteq C \cup D$, let $z.B$ denote the projection of the tuple z on the collection of attributes B, as defined in the in the theory of relational databases. The projection $z.B$ corresponds to a set of objects whose values of attributes in B match $z.B$, that is to the set $\mathbf{B}^{-1}(z) = \{e \in U : \mathbf{B}(e) = z\}$. Clearly, the sets $\mathbf{B}^{-1}(z)$ form a partition of the universe U, i.e. they are disjoint for different restricted tuples $z.B$ and cover the universe U. The partition will be denoted as U/B and its classes will be called *B-elementary sets*. In particular, the $C \cup D$-elementary sets, denoted as $G \in U/C \cup D$, will be referred to as *atoms*. For traditional reasons, the C-elementary sets $E \in U/C$ will be referred to just as *elementary sets* and the D-elementary sets $F \in U/D$ will be called *decision categories*. Each elementary set $E \in U/C$ and each decision category $F \in U/D$ is a union of some atoms. That is, $E = \cup\{G \in U/C \cup D : G \subseteq E\}$ and $F = \cup\{G \in U/C \cup D : G \subseteq F\}$.

Each atom $G \in U/C \cup D$ is assigned a *joint probability* $P(G)$, which is normally estimated from collected data. The mapping $\mathbf{C} \cup \mathbf{D} : U \to \mathbf{C} \cup \mathbf{D}(U)$ can be represented by a *multivalued classification table* consisting of tuples $z \in \mathbf{C} \cup \mathbf{D}(U)$ corresponding to atoms along with their associated joint probabilities. The multivalued classification table summarizes the relationship between classes of objects and attribute values. An example classification table with $C = \{a, b, c\}$, $D = \{d\}$ and joint probabilities P, is shown in Table 1.

¿From our initial assumption and from the basic properties of the probability measure P, follows that for all atoms $G \in U/C \cup D$, we have $0 < P(G) < 1$ and $\sum_{G \in U/C \cup D} P(G) = 1$. Based on the joint probabilities of atoms, probabilities of elementary sets E and decision categories F can be calculated from the classification table by

$$P(E) = \sum_{G \subseteq E} P(G). \tag{1}$$

The probability $P(F)$ of the decision category F will be referred to as *prior probability* of the category F. In the context of the analysis of probabilistic dependencies between attributes, the *conditional probability* of a decision category F, $P(F|E) = \frac{P(F \cap E)}{P(E)}$, conditioned on the occurrence of the elementary set E, is of interest as well. It represents the degree of confidence in the occurrence of the decision category F, given information indicating that E occurred. The conditional probability can be expressed in terms of probabilities of atoms by

$$P(F|E) = \frac{\sum_{G \subseteq F \cap E} P(G)}{\sum_{G \subseteq E} P(G)}. \tag{2}$$

This makes it possible for simple computation of the conditional probabilities from the classification table.

3 Basics of the Variable Precision Rough Set Model

One of the main objectives of rough set theory is the formation and analysis of approximate definitions of otherwise undefinable sets [2]. The approximate or rough definitions, in the form of lower approximation and boundary area of a set, allow for determination of an object's membership in a set with varying degrees of certainty. The lower approximation permits for uncertainty-free membership determination, whereas the boundary defines an area of objects which are not certain, but possible, members of the set. The variable precision model of rough sets (VPRSM)[3] extends upon these ideas by parametrically defining the positive region as an area where the certainty degree of an object's membership in a set is relatively high, the negative region as an area where the certainty degree of an object's membership in a set is relatively low, and by defining the boundary as an area where the certainty of an object's membership in a set is neither high nor low.

The defining criteria in the VPRSM are expressed in terms of conditional probabilities and of the *prior* probability $P(X)$ of the set X in the universe U. In the context the attribute-value representation of sets of the universe U, as described in the previous section, we will assume that the sets of interest are decision categories $X \in U/D$. Two *precision control* parameters are used as follows.

The first parameter, referred to as the *lower limit* l, satisfying the constraint $0 \leq l < P(X) < 1$, represents the highest acceptable degree of the conditional probability $P(X|E)$ to include the elementary set E in the *negative region* of the set X. In other words, the *l-negative region* of the set X, denoted as $NEG_l(X)$ is defined by:

$$NEG_l(X) = \cup\{E : P(X|E) \leq l\} \tag{3}$$

The *l*-negative region of the set X is a collection of objects for which the probability of membership in the set X is deemed to be *significantly lower* than the prior probability $P(X)$, the probability of an object's membership in the set X in the absence of any information about objects of the universe U.

The second parameter, referred to as the *upper limit* u, satisfying the constraint $0 < P(X) < u \leq 1$, defines the *u-positive region* of the set X. The upper limit reflects the least acceptable degree of the conditional probability $P(X|E)$ to include the elementary set E in the positive region, or *u-lower approximation* of the set X. The *u*-positive region of the set X, $POS_u(X)$ is defined as

$$POS_u(X) = \cup\{E : P(X|E) \geq u\}. \tag{4}$$

The u-positive region of the set X is a collection of objects for which the probability of membership in the set X is deemed to be *significantly higher* than the prior probability $P(X)$.

The objects which are not classified as being in the u-positive region nor in the l-negative region belong to the (l, u)-boundary region of the decision category X, denoted as

$$BNR_{l,u}(X) = \cup\{E : l < P(X|E) < u\}. \tag{5}$$

The boundary is a specification of objects about which it is known that their conditional associated probability with respect to the set X, is not significantly different from the prior probability of the set $P(X)$. In the VPRSM *symmetric* case, i.e. if $\beta = u = 1 - l$ [3][13], the *negative* and *positive* regions of the set X, are defined respectively by $NEG_\beta(X) = \cup\{E : P(\neg X|E) \geq \beta\}$ and $POS_\beta(X) = \cup\{E : P(X|E) \geq \beta\}$. The related application-oriented results are reported in [10].

4   Basics of the Bayesian Rough Set Model

The Bayesian rough set model [13] [12] (BRS) can be perceived as the extreme limit model of a series of VPRS models when the parameters l and u approach the prior probability $P(X)$. That is, the BRS positive region $POS^*(X)$ defines an area of the universe where the probability of X is higher than the prior probability. It is an area of certainty improvement or gain with respect to predicting the occurrence of X.

$$POS^*(X) = \bigcup\{E : P(X|E) > P(X)\} \tag{6}$$

The BRS negative region $NEG^*(X)$ defines an area of the universe where the probability of X is lower than the prior probability. It is an area of certainty decrease with respect to predicting the occurrence of X.

$$NEG^*(X) = \bigcup\{E : P(X|E) < P(X)\} \tag{7}$$

The BRS boundary region is an area characterized by the lack of certainty change with respect to predicting X.

$$BND^*(X) = \bigcup\{E : P(X|E) = P(X)\} \tag{8}$$

Information defining the boundary area is unrelated to X, which leads to the same probabilistic distribution of objects belonging to X as in the whole universe U, i.e. $P(X|BND) = P(X)$. This follows from the fact that in the BRS boundary region the target event X is independent, in stochastic sense, with all the elementary events in $BND^*(X)$, that is, for all $E \subseteq BND^*(X)$ we have $P(X \cap E) = P(X)P(E)$.

Table 2. Probabilistic decision table for *u=0.8* and *l=0.1*

a	b	c	$P(E)$	$P(X|E)$	Region
1	1	2	0.23	1.00	**POS**
1	0	1	0.33	0.61	**BND**
2	2	1	0.11	0.27	**BND**
2	0	2	0.01	1.00	**POS**
0	2	1	0.32	0.06	**NEG**

5   Decision Tables Acquired from Data

To describe functional or partial functional connections between attributes of objects of the universe U, Pawlak introduced the idea of decision table acquired from data [2]. The probabilistic decision tables extend this idea into probabilistic domain by forming representations of probabilistic relations between attributes. The extended notion of decision table in case of multiple tables has been studied in depth in [9].

For the given decision category $X \in U/D$ and the set values of the VPRSM lower and upper limit parameters l and u, we define the *probabilistic decision table* $DT_{l,u}^{C,D}$ as a mapping $C(U) \rightarrow \{POS, NEG, BND\}$ derived from the classification table as follows:

The mapping is assigning each tuple of values of condition attribute values $t \in \mathbf{C}(U)$ to its unique designation of one of VPRSM approximation regions $POS_u(X)$, $NEG_l(X)$ or $BND_{l,u}(X)$, the corresponding elementary set E_t is included in, along with associated elementary set probabilities $P(E_t)$ and conditional probabilities $P(X|E_t)$:

$$DT_{l,u}^{C,D}(t) = \begin{cases} (P(E_t), P(X|E_t), POS) \Leftrightarrow E_t \subseteq POS_u(X) \\ (P(E_t), P(X|E_t), NEG) \Leftrightarrow E_t \subseteq NEG_l(X) \\ (P(E_t), P(X|E_t), BND) \Leftrightarrow E_t \subseteq BND_{l,u}(X) \end{cases} \qquad (9)$$

The probabilistic decision table is an approximate representation of the probabilistic relation between condition and decision attributes via a collection of uniform size probabilistic rules corresponding to rows of the table. An example probabilistic decision table derived from the classification Table 1 is shown in Table 2. The probabilistic decision tables are most useful for decision making or prediction when the relation between condition and decision attributes is largely non-deterministic.

6   Probabilistic Dependencies Between Sets

In the presence of probabilistic information, as given by the joint probabilities of atoms, it is possible to evaluate the degree of probabilistic dependency between any elementary set and a decision category.

The adopted dependency measure, called *absolute certainty gain* [14] (*gabs*) is concerned with quantifying the degree of influence the occurrence of an elementary set E has on the likelihood of occurrence of the decision category F. The occurrence of E can increase, decrease, or have no effect on the probability of occurrence of F, which is initially given by its prior probability $P(F)$. The relative degree of variation of the probability of F, due to occurrence of E, is represented by *the absolute gain function* as

$$gabs(F|E) = |P(F|E) - P(F)|, \tag{10}$$

where $| * |$ denotes absolute value function. The values of the absolute gain function fall in the range $0 \leq gabs(F|E) \leq max(P(\neg F), P(F)) < 1$. In addition, let us note that if sets F and E are independent in the probabilistic sense, that is, if $P(F \cap E) = P(F)P(E)$ then $gabs(F|E) = 0$, which is consistent with the intuitive meaning of the independence.

The absolute certainty gain $gabs(F|E)$ can be computed directly from the multivalued classification table because all the prior and conditional probabilities appearing in (10) can be computed from the joint probabilities of tuples. The definition of the absolute certainty gain provides a basis for the definition of the probabilistic dependency measure between attributes, as proposed in the next section.

7   Probabilistic Dependencies Between Attributes

The absolute certainty gain represents the degree of change of the occurrence certainty of a specific decision category in response to an occurrence of a given elementary set. The average degree of change of occurrence certainty of a given decision category due to occurrence of any elementary set is given by the expected gain function [14]:

$$egabs(F|C) = \sum_{E \in U/C} P(E)gabs(F|E) \tag{11}$$

The natural extension of this idea, to measure the degree of connection between condition and decision attributes, is to quantify the average, or expected change of the occurrence certainty of any decision category as a result of an occurrence of any elementary set. The degree of change can be quantified by the expected value $mgabs(D|C)$ of the expected gain functions over all decision categories $F \in U/D$:

$$mgabs(D|C) = \sum_{F \in U/D} P(F)egabs(F|C) \tag{12}$$

The *multivalued expected gain function*, as defined by (12), measures the average degree of increase of the occurrence probability of the decision category $F \in U/D$, or of its complement $\neg F$, relative to its prior probability $P(F)$, as a result of occurrence of an elementary set $E \in U/C$.

The multivalued expected gain function $mgabs$ can also be seen as the measure of the degree of probabilistic dependency between partition U/C of the universe, corresponding to condition attributes, and the partition U/D, corresponding to decision attributes. This follows from the following proposition:

Proposition 1: The expected gain function $mgabs(D|C)$ can be expressed as:

$$mgabs(D|C) = \sum_{F \in U/D} \sum_{E \in U/C} |P(F \cap E) - P(F)P(E)| \tag{13}$$

The formula (13) indicates that $mgabs$ is a measure of average deviation from probabilistic independence between elementary sets and decision categories. The measure can be also expressed in an alternative form, as demonstrated by the following Proposition 2.

Proposition 2: The expected gain function $mgabs(D|C)$ can be expressed as:

$$mgabs(D|C) = \sum_{F \in U/D} P(F) \sum_{E \in U/C} gabs(E|F) \tag{14}$$

For the purpose of normalization of the expected gain function, the following Proposition 3 is useful.

Proposition 3: The multivalued expected gain function falls in the range $0 \leq mgabs(D|C) \leq 2\sum_{F \in U/D} P(F)^2(1 - P(F))$.

Because the strongest dependency occurs when each decision category F is definable, that is when the dependency is functional, this would suggest to use the degree of expected gain in the functional dependency case as a normalization factor to make dependency grades comparable across different classification tables. For that purpose, the λ inter-attribute dependency measure was defined in [14]. Here, it is extended to non-binary decision categories by:

$$\lambda(D|C) - \frac{mgabs(D|C)}{2\sum_{F \in U/D} P(F)^2(1 - P(F))}, \tag{15}$$

to become a normalized measure of dependency between condition attributes C and the decision attributes D. The function reaches its maximum $\lambda(D|C) = 1$ only if the dependency is deterministic (functional). The value of the $\lambda(D|C)$ dependency function can be easily computed from the multivalued classification table since the expected gain and all prior probabilities are directly computable from the table, as demonstrated earlier.

8   Characterization of Independence

The decision category F and the condition attributes C are independent if $egabs(F|C) = 0$. The independence can occur only if $P(F \cap E) = P(F)P(E)$, for all elementary sets $E \in U/C$ and for all decision categories, $F \in U/D$. That is, for the independence between the partition U/D and the partition U/C to hold, all decision categories F must be independent with each elementary set E, which means that $\lambda(D|C) = 0$ in such case.

An interesting question is the characterization attributes that are *neutral* with respect to the relation between attributes C and D. Such attributes, when added to the collection of condition attributes, would have no effect on dependency with the decision attribute. The following Theorem 1 provides partial characterization of such attributes.

Theorem 1: If an attribute a is independent with $C \cup D$ i.e. if $\lambda(C \cup D | \{a\}) = 0$, then $\lambda(D | C \cup \{a\}) = \lambda(D | C)$.

The above theorem suggests that for a new attribute "a", to contribute to the increase of dependency $\lambda(D|C)$, it should be connected, in the stochastic sense, either with condition attributes C or decision attributes D. We also note that the independence is a two-way property, that is, $\lambda(C|D) = 0$ if and only if $\lambda(D|C) = 0$. In particular, $\lambda(C \cup D | \{a\}) = 0$ if and only if $\lambda(\{a\} | C \cup D) = 0$.

9   Reduction of Attributes

The application of the idea of *relative reduct* of attributes, as introduced by Pawlak [2], allows for optimization of representation of classification information by providing a systematic technique for removal of redundant attributes. The notion of reduct is also applicable to the optimization of representation of probabilistic dependencies between attributes in multivalued classification tables. The following theorem demonstrates that the probabilistic dependency measure λ between attributes is *monotonic*, which means that expanding condition attributes C by an extra attribute would never result in the decrease of the degree of dependency with the decision attributes D.

Theorem 2: The λ-dependency is monotonic, that is, for condition attributes C and an attribute a, the following relation holds:

$$\lambda(D|C) \leq \lambda(D|C \cup \{a\}) \tag{16}$$

Based on the Theorem 2, the notion of the *probabilistic reduct* of attributes $RED \subseteq C$ can be defined as a minimal subset of attributes preserving the probabilistic dependency with the decision attributes D. Precisely, the reduct satisfies the following two properties:

1. $\lambda(D|RED) = \lambda(D|C)$;
2. For any attribute $a \in RED$, $\lambda(D|RED - \{a\}) < \lambda(D|RED)$.

The probabilistic reducts can be computed using any methods available for reduct computation in the framework of the original rough set approach (eg. see [2]). The probabilistic reduct provides a method for computing combinations of fundamental factors in a probabilistic relationship.

10   Evaluation of Attributes

Groups of attributes appearing in a reduct can be evaluated with respect to their contribution to the dependency with the target attribute by defining the notion of the probabilistic *significance factor*. The probabilistic significance factor, denoted as $sig_{RED}(B)$, of attribute collection $B \subseteq RED$, represents the relative decrease of the dependency $\lambda(D|RED)$ due to removal of the subset B from the reduct:

$$sig_{RED}(B) = \frac{\lambda(D|RED) - \lambda(D|RED - B)}{\lambda(D|RED)} \qquad (17)$$

Finally, as in the original rough set approach, one can define the probabilistic *core* set of attributes as the ones which form the intersection of all reducts of C, if the intersection is not empty. After [2], any core attribute a satisfies the following inequality:

$$\lambda(D|C) > \lambda(D|C - \{a\}), \qquad (18)$$

which leads to a simple method of core computation.

11   Final Remarks

The article summarizes the basic results of the stochastic approach to rough set theory. The approach generalizes the original Pawlak's theory. The main results of the original theory are preserved whereas the scope of possible applications of the theory is expanded. The generalized model of rough sets benefits from some key results of the probability theory and contributes original, specifically rough set-oriented results. The merge of rough set and probability theory methods creates a novel computational paradigm for data analysis and modelling from data. In applications, the paradigm relies on availability of large databases as data sources and high speed computers to process the data. These two main factors were absent when the probability theory and statistics were originally created. The lack of powerful computation means lead to the development of statistical methods based on assumed or estimated probability distribution functions falling into a number of standard categories, not necessarily closely reflecting the actual data.

The stochastic rough set-based methods, on the other hand, rely entirely on the distributions present in the data and avoid approximate fitting of standard distributions to data. This makes it possible to deal with problems in which distributions are unknown or not matching any standard functions. The benefits of such an approach are the expanded applicability of the analytical methods and perfect accuracy of analytical results and models in relation to data.

Acknowledgment. The research reported in this article was supported by a grant from the Natural Sciences and Engineering Research Council of Canada.

References

1. Pawlak, Z. Rough sets. Intl. Journal of Computer and Information Science, vol. 11, 1982, 341-356.
2. Pawlak, Z. Rough sets - Theoretical Aspects of Reasoning About Data. Kluwer, 1991.

3. Ziarko, W. Variable precision rough sets model. Journal of Computer and Systems Sciences, vol. 46(1), 1993, 39-59.
4. Yao, Y.Y., Wong, S.K.M. A decision theoretic framework for approximating concepts. Intl. Journal of Man-Machine Studies, 37, 1992, 793-809.
5. Wong, S.K.M. Ziarko, W. Comparison of the probabilistic approximate classification and the fuzzy set model. Intl. Journal for Fuzzy Sets and Systems, vol. 21, 1986, 357-362.
6. Wei, L. Zhang, W. Probabilistic rough sets characterized by fuzzy sets. RSFD-GrC'2003, LNAI 2639, Springer Verlag, 173-180.
7. Greco, S. Matarazzo, B. Slowinski, R. Rough membership and Bayesian confirmation measures for parametrized rough sets. RSDGRC '2005, LNAI 3641, Springer Verlag, 2005, 314-324.
8. Zhong, N. Dong, J. Ohsuga, S. Data mining: a probabilistic rough set approach. In Polkowski, L. Skowron, A. (eds) Rough Sets and Knowledge Discovery, Physica Verlag, 1998, 127-146.
9. Inuiguchi, M. Miyajima, T. Variable precision rough set approach to multiple decision tables. RSDGRC '2005, LNAI 3641, Springer Verlag, 2005, 304-313.
10. Muto, Y. Kudo, M. Discernibility-based variable granularity and Kensei representations. RSDGRC '2005, LNAI 3641, Springer Verlag, 2005, 692-700.
11. Yao, Y. Probabilistic approaches to rough sets. Expert Systems, vol. 20(5), 2003, 287-291.
12. Slezak, D. Ziarko, W. The Investigation of the Bayesian rough set model. Intl. Journal of Approximate Reasoning, Elsevier, vol. 40, 2005, 81-91.
13. Ziarko, W. Set approximation quality measures in the variable precision rough set model. Soft Computing Systems, IOS Press, 2001, 442-452.
14. Ziarko, W. Probabilistic rough sets. RSDGRC '2005, Lecture Notes in AI 3641, Springer Verlag, 2005, 283-293.

Zdzisław Pawlak
Commemorating His Life and Work[*]

Zdzisław Pawlak will be remembered as a great human being with exceptional humility, wit and kindness as well as an extraordinarily innovative researcher with exceptional stature. His research contributions have had far-reaching implications inasmuch as his works are fundamental in establishing new perspectives for scientific research in a wide spectrum of fields.

Professor Pawlak's most widely recognized contribution is his brilliant approach to classifying objects with their attributes (features) and his introduction of approximation spaces, which establish the foundations of granular computing and provide frameworks for perception and knowledge discovery in many areas.

Zdzisław Pawlak was born on 10 November 1926 in Łódź, 130 km south-west from Warsaw, Poland[1]. In 1947, Pawlak began his studies in the Faculty of Electrical Engineering at Łódź University of Technology, and in 1949 continued his studies in the Telecommunication Faculty at Warsaw University of Technology. In 1950, he presented in Poland the first project of a computer called GAM 1. He completed his M.Sc. in Telecommunication Engineering in 1951. His publication in 1956 on a new method for random number generation was the first publication abroad in informatics by a researcher from Poland[2]. In 1958, Pawlak completed his doctoral degree from the Institute of Fundamental Technological Research at the Polish Academy of Science with a Thesis on Applications of Graph Theory to Decoder Synthesis. During 1957-1959, Pawlak was also a member of a research team that constructed one of the first computers in Poland called UMC 1. The original arithmetic of this computer with the base "-2" was due to Pawlak. He received his habilitation from the Institute of Mathematics at the Polish Academy of Sciences in 1963. In his habilitation entitled Organization of Address-Less Machines, Pawlak proposed and investigated parenthesis-free languages, a generalization of polish notation introduced by Jan Łukasiewicz[3].

During succeeding years, Pawlak also worked at the Institute of Mathematics at Warsaw University and, in 1965, introduced the foundations for modeling DNA and what has come to be known as molecular computing[4]. He was searching

---

[*] Professor Zdzisław Pawlak, Member of the Polish Academy of Sciences, passed away on 7 April 2006.

[1] Wikipedia summary of the life and work of Z. Pawlak:
`http://pl.wikipedia.org/wiki/Zdzislaw_Pawlak`

[2] Pawlak, Z.: Flip Flop as Generator of Random Binary Digits. Mathematical Tables and Other Aids to Computation 20(53) (1956) 28-30.

[3] Pawlak, Z.: Organization of Address-Less Computers Working in Parenthesis Notation. Zeitschrift für Mathematische Logik und Grundlagen der Mathematik 3 (1965) 243-262; Pawlak, Z.: Organization of Address Less Computers. Polish Scientific Publisher, Warsaw (1965) (the book is in Polish).

[4] Pawlak, Z.: Grammar and Mathematics. (in Polish), PZWS, Warsaw (1965); Gheorghe, M., Mitrana, V.: A formal Language-Based Approach in Biology. Comparative and Functional Genomics 5(1) (2004) 91-94.

S. Greco et al. (Eds.): RSCTC 2006, LNAI 4259, pp. 49–52, 2006.
© Springer-Verlag Berlin Heidelberg 2006

for grammars generating compound biological structures from simpler ones, e.g., proteins from amino acids. He proposed a generalization of traditional grammars used in formal language theory. For example, he considered the construction of mosaics on a plane from some elementary mosaics by using some production rules for the composition. He also presented a language for linear representation of mosaic structures. It was thought that by introducing such grammars, one might better understand protein structure and the processes of their synthesis. Such grammars would give birth to real-life languages to characterize the development of living organisms. Pawlak was interested in developing a formal model of *deoxyribonucleic acid* (DNA), and he proposed a formal model for the genetic code discovered by Crick and Watson. Pawlak's model is regarded by many as the first formal model of DNA. This work on DNA has been cited by others.

Zdzisław Pawlak also proposed a new formal model of a computing machine known as the *Pawlak machine*[5] that is different from the Turing machine and from the von Neumann machine. In 1973, he introduced knowledge representation systems as part of his work on the mathematical foundations of information retrieval [6]. During the early 1980s, he was the head of a research group at the Institute of Computer Science at the Polish Academy of Sciences, where he introduced rough sets and the idea of classifying objects by means of their attributes[7]. Rough set theory has its roots in Zdzisław Pawlak's research on knowledge representation systems during the early 1970s. Rather than attempt exact classification of objects with attributes (features), Pawlak considered an approach to solving the object classification problem in a number of novel ways. First, in 1973, he introduced knowledge representation systems. Then, in 1981,

---

[5] Pawlak, Z.: On the Notion of a Computer. Logic, Methodology and Philosophy of Science 12, North Holland, Amsterdam (1968) 225-242; Pawlak, Z.: Theory of Digital Computers. Mathematical Machines 10 (1969) 4-31; Pawlak, Z.: A Mathematical Model of Digital Computers. Automatentheorie und Formale Sprachen 1973: 16-22; Pawlak, Z., Rozenberg, G., Savitch, W. J.: Programs for Instruction Machines. Information and Control 41(1) (1979) 9-28.

[6] Pawlak, Z.: Mathematical Foundations of Information Retrieval. Proceedings of Symposium of Mathematical Foundations of Computer Science, September 3-8, 1973, High Tartras, 135-136; Pawlak, Z.: Mathematical Foundations of Information Retrieval. Computation Center, Polish Academy of Sciences, Research Report CC PAS Report 101 (1973); Pawlak, Z.: Information Systems Theoretical Foundations. Information Systems 6(3) (1981) 205-218; Pawlak, Z.: Information Systems: Theoretical Foundations. WNT, Warsaw (1983) (the book in Polish); Marek, W., Pawlak, Z.: Information Storage and Retrieval Systems: Mathematical Foundations. Theoretical Computer Science 1 (1976) 331-354.

[7] Pawlak, Z.: Rough Sets. Research Report PAS 431, Institute of Computer Science, Polish Academy of Sciences (1981); Pawlak, Z.: Classification of Objects by Means of Attributes. Research Report PAS 429, Institute of Computer Science, Polish Academy of Sciences, ISSN 138-0648, January (1981); Pawlak, Z.: Rough Sets. International J. Comp. Inform. Science 11 (1982) 341-356; Konrad, E., Orłowska, E., Pawlak, Z.: On Approximate Concept Learning. Report 81-07, Fachbereich Informatik, TU Berlin, Berlin 1981; short version in: Collected Talks, European Conference on Artificial Intelligence 11/5, Orsay/Paris (1982) 17-19.

he introduced approximate descriptions of objects and considered knowledge representation systems in the context of upper and lower classification of objects relative to their attribute values. During the succeeding years, Pawlak refined and amplified the foundations of rough sets and their applications[8] and nurtured worldwide research in rough sets that has led to over 4000 publications[9]. The consequences of this approach to the classification of objects relative to their feature values have been quite remarkable and far-reaching. The work on knowledge representation systems and the notion of elementary sets have profound implications when one considers the problem of approximate reasoning and concept approximation.

Zdzisław Pawlak also invented a new approach to conflict analysis[10].

He has published over 220 scientific papers and supervised over 30 PhD Theses.

For many years, Zdzisław Pawlak had an intense interest in philosophy, especially relative to the connections between rough sets and other forms of sets. It was his venerable habit to point to connections between his own work in rough sets and the works of others in philosophy and mathematics. This is especially true relative to two cardinal notions, namely, sets and vagueness. For the notion of a set, Pawlak calls attention to works by Georg Cantor, Gottlob Frege and Bertrand Russell. Pawlak points out that the notion of a set is not only fundamental for the whole of mathematics but also for natural language, where it is commonplace to speak in terms of collections of such things as books, paintings, people, and their vague properties. In his reflections on structured objects, he points to the work on mereology by Stanisław Leśniewski, where the relation *being a part* replaces the membership relation $\in$[11]. For many years, Pawlak also was interested in vagueness and Gottlob Frege's notion of the boundary of a concept[12]. For Frege, the definition of a concept must unambiguously determine whether or not an object falls under the concept. For a concept without a sharp boundary, one is faced with the problem of determining how close an object must be before it can be said to belong to a concept. Zdzisław Pawlak also points out that mathematics must use crisp, not vague concepts. Hence, mathematics makes

---

[8] see, e.g., Pawlak, Z.: Rough Sets – Theoretical Aspects of Reasoning about Data. Kluwer Academic Publishers, Dordrecht (1991).

[9] see, e.g., Rough Set Database System, `http://rsds.wsiz.rzeszow.pl/pomoc9.html`

[10] Pawlak, Z.: On Conflicts. International Journal of Man Machine Studies 21 (1984) 127-134; Pawlak, Z.: Anatomy of Conflict. Bulletin of the European Association for Theoretical Computer Science 50 (1993) 234-247; Pawlak, Z.: An Inquiry into Anatomy of Conflicts. Journal of Information Sciences 109 (1998) 65-78; Pawlak, Z.: On Conflicts. Polish Sci. Publ., Warsaw (1987) (the book is in Polish).

[11] In 1996, the study of Leśniewski's work has led to rough mereology and the relation *being a part to a degree* (see, e.g., Polkowski, L., Skowron, A.: Rough Mereology: A New Paradigm for Approximate Reasoning. International J. of Approximate Reasoning 15(4) (1996) 333-365).

[12] Frege, G.: Grundgesetzen der Arithmetik, vol. II. Verlag von Hermann Pohle, Jena (1903).

1.1: Treeline Painting by Pawlak

1.2: 1999 Watercape by Pawlak

Fig. 1. Paintings by Zdzisław Pawlak

it possible to reason precisely about approximations of vague concepts. These approximations are temporal and subjective.

Starting in the early 1950s and continuing throughout his life, Zdzisław Pawlak painted the places he visited, especially landscapes and waterscapes of the places he visited in Poland and other parts of the world. A common motif in Pawlak's paintings is the somewhat indefinite separation between objects such as the outer edges of trees and sky (see Fig. 1.1), the outer edges of tree shadows reflected in water and the water itself, and the separation between water and the surrounding land (see Fig. 1.2).

In more recent years, he wrote poems, which are remarkably succinct and very close to his interest in painting. Remarkably, one can find in his theoretical work on rough sets as well as in molecular computing, painting and poetry a common thread, namely, his interest in the border regions of objects that are delineated by considering the attributes (features) of an object.

Professor Zdzisław Pawlak was with us only for a short time and, yet, when we look back at his accomplishments, we realize how greatly he has influenced us with his generous spirit and creative work in many areas such as approximate reasoning, intelligent systems research, computing models, mathematics (especially, rough set theory), molecular computing, pattern recognition, philosophy, art, and poetry.

Zdzisław Pawlak gave generously of his time and energy to help others. His spirit and insights have influenced many researchers worldwide. During his life, he manifested an extraordinary talent for inspiring his students and colleagues as well as many others outside his immediate circle[13].

Andrzej Skowron and James F. Peters

---

[13] The authors wish to thank *all* colleagues who, at various times in the past, have contributed information that has made it possible to write this article.

Pawlak Rough Set Model, Medical Reasoning and Rule Mining

Shusaku Tsumoto

Department of Medical Informatics,
Shimane University, School of Medicine
89-1 Enya-cho, Izumo 693-8501 Japan
`tsumoto@computer.org, hirano@ieee.org`

Abstract. This paper overviews the following two important issues on the correspondence between Pawlak's rough set model and medical reasoning. The first main idea of rough sets is that a given concept can be approximated by partition-based knowledge as upper and lower approximation. Interestingly, thes approximations correspond to the focusing mechanism of differential medical diagnosis; upper approximation as selection of candidates and lower approximation as concluding a final diagnosis. The second idea of rough sets is that a concept, observations can be represented as partitions in a given data set, where rough sets provides a rule induction method from a given data. Thus, this model can be used to extract rule-based knowledge from medical databases. Especially, rule induction based on the focusing mechanism is obtained in a natural way.

1   Introduction

Pawlak shows that knowledge can be captured by data partition and proposes a rough set method where comparison between data partition gives knowledge about classification [1].

Although I thought that Pawlak hit on this concept after the discussion with medical experts from his talk, Pawlak told me that it took a long time for him to reach the idea on rough sets. He had an intuition that an equivalence relation can be applied to computer science, but he had not got the idea on how to achieve it for a long time. I did not ask how long he needs during the conversation, and it was a pity that I cannot ask him again. The discussions with medical experts may be a trigger to rough sets, but the most important turing point is that he captured the idea that an equivalence relation can be regarded as a data partition in a date set, which cannot be overemphasized.

As dedicated to late Professor Pawlak, written for a commemorative session, this paper overviews the following two important issues on the correspondence between Pawlak's rough set model and medical reasoning. The first main idea of rough sets is that a given concept can be approximated by partition-based knowledge as upper and lower approximation. The upper approximation is given by a region which covers all the positive examples, equivalent to the region

S. Greco et al. (Eds.): RSCTC 2006, LNAI 4259, pp. 53–70, 2006.

whose sensitivity of knowledge is equal to 1.0. On the other hand, the lower approximation is given by a region whose accuracy is equal to 1.0, a full positive predictive value. Interestingly, thes approximations correspond to the focusing mechanism of differential medical diagnosis; upper approximation as selection of candidates and lower approximation as concluding a final diagnosis.

The second idea of rough sets is that a concept, observations can be represented as partitions in a given data set, where rough sets provides a rule induction method from a given data. Thus, this model can be used to extract rule-based knowledge from medical databases. Especially, rule induction based on the focusing mechanism is obtained in a natural way. Since the degree of upper and lower approximation can be measured by accuracy and coverage, rule induction method can be achieved by a heuristic search algorithm with two indices, accuracy and coverage.

The paper is organized as follows: Section 2 shows my story, how I encountered rough sets where I met Professor Pawlak. Section 3 provides the brief overview of RHINOS and focusing mechanism. Section 4 presents how rough set gives a framework for automated induction of rules from a given dataset. Section 5 gives an algorithm for mining rules of two diagnosis procedures. Finally, Section 6 concludes this paper.

2   My Story

When I visited a book store *Yaesu Book Center*, which is located near the Tokyo station in 1991, my relationship with rough sets started. I found a Pawlak's book in the bookshelf of foreign books at the 5th floor (In European Style, 6th floor). At a first glance, I feel it very strange, because the subtitle of this book is *Theoretical Aspects of Reasoning About Data*, but the latter half of the book describe many figures and many if-then rules. However, since the title intersts me, I bought Pawlak's book and put it on my desk.

In 1991, I was a neurologist in emergency department of Matsudo City Hospital [2]. Although I had finished my resident course in Chiba University Hospital (one year and half) and Matsudo city hospital and started my career as a neurologist, my mind was occupied by automated knowledge acquisition of if-then rules from data, because I was involved with the project on medical expert system, called *RHINOS* when I was a student of Osaka University, School of Medicine [3] from 1983 to 1989. During this period, I experienced two big movements in Japan. One was the fifth generation computing [4], where logic programming and its programming language, PROLOG, is booming in Japan. We were developing an expert system supporting two-stage differential diagnosis, or focusing mechanism shown in the later section, called RHINOS by using this language, and presented in the conference called *Logic Programming Conference 1985* [5]. During a knowledge acquisition process, interview with an expert of headache, we realized that the differential diagnosis is closely related with set-based reasoning. It suggests that acquisition process should be formalized by using set-theoretical based process. However, we did not have much knowledge at that time. The other one is a rapid progress in hospital information system. When I presented my work on RHINOS at the Jointed conference of Japanese Association of Medical Informatics from 1986 to 1988 , I recognized that all the information in a hospital would be stored as a large database in the near future. Now, twenty years later, this observation came true. Then, I felt that all the knowledge about a hospital can be extracted from the database. Since a database theory is supported by algebra and logic, I thought that knowledge extraction could be achived by using these formal concepts.

On October in 1991, I moved to Division of Medical Informatics, Chiba University Hospital and stated my research on automated knowledge acquisition, which was called rule induction method. Compared with my life in Matsudo City Hospital, I had enough time to read books and started to read Pawlak's book in 1992. When I was reading his book, I was surprised that the theory has a strong concept with the concepts of RHINOS. What an expert on headache had learned from his experience was completely supported by a set-theoretical idea. Moreover, since rough sets give the way how to extract rules from a data, I discovered that this theory can be used to extract RHINOS-based rules from a given datasets. After I read his book, I started to implement my intuition as a PROLOG program, called PRIMEROSE and presented my work to the staff of my division in Chiba University Hospital. However, no one showed his/her interest.

On May in 1993, I moved to Medical Research Institute, Tokyo Medical and Dental University and continued my research on PRIMEROSE [6]. Accidentally, I had found a CFP on RSKD 1993 and sent an email to Dr. Ziarko. He gave me a quick response to my email and encouraged me to send a paper to him, although the deadline had already gone. After he read my paper, he accepted my paper and asked me to come to RSKD in Banff. This conference was very interesting and fruitful, and I really started my career as a *rough setter*.

These communications were my turning point, the most productive one and is still the basis of my research. I met many people: Profs Pawlak, Skowron, Ziarko, Zytkow, Slowinski, Stefanowski, Cercone, Han, T.Y. Lin, Y.Y. Yao and Tony Hu. Without RSKD and Dr. Ziarko's hospitality, my research would have not been so successful; maybe I would neither have received a PhD degree in computer science nor have become a professor of medical informatics. Here, in this opportunity I would like to thank all of my friends for their support, especially, late Professor Z. Pawlak.

3   RHINOS and Focusing Mechanism

3.1   RHINOS

RHINOS is an expert system which diagnoses clinical cases on headache or facial pain from manifestations. In this system, a diagnostic model proposed by Matsumura [3] is applied to the domain, which consists of the following three kinds of reasoning processes: exclusive reasoning, inclusive reasoning, and reasoning about complications.

First, exclusive reasoning excludes a disease from candidates when a patient does not have a symptom which is necessary to diagnose. Secondly, inclusive reasoning suspects a disease in the output of the exclusive process when a patient has symptoms specific to a disease. Finally, reasoning about complications suspects complications of other diseases when some symptoms which cannot be explained by the diagnostic conclusion obtained.

Each reasoning is rule-based, and all the rules needed for diagnostic processes are acquired from medical experts in the following way.

(1)Exclusive Rules. This rule corresponds to exclusive reasoning. In other words, the premise of this rule is equivalent to the necessity condition of a diagnostic conclusion. From the discussion with medical experts, we select the following six basic attributes which are minimally indispensable to defining the necessity condition: *1. Age, 2. Pain location, 3. Nature of the pain, 4. Severity of the pain, 5. History since onset, 6. Existence of jolt headache.* For example, the exclusive rule of common migraine is defined as:

```
In order to suspect common migraine,
the following symptoms are required:
pain location: not eyes,
nature :throbbing or persistent or radiating,
history: paroxysmal or sudden and
jolt headache: positive.
```

One of the reason why we select the six attributes is to solve the interface problem of expert systems: if the whole attributes are considered, we also have to input all the symptoms which are not needed for diagnosis. To make exclusive reasoning compact, the only minimal requirements are chosen. It is notable that this kind of selection can be viewed as the ordering of given attributes, and it is expected that such ordering can be induced from databases. Therefore we intend to formulate induction of exclusive rules by using the whole given attributes. It is because we can acquire the minimal requirements for describing exclusive rules after all the exclusive rules are induced.

(2)Inclusive Rules. The premises of inclusive rules are composed of a set of manifestations specific to a disease to be included. If a patient satisfies one set, we suspect this disease with some probability. This rule is derived by asking the following items for each disease to the medical experts: *1. a set of manifestations by which we strongly suspect a disease. 2. the probability that a patient has the disease with this set of manifestations:SI(Satisfactory Index) 3. the ratio of the patients who satisfy the set to all the patients of this disease:CI(Covering Index) 4. If the total sum of the derived CI(tCI) is equal to 1.0 then end. Otherwise, goto 5. 5. For the patients of this disease who do not satisfy all the collected set of manifestations, goto 1.* Therefore a positive rule is described by a set of manifestations, its satisfactory index (SI), which corresponds to *accuracy measure*, and its covering index (CI), which corresponds to *total positive rate*. Note that SI and CI are given empirically by medical experts.

For example, one of three positive rules for common migraine is given as follows.

```
If history: paroxysmal, jolt headache: yes,
nature: throbbing or persistent,
prodrome: no, intermittent symptom: no,
persistent time: more than 6 hours,
and location: not eye,
then common migraine is suspected with
accuracy 0.9 (SI=0.9) and this rule covers
60 percent of the total cases (CI=0.6).
```

3.2   Focusing Mechanism

One of the characteristics in medical reasoning is a focusing mechanism, which is used to select the final diagnosis from many candidates [7,8]. For example, in differential diagnosis of headache, more than 60 diseases will be checked by present history, physical examinations and laboratory examinations. In diagnostic procedures, a candidate is excluded if a symptom necessary to diagnose is not observed.

This style of reasoning consists of the following two kinds of reasoning processes: exclusive reasoning and inclusive reasoning. Relations of this diagnostic model with another diagnostic model are discussed in [9]. The diagnostic procedure will proceed as follows (Figure 1): first, exclusive reasoning excludes a disease from candidates when a patient does not have a symptom which is necessary to diagnose that disease. Secondly, inclusive reasoning suspects a disease in the output of the exclusive process when a patient has symptoms specific to a disease. These two steps are modelled as usage of two kinds of rules, negative rules (or exclusive rules) and positive rules, the former of which corresponds to exclusive reasoning and the latter of which corresponds to inclusive reasoning. In the next two subsections, these two rules are represented as special kinds of probabilistic rules.

4   Definition of Rules

4.1   Rough Sets

In the following sections, we use the following notations introduced by Grzymala-Busse and Skowron [10], which are based on rough set theory [1]. These notations are illustrated by a small dataset shown in Table 1, which includes symptoms exhibited by six patients who complained of headache.

Let U denote a nonempty, finite set called the universe and A denote a nonempty, finite set of attributes, i.e., $a : U \rightarrow V_a$ for $a \in A$, where V_a is called the domain of a, respectively. Then, a decision table is defined as an information system, $A = (U, A \cup \{d\})$. For example, Table 1 is an information system with $U = \{1, 2, 3, 4, 5, 6\}$ and $A = \{age, location, nature, prodrome, nausea, M1\}$ and $d = class$. For $location \in A$, $V_{location}$ is defined as $\{occular, lateral, whole\}$.

The atomic formulae over $B \subseteq A \cup \{d\}$ and V are expressions of the form $[a = v]$, called descriptors over B, where $a \in B$ and $v \in V_a$. The set $F(B, V)$ of

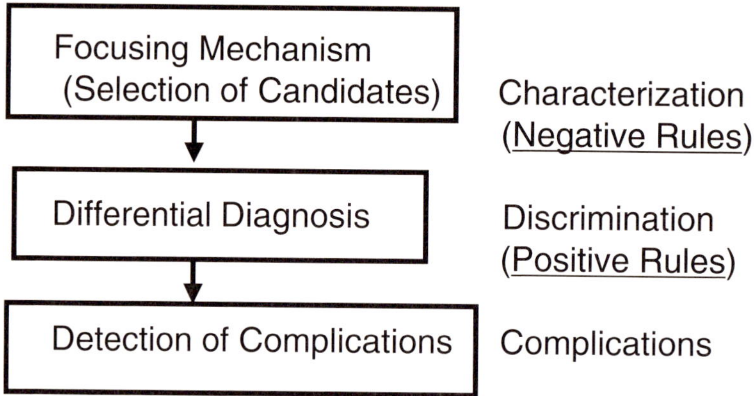

Fig. 1. Illustration of Focusing Mechanism

Table 1. An Example of Dataset

No.	age	location	nature	prodrome	nausea	M1	class
1	50-59	occular	persistent	no	no	yes	m.c.h.
2	40-49	whole	persistent	no	no	yes	m.c.h.
3	40-49	lateral	throbbing	no	yes	no	migra
4	40-49	whole	throbbing	yes	yes	no	migra
5	40-49	whole	radiating	no	no	yes	m.c.h.
6	50-59	whole	persistent	no	yes	yes	psycho

DEFINITIONS. M1: tenderness of M1, m.c.h.: muscle contraction headache, migra: migraine, psycho: psychological pain.

formulas over B is the least set containing all atomic formulas over B and closed with respect to disjunction, conjunction and negation. For example, $[location = occular]$ is a descriptor of B.

For each $f \in F(B, V)$, f_A denote the meaning of f in A, i.e., the set of all objects in U with property f, defined inductively as follows.

1. If f is of the form $[a = v]$ then, $f_A = \{s \in U | a(s) = v\}$
2. $(f \wedge g)_A = f_A \cap g_A$; $(f \vee g)_A = f_A \vee g_A$; $(\neg f)_A = U - f_a$

For example, $f = [location = whole]$ and $f_A = \{2, 4, 5, 6\}$. As an example of a conjunctive formula, $g = [location = whole] \wedge [nausea = no]$ is a descriptor of U and f_A is equal to $g_{location,nausea} = \{2, 5\}$.

4.2   Classification Accuracy and Coverage

Definition of Accuracy and Coverage. By the use of the framework above, classification accuracy and coverage, or true positive rate is defined as follows.

Definition 1. *Let R and D denote a formula in $F(B,V)$ and a set of objects which belong to a decision d. Classification accuracy and coverage(true positive rate) for $R \to d$ is defined as:*

$$\alpha_R(D) = \frac{|R_A \cap D|}{|R_A|} (= P(D|R)), \quad and$$

$$\kappa_R(D) = \frac{|R_A \cap D|}{|D|} (= P(R|D)),$$

where $|S|$, $\alpha_R(D)$, $\kappa_R(D)$ and $P(S)$ denote the cardinality of a set S, a classification accuracy of R as to classification of D and coverage (a true positive rate of R to D), and probability of S, respectively.

Figure 2 depicts the Venn diagram of relations between accuracy and coverage. Accuracy views the overlapped region $|R_A \cap D|$ from the meaning of a relation R. On the other hand, coverage views the overlapped region from the meaning of a concept D.

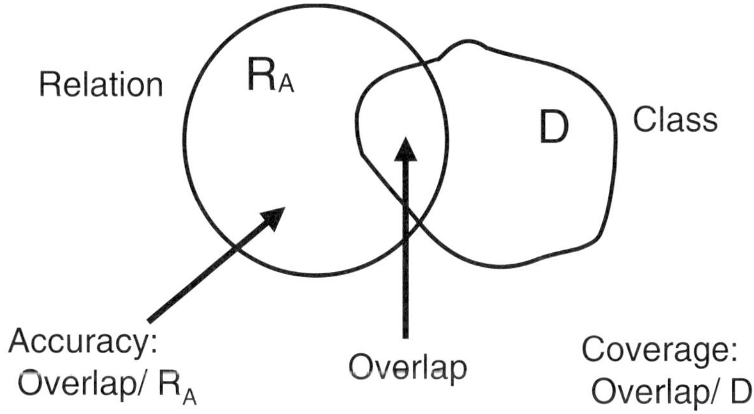

Fig. 2. Venn Diagram of Accuracy and Coverage

In the above example, when R and D are set to $[nau = yes]$ and $[class = migraine]$, $\alpha_R(D) = 2/3 = 0.67$ and $\kappa_R(D) = 2/2 = 1.0$.

It is notable that $\alpha_R(D)$ measures the degree of the sufficiency of a proposition, $R \to D$, and that $\kappa_R(D)$ measures the degree of its necessity. For example, if $\alpha_R(D)$ is equal to 1.0, then $R \to D$ is true. On the other hand, if $\kappa_R(D)$ is equal to 1.0, then $D \to R$ is true. Thus, if both measures are 1.0, then $R \leftrightarrow D$.

4.3   Probabilistic Rules

By the use of accuracy and coverage, a probabilistic rule is defined as:

$$R \xrightarrow{\alpha, \kappa} d \quad s.t. \ R = \wedge_j [a_j = v_k], \alpha_R(D) \geq \delta_\alpha$$
$$\text{and } \kappa_R(D) \geq \delta_\kappa,$$

If the thresholds for accuracy and coverage are set to high values, the meaning of the conditional part of probabilistic rules corresponds the highly overlapped region. Figure 3 depicts the Venn diagram of probabilistic rules with highly overlapped region. This rule is a kind of probabilistic proposition with

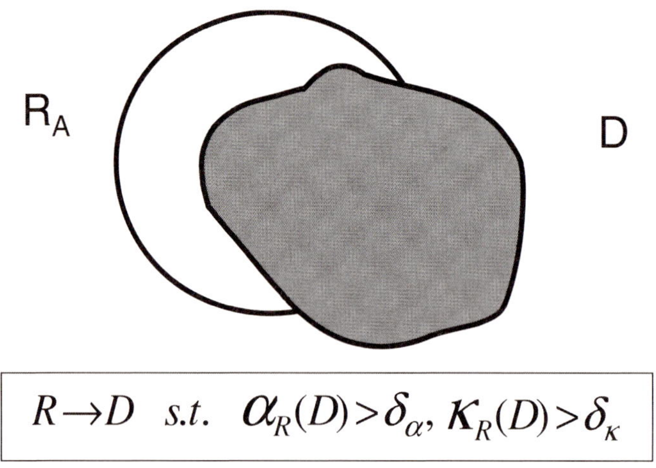

Fig. 3. Venn Diagram for Probabilistic Rules

two statistical measures, which is an extension of Ziarko's variable precision model(VPRS) [11].[1]

It is also notable that both a positive rule and a negative rule are defined as special cases of this rule, as shown in the next subsections.

4.4   Positive Rules

A positive rule is defined as a rule supported by only positive examples, the classification accuracy of which is equal to 1.0. It is notable that the set supporting this rule corresponds to a subset of the lower approximation of a target concept, which is introduced in rough sets [1]. Thus, a positive rule is represented as:

$$R \rightarrow d \quad s.t. \qquad R = \wedge_j [a_j = v_k], \quad \alpha_R(D) = 1.0$$

Figure 4 shows the Venn diagram of a positive rule. As shown in this figure, the meaning of R is a subset of that of D. This diagram is exactly equivalent to the classic proposition $R \rightarrow d$. In the above example, one positive rule of "m.c.h." (muscle contraction headache) is:

$$[nausea = no] \rightarrow m.c.h. \quad \alpha = 3/3 = 1.0.$$

This positive rule is often called a deterministic rule. However, in this paper, we use a term, positive (deterministic) rules, because a deterministic rule which

---

[1] This probabilistic rule is also a kind of *Rough Modus Ponens* [12].

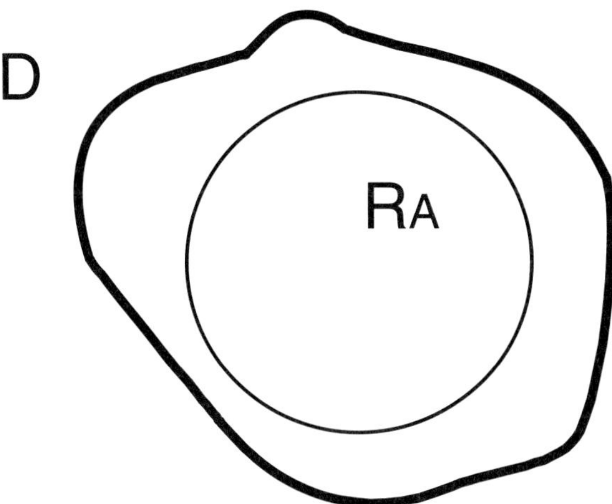

Fig. 4. Venn Diagram of Positive Rules

is supported only by negative examples, called a negative rule, is introduced as in the next subsection.

4.5   Negative Rules

Before defining a negative rule, let us first introduce an exclusive rule, the contrapositive of a negative rule [7]. An exclusive rule is defined as a rule supported by all the positive examples, the coverage of which is equal to 1.0. That is, an exclusive rule represents the necessity condition of a decision. It is notable that the set supporting an exclusive rule corresponds to the upper approximation of a target concept, which is introduced in rough sets [1]. Thus, an exclusive rule is represented as:

$$R \rightarrow d \quad s.t. \qquad R = \vee_j [a_j = v_k], \quad \kappa_R(D) = 1.0.$$

Figure 4 shows the Venn diagram of a exclusive rule. As shown in this figure, the meaning of R is a superset of that of D. This diagram is exactly equivalent to the classic proposition $d \rightarrow R$. In the above example, the exclusive rule of "m.c.h." is:

$$[M1 = yes] \vee [nau = no] \rightarrow m.c.h. \quad \kappa = 1.0,$$

From the viewpoint of propositional logic, an exclusive rule should be represented as:

$$d \rightarrow \vee_j [a_j = v_k],$$

because the condition of an exclusive rule corresponds to the necessity condition of conclusion d. Thus, it is easy to see that a negative rule is defined as the contrapositive of an exclusive rule:

$$\wedge_j \neg [a_j = v_k] \rightarrow \neg d,$$

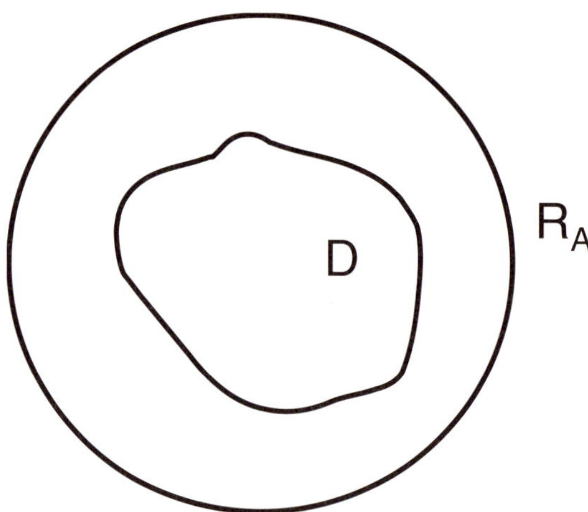

Fig. 5. Venn Diagram of Exclusive Rules

which means that if a case does not satisfy any attribute value pairs in the condition of a negative rules, then we can exclude a decision d from candidates. For example, the negative rule of m.c.h. is:

$$\neg[M1 = yes] \wedge \neg[nausea = no] \rightarrow \neg m.c.h.$$

In summary, a negative rule is defined as:

$$\wedge_j \neg[a_j = v_k] \rightarrow \neg d \quad s.t. \quad \forall[a_j = v_k] \; \kappa_{[a_j=v_k]}(D) = 1.0,$$

where D denotes a set of samples which belong to a class d. Figure 6 shows the Venn diagram of a negative rule. As shown in this figure, it is notable that this negative region is the "positive region" of "negative concept".

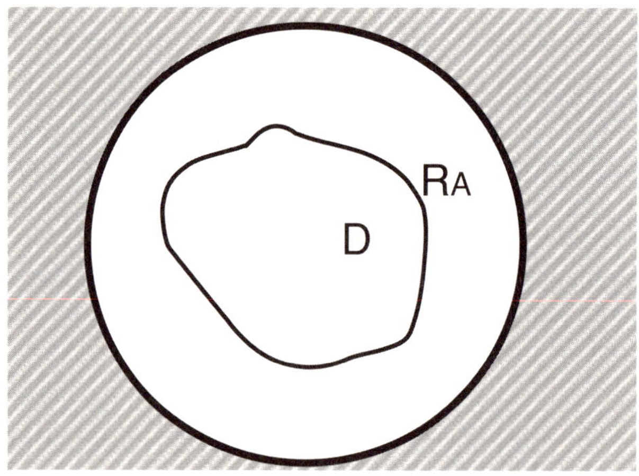

Fig. 6. Venn Diagram of Negative Rules

Negative rules should be also included in a category of deterministic rules, since their coverage, a measure of negative concepts is equal to 1.0. It is also notable that the set supporting a negative rule corresponds to a subset of negative region, which is introduced in rough sets [1].

In summary, positive and negative rules corresponds to positive and negative regions defined in rough sets. Figure 7 shows the Venn diagram of those rules.

5 Algorithms for Rule Induction

The contrapositive of a negative rule, an exclusive rule is induced as an exclusive rule by the modification of the algorithm introduced in PRIMEROSE-REX [7], as shown in Figure 8. This algorithm will work as follows. (1)First, it selects a descriptor $[a_i = v_j]$ from the list of attribute-value pairs, denoted by L. (2) Then, it checks whether this descriptor overlaps with a set of positive examples, denoted by D. (3) If so, this descriptor is included into a list of candidates for positive rules and the algorithm checks whether its coverage is equal to 1.0 or not. If the coverage is equal to 1.0, then this descriptor is added to $R_e r$, the formula for the conditional part of the exclusive rule of D. (4) Then, $[a_i = v_j]$ is deleted from the list L. This procedure, from (1) to (4) will continue unless L is empty. (5) Finally, when L is empty, this algorithm generates negative rules by taking the contrapositive of induced exclusive rules.

On the other hand, positive rules are induced as inclusive rules by the algorithm introduced in PRIMEROSE-REX [7], as shown in Figure 9. For induction of positive rules, the threshold of accuracy and coverage is set to 1.0 and 0.0, respectively.

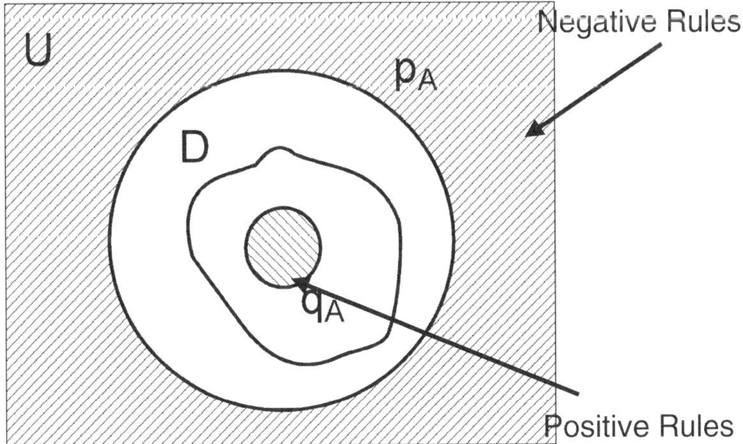

Fig. 7. Positive and Negative Rules as Overview

This algorithm works in the following way. (1) First, it substitutes L_1, which denotes a list of formula composed of only one descriptor, with the list L_{er} generated by the former algorithm shown in Fig. 1. (2) Then, until L_1 becomes empty, the following procedures will continue: (a) A formula $[a_i = v_j]$ is removed from L_1. (b) Then, the algorithm checks whether $\alpha_R(D)$ is larger than the threshold or not. (For induction of positive rules, this is equal to checking whether $\alpha_R(D)$ is equal to 1.0 or not.) If so, then this formula is included a list of the conditional part of positive rules. Otherwise, it will be included into M, which is used for making conjunction. (3) When L_1 is empty, the next list L_2 is generated from the list M.

6 From the Empirical Results: Hierarchical Rules for Decision Support

6.1 Sec: Extension

Empirical validations of rule induction methods are shown in [9]. However, these empirical results are not sufficient to extract "plausible" rules.

For example, rule induction methods introduced in this paper induce the following common rule for muscle contraction headache from databases on differential diagnosis of headache:

$$[location = whole] \wedge [\text{Jolt Headache} = no] \wedge [\text{Tenderness of M1} = yes]$$
$$\rightarrow \text{muscle contraction headache.}$$

This rule is shorter than the following rule given by medical experts.

$[\text{Jolt Headache} = no]$
$\wedge([\text{Tenderness of M0} = yes] \vee [\text{Tenderness of M1} = yes]$
$\qquad \vee [\text{Tenderness of M2} = yes])$
$\wedge [\text{Tenderness of B1} = no] \wedge [\text{Tenderness of B2} = no] \wedge [\text{Tenderness of B3} = no]$
$\wedge [\text{Tenderness of C1} = no] \wedge [\text{Tenderness of C2} = no] \wedge [\text{Tenderness of C3} = no]$
$\wedge [\text{Tenderness of C4} = no]$
$\qquad \rightarrow \text{muscle contraction headache}$

These results suggest that conventional rule induction methods do not reflect a mechanism of knowledge acquisition of medical experts.

$[\text{Jolt Headache} = no]$
$\wedge([\text{Tenderness of M0} = yes] \vee [\text{Tenderness of M1} = yes]$
$\qquad \vee [\text{Tenderness of M2} = yes])$
$\wedge [\text{Tenderness of B1} = no] \wedge [\text{Tenderness of B2} = no]$
$\qquad \wedge [\text{Tenderness of B3} = no]$
$\qquad \wedge [\text{Tenderness of C1} = no] \wedge [\text{Tenderness of C2} = no]$
$\qquad \wedge [\text{Tenderness of C3} = no] \wedge [\text{Tenderness of C4} = no]$
$\qquad \rightarrow \text{muscle contraction headache}$

This rule is very similar to the following classification rule for disease of cervical spine:

procedure *Exclusive and Negative Rules*;
  var
    $L : List$;
      /* A list of elementary attribute-value pairs */
  begin
    $L := P_0$;
    /* P_0: A list of elementary attribute-value pairs given in a database */
    while $(L \neq \{\})$ **do**
      begin
        Select one pair $[a_i = v_j]$ from L;
        if $([a_i = v_j]_A \cap D \neq \phi)$ **then do** /* D: positive examples of a target class d */
          begin
            $L_{ir} := L_{ir} + [a_i = v_j]$;   /* Candidates for Positive Rules */
            if $(\kappa_{[a_i=v_j]}(D) = 1.0)$
            then $R_{er} := R_{er} \wedge [a_i = v_j]$;
              /* Include $[a_i = v_j]$ into the formula of Exclusive Rule */
          end
       $L := L - [a_i = v_j]$;
      end
    Construct Negative Rules:
      Take the contrapositive of R_{er}.
  end *{Exclusive and Negative Rules}*;

Fig. 8. Induction of Exclusive and Negative Rules

procedure *Positive Rules*;
  var
    $i : integer$; $M, L_i : List$;
  begin
    $L_1 := L_{ir}$;
    /* L_{ir}: A list of candidates generated by induction of exclusive rules */
    $i := 1$; $M := \{\}$;
    for $i := 1$ **to** n **do**
    /* n: Total number of attributes given
      in a database */
      begin
        while $(L_i \neq \{\})$ **do**
          begin
            Select one pair $R = \wedge[a_i = v_j]$ from L_i;
            $L_i := L_i - \{R\}$;
            if $(\alpha_R(D) > \delta_\alpha)$
              then **do** $S_{ir} := S_{ir} + \{R\}$;
          /* Include R in a list of the Positive Rules */
             else $M := M + \{R\}$;
          end
        $L_{i+1} := $ (A list of the whole combination of the conjunction formulae in M);
      end
  end *{Positive Rules}*;

Fig. 9. Induction of Positive Rules

[Jolt Headache $= no$]
$\wedge$([Tenderness of M0 $= yes$] $\vee$ [Tenderness of M1 $= yes$]
$\vee$[Tenderness of M2 $= yes$])
$\wedge$([Tenderness of B1 $= yes$] $\vee$ [Tenderness of B2 $= yes$]
$\vee$[Tenderness of B3 $= yes$]
$\vee$[Tenderness of C1 $= yes$] $\vee$ [Tenderness of C2 $= yes$]
$\vee$[Tenderness of C3 $= yes$] $\vee$[Tenderness of C4 $= yes$])
$\rightarrow$ disease of cervical spine

As shown in [9], rules acquired from medical experts are much longer than those induced from databases the decision attributes of which are given by the same experts. This is because rule induction methods generally search for shorter rules, compared with decision tree induction. In the case of decision tree induction, the induced trees are sometimes too deep and in order for the trees to be learningful, pruning and examination by experts are required. One of the main reasons why rules are short and decision trees are sometimes long is that these patterns are generated only by one criteria, such as high accuracy or high information gain. The comparative study in this section suggests that experts should acquire rules not only by one criteria but by the usage of several measures. Those characteristics of medical experts' rules are fully examined not by comparing between those rules for the same class, but by comparing experts' rules with those for another class. For example, a classification rule for muscle contraction headache is given by:

The differences between these two rules are attribute-value pairs, from tenderness of B1 to C4. Thus, these two rules are composed of the following three blocks:

$$A_1 \wedge A_2 \wedge \neg A_3 \rightarrow muscle\ contraction\ headache$$
$$A_1 \wedge A_2 \wedge A_3 \rightarrow disease\ of\ cervical\ spine,$$

where A_1, A_2 and A_3 are given as the following formulae:
$A_1 = $ [Jolt Headache $= no$], $A_2 = $ [Tenderness of M0 $= yes$] $\vee$ [Tenderness of $M1 = yes$] $\vee$ [Tenderness of M2 $= yes$], and $A_3 = $ [Tenderness of C1 $= no$] $\wedge$ [Tenderness of C2 $= no$] $\wedge$ [Tenderness of C3 $= no$] $\wedge$ [Tenderness of C4 $= no$]. The first two blocks (A_1 and A_2) and the third one (A_3) represent the different types of differential diagnosis. The first one A_1 shows the discrimination between muscular type and vascular type of headache. Then, the second part shows that between headache caused by neck and head muscles. Finally, the third formula A_3 is used to make a differential diagnosis between muscle contraction headache and disease of cervical spine. Thus, medical experts first select several diagnostic candidates, which are very similar to each other, from many diseases and then make a final diagnosis from those candidates.

This problem has been solved and reported in [13, 14], where Tsumoto introdouced as induction of hierarchical decision rules.

In [14], the characteristics of experts' rules are closely examined from the viewpoint of hiearchical decision steps. Then, extraction of diagnostic taxonomoy from medical datasets is introduced, which consists of the following three procedures. First, the characterization set of each decision attribute (a given class) is extracted from databases. Then, similarities between characterization sets are calculated. Finally, the concept hierarchy for given classes is calculated from the similarity values.

6.2   Rule Induction with Diagnostic Taxonomy

Intuitive Ideas. When the coverage of R for a target concept D is equal to 1.0, R is a necessity condition of D. That is, a proposition $D \rightarrow R$ holds and its contrapositive $\neg R \rightarrow \neg D$ holds. Thus, if R is not observed, D cannot be a candidate of a target concept. Thus, if two target concepts have a common formula R whose coverage is equal to 1.0, then $\neg R$ supports the negation of two concepts, which means these two concepts belong to the same group. Furthermore, if two target concepts have similar formulae $R_i, R_j \in L_{1.0}(D)$, they are very close to each other with respect to the negation of two concepts. In this case, the attribute-value pairs in the intersection of $L_{1.0}(D_i)$ and $L_{1.0}(D_j)$ give a characterization set of the concept that unifies D_i and D_j, D_k. Then, compared with D_k and other target concepts, classification rules for D_k can be

```
procedure Grouping ;
  var inputs
      Lc : List; /* A list of Characterization Sets */
      Lid : List; /* A list of Intersection */
      Ls : List; /* A list of Similarity */
  var outputs
      Lgr : List; /* A list of Grouping */
  var
      k : integer;        Lg, Lgr : List;
  begin
      Lg := {} ;
      k := n
      /* n: A number of Target Concepts*/
      Sort Ls with respect to similarities;
        Take a set of (Di, Dj), Lmax with maximum similarity values;
        k:= k+1;
        forall (Di, Dj) ∈ Lmax do
          begin
            Group Di and Dj into Dk;
              Lc := Lc − {(Di, L1.0(Di)};
                Lc := Lc − {(Dj, L1.0(Dj)};
                Lc := Lc + {(Dk, L1.0(Dk)};
                Update Lid for DDk;
                Update Ls;
              Lgr := (Grouping for Lc, Lid, and Ls) ;
                Lg := Lg + {{(Dk, Di, Dj), Lg}};
          end
      return  Lg;
  end {Grouping}
```

Fig. 10. An Algorithm for Grouping

obtained. When we have a sequence of grouping, classification rules for a given target concepts are defined as a sequence of subrules.

Algorithms. From these ideas, a rule induction algorithm with grouping target concepts can be described as a combination of grouping (Figure 10) and rule induction(Figure 11).

```
procedure RuleInduction ;
  var inputs
    L_c : List; /* A list of Characterization Sets */
    L_id : List; /* A list of Intersection */
    L_g : List; /* A list of grouping*/ /* {{(D_{n+1},D_i,D_j),{(DD_{n+2},.)...}}} */
    /* n: A number of Target Concepts */
  var
    Q, L_r : List;
  begin
    Q := L_g; L_r := {};
    if  (Q ≠ ∅) then do
      begin
        Q := Q − first(Q);
        L_r := Rule Induction (L_c, L_id, Q);
      end
    (DD_k, D_i, D_j) := first(Q);
    if (D_i ∈ L_c and D_j ∈ L_c) then do
      begin
        Induce a Rule r which discriminate between D_i and D_j;
        r = {R_i → D_i, R_j → D_j};
      end
    else do
      begin
        Search for L_{1.0}(D_i) from L_c;
        Search for L_{1.0}(D_j) from L_c;
        if (i < j) then do
          begin
            r(D_i) := ∨_{R_l∈L_{1.0}(D_j)}¬R_l → ¬D_j;
            r(D_j) := ∧_{R_l∈L_{1.0}(D_j)}R_l → D_j;
          end
        r := {r(D_i), r(D_j)};
      end
    return L_r := {r, L_r} ;
  end {Rule Induction}
```

Fig. 11. An Algorithm for Rule Induction

Pawlak's rough set model corresponds to two-stage differential diagnosis. Then, do we have a model corresponding to multi-stage differential diagnosis ? It will be my future work.

7   Conclusions

This paper discusses the correspondence between Pawlak's rough set model and medical reasoning (two-stage differential diagnosis) and how this idea extends to multi-stage differential diagnosis.

Interestingly, upper and lower approximaiton correspond to the focusing mechanism of differential medical diagnosis; the former approximation as selection of candidates, called characterization and the latter approximation as concluding a final diagnosis, called differentiation. Furthermore, since rough sets provides a rule induction method from a given data, it can be used to extract rule-based knowledge from medical databases. Especially, rule induction based on the focusing mechanism is obtained in a natural way. Since the degree of upper and lower approximation can be measured by accuracy and coverage, rule induction method can be achieved by a heuristic search algorithm with two indices, accuracy and coverage.

From empirical validations of this algorithms and comparison with experts' knowledge, we discovered that expert's reasoning is not two-stage, but multi-stage differential diagnosis. This leads to the extension of rule induction method, called rule induction with diagnostic taxonomy.

Although empirical validations give sufficient performance of the extended algorithms, a corresponding formal model for diagnosis has not been obtained. It will be my future work to investigate the formalization of multi-stage differential diagnosis from set-theoretical viewpoint.

This paper is dedicated to late Professor Pawlak, which overviews my research from 1992 to 2004.

References

1. Pawlak, Z.: Rough Sets. Kluwer Academic Publishers, Dordrecht (1991)
2. Matsudo city hospital (in japanese). (`http:/http://www.intership.ne.jp/~matuhosp/`)
3. Matsumura, Y., Matsunaga, T., Hata, Y., Kimura, M., Matsumura, H.: Consultation system for diagnoses of headache and facial pain: Rhinos. Medical Informatics **11** (1988) 147–157
4. Icot archive. (`http://www.icot.or.jp/English-HomePage.html`)
5. Matsumura, Y., Matsunaga, T., Maeda, Y., Tsumoto, S., Matsumura, H., Kimura, M.: Consultation system for diagnosis of headache and facial pain: "rhinos". In Wada, E., ed.: LP. Volume 221 of Lecture Notes in Computer Science., Springer (1985) 287–298
6. Tsumoto, S., Tanaka, H.: Primerose: Probabilistic rule induction method based on rough set theory. In Ziarko, W., ed.: RSKD. Workshops in Computing, Springer (1993) 274–281
7. Tsumoto, S., Tanaka, H.: Automated discovery of medical expert system rules from clinical databases based on rough sets. In: Proceedings of the Second International Conference on Knowledge Discovery and Data Mining 96, Palo Alto, AAAI Press (1996) 63–69

8. Tsumoto, S.: Modelling medical diagnostic rules based on rough sets. In Polkowski, L., Skowron, A., eds.: Rough Sets and Current Trends in Computing. Volume 1424 of Lecture Notes in Computer Science., Springer (1998) 475–482

9. Tsumoto, S.: Automated extraction of medical expert system rules from clinical databases on rough set theory. Inf. Sci. **112**(1-4) (1998) 67–84

10. Skowron, A., Grzymala-Busse, J.: From rough set theory to evidence theory. In Yager, R., Fedrizzi, M., Kacprzyk, J., eds.: Advances in the Dempster-Shafer Theory of Evidence. John Wiley & Sons, New York (1994) 193–236

11. Ziarko, W.: Variable precision rough set model. J. Comput. Syst. Sci. **46**(1) (1993) 39–59

12. Pawlak, Z.: Rough modus ponens. In: Proceedings of International Conference on Information Processing and Management of Uncertainty in Knowledge-Based Systems 98, Paris (1998)

13. Tsumoto, S.: Extraction of experts' decision rules from clinical databases using rough set model. Intelligent Data Analysis **2**(3) (1998)

14. Tsumoto, S.: Extraction of structure of medical diagnosis from clinical data. Fundam. Inform. **59**(2-3) (2004) 271–285

Algebras of Terms
in Pawlak's Information Systems

J.A. Pomykała

WSM, Warsaw, Poland

Abstract. The notion of information system can be seen as a semantic system, but essentially algebraical in the nature. We show in this note, that it can be treated as a many sorted algebra and that the algebra of terms can be useful in describing and analysing the data in the system.

1 Many Sorted Algebra

In this chapter we recall some basic algebraic notions. We follow Mainke, Tucker [1] and Pomykała [3]. Let me recall first that information system (in the sense of Pawlak) is the following 4-tuple: (O, A, V, f), where O is a set of objects, A is a set of attributes, V is a set of values of attributes, f is a function $f : O \times A \to V$. $V = \{V_a : a \in A\}$ where V_a is a set of values of the attribute a. By the extended system we mean the 3-sorted algebra $(O, A, V, f_1 \ldots f_n)$, where each $f_i : O \times A \to V$.

With every system we can connect approximation algebra

$$\mathrm{Apr} = (\mathbb{O}, \mathbb{E}_1, \ldots, \mathbb{E}_m)(O_p)$$

where $\mathbb{E}_i$ are families of sets of objects and O_p is a set of operations defined using families $\mathbb{E}_i$ and which can be interpreted as an approximation operations.

If the operation F_i is defined only by using elements from the family $\mathbb{E}_k$, we use the symbol $F_i^{(k)}$ or $F_i^{\mathbb{E}_k}$. If the operation $F_i \in O_p$ is defined on the base of families $\mathbb{E}_{i_1}, \ldots, \mathbb{E}_{i_m}$, then we shall write $F_i \in O_p$ and $F_i = F_i^{(i_1, \ldots, i_m)}$.

Example 1.1. Let $\mathbb{E}_1$ be a partition of the family of objects $\mathbb{O}$. Let $\underline{\mathbb{E}}_1$ and $\overline{\mathbb{E}}_1$ be lover and upper approximation operations in the sense of Pawlak. Then $(\mathbb{O}, \underline{\mathbb{E}}_1, \overline{\mathbb{E}}_1)$ is approximation space and the development of the algebra of terms in the respective algebra can be seen as a way to the definition of rough sets.

Example 1.2. Let $\mathbb{E}_1$ be a cover of the family of objects ϑ. Let me recall that I have defined the following operations (cf. [2]) related to $\mathbb{E}_1$: $\underline{I}_1$, $\underline{\mathbb{E}}_1, \underline{\vartheta}_1, \underline{\mathbb{C}}_1$ which are called lower operations related to Kernels, covers, similarity neighbourhoods and connectivity sets, and $\overline{I}_1$, $\overline{\mathbb{E}}_1, \overline{\vartheta}_1, \overline{\mathbb{C}}_1$ which are upper operations (defined dually to lower operations).

In this context the term algebra gives the possibility to find all subsets of the family of objects $\mathbb{O}$, which are in some sense regular or well described. It shows also that the family of rough sets is a special case of this algebra, namely when $\mathbb{E}_i$ are partitions of $\mathbb{O}$.

S. Greco et al. (Eds.): RSCTC 2006, LNAI 4259, pp. 71–76, 2006.

1.1 Algebras of Information Systems

Let the system (O,A,V,F) be given. We connect with it the following algebra A; but first we define the signature Σ:

i) A non-empty set $S = \{O, A, V\}$, the elements of which are called sorts.

ii) An $S^* \times S$ indexed family

$$\langle \Sigma_{w,s} \big| w \in S^*, \ s \in S \rangle$$

of sets, where for the empty word $\lambda \in S^*$ and any sort $s \in S$, each element $c \in \Sigma_{\lambda,s}$ is called a constant symbol of sort s; and for each non-empty word $w = s(1), \dots, s(n) \in S^+$ and sort $s \in S$, each element $\sigma \in \Sigma_{w,s}$ is called an operation or function symbol of type (w, s), sometimes we term w the domain type and n the arity of σ.

Thus we define Σ to be the pair

$$(S, \langle \Sigma_{w,s} : w \in S^*, \ s \in S \rangle).$$

In the sequel we often assume the simple case: $w \in O \times A$ and $s \in V$.

Definition 1.1. B is said to be a Σ subalgebra of A if,and only if, for each sort $s \in S$, $B_s \subseteq A_s$; for each sort $s \in S$ and each constant symbol $c \in \Sigma_{\lambda,s}$, $c_B = c_A$; and for each sort $s \in S$, and non-empty word $w = s(1), \dots, s(n) \in S^+$, and function symbol $\sigma \in \Sigma_{w,s}$ and any $(b_1, b_2, \dots, b_n) \in B^w$ $\sigma_B(b_1, \dots, b_n) = \sigma_A(b_1, \dots, b_n)$.

We write $B \leq A$, if B is a proper subalgebra we write $B < A$.

Definition 1.2. A class K of Σ algebras is said to be closed under the formation of subalgebras iff, whenever $A \in K$ and $B \leq A$ then $B \in K$.

Definition 1.3. Let A be any Σ algebra and $X \subseteq A$ be any subset of A. The subset $\langle X \rangle_A$ of A generated by X is the set $\langle X \rangle_A = \bigcap \{B : X \subseteq B \text{ and } B \leq A\}$ (one-sorted case).

Let me assume that direct product of algebras is defined in the standard way. We recall also that with A, B we associate families of projection functions:

$$U^A = \langle U_s^A : (A \times B)_s \to A_s, \ s \in S \rangle$$

$$U^B = \langle U_s^B : (A \times B)_s \to B_s, \ s \in S \rangle$$

defined by

$$U_s^A(a, b) = a, \quad U_s^B(a, b) = b$$

for each sort $s \in S$ and each pair (a, b). The families U^A, U^B are Σ homomorphisms.

Definition 1.4. Let $\equiv^\phi$, $\equiv^\theta$ be any Σ congruences on a Σ algebra A such that $\equiv^\theta \subseteq \equiv^\phi$. We define the factor congruence $\equiv^{\phi/\theta}$ denoted by $\equiv^\phi / \equiv^\theta$ on $A/ \equiv^\theta$ to be the binary relation given by

$$[a]_\theta \equiv^{\phi/\theta} [b]_\theta \Leftrightarrow a \equiv^\phi b \text{ (see []).}$$

Theorem 1.5. *Let* $\equiv^\phi$, $\equiv^\theta$ *be any* Σ *congruences on a* Σ *algebra* A *such that* $\equiv^\theta \subseteq \equiv^\phi$. *Then the map* $\Psi : \left(A/ \equiv^\theta \right) / \equiv^{\phi/\theta} \to A/ \equiv^\phi$ *defined by*

$$\Psi \left([[a]_\theta]_{\phi/\theta} \right) = [a]_\phi$$

is a Σ *isomorphism.*

Lemma 1.6. *Factor congruence is indeed a congruence.*

2   Algebras of Terms

Let F_0 be a non-empty set of constant symbols for data of sort S, and let F_n for $n \geq 1$ be a set of n-argument function or operator symbols; in particular, if $f \in F_n$ then f has domain type $s \times \ldots \times s$ (n times) and codomain type s.

Let X be a set of variable symbols of sort s. We assume X and the set F_0 of constant symbols are disjoint. The set $T(\Sigma, X)$ of all terms or expressions of sort s is inductively defined by:

(i)   each constant $c \in F_0$ is a term of sort s;
(ii) each variable $x \in X$ is a term of sort s;
(iii) if $t_1, \ldots, t_n$ are terms of sort s and $f \in F_n$ then $f(t_1 t_2 \ldots t_n)$ is a term of sort s;
(iv) nothing else is a term.

The set $T(\Sigma, X)$ is the carrier (if non-empty) for an algebra of terms. The constants of this algebra are the constant symbols $c \in F_0$. The operations of this algebra are the mappings that apply function symbols to terms: for each $f \in F_n$ there is an operation

$$F : T(\Sigma, X)^n \to T(\Sigma, X)$$

defined by

$$F(t_1, \ldots, t_n) = f(t_1, \ldots, t_n)$$

for $t_1, \ldots, t_n \in T(\Sigma, X)$. We denote this algebra by $T(\Sigma, X)$.

The semantics of terms is given by a set A and a map $v : T(\Sigma, X) \to A$, where $v(t)$ is the value of term t.

3   Applications

Let us relax in this section the condition that $f_i : \mathbb{O} \times A \to V$ and let us assume that we have 3 arbitrary sets ϑ, A, V and some functions "working" on these 3 sorts. For example let it be possible that

$$f_1 : \mathbb{O} \times V \to A, \; f_2 : O \times A \to V,$$

$$f_3 : \mathbb{O} \times \mathbb{O} \to \mathbb{O}, \; f_n : V \to A, \; \text{etc.}$$

We define: every set which can be obtained as a term in the term algebra will be called exact. The other sets shall be called not-exact, not describable or not expressible in the given term algebra. In particular we can have exact sets of objects, exact sets of attributes or exact sets of values of attributes in the given algebra of terms. So we can obtain as a terms eg. all red cars in the factory, all blue cars in the database, all attributes which describe fixed family of objects, or as one more example, we can get the term (v_i) which is equal to all (objects, attributes) pairs such that

$$\text{term}\,(v_i) = \{(o,a) : f_k(o,a) = v_i, \; \text{for a function } f_k\}\,.$$

If the algebra considered uses undefined values (null values) then terms containing those values(denoted by special symbols), will be called rough terms. Let me finally propose, for the memory of prof. Z. I. Pawlak, to call sets, which are not exact in the given term algebra T, T-rough sets. In other words we can speak about terms and rough terms is the algebra of terms.

4   On the Notion of Homomorphism

In the many sorted algebras the notion of a homomorphism may be generalized. Here a notion of bidirectional morphism is introduced and an analogon of the first homomorphism theorem is formulated. The considerations of this chapter are inspired by the notion of twisted morphism introduced by Wiweger [5].

4.1   Bidirectional Morphism (cf. [3])

Let us assume that $A = \langle A_s : s \in S \rangle$ and $B = \langle B_s : s \in S \rangle$, are many sorted algebras. Let us assume also that $S = I \cup J$, $I \cap J = \varnothing$ and for every $i \in I, j \in J$ $\Phi_i : A_i \to B_i$, $\Phi_j : B_j \to A_j$. Let f be an operation symbol from the signature of the algebras considered, and let f^A and f^B denote the fundamental operations in the algebras A and B, respectively i.e.

$$f^A : A_{i1} \times \ldots \times A_{in} \times A_{j1} \times \ldots \times A_{jk} \to A_{S0}$$

$$f^B : B_{i1} \times \ldots \times B_{in} \times B_{j1} \times \ldots \times B_{jk} \to B_{S0}$$

where $i1, \ldots, in \in I$, $j1, \ldots, jk \in J$, $so \in S$.

We shall say that f **is preserved by** $\Phi = \langle \Phi_S : s \in S \rangle$ if the following conditions are satisfied:

for all $a_1 \in A_{i1}, \ldots, a_n \in A_{in}, b_1 \in B_{j1}, \ldots, b_k \in B_{jk}$:

a)   if $s_0 \in I$ then $\Phi_{S0}(f^A(a_1, \ldots, a_n, \Phi_{j1}(b_1), \ldots, \Phi_{jk}(b_k))) =$

$$f^B(\Phi_{i1}(a_1), \ldots, \Phi_{in}(a_n), b_1, \ldots, b_k),$$

b)   if $s_O \in J$ then $f^A(a_1, \ldots, a_n, \Phi_{j1}(b_1), \ldots, \Phi_{jk}(b_k)) =$

$$\Phi_{so} f^b(\Phi_{i1}(a_1), \ldots, \Phi_{in}(a_n), b_1, \ldots, b_k).$$

We shall also say that Φ **preserves** f or that Φ **is compatible with** f. The family of mappings $\Phi = \langle \Phi_s : s \in S \rangle$ will be called **a bidirectional (symmetric, or switching) morphism** if, and only if, it is compatible with all the operation symbols, more precisely-with all fundamental operations f^A, f^B in the algebras A, B, respectively. We recall here the convention that f^A, f^B correspond to the same operation symbol f in the signature Σ of the many sorted algebras A, B under consideration. For fixed sets $I, J \subseteq S$, $I \cup J = S$, $I \cap J = \emptyset$ and the algebras A, B of the same signature Φ (over the set of sorts S) we shall denote the family of all bidirectional morphisms with respect to I, J by $\text{Homs}^{I,J}(A, B)$. If Φ is a bidirectional morphism w.r.t. (with respect to) I, J and between A, B then we shall write:

$\Phi : A \, {}^I{=}_J B$ or equivalently $\Phi : B \, {}^J{=}_I A$, sometimes we shall write also $A \, {}^I{=}_J B$.

4.2   Kernel

We modify the notion of kernel in many sorted algebra in the following way. Let A and B be Σ algebras and $\Phi : A \, {}^I{=}_J B$ be a bidirectional homomorphism.

An **A-kernel** of Φ is the binary relation $={}^{A\Phi}$ on A defined by

$$a_1 \equiv^{A\Phi} a_2 \text{ iff } \Phi_i(a_1) = \Phi_i(a_2)$$

whenever $a_1, a_2 \in A_i$, $i \in I$, or

$$a_1 \equiv^{A\Phi} a_2 \text{ iff } a_1 = a_2$$

in case $a_1, a_2 \in A_j$, $j \in J$. In the similar way the notion of B-kernel of Φ is defined. Namely, for all $b_1, b_2 \in B$

$$b_1 \equiv^{B\Phi} b_2 \text{ iff } (b_1 = b_2 \text{ if } b_1, b_2 \in B_i, \ i \in I,$$

$$\text{or } \Phi_j(b_1) = \Phi_j(b_2) \text{ if } b_1, b_2 \in B_j, \ j \in J).$$

It is easy to check that:

Lemma 4.1. *Let $\Phi : A \, {}^I{=}_J B$ be a Σ-bidirectional epimorphism. The kernel $\equiv^{A\Phi}$ is a Σ congruence on A and the kernel $\equiv^{B\Phi}$ is a Σ congruence on B.*

4.3   First Homomorphism Theorem

Given any Σ congruence $\equiv^{A\Phi}$ on a Σ algebra A it is possible to construct a Σ homomorphism nat $: A \to A/\equiv^{A\Phi}$ in the following way:

$$\mathrm{nat}\,(a) = [a]_\equiv$$

nat is called the natural map of the congruence. Now we are prepared to show the generalization of the First Homomorphism Theorem:

Theorem 4.2. *If* $\Phi : A^I =_J B$ *is a* $\Sigma^{I,J}$*-bidirectional epimorphism then the algebras* $A/\equiv^{A\Phi}$ *and* $B/\equiv^{B\Phi}$ *are isomorphic.*

References

1. Mainke, Tucker, *Universal algebra*, chapter in Handbook of logic in Computer Science, ed. S.Abramsky,Dov M.Gabbay, T.S.Meibaum , New York.
2. J. A. Pomykała, *Similarity in relational databases and in information systems theory*, Demonstratio Math., vol. XXXV, No 4, 2002.
3. J. A. Pomykała, *On the notion of homomorphism in many sorted algebras*, Demonstratio Math., vol. XXXVI, No 3, 2003.
4. A. Wiweger, *On topological rough sets*, Bull. Pol. Ac. Sc. Math., vol. 37, No 1–6, 1989.
5. A. Wiweger, *Knowledge Representation Systems, Logical kits and Contexts*, Bull. Pol. Ac.Sc.Math.,vol. 36,No 3-4, 1988
6. Z. Semadeni, On classification, logical educational materials and automata, Colloq.Math., 31(1974), 137-153

Monads Can Be Rough

Patrik Eklund[1] and M.A. Galán[2,*]

[1] Department of Computing Science, Umeå University, Sweden
peklund@cs.umu.se
[2] Department of Applied Mathematics, University of Málaga, Spain
magalan@ctima.uma.es

Abstract. Traditionally, rough sets build upon relations based on ordinary sets, i.e. relations on X as subsets of $X \times X$. A starting point of this paper is the equivalent view on relations as mappings from X to the (ordinary) power set PX. Categorically, P is a set functor, and even more so, it can in fact be extended to a monad (P, η, μ). This is still not enough and we need to consider the partial order $(PX, \leq)$. Given this partial order, the ordinary power set monad can be extended to a *partially ordered monad*. The partially ordered ordinary power set monad turns out to contain sufficient structure in order to provide rough set operations. However, the motivation of this paper goes far beyond ordinary relations as we show how more general power sets, i.e. partially ordered monads built upon a wide range of set functors, can be used to provide what we call *rough monads*.

1 Introduction

Partially ordered monads are monads [9], where the underlying endofunctor is equipped with an order structure. Some additional structure is imposed. Partially ordered monads are useful for various generalized topologies and convergence spaces [3,4], and have also been used for generalisation of Kleene algebras [12,7,2].

Partially ordered monads over the category Set of sets are defined by means of functors from Set to the category acSLAT of almost complete semilattices[1]. A partially ordered monad is a quadruple $(\varphi, \leq, \eta, \mu)$, where $(\varphi, \leq, \eta)$ is a basic triple[2], (φ, η, μ) is a monad[3] (over Set), and further, for all mappings $f, g : Y \to \varphi X$, $f \leq g$ implies $\mu_X \circ \varphi f \leq \mu_X \circ \varphi g$, where $\leq$ is defined argumentwise with respect to the partial ordering of φX. We also require that for each set X, $\mu_X : (\varphi\varphi X, \leq) \to (\varphi X, \leq)$ preserves non-empty suprema.

The classical example of a partially ordered monad is the power set partially ordered monad $(P, \leq, \eta, \mu)$, where PX is the ordinary power set of X and $\leq$ its set inclusion $\subseteq$

---

* Partially supported by Spanish projects TIC2003-09001-C02-01 and TIN2006-15455-C03-01.

[1] An almost complete semilattice is a partially ordered sets $(X, \leq)$ such that the suprema $\sup \mathcal{M}$ of all non-empty subsets $\mathcal{M}$ of X exists.

[2] A *basic triple* ([3]) is a triple $(\varphi, \leq, \eta)$, where $(\varphi, \leq) :$ Set $\to$ acSLAT, $X \mapsto (\varphi X, \leq)$ is a covariant functor, with $\varphi :$ Set $\to$ Set as the underlying set functor, and $\eta : \mathrm{id} \to \varphi$ is a natural transformation.

[3] A *monad* (φ, η, μ) over a category C consists of a covariant functor $\varphi :$ C $\to$ C, together with natural transformations $\eta : id \to \varphi$ and $\mu : \varphi \circ \varphi \to \varphi$ fulfilling the conditions $\mu \circ \varphi\mu = \mu \circ \mu\varphi$ and $\mu \circ \varphi\eta = \mu \circ \eta\varphi = id_\varphi$.

S. Greco et al. (Eds.): RSCTC 2006, LNAI 4259, pp. 77–84, 2006.

making $(PX, \leq)$ a partially ordered set. The unit $\eta : X \to PX$ is given by $\eta(x) = \{x\}$ and the multiplication $\mu : PPX \to PX$ by $\mu(\mathcal{B}) = \cup\mathcal{B}$.

In this paper we will show that partially ordered monads contain sufficient structure for modelling rough sets [10] in a generalized setting with set functors. Even for the ordinary relations, the adaptations through partially ordered monads open up avenues towards an understanding of rough sets in a basic many-valued logic [5] setting. However, the motivation of this paper goes far beyond ordinary relations, and indeed we show how various set functors extendable to partially ordered monads establish the notion of rough monads.

2 Ordinary Relations and Rough Sets

Let R be a relation on X, i.e. $R \subseteq X \times X$. We represent the relation as a mapping $\rho_X : X \to PX$, where $\rho_X(x) = \{y \in X \,|\, xRy\}$. The corresponding inverse relation R^{-1} is represented as $\rho_X^{-1}(x) = \{y \in X \,|\, xR^{-1}y\}$.

Based on indistinguishable relations, *rough sets* are introduced by defining the upper and lower approximation of sets. These approximations represent uncertain or imprecise knowledge. To be more formal, given a subset A of X, the lower approximation of A correspond to the objects that surely (with respect to an indistinguishable relation) are in A.

The lower approximation of A is obtained by

$$A^{\downarrow} = \{x \in X \,|\, \rho(x) \subseteq A\}$$

and the upper approximation by

$$A^{\uparrow} = \{x \in X \,|\, \rho(x) \cap A \neq \emptyset\}.$$

In what follows we will assume that the underlying almost complete semilattice has finite infima, i.e. is a join complete lattice.

Considering P as the functor in its corresponding partially ordered monad we then immediately have

Proposition 1. *The upper and lower approximations of a subset A of X are given by*

$$A^{\uparrow} = \bigvee_{\rho_X(x) \wedge A > 0} \eta_X(x) = \mu_X \circ P\rho_X^{-1}(A)$$

and

$$A^{\downarrow} = \bigvee_{\rho_X(x) \leq A} \eta_X(x),$$

respectively.

Proof. For the upper approximation,

$$\mu_X \circ P\rho_X^{-1}(A) = \bigvee P\rho_X^{-1}(A)$$

$$= \bigvee \{\rho_X^{-1}(y) \mid y \in A\}$$
$$= \{x \in X \mid xRy, \, y \in A\}$$
$$= \bigvee_{\rho_X(x) \wedge A > 0} \eta_X(x) = A^{\uparrow}.$$

And for the lower approximation, since $\eta_X(x) = \{x\}$, we immediately obtain:

$$A^{\downarrow} = \{x \in X \mid \rho(x) \subseteq A\}$$
$$= \bigvee_{\rho_X(x) \leq A} \eta_X(x).$$

The corresponding R-weakened and R-substantiated sets of a subset A of X are given by

$$A^{\Downarrow} = \{x \in X \mid \rho^{-1}(x) \subseteq A\}$$

and

$$A^{\Uparrow} = \{x \in X \mid \rho_X^{-1}(x) \cap A \neq \emptyset\}.$$

Proposition 2. *The R-weakened and R-substantiated sets of a subset A of X are given by*

$$A^{\Uparrow} = \mu_X \circ P\rho_X(A)$$

and

$$A^{\Downarrow} = \bigvee_{\rho_X^{-1}(x) \leq A} \eta_X(x),$$

respectively.

Proof. Similarly as Proposition 1.

The upper and lower approximations, as well as the R-weakened and R-substantiated sets, can be viewed as $\uparrow_X, \downarrow_X, \Uparrow_X, \Downarrow_X : PX \to PX$ with $\uparrow_X (A) = A^{\uparrow}$, $\downarrow_X (A) = A^{\downarrow}$, $\Uparrow_X (A) = A^{\Uparrow}$ and $\Downarrow_X (A) = A^{\Downarrow}$.

3   Inverse Relations

Inverse relations in the ordinary case means to mirror pairs around the diagonal. The following propositions relate inverses to the multiplication of the corresponding monads.

Proposition 3. *In the case of P,*

$$\bigvee_{\rho_X(x) \wedge A > 0} \eta_X(x) = \mu_X \circ P\rho_X^{-1}(A)$$

if and only if

$$\rho_X^{-1}(x) = \bigcup_{\eta_X(x) \leq \rho_X(y)} \eta_X(y).$$

Proof. To see $\Longrightarrow$, let us consider the one element set, $A = \{x\}$. Renaming the variables, by hypothesis we have that $\rho_X(y) \wedge A > 0$, e.g. $x \in \rho_X(y)$, therefore,

$$\bigvee_{\rho_X(y) \wedge A > 0} \eta_X(y) = \bigcup_{x \in \rho_X(y)} \eta_X(y) = \bigcup_{\eta_X(x) \leq \rho_X(y)} \eta_X(y).$$

On the other hand, since A contains only one element, $\mu_X \circ P\rho_X^{-1}(A) = \rho_X^{-1}(x)$. The other implication, $\Longleftarrow$, holds by Proposition 1.

The many-valued extension of P is as follows. Let L be a completely distributive lattice. For $L = \{0, 1\}$ we write $L = 2$. The functor L_{id} is obtained by $L_{id}X = L^X$, i.e. the set of mappings $A : X \to L$. These mappings are usually called *fuzzy sets* (over L). The partial order $\leq$ on $L_{id}X$ is given pointwise. Morphism $f \colon X \to Y$ in $\mathtt{Set}$ are mapped according to

$$L_{id}f(A)(y) = \bigvee_{f(x)=y} A(x).$$

Finally $\eta_X : X \to L_{id}X$ is given by

$$\eta_X(x)(x') = \begin{cases} 1 & \text{if } x' \leq x \\ 0 & \text{otherwise} \end{cases}$$

and $\mu_X : L_{id}X \circ L_{id}X \to L_{id}X$ by

$$\mu_X(\mathcal{M})(x) = \bigvee_{A \in L_{id}X} A(x) \wedge \mathcal{M}(A).$$

Concerning inverse relations, in the case of $\varphi = L_{id}$ we would accordingly define $\rho_X^{-1}(x)(x') = \rho_X(x')(x)$.

Proposition 4. *[1]* $\mathbf{L}_{id} = (L_{id}, \leq, \eta, \mu)$ *is a partially ordered monad.*

Note that $\mathbf{2}_{id}$ is the usual partially ordered power set monad $(P, \leq, \eta, \mu)$.

Proposition 5. *In the case of L_{id},*

$$\mu_X \circ L_{id}\rho_X^{-1}(A)(x) = \bigvee_{x' \in X} (\rho_X(x) \wedge A)(x').$$

Proof. We have

$$\mu_X \circ L_{id}\rho_X^{-1}(A)(x) = \bigvee_{B \in L_{id}X} B(x) \wedge L_{id}\rho_X^{-1}(A)(B)$$

$$= \bigvee_{B \in L_{id}X} B(x) \wedge \left(\bigvee_{\rho_X^{-1}(x')=B} A(x') \right)$$

$$= \bigvee_{B \in L_{id}X} \bigvee_{\rho_X^{-1}(x')=B} B(x) \wedge A(x')$$

$$= \bigvee_{x' \in X} \rho_X^{-1}(x')(x) \wedge A(x')$$

$$= \bigvee_{x' \in X} (\rho_X(x) \wedge A)(x').$$

The generalization from the ordinary power set monad to involving a wide range of set functors and their corresponding partially ordered monads requires an appropriate management of relational inverses and complement. Obviously, for more complicated set functors, the corresponding relational views no longer rest upon 'mirroring over the diagonal'. The general representation of inverses is still an open question and for the the purpose of this paper we specify inverses *in casu*. Inverses and complements in the end need to build upon logic operators in particular concerning negation as derived from implication operators used within basic many-valued logic [5].

4   Monadic Relations and Rough Monads

Let $\Phi = (\varphi, \leq, \eta, \mu)$ be a partially ordered monad. We say that $\rho_X : X \to \varphi X$ is a Φ-*relation* on X, and by $\rho_X^{-1} : X \to \varphi X$ we denote its *inverse*. The inverse must be specified for the given set functor φ.

For any $f \colon X \to \varphi X$, the following condition is required:

$$\varphi f \left(\bigvee_i a_i \right) = \bigvee_i \varphi f(a_i)$$

This condition is valid both for P as well as for L_{id}.

Remark 1. Let ρ_X and ρ_Y be relations on X and Y, respectively. Then the mapping $f : X \to Y$ is a congruence, i.e. $x' \in \rho_X(x)$ implies $f(x') \in \rho_Y(f(x))$, if and only if $Pf \circ \rho_X \leq \rho_Y \circ f$. Thus, congruence is related to kind of weak naturality.

Let $\rho_X : X \to \varphi X$ be a Φ-relation and let $a \in \varphi X$. The Φ-ρ-upper and Φ-ρ-lower approximations, and further the Φ-ρ-weakened and Φ-ρ-substantiated sets, now define rough monads using the following monadic instrumentation:

$$\Uparrow_X (a) = \mu_X \circ \varphi \rho_X(a)$$

$$\downarrow_X (a) = \bigvee_{\rho_X(x) \leq a} \eta_X(x)$$

$$\uparrow_X (a) = \mu_X \circ \varphi \rho_X^{-1}(a)$$

$$\Downarrow_X (a) = \bigvee_{\rho_X^{-1}(x) \leq a} \eta_X(x)$$

Proposition 6. *If $a \leq b$, then $\Uparrow_X a \leq \Uparrow_X b$, $\downarrow_X a \leq \downarrow_X b$, $\uparrow_X a \leq \uparrow_X b$, $\Downarrow_X a \leq \Downarrow_X b$.*

Proof. The proof is straighforward as e.g.

$$\downarrow_X (a) = \bigvee_{\rho_X(x) \leq a} \eta_X(x) \leq \bigvee_{\rho_X(x) \leq b} \eta_X(x) = \downarrow_X (b)$$

and

$$\uparrow_X (a) = \mu_X \circ \varphi \rho_X^{-1}(a) \leq \mu_X \circ \varphi \rho_X^{-1}(b) = \uparrow_X (b).$$

Definition 1. $\rho_X : X \to \varphi X$ *is reflexive if* $\eta_X \leq \rho_X$, *and symmetric if* $\rho = \rho^{-1}$.

Proposition 7. *If ρ is reflexive, $a \leq \Uparrow_X (a)$.*

Proof. By one of the monads conditions wrt multiplication and the fact that for all mappings $f, g : Y \to \varphi X$, $f \leq g$ implies $\mu_X \circ \varphi f \leq \mu_X \circ \varphi g$, we have:

$$a = id_\varphi(a)$$
$$= \mu_X \circ \varphi \eta_X(a)$$
$$\leq \mu_X \circ \varphi \rho_X(a)$$
$$= \Uparrow_X (a)$$

Proposition 8. *ρ is reflexive iff $\downarrow_X (a) \leq a$.*

Proof. If ρ is reflexive, then

$$\downarrow_X (a) = \bigvee_{\rho_X(x) \leq a} \eta_X(x)$$
$$\leq \bigvee_{\rho_X(x) \leq a} \rho_X(x)$$
$$\leq a$$

and, conversely, if $\downarrow_X (a) \leq a$, then we have

$$\eta_X(x) \leq \bigvee_{\rho_X(x') \leq \rho_X(x)} \eta_X(x')$$
$$= \downarrow_X (\rho_X(x))$$
$$\leq \rho_X(x).$$

Proposition 9. *ρ_X^{-1} is reflexive iff $a \leq \uparrow_X (a)$.*

Proof. If ρ_X^{-1} is reflexive, then $\eta_X \leq \rho_X^{-1}$. Therefore, by using monads conditions and properties of the underlying lattice, we obtain

$$a = \mu_X \circ \varphi \eta_X(a) \leq \mu_X \circ \varphi \rho_X^{-1}(a) = \uparrow_X (a).$$

Conversely, we have that $\eta_X(x) \leq \uparrow_X (\eta_X(x))$. Further, by naturality of η_X with respect to ρ_X^{-1}, and by using one of the monad conditions, we have

$$\mu_X \circ \varphi \rho_X^{-1}(\eta_X(x)) = \mu_X \circ \eta_{\varphi X}(\rho_X^{-1}(x)) = \rho_X^{-1}(x).$$

Therefore,

$$\eta_X(x) \leq \uparrow_X (\eta_X(x)) = \mu_X \circ \varphi \rho_X^{-1}(\eta_X(x)) = \rho_X^{-1}(x)$$

which yields the reflexivity of ρ_X^{-1}.

Note that in the case of relations for P and L_{id}, if the relations are reflexive, so are their inverses.

Proposition 10. *If ρ is symmetric, then $\uparrow_X (\downarrow_X (a)) \leq a$.*

Proof. We have

$$
\begin{aligned}
\uparrow_X (\downarrow_X (a)) &= \mu_X \circ \varphi\rho_X^{-1}(\downarrow_X (a)) \\
&= \mu_X \circ \varphi\rho_X^{-1}\Big(\bigvee_{\rho_X(x)\leq a} \eta_X(x) \Big) \\
&= \bigvee_{\rho_X(x)\leq a} \mu_X \circ \varphi\rho_X^{-1}(\eta_X(x)) \\
&= \bigvee_{\rho_X(x)\leq a} \rho_X^{-1}(x) \\
&= \bigvee_{\rho_X(x)\leq a} \rho_X(x) \\
&\leq a.
\end{aligned}
$$

In the particular case of $a = \eta_X(x)$ we have $a \leq \downarrow_X \circ \uparrow_X (a)$. Indeed, by naturality of η_X, and symmetry, we have

$$
\rho_X(x) = \mu_X \circ \varphi\rho_X^{-1}(a).
$$

Therefore,

$$
a = \eta_X(x) \leq \bigvee_{\rho_X(x')\leq \mu_X \circ \varphi\rho_X^{-1}(a)} \eta_X(x') = \downarrow_X (\uparrow_X (a)).
$$

5   Future Work

Algebraic structures of rough sets [6] will be further investigated, both in direction towards topological notions as well as involving logical structures. For instance, relations to topological approaches based on modal-like operators [8] need to be better understood. Concerning algebras, it is important to note that the power set based rough monad, i.e. the ordinary rough sets, fulfill conditions of Boolean algebras where calculi e.g. on inverses are natural and well understood. Going beyond Boolean algebras means dropping complements and the recovery of the notion of complement needs to take other routes, such as those provided by implications in many-valued logic. Further, substructures of partially ordered monads are important for the provision of more examples. It is also interesting to observe how rough sets and their algebraic structures resemble operations on images as found with morphological analysis [11]. Images seen not just as matrices of pixels but, more general, as being placed on a canvas based on rather elaborate set functors which are far more complex than the ordinary power set functor.

Acknowledgement

We would like to thank Jouni Järvinen and Jari Kortelainen for inspiring thoughts on algebras of rough sets. We are grateful also to anonymous referees for valuable comments and suggestions for improvements of this paper.

References

1. P. Eklund, M.A. Galán, W. Gähler, J. Medina, M. Ojeda Aciego, A. Valverde, *A note on partially ordered generalized terms*, Proc. of Fourth Conference of the European Society for Fuzzy Logic and Technology and Rencontres Francophones sur la Logique Floue et ses applications (Joint EUSFLAT-LFA 2005), 793-796.
2. P. Eklund, W. Gähler, *Partially ordered monads and powerset Kleene algebras*, Proc. 10th Information Processing and Management of Uncertainty in Knowledge Based Systems Conference (IPMU 2004).
3. W. Gähler, *General Topology – The monadic case, examples, applications*, Acta Math. Hungar. **88** (2000), 279-290.
4. W. Gähler, P. Eklund, *Extension structures and compactifications*, In: Categorical Methods in Algebra and Topology (CatMAT 2000), 181–205.
5. P. Hájek, *Metamathematics of Fuzzy Logic*, Kluwer Academic Publishers, 1998.
6. J. Järvinen, *On the structure of rough approximations*, Fundamenta Informaticae **53** (2002), 135-153.
7. S. C. Kleene, *Representation of events in nerve nets and finite automata*, In: Automata Studies (Eds. C. E. Shannon, J. McCarthy), Princeton University Press, 1956, 3-41.
8. J. Kortelainen, *A Topological Approach to Fuzzy Sets*, Ph.D. Dissertation, Lappeenranta University of Technology, Acta Universitatis Lappeenrantaensis **90** (1999).
9. E. G. Manes, *Algebraic Theories*, Springer, 1976.
10. Z. Pawlak, *Rough sets*, Int. J. Computer and Information Sciences **5** (1982) 341356.
11. J. Serra. *Image Analysis and Mathematical Morphology*, volume 1. Academic Press, 1982.
12. A. Tarski, *On the calculus of relations*, J. Symbolic Logic **6** (1941), 65-106.

On Testing Membership to Maximal Consistent Extensions of Information Systems

Mikhail Moshkov[1], Andrzej Skowron[2], and Zbigniew Suraj[3,4]

[1] Institute of Computer Science, University of Silesia
Będzińska 39, 41-200 Sosnowiec, Poland
`moshkov@us.edu.pl`
[2] Institute of Mathematics, Warsaw University
Banacha 2, 02-097 Warsaw, Poland
`skowron@mimuw.edu.pl`
[3] Chair of Computer Science, Rzeszów University
Rejtana 16A, 35-310 Rzeszów, Poland
`zsuraj@univ.rzeszow.pl`
[4] Institute of Computer Science, State School of Higher Education in Jarosław
Czarnieckiego 16, 37-500 Jarosław, Poland

Abstract. This paper provides a new algorithm for testing membership to maximal consistent extensions of information systems. A maximal consistent extension of a given information system includes all objects corresponding to known attribute values which are consistent with all true and realizable rules extracted from the original information system. An algorithm presented here does not involve computing any rules, and has polynomial time complexity. This algorithm is based on a simpler criterion for membership testing than the algorithm described in [4]. The criterion under consideration is convenient for theoretical analysis of maximal consistent extensions of information systems.

Keywords: rough sets, information systems, maximal consistent extensions.

1 Introduction

Information systems can be used to represent knowledge about the behavior of concurrent systems. The idea of a concurrent system representation by information systems is due to Zdzisław Pawlak [3]. In this approach, an information system represented by a data table encodes the knowledge about global states of a given concurrent system. Columns of the table are labeled with names of attributes (interpreted as local processes of a given concurrent system). Each row labeled with an object (interpreted as a global state of a given concurrent system) includes a record of attribute values (interpreted as states of local processes). We assume that a given data table includes only a part of possible global states of a concurrent system, i.e., only those which have been observed by us

S. Greco et al. (Eds.): RSCTC 2006, LNAI 4259, pp. 85–90, 2006.

so far. In other words, it contains partial knowledge about a possible system behavior. Such an approach is called the Open World Assumption. This partial knowledge encoded in a data table can be represented by means of rules which can be extracted from the data table. Such knowledge is sufficient to construct a system model of the high quality. The remaining knowledge can be discovered from the constructed model. New knowledge derived from the model encompasses new global states of the system which have not been observed before. Such new states are consistent with the knowledge expressed by the rules extracted from the given data table.

The above approach has been motivation for introducing a notion of consistent extensions of information systems in [5]. A given information system S defines an extension S' of S created by adding to S all new objects including combinations of only known attribute-value pairs, i.e., those pairs which have occurred in S. Among all extensions of a given information system S, the so-called consistent extensions of S play a significant role. A consistent extension S' of S includes only objects, which satisfy all rules true and realizable in S. If the consistent extension S' with the above property is the largest extension of S (with respect to the number of objects) then S' is called a maximal consistent extension of S.

If an information system S describes a concurrent system, the maximal consistent extension of S represents the largest set of global states of the concurrent system consistent with all rules true and realizable in S. This set may include new global states not observed until now. It is – in a certain sense – new knowledge about the concurrent system behavior described by S which is discovered by us.

A crucial problem concerning maximal consistent extensions of information systems is computing such extensions. This problem has been considered in the literature, among others, in [4], [7] and [8]. In [1], [5], [6] some approaches have been presented, where maximal consistent extensions are generated by classical Petri net or colored Petri net models built on the basis of information systems describing concurrent systems. Majority of methods for determining maximal consistent extensions of information systems presented until now in the literature (with the exception of [4]) requires computing all minimal rules (or only a part of them) true and realizable in information systems. Such algorithms characterize exponential complexity. Therefore, elaborating efficient methods became an important research problem. In this paper, some theoretical background for the method of computing maximal consistent extensions of information systems not involving computing any rules in information systems is presented. The method considered in this paper is slightly different from the one considered in [4]. Our method is based on a simpler criterion than the method presented in [4] and is more appropriate for theoretical analysis.

The remaining part of the paper is organized as follows. Main notions are presented in Section 2. Section 3 describes a new algorithm for testing membership to maximal consistent extensions of information systems. Finally, Section 4 consists of some conclusions.

2   Main Notions

Let $S = (U, A)$ be an information system [2] where U is a finite set of objects and A is a set of attributes (functions defined on U). For any $a \in A$, by V_a we denote the set $\{a(u) : u \in U\}$ and we assume that $|V_a| \geq 2$.

We define an information system $S^* = (U^*, A^*)$, where U^* is equal to the Cartesian product $\times_{a \in A} V_a$ and $A^* = \{a^* : a \in A\}$, where $a^*(f) = f(a)$ for $f \in \times_{a \in A} V_a$.

Assuming that for any $u, u' \in U$ if $u \neq u'$ then $Inf_A(u) \neq Inf_A(u')$, where $Inf_A(u) = \{(a, a(u)) : a \in A\}$ we can identify any object $u \in U$ with the object $Inf_A(u) \in U^*$ and any attribute $a \in A$ with the attribute $a^* \in A^*$ defined by $a^*(Inf_A(u)) = a(u)$. Hence, the information system $S = (U, A)$ can be treated as a subsystem of the information system $S^* = (U^*, A^*)$. In the sequel we write a instead a^*.

For any information system $S = (U, A)$ it is defined the set of boolean combinations of descriptors over S [2]. Any descriptor over S is an expression $a = v$ where $a \in A$ and $v \in V_a$. Boolean combinations of descriptors are defined from descriptors using propositional connectives. For any boolean combination of descriptors α it is defined its semantics, i.e., the set $\|\alpha\|_S \subseteq U$ consisting of all objects satisfying α [2]. For example, if α is a formula $\bigwedge_{a \in B}(a = v_a)$, where $B \subseteq A$, $a \in B$, and $v_a \in V_a$ then $\|\alpha\|_S = \{u \in U : a(u) = v_a$ for any $a \in B\}$.

A rule r (over S) is any expression of the form

$$\bigwedge_{a \in B} (a = v_a) \longrightarrow a' = v_{a'}, \tag{1}$$

where $B \subseteq A$, $v_a \in V_a$ for $a \in B$, $a' \in A$, and $v_{a'} \in V_{a'}$.

The rule r (see (1)) is true for $u \in U^*$ if for some $a \in B$ we have $a(u) \neq v_a$ or $a'(u) = v_{a'}$. The rule r (see (1)) is S-true if $\|\bigwedge_{a \in B}(u = v_a)\|_S \subseteq \|u' = v_{a'}\|_S$ and it is S-realizable if $\|\bigwedge_{a \in B}(a = v_a)\|_S \cap \|a' = v_{a'}\|_S \neq \emptyset$.

The set of all S-true and S-realizable rules is denoted by $Rule(S)$.

Now, we can introduce the main concept of this paper, i.e., the maximal extension of S. The maximal extension of S, in symbols $Ext(S)$, is defined by

$$Ext(S) = \{u \in U^* : \text{ any rule from } Rule(S) \text{ is true in } u\}. \tag{2}$$

Let us consider an information system $S = (U, A)$ and $u, u' \in U$. The set of attributes on which u, u' are indiscernible in S is defined by

$$IND_A(u, u') = \{a \in A : a(u) = a(u')\}. \tag{3}$$

Such a set $IND_A(u, u')$ defines a pattern, i.e., the following boolean combination of descriptors over S:

$$T_A(u, u') = \bigwedge_{a \in IND_A(u, u')} (a = a(u)). \tag{4}$$

Now, for a given information system S and any $u^* \in U^* \setminus U$ we define an important for our considerations family of sets $\mathcal{F}(u^*, S)$ by

$$\mathcal{F}(u^*, S) = \{a(\|T_A(u, u^*)\|_S) : a \in A \setminus IND_A(u, u^*) \ \& \ u \in U\}, \qquad (5)$$

where $a(\|T_A(u, u^*)\|_S) = \{a(x) : x \in \|T_A(u, u^*)\|_S\}$, i.e., $a(\|T_A(u, u^*)\|_S)$ is the image under a of the set $\|T_A(u, u^*)\|_S$.

3   Testing Membership to $Ext(S)$

In [4] a polynomial algorithm has been considered, which for a given information system $S = (U, A)$ and a given object u from $U^* \setminus U$ recognizes whether this object belongs to $Ext(S)$ or not. This algorithm is based on a criterion of membership to maximal consistent extension of information system which uses comparison of sets of reducts of a special kind (reducts related to a fixed object and attribute) to a given set of objects and to its one-element extension.

We consider the following problem:

Membership Problem (MP)

INPUT: $S = (U, A)$ and $u^* \in U^* - U$
OUTPUT: 1 if $u* \in Ext(S)$
     0 if $u^* \notin Ext(S)$.

We now present a polynomial algorithm $\mathcal{A}$ for solving the MP problem. Our algorithm is based on a simpler criterion than that presented in [4].

Algorithm $\mathcal{A}$

```
for all u ∈ U
    for all a ∈ A \ IND_A(u, u*)
        begin
            compute a(‖T_A(u, u*)‖_S);
            if |a(‖T_A(u, u*)‖_S)| = 1 then
                begin
                    return(0);
                    Stop
                end
        end
return(1)
```

The correctness of the algorithm $\mathcal{A}$ follows from the following proposition:

Proposition 1. *Let $S = (U, A)$ be an information system and let $u^* \in U^* \setminus U$. Then the following conditions are equivalent:*
(i) $u^* \notin Ext(S)$,
(ii) there exists $X \in \mathcal{F}(u^*, S)$ such that $|X| = 1$.

Proof.

(ii) $\Rightarrow$ (i)

Let us assume that for some one element set X we have $X \in \mathcal{F}(u^*, S)$. Then the following equality holds: $X = a(\|T_A(u, u^*)\|_S)$ for some $a \in A \setminus IND_A(u, u^*)$ and $u \in U$. Hence, the rule r defined by

$$T_A(u, u^*) \longrightarrow a = a(u)$$

is S-true, because $|X| = 1$. We also have $a(u) \neq a(u^*)$ because $a \notin IND_A(u, u^*)$. Hence, r is not true for u^*, so $u^* \notin Ext(S)$.

(i) $\Rightarrow$ (ii)

Let us assume $u^* \notin Ext(S)$. It means that there exists a rule r of the form $\alpha \longrightarrow a = v$, where α is a boolean combination of descriptors over S, which is not true for u^* but is S-true and S-realizable. Hence, $u^* \in \|\alpha\|_{S_*}$ and $a(u^*) \neq v$. The rule r is S-realizable. Hence, for some $u \in U$ we have $u \in \|\alpha\|_S$ and $a(u) = v$. From the definition of $T_A(u, u^*)$ we obtain that $T_A(u, u^*)$ consists of all descriptors from α. Hence, $\|T_A(u, u^*)\|_S \subseteq \|\alpha\|_S$ and in S is true the following rule:

$$T_A(u, u^*) \longrightarrow a = a(u).$$

Let us now consider the set $a(\|T_A(u, u^*)\|_S)$. Since $\|T_A(u, u^*)\|_S \subseteq \|\alpha\|_S$ and $|a(\|\alpha\|_S)| = 1$ we also have $|a(\|T_A(u, u^*)\|_S)| = 1$. The last equality follows from the fact that $|a(\|T_A(u, u^*)\|_S)| \geq 1$ if the set $\|T_A(u, u^*)\|_S$ is non-empty.

Let us consider an example.

Example 1. Let $S = (U, A)$, $A = \{a_1, a_2\}$ and $U = \{(0, 1), (1, 0), (0, 2), (2, 0)\}$. The application of the considered algorithm to each object u from $\{0, 1, 2\}^2 \setminus U$ allows to find the set $Ext(S)$ which is equal to $\{(0, 1), (1, 0), (0, 2), (2, 0), (0, 0)\}$.

4   Conclusions

In this paper, a new method for testing membership to maximal consistent extensions of information systems is proposed. This method significantly differs from the majority of methods presented in the literature, as it does not involve computing any rules. Moreover, the presented method is useful for theoretical analysis of maximal consistent extensions of information systems.

We also plan to extend the presented approach to the case of nondeterministic or probabilistic rules used in the definition of the extension of a given information system. Moreover, filtration methods can be used for selecting relevant rules in constructing models, analogously to methods used for constructing of rule based classifiers.

One of the problem we would like to study is a decision problem for checking if a given information system has consistent extension consisting of at least k new states, where k is a given positive integer.

Acknowledgments

The authors are greatly indebted to anonymous reviewers for useful suggestions. This paper has been partially supported by the Ministry of Scientific Research and Information Technology of the Republic of Poland research grants No. 3 T11C 005 28 and 3 T11C 002 26.

References

1. Pancerz, K., Suraj, Z.: Synthesis of Petri net models: a rough set approach. Fundamenta Informaticae **55**(2) (2003) 149–165
2. Pawlak, Z.: Rough Sets – Theoretical Aspects of Reasoning About Data. Kluwer Academic Publishers, Dordrecht, 1991
3. Pawlak, Z.: Concurrent versus sequential the rough sets perspective. Bulletin of the EATCS **48** (1992) 178–190
4. Rząsa, W., Suraj, Z.: A new method for determining of extensions and restrictions of information systems. Proceedings of the 3rd International Conference on Rough Sets and Current Trends in Computing. Lecture Notes in Artificial Intelligence **2475**, Springer-Verlag (2002) 197–204
5. Skowron, A., Suraj, Z.: Rough sets and concurrency. Bulletin of the Polish Academy of Sciences **41**(3) (1993) 237–254
6. Suraj, Z.: Rough set methods for the synthesis and analysis of concurrent processes. Rough Set Methods and Applications (Studies in Fuzziness and Soft Computing **56**). Edited by L. Polkowski, S. Tsumoto, and T.Y. Lin. Physica-Verlag (2000) 379–488
7. Suraj, Z.: Some remarks on extensions and restrictions of information systems. Rough Sets and Current Trends in Computing. Lecture Notes in Artificial Intelligence **2005**, Springer-Verlag (2001) 204–211
8. Suraj, Z., Pancerz, K.: A new method for computing partially consistent extensions of information systems: a rough set approach. Proceedings of the International Conference on Information Processing and Management of Uncertainty in Knowledge-Based Systems. Paris, France, July 2006, Editions EDK (2006), Vol. III 2618-2625

The Research of Rough Sets in Normed Linear Space

Hui Sun[1] and Qing Liu[1,2]

[1] Department of Computer Science & Technology
Nanchang Institute of Technology, Nanchang 330099, China
sun_hui2006@yahoo.com.cn
[2] Department of Computer Science & Technology
Nanchang University, Nanchang 330029, China

Abstract. As a new mathematical theory, rough sets have been applied to process imprecise, uncertain and incomplete data. The research of rough sets has been fruitful in finite and non-empty sets. Rough sets, however, only serve as a theoretic tool to discretize the real function. As far as the real function research is concerned, the research work to define rough sets in the real function is infrequent. In this paper, we exploit a new method to define rough sets in normed linear space. We put forward an upper and lower approximation definition, and make preliminary research in the properties of rough sets. A new theoretical tool is provided to study the approximation solutions to differential equation and functional variation in normed linear space.This research is significant in that it extends the application of rough sets to a new field.

Keywords: rough sets, normed linear space, upper and lower approximation.

1 Introduction

Rough sets that are applied to process imprecise, uncertain and incomplete data were put forward by Polish mathematician Z.Pawlak in 1982[10]. Rough sets are based on the partition mechanism, according to which, partition means equivalence relation in a given space and equivalence relation means the partition of the space elements. In rough sets, knowledge is interpreted as the partition of the data and the set of each partition is called a concept. The key thinking of the rough set theory is to make use of the known knowledge database, and depict roughly the imprecise or uncertain knowledge with the help of the known knowledge in the knowledge database. This theory differentiates from other theories dealing with uncertain and imprecise data in that it doesn't involve any transcendental information that is beyond the data set. Therefore, it is comparatively objective to depict or deal with the impreciseness of the problem [6, 7, 10, 11, 12, 14]. In recent years,rough set methodology provides a new idea for studying granular computing, thus the scope of our study has been expanded [3, 4, 8, 15, 16, 17, 18, 19, 20].

S. Greco et al. (Eds.): RSCTC 2006, LNAI 4259, pp. 91–98, 2006.

In classical mathematical application, we always attempt to get the exact solution to a problem. If an exact solution is not available, we try to find an approximate one. But in fact, many so-called exact solutions are not accurate whatsoever, for they are nothing but the model solution. The actual problem is always complex, so it is always simplified into some models which are easier to approach. In this sense, some approximate solutions from model are closer to the real situation than the exact solution. For instance, the exact solution to the deformation of simply supported beam with load is not exact. As is known to all, it is not likely that the beam is simply supported in an ideal way on both ends, for there exists somewhat moments on the both ends of the beam. As a result, the displacement of the real situation is always smaller than that of a model. And the model solution to the deformation of the fixed-end beam is always larger than that of the real situation. Thus it is safe to argue that the exact solution from the model is not exact.

Rough sets are a powerful mathematical tool that is applied to deal with uncertain problems. If rough sets are used to deal with the problem of uncertainty between the exact solution and the model solution, the relationship between the exact solution and the model solution can be studied from a new perspective. But heretofore, the research in rough sets mainly concentrates on the discrete set and their extension, even though rough sets are sometimes introduced in the real function studies [5, 6, 12, 13]. But rough sets simply serve as the theoretic tool of function discretization, far from being applied to approach the real situation. The solutions to differential equation and functional variation are mainly in normed linear space. In this paper, we exploit a new method to extend the rough sets to normed linear space. Thus the rough set theory can be applied to study the function in normed linear space, especially that of the approximate solution to problems.

2 The Construction of Rough Sets in Normed Linear Space

Definition 1. *Let U be the normed linear space where there is a basis, $E \subseteq U$ and $E \neq \emptyset$. The set M, composed of all the elements of linear combinations in E, is called subspace spanned from [2].*

Definition 2. *Let the elements in set $E \subseteq U$ be linearly independent. The set that consists of the elements of linear combination under special requirement is called the deduced space of E, which is marked as U'.*

In fact, U' is the linear space spanned from the basis that is linearly independent and $U' \subseteq M \subseteq U$. Sometimes E is called as basis space, U' as approximate solution space, and U as the exact solution space for the sake of convenience.

Note: As far as normed linear space is concerned, what is discussed here is the basis space. In fact, there are good basis sets in the general subspaces of the normed linear space [1].

Definition 3. *Let $\|\,\|_p$ be the L_p norm of U in normed linear space. For function $f \in U, g \in U'$,$\forall \varepsilon > 0$, if $\| f - g \|_p < \varepsilon$, then function g is considered to approximate to f in a way of L_p norm, with ε the given tolerance.*

As for U' , it is difficult to define the equivalence relation directly. So the combination of basis space and solution space are applied to define the equivalence relation R.

Definition 4. *Let U' be the deduced space of $E \subseteq U$, and $U'_i \subseteq U'$ the subspace spanned by some linearly independent basis E_i from E. We define that every multi-dimensional subspace U'_i doesn't include low dimensional subspace, so we have $U'_i \cap U'_j = \varnothing, i \neq j$ and $\cup U'_i = U'$.*

Note: if $U'_i \subseteq U'$ is not a one-dimensional space, U'_i is an open set, or linear manifold, as what is referred by some literatures [2].

Now we would like to make a further explanation for Definition 4. Supposing a basis space be $E = \{a, x, x^2\}$, it is obvious that $\{a, x, x^2\}$ is the linearly independent basis from U , from which a three-dimensional linear space can be spanned. According to Definition 4, the subspaces are as follows

$$U'_1 = \{a\}, U'_2 = \{a_1 x\}, U'_3 = \{a_2 x^2\}, U'_4 = \{a + a_3 x\}$$

$$U'_5 = \{a + a_4 x^2\}, U'_6 = \{a_5 x + a_6 x^2\}, U'_7 = \{a + a_7 x + a_8 x^2\}$$

$$a, a_1, a_2, a_3, a_4, a_5, a_6, a_7, a_8 \neq 0$$

$U'_1 = \{a\}$ is a one-dimensional space, and it is on axis a.

$U'_4 = \{a + a_3 x\}$ is a two-dimentional space spanned by basis a and x,but the subspaces $\{a\}$ and $\{a_3 x\}$ are excluded.

$U'_7 = \{a + a_7 x + a_8 x^2\}$ is a three-dimensional space spanned by basis a, x and x^2,but the three two-dimentional and three one-dimentional subspaces are excluded.

Theorem 1. *The relationship R in U' that is defined by Definition 4 is an equivalence relation.*

Proof. Different class belongs to different subspace, so their elements -functions include different basic functions. As a result, the intersection of different spatial elements is an empty set. In fact, $U'_i \cap U'_j = \varnothing, i \neq j$ results in $[u_i]_R \cap [u_j]_R = \varnothing$. Therefore, relation R is equivalence relation.

Example 1. Suppose that $E = \{a, x, x^2\}$, in which a is a constant and x is the variable in definition domain. All elements are linearly independent, and compose a basis space. U' that derived from the basis in E is $U' = \{a_0, a_1 x, a_2 x^2, a_3 + a_4 x, a_5 + a_6 x^2, a_7 x + a_8 x^2, a_9 + a_{10} x + a_{11} x^2\}$, and $a_i \neq 0, i = 0, 1, 2, ..., 11$.

Obviously, the function in U' is the linear combination of basis in E, and they are located in different subspace. They disjoint from each other. The function in U' is required to meet the given requirements. For instance, if the function value is 0 when $x = 0$, then $U' = \{a_1 x, a_2 x^2, a_7 x + a_8 x^2\}$.

Definition 5. *In a random set $X \subseteq E \subseteq U$, U' is the deduced space of E, and the deduced space of X is $X'(X' \subseteq U')$; $X'$is the linear space spanned by the basis of X; R is equivalence relation defined by Definition 4. In subspace X' of the normed linear space U', R-lower approximations and R-upper approximations are defined as:*

$$R_*(X') = \cup\{Y \in U'/R : Y \subseteq X'\} \tag{1}$$

$$R^*(X') = \cup\{Y \in U'/R : Y \cap (E - X)' = \varnothing\} \tag{2}$$

Then R boundary region of X' is:

$$BN_R(X') = R^*(X') - R_*(X') \tag{3}$$

Lower approximation is the set composed of the subspaces in space X'. Upper approximation is composed of the union of the subspaces which consists of disjoint elements in $(E - X)'$. It is not difficult to prove $R_*(X') \subseteq X' \subseteq R^*(X')$.

If the set is discrete, the lower approximation defined by expression (2) can be easily confirmed to equivalent to that in [10].

Upper approximation means that its function contains the basis in X , as well as that out of X.

3   Example of Rough Sets in Normed Linear Space

In order to have a further understanding of rough sets in normed linear space, here we use an example to illustrate it.

Example 2. Let us consider a mechanics problem [9]. There is a simply supported beam subjected to concentrated force P shown in Fig.1. Let the length of the beam be l, and the displacement curve be $f(x)$. The displacement restriction of the simply supported beam is that there is no displacement at each end.

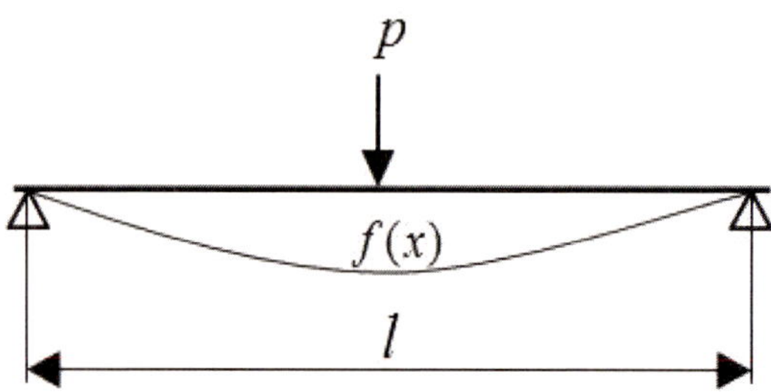

Fig. 1. Two-end simply supported beam subjected to concentrated load

The displacement which satisfies the restriction is called the possible displacement field. Let the accurate solution be $f(x)$, which obviously satisfies the displacement restriction at each end–when $x = 0, x = l$, there is no displacement, that is, $f(0) = f(l) = 0$. If an approximate solution $g(x)$ is used to approximate to the accurate solution, the approximate solution has to satisfy the displacement restriction of the beam, that is

$$g(0) = g(l) = 0 \tag{4}$$

Supposing a polynomial function be used to approximate the accurate solution. Let the basis space be $E = \{x, x^2, x^3, x^4\}$, which forms the approximate solution. The basis in the basis space makes up the space U', and the function cluster are as follows:

$U' = \{\{a_1 x\}, \{a_2 x^2\}, \{a_3 x^3\}, \{a_4 x^4\}, \{a_5 x + a_6 x^2\}, \{a_7 x + a_8 x^3\}, \{a_9 x + a_{10} x^4\}, \{a_{11} x^2 + a_{12} x^3\}, \{a_{13} x^2 + a_{14} x^4\}, \{a_{15} x^3 + a_{16} x^4\}, \{a_{17} x + a_{18} x^2 + a_{19} x^3\}, \{a_{20} x + a_{21} x^2 + a_{22} x^4\}, \{a_{23} x + a_{24} x^3 + a_{25} x^4\}, \{a_{26} x^2 + a_{27} x^3 + a_{28} x^4\}, \{a_{29} x + a_{30} x^2 + a_{31} x^3 + a_{32} x^4\}\}$

Each function is of a sort in its responding subspace and must satisfies the given requirement. Since the function cluster $\{a_1 x\}, \{a_2 x^2\}, \{a_3 x^3\}, \{a_4 x^4\}$ given in this example can not satisfy the requirement, the function cluster should be as following ones to satisfy the requirement:

$$\begin{aligned}
U'/R = &\{\{a_5 x + a_6 x^2\}, \{a_7 x + a_8 x^3\}, \{a_9 x + a_{10} x^4\}, \{a_{11} x^2 + a_{12} x^3\}, \\
&\{a_{13} x^2 + a_{14} x^4\}, \{a_{15} x^3 + a_{16} x^4\}, \{a_{17} x + a_{18} x^2 + a_{19} x^3\}, \\
&\{a_{20} x + a_{21} x^2 + a_{22} x^4\}, \{a_{23} x + a_{24} x^3 + a_{25} x^4\}, \\
&\{a_{26} x^2 + a_{27} x^3 + a_{28} x^4\}, \{a_{29} x + a_{30} x^2 + a_{31} x^3 + a_{32} x^4\}\}
\end{aligned} \tag{5}$$

Let $X = \{x, x^2\}$, then the space satisfying the given requirement derived from $X = \{x, x^2\}$ is $X' = \{\{a_5 x + a_6 x^2\}\}$. According to the lower approximation expression (1), we can get

$$R_*(X') = \cup\{Y \in U'/R : Y \subseteq X'\} = \{\{a_5 x + a_6 x^2\}\} \tag{6}$$

Because of $(E - X) = \{x^3, x^4\}, (E - X)' = \{a_{15} x^3 + a_{16} x^4\}$, we can also get the R-upper approximation according to the upper approximation expression (2):

$$\begin{aligned}
R^*(X') = &\cup \{Y \in U'/R : Y \cap (E - X)' = \varnothing\} = \\
&\{\{a_5 x + a_6 x^2\}, \{a_7 x + a_8 x^3\}, \{a_9 x + a_{10} x^4\}, \{a_{11} x^2 + a_{12} x^3\}, \\
&\{a_{13} x^2 + a_{14} x^4\}, \{a_{17} x + a_{18} x^2 + a_{19} x^3\}, \{a_{20} x + a_{21} x^2 + \\
&a_{22} x^4\}, \{a_{23} x + a_{24} x^3 + a_{25} x^4\}, \{a_{26} x^2 + a_{27} x^3 + a_{28} x^4\}, \\
&\{a_{29} x + a_{30} x^2 + a_{31} x^3 + a_{32} x^4\}\}
\end{aligned} \tag{7}$$

Then R boundary region of X' is

$$BN_R(X') = R^*(X') - R_*(X') =$$

$$\{\{a_7x + a_8x^3\}, \{a_9x + a_{10}x^4\}, \{a_{11}x^2 + a_{12}x^3\}, \{a_{13}x^2 + $$
$$a_{14}x^4\}, \{a_{17}x + a_{18}x^2 + a_{19}x^3\}, \{a_{20}x + a_{21}x^2 + a_{22}x^4\}, \quad (8)$$
$$\{a_{23}x + a_{24}x^3 + a_{25}x^4\}, \{a_{26}x^2 + a_{27}x^3 + a_{28}x^4\},$$
$$\{a_{29}x + a_{30}x^2 + a_{31}x^3 + a_{32}x^4\}\}$$

Through observation, it is not difficult to find out that the lower approximation is the satisfying given requirement function cluster derived from a specified primary function and the upper approximation is the function cluster, in which the functions contain the basis in X space. The function cluster of upper approximation contain more function clusters, because besides the basis in X space, it also contains basis in other spaces.

4   Results of Rough Sets in Normed Linear Space

Theorem 2. *Let $E \subseteq U$ be a known basis space. If the upper approximation equals to the lower approximation, then the basis given by $X \subseteq U$ is the maximum basis satisfying the given requirement and error.*

This theorem shows when the upper approximation equals to the lower approximation, $X \subseteq U$ is the maximum basis satisfying the given requirement. And any other basis in E doesn't accord with the given requirement.

If the lower approximation is null, no basis in $X \subseteq U$ satisfying the requirement exists.

In basis space, the procedure to figure out the minimum basis space according to the given requirement is called reduction.

Reduction can eliminate redundant basis, facilitate constructing approximate solution and reduce the computational work in getting the approximate solution.

When the minimum basis is found, we can construct the approximate solution with lesser amount of parameters, which reduces computational cost.

Example 3. Let the displacement curve of simply supported beam under even load be quadruple polynomial [9]. If the basis space is $E = \{a, x, x^2, x^3, x^4, x^5, \sin(\pi x/l), \sin(2(\pi x/l))\}$ and error $\varepsilon = 0.02$ is given, what is the minimum basis?

Obviously, the linear combination of basis $E = \{x, x^2, x^3, x^4\}$ may compose the solutions satisfying the given error and requirement and so may $E = \{x, x^2, x^3\}$. But the minimum basis in this example is $E = \{\sin(2(\pi x/l))\}$, namely, we can get the proper solution by using only one basis [9].

The approximation computation theory shows that continuous function can be expanded in form of polynomial basis or orthogonal trigonometric function. In general, the front several items in the expansion series plays the most important roles, which means the front several items will meet the needs, especially for the series which converges pretty fast.

Definition 6. *The union of all the reduced minimum basis in the basis space is called the base basis.*

The base basis is the necessary basis when composing the approximate solution.

Observing the basis space $E = \{a, x, x^2, x^3, x^4, x^5, \sin(\pi x/l), \sin(2(\pi x/l))\}$, we get two sorts of basis. One is in type of polynomial functions and the other is in type of orthogonal trigonometric functions. Either type of functions can be used to compose the solution satisfying the given requirement. When polynomial functions are used , the basis $\{x, x^2\}$ is necessary and when orthogonal trigonometric functions are used, the basis $\{\sin(\pi x/l)$ is necessary as well. According to definition 6, we know that the base basis of $E = \{a, x, x^2, x^3, x^4, x^5, \sin(\pi x/l), \sin(2(\pi x/l))\}$ in example 3 is $B = \{x, x^2, \sin(\pi x/l)\}$.

Besides the two sorts of basis above, in fact, we can use wavelet basis to compose the solution to example 3. Through rough set method, we can investigate the structure of approximation solution basis space comprehensively so as to make the investigation of the structure of approximation solution more easily. Traditional methods detach the basis of approximation solution. As for the example 3, traditional methods deal with polynomial functions basis and orthogonal trigonometric functions basis and the wavelet basis individually, but have not put them together. In view of rough sets, more comprehensive and systematic research may be done for the basis of certain problems. Thus, we may get more information of the approximation solution, and provide theoretical direction for composing approximation solution more efficiently.

5   Conclusion

It is a creative attempt to establish rough sets in normed linear space, which has provided a platform and laid a foundation for introducing rough sets to continuous function space. Therefore, the application field for rough sets has been expanded.

There is much work to be done for the further research in rough sets in normed linear space,such as the more properties of rough sets, granular computing on rough sets in normed linear space and so on.

Acknowledgement

This study is supported by the Natural Science Fund of China (NSFC-60173054).

References

1. Hu,S.G.: Applied Functional Analysis(Chinese),Beijing: Science Press(2004).
2. Jiang,Z.J.,Sun,S.L.: Functional Analysis(Second Edition, Chinese). BeiJing:Higher Education Press(2005).
3. Lin,T.Y.: From rough sets and neighborhood systems to information granulation and computing in Words. In: Proceedings of European Congress on Intelligent Techniques and Soft Computing (1997) 1602-1606.

4. Lin,T.Y.: Granular computing on binary relations II: Rough set representations and belief functions. In: Skowron, A., Polkowski, L. (eds): *Rough Sets in Knowledge Discovery.* Physica-Verlag, Berlin (1998).

5. Liu,Z.: Real Function Rough discretize. Journal of Nanjing University, 36(11)(2000)188-191.

6. Liu,Q.: Rough Sets and Rough Reasoning(Third Edition,Chinese). Beijing: Science Press(2005)

7. Liu,Q.,Liu,S.H.,Zheng,F.: Rough logic and its applications in data reduction. *Journal of Software*(In Chinese) 3 (2001) 415-419.

8. Liu,Q.: Granules and reasoning based on granular computing. In: Proceedings of 16th International Conference on Industrial and Engineering Applications of Artificial Intelligence and Expert Systems. Springer, Berlin (2003) 516-526.

9. Oden,J.T.,Ripperger,E.A.: Mechanics of Elastic Structures (Second Edition)(1981).

10. Pawlak,Z.: Rough sets. International Journal of Computer and Information Sciences 11(1982) 341-356.

11. Pawlak,Z.: Rough Sets,Theoretical Aspects of Reasoning about Data, System Theory, Knowledge Engineering and Problem Solving 9, Dordrecht: Kluwer Academic Publishers(1991)

12. Pawlak,Z.: Rough Functions. Bull. Polish Acad. Aci. Tech. 35/5-6(1987) 249-251

13. Pawlak,Z.: Rough sets, Rough Relations and Rough Functions. Fundamenta Informaticae. 8(1996)

14. Pawlak,Z.,skowron,A.: Rough Membership Functions, A Tool for Reasoning with Uncertainty. In: C. Rauszer(ed.),Algebraic Methods in Logic and Computer Science, Banach Center Publications 28,Polish Academy of Sciences, Warsaw(1993)135-150

15. Skowron,A., Stepaniuk,J.,Peters,J.F.: Extracting patterns using information granules. In: Proceedings of International Workshop on Rough Set Theory and Granular Computing. Japan (2001) 135-142.

16. Skowron,A.: Toward intelligent systems: Calculi of information granules. *Bulletin of International Rough Set Society* 1-2 (2001) 9-30.

17. Skowron,A., Swiniarski,R.: Information granulation and pattern recognition. In: Pal, S.K., Polkowski, L., Skowron, A. (eds): *Rough Neurocomputing: Techniques for Computing with Words, Cognitive Technologies.* Springer-Verlag, Berlin (2003).

18. Skowron,A., Stepaniuk,J.: Information granules and rough neurcomputing. In: Pal, S.K., Polkowski, L., Skowron, A. (eds): *Rough Neurocomputing: Techniques for Computing with Words, Cognitive Technologies.* Springer-Verlag, Berlin (2003).

19. Yao,Y.Y., Yao,J.T.: Granular computing as a basis for consistent classification problems. In: Proceedings of PAKDD'02 Workshop on Foundations of Data Mining. Taiwan (2002) 101-106.

20. Yao,Y.Y.: Information granulation and rough set approximation. *International Journal of Intelligence Systems* 16 (2001) 87-104.

Two Kinds of Rough Algebras and Brouwer-Zadeh Lattices

Jian-Hua Dai[1], Hanfei Lv[2], Weidong Chen[1], and Yunhe Pan[1]

[1] Institute of Artificial Intelligence,
Zhejiang University, Hangzhou 310027, P.R. China
`jhdai@126.com, chenwd@zju.edu.cn`
[2] Department of Information Management,
Zhejiang Police Vocational Academy, Hangzhou 310018, P.R. China
`lvhanfei@zjjy.com.cn`

Abstract. Many researchers study rough sets from the point of view of description of the rough set pairs(a rough set pair is also called a rough set), i.e. <lower approximation set, upper approximation set>. Comer [4] showed that all the rough sets in an approximation space constructed a regular double Stone algebra. The constructed algebra is called the rough double Stone algebra in this paper. Pagliani [19] interpreted Rough Set System (all the rough sets in an approximation space in disjoint representation) as a Nelson algebra. The constructed Nelson algebra from an approximation space is called the rough Nelson algebra in this paper. It is showed that a rough double Stone algebra is a Brouwer-Zadeh lattice, and a rough Nelson algebra is a Brouwer-Zadeh lattice also.

1 Introduction

Rough set theory was introduced by Pawlak [21] to account for the definability of a concept with an approximation in an approximation space (U, R), where U is a set, and R is an equivalence relation on U. It captures and formalizes the basic phenomenon of information granulation. The finer the granulation is, the more concepts are definable in it. For those concepts not definable in an approximation space, their lower and upper approximations can be defined.

There have been extensive studies on rough set by algebraic methods [1-20,22,23]. Lin and Liu [18] replaced equivalence relation with arbitrary binary relation, and the equivalence classes are replaced by neighborhood at the same time. By means of the two replacements, they defined more general approximation operators. Yao [23] interpreted Rough set theory as an extension of set theory with two additional unary set-theoretic operators referred to as approximation operators. Such an interpretation is consistent with interpreting modal logic as an extension of classical two-valued logic with two added unary operators. Cattaneo et al.[3] constructed two modal-like unary operators in the frame of de Morgan BZMV algebras. The two operators give rise to rough approximation. In [4], Cattaneo and Ciucci obtianed a de Morgan Brouwer-Zadeh distributive lattice from a Heyting Wajsberg algebra. Modal-like operators were

S. Greco et al. (Eds.): RSCTC 2006, LNAI 4259, pp. 99–106, 2006.

defined generating a rough approximation space. Dai [5,6]introduced molecular lattices into the research on rough sets and constructed structure of rough approximations based on molecular lattices. In [8], Dai et al. also studied the axiomatization of generalized rough set model, i.e. rough set on quasi-ordering.

At the same time, researchers also study rough sets from the point of view of description of the rough set pairs, i.e. <lower approximation set, upper approximation set>. Iwiński [16] suggested a lattice theoretical approach. Iwiński's aim, which was extended by J. Pomykala and J. A. Pomykala [22] later, was to endow the rough seubsets of U with a natural algebraic structure. J. Pomykala and J. A. Pomykala's work was also improved by Comer [4] who noticed that the collection of rough sets of an approximation space is in fact a regular double Stone algebra when one introduced another unary operator, i.e. the dual pseudo-complement operator.In [19], Pagliani investigated rough set systems within the framework Nelson algebras under the assumption of a finite universe. All these algebras have rough sets as their models. They can be called rough algebras.

In this paper, we intend to study the relationships between two kinds of rough algebras, constructed by Comer [4] and Pagliani [19] respectively, and Brouwer-Zadeh algebras.

2   Preliminaries

Let (U, R) be an approximation space, where U is the universe and R is an equivalence relation on U. With each approximation space (U, R), two operators on $\mathcal{P}(U)$ can be defined. For any $X \subseteq U$, then the lower approximation of X and the upper approximation of X are defined as:

$$R_-(X) = \bigcup\{[X]_R | [X]_R \subseteq X\} \tag{1}$$

$$R^-(X) = \bigcup\{[X]_R | [X]_R \cap X \neq \emptyset\} \tag{2}$$

The pair $< R_-(X), R^-(X) >$ is called a rough set. X is termed definable set(also termed exact set) in approximation space (U, R) if and only if $R_-(X) = R^-(X)$. For the sake of simplicity, the lower approximation and upper approximation are also denoted as $\underline{X}$ and $\overline{X}$ respectively. In this paper, we denote the collection of all rough sets of an approximation (U, R) as $\mathcal{RS}(U)$.

Definition 1. [3]*A structure* $(\sum, \vee, \wedge, \neg, \sim, 0)$ *is a distributive Brouwer-Zadeh lattice if*

1. $(\sum, \vee, \wedge, 0)$ *is a (nonempty) distributive lattice with minimum element 0 ;*
2. *The mapping* $\neg : \sum \rightarrow \sum$*is a Kleene orthocomplementation, that is*
    (a) $\neg(\neg a) = a,$
    (b) $\neg(a \vee b) = \neg a \wedge \neg b,$
    (c) $a \wedge \neg a \leq b \vee \neg b.$
3. *The mapping* $\sim : \sum \rightarrow \sum$*is a Brouwer orthocomplementation, that is*
    (a) $a \wedge \sim\sim a = a,$

(b) $\sim (a \vee b) =\sim a \wedge \sim b$,
(c) $a \wedge \sim a = 0$.

4. *The two orthocomplementations are linked by the following interconnection rule:*

$$\neg \sim a =\sim\sim a.$$

The mapping $\neg$ is also called the Łukasiewicz (or fuzzy, Zadeh) orthocomplementation while the mapping $\sim$ is an intuitionistic-like orthocomplementation. The element $1 :=\sim 0 = \neg 0$ is the greatest element of $\sum$.

3   Rough Double Stone Algebras and Brouwer-Zadeh Lattices

Now we study the relationship between the rough double Stone algebra induced from an approximation space (U, R).

Definition 2. *A structure $(L, \vee, \wedge, {}^{*}, {}^{+}, 0, 1)$ is a regular double Stone algebra if*

1. *$(L, \vee, \wedge, {}^{*}, {}^{+} 0, 1)$ is a lattice with least element 0 and greatest element 1;*
2. *$\forall x \in L$ there is an element x^{*}, for any $y \in L$ satisfying*

$$x \wedge y = 0 \; iff \; y \leq x^{*};$$

3. *$\forall x \in L$ there is an element x, for any $y \in L$ satisfying*

$$x \vee y = 1 \; iff \; x^{+} \leq y;$$

4. *$\forall x \in L, x^{*} \vee x^{**} = 1, x^{+} \wedge x^{++} = 0$;*
5. *$x^{*} = y^{*}$ and $x^{+} = y^{+}$ imply $x = y$.*

The element x^{*} is termed pseudo-complement of x, x^{+} is termed dual pseudo-complement of x. The structure L satisfying the conditions 1-4 is called a double Stone algebra. It is called regular, if it additionally satisfies the condition 5. In fact, the condition 5 is equivalent to

$$x \wedge x^{+} \leq x \vee x^{*}.$$

It was shown by J. Pomykala and J. A. Pomykala [22] that the collection of all rough sets of (U, R), denoted as $\mathcal{RS}(U)$, can be made into a Stone algebra expressed as $(\mathcal{RS}(U), \oplus, \otimes, {}^{*}, < \emptyset, \emptyset >, < U, U >)$. The work of J. Pomykala and J. A. Pomykala was improved by Comer [4] who noticed that $\mathcal{RS}(U)$ is in fact a regular double Stone algebra expressed as:

$$(\mathcal{RS}(U), \oplus, \otimes, {}^{*}, {}^{+}, < \emptyset, \emptyset >, < U, U >),$$

where $< \emptyset, \emptyset >$ is the least element and $< U, U >$ is the greatest element. The union operator $\oplus$, join operator $\otimes$, pseudo-complement operator * and the dual pseudo-complement operator ${}^{+}$ are defined as following:

$$< \underline{X}, \overline{X} > \oplus < \underline{Y}, \overline{Y} >=< \underline{X} \cup \underline{Y}, \overline{X} \cup \overline{Y} > \tag{3}$$

$$< \underline{X}, \overline{X} > \otimes < \underline{Y}, \overline{Y} >=< \underline{X} \cap \underline{Y}, \overline{X} \cap \overline{Y} > \tag{4}$$

$$< \underline{X}, \overline{X} >^*=< U - \overline{X}, U - \overline{X} >=< (\overline{X})^c, (\overline{X})^c > \tag{5}$$

$$< \underline{X}, \overline{X} >^+=< U - \underline{X}, U - \underline{X} >=< (\underline{X})^c, (\underline{X})^c > \tag{6}$$

Definition 3. *Let (U, R) be an approximation space. The algebra $(\mathcal{RS}(U), \oplus, \otimes, {}^*, {}^+, < \emptyset, \emptyset >, < U, U >)$ constructed by the approach taken above is called the rough double Stone algebra induced from the approximation space (U, R).*

Proposition 1. *[4] A rough double Stone algebra $(\mathcal{RS}(U), \oplus, \otimes, {}^*, {}^+, < \emptyset, \emptyset >, < U, U >)$is a regular double Stone algebra. Conversely, each regular double Stone algebra is isomorphic to subalgebra of $\mathcal{RS}(U)$ for some approximation space (U, R).*

Theorem 1. *A rough double Stone algebra $(\mathcal{RS}(U), \oplus, \otimes, {}^*, {}^+, < \emptyset, \emptyset >, < U, U >)$is a distributive Brouwer-Zadeh lattice $(\mathcal{RS}(U), \oplus, \otimes, \neg, \sim, < \emptyset, \emptyset >)$ The Kleene orthocomplementation $\neg$ is defined by*

$$\forall a \in \mathcal{RS}(U), \neg a = a^+ \otimes (a \oplus a^*),$$

and the Brouwer orthocomplementation is defined by

$$\forall a \in \mathcal{RS}(U), \sim a = a^*.$$

Proof. (1). It is obvious that $(\mathcal{RS}(U), \oplus, \otimes, < \emptyset, \emptyset >)$ is a distributive lattice with minimum element $< \emptyset, \emptyset >$.

(2). We now prove that $\neg a = a^+ \wedge (a \vee a^*)$ is the Kleene orthocomplementation. Let $a =< A, B >\in \mathcal{RS}(U)$, then $\neg a = a^+ \otimes (a \oplus a^*) =< A^c, A^c > \otimes(< A, B > \oplus < B^c, B^c >) =< A^c \cap (A \cup B^c), A^c \cap (B \cup B^c) >=< A^c \cap B^c, A^c >$. Since $A \subseteq B$, it follows that $B^c \subseteq A^c$. Hence, $\neg a =< B^c, A^c >$.

(a)Let $a =< A, B >\in \mathcal{RS}(U)$, then $\neg\neg a = \neg < B^c, A^c >=< A, B >= a$.

(b)Let $a, b \in \mathcal{RS}(U), a =< A, B >, b =< C, D >$, then $\neg(a \oplus b) = \neg < A \cup C, B \cup D >=< B^c \cap D^c, A^c \cap C^c >=< B^c, A^c > \otimes < D^c, C^c >= \neg a \otimes \neg b$.

(c)Let $a, b \in \mathcal{RS}(U), a =< A, B >, b =< C, D >$, then $a \otimes \neg a =< A, B > \otimes < B^c, A^c >=< A \cap B^c, B \cap A^c >$. Since $A \subseteq B$, it follows that $B^c \subseteq A^c$. Hence, $A \cap B^c = \emptyset$, i.e., $a \otimes \neg a =< \emptyset, B \cap A^c >$. At the same time, $b \oplus \neg b =< C, D > \oplus < D^c, C^c >=< C \cup D^c, D \cup C^c >$. Since $C \subseteq D$, it follows that $D^c \subseteq C^c$. Hence, $D \cup C^c = U$, i.e., $b \oplus \neg b =< C \cup D^c, U >$. It is obvious that $< \emptyset, B \cap A^c > \underline{\le} < C \cup D^c, U >$, i.e., $a \otimes \neg a \le b \oplus \neg b$.

(3). We now prove that $\sim$ is the Brouwer orthocomplementation. Let $a =< A, B >\in \mathcal{RS}(U)$, then we get $\sim a =< A, B >^*=< B^c, B^c >$ by Equation (5).

(a)Let $a =< A, B >\in \mathcal{RS}(U)$, then $\sim\sim a =\sim< B^c, B^c >=< B, B >$. It follows that $a \otimes \sim\sim a =< A, B > \otimes < B, B >=< A, B >= a$.

(b)Let $a, b \in \mathcal{RS}(U), a =< A, B >, b =< C, D >$, then $\sim (a \oplus b) =\sim< A \cup C, B \cup D >=< B^c \cap D^c, B^c \cap D^c >=< B^c, B^c > \otimes < D^c, D^c >=\sim a \otimes \sim b$.

(c)Let $a =< A, B >\in \mathcal{RS}(U)$, then $a \otimes \sim a =< A, B > \otimes < B^c, B^c >=< A \cap B^c, \emptyset >$. Since, $A \subseteq B$, it follows that $B^c \subseteq A^c$, i.e., $A \cap B^c = \emptyset$. Hence, $a \otimes \sim a =< \emptyset, \emptyset >= 0$.

(4). We now consider the relationship between the two orthocomplementations. that $\sim$ is the Brouwer orthocomplementation. Let $a, b \in \mathcal{RS}(U), a =< A, B >, b =< C, D >$, then $\neg \sim a = \neg < B^c, B^c >=< B, B >$. On the other hand, $\sim\sim a =\sim< B^c, B^c >=< B, B >$. It is obvious that $\neg \sim a =\sim\sim a$.

From the above (1)-(4), together with Definition 1, we can prove this theorem.

$$\square$$

4 Rough Nelson Algebras and Brouwer-Zadeh Lattices

Pagliani [19] proposed the disjoint representation of rough sets. Given an approximation space (U, R), let $X \subseteq U$, then the pair $< \underline{X}, \overline{X}^c >$ is called a rough set.

Definition 4. *Let (U, R) be an approximation space, then*

$$\mathcal{RSS}(U) = \{< \underline{X}, \overline{X}^c > | X \subseteq U\}$$

is called the Rough Set System induced by (U, R).

Definition 5. *A structure $(L, \vee, \wedge, \neg, \rightarrow, 0, 1)$ is a Nelson algebra if*

1. *$(L, \vee, \wedge, 0, 1)$ is a distributive lattice with least element 0 and greatest element 1;*
2. *$\neg(x \vee y) = \neg x \wedge \neg y,$*
3. *$\neg\neg x = x,$*
4. *$x \wedge \neg y \leq y \vee \neg y,$*
5. *$x \wedge z \leq \neg x \vee y$ iff $z \leq x \rightarrow y,$*
6. *$x \rightarrow (y \rightarrow z) = (x \wedge y) \rightarrow z.$*

It was shown by Pagliani that the Rough Set System $\mathcal{RSS}(U)$ induced by an approximation space (U, R) can be made into a Nelson algebra expressed as .

$$(\mathcal{RSS}(U), \oplus, \otimes, \neg, \rightarrow, < \emptyset, U >, < \emptyset, U >),$$

where $< \emptyset, U >$ is the least element and $< \emptyset, U >$ is the greatest element. The union operator $\oplus$, join operator $\otimes$, pseudo-complement operator $\neg, \rightarrow$ are defined as following:

$$< \underline{X}, \overline{X}^c > \oplus < \underline{Y}, \overline{Y}^c >=< \underline{X} \cup \underline{Y}, \overline{X}^c \cap \overline{Y}^c > \tag{7}$$

$$< \underline{X}, \overline{X}^c > \otimes < \underline{Y}, \overline{Y}^c >=< \underline{X} \cap \underline{Y}, \overline{X}^c \cup \overline{Y}^c > \tag{8}$$

$$< \underline{X}, \overline{X}^c > \rightarrow < \underline{Y}, \overline{Y}^c >=< (\underline{X})^c \cup \underline{Y}, \underline{X} \cap \overline{Y}^c > \tag{9}$$

$$\neg < \underline{X}, \overline{X}^c >=< \overline{X}^c, \underline{X} > \tag{10}$$

Definition 6. *Let (U, R) be an approximation space. The algebra $(\mathcal{RSS}(U), \oplus, \otimes, \neg, \rightarrow, < \emptyset, U >, < \emptyset, U >)$ constructed by the approach taken above is called the rough Nelson algebra induced from the approximation space (U, R).*

Proposition 2. *[19] A rough Nelson algebra $(\mathcal{RSS}(U), \oplus, \otimes, \neg, \rightarrow, < \emptyset, U >, < \emptyset, U >)$ is a Nelson algebra.*

Theorem 2. *A rough Nelson algebra $(\mathcal{RSS}(U), \oplus, \otimes, \neg, \rightarrow, < \emptyset, U >, < \emptyset, U >)$ is a distributive Brouwer-Zadeh lattice $(\mathcal{RS}(U), \oplus, \otimes, \neg, \sim, < \emptyset, \emptyset >)$. $\neg$ is the Kleene orthocomplementation. The Brouwer orthocomplementation is defined by*

$$\forall a \in \mathcal{RSS}(U), \sim a = a \rightarrow \neg a.$$

Proof. (1). It is obvious that $(\mathcal{RSS}(U)$ is a distributive lattice with minimum element $< \emptyset, U >$.

(2). It is obvious that $\neg$ is the Kleene orthocomplementation.

(3). We now prove that $\sim$ is the Brouwer orthocomplementation. Let $a =< A, B >\in \mathcal{RSS}(U)$, then we get $\sim a =< A, B >\rightarrow \neg < A, B >=< A, B >\rightarrow< B, A >=< A^c \cup B, A \cap A >$. Since $A \subseteq B^c$, it follows that $B \subseteq A^c$. Hence, $\sim a =< A^c, A >$.

(a)Let $a =< A, B >\in \mathcal{RSS}(U)$, then$\sim\sim a =\sim< A^c, A >=< A, A^c >$. It follows that $a\otimes \sim\sim a =< A, B > \otimes < A, A^c >=< A, B \cap A^c >$. Since $A \subseteq B^c$, it follows that $B \subseteq A^c$. Hence,$a\otimes \sim\sim a =< A, B >= a$.

(b)Let $a, b \in \mathcal{RSS}(U), a =< A, B >, b =< C, D >$, then$\sim (a \oplus b) =\sim< A \cup C, B \cap D >=< A^c \cap C^c, A \cup C >=< A^c, A > \otimes < C^c, C >=\sim a\otimes \sim b$.

(c)Let $a =< A, B >\in \mathcal{RSS}(U)$, then$a\otimes \sim a =< A, B > \otimes < A^c, A >=< \emptyset, B\cup A >$. Since,$A \subseteq B^c$, it follows that $B\cup A = U$. Hence, $a\otimes \sim a =< \emptyset, U >= 0$.

(4). We now consider the relationship between the two orthocomplementations. Let $a, b \in \mathcal{RSS}(U), a =< A, B >$, then$\neg \sim a = \neg < A^c, A >=< A, A^c >$. On the other hand, $\sim\sim a =\sim< A^c, A >=< A, A^c >$. It is obvious that $\neg \sim a =\sim\sim a$.

From the above (1)-(4), together with Definition 1, we can prove this theorem. $\square$

5   Conclusion

In this paper, we study the relationship between two kinds of rough algebras and Brouwer-Zadeh lattices. It is showed that a rough double Stone algebra constructed by Comer [4] is a distributive Brouwer-Zadeh lattice, and a rough Nelson algebra constructed by Pagliani [19] is a distributive Brouwer-Zadeh lattice too.

In [7,9], logic systems for rough sets with rough algebraic semantics were studied. In our future work, we will try to construct logic for rough sets in the framework of Brouwer-Zadeh lattices.

Acknowledgements

The work is supported by the 973 National Key Basic Research and Development Program of China(No.2002CB312106), the China Postdoctoral Science Foundation(No.2004035715), the Postdoctoral Science Foundation of Zhejiang Province in China (No. 2004-bsh-023)and the Science&Technology Program of Zhejiang Province in China (No.2004C31098).

References

1. Banerjee, M., Chakraborty, M. K.: Rough sets through algebraic logic. Fundamenta Informaticae, **28**, (1996)211-221.
2. Cattaneo, G., Ciucci, D.: Heyting Wajsberg algebras as an abstract enviroment linking fuzzy and rough sets. Proceedings of 3rd International Conference on Rough Sets and Current Trends in Computing (RSCTC2002), LNAI 2475, Springer-Verlag, Berlin (2004)77-84.
3. Cattaneo, G., Giuntini, R., Pilla, R.: $BZMV^{dM}$ algebras and stonian MV-algebras. Fuzzy Sets and Systems, **108**, (1999)201-222.
4. Comer, S.: On connections between information systems, rough sets and algebraic logic. In: Algebraic methods in logic and computer science. Banach Center Publications (1993)117-124.
5. Dai, J. H.: Generalization of rough set theory using molecular lattices. Chinese Journal of Computers, **27**, (2004)1436-1440(in Chinese).
6. Dai, J. H.: Structure of rough approximations based on molecular lattices. Proceedings of 4th International Conference on Rough Sets and Current Trends in Computing (RSCTC2004), LNAI 3066, Springer-Verlag, Berlin (2004)69-77.
7. Dai, J. H.: Logic for rough sets with rough double Stone algebraic semantics. Proceedings of 10th International Conference on Rough Sets, Fuzzy Sets, Data Mining and Granular Computing (RSFDGrC2005), LNAI 3641, Springer-Verlag, Berlin (2005)141-148.
8. Dai, J. H., Chen, W.D., Pan, Y.H.: A minimal axiom group of rough set based on Quasi-ordering. Journal of Zhejiang University SCIENCE,**7**, (2004)810-815.
9. Dai, J. H., Chen, W.D., Pan, Y.H.: Sequent caculus system for rough sets based on rough Stone algebras. Proc. of IEEE International Conference on Granular Computing (IEEE GrC 2005), IEEE Press, New Jersy (2005)423-426.
10. Dai, J. H., Chen, W.D., Pan, Y.H.: Rousht sets and Brouwer-Zadeh lattices. Proceedings of 1st International Conference on Rough Sets and Knowledge Technology (RSKT2006), LNAI 4062, Springer-Verlag, Berlin (2006)200-207.
11. Dai, J. H., Pan, Y. H.: On rough algebras. Journal of Software,**16**, (2005)1197-1204(in Chinese).
12. Düntsch, I.: Rough relation algebras. Fundamenta Informace,**21**, (1994)321-331.
13. Düntsch, I.: Rough sets and algebra of relations.In: Orlowska, E. (eds.): Incomplete information: Rough set analysis,Physica-Verlag, Herdberg (1998)95-108.
14. Gehrke, M., Walker, E.: On the structure of rough sets. Bulletin of the Polish Academy of Sciences: Mathematics, **40**, (1992)235-255.
15. Iturrioz, L.: Rough sets and 3-valued structures. In: Orlowska, E. (eds.): Logic at work. Springer-Verlag, Herdberg (1998)596-603.
16. Iwiński, T. B.: Algebraic approach to rough sets. Bulletin of the Polish Academy of Sci-ences: Mathematics, **35**, (1987)673-683.

17. Jarvinen, J.: On the structure of rough approximations. Proceedings of 3rd International Conference on Rough Sets and Current Trends in Computing (RSCTC2002), LNAI 2475, Springer-Verlag, Berlin (2002)123-130.
18. Lin, T.Y., Liu, Q.: Rough approximate operators: Axiomatic rough set theory. In: Ziarko, W. P. (eds.): Rough Sets, Fuzzy Sets and Knowledge Discovery. Springer-Verlag, Berlin (1994)256-260.
19. Pagliani, P.: Rough sets and Nelson algebras. Fundamenta Informaticae, **27**, (1996)205-219.
20. Pagliani, P.: Rough set theory and logic-algebraic structures. In: Orlowska, E. (eds.): Incomplete information: Rough set analysis,Physica-Verlag, Herdberg (1998)109-190.
21. Pawlak, Z.: Rough Sets-Theoretical Aspects of Reasoning about Data. Kluwer Academic Publishers, Dordrecht (1991).
22. Pomykala, J., Pomykala, J. A.: The Stone algebra of rough sets. Bulletin of the Polish Academy of Sciences: Mathematics, **36**, (1988)495-508.
23. Yao, Y.Y.: Constructive and algebraic methods of the theory of rough sets. Information Sciences, **109**, (1998)21-47.

Balanced Fuzzy Gates[*]

Wladyslaw Homenda[1] and Witold Pedrycz[2]

[1] Faculty of Mathematics and Information Science
Warsaw University of Technology
Plac Politechniki 1, 00-660 Warszawa, Poland
`homenda@mini.pw.edu.pl`
[2] Department of Electrical and Computer Engineering
University of Alberta, Edmonton, Canada T6G 2G7
and
Systems Research Institute, Polish Academy of Sciences
01-447 Warsaw, Poland
`pedrycz@ece.ualberta.ca`

Abstract. In this paper, we introduce and study a new concept of balanced fuzzy gates. The idea itself is based upon the balanced fuzzy sets forming an essential extension of the generic theory of fuzzy sets. We discuss the topology of the gates and elaborate on several fundamental models of logic connectives. A particular focus is on the two categories of the gates realizing a certain *and* and *or* type of processing. In the sequel presented are architectures of networks built with the use of the logical gates. We offer some design guidelines of the development of the networks and elaborate on the nature of the structural construction.

1   Introduction

In fuzzy sets, and information granules in general, we are concerned with the fundamental concept of membership. More precisely, in fuzzy sets we quantify a degree of membership of a certain element by using numeric values coming from the unit interval. Traditionally, higher membership degrees (located closer to 1) indicate stronger belongingness (membership) of the element to the concept captured by the given fuzzy set. Lower membership degrees assuming values close to zero quantify the fact of a lack of membership. Interestingly enough, there is no generally accepted concept of exclusion neither a suitable mechanism of the quantification of this exclusion itself. With this regard, the previous studies [6,7] have raised this point and offered a concept of the balanced fuzzy sets whose primary intent was to introduce the concept of exclusion and propose some ways of quantification of such effect. The objective of this study is to proceed along this line and develop a collection of generic processing units - balanced gates whose processing exploits the principles of the theory of balanced fuzzy sets.

[*] Support from the State Committee for Scientific Research Grant no 3T11C00926, years 2004-2007 and the Natural Sciences and Engineering Research Council of Canada (NSERC) is gratefully acknowledged.

S. Greco et al. (Eds.): RSCTC 2006, LNAI 4259, pp. 107–116, 2006.

We discuss essential properties of the balanced gates and come up with a sound interpretation of the underlying processing linking those gates to some other existing constructs including digital gates encountered in digital systems and fuzzy gates formed on a basis of fuzzy sets.

The paper is organized as follows. We start with a rationale outlining how the main issues arising around the concept of positive (excitatory), negative (inhibitory) and neutral information. In Section 2, we discuss fuzzy logic gates by presenting the main feature of processing information with the aid of triangular norms. In the sequel, we elaborate on a new category of balanced gates whose processing is governed by extended models of triangular norms. The discussion is augmented by a variety of illustrative material highlighting the performance of the gates. We also elaborate on further buildups coming in the form of networks of balanced gates and augmentations of the gates themselves that result in so-called balanced neurons. Concluding comments are offered in Section 5.

1.1   A Rationale

Logical gates perform discrete information with regard to input, internal and output signal. Such a model of information processing is desired for its simplicity, but it could be applied only for certain information processing. This means that continuous signal/information (say, analog signal, uncertain information) must be turned to discrete information (where we refer to the idea of a certain unit of information or consider digital signal) prior to any processing realized by a system of logical gates. Therefore, any system of logical gates, if applied to uncertain information processing, should come with a meaningful analog-to-discrete conversion mechanism. Such a limitation significantly reduces potential benefits that are associated with the processing of uncertain information.

It would be therefore highly desirable to overcome this limitation by expanding a system of logical gates in such a way so that they could handle continuous signals and then turn output signals into discrete form. The direct and natural way of such expansion could be realized by expanding discrete logical functions, which govern logical gates, to their continuous counterparts. The well known fuzzy extensions of classical fuzzy sets and classical logic are natural candidates for such an expansion. In other words, building continuous versions of logical gates, called fuzzy logic gates, which perform fuzzy connectives *max*, *min* and *not* as well as their generalized counterparts in the form of $t - conorms$ and $t - norms$. Therefore, signal processing would be done based on continuous signals and, after that, output of the system of fuzzy gates would be turned into the required discrete format. Of course, such a system of fuzzy logic gates must include some analogons of classical logical gates and include some extra fuzzy gates which turn continuous signal to the required discrete form.

Both classical logical gates and fuzzy logic gates operate on unipolar model of information processing. Classical logical gates operate only on two truth (logic) values $\{0, 1\}$ which could be interpreted in terms of information processing as certainty of dissatisfaction or satisfaction of some condition, Fuzzy logic gates operate on continuous signals assuming values in the unit interval $[0, 1]$. The scale of the unit interval could be seen as two certainty points with the whole scale of uncertainty of satisfaction of some condition. The scale of uncertainty of satisfaction is represented by the inside $(0, 1)$ of the unit interval. However, the fuzzy extension becomes inadequate in real life applications e.g. [7,14,15]. As pointed out in [7] asymmetry of fuzziness and a lack of negative information in uncertainty modelling (lack of modelling of dissatisfaction of a condition) lead to several expansions of fuzziness, cf. [1,2,3,5].

In this paper, we focus our discussion on a certain generalized model referred to as balanced fuzzy sets. In essence, balanced fuzzy sets form an extension of classical fuzzy sets from the unit interval $[0, 1]$ to the symmetric interval around 0, that is $[-1, 1]$. This expansion is distinguished from other generalizations of fuzzy sets in a special treatment of discrete dissatisfaction. It assumes that fuzziness is a dispersion of discrete satisfaction represented by the value 1 onto the left opened interval $(0, 1]$. It also assumes that discrete dissatisfaction represented by the value 0 is not changed. Balanced expansion of fuzziness keeps fuzziness as dispersed discrete satisfaction and disperses dissatisfaction - still bunch and represented as the value 0 - onto the right opened interval $[-1, 0)$. The value 0 represents a lack of information either about satisfaction or about satisfaction. The balanced extension of fuzziness includes the state of no information and full scale of negative information and brings full symmetry of the model, cf. [5]

The discussion in this paper is aimed at building a model of logical gates formed on a basis of balanced fuzzy sets. Balanced fuzzy gates should subsume fuzzy logic gates as their special cases. In balanced fuzzy gates, signal processing is similar to fuzzy logic gates. Input, internal and output signals of a system of balanced fuzzy gates are positioned in the interval $[-1, 1]$. Then output signals of fuzzy gates are presented to a gate which turns continuous signal to discrete values from the set of $\{-1, 0, 1\}$: certain dissatisfaction, certain lack of information on dissatisfaction/satisfaction and certain satisfaction.

2   Fuzzy Logic Gates

In this section, we briefly recall the essence of fuzzy connectives commonly used in fuzzy sets and then move on to the concept of fuzzy logic gates and elaborate on the idea of the discretizing gates. The discretization of continuous signals is solely based on limit formulas for strong triangular norms.

2.1   Fuzzy Connectives

The fuzzy logic connectives discussed in this paper constitute a formal system in the following form $F = ([0, 1], s, t, n)$. The mapping $n : [0, 1] \to [0, 1], n(x) = 1 - x$ is referred to as negation. In this paper we will not consider generalizations of the negation operator, cf. [8,13]. Connectives s and t are called triangular norms or t-conorm and t-norm, respectively. They are mappings $p : [0, 1] \times [0, 1] \to [0, 1]$ satisfying well known set of axioms: associativity - $p(a, p(b, c)) = p(p(a, b), c)$; commutativity - $p(a, b) = p(b, a)$; monotonicity - $p(a, b) \leq p(c, d)$ for $a \leq c$ and

$b \leq d$; boundary conditions - $s(0, a) = 0$, $t(0, a)$ for $a \in [0, 1]$ - where p stands form both t-conorm and t-norm.

In this paper, we concentrate on so called strong triangular norms which are generated by additive generators. Let us recall that an additive generator of t-conorm is a function $f : [0, 1] \rightarrow [0, \infty]$ which is strictly increasing and continuous. Of course, such conditions guarantee existence of inverse function f^{-1}. For a given additive generator we can define t-conorm as follows: $s(x, y) = f^{-1}(f(x) + f(y))$. Dual t-norm is defined using the De Morgan triple that is $t(x, y) = n(s(n(x), n(y)))$.

Likewise strong triangular norms exhibit interesting limit properties

$$s(x, s(x, \ldots, s(x, x))) = s^n(x) \longrightarrow_{n \rightarrow +\infty} \begin{cases} 0 & x = 0 \\ 1 & x > 0 \end{cases}$$

$$t(x, t(x, \ldots, t(x, x))) = t^n(x) \longrightarrow_{n \rightarrow +\infty} \begin{cases} 0 & x < 1 \\ 1 & x = 1 \end{cases}$$

2.2 Fuzzy Logic Gates

A fuzzy logic gate is a generic computing unit which realizes one of the classical connectives encountered in fuzzy systems, that is negation, t-norm, and t-conorm. From now on, we will consider strong t-norms, strong t-conorms and linear negation.

Example 1. Here we look at the examples of the logical connectives based on the additive generators realized with the aid of the atanh function. To retain some level of uniformity, we will be using this form of the generator throughout all illustrative examples presented in this study (obviously, one could have used some other generator). Thus we have

$$F\_OR(x, y) = s(x, y) = tanh(atanh(x) + atanh(y))$$

$$F\_AND(x, y) = n(F\_OR(n(x), n(y)))$$

Fuzzy logic gates carry our computing on a basis of continuous inputs and outputs. Fuzzy negation forms a straightforward inversion of the input. The resulting characteristics of the fuzzy logic gates are included in Figure 1.

2.3 Discretizing Continuous Signals

We can easily construct fuzzy gates which turn continuous signal to its discrete equivalents. First of all, we can observe that fuzzy logic gates F_NOT, F_OR and F_AND, if restricted to discrete inputs 0 and 1, behave exactly like logical gates NOT, OR and AND:

Secondly, we can build the following two fuzzy logic gates turning analog signal to discrete one. The design of analog-to-discrete fuzzy logic gates involves limit formulas of the strong triangular norms.

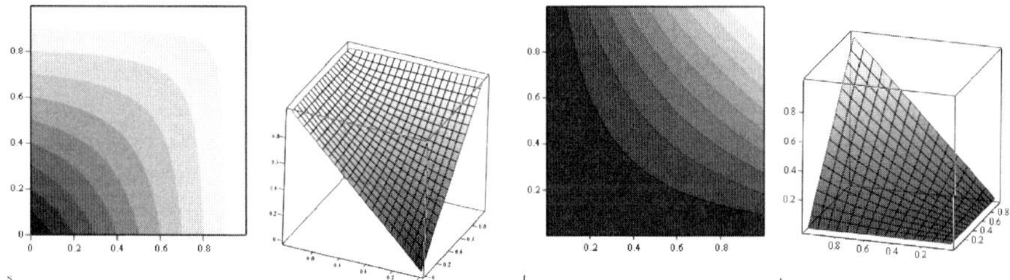

Fig. 1. Contour plots and 3D graphs of the fuzzy logic gates

D_OR	$\parallel$	0	$\nearrow$	1
		0	1	1

D_AND	$\parallel$	0	$\nearrow$	1
		0	0	1

The performance of such gates is illustrated by an iterative process of aggregation of the input signal and the output signal which is presented to the input of the gate by a feedback mechanism. We assume that at starting point such a gate presents input signal to both its inputs. This assumption allows producing an output which - in turn - will be presented to the input of the gate using feedback mechanism. Let us stress that this illustration does not pretend to give technical details of the ensuing hardware realization.

3   Balanced Fuzzy Gates

In this section, we introduce the concept of balanced fuzzy sets and balanced fuzzy connectives. The concept of balanced fuzzy sets will be utilized in construction of balanced fuzzy gates. By analogy to fuzzy logic gates we will discretize continuous signal using limit formulas for strong balanced triangular norms to build respective balanced dicretizing gates.

3.1   Balanced Fuzzy Connectives

Balanced negation, balanced t-conorms and balanced t-norms form an interesting extension of the classical operators of, t-conorms, t-norms and negation. Besides these three operators, we introduce an extra operator which will be referred to as a balanced inversion. Thus, balanced connectives for a formal system $BF = ([-1, 1], N, V, S, T)$, compare Section 2.1. In general, the balanced operators take their arguments from the interval $[-1, 1]$ and produce values in the same interval. Let us stress that the classical operators take their arguments form and produce their values in the unit interval $[0, 1]$. The fuzzy system F is immersed in the balanced system G. This means that balanced connectives restricted to the unit interval are equal to classical connectives.

Balanced negation N and balanced inversion V are mappings:

$$N : [-1, 1] \to [-1, 1] \qquad N(x) = -x$$

$$V : [-1, 1] \to [-1, 1] \qquad V(x) = \begin{cases} 1 - x & x \geq 0 \\ -1 - x & x < 0 \end{cases}$$

The balanced inversion has its "irregular point" for the value 0. Inversion of the value 0 can be assumed either as 1 or as -1. Alternatively, it could be assumed as undefined. None of these assumptions violate properties of balanced connectives. In this discussion we assume the inversion of 0 to be equal to 1 what ensures full immersion of the fuzzy system F into balanced system G, also cf. [6].

The mappings $T : [-1, 1] \times [-1, 1] \to [-1, 1]$ and $S : [-1, 1] \times [-1, 1] \to [-1, 1]$ are balanced t-norm and balanced t-conorm, respectively, assuming that they satisfy the following axioms in the whole domain $[-1, 1] \times [-1, 1]$ unless defined explicitly:

1., 2., 3.   associativity, commutativity and monotonicity
4. $T(1, a) = a$, $S(0, a) = a$ for $a \in [0, 1]$ boundary, conditions
5. $T(x, y) = N(T(N(x), N(y)))$ $S(x, y) = N(S(N(x), N(y)))$ symmetry

As in the case of fuzzy logic connectives, we will consider strong balanced triangular norms. An additive generator of strong balanced t-conorm is a function $f : [-1, 1] \to [-\infty, +\infty]$ which is strictly increasing and continuous. Strong balanced t-conorm is defined by the formula: $S(x, y) = f^{-1}(f(x) + f(y))$. For arguments equal to -1 and 1 we either can assume the value of the balanced t-conorm to be undefined, to be equal to -1 or to be equal to 1. Dual t-norm is defined by applying the De Morgan triple, that is:

$$T(x, y) = \begin{cases} V(S(V(x), V(y))) & x * y \geq 0 \\ 0 & otherwise \end{cases}$$

The essential limit properties of balanced triangular norms come in the form:

$$S(x, S(x, \ldots, S(x, x))) = S^n(x) \longrightarrow_{n \to +\infty} \begin{cases} -1 & x < 0 \\ 0 & x = 0 \\ 1 & x > 0 \end{cases}$$

$$T(x, T(x, \ldots, T(x, x))) = T^n(x) \longrightarrow_{n \to +\infty} \begin{cases} -1 & x = -1 \\ 0 & -1 < x < 1 \\ 1 & x = 1 \end{cases}$$

3.2 Balanced Fuzzy Gates

A fuzzy logic gate is a generic computing unit which realizes one of the classical connectives encountered in fuzzy systems, that is negation, t-norm, and

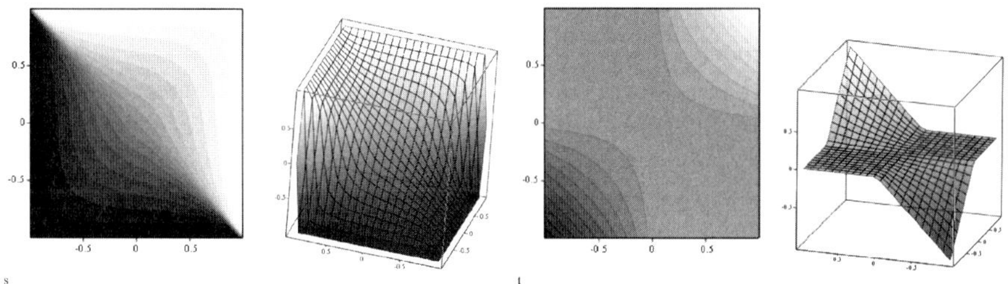

Fig. 2. Contour plots and 3D graphs of the balanced fuzzy gates

t-conorm. From now on, we will consider strong t-norms, strong t-conorms and linear negation.

A balanced fuzzy gate is a computing unit which computes one of the balanced fuzzy connective encountered in the system of balanced fuzzy system that is balanced negation, balanced inversion, balanced t-conorm or balanced t-norm, cf. 3.1. As in the case of fuzzy logic gate, computation of balanced fuzzy gates is analogous to those completed so far, i.e. its inputs and output assume continuous values coming from the interval $[-1, 1]$.

Example 2. As in case of Example 1 we look at the examples of the balanced fuzzy connectives based on the additive generators realized with the aid of the atanh function. Thus we have

$$BF\_OR(x, y) = S(x, y) = tanh(atanh(x) + atanh(y))$$

$$BF\_AND(x, y) = V(F\_OR(V(x), V(y)))$$

The characteristics of the balanced fuzzy gates BF_OR and BF_AND, are displayed in Figure 2.

By analogy to classical logical gates the balanced fuzzy gates for the values -1, 0, and 1 produce the results

BF_NOT	-1	0	1
	1	0	-1

BF_INV	-1	0	1
	0	1	0

BF_AND	-1	0	1
-1	-1	0	0
0	0	0	0
1	0	0	1

BF_OR	-1	0	1
-1	-1	-1	1
0	-1	0	1
1	1	1	1

In this case we have assumed that inversion of 0 (neutral information) is defined as 1. Choosing 1 as the value of inversion of 0 pledges satisfaction of properties including associativity. This assumptions guarantees also that balanced fuzzy gates cast on the unit interval $[0, 1]$ will be equal to fuzzy gates and - in discrete points of 0 and 1 - will be equivalent to logical gates.

Similarly, -1 regarded as an inversion of 0 maintains all properties, but breaks equivalence of the balanced fuzzy gates at discrete points of 0 and 1 with logical gates.

Considering the inversion of the logic value of 0 as a nondeterministic choice between -1 and 1 leads to an interesting solution, which might be interpreted as lack of choice between -1 and 1, i.e. lack of choice between certain negative/positive information. This interpretation leads to natural value of inversion of inversion of 0, which is just 0.

By analogy to fuzzy logic gates we build balanced discretizing gates based on limit formulas. These gates allow for converting continuous signal to its discrete value of -1, 0 or 1.

The discrete balanced fuzzy gates based on limit formulas produce the results as presented here:

BD_OR	-1	$\nearrow$	0	$\nearrow$	1
	-1	-1	0	1	1

BD_AND	-1	$\nearrow$	0	$\nearrow$	1
	-1	0	0	0	1

And, as in case of fuzzy logic gates, we do not pretend to give technical details of hardware realization of such gates.

By analogy with the classical gates we get values of balanced fuzzy gates for discrete arguments:
$BF\_NAND(x, y) = BF\_NOT(BF\_AND(x, y))$,
$BF\_IAND(x, y) = BF\_INV(BF\_AND(x, y))$,
$BF\_NOR(x, y) = BF\_NOT(BF\_OR(x, y))$ and
$BF\_IOR(x, y) = BF\_INV(BF\_OR(x, y))$
assuming that the inversion of 0 becomes equal to 1.

BF_NAND	-1	0	1
-1	1	0	0
0	0	0	0
1	0	0	-1

BF_IAND	-1	0	1
-1	0	1	1
0	1	1	1
1	1	1	0

BF_NOR	-1	0	1
-1	1	1	-1
0	1	0	-1
1	-1	-1	1

BF_IOR	-1	0	1
-1	0	0	0
0	0	1	0
1	0	0	0

The characteristics of systems of the balanced fuzzy gates are included in Figures 3 and 4.

Note that in this case gates BF-IAND and BF-IOR cast on the unit interval $[0, 1]$ are equivalent to the classical gates NAND and NOR, as indicated in the tables above.

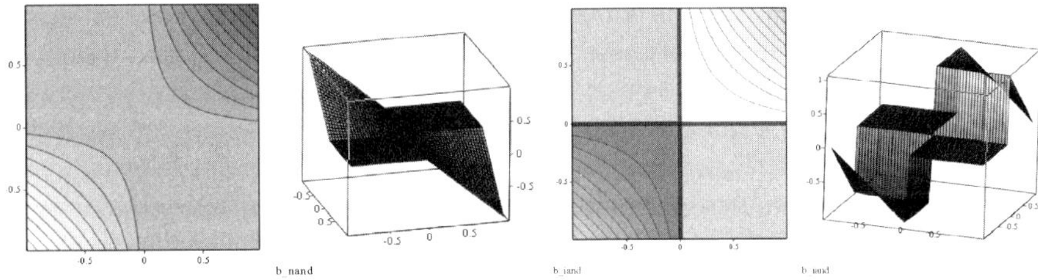

Fig. 3. Contour plots and 3D graphs of the BF_NAND and BF_IAND gates

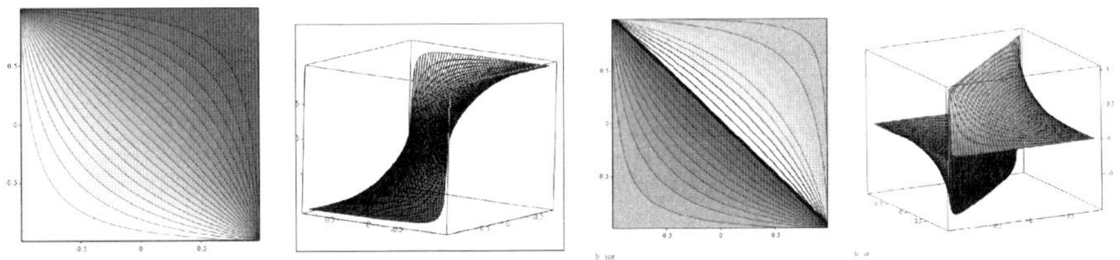

Fig. 4. Contour plots and 3D graphs of the BF_NOR and BF_IOR gates

4 Networks of Balanced Fuzzy Gates and Balanced Neurons: Architectures and Their Developments

The balanced fuzzy gates can be conveniently used as some generic building blocks of architectures of logic networks. Following the fundamental representation result offered by the Shannon theorem being applied to the construction of Boolean functions, we consider here a network composed of two layers of gates. The first layer is formed by the AND gates. In the second layer we consider the use of the OR gates. Here the number of such AND gates depends upon the character of some experimental data we need to capture. Its choice has to be realized experimentally.

In contrast to neurons encountered in "standard" neural networks or neural networks based on logic [4,9], fuzzy logic [10,10] or knowledge [12], the logic gates studied here are not endowed with any connections. Hence the learning of the networks of this category is focused on the selection of the inputs for the individual AND gates located in the first layer of the network. Since such selection is positioned in the realm of combinatorial optimization, one has to confine himself to techniques of evolutionary optimization.

We could move one step forward by developing balanced neurons and form the ensuing structures of the networks composed by them. The difference between the gates and neurons lies in the flexibility of the connections of the neurons. We distinguish between the two categories of the neurons. The OR neurons aggregate or-wise the inputs of the neuron being weighted and-wise by the corresponding connections. For the AND neuron the arrangement of the logic operators is done in a reverse order: each input is combined or-wise with the corresponding weight (connection) and in the sequel these partial results are combined and-wise.

5   Conclusions

In this study, we have introduced the principles of balanced fuzzy gates operating in the framework of the balanced theory of fuzzy sets in which we clearly distinguish between the logic truth values of -1, 0 and 1. The motivation behind this type of membership values helps us develop a sound insight into the nature of processing with the concept of logic inhibition. The generic logic gates (AND and OR) based on this system of logic truth values are essential to support any computing carried out in the presence of inhibitory, neutral and excitatory information. Through detailed visualization of the characteristics of the gates we are able to emphasize the properties of the logic operators. Furthermore we discussed some architectures of the networks composed of logical gates as well as studied some generalizations of the gates in the form of logic neurons.

References

1. Atanassov K. T., Intuitionistic Fuzzy Sets, Fuzzy Sets and Systems, 20 (1986) 87-96.
2. Dubois D., Prade H., Twofold fuzzy sets: an approach to the representation of sets with fuzzy boundaries based on possibility and necessity measures, Journal of Fuzzy Mathematics, Vol. 3, No. 4, 53-76, 1983.
3. Gau W. L., Buehrer D. J., 1993, Vague sets, IEEE Transactions on Systems, Man, and Cybernetics, 23: 610-614
4. Hirota K., Pedrycz W., Logic based neural networks, Inf. Sci., 71(1993) 99-130.
5. Homenda W., Balanced Fuzzy Sets, Information Sciences, in press.
6. Homenda W., Triangular norms, uni- and nullnorms, balanced norms: the cases of the hierarchy of iterative operators, Proc. of the 24th Linz Seminar on Fuzzy Set Theory, Linz, Feb. 4-8, 2003.
7. Homenda W., Pedrycz W., Symmetrization 0f Fuzzy Operators: Notes 0n Data Aggregation, in: Studies in Computational Intelligence, (Eds.), S. K. Halgamuge, L. Wang, ISBN 3-540-26071-4, Springer Verlag, 2005, pp. 1-18.
8. Klement E. P., Mesiar R. and Pap E., Triangular norms, Kluwer Academic Pub., Dordrecht, 2000.
9. Patarnello S., Carnevali P., Learning networks of neurons with Boolean logic, Europhysics Letters, 4, 4, 1987, 503-508.
10. Pedrycz W., Fuzzy neural networks and neurocomputations, Fuzzy Sets and Systems, 56, 1993, 1-28.
11. Pedrycz W., Neurocomputations in relational systems, IEEE Trans.on Pattern Analysis and Machine Intelligence, 13, 1991, 289-296.
12. Pedrycz W., Rocha A., Knowledge-based neural networks, IEEE Trans.on Fuzzy Systems,1, 1993, 254-266.
13. Schweizer B., Sklar A., Probabilistic Metric Spaces, North Holland, New York, 1983.
14. Silvert W., Symmetric Summation: A Class of Operations on Fuzzy Sets, IEEE Trans. System, Man, Cybernetics, 9 (1979) 659-667
15. Yager R.R., Families of OWA operators, Fuzzy Sets and Systems 59 (1993) 125-148.

Triangle Algebras: Towards an Axiomatization of Interval-Valued Residuated Lattices

Bart Van Gasse, Chris Cornelis, Glad Deschrijver, and Etienne Kerre

Fuzziness and Uncertainty Modeling Research Unit,
Department of Applied Mathematics and Computer Science, Ghent University,
Krijgslaan 281 (S9), B-9000 Gent, Belgium
{Bart.VanGasse, Chris.Cornelis, Glad.Deschrijver, Etienne.Kerre}@UGent.be

Abstract. In this paper, we present triangle algebras: residuated lattices equipped with two modal, or approximation, operators and with a third angular point u, different from 0 (false) and 1 (true), intuitively denoting ignorance about a formula's truth value. We prove that these constructs, which bear a close relationship to several other algebraic structures including rough approximation spaces, provide an equational representation of interval-valued residuated lattices; as an important case in point, we consider $\mathcal{L}^I$, the lattice of closed intervals of $[0, 1]$. As we will argue, the representation by triangle algebras serves as a crucial stepping stone to the construction of formal interval-valued fuzzy logics, and in particular to the axiomatic formalization of residuated t-norm based logics on $\mathcal{L}^I$, in a similar way as was done for formal fuzzy logics on the unit interval.

1   Introduction and Preliminaries

Formal fuzzy logics (also: fuzzy logics in the narrow sense) are generalizations of classical logic that allow us to reason gradually. Indeed, in the scope of these logics, formulas can be assigned not only 0 and 1 as truth values, but also elements of $[0,1]$, or, more generally, of a bounded lattice $\mathcal{L}$. The partial ordering of $\mathcal{L}$ then serves to compare the truth values of formulas which can be true to some extent. The best-known examples of formal fuzzy logics are probably Monoidal T-norm based Logic (MTL, Esteva and Godo [10]), Basic Logic (BL, Hájek [13]), Gödel logic (G, [12]) and Łukasiewicz logic (Ł, [15]). For all of these logics, which are fully described in terms of axioms, with the modus ponens as deduction rule, soundness and completeness with respect to a corresponding variety[1] can be proved. For instance, a formula can be deduced in MTL iff it is true (i.e., has truth value 1) in every prelinear residuated lattice; recall that a residuated lattice is a structure $\mathcal{L} = (L, \sqcap, \sqcup, *, \Rightarrow, 0, 1)$ in which $\sqcap, \sqcup, *$ and $\Rightarrow$ are binary operators on L and

---

[1] Recall that a class $\mathcal{K}$ of structures is a variety [13] if there is a set T of identities such that $\mathcal{K}$ is the class of structures in which all identities from T are true.

S. Greco et al. (Eds.): RSCTC 2006, LNAI 4259, pp. 117–126, 2006.

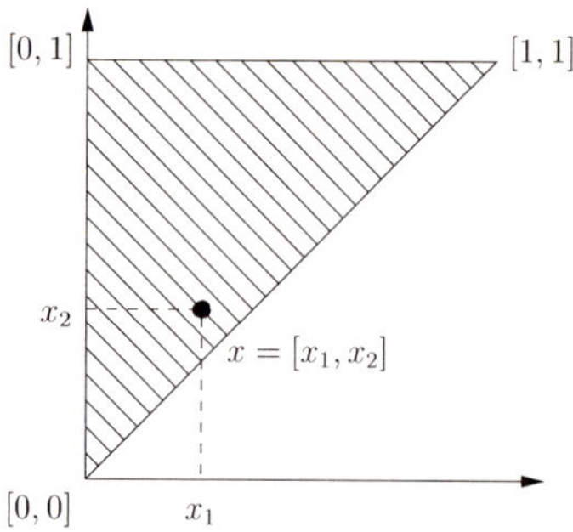

Fig. 1. The lattice $\mathcal{L}^I$

- $(L, \sqcap, \sqcup)$ is a bounded lattice with 0 as smallest and 1 as greatest element,
- $*$ is commutative and associative, with 1 as neutral element, and
- $x * y \leq z$ iff $x \leq (y \Rightarrow z)$ for all x, y and z in L (residuation principle),

and that prelinearity means that $(x \Rightarrow y) \sqcup (y \Rightarrow x) = 1$ for all x and y in L. A prelinear residuated lattice is called an MTL-algebra. The other logics emerge by adding axioms to MTL, and are sound and complete w.r.t. subvarieties of MTL-algebras. For a comprehensive overview of the state-of-the-art on formal fuzzy logics, we refer to [11].

Research on formal fuzzy logics has centered on prelinear residuated structures; indeed, all of the above-mentioned logics presuppose prelinearity. However, while in every residuated lattice $([0, 1], \min, \max, *, \Rightarrow, 0, 1)$ the property holds[2], it is not necessarily preserved for closed intervals of a bounded lattice $\mathcal{L}$; for example, it was shown in [6] that no MTL-algebra exists on the lattice $\mathcal{L}^I = (L^I, \sqcap, \sqcup)$, shown graphically in Figure 1 and defined by

$$L^I = \{[x_1, x_2] \mid (x_1, x_2) \in [0, 1]^2 \text{ and } x_1 \leq x_2\}$$
$$\text{and}$$
$$[x_1, x_2] \sqcap [y_1, y_2] = [\min(x_1, y_1), \min(x_2, y_2)]$$
$$[x_1, x_2] \sqcup [y_1, y_2] = [\max(x_1, y_1), \max(x_2, y_2)],$$

for all $[x_1, x_2]$ and $[y_1, y_2]$ in L^I; and whose partial ordering $\leq_{L^I}$ is given by componentwise extension of $\leq$,

$$[x_1, x_2] \leq_{L^I} [y_1, y_2] \iff x_1 \leq y_1 \text{ and } x_2 \leq y_2.$$

This is not to say that such structures are of no significance for logical purposes. Indeed, note that elements drawn from $\mathcal{L}^I$, or more generally from the lattice of closed intervals of a bounded lattice $\mathcal{L}$, which in this paper we shall call the triangularization of $\mathcal{L}$, carry an attractive and straightforward semantical interpretation as partial, or incomplete, truth values, i.e. they exhibit a lack of

---

[2] Recall that $([0, 1], \min, \max, *, \Rightarrow, 0, 1)$ is a residuated lattice iff $*$ is a left-continuous t-norm on $[0, 1]$ with residuum $\Rightarrow$.

knowledge about a formula's exact truth value; the wider the interval, the greater the uncertainty. Note that the angular point $[0,1]$ in Figure 1 corresponds to "ignorance", or total uncertainty about the exact truth value. This interpretation, together with the relative efficiency of operations defined on them, accounts for the widespread adoption and application of interval-valued truth degrees in knowledge-based systems (see e.g. [16,17]). Moreover, residuated lattices can be constructed on top of triangularizations quite easily, and as extensive research in the context of $\mathcal{L}^I$ (see e.g. [5]) has pointed out, some of them rival their counterparts on $[0,1]$ for the properties they satisfy.

The goal of this paper is to characterize interval-valued residuated lattices (which are residuated lattices on triangularizations) as a variety, i.e. by a set of identities that capture their triangular structure (depicted in Figure 1). This is not only interesting from a purely mathematical stance, it also paves the way for the development of formal interval-valued fuzzy logics, since identities are much more readily axiomatizable than the structural description as triangularizations. A natural and convenient way to obtain this algebraic characterization is the introduction of modal, or approximation, operators. Such operators have been studied from various angles [1,3,13,19] and serve well to describe the incompleteness facet of interval-valued residuated lattices. They give rise to the introduction of triangle algebras in Section 2. In Section 3 we review some related algebraic structures. In Section 4, we prove that every triangle algebra uniquely determines an interval-valued residuated lattice, and vice versa. To illustrate the relevance of these concepts, we relate them to existing work about residuated t-norms (Section 5) on $\mathcal{L}^I$. Finally, Section 6 offers a conclusion and discusses future work.

2 Triangle Algebras

As mentioned in the previous section, we want to construct an algebra that captures the triangular structure of interval-valued residuated lattices (see Definition 3 in Section 4) by a set of appropriate conditions. To this end, we extend the definition of a residuated lattice with a new constant u ("uncertainty") and two new unary connectives ν ("necessity") and μ ("possibility"); intuitively, the elements of a triangle algebra may be thought of as intervals; the formal link with interval-valued residuated lattices will be established in Section 4.

Definition 1. A triangle algebra is a structure $\mathcal{A} = (A, \sqcap, \sqcup, *, \Rightarrow, \nu, \mu, 0, u, 1)$, in which $(A, \sqcap, \sqcup, *, \Rightarrow, 0, 1)$ is a residuated lattice, and in which the following 17 conditions hold ($x \Leftrightarrow y$ is a shorthand notation for $(x \Rightarrow y) \sqcap (y \Rightarrow x)$):

$$
\begin{array}{ll}
T.1\ \nu x \le x & T.1'\ x \le \mu x \\
T.2\ \nu x \le \nu\nu x & T.2'\ \mu\mu x \le \mu x \\
T.3\ \nu(x \sqcap y) = \nu x \sqcap \nu y & T.3'\ \mu(x \sqcap y) = \mu x \sqcap \mu y \\
T.4\ \nu(x \sqcup y) = \nu x \sqcup \nu y & T.4'\ \mu(x \sqcup y) = \mu x \sqcup \mu y \\
T.5\ \nu 1 = 1 & T.5'\ \mu 0 = 0 \\
T.6\ \nu u = 0 & T.6'\ \mu u = 1 \\
T.7\ \nu\mu x = \mu x & T.7'\ \mu\nu x = \nu x
\end{array}
$$

$$T.8 \quad \nu(x \Rightarrow y) \leq \nu x \Rightarrow \nu y$$
$$T.9 \quad (\nu x \Leftrightarrow \nu y) * (\mu x \Leftrightarrow \mu y) \leq (x \Leftrightarrow y)$$
$$T.10 \; \nu x \Rightarrow \nu y \leq \nu(\nu x \Rightarrow \nu y)$$

Remark 1. Suppose $(A, \sqcap, \sqcup, *, \Rightarrow, 0, 1)$ is a residuated lattice such that the negation $\neg$, defined by $\neg x = x \Rightarrow 0$, is involutive (i.e., $\neg\neg x = x$ for every x in A). If there exists an element u in A such that $\neg u = u$, if ν is a unary operator on A that satisfies (T.1–T.6, T.8, T.10), and if $(\nu x \Leftrightarrow \nu y) * (\nu \neg x \Leftrightarrow \nu \neg y) \leq (x \Leftrightarrow y)$, then $(A, \sqcap, \sqcup, *, \Rightarrow, \nu, \mu, 0, u, 1)$ is a triangle algebra if we define $\mu x = \neg \nu \neg x$. In general, however, there need not be a link between ν and μ.

Denote the set of exact elements of a triangle algebra $\mathcal{A}$ by $E(\mathcal{A}) = \{x \in A \mid \nu x = x\}$. By the fact that the following statements are equivalent for all x in A:

1. $x = \nu y$ for some y in A
2. $x = \mu y$ for some y in A
3. $x = \nu x$
4. $x = \mu x$
5. $\nu x = \mu x$

it is clear that $E(\mathcal{A})$ is the direct image of A under ν, as well as under μ. Moreover, this set is invariant under ν and μ, and contains 0 and 1, but not u. It is closed under $\sqcap$, $\sqcup$, $*$ and $\Rightarrow$, and hence it also holds that $\mathcal{E}(\mathcal{A}) = (E(\mathcal{A}), \sqcap, \sqcup, *, \Rightarrow, 0, 1)$ is a residuated lattice.

3 Connections to Other Algebraic Structures

The idea of introducing modal-like operators in residuated lattices and other algebraic structures has also been adopted by other authors, for several purposes.

- Belohlávek and Vychodil [1] defined a so-called "truth stresser" ν for a residuated lattice $(L, \sqcap, \sqcup, *, \Rightarrow, 0, 1)$ as a unary operator on L that satisfies T.1, T.5 and T.8. They used it to model the (truth function of a) unary connective "very true".
- Ono [19] defined modal residuated lattices as structures $(L, \sqcap, \sqcup, *, \Rightarrow, \nu, 0, 1)$, in which $(L, \sqcap, \sqcup, *, \Rightarrow, 0, 1)$ is a residuated lattice and ν a unary operator on L that satisfies T.1, T.2, T.5, and, for all x and y in L, $\nu(x \sqcap y) \leq \nu x$ and $\nu x * \nu y \leq \nu(x * y)$. We can prove, by the residuation principle, that the latter two properties are equivalent to T.8. Hence, in a modal residuated lattice, ν is a truth stresser additionally satisfying T.2; and if $(A, \sqcap, \sqcup, *, \Rightarrow, \nu, \mu, 0, u, 1)$ is a triangle algebra, then $(A, \sqcap, \sqcup, *, \Rightarrow, \nu, 0, 1)$ is a modal residuated lattice.
- A Hájek [13] truth stresser for a residuated lattice $(L, \sqcap, \sqcup, *, \Rightarrow, 0, 1)$ is a unary operator ν on L that satisfies T.1, T.2, T.5, T.8, $\nu(x \sqcup y) \leq \nu x \sqcup \nu y$ (which is in this case equivalent to T.4) and $\nu x \sqcup \neg \nu x = 1$ (weakened law of excluded middle, WLEM) for every x and y in L. Hence, $(L, \sqcap, \sqcup, *, \Rightarrow, \nu, 0, 1)$ is a modal residuated lattice in which T.4 and WLEM are satisfied. Hájek used this truth stresser to establish a faithful imbedding of Boolean logic into his $BL_\triangle$ (Basic Logic BL extended with a Hájek truth stresser $\triangle$).

Triangle algebras do not maintain WLEM as, in many cases, it would imply that $\nu x = 0$ whenever $x \neq 1$. This is not compatible with our interpretation of "necessity of an interval": for example (on $\mathcal{L}^I$), the necessity of $[0.9, 0.9]$ should be greater than the necessity of $[0.2, 0.5]$, it should not be the case that both are $[0, 0]$. However, we do impose several other conditions. T.1'–T.5' are conditions for possibility, dual to T.1–T.5 (in general, we do not require dependency of μ on ν; an example in which this holds is considered in Remark 1). The conditions T.6 and T.6' express the complete lack of knowledge about u: its necessity is 0, but its possibility is 1; T.7 and T.7' are known in modal logics as the S5-principles [18]. Condition T.9 implies that an element of a triangle algebra is completely defined by its necessity and possibility. Indeed: if $\nu x = \nu y$ and $\mu x = \mu y$, then $\nu x \Leftrightarrow \nu y = 1$ and $\mu x \Leftrightarrow \mu y = 1$, so $1 = 1 * 1 \leq x \Leftrightarrow y$, which implies $x = y$. Finally T.10 is a technical condition needed to ensure that triangle algebras correspond to interval-valued residuated lattices.

We adopted the notations ν and μ from Cattaneo and Ciucci [3], who defined these operators on so-called weak Brouwer de Morgan lattices (wBD lattices). A wBD lattice $(L, \sqcap, \sqcup, ', {}^\sim, 0, 1)$ is a bounded distributive lattice $(L, \sqcap, \sqcup)$ equipped with two complementations:

- a de Morgan complementation $'$, which is defined as an involutive unary operator on L that satisfies[3] $(x \sqcup y)' = x' \sqcap y'$, for all x and y in L, and
- a weak Brouwer complementation $\sim$, which is defined as a unary operator satisfying $x \leq x^{\sim\sim}$ and $(x \sqcup y)^\sim = x^\sim \sqcap y^\sim$ for all x and y in L,

for which $x^{\sim\prime} = x^{\sim\sim}$ (interconnection rule).

They defined νx as $x'^\sim$ and μx as $x^{\sim\prime}$. In this structure, T.1, T.1', T.2, T.2', T.3, T.4', T.5, T.5', T.7 and T.7' are always fulfilled, as well as $\mu x = (\nu x')'$. Note that T.3' and T.4 are not always satisfied, because $(x \sqcap y)^\sim$ is not necessarily equal to $x^\sim \sqcup y^\sim$.

Some triangle algebras can be seen as wBD lattices:

Proposition 1. If $\mathcal{A} = (A, \sqcap, \sqcup, *, \Rightarrow, \nu, \mu, 0, u, 1)$ is a distributive triangle algebra, if $'$ is a de Morgan complementation on A such that $\mu x = (\nu x')'$ and if we define $\sim$ by $x^\sim = (\mu x)'$, then $(A, \sqcap, \sqcup, ', {}^\sim, 0, 1)$ is a wBD lattice.

Finally, it can be seen that a triangle algebra $\mathcal{A} = (A, \sqcap, \sqcup, *, \Rightarrow, \nu, \mu, 0, u, 1)$ induces a rough approximation space $\mathcal{R} = (A, E(\mathcal{A}), \nu, \mu)$ (in the sense of Cattaneo [2]) in which

- A is the set of approximable elements,
- $E(\mathcal{A})$ is the set of exact or 'definable' elements,
- $\nu \colon A \to E(\mathcal{A})$ is the inner approximation map, satisfying
  $(\forall x \in E(\mathcal{A}))(\forall y \in A)(x \leq y$ iff $x \leq \nu y)$,
- $\mu \colon A \to E(\mathcal{A})$ is the outer approximation map, satisfying
  $(\forall x \in A)(\forall y \in E(\mathcal{A}))(x \leq y$ iff $\mu x \leq y)$,

and in which for any element x in A, its rough approximation is defined by $(\nu x, \mu x)$. In this case, T.9 ensures that no two different elements have the same rough approximation.

---

[3] In this case, also $(x \sqcap y)' = x' \sqcup y'$ holds for every x and y in L.

4   Connection with Interval-Valued Residuated Lattices

Definition 2. Given a lattice $\mathcal{L} = (L, \sqcap, \sqcup)$, its triangularization is the structure $\mathcal{T}(\mathcal{L}) = (T(\mathcal{L}), \sqcap, \sqcup)$ defined by

- $T(\mathcal{L}) = \{[x_1, x_2] \mid (x_1, x_2) \in L^2 \text{ and } x_1 \leq x_2\}$

and

- $[x_1, x_2] \sqcap [y_1, y_2] = [x_1 \sqcap y_1, x_2 \sqcap y_2]$
- $[x_1, x_2] \sqcup [y_1, y_2] = [x_1 \sqcup y_1, x_2 \sqcup y_2]$

for all $[x_1, x_2]$ and $[y_1, y_2]$ in $T(\mathcal{L})$. The set $D = \{[x, x] \mid x \in L\}$ is called the diagonal of $\mathcal{T}(\mathcal{L})$, and can be seen as a 'copy' of L inside $T(\mathcal{L})$. As an example, note that $\mathcal{L}^I$ is the triangularization of $([0, 1], \min, \max)$.

It is easy to verify that $\mathcal{T}(\mathcal{L})$ is again a lattice. If $\mathcal{L}$ contains a smallest element 0 (resp. a greatest element 1), then $T(\mathcal{L})$ has $[0, 0]$ as smallest element (resp. $[1, 1]$ as greatest element). Moreover, if $\mathcal{L} = (L, \sqcap, \sqcup, *, \Rightarrow, 0, 1)$ is a residuated lattice, then it is always possible to construct a residuated lattice on $\mathcal{T}(\mathcal{L})$; in particular, if we define

$$[x_1, x_2] \odot [y_1, y_2] = [x_1 * y_1, x_2 * y_2] \tag{1}$$

$$[x_1, x_2] \Rightarrow_{\odot} [y_1, y_2] = [(x_1 \Rightarrow y_1) \sqcap (x_2 \Rightarrow y_2), x_2 \Rightarrow y_2] \tag{2}$$

then the structure $(T(\mathcal{L}), \sqcap, \sqcup, \odot, \Rightarrow_{\odot}, [0, 0], [1, 1])$ is a residuated lattice. It is not the only possible way of defining residuated lattices on $T(\mathcal{L})$; Section 5 investigates other possibilities, on L^I. In general, we consider the following construct:

Definition 3. An interval-valued residuated lattice is a residuated lattice $(T(\mathcal{L}), \sqcap, \sqcup, \odot, \Rightarrow_{\odot}, [0, 0], [1, 1])$ on the triangularization $\mathcal{T}(\mathcal{L})$ of a bounded lattice $\mathcal{L}$, in which D is closed under $\odot$ and $\Rightarrow_{\odot}$, i.e., $[x_1, x_1] \odot [y_1, y_1] \in D$ and $[x_1, x_1] \Rightarrow_{\odot} [y_1, y_1] \in D$ for x_1, y_1 in L.

Remark 2. Note that, under our assumptions, $(L, \sqcap, \sqcup, *, \Rightarrow, 0, 1)$, with $*$ and $\Rightarrow$ the restrictions of $\odot$ and $\Rightarrow_{\odot}$ to D, is always a residuated lattice. Our definition of interval-valued residuated lattice excludes those cases, in which $\odot$ and $\Rightarrow_{\odot}$ do not extend corresponding connectives on $\mathcal{L}$.

Proposition 2. If $(T(\mathcal{L}), \sqcap, \sqcup, \odot, \Rightarrow_{\odot}, \nu, \mu, [0, 0], [0, 1], [1, 1])$ is a triangle algebra on a triangularization $(T(\mathcal{L}), \sqcap, \sqcup)$ of a bounded lattice, then $\nu[x_1, x_2] = [x_1, x_1]$ and $\mu[x_1, x_2] = [x_2, x_2]$ for every $[x_1, x_2]$ in $T(\mathcal{L})$.

Proposition 2 makes clear the intended meaning of 'necessity' and 'possibility' of an interval: if $x = [x_1, x_2]$ is the incompletely specified truth value of a formula, then $\nu x = [x_1, x_1]$ and $\mu x = [x_2, x_2]$ represent the minimum, resp. maximum, exact truth value that emerges when the uncertainty is resolved. The next important theorem establishes triangle algebras as the equational representation of interval-valued residuated lattices.

Theorem 1.
If $(A, \sqcap, \sqcup, *, \Rightarrow, \nu, \mu, 0, u, 1)$ is a triangle algebra, then $(A, \sqcap, \sqcup, *, \Rightarrow, 0, 1)$ is iso-morphic to an interval-valued residuated lattice.
Conversely, if $(A, \sqcap, \sqcup, *, \Rightarrow, [0,0], [1,1])$ is an interval-valued residuated lattice and ν and μ are defined by $\nu[x_1, x_2] = [x_1, x_1]$ and $\mu[x_1, x_2] = [x_2, x_2]$, then $(A, \sqcap, \sqcup, *, \Rightarrow, \nu, \mu, [0,0], [0,1], [1,1])$ is a triangle algebra.

We give a sketch of the proof.
For any triangle algebra $\mathcal{A}$, we can define the mapping $\phi\colon A \longrightarrow T(\mathcal{E}(\mathcal{A}))$ as $\phi(x) = [\nu x, \mu x]$. This mapping is an injection because of condition T.9. Be-cause of conditions T.3,T.3',T.4 and T.4' it is a homomorphism from $(A, \sqcap, \sqcup)$ to $(T(\mathcal{E}(\mathcal{A})), \sqcap, \sqcup)$: $\phi(x \sqcap y) = [\nu(x \sqcap y), \mu(x \sqcap y)] = [\nu x \sqcap \nu y, \mu x \sqcap \mu y] = [\nu x, \mu x] \sqcap [\nu y, \mu y] = \phi(x) \sqcap \phi(y)$ and analogously $\phi(x \sqcup y) = \phi(x) \sqcup \phi(y)$. It turns out that ϕ is also a surjection: for every $[x, y]$ in $T(\mathcal{E}(\mathcal{A}))$, $\nu x = x = \mu x$ and $\nu y = y = \mu y$; so

$$[x, y] = [\nu x, \mu x] \sqcup [0, \mu y]$$

$$= [\nu x, \mu x] \sqcup ([0, 1] \sqcap [\nu y, \mu y])$$

$$= \phi(x) \sqcup (\phi(u) \sqcap \phi(y))$$

$$= \phi(x \sqcup (u \sqcap y)).$$

We define on $T(\mathcal{E}(\mathcal{A}))$ the binary operation $\odot$ as $\phi(x) \odot \phi(y) = \phi(x * y)$. It follows immediately from this definition that ϕ is a homomorphism from $(A, *)$ to $(T(\mathcal{E}(\mathcal{A})), \odot)$. Since $(A, \sqcap, \sqcup, *, \Rightarrow, 0, 1)$ is a residuated lattice, we know that $x \Rightarrow y = \sup\{z \in A \mid z * x \leq y\}$, so if we define $x \Rightarrow_\odot y$ as $\sup\{z \in T(\mathcal{E}(\mathcal{A})) \mid z \odot x \leq y\}$, ϕ is also a homomorphism from $(A, \Rightarrow)$ to $(T(\mathcal{E}(\mathcal{A})), \Rightarrow_\odot)$. Thus the structure $(T(\mathcal{E}(\mathcal{A})), \sqcap, \sqcup, \odot, \Rightarrow_\odot, [0,0], [1,1])$ is a residuated lattice, isomorphic to $(A, \sqcap, \sqcup, *, \Rightarrow, 0, 1)$. This means that every triangle algebra $\mathcal{A}$ has the structure of the set of intervals of a residuated lattice (its exact elements).

For the second part of the proof, assume that $(T(\mathcal{L}), \sqcap, \sqcup, \odot, \Rightarrow_\odot, [0,0], [1,1])$ is an interval-valued residuated lattice and that ν and μ are defined by $\nu[x_1, x_2] = [x_1, x_1]$ and $\mu[x_1, x_2] = [x_2, x_2]$. Then it can be proven that $(T(\mathcal{L}), \sqcap, \sqcup, \odot, \Rightarrow_\odot, \nu, \mu, [0,0], [0,1], [1,1])$ satisfies T.1-T.10 and T.1'-T.7'.

5   The Case of $\mathcal{L}^I$

By extension of the corresponding notion on $[0,1]$, t-norms on a bounded lat-tice $(L, \sqcap, \sqcup, 0, 1)$ are defined as increasing, associative, commutative mappings $\mathcal{T}$ that satisfy $\mathcal{T}(1, x) = x$ for x in L. Recall that such a t-norm $\mathcal{T}$ is called residuated if it induces a residuated lattice on L, that is, if $(L, \sqcap, \sqcup, \mathcal{T}, \mathcal{I}_\mathcal{T}, 0, 1)$ is a residuated lattice with $\mathcal{I}_\mathcal{T}(x, y) = \sup\{z \mid z \in L \text{ and } \mathcal{T}(x, z) \leq y\}$. As men-tioned in the introduction, a t-norm on $[0,1]$ is residuated iff it is left-continuous; this property however does not extend to $\mathcal{L}^I$ [8]. While a general characterization of residuated t-norms on $\mathcal{L}^I$ has not yet been found, it was shown in [7] that if

T induces a residuated lattice on $[0, 1]$, then for each α in $[0, 1]$, $\mathcal{T}_{T,\alpha}$ defined by, for $x = [x_1, x_2]$ and $y = [y_1, y_2]$ in L^I,

$$\mathcal{T}_{T,\alpha}(x, y) = [T(x_1, y_1), \max(T(\alpha, T(x_2, y_2)), T(x_1, y_2), T(x_2, y_1))], \qquad (3)$$

induces a residuated lattice on L^I. As the diagonal of $\mathcal{L}^I$ is closed under $\mathcal{T}_{T,\alpha}$ and $\mathcal{I}_{\mathcal{T}_{T,\alpha}}$, Theorem 1 implies that $(L^I, \sqcap, \sqcup, \mathcal{T}_{T,\alpha}, \mathcal{I}_{\mathcal{T}_{T,\alpha}}, \nu, \mu, [0, 0], [0, 1], [1, 1])$ is a triangle algebra.

Two important values of α can be distinguished in Formula (3):

- If $\alpha = 1$, we obtain t-representable t-norms on $\mathcal{L}^I$:
  $\mathcal{T}_{T,1}(x, y) = [T(x_1, y_1), T(x_2, y_2)]$, which can be seen as the straightforward (and most commonly used) extension of T to $\mathcal{L}^I$.
- If $\alpha = 0$, we obtain pseudo t-representable t-norms on $\mathcal{L}^I$:
  $\mathcal{T}_{T,0}(x, y) = [T(x_1, y_1), \max(T(x_1, y_2), T(x_2, y_1))]$. These t-norms are inherently more complex than their t-representable counterparts, but as we shall see below satisfy more relevant properties.

Just like on the unit interval, we can study particular subclasses of residuated t-norms on $\mathcal{L}^I$. To this end, recall that a t-norm $\mathcal{T}$ on $(L, \sqcap, \sqcup, 0, 1)$ is called divisible if $\mathcal{T}(x, \mathcal{I}_{\mathcal{T}}(x, y)) = x \sqcap y$ and involutive if $\mathcal{I}_{\mathcal{T}}(\mathcal{I}_{\mathcal{T}}(x, 0), 0) = x$ for x, y in L, that a BL-algebra is a divisible residuated lattice, and that an MV-algebra is an involutive BL-algebra. On the unit interval, a t-norm induces a BL-algebra iff it is continuous, and an MV-algebra iff it is isomorphic to the Łukasiewicz t-norm T_W defined by $T_W(x, y) = \max(0, x + y - 1)$ for x, y in $[0, 1]$. On $\mathcal{L}^I$, neither a BL-algebra nor an MV-algebra exists (as they are subclasses of MTL-algebras), yet in [21], it was proven that, for a t-norm T on $[0,1]$:

- T is divisible iff for each α in $[0,1]$, $\mathcal{T}_{T,\alpha}$ is weakly divisible, that is, for x, y in L^I,
$$\mathcal{T}(x, \mathcal{I}_{\mathcal{T}}(x, y)) \bigsqcup \mathcal{T}(y, \mathcal{I}_{\mathcal{T}}(y, x)) = x \bigsqcap y$$

- T is involutive iff $\mathcal{T}_{T,0}$ is involutive, hence iff the pseudo t-representable t-norm corresponding to T is involutive; for $\alpha > 0$, $\mathcal{T}_{T,\alpha}$ is never involutive.
- $([0, 1], \min, \max, T, I_T, 0, 1)$ is an MV-algebra iff $(L^I, \sqcap, \sqcup, \mathcal{T}_{T,0}, \mathcal{I}_{\mathcal{T}_{T,0}}, [0, 0], [1, 1])$ is an involutive, weakly divisible residuated lattice.

BL-algebras and MV-algebras are quintessential in formal fuzzy logics as the algebraic counterparts to Basic Logic BL and Łukasiewicz logic Ł (see Section 1). The above results suggest that, in refining the conditions of triangle algebras (which play the same role for $\mathcal{L}^I$ as MTL-algebras do for $([0, 1], \min, \max)$, i.e. they characterize the residuated t-norms) to obtain more powerful structures, we should replace divisibility by weak divisibility.

Note also that the t-norm $\mathcal{T}_{T_W,0}$ on $\mathcal{L}^I$, which seems to satisfy the most useful properties (residuated, weakly divisible, involutive) is not t-representable. At this point, it remains an open question whether every weakly divisible, involutive triangle algebra on $\mathcal{L}^I$ is isomorphic to the triangle algebra induced by $\mathcal{T}_{T_W,0}$.

6   Conclusion and Future Work

In this paper, we established triangle algebras as the variety of interval-valued residuated lattices, in a similar way as MTL-algebras are the variety of prelinear residuated lattices. For our future work, we will use this crucial result to chart the landscape of fuzzy formal logics beyond prelinearity, and, more specifically, to develop a logic that formally characterizes tautologies (true formulas) in interval-valued residuated lattices. Concretely, a follow-up paper introducing "Triangle Logic" (TL) and proving its soundness and completeness w.r.t. triangle algebras is in preparation. Later on, new properties will be imposed on triangle algebras (and corresponding new axioms added to TL) to obtain more specific structures. The intention of these new properties is, amongst others, to characterize (a part of) the class of t-norms on $\mathcal{L}^I$ defined by Formula (3).

Another challenge for the future is to find out if TL (possibly enriched with more axioms) is standard complete, i.e. complete with respect to the corresponding triangle algebras on $\mathcal{L}^I$. In combination with a characterization of these triangle algebras, this would establish a logical calculus for interval truth values that is easy to handle and suitable for use in practical applications. Furthermore also the links with other, comparable theories (see e.g. [4,9,14,20]) will be the subject of further research.

Acknowledgment

Chris Cornelis would like to thank the Research Foundation–Flanders for funding his research.

The comments and suggestions of the reviewers were also greatly appreciated.

References

1. R. Belohlávek, V. Vychodil, **Fuzzy Equational Logic**, Studies in Fuzziness and Soft Computing, Volume 186, (2005)
2. G. Cattaneo, **Abstract Approximation Spaces for Rough Theories**, in: Rough Sets in Knowledge Discovery 1: Methodology and Applications (L. Polkowski and A. Skowron, eds.), Physica-Verlag, (1998), 59–98
3. G. Cattaneo, D. Ciucci, **Intuitionistic Fuzzy Sets or Orthopair Fuzzy Sets?**, Proceedings of the third EUSFLAT Conference Zittau, Germany, (2003), 153–158
4. A. Ciabattoni, G. Metcalfe and F. Montagna, **Adding Modalities to Fuzzy Logics**, Proceedings of the 26th Linz Seminar on Fuzzy Set Theory, Austria, (2005), 27–33
5. C. Cornelis, G. Deschrijver and E.E. Kerre, **Implication in Intuitionistic Fuzzy and Interval-valued Fuzzy Set Theory: Construction, Classification, Application**, International Journal of Approximate Reasoning 35, (2004), 55–95
6. C. Cornelis, G. Deschrijver and E.E. Kerre, **Advances and Challenges in Interval-Valued Fuzzy Logic**, Fuzzy Sets and Systems 157(5), (2006), 622–627
7. G. Deschrijver and E.E. Kerre, **Classes of Intuitionistic Fuzzy t-norms Satisfying the Residuation Principle**, International Journal of Uncertainty, Fuzziness and Knowledge-Based Systems 11, (2003), 691–709

8. G. Deschrijver, C. Cornelis and E.E. Kerre, **On the Representation of Intuitionistic Fuzzy t-norms and t-conorms**, IEEE Transactions on Fuzzy Systems 12, (2004), 45–61

9. F. Esteva, P. Garcia-Calvés, L. Godo, **Enriched Interval Bilattices and Partial Many-Valued Logics: an Approach to Deal with Graded Truth and Imprecision**, International Journal of Uncertainty, Fuzziness and Knowledge-Based Systems, Vol. 2(1), (1994), 37–54

10. F. Esteva, L. Godo, **Monoidal t-norm Based Logic: Towards a Logic for Left-Continuous t-norms**, Fuzzy Sets and Systems 124, (2001), 271–288

11. F. Esteva, L. Godo, A. Garcia-Cerdanya, **On the Hierarchy of t-norm Based Residuated Fuzzy Logics**, in: Beyond Two: Theory and Applications of Multiple Valued Logic (M. Fitting and E. Orlowska, eds.), Physica-Verlag, (2003), 251–272

12. K. Gödel, **Zum intuitionistischen Aussagenkalkül**, Anzeiger der Akademie der Wissenschaften in Wien, (1932), 65-66

13. P. Hajek, **Metamathematics of Fuzzy Logic**, Trends in Logic—Studia Logica Library, Kluwer Academic Publishers, (1998)

14. M. Harlenderova, J. Rachunek, **Modal operators on MV-algebras**, Mathematica Bohemica 131(1), (2006), 39–48

15. J. Łukasiewicz, A. Tarski, **Untersuchungen über den Aussagenkalkül**, Comptes Rendus de la Société des Sciences et des Lettres de Varsovie, (1930), 1–21

16. J.M. Mendel, **Uncertain Rule-Based Fuzzy Logic Systems**, Prentice Hall PTR, Upper Saddle River, New Jersey, (2001)

17. J. Mendel, R. John, F. Liu, **Interval Type-2 Fuzzy Logic Systems Made Simple**, Accepted for publication in IEEE Transactions on Fuzzy Systems, (2005)

18. M. Ohnishi, K. Matsumoto, **Gentzen method in modal calculi, parts I and II**, Osaka Mathematical Journal 9 and 11, (1957), 113–130, (1959), 115–120

19. H. Ono, **Modalities in substructural logic – a preliminary report**, Proceedings of the 39th MLG meeting at Gamagori, Japan, (2005), 36–38

20. J. Rachunek, D. Salounova, **Modal operators on bounded commutative residuated l-monoids**, Mathematica Slovaca, accepted

21. B. Van Gasse, C. Cornelis, G. Deschrijver, E.E. Kerre, **On the Properties of a Generalized Class of T-Norms in Interval-Valued Fuzzy Logics**, New Mathematics and Natural Computation 2, (2006), 29–41

An Approach to Parameterized Approximation of Crisp and Fuzzy Sets

Alicja Mieszkowicz-Rolka and Leszek Rolka

Department of Avionics and Control,
Rzeszów University of Technology,
ul. W. Pola 2, 35-959 Rzeszów, Poland
{alicjamr, leszekr}@prz.edu.pl

Abstract. This paper proposes a concept of parameterized approximation of crisp and fuzzy sets, basing on the notion of rough and fuzzy rough inclusion function. A definition of a single ε-approximation is given. It is suitable for expressing the lower and upper approximations defined in the rough set theory and the variable precision rough set model. A unified form of approximation is especially advantageous in the case of fuzzy information systems. It helps to avoid problems caused by different forms of fuzzy connectives used in the original definition of fuzzy rough sets. The presented parameterized approach to approximation constitutes an easy to implement, straightforward generalization of the variable precision crisp and fuzzy rough set model.

1   Introduction

Rough set theory founded by Pawlak [14] is an effective tool for analysis of decision systems. However, the quality of data obtained from real decision processes is not always sufficient for a successful application of rough sets. Therefore, many extensions of the basic rough set concept have been proposed, by relaxing strong inclusion requirement and admitting of tolerance. It is possible to encompass various extensions of rough sets by a generalized theory. One example is the rough mereology of Polkowski and Skowron [15], based on the mereology of Leśniewski.

Variable precision rough set (VPRS) model, introduced by Ziarko [24], is one of the most significant parameterized extensions of the crisp rough set theory. It has become a starting-point for parameterized probabilistic approaches to rough sets, see e.g., [8,20,25].

Another independent paradigm of imperfect knowledge, originated by Zadeh [23], is the theory of fuzzy sets. Rough sets and fuzzy sets have been found complementary to each other, as they focus on different aspects of uncertainty. Thus, it is an useful idea to combine fuzzy sets with rough sets. The well-known concept of fuzzy rough sets was introduced by Dubois and Prade [5] and developed by many researchers (see, e.g., [7,9,16]). Application of the relaxation idea to fuzzy rough sets was considered in [6,22].

Our previous work [12] aimed at extending the crisp VPRS model to enable analysis of dynamic processes. We also proposed an extensions of the crisp VPRS model in the form of variable precision fuzzy rough set (VPFRS) model [13].

S. Greco et al. (Eds.): RSCTC 2006, LNAI 4259, pp. 127–136, 2006.

The main goal of this paper is to introduce a unified parameterized approach to variable precision crisp and rough set models. We present a different point of view on approximating of sets. Basing on the notion of rough and fuzzy rough inclusion function, a definition of a single ε-approximation is proposed.

Prior to discussing our approach to parameterized crisp and fuzzy approximations, it is necessary to recall crucial notions of the rough set theory and the variable precision rough set model (VPRS).

2　Rough Sets

The idea of rough sets, given by Pawlak [14], introduces two basic notions: the lower and upper approximation of sets. Any crisp subset of an universe U can be approximated by means of an indiscernibility relation $R \subseteq U \times U$.

The lower approximation $\underline{R}(A)$ and upper approximation $\overline{R}(A)$ of a crisp set A are defined as follows

$$\underline{R}(A) = \{x \in U : [x]_R \subseteq A\}, \tag{1}$$

$$\overline{R}(A) = \{x \in U : [x]_R \cap A \neq \emptyset\}, \tag{2}$$

where $[x]_R$ denotes an indiscernibility (equivalence) class which contains the element $x \in U$.

It is possible to define the lower and upper approximations, utilizing solely the notion of set inclusion.

Definition 1. *Given an indiscernibility relation R, the lower approximation $\underline{R}(A)$ and upper approximation $\overline{R}(A)$ of a crisp set A are defined as follows*

$$\underline{R}(A) = \{x \in U : \forall\, S \subseteq [x]_R \wedge S \neq \emptyset,\ S \subseteq A\}, \tag{3}$$

$$\overline{R}(A) = \{x \in U : \exists\, S \subseteq [x]_R \wedge S \neq \emptyset,\ S \subseteq A\}. \tag{4}$$

The only difference between (3) and (4) is the quantifier used, emphasizing two extreme (ideal) cases of approximation obtained by applying the indiscernibility relation R.

We can also define the lower and upper approximations in a similar way, using only the notion of membership in a set.

Definition 2. *Given an indiscernibility relation R, the lower approximation $\underline{R}(A)$ and upper approximation $\overline{R}(A)$ of a crisp set A are defined as follows*

$$\underline{R}(A) = \{x \in U : \forall\, y \in [x]_R,\ y \in A\}, \tag{5}$$

$$\overline{R}(A) = \{x \in U : \exists\, y \in [x]_R,\ y \in A\}. \tag{6}$$

The formulae (3), (4) and (5), (6) emphasize the contrast between all needed elements and some sufficient element in the case of the lower and upper approximations, respectively.

A unified form of the lower and upper approximations is especially important in the case of fuzzy sets. This is because there is no single method of performing basic operations on fuzzy sets. Many fuzzy rough set generalizations are possible, depending on the form of rough set definition which we try to generalize. We extend this idea further in sections 4 and 5.

3   Variable Precision Rough Sets

Inconsistency of information systems, caused by noise and errors, is one of the problems in applications of the rough set theory to analysis of real data. Therefore, it is necessary to admit of some level of misclassification, especially in the case of large information systems.

The idea of relaxation of strong inclusion requirements was introduced by Ziarko [24] with the help of a modified relation of set inclusion. It can be explained using the notion of inclusion degree, $\mathrm{incl}(A, B)$, of a nonempty (crisp) set A in a (crisp) set B, defined as follows

$$\mathrm{incl}(A, B) = \frac{\mathrm{card}(A \cap B)}{\mathrm{card}(A)} \,. \tag{7}$$

To limit the inclusion degree, we can apply a lower limit l and an upper limit u, introduced in the extended version of VPRS [10], which satisfy the requirement

$$0 \leq l < u \leq 1 \,. \tag{8}$$

The crisp VPRS model was generalized recently to a probabilistic rough set approach [18,25], which is based on conditional probability of inclusion.

We retain in our further consideration a non-probabilistic interpretation of VPRS. Basing on the limits l and u which satisfy the constraint (8), one can define the u-lower and the l-upper approximation of any subset A of the universe U by an indiscernibility relation R.

The u-lower approximation of A by R is a set

$$\underline{R_u}(A) = \{x \in U \colon \ \mathrm{incl}([x]_R, A) \geq u\} \,, \tag{9}$$

where $[x]_R$ denotes an indiscernibility class of R containing the element x.

The l-upper approximation of A by R is a set

$$\overline{R_l}(A) = \{x \in U \colon \ \mathrm{incl}([x]_R, A) > l\} \,. \tag{10}$$

The definitions (9) and (10) use the same notion of inclusion degree and can be interpreted as a weakened form of (3) and (4). Not all subsets of an indiscernibility class need to be included in the approximated set, and no subset of the indiscernibility class included in the set is sufficient for the acceptance of the class in the lower and upper approximations, respectively. In this way, we give up the ideals of approximation and admit of some level of misclassification.

In the following discussion, we extend the crisp VPRS model to a parameterized rough set and fuzzy rough set model. The crucial element, upon which our approach will be based, is the degree of set inclusion.

4 Parameterized Approximation of Crisp Sets

In [17], Skowron and Stepaniuk proposed a generalized definition of approximation spaces. They introduced a notion of rough inclusion function, which is defined on the Cartesian product of the powersets $\mathbb{P}(U)$ of the universe U

$$\nu : \mathbb{P}(U) \times \mathbb{P}(U) \to [0,1] \, . \tag{11}$$

Let us adapt the notion of rough inclusion function in order to obtain a new form of parameterized rough set model. We assume that the first parameter represents a nonempty set, and the rough inclusion function should be monotonic with respect to the second parameter

$$\nu(X,Y) \le \nu(X,Z) \quad \text{for any } Y \subseteq Z, \quad \text{where } X, Y, Z \subseteq U \, .$$

Using the rough inclusion function ν, the lower and upper approximations of a crisp set A can be defined by

$$\underline{R}(A) = \{x \in U : \nu([x]_R, A) = 1\} \, , \tag{12}$$

$$\overline{R}(A) = \{x \in U : \nu([x]_R, A) > 0\} \, . \tag{13}$$

The measure of inclusion degree (7), used in the framework of the VPRS model, is an example of rough inclusion function.

Now, we go one step further and propose a parameterized single form of approximation of crisp sets.

Definition 3. *Given an indiscernibility relation R, the ε-approximation $R_\varepsilon(A)$ of a crisp set A is defined as follows*

$$R_\varepsilon(A) = \{x \in U : \nu([x]_R, A) \ge \varepsilon\} \, , \tag{14}$$

where $\varepsilon \in (0, 1]$.

The ε-approximation R_ε has the following properties:

$$
\begin{aligned}
&\text{(P1)} \quad R_\varepsilon(A) = \underline{R}(A) \quad && \text{for } \varepsilon = 1 \, , \\
&\text{(P2)} \quad R_\varepsilon(A) = \overline{R}(A) \quad && \text{for } \varepsilon = 0+ \, , \\
&\text{(P3)} \quad R_\varepsilon(A) = \underline{R}_u(A) \quad && \text{for } \varepsilon = u \, , \\
&\text{(P4)} \quad R_\varepsilon(A) = \overline{R}_l(A) \quad && \text{for } \varepsilon = l+ \, .
\end{aligned}
$$

Furthermore, we can apply the rough inclusion function to introduce a notion called the exactness level of a crisp set.

Definition 4. *The exactness level $\mathrm{exl}(A)$ of a crisp set A is defined by*

$$\mathrm{exl}(A) = \sup\{\varepsilon \in (0,1] : A \subseteq R_\varepsilon(A)\} \, . \tag{15}$$

Any crisp set A is exact ($\underline{R}(A) = \overline{R}(A)$), if and only if $\mathrm{exl}(A) = 1$.

In contrast to the classical rough sets theory, we apply a single definition of approximation. However, it is still possible to determine the lower and upper approximations by using a pair of appropriate values of the ε parameter.

The lower approximation (9) turns out to be the most important notion used for reasoning about data. This is because we are interested in determining the consistent part of the analyzed information system.

The notion of upper approximation has rather a theoretical significance. In fact, if we get a " poor" lower approximation of indiscernibility classes in a given information systems, the approximation quality becomes small. In such a case, the analyzed information system is useless, regardless of the obtained upper approximation. Conversely, in a high quality information system, we can find many exact indiscernibility classes, for which the lower and upper approximations are equal or similar.

The introduced notion (14) is suitable for every case of approximation, depending on the value of the parameter ε used. Basing on our experience [12] from applications of the rough set theory to analysis of process data, we can confirm the need for relaxation of a strong inclusion requirement. It is necessary to repeat the determination of the u-lower approximation (9) for various values of the parameter u. For a series of n ε-approximations of a set A, we have

$$R_{\varepsilon_1}(A) \subseteq R_{\varepsilon_2}(A) \subseteq \ldots \subseteq R_{\varepsilon_n}(A) \quad \text{for} \quad \varepsilon_1 \geq \varepsilon_2 \geq \ldots \geq \varepsilon_n . \tag{16}$$

This property is satisfied due to monotonicity of the inclusion function.

5   Parameterized Approximation of Fuzzy Sets

An extension of the original rough set theory is necessary, if we want to analyze information systems with fuzzy attributes. The notion of fuzzy rough set was proposed by Dubois and Prade [5].

For a given fuzzy set A and a fuzzy partition $\Phi = \{F_1, F_2, \ldots, F_n\}$ on the universe U, the membership functions of the lower and upper approximations of A by Φ are defined by

$$\mu_{\underline{\Phi}(A)}(F_i) = \inf_{x \in U} \mathrm{I}(\mu_{F_i}(x), \mu_A(x)) , \tag{17}$$

$$\mu_{\overline{\Phi}(A)}(F_i) = \sup_{x \in U} \mathrm{T}(\mu_{F_i}(x), \mu_A(x)) , \tag{18}$$

where T and I denote a T-norm operator and an implicator, respectively.

The pair of sets $(\underline{\Phi}F, \overline{\Phi}F)$ is called a fuzzy rough set.

Approximating a fuzzy set A by the family Φ involves the problem of determining the degree of inclusion of one fuzzy set into another. This problem has been widely discussed in the framework of the fuzzy set theory. Many different measures of fuzzy sets inclusion were considered (see, e.g., [4,6,11]). Bandler and Kohout [1,2] applied implication operators for determination of inclusion. An axiomatic approach, given by Sinha-Dougherty [3], can also be based on the generalized Łukasiewicz implicators.

In contrast to various measures, given in the literature, we want to describe inclusion of fuzzy set in a different manner. Instead of using a single value, which expresses the inclusion degree of one fuzzy set into another, we determine inclusion with respect to particular elements of sets. This way we get a fuzzy set rather than a number. This method is particulary helpful in elaborating a variable precision fuzzy rough set model.

Before introducing the details of our approach, we need to recall three basic notions defined in the framework of the fuzzy set theory: support, power, and α-cut of a fuzzy set.

For a given a finite fuzzy subset A of the universe U, with n elements: $\text{power}(A)$ denotes the cardinality of the set A

$$\text{power}(A) = \sum_{i=1}^{n} \mu_A(x_i) \,, \tag{19}$$

support of A, denoted by supp(A), is a crisp set defined as follows

$$\text{supp}(A) = \{x : \mu_A(x_i) > 0\} \,, \tag{20}$$

α-cut of A, denoted by A_α, is a crisp set defined as follows

$$A_\alpha = \{x \in U : \ \mu_A(x) \geq \alpha\} \quad \text{for} \quad \alpha \in [0,1] \,. \tag{21}$$

The basic notion of our VPFRS model is a fuzzy set which describes the inclusion of a fuzzy set A in a fuzzy set B, determined with respect to particular elements (or singletons) of the set A. The obtained fuzzy set will be called the fuzzy inclusion set of A in B, and denoted by $\text{INCL}(A, B)$.

There are many possibilities to define such an inclusion set. According to the above remarks, we apply to this end an implication operator denoted by I. The implication-based inclusion set of a nonempty fuzzy set A in a fuzzy set B, denoted by $\text{INCL}_\text{I}(A, B)$, is defined as follows

$$\mu_{\text{INCL}_\text{I}(A,B)}(x) = \begin{cases} \text{I}(\mu_A(x), \mu_B(x)) & \text{if } \mu_A(x) > 0 \,, \\ 0 & \text{otherwise} \,. \end{cases} \tag{22}$$

By assuming that $\mu_{\text{Incl}_\text{I}(A,B)}(x) = 0$, for $\mu_A(x) = 0$, we take into account the support of the set A. It is useless to consider inclusion for all elements of the universe, because elements form outside of the support of A will do not influence the results of the method presented below.

Another form of the inclusion set definition is obtained, when we use a T-norm operator (e.g. `min`). A T-norm-based inclusion set $\text{INCL}_\text{T}(A, B)$ of a nonempty fuzzy set A in a fuzzy set B is defined as follows

$$\mu_{\text{INCL}_\text{T}(A,B)}(x) = \text{T}(\mu_A(x), \mu_B(x)) \,. \tag{23}$$

When using fuzzy implication, we require that the degree of inclusion with respect to x should be equal to 1, if the inequality $\mu_A(x) \leq \mu_B(x)$ for that x is satisfied

$$\text{I}(\mu_A(x), \mu_B(x)) = 1, \quad \text{if } \mu_A(x) \leq \mu_B(x) \,. \tag{24}$$

The requirement (24) is always satisfied by residual implicators.

Basing on the notion of inclusion set and applying the notion of α-cut (21), we are able to give a fuzzy counterpart of the rough inclusion function (11), which is defined on the Cartesian product of the families $\mathbb{F}(U)$ of all fuzzy subsets of the universe U

$$\nu_\alpha : \mathbb{F}(U) \times \mathbb{F}(U) \to [0,1] \,. \tag{25}$$

Definition 5. *The fuzzy rough α-inclusion function $\nu_\alpha(A, B)$ of any nonempty fuzzy set A in a fuzzy set B is defined as follows*

$$\nu_\alpha(A, B) = \frac{\mathrm{power}(A \cap \mathrm{INCL}(A, B)_\alpha)}{\mathrm{power}(A)} \,, \tag{26}$$

For a given α, the value $\nu_\alpha(A, B)$ expresses how many elements of the nonempty fuzzy set A belong, a least to the degree α, to the fuzzy set B.

It can be shown that the rough inclusion function used in (9) and (10) is a special case of the fuzzy rough inclusion function (26), when we use the implication-based or T-norm-based inclusion set.

Theorem 1. *For any nonempty crisp set A, any crisp set B, and $\alpha \in (0,1]$, it holds that $\nu_\alpha(A, B) = \mathrm{incl}(A, B)$, when the inclusion set $\mathrm{INCL}_\mathrm{I}(A, B)$ or $\mathrm{INCL}_\mathrm{T}(A, B)$ is used.*

Furthermore, we can prove monotonicity of the proposed fuzzy rough inclusion functions.

Theorem 2. *Implication-based or T-norm-based fuzzy rough inclusion function ν_α is monotonic with respect to the second parameter.*

In order to get a general form of fuzzy rough approximation, we introduce a function called *res*, defined on the Cartesian product $\mathbb{P}(U) \times \mathbb{F}(U)$, where $\mathbb{P}(U)$ denotes the powerset of the universe U, and $\mathbb{F}(U)$ the family of all fuzzy subsets of the universe U, respectively

$$\mathrm{res} : \mathbb{P}(U) \times \mathbb{F}(U) \to [0,1] \,. \tag{27}$$

We require that

$\mathrm{res}(\emptyset, Y) = 0 \,,$
$\mathrm{res}(X, Y) \in \{0, 1\}, \quad \text{if } Y \text{ is a crisp set} \,,$
$\mathrm{res}(X, Y) \leq \mathrm{res}(X, Z) \quad \text{for any } Y \subseteq Z, \quad \text{where } X \in \mathbb{P}(U), \text{ and } Y, Z \in \mathbb{F}(U) \,.$

For a given crisp set X and fuzzy set Y, the value of function $\mathrm{res}(X, Y)$ should express the resulting membership degree in the set Y, taking into account not all elements of the universe, but only the elements of the set X. We assume, according to the limit-based approach of Dubois and Prade, the following form of the function `res`

$$\mathrm{res}(X, Y) = \inf_{x \in X} \mu_Y(x) \,. \tag{28}$$

The drawback of the above definition of `res` consists in regarding only one (limit) value of membership degree of elements in the set Y. It is possible to give another definitions, in which many values of membership degree are taken into account.

Definition 6. *For $\varepsilon \in (0,1]$, the ε-approximation $\Phi_\varepsilon(A)$ of a fuzzy set A, by a fuzzy partition $\Phi = \{F_1, F_2, \ldots, F_n\}$, is a fuzzy set on the domain Φ with membership function expressed by*

$$\mu_{\Phi_\varepsilon(A)}(F_i) = \mathrm{res}(S_\varepsilon(F_i, A), \mathrm{INCL}(F_i, A)), \tag{29}$$

where

$$S_\varepsilon(F_i, A) = \mathrm{supp}(F_i \cap \mathrm{INCL}(F_i, A)_{\alpha_\varepsilon}),$$

$$\alpha_\varepsilon = \sup\{\alpha \in [0, 1] : \nu_\alpha(F_i, A) \geq \varepsilon\}.$$

The set $S_\varepsilon(F_i, A)$ is equal to support of the intersection of the class F_i with the part of $\mathrm{INCL}(F_i, A)$, which contains those elements of the approximating class F_i that are included in A at least to the degree α_ε. The resulting membership $\mu_{\Phi_\varepsilon(A)}(F_i)$ is determined using only elements from $S_\varepsilon(F_i, A)$ instead of the whole class F_i. This is accomplished by applying the function res.

It can be shown that applying the definition (28) of the function **res** leads to a simple form of (29)

$$\mu_{\Phi_\varepsilon(A)}(F_i) = \sup\{\alpha \in [0, 1] : \nu_\alpha(F_i, A) \geq \varepsilon\}. \tag{30}$$

In contrast to the approximations (17) and (18), which use two different fuzzy connectives, we have a single unified definition of fuzzy rough approximation. This is important for obtaining a consistent variable precision fuzzy rough set model. Thus, we are able to compare approximations determined for various values of the parameter ε.

To obtain fuzzy rough approximation on the domain of the universe U, we need a fuzzy extension ω, defined by Dubois and Prade [5], which is a mapping from the domain Φ into the domain of the universe U. For any fuzzy set A, the extension $\omega(A)$ is given by

$$\mu_{\omega(A)}(x) = \mu_A(F_i), \quad \text{if } \mu_{F_i}(x) = 1. \tag{31}$$

Example 1. We have a fuzzy set A defined on the universe U

$$A = \{0.2/x_1,\ 0.1/x_2,\ 0.3/x_3,\ 1.0/x_4,\ 1.0/x_5,\ 0.1/x_6,\ 0.0/x_7,\ 1.0/x_8,\\ 1.0/x_9,\ 0.1/x_{10}\},$$

and a fuzzy partition $\Phi = \{F_1, F_2, \ldots, F_n\}$ with the following similarity class F_1

$$F_1 = \{0.0/x_1,\ 0.2/x_2,\ 0.2/x_3,\ 0.1/x_4,\ 1.0/x_5,\ 0.0/x_6,\ 1.0/x_7,\ 0.2/x_8,\\ 1.0/x_9,\ 0.2/x_{10}\}.$$

Let us determine the membership value of the similarity class F_1 in the fuzzy rough ε-approximation of A by Φ.

We get the implication-based inclusion set $\mathrm{INCL}(F_1, A)$ using the Łukasiewicz implication operator: $\mathrm{I}(x, y) = \min(1, 1 - x + y)$

$$\mathrm{INCL}(F_1, A) = \{1.0/x_1,\ 0.9/x_2,\ 1.0/x_3,\ 1.0/x_4,\ 1.0/x_5,\ 1.0/x_6,\ 0.0/x_7,\\ 1.0/x_8,\ 1.0/x_9,\ 0.9/x_{10}\}.$$

Now, we can determine the membership degree of F_1 in the ε-approximation of A, for different values of ε. We start with the limit value of ε equal to 1. It that case, no relaxation of inclusion requirement is allowed. Therefore, we seek for the biggest $\alpha \in [0,1]$, denoted by α_ε, for which

$$\nu_\alpha(F_1, A) = \frac{\mathrm{power}(F_1 \cap \mathrm{INCL}(F_1, A)_\alpha)}{\mathrm{power}(F_1)} \geq 1 \,.$$

We obtain $\alpha_\varepsilon = 0$. This means that we cannot omit any element from the inclusion set $\mathrm{INCL}(F_1, A)$. The membership degree $\mu_{\Phi_\varepsilon(A)}(F_1) = 0$.

Assume now that $\varepsilon = 0.70$. We get $\alpha_\varepsilon = 0.9$.
$\mathrm{INCL}(F_1, A)_{0.9} = \{x_1,\ x_2,\ x_3,\ x_4,\ x_5,\ x_6,\ x_8,\ x_9,\ x_{10}\}$,
$\nu_\alpha(F_1, A) = 2.9/3.9 = 0.744$, the membership degree $\mu_{\Phi_\varepsilon(A)}(F_1) = 0.9$.
Discarding x_7 from $\mathrm{INCL}(F_1, A)$ leads to an increase (from 0.0 to 0.9) of the membership degree of F_1 in the ε-approximation of A.

Similarly, for $\varepsilon = 0.60$, we find that $\alpha_\varepsilon = 1$.
$\mathrm{INCL}(F_1, A)_1 = \{x_1,\ x_3,\ x_4,\ x_5,\ x_6,\ x_8,\ x_9\}$,
$\nu_\alpha(F_1, A) = 2.5/3.9 = 0.641$. The membership degree $\mu_{\Phi_\varepsilon(A)}(F_1) = 1$.

The parameterized fuzzy rough set model presented in this section can be adapted to different needs. This can be done by specifying the form of fuzzy rough inclusion function (26) or changing the way of determining the resulting membership degree (27).

6   Conclusions

Parameterized approximation of crisp and fuzzy sets can be done by applying a single notion of ε-approximation. It is defined using rough or fuzzy rough inclusion function. A unified way of approximation of sets is particulary important in the case of variable precision fuzzy rough set model. It is still possible to retain previous forms of rough sets by using a pair of ε values for obtaining lower and upper approximations of sets. The presented approach can be easy implemented in the form of a computer algorithm. It constitutes a universal tool for applications to analysis of crisp and fuzzy information systems. In future research, the possibility of application of the proposed method in other parameterized approaches to rough sets should be investigated.

References

1. Bandler, W., Kohout, L.: Fuzzy Power Sets and Fuzzy Implication Operators. Fuzzy Sets and Systems **4** (1980) 13–30
2. Burillo, P., Frago, N., Fuentes, R.: Inclusion Grade and Fuzzy Implication Operators. Fuzzy Sets and Systems **114** (2000) 417–429
3. Cornelis, C., Van der Donck, C., Kerre, E.: Sinha-Dougherty Approach to the Fuzzification of Set Inclusion Revisited. Fuzzy Sets and Systems **134** (2003) 283–295
4. De Baets, B., De Meyer, H., Naessens, H.: On Rational Cardinality-based Inclusion Measures. Fuzzy Sets and Systems **128** (2002) 169–183

5. Dubois, D., Prade, H.: Putting Rough Sets and Fuzzy Sets Together. In: Słowiński, R., (ed.): Intelligent Decision Support: Handbook of Applications and Advances of the Rough Sets Theory. Kluwer Academic Publishers, Boston Dordrecht London (1992) 203–232

6. Fernández Salido, J.M., Murakami, S.: Rough Set Analysis of a General Type of Fuzzy Data Using Transitive Aggregations of Fuzzy Similarity Relations. Fuzzy Sets and Systems **139** (2003) 635–660

7. Greco, S., Matarazzo, B., Słowiński, R.: Rough Set Processing of Vague Information Using Fuzzy Similarity Relations. In: Calude, C.S., Paun, G., (eds.): Finite Versus Infinite — Contributions to an Eternal Dilemma. Springer-Verlag, Berlin Heidelberg New York (2000) 149–173

8. Greco, S., Matarazzo, B., Słowiński, R.: Rough Membership and Bayesian Confirmation Measures for Parameterized Rough Sets. [19] 314–324

9. Inuiguchi, M.: Generalizations of Rough Sets: From Crisp to Fuzzy Cases. [21] 26–37

10. Katzberg, J.D., Ziarko, W.: Variable Precision Extension of Rough Sets. Fundamenta Informaticae **27** (1996) 155–168

11. Lin, T.Y.: Coping with Imprecision Information — Fuzzy Logic. Downsizing Expo, Santa Clara Convention Center (1993)

12. Mieszkowicz-Rolka, A., Rolka, L.: Variable Precision Rough Sets: Evaluation of Human Operator's Decision Model. In: Sołdek, J., Drobiazgiewicz, L., (eds.): Artificial Intelligence and Security in Computing Systems. Kluwer Academic Publishers, Boston Dordrecht London (2003) 33–40

13. Mieszkowicz-Rolka, A., Rolka, L.: Variable Precision Fuzzy Rough Sets Model in the Analysis of Process Data. [19] 354–363

14. Pawlak, Z.: Rough Sets: Theoretical Aspects of Reasoning about Data. Kluwer Academic Publishers, Boston Dordrecht London (1991)

15. Polkowski, L.: Toward Rough Set Foundations. Mereological Approach. [21] 8–25

16. Radzikowska, A.M., Kerre, E.E.: A Comparative Study of Fuzzy Rough Sets. Fuzzy Sets and Systems **126** (2002) 137–155

17. Skowron, A., Stepaniuk, J.: Tolerance Approximation Spaces. Fundamenta Informaticae **27** (1996) 245–253

18. Ślęzak, D., Ziarko, W.: Variable Precision Bayesian Rough Set Model. In: Wang, G., Liu, Q., Yao, Y., Skowron, A., (eds.): Rough Sets, Fuzzy Sets, Data Mining, and Granular Computing. Lecture Notes in Artificial Intelligence, Vol. 2639. Springer-Verlag, Berlin Heidelberg New York (2003) 312–315

19. Ślęzak, D., et al., (eds.): Rough Sets and Current Trends in Computing. Lecture Notes in Artificial Intelligence, Vol. 3641. Springer-Verlag, Berlin Heidelberg New York (2005)

20. Ślęzak, D.: Rough Sets and Bayes Factor. In: Peters, J.F., et al., (eds.): Transactions on Rough Sets III. Lecture Notes in Computer Science (Journal Subline), Vol. 3400. Springer-Verlag, Berlin Heidelberg New York (2005) 202–229

21. Tsumoto, S., et al., (eds.): Rough Sets and Current Trends in Computing. Lecture Notes in Artificial Intelligence, Vol. 3066. Springer-Verlag, Berlin Heidelberg New York (2004)

22. Liu, W.N., Yao, J., Yao, Y.: Rough Approximations under Level Fuzzy Sets. [21] 78–83

23. Zadeh, L.: Fuzzy Sets. Information and Control **8** (1965) 338–353

24. Ziarko, W.: Variable Precision Rough Sets Model. Journal of Computer and System Sciences **46** (1993) 39–59

25. Ziarko, W.: Probabilistic Rough Sets. [19] 283–293

Rough Fuzzy Set Approximations in Fuzzy Formal Contexts

Ming-Wen Shao[1,2], Min Liu[1], and Wen-Xiu Zhang[3]

[1] Department of Automation, Tsinghua University, Beijing, 100084, China
shaomingwen1837@163.com, lium@mail.tsinghua.edu.cn
[2] School of Information Technology, Jiangxi University of Finance & Economics,
Nanchang, Jiangxi 330013, P.R. China
[3] Faculty of Science, Xi'an Jiaotong University, Xi'an, Shaan'xi 710049, China
wxzhang@xjtu.edu.cn

Abstract. In the paper, we introduce a new kind of fuzzy formal concept derived from an adjoint pair of operations. Based on the discussed fuzzy formal concepts, a pair of rough fuzzy set approximations in fuzzy formal contexts is introduced. The properties of the proposed approximation operators are examined in details.

Keywords: Approximation operators, concept lattices, formal concepts, rough sets.

1 Introduction

The theory of rough sets, proposed by Pawlak [13], as a method of set approximation, it has continued to flourish as a tool for data mining and data analysis. The basic operators in rough set theory are approximations. Using the concepts of lower and upper approximations, knowledge hidden in information tables may be unraveled and expressed in the form of decision rules. Many authors have generalized the rough set model to rough fuzzy sets and fuzzy rough sets models (see [6,12,15,22,25]).

The theory of formal concept analysis (FCA) proposed by Wille [7,20] have been studied intensively, and obtained results have played an important role in conceptual data analysis and knowledge processing. A formal concept is defined by an (objects, attributes) pair. The set of objects is referred to as the extension, and the set of attributes as the intension, of the formal concept. They uniquely determine each other [7,20]. FCA is based on a formal context, which is a binary relation between a set of objects and a set of attributes with the value 0 and 1. However, in many practical applications, the binary relations are with real values. Burusco [4,5] generalized the model of FCA based on fuzzy formal context. And Belohlavek [1,2,3] proposed fuzzy concepts in fuzzy formal context based on residuated lattice. Moreover, Popescu, Georgescu and Popescu discussed a general approach to fuzzy FCA (see [14,9]).

The combination of formal concept analysis and rough set theory provide more approaches for data analysis. The notions of formal concept and formal

S. Greco et al. (Eds.): RSCTC 2006, LNAI 4259, pp. 137–146, 2006.
© Springer-Verlag Berlin Heidelberg 2006

concept lattice can be introduced into rough set theory by constructing different types of formal concepts [8,23,24]. Rough set approximation operators can be introduced into formal concept analysis by considering different types of definability [26]. Many efforts have been made to compare and combine the two theories [8,10,11,16,21,23,24]. In [17], we defined a pair of rough set approximations within formal contexts based on the notions of the attribute oriented concepts and the object oriented concepts.

In this paper we discussed two kinds of fuzzy concepts, ie. the object oriented fuzzy concept and the attribute oriented fuzzy concept, which are natural generalization to the object oriented concept and the attribute oriented concept in the L-fuzzy formal contexts. Based on the discussed fuzzy formal concepts, a pair of rough fuzzy set approximations in fuzzy formal contexts is introduced. The properties of the proposed approximation operators are examined in details.

2   *L*-Fuzzy Formal Contexts

The notion of residuated lattice provides a very general truth structure for fuzzy logic and fuzzy set theory. In the following, we list its definition and basic properties.

Definition 1. *A residuated lattice is a structure* $(L, \vee, \wedge, \otimes, \rightarrow, 0, 1)$ *such that*

(1) $(L, \vee, \wedge, 0, 1)$ *is a lattice with the least element* 0 *and the greatest element* 1;

(2) $(L, \otimes, 1)$ *is a commutative monoid;*

(3) for all $a, b, c \in L, a \leq b \rightarrow c$ *iff* $a \otimes b \leq c$.

Residuated lattice L is called complete if $(L, \vee, \wedge)$ is a complete lattice. A complete residuated lattice $(L, \vee, \wedge, \otimes, \rightarrow, 0, 1)$ is called involutive if it satisfies $a = a^{\sim\sim}$ (where the negation $\sim$ is defined by $a^{\sim} = a \rightarrow 0$ and we don't distinguish the denotations between $a^{\sim}$ and $\sim a$).

Lemma 1. *The following hold in any complete residuated lattice:*

(1) $a \rightarrow 1 = 1; 1 \rightarrow a = a; a \rightarrow b = 1$ *iff* $a \leq b; 0 \otimes a = a \otimes 0 = 0$;

(2) $\rightarrow$ *is antitone in the first and isotone in the second argument;* $a \leq (a \rightarrow b) \rightarrow b$;

(3) $a \rightarrow b \leq (b \rightarrow c) \rightarrow (a \rightarrow c); a \rightarrow b \leq (c \rightarrow a) \rightarrow (c \rightarrow b); a \rightarrow (b \rightarrow c) = b \rightarrow (a \rightarrow c)$;

(4) $(\bigvee_{i \in I} a_i) \rightarrow a = \bigwedge_{i \in I}(a_i \rightarrow a); a \rightarrow (\bigwedge_{i \in I} a_i) = \bigwedge_{i \in I}(a \rightarrow a_i)$;

(5) $\bigwedge_{i \in I}(a_i \rightarrow b_i) \leq (\bigwedge_{i \in I} a_i) \rightarrow (\bigwedge_{i \in I} b_i); \bigwedge_{i \in I}(a_i \rightarrow b_i) \leq (\bigvee_{i \in I} a_i) \rightarrow (\bigvee_{i \in I} b_i)$;

(6) $\otimes$ *is isotone in both arguments;* $a \otimes b \leq a; a \otimes b \leq b$;

(7) $b \leq a \rightarrow (a \otimes b); (a \rightarrow b) \otimes a \leq b; (a \otimes b) \rightarrow c = a \rightarrow (b \rightarrow c)$;

(8) $a \rightarrow b \leq (a \otimes c) \rightarrow (b \otimes c); (a \rightarrow b) \otimes (b \rightarrow c) \leq (a \rightarrow c)$;

(9) $(\bigvee_{i \in I} a_i) \otimes a = \bigvee_{i \in I} (a_i \otimes a)$; $(\bigwedge_{i \in I} a_i) \otimes a \leq \bigwedge_{i \in I} (a_i \otimes a)$;

(10) $a \leq a^{\sim\sim}$; $a \to b \leq b^{\sim} \to a^{\sim}$; $a \to b^{\sim} = b \to a^{\sim}$.

(11) $(a \otimes b)^{\sim} = a \to b^{\sim} = b \to a^{\sim}$.

Let L be a residuated lattice. An $L - set$ A in an universe set U is any map A: $U \to L$, $A(x)$ being interpreted as the truth degree of the fact " x belongs to A". By L^U denote the set of all $L - set$ in U. The empty set $\emptyset$ and the universe set U in L^U is denoted by $\overline{0}_U$ and $\overline{1}_U$. For all $X_1, X_2 \in L^U$, $X_1 \subseteq X_2$ if and only if $X_1(x) \leq X_2(x)$ ($\forall\ x \in U$). Operations $\vee$ and $\wedge$ on L^U are defined by:

$$(X_1 \vee X_2)(x) = X_1(x) \vee X_2(x),\ (X_1 \wedge X_2)(x) = X_1(x) \wedge X_2(x), \quad \forall X_1, X_2 \in L^U.$$

A L-fuzzy formal context is defined as a tuple (L, U, M, R), where L is a complete residuated lattice, U and M are the object and attribute sets, $R \in L^{U \times M}$ is a L-fuzzy relation between U and M. A L-fuzzy formal context is called involutive if L is an involutive residuated lattice.

Example 1. [4] Let $([0,1], U, M, R)$ be a fuzzy formal context with $U = \{1, 2, 3\}$ and $M = \{a, b, c\}$, the fuzzy relation R defined as Table 1. Let $\to$ be the R_0 implication (see [19]), ie.

$$x \to y = \begin{cases} 1, & x \leq y \\ (1 - x) \vee y & x > y \end{cases}$$

$$x \otimes y = \begin{cases} 0, & x + y \leq 1 \\ x \wedge y, & x + y > 1 \end{cases}$$

Table 1.

R	a	b	c
x_1	0.6	0.6	0.0
x_2	0.9	0.5	0.3
x_3	1.0	0.2	0.7

It can be easily checked that (L, U, M, R) defined in the *Example 1* is an involutive L-fuzzy formal context.

3   The Two Kinds of Generalized Fuzzy Concept Lattices

In this section, we show two kinds of fuzzy concepts, ie. the object oriented fuzzy concept and the attribute oriented fuzzy concept, which are the generalizations to the object oriented concept and the attribute oriented concept in the L-fuzzy formal contexts.

Let (L, U, M, R) be a L-fuzzy formal context, $X \in L^U$, a pair of approximation operators, $^\Diamond$, $^\Box : L^U \longrightarrow L^M$ defined by:

$$X^\Diamond(a) = \bigvee_{x \in U}(X(x) \otimes R(x, a)),$$
$$X^\Box(a) = \bigwedge_{x \in U}(R(x, a) \to X(x)).$$

Analogously, for any $B \subseteq L^M$, a pair of approximation operators, $^\Diamond$, $^\Box :$ $L^M \longrightarrow L^U$ defined by:

$$B^\Diamond(x) = \bigvee_{a \in M}(B(a) \otimes R(x, a)),$$
$$B^\Box(x) = \bigwedge_{a \in M}(R(x, a) \to B(a)).$$

The operators $^\Diamond$, $^\Box$ are relatede by $X^{\sim\Box\sim} = X^\Diamond$, $X^{\sim\Diamond\sim} = X^\Box$, $B^{\sim\Box\sim} = B^\Diamond$ and $B^{\sim\Diamond\sim} = B^\Box$ [18].

Theorem 1. *For any X, X_1, X_2, approximation operators $^\Diamond$, $^\Box$ have the following properties:*

(i) $X_1 \subseteq X_2 \Longrightarrow X_1^\Diamond \subseteq X_2^\Diamond$, $X_1^\Box \subseteq X_2^\Box$;

(ii) $X^{\Box\Diamond} \subseteq X \subseteq X^{\Diamond\Box}$;

(iii) $X^{\Diamond\Box\Diamond} = X^\Diamond$, $X^{\Box\Diamond\Box} = X^\Box$;

(iv) $(X_1 \cap X_2)^\Box = X_1^\Box \cap X_2^\Box$, $(X_1 \cup X_2)^\Diamond = X_1^\Diamond \cup X_2^\Diamond$.

Proof. (i) From $X_1 \subseteq X_2$, we have

$$X_1(x) \otimes R(x, a) \leq X_2(x) \otimes R(x, a),$$
$$R(x, a) \to X_1(x) \leq R(x, a) \to X_2(x).$$

Then, it is evident that $X_1^\Diamond \subseteq X_2^\Diamond, X_1^\Box \subseteq X_2^\Box$.
(ii) On one hand,

$$\begin{aligned}
\forall x \in U, X^{\Box\Diamond}(x) &= \bigvee_{a \in M}(X^\Box(a) \otimes R(x, a)) \\
&= \bigvee_{a \in M}((\bigwedge_{y \in U}(R(y, a) \to X(y)) \otimes R(x, a)) \\
&\leq \bigvee_{a \in M}((R(x, a) \to X(x)) \otimes R(x, a)) \\
&\leq \bigvee_{a \in M} X(x) \\
&= X(x);
\end{aligned}$$

on the other hand,

$$\begin{aligned}
\forall x \in U, X^{\Diamond\Box}(x) &= \bigwedge_{a \in M}(R(x, a) \to X^\Diamond(a)) \\
&= \bigwedge_{a \in M}(R(x, a) \to (\bigvee_{y \in U}(X(y) \otimes R(y, a))) \\
&\geq \bigwedge_{a \in M}(R(x, a) \to (X(x) \otimes R(x, a))) \\
&\geq \bigwedge_{a \in M}(X(x)) \\
&= X(x).
\end{aligned}$$

(iii) From (ii) we have $(X^\Diamond)^{\Box\Diamond} \subseteq (X^\Diamond)$; on the other hand, from (i) and (ii) we have $X^\Diamond \subseteq X^{\Diamond\Box\Diamond}$. Thus, $X^{\Diamond\Box\Diamond} = X^\Diamond$. And $X^{\Box\Diamond\Box} = X^\Box$ can be obtained by the similar proof.

(iv) For any $x \in U$ we have

$$\begin{aligned}
(X_1 \cap X_2)^\square(a) &= \bigwedge_{x \in U}(R(x,a) \to (X_1 \cap X_2)(x)) \\
&= \bigwedge_{x \in U}(\bigwedge_{i=1,2} R(x,a) \to X_i(x)) \\
&= \bigwedge_{i=1,2}(\bigwedge_{x \in U} R(x,a) \to X_i(x)) \\
&= X_1^\square(a) \wedge X_2^\square(a) \\
&= (X_1^\square \cap X_2^\square)(a)
\end{aligned}$$

The proof of $(X_1 \cup X_2)^\Diamond = X_1^\Diamond \cup X_2^\Diamond$ is analogous.

Theorem 2. *For any B, B_1, B_2, approximation operators $^\Diamond$, $^\square$ have the following properties:*

(i) $B_1 \subseteq B_2 \Longrightarrow B_1^\Diamond \subseteq B_2^\Diamond$, $B_1^\square \subseteq B_2^\square$;

(ii) $B^{\square\Diamond} \subseteq B \subseteq B^{\Diamond\square}$;

(iii) $B^{\Diamond\square\Diamond} = B^\Diamond$, $B^{\square\Diamond\square} = B^\square$;

(iv) $(B_1 \cap B_2)^\square = B_1^\square \cap B_2^\square$, $(B_1 \cup B_2)^\Diamond = B_1^\Diamond \cup B_2^\Diamond$.

Proof. It is similar to the proof of Theorem 1.

The object oriented fuzzy concept lattice derived from an adjoint pair of operations was introduced by Georgescu and Popescu [9]. A pair (X, B), $X \subseteq L^U, B \subseteq L^M$, is called an object oriented fuzzy concept if $X = B^\Diamond$ and $B = X^\square$. For two object oriented fuzzy concepts (X_1, B_1) and (X_2, B_2), $(X_1, B_1) \leq (X_2, B_2)$, if and only if $X_1 \subseteq X_2$ (which is equivalent to $B_1 \subseteq B_2$). For a fuzzy set $X \subseteq L^U$, since $(X^{\square\Diamond})^\square = X^\square$, then $(X^{\square\Diamond}, X^\square)$ is an object oriented fuzzy concept. For a fuzzy set $B \subseteq L^M$, we have another object oriented fuzzy concept $(B^\Diamond, B^{\Diamond\square})$.

All the object oriented fuzzy concepts of (L, U, M, R) forms a complete lattice in which infimum and supremum are defined by:

$$\begin{aligned}
(X_1, B_1) \vee (X_2, B_2) &= (X_1 \cup X_2, (B_1 \cup B_2)^{\Diamond\square}), \\
(X_1, B_1) \wedge (X_2, B_2) &= ((X_1 \cap X_2)^{\square\Diamond}, B_1 \cap B_2).
\end{aligned}$$

In the following, we introduce a new kind of fuzzy concept lattice.

A pair (X, B), $X \subseteq L^U, B \subseteq L^M$, is called an attribute oriented fuzzy concept if $X = B^\square$ and $B = X^\Diamond$. For two attribute oriented fuzzy concepts (X_1, B_1) and (X_2, B_2), $(X_1, B_1) \leq (X_2, B_2)$, if and only if $X_1 \subseteq X_2$ (which is equivalent to $B_1 \subseteq B_2$). For a fuzzy set $X \subseteq L^U$, since $(X^{\Diamond\square})^\Diamond = X^\Diamond$, then $(X^{\Diamond\square}, X^\Diamond)$ is an attribute oriented fuzzy concept. For a fuzzy set $B \subseteq L^M$, we have another attribute oriented fuzzy concept $(B^\square, B^{\square\Diamond})$.

All the attribute oriented fuzzy concepts of (L, U, M, R) forms a complete lattice in which infimum and supremum are defined by:

$$\begin{aligned}
(X_1, B_1) \vee (X_2, B_2) &= ((X_1 \cup X_2)^{\Diamond\square}, B_1 \cup B_2), \\
(X_1, B_1) \wedge (X_2, B_2) &= (X_1 \cap X_2, (B_1 \cap B_2)^{\square\Diamond}.
\end{aligned}$$

4   Rough Fuzzy Approximation Operators

In this section, based on above discussed approximation operators we introduced a pair of lower and upper fuzzy approximation operators, which are the generalization to the results presented in [17].

Definition 2. *Let (L, U, M, R) be a L-fuzzy formal context. For any set $X \in L^U$, a pair of lower and upper approximations, $\underline{Apr}(X)$ and $\overline{Apr}(X)$, is defined by*

$$\underline{Apr}(X) = X^{\square\diamond}, \quad \overline{Apr}(X) = X^{\diamond\square}.$$

Operators, $\square\diamond$, $\diamond\square : L^U \longrightarrow L^U$, are referred to as the lower and upper fuzzy approximation operators for fuzzy object sets, and the pair $(\underline{Apr}(X), \overline{Apr}(X))$ is referred to as a generalized rough fuzzy object set.

Theorem 3. *Let (L, U, M, R) be an involutive L-fuzzy formal context. The lower and upper fuzzy approximation satisfy the following properties: for any $X, Y \in L^U$,*

$$(FL_1) \qquad \underline{Apr}(X) =\sim (\overline{Apr}(\sim X)),$$

$$(FU_1) \qquad \overline{Apr}(X) =\sim (\underline{Apr}(\sim X));$$

$$(FL_2) \qquad \underline{Apr}(\emptyset) = \overline{Apr}(\emptyset) = \emptyset,$$

$$(FU_2) \qquad \overline{Apr}(U) = \underline{Apr}(U) = U;$$

$$(FL_3) \qquad \underline{Apr}(X \cap Y) \subseteq \underline{Apr}(X) \cap \underline{Apr}(Y),$$

$$(FU_3) \qquad \overline{Apr}(X \cup Y) \supseteq \overline{Apr}(X) \cup \overline{Apr}(Y);$$

$$(FL_4) \qquad X \subseteq Y \Longrightarrow \underline{Apr}(X) \subseteq \underline{Apr}(Y),$$

$$(FU_4) \qquad X \subseteq Y \Longrightarrow \overline{Apr}(X) \subseteq \overline{Apr}(Y);$$

$$(FL_5) \qquad \underline{Apr}(X \cup Y) \supseteq \underline{Apr}(X) \cup \underline{Apr}(Y),$$

$$(FU_5) \qquad \overline{Apr}(X \cap Y) \subseteq \overline{Apr}(X) \cap \overline{Apr}(Y);$$

$$(FL_6) \qquad \underline{Apr}(X) \subseteq X,$$

$$(FU_6) \qquad X \subseteq \overline{Apr}(X);$$

$$(FL_7) \qquad \underline{Apr}(\underline{Apr}(X)) = \underline{Apr}(X),$$

$$(FU_7) \qquad \overline{Apr}(\overline{Apr}(X)) = \overline{Apr}(X).$$

Proof. Properties (FL_1) and (FU_1) show that approximation operators $\underline{Apr}$ and $\overline{Apr}$ are dual to each other. Properties with the same number may be regarded as dual properties. Thus, we only need to prove one of dual properties with the same number.

For any $X \subseteq U$, we have

$$\sim (\overline{Apr}(\sim X)) = \sim (\sim X)^{\Diamond\Box} = \sim ((\sim X)^{\sim\Box\sim})^{\Box}$$
$$= \sim (X)^{\Box\sim\Box} = (X)^{\Box\sim\Box\sim}$$
$$= (X^{\Box})^{\sim\Box\sim} = X^{\Box\Diamond}$$
$$= \underline{Apr}(X).$$

Thus, (FU_1) follows. And (FL_1) can be directly induced by (FU_1).

For any $x \in U$, we have

$$\overline{Apr}(\emptyset)(x) = \emptyset^{\Diamond\Box}(x)$$
$$= \bigwedge_{a \in M}(R(x,a) \rightarrow \emptyset^{\Diamond}(a))$$
$$= \bigwedge_{a \in M}(R(x,a) \rightarrow (\bigvee_{y \in U}(\emptyset(y) \otimes R(y,a)))$$
$$= \bigwedge_{a \in M}(R(x,a) \rightarrow 0)$$
$$= 0.$$

From Theorem 1 (ii) we have $\underline{Apr}(\emptyset) = \emptyset$. Then, (FL_2) follows.

For any $X, Y \subseteq U$, from Theorem 1 (iv) we have $(X \cap Y)^{\Box\Diamond} = (X^{\Box} \cap Y^{\Box})^{\Diamond}$. Since

$$X^{\Box} \cap Y^{\Box} \subseteq X^{\Box}, \; X^{\Box} \cap Y^{\Box} \subseteq Y^{\Box}$$

then

$$(X^{\Box} \cap Y^{\Box})^{\Diamond} \subseteq X^{\Box\Diamond}, \; (X^{\Box} \cap Y^{\Box})^{\Diamond} \subseteq Y^{\Box\Diamond}$$

which implies (FL_3).

Properties (FL_4) follows directly from Theorem 1 (i).

From Theorem 1 (i) we have

$$X^{\Box} \subseteq (X \cup Y)^{\Box}, \; Y^{\Box} \subseteq (X \cup Y)^{\Box}.$$

And from Theorem 2 (i) we have

$$X^{\Box\Diamond} \subseteq (X \cup Y)^{\Box\Diamond}, \; Y^{\Box\Diamond} \subseteq (X \cup Y)^{\Box\Diamond}.$$

Thus, Property (FL_5) holds.

Properties (FL_6) follows directly from Theorem 1 (ii).

Since $\underline{Apri}(\underline{Apri}(X)) = (X^{\Box\Diamond})^{\Box\Diamond} = X^{\Box\Diamond\Box\Diamond}$, by Theorem 1 (iii) we conclude that (FL_7) holds.

Definition 3. *Let (L, U, M, R) be a L-fuzzy formal context. For any set $B \in L^M$, another pair of lower and upper approximations, $\underline{Apr}(B)$ and $\overline{Apr}(B)$, is defined by*

$$\underline{Apr}(B) = B^{\Box\Diamond}, \quad \overline{Apr}(B) = B^{\Diamond\Box}.$$

Operators, $^{\Box\Diamond}$, $^{\Diamond\Box}$: $L^M \longrightarrow L^M$, are referred to as the lower and upper approximation operators for fuzzy attribute sets, and the pair $(\underline{Apr}(B), \overline{Apr}(B))$ is referred to as a generalized rough fuzzy attribute set.

Theorem 4. *Let (L, U, M, R) be a involutive L-fuzzy formal context. The lower and upper approximation satisfy the following properties: for any $B, C \in L^M$,*

$$(FL_1') \qquad \underline{Apr}(B) = \sim (\overline{Apr}(\sim B)),$$

$$(FU_1') \qquad \overline{Apr}(B) = \sim (\underline{Apr}(\sim B));$$

$$(FL_2') \qquad \underline{Apr}(\emptyset) = \overline{Apr}(\emptyset) = \emptyset,$$

$$(FU_2') \qquad \overline{Apr}(M) = \underline{Apr}(M) = M;$$

$$(FL_3') \qquad \underline{Apr}(B \cap C) \subseteq \underline{Apr}(B) \cap \underline{Apr}(C),$$

$$(FU_3') \qquad \overline{Apr}(B \cup C) \supseteq \overline{Apr}(B) \cup \overline{Apr}(C);$$

$$(FL_4') \qquad B \subseteq C \Longrightarrow \underline{Apr}(B) \subseteq \underline{Apr}(C),$$

$$(FU_4') \qquad B \subseteq C \Longrightarrow \overline{Apr}(B) \subseteq \overline{Apr}(C);$$

$$(FL_5') \qquad \underline{Apr}(B \cup C) \supseteq \underline{Apr}(B) \cup \underline{Apr}(C),$$

$$(FU_5') \qquad \overline{Apr}(B \cap C) \subseteq \overline{Apr}(B) \cap \overline{Apr}(C);$$

$$(FL_6') \qquad \underline{Apr}(B) \subseteq B,$$

$$(FU_6') \qquad B \subseteq \overline{Apr}(B);$$

$$(FL_7') \qquad \underline{Apr}(\underline{Apr}(B)) = \underline{Apr}(B),$$

$$(FU_7') \qquad \overline{Apr}(\overline{Apr}(B)) = \overline{Apr}(B).$$

Proof. It is similar to the proof of Theorem 3.

By the definition of $\underline{Apr}(X)$ and $\overline{Apr}(X)$, we notice that $\underline{Apr}(X)$ is the extent of the object oriented fuzzy concept derived from X, and $\overline{Apr}(X)$ is the extent of the attribute oriented fuzzy concept derived from X. Similarity, $\underline{Apr}(B)$ is the intent of the attribute oriented fuzzy concept derived from B, and $\overline{Apr}(B)$ is the intent of the object oriented fuzzy concept derived from B.

Example 2. In *Example 1*, let $X = (0.3, 0.6, 0.5)$ and $B = (0.5, 0.4, 0.7)$. By calculation we have that

$$\underline{Apr}(X) = X^{\square\lozenge} = (0.0, 0.4, 0.5), \quad \overline{Apr}(X) = X^{\lozenge\square} = (0.5, 0.6, 0.5);$$
$$\underline{Apr}(B) = B^{\square\lozenge} = (0.4, 0.0, 0.5), \quad \overline{Apr}(B) = B^{\lozenge\square} = (0.5, 0.5, 1.0).$$

Theorem 5. *Let (L, U, M, R) be a L-fuzzy formal context, $X \in L^U$, then*

(1) $\underline{Apr}(X) = X$ *iff X is the extent of an object oriented fuzzy concept;*

(2) $\overline{Apr}(X) = X$ *iff X is the extent of an attribute oriented fuzzy concept.*

Proof. Straightforward.

Theorem 6. *Let (L, U, M, R) be a L-fuzzy formal context, $B \in L^A$, then*
(1) $\underline{Apr}(B) = B$ iff A is the intent of an attribute oriented fuzzy concept;
(2) $\overline{Apr}(B) = B$ iff A is the intent of an object oriented fuzzy concept.

Proof. Straightforward.

5   Conclusions

In this paper we discussed two kinds of fuzzy concepts, ie. the object oriented fuzzy concept and the attribute oriented fuzzy concept, which are the generalization to the object oriented concept and the attribute oriented concept in the L-fuzzy formal contexts. The approximation of sets is an important issues in rough set theory. Based on the discussed two kinds of fuzzy concepts, we defined a pair of rough fuzzy set approximations in L-fuzzy formal contexts. The relationship between the proposed approximation operators and model logic is our future research.

Acknowledgments

This paper was supported by the National 973 Program of China (no.2002CB 312200).

References

1. Belohlavek, R.: Lattices of fixed points of fuzzy Galois connections. Math.Logic Quaterly 47 (2001) 111–116.
2. Belohlavek, R.: Fuzzy closure operators. I.J.Math.Anal.Appl 262 (2001), 473–489.
3. Belohlavek, R.: Concept lattice and order in fuzzy logic. Annals of pure and Apll.Logic, 128(1-3) (2004), 277–298.
4. Burusco, A., Fuentes-Gonzalez, R.: Construction of the L-Fuzzy concept lattice. Fuzzy Sets and systems, 97(1998),109–114.
5. Burusco, A., Fuentes-Gonzalez, R.: Concept lattices defined from implication operators. Fuzzy Sets and systems, 114(3)(1998),431–436.
6. Dubois, D., Prade, H.: Twofold fuzzy sets and rough sets-some issuess in knowledge representation. Fuzzy sets and Systems 23(1987) 3–18.
7. Gediga, G., Wille, R.: Formal Concept Analysis. Mathematic Foundations. Springer, Berlin (1999).
8. Gediga, G., Duntsch, I.: Modal-style operators in qualitative data analysis. Rroceedings of the 2002 IEEE International Conference on Data Mining (2002) 155–162.
9. Georgescu, G., Popescu, A.: Non-dual fuzzy connections. Archive for Mathematic Logic, 43(8) (2004) 1009–1039.
10. Hu, K., Sui, Y., Lu, Y., Wang, J., Shi, C.: Concept approximation in concept lattice. Knowledge Discovery and Data Mining, Proceedings of the 5th Pacific-Asia Conference, PAKDD 2001. Lecture Notes in Computer Science 2035 (2001) 167–173.

11. Kent, R. E.: Rough concept analysis: a synthesis of rough sets and formal concept analysis. Fundamenta Informaticae, 27 (1996) 169–181.
12. Morsi, N. N., Yakout, M. M.: Axiomatics for fuzzy rough sets. Fuzzy sets and Systems 100(1998) 327–342.
13. Pawlak, Z.: Rough sets. International Journal of Computer and Information Science 11(1982) 341–356.
14. Popescu, A.: A general approach to fuzzy concept. Math.Logic Quaterly 50(3)(2001) 1–17.
15. Radzikowska, A. M., Kerre, E. E.: A comparative study of fuzzy rough sets. Fuzzy sets and Systems 126(2002) 137–155.
16. Saquer, J., Deogun, J. S.: Formal rough concept analysis. Proceedings of the 7th International Workshop on New directions in Rough Sets, Data Mining, and Granular-Soft. Lecture Notes in Computer Science, Berlin: Springer, 1711 (1999) 91–99.
17. Shao, M. W., Zhang, W. X.: The Set Approximation in Formal Contexts. Lecture Notes in Computer science, Berlin: Springer, 3641 (2005) 43-53.
18. Shao, M. W., Zhang, W. X.: Rough set approximations in fuzzy concept lattices, Manuscript, 2005.
19. Wang, G. J.: Non-Classical Mathematical Logic and Approximate, Science Press, Beijing, 2000.
20. Wille, R.: Restructuring lattice theory: an approach based on hierarchies of concepts. In: *Ordered Sets*, Rival, I.(Ed.), Reidel, Dordrecht-Boston (1982) 445–470.
21. Wolff, K. E.: A conceptual view of knowledge bases in rough set theory. Rough Sets and Current Trends in Computing, Second International Conference, RSCTC 2000. Lecture Notes in Computer Science. Berlin: Springer, 2005 (2001) 220–228.
22. Wu, W. Z., Mi, J. S., Zhang, W. X.: Generalized fuzzy rough sets. Information Sciences 151(2003) 263–282.
23. Yao, Y. Y.: Concept lattices in rough set theory. In: Proceedings of 2004 Annual Meeting of the North American Fuzzy Information Processing Society, (2004) 796–801.
24. Yao, Y. Y.: A comparative study of formal concept analysis and rough set theory in Data analysis. Rough Sets and Current Trends in Computing, Proceedings of 3rd International Conference, RSCTC'04 (2004) 59–68.
25. Yao, Y. Y.: A comparative study of fuzzy sets and rough sets. Information Sciences 109(1998) 227–242.
26. Yao, Y. Y., Chen, Y.: Rough set approximations in formal concept analysis. In: Proceedings of 2004 Annual Meeting of the North American Fuzzy Information Processing Society, (2004) 73–78.

Webpage Classification with ACO-Enhanced Fuzzy-Rough Feature Selection

Richard Jensen and Qiang Shen

Department of Computer Science, The University of Wales, Aberystwyth
{rkj, qqs}@aber.ac.uk

Abstract. Due to the explosive growth of electronically stored information, automatic methods must be developed to aid users in maintaining and using this abundance of information effectively. In particular, the sheer volume of redundancy present must be dealt with, leaving only the information-rich data to be processed. This paper presents an approach, based on an integrated use of fuzzy-rough sets and Ant Colony Optimization (ACO), to greatly reduce this data redundancy. The work is applied to the problem of webpage categorization, considerably reducing dimensionality with minimal loss of information.

1   Introduction

The World Wide Web (WWW) is an information resource, whose full potential may not be realised unless its content is adequately organised and described. However, due to the immense size and dynamicity of the web, manual categorization is not a practical solution to this problem. There is a clear need for automated classification of web content.

Many classification problems involve high dimensional descriptions of input features. It is therefore not surprising that much research has been done on dimensionality reduction [4]. However, existing work tends to destroy the underlying semantics of the features after reduction (e.g. transformation-based approaches) or require additional information about the given data set for thresholding (e.g. entropy-based approaches). A technique that can reduce dimensionality using information contained within the data set and preserving the meaning of the features is clearly desirable. Rough set theory (RST) can be used as such a tool to discover data dependencies and reduce the number of features contained in a dataset by purely structural methods [9]. Given a dataset with discretized attribute values, it is possible to find a subset (termed a *reduct*) of the original attributes using RST that are the most informative; all other attributes can be removed from the dataset with minimal information loss.

Although this is useful, it is more often the case that data is *real-valued*, and this is where traditional rough set theory encounters a problem. In the theory, it is not possible to say whether two attribute values are similar and to what extent they are the same; for example, two close values may only differ as a result of noise, but in RST they are considered to be as different as two values of a different order of magnitude. It is, therefore, desirable to develop these techniques to provide the means

S. Greco et al. (Eds.): RSCTC 2006, LNAI 4259, pp. 147–156, 2006.

of data reduction for crisp and real-value attributed datasets which utilises the extent to which values are similar. This can be achieved through the use of *fuzzy-rough* sets. Fuzzy-rough sets encapsulate the related but distinct concepts of vagueness (for fuzzy sets [17]) and indiscernibility (for rough sets [9]), both of which occur as a result of imprecision, incompleteness and/or uncertainty in knowledge [5].

Ant Colony Optimization (ACO) techniques are based on the behaviour of real ant colonies used to solve discrete optimization problems [1]. These have been successfully applied to a large number of difficult combinatorial problems such as the quadratic assignment and the traveling salesman problems. This method is particularly attractive for feature selection as there seems to be no heuristic that can guide search to the optimal minimal subset (of features) every time. Additionally, it can be the case that ants discover the best feature combinations as they proceed throughout the search space. This paper investigates how ant colony optimization may be applied to the difficult problem of finding optimal feature subsets, using fuzzy-rough sets, for the classification of web content.

The rest of this paper is structured as follows. The second section describes the theory of fuzzy-rough set feature selection. Section 3 introduces the main concepts in ACO and details how this may be applied to the problem of feature selection in general, and fuzzy-rough feature selection in particular. The fourth section describes the system components and experimentation carried out for the purposes of web content classification. Section 5 concludes the paper, and proposes further work in this area.

2   Fuzzy-Rough Feature Selection

The reliance on discrete data for the successful operation of rough set-based feature selection methods such as [2,6,16] can be seen as a significant drawback of the approach. Indeed, this requirement implies an objectivity in the data that is simply not present. For example, in a medical dataset, values such as *Yes* or *No* cannot be considered objective for a *Headache* attribute as it may not be straightforward to decide whether a person has a headache or not to a high degree of accuracy. Again, consider an attribute *Blood Pressure*. In the real world, this is a real-valued measurement but for the purposes of rough set theory must be discretised into a small set of labels such as *Normal, High*, etc. Subjective judgments are required for establishing boundaries for objective measurements.

A better way of handling this problem is the use of fuzzy-rough sets [8]. Subjective judgments are not entirely removed as fuzzy set membership functions still need to be defined. However, the method offers a high degree of flexibility when dealing with real-valued data, enabling the vagueness and imprecision present to be modelled effectively. By employing fuzzy-rough sets, it is possible to use this information to better guide feature selection.

2.1   Fuzzy Equivalence Classes

In the same way that crisp equivalence classes are central to rough sets, *fuzzy* equivalence classes are central to the fuzzy-rough set approach [5]. For typical applications, this means that the decision values and the conditional values may all be fuzzy. The family of normal fuzzy sets produced by a fuzzy partitioning of the universe of discourse can play the role of fuzzy equivalence classes [5].

2.2 Fuzzy Lower and Upper Approximations

The fuzzy lower and upper approximations are fuzzy extensions of their crisp counterparts. Informally, in crisp rough set theory, the lower approximation of a set contains those objects that belong to it with certainty. The upper approximation of a set contains the objects that possibly belong. The definitions given in [5] diverge a little from the crisp upper and lower approximations, as the memberships of individual objects to the approximations are not explicitly available. As a result of this, the fuzzy lower and upper approximations are redefined as:

$$\mu_{\underline{P}X}(x) = \sup_{F \in \mathbb{U}/P} \ min(\mu_F(x), \inf_{y \in \mathbb{U}} max\{1 - \mu_F(y), \mu_X(y)\}) \tag{1}$$

$$\mu_{\overline{P}X}(x) = \sup_{F \in \mathbb{U}/P} \ min(\mu_F(x), \sup_{y \in \mathbb{U}} min\{\mu_F(y), \mu_X(y)\}) \tag{2}$$

The tuple $< \underline{P}X, \overline{P}X >$ is called a fuzzy-rough set.

For an individual feature, a, the partition of the universe by $\{a\}$ (denoted $\mathbb{U}/IND(\{a\})$) is considered to be the set of those fuzzy equivalence classes for that feature. For subsets of feature, the following is used:

$$\mathbb{U}/P = \otimes\{a \in P : \mathbb{U}/IND(\{a\})\} \tag{3}$$

Each set in $\mathbb{U}/P$ denotes an equivalence class. The extent to which an object belongs to such an equivalence class is therefore calculated by using the conjunction of constituent fuzzy equivalence classes, say F_i, $i = 1, 2, ..., n$:

$$\mu_{F_1 \cap ... \cap F_n}(x) - min(\mu_{F_1}(x), \mu_{F_2}(x), ..., \mu_{F_n}(x)) \tag{4}$$

2.3 Fuzzy-Rough Reduction Process

Fuzzy-Rough Feature Selection (FRFS) [7] builds on the notion of the fuzzy lower approximation to enable reduction of datasets containing real-valued features. The process becomes identical to the crisp approach when dealing with nominal well-defined features.

The crisp positive region in the standard RST is defined as the union of the lower approximations. By the extension principle, the membership of an object $x \in \mathbb{U}$, belonging to the fuzzy positive region can be defined by

$$\mu_{POS_P(Q)}(x) = \sup_{X \in \mathbb{U}/Q} \ \mu_{\underline{P}X}(x) \tag{5}$$

Using the definition of the fuzzy positive region, a new dependency function between a set of features Q and another set P can be defined as follows:

$$\gamma'_P(Q) = \frac{|\mu_{POS_P(Q)}(x)|}{|\mathbb{U}|} = \frac{\sum_{x \in \mathbb{U}} \mu_{POS_P(Q)}(x)}{|\mathbb{U}|} \tag{6}$$

As with crisp rough sets, the dependency of Q on P is the proportion of objects that are discernible out of the entire dataset. In the present approach, this corresponds to determining the fuzzy cardinality of $\mu_{POS_P(Q)}(x)$ divided by the total number of objects in the universe.

A new QUICKREDUCT algorithm, based on the crisp version [2], has been developed [7]. It employs the new dependency function γ' to choose which features to add to the current reduct candidate. The algorithm terminates when the addition of any remaining feature does not increase the dependency.

Conventional hill-climbing approaches to feature selection often fail to find maximal data reductions or minimal reducts. Some guiding heuristics are better than others for this, but as no perfect heuristic exists there can be no guarantee of optimality. When maximal data reductions are required, other search mechanisms must be employed. Although these methods also cannot ensure optimality, they provide a means by which the best feature subsets might be found. This motivates the development of feature selection based on ant colony optimization.

3 Ant Colony Optimization-Based Feature Selection

3.1 Swarm Intelligence

Swarm Intelligence (SI) is the property of a system whereby the collective behaviours of simple agents interacting locally with their environment cause coherent functional global patterns to emerge [1]. SI provides a basis with which it is possible to explore collective (or distributed) problem solving without centralized control or the provision of a global model. For example, ants are capable of finding the shortest route between a food source and their nest without the use of visual information and hence possess no global world model, adapting to changes in the environment. Those SI techniques based on the behaviour of ant colonies used to solve discrete optimization problems are classed as Ant Colony Optimization (ACO) techniques [1].

The ability of real ants to find shortest routes is mainly due to their depositing of pheromone as they travel; each ant probabilistically prefers to follow a direction rich in this chemical. The pheromone decays over time, resulting in much less pheromone on less popular paths. Given that over time the shortest route will have the higher rate of ant traversal, this path will be reinforced and the others diminished until all ants follow the same, shortest path (the "system" has converged to a single solution). It is also possible that there are many equally short paths.

ACO is particularly attractive for feature selection as there seems to be no heuristic that can guide search to the optimal minimal subset every time. Additionally, it can be the case that ants discover the best feature combinations as they proceed throughout the search space.

3.2 Feature Selection

The feature selection task may be reformulated into an ACO-suitable problem. ACO requires a problem to be represented as a graph - here nodes represent features, with the edges between them denoting the choice of the next feature. The search for the optimal feature subset is then an ant traversal through the graph where a minimum number of nodes are visited that satisfies the traversal stopping criterion.

A suitable heuristic desirability of traversing between features could be any subset evaluation function - for example, an entropy-based measure [10] or the fuzzy-rough set dependency measure. Depending on how optimality is defined for the particular application, the pheromone may be updated accordingly. For instance, subset minimality and "goodness" are two key factors so the pheromone update should be proportional to "goodness" and inversely proportional to size. How "goodness" is determined will also depend on the application. In some cases, this may be a heuristic evaluation of the subset, in others it may be based on the resulting classification accuracy of a classifier produced using the subset.

The heuristic desirability and pheromone factors are combined to form the so-called probabilistic transition rule, denoting the probability of an ant k at feature i choosing to move to feature j at time t:

$$p_{ij}^{k}(t) = \frac{[\tau_{ij}(t)]^{\alpha} \cdot [\eta_{ij}]^{\beta}}{\sum_{l \in J_i^k} [\tau_{il}(t)]^{\alpha} \cdot [\eta_{il}]^{\beta}} \tag{7}$$

where J_i^k is the set of ant k's unvisited features, η_{ij} is the heuristic desirability of choosing feature j when at feature i and $\tau_{ij}(t)$ is the amount of virtual pheromone on edge (i, j).

Two types of information are available to ants during their graph traversal, local and global, controlled by the parameters β and α respectively. Local information is obtained through a problem-specific heuristic measure. For the purposes of this paper, the fuzzy-rough dependency measure defined in equation (6) is used for this. The extent to which the measure influences an ant's decision to traverse an edge is controlled by the parameter β. This will guide ants towards paths that are likely to result in good solutions. Global knowledge is also available to ants through the deposition of artificial pheromone on the graph edges by their predecessors over time. The impact of this knowledge on an ant's traversal decision is determined by the parameter α. Good paths discovered by past ants will have a higher amount of associated pheromone. How much pheromone is deposited, and when, is dependent on the characteristics of the problem. No other local or global knowledge is available to the ants in the standard ACO model, though the inclusion of such information by extending the ACO framework has been investigated [1]. The choice of α and β is determined experimentally.

Selection Process. The ACO feature selection process begins with the generation of a number of ants, k, which are then placed randomly on the graph (i.e. each ant starts with one random feature). Alternatively, the number of ants to place on the graph may be set equal to the number of features within the data; each ant starts path construction at a different feature. From these initial positions, they traverse edges probabilistically until a traversal stopping criterion is satisfied. The resulting subsets are gathered and then evaluated. If an optimal subset has been found or the algorithm has executed a certain number of times, then the process halts and outputs the best feature subset encountered. If neither condition holds, then the pheromone is updated, a new set of ants are created and the process iterates once more.

Complexity Analysis. The time complexity of the ant-based approach to feature selection is $O(IAk)$, where I is the number of iterations, A the number of original features, and k the number of ants. In the worst case, each ant selects all the features. As the heuristic is evaluated after each feature is added to the reduct candidate, this will result in A evaluations per ant. After one iteration in this scenario, Ak evaluations will have been performed. After I iterations, the heuristic will be evaluated IAk times.

Pheromone Update. Depending on how optimality is defined for the particular application, the pheromone may be updated accordingly. To tailor this mechanism to find fuzzy-rough set reducts, it is necessary to use the fuzzy-rough dependency measure as the stopping criterion. This means that an ant will stop building its feature subset when the dependency of the subset reaches the maximum for the dataset. The pheromone on each edge is then updated according to the following formula:

$$\tau_{ij}(t+1) = (1-\rho).\tau_{ij}(t) + \Delta\tau_{ij}(t) \tag{8}$$

where

$$\Delta\tau_{ij}(t) = \sum_{k=1}^{n}(\gamma'(S^k)/|S^k|) \tag{9}$$

This is the case if the edge (i,j) has been traversed; $\Delta\tau_{ij}(t)$ is 0 otherwise. The value ρ is a decay constant used to simulate the evaporation of the pheromone, S^k is the feature subset found by ant k. The pheromone is updated according to both the fuzzy-rough measure of the "goodness" of the ant's feature subset (γ') and the size of the subset itself. By this definition, all ants update the pheromone. Alternative strategies may be used for this, such as allowing only the ants with the currently best feature subsets to proportionally increase the pheromone.

To show the utility of fuzzy-rough feature selection and to compare the hill-climbing and ant-based fuzzy-rough approaches, the two methods are applied as pre-processors within a webpage classification system. Both methods preserve the semantics of the surviving features after removing redundant ones. This is essential in satisfying the requirement of user readability of the generated knowledge model, as well as ensuring the understandability of the pattern classification process.

4   Web Classification

There are an estimated 1 billion webpages available on the WWW with around 1.5 million webpages being added every day. The task to find a particular webpage, which satisfies a user's requirements by traversing hyper-links, is very difficult. To aid this process, many web directories have been developed - some rely on manual categorization whilst others make decisions automatically. However, as webpage content is vast and dynamic, manual categorization is becoming increasingly impractical. Automatic web content categorization is therefore required to deal with these problems.

Information can be structured within a webpage that may indicate a relatively higher or lower importance of the contained text. For example, terms appearing within a <TITLE> tag would be expected to be more informative than the majority of those appearing within the document body at large. Because of this, keywords are weighted not only according to their statistical occurrence but also to their location within the document itself. These weights are almost always real-valued, which can be a problem for most feature selectors unless data discretization takes place (a source of information loss). This motivates the application of FRFS techniques to this domain.

Initial investigations have been carried out in this area [7], however these employed simplistic methods for classification - the vector space model and the boolean inexact model. The work presented here investigates the utility of more powerful approaches for this task, with the novel use of ACO-assisted feature selection.

4.1 System Overview

A key issue in the design of the system was that of modularity; it should be able to integrate with existing (or new) techniques. The current implementations allow this flexibility by dividing the overall process into several independent sub-modules:

- *Keyword Acquisition.* From the collected webpages, keywords/terms are extracted and weighted according to their perceived importance, resulting in a new dataset of weight-term pairs. These weights are almost always real-valued, hence the problem serves well to test the present work. For this, the TF-IDF metric [12] is used.
- *Keyword Selection.* As the newly generated datasets are too large, mainly due to keyword redundancy, a dimensionality reduction step is carried out using the techniques described previously.
- *Keyword Filtering.* Employed only in testing, this simple module filters the keywords obtained during acquisition, using the reduct generated in the keyword selection module.
- *Classification.* This final module uses the reduced dataset to perform the actual categorization of the test data. Four classifiers were used for comparison, namely C4.5 [10], JRip [3], PART [13] and a fuzzy rule inducer, QSBA [11]. Both JRip and PART are available from [14].

    C4.5 creates decision trees by choosing the most informative features and recursively partitioning the data into subtables based on their values. Each node in the tree represents a feature with branches from a node representing the alternative values this feature can take according to the current subtable. Partitioning stops when all data items in the subtable have the same classification. A leaf node is then created, and this classification assigned.

JRip learns propositional rules by repeatedly growing rules and pruning them. During the growth phase, antecedents are added greedily until a termination condition is satisfied. Antecedents are then pruned in the next phase subject to a pruning metric. Once the ruleset is generated, a further optimization is performed where rules are evaluated and deleted based on their performance on randomized data.

PART generates rules by means of repeatedly creating partial decision trees from data. The algorithm adopts a separate-and-conquer strategy in that it removes instances covered by the current ruleset during processing. Essentially, a rule is created by building a pruned tree for the current set of instances; the leaf with the highest coverage is made into a rule.

QSBA induces fuzzy rules by calculating the fuzzy subsethood of linguistic terms and the corresponding decision variables. These values are also weighted by the use of fuzzy quantifiers. This method utilises the same fuzzy sets as those involved in the fuzzy-rough reduction methods.

4.2 Experimentation and Results

Initially, datasets were generated from large textual corpora collected from Yahoo [15] and separated randomly into training and testing sets, maintaining class distributions. Each dataset is a collection of web documents. Five classification categories were used, namely Art & Humanity, Entertainment, Computers & Internet, Health, Business & Economy. A total of 280 web sites were collected from Yahoo categories and classified into these categories. From this collection of data, the keywords, weights and corresponding classifications were collated into a single dataset.

Table 1 shows the resulting degree of dimensionality reduction, performed via selecting informative keywords, by the standard fuzzy-rough method (FRFS) and the ACO-based approach (AntFRFS). AntFRFS is run several times, and the results averaged both for classification accuracy and number of features selected. It can be seen that both methods drastically reduce the number of original features. AntFRFS performs the highest degree of reduction, with an average of 14.1 features occurring in the reducts it locates.

Table 1. Extent of feature reduction

Original	FRFS	AntFRFS
2557	17	14.10

To see the effect of dimensionality reduction on classification accuracy, the system was tested on the original training data and a test dataset. The results are summarised in table 2. Clearly, the fuzzy-rough methods exhibit better resultant accuracies for the test data than the unreduced method for all classifiers. This demonstrates that feature selection using either FRFS or AntFRFS can greatly aid classification tasks. It is of additional benefit to rule inducers as the induction time is decreased and the generated rules involve significantly fewer features. AntFRFS improves on FRFS in terms of the size of subsets found and resulting testing accuracy for QSBA and PART, but not for C4.5 and JRip. The challenging nature of this particular task can be seen in the overall low accuracies produced by the classifiers (perhaps due to overfitting), though improved somewhat after feature selection. Both fuzzy-rough approaches require a reasonable fuzzification of the input data, whilst the fuzzy sets are herein generated by simple statistical analysis of the dataset with no attempt made at optimizing these sets. A fine-tuned fuzzification will certainly improve the performance of FRFS-based systems. Finally, it is worth noting that the classifications were checked automatically. Many webpages can be classified to more than one category, however only the designated category is considered to be correct here.

Table 2. Classification performance

Classifier	Original Train	Test	FRFS Train	Test	AntFRFS Train	Test
C4.5	95.89	44.74	86.30	57.89	81.27	48.39
QSBA	100.0	39.47	82.19	46.05	69.86	50.44
JRip	72.60	56.58	78.08	60.53	64.84	51.75
PART	95.89	42.11	86.30	48.68	82.65	48.83

5   Conclusion

This paper has presented an ACO-based method for feature selection, with particular emphasis on fuzzy-rough feature selection. This novel approach has been applied to aid classification of web content, with very promising results. In all experimental studies there has been no attempt to optimize the fuzzifications or the classifiers employed. It can be expected that the results obtained with such optimization would be even better than those already observed.

There are many issues to be explored in the area of ACO-based feature selection. The impact of parameter settings should be investigated - how the values of α, β and others influence the search process. Other important factors to be considered include how the pheromone is updated and how it decays. There is also the possibility of using different static heuristic measures to determine the desirability of edges. A further extension would be the use of dynamic heuristic measures which would change over the course of feature selection to provide more search information. Future work will inlcude experimental investigations comparing current rough set-based methods (such as [6,16]) with the proposed approach on benchmark data.

References

1. E. Bonabeau, M. Dorigo, and G. Theraulez. Swarm Intelligence: From Natural to Artificial Systems. Oxford University Press Inc., New York, NY, USA. 1999.
2. A. Chouchoulas and Q. Shen. Rough set-aided keyword reduction for text categorisation. Applied Artificial Intelligence, Vol. 15, No. 9, pp. 843–873. 2001.
3. W.W. Cohen. Fast effective rule induction. In Machine Learning: Proceedings of the 12th International Conference, pp. 115–123. 1995.
4. M. Dash and H. Liu. Feature Selection for Classification. Intelligent Data Analysis, Vol. 1, No. 3, pp. 131–156. 1997.
5. D. Dubois and H. Prade. Putting rough sets and fuzzy sets together. In R. Slowinski (Ed.), Intelligent Decision Support, Kluwer Academic Publishers, pp. 203–232. 1992.
6. J. Han, X. Hu, and T.Y. Lin. Feature Subset Selection Based on Relative Dependency between Attributes. Rough Sets and Current Trends in Computing: 4th International Conference (RSCTC 2004), pp. 176–185. 2004.
7. R. Jensen and Q. Shen. Fuzzy-rough attribute reduction with application to web categorization. Fuzzy Sets and Systems, Vol. 141, No. 3, pp. 469–485. 2004.
8. R. Jensen and Q. Shen. Semantics-Preserving Dimensionality Reduction: Rough and Fuzzy-Rough Based Approaches. IEEE Transactions on Knowledge and Data Engineering, Vol. 16, No. 12, pp. 1457–1471. 2004.
9. Z. Pawlak. Rough Sets: Theoretical Aspects of Reasoning About Data. Kluwer Academic Publishing, Dordrecht. 1991.
10. J.R. Quinlan. *C4.5: Programs for Machine Learning*. The Morgan Kaufmann Series in Machine Learning. Morgan Kaufmann Publishers, San Mateo, CA. 1993.
11. K. Rasmani and Q. Shen. Modifying weighted fuzzy subsethood-based rule models with fuzzy quantifiers. In Proceedings of the 13th International Conference on Fuzzy Systems, pp. 1687–1694. 2004.
12. G. Salton and C. Buckley. Term Weighting Approaches in Automatic Text Retrieval. Information Processing and Management, Vol. 24, No. 5, pp. 513–523. 1988.
13. I.H. Witten and E. Frank. Generating Accurate Rule Sets Without Global Optimization. In Machine Learning: Proceedings of the 15th International Conference, Morgan Kaufmann Publishers, San Francisco. 1998.
14. I.H. Witten and E. Frank. Data Mining: Practical machine learning tools with Java implementations. Morgan Kaufmann Publishers, San Francisco. 2000.
15. Yahoo. www.yahoo.com
16. J. Yao and M. Zhang. Feature Selection with Adjustable Criteria. Rough Sets, Fuzzy Sets, Data Mining, and Granular Computing, 10th International Conference (RSFDGrC 2005), pp.204–213. 2005.
17. L.A. Zadeh. Fuzzy sets. Information and Control, 8, pp. 338–353. 1965.

Association Reducts: Complexity and Heuristics

Dominik Ślęzak

Department of Computer Science, University of Regina
Regina, SK, S4S 0A2 Canada
Polish-Japanese Institute of Information Technology
Koszykowa 86, 02-008 Warsaw, Poland

Abstract. We investigate association reducts, which extend previously studied information and decision reducts in capability of expressing dependencies between groups of attributes in data. We formulate optimization problems related to the most informative associations between groups of attributes. We provide heuristic mechanisms for addressing those problems. We also discuss at more general level how to express approximate dependencies between groups of attributes.

Keywords: Attributes, Reducts, Associations, Approximations.

1   Introduction

Association rules [1] are useful in deriving and representing data-based knowledge. There are many algorithms extracting (in)exact association rules [3], also including methods based on the theory of rough sets [4]. In many applications, however, patterns expressed as combinations of descriptors are too specific and should be reconsidered more globally, at the level of average, approximate relationships between groups of attributes (cf. [2]). Among approaches to such global dependencies [3], there are rough set-based information and decision reducts – irreducible subsets of attributes providing information about other, optionally preset attributes [6,7]. We extend those notions toward *association reducts*, which represent (approximate) determinism between the pairs of subsets of attributes [11,12]. In this way, we formulate analogy for association rules at more global level of groups of attributes instead of specific combinations of their values.

An association reduct is a non-improvable pair (B_l, B_r) of subsets of attributes such that the values of attributes in B_r are determined by those in B_l. Non-improvability means that B_l cannot be reduced and B_r cannot be extended without losing determination of B_r by B_l. Association reducts correspond to families of association rules generated using the values of attributes B_l (B_r) at their left (right) sides. The processes of representation and extraction of most valuable association reducts are, however, conducted at the level of attributes, like in case of information and decision reducts [6,7,8]. In this paper, we adapt theoretical apparatus developed in [9,10] to study complexity, as well as the attribute reduction heuristics developed in [13,14] to deal with that complexity in case of association reducts. It complements [11,12] with regards to solid foundations for multi-attribute dependencies modeled by association reducts.

S. Greco et al. (Eds.): RSCTC 2006, LNAI 4259, pp. 157–164, 2006.

2   Reducts in Information Systems

The theory of rough sets [6] handles data as information systems $\mathbb{A} = (U, A)$, where U consists of objects and A consists of attributes. Every $a \in A$ corresponds to the function $a : U \to V_a$ where V_a is a's value set. For illustration, the following $\mathbb{A} = (U, A)$ has 6 binary attributes and 7 objects (cf. [12]):

$\mathbb{A}$	a	b	c	d	e	f
u_1	1	1	1	1	1	1
u_2	0	0	0	1	1	1
u_3	1	0	1	1	0	1
u_4	0	1	0	0	0	0
u_5	1	0	0	0	0	1
u_6	1	1	1	1	1	0
u_7	0	1	1	0	1	0

Definition 1. *[6] Let information system $\mathbb{A} = (U, A)$ be given. For every subset $B \subseteq A$, we define the binary B-indiscernibility relation*

$$IND(B) = \{(x, y) \in U \times U : \forall_{a \in B}\ a(x) = a(y)\} \tag{1}$$

For every $B, C \subseteq A$, we say that B determines C in $\mathbb{A}$, denoted by $B \Rightarrow C$, iff

$$IND(B) = IND(B \cup C) \tag{2}$$

Condition (2) corresponds to a concept of functional dependency widely applied in databases. In rough set methodology, it is used for an important construction related to attribute selection/reduction, as one of the steps of KDD [3].

Definition 2. *[6] Let $\mathbb{A} = (U, A)$ be given. For every $B \subseteq A$, we say that B is an information reduct in $\mathbb{A}$, if and only if $IND(B) = IND(A)$ (that is $B \Rightarrow A$) and there is no proper $B' \subsetneq B$, for which analogous condition holds.*

Example 1. For $\mathbb{A} = (U, A)$ illustrated above, we have the following information reducts: (we omit brackets for simplicity) $abcf$, $acef$, $adef$, $bcdf$, $bdef$, $cdef$.

A question is whether such reducts represent complete knowledge about dependencies. Consider $adef \Rightarrow bc$. Note that (2) is also satisfied for $ade \Rightarrow bc$ and $aef \Rightarrow b$. The first of them seems to be stronger than $adef \Rightarrow bc$ because less attributes determine the same at the right side. Further, $aef \Rightarrow b$ is not weaker or stronger than $adef \Rightarrow bc$ – it provides complementary information. Consequently, we need a more specific tool to deal with attribute dependencies.

Definition 3. *[11] Let $\mathbb{A} = (U, A)$ be given. For every $B_l, B_r \subseteq A$, $B_l \cap B_r = \emptyset$, we say that the pair (B_l, B_r) forms an association reduct, iff we have $B_l \Rightarrow B_r$ and there is neither proper $B'_l \subsetneq B_l$ nor proper $B'_r \supsetneq B_r$, $B_l \cap B'_r = \emptyset$, for which $B'_l \Rightarrow B_r$ or $B_l \Rightarrow B'_r$ would hold.*

Example 2. For $\mathbb{A} = (U, A)$ illustrated above, we have the following association reducts: (abc, de), (ace, bd), (acf, d), (ade, bc), (aef, b), (bcd, ae), (bde, ac), $(cdef, ab)$, (cdf, a), (cef, b), $(\emptyset, \emptyset)$. The pair $(\emptyset, \emptyset)$ means that $\mathbb{A}$ has no constant attributes $a \in A$, i.e. such that $IND(\{a\}) = IND(\emptyset) = U \times U$ (cf. [12]).

3   Approximate Dependencies

Criterion (2) can be approximated to better adjust methodology to real world data, where exact functional dependencies occur very rarely because of noise and uncertainty. We can imagine a family of approximation thresholds $\theta \in \Theta$, which correspond to inexact, parameterized θ-dependencies of the form

$$B \Rrightarrow_\theta C \qquad B, C \subseteq A,\ \theta \in \Theta \tag{3}$$

For every $\theta \in \Theta$, it should be assumed that θ-dependencies satisfy some reasonable laws, like the following monotonicity properties:

$$\begin{aligned}
\text{IF} \quad X \Rrightarrow_\theta Y \cup Z \quad \text{THEN} \quad X \Rrightarrow_\theta Y \\
\text{IF} \quad X \Rrightarrow_\theta Y \quad \text{THEN} \quad X \cup Z \Rrightarrow_\theta Y
\end{aligned} \tag{4}$$

In particular, properties (4) imply that $X \Rrightarrow_\theta \emptyset$, as well as IF $X \Rrightarrow_\theta Y \cup Z$ THEN $X \cup Z \Rrightarrow_\theta Y$, which is an analogy to the association rules.[1] It may also happen that for some $X \subseteq A$ there is $\emptyset \Rrightarrow_\theta X$. This means that attributes in X are θ-approximately constant over U. (Compare with Example 2.)

In applications, a choice of approximation threshold can be crucial. It is helpful to consider an ordering $\preceq$ over Θ, with the following property:

$$\text{IF} \quad \theta \preceq \vartheta \quad \text{THEN} \quad X \Rrightarrow_\theta Y \Rightarrow X \Rrightarrow_\vartheta Y \tag{5}$$

It is also good to have $\mathbf{O} \in \Theta$, which corresponds to exact dependency (2):[2]

$$\mathbf{O} \preceq \theta \quad \text{AND} \quad X \Rrightarrow_{\mathbf{O}} Y \Leftrightarrow X \Rrightarrow Y \tag{6}$$

Example 3. Consider $\Theta = \{0, 1, 2, \dots\}$, $\mathbf{O} = 0$. Consider the following definition:

$$X \Rrightarrow_\theta Y \ \Leftrightarrow\ |IND(X)| - |IND(X \cup Y)| \leq \theta \tag{7}$$

where $|IND(X)|$ denotes the number of X-indiscernible pairs of objects. Surely, properties (4-6) are satisfied. Analogous condition was used e.g. in [4].

Example 4. Consider $\Theta = [0, +\infty)$, $\mathbf{O} = 0$. Consider the following definition:

$$X \Rrightarrow_\theta Y \ \Leftrightarrow\ H(X \cup Y) - H(X) \leq \theta \tag{8}$$

where $H(X)$ denotes the information entropy of X in $\mathbb{A}$. This condition was used in the original formulation of an association reduct in [11], given that $H(X \cup Y) - H(X)$ is inversely proportional to the geometric average of confidences of association rules with the values of X (Y) at their left (right) sides. Properties (4-6) are satisfied here as well. Statement $\emptyset \Rrightarrow_\theta X \cup Y$ means that $H(X \cup Y) \leq \theta$, which reflects the average of supports of above-mentioned association rules. The same type of θ-dependency was previously used to define approximate information and decision reducts based on entropy [10].

---

[1] Note that the first property in (4) is not true for association rules for non-trivial confidence thresholds. It is reasonable to use it only at the level of global attribute dependencies, and only if the approximation criteria are appropriately defined.

[2] One can claim that equivalence $X \Rrightarrow_{\mathbf{O}} Y \Leftrightarrow X \Rrightarrow Y$ makes sense only for nominal attributes. However, preserving maximum (in)discernibility of values while formulating exact functional dependencies can be extended onto other data types too.

4   Complexity of Reduction

The problems of optimal attribute reduction were studied extensively in the rough set literature (cf. [6,7,8,9,14]). Here, we focus on approximate types:

Definition 4. *Let Θ and $\mathbb{A} = (U, A)$ be given. For every $\theta \in \Theta$ and $B \subseteq A$, we say that B is a θ-information reduct in $\mathbb{A}$, iff $B \Rightarrow_\theta A$ and there is no proper subset $B' \subsetneq B$, for which $B' \Rightarrow_\theta A$ would hold. For every $\theta \in \Theta$ and $B_l, B_r \subseteq A$, $B_l \cap B_r = \emptyset$, we say that (B_l, B_r) is a θ-association reduct in $\mathbb{A}$, iff $B_l \Rightarrow_\theta B_r$, there is no proper subset $B'_l \subsetneq B_l$ for which $B'_l \Rightarrow_\theta B_r$ would hold, and there is no proper superset $B'_r \supsetneq B_r$, $B_l \cap B'_r = \emptyset$, for which $B_l \Rightarrow_\theta B'_r$ would hold.*

Similarly, one can consider various θ-decision reducts (cf. [10,13,15]). Now, the task is to extract from data optimal, most-informative reducts of various types.

Definition 5. *Minimal Θ-Information Reduct Problem (MΘIRP). INPUT: $\theta \in \Theta$ and $\mathbb{A} = (U, A)$. OUTPUT: θ-information reduct of the least cardinality in $\mathbb{A}$.*

Theorem 1. *Let Θ satisfy (6). Then MΘIRP is NP-hard.*[3]

Proof. The search for minimal information reducts was proved to be NP-hard in [9]. Information reducts are identical with **O**-information reducts. So the problem reported in [9] can be polynomially reduced to MΘIRP using $\theta = \mathbf{O}$.

In [12], we discussed representation of all association reducts, extending Boolean characteristics [9]. Indeed, only a full set of association reducts gives complete knowledge about attribute dependencies, derivable using (4). On the other hand, if we need to focus only on reducts providing maximum information, we should reconsider MΘIRP. Namely, we should notice that the smaller B_l and larger B_r we can find, the larger amount of information encoded by (B_l, B_r) is.

Definition 6. *Consider arbitrary function $F : \mathbb{N} \times \mathbb{N} \to \mathbb{R}$ such that*

$$n_1 < n_2 \Rightarrow F(n_1, m) > F(n_2, m) \quad AND \quad m_1 < m_2 \Rightarrow F(n, m_1) < F(n, m_2) \tag{9}$$

F-Optimal Θ-Association Reduct Problem (FΘARP). INPUT: $\theta \in \Theta$ and $\mathbb{A} = (U, A)$. OUTPUT: θ-association reduct (B_l, B_r) maximizing $F(|B_l|, |B_r|)$ in $\mathbb{A}$, different from $(\emptyset, \emptyset)$ if there are any other association reducts in $\mathbb{A}$.

The choice of F, e.g. $F(n, m) = m - n$ or $F(n, m) = m/(n+1)$, surely influences the search results. This is a case also in other areas, e.g. in pattern optimization [5] or multi-criteria decision reduct optimization (see Footnote 3). Similarly to [5], we analyze complexity of $F\Theta$ARP at universal level, for arbitrary F.

Theorem 2. *Let Θ satisfy (6). Let F satisfy (9). Then FΘARP is NP-hard.*

Proof. See the next section. Refer also to Footnote 2.

---

[3] NP-hardness becomes more complicated to prove when θ is not a part of input but, instead, parameterizes the problem's definition [10]. On the other hand, having θ as input better shows the need of adaptive tuning of θ. One can go even further and involve a degree of determinism of the whole A by $B \subseteq A$ into optimization criteria, together with cardinality or any other quality function of B [15].

5   Proof of Theorem 2

We proceed analogously to [9]. We reduce the Minimal Dominating Set Problem (MDSP) to $F\Theta$ARP. MDSP, widely known as NP-hard, is defined by INPUT as undirected graph $\mathcal{G} = (A, E)$, and OUTPUT as the smallest $B \subseteq A$ such that $Cov_\mathcal{G}(B) = A$, where $Cov_\mathcal{G}(B) = B \cup \{a \in A : \exists_{b \in B}(a, b) \in E\}$. To reduce MDSP to $F\Theta$ARP, we construct information system $\mathbb{A}_\mathcal{G} = (U_\mathcal{G}, A_\mathcal{G})$, $U_\mathcal{G} = \{u_1, \dots, u_n, o_1, \dots, o_n, u_*\}$, $A_\mathcal{G} = \{a_1, \dots, a_n, a_*\}$, $n = |A|$, as follows:

$$\begin{aligned}
&a_i(u_j) = 1 \Leftrightarrow i = j \vee (i, j) \in E & &a_i(u_j) = 0 \text{ otherwise} \\
&a_i(o_j) = 1 \Leftrightarrow i = j & &a_i(o_j) = 2 \text{ otherwise} & &(10) \\
&a_i(u_*) = 0, \qquad a_*(u_j) = 0 & &a_*(o_j) = 0, \qquad a_*(u_*) = 1
\end{aligned}$$

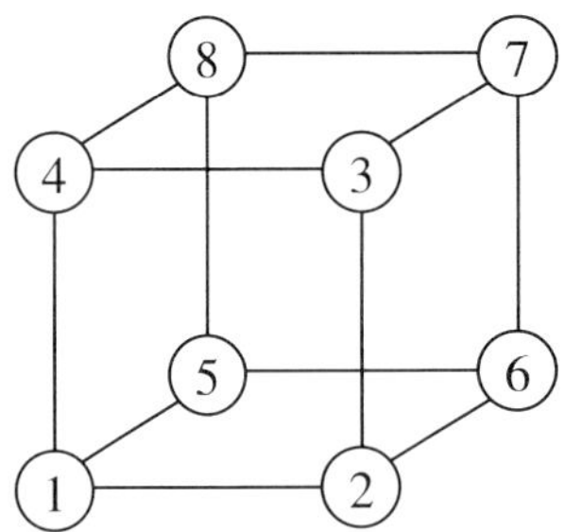

Fig. 1. $\mathcal{G} = (A, E)$ with 8 nodes and $\mathbb{A}_\mathcal{G} = (U_\mathcal{G}, A_\mathcal{G})$ constructed using (10)

$U_\mathcal{G}$	a_1	a_2	a_3	a_4	a_5	a_6	a_7	a_8	a_*
u_1	1	1	0	1	1	0	0	0	0
u_2	1	1	1	0	0	1	0	0	0
u_3	0	1	1	1	0	0	1	0	0
u_4	1	0	1	1	0	0	0	1	0
u_5	1	0	0	0	1	1	0	1	0
u_6	0	1	0	0	1	1	1	0	0
u_7	0	0	1	0	0	1	1	1	0
u_8	0	0	0	1	1	0	1	1	0
o_1	1	2	2	2	2	2	2	2	0
$\vdots$									$\vdots$
o_8	2	2	2	2	2	2	2	1	0
u_*	0	0	0	0	0	0	0	0	1

Lemma 1. *For any $B \subseteq \{a_1, \dots, a_n\}$, $B \Rightarrow \{a_*\}$ holds in $\mathbb{A}_\mathcal{G}$ iff $Cov_\mathcal{G}(B) = A$.*

Proof. Analogous to [9]. See also [10].

Lemma 2. *For any $X, Y \subseteq A_\mathcal{G}$, $X \cap Y = \emptyset$, (X, Y) is an association reduct in $\mathbb{A}_\mathcal{G}$ iff $X = Y = \emptyset$ or $Y = \{a_*\}$ and X is an irreducible dominating set in $\mathcal{G}$, i.e. $Cov_\mathcal{G}(X) = A$ and $Cov_\mathcal{G}(X') \neq A$ for every $X' \subsetneq X$.[4]*

Proof. Values over $o_1, \dots, o_n$ imply that for any $X \subseteq A_\mathcal{G}$ and $Y \subseteq \{a_1, \dots, a_n\}$, $X \cap Y = \emptyset$, there is no $IND(X) = IND(X \cup Y)$, unless $Y = \emptyset$. Hence, the only way to get association reduct $(X, Y) \neq (\emptyset, \emptyset)$ is to put $Y = \{a_*\}$. Then, due to Lemma 1, X needs to satisfy $Cov_\mathcal{G}(X) = A$. Finally, since $(X, \{a_*\})$ is expected to be an association reduct, X must be irreducible.

Now, to complete the proof of Theorem 2, the following observations are enough:

1. Each F satisfying (9), after disregarding $(\emptyset, \emptyset)$, reaches its maximum for the smallest dominating sets. This is because the lower n, the higher $F(n, 1)$.
2. As in Theorem 1, we can consider $\theta = \mathbf{O}$ as input $F\Theta$ARP. Then the solution (B_l, B_r) of $F\Theta$ARP for $\mathbb{A}_\mathcal{G}$ yields B_l as the solution of MDSP for $\mathcal{G}$.

---

[4] Note that for every graph there is always at least one non-empty dominating set.

6   Algorithm for Information Reducts

There are numerous approaches to searching for information and decision reducts (cf. [7,8]). In [13], a simple strategy for entropy-based approximate reducts was suggested. It works on permutations of the sets of attributes, generated randomly or conducted by the order-based genetic algorithms (o-GA) (cf. [14]). Every permutation (individual in o-GA) τ is used as input to a fast procedure resulting with a reduct B_τ. The quality of B_τ (e.g. inversely proportional to $|B_\tau|$) is used to evaluate τ. It is commonly expected (see also Section 8) that valuable reducts are obtained for more permutations. Here, we adapt that method to searching for θ-information reducts, without any special requirements for $\mathbb{A}$ or Θ, just assuming that validity of statements of the form $X \Rightarrow_\theta Y$ can be verified against $\mathbb{A}$ in polynomial time with respect to their size.

Algorithm 1. θ-information reduct calculation (cf. [13,14])

Input: $\mathbb{A} = (U, A)$, $\tau : \{1, ..., n\} \to \{1, ..., n\}$, $n = |A|$
Output: Attribute subset $B_\tau \subseteq A$

   $B_\tau = A$
   for $i = 0$ to $n - 1$ **do**
     if $B_\tau \setminus \{a_{\tau(n-i)}\} \Rightarrow_\theta A$ **then**
       $B_\tau = B_\tau \setminus \{a_{\tau(n-i)}\}$
     end if
   end for
   return B_τ

Proposition 1. *(cf. [13]) Let $\mathbb{A} = (U, A)$ and $\theta \in \Theta$ satisfying (4) be given. For every τ, the result $B_\tau \subseteq A$ of Algorithm 1, is a θ-information reduct. On the other hand, for every θ-information reduct $B \subseteq A$, there exists permutation τ such that the result of Algorithm 1 for τ equals to B.*

Proof. Let τ be given. $B_\tau \Rightarrow_\theta A$ is obvious. Assume that there is $B \subsetneq B_\tau$ such that $B \Rightarrow_\theta A$. We will show that it contradicts the fact that B_τ is the output for τ. Choose the lowest j such that $a_{\tau(n-j)} \in B_\tau \setminus B$. Denote by $B_\tau^j \subseteq A$ the intermediate form of B_τ right before the j-th iteration of Algorithm 1. We have surely $a_{\tau(n-j)} \in B_\tau^j$. We can also assume $B_\tau^j \supseteq B_\tau$. Otherwise, if any element of B_τ has been already removed before, it would immediately negate B_τ as the output for τ. Since $a_{\tau(n-j)} \in B_\tau \setminus B$, there is also $B_\tau^j \setminus a_{\tau(n-j)} \supseteq B$. Given $B \Rightarrow_\theta A$, we get also $B_\tau^j \setminus \{a_{\tau(n-j)}\} \Rightarrow_\theta A$. Consequently, $a_{\tau(n-j)}$ will be removed during the j-th iteration and B_τ will not be the output.

Now, consider θ-information reduct $B \subseteq A$. Put $m = |B|$. Consider τ such that for every $i \leq m$ there is $a_{\tau(i)} \in B$.[5] Then, during first $n - m$ iterations, Algorithm 1 keeps removing attributes because intermediate forms of B_τ still contain B, so $B_\tau \Rightarrow_\theta A$. After the $n-m$'th iteration we get B. We cannot remove any more attributes, for B is a θ-information reduct. Hence, B is the output.

---

[5] B may be empty. This is the case if $\emptyset \Rightarrow_\theta A$, which was discussed below equations (4). Then $B = \emptyset$ is the only θ-information reduct and Proposition 1 is true anyway.

7   Algorithm for Association Reducts

The following procedure enables to use permutations to search for association reducts, analogously to the previously known algorithms [13,14,15]. The main difference here is that each τ yields a pair of attribute subsets $(B_{\tau,l}, B_{\tau,r})$, which can be evaluated by $F(|B_{\tau,l}|, |B_{\tau,r}|)$ while approximating solutions of $F\Theta$ARP.

Algorithm 2. θ-association reduct calculation

Input: $\mathbb{A} = (U, A)$, $\tau : \{1, ..., n\} \to \{1, ..., n\}$, $n = |A|$
Output: The pair of subsets $(B_{\tau,l}, B_{\tau,r}) \subseteq A \times A$, $B_{\tau,l} \cap B_{\tau,r} = \emptyset$

  $B_{\tau,l} = A$, $B_{\tau,r} = \emptyset$
  for $i = 0$ to n **do**
    if $B_{\tau,l} \setminus \{a_{\tau(n-i)}\} \Rrightarrow_\theta B_{\tau,r}$ **then**
      $B_{\tau,l} = B_{\tau,l} \setminus \{a_{\tau(n-i)}\}$
      if $B_{\tau,l} \Rrightarrow_\theta B_{\tau,r} \cup \{a_{\tau(n-i)}\}$ **then**
        $B_{\tau,r} = B_{\tau,r} \cup \{a_{\tau(n-i)}\}$
      end if
    end if
  end for
  return $(B_{\tau,l}, B_{\tau,r})$

Proposition 2. *Let $\mathbb{A} = (U, A)$ and $\theta \in \Theta$ satisfying (4) be given. For every τ, the result $(B_{\tau,l}, B_{\tau,r}) \subseteq A \times A$ of Algorithm 2, is a θ-association reduct. On the other hand, for every θ-association reduct $(B_l, B_r) \subseteq A \times A$, there exists permutation τ such that the result of Algorithm 2 for τ equals to (B_l, B_r).*

Proof. Let τ be given. $B_{\tau,l} \Rrightarrow_\theta B_{\tau,r}$ is obvious. The proof that $B_{\tau,l}$ cannot be reduced is analogous to the corresponding part of Proposition 1, so we omit it.

Given no $B_l \subsetneq B_{\tau,l}$ such that $B_l \Rrightarrow_\theta B_{\tau,r}$, assume that there is $B_r \supsetneq B_{\tau,r}$ such that $B_{\tau,l} \Rrightarrow_\theta B_r$, $B_{\tau,l} \cap B_r = \emptyset$. We show that it contradicts the fact that $(B_{\tau,l}, B_{\tau,r})$ is the output for τ. Take lowest j such that $a_{\tau(n-j)} \in B_r \setminus B_{\tau,r}$. Note that $a_{\tau(n-j)} \notin B_{\tau,l}$. Denote by $(B_{\tau,l}^j, B_{\tau,r}^j)$ intermediate form of $(B_{\tau,l}, B_{\tau,r})$ right before j-th iteration. We have $a_{\tau(n-j)} \notin B_{\tau,r}^j$ and $B_{\tau,r}^j \subseteq B_{\tau,r}$. Otherwise, if any element not in $B_{\tau,r}$ has been already added to the right side, it would immediately negate $(B_{\tau,l}, B_{\tau,r})$ as the output. Since $a_{\tau(n-j)} \in B_r$, there is $B_{\tau,r}^j \cup \{a_{\tau(n-j)}\} \subseteq B_r$. Given $B_{\tau,l} \Rrightarrow_\theta B_r$, we get $B_{\tau,l} \Rrightarrow_\theta B_{\tau,r}^j \cup a_{\tau(n-j)}$. So, $a_{\tau(n-j)}$ will be added to $B_{\tau,r}$ and $(B_{\tau,l}, B_{\tau,r})$ will not be the output.

Now, consider θ-association reduct (B_l, B_r), $B_l \cap B_r = \emptyset$. Put $m_l = |B_l|$, $m_r = |B_r|$, $m_l + m_r \leq n$. Consider τ such that for each $i \leq m_l$ there is $a_{\tau(i)} \in B_l$ and for each $i > n - m_r$ there is $a_{\tau(i)} \in B_r$.[6] In first m_r iterations, attributes move from $B_{\tau,l} \supseteq B_l$ to $B_{\tau,r} \subseteq B_r$, which results in $A \setminus B_r \Rrightarrow_\theta B_r$. During next $n - m_l - m_r$ iterations, attributes are not moved to $B_{\tau,r}$ because B_r is assumed non-extendible. However, they will be removed from $B_{\tau,l} \supseteq B_l$, so after $n - m_l$ steps all together, we get $B_l \Rrightarrow_\theta B_r$. The remaining m_l steps do not change anything because B_l is assumed irreducible. Hence, (B_l, B_r) is the output.

---

[6] As previously, we may have some special cases, like $B_l = \emptyset$ or even $B_l = B_r = \emptyset$.

8 Conclusions

We discussed the problems of searching for optimal approximate association reducts. We continued our work on comparison of association reducts and rules [11], as well as association, decision, and information reducts [12]. Given the current need of analyzing data with huge amounts of attributes, association reducts seem to be well-suited. Still, the proposed heuristics should be implemented and integrated with, e.g., the o-GA framework [14], for experimental verification.

Among challenges, there is analysis of relationships between quality of reducts and amounts of permutations leading to them. In the area of applications, a promising direction is unsupervised analysis of, e.g., gene expression data, in combination with entropy-based methods for grouping numeric attributes [2].

Acknowledgements. Research reported in this paper was supported by the research grant from Natural Sciences and Engineering Research Council of Canada.

References

1. Agrawal, R., Mannila, H., Srikant, R., Toivonen, H., Verkamo, A.I.: Fast discovery of assocation rules. In: Advances in Knowledge Discovery and Data Mining. AAAI/MIT Press (1996) 307–328.
2. Grużdź, A., Ihnatowicz, A., Ślęzak, D.: Interactive gene clustering – a case study of breast cancer microarray data. Information Systems Frontiers 8 (2006) 21–27.
3. Kloesgen, W., Żytkow, J.M. (eds): Handbook of Data Mining and Knowledge Discovery. Oxford University Press (2002).
4. Nguyen, H.S., Nguyen, S.H.: Rough Sets and Association Rule Generation. Fundamenta Informaticae 40/4 (1999) 310–318.
5. Nguyen, S.H., Nguyen, H.S.: Pattern extraction from data. Fundamenta Informaticae 34/1-2 (1998) 129–144.
6. Pawlak, Z.: Rough sets – Theoretical aspects of reasoning about data. Kluwer Academic Publishers (1991).
7. Polkowski, L.: Rough Sets: Mathematical Foundations. Physica Verlag (2002).
8. Polkowski, L., Tsumoto, S., Lin, T.Y. (eds): Rough Set Methods and Applications. Physica Verlag (2000).
9. Skowron, A., Rauszer, C.: The discernibility matrices and functions in information systems. In: Intelligent Decision Support. Handbook of Applications and Advances of the Rough Set Theory. Kluwer Academic Publishers (1992) 311–362.
10. Ślęzak, D.: Approximate Entropy Reducts. Fundamenta Informaticae 53/3-4 (2002) 365–390.
11. Ślęzak, D.: Association Reducts: A Framework for Mining Multi-attribute Dependencies. In: Proc. of ISMIS'2005, Springer (2005) 354–363.
12. Ślęzak, D.: Association Reducts: Boolean Representation. In: Proc. of RSKT'2006, Springer (2006) to appear.
13. Ślęzak, D., Wróblewski, J.: Order-based genetic algorithms for the search of approximate entropy reducts. In: Proc. of RSFDGrC'2003, Springer (2003) 308–311.
14. Wróblewski, J.: Theoretical Foundations of Order-Based Genetic Algorithms. Fundamenta Informaticae 28/3-4 (1996) 423–430.
15. Wróblewski, J.: Ensembles of classifiers based on approximate reducts. Fundamenta Informaticae 47/3-4 (2001) 351–360.

Planning Based on Reasoning About Information Changes

Andrzej Skowron[1] and Piotr Synak[2]

[1] Institute of Mathematics, Warsaw University
Banacha 2, 02-097 Warsaw, Poland
[2] Polish-Japanese Institute of Information Technology
Koszykowa 86, 02-008 Warsaw, Poland

Abstract. We consider the problem of reasoning about information changes in the context of complex concepts approximated hierarchically and actions that can be triggered to change properties of investigated objects. A given object can be in an unwanted state, where some concept is not satisfied to the required degree. We would like to find a plan (sequence of actions to be executed) of object's transformation to a new state which is acceptable. Presented approach is based on reasoning about changes.

Keywords: rough sets, approximate reasoning schemes, hierarchical reasoning, concept approximation, reasoning about changes.

1 Introduction

We consider the problem of reasoning about information changes in the context of complex concepts approximated hierarchically and actions that can be triggered to change properties of investigated objects. The problem of complex concepts approximation has been already intensively studied in the literature [19,1,14,15,16,2,20,4,10,11,3]. Hierarchical reasoning seems to be crucial especially in the case when there is a big gap between description of objects and the concept. For example, it is very difficult to directly reason about the concept "safe situation on the road" just from the low-level sensor measurements. Thus, some methods of hierarchical reasoning using the domain knowledge, e.g., in the form of ontology of concepts, must be adapted to obtain satisfactory approximation of complex concepts (see, e.g., [1,19]). In addition, we consider the case when some set of actions is additionally available. An action can be triggered for a given object to change its properties. We assume to use actions if we detect that the investigated object satisfies a given concept to unsatisfactory degree or it satisfies some unwanted concept. As an example, let us consider an action as some medicine that can be applied to a patient having some disease. We want to apply such medicines that the concept of having disease is not satisfied any longer. Execution of some action corresponds to an application of some transition relation. A sequence of actions defines some kind of a plan.

Let us present some examples of the key problems. We can consider the problem of rules induction. Let x be an investigated object satisfying concept C_1

S. Greco et al. (Eds.): RSCTC 2006, LNAI 4259, pp. 165–173, 2006.

and R be a transition relation that moves/changes x from C_1 to, say, C_2. From the approximation of concept C_1, e.g, by means of AR schemes [13,7,18], and approximation of relation R we obtain approximation of C_1R. On the other hand, from C_1R we can extract approximation of C_2. Let us note, that from approximations of C_1 and R we obtain approximate rules for C_1, $\neg C_1$ and R, $\neg R$, respectively. Thus, finally we also get rules for C_2 and $\neg C_2$.

Next problem is related to the induction of rules of changes. Let x satisfy a given concept C to a degree at least δ. If we apply to x some transition relation R we obtain x' satisfying C to a degree at least $\delta + \Delta\delta$. A basic question is how can we induce rules predicting changes of inclusion degree. We can generalise this problem to the case when we consider not only one particular concept but k-class classification, i.e, $\{C_1, \ldots, C_k\}$, where for a given object we obtain a vector of inclusion degrees $(\delta_1, \ldots, \delta_k)$. Then, how can we induce decision rules describing changes of a vector of inclusion degrees?

2   Hierarchical Reasoning on Complex Concepts

2.1   From Structured Objects to Complex Concepts

One of the fundamental concepts in reasoning is the notion of an object. Objects are some real entities that can be described by some physical observations or measurements. An object can be though identified with some information about it, i.e., with some vector of measurements. From this interpretation it follows that one vector of measurements can describe several objects. From the point of view of this information only, such objects are indiscernible although in fact they can be different. This way of understanding objects is used in the rough set theory [5,6,12], where for a given information system $\mathbb{A} = (U, A)$, the information about an object $x \in U$ is given by means of some attributes from A, i.e., an object x can be identified with the so-called signature of x: $Inf(x) = \{a(x) : a \in A\}$.

In a more complex case, we can consider some structure of an object. Structured or complex objects can consist of some parts which can be constrained by some relations of different nature, e.g., spatial ones. The parts can be built from yet simpler parts and therefore the structure can be hierarchical with many different levels. The relation object–part corresponds in most cases to some spatial or spatio-temporal relation [10]. These problems are considered in rough-mereological approach [8,9] representing some patterns relevant for concept approximation.

For each part of a structured object we can consider some concepts describing its properties. Thus, concepts form also a hierarchical structure and for one structured object we can have several ontologies of concepts [17]. The concepts from the lowest level of such hierarchy describe properties of simple parts. The high-level or complex concepts describe properties of complex objects.

2.2   Structured Reasoning Schemes

Properties of structured (complex) objects can be approximated by means of approximate reasoning schemes (AR schemes) [13,7,18]. Such schemes usually have a tree structure with the root labelled by the satisfiability degree of some feature by a complex object and leaves labelled by the satisfiability degrees of some other features by primitive objects (i.e., the most simple parts of a complex object). An AR scheme can have many levels. Then, from properties of basic parts and relations among them we conclude the properties of more complex parts, and after some levels, the properties of the complex target object.

Any AR scheme is constructed from labelled approximate rules, called productions. Productions can be extracted from data using domain knowledge. We define productions as parameterised implications with premises and conclusions built from patterns sufficiently included in the approximated concept.

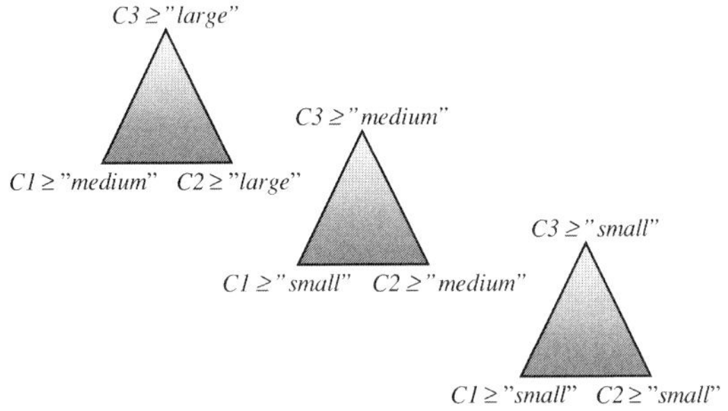

Fig. 1. An example of production as a collection of three production rules

In Figure 1, we present an example of production for some concepts $C1$, $C2$, and $C3$ approximated by three linearly ordered layers *small*, *medium*, and *large*. This production is a collection of three simpler rules, called production rules, with the following interpretation: (1) if inclusion degree to a concept $C1$ is at least *medium* and to a concept $C2$ at least *large* then the inclusion degree to a concept $C3$ is at least *large*; (2) if the inclusion degree to a concept $C1$ is at least *small* and to a concept $C2$ at least *medium* then the inclusion degree to a concept $C3$ is at least *medium*; (3) if the inclusion degree to a concept $C1$ is at least *small* and to a concept $C2$ at least *small* then the inclusion degree to a concept $C3$ is at least *small*.

The concept from the highest level of production is called the target concept of production, whilst the concepts from the lowest level of production are called the source concepts of production. For example, in the case of production from Figure 1, $C3$ is the target concept and $C1$, $C2$ are the source concepts.

One can construct an AR scheme by composing single production rules chosen from different productions from a family of productions for various target concepts. In Figure 2, we have two productions. The target concept of the first production is $C5$ and the target concept of the second production is the concept $C3$. We select one production rule from the first production and one production rule from the second production. These production rules are composed and then a simple AR scheme is obtained that can be treated as a new two-level production rule. Notice that the target pattern of lower production rule in this

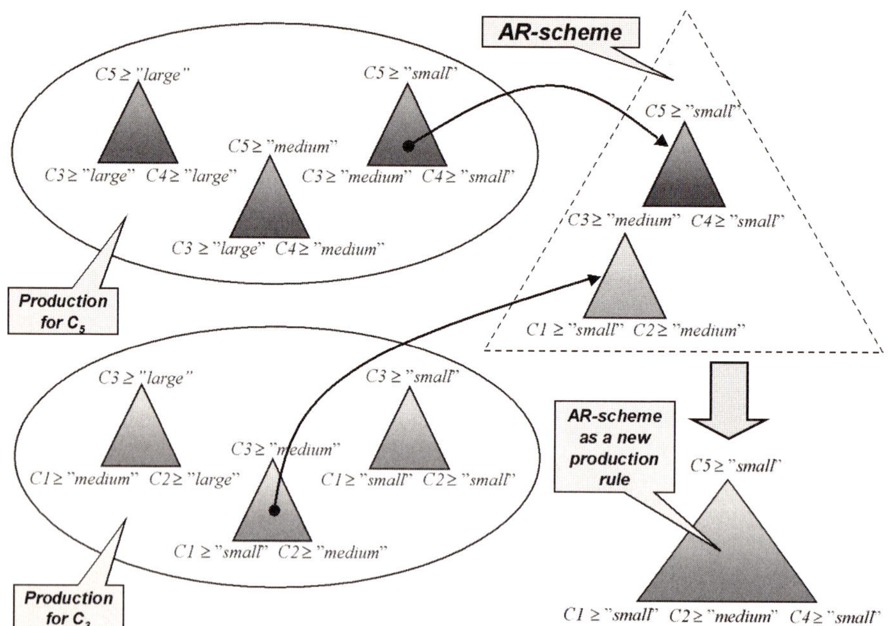

Fig. 2. Synthesis of approximate reasoning scheme

AR scheme is the same as one of the source patterns from the higher production rule. In this case, the common pattern is described as follows: inclusion degree (of some pattern) to a concept $C3$ is at least *medium*.

In this way, we can compose AR schemes into hierarchical and multi-level structures using productions constructed for various concepts.

3   Reasoning Based on Changes

3.1   General Scheme of Reasoning

In this section let us present some general scheme of reasoning about complex concepts that are satisfied to an unsatisfactory degree. Such a case can be a result of some changes of the situation in time and may be required to undertake appropriate actions. Let U be a universe of objects and C be a given concept. For example, we can consider a set of patients as U and a concept of having given disease as C. Let us also denote by $\neg C$ the complementary concept to C – in our example the concept of not having given disease. Now, we can consider some set $X \subseteq U$ of objects included into $\neg C$ to a satisfactory degree, as well as $Y \subseteq U$ – the set of objects well included into C.

A given situation can dynamically be changing in time what we can refer to by states of an object. We can observe that in some states the concept C is satisfied whilst in some other states is $\neg C$. It means that there is additionally some transition relation $R \subseteq U \times U$ responsible for the process of transformation

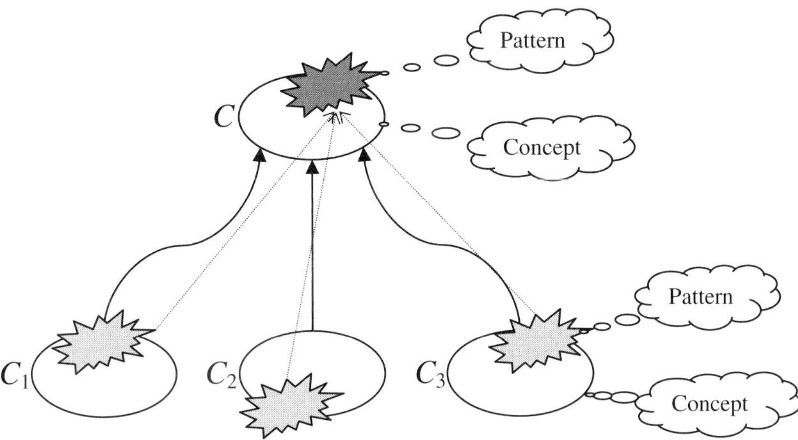

Fig. 3. Approximation of complex concept C by using patterns constructed from patterns approximating low-level concepts C_1, C_2, C_3

of objects from the set X to the set Y. Thus, we can say that $Y = XR = \{y \in U : \exists x \in X \ xRy\}$.

Let us recall that the reasoning about concepts related to X, here $\neg C$, is performed in a hierarchical manner by means of some patterns (see Fig. 3), and classifiers constructed using language of those patterns. In a similar way, one would have to construct a hierarchical classifier for approximation of a concept related to relation R, namely a concept satisfied by relation R to a satisfactory degree. Such a classifier, for a given pair of objects (x, y), where $x \in X, y \in Y$, must take into account: (1) properties of x by means of relevant patterns constructed for X, (2) properties of y by means of relevant patterns constructed for Y, (3) properties of the pair (x, y) by means of relevant patterns constructed for R (note that those patterns can be defined in a language much different from those in the other two cases, e.g., we can consider a closeness between x and y).

Let us emphasise that in general the situation can be much more complex. It can be impossible to approximate such a relation R that directly moves us from set X to Y. We can rather expect to be able to approximate a relation that moves us into "the right direction", i.e., to the state where the change of satisfaction degree of some concept is desired. It means that being in the state where satisfaction degree of concept $\neg C$ is high we have transition that moves us to the state where this degree is lower, i.e, change of degree is negative. We iteratively use several such transition to move in a direction of low satisfiability of $\neg C$ and high satisfiability of C.

The considered problem is related to the following situation: the reasoning about an investigated object leads us to the conclusion that the object does not satisfy a given concept to a satisfactory degree. We would like to impose such a changes that the concept is satisfied. What comes handy is a set of available actions that we can perform to change some properties of an object. The actions are given in the form of rules where premise describes objects to which given action can be applied, and conclusion specifies what will be changed after the action is triggered. In our example we can consider a patient having some disease (thus, satisfying $\neg C$). We would like to undertake some actions to treat the patient so it satisfies C into satisfactory degree. An action could correspond in this case to application of some medicine. A set of action is then a plan of therapy.

We can easily see that there can be induced several transition relations (several paths) that some of their compositions lead a given object from set X to set Y. Let us emphasise, that in each step from the pattern matched by the object and the pattern approximating transition relation we can decode the pattern matched by the transformed object. In this way, we obtain an input pattern for the next step. In each step, an object is transformed to a new state in which the satisfaction degree of a considered concept is better. However, it can appear that one or more steps of one path leads to a worse state. This can be necessary due to necessity of avoiding locally optimal states. Some heuristic search engines, including Genetic Algorithms and Simulated Annealing methods, can be utilised to generate optimal paths. Each path obtained should be additionally verified whether it is feasible. In particular, each step of a path should be verified if there are available actions making possible to realise this step. There should be also considered costs of performing actions realising all steps of a given path. Thus, the cost of a path and the quality of destination (by means of satisfaction degree of considered concept) of state should be evaluated while choosing the optimal path.

3.2   Some Detailed Issues

In this section, let us explain some details related to the possible realisations of the presented ideas. We assume that the investigated objects define some information system $\mathbb{A} = (U, A)$. The considered concept and its complement is denoted by C and $\neg C$, respectively.

Training data and training process. Each object from the training information system contains information about inclusion degrees to concepts C and $\neg C$. There are induced several hierarchical approximate reasoning schemes $\{AR_i\} = \{AR_i^C\} \cup \{AR_i^{\neg C}\}$. The input nodes of the schemes are corresponding to the low-level concepts approximated by means of patterns $\{r_i\}$. The set of patterns used in a given AR scheme depends on the low-level concept used in this scheme, however, any object from U can be tested against any pattern.

Actions and transition relation approximation. One of our assumptions is that we can have an influence on the properties of objects by means of some actions $\{ac_i\}$ we can undertake. Each action can have a cost associated with its execution. In the simplest case, an action can be precisely defined in terms of descriptors over the set of attributes A. Thus, each action can have a form of implication where the premise describes the properties of objects for which the action can be triggered whilst the conclusion defines the changes of object's properties. An example of such action is: "$a_1 = 5$ and $a_5 < 7 \Rightarrow a_1 > 10$ and $\Delta a_8 < 5$", where $a_i \in A$.

In a more complex case, we don't know precise definitions of actions but have some training data describing objects before and after action's execution (for example, we have characteristics of patients before and after application of some medicine). Thus, we also need to induce an AR scheme AR_0 approximating the concept that a given action ac is triggered. AR_0 is then a kind of approximation of transition relation between states of an object where the transition is forced by action ac. The low-level (input) concepts of obtained AR scheme AR_0 are approximated by patterns R_l^{ac} and R_r^{ac} describing properties of objects before and after execution of ac, respectively. Let us also emphasise that some of the low-level concepts can describe properties of pair of objects (x, x'). Those concepts are approximated by yet another set of patterns R_{lr}^{ac}.

In consequence, for a given object x matching patterns R_l^{ac} we can use scheme AR_0 to decode patterns matched by x after we apply action ac. In this way we have some approximation of an action in the language of patterns over the set of attributes A.

Reasoning process. Let x be an investigated object which has been evaluated by induced AR schemes $\{AR_i\}$ as satisfying $\neg C$. It means that it could be recognised by some schemes from $\{AR_i^{\neg C}\}$ (let us denote them by $AR^{\neg C}$) but also by schemes $AR^C \subseteq \{AR_i^C\}$ (in such a case conflict resolving strategies should be involved). The main problem is to find a sequence of actions that should be undertaken in order to transform object x to x' such that x' satisfies C to a satisfactory degree.

One possible way of reasoning is as follows. By examining schemes $AR^{\neg C}$ and $\{AR_i^C\} \setminus AR^C$, as well as the conflict resolving strategy, we can select (1) key schemes that recognised and evaluated x as matching $\neg C$, (2) schemes that could strongly "vote" for C but some of the input concepts were not matched by x good enough. Then, we can decide the way we want to change x. In the first case, we may force x not to match some patterns previously matched, so we can eliminate some schemes from $AR^{\neg C}$. In the second case, we may force x to match some patterns previously not matched, so we can add some "strong" schemes to AR^C.

In either cases, we have some patterns matched by x and some target patterns we would like to be matched by transformed x. Thus, we can try to iteratively combine AR schemes approximating available actions (or combine just actions in the simpler case), starting from patterns matched by x and going forward. Alternatively, we can go backward starting from the target patterns.

Let us denote a very important fact, that approximation of actions can be performed on different levels of generalisation. This is possible because the AR schemes used for approximation are hierarchical structures. Thus, by considering patterns from different levels of AR schemes we can obtain approximation of actions in the language of those patterns, and we can talk about actions as well as meta-actions.

4   Conclusions and Directions for Further Research

In the paper we discussed some problems related to reasoning about information changes in the context of complex concepts approximated hierarchically. Main issue discussed was finding a plan (sequence of actions) of which execution moves an object from some unwanted state to a satisfactory one.

There are several issues that still have to be investigated. One of them is the problem of finding execution plan in the case of classification problem where several decision classes are defined. In such a case we consider a vector of concepts and a vector of inclusion degrees. High number of different combinations of inclusion degree changes (exponential w.r.t. the number of classes) makes the training process not feasible. Some additional techniques, e.g., granulation of the space of inclusion degrees, should be adopted.

Acknowledgements

The research has been supported by the grant 8 T11C 025 19 from the Ministry of Scientific Research and Information Technology of the Republic of Poland and by the Research Center at the Polish-Japanese Institute of Information Technology, Warsaw, Poland.

References

1. Jan G. Bazan, Hoa S. Nguyen, Son H. Nguyen, and Andrzej Skowron. Rough set methods in approximation of hierarchical concepts. In Shusaku Tsumoto, Roman W. Slowinski, Jan Komorowski, and Jerzy W. Grzymala-Busse, editors, *Fourth International Conference on Rough Sets and Current Trends in Computing RSCTC*, volume 3066 of *Lecture Notes in Artificial Intelligence*, pages 346–355, Uppsala, Sweden, June 1-5 2004. Springer-Verlag.

2. M. Ghallab, D. Nau, and P. Traverso. *Automated Planning: Theory and Practice.* Elsevier, Morgan Kaufmann, Cambridge, USA, 2004.

3. J. McCarthy and P. J. Hayes. Some philosophical problems from the standpoint of artificial intelligence. pages 26–45, 1987.

4. Sinh Hoa Nguyen, Jan Bazan, Hung Son Nguyen, and Andrzej Skowron. Layered learning for concept synthesis. *LNCS Transactions on Rough Sets*, 1 (LNCS 3100):193–214, 2004.

5. Zdzisław Pawlak. Information systems - theoretical foundations. *Information Systems*, 6:205–218, 1981.

6. Zdzisław Pawlak. *Rough Sets: Theoretical Aspects of Reasoning about Data*, volume 9 of *D: System Theory, Knowledge Engineering and Problem Solving*. Kluwer Academic Publishers, Dordrecht, The Netherlands, 1991.

7. Lech Polkowski and Andrzej Skowron. Rough mereological approach to knowledge-based distributed AI. In J. K. Lee, J. Liebowitz, and J. M. Chae, editors, *Third World Congress on Expert Systems*, pages 774–781, Soeul, Korea, February 5-9 1996. Cognizant Communication Corporation.

8. Lech Polkowski and Andrzej Skowron. Rough mereology: A new paradigm for approximate reasoning. *International Journal of Approximate Reasoning*, 15(4):333–365, 1996.

9. Lech Polkowski and Andrzej Skowron. Rough mereology in information systems. A case study: Qualitative spatial reasoning. In Lech Polkowski, Tsau Young Lin, and Shusaku Tsumoto, editors, *Rough Set Methods and Applications: New Developments in Knowledge Discovery in Information Systems*, volume 56 of *Studies in Fuzziness and Soft Computing*, chapter 3, pages 89–135. Springer-Verlag/Physica-Verlag, Heidelberg, Germany, 2000.

10. John F. Roddick, Kathleen Hornsby, and Myra Spiliopoulou. YABTSSTDMR - yet another bibliography of temporal, spatial and spatio-temporal data mining research. In K. P. Unnikrishnan and R. Uthurusamy, editors, *SIGKDD Temporal Data Mining Workshop*, pages 167–175, San Francisco, CA, 2001. ACM Press.

11. Yoav Shoham. *Reasoning about change: time and causation from the standpoint of artificial intelligence*. MIT Press, Cambridge, MA, USA, 1988.

12. Andrzej Skowron and Cecylia Rauszer. The discernibility matrices and functions in information systems. In Roman Słowiński, editor, *Intelligent Decision Support - Handbook of Applications and Advances of the Rough Sets Theory*, volume 11 of *D: System Theory, Knowledge Engineering and Problem Solving*, chapter 3, pages 331–362. Kluwer Academic Publishers, Dordrecht, Netherlands, 1992.

13. Andrzej Skowron and Jarosław Stepaniuk. Information granules and rough-neural computing. In Sankar K. Pal, Lech Polkowski, and Andrzej Skowron, editors, *Rough-Neural Computing: Techniques for Computing with Words*, Cognitive Technologies, pages 43–84. Springer Verlag, Heidelberg, Germany, 2004.

14. Andrzej Skowron and Piotr Synak. Complex patterns in spatio-temporal reasoning. In Ludwik Czaja, editor, *Concurrency Specification And Programming CSP*, volume 2, pages 487–499, Czarna, Poland, September 25-27 2003.

15. Andrzej Skowron and Piotr Synak. Complex patterns. *Fundamenta Informaticae*, 60(1-4):351–366, 2004.

16. Andrzej Skowron, Piotr Synak, and James Peters. Spatio-temporal approximate reasoning over hierarchical information maps. In Hans-Dieter Burkhard, editor, *Concurrency Specification And Programming CSP*, volume 2, pages 358–377, Caputh, Germany, September 24-26 2004.

17. Steffen Staab and Rudi Studer, editors. *Handbook on Ontologies*. International Handbooks on Information Systems. Springer, 2004.

18. Jarosław Stepaniuk. Approximation spaces, reducts and representatives. In Lech Polkowski and Andrzej Skowron, editors, *Rough Sets in Knowledge Discovery 2. Applications, Case Studies and Software Systems*, volume 19 of *Studies in Fuzziness and Soft Computing*, chapter 6, pages 109–126. Physica-Verlag, Heidelberg, Germany, 1998.

19. Piotr Synak, Jan G. Bazan, Andrzej Skowron, and James F. Peters. Spatio-temporal approximate reasoning over complex objects. *Fundamenta Informaticae*, 67(1-3):249–269, 2005.

20. W. Van Wezel, R. Jorna, and A. Meystel. *Planning in Intelligent Systems: Aspects, Motivations, and Methods*. John Wiley & Sons, 2006.

Rough Approximation Operators in Covering Approximation Spaces

Tong-Jun Li[1,2]

[1] Institute for Information and System Sciences, Faculty of Science,
Xi'an Jiaotong University, Xi'an, Shaan'xi, 710049, P.R. China
`ltj722@mail.xjtu.edu.cn`
[2] Information College, Zhejiang Ocean University,
Zhoushan, Zhejiang, 316004, P.R. China

Abstract. In this paper, we focus on the study of covering based rough sets in covering approximation spaces. Firstly, two pairs of covering approximation operators are reviewed, their properties are investigated. Secondly, Based on the covering of the covering approximation space, two new coverings of the universe are induced, by which two new pairs of covering approximation operators are constructed. Furthermore, the properties of these operators are examined. Finally, by a comparison of these approximation operators, some conditions are gained under which some or all of these approximation operators are equivalent.

Keywords: Approximation operators, coverings, partitions, rough sets.

1 Introduction

The theory of rough sets is proposed by Pawlak in 1982 [6,7], it is a new mathematical approach to deal with intelligent systems characterized by insufficient and incomplete information, and has been found very successful in many domains.

In the theory of rough sets, based on the knowledge about the universe, a pair of the lower and the upper approximation operators are constructed, with which every subset of the universe can be described. In Pawlak rough set model, the knowledge is determined by an equivalence relation or, equivalently, by a partition of the universe. In order to extend the Pawlak rough set model, many authors replace equivalence relations with general binary relations [4,10,12,16], or replace partitions of the universe with its coverings or its neighborhood systems [1,2,5,8,11,13,15]. If we define a pair of approximation operators by replacing the equivalence classes in Pawlak rough set model with the subsets in a covering, then the lower and the upper approximation operators are not necessarily dual operators. To resolve this problem, Pomykala [8,9] put forward a suggestion, and obtained two pairs of dual approximation operators. In addition, Yao [13,14] discussed this kind of extension by the notion of neighborhood and with granulated view respectively.

Actually, in an approximation space determined by a covering, there are a lot of connections between the objects of the universe, which be hidden in the

S. Greco et al. (Eds.): RSCTC 2006, LNAI 4259, pp. 174–182, 2006.

approximation space. In this paper, by inducing two new coverings from the original covering of the universe, two pairs of new covering lower and upper approximation operators are constructed, Furthermore, we investigate these approximation operators' properties. The relationships among these new operators and the existing covering approximation operators are examined. Finally, we obtain some necessary and sufficient conditions for their equivalence.

2 Review of Covering Approximation Operators

Let U be a finite and nonempty set called the universe, and $\mathcal{C}$ a finite family of nonempty subsets of U. $\mathcal{C}$ is called a covering of U if it satisfies $\bigcup\limits_{C \in \mathcal{C}} C = U$, the ordered pair $(U, \mathcal{C})$ is called a covering approximation space. The covering $\mathcal{C}$ is called a partition of U if it consists of pairwise disjoint subsets of U, then $(U, \mathcal{C})$ is a Pawlak approximation space.

The covering approximation operators is an extension of Pawlak approximation operators. It can be obtained by replacing the equivalence classes with the elements of a covering in granule-oriented definition of Pawlak approximation operators. In order to ensure that the extended lower and upper approximation operators are dual operators, either the lower or the upper approximation operators are extended, and the other one is defined by duality [13,14]. As a result, two pairs of dual approximation operators can be obtained.

(I) $\underline{apr}_{\mathcal{C}}(X) = \cup\{C \in \mathcal{C} : C \subseteq X\}$
$$= \{x \in U : \exists C \in \mathcal{C}(x \in C, C \subseteq X)\},$$
$\overline{apr}_{\mathcal{C}}(X) = \sim \underline{apr}'_{\mathcal{C}}(\sim X)$
$$= \{x \in U : \forall C \in \mathcal{C}(x \in C \Rightarrow C \cap X \neq \emptyset)\}.$$

(II) $\underline{apr}'_{\mathcal{C}}(X) = \sim \overline{apr}'_{\mathcal{C}}(\sim X)$
$$= \{x \in U : \forall C \in \mathcal{C}(x \in C \Rightarrow C \subseteq X)\},$$
$\overline{apr}'_{\mathcal{C}}(X) = \cup\{C \in \mathcal{C} : C \cap X \neq \emptyset\}$
$$= \{x \in U : \exists C \in \mathcal{C}(x \in C, C \cap X \neq \emptyset)\}.$$

The approximation operators $\underline{apr}_{\mathcal{C}}$ and $\overline{apr}_{\mathcal{C}}$ satisfy the following properties:

(L0) $\underline{apr}_{\mathcal{C}}(X) = \sim \overline{apr}_{\mathcal{C}}(\sim X)$,   (U0) $\overline{apr}_{\mathcal{C}}(X) = \sim \underline{apr}_{\mathcal{C}}(\sim X)$;

(L1) $\underline{apr}_{\mathcal{C}}(U) = U$,   (U1) $\overline{apr}_{\mathcal{C}}(\emptyset) = \emptyset$;

(L1$'$) $\underline{apr}_{\mathcal{C}}(\emptyset) = \emptyset$,   (U1$'$) $\overline{apr}_{\mathcal{C}}(U) = U$;

(L2) $X \subseteq Y \Rightarrow \underline{apr}_{\mathcal{C}}(X) \subseteq \underline{apr}_{\mathcal{C}}(Y)$,   (U2) $X \subseteq Y \Rightarrow \overline{apr}_{\mathcal{C}}(X) \subseteq \overline{apr}_{\mathcal{C}}(Y)$;

(L3$'$) $\underline{apr}_{\mathcal{C}}(X \cap Y) \subseteq \underline{apr}_{\mathcal{C}}(Y) \cap \underline{apr}_{\mathcal{C}}(Y)$,

(U3$'$) $\overline{apr}_{\mathcal{C}}(X \cup Y) \supseteq \overline{apr}_{\mathcal{C}}(Y) \cup \overline{apr}_{\mathcal{C}}(Y)$;

(L4) $\underline{apr}_{\mathcal{C}}(X \cup Y) \supseteq \underline{apr}_{\mathcal{C}}(X) \cup \underline{apr}_{\mathcal{C}}(Y)$,

(U4) $\overline{apr}_{\mathcal{C}}(X \cap Y) \subseteq \overline{apr}_{\mathcal{C}}(X) \cap \overline{apr}_{\mathcal{C}}(Y)$;

(L5) $\underline{apr}_{\mathcal{C}}(X) \subseteq X$,   (U5) $X \subseteq \overline{apr}_{\mathcal{C}}(X)$;

(L7) $\underline{apr}_{\mathcal{C}}(X) \subseteq \underline{apr}_{\mathcal{C}}(\underline{apr}_{\mathcal{C}}(X))$,   (U7) $\overline{apr}_{\mathcal{C}}(\overline{apr}_{\mathcal{C}}(X)) \subset \overline{apr}_{\mathcal{C}}(X)$.

Note that $\underline{apr}_{\mathcal{C}}$ and $\overline{apr}_{\mathcal{C}}$ may not satisfy the properties (L3) and (U3):

$$(L3)\ \underline{apr}_{\mathcal{C}}(X \cap Y) = \underline{apr}_{\mathcal{C}}(X) \cap \underline{apr}_{\mathcal{C}}(Y),$$
$$(U3)\ \overline{apr}_{\mathcal{C}}(X \cup Y) = \overline{apr}_{\mathcal{C}}(X) \cup \overline{apr}_{\mathcal{C}}(Y).$$

Some conditions will be given in section 4, under which $\underline{apr}_{\mathcal{C}}$ and $\overline{apr}_{\mathcal{C}}$ satisfy the properties (L3) and (U3).

Besides the properties (L0)–(L5), (U0)–(U5), (L1′) and (U1′), the approximation operators $\underline{apr}'_{\mathcal{C}}$ and $\overline{apr}'_{\mathcal{C}}$ also satisfy the following properties:

$$(L6)\ X \subseteq \underline{apr}'_{\mathcal{C}}(\overline{apr}'_{\mathcal{C}}(X)),\quad (U6)\ \overline{apr}'_{\mathcal{C}}(\underline{apr}'_{\mathcal{C}}(X)) \subseteq X.$$

The following two theorems follows from [13, Theorem 7 and Theorem 8].

Theorem 1. *Let $(U,\mathcal{C})$ be a covering approximation space. Then for all $X \subseteq U$,*

$$\underline{apr}'_{\mathcal{C}}(X) \subseteq \underline{apr}_{\mathcal{C}}(X) \subseteq X \subseteq \overline{apr}_{\mathcal{C}}(X) \subseteq \overline{apr}'_{\mathcal{C}}(X).$$

Theorem 2. *The two pair of lower and upper approximation operators defined by (I) and (II) are equivalent if and only if the covering $\mathcal{C}$ is a partition of U.*

Let $FC(U)$ denote the set of all coverings of U. A relation $\preceq$ on $FC(U)$ can be defined as follows, for $\mathcal{C}_1, \mathcal{C}_2 \in FC(U)$, $\mathcal{C}_1 \preceq \mathcal{C}_2$ if and only if for all $C' \in \mathcal{C}_2$, there exist $C_1, \cdots, C_k \in \mathcal{C}_1$ such that $C' = \bigcup_{i=1}^{k} C_i$. the covering $\mathcal{C}_1$ is finer than $\mathcal{C}_2$, or $\mathcal{C}_2$ is coarser than $\mathcal{C}_1$. It can easily be verified that $\preceq$ is reflexive and translative. Corresponding the relation $\preceq$, the covering approximation operators w.r.t. the coverings in $FC(U)$ have the following properties.

Theorem 3. *Let $(U,\mathcal{C}_1)$ and $(U,\mathcal{C}_2)$ be two covering approximation spaces. Then for any $X \subseteq U$, $\underline{apr}_{\mathcal{C}_2}(X) \subseteq \underline{apr}_{\mathcal{C}_1}(X)$ and $\overline{apr}_{\mathcal{C}_1}(X) \subseteq \overline{apr}_{\mathcal{C}_2}(X)$ if and only if $\mathcal{C}_1 \preceq \mathcal{C}_2$. In special, $\underline{apr}_{\mathcal{C}_2} = \underline{apr}_{\mathcal{C}_1}$ and $\overline{apr}_{\mathcal{C}_1} = \overline{apr}_{\mathcal{C}_2}$ if and only if $\mathcal{C}_1 \preceq \mathcal{C}_2$ and $\mathcal{C}_2 \preceq \mathcal{C}_1$.*

Proof. If $\mathcal{C}_1 \preceq \mathcal{C}_2$, then it immediately follows from Definition (I) that $\underline{apr}_{\mathcal{C}_2}(X) \subseteq \underline{apr}_{\mathcal{C}_1}(X)$ and $\overline{apr}_{\mathcal{C}_1}(X) \subseteq \overline{apr}_{\mathcal{C}_2}(X)$ for all $X \subseteq U$. Conversely, if $\underline{apr}_{\mathcal{C}_2}(X) \subseteq \underline{apr}_{\mathcal{C}_1}(X)$ and $\overline{apr}_{\mathcal{C}_1}(X) \subseteq \overline{apr}_{\mathcal{C}_2}(X)$ for all $X \subseteq U$, then for any $C \in \mathcal{C}_2$,

$$C = \underline{apr}_{\mathcal{C}_2}(C) \subseteq \underline{apr}_{\mathcal{C}_1}(C) = \cup\{A \in \mathcal{C}_1 : A \subseteq C\} \subseteq C,$$

thus, $C = \cup\{A \in \mathcal{C}_1 : A \subseteq C\}$. We can conclude $\mathcal{C}_1 \preceq \mathcal{C}_2$.

3   New Covering Approximation Operators

Let $(U, \mathcal{C})$ be a covering approximation space. In $(U, \mathcal{C})$, every element x of U can be related to some elements of U by different way. here, by using two relations hidden in approximation space $(U, \mathcal{C})$, two coverings of U are constructed as follows.

$$\mathcal{C}^* = \{x^* : x \in U\}, \quad \mathcal{C}^{**} = \{x^{**} : x \in U\},$$

where

$$x^* = \{y \in U : \forall C \in \mathcal{C}(x \in C \Rightarrow y \in C)\},$$
$$x^{**} = \{y \in U : \forall C \in \mathcal{C}(x \in C \Leftrightarrow y \in C)\}.$$

Example 1. Let U and W be two universes, and R a binary relation from U to W. They are given as follows:

$$U = \{1, 2, 3, 4, 5\}, \quad W = \{a, b, c\}, \quad R = \begin{pmatrix} 1\ 1\ 0 \\ 0\ 1\ 0 \\ 0\ 0\ 1 \\ 1\ 0\ 1 \\ 1\ 1\ 0 \end{pmatrix}.$$

Then $Ra = \{x \in U : xRa\} = \{1, 4, 5\}$, similarly we have $Rb = \{1, 2, 5\}$, $Rc = \{3, 4\}$. We can verify that $\mathcal{C}_R = \{Ra, Rb, Rc\}$ is a covering of U, thus $(U, \mathcal{C}_R)$ is a covering approximation space. We can also figure out:

$$1^* = \{1, 5\}, \ 2^* = \{1, 2, 5\}, \ 3^* = \{3, 4\}, \ 4^* = \{4\}, \ 5^* = \{1, 5\},$$

and

$$1^{**} = \{1, 5\}, \ 2^{**} = \{2\}, \ 3^{**} = \{3\}, \ 4^{**} = \{4\}, \ 5^{**} = \{1, 5\}.$$

If we treat the elements in U and W as objects and properties (attributes) respectively, then, for example, the intension of $1Ra$ is that object 1 has property a. Thus $x^*(x \in U)$ consists of all objects having the properties which x has, and x^{**} all objects having the same attributes as x.

It is easy to prove that the following proposition holds.

Proposition 1. *Let $(U, \mathcal{C})$ be a covering approximation space. Then*

(1) *for every $x \in U$, $x \in x^*$,*

(2) *for any $x, y \in U$, $y \in x^* \Rightarrow y^* \subseteq x^*$,*

(3) $\mathcal{C}^*$ *is a covering of U,*

(4) $\mathcal{C}^{**}$ *is a partition of U,*

(5) $\mathcal{C}^{**} \preceq \mathcal{C}^* \preceq \mathcal{C}$.

By definitions (I) and (II) we can construct four pairs of covering lower and upper approximation operators w.r.t the covering $\mathcal{C}^*$ and $\mathcal{C}^{**}$ respectively. By means of Proposition 1 and Theorem 2 the following two theorems can be verified.

Theorem 4. *For all $X \subseteq U$,*

$$\underline{apr}_{\mathcal{C}*}(X) = \{x \in U : x^* \subseteq X\}, \quad \overline{apr}_{\mathcal{C}*}(X) = \{x \in U : x^* \cap X \neq \emptyset\}.$$

Theorem 5. *For all $X \subseteq U$,*

$$\underline{apr}_{\mathcal{C}**}(X) = \underline{apr}'_{\mathcal{C}**}(X) = \{x \in U : x^{**} \subseteq X\},$$
$$\overline{apr}_{\mathcal{C}**}(X) = \overline{apr}'_{\mathcal{C}**}(X) = \{x \in U : x^{**} \cap X \neq \emptyset\}.$$

Theorem 6. *Approximation operators $\underline{apr}_{\mathcal{C}*}$ and $\overline{apr}_{\mathcal{C}*}$ satisfy (L0)–(L5), (U0)–(U5), (L1′), (U1′), (L7) and (U7). Approximation operators $\underline{apr}_{\mathcal{C}**}$ and $\overline{apr}_{\mathcal{C}**}$ satisfy (L0)–(L7), (U0)–(U7), (L1′), (U1′), and the following (L8) and (U8):*

$$\text{(L8)} \ \overline{apr}_{\mathcal{C}**}(X) \subseteq \underline{apr}_{\mathcal{C}**}(\overline{apr}_{\mathcal{C}**}(X)),$$
$$\text{(U8)} \ \overline{apr}_{\mathcal{C}**}(\underline{apr}_{\mathcal{C}**}(X)) \subseteq \underline{apr}_{\mathcal{C}**}(X).$$

4 Connections Among Covering Approximation Operators

Theorem 7. *Let $(U, \mathcal{C})$ be a covering approximation space. For any $X \subseteq U$,*

$$\underline{apr}'_{\mathcal{C}}(X) \subseteq \underline{apr}_{\mathcal{C}}(X) \ \subseteq \underline{apr}_{\mathcal{C}*}(X) \subseteq \underline{apr}_{\mathcal{C}**}(X) \subseteq X$$
$$\subseteq \overline{apr}_{\mathcal{C}**}(X) \subseteq \overline{apr}_{\mathcal{C}*}(X) \subseteq \overline{apr}_{\mathcal{C}}(X) \ \subseteq \overline{apr}'_{\mathcal{C}}(X).$$

Proof. For any $X \subseteq U$, by Theorem 1 we have

$$\underline{apr}'_{\mathcal{C}}(X) \subseteq \underline{apr}_{\mathcal{C}}(X).$$

By using Proposition 1 (5), Theorems 3 and 6, we obtain

$$\underline{apr}_{\mathcal{C}}(X) \subseteq \underline{apr}_{\mathcal{C}*}(X) \subseteq \underline{apr}_{\mathcal{C}**}(X) \subseteq X.$$

By the duality of these operators, we also have

$$X \subseteq \overline{apr}_{\mathcal{C}**}(X) \subseteq \overline{apr}_{\mathcal{C}*}(X) \subseteq \overline{apr}_{\mathcal{C}}(X) \subseteq \overline{apr}'_{\mathcal{C}}(X).$$

Theorem 7 shows that among the two pairs of approximation operators, $\underline{apr}_{\mathcal{C}**}$ and $\overline{apr}_{\mathcal{C}**}$, $\underline{apr}_{\mathcal{C}*}$ and $\overline{apr}_{\mathcal{C}*}$, $\underline{apr}_{\mathcal{C}}$ and $\overline{apr}_{\mathcal{C}}$, and $\underline{apr}'_{\mathcal{C}}$ and $\overline{apr}'_{\mathcal{C}}$, the former give tighter approximations than that of the latter. Moreover, these operators may be pairwise unequal. On account of the restriction of pages, the illustrating examples are omitted.

Let $(U, \mathcal{C})$ be a covering approximation space. Let

$$I_s(\mathcal{C}) = \{\cap \mathcal{C}_0 : \mathcal{C}_0 \subseteq \mathcal{C}\}.$$

Then $I_s(\mathcal{C})$ is called closure system generated by $\mathcal{C}$, where closure system means a class of subsets of U, and satisfies that the intersection of any its subclass belongs to it [3].

Theorem 8. *The following statements are equivalent:*

(1) $\underline{apr}_{\mathcal{C}}$ *and* $\overline{apr}_{\mathcal{C}}$ *satisfy* (L3) *and* (U3) *respectively,*

(2) $\underline{apr}_{\mathcal{C}} = \underline{apr}_{\mathcal{C}^*}$, $\overline{apr}_{\mathcal{C}} = \overline{apr}_{\mathcal{C}^*}$,

(3) $\mathcal{C} \preceq \mathcal{C}^*$,

(4) $\mathcal{C}^* \subseteq \mathcal{C}$,

(5) *For any* $x \in U$, *the minimum element of the family* $\mathcal{C}(x) = \{C \in \mathcal{C} : x \in C\}$ *exists,*

(6) $\mathcal{C} \preceq I_s(\mathcal{C})$.

Proof. $(1) \Rightarrow (2)$: Assume that $\underline{apr}_{\mathcal{C}}$ and $\overline{apr}_{\mathcal{C}}$ satisfy (L3) and (U3). Then for any $X \subseteq U$,

$$\overline{apr}_{\mathcal{C}}(X) = \bigcup_{x \in X} \overline{apr}_{\mathcal{C}}(\{x\}).$$

Since $\overline{apr}_{\mathcal{C}^*}$ satisfies (U3), we also have that for any $X \subseteq U$,

$$\overline{apr}_{\mathcal{C}^*}(X) = \bigcup_{x \in X} \overline{apr}_{\mathcal{C}^*}(\{x\}).$$

By Definition (I) and Theorem 4 we have that for any $x \in U$,

$$
\begin{aligned}
\overline{apr}_{\mathcal{C}}(\{x\}) &= \{y \in U : \forall C \in \mathcal{C}(y \in C \Rightarrow C \cap \{x\} \neq \emptyset)\} \\
&= \{y \in U : \forall C \in \mathcal{C}(y \in C \Rightarrow x \in C)\} \\
&= \{y \in U : x \in y^*\} \\
&= \{y \in U : y^* \cap \{x\} \neq \emptyset\} \\
&= \overline{apr}_{\mathcal{C}^*}(\{x\}).
\end{aligned}
$$

Thus, we can conclude

$$\overline{apr}_{\mathcal{C}}(X) = \overline{apr}_{\mathcal{C}^*}(X), \ \forall X \subseteq U.$$

Similarly, by the duality,

$$\underline{apr}_{\mathcal{C}}(X) = \underline{apr}_{\mathcal{C}^*}(X), \ \forall X \subseteq U.$$

$(2) \Rightarrow (3)$: It follows from Theorem 3.

$(3) \Rightarrow (4)$: Assume that the covering $\mathcal{C}$ be finer than the covering $\mathcal{C}^*$. For any $x \in U$, $x^* \in \mathcal{C}^*$. By the assumption, we have $x^* = \bigcup_{C \in \mathcal{C}, C \subseteq x^*} C$. By $x \in x^*$, there exists a $C \in \mathcal{C}$ such that $x \in C \subseteq x^*$. From the definition of x^*, we can deduce $x^* \subseteq C$. Noticing $C \subseteq x^*$ we have $x^* = C$, thus, $x^* \in \mathcal{C}$. We conclude $\mathcal{C}^* \subseteq \mathcal{C}$.

$(4) \Rightarrow (5)$: Suppose $\mathcal{C}^* \subseteq \mathcal{C}$. Then for any $x \in U$, by $x \in x^*$ we have $x^* \in \mathcal{C}(x)$. It is evident that x^* is included in every set in $\mathcal{C}(x)$. Therefore, we conclude that x^* is the minimum set in $\mathcal{C}(x)$.

$(5) \Rightarrow (6)$: For any $x \in U$, assume that the family $\mathcal{C}(x)$ have the minimum element. $\forall X \in I_s(\mathcal{C})$, for simplicity, we suppose $X = C_1 \cap C_2, C_1, C_2 \in \mathcal{C}$. For any $x \in X = C_1 \cap C_2$, $C_1, C_2 \in \mathcal{C}(x)$. By the assumption there exists a $C_x \in \mathcal{C}$ such that $x \in C_x \subseteq C_1 \cap C_2 = X$. Thus, $X = \bigcup_{x \in X} C_x$. We conclude $\mathcal{C} \preceq I_s(\mathcal{C})$.

$(6) \Rightarrow (1)$: Assume that $\mathcal{C}$ be finer than $I_s(\mathcal{C})$. For any $X, Y \subseteq U$, if $x \in \underline{apr}_\mathcal{C}(X) \cap \underline{apr}_\mathcal{C}(Y)$, then $x \in \underline{apr}_\mathcal{C}(X)$ and $x \in \underline{apr}_\mathcal{C}(Y)$. By Definition (I) there exist $C_1, C_2 \in \mathcal{C}$ such that $x \in C_1 \subseteq X$ and $x \in C_2 \subseteq Y$, that is, $x \in C_1 \cap C_2 \subseteq X \cap Y$. Since $C_1 \cap C_2 \in I_s(\mathcal{C})$, by the assumption, there exists a $C \in \mathcal{C}$ such that $x \in C \subseteq C_1 \cap C_2 \subseteq X \cap Y$. So, $x \in \underline{apr}_\mathcal{C}(X \cap Y)$. Thus

$$\underline{apr}_\mathcal{C}(X) \cap \underline{apr}_\mathcal{C}(Y) \subseteq \underline{apr}_\mathcal{C}(X \cap Y).$$

Noticing $\underline{apr}_\mathcal{C}$ satisfies (L3$'$), we conclude

$$\underline{apr}_\mathcal{C}(X \cap Y) = \underline{apr}_\mathcal{C}(X) \cap \underline{apr}_\mathcal{C}(Y).$$

By the duality, we also have

$$\overline{apr}_\mathcal{C}(X \cup Y) = \underline{apr}_\mathcal{C}(X) \cup \underline{apr}_\mathcal{C}(Y).$$

Theorem 9. *The following statements are equivalent:*

(1) $\underline{apr}_{\mathcal{C}^*} = \underline{apr}_{\mathcal{C}^{**}}$ *and* $\overline{apr}_{\mathcal{C}^*} = \overline{apr}_{\mathcal{C}^{**}}$,

(2) $\mathcal{C}^* \preceq \mathcal{C}^{**}$,

(3) $\mathcal{C}^{**} \subseteq \mathcal{C}^*$.

Proof. The equivalence of (1) and (2) follows from Theorems 3 and 7. With the equivalence of (2) and (3), it is evident that (3) implies (2). Therefore, It is only to prove that (2) implies (3).

Assume that $\mathcal{C}^* \preceq \mathcal{C}^{**}$. For any $x^{**} \in \mathcal{C}^{**}$, by $x \in x^{**}$ and the assumption, there exists a $y \in U$ such that $x \in y^* \subseteq x^{**}$. As $y \in y^* \subseteq x^{**}$, we have that for any $C \in \mathcal{C}$, $x \in C$ is equivalent to $y \in C$. For any $z \in x^{**}$, it is evident that for any $C \in \mathcal{C}$, $x \in C$ is equivalent to $z \in C$. Thus $y \in C$ is equivalent to $z \in C$ for all $C \in \mathcal{C}$, from which we have that $y \in C$ implies $z \in C$ for all $C \in \mathcal{C}$, that is, $z \in y^*$. Thus, $x^{**} \subseteq y^*$. Consequently, by using $y^* \subseteq x^{**}$ we obtain that $x^{**} = y^*$. Therefore, $\mathcal{C}^{**} \subseteq \mathcal{C}^*$.

Theorem 10. *The following statements are equivalent:*

(1) $\underline{apr}_\mathcal{C} = \underline{apr}_{\mathcal{C}^{**}}$ *and* $\overline{apr}_\mathcal{C} = \overline{apr}_{\mathcal{C}^{**}}$

(2) $\mathcal{C} \preceq \mathcal{C}^{**}$,

(3) $\mathcal{C}^{**} \subseteq \mathcal{C}$.

Proof. The equivalence of (1) and (2) follows from Theorems 3 and 7. With the equivalence of (2) and (3), it is evident that (3) implies (2). Therefore, It is only to prove that (2) implies (3).

Suppose that $\mathcal{C} \preceq \mathcal{C}^{**}$. For any $x^{**} \in \mathcal{C}^{**}$, by $x \in x^{**}$ and the assumption, there exists a $C_x \in \mathcal{C}$ such that $x \in C_x \subseteq x^{**}$. For any $y \in x^{**}$ we have that $x \in C$ and $y \in C$ are equivalent for all $C \in \mathcal{C}$. Specially, by $C_x \in \mathcal{C}$ and $x \in C_x$, we have $y \in C_x$. Thus, $x^{**} \subseteq C_x$. Noticing that $C_x \subseteq x^{**}$ we have $x^{**} = C_x$. We conclude $x^{**} \in \mathcal{C}$, which implies $\mathcal{C}^{**} \subseteq \mathcal{C}$.

Theorem 11. *The following statements are equivalent:*

(1) $\underline{apr}'_{\mathcal{C}} = \underline{apr}_{\mathcal{C}} = \underline{apr}_{\mathcal{C}^*} = \underline{apr}_{\mathcal{C}^{**}}$, $\overline{apr}'_{\mathcal{C}} = \overline{apr}_{\mathcal{C}} = \overline{apr}_{\mathcal{C}^*} = \overline{apr}_{\mathcal{C}^{**}}$,

(2) $\underline{apr}'_{\mathcal{C}} = \underline{apr}_{\mathcal{C}}$, $\overline{apr}'_{\mathcal{C}} = \overline{apr}_{\mathcal{C}}$,

(3) $\mathcal{C}$ *is a partition of* U.

Proof. It directly follows from Theorem 2 that (2) and (3) are equivalent. It is evident that (1) implies (2). It is only to prove that (2) implies (1).

Assume $\underline{apr}'_{\mathcal{C}} = \underline{apr}_{\mathcal{C}}$ and $\overline{apr}'_{\mathcal{C}} = \overline{apr}_{\mathcal{C}}$. Then by Theorem 2, $\mathcal{C}$ is a partition of U, by which it is easy to verify that $\mathcal{C} = \mathcal{C}^* = \mathcal{C}^{**}$. Consequently, by the assumption and Definition (I) we conclude that (1) holds.

5   Conclusions

The covering rough set theory is the improvement of Pawlak rough set, and has promising potential for applications to data mining. In this paper, we mainly construct two covering of the universe from the original covering of approximation space, by which we define two pairs of covering lower and upper approximation operators. Furthermore, we investigate their properties, by comparing these operators and the existing covering approximation operators, it is showed that the new approximation operators give tighter approximations than the latter. Finally, some conditions are gained under which some or all of covering approximation operators are equivalent. Naturally, it is interesting to consider possible practical applications of new covering approximation operators, and reliant problems in fuzzy environments are worthy of further research

Acknowledgement

This work was supported by a grant from the National Natural Science Foundation of China (No. 60373078).

References

1. Bonikowski, Z., Bryniariski, E., Skardowska, V.W.: Extension and Intensions in the Rough Set Theory. Information Sciences 107 (1998) 149–167
2. Bonikowski, Z.: Algebraic Structures of Rough Sets in Representative Approximation Spaces. Electronic Notes in Theoretical Computer Science 82 (2003) 1–12
3. Caspard, N., Monjardet, B.: The Lattices of Closure Systems, Closure Operators, and Implicational Systems on a Finite Set: a Survey. Discrete Applied Mathematics 127 (2003) 241–269
4. Li, T.-J., Zhang, W.-X.: Rough Approximations in Formal Contexts. Proceedings of the Fourth International Conference on Machine Learning and Cybernetics, Guangzhou, China, (2005) 3162–3167
5. Orlowska, E.: Semantics Analysis of Inductive Reasoning. Theoretical Computer Science 3 (1986) 81–89

6. Pawlak, Z.: Rough Sets. International Journal of Computer and Information Science 11 (1982) 341–356
7. Pawlak, Z.: Rough Sets: Theoretical Aspects of Reasoning about Data. Kluwer Academic Publisher, Boston, 1991
8. Pomykala, J.A.: Approximation Operations in Approximation Space. Bulletin of the Polish Academy of Sciences: Mathematics 35 (1987) 653–662
9. Pomykala, J.A.: On Definability in the Nondeterministic Information System. Bulletin of the Polish Academy of Sciences: Mathematics 36 (1988), 193–210
10. Slowinski, R., Vanderpooten, D.: A Generalized Definition of Rough Approximations Based on Similarity. IEEE Transactions on Knowledge and Data Engineering 12(2) (2000) 331–336
11. Wu, W.-Z., Zhang, W.-X.: Neighborhood Operator Systems and Appoximations. Infomation Sciences 144 (2002) 201–217
12. Yao, Y.Y.: Constructive and Algebraic Methods of the Theory of Rough Sets. Information Sciences 109 (1998) 21–47
13. Yao, Y.Y.: Relational Interpretations of Neighborhood Operators and Rough Set Approximation Operators. Information Sciences 111 (1998) 239–259
14. Yao, Y.Y.: Rough Sets, Neighborhood Systems, and Granular Computing. Proceedings of the 1999 IEEE Canadian Conference on Electrical and Computer Engineering, Edmonton, Canada, Meng, (ed.), IEEE press, (1999) 1553- 1558
15. Zakowski, W.: Approximations in the Space (U, Π). Demenstratio Mathematica XVI (1983) 761–769
16. Zhang, W.-X., Mi, J.-S.: Incomplete Information System and Its Optimal Selections. Computers and Mathematics with Applications 48 (2004) 691–698

A New Method for Discretization of Continuous Attributes Based on VPRS

Jin-Mao Wei[1,2], Guo-Ying Wang[1], Xiang-Ming Kong[1], Shu-Jie Li[1],
Shu-Qin Wang[3], and Da-You Liu[2]

[1] Institute of Computational Intelligence,
Northeast Normal University, Changchun, Jilin, 130024 China
{weijm374, lisj}@nenu.edu.cn
[2] Open Symbol Computation and Knowledge Engineering Laboratory of
State Education, Jilin University, Changchun, Jilin, 130024, China
[3] School of Mathematics & Statistics, Northeast
Normal University, Changchun,Jilin, 130024, China
wangsq562@nenu.edu.cn

Abstract. A new method for discretization of continuous features based
on the Variable Precision Rough Set theory is proposed and tested in
the process of inducing decision trees. Through rectifying error ratio, the
generalization capability of decision trees is enhanced by enlarging or
reducing the sizes of positive regions. Two ways of computing frequency
and width are deployed to calculate the misclassifying rate of the data,
and thus the negative effect on decision trees is reduced, by which the
discretization points are determined. In the paper, we use some open data
sets to testify the method. The results are compared with that obtained
by C4.5, which shows that the presented method is a feasible way to
discretization of continuous features in applications.

1   Introduction

Discrete values have important roles in AI and machine learning. For example,
in the process of inducing decision trees, the target or decision attribute whose
value is predicted by the learned tree must be discrete value. Besides, the attributes tested for the branch nodes of the tree must be discrete-valued too.
Furthermore, rules with discrete values are normally shorter and more understandable[1]. Continuous data are ordinal data with orders among the values.
Therefore it is certainly not wise to use continuous values to split a node. It is
needed to discretize continuous features either before the decision tree induction
or during the process of the tree building. This can be accomplished by dynamically finding some values of an attribute that partition the continuous value
into a discrete set of intervals. Widely used systems such as C4.5 and CART
deploy various ways to avoid using continuous values directly[2,3]. Vast amounts
of works have been reported regarding discretization of continuous attributes
[4,5,6]. In [4], the author discussed how to handle continuous attributes in large
data bases. In [5], the authors described Chi2, a simple and general algorithm

S. Greco et al. (Eds.): RSCTC 2006, LNAI 4259, pp. 183–190, 2006.

that used the chi-square statistic to discretize numeric attributes repeatedly until some inconsistencies were found in the data, and achieve feature selection via discretization. The empirical results demonstrated that Chi2 is effective in feature selection and discretization of numeric and ordinal attributes. In [6], the authors analyzed the characteristics of the traditional techniques, which makes use of feature merits based on either the information theoretic, or the statistical correlation between each feature and the class. Instead, they assigned merits to features by finding each feature's 'obligation' to the class discrimination in the context of other features. The merits were then used to rank the features, select a feature subset, and discretize the numeric variables. Example sets demonstrated that their approach is an alternative to the traditional methods. Rough Set theory, proposed by Poland mathematician Pawlak in 1982, is a new mathematic tool to deal with vagueness and uncertainty[7]. Rough Set theory is widely used in many applications[8,9]. Some researchers and practitioners have studied discretization methods based on the Rough Set model and got some meaningful results[10,11]. However, the universe U is supposed to be known in the basic Rough Set model. Conclusions induced from the universe only apply to the objects among the universe. Thus, W.Ziarko proposed the Variable Precision Rough Set model(VPRSM) and presented a classification strategy[12]. It is used to make decisions if the error rate is lower than the given threshold. Based on the VPRSM, a method for partitioning continuous attributes is proposed in this paper. It adjusts error ratio parameter in the VPRSM to realize partition. Two ways of computing frequency(numbers of records) and width(value ranges of intervals) are deployed to calculate the misclassification rate of the data. The classification and generalization capabilities of decision trees are both taken into account. Experiments were conducted on some open data sets from the UCI and MLC data repositories. The results are compared with that obtained by the methods of C4.5 and that in paper[11]. It shows that the method proposed in this paper is an effective and simple way to discretization of continuous attributes.

2   Basic Concepts in VPRSM

Given an information system $I = (U, Q, V, f)$, $q \in Q$. U denotes the universe. Q denotes the set of attributes. It is usually divided into two subsets, i.e. C and D, which denote the set of condition attributes and the set of decision attributes respectively. $V = \bigcup_{q \in Q} V_q$ denotes the domain of attributes' value, and f is an information function which associates a unique value of each attribute with every object belonging to U.

Definition 1[10]: Let U denote the universe to be learned, and X and Y denote the non-empty subsets of U. Let:

$$c(X, Y) = \begin{cases} 1 - \frac{|X \cap Y|}{|X|}, & |X| > 0 \\ 0, & |X| = 0 \end{cases} \tag{1}$$

Where $|X|$ is the cardinality of X and $c(X, Y)$ is the relative classification error of the set X with respect to set Y. That is to say, if all elements of set X

were partitioned into set Y then in $c(X, Y) \times 100\%$ of the cases we would make a classification error. Generally, the admissible classification error β must be within the range $0 \leq \beta < 0.5$.

Let $(U, \widetilde{R})$ be an approximation space, and $R^* = \{E_1, E_2, \cdots, E_n\}$ denote the set containing the equivalence classes of the equivalence relation $\widetilde{R}$.

For any subset $X \subseteq U$, the β lower approximation of X with respect to $\widetilde{R}$ is defined as:

$$\underline{R}_\beta X = \bigcup \{E_i \in R^* | C(E_i, X) \leq \beta\} \tag{2}$$

The β lower approximation of X is also called the β positive region of X, denoted as $POS_\beta(X)$.

The β upper approximation of X with respect to $\widetilde{R}$ is defined as:

$$\overline{R}_\beta X = \bigcup \{E_i \in R^* | C(E_i, X) < 1 - \beta\} \tag{3}$$

The β boundary of X with respect to $\widetilde{R}$ is defined as:

$$bnr_\beta X = \bigcup \{E_i \in R^* | \beta < C(E_i, X) < 1 - \beta\} \tag{4}$$

The β negative region of X with respect to $\widetilde{R}$ is defined as:

$$negr_\beta X = \bigcup \{E_i \in R^* | C(E_i, X) \geq 1 - \beta\} \tag{5}$$

Comparing the VPRSM with the initial Rough Set model, we can easily get that the VPRSM will turn to be the Rough Set model when $\beta = 0$.

3   Discretization of Continuous Attributes Based on VPRS

Given $A \subseteq Q$, an equivalence relation $\widetilde{A}$ can be induced. In the context, the set $\{c\}$ and $\{d\}$ are simply referred to as attribute c and d. The induced equivalence relations are referred to as $\widetilde{c}$ and $\widetilde{d}$. Let $X = \{x_1, x_2, \ldots, x_k\}$, $x_1 \leq x_2 \leq \ldots \leq x_k$, be the sorted value set of continuous attribute c. Each x_i corresponds to a unique record in U. Hereunder, we will refer to the ith record as x_i. An ordered partition of X with respect to decision attribute d can be obtained. Denote the partition as $c^* = \{X_1, X_2, \cdots, X_l\}$. For each $x_m \in X_i$ and $x_n \in X_{i+1}$, we have $x_m < x_n$ and $f(x_m, d) \neq f(x_n, d)$. For each $x_m \in X_i$ and $x_n \in X_i, m \neq n$, we have $f(x_m, d) = f(x_n, d)$. The decision attribute value set corresponding to X is $W = \{d_1, d_2, \ldots, d_l\}$, where $d_i \in V_d$. It should be noted that c^* also corresponds to a partition of U. From d_1 to d_l we can also obtain a partition of U, which is denoted as $Y = \{Y_1, Y_2, \cdots, Y_{l'}\}$, $l' \leq l$. For each $x_m \in Y_j$ and $x_n \in Y_j$, we have $f(x_m, d) = f(x_n, d)$. In fact, l' is the number of the possible values of decision attribute. Apparently, Y also corresponds to a partition of the continuous attribute c. It is easy to understand that the partition c^* tends to discretize continuous attribute c into many narrow intervals and hence reduce the generalization ability. The rationale for discretizing continuous attribute c is as follows.

From Y_1 to $Y_{l'}$, we compute the β positive region $POS_\beta(Y_j)$ of Y_j in terms of X_i, that is $POS_\beta(Y_j) = \bigcup_\beta X_i$. Then all of the involved $X_i s$ will form an interval ranging from the minimum value to the maximum value, which can be easily determined from the ordered subsets in $POS_\beta(Y_j)$. The above process can be expressed as:

Given X and Y, we are to classify all elements of set X_i into $POS_\beta(Y_j)$ one by one, then in $C(X_i, Y_j) \times 100\% = \beta_i, (i = 1, 2, \ldots, l)$ of the cases we would make a classification error. Based on the computation of misclassification rate we have:

$$X_i \subseteq_{\beta_i} Y_j, if \beta_i \leq \beta \tag{6}$$

Hence, c is divided into some intervals which are denoted as $S_1, S_2, \ldots, S_M$, $M \leq k$.

In applications, there are some cases that have to be considered:

1): If the decision attribute values $d_1, d_2, \ldots, d_t$ with respect to $x_r = x_{r+1} = \ldots = x_{r+t-1}, (1 \leq r \leq k)$ are different, the most frequent value d_{max} out of all the values of the decision attribute is taken as the decision attribute value with respect to these data.

2): If the decision attribute value corresponding to S_j is the same as that to S_{j+1}, the two intervals are merged.

3): If the obtained intervals still overfit the data, or in other words, M is not smaller enough than k, the generalization capability would be lower than expected. To further solve this problem, we introduce another parameter $0 \leq \alpha \leq 0.5$. If the decision attribute value corresponding to S_j is different from that to S_{j+1}, we calculate the classification error ratio α_j of interval S_{j+1} with respect to interval S_j, that is $C(S_j, S_{j+1})$. As these intervals are successive, we use the width of these intervals in stead of the frequency to calculate α_j. If $\alpha_j \leq \alpha$, the two intervals are merged.

The number of intervals can be changed by adjusting the values of α and β. Based on the above discussion, discretization of continuous features involves two steps as follows:

Frequency Step
Calculate classification error ratio β_i of the value set X_i if it is included in $POS_\beta(Y_j)$.

Width Step
Merge the divisiory intervals by calculating classification error ratio α_j.

The first step guarantees that the system has good distinguishing ability. The second step aims at reducing the number of intervals, when overfitting occurs, in order to enhance the robustness to noise data. The algorithm for discretizing continuous attributes is:

DiscretVPRS

Input: A group of records with continuous attribute c. The items of the data are numbered from Lp to Tp. The ith record's value of attribute c is x_i, the corresponding decision attribute value is d_i. $Y_{d_i} = \{x_r | f(x_r,d)=d_i\}$. The positive region is $POS_\beta(Y_{d_i})$. The error ratio α, β are assigned.

1: Initialize $i = Lp$;

2: Partition the ith record into the positive region;

3: Compare x_i with x_{i+1}. If x_i is equal to x_{i+1}, $i++$, goto 3; else find d_{max} by comparing the decision attribute values;

4: Calculate the partition error ratio β_i. If $i < Tp$, goto 3; else goto 5;

5: Find β_{min}. If $\beta_{min} \leq \beta$, x_r corresponding to β_{min} is adopted as the cut point, and it will partition the whole range under consideration into two discrete intervals S_j, S_{j+1}.

6: Calculate α_j. If $\alpha_j < \alpha$ or the value of the decision attribute corresponding to S_j is the same as that to S_{j+1}, the two intervals are merged into one. If $r = Tp$, goto 7, else assign $r + 1$ to i, goto 2;

7: Number these intervals with 0,1,2,.... and return.

Continuous attributes are discretized dynamically according to the decision attribute in this paper. In the aforementioned discretization process, β_i and α_j are calculated in terms of frequency and width respectively. The time consumed in discretization mostly depends on how many discrete intervals are obtained. In the worst situation, $m = k$, and the maximal degree of time cost is $O(k^2)$. The intervals or the number of discrete values can be changed by adjusting the values of parameter α and β in order to reduce the complexity and enhance the prediction accuracy of the trees. The discrete intervals can also be changed by choosing the values of α and β according to actual needs.

4   Experimental Comparisons of the Methods for Discretizing Continuous Attributes

The proposed method is tested on some databases below. The results are compared with that obtained by C4.5. The methods for building and pruning [13] decision trees are the same as that in C4.5. The databases used in this paper are listed in Table 1 and Table 2(Tr denotes the size of the train set. Te denotes the size of the test set. NCA denotes the number of continuous attributes. NDA denotes the number of decision attribute values).

Firstly, we use the databases in Table 1 (MLC) to test the method proposed in this paper. Assume that the values of α and β are 0.15, 0.5 respectively. The results are listed in Table 3. It shows that the sizes of the decision trees generated by DiscretVPRS are smaller than that by C4.5(Fig. 1) and the estimate accuracy is higher than that by C4.5 (Fig. 2) with respect to most databases. We use the databases in Table 2 and compare the results of DiscretVPRS with that of the method in paper[11]. The results are listed in Table 4. It shows that the classification accuracy of the decision trees built by the proposed method is higher than that reported in paper[11].

Table 1. Databases for experiment 1(MLC)

Name	Tr	Te	NCA	NDA
iris	150	50	4	3
crx	490	200	6	2
wine	118	60	13	3
Cars	261	131	7	3
breast	466	233	10	2
Australian	460	230	6	2
EchoCardiogram	87	44	6	2

Table 2. Databases for experiment 2(UCI)

Name	Tr	NCA	NDA
iris	150	4	3
glass	214	9	7
ecoli	336	7	8

Table 3. Comparison results of 1(MLC)

		C4.5		DiscretVPRS	
		size	errors	size	errors
iris	Tr	9	3 (2.0%)	7	3 (2.0%)
	Te	9	1 (2.0%)	7	2 (4.0%)
crx	Tr	58	24 (4.9%)	44	46 (9.4%)
	Te	58	35 (17.5%)	44	32 (16.0%)
wine	Tr	9	1 (0.8%)	11	1 (0.8%)
	Te	9	9 (15.0%)	11	3 (5.0%)
cars	Tr	35	1 (0.4%)	35	1 (0.4%)
	Te	35	3 (2.3%)	35	2 (1.5%)
breast	Tr	29	6 (1.3%)	11	18 (3.9%)
	Te	29	15 (6.4%)	11	12 (5.2%)
Australian	Tr	58	30 (6.5%)	56	42 (9.1%)
	Te	58	30 (13.0%)	56	30 (13.0%)
Echoca-	Tr	9	15 (17.2%)	9	20 (23.0%)
diogram	Te	9	19 (43.2%)	9	14 (31.8%)

Table 4. Comparison results of 2(UCI)

Name	Error (DiscretVPRS)	Error(method in paper[11])
iris	2.0%	5.5%
glass	15.4%	34.1%
ecoli	16.1%	18.4%

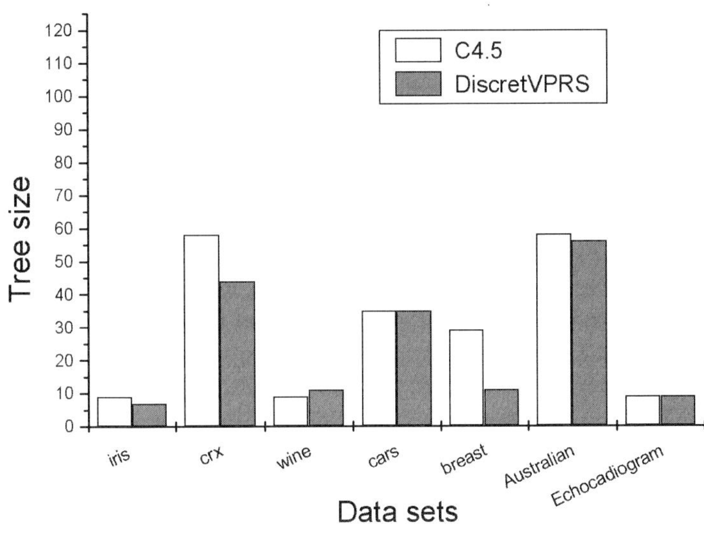

Fig. 1. The sizes of decision trees generated by DiscretVPRS and C4.5

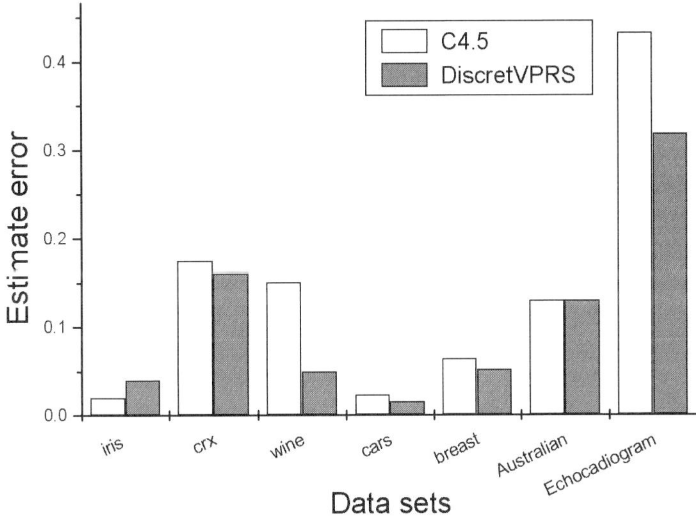

Fig. 2. The estimate accuracy of decision trees generated by DiscretVPRS and C4.5

5   Conclusions

A new method for discretizing continuous attributes based on the Variable Precision Rough Set model is introduced in this paper. The process of discretization involves two steps that first concern the number of records in an interval, called frequency, then the value range of an interval, called width. Both of the steps are based on the concept of β positive region in the VPRSM. No pre-determined M is needed. The classification and generalization capabilities can be promoted by adjusting the values of α and β. Compared to the previous methods for discretization of continuous attributes, the presented approach is easy to be implemented, for it simply needs to count how many records have been included in the positive intervals. Besides, this method is easy to understand from the Rough Set theory point of view, for the goal of classification is to obtain as much explicit information as possible. Experiments show that it is an effective method for discretizing continuous attributes.

References

1. Quinlan J.R.: Simplifying decision trees. J Man-Machine Studies 27(1987) 221-234
2. Hussain F., Liu H., Tan C.L. and Dash M.:Discretization: An Enabling Technique. Data Mining and Knowledge Discovery 6(2002) 393-423
3. Quinlan J.R.: Improved use of continuous attributes in C.45.Journal of Artificial Intelligence Research 4(1996) 77-90
4. Hung Son Nguyen:On efficient handling of continuous attributes in large data bases. Fundamenta Informaticae 48(2001) 61-81
5. Huan Liu,Rudy Setiono: Chi2: Feature Selection and Discretization of Numeric Attributes.Seventh International Conference on Tools with Artificial Intelligence (1995) 388-391
6. Se June Hong: Use of contextual information for feature ranking anddiscretization. IEEE Transactions on Knowledge and Data Engineering 9(1997)718-730
7. Pawlak Z.: Rough sets-theoretical aspects of reasoning about data.Dordrecht:Kluwer Academic Publishers (1991) 9-30
8. Jinmao Wei, Dao Huang: Rough set based decision tree.Proc. of the 4th World Congress on intelligence Control and Automation.Shanghai (2002) 426-431
9. Tao Zhi, Xu Baodong, Wang Dingwei: Knowledge reduction method based on decision attribute support degree. Journal of Northeastern University (Natural Science) 23(2002) 1025-1028
10. N guyen S H, N guyen H S: Some efficient algorithms for Rough Set methods. Proc. of the Conf. On Information Processing and Management of Uncertainty in Knowledge Based Systems (1996) 1451-1456
11. Zhao Jun,Wang Guoyin, WU Zhongfu,Tang Hong, Li Hua: Method of Data Discretization Based on Rough Set Theory . Mini- Micro Systems(Chinese) 25(2004) 60-64
12. Ziarko W: Variable precision rough set model. Journal of Computer and System Sciences 46(1993) 39-59
13. Eibe Frank: Pruning decision trees and Lists. Ph D thesis.Hamilton, New Zealand: University of Waikato, Department of Computer Science (2000) 160-345

On Variable Consistency Dominance-Based Rough Set Approaches

Jerzy Błaszczyński[1], Salvatore Greco[2], Roman Słowiński[1,3],
and Marcin Szeląg[1]

[1] Institute of Computing Science, Poznań University of Technology,
60-965 Poznań, Poland
`{jblaszczynski, rslowinski, mszelag}@cs.put.poznan.pl`
[2] Faculty of Economics, University of Catania,
Corso Italia, 55, 95129 Catania, Italy
`salgreco@unict.it`
[3] Institute for Systems Research, Polish Academy of Sciences,
01-447 Warsaw, Poland

Abstract. We consider different variants of Variable Consistency Dominance-based Rough Set Approach (VC-DRSA). These variants produce more general (extended) lower approximations than those computed by Dominance-based Rough Set Approach (DRSA), (i.e., lower approximations that are supersets of those computed by DRSA). They define lower approximations that contain objects characterized by a strong but not necessarily certain relation with approximated sets. This is achieved by introduction of parameters that control consistency of objects included in lower approximations. We show that lower approximations generalized in this way enable us to observe dependencies that remain undiscovered by DRSA. Extended lower approximations are also a better basis for rule generation. In the paper, we focus our considerations on different definitions of generalized lower approximations. We also show definitions of VC-DRSA decision rules, as well as their application to classification/sorting and ranking/choice problems.

1   Introduction

In this paper we consider different variants of the rough set approach, called Variable Consistency Dominance-based Rough Set Approaches (VC-DRSA). We relate these variants to other approaches presented so far that tend to relax the classical definition of the lower approximation. Lower approximation of set X is a set of objects x which certainly belong to X. Because of the required certainty of the membership of x to X, the condition of inclusion of x to the lower approximation of X is very strict. Upper approximation of X is a set of objects x that possibly belong to X. This means that any object x for which we can detect a relation to X is included in the upper approximation of X. Thus, classical definitions can lead to small lower approximations and large upper approximations. This is why approaches that detect objects having strong but not necessarily certain relation to X have been proposed. Such objects are included into an extended lower approximation. Historically, the first approach that involves extension of lower approximation was introduced by Ziarko [19] and called Variable Precision Rough Set (VPRS) approach. This approach extends classical rough set approach [9] that employs indifference relation to build granules of knowledge. The first definition that followed a similar intuition for Dominance-based Rough Set Approach (DRSA) [4] was presented by Greco et al. [5]. In both these approaches a test based on rough membership function [10] is performed to include objects into an extended lower approximation. Other approaches that extend classical rough set approach are based on the use of the Bayes factor [11] or the confirmation measure [7]. In this paper, however, we focus on approaches that extend DRSA and use different variants of the rough membership function. We present advantages and disadvantages of different variable consistency dominance-based approaches used so far and propose some new variants. Furthermore, we relate the approaches presented here to VPRS. We also show how rules are induced in VC-DRSA.

The paper is organized as follows. In section 2 we introduce elementary notions that are used in DRSA. Section 3 includes presentation of different variable consistency dominance-based approaches proposed so far and new definitions of VC-DRSA that have some desired properties. In section 4 we present decision rules from VC-DRSA perspective. We conclude the paper with a discussion.

2 Information Table, Pairwise Comparison Table and Approximated Sets

One of the basic concepts in DRSA is the information table, defined as a set of objects U, described by a set $G = \{g_1, g_2, \ldots, g_n\}$ of criteria and regular attributes. By a criterion we understand an attribute for which values are ordered according to a scale of preference. In a specific case, scale of preference may be given by a decision maker (DM). Otherwise, it can be interpreted as an order in the domain of attribute introduced into the problem as a part of domain knowledge. We distinguish gain and cost criteria. For gain criterion (e.g. comfort of a car) the greater the value of the criterion, the greater the preference of the DM. For cost criterion (e.g. price of a car) preference of the DM increases along with decrease of the value of such criterion. We distinguish cardinal and ordinal criteria. In case of cardinal criterion (defined on ratio or interval scale) it is possible to specify the degree of the intensity of preference for each difference of evaluations. For ordinal criteria we can only consider order of evaluations, since differences of evaluations are meaningless. By a regular attribute we understand an attribute for which values are not ordered according to preference.

If the set of attributes of the information table is divided into set of condition attributes C and set of decision attributes D, where $C \cup D = G$, then such a table is called decision table. Decision attributes introduce partition of the original set of objects U into decision classes. In order to analyze decision table within DRSA context, we need at least one condition criterion and at least one decision criterion. This requirement is necessary in order to build dominance cones in condition and decision evaluation space. Without loss of generality we will further assume that decision table includes only one decision criterion. Each value of this criterion, appearing in a decision table, represents assignment of an object to a single decision class.

Within DRSA three classes of problems are considered. These are classification (also called sorting), ranking and choice problems. When we solve a classification problem, our goal is to obtain a classifier that will enable us to interpret dependencies observed in analyzed data and to classify new objects. In case of ranking and choice problems, our goal is to obtain a ranking method. However, when the decision problem involves preferences of the DM, then the main goal of all three problems is to induce a preference model of the DM. In DRSA, the preference model is induced from preference information provided by the DM and stored in a decision table. For classification problems decision table is composed of objects assigned to pre-defined, preference-ordered decision classes $Cl_1, Cl_2, \ldots, Cl_m$. Order of decision classes results from complete order in the domain of decision criterion. For ranking or choice problems we start with decision table composed of pairwise comparisons of reference objects. This decision table is called pairwise comparison table (PCT). Each row of PCT corresponds to one pair of objects. Every pair is evaluated on the set of condition attributes. For cardinal criteria, pairs of objects may be characterized by either degrees of the intensity of preference (given by the DM) or simply differences of evaluations (which does not require involvement of the DM). For ordinal criteria and for regular attributes, ordered pairs of values are stored directly in PCT. We consider, in general, that each pair of objects is described by a graded comprehensive preference relation $\succ^h$, where $h \in H$. H being a set of numbercoded degrees of intensity of preference, such that $H \equiv (H^- \cup \{0\} \cup H^+)$, $H \subset [-1, 1]$ and $h \in H^+$ if and only if (iff) $-h \in H^-$ ([3]).

Let us now introduce some basic DRSA notions. Upward (downward) union of decision classes composed of class Cl_t and more (less) preferred classes will be denoted by $Cl_t^{\geq}$ ($Cl_t^{\leq}$). Upward (downward) union of graded comprehensive preference relations composed of relation $\succ^h$ and relations with higher (lower) grades of comprehensive preference will be denoted by $\succ^{\geq h}$ ($\succ^{\leq h}$). Since we want to present general VC-DRSA, that can be applied both to classification and ranking/choice problems, we use symbol X_i, $i \in \{1, 2, \ldots, m\}$ to refer to a single decision class or a single graded comprehensive preference relation, and symbol $X_i^{\geq}$ ($X_i^{\leq}$) to refer to upward (downward) union of decision classes or upward (downward) union of graded comprehensive preference relations. With respect to (w.r.t.) single criterion we will use symbols $\succeq$ and $\preceq$ to indicate weak preference and inverse weak preference, respectively. If $g_i \in G$ is a gain (cost) criterion, then $g_i(x) \succeq g_i(y)$ means that $g_i(x)$ is greater (smaller) than $g_i(y)$.

In order to define rough approximations of unions $X_i^{\geq}$ and $X_i^{\leq}$, we need the concept of dominance relation w.r.t. a subset of condition attributes (criteria and regular attributes) $P \subseteq C$. In case of classification problems, object x is said to dominate object y w.r.t. $P \subseteq C$ ($x\,D_P\,y$) iff for each criterion $g_i \in P$ there is $g_i(x) \succeq g_i(y)$ and for each regular attribute $g_i \in P$ there is $g_i(x) = g_i(y)$.

For ranking and choice problems dominance is defined between pairs of objects (x, y) and (w, z). Furthermore, set P is seen as a union of three sets: P^N, P^O and P^A. These sets are composed of cardinal criteria, ordinal criteria and regular attributes, respectively. Pair (x, y) is said to dominate pair (w, z) w.r.t. $P \subseteq C$ iff at the same time dominance occurs w.r.t. P^N and P^O and indiscernibility occurs w.r.t P^A. For cardinal criteria two situations are possible. Firstly, if differences of evaluations are stored in PCT, then we have $(x, y) \, D_{P^N} \, (w, z)$ iff for each $g_i \in P^N$ there is $\delta_i(x, y) \succeq \delta_i(w, z)$, where $\delta_i(x, y) = g_i(x) - g_i(y)$. Secondly, if the DM expresses his/her preferences w.r.t. P^N in terms of the degrees of the intensity of preference, then we have $(x, y) \, D_{P^N} \, (w, z)$ iff for each $g_i \in P^N$ x is preferred to y at least as strongly as w is preferred to z. Precisely, "at least as strongly" means "in at least the same degree", i.e., for each $g_i \in P^N$ x is preferred to y in degree h_i, w is preferred to z in degree k_i and $h_i \geq k_i$. For the set of ordinal criteria $P^O \subseteq C$, dominance relation $(x, y) \, D_{P^O} \, (w, z)$ occurs iff for each $g_i \in P^O$ there is $g_i(x) \succeq g_i(w)$ and $g_i(y) \preceq g_i(z)$. For the set of regular attributes $P^A \subseteq C$, indifference relation $(x, y) =_{P^A} (w, z)$ occurs iff for each $g_i \in P^A$ there is $g_i(x) = g_i(w)$ and $g_i(y) = g_i(z)$.

We use dominance relation to define dominance cones in the space of condition attributes. For classification problem, given a set of condition attributes $P \subseteq C$ and object x, P-dominating set (positive dominance cone) is defined as $D_P^+(x) = \{y \in U : y \, D_P \, x\}$, while P-dominated set (negative dominance cone) is defined as $D_P^-(x) = \{y \in U : x \, D_P \, y\}$. For ranking or choice problem, we consider pairs of objects in analogous definitions: $D_P^+(x, y) = \{(w, z) \in U \times U : (w, z) \, D_P \, (x, y)\}$ and $D_P^-(x, y) = \{(w, z) \in U \times U : (x, y) \, D_P \, (w, z)\}$.

Dominance cones are building blocks used to define rough approximations of unions $X_i^{\geq}$ and $X_i^{\leq}$, which is described in the next section.

3   Variable Consistency Model of DRSA

One of the most important features of rough set approach is separation of certain and possible knowledge. In (VC-)DRSA this is achieved by defining lower and upper approximations of unions of decision classes $Cl_t^{\geq}$ and $Cl_t^{\leq}$ or unions of graded comprehensive preference relations $\succ^{\geq h}$ and $\succ^{\leq h}$. As mentioned before, these unions are denoted by $X_i^{\geq}$ and $X_i^{\leq}$. To unify the notation for classification and ranking/choice problems, we use symbols x and y to denote either single objects from simple decision table (classification) or pairs of objects from PCT (ranking/choice). This is done because both single objects and pairs of objects are points in multidimensional attribute space. The set of all objects from a simple decision table and the set of all pairs of objects from a PCT are denoted by U. Furthermore, in definitions presented in this section, $P \subseteq C$ is a subset of condition attributes and $|\cdot|$ denotes cardinality of a set. We also use symbol $X_{i-1}^{\leq}$ ($X_{i+1}^{\geq}$) to denote union composed of decision classes (classification) or comprehensive preference relations (ranking/choice), which are less (more) preferred than X_i.

Classical definitions of P-lower approximations, P-upper approximations and P-boundaries of $X_i^{\geq}$ and $X_i^{\leq}$ are the following:

$$\underline{P}(X_i^{\geq}) = \left\{ x \in U : D_P^+(x) \subseteq X_i^{\geq} \right\}, \ \underline{P}(X_i^{\leq}) = \left\{ x \in U : D_P^-(x) \subseteq X_i^{\leq} \right\} \tag{1}$$

$$\overline{P}(X_i^{\geq}) = \bigcup_{x \in X_i^{\geq}} D_P^+(x), \ \overline{P}(X_i^{\leq}) = \bigcup_{x \in X_i^{\leq}} D_P^-(x) \tag{2}$$

$$Bn_P(X_i^{\geq}) = \overline{P}(X_i^{\geq}) - \underline{P}(X_i^{\geq}), \ Bn_P(X_i^{\leq}) = \overline{P}(X_i^{\leq}) - \underline{P}(X_i^{\leq}) \tag{3}$$

In VC-DRSA conditions of inclusion to lower approximations are softened by introduction of consistency level parameter $l \in (0, 1]$, which controls consistency of approximations. In this way lower approximations are extended, because they can include objects which according to the classical definition would not enter the lower approximations. Below we present a survey of variable consistency approaches proposed so far and we analyze their advantages and disadvantages. Finally, we propose new definitions of lower approximations, which solve problems pointed out during analysis. We concentrate only on extended P-lower approximations $\underline{P}^l(X_i^{\geq})$ and $\underline{P}^l(X_i^{\leq})$. For each presented approach P-upper approximations and P-boundaries are defined in the same way:

$$\overline{P}^l(X_i^{\geq}) = U - \underline{P}^l(X_{i-1}^{\leq}), \ \overline{P}^l(X_i^{\leq}) = U - \underline{P}^l(X_{i+1}^{\geq}) \tag{4}$$

$$Bn_P^l(X_i^{\geq}) = \overline{P}^l(X_i^{\geq}) - \underline{P}^l(X_i^{\geq}), \ Bn_P^l(X_i^{\leq}) = \overline{P}^l(X_i^{\leq}) - \underline{P}^l(X_i^{\leq}) \tag{5}$$

The first variable consistency approach was presented in [5]. It involves the following definitions of P-lower approximations of $X_i^{\geq}$ and $X_i^{\leq}$:

$$\underline{P}^l(X_i^{\geq}) = \left\{ x \in X_i^{\geq} : \frac{|D_P^+(x) \cap X_i^{\geq}|}{|D_P^+(x)|} \geq l \right\} \tag{6}$$

$$\underline{P}^l(X_i^{\leq}) = \left\{ x \in X_i^{\leq} : \frac{|D_P^-(x) \cap X_i^{\leq}|}{|D_P^-(x)|} \geq l \right\} \tag{7}$$

According to the above definitions, extended P-lower approximation of considered union consists of those objects x from that union, for which consistency of dominance cone is sufficient (not smaller than l). Definitions (6) and (7) have the advantage that lower approximation of a union is composed of objects from that union only. The disadvantage of these definitions is that it is possible that some object x belongs to extended lower approximation of union $X_i^{\geq}$, while another object $y \in X_i^{\geq}$, dominating object x, does not belong to $\underline{P}^l(X_i^{\geq})$ (analogical situation is possible for $\underline{P}^l(X_i^{\leq})$). We call such a situation: *lack of monotonicity of membership to lower approximation*. It is presented in Fig. 1a. As we may see, $\underline{P}^{0.75}(X_i^{\geq})$ includes object b only, while $\underline{P}^{0.75}(X_{i-1}^{\leq})$ includes object g only.

196   J. Błaszczyński et al.

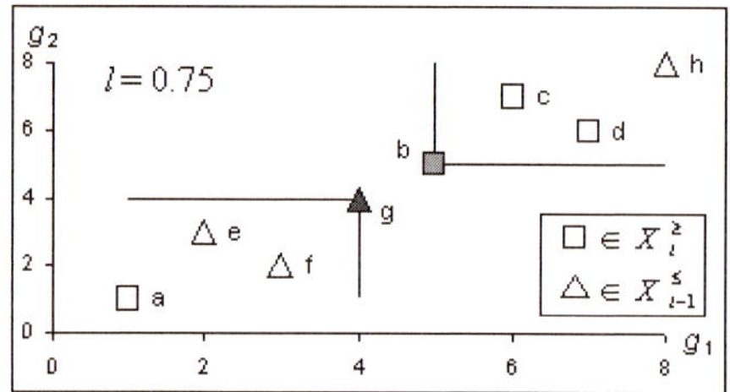

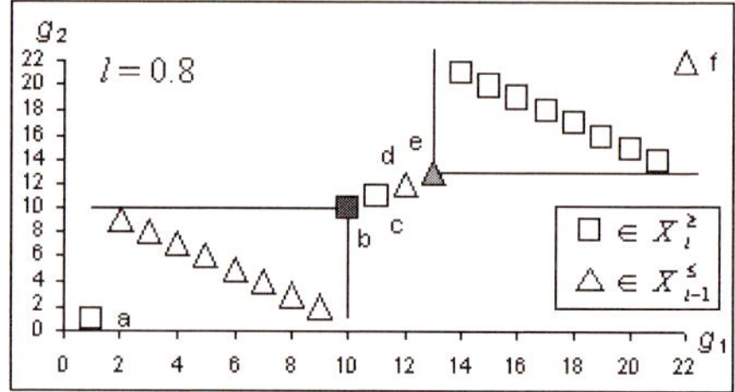

a) Extended P-lower approximations concordant with definitions (6) and (7).

b) Extended P-lower approximations concordant with definitions (6) and (7), with conditions $x \in X_i^\geq$ and $x \in X_i^\leq$ replaced by condition $x \in U$.

Fig. 1. Exemplary data sets described by two condition gain criteria g_1 and g_2. Filled figures correspond to objects from extended P-lower approximations (for $P = C$).

Objects c and d (e and f) do not belong to extended P-lower approximation, although they dominate (are dominated by) object b (object g), because there is object h (object a) which is inconsistent with objects b, c, d (e, f, g).

Slightly different definitions of extended lower approximations were presented in [3,14,16]. The only difference with respect to (6) and (7) is that conditions $x \in X_i^\geq$ and $x \in X_i^\leq$ are replaced by condition $x \in U$. Unfortunately, such definitions of extended lower approximations also suffer from the lack of monotonicity of membership to lower approximation. Moreover, it is possible that extended lower approximation of some union $X_i^\geq$ or $X_i^\leq$ includes (only) objects which are not from the approximated union. This problem is shown in Fig. 1b. As we may observe, lower approximation of union $X_i^\geq$ ($X_{i-1}^\leq$) is composed only of object e (object b), which does not belong to union $X_i^\geq$ ($X_{i-1}^\leq$).

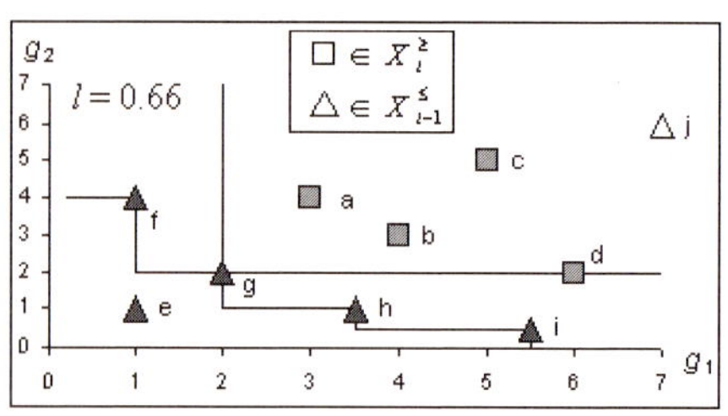

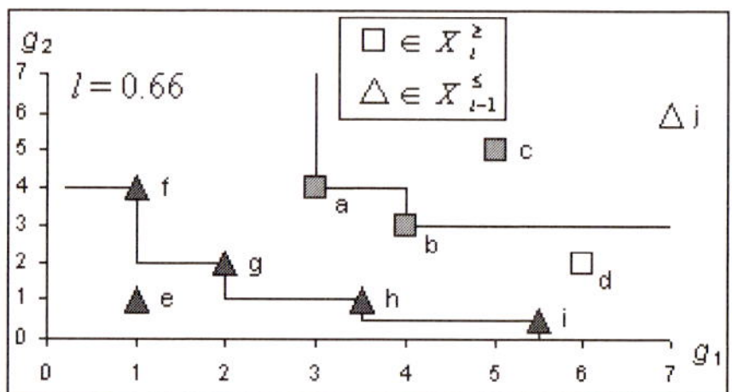

a) Extended P-lower approximations concordant with definition (9), used with definition (8).

b) Extended P-lower approximations concordant with definition (9), used with definition (10).

Fig. 2. Exemplary data sets described by two condition gain criteria g_1 and g_2. Filled figures correspond to objects from extended P-lower approximations (for $P = C$).

The next variable consistency approach was introduced in [15]. This approach involves auxiliary definitions of coefficients $\epsilon_P^{X_i^\geq}(x)$ and $\epsilon_P^{X_i^\leq}(x)$, which we call *robust consistency coefficients*. When considering union $X_i^\geq$ ($X_i^\leq$), for each object $x \in X_i^\geq$ ($x \in X_i^\leq$) robust consistency coefficient $\epsilon_P^{X_i^\geq}(x)$ ($\epsilon_P^{X_i^\leq}(x)$) is defined as follows:

$$\epsilon_P^{X_i^{\geq}}(x) = \max_{y \in D_P^-(x)} \frac{|D_P^+(y) \cap X_i^{\geq}|}{|D_P^+(y)|}, \quad \epsilon_P^{X_i^{\leq}}(x) = \max_{y \in D_P^+(x)} \frac{|D_P^-(y) \cap X_i^{\leq}|}{|D_P^-(y)|} \qquad (8)$$

According to [15], extended P-lower approximations of unions $X_i^{\geq}$ and $X_i^{\leq}$ are defined as:

$$\underline{P}^l(X_i^{\geq}) = \left\{ x \in X_i^{\geq} : \epsilon_P^{X_i^{\geq}}(x) \geq l \right\}, \quad \underline{P}^l(X_i^{\leq}) = \left\{ x \in X_i^{\leq} : \epsilon_P^{X_i^{\leq}}(x) \geq l \right\} \qquad (9)$$

The main advantage of the approach proposed in [15] is the monotonicity of membership to lower approximation, which means that if an object $x \in X_i^{\geq}$ belongs to $\underline{P}^l(X_i^{\geq})$, then each object $y \in X_i^{\geq}$ dominating x also belongs to $\underline{P}^l(X_i^{\geq})$. However, further analysis of the definition from [15] allows us to observe, that it is possible that some objects $x \in X_i^{\geq}$ belong to $\underline{P}^l(X_i^{\geq})$ only because they dominate other objects $y \in X_{i-1}^{\leq}$, for which consistency of positive dominance cone $D_P^+(y)$ is sufficiently large (not smaller than l). This is the case in Fig. 2a, for object d (dominating object g). Such situation should be avoided, as it may cause problems during rule induction process. In our example we can see that object g, causing inclusion of d to $\underline{P}^l(X_i^{\geq})$, does not belong to $\underline{P}^l(X_i^{\geq})$ and consistency of dominance cone $D_P^+(d)$ is not sufficient (only equal to 0.5).

In order to reduce drawbacks of variable consistency approaches presented so far, we introduce a new approach. It is in fact a modification of approach presented in [15]. We keep definition (9) of extended P-lower approximations of unions $X_i^{\geq}$ and $X_i^{\leq}$, but change auxiliary definition (8) for $\epsilon_P^{X_i^{\geq}}(x)$ and $\epsilon_P^{X_i^{\leq}}(x)$ into the following:

$$\epsilon_P^{X_i^{\geq}}(x) = \max_{y \in D_P^-(x) \cap X_i^{\geq}} \frac{|D_P^+(y) \cap X_i^{\geq}|}{|D_P^+(y)|}, \quad \epsilon_P^{X_i^{\leq}}(x) = \max_{y \in D_P^+(x) \cap X_i^{\leq}} \frac{|D_P^-(y) \cap X_i^{\leq}|}{|D_P^-(y)|} \qquad (10)$$

As in [15], our new approach assures monotonicity of membership to lower approximation with respect to objects belonging to $X_i^{\geq}$ and $X_i^{\leq}$, respectively. It also guarantees that extended P-lower approximation of a union $X_i^{\geq}$ $(X_i^{\leq})$ will include objects belonging to that union only. Moreover, we solved the problem mentioned during analysis of the approach presented in [15], which is shown in Fig. 2b - now object d does not belong to the extended P-lower approximation of union $X_i^{\geq}$, while objects a, b and c still belong to this approximation.

To complete the review, let us remind three basic properties of set approximations defined for rough sets in [9].

1. *Rough inclusion* $\underline{P}(X) \subseteq X \subseteq \overline{P}(X)$
2. *Complementarity* $\forall_{X \subseteq U} \ \underline{P}(X) = U - \overline{P}(U - X)$
3. *Monotonicity of the accuracy of approximation*
   $\forall_{X \subseteq U} \forall_{P,R \subseteq C, P \subseteq R} \ \underline{P}(X) \subseteq \underline{R}(X)$ and $\overline{R}(X) \subseteq \overline{P}(X)$

Within DRSA [4] above properties hold considering unions $X_i^{\geq}$ and $X_i^{\leq}$ as set X. Presented here approaches satisfy property 1 (apart from approach presented in [3,14,16]) and 2 (according to definition 4). Property 3 does not hold in any of these approaches. However, this is also the case for other rough set models such as those presented in [7], [11], [12] and [19]. Property 3 requires that with the finer granularity resulting from enlarging the set of considered attributes, lower approximations are not reduced and upper approximations are not enlarged. In VC-DRSA, lower approximations are extended by objects that are strongly related to approximated sets but we are not necessarily certain about their membership to these sets. Required certainty of membership to approximated set is controlled by consistency level l. In approaches discussed here, the certainty of membership is expressed as rough membership function [10], that is not monotone with respect to finer granularity. The value of membership function could decrease when the set of attributes is enlarged. The consequence is that, with a finer granularity, an object previously assigned to the lower approximation could be excluded or an object, previously excluded from the upper approximation, could be included. To satisfy property 3 one can consider the following definition of $\epsilon_P^{X_i^{\geq}}(x)$ and $\epsilon_P^{X_i^{\leq}}(x)$:

$$\epsilon_P^{X_i^{\geq}} = \max_{y \in D_T^-(x) \cap X_i^{\geq}, T \subseteq P} \frac{|D_T^+(y) \cap X_i^{\geq}|}{|D_T^+(y)|}, \quad \epsilon_P^{X_i^{\leq}} = \max_{y \in D_T^+(x) \cap X_i^{\leq}, T \subseteq P} \frac{|D_T^-(y) \cap X_i^{\leq}|}{|D_T^-(y)|} \tag{11}$$

However, computation of extended lower approximations according to definition (9), used together with definition (11), is an NP-hard problem, similar to induction of a set of decision rules or computation of reducts.

4   Induction of Decision Rules in VC-DRSA

Computation of approximations of unions $X_i^{\geq}$ and $X_i^{\leq}$ constitutes the first step of dominance-based rough set analysis of a problem. The next step in this process is induction of decision rules. In this step information that is contained in approximations is generalized and thus transformed into knowledge. We define a decision rule for classification/sorting problem and ranking/choice problem. Decision rule is a logical statement of a simple form "*if* conditions *then* decision". It has different syntax depending on the mentioned above problems that it is defined for. The difference lies in how conditions and decision are defined. Thus, we define a *classification decision rule* and a *ranking decision rule*. However, to define decision rules consistently in the context of VC-DRSA, we need additional notions that are derived from approximations. Let us first note that each union $X_i^{\geq}$ has its complement $X_{i-1}^{\leq}$ and each union $X_i^{\leq}$ has its complement $X_{i+1}^{\geq}$. P-positive regions of unions $X_i^{\geq}$ and $X_i^{\leq}$ are defined as:

$$POS_P^l(X_i^{\geq}) = \bigcup_{x \in \underline{P}^l(X_i^{\geq})} D_P^+(x), \quad POS_P^l(X_i^{\leq}) = \bigcup_{x \in \underline{P}^l(X_i^{\leq})} D_P^-(x) \tag{12}$$

When considering object x, all objects belonging to granule of knowledge $D_P^+(x)$ $(D_P^-(x))$ are comparable (in the sense of dominance relation) to x. According to definition (12), positive region $POS_P^l(X_i^{\geq})$ $(POS_P^l(X_i^{\leq}))$ is composed of all objects that are comparable to objects that belong to $\underline{P}^l(X_i^{\geq})$ $(\underline{P}^l(X_i^{\leq}))$. In DRSA, rules are induced from three types of approximated sets: lower approximations (certain rules), upper approximations (possible rules) and boundaries (approximate rules). In the approach presented here, objects belonging to positive region $POS_P^l(X_i^{\geq})$ $(POS_P^l(X_i^{\leq}))$ are basis for induction of VC-DRSA decision rules for union $X_i^{\geq}$ $(X_i^{\leq})$. Let us note that the concept of positive region used here is similar to positive region proposed by Ślęzak and Ziarko [12]. Ślęzak and Ziarko define positive region as extended lower approximation in Variable Precision Rough Sets and Bayesian Rough Sets.

Basing on the definition of positive regions, we also define P-negative and P-boundary regions of approximated sets as the following:

$$NEG_P^l(X_i^{\geq}) = POS_P^l(X_{i-1}^{\leq}) - POS_P^l(X_i^{\geq}) \tag{13}$$

$$NEG_P^l(X_i^{\leq}) = POS_P^l(X_{i+1}^{\geq}) - POS_P^l(X_i^{\leq}) \tag{14}$$

$$BND_P^l(X_i^{\geq}) = U - POS_P^l(X_i^{\geq}) - NEG_P^l(X_i^{\geq}) \tag{15}$$

$$BND_P^l(X_i^{\leq}) = U - POS_P^l(X_i^{\leq}) - NEG_P^l(X_i^{\leq}) \tag{16}$$

A VC-DRSA decision rule $r_j^{X_i^{\geq}}$ assigning objects to union $X_i^{\geq}$ is meant to cover primarily examples from $\underline{P}^l(X_i^{\geq})$. Thus examples from $\underline{P}^l(X_i^{\geq})$ are the support of rule $r_j^{X_i^{\geq}}$, denoted by $supp(r_j^{X_i^{\geq}})$. Support of rule $r_j^{X_i^{\leq}}$ is defined analogously. Due to the properties of extended lower approximations, rule $r_j^{X_i^{\geq}}$ will probably also cover other objects from $POS_P^l(X_i^{\geq})$. Objects that are covered by rule $r_j^{X_i^{\geq}}$ but do not belong to $\underline{P}^l(X_i^{\geq})$ do not support the rule. Objects from the negative region $NEG_P^l(X_i^{\geq})$ can't be covered by rule $r_j^{X_i^{\geq}}$. We are certain that objects from $NEG_P^l(X_i^{\geq})$ have nothing in common with union $X_i^{\geq}$. Boundary region $BND_P^l(X_i^{\geq})$ is composed of objects for which we have failed to find enough evidence to include them in either $\underline{P}^l(X_i^{\geq})$ or $\underline{P}^l(X_{i-1}^{\leq})$. Objects from the boundary region, in general, also shouldn't be covered by the rule. However, in some cases, this constraint can be softened.

We have shown that positive, negative and boundary regions are important concepts from the perspective of VC-DRSA rules induction. Let us notice, that the following properties hold for these regions of unions $X_i^{\geq}$, $X_i^{\leq}$ and their complements $X_{i-1}^{\leq}$, $X_{i+1}^{\geq}$:

$$BND_P^l(X_i^{\geq}) = BND_P^l(X_{i-1}^{\leq}), \ BND_P^l(X_i^{\leq}) = BND_P^l(X_{i+1}^{\geq}) \tag{17}$$

$$NEG_P^l(X_i^{\geq}) \cap NEG_P^l(X_{i-1}^{\leq}) = \emptyset, \ NEG_P^l(X_i^{\leq}) \cap NEG_P^l(X_{i+1}^{\geq}) = \emptyset \tag{18}$$

The boundary region of approximated union and the boundary region of its complement are equal. This property seems natural since boundary regions consist of objects that we are uncertain to assign either to extended lower approximation of considered union or to extended lower approximation of its complement. Intersection of negative region of approximated union and negative region of its complement is an empty set. This is an important property from both rough set theory perspective and rule induction perspective. The negative region contains objects for which we are sure that they don't belong to considered union. It seems natural that negative regions of complementary unions should not have any common part.

Let us now define decision rules, first for classification/sorting problem and then for ranking/choice problem. In definition of decision rules, we use coefficient α that measures credibility of a rule. Credibility is defined as a ratio of objects that support given rule to all objects that are covered by this rule. We define VC-DRSA decision rules that assign objects to union $X_i^{\geq}$ or $X_i^{\leq}$, with credibility α, $l \leq \alpha \leq 1$.

$$if\ g_{i1}(x) \succeq r_{i1} \wedge \ldots \wedge g_{ip}(x) \succeq r_{ip} \wedge g_{ip+1}(x) = r_{ip+1} \wedge \ldots \wedge g_{iz}(x) = r_{iz}$$
$$then\ x \in X_i^{\geq}\ with\ credibility\ \alpha \quad (19)$$
$$if\ g_{i1}(x) \preceq r_{i1} \wedge \ldots \wedge g_{ip}(x) \preceq r_{ip} \wedge g_{ip+1}(x) = r_{ip+1} \wedge \ldots \wedge g_{iz}(x) = r_{iz}$$
$$then\ x \in X_i^{\leq}\ with\ credibility\ \alpha \quad (20)$$

$$if\ \delta_{i1}(x,y) \succeq r_{i1} \wedge \ldots \wedge \delta_{ik}(x,y) \succeq r_{ik} \wedge$$
$$g_{ik+1}(x) \succeq r_{ik+1} \wedge g_{ik+1}(y) \preceq s_{ik+1} \wedge \ldots \wedge g_{ip}(x) \succeq r_{ip} \wedge g_{ip}(y) \preceq s_{ip} \wedge$$
$$g_{ip+1}(x) = r_{ip+1} \wedge g_{ip+1}(y) = s_{ip+1} \wedge \ldots \wedge g_{iz}(x) = r_{iz} \wedge g_{iz}(y) = s_{iz}$$
$$then\ (x,y) \in X_i^{\geq}\ with\ credibility\ \alpha \quad (21)$$
$$if\ \delta_{i1}(x,y) \preceq r_{i1} \wedge \ldots \wedge \delta_{ik}(x,y) \preceq r_{ik} \wedge$$
$$g_{ik+1}(x) \preceq r_{ik+1} \wedge g_{ik+1}(y) \succeq s_{ik+1} \wedge \ldots \wedge g_{ip}(x) \preceq r_{ip} \wedge g_{ip}(y) \succeq s_{ip} \wedge$$
$$g_{ip+1}(x) = r_{ip+1} \wedge g_{ip+1}(y) = s_{ip+1} \wedge \ldots \wedge g_{iz}(x) = r_{iz} \wedge g_{iz}(y) = s_{iz}$$
$$then\ (x,y) \in X_i^{\leq}\ with\ credibility\ \alpha \quad (22)$$

In order to clarify the description, we distinguish two subsets of C. Namely, subset C^C composed of criteria and subset C^A composed of regular attributes. Furthermore, let us distinguish two subsets of C^C: C^N that includes cardinal criteria and C^O including ordinal criteria. Attributes $g_j, j \in \{i1, i2, \ldots, ip\}$ belong to C^C. Criteria $g_j, j \in \{i1, i2, \ldots, ik\}$ belong to C^N, while criteria $g_j, j \in \{ik+1, ik+2, \ldots, ip\}$ belong to C^O. Attributes $g_j, j \in \{ip+1, ip+2, \ldots, iz\}$ belong to C^A. Moreover, r_i and s_i are values from the domain of attribute g_i. Finally, $\delta_i(x,y)$ denotes either difference of evaluations or degree of the intensity of preference on criterion g_i, depending on problem formulation.

Induction of decision rules is a complex problem and many algorithms have been introduced to solve it. Examples of rule induction algorithms that were presented in the context of the rough set analysis are: by Grzymała-Busse [8], by Skowron [17], by Słowiński and Stefanowski [13], by Stefanowski [18]. Algorithms defined for dominance-based rough set approach are the following: by

Greco et al. [6], by Błaszczyński and Słowiński [1] and by Dembczyński et al. [2]. All these algorithms can be divided into three categories that reflect different induction strategies: generation of a minimal set of decision rules, generation of an exhaustive set of decision rules, generation of a satisfactory set of decision rules. Algorithms from the first category focus on describing objects from approximations by minimal number of minimal rules that are necessary to cover all the objects from the decision table. Algorithms from the second category generate all possible minimal decision rules. The third category includes algorithms that generate all possible minimal rules that satisfy some a priori defined requirements (e.g. maximal rule length).

5 Conclusions

In this paper we have presented several variants of variable consistency dominance-based rough set approach and analyzed their advantages and disadvantages. Among them there are some existing approaches and some new proposals which try to overcome drawbacks of the former ones. We have used notions of positive, negative and boundary regions of unions of decision classes $Cl_t^{\geq}$, $Cl_t^{\leq}$ or unions of graded comprehensive preference relations $\succ^{\geq h}$, $\succ^{\leq h}$. Further, we have investigated properties of defined regions. We have shown that extended lower approximations allows us to discover strong but not necessarily certain dependencies in the analyzed data. Finally, we defined decision rules for classification/sorting and ranking/choice problems that are induced from positive regions, created on the basis of extended lower approximations.

Acknowledgments

The first and the third author wish to acknowledge financial support from the Ministry of Education and Science (grant no. 3T11F 02127). The research of the second author has been supported by Italian Ministry of Education, University and Scientific Research.

References

1. J. Błaszczyński, R. Słowiński, *Incremental Induction of Decision Rules from Dominance-based Rough Approximations.* Electronic Notes in Theoretical Computer Science, **82**, 4, 2003.
2. K. Dembczyński, R. Pindur, R. Susmaga, *Generation of Exhaustive Set of Rules within Dominance-based Rough Set Approach.* Electronic Notes in Theoretical Computer Science, **82**, 4, 2003.
3. P. Fortemps, S. Greco, R. Słowiński, *Multicriteria decision support using rules that represent rough-graded preference relations*, 2005 (submitted).
4. S. Greco, B. Matarazzo, R. Słowiński, *Rough sets theory for multicriteria decision analysis.* European Journal of Operational Research, **129**, 1, 2001, pp. 1-47.

5. S. Greco, B. Matarazzo, R. Słowiński, J. Stefanowski, *Variable Consistency Model of Dominance-based Rough Sets Approach.* In: W. Ziarko, Y. Yao (eds.): *Rough Sets and Current Trends in Computing*, LNAI, vol. 2005, Springler-Verlag, Berlin 2001, pp. 170-181.

6. S. Greco, B. Matarazzo, R. Słowiński, J. Stefanowski, *An algorithm for induction of decision rules consistent with dominance principle.* In: W. Ziarko, Y. Yao (eds.): *Rough Sets and Current Trends in Computing*, LNAI, vol. 2005, Springler-Verlag, Berlin 2001, pp. 304-313.

7. S. Greco, B. Matarazzo, R. Słowiński, *Rough Membership and Bayesian Confirmation Measures for Parameterized Rough Sets.* In: D. Ślęzak, G. Wang, M. S. Szczuka, I. Düntsch, Y. Yao (eds.): *Proceedings RSFDGrC*, 2005, pp. 314-324.

8. J. W. Grzymala-Busse, *LERS - A system for learning from examples based on rough sets.* In: R. Słowiński (ed.): *Intelligent Decision Support. Handbook of Applications and Advances of the Rough sets Theory*, Kluwer Academic Publishers, 1992, pp. 3-18.

9. Z. Pawlak, *Rough sets.* International Journal of Information & Computer Sciences 11, 1982, pp. 341-356.

10. Z. Pawlak, A. Skowron, *Rough membership functions* In: R. R. Yaeger, M. Fedrizzi, and J. Kacprzyk (eds.): *Advances in the Dempster Shafer Theory of Evidence*, John Wiley & Sons, Inc., 1994, pp. 251-271.

11. D. Ślęzak, *Rough Sets and Bayes Factor* Transactions on Rough Sets III, 2005, pp. 202-229.

12. D. Ślęzak, W. Ziarko, *The investigation of the Bayesian rough set model.* International Journal of Approximate Reasoning, 40, 2005, pp. 81-91.

13. R. Słowiński, J. Stefanowski, *RoughDAS and RoughClass software implementations of rough sets approach.* In: R. Słowiński (ed.): *Intelligent Decision Support. Handbook of Applications and Advances of the Rough Sets Theory*, Kluwer Academic Publishers, 1992, pp. 445-456.

14. R. Słowiński, S. Greco, B. Matarazzo, *Mining decision-rule preference model from rough approximation of preference relation.* In: *Proc. 26th IEEE Annual International Conference on Computer Software & Applications*, Oxford, England, 2002, pp. 1129-1134.

15. R. Słowiński, S. Greco, *Inducing Robust Decision Rules from Rough Approximations of a Preference Relation.* In: L. Rutkowski, J. Siekmann, R. Tadeusiewicz, L.A. Zadeh (eds.): *Artificial Intelligence and Soft Computing*, LNAI, vol. 3070, Springer-Verlag, Berlin, Heidelberg, 2004, pp. 118-132.

16. R. Słowiński, S. Greco, B. Matarazzo, *Rough Set Based Decision Support.* Chapter 16 in: E. Burke, G. Kendall (eds.): *Introductory Tutorials on Optimization, Search and Decision Support Methodologies*, Kluwer Academic Publishers, Boston, 2005.

17. A. Skowron, *Boolean Reasoning for Decision Rules Generation.* In: H. J. Komorowski, Z. W. Ras *Proceedings of Methodologies for Intelligent Systems, 7th International Symposium*, ISMIS '93, Trondheim, Norway, pp. 295-305.

18. J. Stefanowski, *On rough set based approaches to induction of decision rules.* In: L. Polkowski, A. Skowron (eds.): *Rough Sets in Data Mining and Knowledge Discovery*, **1**, Physica-Verlag, Heidelberg, 1998, pp. 500-529.

19. W. Ziarko, *Variable Precision Rough Set Model.* J. Comput. Syst. Sci. 46(1), 1993, pp. 39-59.

Variable-Precision Dominance-Based Rough Set Approach

Masahiro Inuiguchi and Yukihiro Yoshioka

Department of Systems Innovation
Graduate School of Engineering Science, Osaka University
1-3, Machikaneyama, Toyonaka, Osaka 560-8531, Japan
inuiguti@sys.es.osaka-u.ac.jp, yoshioka@inulab.sys.es.osaka-u.ac.jp

Abstract. In order to treat the ordinality and the monotonicity between condition and decision attributes in decision tables, the dominance-based rough set approach (DRSA) has been developed. Moreover, to treat the hesitation in evaluation, the variable-consistency dominance-based rough set approach (VC-DRSA) has been proposed. However, the VC-DRSA is not always suitable to treat errors and outliers. In this paper, we propose a new approach called a variable-precision dominance-based approach (VP-DRSA) to be suitable for accommodating errors and outliers.

1 Introduction

Rough sets proposed by Pawlak [1] provide useful tools for reasoning from data. It is applied to various fields such as medicine, engineering, management, economy and so on. It is also useful in decision problems [2,3,4]. When the monotonicity between condition attributes and decision attributes is assumed and some inconsistency is included in the given data, results by the classical rough set approach are often inconsistent with the monotonicity. This is because the nominality of all condition and decision attributes are assumed in the classical rough set approach.

In order to overcome this inexpedience, the dominance-based rough set approach (DRSA) has been proposed by Greco et al. [3,4]. DRSA can treat ordinal condition and decision attributes as well as nominal ones so that the results are inconsistent with the monotonicity. Nevertheless, when a given data includes strong inconsistency, lower approximations become very small and then, we may not obtain useful results.

Some sources of the inconsistency are conceivable: (1) hesitation in evaluation of decision attribute values, (2) errors in recording, measurement and observation, (3) missing condition attributes related to the evaluation of decision attribute values, and so on. To treat the hesitation, the variable-consistency dominance-based rough set approach (VC-DRSA) [5,4] has been proposed. However, to treat errors and missing condition attributes, as far as the authors know, no approach has proposed, so far.

In this paper, we propose an approach to treat errors and missing condition attributes in the frame work of DRSA. For this purpose, we introduce the

S. Greco et al. (Eds.): RSCTC 2006, LNAI 4259, pp. 203–212, 2006.

Table 1. A decision table of student evaluation

Student	Mathematics	Literature	Passing Status
S1	Excellent	Very Good	Yes
S2	Excellent	Medium	Yes
S3	Very Good	Very Good	No
S4	Very good	Good	Yes
S5	Very Good	Bad	Yes
S6	Very Good	Utterly Bad	No
S7	Good	Excellent	Yes
S8	Medium	Excellent	Yes
S9	Medium	Bad	Yes
S10	Bad	Medium	No
S11	Bad	Very Bad	No
S12	Very Bad	Very Bad	No
S13	Very Bad	Utterly Bad	No
S14	Utterly Bad	Medium	No
S15	Utterly Bad	Bad	No
S16	Utterly Bad	Very Bad	No
S17	Utterly Bad	Utterly Bad	No

idea of variable precision rough set approach proposed by Ziarko [6]. Therefore, the proposed approach is called the variable-precision dominance-based rough set approach (VP-DRSA). Corresponding to lower and upper approximations, positive and non-negative regions are defined. Then we define variable-precision dominance-based rough sets as pairs of positive and non-negative regions and examine their properties. Moreover, we show differences among DRSA, VC-DRSA and VP-DRSA using a simple numerical example.

This paper is organized as follows. In Section 2, we review DRSA and VC-DRSA. Using a simple example, we show the inexpediences of DRSA and VC-DRSA. We emphasize that DRSA and VC-DRSA do not always work well when given decision tables include outliers. In order to treat outliers properly, we propose VP-DRSA in Section 3. The properties of positive and non-negative regions in VP-DRSA are investigated. The proposed VP-DRSA is applied to the simple example to show how it analyzes the example appropriately. Finally concluding remarks are given in Section 4.

2   Dominance-Based Rough Set Approach

2.1   Decision Table with Dominance Relations

Consider a decision table $\mathcal{T} = \langle U, C \cup \{d\}, V, \rho \rangle$ shown in Table 1. A decision table $\mathcal{T}$ is characterized by an object set U, a condition attribute set C and a decision attribute d, an attribute value set $V = \bigcup_{a \in C \cup \{d\}} V_a$ (V_a is a set of all values of attribute a) and an information function $\rho : U \times C \cup \{d\} \rightarrow V$. In Table 1, we have $U = \{S1, S2, \ldots, S17\}$, $C = \{\text{Mathematics } (Math), \text{Literature } (Lit)\}$,

$d =$ Passing Status (PS) and $V = \{$Utterly Bad (UB), Very Bad (VB), Bad (B), Medium (M), Good (G), Very Good (VG), Excellent (E), Yes (Y), No (N)$\}$. The information function ρ is characterized by the table so that we know, for example, $\rho(\text{S2}, Math) = \text{E}$ and $\rho(\text{S11}, PS) = \text{N}$.

In cases such as Table 1, we assume that the better condition attribute values are, the better the decision value is. Namely, in Table 1, we assume a student having better evaluations in $Math$ and Lit, he/she can have a better value in PS. However, an inconsistency with this monotonicity is found in Table 1. For example, an inconsistency is found in evaluation between S3 and S9. S3 takes much better evaluations in $Math$ and Lit but a worse result in PS than S9. In cases when inconsistencies are included in given decision tables, the results of the classical rough set approach are often inconsistent with the monotonicity, too. To overcome this inexpedience, the dominance-based rough set approach (DRSA) has been proposed by Greco et al. [3,4]. In DRSA, we can treat nominal and ordinal condition attributes at the same time but in this paper, for the sake of simplicity, we consider a case that all condition attributes are ordinal. By this simplification, we do not loose the essence of the proposed approach.

2.2   DRSA

Let Cl_k, $k = 1, 2, \ldots, n$ be decision classes. Namely, to each decision attribute value v_{d_k}, we define $Cl_k = \{x \in U : \rho(x, d) = v_{d_k}\}$. We assume a total order for decision attribute values such that $v_{d_1} \prec v_{d_2} \prec \cdots \prec v_{d_n}$, where $v_{d_k} \prec v_{d_j}$ means that v_{d_j} is better than v_{d_k}. According to this total order we write $Cl_1 \prec Cl_2 \prec \cdots \prec Cl_n$. We also assume a dominance relation on condition attribute values. A dominance relation with respect to condition attribute p is denoted by $\succ_p$ and "$v_1 \succ_p v_2$" means that v_1 dominates (is better than) v_2. In Table 1, we have N $\prec$ Y for decision attribute and E $\succ_p$ VG $\succ_p$ G $\succ_p$ M $\succ_p$ B $\succ_p$ VB $\succ_p$ UB $(p = Math, Lit)$ for condition attributes.

In order to reflect the weak order and dominance relations, the following upward and downward unions of decision classes are considered:

$$Cl_t^{\geq} = \bigcup_{s \geq t} Cl_s, \qquad Cl_t^{\leq} = \bigcup_{s \leq t} Cl_s. \qquad (1)$$

Then, we have

$$Cl_1^{\geq} = Cl_n^{\leq} = U, \qquad Cl_1^{\leq} = Cl_1, \qquad Cl_n^{\geq} = Cl_n, \qquad (2)$$

$$Cl_t^{\geq} = U - Cl_{t-1}^{\leq}, \qquad Cl_t^{\leq} = U - Cl_{t+1}^{\geq}, \qquad (3)$$

where we define $Cl_0^{\leq} = Cl_{n+1}^{\geq} = \emptyset$ so that the second equalities are valid for $t = 1, 2, \ldots, n$.

On the other hand, using dominance relations on condition attribute values, a dominance relation between objects with respect to a set of condition attributes $P \subseteq C$ is defined by

$$x D_P y \Leftrightarrow \rho(x, p) \succeq_p \rho(y, p) \text{ for all } p \in P, \qquad (4)$$

where $v_1 \succeq_p v_2$ if and only if $v_1 \succ_p v_2$ or $v_1 = v_2$. Then, given $P \subseteq C$ and $x \in U$, we define

$$D_P^+(x) = \{y \in U : yD_px\}, \qquad D_P^-(x) = \{y \in U : xD_py\}. \tag{5}$$

Given $P \subseteq C$, P-lower and P-upper approximations of $Cl_t^{\geq}$ and $Cl_t^{\leq}$ are defined as follows:

$$\underline{P}(Cl_t^{\geq}) = \{x \in U : D_P^+(x) \subseteq Cl_t^{\geq}\}, \quad \overline{P}(Cl_t^{\geq}) = \bigcup\{D_p^+(x) : x \in Cl_t^{\geq}\}, \tag{6}$$

$$\underline{P}(Cl_t^{\leq}) = \{x \in U : D_P^-(x) \subseteq Cl_t^{\leq}\}, \quad \overline{P}(Cl_t^{\leq}) = \bigcup\{D_p^-(x) : x \in Cl_t^{\leq}\}. \tag{7}$$

Using those upper and lower approximations, decision tables with dominance relations can be analyzed in the same way as the classical rough set approach. The properties of P-upper and P-lower approximations are shown in Greco et al. [3,4]. Some of them are shown as follows:

$$\underline{P}(Cl_t^{\geq}) \subseteq Cl_t^{\geq} \subseteq \overline{P}(Cl_t^{\geq}), \qquad \underline{P}(Cl_t^{\leq}) \subseteq Cl_t^{\leq} \subseteq \overline{P}(Cl_t^{\leq}). \tag{8}$$

Moreover, when D_p is reflexive and transitive, we have

$$\underline{P}(Cl_t^{\geq}) = \bigcup\{D_P^+(x) : D_P^+(x) \subseteq Cl_t^{\geq}\}, \tag{9}$$

$$\underline{P}(Cl_t^{\leq}) = \bigcup\{D_P^-(x) : D_P^-(x) \subseteq Cl_t^{\leq}\}. \tag{10}$$

By definition, upper approximations $\overline{P}(Cl_t^{\geq})$ and $\overline{P}(Cl_t^{\leq})$ can be represented by unions of $D_P^+(x)$ and $D_P^-(x)$, respectively. When D_p is reflexive and transitive, lower approximations $\underline{P}(Cl_t^{\geq})$ and $\underline{P}(Cl_t^{\leq})$ can be also represented by unions of $D_P^+(x)$ and $D_P^-(x)$, respectively, as shown in (9) and (10).

2.3 VC-DRSA

The inconsistency with the monotonicity can be understood as the decision maker's hesitation in evaluation. In order to treat the hesitation, Greco et al. [4,5] proposed the variable-consistency dominance-based rough set approach.

The degree of consistency of a fact that an object $x \in U$ belongs to $Cl_t^{\geq}$ with respect to $P \subseteq C$ is defined by

$$\alpha = \frac{|D_P^+(x) \cap Cl_t^{\geq}|}{|D_P^+(x)|}, \tag{11}$$

where $|X|$ stands for the cardinality of a set X. Then, given a consistency level $l \in [0, 1]$, a P-lower approximation of $Cl_t^{\geq}$ with respect to $P \subseteq C$ is defined as a set of objects $x \in Cl_t^{\geq}$ whose consistency degrees are not less than l, i.e.,

$$\underline{P}^l(Cl_t^{\geq}) = \left\{x \in Cl_t^{\geq} : \frac{|D_P^+(x) \cap Cl_t^{\geq}|}{|D_P^+(x)|} \geq l\right\}. \tag{12}$$

Similarly, a P-lower approximation of $Cl_t^{\leq}$ with respect to $P \subseteq C$ is defined by

$$\underline{P}^l(Cl_t^{\leq}) = \left\{ x \in Cl_t^{\leq} : \frac{|D_P^-(x) \cap Cl_t^{\leq}|}{|D_P^-(x)|} \geq l \right\}. \tag{13}$$

By using the duality, P-upper approximations of $Cl_t^{\geq}$ and $Cl_t^{\leq}$ with respect to $P \subseteq C$ can be defined by

$$\overline{P}^l(Cl_t^{\geq}) = U - \underline{P}^l(U - Cl_t^{\geq}) = U - \underline{P}^l(Cl_{t-1}^{\leq})$$
$$= Cl_t^{\geq} \cup \left\{ x \in Cl_t^{\leq} : \frac{|D_P^-(x) \cap Cl_t^{\geq}|}{|D_P^-(x)|} > 1 - l \right\}, \tag{14}$$

$$\overline{P}^l(Cl_t^{\leq}) = U - \underline{P}^l(U - Cl_t^{\leq}) = U - \underline{P}^l(Cl_{t+1}^{\geq})$$
$$= Cl_t^{\leq} \cup \left\{ x \in Cl_t^{\geq} : \frac{|D_P^+(x) \cap Cl_t^{\leq}|}{|D_P^+(x)|} > 1 - l \right\}. \tag{15}$$

P-lower and P-upper approximations in VC-DRSA satisfy

$$\underline{P}^l(Cl_t^{\geq}) \subseteq Cl_t^{\geq} \subseteq \overline{P}^l(Cl_t^{\geq}), \qquad \underline{P}^l(Cl_t^{\leq}) \subseteq Cl_t^{\leq} \subseteq \overline{P}^l(Cl_t^{\leq}). \tag{16}$$

This equation corresponds to (8). However, P-lower and upper approximations in VC-DRSA do not have properties corresponding to (9) and (10). Namely, P-lower and P-upper approximations are not always represented by unions of $D_P^+(x)$ and $D_P^-(x)$.

2.4   Inexpediences of DRSA and VC-DRSA

The following example demonstrates the inexpediences of DRSA and VC-DRSA. We show only P-lower approximations since P-upper approximations can be obtained as the complements of P-lower approximations (see Greco et al. [3,4]).

Example 1.   Consider a decision table given in Table 1. As described already, this decision table include inconsistencies. The data of S3 can be regarded as an outlier. This inconsistency may be caused by some error in recording or observation. Let us see what inexpediences can happen in such cases.

From Table 1, we have $Cl_Y^{\geq} = \{S1, S2, S4, S5, S7, S8, S9\}$ and $Cl_N^{\leq} = \{S3, S6, S10, S11, \ldots, S17\}$. Let $P = C$ then we obtain

$$\underline{P}(Cl_Y^{\geq}) = \{S1, S2, S7, S8\}, \quad \underline{P}(Cl_N^{\leq}) = \{S6, S10, S11, \ldots, S17\}.$$

Based on these results, we can induce the following decision rules:

- if $\rho(x, Math) \succeq_M$ E then $\rho(x, PS) \succeq_{PS}$ Y,
- if $\rho(x, Lit) \succeq_L$ E then $\rho(x, PS) \succeq_{PS}$ Y,
- if $\rho(x, Math) \preceq_M$ B then $\rho(x, PS) \preceq_{PS}$ N,
- if $\rho(x, Lit) \preceq_L$ VB then $\rho(x, PS) \preceq_{PS}$ N.

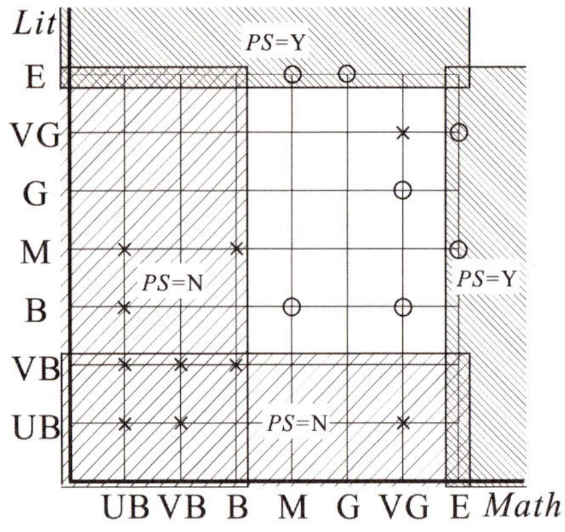

Fig. 1. Decision rules in DRSA

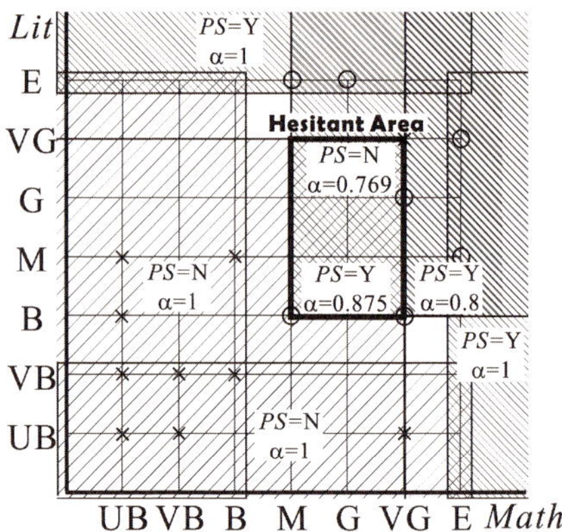

Fig. 2. Decision rules in VC-DRSA

where $\succeq_M$, $\succeq_L$, $\preceq_M$ and $\preceq_L$ denote $\succeq_{Math}$, $\succeq_{Lit}$, $\preceq_{Math}$ and $\preceq_{Lit}$, respectively. The obtained rules can be illustrated on the *Math-Lit* coordinate as in Figure 1. By the existence of an outlier, the P-lower approximation of $Cl_{\overline{Y}}^{\geq}$ becomes small. Thus decision rules induced from $\underline{P}(Cl_{\overline{Y}}^{\geq})$ covers only small areas. A relatively big area on the *Math-Lit* coordinate has no estimated values of PS.

Now let us apply VC-DRSA with $l = 0.75$. We have

$$\underline{P}^{l}(Cl_{\overline{Y}}^{\geq}) = \{S1, S2, S5, S7, S8, S9\}, \quad \underline{P}^{l}(Cl_{\overline{N}}^{\leq}) = \{S3, S6, S10, S11, \ldots, S17\}.$$

Based on these results, we can induce the following decision rules with consistency degrees (see Greco et al. [5] for reference):

- if $\rho(x, Math) \succeq_M$ E then $\rho(x, PS) \succeq_{PS}$ Y $[\alpha = 1]$,
- if $\rho(x, Math) \succeq_M$ VG and $\rho(x, Lit) \succeq_L$ B then $\rho(x, PS) \succeq_{PS}$ Y $[\alpha = 0.8]$,
- if $\rho(x, Lit) \succeq_L$ E then $\rho(x, PS) \succeq_{PS}$ Y $[\alpha = 1]$,
- if $\rho(x, Math) \succeq_M$ M and $\rho(x, Lit) \succeq_L$ B then $\rho(x, PS) \succeq_{PS}$ Y $[\alpha = 0.875]$,
- if $\rho(x, Math) \preceq_M$ VG and $\rho(x, Lit) \preceq_L$ VG then $\rho(x, PS) \preceq_{PS}$ N
$$[\alpha = 0.769],$$
- if $\rho(x, Math) \preceq_M$ B then $\rho(x, PS) \preceq_{PS}$ N $[\alpha = 1]$,
- if $\rho(x, Lit) \preceq_L$ VB then $\rho(x, PS) \preceq_{PS}$ N $[\alpha = 1]$.

These rules are illustrated in Figure 2. By VC-DRSA, we obtained more decision rules which covers large area on the *Math-Lit* coordinate. The conflictions occur in the shaded box with bold edges in Figure 2. This area implies the hesitant area for the decision maker in VC-DRSA. It is large because of the outlier. Moreover, note that $S4 \in Cl_{\overline{Y}}^{\geq}$ which takes better values in both *Math* and *Lit* than S5 and S9 is not included in $\underline{P}^{l}(Cl_{\overline{Y}}^{\geq})$ but S5 and S9 are. A similar strange result can be also found in the obtained decision rules. Namely, the second rule obtained from S5 has stronger condition than the forth rule obtained from S9 but the second takes smaller consistency level than the forth. Such strange results can happen in VC-DRSA applications to decision tables including outliers.

Finally, we note that, under the policy inducing only rules with stronger consistency, this strange result will never appear. This kind of modification in definitions of P-lower and upper approximations can be found in Słowiński and Greco [7]. At any rate, VC-DRSA is applicable to cases when the inconsistency comes from the hesitation in evaluation.

3 VP-DRSA

3.1 Definitions and Properties

In order to treat the inconsistency caused by errors in recording, measurement, observation, and so on, we propose a variable-precision dominance-based rough set approach (VP-DRSA). As a counterpart of consistency degree in VC-DRSA, we define the precision of $x \in Cl_t^{\geq}$ by

$$\beta = \frac{|D_P^-(x) \cap Cl_t^{\geq}|}{|D_P^-(x) \cap Cl_t^{\geq}| + |D_P^+(x) \cap Cl_{t-1}^{\leq}|}. \tag{17}$$

Let us interpret the precision β. For any $y \in D_P^-(x)$, from the dominance relation D_P, we may infer that $\rho(x, d) \succeq_d \rho(y, d)$, i.e., x is included in a decision class not worse than the decision class to which y belongs. Thus for any $y \in D_P^-(x) \cap Cl_t^{\geq}$, we may infer $x \in Cl_t^{\geq}$. Hence $|D_P^-(x) \cap Cl_t^{\geq}|$ is the number of objects which endorses $x \in Cl_t^{\geq}$. On the contrary, by the same consideration, for any $z \in D_P^+(x) \cap Cl_{t-1}^{\leq}$, we may infer $x \in Cl_{t-1}^{\leq} = U - Cl_t^{\geq}$. Hence $|D_P^+(x) \cap Cl_{t-1}^{\leq}|$ is the number of objects which endorses $x \notin Cl_t^{\geq}$. Other objects endorse neither $x \in Cl_t^{\geq}$ nor $x \notin Cl_t^{\geq}$. Therefore, β is the ratio of objects endorsing $x \in Cl_t^{\geq}$ to all objects endorsing $x \in Cl_t^{\geq}$ or $x \notin Cl_t^{\geq}$.

Then, given a precision level $l \in [0, 1]$, corresponding to the P-lower approximation of $Cl_t^{\geq}$, a P-positive region of $Cl_t^{\geq}$ with respect to $P \subseteq C$ is defined as a set of objects $x \in U$ whose degrees of precision are not less than l, i.e.,

$$POS_P^l(Cl_t^{\geq}) = \left\{ x \in U : \frac{|D_P^-(x) \cap Cl_t^{\geq}|}{|D_P^-(x) \cap Cl_t^{\geq}| + |D_P^+(x) \cap Cl_{t-1}^{\leq}|} \geq l \right\}. \tag{18}$$

Similarly, a P-positive region of $Cl_t^{\leq}$ with respect to $P \subseteq C$ is defined by

$$POS_P^l(Cl_t^{\leq}) = \left\{ x \in U : \frac{|D_P^+(x) \cap Cl_t^{\leq}|}{|D_P^+(x) \cap Cl_t^{\leq}| + |D_P^-(x) \cap Cl_{t+1}^{\geq}|} \geq l \right\}. \tag{19}$$

By using the duality, corresponding to P-upper approximations, P-non-negative regions of $Cl_t^{\geq}$ and $Cl_t^{\leq}$ with respect to $P \subseteq C$ can be defined by

$$NNG_P^l(Cl_t^{\geq}) = U - POS_P^l(U - Cl_t^{\geq}) = U - POS_P^l(Cl_{t-1}^{\leq})$$

$$= \left\{ x \in U : \frac{|D_P^-(x) \cap Cl_t^{\geq}|}{|D_P^-(x) \cap Cl_t^{\geq}| + |D_P^+(x) \cap Cl_{t-1}^{\leq}|} > 1 - l \right\}, \tag{20}$$

$$NNG_P^l(Cl_t^{\leq}) = U - POS_P^l(U - Cl_t^{\leq}) = U - POS_P^l(Cl_{t+1}^{\geq})$$

$$= \left\{ x \in U \;\middle|\; \frac{|D_P^+(x) \cap Cl_t^{\leq}|}{|D_P^+(x) \cap Cl_t^{\leq}| + |D_P^-(x) \cap Cl_{t+1}^{\geq}|} > 1 - l \right\}. \quad (21)$$

We can prove that P-positive and P-non-negative regions satisfy

$$POS_P^l(Cl_t^{\geq}) \subseteq NNG_P^l(Cl_t^{\geq}), \qquad POS_P^l(Cl_t^{\leq}) \subseteq NNG_P^l(Cl_t^{\leq}). \quad (22)$$

However, $POS_P^l(Cl_t^{\geq}) \subseteq Cl_t^{\geq}$, $Cl_t^{\geq} \subseteq NNG_P^l(Cl_t^{\geq})$, $POS_P^l(Cl_t^{\leq}) \subseteq Cl_t^{\leq}$ and $Cl_t^{\leq} \subseteq NNG_P^l(Cl_t^{\leq})$ are not always valid. This property is same as the classical variable precision rough sets [6].

When D_p is reflexive and transitive, we have

$$POS_P^l(Cl_t^{\geq}) = \bigcup \left\{ D_P^+(x) \;\middle|\; \frac{|D_P^-(x) \cap Cl_t^{\geq}|}{|D_P^-(x) \cap Cl_t^{\geq}| + |D_P^+(x) \cap Cl_{t-1}^{\leq}|} \geq l \right\}, \quad (23)$$

$$POS_P^l(Cl_t^{\leq}) = \bigcup \left\{ D_P^-(x) \;\middle|\; \frac{|D_P^+(x) \cap Cl_t^{\leq}|}{|D_P^+(x) \cap Cl_t^{\leq}| + |D_P^-(x) \cap Cl_{t+1}^{\geq}|} \geq l \right\}, \quad (24)$$

$$NNG_P^l(Cl_t^{\geq}) = \bigcup \left\{ D_P^+(x) \;\middle|\; \frac{|D_P^-(x) \cap Cl_t^{\geq}|}{|D_P^-(x) \cap Cl_t^{\geq}| + |D_P^+(x) \cap Cl_{t-1}^{\leq}|} > 1 - l \right\}, \quad (25)$$

$$NNG_P^l(Cl_t^{\leq}) = \bigcup \left\{ D_P^-(x) \;\middle|\; \frac{|D_P^+(x) \cap Cl_t^{\leq}|}{|D_P^+(x) \cap Cl_t^{\leq}| + |D_P^-(x) \cap Cl_{t+1}^{\geq}|} > 1 - l \right\}. \quad (26)$$

These properties correspond to (9) and (10) in DRSA. These properties are important to obtain decision rules with fewer conflictions.

Moreover when D_p is reflexive and transitive, we have

$$POS_P^l(POS_P^l(Cl_t^{\geq})) = NNG_P^l(POS_P^l(Cl_t^{\geq})) = POS_P^l(Cl_t^{\geq}), \quad (27)$$

$$POS_P^l(POS_P^l(Cl_t^{\leq})) = NNG_P^l(POS_P^l(Cl_t^{\leq})) = POS_P^l(Cl_t^{\leq}), \quad (28)$$

$$NNG_P^l(NNG_P^l(Cl_t^{\geq})) = POS_P^l(NNG_P^l(Cl_t^{\geq})) = NNG_P^l(Cl_t^{\geq}), \quad (29)$$

$$NNG_P^l(NNG_P^l(Cl_t^{\leq})) = POS_P^l(NNG_P^l(Cl_t^{\leq})) = NNG_P^l(Cl_t^{\leq}). \quad (30)$$

These properties are not always satisfied with P-lower and P-upper approximations in VC-DRSA but with P-lower and P-upper approximations in DRSA.

3.2   Application to Example 1

Let us apply VP-DRSA to Table 1 which is treated in Example 1. As discussed in Example 1, applications of DRSA and VC-DRSA to decision tables including outliers were not very successful. We will see how Table 1 is analyzed appropriately by the proposed VP-DRSA.

Let $l = 0.75$. Then we have

$$POS_P^l(Cl_Y^{\geq}) = \{S1, S2, S3, S4, S7, S8\}, \quad POS_P^l(Cl_N^{\leq}) = \{S6, S10, S11, \ldots, S17\}.$$

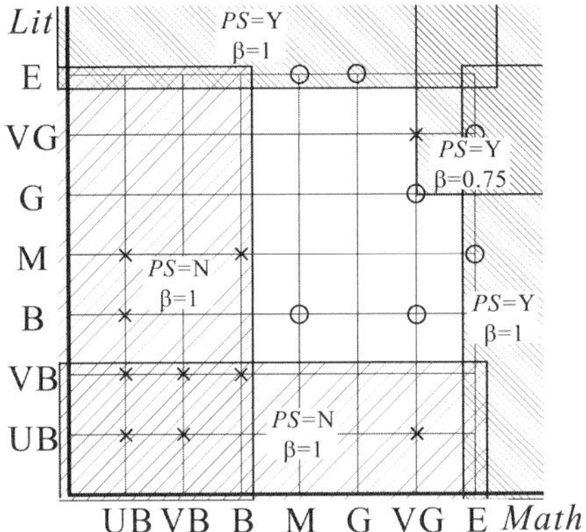

Fig. 3. Decision rules in VP-DRSA

Based on these results, we can induce the following decision rules with degrees of precision:

- if $\rho(x, Math) \succeq_M$ E then $\rho(x, PS) \succeq_{PS}$ Y $[\beta = 1]$,
- if $\rho(x, Math) \succeq_M$ VG and $\rho(x, Lit) \succeq_L$ G then $\rho(x, PS) \succeq_{PS}$ Y $[\beta = 0.75]$,
- if $\rho(x, Lit) \succeq_L$ E then $\rho(x, PS) \succeq_{PS}$ Y $[\beta = 1]$,
- $\rho(x, Math) \preceq_M$ B then $\rho(x, PS) \preceq_{PS}$ N $[\beta = 1]$,
- $\rho(x, Lit) \preceq_L$ VB then $\rho(x, PS) \preceq_{PS}$ N $[\beta = 1]$.

These rules are illustrated in Figure 3. In VP-DRSA, the decision attribute value of the outlier S3 which can be regarded as error data is changed to $PS =$Y by endorsements based on S4, S5 and S9. P-lower approximations in VP-DRSA become larger than that in DRSA. By the change of decision attribute value of S3, an additional decision rule with 0.75 precision is obtained from decision rules in DRSA.

By reduction of l to 0.6, S5 is included in the P-positive region of $Cl_{\overline{Y}}^{\leq}$ in VP-DRSA and another additional decision rule with 0.67 precision, "if $\rho(x, Math)$ $\succeq_M$ VG and $\rho(x, Lit) \succeq_L$ G then $\rho(x, PS) \succeq_{PS}$ Y $[\beta = 0.67]$" is obtained. Even if S5 is added to the P-positive region of $Cl_{\overline{Y}}^{\leq}$, no strange result is obtained. Namely, the precision of S4 is larger than that of S5. On the other hand, by augmentation of l to 0.8, the P-positive region of $Cl_{\overline{Y}}^{\leq}$ in VP-DRSA degenerates to that in DRSA.

4   Concluding Remarks

In this paper, we have proposed a variable-precision dominance-based approach (VP-DRSA) in order to treat inconsistent data caused by errors in recording, measurement, observation and so on. The properties of P-positive and P-non-negative regions are investigated. Inexpediences of DRSA and VC-DRSA are demonstrated using an example. We showed that these inexpediences may be solved by the proposed VP-DRSA.

As the classical variable precision rough set approach [6] is applied to cases when a condition attribute somewhat related to the decision attribute is missing, the proposed VP-DRSA may be applied to the same cases with dominance relations. As DOM-LEM [8], a dominance-based rule induction algorithm is proposed based on DRSA, an extended DOM-LEM algorithm can be designed based on VP-DRSA. Moreover, as the consistency degree used in VC-DRSA is useful for inducing a decision tree (see Giove et al. [9]), the precision used in VP-DRSA may be useful, too.

Acknowledgement

The authors wish to thank anonymous reviewers for their constructive comments. The first author acknowledges that this work has been partially supported by the Grant-in-Aid for Scientific Research (B) No. 17310098.

References

1. Pawlak, Z.: Rough sets, Int. J. Inform. Comp. Sci. **11**(5) (1982) 341–356.
2. Pawlak, Z., Słowiński, R.: Rough set approach to multi-attribute decision analysis, Eur. J. Oper. Res. **72**(3) (1994) 443–459.
3. Greco, S., Matarazzo, B., Słowiński, R.: The use of rough sets and fuzzy sets in MCDM, in: T. Gal, T.J. Stewart and T. Hanne (eds.), Multicriteria Decision Making: Advances in MCDM Models, Algorithms, Theory, and Applications, Kluwer Academic Publishers, Boston (1999) 14.1–14.59.
4. Greco, S., Matarazzo, B., Słowiński, R.: Decision Rule Approach, in: J. Figueira, S. Greco and M. Ehrgott (eds.), Multiple Criteria Decision Analysis, Springer-Verlag, New York (2005) 507–561.
5. Greco, S., Matarazzo, B., Słowiński, R., Stefanowski, J.: Variable consistency model of dominance-based rough set approach, in W. Ziarko, Y. Yao (eds.) Rough Sets and Current Trends in Computing, LNAI 2005, Springer-Verlag, Berlin, (2001) 170–181.
6. Ziarko, W.: Variable precision rough sets model, Journal of Computer and Systems Sciences **46**(1) (1993) 39–59.
7. Słowiński, R., Greco, S.: Inducing robust decision rules from rough approximations of a preference relation, in L. Rutkowski, J. Siekmann, R. Tadeusiewicz, L.A. Zadeh (eds.) Artificial Intelligence and Soft Computing, LNAI 3070, Springer-Verlag, Berlin, (2004) 118–132.
8. Greco, S., Matarazzo, B., Słowiński, R., Stefanowski, J.: An algorithm for induction of decision rules consistent with the dominance principle, in W. Ziarko, Y. Yao (eds.) Rough Sets and Current Trends in Computing, LNAI 2005, Springer-Verlag, Berlin, (2001) 304–313.
9. Giove, S., Greco, S., Matarazzo, B., Słowiński, R.: Variable consistency monotonic decision trees, in J.J. Alpigini, J.F. Peters, A. Skowron, N. Zhong (eds.) Rough Sets and Current Trends in Computing, LNAI 2475, Springer-Verlag, Berlin, (2002) 247–254.

Applying Rough Sets to Data Tables Containing Imprecise Information Under Probabilistic Interpretation

Michinori Nakata[1] and Hiroshi Sakai[2]

[1] Faculty of Management and Information Science,
Josai International University
1 Gumyo, Togane, Chiba, 283-8555, Japan
nakatam@ieee.org
[2] Department of Mathematics and Computer Aided Sciences,
Faculty of Engineering, Kyushu Institute of Technology,
Tobata, Kitakyushu, 804-8550, Japan
sakai@mns.kyutech.ac.jp

Abstract. Rough sets are applied to data tables containing imprecise information under probabilistic interpretation. A family of weighted equivalence classes is obtained, in which each equivalence class is accompanied by the probabilistic degree to which it is an actual one. By using the family of weighted equivalence classes we can derive a lower approximation and an upper approximation. The lower approximation and the upper approximation coincide with those obtained from methods of possible worlds.

Keywords: Rough sets, Imprecise information, Lower and upper approximations.

1   Introduction

Rough sets proposed by Pawlak [15] play a significant role in the field of knowledge discovery and data mining. The framework of rough sets has the premise that data tables consist of perfect information. However, there ubiquitously exists imperfect information containing imprecision and uncertainty in the real world [14]. Under these circumstances, it has been investigated to apply rough sets to data tables containing imprecise information represented by a missing value, an or-set, a possibility distribution etc [1,2,3,6,7,8,9,10,11,12,16,17,18,19,20]. The methods are broadly separated into three ways. The first method is one based on possible worlds [16,17]. In the method, a data table is divided into possible tables that consist of precise values. Each possible table is dealt with in terms of the conventional methods of rough sets to data tables consisting of precise information and then the results from the possible tables are aggregated. The second method is to use assumptions on indiscernibility of missing values [1,2,6,7,8,9,19,20]. Under the assumptions, we can obtain a binary relation for indiscernibility of

S. Greco et al. (Eds.): RSCTC 2006, LNAI 4259, pp. 213–223, 2006.

objects. To the binary relation the conventional methods of rough sets are applied. The third method directly deals with imprecise values under extending the conventional method of rough sets [10, 11, 12, 20]. In the method, imprecise values are dealt with probabilistically or possibilistically [10, 11, 12, 20] and the conventional methods are probabilistically or possibilistically extended. A degree for indiscernibility between any values is calculated.

For the first method, the conventional methods that are already established are applied to each possible table. Therefore, there is no doubt for correctness of the treatment. However, the method has difficulties for knowledge discovery at the level of a set of possible values, although it is suitable for finding knowledge at the level of possible values. This is because the number of possible tables exponentially increases as the number of imprecise attribute values increases.

For the second method, assumptions are used for indiscernibility between a missing value and an exact value and between missing values. One assumption is that a missing value and an exact value are indiscernible with each other [6, 7, 8, 9]. Another assumption is that indiscernibility is directional [1, 2, 19, 20]. Each missing value is discernible with any exact values, whereas each exact value is indiscernible with any missing value, under indiscernibility or discernibility between missing values. In the method, it is not clarified why the assumptions are compromise.

For the third method, first using implication operators, an inclusion degree was calculated between indiscernible sets, which are not an equivalence class, for objects [20]. The correctness criterion is that any extended method must give the same results as the method of possible worlds at the level of possible values [10]. This criterion is commonly used in the field of databases handling imprecise information [5, 4, 21]. Nakata and Sakai have shown that the results in terms of implication operators do not satisfy the correctness criterion and has proposed the method that satisfies the correctness criterion [10, 11, 12]. However, the proposed method has difficulties for definability, because approximations are defined by constructing sets from singletons, where equivalence classes are not used. To overcome the difficulties, the concept of equivalence classes must be extended probabilistically. We introduce weighted equivalence classes in this paper and show how weighted equivalence classes are used to data tables containing imprecise information under probabilistic interpretation[1].

In Section 2, we briefly address the conventional methods of rough sets to data tables containing precise information. In Section 3, methods of possible worlds are mentioned. In the methods, a data table containing imprecise values is divided into possible tables. The conventional methods of rough sets to precise information are applied to each possible table and then the results from the possible tables are aggregated. In Section 4, an extended method of rough sets to data tables containing imprecise values probabilistically interpreted are described in terms of weighted equivalence classes. In Section 5, we present conclusions.

---

[1] See [13] for possibilistic treatment.

2   Rough Sets to Precise Information

In data table t consisting of set of attributes $\mathcal{A}(= \{A_1, \ldots, A_n\})$, indiscernibility relation $IND(X)$ on subset $X \subseteq \mathcal{A}$ of attributes is,

$$IND(X) = \{(o, o') \in t \times t \mid \forall A_i \in X \ \ o[A_i] = o'[A_i]\},$$

where $o[A_i]$ and $o'[A_i]$ denote values of attribute A_i for objects o and o', respectively. Obviously, $IND(X)$ is an equivalence relation. Family $\mathcal{E}(X)$ $(= \{E(X)_o \mid o \in t\})$ of equivalence classes is obtained from the indiscernibility relation, where $E(X)_o$ is the equivalence class containing object o and is expressed in $E(X)_o = \{o' \mid (o, o') \in IND(X)\}$. All equivalence classes obtained from the indiscernibility relation do not cover with each other. This means that the objects are uniquely partitioned.

Using equivalence classes, lower approximation $\underline{Apr}(Y, X)$ and upper approximation $\overline{Apr}(Y, X)$ of $\mathcal{E}(Y)$ by $\mathcal{E}(X)$ are,

$$\underline{Apr}(Y, X) = \{E(X) \mid \exists E(Y) \ E(X) \subseteq E(Y)\},$$
$$\overline{Apr}(Y, X) = \{E(X) \mid \exists E(Y) \ E(X) \cap E(Y) \neq \emptyset\},$$

where $E(X) \in \mathcal{E}(X)$ and $E(Y) \in \mathcal{E}(Y)$ are equivalence classes on sets X and Y of attributes, respectively. These formulas express approximations in terms of a family of equivalence classes. When we express the approximations in terms of a set of objects, the following expressions are used:

$$\underline{apr}(Y, X) = \{o \mid o \in E(X) \wedge \exists E(Y) \ E(X) \subseteq E(Y)\},$$
$$\overline{apr}(Y, X) = \{o \mid o \in E(X) \wedge \exists E(Y) \ E(X) \cap E(Y) \neq \emptyset\}.$$

3   Methods of Possible Worlds

In methods of possible worlds, a table is divided into possible tables, the conventional ways addressed in the previous section are applied to each possible table, and then the results from the possible tables are aggregated. When an imprecise value expressed in an or-set is contained in a data table, the or-set is probabilistically interpreted such that each element in the or-set has an equal probabilistic degree to which it is the actual value. In other words, every or-set is expressed in a uniform probability distribution over the elements contained in the or-set. This leads to that the data table can be expressed in terms of a probability distribution of possible tables pt.

$$t = \{(pt_1, p(pt_1)), \ldots, (pt_n, p(pt_n))\}_p,$$
$$p(pt_i) = 1/n,$$

where subscript p denotes a probability distribution, $p(pt_i)$ denotes the probabilistic degree to which possible table pt_i is the actual one, n is equal to $\Pi_{i=1,m} l_i$,

m is the number of imprecise attribute values, and each of them is expressed in an or-set having $l_i(i = 1, m))$ elements.

Each possible table consists of precise values. A family of equivalence classes is obtained from each possible table pt on set X of attributes. This is possible family $\mathcal{PE}(X)_{pt}$ accompanied by probabilistic degree $p(pt)$. Using possible families of equivalence classes, family $\mathcal{EE}(X)$ of equivalence classes is obtained.

$$\begin{aligned} \mathcal{EE}(X) &= \{(\mathcal{PE}(X)_{pt}, p(pt)) \mid p(pt) > 0\} \\ &= \{(\mathcal{PE}(X), \kappa(\mathcal{PE}(X) \in \mathcal{EE}(X))) \mid \kappa(\mathcal{PE}(X) \in \mathcal{EE}(X)) > 0\}, \end{aligned}$$

where the probabilistic degrees are summed when the same possible family of equivalence classes is obtained from plural possible tables, so probabilistic degree $\kappa(\mathcal{PE}(X) \in \mathcal{EE}(X))$ to which $\mathcal{PE}(X)$ belongs to $\mathcal{EE}(X)$ is:

$$\kappa(\mathcal{PE}(X) \in \mathcal{EE}(X)) = \sum_{\mathcal{PE}(X)_{pt} = \mathcal{PE}(X)} p(pt).$$

$\mathcal{EE}(X)$ has the property:

$$\sum_{\mathcal{PE}(X)} \kappa(\mathcal{PE}(X) \in \mathcal{EE}(X)) = 1.$$

Thus, $\mathcal{EE}(X)$ is considered as a probability distribution over $\mathcal{PE}(X)$.

Equivalence classes consisting of $\mathcal{PE}(X)_{pt}$ in possible table pt are possible equivalence classes on set X of attributes and have probabilistic degree $p(pt)$ to which they are an actual equivalence class. Thus, a family of possible equivalence classes accompanied by a probabilistic degree is obtained for each possible table. The expression for the family of equivalence classes in terms of possible equivalence classes is:

$$\begin{aligned} \mathcal{E}(X) &= \{(E(X), p(pt)) \mid E(X) \in \mathcal{PE}(X)_{pt} \wedge p(pt) > 0\} \\ &= \{(E(X), \kappa(\mathcal{PE}(X) \in \mathcal{EE}(X))) \mid E(X) \in \mathcal{PE}(X) \wedge \kappa(\mathcal{PE}(X) \in \mathcal{EE}(X)) > 0\} \\ &= \{(E(X), \kappa(E(X) \in \mathcal{E}(X))) \mid \kappa(E(X) \in \mathcal{E}(X)) > 0\}, \end{aligned}$$

where the probabilistic degrees are summed when the same possible equivalence class is obtained from plural possible tables, so probabilistic degree $\kappa(E(X) \in \mathcal{E}(X))$ to which $E(X)$ belongs to $\mathcal{E}(X)$ is:

$$\kappa(E(X) \in \mathcal{E}(X)) = \sum_{E(X) \in \mathcal{PE}(X)_{pt}} p(pt) = \sum_{E(X) \in \mathcal{PE}(X)} \kappa(\mathcal{PE}(X) \in \mathcal{EE}(X)).$$

$\mathcal{E}(X)$ has the property:

$$\sum_{E(X)} \kappa(E(X) \in \mathcal{E}(X)) \geq 1.$$

Thus, $\mathcal{E}(X)$ has not properties as a probability distribution and is the family of weighted equivalence classes such that its element is a weighted equivalence classes $(E(X), \kappa(E(X) \in \mathcal{E}(X)))$. When a table has no imprecise value, all the elements in $\mathcal{E}(X)$ have the same weight equal to 1.

The methods addressed in the previous section are applied to each possible table. Let $\underline{Apr(Y, X)}_{pt_i}$ and $\overline{Apr(Y, X)}_{pt_i}$ denote the lower approximation and the upper approximation of $\mathcal{E}(Y)_{pt_i}$ by $\mathcal{E}(X)_{pt_i}$ in possible table pt_i having probabilistic degree $p(pt_i)$. Probabilistic degrees $\kappa(E(X) \in \underline{Apr(Y, X)})_{pt_i}$ and $\kappa(E(X) \in \overline{Apr(Y, X)})_{pt_i}$ to which equivalence class $E(X)$ is contained in $\underline{Apr(Y, X)}$ and $\overline{Apr(Y, X)}$ for each possible table pt_i are obtained, respectively, as follows:

$$\kappa(E(X) \in \underline{Apr(Y, X)})_{pt_i} = \begin{cases} p(pt_i) & \text{if } E(X) \in \underline{Apr(Y, X)}_{pt_i}, \\ 0 & \text{otherwise.} \end{cases}$$

This shows that the probabilistic degree to which equivalence class $E(X)$ is contained in $\underline{Apr(Y, X)}$ is equal to $p(pt_i)$ for possible table pt_i, if the equivalence class is an element in $\underline{Apr(Y, X)}_{pt_i}$. Similarly,

$$\kappa(E(X) \in \overline{Apr(Y, X)})_{pt_i} = \begin{cases} p(pt_i) & \text{if } E(X) \in \overline{Apr(Y, X)}_{pt_i}, \\ 0 & \text{otherwise.} \end{cases}$$

Lower approximation $\underline{Apr(Y, X)}$ and upper approximation $\overline{Apr(Y, X)}$ are:

$$\underline{Apr(Y, X)} = \{(E(X), \kappa(E(X) \in \underline{Apr(Y, X)})) \mid \kappa(E(X) \in \overline{Apr(Y, X)}) > 0\},$$

$$\overline{Apr(Y, X)} = \{(E(X), \kappa(E(X) \in \overline{Apr(Y, X)})) \mid \kappa(E(X) \in \overline{Apr(Y, X)}) > 0\},$$

where probabilistic degrees $\kappa(E(X) \in \underline{Apr(Y, X)})$ and $\kappa(E(X) \in \overline{Apr(Y, X)})$ to which equivalence class $E(X)$ is contained in $\underline{Apr(Y, X)}$ and $\overline{Apr(Y, X)}$ are:

$$\kappa(E(X) \in \underline{Apr(Y, X)}) = \sum_{i=1,n} \kappa(E(X) \in \underline{Apr(Y, X)})_{pt_i},$$

$$\kappa(E(X) \in \overline{Apr(Y, X)}) = \sum_{i=1,n} \kappa(E(X) \in \overline{Apr(Y, X)})_{pt_i}.$$

These formulas show that the summation of the probabilistic degrees obtained from the possible tables is equal to the probabilistic degree for equivalence class $E(X)$.

When the lower approximation and the upper approximation are expressed in terms of a set of objects,

$$\underline{apr(Y, X)} = \{(o, \kappa(o \in \underline{apr(Y, X)})) \mid \kappa(o \in \overline{apr(Y, X)}) > 0\},$$

$$\overline{apr(Y, X)} = \{(o, \kappa(o \in \overline{apr(Y, X)})) \mid \kappa(o \in \overline{apr(Y, X)}) > 0\},$$

where probabilistic degrees $\kappa(o \in \underline{apr(Y, X)})$ and $\kappa(o \in \overline{apr(Y, X)})$ to which object o is contained in $\underline{apr(Y, X)}$ and $\overline{apr(Y, X)}$ are:

$$\kappa(o \in \underline{apr(Y, X)}) = \sum_{E(X) \ni o} \kappa(E(X) \in \underline{Apr(Y, X)}),$$

$$\kappa(o \in \overline{apr(Y,X)}) = \sum_{E(X) \ni o} \kappa(E(X) \in \overline{Apr(Y,X)}).$$

We adopt results from the method of possible worlds as a correctness criterion of extended methods of rough sets to imprecise information. This is commonly used in the field of databases handling imprecise information [5, 4, 21].

Correctness criterion
Results obtained from applying an extended method to a data table containing imprecise information are the same as ones obtained from applying the corresponding conventional method to every possible table derived from that data table and aggregating the results created in the possible tables.

4   Rough Sets to Imprecise Information

When object o takes imprecise values for attributes, we can calculate a degree to which the attribute values are the same as another object o'. The degree is the indiscernibility degree of objects o and o' on the attributes. In this case, a binary relation for indiscernibility between objects is,

$$IND(X) = \{((o,o'), \kappa(o[X] = o'[X])) \mid$$
$$(\kappa(o[X] = o'[X]) \neq 0) \wedge (o \neq o')\} \cup \{((o,o),1)\},$$

where $\kappa(o[X] = o'[X])$ denotes the indiscernibility degree of objects o and o' on set X of attributes and is equal to $\kappa((o,o') \in IND(X))$,

$$\kappa(o[X] = o'[X]) = \bigotimes_{A_i \in X} \kappa(o[A_i] = o'[A_i]),$$

where operator $\bigotimes$ depends on properties of imprecise attribute values. When the imprecise attribute values are probabilistically interpreted, the operator is the product denoted by $\times$.

Unfortunately, we cannot directly obtain the family of equivalence classes from $IND(X)$. This is because any transitivity laws do not hold on $IND(X)$. Therefore, we show another method to obtain the family of equivalence classes on set X of attributes in a table.

Among the elements of $IND(X)$, indiscernible set $S(X)_o$ of objects that are paired with an object o is,

$$S(X)_o = \{o' \mid \kappa((o,o') \in IND(X)) > 0\}.$$

$S(X)_o$ is the greatest possible equivalence class among possible equivalence classes containing objects o. Let $PS(X)_o$ denote the power set of $S(X)_o$. From $PS(X)_o$, family $Poss\mathcal{E}(X)_o$ of possible equivalence classes containing object o is obtained:

$$Poss\mathcal{E}(X)_o = \{E(X) \mid E(X) \in PS(X)_o \wedge o \in E(X)\}.$$

Whole family $Poss\mathcal{E}(X)$ of possible equivalence classes is,

$$Poss\mathcal{E}(X) = \cup_o Poss\mathcal{E}(X)_o.$$

For every possible equivalence class $E(X) \in Poss\mathcal{E}(X)$, probabilistic degree $\kappa(E(X) \in \mathcal{E}(X))$ to which $E(X)$ is an actual one is,

$$\kappa(E(X) \in \mathcal{E}(X)) = \kappa(\wedge_{o \in E(X) \ and \ o' \in E(X)}(o[X] = o'[X])$$
$$\wedge_{o \in E(X) \ and \ o' \notin E(X)}(o[X] \neq o'[X])),$$

where $o \neq o'$, $\kappa(f)$ is the probabilistic degree to which formula f is satisfied, and $\kappa(f) = 1$ when there exists no f. Family $\mathcal{E}(X)$ of weighted equivalence classes consists of $E(X)$ having $\kappa(E(X) \in \mathcal{E}(X)) > 0$, i.e.,

$$\mathcal{E}(X) = \{(E(X), \kappa(E(X) \in \mathcal{E}(X))) \mid \kappa(E(X) \in \mathcal{E}(X)) > 0\}.$$

Proposition 1
When $(E(X), \kappa(E(X) \in \mathcal{E}(X)))$ is an element of $\mathcal{E}(X)$ in table t, there exist possible tables where the families of equivalence classes contain $E(X)$ and the summation of probabilistic degrees that the possible tables have is equal to $\kappa(E(X) \in \mathcal{E}(X))$.

Proposition 2
$\mathcal{E}(X)$ in a table is equal to the union of the families of possible equivalence classes accompanied by a probabilistic degree, where each family of possible equivalence classes is obtained from a possible table created from the table.

Note that the summation of probabilistic degrees is adopted if there exists the same equivalence class accompanied by a probabilistic degree in different possible tables in the union.

Proposition 3
For any object o,

$$\sum_{E(X) \ni o} \kappa(E(X) \in \mathcal{E}(X)) = 1.$$

Using families of weighted equivalence classes, we can obtain lower approximation $\underline{Apr}(Y, X)$ and upper approximation $\overline{Apr}(Y, X)$ of $\mathcal{E}(Y)$ by $\mathcal{E}(X)$. For the lower approximation,

$$\underline{Apr}(Y, X) = \{(E(X), \kappa(E(X) \in \underline{Apr}(Y, X))) \mid \kappa(E(X) \in \underline{Apr}(Y, X)) > 0\},$$
$$\kappa(E(X) \in \underline{Apr}(Y, X)) = \sum_{E(Y)} ((\kappa(E(X) \subseteq E(Y)) \times$$
$$\kappa(E(X) \in \mathcal{E}(X)) \times \kappa(E(Y) \in \mathcal{E}(Y))),$$

where

$$\kappa(E(X) \subseteq E(Y)) = \begin{cases} 1 \text{ if } E(X) \subseteq E(Y), \\ 0 \text{ otherwise.} \end{cases}$$

Proposition 4

If $(E(X), \kappa(E(X) \in \underline{Apr}(Y, X)))$ in table t is an element of $\underline{Apr}(Y, X)$, there exist possible tables where the lower approximations contain $E(X)$ and the summation of probabilistic degrees that the possible tables have is equal to $\kappa(E(X) \in \underline{Apr}(Y, X))$.

Similarly for the upper approximation,

$$\overline{Apr(Y, X)} = \{(E(X), \kappa(o \in \overline{Apr(Y, X)})) \mid \kappa(E(X) \in \overline{Apr(Y, X)}) > 0\},$$

$$\kappa(E(X) \in \overline{Apr(Y, X)}) = \sum_{E(Y)} (\kappa(E(X) \cap E(Y) \neq \emptyset) \times$$

$$\kappa(E(X) \in \mathcal{E}(X)) \times \kappa(E(Y) \in \mathcal{E}(Y))),$$

where

$$\kappa(E(X) \cap E(Y) \neq \emptyset) = \begin{cases} 1 \text{ if } E(X) \cap E(Y) \neq \emptyset, \\ 0 \text{ otherwise.} \end{cases}$$

This formula still requires consideration, however, because probabilistic degrees are duplicately added for intersection. This comes from $\mathcal{E}(Y)$ being not a probability distribution. Thus, using family $\mathcal{EE}(Y)$ of equivalence classes on set Y of attributes, which is a probability distribution expressed in terms of possible families of equivalence classes, the formula of the upper approximation is corrected as follows:

$$\overline{Apr(Y, X)} = \{(E(X), \kappa(o \in \overline{Apr(Y, X)})) \mid \kappa(E(X) \in \overline{Apr(Y, X)}) > 0\},$$

$$\kappa(E(X) \in \overline{Apr(Y, X)}) = \sum_{\mathcal{PE}(Y)} (\kappa(E(X) \cap (\cup_{E(Y) \in \mathcal{PE}(Y)} E(Y)) \neq \emptyset) \times$$

$$\kappa(E(X) \in \mathcal{E}(X)) \times \kappa(\mathcal{PE}(Y) \in \mathcal{EE}(Y))),$$

where

$$\kappa(E(X) \cap (\cup_{E(Y) \in \mathcal{PE}(Y)} E(Y)) \neq \emptyset) = \begin{cases} 1 \text{ if } E(X) \cap (\cup_{E(Y) \in \mathcal{PE}(Y)} E(Y)) \neq \emptyset, \\ 0 \text{ otherwise,} \end{cases}$$

where $\mathcal{PE}(Y)$ is a possible family of equivalence classes, which is accompanied by probabilistic degree $\kappa(\mathcal{PE}(Y) \in \mathcal{EE}(Y))$ to which $\mathcal{PE}(Y)$ is an element of $\mathcal{EE}(Y)$. The upper approximation is easily obtained, because the following proposition holds.

Proposition 5

For the upper approximation, $\overline{Apr(Y, X)} = \mathcal{E}(X)$.

Note that this proposition is valid only for sets X and Y of attributes in the same table.

Proposition 6

If $(E(X), \kappa(E(X) \in \overline{Apr(Y, X)}))$ in table t is an element of $\overline{Apr(Y, X)}$, there exist possible tables where the upper approximations contain $E(X)$ and the summation of probabilistic degrees that the possible tables have is equal to $\kappa(E(X) \in \overline{Apr(Y, X)})$.

For expressions in terms of a set of objects, the same expressions as in Section 3 are used.

Using families of weighted equivalence classes, we can obtain the lower approximation and the upper approximation for two sets Φ and Ψ. We suppose that families $\mathcal{E}(\Psi)$ and $\mathcal{E}(\Phi)$ of weighted equivalence classes are obtained for sets Ψ and Φ, respectively. Let $(E(\Psi), \kappa(E(\Psi) \in \mathcal{E}(\Psi)))$ denote an element of $\mathcal{E}(\Psi)$ and $(E(\Phi), \kappa(E(\Phi) \in \mathcal{E}(\Phi)))$ denote an element of $\mathcal{E}(\Phi)$. Lower approximation $\underline{Apr(\Phi, \Psi)}$ and Upper approximation $\overline{Apr(\Phi, \Psi)}$ of $\mathcal{E}(\Phi)$ by $\mathcal{E}(\Psi)$ are,

$$\underline{Apr(\Phi, \Psi)} = \{(E(\Psi), \kappa(E(\Psi) \in \underline{Apr(\Phi, \Psi)})) \mid \kappa(E(\Psi) \in \underline{Apr(\Phi, \Psi)}) > 0\},$$

$$\kappa(E(\Psi) \in \underline{Apr(\Phi, \Psi)}) = \sum_{E(\Phi)} (\kappa(E(\Psi) \subseteq E(\Phi)) \times \kappa(E(\Psi) \in \mathcal{E}(\Psi)) \times$$
$$\kappa(E(\Phi) \in \mathcal{E}(\Phi))),$$

where

$$\kappa(E(\Psi) \subseteq E(\Phi)) = \begin{cases} 1 \text{ if } E(\Psi) \subseteq E(\Phi), \\ 0 \text{ otherwise.} \end{cases}$$

$$\overline{Apr(\Phi, \Psi)} = \{(E(\Psi), \kappa(E(\Psi) \in \overline{Apr(\Phi, \Psi)})) \mid \kappa(E(\Psi) \in \overline{Apr(\Phi, \Psi)}) > 0\},$$

$$\kappa(E(\Psi) \in \overline{Apr(\Phi, \Psi)}) = \sum_{\mathcal{PE}(\Phi)} (\kappa(E(\Psi) \cap (\cup_{E(\Phi) \in \mathcal{PE}(\Phi)} E(\Phi))) \neq \emptyset) \times$$
$$\kappa(E(\Psi) \in \mathcal{E}(\Psi)) \times \kappa(\mathcal{PE}(\Phi) \in \mathcal{EE}(\Phi))),$$

where

$$\kappa(E(\Psi) \cap (\cup_{E(\Phi) \in \mathcal{PE}(\Phi)} E(\Phi)) \neq \emptyset) = \begin{cases} 1 \text{ if } E(\Psi) \cap (\cup_{E(\Phi) \in \mathcal{PE}(\Phi)} E(\Phi)) \neq \emptyset, \\ 0 \text{ otherwise.} \end{cases}$$

For expressions in terms of a set of objects,

$$\underline{apr(\Phi, \Psi)} = \{(o, \kappa(o \in \underline{apr(\Phi, \Psi)})) \mid \kappa(o \in \underline{apr(\Phi, \Psi)}) > 0\}.$$
$$\kappa(o \in \underline{apr(\Phi, \Psi)}) = \max_{E(\Psi) \ni o} \kappa(E(\Psi) \in \underline{Apr(\Phi, \Psi)}),$$

$$\overline{apr(\Phi, \Psi)} = \{(o, \kappa(o \in \overline{apr(\Phi, \Psi)})) \mid \kappa(o \in \overline{apr(\Phi, \Psi)}) > 0\}.$$
$$\kappa(o \in \overline{apr(\Phi, \Psi)}) = \sum_{E(\Psi) \ni o} \kappa(E(\Psi) \in \overline{Apr(\Phi, \Psi)}),$$

Proposition 7

The lower approximation and the upper approximation that are obtained by the method of weighted equivalence classes coincide ones obtained by the method of possible worlds.

5   Conclusions

We have proposed a method, where weighted equivalence classes are used, to deal with imprecise information expressed in an or-set. The lower approximation and the upper approximation by the method of weighted equivalence classes coincide ones by the method of possible worlds. In other words, this method satisfies the correctness criterion that is used in the field of incomplete databases. This is justification of the method of weighted equivalence classes.

Acknowledgments. This research has been partially supported by the Grant-in-Aid for Scientific Research (C), Japan Society for the Promotion of Science, No. 18500214.

References

1. Greco, S., Matarazzo, B., and Slowinski, R. [1999]Handling Missing Values in Rough Set Analysis of Multi-attribute and Multi-criteria Decision Problem, in N. Zhong, A. Skowron, S. Ohsuga, (eds.), New Directions in Rough Sets, Data Mining and Granular-Soft Computing, Lecture Notes in Artificial Intelligence 1711, pp. 146-157.
2. Greco, S., Matarazzo, B., and Slowinski, R. [2001]Rough Sets Theory for Multicriteria Decision Analysis, European Journal of Operational Research, **129**, 1-47.
3. Grzymala-Busse, J. W. [1991]On the Unknown Attribute Values in Learning from Examples, in Ras, M. Zemankova, (eds.), Methodology for Intelligent Systems, ISMIS '91, Lecture Notes in Artificial Intelligence 542, Springer-Verlag, 368-377.
4. Imielinski, T. [1989]Incomplete Information in Logical Databases, Data Engineering, **12**, 93-104.
5. Imielinski, T. and Lipski, W. [1984]Incomplete Information in Relational Databases, Journal of the ACM, **31**:4, 761-791.
6. Kryszkiewicz, M. [1998]Rough Set Approach to Incomplete Information Systems, Information Sciences, **112**, 39-49.
7. Kryszkiewicz, M. [1998]Properties of Incomplete Information Systems in the framework of Rough Sets, in L. Polkowski and A. Skowron, (ed.), Rough Set in Knowledge Discovery 1: Methodology and Applications, Studies in Fuzziness and Soft Computing 18, Physica Verlag, 422-450.
8. Kryszkiewicz, M. [1999]Rules in Incomplete Information Systems, Information Sciences, **113**, 271-292.
9. Kryszkiewicz, M. and Rybiński, H. [2000]Data Mining in Incomplete Information Systems from Rough Set Perspective, in L. Polkowski, S. Tsumoto, and T. Y. Lin, (eds.), Rough Set Methods and Applications, Studies in Fuzziness and Soft Computing 56, Physica Verlag, 568-580.
10. Nakata, N. and Sakai, H. [2005] Rough-set-based approaches to data containing incomplete information: possibility-based cases, IOS Press, pp. 234-241.
11. Nakata, N. and Sakai, H. [2005]Checking Whether or Not Rough-Set-Based Methods to Incomplete Data Satisfy a Correctness Criterion, Lecture Notes in Artificial Intelligence Vol. 3558, pp. 227-239.
12. Nakata, N. and Sakai, H. [2005] Rough Sets Handling Missing Values Probabilistically Interpreted, Lecture Notes in Artificial Intelligence, Vol. 3641, pp. 325-334.

13. Nakata, N. and Sakai, H. [2006] Rough Sets Approximations to Possibilistic Information, in Proceedings of FUZZ-IEEE 2006, IEEE, pp. 804-811.

14. Parsons, S. [1996] Current Approaches to Handling Imperfect Information in Data and Knowledge Bases, IEEE Transactions on Knowledge and Data Engineering, **83**, 353-372.

15. Pawlak, Z. [1991] Rough Sets: Theoretical Aspects of Reasoning about Data, Kluwer Academic Publishers 1991.

16. Sakai, H. [1998]Some Issues on Nondeterministic Knowledge Bases with Incomplete Information, in: Proceedings of RSCTC'98, Polkowski, L. and Skowron, A., eds., Lecture Notes in Artificial Intelligence Vol. 1424, Springer-Verlag 1998, pp. 424-431.

17. Sakai, H. [1999]An Algorithm for Finding Equivalence Relations from Table Nondeterministic Information, in N. Zhong, A. Skowron, S. Ohsuga, (eds.), New Directions in Rough Sets, Data Mining and Granular-Soft Computing, Lecture Notes in Artificial Intelligence 1711, pp. 64-72.

18. Słowiński, R. and Stefanowski, J. [1989]Rough Classification in Incomplete Information Systems, Mathematical and Computer Modelling, **12**:10/11, 1347-1357.

19. Stefanowski, J. and Tsoukiàs, A. [1999]On the Extension of Rough Sets under Incomplete Information, in N. Zhong, A. Skowron, S. Ohsuga, (eds.), New Directions in Rough Sets, Data Mining and Granular-Soft Computing, Lecture Notes in Artificial Intelligence 1711, pp. 73-81.

20. Stefanowski, J. and Tsoukiàs, A. [2001]Incomplete Information Tables and Rough Classification, Computational Intelligence, **17**:3, 545-566.

21. Zimányi, E. and Pirotte, A. [1997] Imperfect Information in Relational Databases, in Uncertainty Management in Information Systems: From Needs to Solutions, A. Motro and P. Smets, eds., Kluwer Academic Publishers, 1997, pp. 35-87.

Ensembles of Decision Rules for Solving Binary Classification Problems in the Presence of Missing Values

Jerzy Błaszczyński[1], Krzysztof Dembczyński[1], Wojciech Kotłowski[1], Roman Słowiński[1,2], and Marcin Szeląg[1]

[1] Institute of Computing Science, Poznań University of Technology,
60-965 Poznań, Poland
{kdembczynski, jblaszczynski, wkotlowski, rslowinski,
mszelag}@cs.put.poznan.pl

[2] Institute for Systems Research, Polish Academy of Sciences, 01-447 Warsaw, Poland

Abstract. In this paper, we consider an algorithm that generates an ensemble of decision rules. A single rule is treated as a specific subsidiary, base classifier in the ensemble that indicates only one of the decision classes. Experimental results have shown that the ensemble of decision rules is as efficient as other machine learning methods. In this paper we concentrate on a common problem appearing in real-life data that is a presence of missing attributes values. To deal with this problem, we experimented with different approaches inspired by rough set approach to knowledge discovery. Results of those experiments are presented and discussed in the paper.

1   Introduction

Decision rule is a logical expression in the form: *if* [*conditions*], *then* [*decision*]. If an object satisfies conditions of the rule, then it is assigned to the recommended class. Otherwise the object remains unassigned. Decision rules were common in the early machine learning approaches [1,6], widely considered in the rough set approaches to knowledge discovery (see for example, [20,15,23,24]), and within Logical Analysis of Data [3] where they are called patterns. The algorithm described here follows a specific approach to decision rule generation. It treats a single rule as a subsidiary, base classifier in the ensemble that indicates only one of the decision classes.

Ensemble methods became a very popular approach to classification problems. These methods consist in forming an ensemble of classifiers that are simple learning and classification procedures often referred to as base (or weak) learners. The ensemble members (i.e., base learners or classifiers) are applied to a classification task and their individual outputs are then aggregated to one output of the whole ensemble. The aggregation is computed as a linear combination of outputs. The most popular methods that are used as base learners are decision trees, for example C4.5 [21] or CART [5], and decision stumps (that are one level decision trees). There are several approaches to construction of the ensemble, the most popular are bagging [4] and boosting [22,9]. These algorithms have proven to be effective in reducing classification error of a base learner. In other words, a committee of low performance learners creates a powerful and quite simple solution for the classification problem. That is why these methods are often treated as off-the-shelf methods-of-choice.

In our approach, the ensemble of decision rules is constructed using a variation of forward stagewise additive modeling [10]. Similar technique is also used by Friedman and Popescu [13]. However, one can observe substantial differences between their algorithm and the one presented in this paper. In Friedman and Popescu's algorithm, the decision trees are used as base classifiers, and then each node (interior and terminal) of each resulting tree produces a rule. It is setup by the conjunction of conditions associated with all of the edges on the path from the root to that node. Rule ensemble is then fitted by gradient directed regularization [12]. The algorithm presented here generates rules directly. Single rule is created in each iteration of forward stagewise additive modeling. This simpler way is as efficient as other main machine learning methods [2]. Usually, it is enough to generate around 50 rules to achieve satisfying accuracy and, moreover, the rules are easy in interpretation. Our algorithm is also similar to SLIPPER introduced by Cohen and Singer [7]. The difference is that SLIPPER uses AdaBoost [22] schema to produce an ensemble of decision rules. Let us notice that AdaBoost is a specific case of the forward stagewise additive modeling, so the latter is a more general approach [10].

In this paper, we concentrate on a common problem of data analysis. The real-life data has often missing attributes values. There are several approaches to deal with this problem. One of them is to discard objects having missing values, but this could lead to serious depletion of the training data. Another possibility is to replace missing values with the mean, median or mode over non-missing values of objects on a given attribute. The approach adopted here is inspired by rough set theory, within which the problem of missing values were studied in many places (see, for example [14,16,17,18]). There are two problems to be solved. The first one is the way, in which a single rule is generated in the presence of missing values. The second one is the way, in which an unseen object having missing values is classified by a rule. According to [14] and [18] generated rules should remain true when all or some missing values will be replaced by arbitrary values. Such an approach is compatible with knowledge discovery from incomplete information systems. We tried to adapt it to the ensemble of decision rules. In classification procedure, it seems reasonable that only universal selector on a given attribute covers an unseen object with missing value on this attribute. It is so, because, the true value of the object on this attribute is unknown, and we are certain that only universal selector will cover it.

The goal of this paper is to verify experimentally several approaches to deal with missing values that are inspired by rough set theory. The paper is organized as follows. In Section 2, the problem is formulated. Section 3 presents the algorithm for construction of an ensemble of decision rules. In Section 4, approaches taken to deal with missing values are presented. Section 5 contains experimental results. The last section concludes the paper.

2   Problem Statement

Let us define the classification problem in a similar way as in [11,13]. The aim is to predict the unknown value of an attribute y (sometimes called *output, response variable* or *decision attribute*) of an object using the known joint values of other attributes (sometimes called *predictors, condition attributes* or *independent variables*) $\mathbf{x} = (x_1, x_2, \ldots, x_n)$, where some of values may be missing. We consider binary classification problem, and we assume that $y \in \{-1, 1\}$. In other words, all objects for which $y = -1$ constitute decision class Cl_{-1}, and all objects for which $y = 1$ constitute decision class Cl_1. The goal of a learning task is to find a function $F(\mathbf{x})$ using a set of training examples $\{y_i, \mathbf{x}_i\}_1^N$ that classifies accurately objects to these classes. The optimal classification procedure is given by:

$$F^*(\mathbf{x}) = \arg \min_{F(\mathbf{x})} E_{y\mathbf{x}} L(y, F(\mathbf{x}))$$

where the expected value $E_{y\mathbf{x}}$ is over joint distribution of all variables $(y, \mathbf{x})$ for the data to be predicted. $L(y, F(\mathbf{x}))$ is a loss or cost for predicting $F(\mathbf{x})$ when the actual value is y. The typical loss in classification tasks is:

$$L(y, F(\mathbf{x})) = \begin{cases} 0 & y = F(\mathbf{x}), \\ 1 & y \neq F(\mathbf{x}). \end{cases} \tag{1}$$

The learning procedure tries to construct $F(\mathbf{x})$ to be the best possible approximation of $F^*(\mathbf{x})$.

3   Ensembles of Decision Rules

Condition part of a decision rule is represented by a complex $\Phi = \phi_1^\propto \wedge \phi_2^\propto \wedge \ldots \wedge \phi_t^\propto$, where $\phi^\propto$ is a selector and t is a number of selectors in the complex, also referred to as a length of the rule. Selector $\phi^\propto$ is defined as $x_j \propto v_j$, where v_j is a single value or a subset of values from the domain of the j-th attribute; and $\propto$ is specified as $=, \in, \geq$ or $\leq$, depending on the characteristic of the j-th attribute. In other words, complex Φ is a set of selectors that allows to select a subset of objects. Objects covered by complex Φ are denoted by $cov(\Phi)$ and referred to as cover of a complex Φ. Decision part of a rule indicates one of the decision classes and is denoted by $d(\mathbf{x}) = -1$ or $d(\mathbf{x}) = 1$. Let as denote a rule by $r(\mathbf{x}, \mathbf{c})$, where $\mathbf{c}$ represents both complex and decision of the rule, $\mathbf{c} = (\Phi, d(\mathbf{x}))$. Then, the output of the rule may be defined as follows:

$$r(\mathbf{x}, \mathbf{c}) = \begin{cases} d(\mathbf{x}) & \mathbf{x} \in cov(\Phi), \\ 0 & \mathbf{x} \notin cov(\Phi). \end{cases} \tag{2}$$

Algorithm 1. Ensemble of decision rules

> **input** : set of training examples $\{y_i, \mathbf{x}_i\}_1^N$,
> M – number of decision rules to be generated.
> **output**: ensemble of decision rules $\{r_m(\mathbf{x})\}_1^M$.
> $F_0(\mathbf{x}) := \arg\min_{\alpha \in \{-1,1\}} \sum_{i=1}^N L(y_i, \alpha)$; or $F_0(\mathbf{x}) := 0$; //default rule
> $F_0(\mathbf{x}) := \nu \cdot F_0(\mathbf{x})$;
> **for** $m = 1$ *to* M **do**
> $\mathbf{c} := \arg\min_{\mathbf{c}} \sum_{i \in S_m(\eta)} L(y_i, F_{m-1}(\mathbf{x}_i) + r(\mathbf{x}_i, \mathbf{c}))$;
> $r_m(\mathbf{x}) = r(\mathbf{x}, \mathbf{c})$;
> $F_m(\mathbf{x}) = F_{m-1}(\mathbf{x}) + \nu \cdot r_m(\mathbf{x})$;
> **end**
> $ensemble = \{r_m(\mathbf{x})\}_1^M$;

The loss of a single decision rule takes a specific form:

$$L(y, r(\mathbf{x}, \mathbf{c})) = \begin{cases} 0 & y \cdot r(\mathbf{x}, \mathbf{c}) = 1, \\ 1 & y \cdot r(\mathbf{x}, \mathbf{c}) = -1, \\ l & r(\mathbf{x}, \mathbf{c}) = 0, \end{cases} \tag{3}$$

where $0 \geq l \geq 1$ is a penalty for specificity of the rule. It means, the lower the value of l, the smaller the number of objects covered by the rule from the opposite class.

Forward stagewise additive modeling [10] is a general schema that constructs an ensemble. This schema may be suited to the problem of decision rules generation. We have used a variation of it that was also applied by Friedman and Popescu [13]. In their approach, however, base classifiers are decision trees, from which decision rules are produced. Here, the rule is generated directly in each step of Algorithm 1. In this procedure, $L(y_i, F(\mathbf{x}))$ is a loss function, $r_m(\mathbf{x}, \mathbf{c})$ is a decision rule characterized by a set of parameters $\mathbf{c}$ and M is a number of rules to be generated. $S_m(\eta)$ represents a different subsample of size $\eta \leq N$ randomly drawn with or without replacement from the original training data. ν is so called "shrinkage" parameter, usually $0 \leq \nu \leq 1$. Values of ν determine the degree to which previously generated decision rules $r_k(\mathbf{x}, \mathbf{c})$, $k = 1, \ldots, m$, affect the generation of the successive one in the sequence, i.e., $r_{m+1}(\mathbf{x}, \mathbf{c})$.

In the algorithm, in each consecutive iteration m we augment the function $F_{m-1}(\mathbf{x})$ by one additional rule $r_m(\mathbf{x})$ weighted by shrinkage parameter ν. This gives a linear combination of rules $F_m(\mathbf{x})$. The additional rule $r_m(\mathbf{x}) = r(\mathbf{x}, \mathbf{c})$ is chosen to minimize $\sum_{i \in S_m(\eta)} L(y_i, F_{m-1}(\mathbf{x}_i) + r(\mathbf{x}_i, \mathbf{c}))$. $F_0(\mathbf{x})$ corresponds to the default rule in the ensemble generation process. It is set to $F_0(\mathbf{x}) := \arg\min_{\alpha \in \{-1,1\}} \sum_i^N L(y_i, \alpha)$ (i.e., it corresponds to the default rule indicating the majority class) or there is no default rule (then $F_0(\mathbf{x}) := 0$). The default rule is taken with the same "shrinkage" parameter ν as all other rules.

The loss of the linear combination of rules $F_m(\mathbf{x})$ takes the following form in the simplest case:

$$L(y, F_m(\mathbf{x})) = \begin{cases} 0 & y \cdot F_m(\mathbf{x}) > 0, \\ 1 & y \cdot F_m(\mathbf{x}) < 0, \\ l & y \cdot F_m(\mathbf{x}) = 0. \end{cases} \tag{4}$$

Nevertheless, the interpretation of l in the above definition is not as easy as in the case of a single rule. It depends on all other parameters used in Algorithm 1. $L(y, F_m(\mathbf{x}))$ takes value equal to l in two cases. The first case is, when $F_0(\mathbf{x})$ is set to zero (there is no default rule) and no rule generated in m iterations covers object $\mathbf{x}$. The second case is when rules covering object $\mathbf{x}$ indicate equally two classes Cl_{-1} and Cl_1. The interpretation of l is similar to the case of a single rule, when $F_0(\mathbf{x})$ is set to zero and $\nu = 1/M$, for example. Note that $\nu = 1/M$ means that each next rule is more important than all previously generated.

Classification procedure is performed according to:

$$F(\mathbf{x}) = sign(a_0 + \sum_{m=1}^{M} a_m r_m(\mathbf{x}, \mathbf{c})). \tag{5}$$

In other words, it is a linear classifier in a very high dimensional space of derived decision rules that are highly nonlinear functions of the original predictor variables $\mathbf{x}$. Parameters $\{a_m\}_0^M$ can be obtained in many ways. For example, they can be set to fixed values (for example, $a_0=0$ and $\{a_m = 1/M\}_1^M$), computed by some optimization techniques, fitted in cross-validation experiments or estimated in a process of constructing the ensemble (like in AdaBoost [22]).

To perform our experiment, we have used a simple greedy heuristic to construct a single decision rule. It consists in searching for $\mathbf{c}$ such that $L_m = \sum_{i \in S_m(\eta)} L(y_i, F_{m-1}(\mathbf{x}_i) + r(\mathbf{x}_i, \mathbf{c}))$ is minimal. At the beginning, the complex contains an universal selector (i.e., selector that covers all objects). In the next step, a new selector is added to the complex and the decision of the rule is set. The selector and the decision are chosen to give the minimal value of L_m. This step is repeated until L_m is minimized. Remaining settings of the algorithm are as follows. We have decided to generate default rule indicating the majority class. Besides (4), we have tried several formulas for the loss function. The best results were obtained, when we used sigmoidal function:

$$L(y, F_m(\mathbf{x})) = \frac{1}{1 - exp(y \cdot F_m(\mathbf{x}))}, \tag{6}$$

and this formulation was used in the experiment (for a wide discussion on different formulas for loss function see [10]). The "shrinkage" parameter was set to $\nu = 0.5$. Each rule is generated using subsample of size $\eta = N$ drawn with replacement. The classification is performed according to (5), where $a_0 = F_0(\mathbf{x})$ and $\{a\}_1^M$ are set to 1.

4   Missing Values

Decision rule models are well-suited to problems where objects have missing values. A single decision rule involves only a part of attributes. So, the algorithm can seek for such selectors on attributes that "avoid" missing values. In this paper, we have performed the experiment in which we have compared simple, but also effective methods to deal with missing values inspired by rough set approach to knowledge discovery. We assume here that the missing value is interpreted in such a way that its true value is one of all possible values from the domain of the considered attribute. This is consistent with the *disjunctive and exclusive interpretation* of multi-valued information systems given in [8]. While the problem considered in this paper is different from knowledge discovery from incomplete information systems for which rough set approaches are well-suited, there may be observed some similarities. In particular, the linear combination of rules from the ensemble implies a partition of the space of all joint values of the attributes **x** to some regions that might be interpreted as granules of knowledge considered in rough set approaches. These granules contain mainly objects from one class. An object with missing value may belong or not to such a granule, depending on the true value of the attribute with the missing value. It is also possible that the implied granule includes a whole domain of an attribute. Then, objects with missing values on this attribute only are contained in this granule.

There are two problems to be solved. The first one is the way, in which a single rule is generated in the presence of missing values. The second one is the way, in which an unseen object having missing values is classified by a rule. The first problem can be solved in one of the following ways:

(1) objects with missing values are discarded from the further analysis (this is the simplest solution; we implemented it to have comparison with further approaches),

(2) an object with missing values satisfies all selectors built on attributes on which this object has no value,

(3) an object with missing values does not satisfy selectors built on attributes on which this object has no value,

(4) for the rules indicating the same class as the class of an object with missing values: this object does not satisfy selectors build on attributes whose values are missing for it; for the rules indicating an opposite class: this object satisfies the above selectors.

The second problem can be solved in one of the following ways:

(a) an unseen object with missing values satisfies selectors built on attributes on which this object has no value,

(b) an unseen object with missing values does not satisfy selectors built on attributes on which this object has no value.

Approaches (2) and (a) are motivated by the fact that an object having a missing value on an attribute may be treated as indiscernible with other object on this attribute. So, any selector on this attribute is satisfied by this object. One may also take another definition of indiscernibility, where only an universal selector (i.e. selector that covers all objects) on the given attribute covers an object with missing value on this attribute. This definition is used in approaches (3) and (b).

Table 1. Approaches to missing values that were used

Training phase	Testing phase	Abbrev.	Training phase	Testing phase	Abbrev.
(1)	(a)	1-a	(3)	(a)	3-a
(1)	(b)	1-b	(3)	(b)	3-b
(2)	(a)	2-a	(4)	(a)	4-a
(2)	(b)	2-b	(4)	(b)	4-b

Another possible approach is as follows. If a rule contains a selector built on attribute on which an object has a missing value, one may penalize, when this object belongs to opposite class than the class indicated by the rule. Analogously, one may not reward when this object belongs to the class indicated by the rule. This is implemented as described in (4). Then, the loss of the rule increases when covering an object with missing value from the opposite class, and do not decrease when covering an object with missing value from the same class as the decision of the rule.

Let us notice, that in classification procedure, it seems reasonable to proceed according to (b), i.e., only universal selectors on a given attribute covers an object with missing value on this attribute. It is so, because, the true value of the object on the attribute is unknown, and we are certain that only universal selector will cover it.

5   Experimental Results

We designed an experiment to compare performance of the ensemble of decision rules with different approaches to missing values. To conduct this experiment we implemented the method using Weka package [25]. We have decided to compare all combinations of approaches described in Section 4 (see also Table 1).

For purpose of the experiment, we used four data sets taken from UCI [19] repository of machine learning data sets. These sets contain two-class classification problems that have large number of objects with missing values. The data sets that we chosen are presented in Table 2. Hepatitis problem is highly unbalanced, but we have not used any technique to deal with this problem. Labor data contains a relatively small number of objects. We have decided to generate 15, 30, and 60 rules and compare the performance of the algorithm for different number of rules. To estimate classifiers error rates, we used 10-fold cross-validation that we repeated 30 times. Results of the experiment are presented in Tables 3–4. In those tables we show performance of classifiers on factors (given as percents): correctly classified examples (C), true positive in class +1 (TP +1), precision in class +1 (P +1), true positive in class -1 (TP -1), precision in class -1 (P -1).

It is easy to observe that discarding objects with missing values in the case of colic and labor data sets is unacceptable technique. However, for vote and hepatitis problem, where the number of objects with missing values is relatively small, the difference to more advanced techniques is not so visible. For colic

Table 2. Number of attributes and objects for data sets included in the experiment

Data set	Attributes	Objects	Objects from Cl_1	Objects from Cl_{-1}	Objects with missing values
colic	23	368	232	136	361
vote	17	435	267	168	203
labor	17	57	20	37	56
hepatitis	20	155	32	123	75

Table 3. Classification results in percents [%], part 1; C indicates *correctly classified examples*, TP +1 *true positive* in class +1, TP -1 *true positive* in class -1, P +1 *precision* in class +1, P -1 *precision* in class -1

Classifier	colic					vote				
	C	TP +1	TP -1	P +1	P -1	C	TP +1	TP -1	P +1	P -1
15 rules, 1-a	63.04	100.00	0.00	63.04	0.00	94.89	92.52	98.66	99.11	89.22
15 rules, 1-b	63.04	100.00	0.00	63.04	0.00	95.63	94.80	97.00	98.10	92.10
15 rules, 2-a	84.92	91.78	73.22	85.39	83.97	95.57	94.13	97.84	98.56	91.32
15 rules, 2-b	79.58	95.29	52.80	77.54	86.85	95.59	94.80	96.90	98.03	92.09
15 rules, 3-a	84.86	92.03	72.63	85.16	84.29	94.97	92.78	98.42	98.95	89.57
15 rules, 3-b	84.98	92.01	72.99	85.33	84.29	95.63	94.80	97.00	98.10	92.10
15 rules, 4-a	85.57	93.90	71.35	84.84	87.30	95.49	93.92	97.96	98.65	91.05
15 rules, 4-b	85.52	93.76	71.46	84.86	87.06	95.59	94.80	96.90	98.03	92.09
30 rules, 1-a	63.04	100.00	0.00	63.04	0.00	95.26	93.75	97.66	98.45	90.76
30 rules, 1-b	63.04	100.00	0.00	63.04	0.00	95.62	94.80	96.98	98.09	92.10
30 rules, 2-a	85.08	91.67	73.83	85.67	83.91	95.51	94.70	96.82	97.97	91.95
30 rules, 2-b	79.59	94.25	54.58	78.01	84.80	95.54	94.85	96.66	97.87	92.14
30 rules, 3-a	85.14	92.25	73.02	85.37	84.71	95.57	94.52	97.26	98.22	91.75
30 rules, 3-b	85.64	92.14	74.56	86.06	84.78	95.58	94.80	96.86	98.01	92.08
30 rules, 4-a	85.51	93.62	71.67	84.94	86.82	95.39	94.72	96.46	97.74	91.95
30 rules, 4-b	85.69	93.78	71.89	85.06	87.14	95.48	94.90	96.40	97.70	92.21
60 rules, 1-a	63.04	100.00	0.00	63.04	0.00	95.57	94.70	96.96	98.05	91.99
60 rules, 1-b	63.04	100.00	0.00	63.04	0.00	95.56	94.86	96.68	97.89	92.16
60 rules, 2-a	84.64	90.86	74.02	85.65	82.64	95.63	95.35	96.04	97.47	92.87
60 rules, 2-b	80.17	93.65	57.18	78.89	84.11	95.66	95.34	96.14	97.53	92.85
60 rules, 3-a	84.72	92.25	71.87	84.84	84.50	95.61	95.29	96.08	97.50	92.78
60 rules, 3-b	85.76	91.94	75.20	86.35	84.58	95.54	95.09	96.24	97.60	92.49
60 rules, 4-a	85.34	92.5	73.11	85.44	85.12	95.90	95.77	96.10	97.51	93.44
60 rules, 4-b	85.91	93.29	73.31	85.64	86.53	95.74	95.65	95.86	97.36	93.27

problem technique 2-b seems to be the worst. One may see a slight superiority of the 4-b approach. The higher number of rules in this case do not improve the results significantly. It is hard to indicate the best technique in the case of vote data. Also, the performance is good regardless for the number of rules and chosen approach to missing values. We expect that there are some easy to discover general patterns in this problem. The best performance for hepatitis

Table 4. Classification results in percents [%], part 1; C indicates *correctly classified examples*, TP +1 *true positive* in class +1, TP -1 *true positive* in class -1, P +1 *precision* in class +1, P -1 *precision* in class -1

Classifier	hepatitis					labor				
	C	TP +1	TP -1	P +1	P -1	C	TP +1	TP -1	P +1	P -1
15 rules, 1-a	81.74	15.94	98.87	77.40	81.90	38.13	90.00	10.08	35.11	64.91
15 rules, 1-b	81.51	16.68	98.39	74.30	81.96	37.72	90.00	9.45	34.95	63.35
15 rules, 2-a	83.01	29.07	97.04	72.29	84.02	84.21	63.50	95.41	88.19	82.93
15 rules, 2-b	82.82	25.63	97.70	75.74	83.47	74.56	31.83	97.66	89.05	72.71
15 rules, 3-a	82.92	27.10	97.46	73.94	83.71	79.82	66.50	87.04	73.92	82.94
15 rules, 3-b	82.86	25.85	97.71	74.73	83.51	84.39	64.00	95.41	88.44	83.21
15 rules, 4-a	81.81	19.09	98.14	73.52	82.34	81.17	58.83	93.25	82.57	80.77
15 rules, 4-b	81.57	17.72	98.20	72.16	82.10	82.75	58.83	95.68	88.07	81.19
30 rules, 1-a	82.95	27.20	97.46	74.39	83.73	38.13	90.00	10.08	35.11	64.91
30 rules, 1-b	82.99	31.05	96.49	70.99	84.33	38.25	90.00	10.26	35.16	65.36
30 rules, 2-a	83.72	40.02	95.08	68.24	85.92	88.66	76.33	95.32	89.96	88.23
30 rules, 2-b	82.60	34.28	95.16	65.12	84.79	79.59	47.67	96.85	89.60	77.54
30 rules, 3-a	84.37	46.36	94.25	67.99	87.12	82.81	77.83	85.51	74.71	87.75
30 rules, 3-b	82.65	38.13	94.22	63.36	85.43	87.95	74.17	95.41	89.90	87.31
30 rules, 4-a	82.06	29.49	95.72	64.49	83.94	84.39	69.17	92.62	83.59	84.83
30 rules, 4-b	82.13	29.81	95.72	64.84	84.00	84.15	66.33	93.79	85.56	83.84
60 rules, 1-a	83.81	33.98	96.76	74.59	84.93	38.13	90.00	10.08	35.11	64.91
60 rules, 1-b	83.25	33.66	96.13	69.57	84.80	38.13	90.00	10.08	35.11	64.91
60 rules, 2-a	83.03	42.93	93.47	63.18	86.30	90.82	83.50	94.78	89.75	91.45
60 rules, 2-b	83.01	37.62	94.81	65.77	85.40	83.28	60.00	95.86	88.94	81.67
60 rules, 3-a	84.52	55.22	92.15	64.78	88.78	86.14	80.33	89.29	80.58	89.40
60 rules, 3-b	83.23	41.89	93.98	64.46	86.15	90.58	81.67	95.41	90.59	90.62
60 rules, 4-a	81.81	33.34	94.41	60.93	84.50	86.37	74.50	92.80	84.97	87.11
60 rules, 4-b	81.59	31.68	94.57	60.46	84.19	86.78	73.83	93.79	86.58	86.99

problem is achieved by the 3-a technique (particularly, the true positive ratio for class 1 has an acceptable high level). The number of rules in this case plays an important role. For 60 rules the true positive ratio is the highest. In our opinion, it is caused by unbalanced number of objects in decision classes. For the labor problem that contains relatively small number of objects, one may see that the higher the number of rules than the performance is better. The best results for labor are obtained by 2-a and 3-b techniques.

Concluding the above results, for sure, it is not a good idea to discard objects with missing values from the analysis. In some cases, it can lead to unacceptable results. It seems that among the more advanced techniques, we get the worst results for 2-b. When concerning the rest of more advanced techniques, it is hard to point out the best approach. The standard deviations over 30 10-fold cross-validations are relatively small (for colic problem the highest standard deviation was 1.25, for vote problem it is 0.4, for hepatitis problem it is 1.69 and for labor problem it is 3.72). The increase of number of rules, certainly, does not lead to worse results. However, in some cases, it does not improve results significantly, but the cost of computations is higher. Some further investigations are still required.

6 Conclusions and Future Plans

We have described a general algorithm constructing an ensemble of decision rules, for which we have experimented with different methods to deal with missing values. These methods were inspired by rough set approaches to knowledge discovery. It seems that it is hard to point out the best approach. Let us underline that the decision rule models are well-suited to problems where objects have missing values. We plan to use another techniques that deal with missing values. These might be, for example, surrogate selectors by similarity to surrogate splits in CART [5] and the approach used in C4.5 [21].

Acknowledgements. The authors wish to acknowledge financial support from the Ministry of Education and Science (grant no. 3T11F 02127).

References

1. Michalski, R.S.: A Theory and Methodology of Inductive Learning. In Michalski, R.S., Carbonell, J.G., Mitchell, T.M. (eds.): Machine Learning: An Artificial Intelligence Approach. Palo Alto, Tioga Publishing, (1983) 83–129
2. Błaszczyński, J., Dembczyński, K., Kotłowski, W., Słowiński, R., Szeląg, M.: Ensemble of Decision Rules. Research Report RA-011/06, Poznań University of Technology (2006)
3. Boros, E., Hammer, P. L., Ibaraki, T., Kogan, A., Mayoraz, E., Muchnik, I.: An Implementation of Logical Analysis of Data. IEEE Trans. on Knowledge and Data Engineering **12** (2000) 292–306
4. Breiman, L.: Bagging Predictors. Machine Learning **24** 2 (1996) 123–140
5. Breiman, L., Friedman, J. H., Olshen, R. A., Stone, C. J.: Classification and Regression Trees. Wadsworth, (1984)
6. Clark, P., Nibbet, T.: The CN2 induction algorithm. Machine Learning **3** (1989) 261–283
7. Cohen, W. W., Singer, Y.: A simple, fast, and effective rule learner. Proc. of 16th National Conference on Artificial Intelligence (1999) 335–342
8. Düntsch, I., Gediga, G., Orłowska, E.: Relational attribute systems. International Journal of Human-Computer Studies, **55** (2001) 293–309
9. Friedman, J. H., Hastie, T., Tibshirani, R.: Additive logistic regression: a statistical view of boosting. Stanford University Technical Report, `http://www-stat.stanford.edu/~jhf/` (last access: 1.05.2006), August (1998)
10. Friedman, J. H., Hastie, T., Tibshirani, R.: Elements of Statistical Learning: Data Mining, Inference, and Prediction, Springer (2003)
11. Friedman, J. H.: Recent advances in predictive (machine) learning. Stanford University Technical Report, `http://www-stat.stanford.edu/~jhf/` (last access: 1.05.2006), November (2003)
12. Friedman, J. H., Popescu, B. E.: Gradient directed regularization. Stanford University Technical Report, `http://www-stat.stanford.edu/~jhf/` (last access: 1.05.2006), February (2004)

13. Friedman, J. H., Popescu, B. E.: Predictive Learning via Rule Ensembles. Stanford University Technical Report, `http://www-stat.stanford.edu/~jhf/` (last access: 1.05.2006), February (2005)
14. Greco S., Matarazzo, B. and Słowiński, R.: Dealing with missing data in rough set analysis of multi-attribute and multi-criteria decision problems. In Zanakis, S. H., Doukidis, G., Zopounidis C. (eds.): Decision Making: Recent Developments and Worldwide Applications. Kluwer Academic Publishers, Dordrecht (2000) 295–316
15. Grzymala-Busse, J., W.: LERS — A system for learning from examples based on rough sets. In Słowiński, R. (ed.): Intelligent Decision Support, Handbook of Applications and Advances of the Rough Sets Theory. Kluwer Academic Publishers (1992) 3–18
16. Grzymala-Busse, J. W., Hu, M.: A Comaprison of Several Approaches in Missing Attribute Values in Data Mining, LNAI **2005** (2000) 378–385
17. Grzymala-Busse, J. W.: Incomplete Data and Generalization of Indiscernibility Relation, Definability, and Approximation, LNAI **3614** (2005) 244–253
18. Kryszkiewicz, M.: Rough Set approach to incomplete information systems. Information Sciences **112** (1998) 39–49
19. Newman, D. J., Hettich, S., Blake, C. L., Merz, C. J.: (UCI) Repository of machine learning databases. `http://www.ics.uci.edu/~mlearn/MLRepository.html` (last access: 01.05.2006), Dept. of Information and Computer Sciences, University of California, Irvine (1998)
20. Pawlak, Z.: Rough Sets. Theoretical Aspects of Reasoning about Data. Kluwer Academic Publishers, Dordrecht (1991)
21. Quinlan, J. R.: C4.5: Programs for Machine Learning. Morgan Kaufmann (1993)
22. Schapire, R. E., Freund, Y., Bartlett, P., Lee, W. E.: Boosting the margin: A new explanation for the effectiveness of voting methods. The Annals of Statistics **26** 5 (1998) 1651–1686
23. Skowron, A.: Extracting laws from decision tables - a rough set approach. Computational Intelligence **11** (1995) 371–388
24. Stefanowki, J.: On rough set based approach to induction of decision rules. In Polkowski, L., Skowron, A. (eds.): Rough Sets in Knowledge Discovery, Physica-Verlag, Heidelberg (1998) 500–529
25. Witten, I. H., Frank, E.: Data Mining: Practical machine learning tools and techniques, 2nd Edition. Morgan Kaufmann, San Francisco (2005)

Expanding Tolerance RST Models Based on Cores of Maximal Compatible Blocks

Chen Wu[1, 2, 3], Xiaohua Hu[2], Jingyu Yang[1], and Xibei Yang[1]

[1] Dept. of Computer Science and Technology, Nanjing University of Science and Technology, Nanjing 210094 Jiangsu, China
[2] College of Information Science and Technology, Drexel University, Philadelphia, PA 19104, USA
[3] School of Electronics and Information, Jiangsu University of Science and Technology, Zhenjiang, Jiangsu, 212003, China
wuchenzj@gmail.com

Abstract. Based on tolerance relation, this paper proposes three knowledge representation systems and then discusses their properties from a new prospective of cores of maximal compatible blocks. It also discusses the relationships of the three knowledge representation systems with the other two proposed by Kryszkiewicz M. and Wanli C. respectively. It considers the measurements such as the accuracy measurements, the rough entropies of knowledge. It also defines and studies rough entropies of set about knowledge in the three systems and obtains several meaningful theorems.

Keywords: rough set model, incomplete information system, knowledge represented system, entropy.

1   Introduction

Rough Set Theory (RST)[6,7,8] was suggested by Pawlak Z. in 1980s. As an efficient mathematical tool in processing non-deterministic, vagueness, and uncertainty, it has been widely used in the research fields of data mining [1,2], pattern recognition[9], knowledge discovery[5], machine learning[11] ,expert systems and so on. RST , introduced originally by Pawlak Z. is based on the assumption that all objects have deterministic values in each attribute in a complete information system and classifications are made by indiscernibility relations (or called equivalence relations) defined by Pawlak Z. But in incomplete information systems, it is not always possible to form indiscernibility relations due to null values. So the original RST may not be applicable in incomplete information systems in some real applications. Therefore many researchers propose new expanded RST models to transact with, primarily in expanding indiscernibility relation to non-indiscernibility relation such as tolerance relation [4], similarity relation [10], limited tolerance relation, etc. [3,12,14]. Unfortunately, in these expanding models, the result of classification of the universe based on tolerance relation, similarity relation, or limited tolerance relation does not guarantee that any two elements in a class commonly called tolerance class or similarity class are mutually compatible.

S. Greco et al. (Eds.): RSCTC 2006, LNAI 4259, pp. 235–243, 2006.

2 Terminology and Newly Expanded RST Models

We first introduce and define some terms and concepts and then propose some new tolerance RST models, combining several existing work.

Definition 1. An incomplete information system(IIS) is a quadruple $S = < U, AT, V, f >$, where U is a non-empty finite set of objects and AT is a non-empty finite set of attributes, such that for any $a \in AT$: $U \rightarrow V_a$ where V_a is called the value set of attribute a. Attribute domain V_a may contain a null value, meaning unknown or uncertain, denoted by special symbol"*". $V = \underset{a \in AT}{\cup} V_a$ represents the value set of all attributes in S. $a(x)$ represents the value of x at attribute a.

Definition 2.[4] In an incomplete information system $S = <U, AT, V, f>$, each subset of attributes $A \subseteq AT$ determines a binary relation $SIM(A)$ on U:

$$SIM(A) = \{ (x, y) \in U^2 : a(x) = a(y) \vee a(x) = * \vee a(y) = * \text{ for any } a \in A \} . \tag{1}$$

It is called a tolerance relation on U.

It is not difficult to prove that for any $A \subseteq AT$,

$$SIM(A) = \underset{a \in A}{\cap} SIM(\{a\}) . \tag{2}$$

$SIM(A)$ is not necessarily an equivalence relation on U.

Definition 3.[4] Let $A \subseteq AT, x \in U$. $S_A(x) = \{y \in U : (x, y) \in SIM(A)\}$ $\tag{3}$

represents those objects which are possible indiscernible to x in terms of A. $S_A(x)$ is called a tolerance class.

Definition 4.[4] Let $A \subseteq AT, x \in U$. $U/SIM(A) = \{S_A(x): x \in U\}$ $\tag{4}$

is called the set of tolerance classes according to the tolerance relation $SIM(A)$.

$U/SIM(A)$ may not be a partition on U but a covering. It is easy to find that any two elements in $S_A(x)$ are not always compatible. In this sense, we may define another covering on the universe U to overcome that drawback of $U/SIM(A)$.

Definition 5. Let S be an incomplete information system and $A \subseteq AT$, then

$$U//SIM(A) = \max\{X \subseteq U : X \times X \subseteq SIM(A)\} \tag{5}$$

where max is the maximal subsets of U under the partial order of $\subseteq$.

Definition 6. Let S be an incomplete information system, $A \subseteq AT$, then

$$SS_A(x) = X(X \in U//SIM (A), x \in X). \tag{6}$$

$$SU_A(x) = \cup X(X \in U//SIM (A), x \in X). \tag{7}$$

$$SL_A(x) = \cap X(X \in U//SIM (A), x \in X). \tag{8}$$

$$CORE_A (x) = \cap S_A(y)(x \in S_A(y), y \in U). \tag{9}$$

$SS_A(x)$ is actually a maximal compatible block randomly selecting from $U//SIM(A)$ which contains x in it. $SL_A(x)$ is called the compatible core of x under the meaning of $U//SIM(A)$ and $CORE_A(x)$, denoted by <x> in [13], is called the tolerance core of x with the meaning of $U//SIM(A)$. $\{SU_A(x): x \in U\}$, $U//SIM(A) = \{X: X \in U//SIM(A)\} = \{SS_A(x): x \in U\}$, $\{SL_A(x): x \in U\}$ and $\{CORE_A(x): x \in U\}$ are all different knowledge representation systems at different granular levels on U, in addition to $U//SIM(A)$.

Theorem 1. Let S be an incomplete information system and A be a subset of attributes AT, i.e. $A \subseteq AT$, then $SU_A(x) = S_A(x)$.

Proof. i) Assume that for any $y \in SU_A(x)$, then $(x, y) \in SIM(A)$. By section 2, $S_A(x) = \{y \in U: (x,y) \in SIM(A)\}$, there will be $y \in S_A(x)$. Since y is arbitrary, $SU_A(x) \subseteq S_A(x)$. ii) Suppose that for any $y \in S_A(x)$, then $(x, y) \in SIM(A)$ holds. That is to say, there is an X such that $(x,y) \in X^2(X \in U//SIM(A))$, then $y \in \cup X(X \in U//SIM(A), x \in X) = SU_A(x)$. Similarly, since y is arbitrary, then $S_A(x) \subseteq \cup X$ ($X \in U//SIM(A), x \in X$) $= SU_A(x)$. From what have been discussed above, there will be $SU_A(x) = S_A(x)$.

Theorem 2. For any $A \subseteq AT, X \subseteq U$, $X \in U//SIM(A)$ if and only if $X = \underset{y \in X}{\cap} S_A(y)$.

Proof. Suppose that $X \in U//SIM(A)$. Then for $\forall x, y \in X, (x, y) \in SIM(A)$. That is, for $x \in X$ and $\forall y \in X$, $x \in \underset{y \in X}{\cap} S_A(y)$. So $X \subseteq \underset{x \in X}{\cap} S_A(x)$. Assume that $y \in \underset{y \in X}{\cap} S_A(x)$. Then $y \in S_A(x)$ for any $x \in X$, i.e. y is compatible to any element in X. Because $X \in U//SIM(A)$ and any two elements in X are compatible, $(X \cup \{x\})^2 \subseteq SIM(A)$. Because $X \in U//SIM(A)$, $y \in X$. Therefore $\underset{y \in X}{\cap} S_A(x) \subseteq X$. Synthesizing the above two cases, if $X \in U//SIM(A)$ then $X = \underset{y \in X}{\cap} S_A(y)$.

Conversely, assume that $X = \underset{y \in X}{\cap} S_A(y)$. Then for any $y, z \in X$, we must have $(y, z) \in SIM(A)$ because $y \in S_A(z)$ and $z \in S_A(y)$. So $X^2 \subseteq SIM(A)$. Now that we prove that X is maximal. Otherwise, there is an object $o \notin X$ such that $(X \cup \{o\})^2 \subseteq SIM(A)$. This means for any $x \in X, o \in S_A(x)$. So $o \in \underset{y \in X}{\cap} S_A(x) = X$. It contradicts to $o \notin X$. Therefore, X is maximal and $X \in U//SIM(A)$.

Theorem 3. $SL_A(x)= \bigcap\limits_{y\in\cup X\,(X\in U\,//\,SIM\,(A)\wedge x\in X)} S_A(y)$

Proof. Suppose $SL_A(x)=X_1\cap X_2\cap...\cap X_m$, where $X_i\in U//SIM(A)$ and $x\in X_i$ ($i=1,2,...,$ m). Then $X_i= \bigcap\limits_{y\in X_i} S_A(y)$ according to Theorem 2.   So $SL_A(x)=X_1\cap X_2\cap...\cap X_m$

$= \bigcap\limits_{y\in X_1} S_A(y)\cap \bigcap\limits_{y\in X_2} S_A(y)\cap...\cap \bigcap\limits_{y\in X_m} S_A(y)= \bigcap\limits_{y\in\cup X\,(X\in U\,//\,SIM\,(A)\wedge x\in X)} S_A(y)$.

Theorem 4. $CORE_A(x)= \bigcap\limits_{y\in S_A(x)} S_A(y)$

Proof.   Because $CORE_A(x)=\cap S_A(y)(x\in S_A(y),\ y\in U)$, we need only to proof that $\cap S_A(y)(x\in S_A(y),\ y\in U)= \bigcap\limits_{y\in S_A(x)} S_A(y)$. For any given $z\in\cap S_A(y)(x\in S_A(y),\ y\in U)$, we have $z\in S_A(y),\ x\in S_A(y),\ y\in U$. It means $(z,\ y)\in SIM(A),\ (x,\ y)\in SIM(A)$. So $z\in S_A(y),\ y\in S_A(x)$, and then $z\in \bigcap\limits_{y\in S_A(x)} S_A(y)$. Therefore, $CORE_A(x)=\cap S_A(y)(x\in S_A(y),$ $y\in U)\subseteq \bigcap\limits_{y\in S_A(x)} S_A(y)$. Conversely, $\bigcap\limits_{y\in S_A(x)} S_A(y)\subseteq\cap S_A(y)(x\in S_A(y),\ y\in U)$ is also valid.

Theorem 5. $SL_A(x)=CORE_A(x)$.

Proof. Suppose $SL_A(x)=X_1\cap X_2\cap...\cap X_m$, where $X_i\in U//SIM(A)$, and $x\in X_i$ ($i=1,2,...,m$). Then $S_A(x)= SU_A(x)=X_1\cup X_2\cup...\cup X_m$. According to Theorem 3, $SL_A(x)= \bigcap\limits_{y\in\cup X\,(X\in U\,//\,SIM\,(A)\wedge x\in X)} S_A(y) = \bigcap\limits_{y\in X_1\cup X_2\cup...\cup X_m} S_A(y) = \bigcap\limits_{y\in S_A(x)} S_A(y) = CORE_A(x)$.

Theorem 6. $U//SIM(A)=\{X\subseteq U:\ X^2\subseteq SIM(A),\ (\forall x\in U\wedge x\notin X\to(X\cup\{x\})^2$ $\nsubseteq SIM(A))\} =\{X\subseteq U:\ X^2\subseteq SIM(A),\ (\forall x\in X\to\exists y\in U-X\wedge(x,\ y)\notin SIM(A))\}$.

Although $SU_A(x)=S_A(x)$ and $SL_A(x)=CORE(x)$, their construction methods are different and the finding algorithms (see a following paper) vary accordingly.

Definition 7. Let S be an incomplete information system, $X\subseteq U,\ A\subseteq AT$, then for knowledge representation systems mentioned above, upper and lower approximations are defined as follows:

$$\overline{SS}_A(X)=\{\ x\in U:\ SS_A(x)\cap X\neq\varnothing\ \}\}\,. \tag{10}$$

$$\overline{SU}_A(X)=\{x\in U:\ SU_A(x)\cap X\neq\varnothing\ \} \tag{11}$$

$$\overline{SL}_A(X)=\{x\in U:\ SL_A(x)\cap X\neq\varnothing\ \} \tag{12}$$

$$\overline{CORE}_A(X)=\{x\in U:\ CORE_A(x)\cap X\neq\varnothing\ \} \tag{13}$$

$$\underline{SS}_A(X)= \{x\in U : SS_A(x)\subseteq X\} \tag{14}$$

$$\underline{SU}_A(X)= \{x\in U : SU_A(x)\subseteq X\} \tag{15}$$

$$\underline{SL}_A(X) =\{x\in U : SL_A(x)\subseteq X\} \tag{16}$$

$$\underline{CORE}_A(X) =\{x\in U : CORE_A(x)\subseteq X\} \tag{17}$$

We can also introduce the upper approximation and the lower approximation to the tolerance relation in [4] as follows:

$$\overline{S}_A(X)=\{x\in U : S_A(x)\cap X\neq \varnothing \} \tag{18}$$

$$\underline{S}_A(X)= \{x\in U : S_A(x)\subseteq X\} \tag{19}$$

Theorem 7. $\overline{SU}_A(X)= \overline{S}_A(X)$, $\underline{SU}_A(X)= \underline{S}_A(X)$, $\overline{SL}_A(X)= \overline{CORE}_A(X)$, $\underline{SL}_A(X)= \underline{CORE}_A(X)$.

Proof. According to Theorem 1 and Theorem 2, the equations in Theorem 7 can be proved straightforward.

Property 1. Let S be an incomplete information system, $X\subseteq U$, $A\subseteq AT$. Then

$$\text{i)}\ \underline{SU}_A(X)\subseteq\underline{SL}_A(X) \tag{20}$$

$$\text{ii)}\ \overline{SL}_A(X)\subseteq \overline{SU}_A(X) \tag{21}$$

Proof. i) According to Definition 7, we have $SL_A(x) \subseteq SU_A(x)$,   that is to say, if $SU_A(x)\subseteq X$, there must hold $SL_A(x)\subseteq X$; by contradiction, $SL_A(x)\subseteq X$ does not mean $SU_A(x)\subseteq X$, so $\underline{SU}_A(X)\subseteq \underline{SL}_A(X)$ is affirmed.

   ii) Similarly, if $SL_A(x)\cap X \neq \varnothing$, there must be $SU_A(x)\cap X \neq \varnothing$; by contrary, $SU_A(x)\cap X \neq \varnothing$ does not mean $SL_A(x)\cap X \neq \varnothing$, so $\overline{SL}_A(X)\subseteq \overline{SU}_A(X)$. That completes the proof.

   Similar to the properties in the original RST model proposed by Palwak Z. we can obtain the following properties:

Property 2. $\underline{SU}_A(X)\subseteq X\subseteq \overline{SU}_A(X)$ $\tag{22}$

$$A\subset B\Rightarrow \underline{SU}_A(X)\subseteq\underline{SU}_B(X) \tag{23}$$

$$A\subset B\Rightarrow \overline{SU}_A(X)\supseteq \overline{SU}_B(X) \tag{24}$$

Property 3. $\underline{SL}_A(X) \subseteq X \subseteq \overline{SL}_A(X)$ (25)

$$A \subset B \Rightarrow \underline{SL}_A(X) \subseteq \underline{SL}_B(X)$$ (26)

$$A \subset B \Rightarrow \overline{SL}_A(X) \supseteq \overline{SL}_B(X)$$ (27)

Property 4. $\underline{S}_A(X) \subseteq \underline{SS}_A(X)$ (28)

$$\overline{S}_A(X) \supseteq \overline{SS}_A(X)$$ (29)

All these properties can be proved similar to those in the original RST model proposed by Palwak Z.. Owing to the space limitation, the proofs of them are omitted.

3 Accuracy Measurements and Entropies

Definition 8. Let S be an incomplete information system and ψ_1, ψ_2 be two coverings on the universe U. If for any $\mu \in \psi_1$, $\exists v \in \psi_2$ holds that $\mu \subseteq v$ and if for any $v \in \psi_2$, $\exists \mu \in \psi_1$ holds $v \supseteq \mu$, then covering ψ_1 is a refinement of ψ_2, or equivalently speaking, ψ_2 is a coarsening of ψ_1, denoted by $\psi_1 \preceq \psi_2$.

Given two coverings ψ_1 and ψ_2, their meet $\psi_1 \wedge \psi_2$ is the largest covering which is a refinement of both ψ_1 and ψ_2, and their join $\psi_1 \vee \psi_2$ is the smallest covering which is a coarsening of both ψ_1 and ψ_2. Covering ψ_2 has smaller level of granulation for problem solving than covering ψ_1.

Let $\pi_1 = \{SU_A(x): x \in U\} = \{S_A(x): x \in U\}$, $\pi_2 = \{SS_A(x): x \in U)$ and $\pi_3 = \{SL_A(x):x \in U\} = \{CORE_A(x): x \in U\}$. Then they form three different levels of granularity of the universe in the incomplete information system S, named as ψ_1, ψ_2, ψ_3 after eliminating repeated elements, respectively.

Theorem 8. For ψ_1, ψ_2, ψ_3 as mentioned in the above, $\psi_3 \preceq \psi_2 \preceq \psi_1$ holds.

Definition 9. Let S be an incomplete information system, ψ be a covering on the universe U, that is to say, $\psi = \{C_1, C_2, \ldots, C_m\}$ and $\cup_{i=1}^{m} C_i = U$, then the accuracy measurement of subset $X \subseteq U$ is defined as follows:

$$\alpha_\psi = \frac{|\underline{apr}_\psi(X)|}{|\overline{apr}_\psi(X)|},$$ (30)

where $\underline{apr}_\psi(X) = \cup \{C_i : C_i \subseteq X, 1 \leqslant i \leqslant m\}$, $\overline{apr}_\psi(X) = \cup \{C_i : C_i \cap X \neq \varnothing, 1 \leqslant i \leqslant m\}$.

Theorem 9. Let S be an incomplete information system and ψ_1, ψ_2 be two coverings on the universe U, if $\psi_1 \preceq \psi_2$, then $\alpha_{\psi_1} \geq \alpha_{\psi_2}$.

Proof. Suppose that $\psi_1 = \{C_1, C_2, \ldots, C_m\}, \psi_2 = \{D_1, D_2, \ldots, D_n\}$.

i) For $\alpha_{\psi_1} \leq \alpha_{\psi_2}$, then for any j, $D_j \cap X \neq \varnothing$ $(1 \leq j \leq n)$, $\exists\, C_i \subseteq D_j (1 \leq i \leq m)$ and for any i, $C_i \cap X \neq \varnothing$. According to Definition 8, it is clear that $\underline{apr}_{\psi_1}(X) \subseteq \underline{apr}_{\psi_2}(X)$.

ii) It is easy to prove that $\overline{apr}_\psi(X) = (\underline{apr}_\psi(X^c))^c$ where X^c represents the complementation of set X. From this property of rough set theory, $\overline{apr}_{\psi_1}(X) \supseteq \overline{apr}_{\psi_2}(X)$.

According to i) and ii), $\alpha_{\psi_1} \geq \alpha_{\psi_2}$. That completes the proof.

Theorem 9 implies that the accuracy measurement of rough set is monotonously increasing if the level of granularity is decreasing in incomplete information systems.

In an incomplete information system S, for knowledge representation system π_1, the accuracy measurement of the rough set is $\alpha_{\psi_1}(X) = |\underline{SU}_A(X)|/|\overline{SU}_A(X)|$; for knowledge representation system π_2, the accuracy measurement of the rough set is $\alpha_{\psi_2}(X) = |\underline{SS}_A(X)|/|\overline{SS}_A(X)|$ and for knowledge representation system π_3, the accuracy measure of the rough set is $\alpha_{\psi_3}(X) = |\underline{SL}_A(X)|/|\overline{SL}_A(X)|$. It is easy to prove the following theorem.

Theorem 10. $\alpha_{\psi_1}(X) \leq \alpha_{\psi_2}(X) \leq \alpha_{\psi_3}(X)$. $\hspace{2em}$ (31)

Proof. According to Theorem 9, it is obvious that $\alpha_{\psi_1}(X) \leq \alpha_{\psi_2}(X)$ and $\alpha_{\psi_2}(X) \leq \alpha_{\psi_3}(X)$. So $\alpha_{\psi_1}(X) \leq \alpha_{\psi_2}(X) \leq \alpha_{\psi_3}(X)$ must be held.

Definition 10. Let S be an incomplete information system, $A(\subseteq AT)$ be a subset of attributes and ψ be a covering on the universe U, that is to say, $\psi = \{C_1, C_2, \ldots, C_m\}$ and $\bigcup_{i=1}^{m} C_i = U$. Then the rough entropy of the knowledge A is defined as follows:

$$E_\psi(A) = -\sum_{i=1}^{m} \frac{|C_i|}{|U|} \log \frac{1}{|C_i|}.$$ $\hspace{2em}$ (32)

Theorem 11. Let S be an incomplete information system, $\phi_1 = \{C_1, C_2, \ldots, C_m\}$, $\phi_2 = \{D_1, D_2, \ldots, D_n\}$ two coverings on the universe U, $A \subseteq AT$, if $\phi_1 \preceq \phi_2$, then

$$E_{\phi_1}(A) \leq E_{\phi_2}(A).$$ $\hspace{2em}$ (33)

Proof. According to definition 10, for any $C_i \in \psi_1$ $(1 \leq i \leq m)$, there must be $D_j \in \phi_2$ $(1 \leq j \leq n)$ such that $C_i \subseteq D_j$. Then $-\frac{|C_i|}{|U|} \log \frac{1}{|C_i|} \leq -\frac{|D_j|}{|U|} \log \frac{1}{|D_j|}$.

It is easy to extend the right of this inequation for the reason that for any D_j there is a C_i which satisfies $D_j \subseteq C_i$. So

$$-\sum_{i=1}^{m} \frac{|C_i|}{|U|} \log \frac{1}{|C_i|} \leq -\sum_{j=1}^{n} \frac{|D_j|}{|U|} \log \frac{1}{|D_j|},$$

because C_i is marked only once when it appears repeatedly. That completes the proof.

Obviously, π_1, π_2 and π_3 can define different rough entropies of the relative knowledge, such as $E_{\psi_1}(A), E_{\psi_2}(A), E_{\psi_3}(A)$ respectively. From Theorem 8, the rough entropy of knowledge is monotonously decreasing when the level of granularity of the covering is decreasing. Therefore, we obtain the following theorem:

Theorem 12. $E_{\psi_1}(A) \leq E_{\psi_2}(A) \leq E_{\psi_3}(A)$.   (34)

Proof. By Theorem 11, $E_{\psi_1}(A) \leq E_{\psi_2}(A)$ and $E_{\psi_2}(A) \leq E_{\psi_3}(A)$ are held. So It is obvious to have $E_{\psi_1}(A) \leq E_{\psi_2}(A) \leq E_{\psi_3}(A)$.

Definition 11. Let S be an incomplete information system, $A \subseteq AT$ and ψ be a covering on the universe U. Then the rough entropy of $X \subseteq U$ about knowledge A is defined as follows:

$$E_A^{\psi}(X) = E_{\psi}(A) + (1 - \alpha),   (35)$$

where α is the accuracy measurement of X according to covering ψ.

In this way, $E_A^{\psi_1}(X), E_A^{\psi_2}(X), E_A^{\psi_3}(X)$, as different rough entropies of $X \subseteq U$ according to knowledge π_1, π_2 and π_3, respectively, can also be defined.

Theorem 13. $E_A^{\psi_3}(X) \leq E_A^{\psi_2}(X) \leq E_A^{\psi_1}(X)$.   (36)

Proof. Because $E_A^{\psi}(X)$ is an increasing function on ψ and $\psi_3 \preceq \psi_2 \preceq \psi_1$, we can immediately obtain $E_A^{\psi_3}(X) \leq E_A^{\psi_2}(X) \leq E_A^{\psi_1}(X)$.

4 Conclusions

As one of the important formal framework of Granule Computing (GrC), RST and its various expanded models are essential in so many fields of scientific researches. Different levels of granularity have their different use. Five knowledge representation systems $\{S_A(x): x \in U\}$, $\{SU_A(x): x \in U\}$, $\{SS_A(x): x \in U\}$ $\{SL_A(x): x \in U\}$, $\{CORE_A(x): x \in U\}$ are discussed. Two of them, $\{S_A(x): x \in U\}$ and $\{CORE_A(x): x \in U\}$ are directly based on the tolerance classes to the tolerance relation in the incomplete information system S. The other three, $\{SU_A(x): x \in U\}, \{SS_A(x): x \in U\}$ and $\{SL_A(x): x \in U\}$, proposed in this paper, are based on the compatible classes to the compatible relation(a tolerance relation is also a compatible relation). We have proved $\{SU_A(x): x \in U\} = \{S_A(x): x \in U\}$ and $\{SL_A(x): x \in U\} = \{CORE_A(x): x \in U\}$. Therefore only three of the five are really different, having different levels of granularity and are investigated deeply in the paper. Furthermore, measurements such as accuracy measurements, rough entropies of knowledge and rough entropies of set about knowledge to the three different systems are defined and relationships between those measurements are also explored.

Acknowledgement

This work is supported in part by NSF Career Grant IIS 0448023, NSF CCF 0514679, PA Dept of Health Tobacco Settlement Formula Grant (No. 240205 and No. 240196), and PA Dept of Health Grant (No. 239667). We also thank for anonymous reviewers for their comments on the paper.

References

1. Ananthanarayana,V.S., Murty, M. N., Subramanian, D.K.: Tree Structure for Efficient Data Mining Using Rough Sets. Pattern Recognition Letters, 24 (2003) 851-862
2. Chan, C.C.: A Rough Set Approach to Attribute Generalization in Data Mining. Information Sciences. 107 (1998)169-176
3. Chen,W.L., Cheng, J.X., Zhang, C.J.: A Generalization to Rough Set Theory Based on Tolerance Relation, J. computer engineering and applications, 16(2004)26-28
4. Kryszkiewicz,M.: Rough Set Approach to Incomplete Information Systems. Information Sciences, Vol.112,1 (1998) 39-49
5. Mi,J.S., Wu,W.Z., Zhang,W.X.: Approaches to Knowledge Reduction Based on Variable Precision Rough Set Model. Information Sciences. 159 (2004) 255-272
6. Pawlak,Z.: Rough Sets. Int. J.of Computer and Information Sciences. 11(1982) 341-356
7. Pawlak,Z.: Rough Set Theory and Its Applications to Data Analysis. Cybernetics and Systems, Vol 29, 7(1998)661–688
8. Pawlak,Z.: Rough sets and intelligent data analysis. Information Sciences. 147 (2002) 1-12
9. Swiniarski,R.W., Skowron, A.: Rough Set Methods in Feature Selection and Recognition Pattern Recognition Letters, 24 (2003) 833~849
10. Stefanowski,J., Tsoukiàs,A.: Incomplete Information Tables and Rough Classification. J. Computational Intelligence, Vol. 17, 3 (2001) 545-566
11. T Hong,Z.P, Tseng,L.H., Wang, S.L.: Learning Rules from Incomplete Training Examples by Rough Sets. Expert Systems with Applications, 22 (2002) 285-293
12. Wang,G.Y.: Extension of Rough Set under Incomplete Information System. J.ComputerResearch and Development. 39 (2002) 1238-1243
13. Wu,C., Yang,X.B.: Information Granules in General and Complete Covering. Proceedings of 2005 IEEE International Conference on Granular Computing, 675-678
14. Zhu,W., Wang, F.Y.: Reduction and Axiom of Covering Generalized Rough Sets. Information Sciences. 15 (2003) 217-230

Local and Global Approximations for Incomplete Data

Jerzy W. Grzymala-Busse[1,2] and Wojciech Rzasa[3,*]

[1] Department of Electrical Engineering and Computer Science University of Kansas,
Lawrence, KS 66045, USA
[2] Institute of Computer Science, Polish Academy of Sciences,
01–237 Warsaw, Poland
[3] Institute of Mathematics, University of Rzeszow,
35–310 Rzeszow, Poland

Abstract. For completely specified decision tables, where lower and upper approximations are unique, the lower approximation is the largest definable set contained in the approximated set X and the upper approximation of X is the smallest definable set containing X. For incomplete decision tables the existing definitions of upper approximations provide sets that, in general, are not minimal definable sets. The same is true for approximations based on relations that are generalizations of the equivalence relation. In this paper we introduce two definitions of approximations, local and global, such that the corresponding upper approximations are minimal. Local approximations are more precise than global approximations. Global lower approximations may be determined by a polynomial algorithm. However, algorithms to find both local approximations and global upper approximations are NP-hard.

1 Introduction

Recently we observed intensive research activity in two areas: rough set approaches to handle incomplete data, mostly in the form of decision tables with missing attribute values, and attempts to study generalizations of the standard indiscernibility relation. In the latter area concerned relations are not equivalence relations. Our paper contributes to both research areas.

Initially rough set theory was applied to complete data sets (with all attribute values specified). Recently rough set theory was extended to handle incomplete data sets (with missing attribute values) [1,2,3,4,5,6,7,8,9,17,18,19,20].

We will distinguish two types of missing attribute values. The first type of missing attribute value will be called *lost*. A missing attribute value is lost when for some case (example, object) the corresponding attribute value was mistakenly erased or not entered into the data set.

The second type of missing attribute values, called *"do not care" conditions*, are based on an assumption that missing attribute values were initially, when

---

* This research has been partially supported by the Ministry of Scientific Research and Information Technology of the Republic of Poland, grant 3 T11C 005 28.

S. Greco et al. (Eds.): RSCTC 2006, LNAI 4259, pp. 244–253, 2006.

the data set was created, irrelevant. The corresponding cases were classified even though the values of these attribute were not known. A missing attribute value of this type may be potentially replaced by any value typical for that attribute.

For incomplete decision tables there are two special cases: in the first case, all missing attribute values are lost, in the second case, all missing attribute values are "do not care" conditions. Incomplete decision tables in which all attribute values are lost, from the viewpoint of rough set theory, were studied for the first time in [6], where two algorithms for rule induction, modified to handle lost attribute values, were presented. This approach was studied later, e.g., in [18,19], where the indiscernibility relation was generalized to describe such incomplete data. Furthermore, an approach to incomplete data based on relative frequencies was presented in [19]. Another approach, using fuzzy set ideas, was presented in [1].

On the other hand, incomplete decision tables in which all missing attribute values are "do not care" conditions, from the view point of rough set theory, were studied for the first time in [2], where a method for rule induction was introduced in which each missing attribute value was replaced by all values from the domain of the attribute. Originally such values were replaced by all values from the entire domain of the attribute, later, by attribute values restricted to the same concept to which a case with a missing attribute value belongs. Such incomplete decision tables, with all missing attribute values being "do not care conditions", were extensively studied in [8,9], including extending the idea of the indiscernibility relation to describe such incomplete decision tables.

In general, incomplete decision tables are described by characteristic relations, in a similar way as complete decision tables are described by indiscernibility relations [3,4,5].

In rough set theory, one of the basic notions is the idea of lower and upper approximations. For complete decision tables, once the indiscernibility relation is fixed and the concept (a set of cases) is given, the lower and upper approximations are unique.

For incomplete decision tables, for a given characteristic relation and concept, there are three important and different possibilities to define lower and upper approximations, called singleton, subset, and concept approximations [3]. Singleton lower and upper approximations were studied in [8,9,16,18,19]. Note that similar three definitions of lower and upper approximations, though not for incomplete decision tables, were studied in [10,11,12,21,22,23,24].

Our main objective is to study two novel kinds of approximations: local and global. The local approximations are defined using sets of attribute-value pairs called complexes, while the global approximations are formed from characteristic sets. Additionally, lower approximations, local and global, are the maximal sets that are locally and globally definable, respectively, and contained in the approximated set X. Similarly, upper approximations, local and global, are the minimal sets that are locally and globally definable, respectively, containing the approximated set X.

Note that some other rough-set approaches to missing attribute values were presented in [1, 2] as well.

2   Blocks of Attribute-Value Pairs

We assume that the input data sets are presented in the form of a *decision table*. An example of a decision table is shown in Table 1. Rows of the decision table

Table 1. An incomplete decision table

	Attributes			Decision
Case	Temperature	Headache	Nausea	Flu
1	high	?	no	yes
2	very_high	yes	yes	yes
3	?	no	no	yes
4	high	yes	yes	yes
5	high	?	yes	yes
6	normal	yes	no	yes
7	normal	no	yes	no
8	*	yes	*	no

represent *cases*, while columns are labeled by *variables*. The set of all cases will be denoted by U. In Table 1, $U = \{1, 2, ..., 8\}$. Independent variables are called *attributes* and a dependent variable is called a *decision* and is denoted by d. The set of all attributes will be denoted by A. In Table 1, $A = \{Temperature, Headache, Nausea\}$. Any decision table defines a function ρ that maps the direct product of U and A into the set of all values. For example, in Table 1, $\rho(1, Temperature) = high$. A decision table with completely specified function ρ will be called *completely specified*, or, for the sake of simplicity, *complete*. In practice, input data for data mining are frequently affected by missing attribute values. In other words, the corresponding function ρ is incompletely specified (partial). A decision table with an incompletely specified function ρ will be called *incomplete*. Function ρ describing Table 1 is incompletely specified.

For the rest of the paper we will assume that all decision values are specified, i.e., they are not missing. Also, we will assume that lost values will be denoted by "?" and "do not care" conditions by "*". Additionally, we will assume that for each case at least one attribute value is specified.

An important tool to analyze complete decision tables is a block of the attribute-value pair. Let a be an attribute, i.e., $a \in A$ and let v be a value of a for some case. For complete decision tables if $t = (a, v)$ is an attribute-value pair then a *block* of t, denoted $[t]$, is a set of all cases from U that for attribute a have value v. For incomplete decision tables, a block of an attribute-value pair must be modified in the following way:

- If for an attribute a there exists a case x such that $\rho(x, a) = ?$, i.e., the corresponding value is lost, then the case x should not be included in any blocks$[(a, v)]$ for all values v of attribute a,
- If for an attribute a there exists a case x such that the corresponding value is a "do not care" condition, i.e., $\rho(x, a) = *$, then the case x should be included in blocks $[(a, v)]$ for all specified values v of attribute a.

Thus,

$[(\text{Temperature, high})] = \{1, 4, 5, 8\}$,
$[(\text{Temperature, very\_high})] = \{2, 8\}$,
$[(\text{Temperature, normal})] = \{6, 7, 8\}$,
$[(\text{Headache, yes})] = \{2, 4, 6, 8\}$,
$[(\text{Headache, no})] = \{3, 7\}$,
$[(\text{Nausea, no})] = \{1, 3, 6, 8\}$,
$[(\text{Nausea, yes})] = \{2, 4, 5, 7, 8\}$.

For a case $x \in U$ the *characteristic set* $K_B(x)$ is defined as the intersection of the sets $K(x, a)$, for all $a \in B$, where the set $K(x, a)$ is defined in the following way:

- If $\rho(x, a)$ is specified, then $K(x, a)$ is the block $[(a, \rho(x, a))]$ of attribute a and its value $\rho(x, a)$,
- If $\rho(x, a) = ?$ or $\rho(x, a) = *$ then the set $K(x, a) = U$.

For Table 1 and $B = A$,

$K_A(1) = \{1, 4, 5, 8\} \cap U \cap \{1, 3, 6, 8\} = \{1, 8\}$,
$K_A(2) = \{2, 8\} \cap \{2, 4, 6, 8\} \cap \{2, 4, 5, 7, 8\} = \{2, 8\}$,
$K_A(3) = U \cap \{3, 7\} \cap \{1, 3, 6, 8\} = \{3\}$,
$K_A(4) = \{1, 4, 5, 8\} \cap \{2, 4, 6, 8\} \cap \{2, 4, 5, 7, 8\} = \{4, 8\}$,
$K_A(5) = \{1, 4, 5, 8\} \cap U \cap \{2, 4, 5, 7, 8\} = \{4, 5, 8\}$,
$K_A(6) = \{6, 7, 8\} \cap \{2, 4, 6, 8\} \cap \{1, 3, 6, 8\} = \{6, 8\}$,
$K_A(7) = \{6, 7, 8\} \cap \{3, 7\} \cap \{2, 4, 5, 7, 8\} = \{7\}$, and
$K_A(8) = U \cap \{2, 4, 6, 8\} \cap U = \{2, 4, 6, 8\}$.

Characteristic set $K_B(x)$ may be interpreted as the set of cases that are indistinguishable from x using all attributes from B and using a given interpretation of missing attribute values. Thus, $K_A(x)$ is the set of all cases that cannot be distinguished from x using all attributes. In [22] $K_A(x)$ was called a successor neighborhood of x, see also [10, 11, 12, 16, 21, 23, 24].

The characteristic relation $R(B)$ is a relation on U defined for $x, y \in U$ as follows

$$(x, y) \in R(B) \text{ if and only if } y \in K_B(x).$$

The characteristic relation $R(B)$ is reflexive but—in general—does not need to be symmetric or transitive. Also, the characteristic relation $R(B)$ is known if we know characteristic sets $K_B(x)$ for all $x \in U$. In our example, $R(A) = \{(1, 1),$ $(1, 8), (2, 2), (2, 8), (3, 3), (4, 4), (4, 8), (5, 4), (5, 5), (5, 8), (6, 6), (6, 8), (7, 7),$ $(8, 2), (8, 4), (8, 6), (8, 8)\}$. The most convenient way to define the characteristic relation is through the characteristic sets.

For decision tables, in which all missing attribute values are lost, a special characteristic relation was defined in [18], see also, e.g., [17, 19].

For decision tables where all missing attribute values are "do not care" conditions a special characteristic relation was defined in [8], see also, e.g., [9].

3   Definability

Let $B \subseteq A$. For completely specified decision tables, any union of elementary sets of B is called a B-definable set [14]. Definability for completely specified decision tables should be modified to fit into incomplete decision tables. For incomplete decision tables, a union of some intersections of attribute-value pair blocks, in any such intersection all attributes should be different and attributes are members of B, will be called B-*locally definable* sets. A union of characteristic sets $K_B(x)$, where $x \in X \subseteq U$ will be called a B-*globally definable* set. Any set X that is B-globally definable is B-locally definable, the converse is not true. In the example of Table 1, the set $\{7, 8\}$ is A-locally-definable since it is equal to the intersection of [(Temperature, normal)] and [(Nausea, yes)]. Nevertheless, $\{7, 8\}$ is not A-globally-definable.

Obviously, if a set is not B-locally definable then it cannot be expressed by rule sets using attributes from B. This is why it is so important to distinguish between B-locally definable sets and those that are not B-locally definable.

4   Local Approximations

Let X be any subset of the set U of all cases. The set X is called a *concept* and is usually defined as the set of all cases defined by a specific value of the decision. In general, X is not a B-definable set, locally or globally. A set T of attribute-value pairs, where all attributes are distinct, will be called a *complex*. For a set T of attribute-value pairs, the intersection of blocks for all t from T will be denoted by $[T]$.

For incomplete decision tables lower and upper approximations may be defined in a few different ways, see, e.g., [3, 4, 5]. In this paper we introduce a new idea of optimal approximations that are B-locally definable. Let $B \subseteq A$. The *B-local lower* approximation of the concept X, denoted by $L\underline{B}X$, is defined as follows

$$\cup \{[T] \mid T \text{ is a complex of } X, [T] \subseteq X\}.$$

The *B-local upper* approximation of the concept X, denoted by $L\overline{B}X$, is a set with the minimal cardinality containing X and defined in the following way

$$\cup \{[T] \mid T \text{ is a complex of } X, [T] \cap X \neq \emptyset\}.$$

Obviously, the B-local lower approximation of X is unique and it is the maximal B-locally definable set contained in X. Any B-local upper approximation of X is B-locally definable, it contains X, and is, by definition, minimal.

For Table 1

$$L\underline{A}\{1,2,3,4,5,6\} = [(Headache, no)] \cap [(Nausea, no)] = \{3\},$$

so one complex, $\{(Headache, no), (Nausea, no)\}$, is sufficient to describe $L\underline{A}\{1,2,3,4,5,6\}$,

$$L\underline{A}\{7,8\} = [(Temperature, normal)] \cap [(Nausea, yes)] = \{7,8\},$$

so again, one complex, $\{(Temperature, normal), (Nausea, yes)\}$, describes $L\underline{A}\{7,8\}$,

$$L\overline{A}\{1,2,3,4,5,6\} =$$
$$[(Temperature, high)] \cup [(Headache, yes)] \cup [(Nausea, no)] =$$
$$\{1,2,3,4,5,6,8\},$$

therefore, to describe $L\overline{A}\{1,2,3,4,5,6\}$ three complexes are necessary: $\{(Temperature, high)\}$, $\{(Headache, yes)\}$, and $\{(Nausea, no)\}$. Finally,

$$L\overline{A}\{7,8\} = [(Temperature, normal)] \cap [(Nausea, yes)] = \{7,8\}.$$

For the incomplete decision table from Table 1 the local lower approximations for both concepts, $\{1, 2, 3, 4, 5, 6\}$ and $\{7, 8\}$, as well as the upper local approximations for these concepts, are unique. Though the local lower approximations are always unique, the local upper approximations, in general, are not unique. For example, let us consider an incomplete decision table from Table 2.

For Table 2

[(Age, <25)] = {1, 4, 6},
[(Age, 25..35)] = {1, 4, 7},
[(Age, >35)] = {1, 2, 3, 4, 5},
[(Complications, alcoholism)] = {1},
[(Complications, obesity)] = {2, 3},
[(Complications, none)] = {4, 5, 6, 7},
[(Hypertension, mild)] = {1}.
[(Hypertension, severe)] = {2}.
[(Hypertension, no)] = {4, 5, 6, 7}.

Moreover, for Table 2

$$L\underline{A}\{1,2,3,4\} =$$
$$[(Complications, alcoholism)] \cup [(Complications, obesity)] =$$
$$\{1,2,3\},$$

$$L\underline{A}\{5,6,7\} = \emptyset,$$

Table 2. An incomplete decision table

		Attributes		Decision
Case	Age	Complications	Hypertension	Delivery
1	*	alcoholism	mild	pre-term
2	>35	obesity	severe	pre-term
3	>35	obesity	?	pre-term
4	*	none	none	pre-term
5	>35	none	none	full-term
6	<25	none	none	full-term
7	25..35	none	none	full-term

However,

$$\overline{LA}\{1,2,3,4\}$$

is not unique, any of the following sets

$$[(Age, > 35)] = \{1,2,3,4,5\},$$

$$[(Age, < 25)] \cup [(Complications, obesity)] = \{1,2,3,4,6\},$$

or

$$[(Age, 26..35)] \cup [(Complications, obesity)] = \{1,2,3,4,7\}.$$

may serve as local upper approximations of $\{1, 2, 3, 4\}$.

Lastly,

$$\overline{LA}\{5,6,7\} = [(Complications, none)] = \{4,5,6,7\}.$$

Algorithms to compute local lower or upper approximations are NP-hard, since the corresponding problems may be presented in terms of prime implicants, monotone functions, and minimization. A similar result for reducts of complete decision tables is well known [15].

5   Global Approximations

Again, let $B \subseteq A$. Then B-*global lower* approximation of the concept X, denoted by $G\underline{B}X$, is defined as follows

$$\cup\{K_B(x) \mid x \in X, K_B(x) \subseteq X\}.$$

Note that the definition of global lower approximation is identical with the definition of subset (or concept) lower approximation [3,4,5]. The *B-global upper* approximation of the concept X, denoted by $G\overline{B}X$, is a set with the minimal cardinality containing X and defined in the following way

$$\cup\{K_B(x) \mid x \in U, K_B(x) \cap X \neq \emptyset\}.$$

Similarly as for local approximations, a global lower approximation for any concept X is unique. Additionally, both B-global approximations, lower and upper, are B-globally definable. On the other hand, global upper approximations do not need to be unique. For Table 1,

$$G\underline{A}\{1, 2, 3, 4, 5, 6\} = K_A(3) = \{3\},$$

$$G\underline{A}\{7, 8\} = K_A(7) = \{7\},$$

$$G\overline{A}\{1, 2, 3, 4, 5, 6\} =$$
$$K_A(1) \cup K_A(2) \cup K_A(3) \cup K_A(5) \cup K_A(6) = \{1, 2, 3, 4, 5, 6, 8\}.$$

Furthermore,

$$G\overline{A}\{7, 8\}$$

may be computed in four different ways:

(1) as $K_A(1) \cup K_A(7) = \{1, 7, 8\}$,

(2) as $K_A(2) \cup K_A(7) = \{2, 7, 8\}$,

(3) as $K_A(4) \cup K_A(7) = \{4, 7, 8\}$,

(4) or as $K_A(6) \cup K_A(7) = \{6, 7, 8\}$,

all four sets are global upper approximations of the concept $\{7, 8\}$.

In general, local approximations are more precise than global approximations. For any concept X and a subset B of A,

$$L\underline{B}X \supseteq G\underline{B}X$$

and

$$L\overline{B}X \subseteq G\overline{B}X.$$

It is not difficult to find a simple algorithm to compute global lower approximations in polynomial time. Nevertheless, algorithms to compute global upper approximations are NP-hard as well.

6 Conclusions

In this paper we introduced two new kinds of approximations: local and global. These approximations describe optimally approximated sets (lower approximations are maximal, upper approximations are minimal and, at the same time, local approximations are locally definable while global approximations are globally definable).

Note that our global approximations may be used to describe behavior of systems defined by relations that are not equivalence relations, as in [10, 11, 12, 16, 21, 22, 23, 24].

As a final point, optimality comes with the price: algorithms to compute both local upper approximations and global upper approximations are NP-hard.

References

1. Greco, S., Matarazzo, B., and Slowinski, R.: Dealing with missing data in rough set analysis of multi-attribute and multi-criteria decision problems. In *Decision Making: Recent Developments and Worldwide Applications*, ed. by S. H. Zanakis, G. Doukidis, and Z. Zopounidis, Kluwer Academic Publishers, Dordrecht, Boston, London, 2000, 295–316.
2. Grzymala-Busse, J.W.: On the unknown attribute values in learning from examples. Proc. of the ISMIS-91, 6th International Symposium on Methodologies for Intelligent Systems, Charlotte, North Carolina, October 16–19, 1991. Lecture Notes in Artificial Intelligence, vol. 542, Springer-Verlag, Berlin, Heidelberg, New York (1991) 368–377.
3. Grzymala-Busse, J.W.: Rough set strategies to data with missing attribute values. Workshop Notes, Foundations and New Directions of Data Mining, the 3-rd International Conference on Data Mining, Melbourne, FL, USA, November 19–22, 2003, 56–63.
4. Grzymala-Busse, J.W.: Data with missing attribute values: Generalization of idiscernibility relation and rule induction. *Transactions on Rough Sets*, Lecture Notes in Computer Science Journal Subline, Springer-Verlag, vol. 1 (2004) 78–95.
5. Grzymala-Busse, J.W.: Characteristic relations for incomplete data: A generalization of the indiscernibility relation. Proc. of the RSCTC'2004, the Fourth International Conference on Rough Sets and Current Trends in Computing, Uppsala, Sweden, June 1–5, 2004. Lecture Notes in Artificial Intelligence 3066, Springer-Verlag 2004, 244–253.
6. Grzymala-Busse, J.W. and Wang A.Y.: Modified algorithms LEM1 and LEM2 for rule induction from data with missing attribute values. Proc. of the Fifth International Workshop on Rough Sets and Soft Computing (RSSC'97) at the Third Joint Conference on Information Sciences (JCIS'97), Research Triangle Park, NC, March 2–5, 1997, 69–72.
7. Hong, T.P., Tseng L.H. and Chien, B.C.: Learning coverage rules from incomplete data based on rough sets. Proc. of the IEEE International Conference on Systems, Man and Cybernetics, Hague, the Netherlands, October 10–13, 2004, 3226–3231.
8. Kryszkiewicz, M.: Rough set approach to incomplete information systems. Proc. of the Second Annual Joint Conference on Information Sciences, Wrightsville Beach, NC, September 28–October 1, 1995, 194–197.

9. Kryszkiewicz, M.: Rules in incomplete information systems. *Information Sciences* **113** (1999) 271–292.

10. Lin, T.Y.: Neighborhood systems and approximation in database and knowledge base systems. Fourth International Symposium on Methodologies of Intelligent Systems (Poster Sessions), Charlotte, North Carolina, October 12–14, 1989, 75–86.

11. Lin, T.Y.: Chinese Wall security policy—An aggressive model. Proc. of the Fifth Aerospace Computer Security Application Conference, Tucson, Arizona, December 4–8, 1989, 286–293.

12. Lin, T.Y.: Topological and fuzzy rough sets. In *Intelligent Decision Support. Handbook of Applications and Advances of the Rough Sets Theory*, ed. by R. Slowinski, Kluwer Academic Publishers, Dordrecht, Boston, London (1992) 287–304.

13. Pawlak, Z.: Rough Sets. *International Journal of Computer and Information Sciences* **11** (1982) 341–356.

14. Pawlak, Z.: *Rough Sets. Theoretical Aspects of Reasoning about Data.* Kluwer Academic Publishers, Dordrecht, Boston, London (1991).

15. Skowron, A. and Rauszer, C.: The discernibility matrices and functions in information systems. In *Handbook of Applications and Advances of the Rough Sets Theory*, ed. by R. Slowinski, Kluwer Academic Publishers, Dordrecht, Boston, London (1992) 331–362.

16. Slowinski, R. and Vanderpooten, D.: A generalized definition of rough approximations based on similarity. *IEEE Transactions on Knowledge and Data Engineering* **12** (2000) 331–336.

17. Stefanowski, J.: *Algorithms of Decision Rule Induction in Data Mining.* Poznan University of Technology Press, Poznan, Poland (2001).

18. Stefanowski, J. and Tsoukias, A.: On the extension of rough sets under incomplete information. Proc. of the 7th International Workshop on New Directions in Rough Sets, Data Mining, and Granular-Soft Computing, RSFDGrC'1999, Ube, Yamaguchi, Japan, November 8–10, 1999, 73–81.

19. Stefanowski, J. and Tsoukias, A.: Incomplete information tables and rough classification. *Computational Intelligence* **17** (2001) 545–566.

20. Wang, G.: Extension of rough set under incomplete information systems. Proc. of the IEEE International Conference on Fuzzy Systems (FUZZ_IEEE'2002), vol. 2, Honolulu, III, May 12–17, 2002, 1098–1103.

21. Yao, Y.Y.: Two views of the theory of rough sets in finite universes. *International J. of Approximate Reasoning* **15** (1996) 291–317.

22. Yao, Y.Y.: Relational interpretations of neighborhood operators and rough set approximation operators. *Information Sciences* **111** (1998) 239–259.

23. Yao, Y.Y.: On the generalizing rough set theory. Proc. of the 9th Int. Conference on Rough Sets, Fuzzy Sets, Data Mining and Granular Computing (RSFDGrC'2003), Chongqing, China, October 19–22, 2003, 44–51.

24. Yao, Y.Y. and Lin, T.Y.: Generalization of rough sets using modal logics. *Intelligent Automation and Soft Computing* **2** (1996) 103–119.

Missing Template Decomposition Method and Its Implementation in Rough Set Exploration System

Jan G. Bazan[1], Rafał Latkowski[2], and Marcin Szczuka[3]

[1] Institute of Mathematics, University of Rzeszów
Rejtana 16A, 35-959 Rzeszów, Poland
`bazan@univ.rzeszow.pl`
[2] Institute of Informatics, Warsaw University
Banacha 2, 02-097, Warsaw, Poland
`rlatkows@mimuw.edu.pl`
[3] Institute of Mathematics, Warsaw University
Banacha 2, 02-097, Warsaw, Poland
`szczuka@mimuw.edu.pl`

Abstract. We describe a method of dealing with sets that contain missing information in case of classification task. The described method uses multi-stage scheme that induces and combines classifiers for complete parts of the original data. The principles of the proposed Missing Template Decomposition Method are presented together with general explanation of the implementation within the RSES framework. The introduced ideas are illustrated with an example of classification experiment on a real data set.

1 Introduction

The hard task of dealing with data imperfection in inductive learning methods was addressed in the area of data impreciseness by Pawlak in early 80's [9]. He proposed a *Rough Set* approach that made possible to precisely express facts about imprecise data in a formal way. The main concept of rough sets, the *indiscernibility relation*, proved to be very useful for analysis of decision problems concerning objects described in a data table by a set of conditional attributes and a decision attribute [10,11]. However, original definition of the rough set theory does not capture the situation where some of the attribute values are missing. In last twenty years a great research effort has been made in the area of data incompleteness in order to develop methods for inducing classifiers for data with missing attribute values. Some approaches that make handling of missing attribute values possible have been developed within the rough sets framework, see [5,6,14].

One can identify three major approaches to the issue of handling missing data in classification tasks. These are:

- Modification of indiscernibility relation by adopting it to handle missing attribute values (see [6,14]).

S. Greco et al. (Eds.): RSCTC 2006, LNAI 4259, pp. 254–263, 2006.

- Modification of classifier induction algorithms like, e.g., in case of *LEM1* and *LEM2* (see [5]).
- Imputation — replacement of missing values with regular ones (see [3,4]).

The Missing Template Decomposition method (MTD) represents an approach that cannot be strictly classified to any of the three streams of research listed above. It is devised to make it possible to reason on the basis of data with missing attribute values without modification of the inductive learning algorithm itself. The empirical evaluation of core MTD method has been already presented in, e.g, [7] showing that MTD can improve not only the reasoning quality, but also it can reduce complexity of classifier.

In this paper we present a brief description of the principles of Missing Template Decomposition classifier that has been implemented with use of previous experiences (see [7]) and added to the collection of methods that are available within the framework of Rough Set Exploration System (RSES).

The Rough Set Exploration System (RSES) is a free software tool for analysis and exploration of data with use of methods originating in the Rough Set theory. It is being developed for several years and provides a stable platform for experiments with data (see [2]). It can be downloaded from [16].

This paper first presents the general concepts about data, missing values, and templates. Then we introduce the principles of MTD method and the classification method based upon it. The method and its implementation in RSES are illustrated with an example of experiment on *head injury* (`hin`) data.

2   Basic Notions

As usual in Rough Set approach, we start with data set represented in the form of *information system* or, more precisely, the special case of information system called *decision table*.

Information system is a pair of the form $\mathbb{A} = (U, A)$ where U is a *universe* of *objects* and $A = \{a_1, ..., a_m\}$ is a set of *attributes* i.e. mappings of the form $a_i : U \to V_a \cup \{?\}$, where V_a is called *value set* of the attribute a_i and ? denotes missing value. The decision table is also a pair of the form $\mathbb{A} = (U, A \cup \{d\})$ with distinguished attribute d. In case of decision table the attributes belonging to A are called *conditional attributes* or simply *conditions* while d is called *decision*. We will further assume that the set of decision values is finite. The i-th *decision class* is a set of objects $C_i = \{o \in U : d(o) = d_i\}$, where d_i is the i-th decision value taken from decision value set $V_d = \{d_1, ..., d_{|V_d|}\}$.

For any subset of attributes $B \subset A$ *indiscernibility relation* $IND(B)$ for $x, y \in U$ is defined as follows:

$$x \, IND(B) \, y \iff \forall_{a \in B} \, a(x) = a(y). \tag{1}$$

The indiscernibility relation, as an equivalence relation, induces decomposition of objects into *indiscernibility classes* in which all objects are identically described on attributes from subset B. The above, classical definition of indiscernibility relation is capable of handling missing attribute values only in exactly the same way as regular values. We will use K to denote a number of all indiscernibility classes $[x^1]_{IND(B)}, \ldots, [x^K]_{IND(B)}$, and $M \leq K$ to denote a number of inconsistent indiscernibility classes $[x^{j_1}]_{IND(B)}, \ldots, [x^{j_M}]_{IND(B)}$, where an inconsistent indiscernibility class $[x^{j_m}]_{IND(B)}$ contains objects from more than one decision class (i.e., $card(\{d(x) : x \in [x^{j_m}]_{IND(B)}\}) > 1$).

Decision rule is a formula of the form $(a_{i_1} = v_1) \wedge \ldots \wedge (a_{i_k} = v_k) \Rightarrow d = v_d$, where $1 \leq i_1 < \ldots < i_k \leq m$, $v_i \in V_{a_i}$. Atomic subformulae $(a_{i_1} = v_1)$ are called *conditions*. We say that rule r is *applicable* to an object, or alternatively, the object *matches* rule, if its attribute values satisfy the premise of the rule. With the rule we can connect some numerical characteristics such as *matching* and *support* (see [1]).

Missing template t (also called *total template*) of $\mathbb{A}$ is a propositional formula $\bigwedge(a_i \neq ?)$ where $a_i \in A$. An object *satisfies* (matches) a template if for every attribute a_i occurring in the missing template the value of this attribute on considered object is defined (i.e., different from ?). A *width* of template t denoted as $w(t)$ is the number of attributes occurring in the template. A *height* of template t denoted as $h(t)$ is the number of objects satisfying the template. The missing template t induces in natural way a subtable $\mathbb{S}_t = (U_t, A_t \cup \{d\})$ of original information system $\mathbb{A} = (U, A \cup \{d\})$ consisting of set of objects U_t that satisfy the missing template t and set of attributes A_t occurring in the template (c.f. [7]). Obviously, $h(t) = card(U_t)$, $w(t) = card(A_t)$ and the subtable $\mathbb{S}_t$ is complete, i.e. totally described, while all objects satisfying a template are described on attributes occurring in the template.

We will also use a normalization factor $\rho = \frac{card(U)}{card(U_t)} = \frac{card(U)}{h(t)}$ to normalize heuristic measures of different missing templates, D to denote a number of decision classes occurring in subtable $\mathbb{S}_t$, and D_i to denote the number of decision classes occurring in i-th indiscernibility class $[x^i]_{IND(A_t)}$ of $\mathbb{S}_t$.

3   Missing Template Decomposition

The Missing Template Decomposition method (MTD), as it was indicated in introduction, differs from main streams of research on reasoning with incomplete object description. It is meant to meet two requirements. The first one is to adapt many well-known classifier induction methods, that are initially not capable of handling missing attribute values, to the case of incomplete data. In other words, MTD makes it possible to analyze incomplete information systems by previously known and implemented classification methods without the need for their modification. The second requirement is that MTD shall be able to cope with the problem of incomplete data without making an additional assumption of independent random distribution of missing values and without using data imputation methods [3,4]. The second requirement comes from the fact that many real world applications have shown that appearance of missing values may be governed by very complicated dependencies. Missing attribute values are frequently not uniformly distributed, but their distribution is determined by the hidden nature of investigated phenomenon, just like in the case of regular values. Hence, the application of an arbitrary method for data imputation can reduce accuracy of a classifier.

3.1 Classifier Induction

The MTD tries to avoid the necessity of reasoning on data with missing attribute values. The original incomplete data is decomposed into data subsets which contain no missing values. Next, methods for classifier induction are applied to these complete subsets. Finally, a conflict resolving method is used to obtain final solution from partial classifiers constructed on subtables.

In the data decomposition phase the original decision table with missing attribute values is partitioned into a number of decision subtables, which contain no missing values. This data decomposition should reveal patterns in distribution of missing attribute values. Ideally, the complete subtables that are result of the decomposition should correspond to natural subproblems of the whole problem domain. With the help of the concept of total template introduced earlier, we can define data decomposition phase as generation of set of total templates t_1, ..., t_T and extraction of subtables $\mathbb{S}_{t_1}$, ..., $\mathbb{S}_{t_T}$ that satisfy these templates (see Fig. 1).

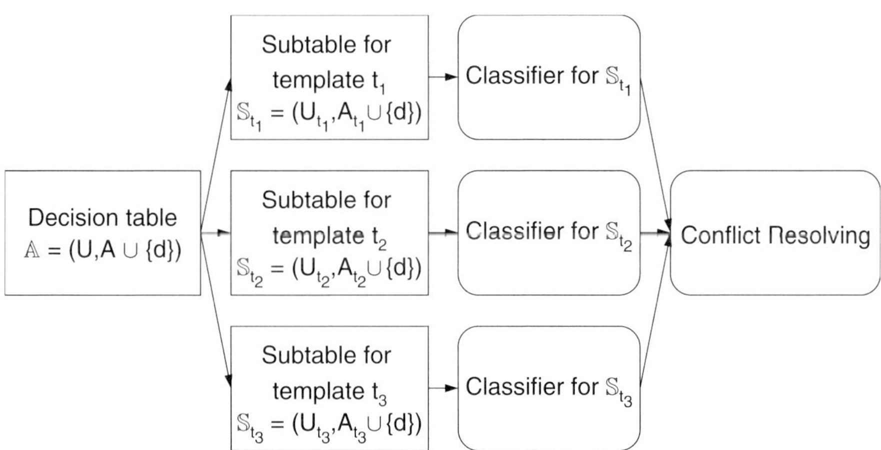

Fig. 1. Missing Template Decomposition Method

Once we have data decomposed into complete decision subtables, we perform classifier induction from these subtables and classifier fusion (refer to figure Fig. 1). For classifier induction one can apply arbitrary method of inductive learning. In our current implementation it is possible to utilize decision tree or decision rules' classifier. For decision tree classifier we can play with two parameters: minimal required confidence (purity) of each leaf and minimal nonterminal node size. For decision rule classifier we can select between optimal exhaustive decision rules (all rules, see [2,12]) and LEM2 rules (see [13]). For classifier fusion we could apply any method for conflict resolution. Current implementation provides standard voting method and decision tree method for this purpose.

The decision subtables $\{\mathbb{S}_t = (U_t, A_t \cup \{d\})\}$ contain exactly the same decision attribute as the original decision table $\mathbb{A} = (U, A \cup \{d\})$. This fact determines the course of classifier induction. All classifiers induced for decision subtables are classifying objects into the same decision classes, but for a given object some of these classifiers may not be applicable. Note, that during classification process the (subtable-induced) classifier is applicable to an object only if this object satisfies total template related to the considered classifier. On the other hand, there may be objects for which more than one classifier is applicable. That is why after classifier induction we need a mechanism for conflict resolution.

Conflict resolving shall result in creation of the final answer. In case of standard voting this answer, depending of requirements, may be obtained in one of two ways. First approach to conflict resolving takes into account only one final decision value (definite decision class assignment) for each partial classifier on the examined object. The object is assigned a decision value that has been selected by majority of partial classifiers. In the second approach, conflict resolving is done on vector of decision class assignment probabilities. The final result (class assignment) is reached by taking the decision with highest cumulative probability.

In the case of conflict resolving with use of decision tree, the tree is induced from a virtual decision table that consist of all classifier answers for objects from training table. Once decision tree is constructed, it is utilized to merge answers from all partial classifiers.

We can briefly summarize the missing template decomposition method as follows:

- Create set of templates $t_1, \ldots, t_T$ for missing values in the following way:
  - Create a temporary set of objects $U' := U$ from the original decision table and repeat two following steps until the temporary set U' becomes empty:
  - Generate the best missing template t_i for objects U' according to a chosen criterion;
  - Remove from the temporary set U' objects that are covered by missing template t_i;
- Create complete decision subtables $\mathbb{S}_{t_1}, \ldots, \mathbb{S}_{t_T}$ that correspond to previously generated set of templates;
- Induce classifiers over complete decision subtables;
- Select a conflict resolving method (or learn a conflict resolving strategy) to get the final answer.

3.2   Data Decomposition Criteria

Subsets $\mathbb{S}_t$ of original decision table $\mathbb{A}$ must satisfy some requirements in order to achieve good quality of inductive reasoning as well as applicability in case of methods that cannot deal with missing attribute values. We expect the decision subtables to exhaustively cover the input table (at least in the terms of objects, i.e., $\bigcup_{i=1}^{T} U_{t_i} = U$). They should contain no missing values. It is also obvious that the quality of inductive reasoning depends on a particular partition and some partitions are better than others.

In current implementation of MTD the search for promising set of total templates $t_1, \ldots, t_T$ is done with help of heuristic functions and genetic algorithm with variable population size. The library utilized by RSES software provides several heuristic functions for total template evaluation. These heuristic functions join properties of standard template evaluation measures with feature selection measures, especially measures based on rough sets. The implemented heuristic functions are of the form $q(t) = w(t)^{\alpha} \cdot h(t) \cdot f(t)^{\beta}$, where $q(t)$ is considered heuristic function, called also quality function of template, $f(t)$ is an additional template evaluation measure, and α, β are exponents for controlling the impact of different components of quality function. Currently there are 8 template evaluation measures implemented in RSES and ready to be used for this purpose. These are:

- S — size measure only, $f(t) = 1$, the template quality function has form $q(t) = w(t)^{\alpha} \cdot h(t)$,
- C — conflict measure that counts conflicts in inconsistent indiscernibility classes, $f(t) = \frac{maxc(t) - c(t)}{maxc(t)}$, where $c(t)$ is a function similar to conflict $c(t) = \rho \cdot \sum_{i=1}^{M} \prod_{d=1}^{D_i} card(\{x \in [x^{j_i}]_{IND(A_t)} : d(x) = d\}))$ and $maxc(t) = \rho \cdot \prod_{d=1}^{D} card(\{x \in U_t : d(x) = d\})$ is a function that estimates maximal possible $c(t)$ value from the top,
- I — inconsistency measure, $f(t) = \frac{h(t) - i(t)}{h(t)}$, where $h(t)$ estimates $i(t)$ value from the top and $i(t) = \rho \cdot \sum_{i=1}^{M} \sum_{d=1}^{D_i} card(\{x \in [x^{j_i}]_{IND(A_t)} : d(x) = d\})$,
- D — average ratio of maximal purity within indiscernibility classes, $f(t) = \frac{1}{K} \sum_{i=1}^{K} \frac{max_{d \in V_d} card(\{x \in [x^i]_{IND(A_t)} : d(x) = d\})}{card(\{x \in [x^i]_{IND(A_t)}\})}$,
- E — proportion of maximal purity within indiscernibility classes to template size, $f(t) = \sum_{i=1}^{K} \frac{max_{d \in V_d} card(\{x \in [x^i]_{IND} : d(x) = d\})}{h(t)}$,
- F — $f(t) = \frac{1}{max(1, c(t))}$, where $c(t)$ is defined above,
- G — $f(t) = \sum_{i=1}^{K} \frac{max_{d \in V_d} card(\{x \in [x^i]_{IND(A_t)} : d(x) = d\})}{card([x^i]_{IND(A_t)})}$ (i.e., $G = K \cdot D$),
- H — $f(t) = \frac{1}{K} \sum_{i=1}^{K} \frac{max_{d \in V_d} card(\{x \in [x^i]_{IND} : d(x) = d\})}{h(t)}$ (i.e., $E = K \cdot H$),
- P — predictive measure, $f(t)$ is an accuracy of decision tree classifier trained and tested on table $\mathbb{S}_t$.

4   Example of Experiment with MTD

To bring the functionality of MTD closer to reader's intuition we present an experiment performed with the RSES' implementation of MTD. Our experiment is carried out with use of `hin` data. It is a set of data describing head injuries data with three possible decision values (moderate disability or good recovery, severe disability, dead or vegetative), 6 conditional attributes and 1000 observations. This dataset was selected because of the quantity of missing information. In the `hin` data table 40.5% of all objects are incomplete (contain at least one ?) and 9.8% of all values are missing. This data was originally split into ten separate train&test pairs for ten fold cross-validation (c.f. [8]), but for simplicity we use only the first pair of train&test datasets.

To begin with, we have to load the training and test data tables into the RSES system (see Fig. 2). Once we have data loaded we can start experiments. In particular we can induce *Missing Template Decomposition Classifier* (*MTD-C*). This is easily done by selecting appropriate option from context menu for an icon representing training table.

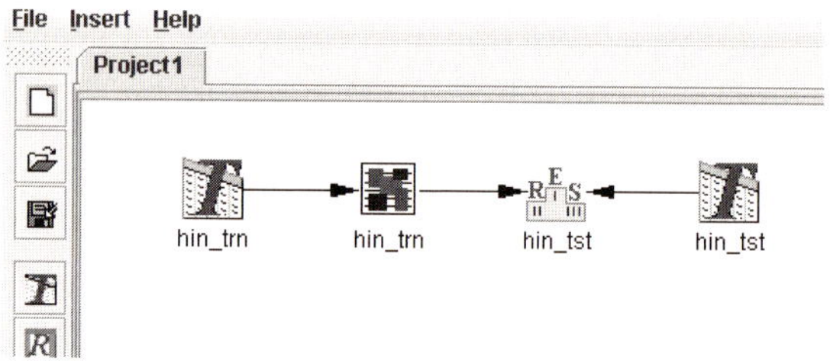

Fig. 2. Simple project diagram of RSES system with decision tables for training and testing, MTD induced from train table and classification results of MTD over test table

Selecting this option causes the RSES system to show the dialog box with settings for MTD, as presented in Fig. 3. Most of these settings were described in the previous section, so here we just briefly point at their location. In the top left part a checkbox for selecting the type of answers gathered from subclassifiers is located. If it is unchecked, then each classifier outputs only one decision value for an object. Checking it causes RSES to use decision probability vectors. Most of the left part of the dialog is related to parameters for missing template generation method. The user can select an additional evaluation function as described previously as well as exponent factors for selecting importance of different components in the the template quality function. There are also settings for genetic algorithm with variable population size that may be used to search for templates. The user can adjust the number of genetic algorithm iterations, probability of including each attribute in initial randomized population, and minimal and maximal population sizes. In the field placed at the bottom left corner the user can select a name for our MTD, which will be used to identify it in RSES project diagram.

The right side of the dialog is devoted to settings for classifiers and conflict resolving method. In the upper part the user can select the algorithm for induction of classifiers for subtables (decision tree, all rules or LEM2 rules) and their settings. Below classifier selection menu there is a section that controls some basic settings for internal discretization algorithms. The internal discretization is required if some attributes in data are numeric and is done automatically for each subtable before rule induction. In our example the head injury data contains no numeric attributes, so discretization is not required. In RSES we have also option of discretizing the entire data table with appropriate algorithm before invoking the MTD module. Finally, the bottom-right part of the dialog is related to selection of conflict resolving method. The user has choice between voting and decision tree learning methods. For decision tree conflict resolution method the user can also specify parameters such as confidence level and minimal size of a leaf.

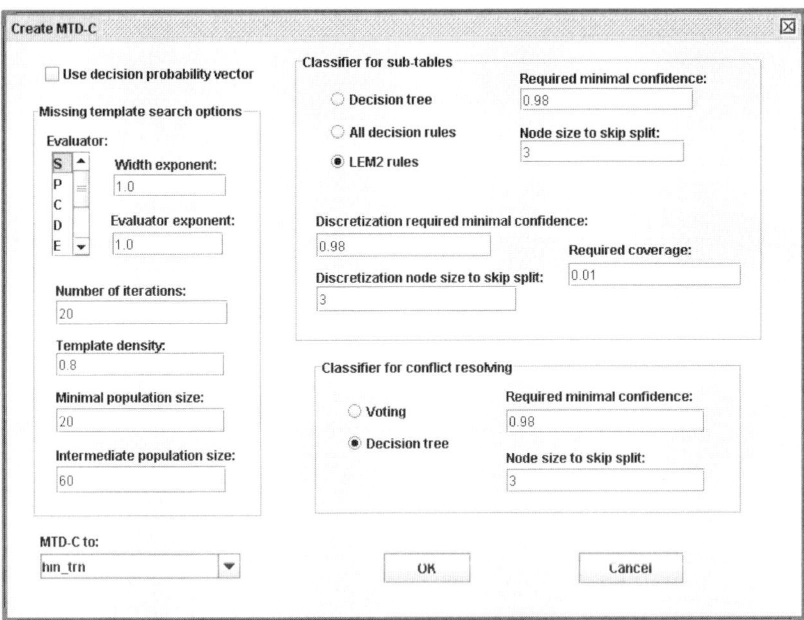

Fig. 3. Configuration dialog of RSES system for Missing Template Decomposition Method

Let us assume that we would like to construct a MTD using the parameter choice presented in Fig. 3. These settings assume no additional template evaluation function $(S = w(h) \cdot h(t))$, LEM2 [1] rule induction algorithm with required coverage factor of 0.01 (1%) for classifier induction and decision tree used for conflict resolving. After clicking OK the RSES system will induce MTD which which will be accessible via a newly created icon within RSES project interface. By double clicking on the MTD icon the user may open the results window and see the "machinery" for constructed MTD classifier. It is possible to display the

---

[1] Please note, that RSES implementation of LEM2 algorithm does not reflect its current status and most recent developements. It is based on description from [13].

set of missing templates as well as induced rule sets and decision tree used for conflict resolving. We can test the accuracy of our MTD model on a test table. The easiest way to do that is by choosing the "Classify/Test table using MTD-C" option from the context menu associated with the previously loaded test table and selecting the name of MTD to be used. The classification results are then stored in the standard RSES object that makes it possible to examine and analyze classification quality.

In the table below we present results of several experiments carried out on `hin` data with use of various classification algorithms available in the RSES system. These results exemplify usefulness of the MTD, at least for this data set. More results of MTD application, as well as more thorough explanation of underlying algorithms can be found in [7].

Description	Accuracy	Precision	Coverage	Classifier Complexity
All rules on original table	0.535	0.581	0.921	734 rules
LEM2 rules on original table	0.426	0.614	0.693	392 rules
All rules on table imputed with most common value	0.475	0.822	0.578	824 rules
LEM2 rules on table imputed with most common value	0.257	0.650	0.396	323 rules
All rules on table imputed with most common value w.r.t. decision class (*)	0.554	0.622	0.891	898 rules
LEM2 rules on table imputed with most common value w.r.t. decision class	0.268	0.628	0.426	289 rules
All Rules (*) shortened with factor 0.7	0.673	0.708	0.950	259 rules
MTD $q = w \cdot h$, All rules, voting	0.554	0.554	1.000	352 rules/4 classifiers
MTD $q = w \cdot h$, All rules, decision trees	0.663	0.663	1.000	352 rules/4 classifiers + 155 tree nodes
MTD $q = w \cdot h$, LEM2 rules (1%), decision tree	0.782	0.782	1.000	8 rules/4 classifiers + 61 nodes

Acknowledgement

This work is partly supported by grant 3T11C00226 from the Polish Ministry of Science and Higher Education.

References

1. Bazan, J.G., Nguyen, H.S., Nguyen, S.H., Synak, P., Wróblewski, J.: Rough set algorithms in classification problem. In Polkowski, L., Tsumoto, S., Lin, T.Y., eds.: Rough Set Methods and Applications, Physica-Verlag (2000) 49–88

2. Bazan, J.G., Szczuka, M.S.: The rough set exploration system. In Peters, J.F., Skowron, A., eds.: Transactions on Rough Sets III. Volume 3400 of Lecture Notes in Computer Science., Springer (2005) 37–56

3. Gediga, G., Düntsch, I.: Maximum consistency of incomplete data via non-invasive imputation. Artificial Intelligence Review **19**(1) (2003) 93–107

4. Grzymała-Busse, J.W., Hu, M.: A comparison of several approaches to missing attribute values in data mining. [15] 378–385

5. Grzymała-Busse, J.W., Wang, A.Y.: Modified algorithms LEM1 and LEM2 for rule induction from data with missing attribute values. In: Proceedings of 5th Workshop on Rough Sets and Soft Computing (RSSC'97) at the 3rd Joint Conference on Information Sciences, Research Triangle Park (NC, USA) (1997) 69–72

6. Kryszkiewicz, M.: Properties of incomplete information systems in the framework of rough sets. [10] 422–450

7. Latkowski, R.: On decomposition for incomplete data. Fundamenta Informaticae **54**(1) (2003) 1–16

8. Lim, T.: Missing covariate values and classification trees. http://www.recursive-partitioning.com/mv.shtml, Recursive-Partitioning.com (2000)

9. Pawlak, Z.: Rough sets. International Journal of Computer and Information Sciences **11** (1982) 341–356

10. Polkowski, L., Skowron, A., eds.: Rough Sets in Knowledge Discovery 1: Methodology and Applications. Physica-Verlag (1998)

11. Polkowski, L., Skowron, A., eds.: Rough Sets in Knowledge Discovery 2: Applications, Case Studies and Software Systems. Physica-Verlag (1998)

12. Skowron, A.: Boolean reasoning for decision rules generation. In Komorowski, H.J., Raś, Z.W., eds.: Methodologies for Intelligent Systems — ISMIS 1993. LNCS 689, Springer (1993) 295–305

13. Stefanowski, J.: On rough set based approaches to induction of decision rules. [10] 500–529

14. Stefanowski, J., Tsoukiàs, A.: Incomplete information tables and rough classification. International Journal of Computational Intelligence **17**(3) (2001) 545–566

15. Ziarko, W., Yao, Y.Y., eds.: Rough Sets and Current Trends in Computing, Second International Conference, RSCTC 2000 Banff, Canada, October 16–19, 2000, Revised Papers. In Ziarko, W., Yao, Y.Y., eds.: RSCTC 2000. LNCS 2005, Springer (2001)

16. The Rough Set Exploration System Homepage
    http://logic.mimuw.edu.pl/~rses

On Possible Rules and Apriori Algorithm in Non-deterministic Information Systems

Hiroshi Sakai[1] and Michinori Nakata[2]

[1] Department of Mathematics and Computer Aided Science,
Faculty of Engineering, Kyushu Institute of Technology,
Tobata, Kitakyushu 804, Japan
`sakai@mns.kyutech.ac.jp`
[2] Faculty of Management and Information Science,
Josai International University,
Gumyo, Togane, Chiba 283, Japan
`nakatam@ieee.org`

Abstract. A framework of rule generation in *Non-deterministic Infor- mation Systems* (*NISs*), which follows rough sets based rule generation in *Deterministic Information Systems* (*DISs*), is presented. We have already coped with *certain rules* and *minimal certain rules*, which are characterized by the concept of *consistency*, in *NISs*. We also introduced *discernibility functions* into *NISs*. In this paper, *possible rules* in *NISs* are focused on. Because of the information incompleteness, huge number of *possible rules* may exist, and we introduce *Min-Max strategy* and *Max-Max strategy* into possible rule generation in *NISs*. Possible rules based on these strategies are characterized by the criteria *minimum support*, *maximum support*, *minimum accuracy* and *maximum accuracy*, and Apriori based algorithm is applied.

Keywords: Rough sets, Non-deterministic information, Possible rules, Apriori algorithm, Min-Max strategy, Max-Max strategy.

1   Introduction

Rough set theory is seen as a mathematical foundation of soft computing. This theory usually handles tables with deterministic information. Many applications of this theory to rule generation, machine learning and knowledge discovery have been presented [1,2,3,4].

We follow rule generation in *DISs* [1,2,3,4] and propose rule generation in *NISs*. *NISs* were proposed by Pawlak, Orłowska and Lipski in order to handle information incompleteness in *DISs*, like null values, unknown values, missing values. From the beginning of the research on incomplete information, *NISs* have been recognized to be the most important framework for handling information incompleteness [5,6]. Therefore, rule generation in *NISs* will also be an important framework for rule generation from incomplete information.

However, very few work deals with rule generation from incomplete information on computers. In [6], Lipski showed a question-answering system besides

S. Greco et al. (Eds.): RSCTC 2006, LNAI 4259, pp. 264–273, 2006.
© Springer-Verlag Berlin Heidelberg 2006

an axiomatization of logic. Grzymala-Busse developed a system named $LERS$, which depends upon $LEM1$ and $LEM2$ algorithms [7,8]. Kryszkiewicz proposed a framework of rules in incomplete information systems [9]. As far as authors know, these are the most important work for handling incomplete information, especially missing values, on computers.

In this paper, we briefly survey a framework of rule generation in $NISs$, and develop possible rule generation in $NISs$.

2   Basic Definitions and Background of This Work

This section summarizes basic definitions and the background of this work.

2.1   Basic Framework

A *Deterministic Information System* (DIS) is a quadruplet $(OB, AT, \{VAL_A| A \in AT\}, f)$. Let us consider two sets $CON \subseteq AT$ which we call *condition attributes* and $DEC \subseteq AT$ which we call *decision attributes*. An object $x \in OB$ is *consistent* (with any distinct object $y \in OB$), if $f(x, A)=f(y, A)$ for every $A \in CON$ implies $f(x, A)=f(y, A)$ for every $A \in DEC$.

A *Non-deterministic Information System* (NIS) is also a quadruplet $(OB, AT, \{VAL_A|A \in AT\}, g)$, where $g : OB \times AT \rightarrow P(\cup_{A \in AT} VAL_A)$ (a power set of $\cup_{A \in AT} VAL_A$). Every set $g(x, A)$ is interpreted as that there is an actual value in this set but this value is not known. For a $NIS=(OB, AT, \{VAL_A| A \in AT\}, g)$ and a set $ATR \subseteq AT$, we name a $DIS=(OB, ATR, \{VAL_A|A \in ATR\}, h)$ satisfying $h(x, A) \in g(x, A)$ a *derived DIS (for ATR) from NIS*. For a set $ATR=\{A_1, \cdots, A_n\} \subseteq AT$ and any $x \in OB$, let $PT(x, ATR)$ denote the Cartesian product $g(x, A_1) \times \cdots \times g(x, A_n)$. We name every element a *possible tuple (for ATR) of* x. For a possible tuple $\zeta=(\zeta_1, \cdots, \zeta_n) \in PT(x, ATR)$, let $[ATR, \zeta]$ denote a formula $\bigwedge_{1 \leq i \leq n}[A_i, \zeta_i]$. Let $PI(x, CON, DEC)$ ($x \in OB$) denote a set $\{[CON, \zeta] \Rightarrow [DEC, \eta]|\zeta \in PT(x, CON), \eta \in PT(x, DEC)\}$. We name an element of $PI(x, CON, DEC)$ a *possible implication (from CON to DEC) of* x.

Now, we define six classes of possible implications, certain rules and possible rules. For any $\tau \in PI(x, CON, DEC)$, let $DD(\tau, x, CON, DEC)$ denote a set $\{\varphi| \varphi$ is such a derived DIS for $CON \cup DEC$ that an implication from x in φ is equal to $\tau\}$. If $PI(x, CON, DEC)$ is a singleton set $\{\tau\}$, we say τ (from x) is *definite*. Otherwise we say τ (from x) is *indefinite*. If a set $\{\varphi \in DD(\tau, x, CON, DEC)| x$ is consistent in $\varphi\}$ is equal to $DD(\tau, x, CON, DEC)$, we say τ is *globally consistent* (GC). If this set is equal to $\{\}$, we say τ is *globally inconsistent* (GI). Otherwise, we say τ is *marginal* (MA). By combining two cases, i.e., '$D(efinite)$ or $I(ndefinite)$' and 'GC, MA or GI', we define six classes, $DGC, DMA, DGI, IGC, IMA, IGI$ in Table 1, for possible implications. A possible implication τ belonging to DGC class is consistent in all derived $DISs$, and this τ is not influenced by the information incompleteness, therefore we name τ a *certain rule*. A possible implication τ' (from object x) belonging to either IGC, DMA or IMA class is consistent in some $\varphi \in DD(\tau', x, CON, DEC)$. Therefore, we name τ' a *possible rule*.

Table 1. Six classes of possible implications in NISs

	GC	MA	GI
$Definite$	DGC	DMA	DGI
$Indefinite$	IGC	IMA	IGI

Now, we give necessary and sufficient conditions for characterizing GC, MA and GI classes. For any $\zeta \in PT(x, ATR)$, we fix the tuple of x to ζ, and define two sets $inf(x, ATR, \zeta)=\{y \in OB | PT(y, ATR)=\{\zeta\}\}$ and $sup(x, ATR, \zeta)=\{y \in OB | \zeta \in PT(y, ATR)\}$. Intuitively, $inf(x, ATR, \zeta)$ implies a set of objects whose tuples are ζ and definite. A set $sup(x, ATR, \zeta)$ implies a set of objects whose tuples may be ζ. In $DISs$, $[x]_{ATR}=inf(x, ATR, \zeta)=sup(x, ATR, \zeta)$ holds, and $\{x\} \subseteq inf(x, ATR, \zeta) \subseteq [x]_{ATR} \subseteq sup(x, ATR, \zeta)$ holds in $NISs$.

Theorem 1 [10]. For a NIS, let us consider a possible implication τ:$[CON, \zeta] \Rightarrow [DEC, \eta] \in PI(x, CON, DEC)$. Then, the following holds.
(1) τ belongs to GC class if and only if $sup(x, CON, \zeta) \subseteq inf(x, DEC, \eta)$.
(2) τ belongs to MA class if and only if $inf(x, CON, \zeta) \subseteq sup(x, DEC, \eta)$.

Proposition 2 [10]. For any NIS, let $ATR \subseteq AT$ be $\{A_1, \cdots, A_n\}$, and let a possible tuple $\zeta \in PT(x, ATR)$ be $(\zeta_1, \cdots, \zeta_n)$. Then, the following holds.
(1) $inf(x, ATR, \zeta)=\cap_i inf(x, \{A_i\}, (\zeta_i))$.
(2) $sup(x, ATR, \zeta)=\cap_i sup(x, \{A_i\}, (\zeta_i))$.

For an implication τ in a DIS, criteria $support(\tau)$ and $accuracy(\tau)$ are applied to defining rules. They are extended to minimum support $minsupp(\tau)$, maximum support $maxsupp(\tau)$, minimum accuracy $minacc(\tau)$ and maximum accuracy $maxacc(\tau)$ in a NIS. These criteria depend upon all derived $DISs$, however we developed an effective method to obtain these criterion values.

Theorem 3 [10]. For a NIS, let us consider a possible implication τ:$[CON, \zeta] \Rightarrow [DEC, \eta] \in PI(x, CON, DEC)$. Let $INACC$ denote a set $[sup(x, CON, \zeta) - inf(x, CON, \zeta)] \cap sup(x, DEC, \eta)$, and let $OUTACC$ denote a set $[sup(x, CON, \zeta) - inf(x, CON, \zeta)] - inf(x, DEC, \eta)$. Then, the following holds.
(1) $minsupp(\tau)=|inf(x, CON, \zeta) \cap inf(x, DEC, \eta)|/|OB|$.
(2) $maxsupp(\tau)=|sup(x, CON, \zeta) \cap sup(x, DEC, \eta)|/|OB|$.
(3) $minacc(\tau)=\frac{|inf(x,CON,\zeta) \cap inf(x,DEC,\eta)|}{|inf(x,CON,\zeta)|+|OUTACC|}$.
(4) $maxacc(\tau)=\frac{|inf(x,CON,\zeta) \cap sup(x,DEC,\eta)|+|INACC|}{|inf(x,CON,\zeta)|+|INACC|}$.

In $minacc(\tau)$, the numerator $inf(x, CON, \zeta) \cap inf(x, DEC, \eta)$ and the denominator $inf(x, CON, \zeta)$ are fixed. We adjust every $y \in [sup(x, CON, \zeta) - inf(x, CON, \zeta)]$ for minimizing $accuracy$. For every $y \in [sup(x, CON, \zeta) - inf(x, CON, \zeta)] - inf(x, DEC, \eta)$, it is possible to obtain a possible implication $[CON, \zeta] \Rightarrow [DEC, \eta']$ $(\eta' \neq \eta)$. This implication is just counted in the denominator, and it is not counted in the numerator. As for $maxacc(\tau)$, it is possible to obtain τ from every $y \in [sup(x, CON, \zeta) - inf(x, CON, \zeta)] \cap sup(x, DEC, \eta)$, This implication is counted both in the denominator and the numerator. Since

Table 2. A Table of NIS_1

OB	P	Q	R	S	T
1	$\{3\}$	$\{1,3\}$	$\{3\}$	$\{2\}$	$\{3\}$
2	$\{2\}$	$\{2,3\}$	$\{1,3\}$	$\{1,3\}$	$\{2\}$
3	$\{1,2\}$	$\{2\}$	$\{1,2\}$	$\{3\}$	$\{1\}$
4	$\{1\}$	$\{3\}$	$\{3\}$	$\{2,3\}$	$\{1,2,3\}$
5	$\{3\}$	$\{1\}$	$\{1,2\}$	$\{3\}$	$\{3\}$

$m/n \leq (m+k)/(n+k)$ $(0 \leq m \leq n,\ n \neq 0,\ k > 0)$ holds, we obtain (4) in Theorem 3.

2.2   Certain Rule Generation in NISs

For certain rule generation, we dealt with the following problem.

Problem 1. For a NIS, let DEC be decision attributes and let η be a tuple of decision attributes values for DEC. Then, find minimal certain rules in the form of $[CON, \zeta] \Rightarrow [DEC, \eta]$.

According to Theorem 1, Problem 1 is reduced to find minimal set of descriptors $[CON, \zeta]$ satisfying $sup(x, CON, \zeta) \subseteq inf(x, DEC, \eta)$. For solving this problem, we followed a discernibility function based method in $DISs$ [11]. We also introduced a revised discernibility function into $NISs$, and realized tool programs [12].

2.3   An Example

An example is picked up in this subsection. This will clarify the rolls of theorems. In order to clarify object x, which an implication τ is extracted from, we employ τ^x, τ_1^x, τ_2^x, $\cdots \tau_n^x$ instead of τ from now on.

Example 1. Let us consider NIS_1 in Table 2. There are 768 derived $DISs$ for all attributes. For $CON=\{P,Q\}$ and $DEC=\{T\}$, there are $24(=2^3 \times 3)$ derived $DISs$. Here, $PT(1, \{P,Q\})=\{(3,1),(3,3)\}$, $PT(1, \{T\})=\{(3)\}$ and $PI(1, \{P,Q\}, \{T\})$ consists of two possible implications τ_1^1 : $[P,3] \wedge [Q,1] \Rightarrow [T,3]$, $[P,3] \wedge [Q,3] \Rightarrow [T,3]$. Since $sup(1, \{P,Q\}, (3,1))=sup(1, \{P\}, (3)) \cap sup(1, \{Q\}, (1))= \{1,5\}$ and $inf(1, \{T\}, (3))=\{1,5\}$, $sup(1, \{P,Q\}, (3,1)) \subseteq inf(1, \{T\}, (3))$ holds. Thus, we know τ_1^1 belongs to IGC class. In object 1, $sup(1, \{P,R,S\}, (3,3,2))= \{1\} \subseteq inf(1, \{T\}, (3))$ also holds. Therefore, it is possible to obtain a minimal certain rule from object 1. The discernibility function $DF(1)=DISC(1,2) \wedge DISC(1,3) \wedge DISC(1,4) =([P,3] \vee [S,2]) \wedge ([P,3] \vee [R,3] \vee [S,2]) \wedge ([P,3])=[P,3]$. Here, $DISC(x,y)=\{[A,\zeta]|y \notin sup(x, \{A\}, (\zeta))\}$. In this way, $[P,3] \Rightarrow [T,3]$ is the unique minimal certain rule from object 1. Now, let us consider criterion values of τ_2^1 : $[Q,3] \Rightarrow [T,3]$ from object 1. $minsupp(\tau_2^1)=|inf(1, \{Q\}, (3)) \cap inf(1, \{T\}, (3))|/5=|\{1,4\} \cap \{1,5\}|/5= |\{1\}|/5=0.2$, and similarly $maxsupp(\tau_2^1)= |\{1,2,4\} \cap \{1,4,5\}|/5= |\{1,4\}|/5=0.4$. Furthermore, $INACC=(\{1,2,4\} - \{1,4\}) \cap \{1,4,5\}=\{\}$ and

$OUTACC=\{2\}-\{1,5\}=\{2\}$ hold, so $minacc(\tau_2^1)=|\{1\}|/(|\{1,4\}|+|\{2\}|)=0.333$, and $maxacc(\tau_2^1)=(|\{1,4\}\cap\{1,4,5\}|+|\{\}|)/(|\{1,4\}|+|\{\}|)=|\{1,4\}|/|\{1,4\}|=1$.

2.4 Rules in DISs and Apriori Algorithm

In $DISs$, rule generation may be defined as the problem below.

Problem 2. Find every implication τ, whose $accuracy(\tau)$ is maximum under the condition $support(\tau) \geq \alpha$ for a fixed value α $(0 < \alpha \leq 1)$.

For solving this problem, an algorithm named *Apriori* was proposed by Agrawal [13]. In this framework, *association rules* in *transaction data* are obtained. The application of the *large itemset* is the key point in Apriori algorithm.

3 Possible Rule Generation in NISs

Now, let us cope with possible rule generation in $NISs$. In this case, there may be huge number of possible implications satisfying condition (2) in Theorem 1. Therefore, we employ criteria $minsupp(\tau)$, $maxsupp(\tau)$, $minacc(\tau)$ and $maxacc(\tau)$ for defining rules, and we follow the method based on Apriori algorithm.

3.1 Two Problems for Possible Rule Generation in NISs

We employ two strategies in the following.

(1) **Min-Max Strategy:** We obtain every possible rule which surely holds in the worst case of a NIS.
(2) **Max-Max Strategy:** We obtain every possible rule which is the most desirable in the best case of a NIS.

In Min-Max strategy, we try to obtain every possible rule, which is credible under the information incompleteness in a NIS. On the other hand, in Max-Max strategy we try to obtain every ideal rule.

Now, we give two problems in this paper.

Problem 3 (Rule generation based on Min-Max Strategy). Find every possible implication τ, whose $minacc(\tau)$ is maximum under the condition $minsupp(\tau) \geq \alpha$ for a fixed value α $(0 < \alpha \leq 1)$.

Problem 4 (Rule generation based on Max-Max Strategy). Find every possible implication τ, whose $maxacc(\tau)$ is maximum under the condition $maxsupp(\tau) \geq \alpha$ for a fixed value α $(0 < \alpha \leq 1)$.

Example 2. Let us consider NIS_1 in Table 2 and $\tau_2^1 : [Q, 3] \Rightarrow [T, 3]$ from object 1, again. Here, $0.2 \leq support(\tau_2^1) \leq 0.4$ and $0.333 \leq accuracy(\tau_2^1) \leq 1$ hold. Let us fix $\alpha=0.3$. In Min-Max strategy, τ_2^1 does not satisfy $minsupp(\tau_2^1) \geq 0.3$, therefore we do not pick up τ_2^1. In Max-Max strategy, τ_2^1 satisfies $maxsupp(\tau_2^1) \geq 0.3$, and $maxacc(\tau_2^1)=1$ (the maximum value) holds. Therefore, we pick up τ_2^1. In this case, Max-Max strategy implicitly relies on a derived DIS^* as follows: A derived DIS^* from NIS_1 such that $g(1,Q)=\{1,3\}$ is replaced with 3, $g(2,Q)=\{2,3\}$ is replaced with 2 and $g(4,T)=\{1,2,3\}$ is replaced with 3.

3.2   A Computational Issue for Solving Problem 3 and 4

According to Theorem 3, the calculation of $minsupp(\tau)$, $minacc(\tau)$, $maxsupp(\tau)$ and $maxacc(\tau)$ for a fixed τ is easy. However, τ depends upon the number of derived $DISs$, and furthermore τ depends upon condition attributes CON ($CON \subseteq 2^{AT-DEC}$). Therefore, it is hard to apply Theorem 3 to every τ sequentially.

For solving this issue, we focus on descriptors $[A, \zeta]$ ($A \in AT$, $\zeta \in VAL_A$). The number of all descriptors is pretty small.

Definition 1. For every descriptor $[A, \zeta]$ ($A \in AT$, $\zeta \in VAL_A$) in a NIS, we define the following.
(1) $descinf([A, \zeta]) = \{x \in OB | \ g(x, A) = \{\zeta\}\}$.
(2) $descinf(\wedge_i [A_i, \zeta_i]) = \cap_i descinf([A_i, \zeta_i])$.
(3) $descsup([A, \zeta]) = \{x \in OB | \ \zeta \in g(x, A)\}$.
(4) $descsup(\wedge_i [A_i, \zeta_i]) = \cap_i descsup([A_i, \zeta_i])$.

Proposition 4. In a NIS, let us suppose $CON = \{A_1, \cdots, A_n\}$, $\zeta = \{\zeta_1, \cdots, \zeta_n\}$ and $\zeta \in PT(x, CON)$. Then, the following holds.
(1) $inf(x, CON, \zeta) = descinf(\wedge_i [A_i, \zeta_i])$ holds, if $PT(x, CON) = \{\zeta\}$.
(2) $inf(x, CON, \zeta) = descinf(\wedge_i [A_i, \zeta_i]) \cup \{x\}$ holds, if $PT(x, CON) \neq \{\zeta\}$.
(3) $sup(x, CON, \zeta) = descsup(\wedge_i [A_i, \zeta_i])$ holds.

The definition of $inf(x, CON, \zeta)$ and $descinf([CON, \zeta])$ is almost the same, however they are not the same. Because, $inf(x, CON, \zeta)$ depends upon object x, but $descinf([CON, \zeta])$ just depends upon the descriptor $[CON, \zeta]$. Therefore, the manipulation on $descinf([CON, \zeta])$ is much simpler than that of $inf(x, CON, \ \zeta)$. As for $sup(x, CON, \zeta)$ and $descsup([CON, \zeta])$, they define the same set for every x. In correspondence with $descinf([CON, \zeta])$, we define $descsup([CON, \zeta])$.

3.3   Calculation of Minsupp and Minacc Based on Descinf and Descsup Information

In this subsection, we show an effective method to calculate $minsupp(\tau)$ and $minacc(\tau)$ based on $descinf$ and $descsup$. This calculation is necessary for solving Problem 3.

Proposition 5. Let $[CON, \zeta]$ be $\wedge_{A \in CON}[A, \zeta_A]$ and $[DEC, \eta]$ be $\wedge_{B \in DEC}[B, \eta_B]$, and let us suppose $x \in descsup([CON, \zeta] \wedge [DEC, \eta])$.
(1) If $x \in descinf([CON, \zeta] \wedge [DEC, \eta])$, it is possible to obtain a possible implication $\tau^x : [CON, \zeta] \Rightarrow [DEC, \eta]$ from object x, which satisfies
$$minsupp(\tau^x) = \frac{|descinf([CON, \zeta] \wedge [DEC, \eta])|}{|OB|}.$$
(2) If $x \in descsup([CON, \zeta] \wedge [DEC, \eta]) - descinf([CON, \zeta] \wedge [DEC, \eta])$, it is possible to obtain a possible implication $\tau^x : [CON, \zeta] \Rightarrow [DEC, \eta]$ from object x, which satisfies
$$minsupp(\tau^x) = \frac{|descinf([CON, \zeta] \wedge [DEC, \eta])| + 1}{|OB|}.$$

Proposition 5 shows us that $minsupp(\tau)$ can be calculated by $descinf$. In Proposition 5, if $x \notin descsup([CON, \zeta] \wedge [DEC, \eta])$, it is impossible to obtain any possible

270   H. Sakai and M. Nakata

Table 3. Descinf and descsup information in Table 2

	$[P,1]$	$[P,2]$	$[P,3]$	$[Q,1]$	$[Q,2]$	$[Q,3]$	$[R,1]$	$[R,2]$	$[R,3]$
$descinf$	{4}	{2}	{1,5}	{5}	{3}	{4}	{}	{}	{1,4}
$descsup$	{3,4}	{2,3}	{1,5}	{1,5}	{2,3}	{1,2,4}	{2,3,5}	{3,5}	{1,2,4}

	$[S,1]$	$[S,2]$	$[S,3]$	$[T,1]$	$[T,2]$	$[T,3]$
$descinf$	{}	{1}	{3,5}	{3}	{2}	{1,5}
$descsup$	{2}	{1,4}	{2,3,4,5}	{3,4}	{2,4}	{1,4,5}

Table 4. Conjunction of descriptors satisfying either CASE 1 or CASE 2 in Table 3

	$[P,3] \wedge [T,3]$	$[Q,1] \wedge [T,3]$	$[R,3] \wedge [T,3]$	$[S,2] \wedge [T,3]$	$[S,3] \wedge [T,1]$	$[S,3] \wedge [T,3]$
$descinf$	{1,5}	{5}	{1}	{1}	{3}	{5}
$descsup$	{1,5}	{1,5}	{1,4}	{1,4}	{3,4}	{4,5}

implication $[CON, \zeta] \Rightarrow [DEC, \eta]$ from object x. Therefore, we employed such a condition that $x \in descsup([CON, \zeta] \wedge [DEC, \eta])$. According to Proposition 5, it is possible to obtain every object, from which we can extract a possible implication satisfying the condition of $minsupp(\tau) \geq \alpha$.

Example 3. Let us consider $descinf$ and $descsup$, which are obtained in NIS_1, in Table 3, and let us consider Problem 3. We set $\alpha{=}0.3$, condition attribute $CON \subseteq \{P, Q, R, S\}$ and decision attribute $DEC{=}\{T\}$. Since $|OB|{=}5$ and $minsupp(\tau){=}|SET|/5 \geq 0.3$, $|SET| \geq 2$ must hold. According to Table 3, we generate Table 4 satisfying either of the following.
(CASE 1) $|descinf([A, \zeta_A] \wedge [T, \eta_T])| \geq 2$ $(A \in \{P, Q, R, S\})$.
(CASE 2) $|descinf([A, \zeta_A] \wedge [T, \eta_T])|{=}1$ and $descsup([A, \zeta_A] \wedge [T, \eta_T]) -$
$\qquad descinf([A, \zeta_A] \wedge [T, \eta_T]) \neq \{\}$ $(A \in \{P, Q, R, S\})$.

The conjunction $[P, 3] \wedge [T, 3]$ in Table 4 means an implication $\tau_3^1, \tau_3^5 : [P, 3] \Rightarrow [T, 3]$. Because $descsup([P, 3] \wedge [T, 3]){=}\{1, 5\}$ holds, τ_3^1 and τ_3^5 come from object 1 and 5, respectively. Since $1, 5 \in descinf([P, 3] \wedge [T, 3])$ holds, $minsupp(\tau_3^1){=}$ $minsupp(\tau_3^5){=}|\{1, 5\}|/5{=}0.4$ holds. Then, the conjunction $[Q, 1] \wedge [T, 3]$ in Table 4 means an implication $\tau_4^1, \tau_4^5 : [Q, 1] \Rightarrow [T, 3]$. Since $5 \in descinf([Q, 1] \wedge [T, 3])$ holds, $minsupp(\tau_4^5){=}|\{5\}|/5{=}0.2$ holds. On the other hand, $1 \in descsup([Q, 1] \wedge [T, 3]) - descinf([Q, 1] \wedge [T, 3])$ holds, so $minsupp(\tau_4^1){=}(|\{5\}| + 1)/5{=}0.4$ holds in object 1.

Now, let us discuss the calculation of $minacc(\tau)$.

Proposition 6. Let us suppose the same condition as in Proposition 5, and let $OUTMINACC$ denote a set $[descsup([CON, \zeta]) - descinf([CON, \zeta])] - descinf([DEC, \eta])$. Then, the following holds.
(1) If $x \in descinf([CON, \zeta] \wedge [DEC, \eta])$, it is possible to obtain a possible implication $\tau^x : [CON, \zeta] \Rightarrow [DEC, \eta]$ from object x, which satisfies
$$minacc(\tau^x){=}\frac{|descinf([CON, \zeta] \wedge [DEC, \eta])|}{|descinf([CON, \zeta])| + |OUTMINACC|}.$$

(2) If $x \in descsup([CON, \zeta] \wedge [DEC, \eta]) - descinf([CON, \zeta] \wedge [DEC, \eta])$, it is possible to obtain a possible implication $\tau^x : [CON, \zeta] \Rightarrow [DEC, \eta]$ from object x, which satisfies

$$minacc(\tau^x) = \frac{|descinf([CON,\zeta] \wedge [DEC,\eta])| + 1}{|descinf([CON,\zeta]) \cup \{x\}| + |OUTMINACC - \{x\}|}.$$

Example 4. Let us continue Example 3. For τ_3^1 and τ_3^5, $descsup([P,3]) = \{1,5\}$, $descinf([P,3]) = \{1,5\}$, $descinf([P,3] \wedge [T,3]) = \{1,5\}$ and $OUTMINACC = [\{1,5\} - \{1,5\}] - \{1,5\} = \{\}$. Since $1,5 \in descinf([P,3] \wedge [T,3])$ holds, $minacc(\tau_3^1) = minacc(\tau_3^5) = |\{1,5\}|/(|\{1,5\}| + |\{\}|) = 1$ is derived. For $\tau_4^3, \tau_4^4 : [S,3] \Rightarrow [T,1]$, $OUTMINACC = [\{2,3,4,5\} - \{3,5\}] - \{3\} = \{2,4\}$ holds. For τ_4^3 from object 3, $minacc(\tau_4^3) = |\{3\}|/(|\{3,5\}| + |\{2,4\}|) = 0.25$ is derived. As for τ_4^4 from object 4, $minacc(\tau_4^4) = (|\{3\}| + 1)/(|\{3,5\} \cup \{4\}| + |\{2,4\} - \{4\}|) = 0.5$ is derived. Since τ_4^4 just satisfies $minsupp(\tau) \geq 0.3$, it is enough to consider $minacc(\tau_4^4)$ for an implication $[S,3] \Rightarrow [T,1]$.

According to the above consideration, we obtain three possible rules, whose $minacc$ is maximum under $minsupp \geq 0.3$, in the following.

$[P,3] \Rightarrow [T,3]$ ($minsupp=0.4$, $minacc=1$) from objects 1 and 5.

$[Q,1] \Rightarrow [T,3]$ ($minsupp=0.4$, $minacc=1$) from object 1.

$[S,2] \Rightarrow [T,3]$ ($minsupp=0.4$, $minacc=1$) from object 4.

In the above procedure, every calculation just depends upon $descinf$ and $descsup$, and the calculation is very simple. The most time-consuming part is to generate conjunctions of descriptors in Table 4.

3.4   Calculation of Maxsupp and Maxacc Based on Descinf and Descsup Information

In this subsection, we show an effective method to calculate $maxsupp(\tau)$ and $maxacc(\tau)$ based on $descinf$ and $descsup$. This calculation is necessary for solving Problem 4. As we have shown, $sup(x, CON, \zeta) - descsup([CON, \zeta])$ holds for every x.

Proposition 7. Let us suppose the same condition as in Proposition 5.
(1) If $x \in descsup([CON, \zeta] \wedge [DEC, \eta])$, it is possible to obtain a possible implication $\tau^x : [CON, \zeta] \Rightarrow [DEC, \eta]$ from object x, which satisfies

$$maxsupp(\tau^x) = \frac{|descsup([CON,\zeta] \wedge [DEC,\eta])|}{|OB|}.$$

Proposition 8. Let us suppose the same condition as in Proposition 5, and let $INMAXACC$ denote a set $[descsup([CON, \zeta]) - descinf([CON, \zeta])] \cap descsup([DEC, \eta])$.
(1) If $x \in descinf([CON, \zeta] \wedge [DEC, \eta])$, it is possible to obtain a possible implication $\tau^x : [CON, \zeta] \Rightarrow [DEC, \eta]$ from object x, which satisfies

$$maxacc(\tau^x) = \frac{|descinf([CON,\zeta]) \cap descsup([DEC,\eta])| + |INMAXACC|}{|descinf([CON,\zeta])| + |INMAXACC|}.$$

(2) If $x \in descsup([CON, \zeta] \wedge [DEC, \eta]) - descinf([CON, \zeta] \wedge [DEC, \eta])$, it is possible to obtain a possible implication $\tau^x : [CON, \zeta] \Rightarrow [DEC, \eta]$ from object x, which satisfies

$$maxacc(\tau^x) = \frac{|descinf([CON,\zeta]) \cap descsup([DEC,\eta]) - \{x\}| + |INMAXACC - \{x\}| + 1}{|descinf([CON,\zeta]) \cup \{x\}| + |INMAXACC - \{x\}|}.$$

Example 5. Let us continue Example 3. For $\tau_3^1 : [P, 3] \Rightarrow [T, 3]$. $maxsupp(\tau_3^1)=$ $|\{1, 5\}|/5{=}0.4$, and $INMAXACC{=}[\{1, 5\} - \{1, 5\}] \cap \{1, 4, 5\}{=}\{\}$. Therefore, $maxacc(\tau_3^1){=}(|\{1, 5\} \cap \{1, 4, 5\}| + |\{\}|)/(|\{1, 5\}| + |\{\}|){=}1$. As for $\tau_4^4 : [S, 3] \Rightarrow$ $[T, 1]$, $maxsupp(\tau_4^4){=}|\{3, 4\}|/5{=}0.4$, and $INMAXACC{=}[\{2, 3, 4, 5\} - \{3, 5\}] \cap$ $\{3, 4\}{=}\{4\}$. Since $4 \in descsup([S, 3] \wedge [T1]) - descinf([S, 3] \wedge [T1])$, condition (2) in Proposition 8 is applied. $maxacc(\tau_4^4){=}(|\{3, 5\} \cap \{3, 4\} - \{4\}| + |\{4\} - \{4\}| +$ $1)/(|\{3, 5\} \cup \{4\}| + |\{4\} - \{4\}|){=}(|\{3\}| + 1)/(|\{3, 4, 5\}|){=}0.666$ is derived.

According to the above consideration, we obtain four possible rules, whose $maxacc$ is maximum under $maxsupp \geq 0.3$, in the following.

$[P, 3] \Rightarrow [T, 3]$ ($maxsupp{=}0.4$, $maxacc{=}1$) from objects 1 and 5.
$[Q, 1] \Rightarrow [T, 3]$ ($maxsupp{=}0.4$, $maxacc{=}1$) from object 1 and 5.
$[R, 3] \Rightarrow [T, 3]$ ($maxsupp{=}0.4$, $maxacc{=}1$) from object 1 and 4.
$[S, 2] \Rightarrow [T, 3]$ ($maxsupp{=}0.4$, $maxacc{=}1$) from object 1 and 4.

3.5   Possible Rule Generation in Two Strategies

In the previous subsection, we showed calculation methods based on $descinf$ and $descsup$. We are now realizing possible rule generation, which depends upon criteria $minsupp$, $minacc$, $maxsupp$ and $maxacc$, below.

An Overview of Possible Rule Generation in Min-Max Strategy
(1) For condition $minsupp(\tau){=}|SET|/|OB| \geq \alpha$, obtain the number NUM of elements in SET satisfying this condition.
(2) Generate conjunctions of descriptors like Table 3 and 4 until $|descsup([CON, \zeta] \wedge [DEC, \eta])|$ is smaller than NUM. If $|descsup([CON, \zeta] \wedge [DEC, \eta])| < NUM$, $minsupp(\tau) < \alpha$ holds. Therefore, it is meaningless to generate the next conjunction.
(3) For every conjunction of descriptors $[CON, \zeta] \wedge [DEC, \eta]$ ($\tau : [CON, \zeta] \Rightarrow$ $[DEC, \eta]$), apply Proposition 5 to calculating $minsupp(\tau)$. If $minsupp(\tau) \geq \alpha$, apply Proposition 6 to calculating $minacc(\tau)$.

As for Max-Max strategy based possible rule generation is also like the above procedure.

We have already proposed a method to calculate $minsupp(\tau), \cdots, maxacc(\tau)$ in Theorem 3. However, this method can be applicable to the fixed τ. In order to apply Theorem 3 to Problem 3 or Problem 4, it is necessary to pick up all τ in a NIS. As we have shown, τ depends upon the number of derived $DISs$, and furthermore τ depends upon condition attributes CON ($CON \subseteq 2^{AT-DEC}$). Therefore, it is hard to pick every τ sequentially. On the other hand, proposed possible rule generation in this paper depends upon the number of conjunctions of descriptors, therefore proposed rule generation will be more effective.

4   Concluding Remarks

We proposed a framework of possible rule generation based on Min-Max and Max-Max strategies in $NISs$. These strategies are usually applied to decision making under the uncertain situation, and we are now including these strategies into *RNIA* (*Rough Non-deterministic Information Analysis*) [10].

We employed *descinf* and *descsup* information and the concept of large itemset in Apriori algorithm. In the current situation, we have not realized tool programs. Toward realizing tool programs, at least it is necessary to consider the following.

(1) To examine the details of rule generation in two strategies.
(2) To examine algorithms for generating conjunctions of descriptors.
(3) To examine the computational complexity of algorithms.
(4) To examine data structure for realizing tool programs.

Acknowledgment. This work is partly supported by the Grant-in-Aid for Scientific Research (C) (No.18500214), Japan Society for the Promotion of Science.

References

1. Z.Pawlak: Rough Sets, Kluwer Academic Publisher, 1991.
2. Z.Pawlak: Some Issues on Rough Sets, Transactions on Rough Sets, Int'l. Rough Set Society, Vol.1, pp.1-58, 2004.
3. J.Komorowski, Z.Pawlak, L.Polkowski and A.Skowron: Rough Sets: a tutorial, Rough Fuzzy Hybridization, Springer, pp.3-98, 1999.
4. Rough Set Software, Bulletin of Int'l. Rough Set Society, Vol.2, pp.15-46, 1998.
5. E.Orłowska(ed.): Incomplete Information: Rough Set Analysis, Physica-Verlag, 1998.
6. W.Lipski: On Semantic Issues Connected with Incomplete Information Data Base, ACM Trans. DBS, Vol.4, pp.269-296, 1979.
7. J.Grzymala-Busse, P.Werbrouck: On the Best Search Method in the LEM1 and LEM2 Algorithms, Incomplete Information: Rough Set Analysis, Phisica-Verlag, pp.75-91, 1998.
8. J.Grzymala-Busse: Data with Missing Attribute Values: Generalization of Indiscernibility Relation and Rule Induction, Transactions on Rough Sets, Int'l. Rough Set Society, Vol.1, pp.78-95, 2004.
9. M.Kryszkiewicz: Rules in Incomplete Information Systems, Information Sciences, Vol.113, pp.271-292, 1999.
10. H.Sakai and A.Okuma: Basic Algorithms and Tools for Rough Non-deterministic Information Analysis, Transactions on Rough Sets, Int'l. Rough Set Society, Vol.1, pp.209-231, 2004.
11. A.Skowron and C.Rauszer: The Discernibility Matrices and Functions in Information Systems, In Intelligent Decision Support - Handbook of Advances and Applications of the Rough Set Theory, Kluwer Academic Publishers, pp.331-362, 1992.
12. H.Sakai and M.Nakata: Discernibility Functions and Minimal Rules in Non-deterministic Information Systems, Lecture Notes in AI, Springer-Verlag, Vol.3641, pp.254-264, 2005.
13. R.Agrawal and R.Srikant: Fast Algorithms for Mining Association Rules, Proc. 20th Very Large Data Base, pp.487-499, 1994.

Generalized Conflict and Resolution Model with Approximation Spaces

Sheela Ramanna[1], James F. Peters[2], and Andrzej Skowron[3]

[1] Department of Applied Computer Science,
University of Winnipeg,
Winnipeg, Manitoba R3B 2E9 Canada
s.ramanna@uwinnipeg.ca
[2] Department of Electrical and Computer Engineering,
University of Manitoba
Winnipeg, Manitoba R3T 5V6 Canada
jfpeters@ee.umanitoba.ca
[3] Institute of Mathematics,
Warsaw University
Banacha 2, 02-097 Warsaw, Poland
skowron@mimuw.edu.pl

Abstract. This paper considers the problem of a generalized model for conflict analysis and resolution. Such a model would be helpful in analyzing and resolving conflict in disputes in both government and industry, where disputes and negotiations about various issues are the norm. The issue here is how to model a combination of situations among agents i) where there are disagreements leading to a conflict situation ii) need for an acceptable set of agreements. The solution to this problem stems from pioneering work on this subject by Zdzisław Pawlak, which provides a basis for a generalized model encapsulating a decision system with complex decisions and an approximation space-based conflict resolution using rough coverage. An example of a requirements scope negotiation for an automated lighting system is presented. The contribution of this paper is a rough set based requirements scope determination model using a generalized conflict model with approximation spaces.

Keywords: Approximation space, conflict analysis, conflict resolution, rough sets, requirements engineering, scope negotiation.

1 Introduction

Conflict analysis and resolution play an important role in government and industry where disputes and negotiations about various issues are the norm. To this end, many mathematical formal models of conflict situations have been proposed and studied, e.g., [4,5,6,11,12,15]. The approach used in this paper, is based on a different kind of relationship in the data. This relationship is not a dependency, but a conflict [16]. Formally, a conflict relation can be viewed as a special kind of discernibility, i.e., negation (not necessarily, classical) of indiscernibility relation

S. Greco et al. (Eds.): RSCTC 2006, LNAI 4259, pp. 274–283, 2006.
© Springer-Verlag Berlin Heidelberg 2006

which is the basis of rough set theory [14]. Thus indiscernibility and conflict are closely related from logical point of view. It is also interesting to note that almost all mathematical models of conflict situations are strongly domain dependent.

Cost effective engineering of complex software systems involves a collaborative process of requirements identification through negotiation. This is one of the key ideas of the Win-Win [1] approach [3] used in requirements engineering. This approach also includes a decision model where a minimal set of conceptual elements, such as win conditions, issues, options and agreements, serves as an agreed upon ontology for collaboration and negotiation defined by the Win-Win process. System requirements (goals) are viewed as conditions. Conflicts arising during system requirements gathering is especially acute due to the nature of the intense collaboration between project stakeholders involved in the process. In particular, determining the scope or the extent of functionality to be developed is crucial.

Recent work in the application of rough sets to handling uncertainty in software engineering can be found in [10,18,19]. However, the basic assumption in all of these papers, is that requirements have already been *decided* and the analysis of gathered requirements data is then performed. This paper extends the earlier work involving the high-level requirements negotiation based on winning conditions [21]. In this paper, the focus is on achieving consensus on detailed set of requirements for each high level requirement that was agreed by all stakeholders. This process is also known as scope negotiation.

The contribution of this paper is a rough set based requirements scope determination model using a generalized conflict model with approximation spaces. Conflict graphs are used to analyze conflict situations, reason about the degree of conflict and explore coalitions. A rough coverage function is used to measure the degree of conformity of sets of similar requirements to negotiation standards. We illustrate our approach in determining scope of a complex engineering system requirements through negotiation.

This paper is organized as follows. An introduction to basic concepts of conflict theory is given Sect. 2. Conflicts, information systems and rough sets are discussed in Sect. 3. A complex conflict model is given in Sect. 4 followed by an illustration of requirements scope negotiation for a home lighting automation system (HLAS) in Sections 5 and 5.1. A generalized conflict model for conflict analysis and conflict resolution considered in the context of approximation spaces is given Sect. 5.2.

2   Basic Concepts of Conflict Theory

The basic concepts of conflict theory that we use in this paper are due to [16]. Let us assume that we are given a finite, non-empty set Ag called the *universe*. Elements of Ag will be referred to as *agents*. Let a *voting function* $v : Ag \rightarrow \{-1, 0, 1\}$, or in short $\{-, 0, +\}$, be a number representing his/her voting result about some issue under negotiation, to be interpreted as *against, neutral*

---

[1] See http://sunset.usc.edu/research/WINWIN

and *favorable*, respectively. The pair $CS = (Ag, V)$, where V is a set of voting functions, will be called a *conflict situation*.

In order to express relations between agents, we define three basic binary relations on the universe: *agreement, neutrality*, and *disagreement*. To this end, for a given voting function v, we first define the following auxiliary function:

$$\phi_v(ag, ag') = \begin{cases} 1, & \text{if } v(ag)v(ag') = 1 \text{ or } v(ag) = v(ag') = 0 \\ 0, & \text{if } v(ag)v(ag') = 0 \text{ and } non(v(ag) = v(ag') = 0) \\ -1, & \text{if } v(ag)v(ag') = -1. \end{cases} \quad (1)$$

This means that, if $\phi_v(ag, ag') = 1$, agents ag and ag' have the same opinion about an issue v (*agree* on issue v); if $\phi_v(ag, ag') = 0$ means that at least one agent ag or ag' has no opinion about an issue v (is *neutral* on v), and if $\phi_v(ag, ag') = -1$, means that both agents have different opinions about an issue v (are in *conflict* on issue v). In what follows, we will define three basic relations R_v^+, R_v^0 and R_v^- on Ag^2 called *agreement, neutrality* and *disagreement* relations respectively, and defined by (i) $R_v^+(ag, ag')$ iff $\phi_v(ag, ag') = 1$; (ii) $R_v^0(ag, ag')$ iff $\phi_v(ag, ag') = 0$; (iii) $R_v^-(ag, ag')$ iff $\phi_v(ag, ag') = -1$. It is easily seen that the *agreement* relation is an *equivalence* relation. Each equivalence class of the agreement relation will be called a *coalition* with respect to v. For the conflict or disagreement relation we have: (i) not $R_v^-(ag, ag)$; (ii) if $R_v^-(ag, ag')$ then $R_v^-(ag', ag)$; (iii) if $R_v^-(ag, ag')$ and $R_v^+(ag', ag'')$ then $R_v^-(ag, ag'')$. For the neutrality relation we have: (i) not $R_v^0(ag, ag)$; (ii) $R_v^0(ag, ag') = R_v^0(ag', ag)$. In the conflict and neutrality relations there are no coalitions. In addition, $R_v^+ \cup R_v^0 \cup R_v^- = Ag^2$. All the three relations R_v^+, R_v^0 , R_v^- are pairwise disjoint. With every conflict situation $cs = (Ag, v)$ relative to a voting function v, we will associate a *conflict graph* CG_v. Examples of conflict graphs are shown in Figure 1. In Figure 1(a), solid lines denote conflicts, dotted line denote agreements, and for simplicity, neutrality is not shown explicitly in the graph.

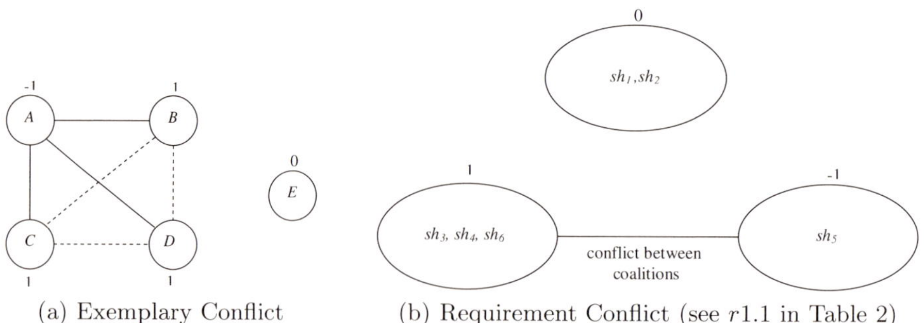

(a) Exemplary Conflict   (b) Requirement Conflict (see $r1.1$ in Table 2)

Fig. 1. Sample Conflict Graphs

As one can see B, C, and D form a coalition. A conflict degree $Con(cs)$ (or $Con_v(cs)$) of the conflict situation $cs = (Ag, v)$ (we write also CS_v instead of cs) is defined by

$$Con(cs) = \frac{\sum_{\{(ag,ag'):\ \phi_v(ag,ag')=-1\}} |\phi_v(ag,ag')|}{2\lceil \frac{n}{2} \rceil \times (n - \lceil \frac{n}{2} \rceil)} \qquad (2)$$

where $n = Card(ag)$. Observe that $Con(cs)$ is a measure of discernibility between agents from Ag relative to the voting function v. For a more general conflict situation $CS = (Ag, V)$ where $V = \{v_1, \ldots, v_k\}$ is a finite set of voting functions each for a different issues the *conflict degree* in CS (*tension generated by V*) can be defined by

$$Con(CS) = \sum_{i=1}^{k} Con(cs_i)/k \qquad (3)$$

where $cs_i = (Ag, v_i)$ for $i = 1, \ldots, k$.

3   Conflicts, Information Systems, and Rough Sets

There are strong relationships between the approach to conflicts and information systems as well as rough sets. In this section, we discuss examples of such relationships. The presented approach in this section seems to be promising for solving problems related to conflict resolution and negotiations (see, e.g.,[24]).

An information system is a table of rows which are labeled by *objects* (*agents*), columns by *attributes* (*issues*) and entries of the table are *values of attributes* (*votes*), which are uniquely assigned to each agent and attribute, i.e. each entry corresponding to row x and column a represents opinion of an agent x about issue a. Formally, an *information system* can be defined as a pair $S = (U, A)$, where U is a nonempty, finite set called the *universe*; elements of U will be called *objects* and A is a nonempty, finite set of *attributes* [14]. Every attribute $a \in A$ is a total function $a : U \to V_a$, where V_a is the set of *values* of a, called the *domain* of a; elements of V_a will be referred to as *opinions*, and $a(x)$ is opinion of agent x about issue a. The above given definition is general, but for conflict analysis we will need its simplified version, where the domain of each attribute is restricted to three values only, i.e. $V_a = \{-1, 0, 1\}$, for every a, meaning *disagreement*, *neutral* and *agreement* respectively. For the sake of simplicity we will assume $V_a = \{-, 0, +\}$. Every information system with the above mentioned restriction will be referred to as a *situation*.

We now observe that any conflict situation $CS = (Ag, V)$ can be treated as an information system where $Ag = \{ag_1, \ldots, ag_n\}$ and $V = \{v_1, \ldots, v_k\}$ with the set of objects Ag (*agents*) and the set V of attributes (*issues*).

The discernibility degree between agents ag and ag' in CS can be defined by

$$disc_{CS}(ag, ag') = \frac{\sum_{\{i:\ \phi_{v_i}(ag,ag')=-1\}} |\phi_{v_i}(ag,ag')|}{k}, \qquad (4)$$

where $ag, ag' \in Ag$. Now, one can consider reducts of CS relative to the discernibility degree defined by $disc_{CS}$. For example, one can consider agents ag, ag' as discernible if

$$disc_{CS}(ag, ag') \geq tr,$$

where tr a given threshold.[2] Any reduct $R \subseteq V$ of CS is a minimal set of voting functions preserving all discernibility in voting between agents that are at least equal to tr. All voting functions from $V - R$ are dispensable with respect to preserving such discernibility between objects. In an analogous way, one can consider reducts of the information system CS^T with the universe of objects equal to $\{v_1, \ldots, v_k\}$ and attributes defined by agents and voting functions by $ag(v) = v(ag)$ for $ag \in Ag$ and $v \in V$. The discernibility between voting functions can be defined, e.g., by

$$disc_{CS^T}(v, v') = |Con(CS_v) - Con(CS_{v'}|, \tag{5}$$

and makes it possible to measure the difference between voting functions v and v', respectively. Any reduct R of CS^T is a minimal set of agents that preserves the differences between voting functions that are at least equal to a given threshold tr.

4   Complex Conflict Model

In this section, we present an extension of the conflict model and we outline an approach to conflict resolution based on such a model. We assume that agents in the complex conflict model are represented by conflict situations $cs = (Ag, v)$, where Ag is the set of lower level agents and v is a voting function defined on Ag for $v \in V$. Hence, agents in the complex conflict model are related to groups of lower level agents linked by a voting function. The voting functions in the complex conflict models are defined on such conflict situations. The set of the voting functions for the complex conflict model is denoted by A. In this, way we obtain an information system (U, A), where U is the set of situations. Observe that any situation $cs = (Ag, v)$ can be represented by a matrix

$$[v(ag)]_{ag \in Ag}, \tag{6}$$

where $v(ag)$ is the result of voting by the agent $ag \in Ag$. We can extend the information system (U, A) to the decision system (U, A, d) assuming, that $d(cs) = Con_v(cs)$ for any $cs = (Ag, v)$. For the constructed decision system (U, A, d) one can use, e.g., the above function(2) to measure the discernibility between compound decision values which correspond to conflict situations in the constructed decision table. The reducts of this decision table relative to decision have a natural interpretation with respect to conflicts. An illustration of conflict analysis with similarity relation can be found in [22].

5   Systems Requirements Identification and Negotiation

A typical system requirements engineering process leads to conflicts between project stakeholders. A stakeholder is one who has a share or an interest in the

---

[2] To compute such reducts one can follow a method presented in [23] assuming that any entry of the discernibility matrix corresponding to (ag, ag') with $disc_{CS}(ag, ag') < tr$ is empty and the remaining entries are families of all subsets of V on which the discernibility between (ag, ag') is at least equal to tr [6].

requirements for a systems engineering project. Let Ag be represented by the set SH (stakeholders). Let V denote the set of requirements. Let $CS = (SH, V)$ where $SH = \{sh_1, \ldots, sh_n\}$ and $V = \{v_1, \ldots, v_k\}$. A complete example of the problem of achieving agreement on high-level system requirements for a home lighting automation system described in [9] can be found in [21]. In this paper, the focus is on achieving consensus on detailed set of requirements for each high level requirement that was agreed by all stakeholders. This is a crucial step as it determines the scope of the project. In other words, the team needs to know the *extent* of functionality that needs to be implemented. In fact, no serious requirements analysis can begin until the scope of project has been determined.

5.1   Example: Determining Scope of System Requirements

As a part of scope negotiation, several parameters need to be determined: level of effort, importance of a requirement, stability, risk, testability to name a few. In this paper, we consider the following negotiation parameters: *Level of Effort* which is a rough estimate of development effort (High, Medium, Low), *Importance* which determines whether a requirement is essential to the project (High, Medium, Low), *Stability* of a requirement which indicates its volatility (Yes, Perhaps, No), *Risk* which indicates whether the requirement is technically achievable (High, Medium, Low) *Testability* indicating whether a requirement is testable (Yes, No). Let $R1$, E, I, S, R, T denote requirement 1, Effort, Importance, Stability, Risk, and Testability, respectively. Specifically, the example illustrates the high level functionality(R1) of Custom Lighting Scene[21] to be included in release of V1.0 of HLAS System. The negotiation parameter values (attributes) assessed by the development team for R1 are given in Table 1.

Table 1. Scope Negotiation

	Negotiation Parameters					
$R1$	E	I	S	R	T	$Conflict\ Degree$
$r1.1$	M	H	N	L	Y	L
$r1.2$	M	H	N	L	Y	M
$r1.3$	H	M	N	M	Y	L
$r1.4$	L	H	Y	L	Y	L
$r1.5$	M	L	P	H	Y	M
$r1.6$	L	H	Y	H	N	H

Assume that R1 includes the following specifications (objects): $r1.1$ - ability to control up to a maximum of 20 custom lighting scenes throughout the residence, $r1.2$ - each scene provides a preset level of illumination (max. of 3) for each lighting bank, $r1.3$ - maximum range of a scene is 20 meters, $r1.4$ - activated using Control Switch, $r1.5$ - activated using Central Control Unit, and $r1.6$ - Ability to control an additional 2 lighting scenes in the yard. The decision attribute is a compound decision denoting the conflict degree which is a result of a matrix given in Table 2.

The voting results of the members drawn from a stakeholders list SH is given in Table 2. The stakeholder list is comprised of builders, electrical contractors and the marketers. Every stakeholder votes on each of the requirements. An algorithm for determining win agreements can be found in [21]. The conflict graph $CG_{r1.1} = (SH, r1.1)$ can be presented in a simplified form as a graph with nodes represented by coalitions and edges representing conflicts between coalitions as shown in Fig. 1(b). From this graph, one can compute the conflict degree using using Eqn. 2 where $Con_{r1.1}(cs) = 0.3$. The degree of conflict for the remaining requirements are $Con_{r1.2}(cs) = 0.44$, $Con_{r1.3}(cs) = 0.2$, $Con_{r1.4}(cs) = 0$, $Con_{r1.5}(cs) = 0.67$, and $Con_{r1.6}(cs) = 0.89$.

Table 2. Voting Results for R1

	Voting Results					
Stakeholder	*r1.1*	*r1.2*	*r1.3*	*r1.4*	*r1.5*	*r1.6*
sh_1	0	1	-1	0	-1	-1
sh_2	0	1	0	0	-1	-1
sh_3	1	-1	0	1	1	-1
sh_4	1	1	0	1	1	-1
sh_5	-1	0	1	1	1	1
sh_6	1	1	-1	1	0	1

5.2   Generalized Conflict Model with Approximation Spaces

This section introduces a generalized model for conflict analysis and conflict resolution that combines earlier work on modeling conflict with approximation spaces. Conflict degree $Con_v(cs)$ for any $cs = (Ag, v)$ plays the role of a decision in Table 1. $Con_v(cs)$ is a subjective value that is a result of voting with the following levels: L (*conflict degree* ≤ 0.3), M ($0.3 \leq$ *conflict degree* ≤ 0.7) and H (*conflict degree* > 0.7). For example, to determine which requirements should be included in product release version V1.0, negotiation must occur at two levels, namely, voting and table. At the voting level (lower level), the basic conflict model is used. At the decision table level, conflicts are evaluated within an approximation space [20], which is the approach used in [17].

Let $DS = (U_{req}, A, d)$, where U_{req}, A, d denote a non-empty set of requirements, a non-empty set of scope negotiation parameters, and an estimated degree of conflict, respectively (see Table 1). Let D_i denote the ith decision, i.e., $D_i = \{u \in U_{req} : d(u) = i\}$, which is set of requirements from U_{reg} with conflict level i. For any boolean combination of descriptors over DS and α, the semantics of α in DS is denoted by $\|\alpha\|_{DS}$, i.e., the set of all objects from U satisfying α [14].

In what follows, $i = L$ and D_L denotes a decision class representing a low degree of conflict between stakeholders. Now, we can define a generalized approximation space $GAS = (U_{req}, N_B, \nu_B)$, where for any objects $r \in U$ the neighborhood $N_B(r)$ is defined by

$$N_B(r) = \| \bigwedge_{a \in B} (a = a(r)) \|_{DS}, \tag{7}$$

and the coverage function ν_B is defined by

$$\nu_B(X, Y) = \begin{cases} \frac{|X \cap Y|}{|Y|}, & \text{if } Y \neq \emptyset, \\ 1, & \text{if } Y = \emptyset, \end{cases} \tag{8}$$

where $X, Y \subseteq U$. This form of specialization of a GAS is called a *lower approximation space* [17]. Assuming that the lower approximation $B_* D_i$ represents an acceptable (standard) level of conflict during negotiation, we are interested in the values

$$\nu_B(N_B(r), B_* D_L), \tag{9}$$

of the coverage function specialized in the context of a decision system DS for the neighborhoods $N_B(r)$ and the standard $B_* D_L$ for conflict negotiation.

Computing the rough coverage value for negotiation parameters extracted from a table such as Table 1 implicitly measures the extent to which standards for release parameters have been followed. What follows is a simple example of how to set up a lower approximation space relative to a scope negotiation table based on the *effort* (E), *risk* (R) and *testability* (T) paramters:

$B = \{E, R, T\}$, $D_L = \{r \in U : d(r) = L\} = \{r1.1, r1.3, r1.4\}$,
$B_* D_L = \{r1.3, r1.4\}$, $N_B(r1.1) = \{r1.1, r1.2\}$, $N_B(r1.3) = \{r1.3\}$,
$N_B(r1.4) = \{r1.4\}$, $N_B(r1.5) = \{r1.5\}$, $N_B(r1.6) = \{r1.6\}$,
$\nu_B(N_B(r1.1), B_* D_L) - 0$, $\nu_B(N_B(r1.3), B_* D_L) = 0.5$, $\nu_B(N_B(r1.4), B_* D_L) -$
0.5, $\nu_B(N_B(r1.5), B_* D_L) = 0$, $\nu_B(N_B(r1.6), B_* D_L) = 0$.

Based on the experimental rough coverage values, we can set a threshold for acceptance. In this case, let $\nu_B \geq 0.5$. Consequently, for the first release version V1.0 of the $HLAS$, requirements r1.3 and r1.4 would be included. On the other hand, if negotiation parameters *effort* (E), *importance* (I) and *stability* (S) are considered, with the same threshold of acceptance, only requirement r1.3 would be included in release version V1.0 as the following calculations show:

$B = \{E, I, S\}$, $D_L = \{r \in U : d(r) = L\} = \{r1.1, r1.3, r1.4\}$, $B_* D_L = \{r1.3\}$
$N_B(r1.1) = \{r1.1, r1.2\}$, $N_B(r1.3) = \{r1.3\}$, $N_B(r1.4) = \{r1.4, r1.6\}$,
$N_B(r1.5) = \{r1.5\}$,
$\nu_B(N_B(r1.1), B_* D_L) = 0$, $\nu_B(N_B(r1.3), B_* D_L) = 1$, $\nu_B(N_B(r1.4), B_* D_L) = 0$,
$\nu_B(N_B(r1.5), B_* D_L) = 0$.

The proposed attempt to assess negotiation offers deeper insight into conflict dynamics whereby one can observe changes to the requirements set based on coverage and level of conflict when different negotiation parameters are selected.

The risk analysis can also be performed using reducts preserving conflicts to a degree and their approximations. It should also be noted that the conflict model discussed in Sect. 4 is more general where any situation will correspond to a set of stakeholders. Analogous to the approach in Sect. 4, we can compute for any such situations conflict degrees and continue with the conflict resolution process. In this situation, we can consider issues for negotiation relative to groups of stakeholders.

6   Conclusion

This paper introduces rough set-based requirements scope determination using a generalized conflict model with approximation spaces. In other words, the generalized conflict model with approximation spaces provides the ability to (i) define a level of conflict that is acceptable, (ii) determine the equivalent set of requirements based on a specified set of negotiation parameters tailored to a specific project, and (iii) select requirements to be included in the system with a measure indicating the extent that standards for release parameters have been followed. The application of rough sets can bring new results in the area related to conflict resolution and negotiations between agents because this make it possible to introduce approximate reasoning about vague concepts into the area.

Acknowledgments. The authors gratefully acknowledge suggestions by Zdzisław Pawlak about conflict graphs. Authors would like to thank Gianpiero Cattaneo for correcting the previous version of the formula (1). The research of Andrzej Skowron, James F. Peters, and Sheela Ramanna is supported by grant 3 T11C 002 26 from the Ministry of Scientific Research and Information Technology of the Republic of Poland, NSERC Canada grants 194376 and 185986, respectively.

References

1. Alpigini, J. J., Peters, J. F., Skowron, A., Zhong, N. (eds.): Third International Conference on Rough Sets and Current Trends in Computing(RSCTC'2002). LNAI, Vol. 2475. Springer-Verlag, Heidelberg Germany (2002)
2. Bazan, J., Osmólski, A., Skowron, A., Ślęzak, D., Szczuka, M., Wróblewski, J.: Rough set approach to the survival analysis. In: Alpigini et al. [1], 522–529.
3. Boehm, B., Grünbacher, P., Kepler, J.: Developing Groupware for Requirements Negotiation: Lessons Learned. IEEE Software, (May/June 2001) 46-55.
4. Casti, J. L. Alternative Realities – Mathematical Models of Nature and Man. John Wiley and Sons (1989)
5. Coombs, C. H., Avrunin, G. S. : The Structure of Conflict. Lawrence Erlbaum Associates (1988)
6. Deja, R., Skowron, A.: On Some Conflict Models and Conflict Resolutions, *Romanian Journal of Information Science and Technology*, 5(1-2) (2002) 69-82.
7. Dunin-Kęplicz, B., Jankowski, A., Skowron, A., Szczuka, M. (eds.): Monitoring, Security, and Rescue Tasks in Multiagent Systems (MSRAS'2004). Advances in Soft Computing. Springer-Verlag, Heidelberg Germany (2005)

8. Easterbrook, S.: Handling Conflict between Domain Descriptions with Computer-Supported Negotiation. *Knowledge Acquisition: An International Journal*, Vol. 3 (1991) 255-289.

9. Leffingwell, D., Widrig, D.: Managing Software Requirements. Addision-Wesley. Boston U.S.A (2003)

10. Li, Z., Ruhe, G.: Uncertainty handling in Tabular-Based Requirements Using Rough Sets. In: Ślęzak, D., Yao, J.T., Peters, J.F., Ziarko, W., Hu, X (eds.): Rough Sets, Fuzzy Sets, Data Mining and Granular Computing. LNAI, Vol. 3642. Springer, Heidelberg Germany (2005) 678-687.

11. Maeda, Y., Senoo, K., Tanaka, H.: Interval density function in conflict analysis. LNAI, Vol. 1711. Springer-Verlag, Heidelberg Germany (1999) 382-389.

12. Nakamura, A.: Conflict logic with degrees. In: Pal, S. K., Skowron. A. (eds.): Rough Fuzzy Hybridization: A New Trend in Decision-Making. Springer-Verlag, Heidelberg Germany (1999) 136-150.

13. Pawlak, Z.: On Conflicts. *Int. J. of Man-Machine Studies*,Vol. 21 (1984) 127-134.

14. Pawlak, Z.: Rough Sets – Theoretical Aspects of Reasoning about Data. Kluwer Academic Publishers (1991)

15. Pawlak, Z.: An inquiry into anatomy of conflicts. *Journal of Information Sciences*, Vol. 109 (1998) 65-78.

16. Pawlak, Z., Skowron, A.: Rough Sets and Conflict Analysis. In: E-Service Intelligence – Methodologies, Technologies and Applications Book series on Computational Intelligence. Springer-Verlag, Berlin Germany (2006) [to appear]

17. Peters, J. F., Henry, C.: Reinforcement Learning with Approximation Spaces. *Fundamenta Informaticae* 71 (2006) 323-349.

18. Ramanna, S.: Approximation Space for Software Models. In: Peters, J.F., Skowron, A. (eds.): *Transactions on Rough Sets I*. LNCS, Vol. 3100. Springer-Verlag, Berlin Germany (2004) 338-354.

19. Peters, J. F., Ramanna, S.: Towards a software change classification system: A rough set approach. *Software Quality Journal*, Vol. 11 (2003) 121-147.

20. Skowron, A., Stepaniuk, J.:Generalized Approximation Spaces. In: Lin, T.Y., Wildberger, A.M. (eds.): Soft Computing. Simulation Councils, San Diego (1995)18-21; see also Tolerance Approximation Spaces, *Fundamenta Informaticae*, Vol. 27(2-3) (1996) 245-253.

21. Ramanna, S., Peters, J.F., Skowron, A · Conflict Analysis and Information Systems: A Rough Set Approach. In: Wang, G., Peters, J.F., Skowron, A.. Yao, Y.Y (eds.): Proceedings of the International Conference on Rough Sets and Knowledge Technology (RSKT 2006), LNAI, Chongqing, China, July 24-26 (2006) [to appear].

22. Ramanna, S., Peters, J.F., Skowron, A.: Analysis of Conflict Dynamics by Risk Patterns. Proceedings of the Workshop on Concurrency, Specification and Programming (CS&P 2006), Germany, September 27-29 (2006) [to appear].

23. Skowron, A. Rauszer, C.: The discernibility matrices and functions in information systems. In: Słowiński, R (ed.): *Intelligent Decision Support - Handbook of Applications and Advances of the Rough Sets Theory, System Theory, Knowledge Engineering and Problem Solving*, Vol. 11 (1992) 331-362.

24. Kowalski, R.: A logic-based approach to conflict resolution (2003) 1-28 (manuscript).

Rough Set Approach to Customer Satisfaction Analysis

Salvatore Greco[1], Benedetto Matarazzo[1], and Roman Słowiński[2]

[1] Faculty of Economics, University of Catania,
Corso Italia, 55, 95129 Catania, Italy
[2] Institute of Computing Science, Poznań University of Technology,
60-965 Poznań, and Institute for Systems Research,
Polish Academy of Sciences, 01-447 Warsaw, Poland

Abstract. Customer satisfaction analysis has become a hot issue in strategic management. The basis of any decision in this field is the analysis of the answers of a sample of customers to a specific questionnaire. Traditionally, using a methodology called conjoint analysis, the data obtained from the questionnaires are used to build a collective utility function representing customer preferences. This utility function permits to measure the satisfaction of the customers and to determine the most critical features relevant for the appreciation of the considered products or services. In this paper, we propose an alternative methodology to analyze the data from the questionnaire. Our approach is based on the rough set methodology and represents the preferences of the customers by means of simple decision rules such as "if feature α is considered good and feature β is considered sufficient, then the overall evaluation of the product is medium". The interpretation of the decision rules is simpler and more direct than the interpretation of the utility function given by conjoint analysis. Moreover, the capacity of representing customer preferences in terms of easily understandable "if ..., then..." statements expressed in the natural language makes our approach particularly interesting for Kansei Engineering. The proposed methodology gives also some indications relative to strategic interventions aimed at improving the quality of the offered products and services. The expected efficiency of these interventions is measured, which is very useful for the definition of proper customer satisfaction strategies. Our approach supplies an integrated support to customer satisfaction oriented management.

1 Introduction

Customer satisfaction analysis aims at determining customer preferences in order to optimize entrepreneurial decisions about strategies for launching new products or about improving the image of existing products. Differently from usual approaches to customer satisfaction analysis [6], we do not represent customer preferences in terms of a utility function expressed in mathematical terms but rather in terms of decision rules expressed in a natural language, such as "if the product is considered good and the purchase process is considered medium, then

S. Greco et al. (Eds.): RSCTC 2006, LNAI 4259, pp. 284–295, 2006.

the global satisfaction is medium". This is obtained by an analysis of the customer satisfaction survey conducted not in usual terms of statistical analysis, but rather in terms of a specific data mining analysis based on a rough set approach. More precisely, we shall use the Dominance-based Rough Set Approach (DRSA) [2,3,10], an extension of the Classical Rough Set Approach (CRSA) [9], in order to handle attributes with preference ordered scales (domains). The preference order is, obviously, of fundamental importance in customer satisfaction analysis. In fact, consider two customers, A and B, and suppose that the evaluations of a (given) product with respect to a set of relevant features (attributes) given by A are better than the evaluations given by B. In this case, it is reasonable to expect that also the comprehensive evaluation of this product by customer A is better (or at least not worse) than the evaluation made by customer B. Thus, we can state a general dominance principle which says that better (or, at least, not worse) evaluations on single features of the considered product should imply a better (or, at least, not worse) comprehensive evaluation of the product. This means that if in the above example customer A gives a comprehensive evaluation of the considered product worse than customer B, this can be considered as an inconsistency with the dominance principle. However, within CRSA the two evaluations will be considered as just discernible and no inconsistency will be stated. Motivated by the above considerations, we propose to apply the DRSA to customer satisfaction analysis. Moreover, we propose a methodology to evaluate proper strategies to improve customer satisfaction. This is based on the application of a new class of interestingness measures, which evaluate the efficiency of intervention based on rules induced from data [1]. Let us also observe that our rough set approach to analysis of customer preferences can become very useful for Kansei Engineering. Kansei Engineering is a "translating technology of consumer's feeling and image for a product into design elements" [8]. Since Kansei Engineering uses verbal language for requirement elicitation, an important characteristic of our approach is the representation of customer preferences in terms of "if..., then ..." statements in a natural language.

The article is organized as follows. In the next section we recall basic concepts of DRSA. In the third section we remember the intervention measures. In the fourth section, we propose the main steps of a customer satisfaction analysis based on the use of DRSA and intervention measures. The last section contains conclusions.

2   Dominance-Based Rough Set Approach

For algorithmic reasons, information about objects is represented in the form of an information table. The rows of the table are labelled by objects, whereas columns are labelled by attributes and entries of the table are attribute-values. Formally, by an information table we understand the 4-tuple $S = <U, Q, V, f>$, where U is a finite set of objects, Q is a finite set of attributes, and V is a domain of the attribute q, and $f : U \times Q \to V$ is a total function such that $f(x, q) \to V_q$ for every $q \in Q$, $x \in U$, called an information function [9]. The set

Q is, in general, divided into set C of condition attributes and set D of decision attributes. Assuming that all condition attributes $q \in C$ are criteria, let $\succeq_q$ be a weak preference relation on U with respect to criterion q such that $x \succeq_q y$ means "x is at least as good as y with respect to criterion q". We suppose that $\succeq_q$ is a complete preorder, i.e. a strongly complete and transitive binary relation, defined on U on the basis of evaluations $f(\cdot, q)$. Furthermore, assuming that the set of decision attributes D (possibly a singleton $\{d\}$) makes a partition of U into a finite number of decision classes, let $Cl = \{Cl_t, t \in T\}$, $T = \{1, ..., n\}$, be a set of these classes such that each $x \in U$ belongs to one and only one class $Cl_t \in Cl$. We suppose that the classes are preference ordered, i.e. for all $r, s \in T$, such that $r > s$, the objects from Cl_r are preferred to the objects from Cl_s. More formally, if $\succeq$ is a comprehensive weak preference relation on U, i.e. if for all $x, y \in U$, $x \succeq y$ means "x is at least as good as y", we suppose:

$$[x \in Cl_r, y \in Cl_s, r > s] \Rightarrow [x \succeq y \ and \ not \ y \succeq x]$$

The above assumptions are typical for consideration of a multiple-criteria sorting problem. The sets to be approximated are called *upward union* and *downward union* of classes, respectively:

$$Cl_t^{\geq} = \bigcup_{s \geq t} Cl_s, \quad Cl_t^{\leq} = \bigcup_{s \leq t} Cl_s, \ t = 1, ..., n.$$

The statement $x \in Cl_t^{\geq}$ means "x belongs to at least class Cl_t", while $x \in Cl_t^{\leq}$ means "x belongs to at most class Cl_t".

Let us remark that $Cl_1^{\geq} = Cl_n^{\leq} = U$, $Cl_n^{\geq} = Cl_n$ and $Cl_1^{\leq} = Cl_1$. Furthermore, for $t = 2, ..., n$, we have:

$$Cl_{t-1}^{\leq} = U - Cl_t^{\geq} \ and \ Cl_t^{\geq} = U - Cl_{t-1}^{\leq}.$$

In the following, in order to gain some more flexibility, we present the variable consistency DRSA model [4] which has its counterpart within the CRSA in the variable precision rough set approach [12,13]. Let us define now the dominance relation. We say that "x dominates y with respect to $P \subseteq C$", denoted by xD_Py, if $x \succeq_q y$ for all $q \in P$.

Given a set of criteria $P \subseteq C$ and $x \in U$, the "granules of knowledge" used for approximation in DRSA are:

− a set of objects dominating x, called *P-dominating set*,

$$D_P^+(x) = \{y \in U : yD_Px\},$$

− a set of objects dominated by x, called *P-dominated set*,

$$D_P^-(x) = \{y \in U : xD_Py\}.$$

For any $P \subseteq C$ we say that $x \in U$ belongs to $Cl_t^{\geq}$ with no ambiguity at consistency level $l \in (0, 1]$, if $x \in Cl_t^{\geq}$ and at least $l \times 100\%$ of all objects $y \in U$ dominating x with respect to P also belong to $Cl_t^{\geq}$, i.e.

$$\frac{card(D_P^+(x) \cap Cl_t^{\geq})}{card(D_P^+(x))}$$

The level l is called consistency level because it controls the degree of consistency between objects qualified as belonging to without any ambiguity. In other words, if $l < 1$, then $(1 - l) \times 100\%$ of all objects $y \in U$ dominating x with respect to P do not belong to $Cl_t^{\geq}$ and thus contradict the inclusion of x in $Cl_t^{\geq}$. Analogously, for any $P \subseteq C$ we say that $x \in U$ belongs to $Cl_t^{\leq}$ with no ambiguity at consistency level $l \in (0, 1]$, if $x \in Cl_t^{\leq}$ and at least $l \times 100\%$ of all objects $y \in U$ dominated by x with respect to P also belong to $Cl_t^{\leq}$, i.e.

$$\frac{card(D_P^-(x) \cap Cl_t^{\leq})}{card(D_P^-(x))}$$

Thus, for any $P \subseteq C$, each object $x \in U$ is either ambiguous or non-ambiguous at consistency level l with respect to the upward union $Cl_t^{\geq}$ ($t = 2, ..., n$) or with respect to the downward union $Cl_t^{\leq}$ ($t = 1, ..., n - 1$). The concept of non-ambiguous objects at some consistency level l leads naturally to the definition of P-lower approximations of the unions of classes $Cl_t^{\geq}$ and $Cl_t^{\leq}$

$$\underline{P}^l(Cl_t^{\geq}) = \left\{ x \in Cl_t^{\geq} : \frac{card(D_P^+(x) \cap Cl_t^{\geq})}{card(D_P^+(x))} \geq l \right\},$$

$$\underline{P}^l(Cl_t^{\leq}) = \left\{ x \in Cl_t^{\leq} : \frac{card(D_P^-(x) \cap Cl_t^{\leq})}{card(D_P^-(x))} \geq l \right\}.$$

Given $P \subseteq C$ and consistency level l, we can define the P-upper approximations of $Cl_t^{\geq}$ and $Cl_t^{\leq}$, denoted by $\overline{P}^l(Cl_t^{\geq})$ and $\overline{P}^l(Cl_t^{\leq})$, by complementation of $\underline{P}^l(Cl_t^{\geq})$ and $\underline{P}^l(Cl_t^{\leq})$ with respect to U:

$$\overline{P}^l(Cl_t^{\geq}) = U - \underline{P}^l(Cl_{t-1}^{\leq}),$$

$$\overline{P}^l(Cl_t^{\leq}) = U - \underline{P}^l(Cl_{t+1}^{\geq}).$$

$\overline{P}^l(Cl_t^{\geq})$ can be interpreted as the set of all the objects belonging to $Cl_t^{\geq}$, possibly ambiguous at consistency level l. Analogously, $\overline{P}^l(Cl_t^{\leq})$ can be interpreted as the set of all the objects belonging to $Cl_t^{\leq}$, possibly ambiguous at consistency level l.

The dominance-based rough approximations of upward and downward unions of classes can serve to induce a generalized description of objects contained in the information table in terms of "if..., then..." decision rules. Assuming that for each $q \in C$, $V_q \subseteq \mathbf{R}$ (i.e. V_q is quantitative) and that for each $x, y \in U$, $f(x, q) \geq f(y, q)$ implies $x \succeq_q y$ (i.e. V_q is preference ordered), the following two basic types of variable-consistency decision rules can be considered:

1. $D_\geq$-decision rules with the following syntax:
   "if $f(x, q1) \geq r_{q1}$ and $f(x, q2) \geq r_{q2}$ and ... $f(x, qp) \geq r_{qp}$, then $x \in Cl_t^\geq$ with confidence α (i.e. in fraction α of considered cases),
   where $P = \{q1, ..., qp\} \subseteq C$, $(r_{q1}, ..., r_{qp}) \in V_{q1} \times V_{q2} \times ... \times V_{qp}$ and $t \in T$;
2. $D_\leq$-decision rules with the following syntax:
   "if $f(x, q1) \leq r_{q1}$ and $f(x, q2) \leq r_{q2}$ and ... $f(x, qp) \leq r_{qp}$, then $x \in Cl_t^\leq$ with confidence α,
   where $P = \{q1, ..., qp\} \subseteq C$, $(r_{q1}, ..., r_{qp}) \in V_{q1} \times V_{q2} \times ... \times V_{qp}$ and $t \in T$.

3 Efficiency Measures for Interventions Based on Decision Rules

We are considering decision rules induced from data organized in a decision table. The decision table is composed of a finite set U of objects described by a finite set Q of attributes used for object description. The attributes are divided into condition attributes (independent variables) and decision attribute (dependent variable). Formally, let DT be a decision table represented as follows:

$$DT = \langle U, C \cup \{d\} \rangle$$

where U is a set of objects, C is a set of condition attributes q such that $q : U \rightarrow V_q$ for every $q \in C$. Set V_q is a domain of q. $d \notin C$ is a decision attribute that partitions objects from U into a set of decision classes (concepts) $D = \{\Psi_j : j = 1, ..., k\}$. A decision rule r expresses the relationship between condition attribute(s) and a decision class $\Psi \in D$. It can be represented in the form of consequence relation:

$$\Phi \rightarrow \Psi$$

where $\Phi = \Phi_1 \wedge \Phi_2 \wedge ... \wedge \Phi_m$ is a condition part and Ψ a decision part of the rule, $\Phi_1 \in V_{q1}$, $\Phi_2 \in V_{q2}$, ..., $\Phi_m \in V_{qm}$, $q1, q2, ..., qm \in C$, $\Psi \in D$. Several different measures are associated with the rule, quantifying various properties of the rule. To define these measures, we take into account the set-theoretic interpretation of rules. Let $m(\Phi)$ denote the set of objects of U that satisfy the conditions expressed by Φ. Similarly, the set $m(\Psi)$ consists of objects belonging to decision class Ψ. Then, one can define an index, called confidence (or certainty) of the rule, represented as follows:

$$conf\,(r, U) = \frac{|m(\Phi) \cap m(\Psi)|}{|m(\Phi)|}$$

where $|\cdot|$ denotes the cardinality of a set, i.e. $|m(\Phi) \cap m(\Psi)|$ denotes the number of objects satisfying both parts Φ and Ψ, and $|m(\Phi)|$ is the number of objects satisfying the condition part only. The range of this measure is $0 \leq conf\,(r, U) \leq 1$: it shows the degree to which Ψ is related to Φ and can be interpreted as the probability of assignment to decision class Ψ when condition Φ holds. Moreover, each decision rule is characterized by its strength, defined by the number of objects satisfying condition and decision part of the rule, i.e. the absolute number of objects supporting the rule:

$$strength(r) = |m(\Phi) \cap m(\Psi)|\,.$$

Intervention is a modification (manipulation) of a universe made with the aim of getting a desired result. For example, in the customer satisfaction context, the universe is a set of customers and the intervention is a strategy (promotion campaign) modifying perception of a product's feature so as to increase customer satisfaction. Decision rules can help in setting up efficient interventions. Decision rules and their measures (confidence and support) can be used, moreover, to estimate the expected effects of an intervention. The idea is the following [1]. Let us consider decision rule $r \equiv \Phi \to \Psi$ with confidence $conf\,(r, U)$ and suppose that we want to make an intervention to increase the number of objects in universe U' satisfying Ψ. An example in the customer satisfaction context is the following. Let Φ be the condition "satisfaction at least good with respect to feature i" and Φ be the decision "comprehensive satisfaction at least medium". Then, $\Phi \to \Psi$ is the decision rule $r \equiv$ "if the satisfaction of customer x is at least good with respect to feature i, then comprehensive satisfaction of customer x is at least medium", with confidence $conf\,(r, U)$. Suppose to pursue a strategy $Str \equiv$ "obtain a satisfaction at least good with respect to feature i by customer satisfaction x if x has not it and she has not a comprehensive satisfaction at least medium". The question is: what is the expected increase (in %) of the population of customers with a satisfaction at least medium after application of treatment Str? U' is the universe (possibly, $U' \neq U$) where the strategy is activated. The set of objects having property Γ in universe U' is denoted by $m'(\Gamma)$. Therefore, $m'(\Phi)$ is the set of objects having property Φ in universe U'. Analogous interpretation holds for $m'(\neg\Phi)$, $m'(\Psi)$, $m'(\neg\Psi)$, $m'(\Phi \wedge \Psi)$, and so on. After applying strategy Str, universe U' will be transformed to universe U''. The set of objects having property Γ in universe U'' is denoted by $m''(\Gamma)$. Therefore, $m''(\Phi)$ is the set of objects having property Φ in universe U''. Analogous interpretation holds for $m''(\neg\Phi)$, $m''(\Psi)$, $m''(\neg\Psi)$, $m''(\Phi \wedge \Psi)$, and so on. We suppose that universe U' and U'' are homogeneous with universe U. This means that the decision rule $r \equiv \Phi \to \Psi$ holding in U with confidence $conf\,(r, U)$, holds also in the transition from U' to U'' in the following sense: if we modify condition $\neg\Phi$ to condition Φ in the set $m'(\neg\Phi \wedge \neg\Psi)$, we may reasonably expect that $conf\,(r, U) \times |m'(\neg\Phi \wedge \neg\Psi|$ elements from $m'(\neg\Phi \wedge \neg\Psi)$ will enter decision class Ψ in universe U''. With respect to our example, this means that in universe U'' the number of customers with a satisfaction at least medium after activation of strategy Str is

$$|m''(\Psi)| = |m'(\Psi)| + |m'(\neg\Phi \wedge \neg\Psi)| \times conf\,(r, U)$$

$$=$$

$$|m'(\Psi)| + |m'(\neg\Phi \wedge \neg\Psi)| \times \frac{|m(\Phi \wedge \Psi|}{|m(\Phi|}\,.$$

The increment of the number of customers with a satisfaction at least medium due to activation of strategy Str on U' is

$$\Delta(\Psi) = |m''(\Psi)| - |m'(\Psi)| = |m'(\neg\Phi \wedge \neg\Psi)| \times \frac{|m(\Phi \wedge \Psi|}{|m(\Phi|}.$$

Therefore, the expected relative increment of satisfied customers due to strategy Str is given by:

$$\delta(\Psi) = \frac{|m''(\Psi)|}{|U'|} - \frac{|m'(\Psi)|}{|U'|} = \frac{|m'(\neg\Phi) \cap m'(\neg\Psi)|}{|U'|} \times conf(r, U).$$

Let us remark that there has been a rich discussion about interestingness measures for decision rules in data mining (see e.g. [7,11,5]). These measures are defined, however, in terms of characteristics of the universe U where the rules come from. If we consider an intervention in universe U', which may be different from U, then we need an interestingness measure expressed not only in terms of characteristics of U but also in terms of characteristics of U'. This proposal aims at satisfying this requirement.

4   Customer Satisfaction Analysis Using DRSA

The main steps of an exhaustive customer satisfaction analysis based on the rough set approach are the following. First of all, one have to select a proper set of features $F = \{f_1, ..., f_n\}$ of the considered product. With respect to each feature $f_i \in F$, the customers in a sample $Cust = \{cust_1, ..., cust_m\}$ are asked to express their level of satisfaction choosing this level from a set $Sat = \{sat_1, ..., sat_n\}$, such that $sat_i > sat_j$ means that the level of satisfaction denoted by sat_i is greater than the level of satisfaction denoted by sat_j. Generally, satisfaction is expressed on a five level scale, such that $sat_1 = very\ bad$, $sat_2 = bad$, $sat_3 = medium$, $sat_4 = good$, $sat_5 = very\ good$. The customers in the sample are also requested to express a level of their comprehensive satisfaction cs on the same scale of the satisfaction as for single features. Thus, we have a function $\varphi : Cust \times F \cup \{cs\} \rightarrow Sat$ such that for each $cust_h \in Cust$ and for each feature $f_i \in F$, $\varphi(cust_h, f_i)$ expresses the level of satisfaction of customer $cust_h$ with respect to feature f_i and $\varphi(cust_h, cs)$ expresses the level of comprehensive satisfaction cs. In this context, the DRSA can be applied for building a decision table using the following correspondence:

- the universe is the sample of customers, such that $U = Cust$,
- the set of condition attributes corresponds to the set of features, and the comprehensive satisfaction is the decision attribute, such that $C = F$, $D = cs$ and $Q = F \cup \{cs\}$,
- the domain of each attribute, both condition attribute and decision attribute, is the set of satisfaction levels, such that $V = Sat$,
- the total information function f corresponds to function φ,

– the set of decision classes $Cl = \{Cl_t, t \in T\}$, $T = \{1, ..., n\}$, corresponds to the set of satisfaction levels of the decision attribute, such that $Cl = Sat$.

Let us remark that all features $f_i \in F$ are criteria, and the weak relation $\succeq_i$ on $Cust$ with respect to feature f_i is a preorder on $Cust$ having the following semantics: for all $cust_h, cust_k \in Cust$, $cust_h \succeq_i cust_k$ means "with respect to feature f_i, the level of satisfaction of $cust_h$ is at least as good as the level of satisfaction of $cust_k$". Let us observe that

$$cust_h \succeq_i cust_k \Leftrightarrow \varphi(cust_h, f_i) \geq \varphi(cust_k, f_i).$$

Moreover, the comprehensive preference relation $\succeq$ on $Cust$ is defined as follows: for all $cust_h, cust_k \in Cust$, $cust_h \succeq cust_k$ means "with respect to comprehensive satisfaction, the level of satisfaction of $cust_h$ is at least as good as the level of satisfaction of $cust_k$". Let us observe that

$$cust_h \succeq cust_k \Leftrightarrow \varphi(cust_h, cs) \geq \varphi(cust_k, cs).$$

The data of the questionnaires so interpreted can be analyzed using DRSA, giving rough approximations and decision rules. The following types of decision rules are considered:

1. $D_\geq$-decision rules having the following syntax
   if $\varphi(cust, f_{q1}) \geq r_{q1}$ and $\varphi(cust, f_{q2}) \geq r_{q2}$ and ... $\varphi(cust, f_{q2}) \geq r_{qp}$, then $\varphi(cust, cs) \geq r_{cs}$ with confidence α, where $P = \{f_{q1}, ..., f_{qp}\} \subseteq F$ and $(r_{q1}, ..., r_{qp}, r_{cs}) \in Sat^{p+1}$,
   and the following semantics
   "if the satisfaction with respect to feature f_{q1} is at least of level r_{q1} and the satisfaction with respect to feature f_{q2} is at least of level r_{q2} and ... the satisfaction with respect to feature f_{qp} is at least of level r_{qp}, then the comprehensive evaluation is at least of level r_{cs} in the $(\alpha \times 100)\%$ of the cases";
2. $D_<$-decision rules having the following syntax
   if $\varphi(cust, f_{q1}) \leq r_{q1}$ and $\varphi(cust, f_{q2}) \leq r_{q2}$ and ... $\varphi(cust, f_{q2}) \leq r_{qp}$, then $\varphi(cust, cs) \leq r_{cs}$ with confidence α, where $P = \{f_{q1}, ..., f_{qp}\} \subseteq F$ and $(r_{q1}, ..., r_{qp}, r_{cs}) \in Sat^{p+1}$,
   and the following semantics
   "if the satisfaction with respect to feature f_{q1} is at most of level r_{q1} and the satisfaction with respect to feature f_{q2} is at most of level r_{q2} and ... the satisfaction with respect to feature f_{qp} is at most of level r_{qp}, then the comprehensive evaluation is at most of level r_{cs} in the $(\alpha \times 100)\%$ of the cases".

The set of rules so obtained can be selected as the basis of a marketing strategy, aiming at improving or not deteriorating the customer satisfaction as follows:

1. An aggressive strategy aiming at improving customer satisfaction, can be based on the $D_\geq$-decision rules

if $\varphi(cust, f_{q1}) \geq r_{q1}$ and $\varphi(cust, f_{q2}) \geq r_{q2}$ and ... $\varphi(cust, f_{q2}) \geq r_{qp}$, then $\varphi(cust, cs) \geq r_{cs}$ with confidence α;

this strategy has as target all such customers that $\varphi(cust, f_{q1}) < r_{q1}$ or $\varphi(cust, f_{q2}) < r_{q2}$ or ... $\varphi(cust, f_{qp}) < r_{qp}$ and $\varphi(cust, cs) < r_{cs}$ and aims at obtaining $\varphi(cust, f_{q1}) \geq r_{q1}$ and $\varphi(cust, f_{q2}) \geq r_{q2}$ and ... $\varphi(cust, f_{qp}) \geq r_{qp}$, such that the final goal of obtaining $\varphi(cust, cs) \geq r_{cs}$ is reached;

2. A defensive strategy aiming at not deteriorating customer satisfaction, can be based on the $D_{\leq}$-decision rules

if $\varphi(cust, f_{q1}) \leq r_{q1}$ and $\varphi(cust, f_{q2}) \leq r_{q2}$ and ... $\varphi(cust, f_{q2}) \leq r_{qp}$, then $\varphi(cust, cs) \leq r_{cs}$ with confidence α;

this strategy has as target all such customers that $\varphi(cust, f_{q1}) > r_{q1}$ or $\varphi(cust, f_{q2}) > r_{q2}$ or ... $\varphi(cust, f_{qp}) > r_{qp}$ and $\varphi(cust, cs) > r_{cs}$ and aims at mantaining $\varphi(cust, f_{q1}) > r_{q1}$ or $\varphi(cust, f_{q2}) > r_{q2}$ or ... $\varphi(cust, f_{qp}) > r_{qp}$, such that the final goal of mantaining $\varphi(cust, cs) > r_{cs}$ is reached.

In a first step, the rules on which the marketing strategy should be based are chosen, using the efficiency measures for interventions recalled in the previous section. In the specific context of customer satisfaction analysis, these efficiency measures have the following interpretation:

1. In case of an aggressive strategy based on the $D_{\geq}$-decision rules

if $\varphi(cust, f_{q1}) \geq r_{q1}$ and $\varphi(cust, f_{q2}) \geq r_{q2}$ and ... $\varphi(cust, f_{q2}) \geq r_{qp}$, then $\varphi(cust, cs) \geq r_{cs}$ with confidence α,

we have that

- U is the sample of customers where the analysis was performed and U' is the whole market
- Φ is the condition "$\varphi(cust, f_{q1}) \geq r_{q1}$ and $\varphi(cust, f_{q2}) \geq r_{q2}$ and ... $\varphi(cust, f_{q2}) \geq r_{qp}$" and Ψ is the consequence "$\varphi(cust, cs) \geq r_{cs}$"
- $m(\Phi)$ and $m'(\Phi)$ are the sets of customers satisfying condition Φ in the sample and in the whole market, respectively,
- $m(\Psi)$ and $m'(\Psi)$ are the sets of customers for which consequence Ψ holds in the sample and in the whole market, respectively,

such that the efficiency measure

$$\delta(\Psi) = \frac{|m'(\neg\Phi) \cap m'(\neg\Psi)|}{|U'|} \times \frac{|m(\Phi) \cap m(\Psi)|}{|m(\Phi|} = \frac{|m'(\neg\Phi) \cap m'(\neg\Psi)|}{|U'|} \times \alpha$$

represents the percentage of customers in the whole market whose satisfaction could reach at least level r_{cs} as effect of the strategy at hand;

2. In case of a defensive strategy based on the $D_{\leq}$-decision rules

if $\varphi(cust, f_{q1}) \leq r_{q1}$ and $\varphi(cust, f_{q2}) \leq r_{q2}$ and ... $\varphi(cust, f_{q2}) \leq r_{qp}$, then $\varphi(cust, cs) \leq r_{cs}$ with confidence α,

we have that

- Φ is the condition "$\varphi(cust, f_{q1}) \leq r_{q1}$ and $\varphi(cust, f_{q2}) \leq r_{q2}$ and ... $\varphi(cust, f_{q2}) \leq r_{qp}$" and Ψ is the consequence "$\varphi(cust, cs) \leq r_{cs}$"
- U, U', $m(\Phi)$ and $m'(\Phi)$, $m(\Psi)$ and $m'(\Psi)$, have the same meanong as in above point 1)

such that the efficiency measure $\delta(\Psi)$, formulated as in above point 1) represents the percentage of customers in the whole market whose satisfaction could reach at most level r_{cs} if the strategy at hand was not realized.

The percentages given by the efficiency measure $\delta(\Psi)$, both in case of an aggressive strategy and in case of a defensive strategy, constitute a first step of the analysis. We explain this point for the case of an aggressive strategy. We have

$$\delta(\Psi) = \frac{|m'(\neg\Phi) \cap m'(\neg\Psi)|}{|U'|} \times \frac{|m(\Phi) \cap m(\Psi)|}{|m(\Phi|},$$

but the percentage increase $\delta(\Psi)$ can be obtained only under condition that all the customers in the set $m'(\neg\Phi) \cap m'(\neg\Psi)$ are transformed, due to the strategy, in such customers that condition Φ holds for them. In simpler terms, the hypothesis is that all the customers for whom $\varphi(cust, f_{q1}) < r_{q1}$ or $\varphi(cust, f_{q2}) < r_{q2}$ or ... $\varphi(cust, f_{q2}) < r_{qp}$, after application of the strategy become customers for whom $\varphi(cust, f_{q1}) \geq r_{q1}$ and $\varphi(cust, f_{q2}) \geq r_{q2}$ and ... $\varphi(cust, f_{q2}) \geq r_{qp}$. Very often, this is not realistic. For example, if one considers rule $r^* \equiv \Phi \rightarrow \Psi$, where rule condition Φ is "satisfaction with respect to feature f_{i1} is at least good and satisfaction with respect to feature f_{i2} is at least medium", one has that among the customers for whom condition Φ does not hold, there are customers for whom satisfaction with respect to features f_{i1} and f_{i2} is very bad. Therefore, it is questionable that for those customers a strategy can change so radically their evaluations such that at the end condition Φ holds for all of them. In this case, it would rather be reasonable to address the strategy not to all the customers for whom condition Φ does not hold, but to a subset of these customers who are not far from satisfying condition Φ. These customers can be characterized by initial closeness conditions consisting in satisfaction profiles such as "$\varphi(cust, f_{t1}) \geq r'_{t1}$ and $\varphi(cust, f_{t2}) \geq r'_{t2}$ and ... $\varphi(cust, f_{th}) \geq r'_{th}$" where $\{f_{t1}, ..., f_{th}\} \subseteq F$ with $r'_{ti} \geq r_{ti}$ but close each other, for all $f_{ti} \in \{f_{q1}, ..., f_{qp}\}$. Let us remark that not necessarily $\{f_{t1}, ..., f_{th}\} \subseteq \{f_{q1}, ..., f_{qp}\}$, that is features not considered in the decision rule on which the strategy is based can be considered in the initial closeness condition. Considering the above rule r^*, one initial closeness condition can be $\Phi_1=$"satisfaction with respect to feature f_{i1} is at least medium and satisfaction with respect to feature f_{i2} is at least medium". In this case, the efficiency measure should be modified to take into account the initial closeness condition, and in this way we obtain

$$\delta(\Psi) = \frac{|m'(\Phi_1) \cap m'(\neg\Phi) \cap m'(\neg\Psi)|}{|U'|} \times \frac{|m(\Phi) \cap m(\Psi)|}{|m(\Phi|},$$

One can consider also multiple initial closeness conditions. For example, considering the above rule r^*, another initial closeness condition could be $\Phi_2=$"satisfaction with respect to feature f_{i2} is at least medium and satisfaction with respect to feature f_{i4} is at least medium". When we have multiple initial closeness conditions $\Phi_1, \ldots, \Phi_v$, the efficiency measure becomes

$$\delta(\Psi) = \frac{|[\cup_{i=1}^{v} m'(\Phi_i)] \cap m'(\neg\Phi) \cap m'(\neg\Psi)|}{|U'|} \times \frac{|m(\Phi) \cap m(\Psi)|}{|m(\Phi|}.$$

There is another important aspect to be taken into account to make more realistic the efficiency measure $\delta(\Psi)$. In fact, even considering the initial conditions, it is reasonable to expect that the strategy does not give the expected results for all the customers to whom the strategy is directed. Thus, it is convenient to introduce a parameter λ expressing the percentage of customers in the set to whom the strategy is addressed, i.e. the set $[\cup_{i=1}^{v} m'(\Phi_i)] \cap m'(\neg\Phi)$, for which the strategy is expected to modify the condition. Thus, if $m''(\Phi)$ represents the set of customers satisfying condition Φ in the universe U'', being the universe U' transformed by application of the strategy, the parameter λ should give a reasonable estimation of the ratio $\frac{|m''(\Phi)-m'(\Phi)|}{|[\cup_{i=1}^{v} m'(\Phi_i)] \cap m'(\neg\Phi)|}$ (verifiable ex post only). Thus, the definitive efficiency measure should be:

$$\delta(\Psi) = \frac{|[\cup_{i=1}^{v} m'(\Phi_i)] \cap m'(\neg\Phi) \cap m'(\neg\Psi)|}{|U'|} \times \frac{|m(\Phi) \cap m(\Psi)|}{|m(\Phi|} \times \lambda.$$

such that, if λ is correctly estimated, one have

$$\delta(\Psi) = \frac{|[\cup_{i=1}^{v} m'(\Phi_i)] \cap m'(\neg\Phi) \cap m'(\neg\Psi)|}{|U'|} \times \frac{|m(\Phi) \cap m(\Psi)|}{|m(\Phi|} \times \frac{|m''(\Phi) - m'(\Phi)|}{|[\cup_{i=1}^{v} m'(\Phi_i)] \cap m'(\neg\Phi)|}.$$

5   Conclusions

We presented a rough set approach to customer satisfaction analysis. This approach aims at representing customer preferences expressed on a questionnaire in terms of simple decision rules such as "if feature f_i is considered good and feature f_j is considered sufficient, then the overall evaluation of the product is medium". The interpretation of the decision rules is simpler and more direct than the interpretation of the utility function that is supplied by usual customer satisfaction analysis based on conjoint analysis. Moreover, our approach permits to evaluate the expected efficiency of some strategies based on the induced decision rules. Thus, strategic intervention related to rules with higher expected efficiency can be recommended as the most promising for improving the quality of the offered products and services. In this perspective, our approach supplies an integrated support to customer satisfaction oriented management. Finally, the capacity of representing customer preferences in terms of easily understandable "if ..., then..." statements expressed in the natural language makes our approach particularly interesting for Kansei Engineering.

Acknowledgements. The research of the first two authors has been supported by the Italian Ministry of Education, University and Scientific Research (MIUR). The third author wishes to acknowledge financial support from the Polish Ministry of Education and Science (grant no. 3T11F 02127).

References

1. Greco, S., Matarazzo, B., Pappalardo, N., Słowiński, R., Measuring expected effects of interventions based on decision rules. *Journal of Experimental & Theoretical Artificial Intelligence*, 17 (2005) no. 1-2, 103-118.
2. Greco, S., Matarazzo, B., Słowiński, R., Rough set theory for multicriteria decision analysis, *European Journal of Operational Research*, 129 (2001) 1-47.
3. Greco, S., Matarazzo, B., Słowiński R., Decision rule approach, in: J. Figueira, S. Greco, M. Erghott (eds.), *Multiple Criteria Decision Analysis: State of the Art Surveys*, Springer, Berlin, 2005, pp. 507-563.
4. Greco, S., Matarazzo, B., Słowiński, R., Stefanowski, J., Variable Consistency Model of Dominance-based Rough Sets Approach, in: W. Ziarko, Y. Yao (eds.), *Rough Sets and Current Trends in Computing*, LNAI, vol. 2005, Springler-Verlag, Berlin 2001, pp. 170-181.
5. Greco, S., Pawlak, Z., Słowiński, R., Can Bayesian confirmation measures be useful for rough set decision rules? *Engineering Applications of Artificial Intelligence*, 17 (2004) 345-361.
6. Green P. E., Srinivasan, V., Conjoint Analysis in Consumer Research: Issues and Outlook, *The Journal of consumer Research*, 5 (1978) no. 2, 103-123.
7. Hilderman, R.J., Hamilton, H.J., *Knowledge Discovery and Measures of Interest* , Kluwer Academic Publishers, Boston, 2001.
8. Nagamachi, M., Kansei Engineering: A new ergonomic consumer-oriented technology for product development, *International Journal of Industrial Ergonomics*, 15 (1995) no. 1, 3 - 11.
9. Pawlak, Z., *Rough Sets*, Kluwer, Dordrecht, 1991.
10. Słowiński, R., Greco, S., Matarazzo, B., Rough Set Based Decision Support, Chapter 16 in: E. Burke, G. Kendall (eds.), *Introductory Tutorials on Optimization, Search and Decision Support Methodologies*, Kluwer Academic Publishers, Boston, 2005, pp. 475-527.
11. Yao Y.Y., Zhong. N., An analysis of quantitative measures associated with rules, in: *Proceedings of the Third Pacific-Asia Conference on Knowledge Discovery and Data Mining*, LNAI 1574, Springer-Verlag, Berlin, 1999, pp. 479 - 488.
12. Ziarko W., Variable precision rough sets model, *Journal of Computer and Systems Sciences*, 46 (1993) no. 1, 39-59.
13. Ziarko W., Rough sets as a methodology for data mining, in: L. Polkowski, A. Skowron (eds.), *Rough Sets in Data Mining and Knowledge Discovery*, vol. 1, Physica-Verlag, Heidelberg, 1998, pp. 554-576.

Utility Function Induced by Fuzzy Target in Probabilistic Decision Making

Van-Nam Huynh, Yoshiteru Nakamori, and Tu-Bao Ho

School of Knowledge Science
Japan Advanced Institute of Science and Technology
Nomi, Ishikawa, 923-1292, JAPAN
{huynh, nakamori, bao}@jaist.ac.jp

Abstract. It is widely accepted that a common precept for the choice under uncertainty is to use the expected utility maximization principle, which was established axiomatically. Recently, a formal equivalence between this principle of choice and the target-based principle, that suggests that one should select an action which maximizes the (expected) probability of meeting a (probabilistic) uncertain target, has been established and extensively discussed. In this paper, we discuss the issue of how to bring fuzzy targets within the reach of the target-based model for a class of decision making under uncertainty problems. Two methods for inducing utility functions from fuzzy targets are discussed and illustrated with an example taken from the literature.

1 Introduction

A classical problem in decision analysis under uncertainty is to rank a set of acts defined on a state space S, where, due to the uncertainty in the state of nature, each act a may lead to different outcomes taking from a set of outcomes D, usually associated with a random outcome $X_a : S \rightarrow D$. The decision maker (DM) must then use some ranking procedure over acts for making decisions. The most commonly-used ranking procedure is based on the expected utility model. The DM defines a utility function U over D and then ranks an act a by its expected utility $EU(X_a)$. Note that the utility function U is bounded and unique up to increasing affine transformations (or *cardinal*, for short) [13].

Another ranking procedure is the DM establishes some *target* t and then ranks an act a by the probability $P(X_a \succeq t)$ that it meets the target [11]. Although simple and appealing from this target-based point of view, the DM may not know for sure which target he should select. Then he could define some random variable T as his uncertain target (or, *benchmark*) instead and rank an act a by the probability $P(X_a \succeq T)$ that it meets the uncertain target T (or, it outperforms the benchmark), provided that the target T is stochastically independent of the random outcomes to be evaluated. We call this procedure *target-based* or *benchmarking*.

Interestingly, these two different procedures are shown to be both mathematically and observationally equivalent [10]. In particular, Castagnoli and Li-Calzi [4] discussed a formal equivalence of von Neumann and Morgenstern's

S. Greco et al. (Eds.): RSCTC 2006, LNAI 4259, pp. 296–305, 2006.

expected utility model and the target-based model with reference to preferences over lotteries. Later, a similar result for Savage's expected utility model with reference to preferences over acts was established by Bordley and LiCalzi [2]. Despite the differences in approach and interpretation, both target-based procedure and utility-based procedure essentially lead to only one basic model for decision making. It should be worth, however, emphasizing that while both target-based and utility-based decision making demand an understanding of probabilities, the utility-based model additionally requires a comprehension of cardinal utilities. More details on the formal connection between the utility-based approach and the target-based approach in decision analysis with uncertainty can be referred to, e.g., [3,5,10].

In this paper, we study the problem of how to transform fuzzy targets so as to allow the application of the target-based decision model for a class of decision making under uncertainty problems. Note that while assessing probabilistic uncertain targets may require statistical evidence, fuzzy targets can be assessed according to feelings or attitude of the DM. In many situations, where due to a lack of information, defining fuzzy targets is much easier and intuitively natural than directly defining random targets. We will discuss two methods for inducing utility functions from fuzzy targets and illustrate with an example taken from the literature. Different attitudes of the DM on target will be also discussed in relation to the concept of risk attitude.

2   Target-Based Interpretation of Expected Utility Value

In this paper we discuss the problem of decision making under uncertainty (DMUU) which is described using the decision matrix shown in Table 1. In this matrix, $A_i(i = 1, \ldots, n)$ represent the acts available to a decision maker, one of which must be selected. The elements $S_j(j = 1, \ldots, m)$ correspond to the possible values/states associated with the so called state of nature S. Each element c_{ij} of the matrix is the payoff the DM receives if the act A_i is selected and state S_j occurs. The uncertainty associated with this problem is generally a result of the fact that the value of S is unknown before the DM must choose an act A_i. Let us consider the decision problem as described in Table 1 with assuming a probability distribution $P_{\mathcal{S}}$ over $\mathcal{S} = \{S_1, \ldots, S_m\}$. Here, we restrict ourselves to a bounded domain of the payoff variable that $D = [c_{min}, c_{max}]$.

As is well-known, the most commonly used method for valuating acts A_i to solve the DMUU problem described by Table 1 is to use the expected utility value:

$$v(A_i) \triangleq EU_i = \sum_{j=1}^{m} P_{\mathcal{S}}(S_j)U(c_{ij}) \tag{1}$$

where U is a utility function defined over D.

On the other hand, each act A_i can be formally considered as a random payoff having the probability distribution P_i defined, with an abuse of notation, as follows:

$$P_i(A_i = x) = P_{\mathcal{S}}(\{S_j : c_{ij} = x\}) \tag{2}$$

Table 1. Decision Matrix

Acts	State of Nature		
	S_1	S_2 $\ldots$	S_m
A_1	c_{11}	c_{12} $\ldots$	c_{1m}
A_2	c_{21}	c_{22} $\ldots$	c_{2m}
$\vdots$	$\vdots$	$\vdots$ $\ddots$	$\vdots$
A_n	c_{n1}	c_{n2} $\ldots$	c_{nm}

Then, the target-based model [2] suggests using the following value function

$$v(A_i) \triangleq P(A_i \succeq T)$$
$$= \sum_x P(x \succeq T) P_i(A_i = x)$$
$$= \sum_{j=1}^{m} P_{\mathcal{S}}(S_j) P(c_{ij} \succeq T) \tag{3}$$

where the random target T is stochastically independent of any random payoffs A_i, and $P(x \succeq T)$ is the cumulative distribution function (c.d.f., for short) of the target T.

Recall that the utility function U is bounded and increasing. Thus, after having normalized its range to the unit interval $[0, 1]$, U has all the properties of a cumulative distribution function over the payoff domain D. As shown in [2], by a standard probability-theoretic argument, one can associate to the c.d.f. U a random payoff T stochastically independent of A_i and then view $U(x)$ as the probability that x meets the target T, i.e. $U(x) = P(x \succeq T)$. This makes (1) and (3) formally identical. In other words, the target-based decision model with decision function $v(A_i)$ in (3) above is equivalent to the expected utility model defined by (1).

In the next section, we will discuss how to develop the assessment procedure for $U(x)$ in the case that the DM can only assess his target in terms of a possibility distribution instead.

3   Utility Functions Induced from Fuzzy Targets

Before discussing about the problem of decision making using fuzzy targets, it is necessary to recall that when expressing the value of a variable as a fuzzy set, we are inducing a possibility distribution [18] over the domain of the variable. Formally, the soft constraint imposed on a variable V in the statement "V is F", where F is a fuzzy set, can be considered as inducing a possibility distribution Π on the domain of V such that $F(x) = \Pi(x)$, for each x. Here, by a fuzzy target we mean a possibility variable T over the payoff domain D represented by a possibility distribution $\mu_T : D \to [0,1]$. For simplicity, we also assume further that T is normal, convex and has a piecewise continuous function with $\mathrm{supp}(T) = [c_{min}, c_{max}]$, where $\mathrm{supp}(T)$ denotes the support of T.

Let us turn back to the DMUU problem described in Table 1. In a target-based decision model, assume now that the DM establishes a fuzzy target T which reflects his attitude. Then, according to the optimizing principle, after assessed the target the DM would select an act as the best that maximizes the expected probability of meeting the target defined by

$$v(A_i) = \sum_{j=1}^{m} P_S(S_j)\mathbb{P}(c_{ij} \succeq T) \tag{4}$$

where $\mathbb{P}(c_{ij} \succeq T)$ is a formal notation indicating the *probability of meeting the target* of value c_{ij} or, equivalently, the utility $U(c_{ij}) \triangleq \mathbb{P}(c_{ij} \succeq T)$ in the utility-based language.

3.1   Simple Normalization

A direct and simple way to define $\mathbb{P}(c_{ij} \succeq T)$ is making use of Yager's method [16] for converting a possibility distribution into an associated probability distribution via the simple normalization. Particularly, the possibility distribution μ_T of the target T is first converted into its associated probability distribution, denoted by P_T, as follows

$$P_T(t) = \frac{\mu_T(t)}{\int_{c_{min}}^{c_{max}} \mu_T(t)dt}$$

Then $\mathbb{P}(c_{ij} \succeq T)$ is defined as the c.d.f. as usual by

$$\mathbb{P}(c_{ij} \succeq T) \triangleq U_1^T(c_{ij}) = \int_{c_{min}}^{c_{ij}} P_T(t)dt \tag{5}$$

It should be noted that this definition of $\mathbb{P}(c_{ij} \succeq T)$ is also formally used, but without a probabilistic interpretation, for the so-called *satisfaction function* $S(T < c_{ij})$ in [9] for the comparison between a fuzzy number T with a crisp number c_{ij}. A formulation of DMUU using fuzzy targets based on this approach has been discussed in [7].

3.2 α-Cut Based Method

Here we propose another method for inducing the utility function associated with $\mathbb{P}(c_{ij} \succeq T)$ based on the α-cut representation. In fuzzy set theory, the concept of α-cuts plays an important role in establishing the relationship between fuzzy sets and crisp sets. As is well known, each fuzzy set can be uniquely represented by the family of all of its α-cuts. Intuitively, each α-cut A_α of a fuzzy set A can be viewed as a crisp approximation of A at the level $\alpha \in (0,1]$.

It is necessary to recall here that in the case where a fuzzy set A has a discrete membership function, i.e.

$$A = \{(x_i, \mu_A(x_i))\}, \text{ for } x_i \in \mathbb{R} \text{ and } i = 1, \ldots, N$$

with N being a finite positive integer, Dubois and Prade [6] pointed out that the family of its α-cuts forms a nested family of focal elements in terms of Dempster-Shafer theory [14]. In particular, assuming the range of the membership function μ_A, denoted by $\mathrm{rng}(\mu_A)$, is $\mathrm{rng}(\mu_A) = \{\alpha_1, \ldots, \alpha_k\}$, where $\alpha_i > \alpha_{i+1} > 0$, for $i = 1, \ldots, k - 1$, then the body of evidence induced from A with the basic probability assignment, denoted by m_A, is defined as

$$m_A(X) = \begin{cases} \alpha_i - \alpha_{i+1}, & \text{if } X = A_{\alpha_i} \\ 0, & \text{otherwise} \end{cases}$$

with $\alpha_{k+1} = 0$ by convention. In this case the normalization assumption of A insures the body of evidence does not contain the empty set. Interestingly, this view of fuzzy sets has been used by Baldwin in [1] to introduce the so-called mass assignment of a fuzzy set, and to provide a probabilistic semantics for fuzzy sets.

From the perspective of this interpretation of fuzzy sets, we now consider a finite approximation of the fuzzy target T having a continuous-type membership function as above. Assuming uniform sampling and that sample values are taken at membership grades $\alpha_1 = 1 > \alpha_2 > \ldots > \alpha_{k-1} > \alpha_k > \alpha_{k+1} = 0$, we can approximately represent T as a body of evidence (equivalently, a random set)

$$\mathcal{F}_T = \{(T_{\alpha_i} : \alpha_i - \alpha_{i+1})\}_{i=1}^k \tag{6}$$

where T_{α_i} are intervals, denoted by $T_{\alpha_i} = [t_l(\alpha_i), t_r(\alpha_i)]$, as T is convex.

According to the probabilistic interpretation of (6), we can now approximate $\mathbb{P}(x \succeq T)$ by

$$\mathbb{P}(x \succeq T) \cong \Delta\alpha \sum_{i=1}^{k} P(x \succeq T_{\alpha_i}) \tag{7}$$

where $\Delta\alpha$ is the separation between any two adjacent levels, and

$$P(x \succeq T_{\alpha_i}) = \begin{cases} 0, & \text{if } x \leq t_l(\alpha_i) \\ \frac{x - t_l(\alpha_i)}{t_r(\alpha_i) - t_l(\alpha_i)}, & \text{if } t_r(\alpha_i) \leq x \leq t_r(\alpha_i) \\ 1, & \text{if } x \geq t_r(\alpha_i) \end{cases}$$

i.e. the c.d.f. of the random variable having a uniform distribution over T_{α_i} that is viewed as an approximation of T at level α_i.

Clearly, the right side of the expression (7) is the Riemann sum of the function $f(\alpha) = P(x \succeq T_\alpha)$ over $[0, 1]$ with respect to the partition $\alpha_1, \ldots, \alpha_{k+1}$. Thus, we now generally define $\mathbb{P}(x \succeq T)$ as

$$\mathbb{P}(x \succeq T) = \int_0^1 P(x \succeq T_\alpha)d\alpha \tag{8}$$

The approximation in (7) of the integral in (8) improves the finer the sample of membership grades.

Returning to our DMUU problem described as above we obtain the following utility function induced from the fuzzy target T:

$$\mathbb{P}(c_{ij} \succeq T) \triangleq U_2^T(c_{ij}) = \int_0^1 P(c_{ij} \succeq T_\alpha)d\alpha \tag{9}$$

3.3   Example of Fuzzy Targets and Risk Attitude

Let us now consider four fuzzy targets which correspond to prototypical attitudes of DM on target assessment. The first one expresses a *neutral* behavior of the DM on target and is represented by the possibility distribution $T_{neutral}(x) = 1$ for $c_{min} \leq x \leq c_{max}$, and $T_{neutral}(x) = 0$ otherwise. Then, it is easily shown that both methods for inducing utility yield the same value function for (4):

$$v(A_i) = \sum_{j=1}^{m} \frac{c_{ij} - c_{min}}{c_{max} - c_{min}} P_{\mathcal{S}}(S_j)$$

which is equivalent to the expected value model.

The second is called the *optimistic target*. This target would be set by a DM who has an aspiration towards the maximal payoff. Formally, the optimistic fuzzy target, denoted by T_{opt}, is defined as follows

$$T_{opt}(x) = \begin{cases} \frac{x - c_{min}}{c_{max} - c_{min}}, & \text{if } c_{min} \leq x \leq c_{max} \\ 0, & \text{otherwise} \end{cases}$$

Fig. 1 graphically depicts the membership function $T_{opt}(x)$ along with the utility functions $U_1^{T_{opt}}(x)$ and $U_2^{T_{opt}}(x)$ corresponding to this target.

The third target is called the *pessimistic target*. This target is characterized by a DM who believes bad things may happen and has a conservative assessment of the target, which correspond to ascribing high possibility to the uncertain target being a low payoff. The membership function of this target is defined by

$$T_{pess}(x) = \begin{cases} \frac{c_{max} - x}{c_{max} - c_{min}}, & \text{if } c_{min} \leq x \leq c_{max} \\ 0, & \text{otherwise} \end{cases}$$

The portraits of related functions corresponding to the pessimistic target is shown in Fig. 2.

Consider now the fourth target linguistically represented as "*about c_0*" whose membership function is defined by

$$T_{\tilde{c}_0}(x) = \begin{cases} \frac{x - c_{min}}{c_0 - c_{min}}, & c_{min} \leq x \leq c_0 \\ \frac{c_{max} - x}{c_{max} - c_0}, & c_0 \leq x \leq c_{max} \\ 0, & \text{otherwise} \end{cases}$$

where $c_{min} < c_0 < c_{max}$. This fuzzy target characterizes the situation at which the DM establishes a modal value c_0 as the most likely target and assesses the

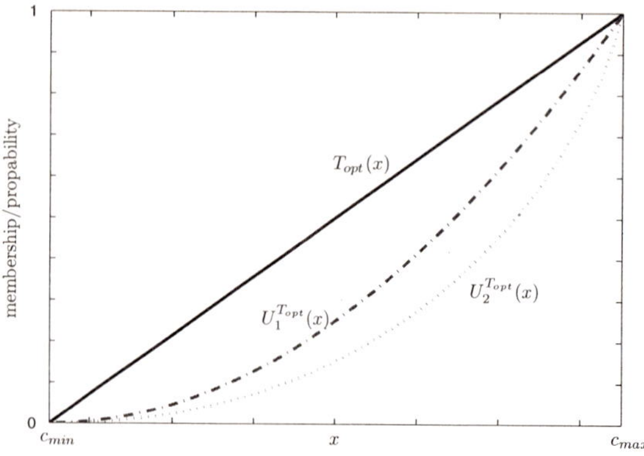

Fig. 1. Optimistic target

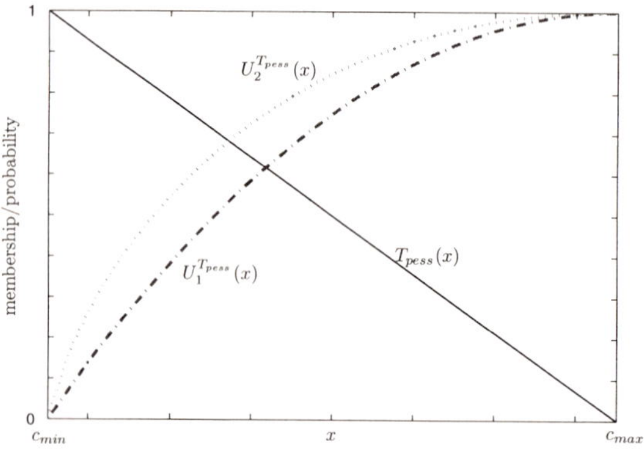

Fig. 2. Pessimistic target

possibilistic uncertain target as distributed around it. We call this target the *unimodal*. Fig. 3 graphically illustrates for this situation.

Looking at Figs. 1–3, we see that the portraits of the utility functions $U_1^T(x)$ and $U_2^T(x)$ have similar shapes for each corresponding target. However, the behavior of the utility function $U_1^T(x)$ is steeper towards the modal value of the corresponding targets than that of the utility function $U_2^T(x)$. This practically implies that the value function $v(\cdot)$ defined with utility function $U_2^T(x)$ reflects a stronger decision attitude towards the target than that defined with utility function $U_1^T(x)$ as shown in the example below.

As we have seen from Fig. 1, the optimistic target T_{opt} leads to the convex utility functions and therefore, exhibits a risk-seeking behavior. This is because of having an aspiration towards the maximal payoff, the DM always feels loss over the whole domain except the maximum, which would produce more risk-seeking behavior globally. By contrast, Fig. 2 shows that the pessimistic target induces

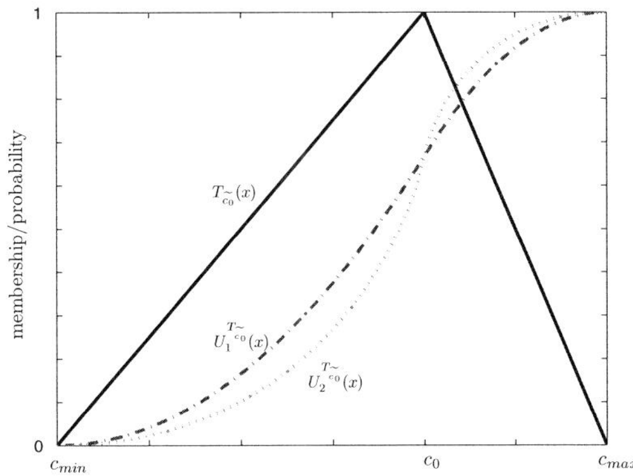

Fig. 3. Unimodal target

the concave utility functions and thus equivalently corresponds to global risk-aversion behavior. More interestingly, the unimodal target induces the utility functions that are equivalent to the S-shape utility function of Kahneman and Tversky's prospect theory [8], according to which people tend to be risk averse over gains and risk seeking over losses. In the fuzzy target-based language, as the DM assesses his uncertain target as distributed around the modal value, he feels loss (respectively, gain) over payoff values that are coded as negative (respectively, positive) changes with respect to the modal value. This would lead to the behavior consistent with that described in the prospect theory. A link of this behavior to unimodal probabilistic targets has been established by LiCalzi in [10]. Further, it has been also suggested in the literature that this sort of target be the most natural one to occur.

4   An Illustrated Example

Let us consider the following example from Samson [12] to illustrate the point discussed above. In this example, payoffs are shown in thousands of dollars for a problem with three acts and four states as described in Table 2. It is also assumed [12] a proper prior over the four possible states of $p_1 = 0.2$, $p_2 = 0.4$, $p_3 = 0.3$, $p_4 = 0.1$.

Table 3 shows the computational results of two value functions with different fuzzy targets for acts, where

$$v_1(A_i) = \sum_{j=1}^{m} p_j U_1^T(c_{ij}) \text{ and } v_2(A_i) = \sum_{j=1}^{m} p_j U_2^T(c_{ij})$$

From the result shown in Table 3, we see that both value functions $v_1(\cdot)$ and $v_2(\cdot)$ suggest the same solution for the selection problem. That is, the act A_2 is the preferred choice according to a DM who has a neutral (equivalently, who abides by the expected value) or optimistic-oriented behavior about targets, a

Table 2. The Payoff Matrix

Acts	States			
	1	2	3	4
A_1	400	320	540	600
A_2	250	350	700	550
A_3	600	280	150	400

Table 3. The Target-Based Value Functions

Targets	Value Functions					
	$v_1()$			$v_2()$		
	A_1	A_2	A_3	A_1	A_2	A_3
Neutral	0.51	**0.55**	0.30	0.51	**0.55**	0.30
Optimist	0.3	**0.41**	0.18	0.20	**0.37**	0.13
Pessimist	**0.72**	0.7	0.43	**0.82**	0.79	0.51
$\widetilde{300}$	**0.62**	0.59	0.33	**0.69**	0.63	0.33
$\widetilde{425}$	**0.50**	**0.50**	0.27	**0.48**	0.47	0.25
$\widetilde{550}$	0.40	**0.45**	0.23	0.35	**0.42**	0.22

DM having pessimistic-oriented behavior about targets selects A_1 as his preferred choice. Especially, in the case of symmetrical unimodal target $\widetilde{425}$, the acts A_1 and A_2 are almost indifferent to a DM who use $v_1(\cdot)$, while A_1 slightly dominates A_2 if using $v_2(\cdot)$. In addition, though the act A_3 is not selected in all cases, its value is much improved with respect to a pessimistic-oriented decision maker. However, the computational results of these two functions are different except, obviously, for the case of the neutral target. Especially, it is of interest to see that the spread of the difference of the value function $v_2(\cdot)$ between opposite-oriented targets is much larger than that of the value function $v_1(\cdot)$. This illustrates that the target-based decision model using $U_2^T(\cdot)$ reflects a stronger decision attitude towards the target than that using $U_1^T(\cdot)$.

5   Conclusion

In this paper, we have discussed two methods for inducing utility functions from fuzzy targets for DMUU using a target-based language. It should be noted that the target-based approach has some appealing features because thinking of targets is quite natural in many situations. We have also related different attitudes of the DM on target with the corresponding attitudes towards risk in decision analysis with uncertainty. For further research, we are planning to study a target-based framework of attitudinal decision making with uncertainty as developed recently by Yager [17]. Moreover, the target-based formulation for the problem of decision making in the face of uncertainty about the state of nature and imprecision about payoffs are being also considered.

References

1. J. F. Baldwin. The management of fuzzy and probabilistic uncertainties for knowledge based systems, in: S. A. Shapiro (Ed.), *The Encyclopaedia of AI*, New York: Wiley, 1992, pp. 528–537.
2. R. Bordley, M. LiCalzi. Decision analysis using targets instead of utility functions, *Decisions in Economics and Finance* 23(1) (2000) 53–74.
3. R. Bordley. Foundations of target-based decision theory, in: H. W. Brachinger, P. A. Monney (Eds.), *Decision Analysis*. From: Encyclopedia of Life Support Systems (EOLSS), Eolss Publishers, Oxford, 2002.
4. E. Castagnoli, M. LiCalzi. Expected utility without utility, *Theory and Decision* **41**(3) (1996) 281-301.
5. E. Castagnoli, M. LiCalzi. Benchmarking real-valued acts, *Games and Economic Behavior*, in press.
6. D. Dubois, H. Prade. Properties of measures of information in evidence and possibility theories, *Fuzzy Sets and Systems* **24** (1987) 161–182.
7. V. N. Huynh, Y. Nakamori, M. Ryoke, T. B. Ho. A fuzzy target based model for decision making under uncertainty, *FUZZ–IEEE 2006*, accepted.
8. D. Kahneman, A. Tversky. Prospect theory: An nnalysis of decision under risk, *Econometrica* **47**(2) (1979) 263–291.
9. H. Lee-Kwang, J.-H. Lee. A method for ranking fuzzy numbers and its application to decision-making, *IEEE Transactions on Fuzzy Systems* **7**(6) (1999) 677–685.
10. M. LiCalzi. A language for the construction of preferences under uncertainty, *Revista de la Real Academia de Ciencias Exactas, Físicas y Naturales* **93** (1999) 439–450.
11. C. F. Manski. Ordinal utility models of decision making under uncertainty, *Theory and Decision* **25** (1988) 79–104.
12. D. Samson. *Managerial Decision Analysis*. Chicago: Irwin Publishing Co., 1988.
13. L. J. Savage. *The Foundations of Statistics*. New York: John Wiley and Sons, 1954.
14. G. Shafer. *A Mathematical Theory of Evidence*. Princeton: Princeton University Press, 1976.
15. J. Von Neumann, O. Morgenstern. *Theory of Games and Economic Behavior*. Princeton University Press: Princeton, 1944.
16. R. R. Yager, M. Detyniecki, B. Bouchon-Meunier. A context-dependent method for ordering fuzzy numbers using probabilities, *Information Sciences* **138**(1–4) (2001) 237–255.
17. R. R. Yager. Including decision attitude in probabilistic decision making, *International Journal of Approximate Reasoning* **21** (1999) 1–21.
18. L. A. Zadeh. Fuzzy sets as a basic for a theory of possibility, *Fuzzy Sets and Systems* **1** (1978) 3–28.

Dominance-Based Rough Set Approach to Decision Involving Multiple Decision Makers

Salvatore Greco[1], Benedetto Matarazzo[1], and Roman Słowiński[2]

[1] Faculty of Economics, University of Catania,
Corso Italia, 55, 95129 Catania, Italy
[2] Institute of Computing Science, Poznań University of Technology,
60-965 Poznań, and Institute for Systems Reserch,
Polish Academy of Sciences, 01-447 Warsaw, Poland

Abstract. In this paper we present a rough set approach to decisions with multiple decision makers. Since preference order is a crucial feature of data concerning decision situations, and classical rough set approach is not able to deal with it, we are using Dominance-based Rough Set Approach (DRSA) where indiscernibility relation of the classical approach has been substituted by dominance relation. To deal with decision of multiple decision makers we extend DRSA by introducing specific concepts related to dominance with respect to minimal profiles of evaluations given by multiple decision makers. This extension provides also a general methodology for rough approximations of partial preorders.

1 Introduction

In many real-life decision problems, potential actions described by multiple criteria are evaluated by multiple decision makers. Then, it is important to characterize conditions for a consensus between the decision makers. Different approaches were considered within this context, however, they were concentrated on converging toward a consensus defined as an output minimizing dissimilarities (or maximizing similarities) between decision makers, using a particular metric in the space of evaluations (see e.g. [5], [6], [4]). For this reason, the research in this field has been focused on supporting negotiations between decision makers. Instead of this, we propose to define conditions for a given scenario of a consensus, expressed in terms of decision rules induced from examples of evaluations provided by multiple decision makers. The decision rules are logical *"if. . . , then. . . "* statements relating conditions defined in multiple criteria space with decisions defined in multiple decision makers evaluation space.

For example, consider a multiple criteria decision problem concerning students described by scores (from 0 to 20) in such subjects (criteria) as mathematics (M), physics (Ph) and literature (L), and evaluated by a committee composed of three professors (decision makers), P1, P2, P3. Suppose that each professor is giving a comprehensive evaluation of each student on three-level scale {Bad, Medium, Good}, taking into account the scores gained by the students in M, Ph and L. Suppose, moreover, that decisions of P1, P2, P3 have to be aggregated so as

S. Greco et al. (Eds.): RSCTC 2006, LNAI 4259, pp. 306–317, 2006.

to designate students which will be finally accepted for a higher-level program. The aggregate decision represents a consensus between professors. Let us consider a possible consensus which is reached when at least two of three professors evaluate a student as comprehensively at least Medium, and the remaining professor evaluates this student as comprehensively Good. Thus, the corresponding minimal profiles [E1, E2, E3] of comprehensive evaluations given, respectively, by P1, P2 and P3 are: [Medium, Medium, Good], [Medium, Good, Medium], [Good, Medium, Medium]. Characterization of this consensus in terms of scores obtained by students in M, Ph and L can be made by means of rules of the type: "if student x gained at least 15 in M, and at least 18 in L, then x is accepted", or "if student x gained at most 10 in M, and at most 13 in Ph, then x is not accepted". These rules are induced from a decision table including both the scores in M, Ph, L, and the comprehensive evaluations by P1, P2 and P3.

Remark that data used for induction of decision rules characterizing a supposed consensus are preference ordered. For this reason we cannot apply the classical rough set approach based on indiscernibility (see [7]), but rather the Dominance-based Rough Set Approach (DRSA) which we proposed (see e.g. [1],[2], [3], [8]) for analysis of preference ordered data. To deal with decision involving multiple decision makers, we have to extend DRSA by introducing specific concepts related to dominance with respect to minimal profiles of evaluations given by multiple decision makers.

The paper is organized as follows. In section 2, we recall main elements of DRSA. In section 3, we introduce definitions extending DRSA to the case of multiple decision makers. In section 4, we investigate some properties of the proposed approach, in particular, properties of dominance between sets of vectors of comprehensive evaluations. The paper ends with conclusions.

2   Reminder of Dominance-Based Rough Set Approach

Let us recall some main elements of DRSA. For algorithmic reasons, information about objects of the decision (also called actions) is represented in the form of an information table. The rows of the table are labelled by *objects*, whereas columns are labelled by *attributes* and entries of the table are *attribute-values*. Formally, by an *information table* we understand the 4-tuple $S=< U,Q,V,f >$, where U is a finite set of objects, Q is a finite set of *attributes*, $V = \bigcup_{q \in Q} V_q$ and V_q is a domain of the attribute q, and $f\colon U \times Q \to V$ is a total function such that $f(x,q) \in V_q$ for every $q \in Q$, $x \in U$, called an *information function*. The set Q is, in general, divided into set C of *condition attributes* and set D of *decision attributes*. Information table for which condition and decision attributes are distinguished is called *decision table*.

We are considering condition attributes with domains (scales) ordered according to decreasing or increasing preference – such attributes are called *criteria*. For criterion $q \in Q$, $\succeq_q$ is a *weak preference* relation (also called outranking relation) on U such that $x \succeq_q y$ means "x is at least as good as y with respect to criterion q". We suppose that $\succeq_q$ is a total preorder, i.e. a strongly complete and transitive binary relation, defined on U on the basis of evaluations $f(\cdot,q)$. We assume, without loss of generality, that the preference is increasing with the value of $f(\cdot,q)$ for every criterion $q \in C$.

Furthermore, we assume that the set of decision attributes D is a singleton $\{d\}$. Decision attribute d makes a partition of U into a finite number of decision classes, $\textbf{\textit{Cl}}=\{Cl_t, t \in T\}$, $T = \{1, ..., n\}$, such that each $x \in U$ belongs to one and only one class $Cl_t \in \textbf{\textit{Cl}}$. We suppose that the classes are preference-ordered, i.e. for all $r,s \in T$, such that $r > s$, the objects from Cl_r are preferred to the objects from Cl_s. More formally, if $\succeq$ is a *comprehensive weak preference relation* on U, i.e. if for all $x,y \in U$, $x \succeq y$ means "x is at least as good as y", we suppose: $[x \in Cl_r, y \in Cl_s, r > s] \Rightarrow [x \succeq y$ and *not* $y \succeq x]$. The above assumptions are typical for consideration of a *multiple-criteria classification problem* (also called multiple-criteria sorting problem).

The sets to be approximated are called *upward union* and *downward union* of classes, respectively:

$$Cl_t^{\geq} = \bigcup_{s \geq t} Cl_s, \quad Cl_t^{\leq} = \bigcup_{s \leq t} Cl_s, \quad t = 1, ..., n.$$

The statement $x \in Cl_t^{\geq}$ means "x belongs to at least class Cl_t", while $x \in Cl_t^{\leq}$ means "x belongs to at most class Cl_t".

The key idea of the rough set approach is representation (approximation) of knowledge generated by decision attributes, by "*granules of knowledge*" generated by condition attributes.

In DRSA, where condition attributes are criteria and decision classes are preference ordered, the represented knowledge is a collection of *upward* and *downward unions of classes* and the "granules of knowledge" are sets of objects defined using a dominance relation.

We say that x *dominates* y with respect to $P \subseteq C$ (shortly, x *P-dominates* y), denoted by $x D_P y$, if for every criterion $q \in P$, $f(x, q) \geq f(y, q)$. P-dominance is reflexive.

Given a set of criteria $P \subseteq C$ and $x \in U$, the "granules of knowledge" used for approximation in DRSA are:

- a set of objects dominating x, called *P-dominating set*,
  $D_P^+(x) = \{y \in U: y D_P x\}$,
- a set of objects dominated by x, called *P-dominated set*,
  $D_P^-(x) = \{y \in U: x D_P y\}$.

Let us recall that the *dominance principle* (or Pareto principle) requires that an object x dominating object y on all considered criteria (i.e. x having evaluations at least as good as y on all considered criteria) should also dominate y on the decision (i.e. x should be assigned to at least as good decision class as y). This principle is the only objective principle that is widely agreed upon in the multicriteria comparisons of objects.

The *P-lower approximation* of $Cl_t^{\geq}$, denoted by $\underline{P}\,Cl_t^{\geq}$, and the *P-upper approximation* of $Cl_t^{\geq}$, denoted by $\overline{P}(\,Cl_t^{\geq}\,)$, are defined as follows ($t{=}1,...,n$):

$$\underline{P}(\,Cl_t^{\geq}\,) = \{x \in U : D_P^+(x) \subseteq Cl_t^{\geq}\,\},$$
$$\overline{P}(\,Cl_t^{\geq}\,) = \{x \in U : D_P^-(x) \cap Cl_t^{\geq} \neq \emptyset\} = \bigcup_{x \in Cl_t^{\geq}} D^+(x),$$

Analogously, one can define the *P-lower approximation* and the *P-upper approximation* of $Cl_t^{\leq}$ as follows ($t{=}1,...,n$):

$$\underline{P}(\,Cl_t^{\leq}\,) = \{x \in U : D_P^-(x) \subseteq Cl_t^{\leq}\,\},$$
$$\overline{P}(\,Cl_t^{\leq}\,) = \{x \in U : D_P^+(x) \cap Cl_t^{\leq} \neq \emptyset\} = \bigcup_{x \in Cl_t^{\leq}} D^-(x),$$

The P-lower and P-upper approximations so defined satisfy the following *inclusion properties* for each $t \in \{1,\ldots,n\}$ and for all $P \subseteq C$:

$$\underline{P}(\,Cl_t^{\geq}\,) \subseteq Cl_t^{\geq} \subseteq \overline{P}(\,Cl_t^{\geq}\,), \quad \underline{P}(\,Cl_t^{\leq}\,) \subseteq Cl_t^{\leq} \subseteq \overline{P}(\,Cl_t^{\leq}\,).$$

The $P-$lower and $P-$upper approximations of $Cl_t^{\geq}$ and $Cl_t^{\leq}$ have an important *complementarity property*, according to which, $\underline{P}(\,Cl_t^{\geq}\,) = U{-}\overline{P}(Cl_{t-1}^{\leq})$, $t{=}2,...,n$.

The dominance-based rough approximations of upward and downward unions of classes can serve to induce "*if...*, *then...*" decision rules. It is meaningful to consider the following five types of decision rules:

1. *Certain* $D_{\geq}$*-decision rules:* if $x_{q1} \succeq_{q1} r_{q1}$ and $x_{q2} \succeq_{q2} r_{q2}$ and $\ldots x_{qp} \succeq_{qp} r_{qp}$, then $x \in Cl_t^{\geq}$, where for each $w_q, z_q \in X_q$, "$w_q \succeq_q z_q$" means "w_q is <u>at least</u> as good as z_q"
2. *Possible* $D_{\geq}$*-decision rules:* if $x_{q1} \succeq_{q1} r_{q1}$ and $x_{q2} \succeq_{q2} r_{q2}$ and $\ldots x_{qp} \succeq_{qp} r_{qp}$, then x possibly belongs to $Cl_t^{\geq}$
3. *Certain* $D_{\leq}$*-decision rules:* if $x_{q1} \preceq_{q1} r_{q1}$ and $x_{q2} \preceq_{q2} r_{q2}$ and $\ldots x_{qp} \preceq_{qp} r_{qp}$, then $x \in Cl_t^{\leq}$, where for each $w_q, z_q \in X_q$, "$w_q \preceq_q z_q$" means "w_q is <u>at most</u> as good as z_q"
4. *Possible* $D_{\leq}$*-decision rules:* if $x_{q1} \preceq_{q1} r_{q1}$ and $x_{q2} \preceq_{q2} r_{q2}$ and $\ldots x_{qp} \preceq_{qp} r_{qp}$, then x possibly belongs to $Cl_t^{\leq}$
5. *Approximate* $D_{\geq\leq}$*-decision rules:* if $x_{q1} \succeq_{q1} r_{q1}$ and... $x_{qk} \succeq_{qk} r_{qk}$ and $x_{qk+1} \preceq_{qk+1} r_{qk+1}$ and ... $x_{qp} \preceq_{qp} r_{qp}$, then $x \in Cl_s^{\geq} \cap Cl_t^{\leq}$.

3   DRSA for Multiple Decision Makers – Definitions

We are considering a *decision table* with a finite set of *objects* $U{=}\{a,b,\ldots,x,y,\ldots\}$, called *universe*, a finite set of *criteria* $C{=}\{1,\ldots,q,\ldots,m\}$, and a finite set of *decision makers* $H{=}\{1,\ldots,i,\ldots,h\}$, corresponding to h *decision attributes*.

We suppose that each decision maker $i \in H$ has a preference order on the universe U and that this preference order is represented by a finite set of preference ordered classes

$$\boldsymbol{Cl}_i = \{ Cl_{t,i},\ t \in T_i \}, \quad T_i = \{1,\ldots,n_i\},$$

such that

$$\bigcup_{t=1}^{n_i} Cl_{t,i} = U, \quad Cl_{t,i} \cap Cl_{r,i} = \emptyset \text{ for all } r,t \in T_i,$$

and if $x \in Cl_{r,i}$, $y \in Cl_{s,i}$ and $r > s$, then x is better than y for decision maker i.

For a single decision maker $i \in H$, the sets to be approximated are the *upward* and *downward unions* of decision classes $(t=1,\ldots,n_i)$:

$$Cl_{t,i}^{\geq} = \bigcup_{s \geq t} Cl_{s,i} \text{ (at least class } Cl_{t,i}), \quad Cl_{t,i}^{\leq} = \bigcup_{s \leq t} Cl_{s,i} \text{ (at most class } Cl_{t,i}).$$

Thus, considering a single decision maker, DRSA does not need any extension, because the only difference is that instead of considering only one set of preference ordered classes, we have multiple sets of preference ordered classes such that one set corresponds to one decision maker.

If we want to consider the set of decision makers H as a whole, we need to introduce some new concepts:

- *upward multi-union with respect to one configuration*
  $[t(1),\ldots,\ t(h)]$, $(t(i) \in T_i,\ \text{for all } i \in H)$:

$$Cl_{[t(1),\ldots t(h)]}^{\geq} = \bigcap_{i \in H} Cl_{t(i),i}^{\geq},$$

- *downward multi-union with respect to one configuration*
  $[t(1),\ldots,t(h)]$, $(t(i) \in T_i,\ \text{for all } i \in H)$:

$$Cl_{[t(1),\ldots,t(h)]}^{\leq} = \bigcap_{i \in H} Cl_{t(i),i}^{\leq}$$

- *upward mega-union with respect to a set of k configurations*
  $\{[t_1(1),\ldots,t_1(h)],\ldots,[t_k(1),\ldots,t_k(h)]\}$, $k=1,\ldots,\prod_{i=1}^{h} n_i$

$$Cl_{\{[t_1(1),\ldots,t_1(h)],\ldots,[t_k(1),\ldots,t_k(h)]\}}^{\geq} = \bigcup_{r=1}^{k} Cl_{[t_r(1),\ldots,t_r(h)]}^{\geq},$$

- *downward mega-union with respect to a set of k configurations*
  $\{[t_1(1),\ldots,t_1(h)],\ldots,[t_k(1),\ldots,t_k(h)]\}$, $k=1,\ldots,\prod_{i=1}^{h} n_i$

$$Cl_{\{[t_1(1),\ldots,t_1(h)],\ldots,[t_k(1),\ldots,t_k(h)]\}}^{\leq} = \bigcup_{r=1}^{k} Cl_{[t_r(1),\ldots,t_r(h)]}^{\leq}.$$

In the above concepts, *configuration* means an evaluation profile, which is a vector of names of decision classes used by particular decision makers; e.g. [Bad, Medium, Average] is a configuration of class names of three decision makers.

The meaning of an *upward multi-union* is such that it includes objects which were assigned by particular decision makers to <u>at least</u> as good decision classes as those indicated in the corresponding configuration; e.g. for configuration [Bad, Medium, Average], the upward multi-union includes all those objects which were qualified as at least Bad by the first decision maker, as at least Medium by the second decision maker, and as at least Average by the third decision maker. The meaning of a *downward multi-union* is analogous, i.e. it includes objects which were assigned by particular decision makers to <u>at most</u> as good decision classes as those indicated in the corresponding configuration.

While the maximum number of all possible configurations is equal to the number of all possible combinations of class names by particular decision makers, i.e. $\prod_{i=1}^{h} n_i$, the number k of configurations considered in mega-unions can be, of course, smaller.

Given k configurations, an *upward mega-union* is a sum of upward multi-unions corresponding to the k configurations; e.g. for 2 configurations [Bad, Medium, Average] and [Medium, Bad, Average], the upward mega-union includes all those objects which were qualified as at least Bad by the first decision maker, as at least Medium by the second decision maker, and as at least Average by the third decision maker, plus all those objects which were qualified as at least Medium by the first decision maker, as at least Bad by the second decision maker, and as at least Average by the third decision maker. The meaning of a *downward mega-union* is analogous, i.e. it is a sum of downward multi-unions corresponding to the k configurations.

Using the concept of a mega-union, one can model a collective decision of majority type. E.g., in a simple case of three decision makers and YES/NO voting decisions for the objects, a "majority" mega-union is a set of objects such that at least two decision makers voted YES for them.

With respect to approximations of multi-unions, the following principle of coherence can be stated: for any $P \subseteq C$,

- $x \in U$ belongs to $Cl^{\geq}_{[t(1),...t(h)]}$ *without any inconsistency* if $x \in Cl^{\geq}_{[t(1),...t(h)]}$ and, for all $y \in U$ dominating x on P, also y belongs to $Cl^{\geq}_{[t(1),...t(h)]}$, i.e. $D_P^+(x) \subseteq Cl^{\geq}_{[t(1),...t(h)]}$,
- $x \in U$ *could* belong to $Cl^{\geq}_{[t(1),...t(h)]}$ if there existed at least one $y \in Cl^{\geq}_{[t(1),...t(h)]}$ such that x dominates y on P, i.e. $x \in D_P^+(y)$.

For any $P \subseteq C$, the set of all objects belonging to $Cl^{\geq}_{[t(1),...t(h)]}$ without any inconsistency constitutes the P-lower approximation of upward multi-union $Cl^{\geq}_{[t(1),...t(h)]}$,

$$\underline{P}\left(Cl^{\geq}_{[t(1),...,t(h)]}\right) = \left\{ x \in U : D_P^+(x) \subseteq Cl^{\geq}_{[t(1),...t(h)]} \right\}.$$

The set of all objects that could belong to $Cl^{\geq}_{t,i}$ constitutes the P-upper approximation of upward multi-union $Cl^{\geq}_{[t(1),...t(h)]}$,

$$\overline{P}\left(Cl^{\geq}_{[t(1),\ldots t(h)]}\right) = \bigcup_{x \in Cl^{\geq}_{[t(1),\ldots t(h)]}} D_P^+(x).$$

The definitions of P-lower approximation and P-upper approximation of downward multi-union $Cl^{\leq}_{[t(1),\ldots t(h)]}$ can be obtained following the same reasoning and, therefore, we have

$$\underline{P}\left(Cl^{\leq}_{[t(1),\ldots,t(h)]}\right) = \left\{x \in U : D_P^-(x) \subseteq Cl^{\leq}_{[t(1),\ldots t(h)]}\right\},$$

$$\overline{P}\left(Cl^{\leq}_{[t(1),\ldots t(h)]}\right) = \bigcup_{x \in Cl^{\leq}_{[t(1),\ldots t(h)]}} D_P^-(x).$$

Theorem 1. *For all $P \subseteq C$ and for any configuration $[t(1),\ldots,t(h)]$, $(t(i) \in T_i$, for all $i \in H)$,*

$$\underline{P}\left(Cl^{\geq}_{[t(1),\ldots,t(h)]}\right) = \bigcap_{i=1}^{h}\underline{P}\left(Cl^{\geq}_{t(i),i}\right), \quad \overline{P}\left(Cl^{\geq}_{[t(1),\ldots t(h)]}\right) \subseteq \bigcup_{i=1}^{h}\overline{P}\left(Cl^{\geq}_{t(i),i}\right),$$

$$\underline{P}\left(Cl^{\leq}_{[t(1),\ldots,t(h)]}\right) = \bigcap_{i=1}^{h}\underline{P}\left(Cl^{\leq}_{t(i),i}\right), \quad \overline{P}\left(Cl^{\leq}_{[t(1),\ldots t(h)]}\right) \subseteq \bigcup_{i=1}^{h}\overline{P}\left(Cl^{\leq}_{t(i),i}\right).$$

Similarly to multi-unions, we can express the following principle of coherence with respect to mega-unions: for any $P \subseteq C$,

- $x \in U$ belongs to upward mega-union $Cl^{\geq}_{\{[t_1(1),\ldots,t_1(h)],\ldots,[t_k(1),\ldots,t_k(h)]\}}$ *without any inconsistency if* $x \in Cl^{\geq}_{\{[t_1(1),\ldots,t_1(h)],\ldots,[t_k(1),\ldots,t_k(h)]\}}$ and for all $y \in U$ dominating x on P, also y belongs to $Cl^{\geq}_{\{[t_1(1),\ldots,t_1(h)],\ldots,[t_k(1),\ldots,t_k(h)]\}}$, i.e. $D_P^+(x) \subseteq Cl^{\geq}_{\{[t_1(1),\ldots,t_1(h)],\ldots,[t_k(1),\ldots,t_k(h)]\}}$,
- $x \in U$ *could* belong to $Cl^{\geq}_{\{[t_1(1),\ldots,t_1(h)],\ldots,[t_k(1),\ldots,t_k(h)]\}}$ if there existed at least one $y \in Cl^{\geq}_{\{[t_1(1),\ldots,t_1(h)],\ldots,[t_k(1),\ldots,t_k(h)]\}}$ such that x dominates y on P, i.e. $x \in D_P^+(y)$.

Now, we can define rough approximations of mega-unions. For any $P \subseteq C$, the set of all objects belonging to $Cl^{\geq}_{\{[t_1(1),\ldots,t_1(h)],\ldots,[t_k(1),\ldots,t_k(h)]\}}$ without any inconsistency constitutes the P-lower approximation of the upward mega-union,

$$\underline{P}\left(Cl^{\geq}_{\{[t_1(1),\ldots,t_1(h)],\ldots,[t_k(1),\ldots,t_k(h)]\}}\right) =$$

$$\left\{x \in U : D_P^+(x) \subseteq Cl^{\geq}_{\{[t_1(1),\ldots,t_1(h)],\ldots,[t_k(1),\ldots,t_k(h)]\}}\right\}.$$

The set of all objects that could belong to $Cl^{\geq}_{\{[t_1(1),\ldots,t_1(h)],\ldots,[t_k(1),\ldots,t_k(h)]\}}$ constitutes the P-upper approximation of the upward mega-union,

$$\overline{P}\left(Cl^{\geq}_{\{[t_1(1),\ldots,t_1(h)],\ldots,[t_k(1),\ldots,t_k(h)]\}}\right) = \bigcup_{x \in Cl^{\geq}_{\{[t_1(1),\ldots,t_1(h)],\ldots,[t_k(1),\ldots,t_k(h)]\}}} D_P^+(x).$$

The definitions of P-lower approximation and P-upper approximation of downward mega-union $Cl^{\leq}_{\{[t_1(1),...,t_1(h)],...,[t_k(1),...,t_k(h)]\}}$ can be obtained following the same reasoning and, therefore, we have

$$\underline{P}\left(Cl^{\leq}_{\{[t_1(1),...,t_1(h)],...,[t_k(1),...,t_k(h)]\}}\right) =$$

$$\left\{x \in U : D^-_P(x) \subseteq Cl^{\leq}_{\{[t_1(1),...,t_1(h)],...,[t_k(1),...,t_k(h)]\}}\right\},$$

$$\overline{P}\left(Cl^{\leq}_{\{[t_1(1),...,t_1(h)],...,[t_k(1),...,t_k(h)]\}}\right) = \bigcup_{x \in Cl^{\leq}_{\{[t_1(1),...,t_1(h)],...,[t_k(1),...,t_k(h)]\}}} D^-_P(x).$$

Theorem 2. *For all $P \subseteq C$ and for all mega-unions $\{[t_1(1), \ldots, t_1(h)], \ldots, [t_k(1), \ldots, t_k(h)]\}$, $(t_r(i) \in T_i$ for all $r = 1, \ldots, k)$*

$$\underline{P}\left(Cl^{\geq}_{\{[t_1(1),...,t_1(h)],...,[t_k(1),...,t_k(h)]\}}\right) \supseteq \bigcup_{r=1}^{k} \underline{P}\left(Cl^{\geq}_{[t_r(1),...,t_r(h)]}\right),$$

$$\overline{P}\left(Cl^{\geq}_{\{[t_1(1),...,t_1(h)],...,[t_k(1),...,t_k(h)]\}}\right) = \bigcup_{r=1}^{k} \overline{P}\left(Cl^{\geq}_{[t_r(1),...,t_r(h)]}\right),$$

$$\underline{P}\left(Cl^{\leq}_{\{[t_1(1),...,t_1(h)],...,[t_k(1),...,t_k(h)]\}}\right) \supseteq \bigcup_{r=1}^{k} \underline{P}\left(Cl^{\leq}_{[t_r(1),...,t_r(h)]}\right),$$

$$\overline{P}\left(Cl^{\leq}_{\{[t_1(1),...,t_1(h)],...,[t_k(1),...,t_k(h)]\}}\right) = \bigcup_{r=1}^{k} \overline{P}\left(Cl^{\leq}_{[t_r(1),...,t_r(h)]}\right).$$

In the case of DRSA for multiple decision makers, the syntax of the five types of decision rules presented in section 2 does not change in the condition part, however, in the decision part there are, in general, upward or downward mega-unions.

4 DRSA for Multiple Decision Makers – Properties

In this section we investigate some fundamental properties of DRSA adapted to the presence of multiple decision makers.

Let us point out the following remarks:

1. Each upward union $Cl^{\geq}_{t,i}$ can be seen as an upward multi-union:
   $$Cl^{\geq}_{t,i} = Cl^{\geq}_{[1,...,t(i),...,1]}.$$
2. Each downward union $Cl^{\leq}_{t,i}$ can be seen as a downward multi-union:
   $$Cl^{\leq}_{t,i} = Cl^{\leq}_{[m_1,...,t(i),...,m_h]}.$$
3. Each upward multi-union $Cl^{\geq}_{[t(1),...,t(h)]}$ can be seen as an upward mega-union: $Cl^{\geq}_{[t(1),...,t(h)]} = Cl^{\geq}_{\{[t(1),...,t(h)]\}}.$

4. Each downward multi-union $Cl^{\leq}_{\overline{[t(1),...,t(h)]}}$ can be seen as a downward mega-union: $Cl^{\leq}_{\overline{[t(1),...,t(h)]}} = Cl^{\leq}_{\overline{\{[t(1),...,t(h)]\}}}$.
5. For above 1)-4), we can consider only mega-unions, because all results holding for mega-unions hold also for multi-unions and single decision makers.

Let us consider the property of inclusion and the associated order relation between upward or downward unions, multi-unions and mega-unions.

Let us start with simple upward unions. There is an isomorphism between inclusion relation $\subseteq$ on the set of all upward unions $\boldsymbol{Cl}^{\geq} = \left\{ Cl^{\geq}_t , t \in T \right\}$, and order relation $\geq$ on the set of class indices $T = \{1,..,n\}$, expressed as follows: for each $r,s \in T$,

$$Cl^{\geq}_r \subseteq Cl^{\geq}_s \Leftrightarrow r \geq s.$$

Observe that inclusion relation $\subseteq$ on $\boldsymbol{Cl}^{\geq}$ is a complete preorder, i.e. it is strongly complete (for each $r,s \in T$, $Cl^{\geq}_r \subseteq Cl^{\geq}_s$ or $Cl^{\geq}_s \subseteq Cl^{\geq}_r$) and transitive (for each $r,s,t \in T$, $Cl^{\geq}_r \subseteq Cl^{\geq}_s$ and $Cl^{\geq}_s \subseteq Cl^{\geq}_t$ imply $Cl^{\geq}_r \subseteq Cl^{\geq}_t$).

An analogous isomorphism holds for inclusion relation $\subseteq$ on the set of all downward unions $\boldsymbol{Cl}^{\leq} = \left\{ Cl^{\leq}_t , t \in T \right\}$, and order relation $\leq$ on the set of class indices $T = \{1,..,n\}$, expressed as follows: for each $r,s \in T$,

$$Cl^{\leq}_r \subseteq Cl^{\leq}_s \Leftrightarrow r \leq s.$$

Obviously, inclusion relation $\subseteq$ on $\boldsymbol{Cl}^{\leq}$ is again a complete preorder.

There is also an isomorphism between inclusion relation $\subseteq$ on the set of all upward multi-unions $\boldsymbol{Cl}^{\geq\Pi} = \left\{ Cl^{\geq}_{[t(1),...t(h)]}, [t(1),...,t(h)] \in \prod_{i=1}^{h} T_i \right\}$, and order relation $\geq$ on the Cartesian product of class indices $\prod_{i=1}^{h} T_i$, expressed as follows: for each $\boldsymbol{t}^1 = \left[t^1(1),...,t^1(h) \right]$, $\boldsymbol{t}^2 = \left[t^2(1),...,t^2(h) \right] \in \prod_{i=1}^{h} T_i$,

$$Cl^{\geq}_{\boldsymbol{t}^1} \subseteq Cl^{\geq}_{\boldsymbol{t}^2} \Leftrightarrow \boldsymbol{t}^1 \geqq \boldsymbol{t}^2.$$

In the multiple criteria context (criteria correspond to decision makers' evaluations), the order relation $\geqq$ is the dominance relation.

Observe that inclusion relation $\subseteq$ on $\boldsymbol{Cl}^{\geq\Pi}$ is a partial preorder, i.e. it is reflexive (for each $\boldsymbol{t} = [t(1),...,t(h)] \in \prod_{i=1}^{h} T_i$, $Cl^{\geq}_{\boldsymbol{t}} \subseteq Cl^{\geq}_{\boldsymbol{t}}$) and transitive.

An analogous isomorphism holds for inclusion relation $\subseteq$ on the set of all downward multi-unions $\boldsymbol{Cl}^{\leq\Pi} = \left\{ Cl^{\leq}_{[t(1),...t(h)]}, [t(1),...,t(h)] \in \prod_{i=1}^{h} T_i \right\}$, and order relation $\leq$ on the Cartesian product of class indices $\prod_{i=1}^{h} T_i$, expressed as follows: for each $\boldsymbol{t}^1 = \left[t^1(1),...,t^1(h) \right]$, $\boldsymbol{t}^2 = \left[t^2(1),...,t^2(h) \right] \in \prod_{i=1}^{h} T_i$,

$$Cl^{\leq}_{\boldsymbol{t}^1} \subseteq Cl^{\leq}_{\boldsymbol{t}^2} \Leftrightarrow \boldsymbol{t}^1 \leqq \boldsymbol{t}^2.$$

Obviously, inclusion relation $\subseteq$ on $\boldsymbol{Cl}^{\leq\Pi}$ is again a partial preorder. Observe that for all $\boldsymbol{t}^1, \boldsymbol{t}^2 \in \prod_{i=1}^{h} T_i$, $\boldsymbol{t}^1 \geqq \boldsymbol{t}^2 \Leftrightarrow \boldsymbol{t}^2 \leqq \boldsymbol{t}^1$. This implies that

$$Cl_{\boldsymbol{t}^1}^{\geq} \subseteq Cl_{\boldsymbol{t}^2}^{\geq} \Leftrightarrow Cl_{\boldsymbol{t}^2}^{\leq} \subseteq Cl_{\boldsymbol{t}^1}^{\leq}.$$

Let us finally pass to upward mega-unions. In this case, it is useful to consider another type of order relations, denoted by $\langle\geq\rangle$ and $\langle\leq\rangle$, defined in the power set of h-dimensional real space $2^{\boldsymbol{R}^h}$. For all $\langle\boldsymbol{x}^1\rangle = \left\{ \left[x_1^{1,1}, ..., x_h^{1,1}\right], ..., \left[x_1^{1,k_1}, ..., x_h^{1,k_1}\right] \right\}$, $\langle\boldsymbol{x}^2\rangle = \left\{ \left[x_1^{2,1}, ..., x_h^{2,1}\right], ..., \left[x_1^{2,k_2}, ..., x_h^{2,k_2}\right] \right\} \in 2^{\boldsymbol{R}^h}$,

$$\langle\boldsymbol{x}^1\rangle \,\langle\geq\rangle\, \langle\boldsymbol{x}^2\rangle \Leftrightarrow \forall \left[x_1^{1,i}, ..., x_h^{1,i}\right] \in \langle\boldsymbol{x}^1\rangle \,\exists\, \left[x_1^{2,j}, ..., x_h^{2,j}\right] \in \langle\boldsymbol{x}^2\rangle,$$

such that $\left[x_1^{1,i}, ..., x_h^{1,i}\right] \geqq \left[x_1^{2,j}, ..., x_h^{2,j}\right]$, $i = 1, ..., k_1$, $j = 1, ..., k_2$, as well as

$$\langle\boldsymbol{x}^2\rangle \,\langle\leq\rangle\, \langle\boldsymbol{x}^1\rangle \Leftrightarrow \forall \left[x_1^{2,j}, ..., x_h^{2,j}\right] \in \langle\boldsymbol{x}^2\rangle \,\exists\, \left[x_1^{1,i}, ..., x_h^{1,i}\right] \in \langle\boldsymbol{x}^1\rangle,$$

such that $\left[x_1^{2,j}, ..., x_h^{2,j}\right] \leqq \left[x_1^{1,i}, ..., x_h^{1,i}\right]$, $i = 1, ..., k_1$, $j = 1, ..., k_2$.

Let us observe that order relations $\langle\geq\rangle$ and $\langle\leq\rangle$ on $2^{\boldsymbol{R}^h}$ are independent in the sense that for all $\langle\boldsymbol{x}^1\rangle, \langle\boldsymbol{x}^2\rangle \in 2^{\boldsymbol{R}^h}$, $\langle\boldsymbol{x}^1\rangle \,\langle\geq\rangle\, \langle\boldsymbol{x}^2\rangle$ is not equivalent to $\langle\boldsymbol{x}^2\rangle \,\langle\leq\rangle\, \langle\boldsymbol{x}^1\rangle$. Consider, for example, the case where $h=2$, $\langle\boldsymbol{x}^1\rangle = \{[3,3]\}$ and $\langle\boldsymbol{x}^2\rangle = \{[1,2], [4,1]\}$; then $\langle\boldsymbol{x}^1\rangle \,\langle\geq\rangle\, \langle\boldsymbol{x}^2\rangle$ because for $[3,3]$ in $\langle\boldsymbol{x}^1\rangle$ there exists $[1,2]$ in $\langle\boldsymbol{x}^2\rangle$ such that $[3,3] \geqq [1,2]$, but $\langle\boldsymbol{x}^2\rangle \,\langle\leq\rangle\, \langle\boldsymbol{x}^1\rangle$ does not hold because for $[4,1]$ in $\langle\boldsymbol{x}^2\rangle$ there is no vector $\boldsymbol{x}^{1,i} \in \langle\boldsymbol{x}^1\rangle$ such that $[4,1] \leqq \boldsymbol{x}^{1,i}$ (in fact, $[4,1] \leqq [3,3]$ is not true).

We can define now an isomorphism between inclusion relation $\subseteq$ in the set of all upward mega-unions

$$\boldsymbol{Cl}^{\geq 2^{\Pi}} = \left\{ Cl_{\{[t_1(1),...,t_1(h)],...,[t_k(1),...,t_k(h)]\}}^{\geq}, \right.$$

$$\left. [t_1(1), ..., t_1(h)], ..., [t_k(1), ..., t_k(h)] \in \prod_{i=1}^{h} T_i \right\},$$

and order relation $\langle\geq\rangle$ in the power set of Cartesian product of class indices $2^{\prod_{i=1}^{h} T_i}$, expressed as follows: for each

$$\langle\boldsymbol{t}^1\rangle = \left\{ \left[t_1^1(1), ..., t_1^1(h)\right], ..., \left[t_{k_1}^1(1), ..., t_{k_1}^1(h)\right] \right\},$$

$$\langle\boldsymbol{t}^2\rangle = \left\{ \left[t_1^2(1), ..., t_1^2(h)\right], ..., \left[t_{k_2}^2(1), ..., t_{k_2}^2(h)\right] \right\} \in 2^{\prod_{i=1}^{h} T_i},$$

$$Cl_{\langle\boldsymbol{t}^1\rangle}^{\geq} \subseteq Cl_{\langle\boldsymbol{t}^2\rangle}^{\geq} \Leftrightarrow \langle\boldsymbol{t}^1\rangle \,\langle\geq\rangle\, \langle\boldsymbol{t}^2\rangle.$$

Observe that inclusion relation $\subseteq$ in $\boldsymbol{Cl}^{\geq 2^\Pi}$ is a partial preorder, i.e. it is reflexive and transitive.

An analogous isomorphism holds for inclusion relation $\subseteq$ on the set of all downward mega-unions

$$\boldsymbol{Cl}^{\leq 2^\Pi} = \Big\{ Cl^{\leq}_{\{[t_1(1),\dots,t_1(h)],\dots,[t_k(1),\dots,t_k(h)]\}} ,$$

$$[t_1(1),\dots,t_1(h)],\dots,[t_k(1),\dots,t_k(h)] \in \prod_{i=1}^{h} T_i \Big\},$$

and order relation $\langle\leq\rangle$ in the power set of Cartesian product of class indices $2^{\prod\limits_{i=1}^{h} T_i}$, expressed as follows: for each

$$\langle\boldsymbol{t}^1\rangle = \left\{ \left[t_1^1(1),\dots,t_1^1(h)\right],\dots,\left[t_{k_1}^1(1),\dots,t_{k_1}^1(h)\right] \right\},$$

$$\langle\boldsymbol{t}^2\rangle = \left\{ \left[t_1^2(1),\dots,t_1^2(h)\right],\dots,\left[t_{k_2}^2(1),\dots,t_{k_2}^2(h)\right] \right\} \in 2^{\prod\limits_{i=1}^{h} T_i},$$

$$Cl^{\leq}_{\langle\boldsymbol{t}^1\rangle} \subseteq Cl^{\leq}_{\langle\boldsymbol{t}^2\rangle} \Leftrightarrow \langle\boldsymbol{t}^1\rangle \,\langle\leq\rangle\, \langle\boldsymbol{t}^2\rangle.$$

Obviously, inclusion relation $\subseteq$ in $\boldsymbol{Cl}^{\leq 2^\Pi}$ is again a partial preorder, however, according to observation made above, $Cl^{\geq}_{\langle\boldsymbol{t}^1\rangle} \subseteq Cl^{\geq}_{\langle\boldsymbol{t}^2\rangle}$ is not equivalent to $Cl^{\leq}_{\langle\boldsymbol{t}^2\rangle} \subseteq Cl^{\leq}_{\langle\boldsymbol{t}^1\rangle}$.

The rough approximations defined within DRSA adapted to the presence of multiple decision makers satisfy all basic properties of classical rough approximations, e.g. for upward mega-unions: for all $P \subseteq R \subseteq C$ and for all $\langle\boldsymbol{t}\rangle \in 2^{\prod\limits_{i=1}^{h} T_i}$,

- rough inclusion: $\underline{P}\left(Cl^{\geq}_{\langle\boldsymbol{t}\rangle}\right) \subseteq Cl^{\geq}_{\langle\boldsymbol{t}\rangle} \subseteq \overline{P}\left(Cl^{\geq}_{\langle\boldsymbol{t}\rangle}\right)$,
- complementarity: $\underline{P}\left(Cl^{\geq}_{\langle\boldsymbol{t}\rangle}\right) = U - \overline{P}\left(Cl^{\leq}_{\langle\boldsymbol{t}'\rangle}\right)$, where $Cl^{\leq}_{\langle\boldsymbol{t}'\rangle} = U - Cl^{\geq}_{\langle\boldsymbol{t}\rangle}$,
- monotonicity: $\underline{P}\left(Cl^{\geq}_{\langle\boldsymbol{t}\rangle}\right) \subseteq \underline{R}\left(Cl^{\geq}_{\langle\boldsymbol{t}\rangle}\right)$, $\overline{P}\left(Cl^{\geq}_{\langle\boldsymbol{t}\rangle}\right) \supseteq \overline{R}\left(Cl^{\geq}_{\langle\boldsymbol{t}\rangle}\right)$.

5 Conclusions

We presented an extension of DRSA to the case of multiple decision makers. It required a new definition of dominance with respect to profiles of evaluations made by the multiple decision makers. The approach can be used to support decision of multiple decision makers because it permits to characterize conditions for reaching a consensus. These conditions are expressed in terms of decision rules. Premises of these rules are formulated in original multiple criteria evaluation space, and conclusions in the space of evaluations by multiple decision makers. Our approach differs from existing approaches to decision involving multiple decision makers, because we are not searching for concordant decision rules of multiple decision makers, considered as individuals (see [4]), but we rather characterize conditions for a consensus attainable by multiple decision makers considered as a whole. Such a perspective permits to handle interactions between decision makers.

Let us finally remark that the presented extension of DRSA can be used to solve a more general problem of data analysis, requiring rough approximation of partial preorders.

Acknowledgements. The research of the first two authors has been supported by the Italian Ministry of Education, University and Scientific Research (MIUR). The third author wishes to acknowledge financial support from the Polish Ministry of Science and Higher Education (grant no. 3T11F 02127).

References

1. S. Greco, B. Matarazzo, R. Słowiński (1999): The use of rough sets and fuzzy sets in MCDM, chapter 14 in: T. Gal, T. Hanne, T. Stewart (eds.), *Advances in Multiple Criteria Decision Making*, Kluwer Academic Publishers, Dordrecht, pp. 14.1-14.59.
2. S. Greco, B. Matarazzo, R. Słowiński (2001), Rough sets theory for multicriteria decision analysis, *European Journal of Operational Research*, 129, 1, 1-47.
3. S. Greco, B. Matarazzo, R. Słowiński (2005): Decision rule approach, chapter 13 in: J. Figueira, S. Greco, M. Ehrgott (eds.), *Multiple Criteria Decision Analysis, State of the art Surveys*, Springer-Verlag, pp. 507-561.
4. M. Inuiguchi, T. Miyajima (2006): Rough set based rule induction from two decision tables. *European Journal of Operational Research* (to appear).
5. T. Jelassi, G.E. Kersten, S. Zionts (1990): An introduction to group decision and negotiation support, in: C. Bana e Costa (ed.), *Readings in Multiple Criteria Decision Aid*, Springer Verlag, Heidelberg, pp. 537-568.
6. H. Nurmi, J. Kacprzyk, M. Fedrizzi (1996): Probabilistic, fuzzy and rough concepts in social choice. *European Journal of Operational Research*, 95, 2, 264-277.
7. Z. Pawlak (1990): *Rough Sets. Theoretical Aspects of Reasoning about Data*, Kluwer Academic Publishers, Dordrecht.
8. R. Słowiński, S. Greco, B. Matarazzo (2005): Rough set based decision support, chapter 16 in: E.K. Burke and G. Kendall (eds.), *Search Methodologies: Introductory Tutorials in Optimization and Decision Support Techniques*, Springer-Verlag, New York, pp. 475-527.

Quality of Rough Approximation in Multi-criteria Classification Problems

Krzysztof Dembczyński[1], Salvatore Greco[2], Wojciech Kotłowski[1],
and Roman Słowiński[1,3]

[1] Institute of Computing Science, Poznań University of Technology,
60-965 Poznań, Poland
{kdembczynski, wkotlowski, rslowinski}@cs.put.poznan.pl
[2] Faculty of Economics, University of Catania, 95129 Catania, Italy
salgreco@unict.it
[3] Institute for Systems Research, Polish Academy of Sciences, 01-447 Warsaw, Poland

Abstract. Dominance-based Rough Set Approach (DRSA) has been proposed to deal with multi-criteria classification problems, where data may be inconsistent with respect to the dominance principle. In this paper, we consider different measures of the quality of approximation, which is the value indicating how much inconsistent the decision table is. We begin with the classical definition, based on the relative number of inconsistent objects. Since this measure appears to be too restrictive in some cases, a new approach based on the concept of generalized decision is proposed. Finally, motivated by emerging problems in the presence of noisy data, the third measure based on the object reassignment is introduced. Properties of these measures are analysed in light of rough set theory.

1   Introduction

The multi-criteria classification problem consists in assignment of objects from a set A to pre-defined *decision classes* Cl_t, $t \in T = \{1, \ldots, n\}$. It is assumed that the classes are preference-ordered according to an increasing order of class indices, i.e. for all $r, s \in T$, such that $r > s$, the objects from Cl_r are strictly preferred to the objects from Cl_s. The objects are evaluated on a set of *condition criteria* (i.e., attributes with preference-ordered domains). It is assumed that there exists a semantic correlation between evaluation of objects on criteria and their assignment to decision classes, i.e. a better evaluation of an object on a criterion with other evaluations being fixed should not worsen its assignment to a decision class.

In order to support multi-criteria classification, one must construct a preference model of the Decision Maker (DM). The construction of the preference model requires some *preference information* from the DM. One possible way is to induce the preference model from a set of exemplary decisions (assignments of objects to decision classes) made on a set of selected objects called *reference objects*. The reference objects are those relatively well-known to the DM who

S. Greco et al. (Eds.): RSCTC 2006, LNAI 4259, pp. 318–327, 2006.

is able to assign them to pre-defined classes. In other words, the preference information comes from observation of DM's acts (comprehensive decisions). It is concordant with a paradigm of artificial intelligence and, in particular, of inductive learning. Moreover, the induced model can be represented in intelligible way, for example as a set of decision rules.

The reference objects and their evaluations and assignments are often presented in a *decision table* $S = \langle U, C, D \rangle$, where $U \subseteq A$ is a finite, non-empty set of reference objects, C is a set of condition criteria, and D is a set of decision criteria that contain information on assignment of objects to decision classes. D is often a singleton ($D = \{d\}$), where d is shortly called *decision*. C and D are disjoint, finite and non-empty sets that jointly constitute a set of all criteria Q. It is assumed, without loss of generality, that the domain of each criterion $q \in Q$, denoted by V_q, is numerically coded with an increasing order of preference. The domains of criteria may correspond to cardinal or ordinal scales, however, we are exploiting the ordinal information (the weakest) only, whatever is the scale. The domain of decision d is a finite set ($T = \{1, \ldots, n\}$) due to a finite number of decision classes. Evaluations and assignments of objects on any criterion ($q \in Q$) are defined by an *information function* $f(x, q)$, $f : U \times Q \to V$, where $V = \bigcup_{q \in Q} V_q$.

There is, however, a problem with inconsistency often present in the set of decision examples. Two decision examples are inconsistent with respect to, so-called, *dominance principle*, if there exists an object not worse than another object on all considered criteria, however, it has been assigned to a worse decision class than the other. To deal with these inconsistencies, it has been proposed to construct the preference model in the form of a set of decision rules, after adapting rough set theory [7,8,9] to preference ordered data. Such an adaptation has been made by Greco, Matarazzo and Słowiński [4,5,6]; it consists in substituting the classical indiscernibility relation by a dominance relation, which permits taking into account the preference order in domains (scales) of criteria. The extended rough set approach is called Dominance-based Rough Set Approach (DRSA) - a complete overview of this methodology is presented in [10].

Using the rough set approach to the analysis of preference information, we obtain the lower and the upper (rough) approximations of unions of decision classes. The difference between upper and lower approximations shows inconsistent objects with respect to the dominance principle. The rough approximations are then used in induction of decision rules representing, respectively, certain and possible patterns of DM's preferences. The preference model in the form of decision rules explains a decision policy of the DM and permits to classify new objects in line of the DM's preferences.

The ratio of the cardinality of all consistent objects to the cardinality of all reference objects is called quality of approximation. This ratio is very restrictive, because in the extreme case, if there existed one object having better evaluations on condition criteria than all the other objects from U and if it was assigned to the worst class being a singleton, this ratio would decrease to 0. In the paper, we consider two other measures of the quality of approximation. The first, based on the generalized decision, is more resistant to local inconsistencies, but still in the extreme case described above, its value would decrease to 0. The second, motivated by emerging problems in the presence of noisy data, is free of this disadvantage and is resistant to local inconsistencies. Its definition is based on the concept of object reassignment. All these measures are monotonically non-decreasing with the number of condition criteria considered.

The article is organized in the following way. Section 2 describes main elements of Dominance-based Rough Set Approach. Section 3 describes the classical ratio of quality of approximation and the ratio based on generalized decision. In Section 4, the third measure and its properties are presented. The last section concludes the paper.

2   Dominance-Based Rough Set Approach

Within DRSA, the notions of *weak preference* (or *outranking*) relation $\succeq_q$ and P-dominance relation D_P are defined as follows. For any $x, y \in U$ and $q \in Q$, $x \succeq_q y$ means that x is at least as good as (*is weakly preferred to*) y with respect to criterion q. With respect to assumptions taken in the previous section, it is $x \succeq_q y \Leftrightarrow f(x, q) \geq f(y, q)$. Moreover, taking into account more than one criterion, we say that x dominates y with respect to $P \subseteq Q$ (shortly x P-dominates y), if $x \succeq_q y$ for all $q \in P$. The weak preference relation $\succeq_q$ is supposed to be a complete pre-order and, therefore, the P-dominance relation D_P, being the intersection of complete pre-orders $\succeq_q$, $q \in P$, is a partial pre-order in the set of reference objects. The dominance principle can be expressed as follows, for $x, y \in U$, and $P \subseteq C$:

$$xD_Py \Rightarrow xD_{\{d\}}y, \text{ i.e.,} \quad (\forall_{q \in P} \ f(x, q) \geq f(y, q)) \Rightarrow f(x, d) \geq f(y, d). \quad (1)$$

The rough approximations concern granules resulting from information carried out by the decision criterion. The approximation is made using granules resulting from information carried out by condition criteria. These granules are called *decision* and *condition* granules, respectively. The decision granules can be expressed by unions of decision classes:

$$Cl_t^{\geq} = \{y \in U : f(y, d) \geq t\} \quad (2)$$
$$Cl_t^{\leq} = \{y \in U : f(y, d) \leq t\}. \quad (3)$$

The condition granules are P-dominating and P-dominated sets defined, respectively, as:

$$D_P^+(x) = \{y \in U : yD_Px\} \quad (4)$$
$$D_P^-(x) = \{y \in U : xD_Py\}. \quad (5)$$

Let us remark that both decision and condition granules are cones in decision and condition spaces, respectively. The origin of a decision cone is a class index $t \in T$, while the origin of a condition cone is an object $x \in U$. The dominating cones are open towards increasing preferences, and the dominated cones are open towards decreasing preferences.

P-lower dominance-based rough approximations of $Cl_t^{\geq}$ and $Cl_t^{\leq}$ are defined for $P \subseteq C$ and $t \in T$, respectively, as follows:

$$\underline{P}(Cl_t^{\geq}) = \{x \in U : D_P^+(x) \subseteq Cl_t^{\geq}\}, \tag{6}$$

$$\underline{P}(Cl_t^{\leq}) = \{x \in U : D_P^-(x) \subseteq Cl_t^{\leq}\}. \tag{7}$$

P-upper dominance-based rough approximations of $Cl_t^{\geq}$ and $Cl_t^{\leq}$ are defined for $P \subseteq C$ and $t \in T$, respectively, as follows:

$$\overline{P}(Cl_t^{\geq}) = \{x \in U : D_P^-(x) \cap Cl_t^{\geq} \neq \emptyset\}, \tag{8}$$

$$\overline{P}(Cl_t^{\leq}) = \{x \in U : D_P^+(x) \cap Cl_t^{\leq} \neq \emptyset\}, \tag{9}$$

Consider the following definition of P-generalized decision for object $x \in U$:

$$\delta_P(x) = \langle l_P(x), u_P(x) \rangle, \text{ where,} \tag{10}$$

$$l_P(x) = \min\{f(y,d) : y D_P x, y \in U\}, \tag{11}$$

$$u_P(x) = \max\{f(y,d) : x D_P y, y \in U\}. \tag{12}$$

In other words, the P-generalized decision reflects an interval of decision classes to which an object may belong due to inconsistencies with the dominance principle caused by this object. $l_P(x)$ is the lowest decision class, to which belong an object P-dominating x; $u_P(x)$ is the highest decision class, to which belong an object P-dominated by x. Obviously, $l_P(x) \leq u_P(x)$ for every $P \subseteq C$, $x \in U$ and if $l_P(x) = u_P(x)$, then object x is consistent with respect to the dominance principle in the decision table.

Let us remark that the dominance-based rough approximations may be expressed using P-generalized decision:

$$\underline{P}(Cl_t^{\geq}) = \{x \in U : l_P(x) \geq t\}, \tag{13}$$

$$\overline{P}(Cl_t^{\geq}) = \{x \in U : u_P(x) \geq t\}, \tag{14}$$

$$\underline{P}(Cl_t^{\leq}) = \{x \in U : u_P(x) \leq t\}, \tag{15}$$

$$\overline{P}(Cl_t^{\leq}) = \{x \in U : l_P(x) \leq t\}. \tag{16}$$

The lower and the upper rough approximations are then used in induction of decision rules representing, respectively, certain and possible patterns of DM's preferences. These rules are used in classification of new objects. In general, a new object is covered by several rules indicating rough approximations of upward and downward unions of decision classes. Intersection of the outputs of the rules gives an interval of decision classes to which an object is assigned. In many cases the object is assigned to only one class resulting from the intersection of the matching rules.

3 Quality of Approximation

Let us begin with very restrictive definition of the quality of approximation. The quality of approximation is defined as a ratio of the number of objects from the decision table that are consistent with respect to the dominance principle, to the number of all objects from this decision table. A set of consistent objects can be defined in the following way, for any $P \subseteq C$:

$$\{x \in U : u_P(x) = l_P(x)\}. \tag{17}$$

The same may be expressed, equivalently, by:

$$\bigcup_{t \in T}\{x \in U : D_P^-(x) \subseteq Cl_t^{\leq} \wedge D_P^+(x) \subseteq Cl_t^{\geq}\} =$$
$$= U - \left(\bigcup_{t \in T} Bn_P^{\geq t}\right) = U - \left(\bigcup_{t \in T} Bn_P^{\leq t}\right),$$

where $Bn_P^{\geq t} = \overline{P}(Cl_t^{\geq}) - \underline{P}(Cl_t^{\geq})$, and $Bn_P^{\leq t} = \overline{P}(Cl_t^{\leq}) - \underline{P}(Cl_t^{\leq})$, are, so-called, *boundary regions*.

The *quality of approximation* can be defined as:

$$\gamma(P) = \frac{card\left(\{x \in U : u_P(x) = l_P(x)\}\right)}{card\,(U)}. \tag{18}$$

This definition is very restrictive, because in the extreme case, if there existed one object dominating all the other objects from U while being assigned to the lowest possible class, and if the lowest possible class was a singleton including this object, $\gamma(P)$ would decrease to 0, even if the other objects from U were perfectly consistent. It is not true, however, that $\gamma(P)$ does not count the relative number of objects which can be captured by deterministic rules (i.e., induced from the lower approximations of unions of decision classes), what was pointed by Düntsch and Gediga in [3]. This is in fact, the relative number of objects that are covered by these rules in the following way. When deterministic rules induced from lower approximations of upward and downward unions of decision classes are applied to an object, then the object is assigned by these rules to an interval of decision classes to which it may belong. For a consistent object this interval boils down to a single class. The relative number of these objects is just shown by $\gamma(P)$.

It is easy to show that, for any $P \subseteq R \subseteq C$, there holds:

$$\gamma(P) \leq \gamma(R). \tag{19}$$

In other words, $\gamma(P)$ possesses a monotonicity property well-known in rough set theory.

An improved ratio of the quality of approximation can be based on P-generalized decision. The *quality of approximation based on P-generalized decision* is defined as:

$$\eta(P) = 1 - \frac{\sum_{x \in U}(u_P(x) - l_P(x))}{(n-1) \cdot card(U)}, \tag{20}$$

where n is the number of decision classes, and it is assumed that the domain of decision criterion is numbercoded and class indices are consecutive.

It is easy to see that $\eta(P) \in [0,1]$. The ratio expresses an average relative width of P-generalized decisions of reference objects. It is resistant to local inconsistencies, i.e. inconsistencies appearing between objects with similar evaluations and assignments. In fact, this ratio is equivalent to the formulation given by Düntsch and Gediga [3], however, differently motivated.

Theorem 1. *$\eta(P)$ is equivalent to the quality of approximation*

$$\gamma_{OO}(P) = \frac{\sum_{t=2}^{n} card(\underline{P}(Cl_t^{\geq})) + \sum_{t=1}^{n-1} card(\underline{P}(Cl_t^{\leq}))}{\sum_{t=2}^{n} card(Cl_t^{\geq}) + \sum_{t=1}^{n-1} card(Cl_t^{\leq})}, \tag{21}$$

defined in [3].

Proof. Taking into account that $U = Cl_t^{\geq} + Cl_{t-1}^{\leq}$, $t = 2, \ldots, n$, $\gamma_{OO}(P)$ may be expressed as follows:

$$\gamma_{OO}(P) = \frac{\sum_{t=2}^{n}(card(\underline{P}(Cl_t^{\geq})) + card(\underline{P}(Cl_{t-1}^{\leq})))}{(n-1) \cdot card(U)}. \tag{22}$$

Further, we have:

$$\gamma_{OO}(P) = \frac{\sum_{t=2}^{n} \left(card(\{x \in U : l_P(x) \geq t\}) + card(\{x \in U : u_P(x) \leq t-1\})\right)}{(n-1) \cdot card(U)}$$

$$= \frac{\sum_{x \in U} (l_P(x) - 1 + n - u_P(x))}{(n-1) \cdot card(U)} = \frac{\sum_{x \in U} ((n-1) - (u_P(x) - l_P(x)))}{(n-1) \cdot card(U)}$$

$$= \frac{(n-1) \cdot card(U) - \sum_{x \in U} (u_P(x) - l_P(x))}{(n-1) \cdot card(U)} = 1 - \frac{\sum_{x \in U} (u_P(x) - l_P(x))}{(n-1) \cdot card(U)} \qquad \square$$

An interesting interpretation of (22) is that this ratio is also the average of the quality of approximations for $n-1$ binary classification problems for consecutive unions of decision classes ($Cl_1^{\leq}$ against $Cl_2^{\geq}$, $Cl_2^{\leq}$ against $Cl_3^{\geq}$, ..., $Cl_{n-1}^{\leq}$ against $Cl_n^{\geq}$).

It is easy to see that for any $P \subseteq R \subseteq C$, there holds:

$$\eta(P) \leq \eta(R).$$

4   Quality of Approximation Based on Reassignment of Objects

The measures of approximation described above were based on the notions of lower and upper approximations of the unions of classes. The common idea behind these definitions was the fact that a decision interval for a given object $x \in U$ is calculated taking into account all the other objects from U, dominating or being dominated by x. The problem is that it is enough to introduce one more object dominating x, with the class assignment lower than x (alternatively, being dominated by x, with higher class assignment) to enlarge the decision interval, thus lowering the measures of approximation.

The key idea of the new measure is the following. The *quality of approximation based on reassignment of objects* is the minimal number of objects in U that must be reassigned to make the reference objects from U consistent, i.e. satisfying the dominance principle (1). Formally, it is defined as:

$$\zeta(P) = \frac{m - L}{m} \tag{23}$$

where L is the minimal number of objects from U that have to be reassigned consistently and $m = card(U)$. It is easy to see that $\zeta(P) \in [0, 1]$, but one can give tighter lower bound: $\zeta(P) \geq \frac{m_{\max}}{m}$, where $m_{\max}$ is the number of objects belonging to the largest class. Notice that $\zeta(P) = 1$ iff set U is consistent for $P \subseteq C$.

To compute L one can formulate a linear programming problem. Similar problem was considered in [1] in the context of specific binary classification that has much in common with multi-criteria classification. The method presented in [1] is called *isotonic separation*. Here we formulate more general problem, used for different goal (measuring the quality of approximation), however the idea behind the algorithm for finding the optimal solution remains similar.

To formulate the problem in a linear form, for each object x_i, $i \in \{1, \ldots, m\}$, we introduce $n - 1$ binary variables d_{it}, $t \in \{1, \ldots, n\}$, with the following interpretation: $d_{it} = 1$ iff object $x_i \in Cl_t^{\geq}$. Such interpretation implies the following conditions:

$$\text{if } t' > t \text{ then } d_{it'} \leq d_{it} \tag{24}$$

for all $i \in \{1, \ldots m\}$ (otherwise it would be possible that there exists object x_i belonging to the $Cl_{t'}^{\geq}$, but not belonging to $Cl_t^{\geq}$, where $t' > t$). Moreover, we give a new value of decision f_i^* to object x_i according to the rule: $f_i^* = \max_{d_{it}=1}\{t\}$ (the highest t, for which we know that x_i belongs to $Cl_t^{\geq}$).

Then, for each object $x_i \in U$ with the initial class assignment $f_i = f(x_i, d)$, the cost function can be formulated as below:

$$L(x_i) = (1 - d_{i,f_i}) + d_{i,f_i+1} \tag{25}$$

Indeed, for $t = f_i + 1$, $d_{it} = 1$ means wrong assignment (to the class higher than f_i). For $t = f_i$, $d_{it} = 0$ means also wrong assignment, to the class lower than f_i. Moreover, according to (24), only one of those conditions can appear at the same time and one of those conditions is necessary for x_i to be wrongly assigned. Thus the value of decision for x_i changes iff $L(x_i) = 1$.

According to (1), the following conditions must be satisfied for U to be consistent:

$$d_{it} \geq d_{jt} \qquad \forall i, j: x_i D_P x_j \quad 1 \leq t \leq n \tag{26}$$

Finally we can formulate the problem in terms of integer linear programming:

$$\text{minimize} \quad L = \sum_{i=1}^{m} L(x_i) = \sum_{i=1}^{m} (1 - d_{i,f_i} + d_{i,f_i+1})) \tag{27}$$

$$\text{subject to} \quad d_{it'} \leq d_{it} \quad 1 \leq i \leq m, \quad 1 \leq t < t' \leq n$$
$$d_{it} \geq d_{jt} \quad 1 \leq i, j \leq m, \quad x_i D_P x_j, \quad 1 \leq t \leq n$$
$$d_{it} \in \{0, 1\} \quad 1 \leq i \leq m, \quad 1 \leq t \leq n$$

The matrix of constraints in this case is totally unimodular, because it contains in each row either two values 1 and -1 or one value 1, and the right hand sides of the constraints are integer. Thus, we can relax the integer condition:

$$0 \leq d_{it} \leq 1 \quad 1 \leq i \leq m, \quad 1 \leq t \leq n \tag{28}$$

and get a linear programming problem. This property was previously applied in isotonic separation method for two class problems [1]. In this paper, the authors give also a way for further reduction of the problem size. Here we prove a more general result using the language of DRSA.

Theorem 2. *There always exists an optimal solution of (27), $f_i^* = \max_{d_{it}=1}\{t\}$, for which the following condition holds: $l_P(x_i) \leq f_i^* \leq u_P(x_i)$, $1 \leq i \leq m$.*

Proof. First, notice that all the constraints in (27) are equivalent to introducing a new (optimal) class assignment variable $f_i^* = \max_{d_{it}=1}\{t\}$ and constraints $f_i^* \geq f_j^*$ for all x_i, x_j such that $x_i D_P x_j$.

Now, assume we have an optimal solution f_i^*, $i \in \{1, \ldots, m\}$. Assume also, that for some $I \subseteq \{1, \ldots, m\}$, $f_i^* < l_P(x_i)$, $i \in I$, and for some $J \subseteq \{1, \ldots, m\}$, $f_i^* > u_P(x_i)$, $j \in J$, holds. The solution can be modified to obtain new solution $f_i^{**} = l_P(x_i)$ for $i \in I$, $f_i^{**} = u_P(x_i)$ for $i \in J$ and $f_i^{**} = f_i^*$, $i \notin I \cup J$, which will not have higher cost than f^*. We will prove that the new solution f^{**} is also feasible (i.e. satisfies all the constraints), therefore, being optimal solution of the problem (27).

Thus, we must prove that for each $x_i, x_j \in U$, the following condition holds:

$$x_i D_P x_j \Rightarrow f_i^{**} \geq f_j^{**} \tag{29}$$

The proof consist of three parts. First, we consider object x_i, where $i \in I$. Then, we take into account $i \in J$. Finally, we check the consistency for $i \notin I \cup J$.

First, notice that for all $i \in I$, $f_i^{**} > f_i^*$, and for all $i \in J$, $f_i^{**} < f_i^*$.

Consider $i \in I$. Then, (29) holds for all $j \in \{1, \ldots, m\}$, since if $j \in I$, then $f_i^{**} = l_P(x_i)$, $f_j^{**} = l_P(x_j)$, and according to the definition of $l_P(x)$ it holds that $l_P(x_i) \geq l_P(x_j)$ for $x_i D_P x_j$. If $j \notin I$, then $f_i^{**} > f_i^* \geq f_j^* \geq f_j^{**}$.

Now, consider $i \in J$. Then, (29) holds for all $j \in \{1, \ldots, m\}$, since $f_i^{**} = u_P(x_i)$, $f_j^{**} \leq u_P(x_j)$, and according to the definition of $u_P(x)$, it holds that $u_P(x_i) \geq u_P(x_j)$ for $x_i D_P x_j$, so $f_i^{**} = u_P(x_i) \geq u_P(x_j) \geq f_j^{**}$.

Finally, consider $i \notin I \cup J$. Then, (29) holds for all $j \in \{1, \ldots, m\}$, since if $j \in I$, then $f_i^{**} \geq l_P(x_i) \geq l_P(x_j) = f_j^{**}$. If $j \notin I$, then $f_i^{**} = f_i^* \geq f_j^* = f_j^{**}$. Thus, we proved the theorem. $\qquad\square$

Theorem 2 enables a strong reduction of the number of variables. For each object x_i, variables d_{it} can be set to 1 for $t \leq l_P(x_i)$, and to 0 for $t > u_P(x_i)$, since

Table 1. Example of decision table; q_1, q_2 are criteria, d is decision criterion

U	q_1	q_2	d	U	q_1	q_2	d
x_1	23	48	4	x_7	16	10	1
x_2	44	48	4	x_8	20	30	2
x_3	45	44	2	x_9	6	14	1
x_4	26	28	3	x_{10}	9	16	1
x_5	30	26	3	x_{11}	5	9	2
x_6	24	33	3	x_{12}	15	11	1

there exists an optimal solution with such values of the variables. In particular, if an object x is consistent (i.e. $l_P(x) = u_P(x)$), the class assignment for this object remains the same.

The introduced ratio of the quality of approximation $\zeta(P)$ satisfies also the monotonicity property, as stated by the following theorem.

Theorem 3. *For any $P \subseteq R \subseteq C$, it holds:*

$$\zeta(P) \leq \zeta(R)$$

Proof. It results from the fact that for any $P \subseteq R \subseteq C$ and any $x, y \in U$, $x D_{RY} \Rightarrow x D_P y$. Thus, any constraint in the optimization problem (27) for set R must also appear in the optimization problem for set P, so the feasible region (set of solutions satisfying all the constraints) for R includes the feasible region for P. Thus, the minimum of L for R cannot be greater than the minimum of L for P. $\qquad\square$

Finally, we should notice that the measure $\zeta(P)$ is more robust to the noise than $\gamma(P)$ and $\eta(P)$. Randomly changing an assignment of an object in the decision table will not change $\zeta(P)$ by more than $\frac{1}{m}$.

In Table 1, there is an example of decision table. If we consider set $U_1 = \{x_1, x_2, x_3, x_4, x_5, x_6\}$ with classes $\{Cl_2, Cl_3, Cl_4\}$ then we have $\gamma(P) = \frac{1}{3}$, $\eta(P) = \frac{2}{3}$, $\zeta(P) = \frac{5}{6}$. However, for the set $U_2 = \{x_7, x_8, x_9, x_{10}, x_{11}, x_{12}\}$ and classes $\{Cl_1, Cl_2\}$ we have $\gamma(P) = \frac{1}{6}$, $\eta(P) = \frac{1}{6}$, but $\zeta(P) = \frac{5}{6}$. Taking into account the whole decision table $U = U_1 \cup U_2$, we obtain $\gamma(P) = \frac{1}{4}$, $\eta(P) = \frac{3}{4}$, $\zeta(P) = \frac{5}{6}$.

5   Conclusions

The paper discusses different measures of the quality of approximation in the multi-criteria classification problem. There seems to be no one best way of calculating such a coefficient from the dataset. However, each measure can be characterized by showing its advantages and drawbacks. The classical measure is simple and intuitively clear, however, for real-life data it might be too restrictive in use. The second one, based on the generalized decision concept, measures the width of decision ranges, thus allowing some local inconsistencies with small decrease of quality of approximation. However, both may boil down to 0 only because of one object being maximally inconsistent with the rest of reference objects. The third measure based on the objects reassignment, is more robust to noise, unfortunately the coefficient cannot be given explicitly, but has to be found in result of solving an optimization problem. All the proposed measures satisfy the monotonicity property typical for rough set theory.

Acknowledgements. The first, the third and the fourth author wish to acknowledge financial support from the Ministry of Education and Science (grant no. 3T11F 02127). The research of the second author has been supported by Italian Ministry of Education, University and Scientific Research (MIUR).

References

1. Chandrasekaran, R., Ryu, Y. U., Jacob, V., Hong, S.: Isotonic separation. IN-FORMS J. Comput. **17** (2005) 462–474
2. Dembczyński, K., Greco, S., Słowiński, R.: Second-order Rough Approximations in Multi-criteria Classification with Imprecise Evaluations and Assignments, LNAI, **3641** (2005) 54–63
3. Düntsch, I., Gediga, G.: Approximation quality for sorting rules. Computational Statistics & Data Analysis, **40** 3 (2002) 499–526
4. Greco S., Matarazzo, B., Słowiński, R.: Rough approximation of a preference relation by dominance relations. European Journal of Operational Research, **117** (1999) 63–83
5. Greco S., Matarazzo, B., Słowiński, R.: Rough sets theory for multicriteria decision analysis. European Journal of Operational Research, **129** 1 (2001) 1–47
6. Greco S., Matarazzo, B., Słowiński, R.: Rough sets methodology for sorting problems in presence of multiple attributes and criteria. European Journal of Operational Research, **238** (2002) 247–259
7. Pawlak, Z.: Rough sets. International Journal of Information & Computer Sciences, **11** (1982) 341–356
8. Pawlak, Z., Rough Sets. Theoretical Aspects of Reasoning about Data. Kluwer Academic Publishers, Dordrecht (1991)
9. Polkowski, L.: Rough Sets: Mathematical Foundations. Physica-Verlag, Heidelberg (2002)
10. Słowiński, R., Greco S., Matarazzo, B.: Rough Set Based Decision Support. Chapter 16 [in]: Burke, E., Kendall, G. (eds.): Introductory Tutorials on Optimization, Search and Decision Support Methodologies. Springer-Verlag, Boston (2005)

Rough-Set Multiple-Criteria ABC Analysis

Ye Chen[1], Kevin W. Li[2], Jason Levy[3], Keith W. Hipel[1], and D. Marc Kilgour[4]

[1] Department of Systems Design Engineering, University of Waterloo, Waterloo,
Ontario, N2L 3G1, Canada
`y3chen@uwaterloo.ca, kwhipel@uwaterloo.ca`
[2] Odette School of Business, University of Windsor, Windsor, Ontario, N9B 3P4,
Canada
`kwli@uwindsor.ca`
[3] Department of Applied Disaster and Emergency Studies, Brandon University,
Brandon, Manitoba, R7A 6A9, Canada
`Levyj@brandonu.ca`
[4] Department of Mathematics, Wilfrid Laurier University, Waterloo, Ontario,
N2L 3C5, Canada
`mkilgour@wlu.ca`

Abstract. Multiple-criteria ABC (MCABC) analysis is conducted using a dominance-based rough set approach. ABC analysis, a well-known technique for inventory planning and control, divides stock-keeping units (SKUs) into three classes according to annual dollar usage. But MCABC analysis offers more managerial flexibility by including other criteria, such as lead time and criticality, in the classification of SKUs. The objective of this paper is to propose an MCABC method that uses the dominance-based rough set approach to generate linguistic rules that represent a decision-maker's preferences based on the classification of a test data set. These linguistic rules are then used to classify all SKUs. A case study demonstrates that the procedure is feasible.

1   Introduction

In response to demands for mass customization, firms tend to increase inventories of components, work-in-progress, and spare parts [18]. The different items in an inventory system, referred to as stock-keeping units (SKUs), typically number in the thousands. Corner convenience stores, for instance, often have several thousand SKUs. In such a large inventory system, specific control schemes for individual SKUs are simply not practical, as they would leave no resources for other management activities [4]. Instead, a general practice in industry is to aggregate SKUs into several groups and apply control policies that are uniform across each group [1].

One commonly used approach to classifying SKUs is ABC analysis. In the traditional ABC analysis, SKUs are ranked in descending order of annual dollar usage, the product of unit price and annual demand. The top few SKUs, with the highest annual dollar usage, are placed in group A, which will receive the most management attention; the SKUs with least annual dollar usage are placed

S. Greco et al. (Eds.): RSCTC 2006, LNAI 4259, pp. 328–337, 2006.

in group C and will receive the least management attention; and the remaining SKUs are placed in group B. Traditional ABC analysis can be seen as an implementation of Pareto's famous observation about the uneven distribution of national wealth [12]: the majority of national wealth is controlled by a few, and the majority of the population controls only a small portion of the wealth. Applications similar to ABC analysis are found in many managerial areas [19]; for instance, in marketing it is often observed that the majority of sales come from a few important customers, while a significant proportion of total sales is due to a large number of very small customers.

Classical ABC analysis has been criticized because of the amount of attention management pays to an SKU depends on only one criterion, the annual dollar usage of the SKU at the time of classification, [8]. However, other attributes of an SKU should sometimes play a significant role in prioritization. For instance, suppose that two SKUs are virtually identical except that one is easy to replace while the other is unique and has only one specific supplier. Surely the SKU with higher substitutability should receive less management attention. Other criteria that could be accounted for include obsolescence, reparability, criticality, and lead time [6], [7]. To carry out multiple criteria classification of SKUs, a variety of approaches has been proposed, including a bi-criteria matrix approach [6], [7], the analytic hierarchical process (AHP) [8], [14], artificial neural networks [13], and a case-based distance model [2]. This article shows how rough sets can be applied to multiple-criteria ABC analysis (MCABC). Specifically, the dominance approach, a recent advance in rough set theory [9], can extract information about a decision-maker's preferences from the classification of test data and generate a set of decision rules to classify other SKUs consistently.

The rest of the paper is organized as follows. Section 2 provides background pertaining to multiple criteria decision analysis, while Section 3 describes the rough set approach to MCABC. An illustrative example is furnished in Section 4, followed by some concluding remarks in Section 5.

2   Multiple Criteria Decision Analysis

Multiple criteria decision analysis (MCDA) is a set of techniques to assist a single decision maker (DM) to *choose*, *rank*, or *sort* a finite set of alternatives according to two or more criteria [16]. The first step of MCDA is to establish the basic structure of the decision problem: define the objectives, arrange them into criteria, identify all possible alternatives, and measure the consequences of each alternative on each criterion. A consequence is a direct measurement of the success of an alternative against a criterion (e.g. cost in dollars). Note that a consequence is usually a physical measurement or estimate; it should not include preferential information.

Figure 1 shows the basic structure of an MCDA problem. In this figure, $\mathbf{N} = \{N^1, N^2, \cdots, N^i, \cdots, N^n\}$ is the set of alternatives, and $\mathbf{Q} = \{1, 2, \cdots, j, \cdots, q\}$ is the set of criteria. The consequence of alternative N^i over criterion j is denoted $c_j(N^i)$, which can be shortened to c_j^i when there is no possibility of confusion. Note that there are $n > 1$ alternatives and $q > 1$ criteria.

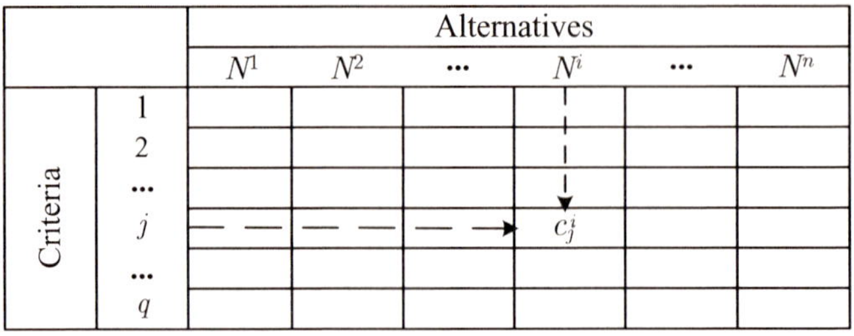

		Alternatives					
		N^1	N^2	...	N^i	...	N^n
Criteria	1						
	2						
	...						
	j				c^i_j		
	...						
	q						

Fig. 1. The structure of MCDA, adapted from [3]

There are several approaches that a DM may take to the decision structure represented by Figure 1. Roy [16] suggested that MCDA can be organized into three **problématiques**, or fundamental problems, as follows:

- α, **Choice problématique.** Choose the best alternative from **N**.
- β, **Sorting problématique.** Sort the alternatives of **N** into predefined, relatively homogeneous groups, arranged in preference order.
- γ, **Ranking problématique.** Rank the alternatives of **N** from best to worst.

MCABC is a special kind of sorting problématique: the alternatives are SKUs, and they are to be arranged into three groups, **A**, **B** or **C**. The preference order **A** $\succ$ **B** $\succ$ **C** signifies that an SKU in **A** is to receive more management attention than an SKU in **B**, for instance. It is understood that SKUs in the same group are to receive equal management attention, in this sense, they are indifferent.

The DM's preferences are crucial to the solution of any MCDA problem; moreover, different ways of expressing them may lead to different results. Pareto-Superiority [12] may be used to identify some inferior alternatives, but almost always a more elaborate preference construction is needed to carry out any of the problématiques. Generally speaking, there are two kinds of preference expressions: *values*, which are preferences on consequences, and *weights*, which are preferences on criteria.

After the structure of an MCDA problem has been determined and the DM's preferences acquired, a model must be constructed that aggregates preferences and thereby permits the chosen problématique to be implemented. Some methods, such as multiattribute utility theory (MAUT) [11], are explicit models which can be analyzed directly; others, including Outranking methods [16], allow analyses to be based in part on explicit functions; still others, such as rough set theory [9], address the problem using implicit linguistic rules.

3   A Rough Set Approach to MCABC

Pawlak [15] introduced Rough Sets as a tool to describe dependencies among attributes and to evaluate the significance of individual attributes. Because of its ability to handle the inherent uncertainty or vagueness of data, rough set theory complements probability theory, evidence theory, fuzzy set theory, and other approaches. Recent advances in rough set theory have made it a powerful tool for data mining, pattern recognition, and information representation.

An important principle of rough sets is that all relevant information about alternatives, which may include both condition and decision attributes, can be expressed in a data set [15]. Condition attributes refer to the characteristics of the alternatives; for instance, condition attributes describing a firm can include size, financial characteristics (profitability, solvency, liquidity ratios), market position, and so on. Decision attributes define a partition of the alternatives into groups reflecting the condition attributes in some way. In terms of MCDA, condition and decision attributes are regarded as criteria and decision choices, respectively.

3.1   A Dominance-Based Rough Set Theory for MCABC

As pointed out in [9], the original rough set approach cannot efficiently extract knowledge from the analysis of a case set. In MCDA problems, preferences over groups and indiscernibility or similarity must be replaced by the *dominance* relation.

To apply rough set theory to MCABC, we treat SKUs as alternatives and relevant data about SKUs as criteria (conditions). We select a non-empty case set $\mathbf{T} \subseteq \mathbf{N}$ and ask the DM to decide how to partition the case set into three non-overlapping classes $\mathbf{A}'$, $\mathbf{B}'$ and $\mathbf{C}'$, with preference order $\mathbf{A}' \succ \mathbf{B}' \succ \mathbf{C}'$. (Typically, $\mathbf{T}$ is much smaller than $\mathbf{N}$. For convenience, we assume that $\mathbf{T} = \{N^1, \ldots, N^m\}$.) Then we use rough set theory to extract a set of linguistic rules $\mathbf{R}$ that capture preferential information in the case set classification, and apply $\mathbf{R}$ to all of $\mathbf{N}$ to extend $\mathbf{A}'$ to $\mathbf{A}$, $\mathbf{B}'$ to $\mathbf{B}$, and $\mathbf{C}'$ to $\mathbf{C}$. Thus, $\mathbf{N}$ is sorted into three classes $\mathbf{A}$, $\mathbf{B}$, and $\mathbf{C}$ with preference order $\mathbf{A} \succ \mathbf{B} \succ \mathbf{C}$. The classification produced by the DM is shown in Figure 2.

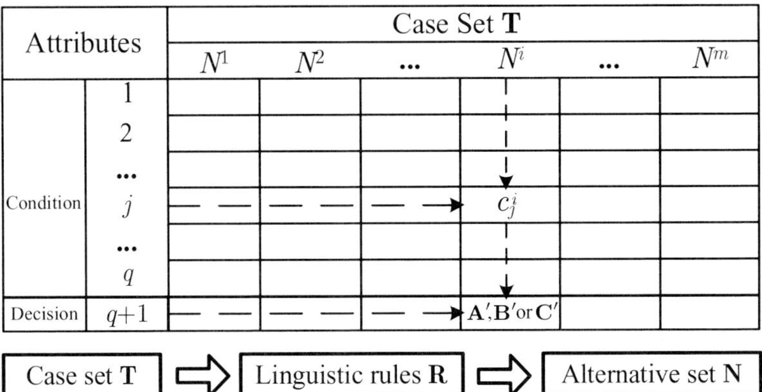

Fig. 2. The structure of the case set

Let S_j be preference with respect to criterion $j \in \mathbf{Q}$, such that $N^i S_j N^l$ means "N^i is at least as good as N^l with respect to criterion j", where $N^i, N^l \in \mathbf{T}$ are alternatives. We assume that S_j is a complete preorder, i.e. a strongly complete and transitive binary relation, and that $\mathbf{S} = (S_1, S_2, \ldots, S_q)$ is a comprehensive preference relation on $\mathbf{N}$, i.e. $N^i \mathbf{S} N^l$ means $N^i S_j N^l$ for every criterion $j \in Q$, for $N^i, N^l \in \mathbf{N}$.

The *upward union* and *downward union* with respect to the classes in the test set is defined next. Upward unions are denoted by subscript "$\geq$", and downward unions by subscript "$\leq$".

- $\mathbf{C}'_{\geq} = \mathbf{C}' \cup \mathbf{B}' \cup \mathbf{A}'$; $\mathbf{C}'_{\leq} = \mathbf{C}'$.
- $\mathbf{B}'_{\geq} = \mathbf{B}' \cup \mathbf{C}'$; $\mathbf{B}'_{\leq} = \mathbf{C}' \cup \mathbf{B}'$.
- $\mathbf{A}'_{\geq} = \mathbf{A}'$; $\mathbf{A}'_{\leq} = \mathbf{C}' \cup \mathbf{B}' \cup \mathbf{A}'$.

For example, $\mathbf{C}'_{\geq}$ consists of those test items that at least belong to group $\mathbf{C}'$, and $\mathbf{C}'_{\leq}$ those test items that at most belong to group $\mathbf{C}'$.

N^i dominates N^l with respect to criterion set $\mathbf{P} \subseteq \mathbf{Q}$ and written as $N^i D_{\mathbf{P}} N^l$, iff $N^i S_j N^l$ for all $j \in \mathbf{P}$. Relative to N^i, the $\mathbf{P}$-dominating set is defined by

$$D_{\mathbf{P}}^{+}(N^i) = \{N^l \in \mathbf{T} : N^l D_{\mathbf{P}} N^i\},$$

and the $\mathbf{P}$-dominated set by

$$D_{\mathbf{P}}^{-}(N^i) = \{N^l \in \mathbf{T} : N^i D_{\mathbf{P}} N^l\}.$$

With respect to $\mathbf{P} \subseteq \mathbf{Q}$, we say that N^i belongs to $\mathbf{G}'_{\geq}$ unambiguously, where $\mathbf{G}' = \mathbf{A}'$, $\mathbf{B}'$ or $\mathbf{C}'$, iff $N^i \in \mathbf{G}'_{\geq}$ and, for any $N^l \in D_{\mathbf{P}}^{+}(N^i)$, $N^l \in \mathbf{G}'_{\geq}$. More generally, the $\mathbf{P}$-lower approximation to $\mathbf{G}'_{\geq}$ is

$$\underline{\mathbf{P}}(\mathbf{G}'_{\geq}) = \left\{ N^i \in \mathbf{T} : D_{\mathbf{P}}^{+}(N^l) \subseteq \mathbf{G}'_{\geq} \right\},$$

and the $\mathbf{P}$-upper approximation to $\mathbf{G}'_{\geq}$ is

$$\overline{\mathbf{P}}(\mathbf{G}'_{\geq}) = \bigcup_{A^l \in \mathbf{G}'_{\geq}} D_{\mathbf{P}}^{+}(N^l).$$

Similarly, the $\mathbf{P}$-lower approximation to $\mathbf{G}'_{\leq}$ is

$$\underline{\mathbf{P}}(\mathbf{G}'_{\leq}) = \left\{ N^l \in \mathbf{N}' : D_{\mathbf{P}}^{-}(N^l) \subseteq \mathbf{G}'_{\leq} \right\},$$

and the $\mathbf{P}$-upper approximation to $\mathbf{G}'_{\leq}$ is

$$\overline{\mathbf{P}}(\mathbf{G}'_{\leq}) = \bigcup_{N^l \in \mathbf{G}'_{\leq}} D_{\mathbf{P}}^{-}(N^l).$$

The $\mathbf{P}$-boundaries ($\mathbf{P}$-doubtful regions) of $\mathbf{G}'_{\leq}$ and $\mathbf{G}'_{\geq}$ are

$$BN_{\mathbf{P}}(\mathbf{G}'_{\leq}) = \overline{\mathbf{P}}(\mathbf{G}'_{\leq}) - \underline{\mathbf{P}}(\mathbf{G}'_{\leq}),$$

$$BN_{\mathbf{P}}(\mathbf{G}'_{\geq}) = \overline{\mathbf{P}}(\mathbf{G}'_{\geq}) - \underline{\mathbf{P}}(\mathbf{G}'_{\geq}).$$

The quality of the sorting of the case set $\mathbf{T}$ with respect to $\mathbf{P} \subseteq \mathbf{Q}$ is

$$\gamma_{\mathbf{P}}(\mathbf{G}') = \frac{\left| \mathbf{N} - \left\{ \left(\bigcup_{\mathbf{I}'=\mathbf{A}',\mathbf{B}',\mathbf{C}'} BN_{\mathbf{P}}(\mathbf{I}'_\leq) \right) \cup \left(\bigcup_{\mathbf{I}'=\mathbf{A}',\mathbf{B}',\mathbf{C}'} BN_{\mathbf{P}}(\mathbf{I}'_\geq) \right) \right\} \right|}{m},$$

where m is the size (cardinality) of the case set $\mathbf{T}$. Thus, $\gamma_{\mathbf{P}}(\mathbf{G}')$ represents the proportion of alternatives in the case set $\mathbf{T}$ that are accurately sorted using only the criteria in $\mathbf{P}$.

Each minimal subset $\mathbf{P} \subseteq \mathbf{Q}$ such that $\gamma_{\mathbf{P}}(\mathbf{T}) = \gamma_{\mathbf{Q}}(\mathbf{T})$ is called a *reduct* of $\mathbf{Q}$. A case set $\mathbf{T}$ can have more than one reduct; the intersection of all reducts is called the *core*.

3.2   Decision Rules for MCABC

The approximations obtained through dominance can be used to construct decision rules capturing preference information contained in the classification of a case set [9]. Assume that all criteria are benefit criteria, i.e. that $c_j(N^i) \geq c_j(N^l)$ implies $N^i S_j N^l$ for all $j \in \mathbf{Q}$ and $N^i, N^l \in \mathbf{N}$. Then three types of decision rule can be generated from a non-empty set of criteria $\mathbf{P} \subseteq \mathbf{Q}$ and used to sort $\mathbf{N}$ into $\mathbf{G}$ and $\mathbf{H}$, respectively, where $\mathbf{G}, \mathbf{H} \in \{\mathbf{A}, \mathbf{B}, \mathbf{C}\}$, as required.

- $\mathbf{R}_\geq$ decision rules, which have the syntax

  $$\text{If } c_j(N^i) \geq r_j \text{ for all } j \in \mathbf{P}, \text{ then } N^i \in \mathbf{G}_\geq,$$

  where, for each $j \in \mathbf{P}$, $r_j \in \mathbb{R}$ is a consequence threshold for criterion j. Rules of this form are supported only by alternatives from the $\mathbf{P}$-lower approximations of class $\mathbf{G}'_\geq$.
- $\mathbf{R}_\leq$ decision rules, which have the syntax

  $$\text{If } c_j(N^i) \leq r_j \text{ for all } j \in \mathbf{P}, \text{ then } N^i \in \mathbf{G}_\leq,$$

  where, for each $j \in \mathbf{P}$, $r_j \in \mathbb{R}$ is a consequence threshold for criterion j. Rules of this form are supported only by alternatives from the $\mathbf{P}$-lower approximations of class $\mathbf{G}'_\leq$.
- $\mathbf{R}_{\geq\leq}$ decision rules, which have the syntax

  $$\text{If } c_j(N^i) \geq r_j \text{ for all } j \in \mathbf{O} \text{ and } c_j(N^i) \leq r_j \text{ for all } j \in \mathbf{P} - \mathbf{O},$$

  $$\text{then } N^i \in \mathbf{G}' \cup \mathbf{H}',$$

  where $\mathbf{O} \subseteq \mathbf{P}$ such that both $\mathbf{O}$ and $\mathbf{P} - \mathbf{O}$ are non-empty, and $r_j \in \mathbb{R}$ is a consequence threshold for criterion j for each $j \in \mathbf{P}$. Rules of this form are supported only by alternatives from the $\mathbf{P}$-boundaries of the unions of the classes $\mathbf{G}'_\geq$ and $\mathbf{H}'_\leq$.

A set of decision rules is *complete* if, when it is applied to all alternatives in the case set $\mathbf{T}$, consistent alternatives are re-classified to their original groups and inconsistent alternatives are classified to groups referring to this inconsistency. A set of decision rules is *minimal* if it is complete and non-redundant, i.e. exclusion of any rule makes the set incomplete [9]. Fortunately, software is available (see below) that produces sets of minimal decision rules.

4   Application

4.1   Background

We now use a case study on a hospital inventory system, based on data in [8], to demonstrate the proposed procedure. In the reference, 47 disposable SKUs used in a respiratory therapy unit are classified using AHP [17] for MCABC analysis. Table 1 lists data on the SKUs, referred to as S1 through S47. Four criteria are considered to be relevant to the MCABC analysis: (1) average unit cost ($), ranging from $5.12 to $210.00; (2) annual dollar usage ($), ranging from $25.38 to $5840.64; (3) criticality, described by a linguistic variable, which can equal h, for high or very critical), m, for moderate or important, and l, for low or non-critical; (4) lead time (weeks), the normal time to receive replenishment after an order is placed, ranging from 1 to 7 weeks. We employ the dominance-based rough set approach described above to analyze these results obtained by AHP and generate linguistic rules to demonstrate the DM's subjective judgement. These rules can then be used to classify remaining SKUs in the inventory system.

4.2   Analysis Procedures

The software 4eMka2 [10] was employed to carry out the calculations and the analysis procedures, as follows:

(1) Criteria Specification: All criteria were interpreted to be benefit criteria. For a product buyer such as a hospital, lead time is a gain criterion since the greater the lead time, the higher the level of management attention required. Average unit cost and annual dollar usage were identified as continuous criteria, while criticality and lead time were identified as discrete criteria.

(2) Input Data: All data in Table 1 were input into the software for training.

(3) Calculation of Unions: All upward unions, downward unions, and boundaries for each class, $\mathbf{A'}$, $\mathbf{B'}$, and $\mathbf{C'}$, were calculated by the software. There were no cases in each group boundary, indicating that the case set had been classified consistently.

(4) Rule Generation: As shown in Figure 3, 17 rules were generated based on the algorithm to construct a minimal cover. These rules can help a DM to identify and explain his or her preferences using natural language. The DM can check and update them as necessary and then apply them to classify any remaining SKUs.

(5) Classification Precision: All items in the case set were re-classified using the rules generated. The reclassification results were used to assess classification precision. The rules generated successfully re-classified all items in the case study into the "correct" group. Therefore, the DM's is likely to be satisfied that the rules represent preferences accurately.

The original rough set approach is also applied to the problem, resulting in the generation of 54 rules. The number of rules obtained by the original method is much larger than the number generated by our proposed method, since many

Table 1. Listing of SKUs with multiple criteria, adapted from [8]

SKUs	Criteria				
	Average unit cost (\$)	Annual dollar usage (\$)	Critical factor	Lead time (week)	Group
S1	49.92	5840.64	h	2	A
S2	210.00	5670.00	h	5	A
S3	23.76	5037.12	h	4	A
S4	27.73	4769.56	l	1	C
S5	57.98	3478.80	m	3	B
S6	31.24	2936.67	m	3	C
S7	28.20	2820.00	m	3	C
S8	55.00	2640.00	l	4	C
S9	73.44	2423.52	h	6	A
S10	160.50	2407.50	m	4	B
S11	5.12	1075.20	h	2	B
S12	20.87	1043.50	m	5	B
S13	86.50	1038.00	h	7	A
S14	110.40	883.20	m	5	B
S15	71.20	854.40	h	3	A
S16	45.00	810.00	m	3	C
S17	14.66	703.68	m	4	B
S18	49.50	594.00	m	6	A
S19	47.50	570.00	m	5	B
S20	58.45	467.60	m	4	B
S21	24.40	463.60	h	4	A
S22	65.00	455.00	m	4	B
S23	86.50	432.50	h	4	A
S24	33.20	398.40	h	3	A
S25	37.05	370.50	l	1	C
S26	33.84	338.40	l	3	C
S27	84.03	336.12	l	1	C
S28	78.40	313.60	l	6	C
S29	134.34	268.68	l	7	B
S30	56.00	224.00	l	1	C
S31	72.00	216.00	m	5	B
S32	53.02	212.08	h	2	B
S33	49.48	197.92	l	5	C
S34	7.07	190.89	l	7	C
S35	60.60	181.80	l	3	C
S36	40.82	163.28	h	3	B
S37	30.00	150.00	l	5	C
S38	67.40	134.80	m	3	C
S39	59.60	119.20	l	5	C
S40	51.68	103.36	l	6	C
S41	19.80	79.20	l	2	C
S42	37.70	75.40	l	2	C
S43	29.89	59.78	l	5	C
S44	48.30	48.30	l	3	C
S45	34.40	34.40	l	7	B
S46	28.80	28.80	l	3	C
S47	8.46	25.38	l	5	C

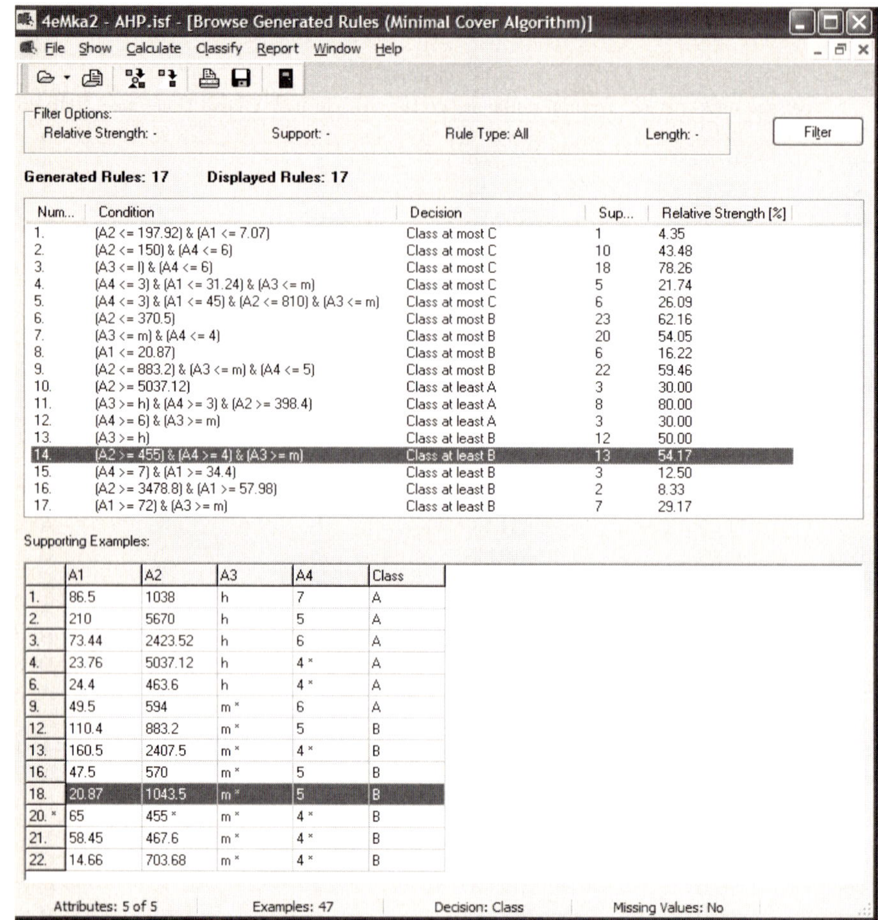

Fig. 3. The rules generated by 4eMka2

of the rules can be merged under the dominance relationships. This indicates that the dominance-based rough set approach is more efficient than the original method to handle problems involving DMs' preferences.

5   Conclusions

Classical ABC analysis is a straightforward technique to achieve cost-effective inventory management by categorizing SKUs into three groups according to annual dollar usage and then applying similar inventory management procedures throughout each group. However, management can often be made more effective by making the classification of SKUs reflect additional criteria, such as lead time and criticality. MCABC furnishes an inventory manager with the flexibility to account for more factors in classifying SKUs. In this paper a dominance-based rough set approach is proposed to solve MCABC problems, under the umbrella of MCDA theory. A case study is used to demonstrate the procedure; it is shown that the results are comparable with those obtained using the AHP method, confirming the applicability of this approach. Future research could be executed to compare the sorting abilities of this method with other sorting methods, such as methods described by Doumpos and Zopounidis [5].

References

1. Chakravarty, A. K.: Multi-item inventory aggregation into groups, Journal of Operational Research Society, **32** (1981) 19–26.
2. Chen, Y., Li, K.W., Kilgour, D.M., Hipel, K.W.: A Case-based distance model for multiple criteria ABC analysis, Computers and Operations Research, in press, (2006).
3. Chen, Y., Kilgour, D.M., Hipel, K.W.: Multiple criteria classification with an application in water resources planning, Computers and Operations Research, **33** (2006) 3301–3323.
4. Cohen, M. A., Ernst, R.: Multi-item classification and generic inventory stock control policies, Production and Inventory Management Journal, **29** (1988) 6–8.
5. Doumpos, M., Zopounidis, C.: Multicriteria decision aid classification methods, Kluwer, Dordrecht, 2002.
6. Flores, B.E., Whybark, D.C.: Multiple criteria ABC analysis, International Journal of Operations and Production Management, **6** (1986) 38–46.
7. Flores, B.E., Whybark, D.C.: Implementing multiple criteria ABC analysis, Journal of Operations Management, **7** (1987) 79–84.
8. Flores, B. E., Olson, D. L., Dorai, V. K.: Management of multicriteria inventory classification, *Mathematical and Computer Modeling*, **16** (1992) 71–82.
9. Greco, S., Matarazzo, B., Slowinski, R.: Rough set theory for multicriteria decision analysis, European Journal of Operational Research, **129** (2001) 1–47.
10. Institute of Computing Sceience, Poznan University of Technology, Poland, 4eMka2 software, http://idss.cs.put.poznan.pl/site/4emka.html, accessed on March 18, 2006.
11. Keeney R.L., Raiffa, H.: Decision with multiple objectives: preferences and value tradeoffs, Wiley, New York, 1976.
12. Pareto, V.: Mannual of Political Economy (English translation), A. M. Kelley Publishers, New York, 1971.
13. Partovi, F. Y., Anandarajan M.: Classifying inventory using an artificial neural network approach, Computers and Industrial Engineering, **41** (2002) 389–404.
14. Partovi, F. Y., Hopton, W. E.: The analytic hierarchy process as applied to two types of inventory problems, Production and Inventory Management Journal, **35** (1994) 13–19.
15. Pawlak, Z.: Rough Sets, International Journal of Computer and Information Sciences, **11** (1982) 341–356.
16. Roy, B.: Multicriteria methodology for decision aiding, Kluwer, Dordrecht, 1996.
17. Saaty, T. L.: The Analytic Hierarchy Process, McGraw Hill, New York, 1980.
18. Silver, E. A., Pyke, D. F., Peterson, R.: Inventory management and production planning and scheduling, 3rd edition, Wiley, New York, 1998.
19. Swamidass, P.M.: ABC analysis or ABC classification, In P.M. Swamidass, Encyclopedia of production and manufacturing management, Vol. 1-2, Kluwer Academic Publishers, Boston, 2000.

A Method of Generating Decision Rules in Object–Oriented Rough Set Models

Yasuo Kudo[1] and Tetsuya Murai[2]

[1] Dept. of Computer Science and Systems Eng., Muroran Institute of Technology
Mizumoto 27-1, Muroran 050-8585, Japan
`kudo@csse.muroran-it.ac.jp`
[2] Graduate School of Information Science and Technology, Hokkaido University
Kita 14, Nishi 9, Kita-ku, Sapporo 060-0814, Japan
`murahiko@main.ist.hokudai.ac.jp`

Abstract. We propose a method of decision rule generation in object–
oriented rough set models proposed by Kudo and Murai. The object–
oriented rough set model is an extension of the "traditional" rough set
theory by introducing object–oriented paradigm used in computer science. The object–oriented rough set model treats objects as instances of
some classes, and illustrate structural hierarchies among objects based on
is-a relationship and has-a relationship. In this paper, we introduce decision rules in the object–oriented rough set model, and revise discernibility
matrices proposed by Skowron and Rauser to generate decision rules in
the object–oriented rough set model.

1 Introduction

Rough set theory [1,2] provides a basis of approximation and reasoning about
data. In the aspect of approximation, the basic concepts are lower and upper
approximations by indiscernibility relations, which illustrate set-theoretic approximations of any given subsets of objects. On the other hand, in the aspect
of reasoning about data, the basic concepts are *reducts* and *decision rules* based
on a given decision tables which represent data by combination of attributes and
its values. In the given decision table, the set of attributes are divided into the set
of condition attributes and the set of decision attributes that provide decision
classes. Decision rules are "if–then" rules that describe certain characteristics
of combination between values of condition attributes and decision attributes.
Reducts are minimal sets of condition attributes to classify all objects into decision classes correctly. Reducts also provide antecedents of decision rules. many
methods have been proposed to calculate reducts (for detail, see [2]).

Kudo and Murai have proposed object–oriented rough set models [3], and have
extended the object–oriented rough set models to treat incomplete information
[4]. The object–oriented rough set model is an extension of the "traditional"
rough set theory by introducing object–oriented paradigm (cf. [5]) used in computer science, and the object–oriented rough set model illustrates hierarchical

S. Greco et al. (Eds.): RSCTC 2006, LNAI 4259, pp. 338–347, 2006.

structures between classes, names and objects based on is-a and has-a relationships. However, in the previous papers [3,4], formulation of the object–oriented rough set model was concentrated to the aspect of approximation, and reasoning about objects has not been discussed.

In this paper, we consider reasoning about objects in the object–oriented rough set model. Thus, we introduce decision rules in the object–oriented rough set model, and revise discernibility matrices proposed by Skowron and Rauser [6] to generate decision rules in the object–oriented rough set model. Moreover, we illustrate an example of decision rule generation.

2   The Object–Oriented Rough Set Model

We briefly review the object–oriented rough set model. First, we describe the concept of class, name and object. Next, we illustrate well-defined structures as a basic framework of the object–oriented rough set model. Moreover, we introduce equivalence relations based on "equivalence as instances". Note that the contents of this section are entirely based on the authors' previous papers [3,4].

2.1   Class, Name, Object

Formally, a *class structure* $\mathcal{C}$, a *name structure* $\mathcal{N}$ and a *object structure* $\mathcal{O}$ are defined by the following triples, respectively:

$$\mathcal{C} = (C, \ni_C, \sqsupseteq_C), \ \ \mathcal{N} = (N, \ni_N, \sqsupseteq_N), \ \ \mathcal{O} = (O, \ni_O, \sqsupseteq_O),$$

where C, N and O are finite and disjoint non-empty sets such that $|C| \leq |N|$ ($|X|$ is the cardinality of X). Each element $c \in C$ is called a *class*. Similarly, each $n \in N$ is called a *name*, and each $o \in O$ is called an *object*. The relation $\supset_X$ $(X \subset \{C, N, O\})$ is an acyclic binary relation on X, and the relation $\sqsupseteq_X$ is a reflexive, transitive, and asymmetric binary relation on X. Moreover, $\ni_X$ and $\sqsupseteq_X$ satisfy the following property:

$$\forall x_i, x_j, x_k \in X, \ x_i \sqsupseteq_X x_j, \ x_j \ni_X x_k \ \Rightarrow \ x_i \ni_X x_k. \tag{1}$$

The class, name and object structures have the following characteristics, respectively:

- The class structure illustrates abstract data forms and those hierarchical structures based on part / whole relationship (has-a relation) and specialized / generalized relationship (is-a relation).
- The name structure introduces numerical constraint of objects and those identification, which provide concrete design of objects.
- The object structure illustrates actual combination of objects.

Two relations $\ni_X$ and $\sqsupseteq_X$ on $X \in \{C, N, O\}$ illustrate hierarchical structures among elements in X. The relation $\ni_X$ is called a *has-a relation*, which illustrates part / whole relationship. $x_i \ni_X x_j$ means "x_i has-a x_j", or "x_j is a part of x_i".

For example, $c_i \ni_C c_j$ means that "the class c_i has a class c_j", or "c_j is a part of c_i". On the other hand, the relation $\sqsupseteq_X$ is called an *is-a relation*, which illustrates specialized / generalized relationship. $x_i \sqsupseteq_X x_j$ means that "x_i is-a x_j". For example, $\sqsupseteq_C$ illustrates relationship between superclasses and subclasses, and $c_i \sqsupseteq_C c_j$ means that "c_i is a superclass of c_j", or "c_j is a subclass of c_i".

2.2 Well–Defined Structures

Each object $o \in O$ is defined as an instance of some class $c \in C$, and the class of o is identified by the *class identifier* function. The class identifier id_C is a *p-morphism* between $\mathcal{O}$ and $\mathcal{C}$ (cf. [7], p.142), that is, the function $id_C : O \longrightarrow C$ satisfies the following conditions:

1. $\forall o_i, o_j \in O, o_i \ni_O o_j \Rightarrow id_C(o_i) \ni_C id_C(o_j)$.
2. $\forall o_i \in O, \forall c_j \in C, id_C(o_i) \ni_C c_j \Rightarrow \exists o_j \in O$ s.t. $o_i \ni_O o_j$ and $id_C(o_j) = c_j$,

and the same conditions are also satisfied for $\sqsupseteq_O$ and $\sqsupseteq_C$. $id_C(o) = c$ means that the object o is an instance of the class c.

The object structure $\mathcal{O}$ and the class structure $\mathcal{C}$ are also connected through the name structure $\mathcal{N}$ by the *naming function* $nf : N \longrightarrow C$ and the *name assignment* $na : O \longrightarrow N$. The naming function provides names to each class, which enable us to use plural instances of the same class simultaneously. On the other hand, the name assignment provides names to every objects, which enable us to identify objects by names.

Formally, the naming function $nf : N \longrightarrow C$ is a surjective p-morphism between $\mathcal{N}$ and $\mathcal{C}$, and satisfies the following *name preservation constraint*:

- For any $n_i, n_j \in N$, if $nf(n_i) = nf(n_j)$, then $H_N(c|n_i) = H_N(c|n_j)$ is satisfied for all $c \in C$,

where $H_N(c|n) = \{n_j \in N \mid n \ni_N n_j, f(n_j) = c\}$ is the set of names of c that n has. The requirement that nf is a surjective p-morphism means that there is at least one name for each class, and structures between names reflect all structural characteristics between classes. The name preservation constraint requires that, for any class $c_i, c_j \in C$ such that $c_i \ni_C c_j$, and any name $n \in N$ with $nf(n) = c_i$, all names of the parts of c are uniquely determined. Thus, the number of names of c_j is fixed as $m = |H_N(c_j|n)|$, and we can simply say that "the class c_i has m objects of the class c_j".

On the other hand, the name assignment $na : O \longrightarrow N$ is a p-morphism between $\mathcal{O}$ and $\mathcal{N}$, and satisfies the following *uniqueness condition*:

- For any $x \in O$, if $H_O(x) \neq \emptyset$, the restriction of na into $H_O(x)$:
  $na|_{H_O(x)} : H_O(x) \longrightarrow N$ is injective,

where $H_O(x) = \{y \in O \mid x \ni_O y\}$ is the set of objects that x has. $na(x) = n$ means that the name of the object x is n. The uniqueness condition requires that all distinct parts $y \in H_O(x)$ have different names.

We say that $\mathcal{C}$, $\mathcal{N}$ and $\mathcal{O}$ are *well-defined* if and only if there exist a naming function $nf : N \longrightarrow C$ and a name assignment $na : O \longrightarrow N$ such that

$$id_C = nf \circ na, \tag{2}$$

that is, $id_C(x) = nf(na(x))$ for all $x \in O$.

In this paper, we concentrate well-defined class, name and object structures. In well-defined structures, if a class c_i has m objects of a class c_j, then any instance o_i of the class c_i has exactly m instances $o_{j1}, \cdots, o_{jm}$ of the class c_j [3]. This good property enables us the following description for clear representation of objects. Suppose we have $o_1, o_2 \in O$, $n_1, n_2 \in N$, and $c_1, c_2 \in C$ such that $o_1 \ni_O o_2$, and $na(o_i) = n_i$, $nf(n_i) = c_i$ for $i \in \{1, 2\}$. We denote $o_1.n_2$ instead of o_2 by means of "the instance of c_2 named n_2 as a part of o_1".

Example 1. We use the same settings with examples of the object–oriented rough set model in [3]. Let $\mathcal{C} = (C, \ni_C, \sqsupseteq_C)$ be a class structure with $C = \{$PC, DeskTopPC, 2CPU − DTPC, CPU, Memory, HDD, Clock, MSize, HSize$\}$, and we have the following relationships:

<table>
<tr><td>Is-a relation:</td><td>Has-a relation:</td></tr>
<tr><td>DeskTopPC $\sqsupseteq_C$ PC,</td><td>PC $\ni_C$ CPU, PC $\ni_C$ Memory,</td></tr>
<tr><td>2CPU − DTPC $\sqsupseteq_C$ DeskTopPC,</td><td>DeskTopPC $\ni_C$ HDD, CPU $\ni_C$ Clock,</td></tr>
<tr><td>2CPU − DTPC $\sqsupseteq_C$ PC,</td><td>Memory $\ni_C$ MSize, HDD $\ni_C$ HSize,</td></tr>
<tr><td>$\cdots$.</td><td>$\cdots$.</td></tr>
</table>

By the property (1), these relations illustrate connections between classes, for example, "2CPU-DTPC is-a PC" and "PC has-a CPU" imply "2CPU-DTPC has-a CPU".

Next, let $\mathcal{N} = (N, \ni_N, \sqsupseteq_N)$ is a name structure with $N = \{$pc, desk_top_pc, 2cpu_dtpc, cpu, cpu2, memory, hdd, clock, msize, hsize$\}$ and the following relationships:

<table>
<tr><td>Is a relation:</td><td>Has-a relation:</td></tr>
<tr><td>desk_top_pc $\sqsupseteq_N$ pc,</td><td>desk_top_pc $\ni_N$ cpu</td></tr>
<tr><td>2cpu_dtpc $\sqsupseteq_N$ desk_top_pc,</td><td>2cpu_dtpc $\ni_N$ cpu, 2cpu_dtpc $\ni_N$ cpu2,</td></tr>
<tr><td>$\cdots$.</td><td>cpu $\ni_N$ clock, memory $\ni_N$ msize,</td></tr>
<tr><td></td><td>$\cdots$.</td></tr>
</table>

Moreover, suppose we have a naming function $nf : N \longrightarrow C$ such that

$$
\begin{aligned}
&nf(\mathrm{pc}) = \mathsf{PC},\ nf(\mathrm{desk\_top\_pc}) = \mathsf{DeskTopPC},\\
&nf(\mathrm{2cpu\_dtpc}) = \mathsf{2CPU - DTPC},\ nf(\mathrm{cpu}) = nf(\mathrm{cpu2}) = \mathsf{CPU},\\
&nf(\mathrm{memory}) = \mathsf{Memory},\ nf(\mathrm{hdd}) = \mathsf{HDD},\\
&nf(\mathrm{clock}) = \mathsf{Clock},\ nf(\mathrm{msize}) = \mathsf{MSize},\ nf(\mathrm{hsize}) = \mathsf{HSize}.
\end{aligned}
$$

Note that we have $H_N(\mathsf{CPU}|\mathrm{2cpu\_dtpc}) = \{\mathrm{cpu}, \mathrm{cpu2}\}$, and $H_N(\mathsf{Clock}|\mathrm{cpu}) = H_N(\mathsf{Clock}|\mathrm{cpu2}) = \{\mathrm{clock}\}$. Thus, for example, 2CPU-DTPC class has two objects of the CPU class, called "cpu" and "cpu2", respectively, one object "memory" of the Memory class, and one object "hdd" of the HDD class.

Finally, let $\mathcal{O} = (O, \ni_O, \sqsupseteq_O)$ be an object structure with the following is-a and relationships:

Is-a relation:
$x \sqsupseteq_O x$, $\forall x \in O$, and
pc3 $\sqsupseteq_O$ pc1, pc3 $\sqsupseteq_O$ pc2.

Has-a relation:
pc$i$ $\ni_O$ ci,   pc$i$ $\ni_O$ mi,   pc$i$ $\ni_O$ hi, $i \in \{1, 2, 3\}$,
pc3 $\ni_O$ c4,
ci $\ni_O$ 2.4GHz, $i \in \{1, 3, 4\}$,   c2 $\ni_O$ 3.0GHz,
m1 $\ni_O$ 512MB,   mi $\ni_O$ 1GB, $i \in \{2, 3\}$,
hi $\ni_O$ 40GB, $i \in \{1, 2\}$,   h3 $\ni_O$ 80GB.

Moreover, let $na : O \longrightarrow N$ be the following name assignment:

$$na(\text{pc1}) = na(\text{pc2}) = \text{desk\_ top\_ pc},\quad na(\text{pc3}) = \text{2cpu\_dtpc},$$
$$na(\text{c1}) = na(\text{c2}) = na(\text{c3}) = \text{cpu},\quad na(\text{c4}) = \text{cpu2},$$
$$na(\text{m1}) = na(\text{m2}) = na(\text{m3}) = \text{memory},$$
$$na(\text{h1}) = na(\text{h2}) = na(\text{h3}) = \text{hdd},$$
$$na(\text{2.4GHz}) = na(\text{3.0GHz}) = \text{clock},$$
$$na(\text{512MB}) = na(\text{1GB}) = \text{msize},\quad na(\text{40GB}) = na(\text{80GB}) = \text{hsize}.$$

We define the class identifier $id_C : O \longrightarrow C$ by $id_C = nf \circ na$.

This object structure $\mathcal{O}$ illustrates the following situation: There are three objects pc1, pc2 and pc3. pc1 and pc2 are instances of the DeskTopPC class, and pc3 is an instance of the the 2CPU-DTPC class. pc1 and pc2 have one instance of the CPU class, c1 = pc1.cpu and c2 = pc2.cpu, respectively. On the other hand, pc3 has two instances of the CPU class, c3 = pc3.cpu and c4 = pc3.cpu2, respectively. Moreover, each pc$i$ ($i = 1, 2, 3$) has just one instance mi of the Memory class, and just one instance hi of the HDD class. Each cpu has its clock (2.4GHz or 3.0GHz), each memory has its size (512MB or 1GB), and each hard disk drive has its size (40GB or 80GB).

2.3   Indiscernibility Relations in the Object – Oriented Rough Set Model

All equivalence relations in object–oriented rough set models are based on the concept of equivalence as instances. In [3], to evaluate equivalence of instances, an equivalence relation $\sim$ on O are recursively defined as follows:

$$x \sim y \iff \begin{array}{l} x \text{ and } y \text{ satisfy the following two conditions:}\\ 1.\ id_C(x) = id_C(y), \text{ and,}\\ 2.\ \begin{cases} x.n \sim y.n,\ \forall n \in H_N(na(x)) & \text{if } H_N(na(x)) \neq \emptyset,\\ Val(x) = Val(y) & \text{otherwise,} \end{cases} \end{array} \tag{3}$$

where $H_N(na(x))$ is the set of names that $na(x)$ has. $Val(x)$ is the "value" of the "value object" x. Because C is a finite non-empty set and $\ni_C$ is acyclic, there is at least one class c such that c has no other class c', that is, $c \not\ni_C c'$ for any $c' \in C$. We call such class c an *attribute*, and denote the set of attributes by AT. For any object x, if $id_C(x) = a$ and $a \in AT$, we call such object x a *value object* of the attribute a. The value object x as an instance of the attribute a represents a "value" of the attribute.

$x \sim y$ means that the object x is equivalent to the object y as an instance of the class $id_C(x)$. Using the equivalence relation $\sim$, an equivalence relation $\sim_B$ with respect to a given subset $B \subseteq N$ of names is defined as follows:

$$x \sim_B y \iff \begin{array}{l} x \text{ and } y \text{ satisfy the following two conditions:} \\ 1 \ \ B \cap H_N(na(x)) = B \cap H_N(na(y)), \text{ and,} \\ 2. \ \forall n[n \in B \cap H_N(na(x)) \Rightarrow x.n \sim y.n]. \end{array} \qquad (4)$$

$x \sim_B y$ means that x and y are equivalent as instances of the class $id_C(x)$ in the sense that, for all $n \in B \cap H_N(na(x))$, x and y have equivalent instances of the class $id_C(x.n)$. Equivalence classes $[x]_{\sim_B}$ by $\sim_B$ are usually defined. Note that, in the "traditional" rough set theory, all equivalence classes concern the same attributes. On the other hand, each equivalence class of the object–oriented rough set model may concern different classes. In particular, if $B \cap H_N(na(x)) = \emptyset$, the equivalence class $[x]_{\sim_B}$ is the set of objects that are not concerned any class $nf(n), n \in B$ at all.

Example 2. This example is continuation of example 1, and has used in [4]. Suppose $B = \{cpu\}$. Using the equivalence relation $\sim$ defined by (3), we construct the equivalence relation $\sim_B$ by (4), and the resulted equivalence classes by $\sim_B$ are as follows:

$$[pc1]_{\sim_B} = \{pc1, pc3\}, \ [pc2]_{\sim_B} = \{pc2\}, \ [c1]_{\sim_B} = O - \{pc1, pc2, pc3\}.$$

The equivalence classes $[pc1]_{\sim_B}$ and $[pc3]_{\sim_B}$ correspond to the set of personal computers that have "2.4GHz CPU" and the singleton set of the personal computer that has "3.0GHz CPU", respectively. On the other hand, $[c1]_{\sim}$ represents the set of objects that have no CPU.

3   Decision Rules and Discernibility Matrices in the Object–Oriented Rough Set Model

3.1   Decision Rule

We extend decision rules in "traditional" rough set theory into the object–oriented rough set model. Suppose $\mathcal{C} = (C, \ni_C, \sqsupseteq_C)$, $\mathcal{N} = (N, \ni_N, \sqsupseteq_N)$, and $\mathcal{O} = (O, \ni_O, \sqsupseteq_O)$ be the well-defined class, name and object structures, respectively. Similar to the decision table in rough set theory, we divide the set of names N into the following two parts: the set of names that may appear in antecedents of decision rules (called condition names) N_{CON}, and the set of names that may appear in conclusions of decision rules (called decision names) N_{DEC}. Note that $N = N_{CON} \cup N_{DEC}$ and $N_{CON} \cap N_{DEC} = \emptyset$. The decision names provide *decision classes* as equivalence classes $[x]_{\sim_{N_{DEC}}}$ based on the equivalence relation $\sim_{N_{DEC}}$ by (4). Decision rules in the object–oriented rough set model are defined as follows.

Definition 1. *A decision rule in the object–oriented rough set model has the following form:*

$$c \wedge c.n_1 \sim o.n_1 \wedge \cdots \wedge c.n_i \sim o.n_i \Rightarrow c.m_1 \sim o.m_1 \wedge \cdots \wedge c.m_j \sim o.m_j, \quad (5)$$

where $c \in C$, $o \in O$ such that $id_C(o) = c$, $n_1, \cdots, n_i \in N_{CON} \cap H_N(na(o))$ $(i \geq 0)$ and $m_1, \cdots, m_j \in N_{DEC} \cap H_N(na(o))$ $(j \geq 1)$. We call this rule a decision rule of the class c by the object o, and denote $DR(c; o)$.

The decision rule $DR(c; o)$ means that, for any object $o' \in O$, if o' is an instance of c and each part $o'.n_k$ is equivalent to $o.n_k$ $(k \leq i)$, then all parts $o'.m_l$ are also equivalent to $o.m_l$ $(l \leq j)$, respectively. Thus, $DR(c; o)$ describes a certain property about combination of objects as an instance of the class c.

As a special case, we allow rules that have no condition names, that is, the case of $i = 0$ in (5) as follows:

$$c \Rightarrow c.m_1 \sim o.m_1 \wedge \cdots \wedge c.m_j \sim o.m_j.$$

This rule illustrates that all instances o' of the class c have some parts $o'.m_k$ $(1 \leq k \leq j)$ that are equivalent to $o.m_k$, respectively. On the other hand, we require that there is at least one name $m \in N_{DEC}$ such that $m \in H_N(na(o))$. This means that any object that has no decision name are not the target of decision rule generation.

3.2 Discernibility Matrix

To generate decision rules in the object–oriented rough set model, we need to determine classes and names that appear actually in antecedents of decision rules. In "traditional" rough set theory, antecedents of decision rules are constructed from *reducts* which are minimal sets of attributes to approximate all decision classes. Here, to construct all "reducts" in the object–oriented rough set model, we revise the discernibility matrix for "traditional" rough set theory proposed by Skowron and Rauser [6].

Definition 2. *A discernibility matrix of the object–oriented rough set model is a $k \times k$ matrix whose element δ_{ij} at the i-th row and the j-th column is defined as follows:*

$$\delta_{ij} = \begin{cases} \{id_C(o_i)\} & \begin{array}{l} \text{if } id_C(o_i) \neq id_C(o_j) \text{ and} \\ \exists m \in N_{DEC} \cap H_N(na(o_i)) \\ \text{s. t. } o_i.m \not\sim o_j.m, \end{array} \\[2em] \left\{ id_C(o_i).n \,\middle|\, \begin{array}{l} n \in H_N(na(o_i)), \\ n \in N_{CON}, \\ o_i.n \not\sim o_j.n \end{array} \right\} & \begin{array}{l} \text{if } id_C(o_i) = id_C(o_j) \text{ and} \\ \exists m \in N_{DEC} \cap H_N(na(o_i)) \\ \text{s. t. } o_i.m \not\sim o_j.m, \end{array} \\[2em] \emptyset & \text{otherwise,} \end{cases} \quad (6)$$

where k is the number of objects, that is, $|O| = k$. $o_i.n \not\sim o_j.n$ means that $o_i.n$ is not equivalent to $o_j.n$.

The element δ_{ij} is the set of classes that we should check to distinguish the object o_i and the object o_j. Thus, when we need to distinguish o_i and o_j, we check the class $id_C(o_i)$ and $id_C(o_j)$ firstly, and if these classes are not equal, we can distinguish these objects. Otherwise, we need to compare parts $o_i.n$ and $o_j.n$ such that $n \in N_{CON} \cap H_N(na(o_i))$. Note that, different from the "traditional" discernibility matrix, we have generally $\delta_{ij} \neq \delta_{ji}$ in the revised discernibility matrix.

Similar to the case of calculating reducts by the "traditional" discernibility matrix, we construct reducts of the object–oriented rough set model. First, for each element δ_{ij} in the revised discernibility matrix, we construct the following formula $L(\delta_{ij})$:

$$L(\delta_{ij}) \equiv \begin{cases} c & \text{if } \delta_{ij} = \{c\}, \\ c.n_1 \vee \cdots \vee c.n_l & \text{if } \delta_{ij} = \{c.n_1, \cdots, c.n_l\}, \\ \top & \text{if } \delta_{ij} = \emptyset. \end{cases} \tag{7}$$

The intention of $L(\delta_{ij})$ is that, for example the case of $L(\delta_{ij}) \equiv c.n_1 \vee \cdots \vee c.n_l$, we can distinguish o_i and o_j by checking at least one of $c.n_s$ $(1 \leq s \leq l)$.

Next, connecting all formulas $L(\delta_{ij})$ by the logical product, we get a formula $\bigwedge_{i=1}^{k} \bigwedge_{j=1}^{k} L(\delta_{ij})$. This formula is the conjunctive normal form. Thus, finally, we transform this formula to the disjunctive normal form that is logically equivalent to $\bigwedge_{i=1}^{k} \bigwedge_{j=1}^{k} L(\delta_{ij})$ with no redundant expression as follows:

$$\bigwedge_{i=1}^{k} \bigwedge_{j=1}^{k} L(\delta_{ij}) \equiv \bigvee_{s=1}^{m} \bigwedge_{t=1}^{s_t} c_{st},$$

where each conjunction $\bigwedge_{t=1}^{s_t} c_{lt}$ describes a *reduct* of the object–oriented rough set model $R = \{c_{l1}, \cdots, c_{ls_t}\}$. This is because, for each element δ_{ij} of the revised discernibility matrix, R contains at least one expression c or $c.n$ such that $c \in \delta_{ij}$ or $c.n \subset \delta_{ij}$.

3.3   A Method of Generating Decision Rules

Let R be a reduct of the object–oriented rough set model. We construct decision rules from the reduct and each object in decision classes. However, for each object o in any decision class $[x]_{\sim N_{DEC}}$, not all classes $c \in R$ and $c.n \in R$ are concerned with o. Thus, for each object $o \in [x]_{\sim N_{DEC}}$ such that $id_C(o) = c$, we construct a decision rule $DR(c; o)$ in the object–oriented rough set model as follows:

1. Select the class c such that $id_C(o) = c$ and all classes $c.n_s$ from the reduct R.
2. Construct an expression $c.n_s \sim o.n_s$ for each selected $c.n_s$ and the object o, and connect the class c and these expressions by $\wedge$ as follows:
   (Antecedents) $c \wedge c.n_1 \sim o.n_1 \wedge \cdots \wedge c.n_l \sim o.n_l$
3. Construct an expression $c.m_t \sim o.m_t$ for each $c.m_t$ such that $m_t \in N_{DEC} \cap H_N(na(o))$, and connect the class c and these expressions by $\wedge$ as follows:
   (Conclusions) $c \wedge c.m_1 \sim o.m_1 \wedge \cdots \wedge c.m_u \sim o.m_u$

4. Construct the decision rule $DR(c : o)$ by connecting antecedents and conclusions by $\Rightarrow$ as follows:
$$c \wedge c.n_1 \sim o.n_1 \wedge \cdots \wedge c.n_l \sim o.n_l \Rightarrow c \wedge c.m_1 \sim o.m_1 \wedge \cdots \wedge c.m_u \sim o.m_u$$

Example 3. Suppose we have $N_{DEC} = \{\text{cpu}\}$ and $N_{CON} = N - \{\text{cpu}\}$. Thus, similar to example 2, we have three decision classes by the equivalence relation $\sim_{N_{DEC}}$: $[\text{pc1}] = \{\text{pc1, pc3}\}$ as the set of objects with "2.4GHz CPU", $[\text{pc2}] = \{\text{pc2}\}$ as the set of object with "3.0GHz CPU", and $[\text{c1}]$ as the set of objects that have no CPU. We consider to generate decision rules for $[\text{pc1}]$ and $[\text{pc2}]$. First, we construct a discernibility matrix to distinguish members of $[\text{pc1}]$ and $[\text{pc2}]$. Table 1 illustrates the discernibility matrix to distinguish $[\text{pc1}]$ and $[\text{pc2}]$.

Table 1. Discernibility matrix in the object–oriented rough set model

	pc1	pc2	pc3
pc1	$\emptyset$	{DeskTopPC.memory}	$\emptyset$
pc2	{DeskTopPC.memory}	$\emptyset$	{DeskTopPC}
pc3	$\emptyset$	{2CPU-DTPC}	$\emptyset$

We omit any objects that are not the instances of either DeskTopPC or 2CPU-DTPC. This is because we have $\delta_{ij} = \emptyset$ for such objects o_i and o_j.

Next, we construct reducts for decision classes. By this discernibility matrix, we have one reduct {DeskTopPC, 2CPU-DTPC, DeskTopPC.memory}.

Finally, using the reducts, we generate decision rules $DR(\text{DeskTopPC}; \text{pc}i)$ ($i \in \{1, 3\}$) and $DR(\text{2CPU-DTPC}; \text{pc2})$. as follows:

1. DeskTopPC$\wedge$ DeskTopPC.memory $\sim$ m1 $\Rightarrow$ DeskTopPC.cpu $\sim$ c1.
2. 2CPU-DTPC $\Rightarrow$ 2CPU-DTPC.cpu $\sim$ c2.
3. DeskTopPC$\wedge$ DeskTopPC.memory $\sim$ m3 $\Rightarrow$ DeskTopPC.cpu $\sim$ c3,

where mi=pc$i$.memory and ci=pc$i$.cpu.

These three rules illustrate certain characteristics about combination of objects in the given object structure $\mathcal{O}$. For example, the rule 1 means that if an object is an instance of the DeskTopPC class, and its memory is equivalent to the object $m1$, that is, the size of memory is 512MB, then the CPU of the object is equivalent to $c1$, that is, the clock of the CPU is 2.4GHz. The other rules are also interpreted similarly.

4   Discussion and Conclusion

In this paper, we have proposed a method to generate decision rules in the framework of object–oriented rough set model [3]. First, we have introduced decision rules in the object–oriented rough set model, and revised discernibility matrices proposed by Skowron and Rauser [6] to generate decision rules in the object–oriented rough set model. Moreover, we have illustrated an example of decision rule generation.

As introduction of the object–orientation into rough set theory, in the previous papers [3,4] and this paper, we have only treated the aspects of *data* of objects as representation of hierarchical structures, however we have not treated the concepts of *methods* of objects. According to [5], an object is an encapsulation of state (data values) and behavior (operations), and an object will exhibit its behavior by invoking a method (similar to executing a procedure) in response to a message (cf. [5], p.22). We think that methods in the object–oriented rough set model will correspond to manipulation of objects, which is one of the most interesting improvement of the object–oriented rough set model.

We also consider the following future issues: More refinement of theoretical aspects of the proposed method, application of the proposed method to actual object–oriented databases, and development of rule generation systems in the object–oriented rough set model based on the proposed method.

Acknowledgments

We would like to express appreciation to reviewers for their helpful comments. This research is partially supported by the Grant-in-Aid for Young Scientists (B) (No.17700222-1), The Ministry of Education, Culture, Sports, Science and Technology, Japan.

References

1. Pawlak, Z.: Rough sets. International Journal of Computer and Information Science **11** (1982) 341–356
2. Pawlak, Z.: Rough Sets: Theoretical Aspects of Reasoning about Data. Kluwor Academic Publisher (1991)
3. Kudo, Y., Murai, T.: A theoretical formulation of object–oriented rough set models. Journal of Advanced Computational Intelligence and Intelligent Informatics **10**(5) (to appear)
4. Kudo, Y., Murai, T.: A note on treatment of incomplete information in object–oriented rough sets. In: Proceedings of the Joint 3rd International Conference on Soft Computing and Intelligent Systems and 7th International Symposium on advanced Intelligent Systems. (to appear)
5. Budd, T.A.: An Introduction of Object – Oriented Programming, 2nd Edition. Addison Wesley Longman (1997)
6. Skowron, A., Rauser, C.M.: The dicernibility matrix and functions in information systems. In Słowiński, R., ed.: Intelligent Decision Support: Handbook of Application and Advances of the Rough Set Theory. Kluwer Academic Publisher (1992) 331–362
7. Popkorn, S.: First Steps in Modal Logic. Cambridge University Press (1994)

Knowledge Reduction in Set-Valued Decision Information System

Xiao-Xue Song[1,2] and Wen-Xiu Zhang[1]

[1] Institute for Information and System Sciences, Faculty of Science
Xi'an Jiaotong University, Xi'an, Shaan'xi, 710049, P.R. China
[2] Department of Computer, Xianyang Normal College, Xianyang,
Shaan'xi, 712000, P.R. China
sxx1669@163.com (X.-X.Song)
hrli2951@mailst.xjtu.edu.cn (H.-R. Li)

Abstract. Reduction is one of the key problem in rough set theory due to its applications in data mining, rule induction, classification, etc.. In this paper the reductions for a set-valued decision information system(DIS) are studied. The judgment theorem and the discernibility matrix of the generalized decision reduct in a set-valued DIS are given, and the relationships among the generalized decision reduct and alternative types of knowledge reduction in set-valued DIS are investigated. It is proved that the reduct in the consistent set-valued DIS is equivalent to the generalized decision reduct, and the possible reduct in the inconsistent set-valued DIS is equivalent to the generalized decision reduct. The judgment theorem and the discernibility matrix associated with the possible reduct are also established.

1 Introduction

Rough Set theory(see [7]), a new mathematical approach to deal with inexact, uncertain or vague knowledge, has recently received wide attention on the research areas in both of the real-life applications and the theory itself.

The rough set theory that based on the conventional indiscernibility relation is not useful for analyzing incomplete information. When the precise values of some of the attributes in an information system are not known, i.e., missing or known partially, then such a system is called an incomplete information system(IIS). Such a situation can be described by a set-valued information system in which the attribute value function f_a is defined as a mapping from U to the power set of V_a, i.e., $f_a : U \longrightarrow 2^{V_a}$, called a set-valued function. The missing values can be represented by the set of all possible values for the attribute. In this paper, we discuss the incomplete information systems in which the attribute value for an object is the subset of the attribute's domains.

Reduction is one of the hot research topics of rough set. Many useful results had been reported (see [1-6],[8-11]). In [11], *Variable Precision Rough Set Model* (VPRS) was presented, in which concept approximations are parameterized. The VPRS model was meant to overcome the problem of noise in data. In [4], two

S. Greco et al. (Eds.): RSCTC 2006, LNAI 4259, pp. 348–357, 2006.

new types of attribute reduction based on VPRS, β lower distribution reduct and β upper distribution reduct, are introduced. It has been proved that for certain parameter β, the β lower distribution reduct is equivalent to the maximum distribution reduct, whereas the β upper distribution reduct is equivalent to the possible reduct. In [6] the notions of α-reduct and α-relative reduct for decision tables were defined. The α-reduct allows occurrence of additional inconsistency that is controlled by means of α parameter. The notion of *dynamic reducts* was distributed and tested experimentally in [1]. In [2], generalized decision and generalized decision reduct was taken into account by M.Kryszkiewicz, it provides a decision maker with more flexible selection of decision behavior.

The main objective of the paper was to discuss the reductions of a set-valued decision information system(DIS) and find the relationships of these knowledge reductions in set-valued DIS. The judgment theorem and the discernibility matrix of the generalized decision reduct in a set-valued DIS are given. It is proved that both of the reduction in the consistent set-valued DIS and the possible reduction in the inconsistent set-valued DIS are equivalent to the generalized decision reduct. The judgment theorem and the discernibility matrix associated with the possible reduct are also established.

The paper is organized as follows. Section 2 presents basic notions of a set-valued information system. In section 3 the generalized decision reduct in a set-valued DIS is discussed, the judgment theorem and the discernibility matrix associated with the generalized decision reduct are given. In section 4 we discuss the consistent set-valued DIS. The properties and the approach to reduction for a consistent set-valued DIS are given. In section 5 the inconsistent set-valued DIS is discussed, and the relationship between the possible reduct and the generalized decision reduct is given. A final section contains conclusions.

2   Set-Valued Decision Information System

A set-valued decision information system (DIS) (see [10]) is a quinary $\varphi = (U, A, F, d, g_d)$, where $U = \{x_1, x_2, \cdots, x_n\}$ is a nonempty finite set of objects called universe and $A = \{a_1, a_2, \cdots, a_m\}$ is a nonempty finite set of attributes, are called condition attributes, $d \notin A$ is a decision attribute, $F = \{f_l : l \leq m\}, where\ f_l : U \longrightarrow \mathcal{P}_0(V_l)(l \leq m)$ is an attribute value function, V_l is a domain of attribute a_l, $\mathcal{P}_0(V_l)$ is the whole nonempty subset of V_l, $g_d : U \longrightarrow V_d$ is a specific attribute value function, $V_d = \{1, 2, \cdots, r\}$ is a finite domain of g_d.

Let (U, A, F, d, g_d) be a set-valued DIS, $\forall B \subseteq A$, define a relation as follow:

$$R_B^{\cap} = \{(x, y) \in U \times U : f_a(x) \cap f_a(y) \neq \emptyset \quad (\forall a \in B)\}.$$

The relation is called a similarity relation or a tolerance relation ,and note

$$[x]_B^{\cap} = \{y \in U : (x, y) \in R_B^{\cap}\} = \{y \in U : f_a(x) \cap f_a(y) \neq \emptyset \quad (\forall a \in B)\}$$

called tolerance class.

Let

$$R_d = \{(x, y) \in U \times U : g_d(x) = g_d(y)\}.$$

Obviously, $R_B^\cap$ is reflexive and symmetric, but not transitive, so it is not an equivalence relation, we call it a tolerance relation; R_d is an equivalence relation.

We can easily proof if objects x and y have Kryszkiewicz's tolerance relation $SIM(B)$, i.e.,

$$SIM(B) = \{(x,y) \in U \times U : \forall a \in B, f_a(x) = f_a(y) \ or \ f_a(x) = * \ or \ f_a(y) = *\},$$

then x and y are also possess the relation $R_B^\cap$. This shows $R_B^\cap$ is an extension to Kryszkiewicz's tolerance relation $SIM(B)$.

Proposition 1.   Let (U, A, F, d, g_d) be a set-valued DIS, $\forall B \subseteq A$, $R_B^\cap$ is a similarity relation defined as above, then we have:

(1) *if $B_1 \subseteq B_2 \subseteq A$, then $R_{B_1}^\cap \supseteq R_{B_2}^\cap \supseteq R_A^\cap$;*
(2) *if $B_1 \subseteq B_2 \subseteq A$, then $[x]_{B_1}^\cap \supseteq [x]_{B_2}^\cap \supseteq [x]_A^\cap$;*
(3) $\mathcal{I} = \{[x]_B^\cap : x \in U\}$ *constitute a covering of U,*

Let $U/R_B^\cap$ denote classification, which is the family set $\{[x]_B^\cap \mid x \in U\}$. Any element from $U/R_B^\cap$ will be called a tolerance class.

Example 1.   A set-valued DIS is presented in Table 1.

Table 1. A Set-Valued Decision Information System

U	a_1	a_2	a_3	a_4	d
x_1	{1}	{1}	{0}	{0}	1
x_2	{0}	{1,2}	{0}	{0}	1
x_3	{1,0}	{1,2}	{1}	{0}	0
x_4	{1}	{1,2}	{0}	{1}	1
x_5	{1,0}	{1,2}	{0}	{1}	2
x_6	{0}	{2}	{0}	{1,0}	1

From Table 1, one can obtain:

$$[x_1]_A^\cap = \{x_1\}, \ [x_2]_A^\cap = \{x_2, x_6\}, \ [x_3]_A^\cap = \{x_3\},$$

$$[x_4]_A^\cap = \{x_4, x_5\}, \ [x_5]_A^\cap = \{x_4, x_5, x_6\}, \ [x_6]_A^\cap = \{x_2, x_5, x_6\};$$

$$U/R_d = \{D_1, D_2, D_3\}, \quad where \ D_1 = \{x_1, x_2, x_4, x_6\}, D_2 = \{x_3\}, D_3 = \{x_5\}.$$

3   Generalized Decision Reduct

Let (U, A, F, d, g_d) be a set-valued DIS, $\forall B \subseteq A$, $R_B^\cap$ is a similarity relation defined as above.

The generalized decision function in a set-valued DIS $\partial_B^\cap : U \to P(V_d), B \subseteq A$, is definied as follows:

$$\partial_B^\cap(x) = \{i \mid i = d(y) \ and \ y \in [x]_B^\cap\}$$

If $card(\partial_A^\cap(x)) = 1$ for any $x \in U$ then DIS is consistent, otherwise it is inconsistent.

Reduction of knowledge that preserves generalized decision for all objects in DIS is lossless from the point of making decision.

Definition 1.   A set $B \subseteq A$ is a generalized decision consistent set of the set-valued DIS if $\partial_B^\cap = \partial_A^\cap$ for all $x \in U$. If B is a generalized decision consistent set, and no proper subset of B is generalized decision consistent, then B is referred to as a generalized decision reduct of the set-valued DIS.

We denote $\mathcal{D}_\partial^\cap = \{D_\partial^\cap(x_i, x_j), \ x_i, x_j \in U\}$, where

$$D_\partial^\cap(x_i, x_j) = \begin{cases} \{a \in A \mid (x_i, x_j) \notin R_a^\cap\} = \{a \in A \mid f_a(x_i) \cap f_a(x_j) = \emptyset\}, & d(x_j) \notin \partial_A^\cap(x_i), \\ \emptyset, & d(x_j) \in \partial_A^\cap(x_i). \end{cases}$$

$\mathcal{D}_\partial^\cap$ is called the discernibility matrix of set-valued DIS with respect to $\partial_A^\cap$.

Proposition 2.   Let $\varphi = (U, A, F, d, g_d)$ be a Set-valued DIS, $B \subseteq A$, and $\mathcal{D}_\partial^\cap = \{D_\partial^\cap(x_i, x_j), \ x_i, x_j \in U\}$ be the discernibility matrix of set-valued DIS with respect to $R_A^\cap$, then

$$B \cap D_\partial^\cap(x_i, x_j) \neq \emptyset \ (D_\partial^\cap(x_i, x_j) \neq \emptyset) \ iff \ \partial_B^\cap = \partial_A^\cap.$$

Proof: Since $[x]_B^\cap \supseteq [x]_A^\cap$ for any $B \subseteq A$, so we have $\partial_B^\cap(x_i) \supseteq \partial_A^\cap(x_i)$. Hence we only need to prove

$$B \cap D_\partial^\cap(x_i, x_j) \neq \emptyset \ (D_\partial^\cap(x_i, x_j) \neq \emptyset) \ iff \ \partial_B^\cap \subseteq \partial_A^\cap.$$

($\to$)   Suppose $B \cap D_\partial^\cap(x_i, x_j) \neq \emptyset \ (D_\partial^\cap(x_i, x_j) \neq \emptyset)$.

If for any $x_i' \in [x_i]_B^\cap$ and $x_i' \notin [x_i]_A^\cap, d(x_i') \notin \partial_A^\cap(x_i)$, then we have $D_\partial^\cap(x_i, x_i') \neq \emptyset$. So $B \cap D_\partial^\cap(x_i, x_i') \neq \emptyset$. However, according to $x_i' \in [x_i]_B^\cap$ we can get $(x_i, x_i') \in R_B^\cap$, that is $f_b(x_i) \cap f_b(x_i') \neq \emptyset (\forall b \in B)$. Then $B \cap D_\partial^\cap(x_i, x_i') = \emptyset$. This is a contradiction.

Hence, for $B \cap D_\partial^\cap(x_i, x_j) \neq \emptyset \ (D_\partial^\cap(x_i, x_j) \neq \emptyset)$, if $x_i' \in [x_i]_B^\cap$ and $x_i' \notin [x_i]_A^\cap$, then $d(x_i') \in \partial_A^\cap(x_i)$. So $\partial_B^\cap(x_i) \subseteq \partial_A^\cap(x_j)$.

($\Leftarrow$)   Suppose $\partial_B^\cap \subseteq \partial_A^\cap$. If $d(x_j) \notin \partial_A^\cap(x_i)$, then $d(x_j) \notin \partial_B^\cap(x_i)$, that is $x_j \notin [x_i]_B^\cap$. Thus there exists $b \in B$ such that $(x_i, x_j) \notin R_b^\cap$, we have $b \in D_\partial^\cap(x_i, x_j)$. Therefore $B \cap D_\partial^\cap(x_i, x_j) \neq \emptyset \ (D_\partial^\cap(x_i, x_j) \neq \emptyset)$.

Let $\vee D_\partial^\cap(x_i, x_j)$ be a Boolean expression that is equal to 1 if $D_\partial^\cap(x_i, x_j) = \emptyset$. Otherwise, $\vee D_\partial^\cap(x_i, x_j)$ is a disjunction of variables corresponding to attributes contained in $D_\partial^\cap(x_i, x_j)$.

Let $\Delta = \wedge_{(x_i, x_j) \in U \times U} \vee D_\partial^\cap(x_i, x_j)$, Δ is referred to the generalized decision discernibility function for a set-valued DIS.

Discernibility function is monotonic Boolean function and its prime implication determine reductions uniquely.

Example 2. In Table 2 we place the values of generalized decision function based on the set-valued DIS described by Table 1.

Table 2. The values of generalized decision function

U	a_1	a_2	a_3	a_4	d	$\partial_A^\cap$
x_1	$\{1\}$	$\{1\}$	$\{0\}$	$\{0\}$	1	$\{1\}$
x_2	$\{0\}$	$\{1,2\}$	$\{0\}$	$\{0\}$	1	$\{1\}$
x_3	$\{1,0\}$	$\{1,2\}$	$\{1\}$	$\{0\}$	0	$\{0\}$
x_4	$\{1\}$	$\{1,2\}$	$\{0\}$	$\{1\}$	1	$\{1,2\}$
x_5	$\{1,0\}$	$\{1,2\}$	$\{0\}$	$\{1\}$	2	$\{1,2\}$
x_6	$\{0\}$	$\{2\}$	$\{0\}$	$\{1,0\}$	1	$\{1,2\}$

From Table 2, we can obtain the set-valued DIS described by Table 1 is inconsistent.

Table 3 is the discernibility matrix of the set-valued DIS described by Table 1:

Table 3. The discernibility matrix of set-valued DIS described by Table 1

$x \backslash y$	x_1	x_2	x_3	x_4	x_5	x_6
x_1			a_3		a_4	
x_2			a_3		a_4	
x_3	a_3	a_3		$a_3 a_4$	$a_3 a_4$	a_3
x_4			$a_3 a_4$			
x_5			$a_3 a_4$			
x_6			a_3			

From Table 3, we have

$$\Delta = a_3 \wedge a_4 \wedge (a_3 \vee a_4) = a_3 \wedge a_4.$$

Thus, B=$\{a_3, a_4\}$ is a reduction for the set-valued DIS presented by Table 1. From Table 1, we have:

$$[x_1]_B^\cap = \{x_1, x_2, x_6\}, \ [x_2]_B^\cap = \{x_1, x_2, x_6\}, \ [x_3]_B^\cap = \{x_3\},$$

$$[x_4]_B^\cap = \{x_4, x_5, x_6\}, \ [x_5]_B^\cap = \{x_4, x_5, x_6\}, \ [x_6]_B^\cap = \{x_1, x_2, x_4, x_5, x_6\}.$$

One can easily obtain $\partial_B^\cap = \partial_A^\cap$.

4   The Reduct in a Consistent Set-Valued DIS

If $card(\partial_A^\cap(x)) = 1$ for any $x \in U$ then a set-valued DIS is called a consistent set-valued DIS.

Proposition 3. Let (U, A, F, d, g_d) be a set-valued DIS, then

$$card(\partial_A^{\cap}(x)) = 1(\forall x \in U) \text{ iff } R_A^{\cap} \subseteq R_d.$$

Proof: $R_A^{\cap} \subseteq R_d \Leftrightarrow [x]_A^{\cap} \subseteq [x]_d^{\cap} \Leftrightarrow card(\partial_A^{\cap}(x)) = 1(\forall x \in U).$

Definition 2. A set $B \subseteq A$ is a consistent set of the consistent set-valued DIS if $R_B^{\cap} \subseteq R_d$, and in addition $\forall B' \subset A, R_{B'}^{\cap} \not\subseteq R_d, B$ is called the reduct of the consistent set-valued DIS. Thus, a reduction of the consistent set-valued DIS is a minimal attribute subset satisfying $R_B^{\cap} \subseteq R_d$.

We denote $\mathcal{D}_d^{\cap} = \{D_d^{\cap}(x_i, x_j), \ x_i, x_j \in U\}$, where

$$D_d^{\cap}(x_i, x_j) = \begin{cases} \{a \in A : f_a(x_i) \cap f_a(x_j) = \emptyset\}, & d(x_i) \neq d(x_j), \\ \emptyset, & d(x_i) = d(x_j). \end{cases}$$

$\mathcal{D}_d^{\cap}$ is called the discernibility matrix of the consistent set-valued DIS with respect to $R_A^{\cap}$.

Proposition 4. Let $\varphi = (U, A, F, d, g_d)$ be a consistent Set-valued DIS, $B \subseteq A$, and $\mathcal{D}_d^{\cap} = \{D_d^{\cap}(x_i, x_j), \ x_i, x_j \in U\}$ is the discernibility matrix of consistent set-valued DIS, then

$$B \cap D_d^{\cap}(x_i, x_j) \neq \emptyset \ (D_d^{\cap}(x_i, x_j) \neq \emptyset) \text{ iff } R_B^{\cap} \subseteq R_d.$$

Proof:$R_B^{\cap} \subseteq R_d \Leftrightarrow if \ (x_i, x_j) \notin R_d^{\cap} \ then \ (x_i, x_j) \notin R_B^{\cap} \Leftrightarrow if \ D_d^{\cap}(x_i, x_j) \neq \emptyset \ then \ (x_i, x_j) \notin R_B^{\cap}, \ that \ is \ \exists a_l \in B \ such \ that \ a_l \in D_d^{\cap}(x_i, x_j) \Leftrightarrow B \cap D_d^{\cap}(x_i, x_j) \neq \emptyset \ when \ D_d^{\cap}(x_i, x_j) \neq \emptyset.$

Proposition 5. Let $\varphi = (U, A, F, d, g_d)$ be a consistent Set-valued DIS, i.e., $card(\partial_A^{\cap}(x)) = 1 \ (\forall x \in U \ ), B \subseteq A$, then

$$R_B^{\cap} \subseteq R_d \text{ iff } \partial_B^{\cap}(x) = \partial_A^{\cap}(x) \ (\forall x \in U).$$

Proof:($\Leftarrow$) Suppose $\partial_B^{\cap}(x) = \partial_A^{\cap}(x)$. So $card(\partial_B^{\cap}(x)) = 1$. By Proposition 3, we conclude that $R_B^{\cap} \subseteq R_d$.
($\Rightarrow$) Suppose $R_B^{\cap} \subseteq R_d$, then we obtain $card(\partial_B^{\cap}(x)) = card(\partial_A^{\cap}(x)) = 1$.
On the other hand, $[x]_A^{\cap} \subseteq [x]_B^{\cap}$ for $B \subseteq A$, so $\partial_B^{\cap}(x) \supseteq \partial_A^{\cap}(x)$.Therefore $\partial_B^{\cap}(x) = \partial_A^{\cap}(x)$.

From Proposition 5, we can obtain Definition 2 is equivalent to Definition 1 for a consistent set-valued DIS.

Let $\Delta' = \wedge_{(x_i, x_j) \in U \times U} \vee D_d^{\cap}(x_i, x_j)$, Δ' is referred to the discernibility function for a consistent set-valued DIS. Δ' determines reductions uniquely for the consistent set-valued DIS. .

Table 4. A Consistent Set-Valued DIS

U	a_1	a_2	a_3	a_4	d
x_1	{1}	{1}	{0}	{0}	2
x_2	{0}	{1,2}	{0}	{0}	1
x_3	{1,0}	{1,2}	{1}	{0}	0
x_4	{1}	{1,2}	{0}	{1}	1
x_5	{1,0}	{1,2}	{0}	{1}	1
x_6	{0}	{2}	{0}	{1,0}	1

Example 3. Table 4 describes a consistent set-valued DIS.

From Table 4, one can obtain:

$$[x_1]_A^{\cap} = \{x_1\}, \ [x_2]_A^{\cap} = \{x_2, x_6\}, \ [x_3]_A^{\cap} = \{x_3\},$$

$$[x_4]_A^{\cap} = \{x_4, x_5\}, \ [x_5]_A^{\cap} = \{x_4, x_5, x_6\}, \ [x_6]_A^{\cap} = \{x_2, x_5, x_6\};$$

$$U/R_d = \{D_1, D_2, D_3\}, \quad where \ D_1 = \{x_1\}, D_2 = \{x_3\}, D_3 = \{x_2, x_4, x_5, x_6\}.$$

So we have $card(\partial_A^{\cap}(x)) = 1 \ (\forall x \in U)$.

Table 5 is the discernibility matrix of the consistent set-valued DIS described by Table 4.

Table 5. The discernibility matrix of the set-valued DIS described by Table 4

$x \backslash y$	x_1	x_2	x_3	x_4	x_5	x_6
x_1		a_1	a_3	a_4	a_4	$a_1 a_2$
x_2	a_1		a_3			
x_3	a_3	a_3		a_3	$a_3 a_4$	a_3
x_4	a_4		$a_3 a_4$			
x_5	a_4		$a_3 a_4$			
x_6	$a_1 a_2$		a_3			

From Table 5, we have

$$\Delta' = a_1 \wedge a_3 \wedge a_4 \wedge (a_1 \vee a_2) \wedge (a_3 \vee a_4) = a_1 \wedge a_3 \wedge a_4.$$

Thus, B=$\{a_1, a_3, a_4\}$ is a reduct for the consistent set-valued DIS presented by Table 4.

From Table 4, we have:

$$[x_1]_B^{\cap} = \{x_1\}, \ [x_2]_B^{\cap} = \{x_2, x_6\}, \ [x_3]_B^{\cap} = \{x_3\}, \ [x_4]_B^{\cap} = \{x_4, x_5\},$$

$$[x_5]_B^{\cap} = \{x_4, x_5, x_6\}, \ [x_6]_B^{\cap} = \{x_2, x_5, x_6\}.$$

One can easily observe $R_B^{\cap} \subseteq R_d$.

5   The Reduction in an Inconsistent Set-Valued DIS

If $card(\partial_A^\cap(x)) \neq 1$ for any $x \in U$ then a set-valued DIS is called an inconsistent set-valued DIS.

Definition 3. Let $\varphi = (U, A, F, d, g_d)$ be an inconsistent Set-valued DIS, $V_d = \{1, 2, \cdots, r\}$ is a finite domain of the condition attribute d, R_d is an equivalence relation, $U/R_d = \{D_1, D_2, \cdots, D_r\}$. Note

$$\delta_B^\cap(x_i) = \{D_j; \ [x_i]_B^\cap \cap D_j \neq \emptyset \ (x_i \in U)\}.$$

A set $B \subseteq A$ is a possible consistent set of the inconsistent set-valued DIS if $\delta_B^\cap = \delta_A^\cap$ for all $x \in U$. If B is a possible consistent set, and no proper subset of B is possible consistent, then B is referred to as a possible reduct of the inconsistent set-valued DIS. A possible consistent set of the set-valued DIS preserves all possible decision classes.

Lemma 6. Let $\varphi = (U, A, F, d, g_d)$ be an inconsistent Set-valued DIS, define a map as follow:

$$g: \ U/R_d \rightarrow V_d, \ g(D_i) = d(x_j), \forall x_j \in D_i,$$

then $\partial_A^\cap(x_i) = g(\delta_A^\cap(x_i))$, where $\delta_A^\cap(x_i) = \{D_1, D_2, \cdots, D_l\}$, $g(D_1, D_2, \cdots, D_l) = (g(D_1), g(D_2), \cdots, g(D_l))$.
Proof:Let $d(y) \in \partial_A^\cap(x_i)$, then $\exists x_j \in [x_i]_A^\cap$, such that $d(x_j) = d(y)$. For $x_j \in [x_i]_A^\cap \subseteq U$, $\exists \ unique \ D_j$, such that $x_j \in D_j$, then $D_j \cap [x_i]_A^\cap \neq \emptyset$, so $D_j \in \delta_A^\cap(x_i)$. That is $d(y) = d(x_j) = g(D_j)$ and $g(D_j) \in g(\delta_A^\cap(x_i))$.Therefore $\partial_A^\cap(x_i) \subseteq g(\delta_A^\cap(x_i))$

On the other hand, let $x_i \in U$, $\forall D_j \in \delta_A^\cap(x_i)$, $D_j \cap [x_i]_A^\cap \neq \emptyset$. So $\exists y \in [x_i]_A^\cap \ and \ y \in D_j$. Hence $g(D_j) = d(y) \ and \ d(y) \in \partial_A^\cap(x_i)$. That is $g(\delta_A^\cap(x_i)) \subseteq \partial_A^\cap(x_i)$

Therefore $\partial_A^\cap(x_i) = g(\delta_A^\cap(x_i))$.

We denote $\mathcal{D}_\delta^\cap = \{D_\delta^\cap(x_i, x_j), \ x_i, x_j \in U\}$, where

$$D_\delta^\cap(x_i, x_j) = \begin{cases} \{a \in A : (x_i, x_j) \notin R_a^\cap\} = \{a \in A : f_a(x_i) \cap f_a(x_j) = \emptyset\}, & d(x_j) \notin g(\delta_A^\cap(x_i)), \\ \emptyset, & d(x_j) \in g(\delta_A^\cap(x_i)). \end{cases}$$

$\mathcal{D}_\delta^\cap$ is called the discernibility matrix of an inconsistent set-valued DIS with respect to $\delta_A^\cap$.

Proposition 7. Let $\varphi = (U, A, F, d, g_d)$ be an inconsistent Set-valued DIS, $B \subseteq A$, and $\mathcal{D}_\delta^\cap = \{D_\delta^\cap(x_i, x_j), \ x_i, x_j \in U\}$ is the discernibility matrix of set-valued DIS, then

$$B \cap D_\delta^\cap(x_i, x_j) \neq \emptyset \ (D_\delta^\cap(x_i, x_j) \neq \emptyset) \text{ iff } \delta_B^\cap = \delta_A^\cap.$$

Proof: It is immediately from lemma 6 and Proposition 2.

Remark. From Lemma 6, Proposition 7 and Proposition 2, we can immediately conclude that the possible consistent set of an inconsistent set-valued DIS is equivalent to the generalized decision consistent set of the inconsistent set-valued DIS.

Example 4. The values of $\partial_A^{\cap}$ and $\delta_A^{\cap}$ based on the set-valued DIS described by Table 1 is given as Table 6, where $D_1 = \{x_1, x_2, x_4, x_6\}, D_2 = \{x_3\}, D_3 = \{x_5\}$.

Table 6. The values of $\partial_A^{\cap}$ and $\delta_A^{\cap}$ from Table 1

U	$\partial_A^{\cap}$	$\delta_A^{\cap}$
x_1	$\{1\}$	D_1
x_2	$\{1\}$	D_1
x_3	$\{0\}$	D_2
x_4	$\{1,2\}$	D_1, D_3
x_5	$\{1,2\}$	D_1, D_3
x_6	$\{1,2\}$	D_1, D_3

Obviously, $g(D_1) = 1, g(D_2) = 0, g(D_3) = 2$. So we have $g(\delta_A^{\cap}(x_i)) = \partial_A^{\cap}(x_i)$ $(\forall x_i \in U)$.

6   Conclusion

One fundamental aspect of rough set theory involves the searching for some particular subsets of condition attributes. The information for classification or decision making provided by such one subset is the same as the information provided by the condition attribute set. Such subsets are called reducts. To acquire brief decision rules from the decision table, knowledge reduction is needed. However, much study on reduction was based on complete information system or consistent information system.

In this paper we discuss the reductions of a set-valued decision information system(DIS). The judgment theorem and the discernibility matrix of alternative types of knowledge reduction in set-valued DIS are given. The relationships of the various knowledge reduction in set-valued DIS are investigated. It is proved that the reduct in the consistent set-valued DIS is equivalent to the generalized decision reduct, and the possible reduct in the inconsistent set-valued DIS is equivalent to the generalized decision reduct.

Acknowledgment. The paper was supported by the National 973 Program of China(no.2003CB312206).

References

1. Bazan, J.: A Comparison of Dynamic and Non-dynamic Rough Set Methods for Extracting Laws From Decision Tables. In: Polkowski, L., Skowron, A. (eds.): Rough Sets in Knowledge Discovery. Physica-Verlag, Heidelberg (1998) 321-365
2. Kryszkiewicz, M.:Comparative Study of Alternative Types of knowledge Reduction in inconsistent systems. International Journal of Intelligent Systems. **16** (2001) 105-120
3. Liu, Q., Liu, S.H., Zheng, F.: Rough Logic and its Applications in Data Reduction. (in Chinese) Journal of Software. **12** (2001) 415–419
4. Mi, J.S., Wu, W.Z., Zhang, W.X.: Approaches to Knowledge Reduction Based on Variable Precision Rough Set Model. Information Sciences. **159** (2004) 255-272
5. Miao, D.Q., Hu, G.R.: A Heuristic Algorithm for Reduction of Knowledge. (in Chinese) Journal of Computer Research and Development. **36** (1999) 681–684
6. Nguyen, H.S., Slezak, D.: Approximate reducts and association rules correspondence complexity results. In: Zhong, N., Skowron, A., Oshuga, S. (eds): Proc of RSFDGrC'99. Yamaguchi, Japan. LNAI 1711. (1999) 137-145
7. Pawlak, Z.: Rough Sets: Theoretical Aspects of Reasoning about Data. Boston: Kluwer Academic Publishers (1991)
8. Wang, G.Y.(ed.): Rough Set Theory and Knowledge acquirement. Xi'an JiaoTong University Press, Xi'an, (2001)(in chinese)
9. Yao, Y.Y.: Generalized rough Set Models. In: Polkowski, L., Skowron, A. (eds.): Rough Sets in Knowledge Discovery. Physica-Verlag, Heidelberg (1998) 286-318
10. Zhang, W.X., Leung, Y., Wu, W.Z.(eds.) Information Systems and knowledge Discovery. Science Press, Beijing, (2003)(in chinese)
11. Ziarko, W.: Variable Precision Rough Set Model. Journal of Computer and System Science. 46 (1993) 39-59

Local Reducts and Jumping Emerging Patterns in Relational Databases*

Pawel Terlecki and Krzysztof Walczak

Institute of Computer Science, Warsaw University of Technology,
Nowowiejska 15/19, 00-665 Warsaw, Poland
P.Terlecki, K.Walczak@ii.pw.edu.pl

Abstract. This paper refers to the notion of minimal pattern in relational databases. We study the analogy between two concepts: a local reduct, from the rough set theory, and a jumping emerging pattern, originally defined for transactional data. Their equivalence within a positive region and similarities between eager and lazy classification methods based on both ideas are demonstrated. Since pattern discovery approaches vary significantly, efficiency tests have been performed in order to decide, which solution provides a better tool for the analysis of real relational datasets.

1   Introduction

Many definitions of knowledge discovery emphasize the importance of patterns in information modeling. There are at least three important reason for this. First of all, patterns are a useful tool in many practical problems, mainly in classification. Secondly, they can be easily understood by the human mind. Unlike neural networks, support vector machines or Bayesian classifiers, the most expressive patterns do not need any additional visualization to be comprehended and evaluated. Last but not least, the simple structure of a pattern and the intensive development of concise representations make them a convenient and powerful tool in knowledge processing and storing.

Many experiments demonstrated the accuracy of rule-based classifiers [1]. However, there are no criteria applicable to all types of data and different sorts of patterns are still being proposed to produce better rules. Notwithstanding this variety, we can figure out some common features, like their highly discriminative power, not overfitting to training data or avoiding exponential result sets.

In this paper, we focus on patterns in relational databases. One of the most elegant descriptions for this kind of data is provided by the rough set theory. Basic concepts triggered intensive research which has brought many methods suitable for practical application. The most accurate classifiers are based on the notion of a local reduct, i.e. a minimal set of attributes capable of distinguishing one particular object from objects belonging to other classes as well as the

---

* The research has been partially supported by grant No 3 T11C 002 29 received from Polish Ministry of Education and Science.

S. Greco et al. (Eds.): RSCTC 2006, LNAI 4259, pp. 358–367, 2006.

total set of attributes. This approach allows to induce minimal patterns and corresponding rules that describe a class in a very general manner.

In contrast to these classic solutions, we observe a fast development of methods for transaction databases. The most popular solutions make use of class association rules (CAR) and emerging patterns. Such classifiers as JEP-C, CAEP, DeEP or EJEP-C have already proved their high accuracy in many experiments [1]. Our study focuses on jumping emerging patterns (JEPs), the idea very similar to minimal patterns based on local reducts. A JEP is a pattern that is present in one class and absent in others. In particular, the minimal ones give a possibly general and concise description of each class in contrast to the rest.

As it was mentioned above, a JEP is originally defined by means of the traditional formal apparatus of transaction databases. Nevertheless, it is often used to deal with relational data transformed to a transactional form [2]. Now, the question emerges what the differences are between classification algorithms associated with the concept of a local reduct and a JEP. Another question is which of these approaches allows to discover the set of minimal patterns more efficiently, when relational data is concerned. Our intuition is that algorithms which operate on this kind of data can take advantage of information held in attributes in order to differentiate objects, whereas methods using the transactional approach fail to account for the actual relation between items associated with the same attribute. In addition, the space of attribute sets is often much smaller than the respective space of itemsets, which also depends on attribute value domains. For these reasons, we expect that, at least for large datasets, the efficiency of methods from both streams will be significantly different.

The text is organized as follows. Section 2 provides a formal background for the rough set theory, EPs and a relational-to-transactional transformation. In Sect. 3, we prove the similarity between minimal patterns obtained from local reducts and JEPs. Then, in Sect. 4 basic classification methods from both streams are compared. We discuss popular eager and lazy methods, taking into account differences in the way of selecting minimal patterns and aggregating them in order to obtain a decision. Section 5 explains the main issues of the two methods of minimal pattern discovery: the rough set approach and JEP-Producer. Implementation remarks are discussed in Sect. 6. Our testing procedure and results are presented in Sect. 7. The paper is summarized in Sect. 8.

2 Preliminaries

2.1 Elements of Rough Set Theory

Let a decision table be a triple $(\mathcal{U}, \mathcal{C}, d)$, where $\mathcal{U}$(universum) is a non-empty, finite set of objects, $\mathcal{C}$ is a non-empty finite set of condition attributes and d is a decision attribute. A set of all attributes is denoted by $\mathcal{A} = \mathcal{C} \cup \{d\}$. The domain of an attribute $a \in \mathcal{A}$ is denoted by V_a and its value for an object $u \in \mathcal{U}$ is denoted by a(u). In particular, $V_d = \{k_1, .., k_{|V_d|}\}$ and the decision attribute induces a partition of $\mathcal{U}$ into decision classes $\{U_k\}_{k \in V_d}$. Hereinafter, we use the term *attribute* to denote a condition attribute.

Consider $B \subseteq \mathcal{A}$. An indiscernibility relation $IND(B)$ is defined as follows:

$$IND(B) = \{(u,v) \in \mathcal{U} \times \mathcal{U} : \forall_{a \in B} \, a(u) = a(v)\}$$

Since $IND(B)$ is an equivalence relation, it induces a partition of $\mathcal{U}$ denoted by $\mathcal{U}/IND(B)$. Let $B(u)$ be a block of the partition containing $u \in \mathcal{U}$. A B-lower approximation of a set $X \subseteq \mathcal{U}$ is defined as follows: $B_*(X) = \{u \in \mathcal{U} \mid B(u) \subseteq X\}$, and a B-positive region with respect to a decision attribute d is defined by:

$$POS(B,d) = \bigcup_{X \in \mathcal{U}/IND(\{d\})} B_*(X)$$

We say that a decision table is consistent or deterministic if $POS(\mathcal{C}, d) = \mathcal{U}$. Otherwise, we call it inconsistent or non-deterministic. A local reduct for an object $u \in \mathcal{U}$ (a reduct relative to an object and a decision) is a minimal attribute set $B \subseteq \mathcal{C}$ such that $\forall_{k \in V_d}(\mathcal{C}(u) \cap U_k = \emptyset \implies B(u) \cap U_k = \emptyset)$. It means that the object u can be differentiated by means of B from all the objects from other classes as accurately as by the complete available description $\mathcal{C}$. The set of all local reducts for an object u is denoted by $REDLOC(u,d)$.

Lemma 1 ([3]). *$B \in REDLOC(u,d)$ for $u \in POS(\mathcal{C},d) \iff B$ is a minimal set such that $B(u) \subseteq U_{d(u)}$.*

2.2 Emerging Patterns

Let a decision transaction database be a tuple $(\mathcal{D}, \mathcal{N}, \mathcal{I}, \mathcal{Z})$, where $\mathcal{D} \subseteq \{(n,t) \in \mathcal{N} \times 2^{\mathcal{I}} : \forall_{(n',t') \in \mathcal{N} \times 2^{\mathcal{I}}} n = n' \implies t = t'\}$ is a set of transactions (database), $\mathcal{N}$ is a non-empty set of transaction identifiers, $\mathcal{I}$ is a non-empty set of items and $\mathcal{Z}$ is a function $\mathcal{Z} : \mathcal{D} \mapsto V_Z$, where V_Z is the set of decision class labels. The function $\mathcal{Z}$ splits the database $\mathcal{D}$ into decision classes $D_k = \mathcal{Z}^{-1}(k)$, for $k \in V_Z$. In addition, for $D \subseteq \mathcal{D}$, we define a complement database $D' = \mathcal{D} - D$. An itemset $X \in 2^{\mathcal{I}}$ is a set of items and its support in a database $D \subseteq \mathcal{D}$ is defined as $supp_D(X) = \frac{|(n,t) \in D : X \subseteq t|}{|D|}$. Given two databases $D_1, D_2 \subseteq \mathcal{D}$, we define a jumping emerging pattern (JEP) from D_1 to D_2 as an itemset X for which $supp_{D_1}(X) = 0$ and $supp_{D_2}(X) \neq 0$. A set of all JEPs from D_1 to D_2 is called a JEP space and denoted by $JEP(D_1, D_2)$.

2.3 Convexity of JEP Space

One of the most useful features of jumping emerging patterns is the possibility to store a JEP space in a concise manner.

Consider a set S. A collection $F \subseteq 2^S$ is a convex space iff $\forall_{X,Z \in F} \forall_{Y \in 2^S} X \subseteq Y \subseteq Z \Rightarrow Y \in F$. A border is an ordered pair $< \mathcal{L}, \mathcal{R} >$ such that $\mathcal{L}, \mathcal{R} \subseteq P(S)$ are antichains and $\forall_{X \in \mathcal{L}} \exists_{Z \in \mathcal{R}} X \subseteq Z$. $\mathcal{L}$ and $\mathcal{R}$ are called a left and a right bound, respectively. A border $< \mathcal{L}, \mathcal{R} >$ represents a set interval $[\mathcal{L}, \mathcal{R}] = \{Y \in P(S) : \exists_{X \in \mathcal{L}} \exists_{Z \in \mathcal{R}} X \subseteq Y \subseteq Z\}$. The left and right bounds consist, respectively, of minimal elements and maximal elements of a set, assuming inclusion relation. It can be demonstrated [2] that every convex space has a unique border.

Consider a decision transaction database $(\mathcal{D}, \mathcal{N}, \mathcal{I}, \mathcal{Z})$ and two databases $D_1, D_2 \subseteq \mathcal{D}$. According to [2] a collection $JEP(D_1, D_2)$ is a convex space. Thus, for $k \in V_Z$, we use a border $< \mathcal{L}_k, \mathcal{R}_k >$ to represent a JEP space $JEP(D'_k, D_k)$.

Lemma 2 ([2]). $\forall_{J \in 2^\mathcal{I}} J$ *is minimal in* $JEP(D'_k, D_k) \Longleftrightarrow J \in \mathcal{L}_k$.

2.4 Relational to Transactional Transformation

One can analyze relational data by means of methods formulated for transaction databases. In our study, we consider a decision transaction database build for a given decision table. For brevity, we use the following notations introduced in [4]: $patt(u, B) = \{(a, a(u))\}_{a \in B}$, where $u \in \mathcal{U}$ and $B \subseteq \mathcal{C}$, and $attr(X) = \{a \in \mathcal{C} : (a, v) \in X \wedge v \in V_a\}$, for an itemset $X \subset \{(a, v)\}_{a \in \mathcal{C}, v \in V_a}$. Without loss of generality, we assume that a universum can be linearly ordered $\mathcal{U} = \{u_1, .., u_{|\mathcal{U}|}\}$.

Definition 1. *A decision transaction database for a decision table* $(\mathcal{U}, \mathcal{C}, d)$ *is a decision transaction database* $(\mathcal{D}, \mathcal{N}, \mathcal{I}, \mathcal{Z})$, *such that*

- $\mathcal{D} = \{\varphi(u)\}_{u \in \mathcal{U}}$, *where* $\varphi : \mathcal{U} \mapsto \mathcal{D}$, $\forall_{i \in \{1..|\mathcal{U}|\}} \varphi(u_i) = (i, patt(u_i, \mathcal{C}))$
- $\mathcal{N} = \mathbb{N}$ *(positive integers)*
- $\mathcal{I} = \{(a, v)\}_{a \in \mathcal{C}, v \in V_a}$
- $V_\mathcal{Z} = V_d$ *and* $\forall_{u \in U} \mathcal{Z}(\varphi(u)) = d(u)$

Notice that φ is a bijection, so it is possible to transform the result obtained by some methods for transaction data back to relational form.

3 Relations Between Concepts

Hereinafter, we consider a decision table $\mathcal{DT} = (\mathcal{U}, \mathcal{C}, d)$ and a decision transaction database $\mathcal{RDDT} = (\mathcal{D}, \mathcal{N}, \mathcal{I}, \mathcal{Z})$ for $\mathcal{DT}$. For $u \in \mathcal{U}$, a set of all local reducts for the object u is represented by $REDLOC(u, d)$ and for $k \in V_d$ a JEP space $JEP(D'_k, D_k)$ is represented by the border $< \mathcal{L}_k, \mathcal{R}_k >$.

Rough set reducts and emerging patterns are strongly related concepts. Our previous paper [4] demonstrates the relations between global reducts and JEPs. According to that work, every global reduct P generates with object $u \in \mathcal{U}$ a pattern $patt(u, P)$ that belongs to $JEP(D'_{d(u)}, D_{d(u)})$. The following theorem considers a similar relation for local reducts. It says that every local reduct generates with object $u \in POS(\mathcal{C}, d)$ a jumping emerging pattern that is minimal, i.e. it belongs to $\mathcal{L}_{d(u)}$, the left bound of the border of a space $JEP(D'_{d(u)}, D_{d(u)})$.

Notice that for a consistent decision table this relation holds for each $u \in \mathcal{U}$. Thus, we can use algorithms originating in either rough set theory or emerging patterns approach to compute the set of minimal patterns.

Theorem 1. *Let* $\mathcal{DT} = (\mathcal{U}, \mathcal{C}, d)$ *be a decision table and* $\mathcal{RDDT} = (\mathcal{D}, \mathcal{N}, \mathcal{I}, \mathcal{Z})$ *a decision transaction database for* $\mathcal{DT}$.

$\forall_{u \in POS(\mathcal{C}, d)} \forall_{P \subseteq \mathcal{C}} P \in REDLOC(u, d) \Longleftrightarrow patt(u, P) \in \mathcal{L}_{d(u)}$.

Proof. Let $P, B \in \mathcal{C}$, $u \in POS(\mathcal{C}, d)$ and $k = d(u)$.

Consider first $B(u) \subseteq U_k \iff patt(u, B) \in JEP(D'_k, D_k)$ (1). We have $B(u) \subseteq U_k \iff u \in B_*(U_k) \iff u \in POS(B, d) \cap U_k$. But, according to Theorem 1 from [4], we have: $u \in POS(B, d) \cap U_k \iff patt(u, B) \in \{J \in JEP(D'_k, D_k) : attr(J) = B\} \iff patt(u, B) \in JEP(D'_k, D_k)$.

Consider $P \in REDLOC(u, d) \implies patt(u, P) \in \mathcal{L}_k$. Let $P \in REDLOC(u, d)$. According to Lemma 1, we have: $P \in REDLOC(u, d) \iff P$ is minimal in $\{B \subseteq \mathcal{C} : B(u) \subseteq U_k\}$. Consider $R \subset P$. It means that $R(u) \not\subseteq U_k$, and, according to (1), we obtain $patt(u, R) \notin JEP(D'_k, D_k)$. Summing up, according to (1) we have $patt(u, P) \in JEP(D'_k, D_k)$ and for any $J \subset patt(u, P)$ we have $J \notin JEP(D'_k, D_k)$. Thus, $patt(u, P)$ is minimal in $JEP(D'_k, D_k)$ and, according to Lemma 2, we have $patt(u, P) \in \mathcal{L}_k$.

Consider $P \in REDLOC(u, d) \impliedby patt(u, P) \in \mathcal{L}_k$. Let $patt(u, P) \in \mathcal{L}_k$. According to Lemma 2, we have: $patt(u, P) \in \mathcal{L}_k \iff patt(u, P)$ is minimal in $JEP(D'_k, D_k)$. Consider $R \subset P$. It means that $patt(u, R) \subset patt(u, P) \implies patt(u, R) \notin JEP(D'_k, D_k)$, and, according to (1), we obtain $R(u) \not\subseteq U_k$. Summing up, according to (1) we have $P \in \{B \subseteq \mathcal{C} : B(u) \subseteq U_k\}$ and for any $R \subset P$ we have $R(u) \not\subseteq U_k$. Thus, P is minimal in $\{B \subseteq \mathcal{C} : B(u) \subseteq U_k\}$ and, according to Lemma 1, we have $P \in REDLOC(u, d)$.

4   Classification Based on Minimal Patterns

The rough set theory and emerging patterns are often used to build efficient classifiers. Although both approaches use different formal apparatus, they often employ similar algorithmic ideas.

A rough set is a convenient tool for representing approximate concepts. In particular, one of its major applications is to express the classification hypothesis provided by a decision table. Most of rough set classifiers are rule-based and make use of the notion of a reduct and its derivatives. The rule set of a classifier results from the set of reducts used against the objects in a decision table. On the other hand, classifiers based on emerging patterns operate on sets of patterns induced for each decision class. Patterns are discovered according to their characteristics in a transaction database, e.g. minimal support in a positive or negative class, minimal growth-rate, minimal chi-square test value etc.

A classification function is defined as a function $f : \mathcal{U} \mapsto V_d$, such that $f(u) = argmax_{k \in V_d} score(u, k)$, for $u \in \mathcal{U}$, where $score$ is a class scoring function $score : \mathcal{U} \times V_d \mapsto \mathbb{R}$. The form of the class scoring function depends on a particular method. For a rule-based classifier, it is determined by the set of rules and the way of aggregating their significance. In fact, a decision rule $\bigwedge_{a \in P}(a = v_a) \implies v_d$ can be equivalently expressed by $\{(a, v_a)\}_{a \in P} \implies v_d$, for some $P \subseteq \mathcal{C}$, $v_a \in V_a$ for each $a \in P$ and $v_d \in V_d$. Thus, for the sake of this study, we assume that a rule-based classifier operates on a collection of pattern sets $\{P_k\}_{k \in V_d}$ induced for respective classes. Moreover, we use two following notations analogical to [5]. A set of all patterns assigned to a class $k \in V_d$ and matching an object $u \in \mathcal{U}$ is denoted by $MatchPatterns(u, k) = \{R \in P_k : R \subseteq patt(u, \mathcal{C})\}$. On the other hand, a set of all objects that supports a given pattern is represented by $SupportSet(R) = \{u \in \mathcal{U} : R \subseteq patt(u, \mathcal{C})\}$. Thanks to the two-way nature of the relational-to-transactional transformation, these expressions remain true also when we operate on a respective decision transaction database.

In this study, we limit our interest to classifiers based on minimal patterns. The following sections provide a comparison of methods originating in both families. Our purpose is to demonstrate the analogical solutions and point out the main differences. Comparative accuracy tests can be found in [1,3].

4.1   Pattern Selection Methods

The rough set approach based on the concept of a local reduct is presented in [3,6]. It discovers the set $REDLOC(u, d)$ for each $u \in \mathcal{U}$ in the decision table $DT = (\mathcal{U}, \mathcal{C}, d)$ and then uses it to generate the pattern set collection $\{P_k\}_{k \in V_d}$, where $P_k = \{patt(u, R) : u \in U_k \wedge R \in REDLOC(u, d)\}$ for $k \in V_d$. A similar idea can be found in JEP-C (e.g. [1]) which computes JEP spaces for each class in the respective decision transaction database in order to obtain the collection $\{\mathcal{L}_k\}_{k \in V_d}$. According to Theorem 1, both collections are equal when DT is consistent. Otherwise, every object from outside of the positive region can generate emerging patterns that are not jumping and cannot be generalized in order to obtain JEP. In fact, JEP-C induces patterns only from the positive region of a decision data, i.e. it considers the decision transaction database for the table $(POS(\mathcal{U}), \mathcal{C}, d)$.

This difference remains true also for other propositions based on JEPs, like DeEP or DeEP-NN [7]. The assumption about consistency holds for many real data sets, especially with a large number of attributes; however, in general, the inability to make inference from non-positive data can be a weakness of the classifiers of this type. In particular, they are more prone to noisy data than approaches based on local reducts or other types of patterns, e.g. EP, chi-EP.

One of the improvements of the local reduct-based method, described in [6], is to decrease the size of a rule set by selecting the minimal set of patterns that covers the universum. The main arguments behind this idea refer to the minimum description length principle, classification efficiency and the possible generality of a discovered subset of patterns. Since this step involves solving a set covering problem, in many cases heuristic methods are employed to find a suboptimal solution. As a matter of fact, there is no such proposition for emerging patterns, however, this strategy can be applied in the similar manner. Since, the sets of jumping emerging patterns P_k are exclusive, we can solve k set covering problems, one for each class U_k, instead of dealing with $\mathcal{U}$ at once. It also means that, for inconsistent decision tables, one can obtain a more concise pattern set, when using an approach based on local reducts.

4.2   Class Scoring

Let us consider a pattern set collection $\{P_k\}_{k \in V_d}$, where P_k contains minimal patterns chosen according to some criteria. In order to complete the picture of rule-based classifiers, popular scoring functions will be discussed. The approaches are divided into two groups depending on what is aggregated to obtain a decision.

In the first group, the algorithm takes into account a set of training objects that support any of the patterns matching a testing object. This approach is commonly used in lazy classifiers. The scoring function for lazy local reduct classification has the form: $strength(u, k) = |\bigcup_{R \in MatchPatterns(u,k)} SupportSet(R)|$. A similar idea is proposed in DeEP classifier [7], however, the number of matching objects is related to the cardinality of a respective class, i.e: $compactScore(u, k) = \frac{strength(u,k)}{D_k}$. The second formula seems to be more adequate in case of an object disproportion within the classes U_k or pattern sets P_k, both for $k \in V_d$.

The second concept focuses on direct aggregation of patterns matching a testing object. A good example is the scoring function used in JEP-C (e.g. [1]) defined as: $collectiveImpact(u, k) = \sum_{R \in MatchPatterns(u,k)} supp_{D_k}(R)$. On the other hand, eager classifiers based on local reducts employ the notion of an approximation space in order to produce a classification result. In the beginning, for a testing object u the algorithm finds a set of all patterns matching u, denoted by $\mathcal{R}$. Then, for each pattern $R \in \mathcal{R}$, the objects of $SupportSet(R)$ are analyzed in order to obtain a partial decision for this pattern. Finally, the partial results are aggregated to indicate a decision class. Although this approach is very general, in the most common case, it becomes similar to $collectiveImpact$. In fact, when we assume consistency, each pattern indicates only one class. Therefore, for a frequency-wise aggregating strategy, both classifiers are equivalent.

In practice, the result of pattern aggregation can be strongly influenced by a disproportion in the number of minimal patterns $|P_k|$ in particular classes. One of the solutions was proposed originally for CAEP (e.g. [1]) and involves dividing a score by the base score for the respective class. The base score for a class $k \in V_d$ is a selected percentile of the distribution of scores for a training data $\{score(u, k) : u \in U_k\}$, e.g. 50-80th within these scores. Last but not least, when we sum the supports of selected patterns, we use the assumption of their independent occurrence in data and ignore possible correlations that can be observed in a training set. As a result, the score can be overestimated.

5   Minimal Pattern Discovery

Due to their generality and sharp discriminating power, minimal patterns are a good basis to build accurate classifiers. However, discovering the collection of all minimal patterns for each class of a decision table can be a time-consuming task. In general, the resulting pattern sets might have an exponential cardinality, which suggests the non-polynomial complexity of any possible algorithm. This opinion is also strengthened by the NP-hardness of finding the decision rule of a minimal cardinality [3]. Moreover, even if the result is not large, there is still a possibility that temporary collections involved in computation can be exponentially large. To efficiently solve the problem for real data sets, much attention should be dedicated to identifying and optimizing the most frequent operations and to using economical data structures. In fact, there are many propositions concerning the discovery of minimal rules and patterns [8,5]. In our study, we compare the efficiency of a local reduct approach with two different reduct computation methods [6,9] and JEP-Producer based on a border differential operation [2].

The rough set algorithm consists of two stages. First, for each object $u \in \mathcal{U}$, the set of local reducts $REDLOC(u, d)$ is computed. Then, for each local reduct $R \in REDLOC(u, d)$, a minimal pattern $patt(u, R)$ is added to the pattern set $P_{d(u)}$. Local reduct discovery determines a total time. For a wider view, we selected two reduct computation algorithms. Both methods employ a discernibility matrix [5], the structure that contains for each object pair a set of such attributes that can individually discern these objects. Then, for efficiency, one computes the discernibility vector of minimal attribute sets from this matrix. The first tested algorithm is a classic approach (e.g. [6]), based on finding all prime implicants of a monotonous boolean function. The elements of a discernibility vector are examined successively and the set of reducts is updated in every iteration. For comparison, we propose a novel apriori-based method [9]. In this approach, the search space is traversed according to an apriori scheme and the notion of attribute set dependence is used to form a pruning border.

As far as transaction databases are concerned, we study a JEP-based method. In the beginning, a decision transaction database is computed for a given decision table. Then, for each class k, we compute a space $JEP(D'_k, D_k)$ by means of JEP-Producer. Actually, the purpose is to find the left bound of this space, since, according to Theorem 2 from [4], the right bound is trivially equal to $\{t : (n, t) \in D_k\}$. First, the spaces for both classes, referred to as a positive and negative space, are equal to the respective horizontal spaces [2]. To obtain a resulting space, a border differential procedure is performed. This routine is iterative, the sets of the right bound of the positive space are examined successively. If the considered set belongs to the negative space, a specific differential procedure, named BORDER-DIFF, is called in order to correct the bounds of the positive space [2]. Finally, the set of minimal patters is equal to the left bound of the resulting space. The execution time depends mostly on the border computation.

6   Implementation Issues

One of major problems in comparing the efficiency of different algorithms is to choose an adequate methodology. Generally, in sophisticated procedures it is hard to describe the complexity in a theoretical manner. Even more troublesome is to find operations common for different approaches so as to make a reliable comparison. The algorithms studied in our paper operate on sets of attributes or items and on collections and vectors of these sets. Thus, the crucial thing is to base their implementation on the same data structures. Actually, many set implementations have been studied [10], in particular: a byte array, a bit array or a balanced tree. We tested algorithms using all these three approaches. For the comparison, we chose the first one due to its simplicity, high efficiency and absence of optimizations that can disturb the result. More specifically, the current size of a set is stored instead of being computed on-demand. It appears important e.g. when a collection of sets is stored as cardinality-wise buckets [2].

Our implementation is coded in Java 1.5. In particular, the collection of sets is represented by a balanced tree based on the class java.util.TreeSet and a vector of sets by java.util.ArrayList. The local reduct computation is based on [6,5,9] and JEP-Producer is implemented with optimization remarks described in [2].

7   Efficiency Tests

The algorithms have been tested against consistent decision tables from [11]. We repeated executions for each data set and each method to obtain a reliable average execution time. Tests have been performed on Intel Pentium M 2.13GHz with 2GB of RAM, switched to a stable maximum performance, using the Windows XP operating system and Sun JRE 1.5.0.06.

For small datasets (lymn, zoo) all methods have similar efficiency. The classic approach scales worse than the apriori method with the number of attributes (dna, lung, mushroom). On the other hand, JEP-Producer is slower for a high number of items (dna, geo, lung, mushroom), which depends on attributes and their domain values. The results for large universums (krkopt, mushroom, nursery) suggest that JEP-Producer tends to be significantly slower than rough set approaches. Based on the tested datasets the apriori-like method [9] seems to be more appropriate, when a large number of objects or attributes is concerned.

Table 1. Experimental results summary (time in ms)

Dataset	Obj.	Attr.	Items	Red. classic time	Red. apriori time	JEP-Producer time
car	1728	6	25	880	917	5276
dna	500	20	80	3682802	72109	468937
geo	402	10	78	369	338	1796
house	435	16	48	6120	3823	3224
krkopt	28056	6	43	355052	274593	2946906
lung	32	55	220	6653937	25453	2426344
lymn	148	18	59	2406	1301	1401
tic-tac-toe	958	9	27	2276	2729	2396
zoo	101	16	39	114	114	109
nursery	12960	8	27	102823	103750	516807
mushroom	8124	22	117	117568	81854	1180822

8   Conclusions

In the paper, we have discussed the concept of minimal patterns in relational data. We have focused on two similar ideas: minimal patterns obtained from local reducts and jumping emerging patterns. As far as relational data is concerned, we have demonstrated the equivalence between both types of patterns in a positive region. Moreover, similarities are present in classification methods originating in both streams. The pattern sets used in JEP-C and DeEP are equivalent to sets induced for positive objects in respective eager and lazy local reduct methods.

On the contrary, results for methods of minimal pattern discovery vary significantly due to differences in the form of data. Efficiency tests performed for large consistent decision tables confirmed the intuition that methods using the information held in attributes outperform the solutions operating on a more general, transactional form of data, like JEP-Producer. Nevertheless, all the methods behave similarly for small datasets and time differences are not unequivocal. The results suggest that rough set methods seem more appropriate in the analysis of large relational data. In particular, an apriori-like algorithm appears more efficient than a classic method that minimizes an indiscernibility function.

In our opinion both modes of reasoning of thought bring a number of interesting ideas that can be interchanged in order to develop more efficient methods for the analysis of relational and transactional data.

References

1. H. Fan, *Efficient Mining of Interesting Emerging Patterns and Their Effective Use in Classification.* University of Melbourne: PhD thesis, 2004.
2. G. Dong and J. Li, "Mining border descriptions of emerging patterns from dataset pairs," *Knowl. Inf. Syst.*, vol. 8, no. 2, pp. 178–202, 2005.
3. J. Wroblewski, *The Adaptive Methods for Object Classification.* Warsaw University, Institute of Informatics: PhD thesis, 2002.
4. P. Terlecki and K. Walczak, "On the relation between rough set reducts and jumping emerging patterns," *Information Sciences*, 2006 (to be published).
5. A. Skowron and C. Rauszer, "The discernibility matrices and functions in information systems," in *Intelligent Decision Support* (R. Slowinski, ed.), (Dordrecht, The Netherlands), pp. 331–362, Kluwer Academic Publishers, 1992.
6. J. Bazan, H. S. Nguyen, S. H. Nguyen, P. Synak, and J. Wroblewski, "Rough set algorithms in classification problem," *Rough set methods and applications: new developments in knowl. disc. in inf. syst.*, pp. 49–88, 2000.
7. J. Li, G. Dong, K. Ramamohanarao, and L. Wong, "Deeps: A new instance-based lazy discovery and classification system," *Mach. Learn.*, vol. 54, no. 2, pp. 99–124, 2004.
8. N. Shan and W. Ziarko, "An incremental learning algorithm for constructing decision rules," in *Rough Sets, Fuzzy Sets and Knowledge Discovery* (W. Ziarko, ed.), pp. 326–334, Springer Verlag, Berlin, 1994.
9. P. Terlecki and K. Walczak, "Attribute set dependence in apriori-like reduct computation," in *Rough Sets and Knowl. Techn.*, 2006 (to be published).
10. M. Jürgens and H.-J. Lenz, "Tree based indexes vs. bitmap indexes - a performance study.," *Int. Journal of Cooperative Inf. Syst.*, vol. 10, no. 3, pp. 355–376, 2001.
11. C. B. D.J. Newman, S. Hettich and C. Merz, "UCI repository of machine learning databases," 1998.

Mining Rough Association from Text Documents

Yuefeng Li[1] and Ning Zhong[2]

[1] School of Software Engineering and Data Communications
Queensland University of Technology, Brisbane, QLD 4001, Australia
[2] Department of Systems and Information Engineering
Maebashi Institute of Technology, Japan
y2.li@qut.edu.au, zhong@maebashi-it.ac.jp

Abstract. It is a big challenge to guarantee the quality of association rules in some application areas (e.g., in Web information gathering) since duplications and ambiguities of data values (e.g., terms). This paper presents a novel concept of rough association rules to improve the quality of discovered knowledge in these application areas. The premise of a rough association rule consists of a set of terms (items) and a weight distribution of terms (items). The distinct advantage of rough association rules is that they contain more specific information than normal association rules. It is also feasible to update rough association rules dynamically to produce effective results. The experimental results also verify that the proposed approach is promising.

1 Introduction

One of the important issues for Web information gathering is to apply data mining techniques within Web documents to discover some interesting patterns for user information needs. The motivation arises while we determine the interesting and useful Web pages or text documents to a specified topic. It is easier for users to answer which of Web pages or documents are relevant to the specified topic rather than describe what the specified topic they want. The challenging issue is how to use the discovered patterns effectively for such problem.

Data mining has been used in Web text mining, which refers to the process of searching through unstructured data on the Web and deriving meaning from it [6] [8] [12]. One of main purposes of text mining is association discovery [3], where the association between a set of terms and a category (e.g., a term or a set of terms) can be described as association rules. The current association discovery approaches include maximal patterns [7] [11], sequential patterns [22] and closed sequential patterns [23] [24].

The association discovery approaches only discuss relationship between terms in a broad-spectrum level. They pay no attention to the duplications of terms in a transaction (e.g., a document) and labeled information in the training set. The consequential result is that the effectiveness of the systems is worse than the traditional information retrieval. The objective of this paper is to improve the effectiveness of association discovery by presenting the concept of rough association rules, where the premise (antecedent) of a rough association rule consists of a set of

S. Greco et al. (Eds.): RSCTC 2006, LNAI 4259, pp. 368–377, 2006.
© Springer-Verlag Berlin Heidelberg 2006

terms and a weight distribution of terms, which normalizes frequencies in documents. We also present a mining algorithm for discovery of the rough association rules in this paper.

The distinct advantage of rough association rules is that we can take away uncertainties from discovered knowledge through updating supports and weight distributions of association rules. We also establish a method for updating rough association rules according to negative association discovery. This research is significant since it takes one more step further to association discovery for text mining.

2   Information Table

Formally the association discovery can be described as an information table $(\mathcal{D}, V^{\mathcal{D}})$, where $\mathcal{D}$ is a set of documents in which each document is a set of terms (may include duplicate terms); and $V^{\mathcal{D}} = \{t_1, t_2, \ldots, t_n\}$ is a set of selected terms from $\mathcal{D}$.

A set of terms X is referred to as a *termset* if $X \subseteq V^{\mathcal{D}}$. Let X be a termset, we use $[X]$ to denote the *covering set* of X, which includes all documents d such that $X \subseteq d$, i.e., $[X] = \{d \mid d \in \mathcal{D}, X \subseteq d\}$.

If we view each document as a transaction, *an association rule* between *termset X* and *termset Y* is a rule of the form $X \rightarrow Y$. Its support degree is $|[X \cup Y]|$, and its confidence is $|[X \cup Y]| / |[X]|$, where $|A|$ denotes the number of elements in A.

3   Decision Rules

Two important factors are missed in the information table: the duplications of terms in a document and labeled information. To consider both factors, we use a decision table to replace the information table.

We now assume that $\mathcal{D}$ consists of a set of positive documents, $\mathcal{D}^+$; and a set of negative documents, $\mathcal{D}^-$. For example, Table 1 depicts a set of labeled documents that frequently citied ($min\_sup = 20$) for a specified topic "Economic espionage".

Table 1. An example of labeled documents

Document	*Termset*	*POS*	N_d
d_1	GERMAN VW GERMAN	yes	80
d_2	US US ECONOM ESPIONAG	yes	140
d_3	US BILL ECONOM ECONOM ESPIONAG ECONOM	yes	40
d_4	US ECONOM ESPIONAG BILL	yes	450
d_5	GERMAN MAN VW ESPIONAG	yes	20
d_6	GERMAN GERMAN MAN VW ESPIONAG	yes	200
d_7	GERMAN VW GERMAN VM	no	20
d_8	US ECONOM	no	50

In this example, $\mathcal{D}^+ = \{d_1, d_2, d_3, d_4, d_5, d_6\}$; $\mathcal{D}^- = \{d_7, d_8\}$; $V^{\mathcal{D}} = \{t_1, t_2, t_3, t_4, t_5, t_6, t_7\}$ = {GERMAN, VW, US, ECONOM, BILL, ESPIONAG, MAN}; N_d is the frequency of the document citied for the specified topic; and *POS*=yes denotes the document positive, otherwise negative.

Table 2 demonstrates the corresponding decision table $(\mathcal{D}, A_C, A_D)$, where the set of objects $\mathcal{D} = \{d_1, d_2, d_3, d_4, d_5, d_6, d_7, d_8\}$; the set of *condition attributes* $A_C = \{t_1, t_2, t_3, t_4, t_5, t_6, t_7\}$, and the set of *decision attributes* $A_D = \{POS\}$.

Table 2. An example of labeled documents

Doc	t_1	t_2	t_3	t_4	t_5	t_6	t_7	**POS**
d_1	2	1	0	0	0	0	0	*yes*
d_2	0	0	2	1	0	1	0	*yes*
d_3	0	0	3	1	1	1	0	*yes*
d_4	0	0	1	1	1	1	0	*yes*
d_5	1	1	0	0	0	1	1	*yes*
d_6	2	1	0	0	0	1	1	*yes*
d_7	2	2	0	0	0	0	0	*no*
d_8	0	0	1	1	0	0	0	*no*

Every object (document) in the decision table can be mapped into a decision rule (a sort of association rules) [19]: either a *positive* decision rule (*POS*=yes) or a *negative* decision rule (*POS*=no). So we can obtain eight decision rules, e.g., d_1 in Table 2 can be read as the following rule:

$$(\text{GERMAN}, 2) \wedge (\text{VW}, 1) \rightarrow yes$$

where each pair (*term, frequency*) denotes a term frequency pair.

Let $termset(d) = \{t_1, \ldots, t_k\}$, formally every document d determines a sequence:

$$(t_1, f(t_1, d)), \ldots, (t_k, f(t_k, d)), POS(d).$$

The sequence can determine a decision rule:

$$(t_1, f(t_1, d)) \wedge \ldots \wedge (t_k, f(t_k, d)) \rightarrow POS(d)$$

or in short $d(A_C) \rightarrow d(A_D)$.

Algorithm 3.1 describes Pawlak's idea for the discovery of decision rules ([19] or [16]). If we assume the basic operation is the comparison between two objects (i.e., $d(A_C) = d'(A_C)$), then the time complexity is $(n-1) \times n = O(n^2)$, where n is the number of objects in the decision table. It also needs a similar algorithm to determine interesting rules for Pawlak's method.

Algorithm 3.1 (Pawlak's Method)
Input parameters: $\mathcal{D}$, A_C, A_D and $V^{\mathcal{D}}$.
Output: Decision rules.
Method:
1. let $UN = 0$;
2. for (each $d \in \mathcal{D}$) $UN = UN + N_d$;
3. for (each $d \in \mathcal{D}$)
      $\{$ $strength(d) = N_d/UN$, $CN = N_d$;
        for (each $d' \in \mathcal{D}$ and $d' \neq d$)
           if $(d(A_C) = d'(A_C))$ $CN = CN + N_{d'}$;
      $certainty\_factor(d) = N_d/CN$; $\}$.

We can obtain a lot of decision rules as showed in the above example. However there exists ambiguities whist we use the decision rules for determining other relevance information for the specified topic. For example, give an instance of a piece of information that contains only four terms t_3, t_4, t_5 and t_6; but we can found two rules' premises (d_3 and d_4) match this instance.

To remove such ambiguities, we present the concept of rough association rules in next section.

4 Rough Association Rules

For every attribute $a \in A_C$, its domain is denoted as V_a; especially in the above example, V_a is the set of all natural numbers. Also A_C determines a binary relation $I(A_C)$ on $\mathcal{D}$ such that $(d_i, d_j) \in I(A_C)$ if and only if $a(d_i) > 0$ and $a(d_j) > 0$ for every $a \in A_C$, where $a(d_i)$ denotes the value of attribute a for object $d_i \in \mathcal{D}$.

It is easy to prove that $I(A_C)$ is an equivalence relation, and the family of all equivalence classes of $I(A_C)$, that is a partition determined by A_C, is denoted by $\mathcal{D}/A_C$. The classes in $\mathcal{D}/A_C$ are referred to A_C-granules (or called the set of condition granules). The class which contains d_i is called A_C-granule induced by d_i, and is denoted by $A_C (d_i)$. We also can obtain an A_D-granules $\mathcal{D}/A_D$ (or called the set of decision granules) in parallel.

For example, using Table 2, we can get the set of condition granules, $\mathcal{D}/A_C = \{\{d_1, d_7\}, \{d_2\}, \{d_3, d_4\}, \{d_5, d_6\}, \{d_8\}\}$, and the set of decision granules, $\mathcal{D}/A_D = \{POS = yes, POS = no\} = \{\{d_1, d_2, d_3, d_4, d_5, d_6\}, \{d_7, d_8\}\}$, respectively. In the following we let $\mathcal{D}/A_C = \{cd_1, cd_2, cd_3, cd_4, cd_5\}$ and $\mathcal{D}/A_D = \{dc_1, dc_2\}$.

We also need to consider the weight distributions of terms for the condition granules in order to consider the factor of duplications of terms in documents. Let cd_i be $\{d_{i1}, d_{i2}, \ldots, d_{im}\}$, we can obtain a weigh distribution about the terms in these documents for granule cd_i using the following equation:

$$weight(a_j) = \frac{a_j(cd_i)}{\sum_{a \in A_C} a(cd_i)} \tag{4.1}$$

where we use a *merge* operation to assign a value to condition granules' attributes:
$$a(cd_i) = a(d_{i1}) + a(d_{i2}) + \ldots + a(d_{im})$$
for all $a \in A_C$.

Table 3 illustrates a set of condition granules we obtain from Table 2 according to the above definitions, where each condition granule consists of a *termset* and a weight distribution. For example, $cd_1 = <\{t_1, t_2\}, (4/7, 3/7, 0, 0, 0, 0, 0)>$ or in short $cd_1 = \{(t_1, 4/7), (t_2, 3/7)\}$.

Using the associations between condition granules and decision granules, we can rewrite the eight decision rules in Table 2 (see N_d in Table 1) as follows:

$cd_1 \rightarrow \{(POS=yes, 80/100), (POS=no, 20/100)\}$; $cd_2 \rightarrow \{(POS=yes, 140/140)\}$
$cd_3 \rightarrow \{(POS=yes, 490/490)\}$; $cd_4 \rightarrow \{(POS=yes, 220/220)\}$
$cd_5 \rightarrow \{(POS=no, 50/50)\}$.

Table 3. Condition granules

Condition granule	t_1	t_2	t_3	t_4	t_5	t_6	t_7
cd_1	4/7	3/7					
cd_2			1/2	1/4		1/4	
cd_3			2/5	1/5	1/5	1/5	
cd_4	1/3	2/9				2/9	2/9
cd_5			1/2	1/2			

Formally the associations can be represented as the following mapping: $\Gamma : \mathcal{D}/A_C \to 2^{(\mathcal{D}/A_D) \times [0,1]}$, where $\Gamma(cd_i)$ is the set of conclusions for premise cd_i ($i = 1$, ..., $|\mathcal{D}/A_C|$), which satisfies $\sum_{(fst,snd) \in \Gamma(cd_i)} snd = 1$ for all $cd_i \in \mathcal{D}/A_C$.

Now we consider the support degree for each condition granule. The obvious way is to use the cited numbers in the decision table, that is, $NC(cd_i) = \sum_{d \in cd_i} N_d$ for every condition granule cd_i. By normalizing, we can get a support function sup on $\mathcal{D}/A_C$ such that $sup(cd_i) = \dfrac{NC(cd_i)}{\sum_{cd_j \in D/A_C} NC(cd_j)}$ for all $cd_i \in \mathcal{D}/A_C$.

Given a condition granule cd_i, let $\Gamma(cd_i) = \{(fst_{i,1}, snd_{i,1}), ..., (fst_{i,|\Gamma(cd_i)|}, snd_{i,|\Gamma(cd_i)|})\}$ We call "$cd_i \to fst_{i,j}$" a *rough association rule*, its *strength* is $sup(cd_i) \times snd_{i,j}$ and its *certainty factor* is $snd_{i,j}$, where $1 \le j \le |\Gamma(cd_i)|$.

From the above definitions, we have $snd_{i,j} = \dfrac{|cd_i \cap fst_{i,j}|}{|cd_i|}$ that proves the above definitions about strengths and certainty factors are the generalization of Pawlak's definitions about decision rules. Fig. 1 illustrates the data structure for the representation of associations between condition granules and decision granules.

sup	$\mathcal{D}/A_C$		$\Gamma(cd_i)$	
0.10	cd_1	$\to$	$(dc_1, 0.8)$	$(dc_2, 0.2)$
0.14	cd_2	$\to$	$(dc_1, 1)$	
0.49	cd_3	$\to$	$(dc_1, 1)$	
0.22	cd_4	$\to$	$(dc_1, 1)$	
0.05	cd_5	$\to$	$(dc_2, 1)$	

Fig. 1. The data structure for associations between condition granules and decision granules

5   Mining Algorithms

In this section, we first present an algorithm (see Algorithm 5.1) to find the set of rough association rules. We also analyse the proposed algorithm and compare it with Pawlak's Method.

The time complexity of Algorithm 5.1 is determined by step 3 since steps 4, 5, and 6 all traverse the data structure, where $|\mathcal{D}/A_C| \leq n$; the number of pairs in all $\Gamma(cd_i)$ $(i = 1, \ldots, |\mathcal{D}/A_C|)$ is just n; and n is the number of objects in the decision table.

In step 3, checking if ($\exists cd \in \mathcal{D}/A_C$ such that $termset(d) = termset(cd)$) takes $O(|\mathcal{D}/A_C|)$, so the time complexity of the algorithm is $O(n \times |\mathcal{D}/A_C|)$, where the basic operation is still the comparison between objects. Algorithm 5.1 is better than Algorithm 3.1 in time complexity since $|\mathcal{D}/A_C| \leq n$.

A decision rule "$cd_i \rightarrow fst_{i,j}$" is an *interesting rule* if $P(fst_{i,j} \mid cd_i) - P(fst_{i,j})$ is greater than a suitable constant.

From the definition of mapping Γ, we have $P(fst_{i,j} \mid cd_i) = snd_{i,j}$. To decide the probability on the set of decision granules, we present the following function:

$$P:\ \mathcal{D}/A_D \rightarrow [0,1] \ \text{ such that } \ P(dc) = \sum_{cd_i \in (D/A_C),(fst,snd) \in \Gamma(cd_i)} sup(cd_i) \times snd$$

We can prove that P is a probability function on $\mathcal{D}/A_D$. The algorithm of determining P is only to traverse the data structure as showed in Figure 1.

Algorithm 5.1 (Rough Association Mining Approach)
Input parameters: $\mathcal{D}$, A_C, A_D and $V^{\mathcal{D}}$.
Output: Rough association rules.
Method:

1.   let $UN = 0$, $\mathcal{D}/A_C = \varnothing$;
2.   for (each $d \in \mathcal{D}$) $UN = UN + N_d$;
3.   for each $d \in \mathcal{D}$ // create the data structure as shown in Figure 1.
          if ($\exists\ cd \in \mathcal{D}/A_C$ such that $termset(d) = termset(cd)$)
              { *merge $d(A_C)$ to cd, insert $d(A_D)$ to* $\Gamma(cd)$; }
          else
              { *add($d(A_C)$) into* $\mathcal{D}/A_C$, $\Gamma(d(A_C)) = d(A_D)$; }
4.   for ($i = 1$ to $|\mathcal{D}/A_C|$)
          { $sup(cd_i) = (1/UN) \times (\sum_{(fst,snd) \in \Gamma(cd_i)} snd$);
             calculate weights for cd_i using Eq. (4.1); }
5.   for ($i = 1$ to $|\mathcal{D}/A_C|$) // normalization
          { $temp = 0$;
            for ($j = 1$ to $|\Gamma(cd_i)|$) $temp = temp + snd_{i,j}$;
            for ($j = 1$ to $|\Gamma(cd_i)|$) $snd_{i,j} = snd_{i,j} \div temp$; }
6.   for ($i = 1$ to $|\mathcal{D}/A_C|$) // calculate rule strengths and certainty factors
          for ($j = 1$ to $|\Gamma(c_i)|$)
             { $strength(cd_i \rightarrow fst_{i,j}) = sup(cd_i) \times snd_{i,j}$;
             $certainty\_factor(cd_i \rightarrow fst_{i,j}) = snd_{i,j}$; }.

---

6 Updating Rough Association Rules

Indeed not all association rules are useful for a particular application. For example, most people usually use positive decision rules to determine documents' relevance.

However, the consequential result of using the positive rules is that many irrelevant documents may be marked in relevance [15]. That guides us to refine positive decision rules through considering negative decision rules.

Give a negative rule "$cd \rightarrow (dc_2, x)$", let $termset(cd) = \{t_1, t_2, ..., t_m\}$. We use the following procedure to update positive rough association rules in our experiments:

for ($i = 1$ to $|\mathcal{D}/A_C|$)
    if ($termset(cd_i) \subseteq termset(cd)$)
        deduct half *support* from cd_i;
    else if ($termset(cd_i) \cap termset(cd) \neq \varnothing$)
        shift half *weight* from all terms in the intersection to cd_i's rest terms;

For example, "$cd_5 \rightarrow (dc_2, 1)$" is a negative rule in Figure 1 and it does not include any condition granules but we have

$$termset(cd_2) \cap termset(cd_5) = termset(cd_3) \cap termset(cd_5) = \{t_3, t_4\} \neq \varnothing.$$

The *shifting* operation includes two steps:

1. take half weight from every term in $termset(cd_i) \cap termset(cd)$;
2. distribute the total of the half weighs to all terms in $termset(cd_i)\text{-}termset(cd)$;

For example, we have $cd_3 = \{(t_3, 2/5), (t_4, 1/5), (t_5, 1/5), (t_6, 1/5)\}$ and $cd_5 = \{(t_3, 1/2), (t_4, 1/2)\}$ in Table 3. To implement the shifting operation, we firstly take half weight from t_3 and t_4 in cd_3 respectively, and the total is $(2/10 + 1/10) = 3/10$. We also distribute the total to t_5 and t_6 as follows:

$$weight(t_5) = weight(t_6) = 1/5 + \{ [(3/10)*(1/5)] \div (1/5 + 1/5)\} = 7/20.$$

The *shifting* operation can be used to update the weight distributions of cd_2 and cd_3 in Table 3. Table 4 illustrates the result of shifting weights for condition granules cd_2 and cd_3, where cd_5 is the negative rule.

Table 4. Shifting weights in some condition granules

Condition granule	t_1	t_2	t_3	t_4	t_5	t_6	t_7
cd_1	4/7	3/7					
cd_2			1/4	1/8		5/8	
cd_3			1/5	1/10	7/20	7/20	
cd_4	1/3	2/9				2/9	2/9
cd_5			1/2	1/2			

7 Evaluations

In this section, we evaluate the proposed method. We use a standard data collection, TREC2002 (filtering track) data collection (Text REtrieval Conference, see http://trec.nist.gov/), which included Reuters Corpus articles from 1996-08-20 to 1997-08-19. In the experiment, we test 20 topics: R101, 102, ..., to R120, which include about ten thousands different XML documents.

The proposed testing is compared to normal association rule mining that discards information about the frequency of the terms in the document and decision rule mining. We use both *top 25 precision* and *breakeven point* which are two methods used in Web mining for testing effectiveness, where a breakeven point is a point in the precision and recall curve with the same x coordinate and y coordinate. The greater both the top 25 precision and the breakeven point, the more effective the model is.

The selected terms V^D were chosen by removing stop words, stemming the documents using the porter stemming algorithm and then taking the top 150 terms chosen by *tf*idf* weights.

Given a testing document, d, we use the following equation to determine its relevance:

$$rel(d) = \sum_{term \in V^D} weight_i(term) \times \delta(term, d)$$

where $\delta(x, y) = \begin{cases} 1 & if\ x \in y \\ 0 & otherwise \end{cases}$, $i = 1$ denotes "rough association rules" or 2 means "association rule" and

$$weight_1(term) = \sum_{cd \in D/A_C, (term, w) \in cd} sup(cd) \times w$$

$$weight_2(term) = \sum_{cd \in D/A_C, (term, w) \in cd} sup(cd)$$

for all *term* $\in V^D$.

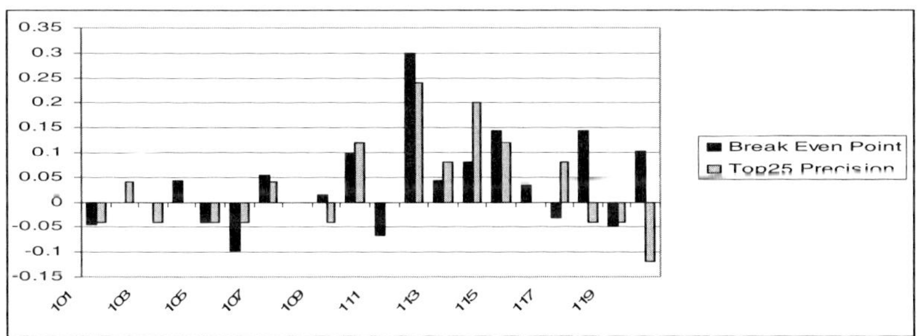

Fig. 2. Difference between models

Figure 2 shows the difference of rough association mining and association rule mining in Break Even Point and Top 25 Precision for the 20 topics. The positive values (the bars above the horizontal axis) mean the rough association mining performed better than association mining. The negative values (the bars below the horizontal axis) mean the association mining performed better than rough association mining.

It is no less impressed by the performance of the rough association rule mining since both top 25 precision and breakeven points gain a significant increase. On average the rough association rule mining increased the Break Even Point and Top 25 Precision by 13.9% = (0.49-0.43)/0.43 and 10.2% = (0.54-0.49)/0.49, respectively.

8 Related Works

Web information gathering (IG) systems tend to find useful information from the huge size of Web related data sources to meet their user information needs. The key issue regarding the effectiveness of IG is automatic acquiring of knowledge from text documents for describing user profiles [14] [17]. It is also a fundamental issue in Web personalization [4].

Traditional information retrieval (IR) techniques can be used to provide simple solutions for this problem. We can classify the methods into two categories: single-vector models and multi-vector models. The former models produce one term-weight vector to represent the relevant information for the topic [2] [10] [5] [21]. The later models produce more than one vector [18] [13]. IR based techniques can be used to obtain efficient systems. This is the distinct merit of IR-based techniques. However, the main drawback of IR-based models is that it is hard to interpret the meaning of vectors, and hence the correlation between vectors cannot be explained using user acceptable concepts.

Text mining tries to derive meaning from documents. Association mining has been used in Web text mining for such purpose for association discovery, trends discovery, event discovery, and text classification [6] [9] [12]. To compare with IR-based models, data mining-based Web text mining models do not use term independent assumption [1]. Also, Web mining models try to discover some unexpected useful data [3]. The disadvantage of association rule mining is that the discovered knowledge is very general that makes the performance of text mining systems ineffectively [24].

Rough set based decision rule mining [19] [16] [20] could be a promising method for association rule generation. However, there exists ambiguities whist we use the decision rules for determining other relevance information for specified topics. Rough association rule mining can be used to overcome these disadvantages.

9 Conclusions

In this paper, we present a new concept of rough association rules to improve of the quality of association discovery for text mining. To compare with the traditional association mining, the rough association rules include more specific information and can be updated dynamically to produce more effective results.

We have verified that the new algorithm is faster than Pawlak's decision rules mining algorithm. We also show that the proposed approach gains a better performance on both precision and recall. This research is significant since it takes one more step further to the development of association rule mining.

References

[1] M. L. Antonie and O. R. Zaiane, Text document categorization by term association, 2nd *IEEE International Conference on Data Mining*, Japan, 2002, 19-26.

[2] R. Baeza-Yates and B. Ribeiro-Neto, *Modern Information Retrieval*, Addison Wesley, 1999.

[3] G. Chang, M.J. Healey, J. A. M. McHugh, and J. T. L. Wang, *Mining the World Wide Web: an information search approach*, Kluwer Academic Publishers, 2001.

[4] M. Eirinaki and M. Vazirgiannis, Web mining for web personalization, *ACM Transactions on Internet Technology*, 2003, **3(1):** 1-27.

[5] D. A. Evans, et al., CLARIT experiments in batch filtering: term selection and threshold optimization in IR and SVM Filters, *TREC02*, 2002.

[6] R. Feldman and H. Hirsh, Mining associations in text in presence of background knowledge, 2nd *ACM SIGKDD*, 1996, 343-346.

[7] R. Feldman, et. al., Maximal association rules: a new tool for mining for keyword co-occurrences in document collection, *KDD97*, 1997, 167-170.

[8] R. Feldman, et. al., Text mining at the term level, in *Lecture Notes in Artificial Intelligence* 1510, Springer, 65-73.

[9] R. Feldman, I. Dagen, and H. Hirsh, Mining text using keywords distributions, *Journal of Intelligent Information Systems*, 1998, **10(3):** 281-300.

[10] D. A. Grossman and O. Frieder, *Information retrieval algorithms and heuristics*, Kluwer Academic Publishers, Boston, 1998.

[11] J. W. Guan, D. A. Bell, D. Y. Liu, The rough set approach to association rules, in: 3rd *IEEE International Conference on Data Mining*, 2003, Melbourne, Florida, USA, 529-532.

[12] J. D. Holt and S. M. Chung, Multipass algorithms for mining association rules in text databases, *Knowledge and Information Systems*, 2001, **3:** 168-183.

[13] X. Li and B. Liu, Learning to classify texts using positive and unlabeled data, *IJCAI*, 2003, 587-592.

[14] Y. Li and N. Zhong, Web mining model and its applications on information gathering, *Knowledge-Based Systems*, 2004, **17:** 207-217.

[15] Y. Li and N. Zhong, Capturing evolving patterns for ontology-based, *IEEE/WIC/ACM International Conference on Web Intelligence*, 2004, Beijing, China, 256-263.

[16] Y. Li and N. Zhong, Interpretations of association rules by granular computing, 3rd *IEEE International Conference on Data Mining*, 2003, Melbourne, Florida, USA, 593-596.

[17] Y. Li and N. Zhong, Mining ontology for automatically acquiring Web user information needs, *IEEE Transactions on Knowledge and Data Engineering*, 2006, **18(4):** 554-568.

[18] J. Mostafa, W. Lam and M. Palakal, A multilevel approach to intelligent information filtering: model, system, and evaluation, *ACM Transactions on Information Systems*, 1997, **15(4):** 368-399.

[19] Z. Pawlak, In pursuit of patterns in data reasoning from data, the rough set way, 3rd *International Conference on Rough Sets and Current Trends in Computing*, USA, 2002, 1-9.

[20] Z. Pawlak and A. Skowron, Rough sets and Boolean reasoning, to appear in: *Information Science*, 2006.

[21] S. Robertson, and D. A. Hull, The TREC-9 filtering track final report, *TREC-9*, 2000.

[22] F. Sebastiani, Machine learning in automated text categorization, *ACM Computing Surveys*, 2002, **34(1):**1-47.

[23] P. Tzvetkov, X. Yan and J. Han, TSP: Mining top-K closed sequential patterns, in: *Proceedings of 3rd IEEE International Conference on Data Mining*, 2003, Melbourne, Florida, USA, 347-354.

[24] S.-T. Wu, Y. Li, Y. Xu, B. Pham and P. Chen, Automatic pattern taxonomy exatraction for Web mining, *IEEE/WIC/ACM International Conference on Web Intelligence*, 2004, Beijing, China, 242-248.

NetTRS Induction and Postprocessing of Decision Rules

Marek Sikora and Marcin Michalak

Silesian University of Technology, Institute of Computer Sciences, 44-100 Gliwice,
Poland
{Marek.Sikora, Marcin.Michalak}@polsl.pl

Abstract. The internet service NetTRS that enable to induction, evaluation, and postprocessing of decision rules is presented in the paper.
The TRS library is the main part of the service. The TRS library makes
possible, among others, induction of decision rules by means of tolerance
rough sets model.

1   Introduction

Tolerance Rough Sets (TRS) library was created as a tool for data analysis,
using tolerance rough sets model [12]. The final result of data analysis is a
set of rules, that describes patterns discovered in analysed data. Sets of rules,
obtained as a results of not trivial data sets analysis, are rather big, that causes
some difficulties in interpretation and adapting those rules in practice. Hence
TRS library offers many heuristic algorithms implemented in, which allow to
reduce the number of generated rules. Most of them can be found in literature
described in detail [7],[8],[10], therefore only short descriptions of algorithms are
written below.

Library is equipped with a simple script interpreter. Script is a set of commands written in special ,,language" and allows to execute experiments (analysis) faster. The results of those experiments are stored in text files and contains:
obtained sets of rules (with their quality measure value) and classification results. The library - for the sake of its experimental nature - accepts train, test
and tune data sets in specific text format.

NetTRS environment (service) makes TRS library accessible via Internet. New
data analysis task (also called an ,,experiment") defining consists in uploading
train, test and tune data files to service and setting parameters of available
algorithms. On the basis of their parameters the controlling script is generated,
that later is interpreted by the library. The results of analysis are stored in text
files and can be viewed in web browser window or can be downloaded to a local
computer.

In the following chapters service functionality and technical aspects are briefly
described.

S. Greco et al. (Eds.): RSCTC 2006, LNAI 4259, pp. 378–387, 2006.

2   System Functionality

2.1   Tolerance Thresholds

TRS library allows to generate decision rules from relative reducts [13] or using one of two algorithms: MODLEM [14] or RMatrix [8]. In the case of rules induction form relative reducts it is necessary to determine tolerance thresholds. There are two ways of tolerance threshold vector searching, implemented in TRS library:

- searching by a genetic algorithm [15]; in this case, for conditional attributes set $\{a1, \ldots, am\}$, tolerance threshold vector $(\varepsilon_{a1}, \ldots, \varepsilon_{am})$ is searched, that for every $i \neq j$ tolerance thresholds $\varepsilon_{ai}, \varepsilon_{aj}$ can be different
- using a climbing strategy; in this case, for a set of conditional attributes $\{a1, .., am\}$, tolerance threshold vector $(\varepsilon_{a1}, \ldots, \varepsilon_{am})$ is searched, that for every $i \neq j$, $\varepsilon_{ai} = \varepsilon_{aj}$; optimal vector searching starts with vector $(0, \ldots, 0)$, thresholds are increased by user defined value (0.1 by default), after increasing the new vector is evaluated and the vector with highest evaluation is admitted as the optimal one

In each case user can choose one from various criteria of threshold optimality, applying standard criterion given by Stepaniuk [15] or criteria adapted from decision rules quality measures.

For a given decision table $DT = (U, A \cup \{d\})$, where U is a set of objects, and A is a set of conditional attributes, standard tolerance threshold vector quality measure is defined in the following way:

$$w\gamma(d) + (1 - w)\nu_{SRI}(R_d, R_{IA}) \tag{1}$$

where $\gamma = \frac{|POS(d)|}{|U|}$, $POS(d)$ is a positive region of the decision table DT, $R_d = \{< x, y >\in U \times U : d(x) = d(y)\}$, $R_{IA} = \{< x, y >\in U \times U : y \in IA(x)\}$, $\nu_{SRI}(X, Y)$ is a standard rough inclusion [6] and $IA(x)$ is a set of objects similar to x in given tolerance threshold vector.

We expect from tolerance thresholds vector, that most of all objects from the same decision class (R_d) will be admitted as similar (R_{IA}). Then, for a given tolerance thresholds vector, R_d, $\neg R_d$, R_{IA}, and $\neg R_{IA}$ can be determined. On the basis of them quality measures that evaluate tolerance thresholds vector can be built, similarly as it takes place in the case of rule quality measures [9]. TRS library has some adapted measures for evaluation of tolerance threshold vector (WS, Pearson, Cohen, Coleman, IKIB, Gain, J-measure, Brazdil, IREP).

Distance between attributes values is calculated in two ways: using the *diff* measure [15] for a numeric attributes and the *vdm* measure [15] for a symbolic ones. Standard rough set model can be obtained by setting all threshold values $\varepsilon_{ai} = 0$.

2.2   Rules

TRS library generates decision rules in the following form (2):

$$\text{IF } a_1 \in V_{a1} \text{ and } \ldots \text{ and } a_k \in V_{ak} \text{ THEN } d = v_d \tag{2}$$

where $\{a_1, \ldots, a_k\} \subseteq A$, d is the decision attribute, $V_{ai} \subseteq D_{ai}$, $v_d \subseteq D_d$, where D_a is the domain of an attribute $a \in A$. Expression $a \in V$ is called a conditional descriptor and a set of objects with the same value of decision attribute is called decision class (denoted as $X_v = \{x \in U : d(x) = v\}$).

Decision rules, given in the form (2), can be inducted in a few ways:

- by the local relative reducts [13]; in this case, decision rules are generated on the basis of discernibility matrix; there are three different algorithm variants: all rules (from each objects all relative reducts are generated and from each reduct one decision rule is obtained), one rule (from each object only one relative reduct is generated - the shortest one - that is used for the rule creation, the shortest reduct is determined by the modified Johnson algorithm [5]); from each object given by the user rules number is generated, in this case the randomized algorithm is used [5];
- by the RMatrix algorithm, that also uses discernibility matrix, but takes into consideration rule quality measure to control rules induction process; each decision rule is built around the object–generator, that has assigned one row (column) in the discernibility matrix; the algorithm uses attributes ranking, in the consideration of their appearance frequency in analysed row (column) cells; rule induction starts from the first attribute (first conditional descriptor) in the ranking, adding next conditional description makes the rule more accurate but also decreases its coverage; each time the descriptor is added the new rule is evaluated by the rule quality measure; the final rule is the one with the highest value of that measure; the detailed description of this algorithm can be found in [8];
- by the MODLEM algorithm; in this case the tolerance thresholds searching is not needed, because this algorithm uses non discretized data; the standard version of the MODLEM algorithm rules induction is finished by getting the maximal possible accuracy that can be achieved in given decision table; it usually leads to creation quite a big number of decision rules; TRS library limits number of decision rules by using rule quality measures during rule induction; the rule is evaluated after every descriptor adding/modifying; the final rule is the one with the best evaluation; rule induction process ends in the moment, when the rule quality decreases; the detailed description of the MODLEM algorithm can be found in [14], the modification is described in [11].

2.3   Rules Generalization and Filtration

Apart from the number of generated rules (either all minimal rules are obtained or the heuristic algorithm is used) it is common, that the set of generated decision rules is large, what decreases its describing ability. TRS library owns some algorithms implemented in, that are responsible for the generated rules set postprocessing. The main target of postprocessing is to limit the number of decision rules (in other words: to increase their describing ability) but with keeping their good classification quality simultaneously.

TRS library developed postprocessing in two ways: rules generalization (rules shortening and rules joining) and rules filtering (rules, that are not needed in view of certain criterion, are removed from the final rules set).

Shortening a decision rule consists in removing some conditional descriptors from the conditional part of the rule. Every unshortened decision rule has an assigned quality measure value. The shortening process takes time as long as the new rule quality decreases below defined by the user threshold. The threshold of quality is defined for each decision class separately. The order of descriptors removing is set in accordance with a climbing strategy.

Rules joining consists in obtaining one more general rule from two (or more) less general rules. The joining algorithm implemented in TRS library bases on following assumptions: only rules from the same decision class can be joined, two rules can be joined if their conditional parts are built from the same conditional attributes or if one rule conditional attributes set is a subset of the second rule.

Rules joining process consists in joining sets of values of corresponding conditional descriptors. If conditional descriptor (a, V_a^1) occurs in the conditional part of $\varphi_1 \rightarrow \psi$ rule and descriptor (a, V_a^2) occurs in the conditional part of $\varphi_2 \rightarrow \psi$ rule, then - as the result of joining process - the final conditional descriptor (a, V_a) has the following properties: $V_a^1 \subseteq V_a$ and $V_a^2 \subseteq V_a$.

Controlling of the rules joining process bases on the following rules: the ,,basis" one, to which the other rule is joined, is the rule with higher value of the quality measure; conditional descriptors are joined sequentially; the order of descriptors joining is determined by the value of new rule r quality measure; the best descriptor to be joined is determined by the climbing strategy; the process stops when the new rule recognizes all positive training examples, recognized by rules r_1 and r_2.

The new decision rule replaces two joined rules in the description of the decision class, if its quality is not less than the quality of the basis rule. The detailed description of this algorithm can be found in [7].

Decision rules filtration process consists in removing some rules from a decision class description, that are useless according to defined criterion. There are two kinds of algorithms implemented in the TRS library: not considering and considering classification accuracy of filtered rules set.

First approach is represented by the ,,*From coverage*" algorithm. The first step of this algorithm is to generate a rules ranking, then the train set coverage building starts from the best rule. The following rules are added according to their position in ranking. When the final rules set covers all train examples, all remaining rules are rejected.

The second approach is represented by two algorithms: ,,*Forward*" and ,,*Backward*". Both of them, besides the rules ranking generated in the basis of selected rule quality measure, take into consideration the result of all rules classification accuracy. To guarantee the independence of the filtration result the separate tuning set of examples is applied.

In the case of ,,*Forward*" algorithm, each decision class initial description contains only one decision rule - the best one. Then, to each decision class description single rules are added. If the decision class accuracy increases, the added rule remains in this description, otherwise next decision rule is considered. The order of rules is defined by the rule quality measure. The process of adding rules to the decision class description stops when the obtained rules set has the same classification accuracy as the initial, or when all rules have been already considered.

The ,,*Backward*" algorithm is based on the opposite conception. From each decision class description decision rules are removed, with effect from the weakest ones. The order of rules removing is given by the rule quality measure. Keeping the difference between accuracy of the most and the least decision class guarantees, that the filtered rules set keeps the same sensitivity as the initial.

Also a simple algorithm, that removes rule, which quality is less then defined by user threshold, is implemented in TRS library. All mentioned filtration algorithms are described in [10].

2.4   Classification

Classification is considered as a process of assigning objects to corresponding decision classes.

TRS library uses a ,,*voting mechanism*" to perform objects classification process. Each decision rule has an assigned kind of confidence grade (simply: this is a value of the rule quality measure). The TRS library classification process consists in summing up confidence grades of all rules from each decision class, that recognize a test object (3). Test object is assigned to the decision class, that has the highest value of mentioned sum. Sometimes it happens, that object is not recognized by any rule from given decision classes descriptions. In case of that, it is possible to calculate a distance between the object and the rule, and admit that rules close enough to the object recognizes it.

$$conf(X_v, u) = \sum_{r \in RUL_{X_v}(DT), dist(r,u) \leq \varepsilon} (1 - dist(r, u)) \cdot q(r) \tag{3}$$

In the formula (3) $dist(r, u)$ is a distance between the test object u and the rule r (Euclidean or Hamming), ε is a maximal acceptable distance between the object and the rule (especially when $\varepsilon = 0$ classification takes place only by the rules, that accurately recognizes the test object), $q(r)$ is voice strength of the rule.

2.5   Rule Quality Measures

Most of mentioned algorithms use rule quality measures. They make possible to evaluate rules quality, joining the evaluation of its accuracy and coverage. From the theory of probability point of view the dependence presented by the decision rule, that is accurate and is characterized by the large coverage, describes a general regularity extracted from data.

It is common to use measures, that are based on the contingency table. The contingency table for the rule $\varphi \to \psi$ is usually shown as a square matrix as follows:

$$\begin{array}{cc|c} n_{\varphi\psi} & n_{\varphi\neg\psi} & n_{\varphi} \\ n_{\neg\varphi\psi} & n_{\neg\varphi\neg\psi} & n_{\neg\varphi} \\ \hline n_{\psi} & n_{\neg\psi} & \end{array}$$

where:

$n_{\varphi} = n_{\varphi\psi} + n_{\varphi\neg\psi} = |U_{\varphi}|$ — number of objects recognizing the rule $\varphi \to \psi$,
$n_{\neg\varphi} = n_{\neg\varphi\psi} + n_{\neg\varphi\neg\psi}$ — number of objects not recognizing the rule $\varphi \to \psi$,
$n_{\psi} = n_{\varphi\psi} + n_{\neg\varphi\psi} = |U_{\psi}|$ — number of objects from decision class, described by the rule $\varphi \to \psi$, $n_{\neg\psi} = n_{\varphi\neg\psi} + n_{\neg\varphi\neg\psi}$ — number of objects form another decision classes, $n_{\varphi\psi} = |U_{\varphi} \cup U_{\psi}|$, $n_{\varphi\neg\psi} = |U_{\varphi} \cup U_{\neg\psi}|$, $n_{\neg\varphi\psi} = |U_{\neg\varphi} \cup U_{\psi}|$, $n_{\neg\varphi\neg\psi} = |U_{\neg\varphi} \cup U_{\neg\psi}|$.

TRS library has the following popular quality measures implemented in: *Accuracy, Coverage, WS* (proposed by Michalski), *Brazdil, Cohen, Coleman, Gain, IKIB, Pearson, IREP*. Those measures properties are described in details in [4], [1], [10], so no measure formulas are presented in this paper.

TRS library gives a possibility to calculate values of above measures for objects that are uniquely covered by the rule. There is also the other measure implemented in the library, called „mixed measure" and defined in the following way:

$$q(r)_{new} = q(r)_{unique}/q(r)_{normal} \tag{4}$$

where: $q(r)_{unique}$ — q measure value, that takes into consideration only objects, that uniquely recognizes r rule, $q(r)_{normal}$ — q measure value calculated typically.

The number of conditional descriptors, contained in the conditional part of the decision rule, is very important from the interpretation of dependencies (described by the rule) point of view. The library allows to evaluate the decision rule from the point of view of its conditional descriptors number; the evaluation is higher as the number of conditional descriptors decreases. It is also possible to evaluate a decision rules, considering both of them: rule quality and length.

TRS library makes possible, besides applying rules quality measures to rules induction and postprocessing, to create a ranking of a given rules set get by a given rule quality measure.

3   Technical Aspects and System Overview

System NetTRS is implemented with ASP.NET technology. At present, only by the Internet Explorer web browser window the system is available.

User interface consists of a web sites set. Some of them are responsible for a new data analysis task defining (Fig. 1) and some of them show the user results of previous experiments and make possible to download them to the local computer.

The separate system layer is responsible for a consecutive realization of all data analysis tasks, defined by all users. This layer deals with transferring data analysis results to the user interface layer. When the data analysis process reaches the end, all files (data and result) are compressed to one file, that is transferred to the mentioned layer.

3.1 Data Analysis Tasks Defining and Setting Parameters

The system web pages set has a ,,tabbed" structure. On the first tab *Analysis* (Fig. 1) user defines a type of new experiment (one of three common known testing methodologies are available: train and test, 5 – fold CV and 10 – fold CV). After *Files upload* option selecting, the website that makes possible to select train, test and tune files is shown.

The following options on the *Analysis* tab setting (*Reducts and rules generating*, *Rules generalization* and so on) gives the user a possibility to set all parameters of all indicated algorithms, that are used during data analysis process. Fig. 2 shows a configuration website that sets parameters of shortening and joining rules algorithms.

When all required data files are uploaded, *Script* tab becomes enable, that contains parameters of all defined algorithms within the framework of one experiment. The task becomes queued when user presses the button *Upload* on the *Script* tab.

Since user can defined more than one data analysis, the *Current state* tab allows to monitor which tasks remain still in queue.

All user defined experiments are executed by the *TRSExecutor* program on the server side, that cyclically reads them from the database, which stores all data about users, their experiments and results of those experiments. The *TRSExecutor* program starts the executable version of TRS library and transmits the control script describing the current experiment. When all calculations connected with an experiment are finished, all result files and data files are compressed to the one archive, that is available for the user on the *Results* tab.

As user defined consecutive experiments are finished, their results appears on the *Results* tab. User can view them in the web browser window or download them as the compressed archive file and analyse them on the local computer.

The primary result file, generated by TRS library, is a text file with a default name out.txt. It contains, depending on algorithms chosen during data analysis definition, originally generated decision rules, rules after shortening process, rules after joining, rules after filtering and classification results. The content of this file can be viewed after the *View* button click, on the *Results* tab. TRS library generates also some auxiliary files, that contain rules rankings and rules with their quality measure values. As it was mentioned above, all files connected with a single experiment (both: data and results) are compressed to the one file and made available for the user.

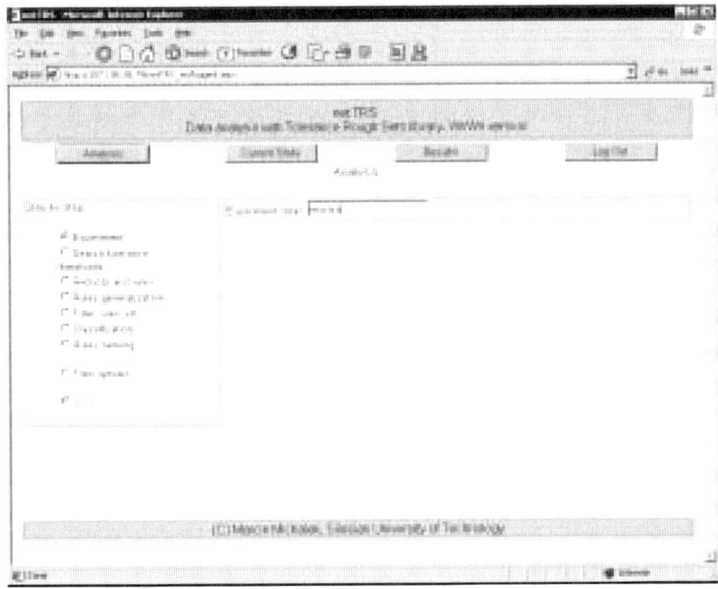

Fig. 1. New experiment labelling

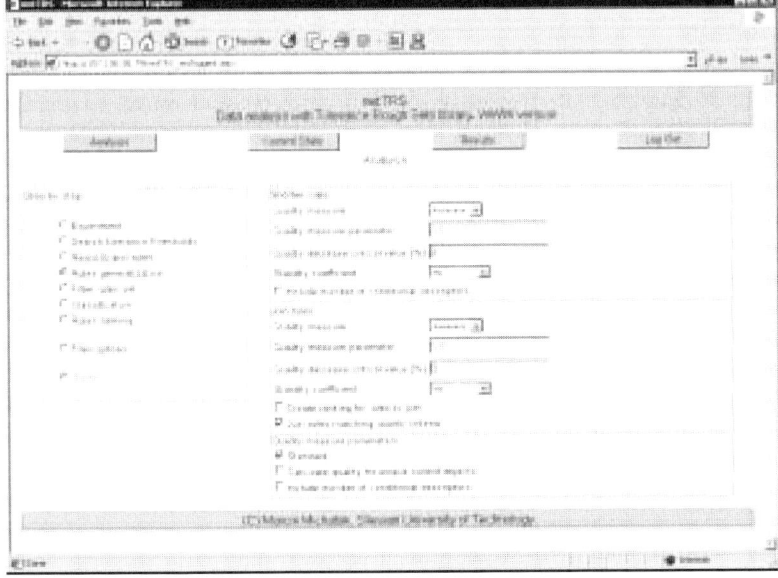

Fig. 2. Rules generalization algorithms side

4 Conclusions

This paper describes web application, that makes possible to use some of algorithms that are implemented in TRS library. Both, the library and the system, still have experimental character only. At present, the system has a poor user interface there is no possibility for data management but it is one of the first systems, by means of which user can perform experiments (analyse data) with no need of their implementation. The functionality of the service differs from other known tools for rules induction (RSES [2], WEKA, Rosetta).

The further works, that take into consideration functionality of mentioned tools, will focus on user interface development, implementation of scattering functions (similar as in the DIXER system [3]) and parallel computing. The scattering and paralleling functionality will be added to TRS library, the NetTRS system will work as today with a new module, that will distribute experiments between servers.

It is necessary to have an account to log into the server:

www.nettrs.polsl.pl/nettrs (http://157.158.55.79/nettrs)

It can be obtained, after contact to service administrator:

Marcin.Michalak@polsl.pl

References

1. An, A., Cercone, N.: Rule quality measures for rule induction systems description and evaluation. Computational Intelligence, Vol. 17, No. 3, 2001, pp. 409-424
2. Bazan, J., Szczuka, M., Wrblewski, J.: A new version of rough set exploration system. Lecture Notes in Computer Sciences, Vol. 2475, Springer, 2002, pp. 14-16. (RSCTC 2002)
3. Bazan, J., Latkowski, R., Szczuka, M.: DIXER distributed executor for rough set exploration system. Lecture Notes in Artificial Intelligence, Vol. 3642, Springer-Verlag, Berlin Heidelberg, 2005, pp. 39-47. (RSFDGrC 2005)
4. Bruha, I.: Quality of Decision Rules: Definitions and Classification Schemes for Multiple Rules. Nakhaeizadeh G., Taylor C. C. (ed.) Machine Learning and Statistics, The Interface. John Wiley and Sons, 1997
5. Nguyen, H. S., Nguyen, S. H.: Some Efficient Algorithms for Rough Set Methods. Proceedings of the Sixth International Conference, Information Processing and Management of Uncertainty in Knowledge-Based Systems, vol. 2, Granada, Spain, 1996, 1451-1456
6. Pawlak, Z.: Rough Sets. Theoretical aspects of reasoning about data. Dordrecht: Kluwer, 1991
7. Sikora, M.: An algorithm for generalization of decision rules by joining. Foundation on Computing and Decision Sciences, Vol. 30, No. 3, 2005
8. Sikora, M.: Approximate decision rules induction algorithm using rough sets and rule-related quality measures. Theoretical and Applied Informatics, No. 4, 2004
9. Sikora, M., Proksa, P.: Algorithms for generation and filtration of approximate decision rules, using rule-related quality measures. Bulletin of International Rough Set Society, vol. 5, no. 1/2, (RSTGC-2001), 2001

10. Sikora, M.: Filtering of decision rules sets using rules quality measures. Studia Informatica Vol. 46, No. 4, Gliwice 2001
11. Sikora, M., Proksa, P.: Induction of decision and association rules for knowledge discovery in industrial databases. ICDM-2004, Alternative Techniques for Data Mining Workshop, November 1-4, UK, 2004
12. Skowron, A., Stepaniuk, J.: Tolerance approximation spaces. Fundamenta Informaticae 27, 1996, pp. 245-253
13. Skowron, A., Rauszer, C.: The Discernibility Matrices and Functions in Information systems. In: Sowiski R. (ed.) Intelligent Decision Support. Handbook of Applications and Advances of the Rough Sets Theory. Dordrecht: Kluwer, 1992, 331-362
14. Stefanowski, J.: Rough set based rule induction techniques for classification problems. Proc. 6-th European Congress of Intelligent Techniques and Soft Computing, vol.1 Achen Sept. 7-10, 1998, 107-119
15. Stepaniuk, J.: Knowledge Discovery by Application of Rough Set Models. Institute of Compuer Sciences Polish Academy of Sciences, Reports, no. 887, Warszawa, 1999

Outlier Detection Based on Rough Membership Function

Feng Jiang[1,2], Yuefei Sui[1], and Cungen Cao[1]

[1] Key Laboratory of Intelligent Information Processing, Institute of Computing
Technology, Chinese Academy of Sciences, Beijing 100080, P.R. China
[2] Graduate School of Chinese Academy of Sciences, Beijing 100039, P.R. China
jiangkong@163.net, {yfsui, cgcao}@ict.ac.cn

Abstract. In recent years, much attention has been given to the problem of outlier detection, whose aim is to detect outliers — individuals who behave in an unexpected way or have abnormal properties. Outlier detection is critically important in the information-based society. In this paper, we propose a new definition for outliers in rough set theory which exploits the rough membership function. An algorithm to find such outliers in rough set theory is also given. The effectiveness of our method for outlier detection is demonstrated on two publicly available databases.

Keywords: Outlier detection, rough sets, rough membership function.

1 Introduction

Usually, knowledge discovery tasks can be classified into four general categories: (a) dependency detection, (b) class identification, (c) class description, and (d) outlier/exception detection [1]. In contrast to most KDD tasks, such as clustering and classification, outlier detection aims to find small groups of data objects that are exceptional when compared with the rest large amount of data, in terms of certain sets of properties. For many applications, such as fraud detection in E-commerce, it is more interesting to find the rare events than to find the common ones, from a knowledge discovery standpoint. While there is no single, generally accepted, formal definition of an outlier, Hawkins' definition captures the spirit: "an outlier is an observation that deviates so much from other observations as to arouse suspicions that it was generated by a different mechanism" [1, 2]. With increasing awareness on outlier detection in literatures, more concrete meanings of outliers are defined for solving problems in specific domains [1, 6-13].

Rough set theory introduced by Z. Pawlak [3-5], as an extension of naive set theory, is for the study of intelligent systems characterized by insufficient and incomplete information. It is motivated by practical needs in classification and concept formation. In recent years, there has been a fast growing interest in rough set theory.

In this paper, we aim to use the rough membership function of rough set theory for outlier detection. The rough membership function expresses how strongly an object belongs to a given set of objects in view of available information about the

S. Greco et al. (Eds.): RSCTC 2006, LNAI 4259, pp. 388–397, 2006.

object expressed by indiscernibility relations. Our basic idea is that objects whose degrees of membership wrt a given set of objects are small have more likelihood of being an outlier. Our definition for outliers follows the spirit of Hawkins' definition. That is, given an information system and a set of indiscernibility relations in it, if the values of rough membership function of an object wrt a given subset of universe under these indiscernibility relations are always small, then we consider that object as not behaving normally and call it an outlier wrt the given subset of universe.

The paper is organized as follows. In the next section, we introduce some preliminaries that are relevant to this paper. In section 3 we give some definitions concerning RMF(rough membership function)-based outliers in information systems of rough set theory. An algorithm to find RMF-based outliers is also given. Experimental results are given in section 4 and section 5 concludes the paper.

2   Preliminaries

In rough sets, an information system is a quadruple $IS = (U, A, V, f)$, where:

(1) U is a non-empty finite set of objects;

(2) A is a non-empty finite set of attributes;

(3) V is the union of attribute domains, i.e., $V = \bigcup_{a \in A} V_a$, where V_a denotes the domain of attribute a;

(4) $f : U \times A \to V$ is an information function such that for any $a \in A$ and $x \in U$, $f(x, a) \in V_a$.

Each subset $B \subseteq A$ of attributes determines a binary relation $IND(B)$, called indiscernibility relation, defined as follows:

$$IND(B) = \{(x, y) \in U \times U : \ \forall a \in B \ (f(x, a) = f(y, a))\} \tag{1}$$

Given any $B \subseteq A$, relation $IND(B)$ induces a partition of U, which is denoted by $U/IND(B)$, where an element from $U/IND(B)$ is called an equivalence class or elementary set. For every element x of U, let $[x]_B$ denote the equivalence class of relation $IND(B)$ that contains element x.

Let $B \subseteq A$ and $X \subseteq U$, the B-lower and B-upper approximation of X is defined respectively as follows

$$\underline{X}_B = \bigcup \{[x]_B \in U/IND(B) : [x]_B \subseteq X\} \tag{2}$$

$$\overline{X}_B = \bigcup \{[x]_B \in U/IND(B) : [x]_B \cap X \neq \emptyset\} \tag{3}$$

The pair $(\underline{X}_B, \overline{X}_B)$ is called the rough set with respect to X. The set $BN_B(X) = \overline{X}_B - \underline{X}_B$ is called the B-boundary region of X.

In classical set theory, either an element belongs to a set or it does not. In the case of rough sets, the notion of membership is different. A rough membership function is usually defined as follows [5].

Definition 2.1. Let $IS = (U, A, V, f)$ be an information system, $B \subseteq A$, $X \subseteq U$. The function $\mu_X^B : U \to [0, 1]$ such that for any $x \in U$

$$\mu_X^B(x) = \frac{|[x]_B \cap X|}{|[x]_B|} \tag{4}$$

is called a rough membership function (RMF), where $[x]_B$ denotes the indiscernibility class of relation $IND(B)$ that contains element x, $|M|$ denotes the cardinality of set M.

The following proposition collects the basic properties for the rough membership function of definition 2.1 [5].

Proposition 2.2. The rough membership function μ_X^B of definition 2.1 has the following properties

(1) $\mu_X^B(x) = 1$ iff $x \in \underline{X}_B$;
(2) $\mu_X^B(x) = 0$ iff $x \in U - \overline{X}_B$;
(3) $0 < \mu_X^B(x) < 1$ iff $x \in BN_B(X)$;
(4)   if $(x, y) \in IND(B)$ then $\mu_X^B(x) = \mu_X^B(y)$;
(5) $\mu_X^B(x) = 1 - \mu_{U-X}^B(x)$;
(6) $\mu_{X \cup Y}^B(x) \geq \max\{\mu_X^B(x), \mu_Y^B(x)\}$;
(7) $\mu_{X \cap Y}^B(x) \leq \min\{\mu_X^B(x), \mu_Y^B(x)\}$;
(8)   If X is a family of pair wise disjoint sets of U, then for any $x \in U$,
$$\mu_{\cup X}^B(x) = \sum_{x \in X} \mu_X^B(x).$$

In definition 2.1, the domain of the rough membership function is the universe U. In this paper, in order to be used in outlier detection, a slightly different definition for rough membership function is taken. That is, the domain of the rough membership function is a given subset X of the universe U, not the universe U itself. Correspondingly, the basic properties for the rough membership function will differ from those in proposition 2.2. We use another proposition to represent them.

Proposition 2.3. The rough membership function μ_X^B has the following properties

(1) $\mu_X^B(x) = 1$ iff $x \in \underline{X}_B$;
(2) $\mu_X^B(x) > 0$;
(3) $\mu_X^B(x) < 1$ iff $x \in X - \underline{X}_B$;
(4)   if $(x, y) \in IND(B)$ then $\mu_X^B(x) = \mu_X^B(y)$;
(5)   if $IND(B) \cap (X \times (U - X)) = \emptyset$ then $\mu_X^B(x) = 1$;
(6)   given $X, Y \subseteq U$, for any $x \in X \cap Y$,
$$\mu_{X \cup Y}^B(x) = \mu_X^B(x) + \mu_Y^B(x) - \frac{|[x]_B \cap X \cap Y|}{|[x]_B|};$$
(7)   given $X, Y \subseteq U$, for any $x \in X \cap Y$,
$$\mu_{X \cap Y}^B(x) = \mu_X^B(x) + \mu_Y^B(x) - \frac{|[x]_B \cap (X \cup Y)|}{|[x]_B|};$$
(8)   given $X_1, X_2 \subseteq U$ and $X_1 \subseteq X_2$, for any $x \in X_1$, $\mu_{X_1}^B(x) \leq \mu_{X_2}^B(x)$.

3   RMF-Based Outlier Detection

3.1   Degree of Outlierness

Most current methods for outlier detection give a binary classification of objects: is or is not an outlier, e.g. the distance-based outlier detection. However, for many scenarios, it is more meaningful to assign to each object a degree of being an outlier. Given a degree of outlierness for every object, the objects can be ranked according to this degree, giving the data mining analyst a sequence in which to analyze the outliers.

Therefore, Breunig et al. introduced a novel notion of local outlier in which the degree to which an object is outlying is dependent on the density of its local neighborhood, and each object can be assigned a *Local Outlier Factor (LOF)* which represents the likelihood of that object being an outlier [6]. LOF is local in that the degree depends on how isolated the object is with respect to the surrounding neighborhood.

3.2   Definition of RMF-Based Outliers

It should be noted that our definition for RMF-based outliers has a characteristic that is ignored by most current definitions for outliers. That is, for a given data set (universe) U, we do not have to detect outliers just in U by checking all elements of U. In fact we may consider detecting outliers wrt any subset X of U, where X maybe a particular subset of U which we are interested in or anything else which we are willing to separate from other elements of U.

Similar to Breunig's method, we define a *rough outlier factor (ROF)*, which indicates the degree of outlierness for every object wrt a given subset of universe.

Definition 3.1 [Rough Outlier Factor]. Let $IS = (U, A, V, f)$ be an information system, $X \subseteq U$ and $X \neq \emptyset$. For any $x \in X$, the *rough outlier factor of x* wrt X in IS is defined as

$$ROF_X(x) = 1 - \frac{\sum_{a \in A} \left(\mu_X^{\{a\}}(x) \times W_X^{\{a\}}(x) \right)}{|A|} \tag{5}$$

where $\mu_X^{\{a\}} : X \rightarrow (0, 1]$ is a rough membership function whose domain is set X, for every singleton subset $\{a\}$ of A; and for every singleton subset $\{a\}$ of A, $W_X^{\{a\}} : X \rightarrow (0, 1]$ is a weight function such that for any $x \in X$, $W_X^{\{a\}}(x) = |[x]_{\{a\}} \cap X| \, / \, |X|$. $[x]_{\{a\}} = \{u \in U : f(u, a) = f(x, a)\}$ denotes the indiscernibility class of relation $IND(\{a\})$ that contains element x and $|M|$ denotes the cardinality of set M.

The weight function $W_X^{\{a\}}$ in the above definition expresses such an idea that outlier detection always concerns the minority of objects in the data set and the minority of objects are more likely to be outliers than the majority of objects. Since from the above definition, we can see that the less the weight, the more the rough outlier factor, the minority of objects should have less weight than the majority of objects. Therefore if the objects in X that are indiscernible with x under relation $IND(\{a\})$ are few, that is, the percentage of objects in X that are indiscernible with x is small, then we consider x belonging to the minority of objects in X, and assign a small weight (i.e. that percentage) to x.

Actually, definition 3.1 is an example of using inverse (Bayesian) probabilities in rough sets. In a series of papers, Slezak and Ziarko introduced inverse probabilities to rough sets, and proposed the Rough Bayesian model and the Variable Precision Bayesian Rough Set (VPBRS) model, respectively [14, 15].

In definition 3.1, we only consider every singleton subset $\{a\}$ of A. Since if all subsets of A are used for defining the rough outlier factor, then the time complexity of our method may be too expensive.

Definition 3.2 [Rough Membership Function-based Outliers]. Let $IS = (U, A, V, f)$ be an information system, $X \subseteq U$ and $X \neq \emptyset$. Let μ be a given threshold value, for any $x \in X$, if $ROF_X(x) > \mu$ then x is called a *rough membership function(RMF)-based outlier* wrt X in IS, where $ROF_X(x)$ is the rough outlier factor of x wrt X in IS.

Algorithm 3.1

Input: information system $IS = (U, A, V, f)$ and a subset X of U, where
    $|U| = n$, $|X| = n_X$ and $|A| = m$; threshold value μ
Output: a set E of RMF-based outliers wrt X in IS

---

(1) For every $a \in A$
(2) {
(3)   Sort all objects from U and X according to a given order (e.g. the
(4)   lexicographical order) on domain V_a of attribute a [14];
(5)   For every $x \in X$
(6)   {
(7)   Determine the indiscernibility class $[x]_{\{a\}}$;
(8)   Calculate $\mu_X^{\{a\}}(x)$, the value of rough membership function of
(9) x wrt X under indiscernibility relation $IND(\{a\})$;
(10)   Assign a weight $W_X^{\{a\}}(x)$ to x
(11)   }
(12) }
(13) For every $x \in X$
(14) {
(15)   Calculate $ROF_X(x)$, the rough outlier factor of x wrt X;
(16)   If $ROF_X(x) > \mu$ then $E = E \cup \{x\}$
(17) }
(18) Return E.

In algorithm 3.1, we use a method proposed by Nguyen et al. [16] to calculate the partition induced by an indiscernibility relation in an information system.

In the worst case, the time complexity of algorithm 3.1 is $O(m \times nlogn)$, and its space complexity is $O(m \times n)$, where m and n are the cardinalities of A and U respectively.

4   Experimental Results

4.1   Experiment Design

In our previous papers [7, 8], we have proposed two different methods for outlier detection in rough set theory. In our experiment, we compare the performance of RMF-based outlier detection with these two methods on identifying true outliers.

In [8], we introduced distance-based outlier detection to rough set theory. Since in distance-based outlier detection, being an outlier is regarded as a binary property, we revise the definition of distance-based outlier detection by introducing a *distance outlier factor (DOF)* to indicate the degree of outlierness for every object wrt a given subset of universe in an information system.

Definition 4.1 [Distance Outlier Factor]. Given an information system $IS = (U, A, V, f)$ and $X \subseteq U$. For any object $x \in X$, the percentage of the objects in X lie greater than d from x is called the *distance outlier factor of x* wrt X in IS, denoted by

$$DOF_X(x) = \frac{|\{y \in X : dist(x,y) > d\}|}{|X|} \tag{6}$$

where $dist(x,y)$ denotes the distance between object x and y under a given distance metric in rough set theory (In our experiment, the overlap metric in rough set theory is adopted [8]), d is a given parameter (In our experiment, we set $d = |A|\,/2$), and $|X|$ denotes the cardinality of set X.

In [7], we firstly defined the notions of *inner boundary* and *boundary degree*. Then we defined the notion of *exceptional degree* for every object in a given data set. Similar to ROF and DOF, the exceptional degree of an object indicates the degree of outlierness. Here we call the method in [7] *boundary-based outlier detection*. And in order to compare boundary-based method with other methods, we revise the definition for boundary degree in [7].

Definition 4.2 [Boundary Degree]. Given an information system $IS = (U, A, V, f)$ and $X \subseteq U$ $(X \neq \emptyset)$, where $A = \{a_1, ..., a_m\}$. Let $IB = \{IB_1, IB_2, ..., IB_m\}$ be the set of all inner boundaries of X under each relation $IND(\{a_i\})$, $1 \leq i \leq m$. For every object $x \in X$, the *boundary degree* of x wrt X in IS is defined as:

$$BD_X(x) = \sum_{i=1}^{m} \left(f(x, IB_i) \times W_X^{\{a_i\}} \right) \tag{7}$$

where f is a characteristic function for set IB_i; $W_X^{\{a_i\}} : X \to [0,1)$ is a weight function such that for any $x \in X$, $W_X^{\{a_i\}}(x) = 1 - (|[x]_{\{a_i\}} \cap X| \,/\, |X|)$, $1 \leq i \leq m$. $|M|$ denotes the cardinality of set M.

4.2 Lymphography Data

Next we demonstrate the effectiveness of RMF-based method against distance-based and boundary-based methods on two data sets. The first is the lymphography data set, which can be found in the UCI machine learning repository [9]. It contains 148 instances (or objects) with 19 attributes (including the class attribute). The 148 instances are partitioned into 4 classes: "normal find" (1.35%), "metastases" (54.73%), "malign lymph" (41.22%) and "fibrosis" (2.7%). Classes 1 and 4 ("normal find" and "fibrosis") are regarded as rare classes.

Aggarwal et. al. proposed a practicable way to test the effectiveness of an outlier detection method [10, 13]. That is, we can run the outlier detection method on a given data set and test the percentage of points which belonged to one of the rare classes (Aggarwal considered those kinds of class labels which occurred in less than 5 % of the data set as rare labels [10]). Points belonged to the rare class are considered as outliers. If the method works well, we expect that such abnormal classes would be over-represented in the set of points found.

In our experiment, data in the lymphography data set is input into an information system $IS_L = (U, A, V, f)$, where U contains all the 148 instances of lymphography data set and A contains 18 attributes of lymphography data set (not including the class attribute). We consider detecting outliers (rare classes) wrt four subsets $X_1, ..., X_4$ of U, respectively, where

(1) $X_1 = \{x \in U : f(x, \text{bl\_affere}) = 1\}$;
(2) $X_2 = \{x \in U : f(x, \text{early\_uptake}) = 1 \ \vee \ f(x, \text{bl\_affere}) = 2\}$;
(3) $X_3 = \{x \in U : f(x, \text{spec\_froms}) = 3 \ \vee \ f(x, \text{dislocation}) = 1\}$;
(4) $X_4 = \{x \in U : f(x, \text{changes\_lym}) = 2 \ \vee \ f(x, \text{exclusion}) = 2\}$.

X_1 contains those objects of U whose values on attribute "bl_affere" equal 1; ... Moreover, we use R_{X_i} to denote the set of all objects in X_i that belong to one of the rare classes (class 1 or 4), $1 \leq i \leq 4$.

The experimental results are summarized in table 1 and table 2.

In table 1 and table 2, "RMF", "RBD", "DIS" denote RMF-based, boundary-based and distance-based outlier detection methods, respectively. For every objects in X_i, the degree of outlierness wrt X_i is calculated by using the three outlier detection methods, respectively. For each outlier detection method, the "Top Ratio (Number of Objects)" denotes the percentage (number) of the objects selected from X_i whose degrees of outlierness wrt X_i calculated by the method are higher than those of other objects in X_i. And if we use $Y_i \subseteq X_i$ to contain all those objects selected from X_i, then the "Number of Rare Classes Included" is the number of objects in Y_i that belong to one of the rare classes. The "Coverage" is the ratio of the "Number of Rare Classes Included" to the number of objects in X_i that belong to one of the rare classes (i.e. $|R_{X_i}|$), $1 \leq i \leq 4$ [13].

Table 1. Experimental Results wrt X_1, X_2 in IS_L

| $X_1:\ |X_1| = 66,\ |R_{X_1}| = 4$ | | | | $X_2:\ |X_2| = 102,\ |R_{X_2}| = 5$ | | | |
| Top Ratio (Number of Objects) | Number of Rare Classes Included (Coverage) | | | Top Ratio (Number of Objects) | Number of Rare Classes Included (Coverage) | | |
	RMF	RBD	DIS		RMF	RBD	DIS
2%(1)	1(25%)	1(25%)	1(25%)	2%(2)	2(40%)	1(20%)	2(40%)
4%(3)	2(50%)	2(50%)	3(75%)	3%(3)	3(60%)	1(20%)	3(60%)
6%(4)	3(75%)	2(50%)	4(100%)	4%(4)	4(80%)	2(40%)	4(80%)
9%(6)	4(100%)	2(50%)	4(100%)	5%(5)	4(80%)	3(60%)	5(100%)
15%(10)	4(100%)	2(50%)	4(100%)	6%(6)	5(100%)	3(60%)	5(100%)
20%(13)	4(100%)	3(75%)	4(100%)	9%(9)	5(100%)	4(80%)	5(100%)
65%(43)	4(100%)	4(100%)	4(100%)	15%(15)	5(100%)	5(100%)	5(100%)

Table 2. Experimental Results wrt X_3, X_4 in IS_L

| $X_3:\ |X_3| = 105,\ |R_{X_3}| = 5$ | | | | $X_4:\ |X_4| = 132,\ |R_{X_4}| = 4$ | | | |
| Top Ratio (Number of Objects) | Number of Rare Classes Included (Coverage) | | | Top Ratio (Number of Objects) | Number of Rare Classes Included (Coverage) | | |
	RMF	RBD	DIS		RMF	RBD	DIS
3%(3)	3(60%)	3(60%)	3(60%)	1%(1)	1(25%)	1(25%)	1(25%)
4%(4)	3(60%)	3(60%)	4(80%)	2%(3)	3(75%)	2(50%)	3(75%)
5%(5)	4(80%)	3(60%)	4(80%)	3%(4)	3(75%)	2(50%)	3(75%)
8%(8)	5(100%)	3(60%)	5(100%)	4%(5)	3(75%)	3(75%)	3(75%)
11%(12)	5(100%)	4(80%)	5(100%)	5%(7)	4(100%)	4(100%)	4(100%)
24%(25)	5(100%)	5(100%)	5(100%)				

From table 1 and table 2, we can see that for the lymphography data set, RMF-based and distance-based methods perform markedly better than boundary-based method. And the performances of RMF-based and distance-based methods are very close, though the former performs a little worse than the latter.

4.3 Wisconsin Breast Cancer Data

The Wisconsin breast cancer data set is found in the UCI machine learning repository [9]. The data set contains 699 instances with 9 continuous attributes. Here we follow the experimental technique of Harkins et al. by removing some of the *malignant* instances to form a very unbalanced distribution [11-13]. The resultant data set had 39 (8%) *malignant* instances and 444 (92%) *benign* instances. Moreover, the 9 continuous attributes in the data set are transformed into categorical attributes, respectively[1] [13].

Data in the Wisconsin breast cancer data set is also input into an information system $IS_W = (U', A', V', f')$, where U' contains all the 483 instances of the data set and A' contains 9 categorical attributes of the data set (not including

---

[1] The resultant data set is public available at:
http://research.cmis.csiro.au/rohanb/outliers/breast-cancer/

the class attribute). We consider detecting outliers (*malignant* instances) wrt four subsets $X'_1, ..., X'_4$ of U', respectively, where
(1) $X'_1 = \{x \in U' : f'(x, \text{Clump\_thickness}) = 5\}$;
(2) $X'_2 = \{x \in U' : f'(x, \text{Unif\_Cell\_Shape}) = 3\}$;
(3) $X'_3 = \{x \in U' : f'(x, \text{Clump\_thickness}) = 1 \vee f'(x, \text{Bland\_Chromatine}) = 3\}$;
(4) $X'_4 = \{x \in U' : f'(x, \text{Mitoses}) = 1\}$.

We use $R_{X'_i}$ to denote the set of objects in X'_i that are *malignant*, $1 \leq i \leq 4$. The experimental results are summarized in table 3 and table 4.

Table 3. Experimental Results wrt X'_1, X'_2 in IS_W

$X'_1 :$ $|X'_1| = 87, |R_{X'_1}| = 4$			$X'_2 :$ $|X'_2| = 34, |R_{X'_2}| = 4$		
Top Ratio (Number of Objects)	Number of *Malignant* Instances Included (Coverage)		Top Ratio (Number of Objects)	Number of *Malignant* Instances Included(Coverage)	
	RMF	RBD	DIS		RMF	RBD	DIS
2%(2)	2(50%)	2(50%)	2(50%)	5%(2)	2(50%)	1(25%)	2(50%)
3%(3)	3(75%)	3(75%)	2(50%)	10%(3)	3(75%)	2(50%)	3(75%)
5%(4)	3(75%)	3(75%)	3(75%)	12%(4)	4(100%)	3(75%)	3(75%)
7%(6)	4(100%)	3(75%)	4(100%)	15%(5)	4(100%)	4(100%)	4(100%)
8%(7)	4(100%)	4(100%)	4(100%)				

Table 4. Experimental Results wrt X'_3, X'_4 in IS_W

$X'_3 :$ $|X'_3| = 232, |R_{X'_3}| = 9$			$X'_4 :$ $|X'_4| = 454, |R_{X'_4}| = 23$		
Top Ratio (Number of Objects)	Number of *Malignant* Instances Included (Coverage)		Top Ratio (Number of Objects)	Number of *Malignant* Instances Included (Coverage)	
	RMF	RBD	DIS		RMF	RBD	DIS
1%(2)	2(22%)	2(22%)	2(22%)	1%(5)	4(17%)	4(17%)	4(17%)
2%(5)	4(44%)	4(44%)	3(33%)	2%(9)	8(35%)	7(30%)	6(26%)
3%(7)	6(67%)	6(67%)	5(56%)	3%(14)	12(52%)	11(48%)	10(43%)
4%(9)	7(78%)	6(67%)	6(67%)	4%(18)	14(61%)	13(57%)	12(52%)
5%(12)	8(89%)	7(78%)	8(89%)	5%(23)	17(74%)	18(78%)	15(65%)
6%(14)	9(100%)	7(78%)	9(100%)	6%(27)	20(87%)	20(87%)	18(78%)
7%(16)	9(100%)	9(100%)	9(100%)	7%(32)	22(96%)	21(91%)	23(100%)
				8%(36)	23(100%)	21(91%)	23(100%)
				10%(45)	23(100%)	22(96%)	23(100%)
				12%(54)	23(100%)	23(100%)	23(100%)

Table 3 and table 4 are similar to table 1 and table 2. From table 3 and table 4, we can see that for the Wisconsin breast cancer data set, RMF-based method always performs the best among the three outlier detection methods, except in the case when "Top Ratio" is 7% for X'_4. And the performances of RMF-based and distance-based methods are very close.

5   Conclusion

Finding outliers is an important task for many KDD applications. In this paper, we present a new method for outlier definition and outlier detection, which exploits the rough membership function of rough set theory. The main idea is that objects whose degrees of membership wrt a given subset of universe are small have more likelihood of being an outlier. Experimental results on real data sets demonstrate the effectiveness of our method for outlier detection.

Acknowledgements. This work is supported by the Natural Science Foundation (grants no. 60273019, 60496326, 60573063 and 60573064), and the National 973 Programme (grants no. 2003CB317008 and G1999032701).

References

1. Knorr, E. and Ng, R.: Algorithms for Mining Distance-based Outliers in Large Datasets. In: *Proc. of the 24th VLDB Conf.*, New York (1998) 392-403
2. Hawkins, D.: *Identifications of Outliers*. Chapman and Hall, London (1980)
3. Pawlak, Z.: "Rough sets", *International Journal of Computer and Information Sciences*, **11** (1982) 341–356
4. Pawlak, Z.: *Rough sets: Theoretical Aspects of Reasoning about Data*. Kluwer Academic Publishers, Dordrecht (1991)
5. Pawlak, Z. and Skowron, A.: Rough membership functions. In: *Advances in the Dempster-Shafer Theory of Evidence*. John Wiley Sons, New York, (1994) 251-271
6. Breunig, M. M., Kriegel, H-P., Ng, R. T. and Sander, J.: LOF: identifying density-based local outliers. In: *Proc. of the 2000 ACM SIGMOD Int. Conf. on Management of Data*, Dallas (2000) 93-104
7. Jiang, F., Sui, Y. F. and Cao, C. G.: Outlier Detection Using Rough Set Theory. In: *RSFDGrC (2)*. LNAI 3642, Regina (2005) 79-87
8. Jiang, F., Sui, Y. F. and Cao, C. G.: Some Issues about Outlier Detection in Rough Set Theory. Submitted to Special Issues on Rough Sets in China in LNCS Transactions on Rough Sets
9. Bay, S. D.: The UCI KDD repository, 1999. http://kdd.ics.uci.edu.
10. Aggarwal, C. C. and Yu, P. S.: Outlier detection for high dimensional data. *Proc. of the 2001 ACM SIGMOD Int. Conf. on Managment of Data*, California, 37-46
11. Harkins, S., He, H. X., Willams, G. J. and Baxter, R. A.: Outlier detection using replicator neural networks. In: *Proc. of the 4th Int. Conf. on Data Warehousing and Knowledge Discovery*, France (2002) 170-180
12. Willams, G. J., Baxter, R. A., He, H. X., Harkins, S. and Gu, L. F.: A Comparative Study of RNN for Outlier Detection in Data Mining. ICDM 2002, Japan, 709-712
13. He, Z. Y., Deng, S. C. and Xu, X. F.: An Optimization Model for Outlier Detection in Categorical Data. In: ICIC(1) 2005, Hefei, China (2005) 400-409
14. Slezak, D. and Ziarko, W.: The investigation of the Bayesian rough set model. *Int. J. Approx. Reasoning* (2005) 40(1-2): 81-91
15. Slezak, D. and Ziarko, W.: Variable Precision Bayesian Rough Set Model. RSFD-GrC 2003: 312-315
16. Nguyen, S. H. and Nguyen,. H. S.: Some efficient algorithms for rough set methods. In: *IPMU'96*, Granada, Spain (1996) 1451-1456

An Approach to a Rough Set Based Disease Inference Engine for ECG Classification

S. Mitra[1], M. Mitra[1], and B.B. Chaudhuri[2]

[1] Department of Applied Physics, Faculty of Technology, University of Calcutta,
Kolkata, India
[2] Computer Vision and Pattern Recognition Unit, Indian Statistical Institute,
Kolkata, India
{S.Mitra, susa68}@hotmail.com

Abstract. An inference engine for classification of ECG signals is developed with the help of a rule based rough set decision system. For this purpose an automated ECG data extraction system from ECG strips is being developed by using few image processing techniques. Filtering techniques are used for removal of noises from recorded ECG. A knowledge base is developed after consultation of different medical books and feedback of reputed cardiologists regarding ECG interpretation and selection of essential time-plane features of ECG signal. An algorithm for extraction of different time domain features is also developed with the help of differentiation techniques and syntactic approaches. Finally, a rule-based roughest decision system is generated from these time-plane features for the development of an inference engine for disease classification.

Keywords: Rough set, rule based, decision system, electrocardiogram (ECG).

1 Introduction

In past, there have been many approaches to generate automatic diagnostic ECG classification based on the 12-lead electrocardiogram. The morphological diagnosis of ECGs is a pattern recognition procedure. The way the clinician does this is not clearly elucidated. Nevertheless, several models aimed at achieving identical results by automatic means are employed. While in the doctor's case this is not exactly so, the computer task for ECG interpretation comprises two distinct and sequential phases: feature extraction and classification. A set of signal measurements containing information for the characterization of the waveform is first obtained. These waveform descriptors are then used to allocate the ECG to one or more diagnostic classes in the classification phase. The classifier can embody rules-of-thumb used by the clinician to decide between conflicting ECG diagnosis and formal or fuzzy logic as a reasoning tool (heuristic classifiers). On the other hand, it can use complex and even abstract signal features as waveform descriptors and different discriminant function models for class allocation (statistical classifiers). More recently, artificial neural network techniques have also been used for signal classification [1,5,6,7].

S. Greco et al. (Eds.): RSCTC 2006, LNAI 4259, pp. 398–407, 2006.

The biological variability, the lack of standards in the definition of measurements and diagnostic criteria make the classification problem a complex task. Two basic methods of the diagnostic process are described: the statistical model and the deterministic approach. In particular, a model for ECG classification is illustrated where the imprecise knowledge of the state of cardiac system and the vague definition of the pathological classes are taken care of by means of the fuzzy set formalism [3]. Fuzzy adaptive resonance theory mapping (ARTMAP) is also used to classify cardiac arrhythmias[2]. A classifier is developed based on wavelet transforms for extracting features and then using a radial basis function neural network (RBFNN) to classify the arrhythmia[4]. A hybrid neuro-fuzzy system was used for ECG classification of myocardial infarction [8].

For the past few years, rough set theory[10,11] and granular computation has proven to be another soft computing tool which, in various synergetic combination with fuzzy logic, artificial neural networks and genetic algorithms provides a stronger frame work to achieve tractability, low cost solution, robustness and close resembles with human like decision making. For example, rough-fuzzy integration forms the basis of the computational theory of perceptions (CPT), recently explained by Zadeh, where perceptions are considered to have fuzzy boundaries and granular attribute values. Similarly to describe different concept or classes, crude domain knowledge in the form of rules are extracted with the help of rough neural synergistic integration and encoded them as network parameters. Hence the initial knowledge base network for efficient learning is built. As the methodology has matured, several interesting applications of the theory have surfaced, also in medicine. Pawlak [12] used rough set theory in Bayes' theorem and showed that it can apply for generating rule base to identify the presence or absence of disease. Discrete Wavelet Transform and rough set theory were used for classification of arrhythmia[9]. So, rough set theory is now becoming the most useful tool for soft computing and decision making. For this reason a rule-based roughest decision system is generated for the development of an inference engine for disease identification from the time-plane features analysis of ECG signals.

2 Materials and Methods

The block diagram of the developed system is given in fig.1. The detail methodologies are given below in step by step.

2.1 Development of ECG Data Extraction System

For development of the off-line data extraction system[GUI based], those paper records are scanned by flat-bed scanner (HP Scanjet 2300C) to form TIFF formatted image database. Those images are then processed by some image processing techniques which are applied by a new manner by us. These TIFF formatted gray tone images are converted into two tone binary images with the help of a global thresholding technique. This method almost remove the background noise i.e, the grid lines of ECG papers from the actual ECG signal. The rest dotted portion of the

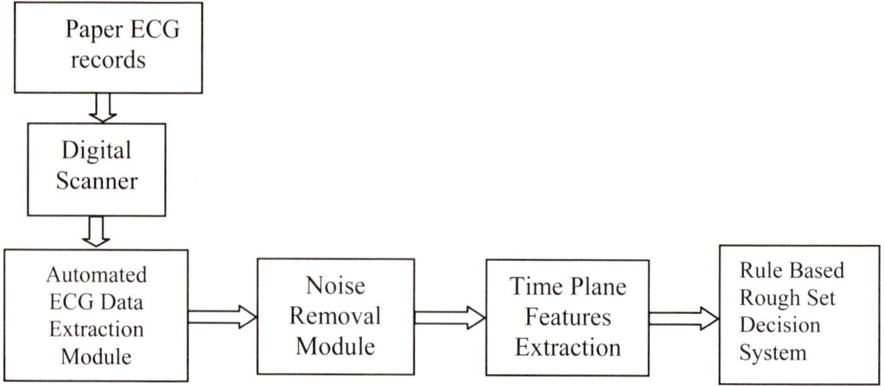

Fig. 1. Block Diagram of the Proposed System

background noise are removed by using component leveling[13]. Then the thinning algorithm is applied to avoid repetition of co-ordinate information in the dataset (fig.2). The pixel to pixel co-ordinate information is extracted and calibrated according to the electrocardiographic paper to form ASCII datafile. A Time (in sec.) Vs. mili volt data-file is obtained for each of 12 lead ECG signal after each processing. The present database contains 70 normal and 75 diseased subjects out of which 40 patients have acute myocardial infarction (MI) and rest 35 patients have Myocardial Ischemia.

2.2 Removal of Noises from ECG Signals

Electrocardiographic signals may be corrupted by different types of noises [23]. Typical examples are: 1. power line Interference, 2. electrode contact noise, 3. motion artifacts, 4. muscle contraction (electrmyographic,EMG), 5. baseline drift and ECG amplitude modulation with respiration, and 6. electrosurgical noise.

All the noises are simulated by a software package Cool Edit Pro offered by Syntrillium Software Corporation. This is done to get a realistic situation for the algorithm. The EMG is simulated by adding random noise(white noise) to the ECG. An FIR filter depending upon Savitzky-Golay algorithm is developed to remove EMG like white noises from the ECG signals. 50Hz sinusoid is modeled as power line interference and added with ECG. The base line drift due to respiration was modeled as a sinusoid of frequency 0.15 to 0.4 Hz. A 50 Hz Notch filter is designed for rejection of frequency band due to power line oscillation. Then a high pass filter of critical frequency 0.6 Hz is developed to block the low frequency noise signal that causes the base line shift. Both these FIR filters are designed by the Cool Edit Pro software. The abrupt base line shift is simulated by adding a dc bias for a given segment of the ECG. This noise can be blocked with the help of the high pass filter described above.

Since, motion artifact is similar as baseline drift in respiration, it was not specifically modeled. All of these noises are added to the ECG signal to simulate the composite noise. This ECG signal corrupted by composite noise is passed through all the filters described above to get almost noise free ECG signal. All types of noise levels are varied from 10% to 30% and the generated filters gave good response in all the cases.

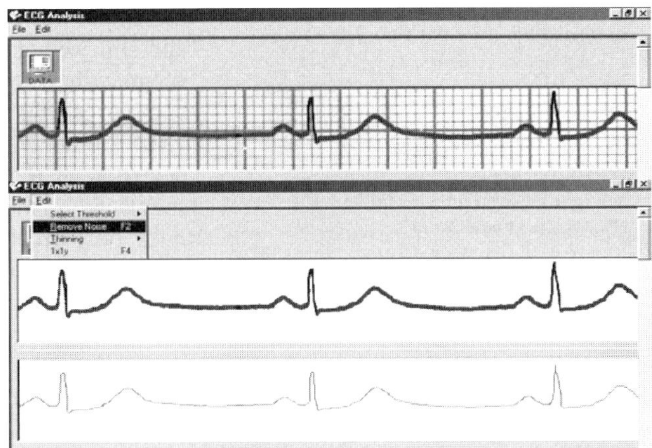

Fig. 2. Original ECG Image [upper], ECG Signal after Removal of Background Noise[middle], ECG signal after thinning[lower]

2.3 Time-Plane Features Extraction

To extract the time based features from ECG signals the accurate detection of the R-R interval between two consecutive ECG waves is very much important. For this purpose, the 2nd order derivative of the captured signal is being computed by using 5-point Lagrangian interpolation formulas for differentiation [14]. The formula is given below :

$$ f_0' = \frac{1}{12h} \left(f_{-2} - 8f_{-1} + 8f_1 - f_2 \right) + \frac{h^4}{30} f^{\,v}(\xi) \tag{1} $$

ξ lies between the extreme values of the abscissas involved in the formula. After squaring the values of 2nd order derivative, a square-derivative curve having only high positive peaks of small width at the QRS complex region can be obtained (fig. 5). A small window of length (say W) was taken to detect the area of this curve and we obtained maximum area at those peak regions.

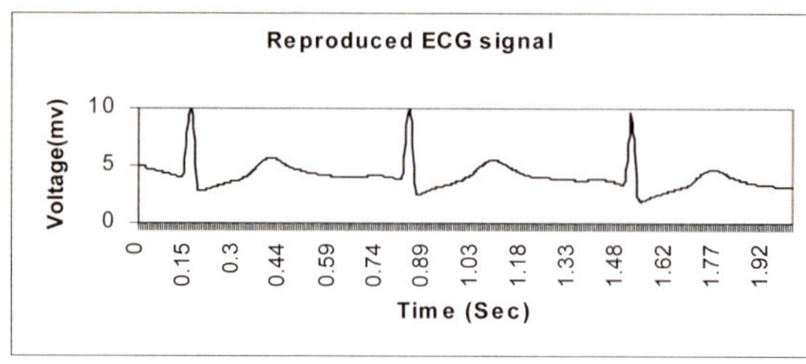

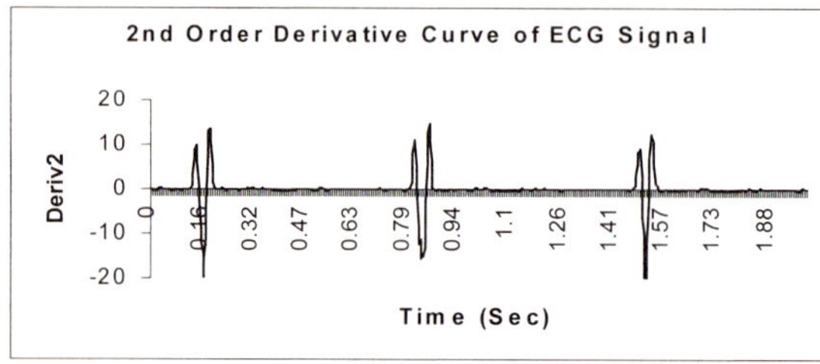

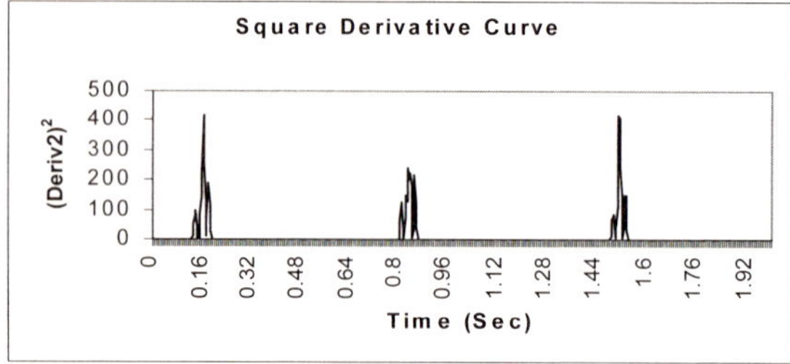

Fig. 3. QRS complex or R-R interval Detection

The local maxima of these peak regions are considered as R-peak. For this experiment the W is set as ~0.07 sec. The system was tested for both noise free and noisy signals. The levels of all type of noises are increased from 0% to 30% and still we achieved 99.4% accuracy in detection of QRS complexes.

In order to accurate detection of P wave and ST segments, isoelectric line must be correctly identified. Most methods are based upon the assumption that the isoelectric level of the signal lies on the area ~80 ms left of the R-peak, where the first derivative becomes equal.

In particular let $y_1, y_2, ..., y_n$ be the samples of a beat, $y_1', y_2', ..., y_{n-1}'$ be their first differences and y_r the sample where the R-peak occurs. The isoelectric level samples y_b are then defined if either of the two following criteria is satisfied:

$$\left| y'_{r-j-int(0.08f)} \right| = 0, j=1,2,....,0.01f \quad \text{or}$$

$$\left| y'_{r-j-int(0.08f)} \right| \le \left| y'_{r-i-int(0.08f)} \right|, \quad i, j = 1,2,....,0.02f \tag{2}$$

where f is the sampling frequency.

After detection of baseline the location of P wave is determined from the first derivative of the samples.

The R wave can be detected very reliably and for this reason, it is used as the starting point for ST segment processing, and for T wave detection. In most algorithms dealing with ST segment processing it is assumed that the ST segment begins at 60 ms after the R-peak in normal sinus rhythm. In the case of tachycardia (RR-interval <600 ms), the beginning of the ST segment is marked at 40 ms after the R peak. The ST-segment duration has beat-to-beat variability, but since this is not easily determined, many algorithms assume that ST has a predefined length of 160 ms (this means that the end point is 220 ms after R-peak in the normal case and 200 ms otherwise).

Other algorithms follow the Bazzet formula, that links the ST segment duration with the RR interval duration. The above mentioned ST segment limits are in general agreement with the recommendation the European ST-T database and with the observations in [15,16,17].

Our algorithm adopted the first assumption and once getting the beginning it computes the slope of the ST segments and also detects the zero crossings. Depending on the zero crossings and shape of the each wave a syntactic approach is developed for detection of P, Q, R ,S and T waves. For getting QRS complex we achieved 99.4% accuracy, for T waves the accuracy is 96.7% and for P waves the accuracy obtained 92.2%.

2.4 Development of Knowledgebase

A knowledge base regarding ECG interpretation is also developed from the opinion of the reputed cardiologists of different hospitals and clinical centers. For this purpose we select 20 doctors and gave them different sample questions about ECG interpretation. From their feedback and after consultation of different medical books[20,21,22] we have selected 12 time plane features for disease identification. They are listed below:

1.Heart Rate, 2. PR interval, 3.P wave height, 4. P wave width, 5. QRS width, 6. QRS voltage, 7..QTc= (QT interval/ Sqrt RR interval), 8. Abnormal Q wave, 9. R wave Progression, 10. ST segment, 11. Reciprocity in T wave, and 12. T wave.

2.5 Development of Inference Engine

A rule-based roughest decision system is generated for the development of an inference engine for disease identification from the time-plane features analysis of ECG signals. The most popular and widely used rough-set software tool box is ROSETTA[18,19,the URL for downloading is http://www.idi.ntnu.no/~aleks/rosetta/rosetta.html]. This software supports different options of generating decision tables, reducts, discretization techniques, decision algorithms and classifications. For this reason we used this software for our experiment. Learning samples are processed in the following way. First a knowledge base is acquired for the data set. Knowledge base consists of objects, which are represented using conditional attributes and decision parameters. All the time plane features described above are get their specific attributes according to knowledgebase and used as the input parameters of the Decision table, a portion of which is given in table 1.

Consequently, the acquired data are quantized to convert real attribute values into discretized form allowing further rule processing. Based on the discrete values, attributes are analyzed in terms of discernibility investigation. Sets of attributes allowing partition of object classes are then revealed. These sets are called reducts.

The ROSETTA system supports a variety of quantization as well as reduct and rule generation procedures however the details of these lie beyond the scope of this report. For the purpose of our experiments the following processing parameters were used:

- Equal frequency binning using 3 intervals is used for discretization.
- Object related genetic algorithm producing a set of rules via minimal attribute subsets that discern object classes; reducts and rules are generated upon analysis of all learning patterns.

These processing parameters were chosen during a preliminary research aimed at optimizing the system efficiency and generation ability.

3   Result

In this experiment total 23 rules [fig.4] are generated. Intuitively a "strong" rule is both accurate and has a high coverage. The accuracy of a rule reflects how trustworthy its consequent is. A portion of the generated rule set and the confusion matrix which is generated using standard voting classifier are given below in the figures 4 & 5. We consider both LHS and RHS coverage factor for the selection of the optimum ruleset. For example the rule 1 of fig.4 gives the decision according to LHS coverage factor that only 31.4% patients having ECG where Abnormal Q wave present(P) are suffering from the disease Myocardial Infarction(MI). Whereas from the inverse decision rule, considering RHS coverage factor it can be conclude that 100% patients suffering from MI having ECG where abnormal Q wave present. So, inverse decision rule give more strong explanation of the generated decision. Obviously, rule 4 having highest LHS and RHS coverage factor will be the strongest. The first 7 rule sets with high accuracy and coverage factor (both LHS and RHS) are taken for the generation of rule based classifier of disease. Both trained and untrained samples for all the three sets of dataset (e.g. Normal, Ischemia and Myocardial Infarction) are fed to the Inference system and the result obtained is given in table 2. The numbers given in brackets in table 2 represent the number of properly classified samples versus all tested samples. The confusion matrix, generated by using the standard voting classifier offered by the ROSETTA software toolbox, predicts cent percent accuracy for all the three set of trained data. Table 2 supports this

	Rule	LHS Supp	RHS Sup	RHS Accu	LHS Coverage	RHS Coverag	RHS Stability	L
1	Abn_Q_waves(P) => Disease(MI)	27	27	1.0	0.313953	1.0	1.0	1
2	Heart_Rate(N) AND ST_segments(E) AND Reciprocity(Ab) => Disease(ISC)	21	21	1.0	0.244186	1.0	1.0	3
3	Abn_Q_waves(Ab) AND ST_segments(E) => Disease(ISC)	21	21	1.0	0.244186	1.0	1.0	2
4	ST_segments(I) => Disease(N)	38	38	1.0	0.44186	1.0	1.0	1
5	Reciprocity(P) => Disease(MI)	23	23	1.0	0.267442	0.851852	1.0	1
6	PR_interval(N) AND ST_segments(E) AND Reciprocity(Ab) => Disease(ISC)	17	17	1.0	0.197674	0.809524	1.0	3
7	R_wave_Prog(N) AND ST_segments(E) => Disease(ISC)	16	16	1.0	0.186047	0.761905	1.0	2
8	PR_interval(A) AND R_wave_Prog(A) => Disease(MI)	12	12	1.0	0.139535	0.444444	1.0	2
9	Heart_Rate(B) => Disease(MI)	10	10	1.0	0.116279	0.37037	1.0	1
10	Heart_Rate(T) => Disease(N)	14	14	1.0	0.162791	0.368421	1.0	1
11	R_wave_Prog(A) AND Abn_Q_waves(Ab) => Disease(ISC)	5	5	1.0	0.05814	0.238095	1.0	2
12	PR_interval(N) AND R_wave_Prog(A) AND Reciprocity(Ab) => Disease(ISC)	5	5	1.0	0.05814	0.238095	1.0	3
13	Heart_Rate(N) AND R_wave_Prog(A) AND Reciprocity(Ab) => Disease(ISC)	5	5	1.0	0.05814	0.238095	1.0	3
14	PR_interval(A) AND R_wave_Prog(N) => Disease(ISC)	4	4	1.0	0.046512	0.190476	1.0	2
15	PR_interval(A) AND Abn_Q_waves(Ab) => Disease(ISC)	4	4	1.0	0.046512	0.190476	1.0	2
16	Heart_Rate(N) AND PR_interval(A) AND Reciprocity(Ab) => Disease(ISC)	4	4	1.0	0.046512	0.190476	1.0	3
17	ST_segments(D) => Disease(MI)	4	4	1.0	0.046512	0.148148	1.0	1
18	R_wave_Prog(A) AND T_waves(-) => Disease(MI)	4	4	1.0	0.046512	0.148148	1.0	2
19	QRS_width(A) => Disease(MI)	4	4	1.0	0.046512	0.148148	1.0	1
20	R_wave_Prog(N) AND T_waves(-) => Disease(ISC)	2	2	1.0	0.023256	0.095238	1.0	2
21	Reciprocity(Ab) AND T_waves(-) => Disease(ISC)	2	2	1.0	0.023256	0.095238	1.0	2
22	ST_segments(E) AND T_waves(-) => Disease(ISC)	2	2	1.0	0.023256	0.095238	1.0	2
23	Abn_Q_waves(Ab) AND T_waves(-) => Disease(ISC)	2	2	1.0	0.023256	0.095238	1.0	2

Fig. 4. A Portion of Generated Rule Set

Rosetta - [CONFUSION MATRIX]

File   Edit   View   Window   Help

		Predicted			
		MI	N	ISC	
Actual	MI	27	0	0	1.0
	N	0	38	0	1.0
	ISC	0	0	21	1.0
		1.0	1.0	1.0	1.0
ROC	Class	N			
	Area	1.0			
	Std. error	0.0			
	Thr. (0, 1)	0.628			
	Thr. acc.	0.628			

Fig. 5. Confusion Matrix Output for Standard Voting Classifier

Table 1. A portion of decision table

Heart Rate	PR Interval	P Wave height	P wave width	QRS width	QTc	QRS voltage	R Wave Prog	Abn. Q waves	ST Segment	Reciprocity	T waves	Disease
String	String	String	String	String	String	String	String	String	String	String	String	String
N	N	N	N	N	N	N	A	P	E	P	+	MI
B	N	N	N	A	N	N	A	P	E	P	+	MI
N	A	N	N	A	N	N	A	P	E	P	-	MI
N	N	N	N	N	N	N	N	Ab	I	Ab	+	N
N	N	N	N	N	N	N	N	Ab	I	Ab	+	N
N	N	N	N	N	N	N	N	Ab	I	Ab	+	N
N	A	N	N	N	N	N	N	Ab	E	Ab	+	ISC
N	N	N	N	N	N	N	N	Ab	E	Ab	+	ISC
N	N	N	N	N	N	N	N	Ab	E	Ab	+	ISC

prediction. Only one untrained ischemic dataset is wrongly classified to unrecognized set since the PR interval of that data was abnormal. Still, the present system is tested by three types of ECG data samples and encouraging result is obtained. In future the system will be tested by more number of samples and few other types of diseases.

4   Conclusion

The suitability of rough set theory in ECG analysis has been tested in this paper. To do so, an automated off-line data acquisition package is developed to extract the ECG signals from paper records. Six different types of noises may corrupt those extracted ECG signals. So different techniques are adopted for making those signals almost noise free. We use Cool Edit Pro software for simulating different noises and then

Table 2. Result obtained from rule based rough set decision system

Type of Samples	No. of Trained Samples	No. of Untrained Samples	Accuracy for Trained Samples	Accuracy for Untrained Samples
Normal	38	32	100% (38/38)	100% (32/32)
Ischemia	21	14	100% (21/21)	93% (13/14)
MI	27	13	100%(27/27)	100% (13/13)

generated the appropriate filters to remove them. A knowledge base about the time plane features and ECG interpretation is developed from various medical books and from the feed back of different reputed cardiologists. The time-plane features of ECG signals are extracted from each of the 12 lead ECG signals with the help of syntactic approaches. A rule-based rough set decision system is developed from these time-plane features to make an inference engine for disease identification. At present, the system is tested with three types of ECG data- Normal, Myocardial Ischemia and Myocardial Infarction. An accuracy of 100% is obtained for both trained and untrained dataset for Normal and Myocardial Infarction whereas for Ischemia 100% accuracy is obtained for trained dataset and 93% for untrained sample is obtained. In future the system will be tested with large number and different types of dataset.

Acknowledgement. The present paper is part of the research work on Digital Time Database Generation and Disease Identification from Paper ECG Records funded by Council of Scientific and Industrial Research(CSIR), Govt. of India.

References

1. Abreu-Lima C, de Sa, JP. : Automatic classifiers for the interpretation of electrocardiograms, Rev Port Cardiol ,May;17(5) (1998) 415-428
2. Ham FM, Han S, Classification of cardiac arrhythmias using fuzzy ARTMAP, IEEE Trans Biomed Eng , Apr;43(4) (1996) 425-430
3. Degani R, Computerized electrocardiogram diagnosis: fuzzy approach, Methods Inf Med ,Nov;31(4) (1992) 225-233
4. al-Fahoum AS, Howitt I., Combined wavelet transformation and radial basis neural networks for classifying life-threatening cardiac arrhythmias, Med Biol Eng Comput., Sep;37(5) (1999) 566-573
5. Degani R., Computerized Electrocardiogram Diagnosis: Fuzzy ApproachMethods of Inform. Med., 31 (1992) 225–233
6. Bortolan G., Brohet C., and Fusaro S., Possibilities of using neural networks for ECG classification, J. Electrocardiol., 29 (1996) 10–16
7. Silipo R., Bartolan G., Neural and traditional techniques in diagnostic ECG classification, in Proc. ICASSP, 1997.
8. Bozzola P ., et al., Ahybrid neuro-fuzzy system for ECG classification of myocardial infarction, in Comput. Cardiol., Indianapolis, IN, 1996.
9. King M.J.,.Han J.S, .Park K.H, et al., Classification of Arrhythmia based on discrete wavelet transform and roughest theory, Intl. Conf. Control , Automation and System, ICCAS,2001.

10. Zdzislaw Pawlak. Rough sets. International Journal of Information and Computer Science, vol. 11(5), pp. 341–356, 1982.
11. Zdzislaw Pawlak. Rough Sets: Theoretical Aspects of Reasoning about Data, volume 9 of Series D: System Theory, Knowledge Engineering and Problem Solving. Kluwer Academic Publishers, Dordrecht, The Netherlands, 1991.
12. Zdzislaw Pawlak, Bayes' Theorem Revised – The Rough Set View, New Frontiers in Artificial Intelligence : Joint JSAI 2001 Workshop Post-Proceedings, Lecture Notes in Computer Science, vol. 2253, pp. 240-250, 2001.
13. Gonzalez, R.C, Woods R.E, Digital Image Processing, 3rd edn, pp. 491 - 495, Addison Wesley Longman,Inc., 2000.
14. Hildebrand F.B., Introduction To Numerical Analysis, T M H edn., pp. 82-84, Tata Mcgraw-Hill Publishing Company Ltd.
15. Maglaveras N., Stamkopoulos T, Pappas C., Strintzis M., An adaptive back-propagation neural network for real-time ischemia episodes detection. Development and performance analysis using the European ST-T database, IEEE Trans. Biomed.Eng., vol. 45 (7), pp. 805–813, 1998.
16. Silipo R., Laguna P., Marchesi C, Mark R.G., ST-T segment change recognition using artificialneural networks and principal component analysis, Computers in Cardiology, IEEE Comput. Soc.Press, pp. 213–216, 1995.
17. Jager F, Mark R.G., Moody G.B., Divjak S., Analysis of transient ST segment changes during ambulatory monitoring using the Karhunen-Loeve transform, Computers in Cardiology, IEEE Comput. Soc. Press, pp. 691–694, 1992.
18. Polkowski L., Skowron A., Rough Sets in Knowledge Discovery, Physica – Verlag, Wurzburg, Wein, 1998.
19. φhrm, Discernibility and Rough Sets in Medicine : Tools and Applications, Ph.D. Thesis, Department of Computer and Information Science, Norwegian University of Science and Technology, Trondheim, NTNU Report, 1999:133, IDI Report 1999.
20. Goldman M.J., Principles of Electrocardiography, 11th Edn., Marugen Asia (Pvt.) Ltd.
21. Hampton J.R.,The ECG Made Easy, 5th edn., Churchill Livingstone.
22. Ary L. Goldberger, Clinical Electrocardiography, A Simlified Approach, 6th Edn., Harcourt India Pvt. Ltd.
23. Friesen G.M.,. Jennett T.C, Jadallah M.A., Yates S.L., Quint S.R., Nagle H.T., "A Comparison of the Noise Sensitivity of Nine QRS Detection Algorithms", *IEEE Trans. Biomed. Eng.*, vol. 37, no. 1, pp. 85-98, 1990.

Attribute Selection for EEG Signal Classification Using Rough Sets and Neural Networks

Kenneth Revett[1], Marcin Szczuka[2],
Pari Jahankhani[1], and Vassilis Kodogiannis[1,3]

[1] Mechatronics Group, Harrow School of Computer Science,
Univ. of Westminster, London HA1 3TP, UK
{parij, revettk}@wmin.ac.uk
[2] Institute of Mathematics, Warsaw University
Banacha 2, 02-097, Warsaw, Poland
szczuka@mimuw.edu.pl
[3] Centre of Systems Analysis and the Mechatronics Group,
School of Computer Science, Univ. of Westminster, London HA1 3TP, UK
kodogiv@wmin.ac.uk

Abstract. This paper describes the application of rough sets and neural network models for classification of electroencephalogram (EEG) signals from two patient classes: normal and epileptic. First, the wavelet transform (WT) was applied to the EEG time series in order to reduce the dimensionality and highlight important features in the data. Statistical measures of the resulting wavelet coefficients were used for the classification task. Employing rough sets, we sought to determine which of the acquired attributes were necessary/informative as predictors of the decision classes. The results indicate that rough sets was able to accurately classify the datasets with an accuracy of almost 100%. The resulting rule sets were small, with an average cardinality of 6. These results were confirmed using standard neural network based classifiers.

1 Introduction

Electroencephalography (EEG) provides a direct measure of cortical activity with millisecond temporal resolution in a non-invasive manner. The technique is widely used in clinical neurophysiological settings and has provided a wealth of diagnostic information for a wide range of neurological deficits [5,7]. Although the underlying technology has not radically changed since its introduction by Hans Berger in 1924, the amount of data that is generated by EEG studies has increased exponentially. Laboratories routinely use 100-electrode arrays and record for more than 24 hours at a sampling rate of over 100 Hz. In response to this wealth of important data generated by EEG studies, many laboratories around the world have developed various techniques for automating the extraction of diagnostically relevant information.

The current trend in EEG analysis employs a multi-stage process: in the first stage, Discrete Wavelet Transforms (DWT) are used as a pre-processing step to decompose the time series into a number of subbands through a process that is

S. Greco et al. (Eds.): RSCTC 2006, LNAI 4259, pp. 408–417, 2006.

essentially a series of low and high pass filters. This pre-processing step effectively performs a dimensionality reduction of the data in preparation for subsequent analysis. In the next phase, a series of attributes are generated from the DWT processed dataset, which is used as input to a classification system. In the present case, we are seeking to produce a classifier that is capable of distinguishing a normal EEG recording from one containing an epileptic seizure segment. This is not a novel task, as many literature reports have presented a variety of techniques. Neural networks and statistical pattern recognition methods have been applied to EEG analysis. Neural Network (NN) detection systems have been proposed by a number of researchers. Pradhan et al. [10] used the raw EEG as an input to a neural network while Weng and Khorasani [11] used an adaptive structure neural network, but his results show a poor false detection rate. Petrosian et al. [9] showed that the ability of specifically designed and trained recurrent neural networks (RNN) combined with wavelet pre-processing, to predict the onset of epileptic seizures both on scalp and intracranial recordings only one-channel of electroencephalogram. In order to provide faster and efficient algorithm, Folkers et al. [4] proposed a versatile signal processing and analysis framework for bioelectrical data and in particular for neural recordings and 128-channel EEG.

In our approach, we are using rough sets to determine which attributes are the most relevant for the classification task. Ningler et al. [8] have applied rough sets to classify EEG-signals with respect to intraoperative awareness, with a reasonable degree of success (90% classification accuracy). They did not however relate these resulting attributes to any underlying phenomenon, as is evidenced by their very large rule set (475 for the crisp and 13,424 for the fuzzy discretisation methods respectively). We applied rough sets to a set of attributes (measures of dispersion from the DWT pre-processing step) in order to determine which attributes were critical in the classification process. We validated the results using 5-fold cross validation, as well as through three neural network classifiers – the feed-forward error back-propagation network, the Radial Basis Function (RBF) network, and the Local Transfer Function Classifier (LTF-C). This validation was performed in a two-stage process (for Multi Layered Perceptron (MLP) only). We first trained and tested the neural networks on the full dataset (containing 20 attributes), we then performed attribute dimensionality reduction using rough sets, and then tested the neural networks with the remaining attributes generated from the rough sets analysis. We used the LTF-C neural network and a modified k-NN classifier as independent measures of the accuracy of the results we obtained with rough sets. To our knowledge, this is the first paper reporting this type of analysis within the context of EEG analysis.

2 Data Acquisition and Pre-processing

We have used publicly available datasets described in Andrzejak et al. [1]. The complete data set consists of five sets (denoted A–E) each containing 100 single-channel (100 electrodes) EEG recordings of 5 separate patient classes. For this study we focused on sets labelled A and E in [1]: the normal and epileptic seizure session recordings. These segments were selected and cut out from continuous multi-channel EEG recordings (i.e. 23.6 seconds of recording time) after visual inspection for artifacts, e.g., due to muscle activity or eye movements. In Figure 2, the panel labelled 'Set A' corresponded to the normal class and panel 'Set E' is an example of epileptic seizure class. All EEG signals were recorded with the same 128-channel amplifier system, using an average common reference. The data were digitised at 173.61 Hz using 12-bit resolution. The data was band-pass filtered at 0.53–40 Hz (12dB/oct). Each EEG dataset consisted of 4,096 data points and a rectangular window of 256 discrete data points (16 windows per electrode) was selected.

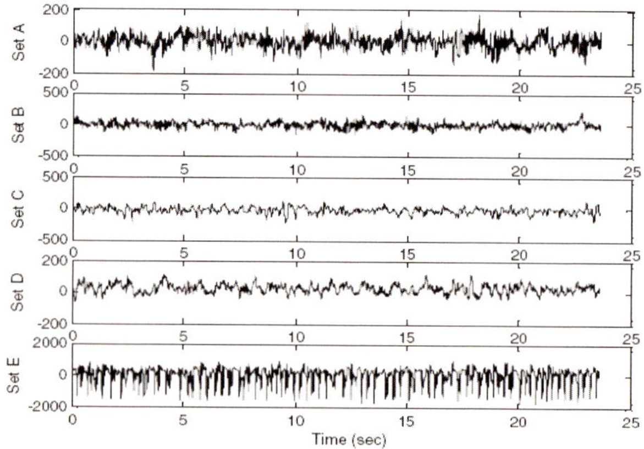

Fig. 1. Examples of five different sets of EEG signals taken from different subjects

Selection of suitable wavelet and the number of decomposition levels is very important in analysis of signals using the DWT. The number of decomposition levels is chosen based on the dominant frequency components of the signal. The levels are chosen such that those parts of the signal that correlate well with the frequencies necessary for classification of the signal are retained in the wavelet coefficients. In the present study, since the EEG signals do not have any useful frequency components above 30 Hz, the number of decomposition levels was chosen to be 4. Thus, the EEG signals were decomposed into details D1–D4 and one final approximation, A4. Usually, tests are performed with different types of wavelets and the one which gives maximum efficiency is selected for the particular application. The smoothing feature of the Daubechies wavelet of order 2 (db2) made it more appropriate to detect changes of EEG signals. Hence, the wavelet coefficients were computed using the db2 in the present study. Figure 2 shows approximation (A1–A4) and details (D1–D4) of an epileptic EEG signal.

The detail wavelet coefficients (D1–D4) at the first, second, third, and fourth levels (129+66+34+18 coefficients) and the approximation wavelet coefficients (A4) at the fourth level (18 coefficients) were generated. We have 100 electrodes and 16 windows per electrode, yielding a total of 1,600 segments per class.

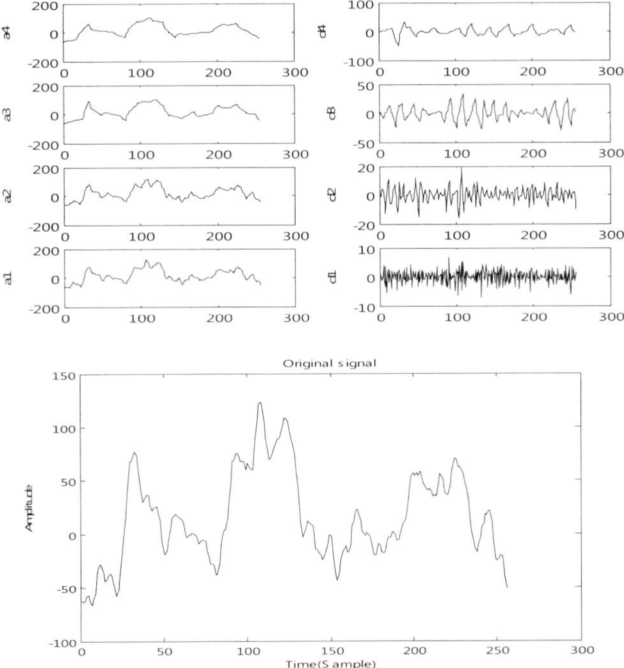

Fig. 2. Approximate and detailed coefficients of EEG signals taken from epileptic subject

The extracted wavelet coefficients provide a compact representation that shows the energy distribution of the EEG signal in time and frequency. For each set of detail coefficients (D1-D4) and the approximation wavelet coefficients (A4) we calculate four values: maximum, minimum, mean and standard deviation. That yields a final set of 20 real valued attributes for each class (following the ideas from [6]).

3   Classification Methods

In this study, we employed a combination of neural network based classification algorithms in conjunction with rough sets. Initially, we trained an MLP and RBF neural network to classify the 2 EEG classes (A and E). This was accomplished through the standard back-propagation learning algorithm and the orthogonal least squares algorithm was used to train the RBF network. The LTF-C algorithm uses a modified version of the RBF algorithm, which is explained in detail below. We next briefly describe the rough sets and neural network based classifier, before presenting the main results of this study.

3.1   Rough Sets

Rough Set (RS) theory is a main topic of this conference and that our study uses only some very basic and well known RS tools we restrict ourselves to introducing only these RS notions that we further make use of. As the capacity of this paper is very limited, we make only a basic description of these concepts.

The first step in the process of mining any dataset using rough sets is to transform the data into a decision table. In a decision table (DT), each row consists of an observation (also called an object) and each column is an attribute, one of which is the decision attribute for the observation. In our case the decision table consists of 8000 rows and each row contains a vector of 20 numbers (values of 20 numerical conditional attributes) labelled with one of 5 decision values (A-E). Objects that share the same decision value are said to belong to one *decision class*. Attributes other than decision will be referred to as *conditional attributes* or simply *conditions*.

Luckily enough, thanks to the fact that data table is generated by a controlled pre-processing algorithm, we have no missing values and no errors which is not commonplace in medical data sets. The table is consistent, i.e. there are no two rows that have the same conditional part and different decisions.

One of most characteristic features of our data set is that all conditional attributes are numeric (floating point numbers). In order to apply some of the RS methods to such data table one have to perform *discretisation*.

Discretisation refers to partitioning attributes into intervals – tantamount to searching for "cuts" in the range of attribute. All values that lie within a given range (between two cuts) are mapped onto the same value, transforming interval into categorical data. In this study we apply discretisation method based on Maximal Discernibility (MD) heuristics that makes use of the core RS notion of *discernibility* between decision classes. Details of this method and its implementation in RSES are given in [2,3].

The ultimate goal we want to achieve with our RS toolkit is to construct a *classifier* – that is a procedure which when given an unlabelled object is capable of assigning a proper decision value. In particular, we will be dealing with classifiers that are based on *decision rules*, i.e., formulae of the form:

$$(a_i = v_i) \wedge \ldots \wedge (a_i = v_i) \Rightarrow (d = v)$$

where atomic sub-formula $(a_i = v_i)$ is called *descriptor* or *condition*. We say that rule r is *applicable* to an object, or alternatively, the object *matches* rule, if its attribute values satisfy the premise of this rule. With the rule we can associate some numerical characteristics derived from the underlying data table DT. $Supp(r)$ is equal to the number of objects from table for which rule r applies correctly, i.e., the premise of rule is satisfied and the decision given by rule is similar to the one preset in decision table. $Match(r)$ is the number of objects in the table for which rule r applies in general. Analogously the notion of matching set for a rule or collection of rules may be introduced (see [3]).

The notions of matching and supporting set are common to all classifiers, not only decision rules. For a classifier Cl we will denote by $Supp(Cl)$ the set of objects that support classifier, i.e., the set of objects for which classifier gives the answer (decision) identical to that we already have. Similarly, $Match(Cl)$ is the set of objects that are recognized by Cl. Support and matching make it possible to introduce two measures that are used in our study for classifier scoring. These are *Accuracy* and *Coverage*, defined as follows:

$$Accuracy_{DT}(Cl) = \frac{|Supp(Cl)|}{|DT|}; \quad Coverage_{DT}(Cl) = \frac{|Match(Cl)|}{|DT|}$$

where $|DT|$ denotes number of objects in our data table.

3.2 MLP, RBF, and LTF-C Networks

The Multilayer Perceptron Network (MLP), which has the ability to learn and generalise, smaller training set requirements, fast operation, ease of implementation and therefore most commonly used neural network architectures, have been adapted for describing the alertness level of arbitrary subject. We have used in this case, the classic gradient descent learning scheme for the training of this particular network.

The second classification scheme utilised here is a Radial Basis Function Network (RBF) scheme. RBF networks train rapidly, usually orders of magnitude faster than MLP, while exhibiting none of its training pathologies such as paralysis or local minima problems. Such a system consists of three layers (input, hidden, output). The activation of a hidden neuron is determined in two steps: The first is computing the distance (usually by using the Euclidean norm) between the input vector and a centre c_i that represents the ith hidden neuron. Second, a function h that is usually bell-shaped is applied, using the obtained distance to get the final activation of the hidden neuron. In this case the Gaussian function $G(x)$ was used. The parameter σ is called unit width and is determined using the heuristic rule "global first nearest-neighbour". The activation of a neuron in the output layer is determined by a linear combination of the fixed nonlinear basis functions, i.e. here $\phi_i(x) = G(\|x - c_i\|)$ and w_i are the adjustable weights that link the output nodes with the appropriate hidden neurons. The orthogonal least squares (OLS) method has been employed as a forward selection procedure that constructs RBF networks in a rational way. The algorithm chooses appropriate RBF centres one by one from training data points until a satisfactory network is obtained.

The last classification scheme utilised in this study was based on the Linear Transfer Function Classifier (LTF-C) scheme in the version implemented in RSES. LTF-C (cf. [12]) is a neural network solving classification problems. Its architecture is very similar to this of RBF – the network has a hidden layer with Gaussian neurons connected to an output layer of linear units. The number of inputs corresponds to the number of attributes while the number of linear neurons in output layers equals the number of decision classes. There are some additional restrictions on values of output weights that enable to use an entirely different training algorithm and to obtain very high accuracy in real-world problems. The training algorithm of LTF-C comprises four types of modifications of the network, performed after every presentation of a training object. Namely the network can: change positions (means) of Gaussians in hidden layer, change widths (deviations) of Gaussians separately for each hidden neuron and attribute, insert new hidden neurons, and remove unnecessary hidden neurons.

As one can see, the LTF-C structure is dynamical. The training process starts with an empty hidden layer, adding new hidden neurons when the accuracy is insufficient and removing the units which do not positively contribute to the calculation of correct network decisions. This feature of LTF-C enables automatic choice of the best network size, which is much easier than setting the number of hidden neurons manually.

4   Results

As previously indicated, we initially trained the MLP, RBF, and LTF-C networks to classify the two EEG time series using 20 inputs and a binary decision class (either A or E) for the output. We used a 50/50 rule where 50% of the data (half of 3,200 objects in total) were used for training and the rest was used for testing. This train-and-test scheme was selected for the sake of obtaining results that are directly comparable with those existing before. More sophisticated testing schemes are planned for the follow-up of the currently presented study. The results in Table 1 represent the training and testing accuracy of the neural network classifiers.

Table 1. The classification accuracy of the MLP, RBF and LTF-C on the 2 classes EEG testing data. The values in parentheses represent training accuracy.

	MLP	RBF	LTF-C
Class A	(95.1) 94.3%	(96.1)95.2%	(100) 99.8%
Class E	(96.5) 93.8%	(97.3)96.8%	(100) 99.8%

Relatively high quality obtained by neural network models without any special fine-tuning was an indicator that they may exist a simple regularity in the data that makes it possible to discern between classes A and E. To find out what kind of regularity may that be and what possible use we may have of it for our study, we turned to rough set methodology. Using some typical rough set based algorithm implemented in the Rough set Exploration System (RSES, see [11]) we started to search for a set of simple description rules discriminating between classes A and E. Since the considered data set has all conditional attributes represented numerically, the discretisation procedure has been applied. The use of discretisation, reduct and rule calculation has resulted in a very interesting and somehow surprising results. Since rough set methods we have used concentrate on maximising discernibility and minimising (reducing) the dimensionality of derived model, they tend to provide a concise description. In our case this these descriptions have in fact become ultra-compact. As it turns out the DWT data contains several attributes that have very high discriminative abilities with regard to classes A and E. Some attributes make it possible to construct a set of rules with only a single condition (on this attribute) and almost perfect accuracy on the entire data set. The table below presents a simple summary of the identified attributes.

Table 2. Qualities of selected single-attribute rule sets for classes A and E

Attribute	No. of rules	Accuracy	Attribute	No. of rules	Accuracy
Max. D2	2	99.8%	Min. D4	2	99.9%
Min. D2	10	99.6%	Max D4	2	100%
St. dev. D2	14	99.2%	Min. A4	6	99.9%
Min D3	8	99.9%	Max A4	10	99.7%
Max D3	2	99.9%	St. dev. A4	2	99.9%
St. dev. D3	2	99.8%			

Note that a single attribute Max D4 is sufficient to create a perfect classifier if we only discern between classes A and E. Such classifier would consist of only two 100% correct decision rules:

```
If Max D4 < 173.1838 then Decision = A;
If Max D4 > 173.1838 then Decision = E;
```

Also, the results in table show that basically for all listed attribute there is only a handful of outliers that prevents each of them from being 100% correct. These errors are in fact almost entirely dependant on the random split. Inasmuch as experiments have shown that classes A and E are easily discernible we decided to investigate how different is the situation if we not only focus on these two classes. In the more realistic setting we will not know in advance whether the given measurement comes from the patient from class A/E or any of the other (B,C,D). Therefore, even if we focus on A and E, we still have to be able to discern between A, E and the rest. If it proves possible to do so, then we may attempt to construct a decision support system that at the same time tells us whether a given data example is in our focus group (A+E) or not and whether it is a healthy (A) or epileptic (E) patient.

We have staged an experiment with use of various classifiers implemented in RSES in order to verify how well can we differentiate classes A and E from the rest. The training and verification in this experiment was performed on the entire 8000 rows (all classes). As in the previous experiments the data was randomly halved in order to create training and test samples. Once again we have used LTF-C and a rule-based RS classifier from RSES (see see [11] for details). For reference we have also applied a modified *k-Nearest Neighbours* (k-NN) classifier from RSES. The k-NN classifier is known to provide very good results, however, without giving an explanation. The results were rather encouraging. Classes A and E are not only well discernable from each other, but also significantly different from the rest of data set (B+C+D). Table 3 presents overview of the results. Since the methods used are always 100% accurate on training sample we only show average results on test cases.

We have also performed an initial attempt to construct classifier for all 5 types of patients. As expected, the performance of such classifier is significantly lower (on average more than 10%). Rule based methods tend to have problems with unseen cases (low coverage). It is quite visible that the three sets B, C, and D

Table 3. Classification results for classes A, B+C+D, and E on test set

Classifier	Classifier details	Avg. accuracy	Avg. coverage
Modified k-NN	Reference result	99.4%	100%
LTF-C	Neural network	98%	100%
Decision rules (all)	Up to 13000 rules	97.2%	99%
Decision rules (LEM)	200-220 rules	98.7%	95.2%
Decision rules (LEM)	270-290 rules	98.5%	96.5%

are more complicated and vague than A and E. Constructing a proper classifier for the entire dataset is on our task list for next stage of this study.

Notice: *All the experimental results presented in this section have been averaged over several repetitions in order to avoid presentation of random, insignificant and non-replicable outputs.*

5   Conclusions

In this study, we examined the difference(s) between normal and epileptic EEG time series. After extracting the DWT coefficients, we used four measures of dispersion to as attributes for subsequent classification. The results of the neural network (MLP and RBF) classification were high, comparable to other published results on similar datasets. We then sought to perform dimensionality reduction through the rough sets paradigm. The results from this analysis indicated that the statistical attributes (20 in all) contained a considerable amount of redundancy. Rough sets was able to reduce the dimensionality of the attributes to a single one – Max D4 (see Table 2). With this single attribute, only 2 rules were generated which provided 100% classification accuracy. This result was confirmed with independent methods such as a modified k-NN and the LTF-C. We also used this single attribute to re-test the original MLP network that were trained on the full dataset and the resulting classification accuracy was not reduced using the single attribute (Max D4). The resulting classification accuracy was in fact somewhat higher (98%) than when trained on the full set of attributes.

These results indicate that there is the potential for considerable redundancy with attribute selection in this particular domain. Our results indicate that preprocessing the data using rough sets is an effective way of eliminating this potential redundancy in attribute selection. With a minimal attribute set, one can then begin to find more exacting correlations between the behaviour of attributes and the underlying phenomenon. In this particular case, Max D4 was the primary attribute for distinguishing normal from epileptic EEG recordings. The 4th level represents the most refined sampling performed on this data. We are planning to investigate this result in future work – but in this instance one can hypothesise that the increased sampling rate provides significant information. The 'Max' represents the maximal value within the window – and one could reasonably explain this result in terms of the reported spiking that occurs in epileptic seizures.

The results from this preliminary study will be expanded to include a more complete range of pathologies. In this work, we focused on the extremes that are found within the EEG spectrum – normal and epileptic time series. These two series were chosen as they would more than likely lead to the maximal dispersion between the 2 signals and be amenable for training of the classifiers. In the next stage of this research, we have datasets that are intermediate in the signal changes they present. This will provide a more challenging set of data to work with – and will allow us to refine our learning algorithms and/or approaches to the problem of EEG analysis.

Acknowledgements. The authors wish to thank the authors of EEG dataset which is publicly available at
http://www.meb.uni-bonn.de/epileptologie/science/physik/eegdata.html.
Marcin Szczuka is partly supported by Polish grant 3T11C02226.

References

1. Andrzejak R. G., Lehnertz K., Mormann F., Rieke C., David P., Elger C. E., Indications of nonlinear deterministic and finite-dimensional structures in time series of brain electrical activity. *Phys. Rev. E*, 64, pp. 1-8, 2001.
2. Bazan J., Nguyen H.S., Nguyen S.H., Synak P., Wróblewski J., Rough set algorithms in classification problems. *Studies in Fuzziness and Soft Computing* vol 56,. Physica-Verlag, Heidelberg, pp. 49-88, 2000.
3. Bazan J., Szczuka M., The Rough Set Exploration System. Transactions on Rough Sets III, **LNCS** 3400, Springer, pp.37-56, 2005. http://logic.mimuw.edu.pl/~rses
4. Folkers A., Mosch F., Malina T., Hofmann U. G., Realtime bioelectrical data acquisition and processing from 128 channels utilizing the wavelet-transformation. *Neurocomputing*, 52–54, pp. 247-254, 2003.
5. Glover Jr. J.R., Raghaven N., Ktonas P.Y., Frost Jr. J.D., Context-based automated detection of eleptogenic sharp transients in the EEG, *IEEE Tans. Biomed. Eng.*, 36(5), pp. 519-527, 1989.
6. Guler I., Ubeyli E.D., Application of adaptive neuro-fuzzy inference system for detection of electrocardiographic changes in patients with partial epilepsy using feature extraction. *Expert Syst. Appl.*, 27(3), pp. 323-30, 2004.
7. Nigam V.P., Graupe D.A, Neural-network-based detection of epilepsy, *Neurological Research*, vol. 26:1, pp. 55-60, 2004.
8. Ningler M., Stockmanns G., Schneider G., Dressler O., Kochs E.F., Rough Set-based Classification of EEG-signals to detect Intraoperative Awareness, Proc. of RSCTC2004, **LNAI** 3066, Springer, pp. 825-834, 2004.
9. Petrosian A., Prokhorov D., Homan R., Dashei R., Wunsc, D., Recurrent neural network based prediction of epileptic seizures in intra and extracranial EEG. *Neurocomputing*, 30, pp. 201–218, 2000.
10. Pradhan N., Sadasivan P. K., Arunodaya G. R., Detection of seizure activity in EEG by an artificial neural network. *Computers and Biomedical Research*, 29, pp. 303–313, 1996.
11. Weng W., Khorasani K., An adaptive structure neural network with application to EEG automatic seizure detection. Neural Networks, 9, pp. 1223-1240, 1996
12. Wojnarski M., LTF-C: Architecture, training algorithm and applications of new neural classifier. *Fundamenta Informaticae*, 54(1), pp. 89-105, 2003.

Automatic Planning of Treatment of Infants with Respiratory Failure Through Rough Set Modeling

Jan G. Bazan[1], Piotr Kruczek[2], Stanislawa Bazan-Socha[3],
Andrzej Skowron[4], and Jacek J. Pietrzyk[2]

[1] Institute of Mathematics, University of Rzeszów
Rejtana 16A, 35-959 Rzeszów, Poland
[2] Department of Pediatrics, Collegium Medicum, Jagiellonian University
Wielicka 265, 30-663 Cracow, Poland
[3] Department of Internal Medicine, Collegium Medicum, Jagiellonian University
Skawinska 8, 31-066 Cracow, Poland
[4] Institute of Mathematics, Warsaw University
Banacha 2, 02-097 Warsaw, Poland

Abstract. We discuss an application of rough set tools for modeling networks of classifiers induced from data and ontology of concepts delivered by experts. Such networks allow us to develop strategies for automated planning of a treatment of infants with respiratory illness. We report results of experiments with the networks of classifiers used in automated planning of the treatment of newborn infants with respiratory failure. The reported experiments were performed on medical data obtained from the Neonatal Intensive Care Unit in the Department of Pediatrics, Collegium Medicum, Jagiellonian University.

Keywords: Automated planning, concept approximation, dynamical system, ontology of concepts, respiratory failure, rough sets.

1 Introduction

This paper investigates medical planning in the context of a complex dynamical system (see, e.g., [1,3,6,2,4]). A *complex dynamical system* (also called as an *autonomous multiagent system* [2] or *swarm* [9]) is a system of complex objects that are changing (adapting), interacting, and learning over time. Such objects are usually linked by some dependencies, sometimes can cooperate between themselves and are able to perform flexible autonomous complex actions (operations, changes). For example, one can consider *road traffic* as a complex dynamical system represented by a road simulator (see e.g. [2]). Another example can be taken from medical practice. This second example concerns the treatment of infants with respiratory failure, where a given patient is treated as a complex dynamical system, while diseases of a patient are treated as complex objects changing and interacting over time (see [4] and Section 2).

S. Greco et al. (Eds.): RSCTC 2006, LNAI 4259, pp. 418–427, 2006.

The prediction of behaviors of a complex object evaluated over time is usually based on some historical knowledge representation used to store information about changes in relevant features or parameters. This information is usually represented as a data set and has to be collected during long-term observation of a complex dynamic system. For example, in case of the treatment of the infants with respiratory failure, we associate the object parameters mainly with values of arterial blood gases measurements and the X-ray lung examination. A single action is often not sufficient for changing the complex object in the expected direction. Therefore a sequence of actions need to be used instead of a single action during medical treatment. Hence, methods of automated planning are necessary during monitoring of a given complex dynamic system (see [7,10]).

This paper is organized as follows. In Section 2, some medical knowledge about the treatment of the infants with respiratory failure is given. The basic concept of a planning rule is given in Section 3. The automated planning of actions for groups of complex objects realized using *planning graphs for a group of objects* is considered in Section 4. Experimental results using the proposed tools for automated planning, are presented in Section 5.

2   Neonatal Respiratory Failure

The new possibilities in medical intensive care have appeared during last decades thanks to the progress in medical and technical sciences. This progress allowed us to save the live of prematurely born infants including the smallest born between 20th and 24th week of gestation with the birth weight above 500g.

Prematurely born infants demonstrate numerous abnormalities in their first weeks of life. Their survival, especially without severe multiorgan complications is possible with appropriate treatment. Prematurity can be characterized as inappropriate maturity of systems and organs leading to their dysfunction after birth.

The respiratory system dysfunction appearing in the first hours of life and leading to respiratory failure is the most important single factor limiting survival of our smallest patients. The respiratory failure is defined as inappropriate blood oxygenation and accumulation of carbon dioxide and is diagnosed based on arterial blood gases measurements. Clinical symptoms - increased rate of breathing, accessory respiratory muscles use as well as X-ray lung examination are also included in assessment of the severity of respiratory failure.

The most important cause of respiratory failure in prematurely born infants is RDS (respiratory distress syndrome). RDS results from lung immaturity and surfactant deficiency. The other co-existing abnormalities such as PDA (patent ductus arteriosus), sepsis (generalized reaction on infection leading to multiorgan failure) and Ureaplasma lung infection (acquired during pregnancy or birth) may exacerbate the course of respiratory failure. Each of these conditions can be treated as an unrelated disease requiring separate treatment. However, these abnormalities very often co-exist, so it is sometimes necessary to treat combinations such as RDS + PDA + sepsis. In a holistic, therapeutic approach, it is important to synchronize the treatment of co-existing abnormalities in an effort to combat respiratory failure.

Effective care of prematurely born infants entails consideration of all co-existing abnormalities such as infections (both congenital and acquired), water-electrolyte and acid-base imbalance, circulatory, kidney problems. All of these factors are related and influence one another. The care of prematurely born infants during their first days of life requires continuous analysis of many parameters. These parameters can be divided into stationary (e.g., gestational age, birth weight, Apgar score) and continuous (changing over time). Parameter values can be obtained from various monitoring devices (e.g., oxygen hemoglobin saturation (SAT), blood pressure, temperature, lung mechanics) either on a discrete (e.g. blood gases) or continuous basis. Neonatal care includes assessment of a number of sources of information such as ultrasound scans of the brain, echocardiography and chest X-ray. Global analysis should also include current methods of treatment used for particular patients. These methods may have qualitative (e.g., administration of medication) or quantitative (e.g., respiratory settings) characteristics. It should also be observed that assessment of a patient's state is very often performed hurriedly under stress conditions.

Computerized data analysis may provide support for a physician during daily diagnostic-therapeutic processes both in collecting and storing patient data using a number of tools (e.g., Neonatal Information System) and as a means of quick, automatic and intelligent analysis of patient data. This approach might allow for computer presentation of some information based on the observed patterns, which might be helpful in automating the planning of treatment.

The aim of this paper is to present some computer tools for automated planning of the treatment (see, e.g., [7,10]). In this approach, a given patient is treated as a complex dynamical system, while patient diseases (e.g., RDS, PDA, sepsis, Ureaplasma and respiratory failure) are treated as complex objects changing and interacting over time (see Section 4). Respiratory failure is very complex because it is a consequence of RDS, PDA, sepsis or Ureaplasma. Our task is to facilitate automatic planning for sequences of medical actions required to treat a given patient.

3   The Automatic Planning for Complex Objects

In this research, we discuss some rough set [8] tools for automated planning as part of a system for modeling networks of classifiers. Such networks are constructed using an ontology of concepts delivered by experts[1].

The basic concept we use is a *planning rule*. Let $s_l, s_{r_1} \ldots s_{r_k}$ denote states of a complex object and a denotes an action that causes a transition to some another state. A planning rule proposed by a human expert such as a medical doctor has the following simplified form: $(s_l, a) \rightarrow s_{r_1}|s_{r_2} \ldots |s_{r_k}$. Such rule can be used to change the state s_l of a complex object, using the action a to some state from the right hand side of a rule. But the result of applying such a rule is

---

[1] The ontology focuses on bases for concept approximation (see, e.g., [5]).

nondeterministic, because there are usually many states on the right hand side of a planning rule.

A set of planning rules can be represented by a *planning graph*. There are two kinds of nodes in planning graphs: *state nodes* represented by ovals and *action nodes* represented by rectangles (see, e.g., Figure 1). The connections between nodes represent temporal dependencies, e.g., the connection between the state node s_1 and the action node a_1 says that in state s_1 of a complex object, action a_1 can be performed while the connection between a_1 and state node s_2 means that after performing action a_1 in s_1 the status of the complex object can be changed from s_1 to s_2. Figure 1 shows how planning rules can be joined to obtain a planning graph.

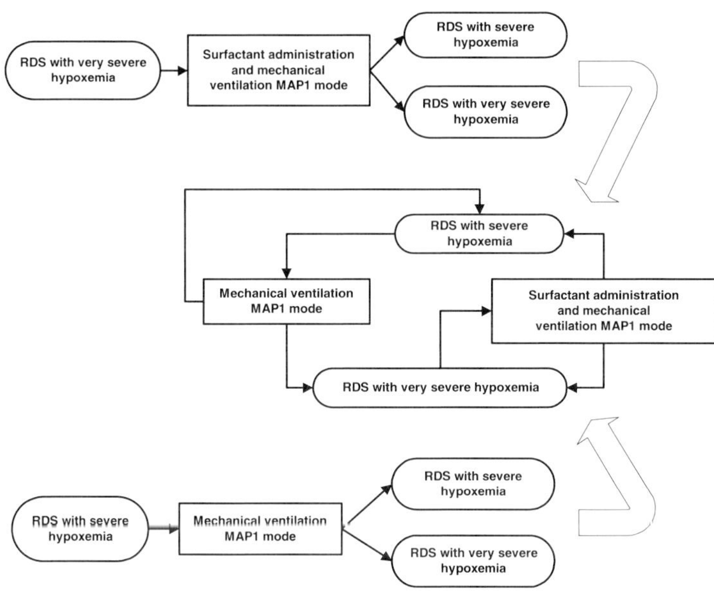

Fig. 1. Planning Rules in a Planning Graph

Notice, that any state from the planning graph can be treated as a complex concept specified by a human expert in natural language. Such concepts can be approximated by approximate reasoning schemes (AR-schemes, for short) using data sets and domain knowledge accumulated for a given complex dynamical system (see [1,2,4]). Hence, it is possible to identify the initial state at the beginning of planning for a particular complex object.

The output for the planing problem for a single complex object is a path in the planning graph from the initial node-state to the *expected (target) node-state*. Such a path can be treated as a plan of action that should be performed beginning from the given complex object in order to change its state to the expected status.

In practice, it is often the case that a generated plan must be compatible with the plan proposed by a human expert (e.g., the treatment plan should be compatible with the plan suggested by human experts from a medical clinic). It is strongly recommended that the method of the verification and evaluation of generated plans should be based on the similarity between the generated plan and the plan proposed by human experts (see Section 5). Hence, the usage of special tools that make it possible to resolve conflicts (nondeterminism) of actions in planning rules is needed. Therefore, in this paper we propose a family of classifiers constructed for all state-nodes from a planning graph. These classifiers are constructed on the basis of decision rules computed for a special decision table called a *resolving table*. The resolving table is constructed for any state-nodes from the planning graph and stores information about objects of a given complex dynamical system satisfying the concept from the current state-node. Any row of this table represents information about parameters of a single object registered at a given time. Condition attributes (features) from this table are defined by human experts and have to be computed on the basis of information included in the description of the current state of a complex object as well on some previous states or actions obtained from the near or far history of an object. It should be emphasized that the definition of such condition attributes should facilitate easy update of attribute values during the construction of a given plan according to performed actions and new states of a complex object. The proposed approach should be accompanied by some kind of simulation during plan construction. The decision attribute of the resolving table is defined as the action that has been performed for a given training object combined with the real effect of this action for an object. Next, we construct rule based classifiers for all states, i.e., for all associated resolving tables. In addition, these classifiers make it possible to obtain a list of actions and states after usage of actions with their weights in descending order. This is very important in generating plans for groups of objects (see Section 4).

4   Automatic Planning for Groups of Complex Objects

In this section, we present a generalization of the method for automated planning described in Section 3. For a group of objects, we define a graph that we call a *planning graph for a group of objects*. This new graph is similar to a planning graph for a single object (see Section 3). There are two kinds of nodes in this graph, namely, *states nodes* (denoted by ovals) that represent the current state of a group of objects specified as complex concepts by a human expert in natural language, and *action nodes* (denoted by rectangles) that represent so-called *meta actions* defined for groups of objects by a human expert. Meta actions are performed over a longer period called a *time window* [2].

In Figure 2, we present an exemplary planning graph for a group of four diseases: sepsis, Ureaplasma, RDS and PDA, related to the planning of the treatment of the infant during the respiratory failure. This graph was created on

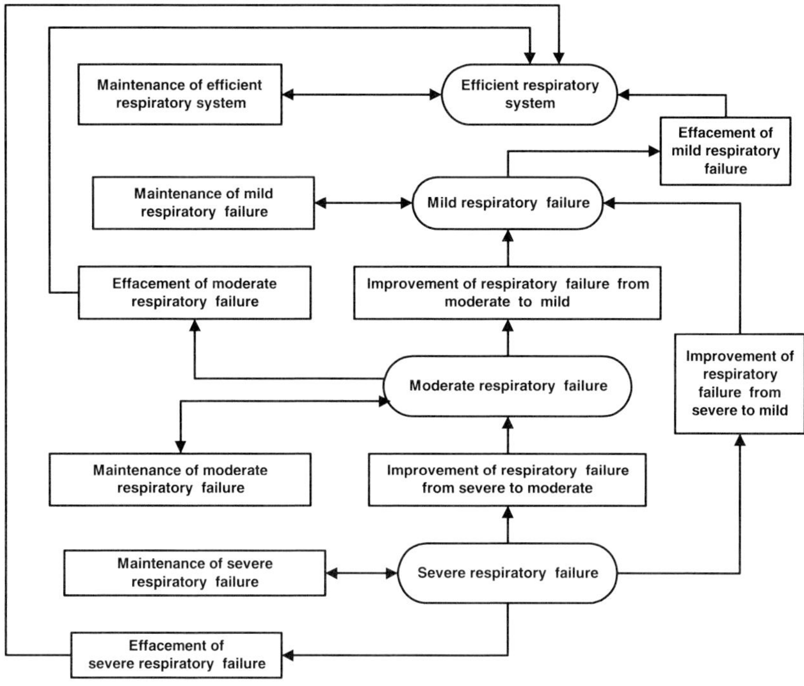

Fig. 2. A planning graph for the treatment of infants during the respiratory failure

the basis of observation of medical data sets (see Section 5) and with support of human experts.

Notice that any state-node from a planning graph for groups of objects can be treated as a complex concept that is specified by a human expert in natural language. Such concepts can be approximated by AR-schemes using data sets and the domain knowledge accumulated for a given complex dynamical system (see [1,2,4]). As a result, it is possibly to recognize an initial state at the beginning of planning for a particular group of complex objects.

At the beginning of planning for a group of objects, we assign the current state of a group of objects. As mentioned earlier, this can be done by AR-schemes that have been constructed for all states from the planning graph. Next, we plan a sequence of actions that can transform a group of objects from the current state to the target state (more expected, safer or more comfortable). For example, in the case of the treatment of infants with respiratory failure, if the infant is suffering from severe respiratory failure, we try to change the patient status using some methods of treatment to change its status to moderate or mild respiratory failure (see Figure 2).

So, our system can propose many plans on the basis of connections in a planning graph for groups of objects starting from the current state. Next, the proposed system chooses a plan that seems to be the most effective. However, it is necessary to make sure that the proposed plan can be realized on the level of any object belonging to a group. In other words, for any object from the group a specific plan should be constructed that leads to a given meta action from the level of the group. Besides, all constructed plans for objects belonging to a group should be compatible.

Therefore, during planning a meta action for a group of objects, we use a special tool for verifying the compatibility of plans generated for all members of a group. This verification can be performed by using some special decision rules that we call *elimination rules*. Such rules make it possible to eliminate combination of plans that are not compatible relative to domain knowledge. This is possible because elimination rules describe all important dependencies between plans that are joined together. If any combination of plans is not consistent with any elimination rule, then it is eliminated. A set of elimination rules can be specified by human experts or can be computed from data sets. In both of these cases, we need a set of attributes (features) defined for a single plan that are used for the explaining elimination rules. Such attributes are specified by human experts on the basis of domain knowledge and they describe some important features of the plan (generated for single complex object) with respect to proper joining a plan with plans generated for other members of a group.

These features are used as a set of attributes in the special table that we call *an elimination table*. Any row of an elimination table represents information about features of plans assigned for complex objects belonging to an exemplary group of objects from the training data. We propose the following method of calculation the set of elimination rules on the basis of the elimination table.

For any attribute from an elimination table, we compute the set of rules treating this attribute as a decision attribute. In this way, we obtain a set of dependencies in the elimination table explained by decision rules. In practice, it is necessary to filter elimination rules to remove the rules with low support because such rules can be too strongly matched to the training data. The resulting set of elimination rules can be used as a filter of inconsistent combinations of plans generated for members of groups. Any combination of plans is eliminated when there exists an elimination rule that is not supported by features of a combination while the combination matches a predecessor of this rule. In other words, a combination of plans is eliminated when the combination matches to the predecessor of some elimination rule and does not match the successor of a rule.

If the combination of plans for members of the group is consistent (it was not eliminated by elimination rules), we should check if the execution of this combination allow us to achieve the expected meta action from the level of group of objects. This can be done by a special classifier constructed for a table called as an *action table*. The structure of an action table is similar to the structure of an elimination table, i.e., attributes are defined by human experts, where rows represent information about features of plans assigned for complex objects belonging to exemplary groups of objects from the training data. In addition, we add to this table a decision attribute. Values of decision attributes represent names of meta actions which will be realized as an effect of the execution of plans described in the current row of a training table. The classifier computed for an action table makes it possible to predict the name of a meta action for a given combination of plans from the level of members of a group. The last step is the selection of combinations of plans that makes it possible to obtain a target meta action with respect to a group of objects.

It was mentioned in Section 3 that the resolving classifier used for the generation of a next action during the planning for a single object, gives us the list of actions (and states after usage of action) with their weights in descending order. This makes it possible to generate many alternative plans for any single object and many alternative combinations of plans for a group of objects. Therefore, the chance of finding an expected combination of plans from a lower level to realize a given meta action (from the higher level) is relatively high.

After planning the selected meta action from the path of action from the planning graph (for a group of objects), the system begins the planning of the next meta action from this path. The planning is stopped, when the planning of the last meta action from this path is finished.

5   Experimental Results

To verify the effectiveness of the proposed methods of automated planning, we have implemented algorithms in a *Automated Planning* library (AP-lib), which is an extension of the RSES-lib 2.1 library forming the computational kernel of the RSES system[2].

Experiments have been performed on medical data sets obtained from Neonatal Intensive Care Unit in Department of Pediatrics, Collegium Medicum, Jagiellonian University, Cracow. The data were collected between 2002 and 2004 using computer database NIS (Neonatal Information System). Detailed information about treatment of 340 newborns are available in the data set that includes perinatal history, birth weight, gestational age, lab tests results, imagine techniques results, detailed diagnoses during hospitalization, procedures and medication were recorded for the each patient. The study group included prematurely born infants with the birth weight $\leq 1500g$, admitted to the hospital before the end of 2 days of life. Additionally, children suffering from respiratory failure but without diagnosis of RDS, PDA, sepsis or ureaplasma infection during their entire clinical course, were excluded from the study group.

In our experiments we used one data table extracted from the NIS system, that consists of 11099 objects. Each object of this table describes parameters of one patient in single time point. There were prepared 7022 situations on the basis of this data table, when the plan of treatment has been proposed be human experts during the realistic clinical treatment.

As a measure of planning success (or failure) in our experiments, we use a special hierarchical classifier that can predict the similarity between two plans as a number between 0.0 and 1.0. This classifier has been constructed on the basis of a special ontology specified by human experts (see Figure 3) and data

---

[2] See RSES Homepage at `logic.mimuw.edu.pl/~rses`

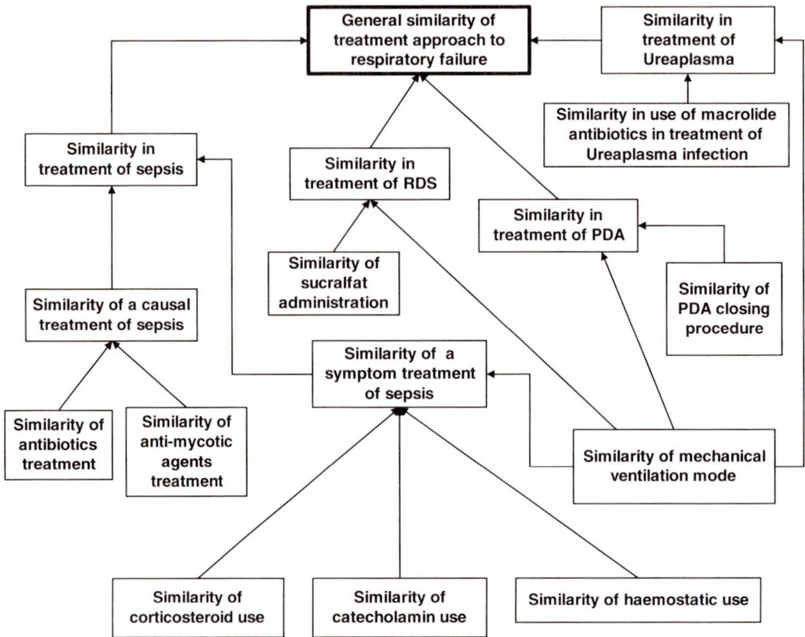

Fig. 3. An Ontology of Similarity between Plans

sets. It is important to mention that besides the ontology, experts provided exemplary data (values of attributes) for the purpose of concept approximation from the ontology. The methods of construction of such classifiers are based on AR schemes and were described in [1]. We use this classifier to determine the similarity between plans generated by our methods of automated planning and plans proposed be human experts during realistic clinical treatment. A training set consists of 4052 situations (when plans of treatment have been assigned), whereas a testing set consists of 2970 situations when plans have been generated by an automated method and comparable expert plans were known. The average similarity between plans for all tested situations was about 0.82, while the coverage of tested situations by generated plans was about 88 percent.

6   Conclusion

In this paper, we discussed some rough set tools for automated planning that are developed for a system for modeling networks of classifiers. The performed experiments show that the similarity between the plan of treatment generated automatically and the plan proposed by human experts during the real clinical treatment is sufficiently high. Therefore, we conclude that our methods have promise as useful tools in medical practice. In our further work, we would like to increase the recognition of similarity between plans of the treatment (generated automatically and proposed by human experts) and to improve the coverage of tested situations by the generated plans.

Acknowledgement

The authors wish to thank professor James Peters for his insights and many helpful comments and corrections for this article. The research has been supported by the grant 3 T11C 002 26 from Ministry of Scientific Research and Information Technology of the Republic of Poland.

References

1. Bazan J., Skowron A.: Classifiers based on approximate reasoning schemes. In Dunin-Keplicz, B., Jankowski, A., Skowron, A., and Szczuka, M. (Eds.): Monitoring, Security, and Rescue Tasks in Multiagent Systems MSRAS, *Advances in Soft Computing* Springer, Heidelberg, (2005) 191-202.
2. Bazan J., Peters, J., F., Skowron, A.: Behavioral pattern identification through rough set modeling. In *Proceedings of RSFDGrC'2005*, LNAI **3641**. Springer, Heidelberg, Germany (2005) 688–697.
3. Bazan, J., Nguyen, Hoa, S., Nguyen, Son, H., Skowron, A.: Rough set methods in approximation of hierarchical concepts. In *Proceedings of RSCTC'2004*, LNAI **3066**. Springer, Heidelberg, Germany (2004) 346–355.
4. Bazan, J., G., Kruczek, P., Bazan-Socha, S., Skowron, A., Pietrzyk, J., J.: Risk Pattern Identification in the Treatment of Infants with Respiratory Failure Through Rough Set Modeling, In *Proceedings of IPMU'2006*, Paris, France, July 2-7 (2006) 2650–2657.
5. Jarrar, M.: Towards Methodological Principles for Ontology Engineering. Ph.D. Thesis, Supervisor: Meersman, R., Vrije Universiteit Brussel (2005).
6. Nguyen, Hoa, S., Bazan, J., Skowron, A., Nguyen, Son, H.: Layered learning for concept synthesis. In LNCS **3100**, Transactions on Rough Sets, **I**, Springer, Heidelberg, Germany (2004) 187–208.
7. M. Ghallab, D. Nau, P. Traverso: *Automated Planning: Theory and Practice*. Elsevier, Morgan Kaufmann, CA (2004).
8. Pawlak, Z.: *Rough Sets: Theoretical Aspects of Reasoning about Data. Volume 9 of System Theory, Knowledge Engineering and Problem Solving*. Kluwer Academic Publishers, Dordrecht, The Netherlands (1991).
9. Peters, J.F.: Rough ethology: Towards a Biologically-Inspired Study of Collective Behavior in Intelligent Systems with Approximation Spaces, *Transactions on Rough Sets* III (2005) 153-174.
10. Van Wezel, W., Jorna, R., Meystel, A.: *Planning in Intelligent Systems: Aspects, Motivations, and Methods*. John Wiley & Sons, Hoboken, New Jersey (2006).

Developing a Decision Model for Asthma Exacerbations: Combining Rough Sets and Expert-Driven Selection of Clinical Attributes

Ken Farion[1], Wojtek Michalowski[2], and Szymon Wilk[3]

[1] Children's Hospital of Eastern Ontario, Ottawa, Canada
farion@cheo.on.ca
[2] University of Ottawa, Ottawa, Canada
wojtek@management.uottawa.ca
[3] Poznan University of Technology, Poznan, Poland
szymon.wilk@cs.put.poznan.pl

Abstract. The paper describes the development of a clinical decision model to help Emergency Department physicians assess the severity of pediatric asthma exacerbations. The model should support an early identification (at 2 hours) of those patients who are having a mild attack and those who are having a moderate/severe attack. A comprehensive approach combining rough sets and expert-driven manual feature selection was applied to develop a rule-based decision model from retrospective data that described asthmatic patients visiting the Emergency Department. The experiment involved creating the following four potential decision models differentiated by the subsets of clinical attributes that were considered: Model A using all attributes collected in the retrospective chart study; Model B using only attributes describing the patient's history; Model C using only attributes describing the triage and repeated assessments; and Model D using attributes from Model C expanded with some of the attributes from Model B identified by expert clinical knowledge. Model D offered the highest assessment accuracy when tested on an independent retrospective data set and was selected as the decision model for asthma exacerbations.

Keywords: rough sets; asthma exacerbations; decision rules; manual feature selection; decision model.

1 Introduction

Asthma exacerbations are one of most common reasons for children to be brought to the Emergency Department (ED). These visits, and the subsequent hospitalizations required by a large proportion of these patients, account for nearly 65% of all direct costs of asthma care. Children with asthma, compared to their non-asthmatic counterparts, use more prescriptions and require more ambulatory care visits, ED visits and hospitalizations [1].

Management guidelines for children with asthma exacerbations coming to the ED are aimed at three levels of attack severity: mild, moderate, and severe [2].

S. Greco et al. (Eds.): RSCTC 2006, LNAI 4259, pp. 428–437, 2006.
© Springer-Verlag Berlin Heidelberg 2006

Early identification of the severity of an asthma exacerbation has implications for the child's management in the ED. Patients with a mild attack are usually discharged home following a brief course of treatment (less than 4 hours) and resolution of symptoms, patients with a moderate attack receive more aggressive treatment over an extended observation in the ED (up to 12 hours), and patients with a severe attack receive maximal therapy before ultimately being transferred to an in-patient hospital bed for ongoing treatment (after about 16 hours in the ED).

In clinical practice, a decision on the severity and subsequent disposition of an attack is ideally made as soon as possible after arrival of the patient to the ED to ensure key therapies have been instituted. Underestimation of severity may result in inadequate treatment, premature discharge and a possible return visit, while overestimation of severity may result in an extended ED stay and unnecessary utilization of hospital resources. As information available on arrival is not sufficient for accurate disposition [3], disposition decisions are made later in the management process – usually between 1 and 4 hours. In our research we assumed the decision would be made at 2 hours [4]. One the one hand, is early enough to provide adequate therapies, and on the other hand, clinical information available at that time allows for accurate dispositions.

There have been many attempts to identify pertinent risk factors associated with pediatric asthma [5] and to develop prediction models [6] or severity scores [7] for asthma exacerbations. However, to date, no clear clinical decision model or widely used asthma score exists. In this paper, we discuss the development of a decision model to support physicians in making early disposition decisions about asthma exacerbations and discerning between two groups of patients: those with mild attacks and those with moderate/severe attacks. We dichotomized the original severity categories into two outcomes because of the importance of early identification of patients with a mild attack that can be safely discharged home while ensure that patients with moderate or severe attacks are identified to receive maximum therapy (e.g., systemic steroids). We used data transcribed from the ED charts in a retrospective study to construct four rule-based decision models using clinical attributes suggested by a medical expert and clinical practice guidelines. Models were verified on an independent testing data set acquired through the same retrospective chart study.

The paper is organized as follows. We start with a description of the retrospective chart data. Then we present our approach to developing decision models that combines rough sets with manual feature selection driven by expert clinical knowledge. This is followed by a description of considered models and the results of their preliminary evaluation leading to the selection of the best one. Finally, we conclude with a discussion.

2   Retrospective Chart Study

The data used to develop the decision model were collected through a retrospective chart review of patients presenting to the ED of the Children's Hospital of

Eastern Ontario (CHEO) between November 2000 and September 2003. This clinical center appropriately represents a potential sample of pediatric patients with asthma, and the collected data can be considered a representative picture of the asthma exacerbations amongst the pediatric population.

The processed pediatric asthma workflow is as follows. First, when child with asthma exacerbation arrives at the ED, a triage nurse gathers basic information on the patient's presenting complaint and evaluates the child's general condition. At this point the patient's breathing is also assessed for the first time (the first assessment is labeled as the triage assessment). After this first assessment the patient is registered, and then awaits a physician evaluation. During this physician-led evaluation, more information about child's condition is collected, including the patient's history, social environment, presence of known risk factors signifying more serious disease, outcomes of previous exacerbations, and the length and severity of symptoms during this exacerbation. At this point, the physician begins management of the asthma exacerbation, including repeated bronchodilator treatments at intervals from every few minutes (continuous) to every few hours, along with systemic corticosteroids for most patients. All management decisions are recorded in patient's ED chart. Moreover, throughout the patient's ED stay, he/she is reassessed by the physician or by the ED nurse to check response to treatments. Depending on a variety of external factors (patient's condition, clinicians' workload, etc), these re-assessments are performed at irregular intervals and they are partially or completely recorded in the chart.

Table 1 lists commonly evaluated and documented clinical attributes associated with asthma exacerbations that could be transcribed from ED charts. Attributes #1–#22 were collected during registration and physician evaluation and they describe patient's history, attributes #23–#32 were collected during the triage assessment and repeated assessments. We considered two sets of these attributes – the first set characterizes the state of the patient on arrival and it was collected during the triage assessment, and the other set presents the patient's most complete picture recorded in a repeated assessment within an interval of 100 and 140 minutes from arrival. Finally, attribute #33 was calculated as the number of bronchodilator treatments (i.e., masks) provided to the patient between the triage and repeated assessment being considered.

Each patient's data was reviewed and a patient was assigned to one of the two groups using asthma exacerbation severity category documented in the ED chart and confirmed later by lack of a subsequent visit to the ED. This procedure allowed us to identify those patients where the initial ED visit resulted in a premature discharge and subsequent readmission to the ED. In this sense we considered the confirmed severity group as a gold standard during development of decision models.

A final sample of 239 ED patient visits for asthma exacerbations was identified during the study period. Basic characteristics of this population are given in Table 2. Although the distribution of visits between both decision groups is fairly well balanced, it can be seen that more patients treated in the ED experienced moderate/severe attacks.

Table 1. Clinical attributes

#	Attribute	Domain
	Registration and physician evaluation	
1	Patient age	< 3 years, 3 – 7 years, ≥ 7 years
2	Primary care	family doctor, pediatrician, other, none
3	Chest clinic	yes, no
4	Current inhaled steroids	< 1 week, 1 – 4 weeks, ≥ 4 weeks, as necessary, none
5	Age of first symptoms	< 1 year, 1 – 3 years, ≥ 3 years
6	Previous oral steroids	< 1 month, 1 – 3 months, 3 – 12 months, ≥ 12 months
7	Previous ED last year	1 visit, 2 visits, 3 visits, ≥ 4 visits, none
8	Previous admission	floor, ICU, none
9	Smokers in environment	yes, no
10	Dander in environment	yes, no
11	Carpets in environment	yes, no
12	Allergies to environment	yes, no
13	Allergies to pets	yes, no
14	Allergies to food	yes, no
15	History of atopy	yes, no
16	Family history of asthma	yes, no
17	Allergy exposure	yes, no
18	URTI symptoms	yes, no
19	Fever	yes, no
20	Duration of symptoms	< 12 hours, 12 – 48 hours, ≥ 48 hours
21	Bronchodilators in last 24h	1 – 3, 3 – 6, ≥ 6, none
22	Arrival to the ED	ambulance, parents
	Triage assessment/Repeated assessment	
23	Temperature	< 38 C, 38 – 39 C, > 39 C
24	Respiratory rate	normal, mild abnormal, abnormal
25	Heart rate	normal, mild abnormal, abnormal
26	Oxygen saturation	< 88, 88 – 93, 93 – 95, ≥ 95
27	Air entry	good, reduced
28	Distress	none, mild, moderate, severe
29	Skin color	pink, pale, dusky
30	Expiratory wheeze	present, absent
31	Inspiratory wheeze	present, absent
32	Retractions	present, absent
	Treatment summary	
33	Number of treatments received	number

As expected, the majority of charts had incomplete data. Only three clinical attributes (all describing demographics and history) were specified on all charts – they were #1, #2, and #3 (also attribute #33 was provided for all visits, however, it was calculated from information available in charts). Moreover, nine

Table 2. Characteristic of the learning data

Characteristics	Value
Mean age	5.7 years
% of visits in the mild group	41.0%
% of visits in the moderate/severe group	59.0%

attributes (#9–#11 and #17 for the registration and physician evaluation; #30–#32 for the triage assessment; #23 and #28 for the repeated assessment) had missing values for more than 60% of collected visits. We excluded these attributes from the analysis.

3   Development of a Decision Model

In order to develop potential decision models we used a rough set approach with cumulative indiscernibility relation [8] that allows dealing with incomplete data without prior preprocessing (e.g., replacing missing values of attributes by known ones or removing incomplete cases). This approach supports evidence-based medical decision making [9] since data used for constructing the decision model are not changed.

Cumulative indiscernibility relation assumes that a missing value of an attribute is equivalent to any other value of this attribute. This simplification does not distinguish between situations where values were collected but not recorded and where values were not collected as it was deemed unnecessary by the physician. However, this distinction can be rarely inferred from retrospective chart study, making this approach suitable for analyzing clinical data transcribed from charts (written medical records are rarely standardized in format and content). It has been also successfully applied in other clinical studies [10,11].

Rough set theory offers a methodology for finding important attributes in the form of a core and reducts. However, for data described by a large number of attributes, also the number of reducts may be very large making selection of attributes difficult and ambiguous [12]. Therefore, we decided against automated feature selection as an approach that does not consider knowledge about a problem domain, and instead used expert-driven manual selection. This approach has proved successful for other clinical problems [13].

The experiment involved using the entire set of clinical attributes transcribed from charts and three subsets of attributes selected according to clinical knowledge. For each of the sets of attributes, we induced decision rules using the modified LEM2 algorithm that ensured robustness of created rules (each rule had to cover at least one case with known values of attributes in the rule's conditions). Generated sets of rules were then coupled with a distance-based classification strategy [14] to form rule-based decision models. Finally, we obtained the following four potential decision models:

1. Model A using all clinical attributes included in the analysis (a baseline model),
2. Model B using clinical attributes collected during registration and physician evaluation (attributes #1–#22),
3. Model C using clinical attributes collected during triage and repeated assessment together with the number of bronchodilator treatments (two sets of attributes #23–#32 and attribute #33),
4. Model D using clinical attributes from Model C and extended by the attributes from Model B as per asthma guidelines [2] . Specifically we included the following additional attributes:
   - Age of first symptoms (attribute #5),
   - Duration of symptoms (attribute #20),
   - Timing since last oral steroids (attribute #6),
   - Possible allergens (attributes #12–#14),
   - Family history of asthma (attribute #16),
   - Social status of the patient (attributes #2 and #22) - patients coming from poorer families would likely not have a family physician and would be brought to the ED by ambulance).

4   Evaluation of Decision Models

In order to evaluate the quality of the four decision models, we conducted an experiment that compared their performance on new retrospective chart data. Data transcribed from the ED charts were used as input to a decision model, and the suggested dichotomized evaluation of a severity of asthma exacerbation was considered as an output and compared to the gold standard (verified severity group).

The potential decision models were evaluated on an independent data set describing 123 visits to the ED of CHEO between October 2003 and July 2004. The transcription process followed the same regimen as described for the retrospective learning data. General characteristics of the testing data are given in Table 3. Compared to the learning data (see Table 2), the percentage of patients with moderate/severe attacks decreased and the distribution of visits between groups became almost even (with slightly greater number of patients with mild attacks).

Results of the evaluation are presented in Table 4. Compared to the baseline Model A, Model B exhibited decreased accuracies for both dichotomized groups, thus suggesting that the corresponding set of attributes did not include information required for reliable prediction of severity. Model C was found to be much more accurate – it preserved accuracy in the moderate/severe group and significantly increased accuracy for the mild group (increase of 20%). Overall accuracy for Model C was also higher than for the baseline model. This implies that the attributes characterizing assessments and treatment allowed us to identify relatively well patients with mild asthma exacerbation, while there was still not enough information to identify patients from the other group (this group was underestimated).

Table 3. Characteristic of the testing data

Characteristics	Value
Mean age	6.0 years
% of visits in the mild group	52.8%
% of visits in the moderate/severe group	47.2%

Table 4. Accuracy of classification for considered decision models

Group	Model			
	A	B	C	D
Mild	60.0%	43.1%	81.5%	78.5%
Moderate/severe	63.8%	58.6%	62.1%	74.1%
Overall	61.8%	50.4%	72.4%	76.4%

Finally, Model D improved accuracy in the moderate/severe group (increase of 12%) and only slightly lowered accuracy for the mild group (decrease of 3%). Overall accuracy of this model was the highest, proving the importance of expanding the triage and repeated assessment set of the attributes with those suggested in the guidelines.

To further validate the results, we used McNemar's test [15] to verify statistical significance of differences in performance of potential models. The McNemar's test is often used in clinical problems to compare individual outcomes before and after intervention and in our experiment we used the test to compare classification outcomes of paired models associated with the same patient records from the testing set. The results of the McNemar's statistic are given in Table 5 and they show that statistically significant classification differences were obtained for all pairs except Model A and B and Model C and D (significance 0.95, threshold 3.841), and the largest values of McNemar's statistic were obtained for Model B and C and for Model B and D pairwise comparisons. Considering the best prediction accuracy of Model D, McNemar statistic provided additional argument for selecting this decision model for predicting the severity of asthma exacerbations.

Table 5. McNemar's statistics

	Model B	Model C	Model D
Model A	2.817	3.892	6.881
Model B	–	10.090	16.569
Model C	–	–	0.552

5   Discussion

Data transcribed retrospectively from patient charts is usually characterized by a large number of clinical attributes with many of them being considered by the physician in a specific context (e.g., when a severe problem is suspected). It means that values of these attributes are evaluated and recorded only for specific patients and appear only on a fraction of charts. Moreover, some attributes may be checked by the physician during examination, but as they were deemed unnecessary (e.g., their values would not contribute to a decision), they might be not recorded either. A fact that there is a large number of attributes and that many charts include incomplete information, makes development of a decision model a difficult and challenging task [16] as a model may be prone to superfluous information and offer poor performance in clinical practice. Therefore, the development of a decision model should start with identification of those attributes that are the most explanatory but also that make the most sense from a clinical perspective. Values of selected attributes may still be incomplete, so methods employed to develop a decision model should be capable to handle such a situation.

The rough set approach with cumulative indiscernibility relation [8] used in this study handles incomplete data in a manner that is consistent with those reported in literature [17] that suggest that the most promising results in terms of accuracy of prediction are obtained when missing values are handled directly or when incomplete cases are removed from the analysis (the latter approach is rarely feasible for medical data sets transcribed from charts as it would result in excluding a significant number of available cases).

Direct processing of missing values is also in line with principles of evidence-based decision making, where clinical decisions have to be made using the best available knowledge. Modifications of clinical data, where missing values are replaced by automatically selected known values, could result in creating artificial patterns that might be captured by a decision model developed from such data, thus significantly limiting its clinical reliability. The approach we have used allowed us to avoid this trap, and it also ensured robustness of discovered patterns (each rule was supported by at least one case with known values of attributes referenced by this rule, thus it was supported by a complete evidence).

Rough sets offer techniques and evaluation measures for automatic selection of attributes, but we argue that whenever it is possible, attributes should be evaluated and selected according to expert knowledge and clinical experience. As physicians often tend to consider too many clinical attributes, it is reasonable to compare their selection against practice guidelines to possibly limit the number of selected attributes. Even if an automatic feature selection is used and a created decision model provides good predictive performance, the selected attributes should be verified by an expert in order to ensure that they are appropriate from a clinical perspective. Otherwise, the clinical applicability of a developed model may be very limited.

Our study demonstrated that rough sets combined with manual feature selection based on expert knowledge proved to be a valid methodology for developing a rule-based decision model for asthma exacerbations. The model that offered the highest predictive accuracy and thus was finally selected, was based on attributes characterizing assessments and treatments combined with those describing patient's history and identified in the practice guideline reflecting expert knowledge. The study confirmed that data transcribed retrospectively from charts often includes superfluous information that may result in less accurate decision models, and thus prior selection of attributes is of high importance. It also demonstrated that manual feature selection based on expert knowledge is an important success factor.

The decision model for asthma exacerbations has not been validated in clinical practice, however, we plan to embed it in a decision support module for the MET (Mobile Emergency Triage) system [18]. MET with a module for triaging pediatric abdominal pain successfully underwent a 7-month clinical trial in the ED at CHEO [19]. The decision model in the abdominal pain module was developed using the rough set approach with cumulative indiscernibility relation. Results from the prospective clinical trial demonstrated that our model has classification accuracy similar to the accuracy of physicians. We plan to conduct a similar clinical trial of the MET system with the asthma module.

Acknowledgments

The research reported in this paper was supported by the grants from the Natural Sciences and Engineering Research Council of Canada, Canadian Institutes of Health Research and the State Committee for Scientific Research of Poland.

References

1. Lozano, P., Sullivan, S., Smith, D., Weiss, K.: The economic burden of asthma in us children: Estimates from the national medical expenditure survey. Journal of Allergy and Clinical Immunology **104** (1999) 957–63
2. National Asthma Education and Prevention Program: Guidelines for the diagnosis and management of asthma. NIH publication no. 97-4051, National Heart, Lung and Blood Institute (2002)
3. Kelly, A., Kerr, D., Powell, C.: Is severity assessment after one hour of treatment better for predicting the need for admission in acute asthma? Respiratory Medicine **98**(8) (2004) 777–781
4. Schuh, S., Johnson, D., Stephens, D., Callahan, S., Canny, G.: Hospitalization patterns in severe acute asthma in children. Pediatric Pulmonology **23**(3) (1997) 184–92
5. Gaspar, A., Morais-Almeida, M., Pires, G., Prates, S., Camara, R., Godinho, N., Arede, C., Rosado-Pinto, J.: Risk factors for asthma admissions in children. Allergy and Asthma Proceedings **23** (2002) 295–301
6. Keogh, K.A., Macarthur, C., Parkin, P.C., Stephens, D., Arseneault, R., Tennis, O., Bacal, L., Schuh, S.: Predictors of hospitalization in children with acute asthma. Journal of Pediatrics **139** (2001) 273–277

7. Ortega, A., Belanger, K., Bracken, M., Leaderer, B.: A childhood asthma severity scale: symptoms, medications, and health care visits. Annuals of Allergy, Asthma and Immunology **86** (2001) 405–413
8. Greco, S., Matarazzo, B., Slowinski, R.: Dealing with missing data in rough set analysis of multi-attribute and multi-criteria decision problems. In Zanakis, S., Doukidis, G., Zopounidis, C., eds.: Decision Making: Recent Developments and Worldwide Applications. Kluwer Academic Publishers (2000) 295–316
9. Sackett, D., Rosenberg, W., Gray, J., Haynes, R., Richardson, W.: Evidence based medicine: what it is and what it isn't. British Medical Journal **312** (1996) 7–12
10. Wilk, S., Slowinski, R., Michalowski, W., Greco, S.: Supporting triage of children with abdominal pain in the emergency room. European Journal of Operational Research **160**(3) (2005) 696–709
11. Michalowski, W., Wilk, S., Farion, K., Pike, J., Rubin, S., Slowinski, R.: Development of a decision algorithm to support emergency triage of scrotal pain and its implementation in the MET system. INFOR **43**(4) (2005) 287–301
12. Flinkman, M., Michalowski, W., Nilsson, S., Slowinski, R., Susmaga, R., Wilk, S.: Use of rough sets analysis to classify siberian forest ecosystems according to net primary production of phytomass: Siberian forest case study. INFOR **3**(38) (2000) 145–161
13. Wang, J., Bo, T., Jonassen, I., Myklebost, O., Hovig, E.: Tumor classification and marker gene prediction by feature selection and fuzzy c-means clustering using microarray data. BMC Bioinformatics **4** (2003) 60 (electronic)
14. Stefanowski, J.: Classification support based on the rough sets. Foundations of Computing and Decision Sciences **18**(3-4) (1993) 371–380
15. Everitt, B.: The analysis of contingency tables. Chapman and Hall, London (1977)
16. John, G.H., Kohavi, R., Pfleger, K.: Irrelevant features and the subset selection problem. In: Proceedings of the 11th International Conference on Machine Learning. (1994) 121–129
17. Grzymala-Busse, J.W., Hu, M.: A comparison of several approaches to missing attribute values in data mining. In Ziarko, W., Yao, Y.Y., eds.: Rough Sets and Current Trends in Computing. Volume 2005 of Lecture Notes in Computer Science., Springer (2000) 378–385
18. Michalowski, W., Slowinski, R., Wilk, S.: MET system: A new approach to m-health in emergency triage. Journal on Information Technology in Healthcare **2**(4) (2004) 237–249
19. Farion, K., Michalowski, W., Slowinski, R., Wilk, S., Rubin, S.: Rough set methodology in clinical practice: Controlled hospital trial of the MET system. In Tsumoto, S., Slowinski, R., Komorowski, J., Grzymala-Busse, J., eds.: Rough Sets and Current Trends in Computing. 4th International Conference, RSCTC 2004. Volume 3066 of LNAI., Uppsala, Sweden, Springer-Verlag (2004) 805–814

A GrC-Based Approach to Social Network Data Protection[*]

Da-Wei Wang, Churn-Jung Liau, and Tsan-sheng Hsu

Institute of Information Science, Academia Sinica, Taipei 115, Taiwan
{wdw, liaucj, tshsu}@iis.sinica.edu.tw

Abstract. Social network analysis is an important methodology in sociological research. Although social network data is very useful to researchers and policy makers, releasing it to the public may cause an invasion of privacy. In this paper, we generalize the techniques used to protect private information in tabulated data, and propose some safety criteria for assessing the risk of breaching confidentiality by releasing social network data. We assume a situation of data linking, where data is released to a particular user who has some knowledge about individual nodes of a social network. We adopt description logic as the underlying knowledge representation formalism and consider the safety criteria in both open-world and closed-world contexts.

1   Introduction

Social network analysis (SNA) is a methodology used extensively in social and behavioral sciences, as well as in political science, economics, organization theory, and industrial engineering[6]. Though the analysis of social network data is valuable to researchers and policy makers, there may be a risk of privacy invasion. In SNA, researchers usually collect data by social surveys. Respondents to the surveys are typically anonymous; however, previous research on tabulated data has shown that simply ensuring the anonymity of respondents may not be sufficient to protect their privacy. The key point is that respondents could be re-identified by linking the anonymous data with some publicly available databases [2,3,4,8,9].

While each data record in a data table is completely defined by the attribute values of an individual[1], a social network also contains relational data between individuals. In this sense, a social network is more general than a data table. In this paper, we provide a formal model of a situation where personal information not only contains attribute values, but also relational links to other individuals.

Several methods have been developed for tabulated data protection [8,4,9]. The main idea is to group the individuals with the same combination of public attribute values into a *bin*, or an *information granule*. Some qualitative and

---

[*] This work was partially supported by the Taiwan Information Security Center (TWISC) and NSC (Taiwan). NSC Grants: 94-2213-E-001-030 (D.W. Wang), 95-2221-E-001-029-MY3 (C.J. Liau), and 94-2213-E-001-014 (T-s. Hsu).
[1] An individual refers to a person whose privacy should be protected.

S. Greco et al. (Eds.): RSCTC 2006, LNAI 4259, pp. 438–447, 2006.

quantitative safety criteria are then defined, according to the distribution of the confidential attribute values of individuals in the same information granule. In a social network, two individuals with the same public attribute values may still be distinguishable by their relationship with other individuals. Thus, to formulate information granules for social networks, we have to consider the attributes of individuals and the relationships between individuals. By generalizing the definition of information granules, we can extend the analysis for tabulated data to social network data.

The remainder of the paper is organized as follows. In the next section, we review a basic description logic. In Section 3, we discuss the representation of a social network with description logic languages. In such a representation, the social network data is transformed into an ABox, or an interpretation of the description logic based on the open-world or closed-world assumption. In Section 4, the transformations are described in detail and some safety criteria are defined. Finally, in Section 5, we present our conclusions.

2 Description Logic—A Review

Description logic (DL) was originally a subset of first-order logic specially designed for knowledge representation[2]. In this section, we introduce a basic DL called $\mathcal{AL}$ (attributive language).

2.1 Basic Syntax and Semantics

The language $\mathcal{AL}$ was first introduced in [5]. The alphabets of $\mathcal{AL}$ consist of two disjoint sets, the elements of which are called concept names (atomic concepts) and role names (atomic roles) respectively. Following the notations in [1], we use the letters A and B for atomic concepts, the letter R for atomic roles, and the letters C and D for concept terms. The concept terms of $\mathcal{AL}$ are formed according to the following syntactic rule:

$$C ::= A \mid \top \mid \bot \mid \neg A \mid C \sqcap D \mid \forall R : C \mid \exists R : \top.$$

Note that, in $\mathcal{AL}$, negation can only be applied to atomic concepts, and only the top concept is allowed in the scope of an existential quantification.

The Tarskian semantics for $\mathcal{AL}$ assigns sets to concept names and binary relations to role names. Formally, an interpretation of $\mathcal{AL}$ is a pair $I = (\Delta^I, \llbracket \cdot \rrbracket_I)$, where Δ^I is a non-empty set called the domain of the interpretation and $\llbracket \cdot \rrbracket_I$ is an interpretation function that assigns to each concept name a subset of Δ^I and to each role name a subset of $\Delta^I \times \Delta^I$. For brevity, we usually drop the subscript and superscript I. The domain of $\llbracket \cdot \rrbracket$ can then be extended to all concept terms by induction as usual. In particular, we have

$$\llbracket \forall R : C \rrbracket = \{x \in \Delta \mid \forall y((x, y) \in \llbracket R \rrbracket \Rightarrow y \in \llbracket C \rrbracket)\}.$$

---

[2] Most of the notations and definitions in this section follow those introduced in [1].

2.2   Knowledge Representation by DL

Within a knowledge base one can distinguish between intensional knowledge (i.e., general knowledge about the problem domain) and extensional knowledge, which is specific to a particular problem. A DL knowledge base is similarly comprised of two components — a "TBox" and an "ABox". The TBox consists of *terminological axioms* [3] that have the form

$$C \sqsubseteq D \ (R \sqsubseteq S) \quad \text{or} \quad C \equiv D \ (R \equiv S),$$

where C, D are concepts (and R, S are roles). An equality whose left-hand side is an atomic concept is called a definition, which is used to introduce a symbolic name for a complex description. An atomic concept not occurring on the left-hand side of an axiom is called *primitive*. A finite set of Definitions Σ is called a terminology, or TBox, if no symbolic name is defined more than once; that is, if for every atomic concept A, there is at most one axiom in Σ whose left-hand side is A. An interpretation $I = \langle \Delta, \| \cdot \| \rangle$ satisfies the axiom $C \equiv D$ (resp. $C \sqsubseteq D$) iff $\|C\| = \|D\|$ (resp. $\|C\| \subseteq \|D\|$).

An ABox contains the world description in the form of *assertional axioms*

$$C(a) \quad \text{or} \quad R(a,b),$$

where C is a concept term , R is a role name, and a, b are constants for naming the individuals in the world. The domain of the interpretation function $\| \cdot \|$ is extended to the constants occurring in an ABox such that $\|a\| \in \Delta$ for any constant a. We assume that distinct individual names denote distinct objects (the unique name assumption). For the purpose of distinction, an *extended interpretation* is used to give a full assignment of meanings to constants, concepts, and roles. An extended interpretation $I = \langle \Delta, \| \cdot \| \rangle$ satisfies an assertion $C(a)$ (resp. $R(a,b)$) iff $\|a\| \in \|C\|$ (resp. $(\|a\|, \|b\|) \in \|R\|$). I satisfies the ABox Φ if it satisfies each assertion in Φ. It is also said that I is a model of the assertion or the ABox. An assertion φ is a logical consequence of an ABox Φ, written as $\Phi \models \varphi$, if for every interpretation I, $I \models \Phi$ implies $I \models \varphi$.

3   DL-Based Representation of Social Network Data

To represent social network data, we partition the atomic concepts (resp. roles) into two disjoint sets. The first set contains the *easily-known* (EK) atomic concepts (resp. roles), and the second consists of the *sensitive* atomic concepts (resp. roles). Let $\mathcal{L}$ be a DL language[4]. We use $\mathcal{L}^e$ to denote the sub-language of concept terms, which is composed of EK atomic concepts and roles only. The sub-language of other concept terms, i.e., $\mathcal{L} - \mathcal{L}^e$ is denoted by $\mathcal{L}^s$.

---

[3] For this reason, DL is also known as terminological logic or concept logic.

[4] Though we have only exemplified a DL language in the $\mathcal{AL}$ family, the results in this paper do not depend on the choice of any particular DL language.

In this paper, we assume that there is a set of actual individuals $\{a_1, a_2, \cdots, a_m\}$ whose data is available in the data center and represented as an *actual* social network. For privacy reasons, the data center must mask off the identities of the actual individuals, so it is assumed that the actual individuals are replaced by nominal constants $u_1, u_2, \cdots, u_m$ in the released network data. The data center would like to release an anonymous network, obtained from a part or the whole of the actual social network by masking off the identities of the actual individuals.

Formally, an *anonymous social network* (based on a DL language $\mathcal{L}$) is defined as a labeled graph $G = (V, E, l)$, where V is a set of nodes, $E \subseteq V \times V$ is a set of edges between the nodes, and l assigns a subset of atomic concepts to each node and a subset of atomic roles to each edge. We can mark each vertex of G distinctly with a nominal constant u_i. Without loss of generality, and by slightly abusing the notation, we can identify V by $\{u_1, u_2, \cdots, u_m\}$.

The basic assumption is that a particular user[5] may know (though perhaps only partially) some information about the actual individuals before the anonymous network is released, and wants to obtain the private data of these individuals by linking his *a priori* knowledge to the released social network data. The data administrator needs to assess the possibility that the user could link his *a priori* knowledge to the released social network data to discover any individual's private information. Thus, it is important to model the user's *a priori* knowledge. However, the data administrator may not know the user's *a priori* knowledge. In such cases, the data administrator makes the worst-case assumption that all easily known information about the individuals is known to the user. Therefore, from the data administrator's perspective, the user's knowledge is represented as an ABox in which only concepts and roles from $\mathcal{L}^e$ and actual individuals appear. In addition, we assume that both the user and the data administrator use a common ontology, i.e., a TBox, to represent the background knowledge of the problem domain.

4 Privacy Protection in Data Linking

We now consider the DL-based representation of the released anonymous network, and formulate the notion of information granules based on that representation. There are two possible interpretations of the released anonymous network. One is based on the closed-world assumption (CWA) and the other on the open-world assumption (OWA). By CWA, we mean that the anonymous network $G = (V, E, l)$ is complete in the sense that if $C \notin l(u)$, then u has the property $\neg C$; and if $R \notin l(u, v)$, u is not R-related to v. Thus, from the anonymous network $G = (V, E, l)$, we can obtain an interpretation I_G. In OWA, on the other hand, the anonymous network $G = (V, E, l)$ may be incomplete, so if $C \notin l(u)$, then u may have the property C or $\neg C$, and analogously for the roles. Thus, the social network can only be represented as an ABox, since DL typically adopts open-world semantics for the interpretation of an ABox.

---

[5] In this paper, "user" or "users" refers to anyone receiving social network data and having the potential to breach the privacy of individuals.

In general, DL-based social network representations adopt the open-world assumption. However, in some special cases when only primitive concepts are considered, the CWA enables a more efficient representation of knowledge, since only positive information is needed.

In the following, we first present the safety criteria for CWA and then those for OWA. We also have to represent the user's knowledge available to the data administrator. In practice, the user's knowledge is rarely complete, so we always represent it by an ABox. Let Φ denote such an ABox throughout this section. The individual constants occurring in the ABox for the user's knowledge are the actual ones. It is assumed that the concepts and roles appearing in the ABox are all from $\mathcal{L}^e$, and the set of actual individuals occurring in the ABox is $\mathcal{A}$. Note that it is possible that the cardinality of $\mathcal{A}$ is less than the number of anonymous individuals in the social network, since the user may not have information about all actual individuals.

4.1 Social Networks in a Closed World

CWA has been adopted in much of the database literature. It is efficient for data representation, since only positive information is explicitly represented. However, due to an obvious technical reason, CWA is only applicable when the social network $G = (V, E, l)$ is restricted to a special form, where each element of $l(u)$ is primitive for all $u \in V^6$. In this subsection, we assume that the released social network meets this special restriction.

With CWA, an anonymous network can be transformed into an interpretation of DL. Formally, given a social network $G = (V, E, l)$ based on a DL language $\mathcal{L}$, we construct an interpretation $I_G = (V, \|\cdot\|_{I_G})$ such that

1. the domain of the interpretation is the set of anonymous individuals V
2. $u \in \|A\|_{I_G}$ iff $A \in l(u)$ for each primitive concept A
3. $(u, v) \in \|R\|_{I_G}$ iff $R \in l((u, v))$ for each atomic role R
4. the interpretation of other non-primitive atomic concepts is determined by the axioms in the TBox of our problem domain.

Let Φ be an ABox representing the user's knowledge. Then, an extended interpretation $I = (V, \|\cdot\|_I)$ for Φ is said to be an extension of the interpretation I_G, written as $I_G \rhd I$, if $\|A\|_I = \|A\|_{I_G}$ for each concept name A and $\|R\|_I = \|R\|_{I_G}$ for each role name R. The set of G-based models for Φ is defined as

$$Mod(\Phi, G) = \{I \mid I_G \rhd I \text{ and } I \models \Phi\}. \tag{1}$$

Note that a G-based model maps each actual individual appearing in Φ to a nominal constant in G. Such a mapping provides the user with a possible re-identification of these individuals in the anonymous network.

---

[6] If $B \equiv C \sqcup D$ is an axiom in the background TBox and $B \in l(u)$, but $C, D \notin l(u)$, then we obviously can not assume $\neg C \in l(u)$ and $\neg D \in l(u)$ simultaneously without contradiction.

4.2 Safety Criteria Under CWA

Once the G-based models for the user's knowledge Φ are available, we can define different criteria to safeguard confidentiality when releasing an anonymous social network to a particular user.

The first safety criterion is the *granule size (bin size)* criterion, which was proposed in some pioneering works [4,8]. First, we define a granule for each actual individual $a \in \mathcal{A}$ as the set of possible anonymous individuals corresponding to a. Thus, the granule (or bin) for an actual individual $a \in \mathcal{A}$ with respect to G and Φ is formally defined as

$$[a]_G^\Phi = \{ \llbracket a \rrbracket_I \mid I \in Mod(\Phi, G) \}. \tag{2}$$

The pair (Φ, G) is said to satisfy the *k-anonymity criterion* if for each $a \in \mathcal{A}$, $|[a]_G^\Phi| \geq k$, where $|\cdot|$ denotes the cardinality of a set. The rationale behind the criterion is that the more individuals there are in a granule, the less likely it is that the user can re-identify to whom the anonymous individuals correspond.

It is shown in [3] that the granule size criterion may be not sufficient for privacy protection. Even though the user can not re-identify the anonymous individuals, he can sometimes deduce the sensitive information common to all individuals in a granule. To formulate a safety criterion for this situation, we assume $\mathcal{SC} \subseteq \mathcal{L}^s$ to be a set of sensitive concepts that we would like to prevent users from knowing. Because the G-based models for Φ in fact determine all possible correspondence between the actual individuals and the anonymous individuals, an actual individual a is known to have the property C if $I \models C(a)$ for all $I \in Mod(\Phi, G)$. Hence, (Φ, G) satisfies the *epistemic safety* criterion if for every $a \in \mathcal{A}$ and $C \in \mathcal{SC}$, there exists $I \in Mod(\Phi, G)$ such that $I \not\models C(a)$. It can be easily shown that (Φ, G) satisfies the epistemic safety criterion if $[a]_G^\Phi \not\subseteq \llbracket a \rrbracket_{I_G}$ for every $a \in \mathcal{A}$ and $C \in \mathcal{SC}$.

The two above-mentioned criteria are purely qualitative. Two quantitative criteria, called the *average benefit* and the *total cost* criteria, have been proposed for tabulated data[9]. These criteria can also be generalized to the current setting. In the average benefit model, we measure a privacy breach by estimating the average benefit the user can gain after receiving the anonymous social network. This is based on the assumption that the individuals' private information is valuable to the user; therefore, from the privacy protection viewpoint, the larger the average benefit, the less safe the social network data will be. On the other hand, the total cost model measures data safety by estimating the effort the user must expend to find the private information of every individual after receiving the anonymous social network. Thus, the higher the total cost, the harder it is for the user to find the individuals' private information.

The average benefit model is based on the information-theoretic measure of entropy[7]. For each sensitive concept $C \in \mathcal{SC}$, the *a priori* probability of an arbitrary individual satisfying C is denoted by $Pr(C)$. It is sometimes assumed that value of $Pr(C)$ can be obtained from some external knowledge sources, and is therefore available to both the user and the data center. If the assumption fails, the value of $Pr(C)$ can be estimated by

$$Pr(C) = \frac{|\{u \in V \mid C \in l(u)\}|}{m}. \tag{3}$$

After receiving the released anonymous network data, the user knows the *a posteriori* probability of an actual individual a satisfying a sensitive concept C. This is defined by

$$Pr_a(C) = \frac{|\{I \in Mod(\Phi, G) \mid I \models C(a)\}|}{|(Mod(\Phi, G)|}. \tag{4}$$

The user's information gain about a regarding the sensitive concept C is thus

$$IG_a(C) = \max(\frac{\log Pr(C) - \log Pr_a(C)}{\log Pr(C)}, 0). \tag{5}$$

Hence, the user's average information gain regarding C is defined as

$$IG(C) = \frac{\sum_{a \in A} IG_a(C)}{|\mathcal{A}|}. \tag{6}$$

Let us further assume $bef : \mathcal{SC} \rightarrow \Re^+ \cup \{0\}$ is a function that maps each sensitive concept C to the corresponding benefit the user can gain when he obtains some information about C. The value $bef(C)$ can also be seen as the degree of damage caused to an individual if it becomes known that he has the property C. Then, the average benefit to a user by receiving the social network data is $\mathcal{B} = \sum_{C \in \mathcal{SC}} bef(C) \cdot IG(C)$. The larger the value of $\mathcal{B}$, the greater the amount of private information that is leaked.

Let us now turn to the total cost model, which estimates the cost to the user for completely knowing the private information of all individuals. It is assumed that the user can conduct an investigation of the actual individuals to determine whether any of them have the property C. If the user does not have any knowledge about these individuals, he has to investigate all of them. However, by utilizing the knowledge deduced from the released anonymous network, he could discover the private information of all individuals without investigating all of them. The total cost is based on the number of individuals he has to investigate in order to discover the private information of all individuals.

A constructive procedure is used to determine the total cost. Since each model in $Mod(\Phi, G)$ stands for a possible correspondence between the actual and the anonymous individuals, the user can increase his knowledge by eliminating the impossible models via investigation.

Let us first fix a sensitive concept C. Then, for each actual individual $a \in \mathcal{A}$ and class of interpretations $\mathcal{M}$, define $\mathcal{M}_a^+ = \{I \in \mathcal{M} \mid I \models C(a)\}$ and $\mathcal{M}_a^- = \{I \in \mathcal{M} \mid I \not\models C(a)\}$.

Next, we enumerate all possible investigation sequences by using the investigation tree. Each node of the investigation tree denotes a string of actual individuals, which represents a sequence of individuals who have been investigated on that node. Thus, the root node is denoted by the empty string ϵ. Let us define $\mathcal{M}_\epsilon = Mod(\Phi, G)$, $A_\epsilon = \mathcal{A}$, and $p_\epsilon = 1$. Then, for each node denoted by $\lambda = \lambda' \cdot a$ such that $a \in A_{\lambda'}$, define

$$\mathcal{M}_\lambda = \begin{cases} (\mathcal{M}_{\lambda'})_a^+, & \text{if } C(a) \text{ holds} \\ (\mathcal{M}_{\lambda'})_a^-, & \text{if } C(a) \text{ does not hold}, \end{cases}$$

$$A_\lambda = \{a \in A_{\lambda'} \mid (\mathcal{M}_\lambda)_a^+ \neq \emptyset \wedge (\mathcal{M}_\lambda)_a^- \neq \emptyset\},$$

and

$$p_\lambda = p_{\lambda'} \cdot \frac{1}{|A_{\lambda'}|}.$$

Intuitively, $\mathcal{M}_\lambda$ and A_λ respectively denote the set of remaining possible models and the set of individuals whose C-membership is not yet known; and p_λ denotes the probability that the actual investigation sequence is λ. On each internal node λ, we assume that the next individual to be investigated is chosen uniformly from A_λ.

A node denoted by λ is a leaf node if $A_\lambda = \emptyset$. Let $\mathcal{P}$ denote the set of all leaf nodes. Then, the expected number of investigations by the user is

$$IV_C = \sum_{\lambda \in \mathcal{P}} p_\lambda \cdot len(\lambda), \tag{7}$$

where $len(\lambda)$ denotes the length of the string λ.

The rationale for taking the cost as a safety criterion is to prevent the user substantially reducing his investigation costs after receiving the released network data. To measure the extent of privacy leakage, we should consider the minimal effort the user must expend to find some private information; therefore, the expected total cost for the user to discover some private information after receiving the social network data should be $\mathcal{D} = \min_{C \in \mathcal{SC}} IV_C$. The larger the value of $\mathcal{D}$, the harder it is to breach privacy.

4.3   Social Networks in an Open World

An anonymous social network $G = (V, E, l)$ under OWA can be transformed into an ABox Φ_G as follows:

$$\Phi_G = \{A(u) \mid A \in l(u), u \in V\}$$
$$\cup \ \{R(u, v) \mid R \in l((u, v)), (u, v) \in E\}.$$

Consequently, we have an ABox, Φ, for the user's knowledge and an ABox, Φ_G, for the anonymous social network G. The user seeks a mapping from $\mathcal{A}$ to $V = \{u_1, \cdots, u_m\}$. Let $\iota : \mathcal{A} \to V$ be a 1-1 mapping; then $\iota(\Phi_G)$ is the resultant ABox obtained from Φ_G by replacing each anonymous individual u occurring in Φ_G with $\iota^{-1}(u)$. The mapping ι is said to be a (Φ, G)-*possible matching* if $\iota(\Phi_G) \cup \Phi$ is consistent with respect to the background TBox. Sometimes, we simply call it a possible matching.

4.4 Safety Criteria for OWA

Once the notion of possible matchings is given, the definition of the granule size criterion is analogous to that under CWA. In fact, each G-based model corresponds exactly to a 1-1 mapping between $\mathcal{A}$ and V, which makes all assertions in Φ true. Under OWA, the granule (or bin) for an actual individual $a \in \mathcal{A}$ with respect to G and Φ is formally defined as

$$[a]_G^\Phi = \{\iota(a) \mid \iota \text{ is a possible matching}\}. \tag{8}$$

The pair (Φ, G) is said to satisfy the k-anonymity criterion if for each $a \in \mathcal{A}$, $|[a]_G^\Phi| \geq k$.

It is easy to define the epistemic safety criterion. Formally, (Φ, G) satisfies the epistemic safety criterion if for every $a \in \mathcal{A}$ and $C \in \mathcal{SC}$, there exists a possible matching ι such that $\iota(\Phi_G) \cup \Phi \not\models C(a)$.

For the average benefit model, the *a priori* probability $Pr(C)$ may be still estimated by (3) or obtained from some external source. However, the *a posteriori* probability of an actual individual a satisfying a sensitive concept C is changed to

$$Pr_a(C) = \frac{|\{\iota \mid \iota(\Phi_G) \cup \Phi \models C(a)\}|}{\text{the number of possible matchings}}. \tag{9}$$

The definitions of $IG_a(C)$ and $IG(C)$ are then exactly same as those given in (5) and (6) respectively.

We still use the investigation tree for the total cost model. For the root node, let $\mathcal{M}_\epsilon$ denote the set of all possible matchings, Φ_ϵ be the empty set, and A_ϵ and p_ϵ be defined as above. Then, for each node denoted by $\lambda = \lambda' \cdot a$ such that $a \in A_{\lambda'}$, let

$$\mathcal{M}_\lambda = \begin{cases} \mathcal{M}_{\lambda'} - (\mathcal{M}_{\lambda'})_a^-, & \text{if } C(a) \text{ holds} \\ \mathcal{M}_{\lambda'} - (\mathcal{M}_{\lambda'})_a^+, & \text{if } C(a) \text{ does not hold,} \end{cases}$$

where $(\mathcal{M}_{\lambda'})_a^+ = \{\iota \in \mathcal{M}_{\lambda'} \mid \iota(\Phi_G) \cup \Phi \cup \Phi_{\lambda'} \models C(a)\}$ and $(\mathcal{M}_{\lambda'})_a^- = \{\iota \in \mathcal{M}_{\lambda'} \mid \iota(\Phi_G) \cup \Phi \cup \Phi_{\lambda'} \models \neg C(a)\}$,

$$\Phi_\lambda = \begin{cases} \Phi_{\lambda'} \cup \{C(a)\}, & \text{if } C(a) \text{ holds} \\ \Phi_{\lambda'} \cup \{\neg C(a)\}, & \text{if } C(a) \text{ does not hold,} \end{cases}$$

$$A_\lambda = A_{\lambda'} - \{b \in A_{\lambda'} \mid \mathcal{M}_\lambda = (\mathcal{M}_\lambda)_b^+ \vee \mathcal{M}_\lambda = (\mathcal{M}_\lambda)_b^-\},$$

and p_λ be defined as above. The intuitive meanings of $\mathcal{M}_\lambda$, A_λ, and p_λ are analogous to those of the CWA case, except that possible models are replaced by possible matchings. Note that $\mathcal{M}_\lambda = (\mathcal{M}_\lambda)_b^+ \vee \mathcal{M}_\lambda = (\mathcal{M}_\lambda)_b^-$ means that the C-membership of b can be inferred from the known facts, so the investigation of b is not necessary. In addition, Φ_λ contains the known facts discovered through the investigation of individuals in λ. The definitions of IV_C and $\mathcal{D}$ then follow exactly the same form as above.

5   Conclusion

In this paper, we generalize the privacy protection problem of microdata release in tabulated form to the social network form. A social network not only contains the attribute data of each individual, but also relational data between individuals. Therefore, the problem is more complicated than that encountered in tabulated data protection. We resolve it by employing a DL-based representation for social network data.

The safety criteria proposed in this paper enable a data center to assess the risk of breaching confidentiality by releasing social network data. However, some preventive action should be taken when the assessment shows that the direct release of the data is not safe. For tabulated data, some techniques such as generalization, suppression, and random perturbation have been studied extensively [4,3,9]. In our future work, we will explore how to apply these techniques to social network data.

Another research problem is how to protect sensitive roles. In this paper, the safety criteria are mainly defined with respect to the protection of sensitive concepts. The protection of sensitive roles can be achieved indirectly. For example, if the data center wants to prevent the user from knowing $R(a,b)$, then it is sufficient to protect the sensitive concept $\exists R : \top$ for a. However, the criteria may be unnecessarily strict if it does not matter whether a is R-related to anyone else apart from the particular b; therefore, the safety criteria can be further relaxed if defined with respect to the protection of roles directly.

References

1. F. Baader and W. Nutt. "Basic description logics". In F. Baader *et al.*, editor, *Description Logic Handbook*, pages 47–100. Cambridge University Press, 2002.
2. Y.C. Chiang, T.-s. Hsu, S. Kuo, C.J. Liau, and D.W. Wang. Preserving confidentiality when sharing medical database with the Cellsecu system. *International Journal of Medical Informatics*, 71:17–23, 2003.
3. T.-s. Hsu, C.-J. Liau, and D.-W. Wang. A logical model for privacy protection. In *Proc. of the 4th ISC*, LNCS 2200, pages 110–124. Springer-Verlag, 2001.
4. P. Samarati. "Protecting respondents' identities in microdata release". *IEEE Transactions on Knowledge and Data Engineering*, 13(6):1010–1027, 2001.
5. M. Schmidt-Schauß and G. Smolka. "Attributive concept descriptions with complements". *Artificial Intelligence*, 48(1):1–26, 1991.
6. J. Scott. *Social Network Analysis: A Handbook*. SAGE Publications, 2 edition, 2000.
7. C.E. Shannon. "The mathematical theory of communication". *The Bell System Technical Journal*, 27(3&4):379–423,623–656, 1948.
8. L. Sweeney. k-anonymity: a model for protecting privacy. *International Journal on Uncertainty, Fuzziness and Knowledge-based Systems*, 10(5):557–570, 2002.
9. D.W. Wang, C.J. Liau, and T.-s. Hsu. Medical privacy protection based on granular computing. *Artificial Intelligence in Medicine*, 32(2):137–149, 2004.

An Interpretation of Flow Graphs by Granular Computing

Jigui Sun[1,2], Huawen Liu[1,2], Changsong Qi[1,3], and Huijie Zhang[1,4]

[1] College of Computer Science, Jilin University, Changchun 130012, China
JgSun@jlu.edu.cn, Huaw.Liu@gmail.com
[2] Key Laboratory of Symbolic Computation and Knowledge Engineering of Ministry
of Education, Changchun 130012, China
[3] Department of Computer, Tonghua Normal College, Tonghua 134002, China
ChangSongQi@email.jlu.edu.cn
[4] College of Computer, Northeast Normal University, Changchun 130021, China
Zhanghj167@nenu.edu.cn

Abstract. Flow graph (FG) is a unique approach in data mining and data analysis mainly in virtue of its well-structural characteristics of network, which is naturally consistent with granular computing (GrC). Meanwhile, GrC provides us with both structured thinking at the philosophical level and structured problem solving at the practical level. The main objective of the present paper is to develop a simple and more concrete model for flow graph using GrC. At first, FG will be mainly discussed in three aspects under GrC, namely, granulation of FG, some relationships and operations of granules. Moreover, as one of advantages of this interpretation, an efficient approximation reduction algorithm of flow graph is given under the framework of GrC.

Keywords: Flow graph, granular computing, data mining.

1 Introduction

Since flow graph(shortly, FG) has been proposed by Pawlak is his initiated paper [8], series of related papers, such as [4,5,6,7,9,10,11], continuously have been put forward to place emphasis upon its importance in data analysis. As a new mathematical model of finding and mining knowledge, FG has some characteristics, such as intuitional representation, straightforward computation, explicit relations and parallel processing. Moreover, FG has tight relationships with Bayes' theorem, rough sets and decision systems in theory aspects and these works pave the way for its application in many field [7]. For example, Palwak first discuss the relations between probability theory and FG in [9]. Butz et al. [1] have shown that flow graph inference algorithm has exponential complexity. Then, FG was linked up with decision systems in [4,5] and [6], and tied up with rough sets in his recent paper [10].

Although FG has some merits in data mining, some undesirable effects also exist in it. For example, it can not exactly or precisely depict the relationships

S. Greco et al. (Eds.): RSCTC 2006, LNAI 4259, pp. 448–457, 2006.

among nodes in network account for the fact that FG is only based on information flow distribution and represents relationships among nodes in quantity of flow. Therefore, Sun et al. introduced an extension of flow graph(in short, EFG) in [15] to tackle with this problem.

Due to its well-structural network, EFG is consistent with granular computing(GrC) in nature. Meanwhile, GrC, which is motivated by the practical needs for simplification, clarity, low cost, approximation, and tolerance of uncertainty, is more about a philosophical way of thinking and a practical methodology of problem solving deeply rooted in human mind. By effectively using levels of granularity, GrC provides a systematic, natural way to analyze, understand, represent, and solve real world problems [18]. In this paper, we will investigate to joint EFG with GrC. However, granulation of the universe, relationships of granules and computing with granules are three fundamental issues of granular computing [19]. Without loss of generality, we will first discuss granulation of EFG in details, and then involve some relationships of granules and GrC methods describe its ability to switch among different granularities in problem solving. What's more, an approximation reduction algorithm about EFG based on the model of GrC will be represented after decomposition and composition of granules are introduced in order to prove its utility values of the interpretation.

The structure of the rest is organized as follows. Section 2 briefly introduces necessary notions of flow graph and its extension. In Section 3, granulation of EFG will be proposed. Section 4 presents decomposition and composition operations on granules and an approximation reduction algorithms about EFG under the framework of GrC will be given in Section 5. Finally, some concluding remarks are shown in Section 6.

2   Flow Graphs

In this section, some concepts of flow graph and its extension will be recalled briefly. More notations can be consulted [11] and [15].

A flow graph (FG) is a *directed, acyclic, finite* graph $G = (N, B, \varphi)$, where N is a set of *nodes*, $B \subseteq N \times N$ is a set of *directed branches*, $\varphi : B \to R^+$ is a *flow function* and R^+ is the set of non-negative reals [11]. If $(n_i, n_j) \in B$ then n_i is an *input* of n_j and n_j is an *output* of n_i. $\varphi(n_i, n_j)$ is the *throughflow* from n_i to n_j. $I(n_i), O(n_i)$ are the sets of all inputs or outputs of n_i, respectively.

However, FG is a quantificational graph, that is, it represents simple relations among nodes using information flow distribution. As a result, FG can not exactly determine the nature of relationships among nodes. Therefore, we have proposed an extension of FG in [15] according to the information or objects flowing in the network.

An extension of flow graph (EFG) is a *directed, acyclic, finite* graph $G=(E, N, B, \varphi, \alpha, \beta)$, where E is the set of *objects* flowing in the graph, N is a set of *nodes*, $B \subseteq N \times N$ is a set of *directed branches*, $\varphi : B \to 2^E$ is the set of *objects* which flow through branches and $\alpha, \beta : B \to [0,1]$ are threshold of *certainty* and *decision*, respectively. If $(n_i, n_j) \in B$ then n_i is *input(father)* of n_j and n_j

is *output(child)* of n_i. and $I(n_i), O(n_i)$ are respectively the sets of *fathers* and *children* of node n_i. Node n_i is called a *root* if $I(n_i) = \emptyset$ holds. Similarly, n_i is a *leaf* if $O(n_i) = \emptyset$ holds. The *inflow* and *outflow* of node are respectively defined as

$$\varphi_+(n_i) = \bigcup_{n_j \in I(n_i)} \varphi(n_j, n_i) \ \ and \ \ \varphi_-(n_i) = \bigcup_{n_j \in O(n_i)} \varphi(n_i, n_j). \tag{1}$$

Moreover, we assume that for any internal node n_i, $\varphi(n_i) = \varphi_+(n_i) = \varphi_-(n_i)$. *Input* and *output* of G are defined $I(G) = \{n_i \in N | I(n_i) = \emptyset\}$, $O(G) = \{n_i \in N | O(n_i) = \emptyset\}$.

Let G be an EFG, the *certainty* and *coverage* factors of $(n_i, n_j) \in B$ are

$$cer(n_i, n_j) = |\varphi(n_i, n_j)| / |\varphi(n_i)| \ \ and \ \ cov(n_i, n_j) = |\varphi(n_i, n_j)| / |\varphi(n_j)|. \tag{2}$$

respectively, where $|X|$ is the cardinality of X, $\varphi(n_i) \neq \emptyset$ and $\varphi(n_j) \neq \emptyset$.

In EFG, an sequence of nodes $n_1, ..., n_m$ will be called a *directed path* from n_1 to n_m, denoted by $[n_1...n_m]$, if $(n_i, n_{i+1}) \in B$ for $1 \leq i \leq m - 1$ and $\bigcap_{i=1}^{m} \varphi(n_i, n_{i+1}) \neq \emptyset$. Furthermore, the *support*, *certainty* and *coverage* of the path $[n_1...n_m]$ are $\varphi(n_1...n_m) = \bigcap_{i=1}^{m} \varphi(n_i, n_{i+1})$,

$$cer(n_1...n_m) = \frac{|\varphi(n_1...n_m)|}{|\varphi(n_1...n_{m-1})|} \ \ and \ \ cov(n_1...n_m) = \frac{|\varphi(n_1...n_m)|}{|\varphi(n_m)|} \tag{3}$$

respectively, where $\varphi(n_1...n_{m-1}) \neq \emptyset$ and $\varphi(n_m) \neq \emptyset$.

For an EFG G, if we only cast our lights on quantity of objects flowing through branches in G rather than concrete objects, i.e. $|\varphi(n_i, n_j)| / |E|$, and $\alpha = 0, \beta = 0$, the EFG can be transformed into an FG and, what's more, an approximate FG [11] can be obtained from the EFG by adjusting the value of α or β.

For the sake of simplicity, in this paper, we assume that nodes with same attribute form a layer and an EFG are arranged in several layers, denoted by a set L, where $L = CL \cup \{O(G)\}$ and $CL, \{O(G)\}$ are *condition* and *decision layers(output* of EFG), respectively. In each layer, there does not exist any branch among nodes and one object only belongs to one node. What's more, the throughflow of (n_i, n_j) is not empty if $(n_i, n_j) \in B$ in EFG, namely, $\varphi(n_i, n_j) \neq \emptyset$.

Example 1. Let us consider an EFG $G = (E, N, B, \varphi, \alpha, \beta)$ presented in Fig. 1, where $E = \{p_1, p_2, p_3, p_4, p_5, p_6\}$, $N = \{n_{01}, n_{11}, n_{12}, n_{13}, n_{21}, n_{22}, n_{31}, n_{32}\} \cup \{n_{41}, n_{42}\}$, $\alpha = 0, \beta = 0, CL = \{l_0, l_1, l_2, l_3\}, O(G) = l_4$ and B, φ as shown in Fig. 1.

In Fig. 1, the root of G is n_{01} and leaves are n_{41} and n_{42}. The throughflow of branch (n_{21}, n_{32}) and node n_{21} are $\varphi(n_{21}, n_{32}) = \{p_3\}, \varphi_+(n_{21}) = \varphi_-(n_{21}) = \varphi(n_{21}) = \{p_2, p_3, p_5\}$. In addition, the sequence of $n_{01}, n_{12}, n_{21}, n_{32}$ is a path and its degrees of certainty and coverage are $cer(n_{01}, n_{12}, n_{21}, n_{32}) = 1, cov(n_{01}, n_{12}, n_{21}, n_{32}) = 1/4$, respectively. $\qquad \square$

3   Granulation of EFG

As a tool of data analysis in data mining, FG has been interpreted by decision algorithms, probability and rough sets [10]. However, we will investigate EFG with

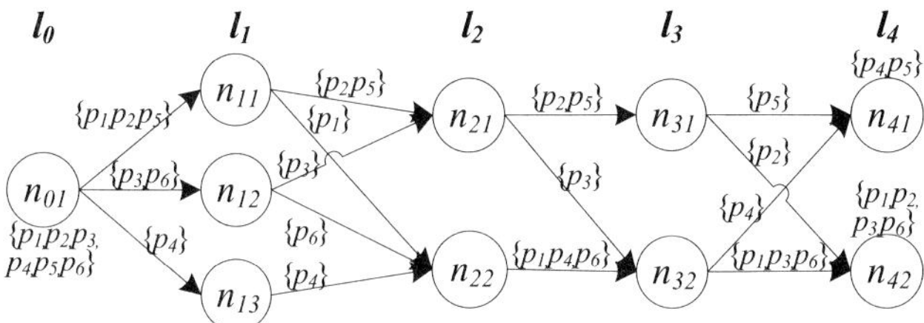

Fig. 1. An EFG G

GrC in this paper, for EFG has an excellent construction features in describing information flow. The first step is granulation of EFG illustrated as follows.

With respect to a layer $l \in L$ in EFG, two objects x, y may flow through the same node n, i.e., $x, y \in \varphi(n)$. In this case, one can not distinguish x and y according to n in l. This means that x, y can be grouped into a *granule*, that is, a granule $g(n)$ in EFG is formally represented as a pair $(n, m(n))$ [11], where n is a descriptor (node) and $m(n)$ denotes the meanings of $g(n)$. Moreover, one can get

$$m(n) = \{x \in E | x \in \varphi(n)\} = \varphi(n) \tag{4}$$

for $n \in N$, namely, the meanings of the granule $g(n)$ consist of all objects flowing through n. Hereafter, we simply denote $m(n)$ as $\varphi(n)$. In addition, the family of granules $F(\{l\}) = \{g(n) | m(n) \neq \emptyset, \forall n \in l\}$ forms a partition of E, denoted by E/l. The corresponding equivalence relation R_l on E is

$$x R_l y \Leftrightarrow x \in m(n) \wedge y \in m(n) \wedge n \in l. \tag{5}$$

Thus, the equivalence class of x with reference to R_l is $[x]_{R_l} = \{y \in E | x R_l y\}$ and each $[x]_{R_l}$ is a granule, i.e., $g(n) = (n, [x]_n)$, where $n \in R_l$.

A granule $g(n)$ will be called an *element granule* if n is an single node in EFG. According to (1), we know that

$$m(n \wedge n') \Leftrightarrow \varphi(n \wedge n') \Leftrightarrow \varphi(n) \cap \varphi(n') \Leftrightarrow m(n) \cap m(n'). \tag{6}$$

Hence, a granule can also be comprised of several granules or element granules in a manner of

$$g(n \wedge n') = (n \wedge n', m(n \wedge n')) = (n \wedge n', m(n) \cap m(n')) = g(n) \cap g(n') \tag{7}$$

where $l, l' \in L$ and $n \in l, n' \in l'$. Moreover, the family of granules $F(\{l, l'\}) = \{g(n \wedge n') | m(n \wedge n') \neq \emptyset, \forall n \in l, n' \in l'\}$ is a partition of E. The corresponding equivalence relation is $R_{\{l,l'\}} = R_l \cap R_{l'}$, namely, $x R_{\{l,l'\}} y \Leftrightarrow x \in m(n) \wedge y \in m(n) \wedge n \in l \wedge x \in m(n') \wedge y \in m(n') \wedge n' \in l'$. Hence, granules in the partition $F(\{l, l'\})$ are smaller than granules in $F(\{l\})$ and $F(\{l'\})$, that is, granules in $F(\{l, l'\})$ are finer than those in $F(\{l\})$ and $F(\{l'\})$. Generally, for a subset of layers $L' \subseteq L$, the equivalence relation is $R_{L'} = \bigcap_{l \in L'} R_l$ such that $x R_{L'} y \Leftrightarrow \wedge_{l \in L'} x \in m(n) \wedge y \in m(n) \wedge n \in l$, and each granule is $g(\wedge_{n_i \in l, l \in L'} n_i)$, whose meanings is $m(\wedge_{n_i \in l, l \in L'} n_i) = \bigcap_{n_i \in l, l \in L'} m(n_i)$.

In terms of the definition of directed path in EFG, we observe the fact that for each path $[n_1, ..., n, n']$, the throughflow is

$$\varphi(n_1, ..., n, n') = \varphi(n_1, ..., n) \cap \varphi(n, n') = \varphi(n_1, ..., n) \cap \varphi(n'), \qquad (8)$$

that is, the longer of the path, the less of its throughflow. Consequently, one can obtained that a path is a granule from (7) and (8) in nature. In other words, a granule can be denoted by a path starting from the root. Furthermore, all paths with the same length form a partition of E if their first nodes are the root of EFG.

Example 2. (**cont.**) In Fig.1, the partitions or granules of E by l_0, l_1, l_2, l_3, l_4 are
$l_0 : g(n_{01}) = \{p_1, p_2, p_3, p_4, p_5, p_6\}$
$l_1 : g(n_{11}) = \{p_1, p_2, p_5\}, \quad g(n_{12}) = \{p_4\}, \quad g(n_{13}) = \{p_3, p_6\}$
$l_2 : g(n_{21}) = \{p_2, p_3, p_5\}, \quad g(n_{22}) = \{p_1, p_4, p_6\}$
$l_3 : g(n_{31}) = \{p_2, p_5\}, \quad g(n_{32}) = \{p_1, p_3, p_4, p_6\}$
$l_4 : g(n_{41}) = \{p_1, p_2, p_3, p_6\}, \quad g(n_{42}) = \{p_4, p_5\}$
Let $L' = \{l_1, l_2\}$, $L'' = \{l_1, l_2, l_3\}$, then the granules with respect to L' and L'' are
$L' : g(n_{11} \wedge n_{21}) = \{p_2, p_5\}, \quad g(n_{11} \wedge n_{22}) = \{p_1\}, \quad g(n_{12} \wedge n_{22}) = \{p_4\},$
$\quad g(n_{13} \wedge n_{21}) = \{p_3\}, \quad g(n_{13} \wedge n_{22}) = \{p_6\}$
$L'' : g(n_{11} \wedge n_{21} \wedge n_{31}) = \{p_2, p_5\}, \quad g(n_{11} \wedge n_{22} \wedge n_{32}) = \{p_1\},$
$\quad g(n_{12} \wedge n_{22} \wedge n_{32}) = \{p_4\}, \quad g(n_{13} \wedge n_{21} \wedge n_{32}) = \{p_3\},$
$\quad g(n_{13} \wedge n_{22} \wedge n_{32}) = \{p_6\}.$ □

4   Decomposition and Composition of Granules

In GrC, granules must have the capabilities of decomposition and composition in problem-solving which can traverse views among different levels of granularity. However, there is no exception to the granules in EFG.

Granule decomposition deals with the change from a coarse granularity to a fine granularity to provide more details to further classified objects into a group, whereas granule composition deals with the shift from a fine granularity to a coarse granularity to discard certain details and make distinct objects no longer differentiable [18]. In other words, the meaning of granules decomposition is that the problem has been divided into a sequence of more manageable and smaller subtasks to reduce an overall computing effort, while combination integrate subproblems into a whole to provide with a better insight into its essence rather than get buried in all unnecessary details where granulation serves as an abstraction mechanism that omits irrelevant details of the problem.

According to the analysis in section 3, we notice the fact that the granule model of EFG is a partition one [17] and operations can be attained under the framework of quotient space theory [20]. In the granule model of EFG, a directed path represents a granule and the longer the path, the finer the granule. Thus a nested granulations hierarchy is constituted by all granularities corresponding to paths originating from the root. In this hierarchy, the granules (or the paths) from the root to each levels form a partition of E. Furthermore, the granules in the i-th level are finer than those in j-th level in the light of (7) and (8), where $i > j$. Based on this principle, granules decomposition (or composition) can be implemented in top-down (or bottom-up) method. For convenience, we only involve the granularities corresponding to paths stemming from the root in this paper.

Definition 1. *[17] In GrC model of EFG, granules decomposition is a mapping $Dec : 2^{E/l} \to 2^{E/l'}$, such that $Dec([x]_{R_l}) = \bigcup_{y \in [x]_{R_l}} \{[y]_{R_{l'}}\}$ and $Dec(X) = \bigcup_{[x]_{R_l} \in X} Dec([x]_{R_l})$ for $X \subseteq E/l$, where E is the set of objects, $[x]_{R_l}$ is the equivalence class (or a granule) of x with reference to R_l and l' is the next level of l.*

By the decomposition function, a granule in high levels can be split into several disjoint finer granules in the next levels, that is, more details can be obtained about the granule. Reversely, a coarser granule can be built in a higher abstract level regardless of some inessential information by a combination operation which converses a granule or equivalence class into a point in higher level.

Definition 2. *In GrC model of EFG, granules composition is a mapping $Com : 2^{E/l'} \to 2^{E/l}$, such that $Com([x]_{R_{l'}}) = \bigcup_{y \in [x]_{R_{l'}}} \{[y]_{R_l}\}$ and $Com(X) = \bigcup_{[x]_{R_{l'}} \in X} Com([x]_{R_{l'}})$ for $X \subseteq E/l'$, where E is the set of objects, $[x]_{R_l}$ is the equivalence class (or a granule) of x with reference to R_l and l' is the next level of l.*

However, Dec and Com are work under a partition of granule model, so they are the special cases of binary neighborhood relation [2]. What's more, we immediately have $[x]_{R_l} \in Dec(Com([x]_{R_l}))$, $[x]_{R_l} = Com(Dec([x]_{R_l}))$ in terms of the Def. 1, 2 and (7), (8).

5   Reduction of EFG

An simplification of EFG can bring some predominance, such as low costs and rapid reasoning, in data analysis. In this section, we will present an EFG reduction algorithm based on GrC. Above all, some definitions about reductions of EFG and path will be given as follows.

Definition 3. *Let $[n_1, ..., n_k]$ be a path in an EFG, we will say n_i is dispensable with respect to $O(G)$ if $\varphi(n_1, ..., n_k) = \varphi(n_1, ..., n_{i-1}, n_{i+1}, ..., n_k)$, where $1 \leq i \leq k$, otherwise n_i is indispensable. If there is no dispensable nodes in $[n_1, ..., n_k]$, then $[n_1, ..., n_k]$ is called a minimal reduction path.*

Definition 4. *Let G be an EFG, we will say G is a minimal reduction EFG if all paths in G are minimal reduction paths.*

Before giving the algorithm, we retrospect some conception about rule. The relation between flow graphs and decision algorithms is first given by Pawlak in [6] where every branches $(n, n') \in B$ is interpreted as a decision rule $n \to n'$

Algorithm 1. Approximation reduction algorithm of EFG (ARAEFG)

Input : An EFG $G = (E, N, B, \varphi, \alpha, \beta)$.
Output: An approximation reduction of EFG $G' = (E, N', B', \varphi, \alpha, \beta)$.
$GS = \{g(I(G))\}; DGS = \{g(O(G))\}; B' = \emptyset; N' = I(G) \cup O(G);$
for $\forall g(n_1 \wedge ... \wedge n_i) \in GS$ **do**

    $IsExistDispensableNode = False;$ //whether exists a dispensable node
    if $\exists g(n) \in DGS$ and $|m(n_1 \wedge ... \wedge n_j) \cap m(n)|/|m(n_1 \wedge ... \wedge n_j)| \geq \beta$ **then**
        // $g(n_1 \wedge ... \wedge n_i) \rightarrow g(n)$ is an approximation rule
        $B' = B' \cup \{(n_i, n)\};$
    else
        for $\forall (n_i, n_j) \in B$ and $m(n_1 \wedge ... \wedge n_i) \cap m(n_j) \neq \emptyset$ **do**
            if $m(n_1 \wedge ... \wedge n_i) \cap m(n_j) = m(n_1 \wedge ... \wedge n_i)$ **then**
                $IsExistDispensable = True;$ // n_j is dispensable
                for $\forall (n_j, n_t) \in B$ **do**
                    $B = B \cup (n_i, n_t);$
                end
            else
                $B' = B' \cup \{(n_i, n_j)\}; N' = N' \cup \{n_j\};$
                if $n_j \notin O(G)$ **then**
                    $m(n_1 \wedge ... \wedge n_i \wedge n_j) = m(n_1 \wedge ... \wedge n_i) \cap m(n_j);$
                    $GS = GS \cup g(n_1 \wedge ... \wedge n_i \wedge n_j);$
                end
            end
        end
    end
    if $IsExistDispensableNode = False$ **then**
        $GS = GS - \{g(n_1 \wedge ... \wedge n_i)\};$
    end
end

---

and each paths $[n_1, .., n_k]$ is a sequence of decision rules $n_1 \rightarrow n_2, .., n_{k-1} \rightarrow n_k$, in short $n_1, .., n_{k-1} \rightarrow n_k$. However, the rules in this paper will be slightly different from those in [6] on the measurement.

In the framework of GrC, a granule represents a path from the root to one node such that each element in the granule is an object flowing through the path. We will say an object x satisfy a granule $g(n)$, if x flow through the corresponding path n, namely, $x \in \varphi(n)$. Under this interpretation, the meaning of granule $g(n_1 \wedge .. \wedge n_k)$ is the throughflow of the path $[n_1, .., n_k]$ determining a rule $n_1, .., n_{k-1} \rightarrow n_k$, that is, the set of *support* of $n_1, .., n_{k-1} \rightarrow n_k$ is $\varphi(n_1..n_k)$. What's more, the *certainty* and *coverage coefficients* of $n_1, .., n_{k-1} \rightarrow n_k$ are certainty and coverage degrees of the path $[n_1, .., n_k]$, i.e.

$$cer(n_1...n_{k-1} \rightarrow n_k) = \frac{|m(n_1 \wedge ... \wedge n_{k-1}) \cap m(n_k)|}{|m(n_1 \wedge ... \wedge n_{k-1})|} = \frac{|\varphi(n_1...n_{k-1}) \cap \varphi(n_k)|}{|\varphi(n_1...n_{k-1})|} = cer(n_1...n_k),$$

$$cov(n_1...n_{k-1} \rightarrow n_k) = \frac{|m(n_1 \wedge ... \wedge n_{k-1}) \cap m(n_k)|}{|m(n_k)|} = \frac{|\varphi(n_1...n_{k-1}) \cap \varphi(n_k)|}{|\varphi(n_k)|} = cov(n_1...n_k),$$

respectively, where $\varphi(n_1...n_{k-1}) \neq \emptyset$ and $\varphi(n_k) \neq \emptyset$. However, these quantities consistent with those in [19]. A rule $n \to n'$ is certainty if $cer(n \to n')=1$, namely, $\varphi(n) \subseteq \varphi(n')$. However, it is too rigid to the real-life world filled with noise data. So an variable degree of certainty rule will be introduced naturally.

Definition 5. *[21] A rule $n \to n'$ is approximation certainty if $cer(n \to n') \geq \beta$, where $0< \beta \leq 1$.*

Based on this principle, an approximation reduction algorithm about EFG (ARAEFG) is shown as Alg. 1. In ARAEFG, notions of GS, DGS denote the set of granules of paths originating from the roots and the set of element granules of leaves, respectively.

The time complexity of ARAEFG is $O(M^L)$ which is lower than those in [15] where the time complexity of nodes reduction algorithm of EFG is $O(M^{2L})$, where $L = |CL|$ and M is the maximal number of branches among layers. To improve the performance, some heuristic strategies, such as the priority of layers with most nodes [3], can also be employed.

Example 3. **(cont.)** Let G be an EFG depicted in Fig. 1 and $\beta = 1$, the steps of the algorithm are shown in Table 1 and the result, namely, the approximation reduction EFG G' of G, is illustrated in Fig. 2, after the ARAEFG has been used. $\qquad\qquad\square$

Table 1. The steps of the Algorithm 1

Loop	*State*
0	$GS=\{g(n_{01})\}$; $N'=\{n_{01}, n_{41}, n_{42}\}$; $B'=\{\}$;
1	$GS=\{g(n_{01}\wedge n_{13}), g(n_{01}\wedge n_{12}), g(n_{01}\wedge n_{11})\}$; $N' = \{n_{01}, n_{41}, n_{42}, n_{13}, n_{12}, n_{11}\}$; $B'=\{(n_{01}, n_{13}), (n_{01}, n_{12}), (n_{01}, n_{11})\}$;
2	$GS=\{g(n_{01}\wedge n_{12}), g(n_{01}\wedge n_{11})\}$; $N'=\{n_{01}, n_{41}, n_{42}, n_{13}, n_{12}, n_{11}\}$; $B'=\{(n_{01}, n_{13}),(n_{01}, n_{12}),(n_{01}, n_{11}),(n_{13}, n_{41})\}$;
3	$GS=\{g(n_{01}\wedge n_{11})\}$; $N'=\{n_{01}, n_{41}, n_{42}, n_{13}, n_{12}, n_{11}\}$; $B'=\{(n_{01}, n_{13}),(n_{01}, n_{12}),(n_{01}, n_{11}),(n_{13}, n_{41}),(n_{12}, n_{42})\}$;
4	$GS=\{g(n_{01}\wedge n_{11}\wedge n_{22}), g(n_{01}\wedge n_{11}\wedge n_{21})\}$; $N'=\{n_{01}, n_{41}, n_{42}, n_{13}, n_{12}, n_{11}, n_{22}, n_{21}\}$; $B'=\{(n_{01}, n_{13}),(n_{01}, n_{12}),(n_{01}, n_{11}),(n_{13}, n_{41}),(n_{12}, n_{42}),(n_{11}, n_{22}),(n_{11}, n_{21})\}$;
5	$GS=\{g(n_{01}\wedge n_{11}\wedge n_{21})\}$; $N'=\{n_{01}, n_{41}, n_{42}, n_{13}, n_{12}, n_{11}, n_{22}, n_{21}\}$; $B'=\{(n_{01}, n_{13}),(n_{01}, n_{12}),(n_{01}, n_{11}),(n_{13}, n_{41}),(n_{12}, n_{42}),(n_{11}, n_{22}),(n_{11}, n_{21}),$ $(n_{22}, n_{42})\}$;
6	$GS=\{g(n_{01}\wedge n_{11}\wedge n_{21})\}$; $N'=\{n_{01}, n_{41}, n_{42}, n_{13}, n_{12}, n_{11}, n_{22}, n_{21}\}$; $B'=\{(n_{01}, n_{13}),(n_{01}, n_{12}),(n_{01}, n_{11}),(n_{13}, n_{41}),(n_{12}, n_{42}),(n_{11}, n_{22}),(n_{11}, n_{21}),$ $(n_{22}, n_{42})\}$;
7	$GS=\{\}$; $N'=\{n_{01}, n_{41}, n_{42}, n_{13}, n_{12}, n_{11}, n_{22}, n_{21}\}$; $B'=\{(n_{01}, n_{13}),(n_{01}, n_{12}),(n_{01}, n_{11}),(n_{13}, n_{41}),(n_{12}, n_{42}),(n_{11}, n_{22}),(n_{11}, n_{21}),$ $(n_{22}, n_{42}),(n_{21}, n_{42}),(n_{21}, n_{42})\}$;

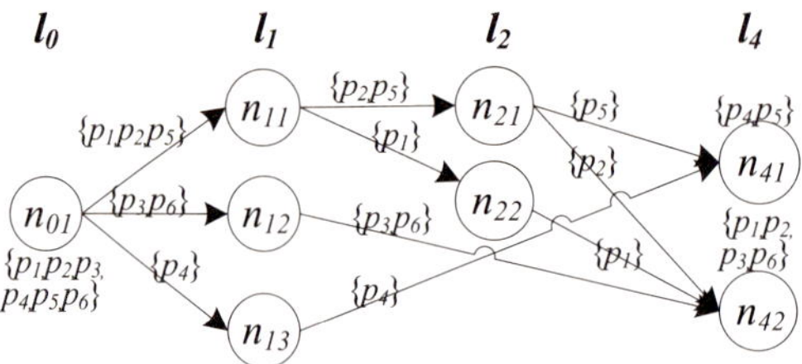

Fig. 2. An approximation EFG G' of the G

6   Conclusion

The main purpose of this paper can be described as providing an interpretation of flow graphs using GrC. This is done in two steps: First, a model of GrC in the context of the extension of flow graph is proposed. In this framework, nodes have been interpreted as element granules and a path denotes a granule. Besides the meaning of granule is presented by the throughflow of the path corresponding to the granule, the dependency of granules can measured by certainty and coverage degree of paths. Under this interpretation, a partition model has been built. Moreover, the operations of decomposition and composition about granules, which can transform granules from one view to another easily, have been given. To illustrate its availabilities which this interpretation brings forth, an approximation reduction algorithm of EFG, based on granular computing, has also been introduced at the end of this paper. This algorithm has higher performance than the nodes reduction approach which we have proposed before.

However, some more virtues under this model are still in their early states of research and our future works will be carried on exploring them.

Acknowledgment

This work is supported by the National NSF of China(60473003), Ministry of Education Program for New Century Excellent Talents in University(NECT) and Doctor Point Founds of Educational Department(20050183065). The 4th author was supported by the Science Foundation for Young Teachers of Northeast Normal University(20051003).

The authors also expresse their sincere thanks to the anonymous referees for their careful reading, critical remarks and the constructive suggestions which greatly improved the exposition of the paper.

References

1. Butz, C.J., Yan, W., Yang, B.: The Computational Complexity of Inference using Rough Set Flow Graphs. In: [14], (2005) 335-344
2. Lin, T.Y.: Granular Computing on Binary Relations I: Data Mining and Neighborhood Systems. In: Skoworn, A., Polkowski, L., eds., *Rough Sets In Knowledge Discovery*, Springer-Verlag, (1998) 107-121

3. Lin, T.Y., Yin, P.: Heuristically Fast Finding of the Shortest Reducts. In: [16], (2004) 465-470
4. Pawlak, Z.: Decision Networks. In: [16], (2004) 1-7
5. Pawlak, Z.: Decisions rules and flow networks. *European Journal of Operational Research*, **154** (2004) 184-190
6. Pawlak, Z.: Flow graphs and decision algorithms. In: Wang, G.Y., et al, Eds., *Rough Sets,Fuzzy Sets,Data Mining and Granular Computing.* Springer, (2003) 1-11
7. Pawlak, Z.: Flow Graphs and Data Mining. In: Peters, J.F., Skowron, A., Eds., *Transactions on Rough Sets III*, Springer, (2005) 1-58
8. Pawlak, Z.: In Pursuit of Patterns in Data Reasoning from Data - The Rough Set Way. In: Proceedings of the 3rd of Rough Sets and Current Trends in Computing, (2002) 1-9
9. Pawlak, Z.: Probability,truth and flow graphs. In: Proceedings of the Workshop on Rough Sets in Knowledge Discovery and Soft Computing at ETAPS, (2003) 1-9
10. Pawlak, Z.: Rough Sets and Flow Graphs. In: [14], (2005) 1-11
11. Pawlak, Z.: Some Issues on Rough Sets. In: [12], (2004) 1-58
12. Peters, J.F., Skowron, A.(Eds.):*Transactions on Rough Sets I.* Springer-Verlag, Berlin (2004)
13. Skowron, A., Stepaniuk, J.: Information granules : towards foundations of granular computing. *International Journal of Intelligent Systems*, **16** (2001) 57-85
14. Ślęzak, D., et al.(Eds.): *Rough Sets, Fuzzy Sets, Data Mining and Granular Computing*, Springer-Verlag, Berlin (2005)
15. Sun, J., Liu, H., Zhang, H.: An Extension of Pawlak's Flow Graphs. In: Proceedings of the 1st International Conference on Rough Sets and Knowledge Technology. Chongqing, China(to appear) (2006)
16. Tsumoto, S., Słowiński, R., Komorowski, J.(Eds.): *Rough Sets and Current Trends in Computing.* RSCTC 2004, Springer (2004)
17. Yao, Y.Y.: A partition model of granular computing. In: [12], (2004) 232-253
18. Yao, Y.Y.: Perspectives of Granular Computing. In: Proceedings of 2005 IEEE International Conference on Granular Computing, **1** (2005) 85-90
19. Yao, Y.Y., Zhong, N.: Granular computing using information tables. In: Lin, T.Y., Yao, Y.Y., Zadeh, L.A., Eds., *Data Mining, Rough Sets and Granular Computing*, Physica-Verlag, Heidelberg (2002) 102-124
20. Zhang, L., Zhang, B.: The quotient space theory of problem solving, In: Wang, G.Y., et al, Eds., *Rough Sets,Fuzzy Sets,Data Mining and Granular Computing.* Springer (2003) 11-15
21. Zhang, C., Zhang, S.(Eds.): *Association Rule Mining: models and algorithms.* LNAI 2307, Springer-Verlag, Berlin (2002)

Attribute Reduction Based on Granular Computing[*]

Jun Hu[1,2], GuoYin Wang[1,2], QingHua Zhang[2,3], and XianQuan Liu[2,3]

[1] School of Electronic Engineering,
XiDian University,
Xi'an, Shaanxi, 710071, P.R. China
[2] Institute of Computer Science and Technology,
Chongqing University of Posts and Telecommunications,
Chongqing, 400065, P.R. China
[3] School of Information Science and Technology,
Southwest Jiaotong University,
Chengdu, Sichuan, 610031, P.R. China
{hujun, wanggy, zhangqh, liuxq}@cqupt.edu.cn

Abstract. Attribute reduction is a very important issue in data mining and machine learning. Granular computing is a new kind of soft computing theory. A novel method for encoding granules using bitmap technique is proposed in this paper. A new attribute reduction method based on granular computing is also developed with this encoding method. It is proved to be efficient.

Keywords: Granular computing, rough set, attribute reduction, bitmap technique.

1 Introduction

Attribute reduction is a very important issue in data mining and machine learning. It can reduce redundant attributes, simplify the structure of an information system, speed up the following process of rule induction, reduce the cost of instance classification, and even improve the performance of the generated rule systems. There are many methods for attribute reduction in rough set theory. Rough set theory was developed by Pawlak in 1982[1]. For its ability to process inconsistent and imperfect information, it has been applied successfully in many fields in the past years. A lot of attribute reduction algorithms based on rough set theory have been developed in the last decades, which can be classified into two categories: (1)attribute reduction from the view of algebra[2][3]; (2)attribute reduction from the view of information[4][5]. The challenging issues of

[*] This paper is supported by National Natural Science Foundation of P. R. China (No.60373111, No.60573068), Program for New Century Excellent Talents in University (NCET), Science & Technology Research Program of Chongqing Education Commission(No.040505), and Natural Science Foundation of Chongqing University of Posts and Telecommunications(A2006-56).

S. Greco et al. (Eds.): RSCTC 2006, LNAI 4259, pp. 458–466, 2006.

these methods are multiple computation for equivalent classes and huge number of objects. The major objective of this paper is to design an encoding method for granules based on bitmap, and develop an efficient method for attribute reduction.

The rest of this paper is organized as follows: basic concepts of granular computing are introduced in section 2. In section 3, an encoding method for granules using bitmap technique is developed. A new method for attribute reduction based on granular computing is proposed in section 4. Then section 5 try to prove the efficiency of this method by a simple simulation. At last this paper is concluded in section 6.

2 Basic Concepts of Granular Computing

In many cases, it is impossible or unnecessary to distinguish individual objects or elements in a universe, which force us to think of a subset of the universe as one unit, instead of many individuals. In other words, one has to consider groups, classes, or clusters of elements. They are referred to as granules. The concept of information granule was first introduced by Zadeh in 1979[6]. Information granules arise in the process of abstraction of data and derivation of knowledge from information[7].

Granular Computing (GrC) is an emerging conceptual and computing paradigm of information processing. As the name stipulates, GrC concerns processing with information granules. Ever since the introduction of the term of GrC by T.Y Lin in 1997[8], a rapid development of this topic has been observed. Many models and methods for granular computing have been proposed and studied[9][10][11].

Although there does not exist a general agreement about what is GrC, nor is there a unified model, the basic notions and principles are the same. Granular computing focuses on problem solving based on the commonsense concepts of granule, granularity, granulated view, and hierarchy. The objective of granular computing is to translate problems into a hierarchy structure, and search the solution by order relations. This method is also consistent with human problem solving experiences. It is a method simulating human problem solving.

3 Encoding Granules with Bitmap Technique

The construction of granular computing and computation with granules are the two basic issues of GrC. The former deals with the formation, representation, and interpretation of granules, while the later deals with the utilization of granules in problem solving[12]. The bitmap technique was proposed in the 1960's[13] and has been used by a variety of products since then. Recently, many attempts have been paid to applying bitmap techniques in knowledge discovery algorithms[14][15], for bitmaps improve the performance and reduce the storage requirement. In this section, we will introduce a method for encoding granules using bitmap.

3.1 Partition Matrix

It is convenient to describe a finite set of objects called the universe by a finite set of attributes in an information table[16]. Formally, an information table can be expressed as: $S(U, At, L, \{V_a \mid a \in At\}, \{I_a \mid a \in At\})$, where U is a finite nonempty set of objects, At is a finite nonempty set of attributes, L is a language defined using attributes in At, V_a is a nonempty set of values for $a \in At$, $I_a : U \to V_a$ is an information function. Each information function I_a is a total function that maps an object of U to exactly one value in V_a[17]. An information table could be encoded using bitmap, called encoding information table.

Table 1 is an example of information table.

Table 1. An information table

Object	Height	Hair	Eyes	Class
O_1	short	blond	blue	+
O_2	short	blond	brown	-
O_3	tall	red	blue	+
O_4	tall	dark	blue	-
O_5	tall	dark	blue	-
O_6	tall	blond	blue	+
O_7	tall	dark	brown	-
O_8	short	blond	brown	-

The encoding rule is as follows:

1. For every attribute $a \in At$, the code length of a is equal to the cardinality of V_a;

2. Every bit of the code denotes a value in V_a;

3. For every attribute value, its code can be represented by a $\mid V_a \mid$-length bitmap, in which the corresponding bit is set to be 1, other bits 0.

For example, the cardinality of *Height* is 2, so the length of its code is two. Let the first bit denote *short* and the second bit *tall*. The attribute value *tall* will be encoded as 01, and *short* as 10. According to this rule, the information table shown in Table 1 could be encoded like Table 2.

Each subset A of At determines an equivalent relation on U, in which two objects are equivalent iff they have exact the same values under A[18]. An equivalence relation divides a universal set into a family of pair-wise disjoint subsets, called the partition of the universe. Here we use a matrix to represent a partition induced by an attribute. For an attribute $a \in At$ in an information system S, the partition matrix can be defined as $P(a) = \{P_a(i,j)\}_{n \times n}, 1 \leq i, j \leq n = \mid U \mid$, where

$$P_a(i,j) = \begin{cases} 1, & I_a(i) = I_a(j) \\ 0, & else \end{cases} \tag{1}$$

To generate the partition matrix on an attribute, the traditional way, according to above definition, is to compare the attribute values and $P_a(i,j)$ is set to

Table 2. Encoded information table

Object	Height	Hair	Eyes	Class
O_1	10	100	10	10
O_2	10	100	01	01
O_3	01	010	10	10
O_4	01	001	10	01
O_5	01	001	10	01
O_6	01	100	10	10
O_7	01	001	01	01
O_8	10	100	01	01

be 1 if the object i and j have the same value on attribute a, otherwise $P_a(i,j)$ is set to be 0. Here we could have another way using bitmap. In terms of the definition of the encoded information table, if two objects have the same value on an attribute, then they have the same code value on this attribute. To judge whether two objects have the same code value, the logic operation AND can be applied, i.e. $P_a(i,j)$ is set to be 1 for the result of non-zero, otherwise is set to be 0. Because the partition is symmetrical, it can be simplified to reduce the storage. For example, Table 3 is the partition matrix on *Height*, and Table 4 is the partition matrix on *Eyes*.

Table 3. Partition matrix on *Height*

P_{Height}	O_1	O_2	O_3	O_4	O_5	O_6	O_7	O_8
O_1	1							
O_2	1	1						
O_3	0	0	1					
O_4	0	0	1	1				
O_5	0	0	1	1	1			
O_6	0	0	1	1	1	1		
O_7	0	0	1	1	1	1	1	
O_8	1	1	0	0	0	0	0	1

Table 4. Partition matrix on *Eyes*

P_{Eyes}	O_1	O_2	O_3	O_4	O_5	O_6	O_7	O_8
O_1	1							
O_2	0	1						
O_3	1	0	1					
O_4	1	0	1	1				
O_5	1	0	1	1	1			
O_6	1	0	1	1	1	1		
O_7	0	1	0	0	0	0	1	
O_8	0	1	0	0	0	0	1	1

Having the partition matrix on each attribute, the partition matrix on a subset of At can be further computed. For a subset A of At, the partition matrix $P(A) = \{P_A(i,j)\}_{n \times n}, 1 \leq i, j \leq n = \mid U \mid$, can be computed using the following formula:

$$P_A(i,j) = P_{a_1}(i,j)\,AND\,P_{a_2}(i,j)\,AND...AND\,P_{a_m}(i,j),\ a_1, a_2...a_m \in A \quad (2)$$

For instance, we can get the partition on {*Height, Eyes*} based on the above two partition matrixes. It is shown in Table 5.

For convenience, we complement the partition matrix by symmetry. A partition matrix represents the equivalence relation holding between all the objects. In each line or column of a partition matrix, the subset consists of all objects which

Table 5. Partition matrix on $\{Height, Eyes\}$

$P_{\{Height,Eyes\}}$	O_1	O_2	O_3	O_4	O_5	O_6	O_7	O_8
O_1	1	0	0	0	0	0	0	0
O_2	0	1	0	0	0	0	0	1
O_3	0	0	1	1	1	1	0	0
O_4	0	0	1	1	1	1	0	0
O_5	0	0	1	1	1	1	0	0
O_6	0	0	1	1	1	1	0	0
O_7	0	0	0	0	0	0	1	0
O_8	0	1	0	0	0	0	0	1

are equivalent to the object denoted by the line. In other words, every line or column represents an equivalence class. Using partition matrix, we can easily get all equivalent classes, for example, $U/\{Height, Eyes\} = \{\{O_1\}, \{O_2, O_8\}, \{O_3, O_4, O_5, O_6\}, \{O_7\}\}$. Moreover, the computing process is incremental, that is, we can get the partition on $\{Height, Eyes\}$ step by step.

3.2   Computation with Encoded Granules

In the partition model, a granule is a subset of the universe. The objects in a granule are gathered together by indiscernibility. On the other hand, a formula put the objects satisfying the formula in a granule. Therefore, we have a formal description of a granule. A definable granule in an information table is a pair $(\phi, m(\phi))$, where $\phi \in L$, and $m(\phi)$ is the set of all objects having the property expressed by the formula ϕ. In other words, ϕ can be viewed as the description of the set of objects $m(\phi)$. For $\phi, \psi \in L$, the following properties hold[16]:

(1) $m(\neg\phi) = \neg m(\phi)$
(2) $m(\phi \wedge \psi) = m(\phi) \cap m(\psi)$
(3) $m(\phi \vee \psi) = m(\phi) \cup m(\psi)$

Suppose the cardinalities of $m(\phi), m(\psi)$ and U are p, q and n respectively. The time complexities for calculating $m(\phi), m(\phi \wedge \psi)$ and $m(\phi \vee \psi)$ are $O(pn), O(pq)$ and $O(pq)$ respectively using traditional set operation. In the following paragraph, an encoding method for granules will be introduced. The time complexities of the above three computations will be reduced obviously with it.

Suppose the number of objects in the universe is n, then the length of code is n, and every bit denotes an object in the universe. Given a granule, if an object of the universe belongs to the granule, then the corresponding bit is set to be 1, otherwise, 0. A granule encoded by this rule is called as an encoded granule. According to the definition, the empty set is encoded by $\underbrace{00...0}_{n}$, and the universe $\underbrace{11...1}_{n}$, labeled as G_ϕ and G_U respectively.

Using encoded granules, the set operation of granules can be translated into logic operation (AND, OR, NOT, XOR) on codes of encoded granules.

Let $(\phi, m(\phi))$ and $(\psi, m(\psi))$ be two granules, and their codes is $a_1 a_2 ... a_n$, $b_1 b_2 ... b_n$, where n is the cardinality of the universe. The complement, intersection and union are defined as:

(1) $m(\neg\phi) = NOT\ a_1 a_2 ... a_n$
(2) $m(\phi \wedge \psi) = a_1 a_2 ... a_n\ AND\ b_1 b_2 ... b_n$
(3) $m(\phi \vee \psi) = a_1 a_2 ... a_n\ OR\ b_1 b_2 ... b_n$

Based on the above analysis, if we use set operation, the time complexity of complement, intersection and union are $O(np), O(pq)$ and $O(pq)$, while the time complexity is $O(p), O(p+q)$ and $O(p+q)$ respectively using logic operation.

We often need to determine whether a granule is included in another granule. If we check every object one by one, the complexity is $O(pq)$. Here we can get a simplified method with encoded granules, and its complexity is $O(p+q)$. If $((\phi, m(\phi))\ AND\ (\psi, m(\psi)))\ XOR\ (\phi, m(\phi)) = 0$, $(\phi, m(\phi))$ is included in $(\psi, m(\psi))$. For example, $\{O_2, O_4\}$ and $\{O_2, O_4, O_5\}$ are encoded as 01010000 and 01011000 respectively. Because (01010000 AND 01011000) XOR 01010000 $= 0$, we can conclude that $\{O_2, O_4\}$ is included in $\{O_2, O_4, O_5\}$, while needn't to check every object one by one. So, this method is more efficient than the traditional way.

Each equivalent class is a subset of the universe. It is a granule also. Therefore, every equivalent class can be encoded using the method developed in the last section. For example, $\{10000000, 01000001, 00111100, 00000010\}$ is the code of $U/\{Height, Eyes\}$. Comparing these codes with Table 5, we can find that each line or column of a partition matrix is a code of an equivalent class.

In conclusion, the partition matrix not only describes the relationship between objects, but also gives the codes of equivalent classes. In this way, the challenging issues of attribute reduction can be solved by partition matrix and encoded granules.

4   Attribute Reduction Based on Granular Computing

Attribute reduction aims to find minimal subsets of attributes, each of which has the same discrimination power as the entire attributes. A minimal subset of attributes is called a reduction if it cannot be further reduced without affecting the essential information. Owning to the limitation of space, the basic concepts about attribute reduction is omitted here, but one can consult them in [19].

Attribute reductions based on algebra and information views were discussed in [18]. Although their definitions are different, both of them need to compute equivalent classes, so we can use the methods developed in the last section. Moreover, the set operation can be replaced by logic operation, which could improve the performance.

Let S be an information system. Using partition matrix we can get the codes of equivalent classes on condition attributes and decision attributes. Suppose they are $\{C_1, C_2, ..., C_i\}$ and $\{D_1, D_2, ..., D_j\}$, we can develop the following algorithm to compute the positive region of C with respect to D.

Algorithm 1 (Computing Positive region of C with respect to D)
Input: $IND(C) = \{C_1, C_2, ..., C_i\}$ and $IND(D) = \{D_1, D_2, ..., D_j\}$
Output: The positive region of C with respect to D, $POS_C(D)$
Step 1: Let $POS_C(D) = G_\phi$
Step 2: If $IND(C) \neq \phi$, then select an element C_m from $IND(C)$, let $IND(C) = IND(C) - \{C_m\}$, $T = IND(D)$. Otherwise go to Step 5
Step 3: If $T \neq \phi$, then select an element D_n from $IND(D)$, let $T = T - \{D_n\}$, $t = C_m\ AND\ D_n$
Step 4: If $t = 0$, then go to Step 3. Otherwise if $t\ XOR\ C_m = 0$, then let $POS_C(D) = POS_C(D)\ OR\ C_m$. Go to Step 2
Step 5: End

According to the definition of attribute reduction in the algebra view, here we can develop a new attribute reduction algorithm.

Algorithm 2 (Attribute Reduction Based on Granular Computing, $ARBGrC$)
Input: An information system S
Output: A reduction of condition attribute C, $RED(C)$
Step 1: Let $RED(C) = \phi$, $A = C$, compute the significance of each attribute $a \in A$, and sort the set of attributes based on significance
Step 2: Compute $POS_C(D)$ with Algorithm 1
Step 3: Compute $POS_{RED(C)}(D)$ with Algorithm 1
Step 4: If $(POS_{RED(C)}(D)\ XOR\ POS_C(D))=0$, then let $A = RED(C)$, go to Step 6
Step 5: Select an attribute a from A with the highest significant value, $RED(C) = RED(C) \cup \{a\}$, $A = A - \{a\}$, go to Step 3
Step 6: If $A = \phi$, then go to Step 8. Otherwise, select an attribute a from A, $A = A - \{a\}$
Step 7: Compute $POS_{RED(C)-\{a\}}(D)$ with Algorithm 1, if $POS_C(D)\ XOR$ $POS_{RED(C)-\{a\}}(D) = 0$, then let $RED(C) = RED(C) - \{a\}$. go to Step 6
Step 8: End

The time complexity of $ARBGrC$ is $O(mn^2)$, where n is the number of objects and m is the number of attributes.

5   Simulation Result

In order to test the efficiency of $ARBGrC$ algorithm, we compare it with other two algorithms. One is the algorithm introduced in [19] whose time complexity is $O(m^2n^2)$, the other is the algorithm developed in [20] whose time complexity is $O(m^2nlogn)$. These two algorithms are labeled as Algorithm 3 and Algorithm 4 respectively in Table 6. We implement all algorithms using Visual C++6.0. Some classical data sets from UCI used by many other researchers are used in our experiment. To make the test result more validity, every algorithm on each data set was tested 100 times, and the time consuming is their average. For the reason of simplification, we might suppose NI is the number of instances, NOA is the number of original attributes, NAR is the number of attributes after reduction and TC is the time consuming. The experiment results are shown in Table 6.

Table 6. Test result for different algorithms

Data set	NI	NOA	Algorithm 3		Algorithm 4		ARBGrC	
			NAR	TC(s)	NAR	TC(s)	NAR	TC(s)
Zoo	101	16	5	0.0745323	5	0.0236871	5	0.0199314
Glass	214	9	8	0.1363940	8	0.0436963	8	0.0439632
Wine	178	13	2	0.1882960	2	0.1238230	2	0.0251350
Bupa	345	6	3	0.3069120	3	0.1986720	3	0.0435812
Letter-recognition	5000	16	9	202.7750	10	138.4930	9	58.9536

From the experiment, we can find that the results are almost the same in NAR, while different in TC. More concretely, these three algorithms have the same NAR, except that Algorithm 4 got 10 attributes on Letter-recognition, while the other two algorithms got 9 attributes. Moreover, Algorithm 4 has higher speed than Algorithm 3, and $ARBGrC$ consumes less time than Algorithm 4 except on Glass. From the view of time complexity, Algorithm 4 and $ARBGrC$ are better than Algorithm 3, but it is difficult to say which one is better than the other of these two algorithms. Theoretically, Algorithm 4 is better than $ARBGrC$ when $n/\log_2 n$ is greater than m, while $ARBGrC$ is better than Algorithm 4 when m is greater than $n/\log_2 n$. However, from the view of computing method, bitmap technique is applied in $ARBGrC$, which is machine oriented, and makes the computing positive region process incremental, avoiding computing repeatedly. For this reason, $ARBGrC$ is more effective than the other two algorithms in time consuming.

6   Conclusion

As a new general computation theory, granular computing has appeared in many related fields. Granule is everywhere, such as classes, clusters, subsets, groups and intervals. Computing with granules can improve the performance, and reduce the time complexity, etc. An encoding method for granules using bitmap is proposed in this paper. Based on it, a new method of attribute reduction is developed. Compared with former methods, this method translates the set operation into logic operation, which improves the performance. This method can be also used in other fields, such as distributed data processing, and this will be our future work.

References

1. Pawlak,Z.: Rough set. *International Journal of Computer and Information Sciences.* 11(1982)341-356
2. Hu,X.H.: Mining Knowledge Rules from Database: A Rough Set Approach. Proceedings of the Twelfth International Conference on Data Engineering. (1996)96-105

3. Chang,L.Y., Wang,G.Y., and Wu,Y.: An Approach for Attribute Reduction and Rule Generation Based on Rough Set Theory. *Chinese Journal of Software.* 10(1999)1206-1211

4. Wang,G.Y., Yu,H., and Yang,D.C.: Decision Table Reduction Based on Conditional Information Entropy. *Chinese Journal of Computers.* 25(2002)759-766

5. Wang,G.Y., Yu,H., Yang,D.C., and Wu,Z.F.: Knowledge Reduction Based on Rough Set and Information Entropy. The 5th World Multi-Conference on Systemics and Informatics. (2001)555-560

6. Zadeh,L.A.: Fuzzy sets and information granularity. In Advances in Fuzzy Set Theory and Applications, Gupta, N., Ragade, R., Yager, R. (Eds.). North-Holland, Amsterdam. (1979)3-18

7. Pedrycz,W.: *Granular computing: An Introduction.* Kluwer Academic Publishers(2001)

8. Lin,T.Y.: Granular computing, announcement of the BISC Special Interest Group on Granular Computing(1997)

9. Zadeh,L.A.: Towards a theory of fuzzy information granulation and its centrality in human reasoning and fuzzy logic. *Fuzzy Sets and Systems.* 90(1997)111-127

10. Yao,Y.Y.: A partition model of granular computing. LNCS Transactions on Rough Sets. (2004)232-253

11. Ma,J.M.: A covering model of granular computing. Proceedings of the Fourth International Conference on Machine Learning and Cybernetics, Guangzhou. (2005)1625-1630

12. Yao,Y.Y.: Granular computing: basic issues and possible solutions. Proceedings of the 5th Joint Conference on Information Sciences. (2000)186-189

13. Bertino,E., etc.: *Indexing techniques for advanced database system.* Kluwer Academic Publisher(1997)

14. Lin,T.Y.: Data mining and machine oriented modeling: a granular computing approach. *Journal of Applied Intelligence.* 10(2000) 113-124

15. Louie,E., Lin,T.Y.: Finding association rules using fast bit computation: machine-oriented modeling. Proceedings of the 12th International Symposium on Foundations of Intelligent Systems. (2000)486-494

16. Pawlak,Z.: *Rough Sets, Theoretical Aspects of Reasoning about Data.* Kluwer Academic Publishers, Dordrecht(1991)

17. Yao,Y.Y.: Modeling data mining with granular computing. Proceedings of the 25th Annual International Computer Software and Applications Conference. (2001)638-643

18. Wang,G.Y., Zhao,J., An,J.J., Wu,Y.: Theoretical Study on Attribute Reduction of Rough Set Theory: in Algebra View and Information View. Third International Conference on Cognitive Informatics. (2004) 148-155

19. Wang,G.Y.: *Rough Set Theory and Knowledge Acquisition.* Xi'an: Xi'an Jiaotong University Press(2001)

20. Liu,S.H., Sheng,Q.J., Wu,B., Shi,Z.Z., Hu,F.: Research on Efficient Algorithms for Rough Set Methods. *Chinese Journal of Computers.* 26(2003)524-529

Methodological Identification of Information Granules-Based Fuzzy Systems by Means of Genetic Optimization

Sung-Kwun Oh[1], Keon-Jun Park[1], and Witold Pedrycz[2]

[1] Department of Electrical Engineering, The University of Suwon, San 2-2 Wau-ri,
Bongdam-eup, Hwaseong-si, Gyeonggi-do, 445-743, South Korea
ohsk@suwon.ac.kr
[2] Department of Electrical and Computer Engineering, University of Alberta, Edmonton,
AB T6G 2G6, Canada and Systems Research Institute, Polish Academy of Sciences, Warsaw,
Poland

Abstract. In this study, we introduce an information granules-based fuzzy systems and a methodological identification by means of genetic optimization to carry out the model identification of complex and nonlinear systems. Information granulation realized with Hard C-Means clustering help determine the initial parameters of fuzzy model such as the initial apexes of the membership functions in the premise part and the initial values of polynomial functions in the consequence part of the fuzzy rules. And the initial parameters are tuned effectively with the aid of the genetic algorithms and the least square method. The design methodology emerges as a hybrid structural optimization and parametric optimization. Especially, genetic algorithms (GAs) and HCM clustering are used to generate the structurally as well as parametrically optimized fuzzy model. To identify the structure and parameters of fuzzy model we exploit the methodologies of a respective and consecutive identification by means of genetic algorithms. The proposed model is contrasted with the performance of the conventional fuzzy models in the literature.

1 Introduction

Fuzzy modeling has been a focal point of the technology of fuzzy sets from its very inception. Fuzzy modeling has been studied to deal with complex, ill-defined, and uncertain systems in many other avenues. The researches on the process have been exploited for a long time. Linguistic modeling [2], [3] and fuzzy relation equation-based approach [4], [5] were proposed as primordial identification methods for fuzzy models. The general class of Sugeno-Takagi models [6] gave rise to more sophisticated rule-based systems where the rules come with conclusions forming local regression models. While appealing with respect to the basic topology (a modular fuzzy model composed of a series of rules) [7], [8], these models still await formal solutions as far as the structure optimization of the model is concerned, say a construction of the underlying fuzzy sets—information granules being viewed as basic building blocks of any fuzzy model. Some enhancements to the model have been proposed by Oh and Pedrycz [9], yet the problem of finding "good" initial parameters of the fuzzy sets in the rules remains open.

S. Greco et al. (Eds.): RSCTC 2006, LNAI 4259, pp. 467–476, 2006.

This study concentrates on the central problem of fuzzy modeling that is a development of information granules-fuzzy sets. Taking into consideration the essence of the granulation process, we propose to cast the problem in the setting of clustering techniques and genetic algorithms. The design methodology emerges as a hybrid structural optimization (based on Hard C-Means (HCM) clustering and genetic optimization) and parametric optimization (based on least square method (LSM), as well as HCM clustering and genetic optimization). Information granulation with the aid of HCM clustering help determine the initial parameters of fuzzy model such as the initial apexes of the membership functions and the initial values of polynomial function being used in the premise and consequence part of the fuzzy rules. And the initial parameters are tuned (adjusted) effectively by means of the genetic algorithms and the least square method. And to identify the structure and parameters of fuzzy model we exploit two methodologies of a respective and consecutive identification by means of genetic algorithms. The proposed model is through intensive numeric experimentation.

2   Information Granules

Roughly speaking, information granules (IG) [10], [11] are viewed as related collections of objects (data point, in particular) drawn together by the criteria of proximity, similarity, or functionality. Granulation of information is an inherent and omnipresent activity of human beings carried out with intent of gaining a better insight into a problem under consideration and arriving at its efficient solution. In particular, granulation of information is aimed at transforming the problem at hand into several smaller and therefore manageable tasks. In this way, we partition this problem into a series of well-defined subproblems (modules) of a far lower computational complexity than the original one. The form of information granulation themselves becomes an important design feature of the fuzzy model, which are geared toward capturing relationships between information granules.

It is worth emphasizing that the HCM clustering has been used extensively not only to organize and categorize data, but it becomes useful in data compression and model identification. For the sake of completeness of the entire discussion, let us briefly recall the essence of the HCM algorithm [12].

We obtain the matrix representation for hard c-partition, defined as follows.

$$M_C = \left\{ \mathbf{U} \mid u_{gi} \in \{0,1\}, \ \sum_{g=1}^{c} u_{gi} = 1, \ 0 < \sum_{i=1}^{m} u_{gi} < m \right\} \tag{1}$$

[Step 1] Fix the number of clusters $c(2 \leq c < m)$ and initialize the partition matrix $\mathbf{U}^{(0)} \in M_C$

[Step 2] Calculate the center vectors $\mathbf{v}_g$ of each cluster:

$$\mathbf{v}_g^{(r)} = \{v_{g1}, \ v_{g2}, \cdots, \ v_{gk}, \cdots, \ v_{gl}\} \tag{2}$$

$$v_{gk}^{(r)} = \sum_{i=1}^{m} u_{gi}^{(r)} \cdot x_{ik} \left/ \sum_{i=1}^{m} u_{gi}^{(r)} \right. \tag{3}$$

Where, $[u_{gi}] = \mathbf{U}^{(r)}$, $g = 1, 2, \ldots, c$, $k = 1, 2, \ldots, l$.

[Step 3] Update the partition matrix $\mathbf{U}^{(r)}$; these modifications are based on the standard Euclidean distance function between the data points and the prototypes,

$$d_{gi} = d(\mathbf{x}_i - \mathbf{v}_g) = \left\| \mathbf{x}_i - \mathbf{v}_g \right\| = \left[\sum_{k=1}^{l} (x_{ik} - v_{gk})^2 \right]^{1/2} \tag{4}$$

$$u_{gi}^{(r+1)} = \begin{cases} 1 & d_{gi}^{(r)} = \min\{d_{ki}^{(r)}\} \text{ for all } k \in c \\ 0 & \text{otherwise} \end{cases} \tag{5}$$

[Step 4] Check a termination criterion. If

$$\| \mathbf{U}^{(r+1)} - \mathbf{U}^{(r)} \| \leq \varepsilon \quad \text{(tolerance level)} \tag{6}$$

Stop ; otherwise set $r = r + 1$ and return to **[Step 2]**

3   Information Granules-Based Fuzzy Systems

The identification procedure for fuzzy models is usually split into the identification activities dealing with the premise and consequence parts of the rules. The identification completed at the premise level consists of two main steps. First, we select the input variables x_1, x_2, …, x_k of the rules. Second, we form fuzzy partitions of the spaces over which these individual variables are defined. The identification of the consequence part of the rules embraces two phases, namely 1) a selection of the consequence variables of the fuzzy rules, and 2) determination of the parameters of the consequence (conclusion part). And the least square error method used at the parametric optimization of the consequence parts of the successive rules.

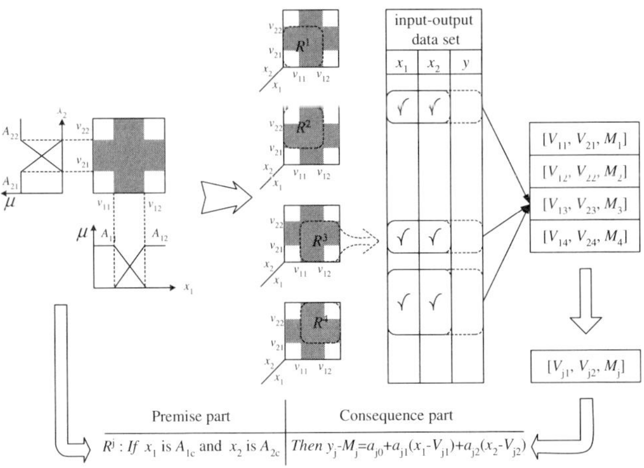

Fig. 1. IG-based fuzzy systems; illustrate is a case of the two-input single-output system

In this study, we carry out the modeling using characteristics of experimental data. The HCM clustering addresses this issue. Subsequently we design the fuzzy model by considering the centers (prototypes) of clusters. In this manner the clustering help us determine the initial parameters of fuzzy model such as the initial apexes of the membership functions in the premise and the initial values of polynomial function in the consequence part of the fuzzy rules. The design process of fuzzy model based on information granules for two-input single-output system is visualized in figure 1. Here, V_{jk} and M_j is a center value of the input and output data, respectively.

3.1 Premise Identification

In the premise part of the rules, we confine ourselves to a triangular type of membership functions whose parameters are subject to some optimization. The HCM clustering helps us organize the data into cluster so in this way we capture the characteristics of the experimental data. In the regions where some clusters of data have been identified, we end up with some fuzzy sets that help reflect the specificity of the data set. In the sequel, the modal values of the clusters are refined (optimized) using genetic optimization, and genetic algorithms (GAs), in particular.

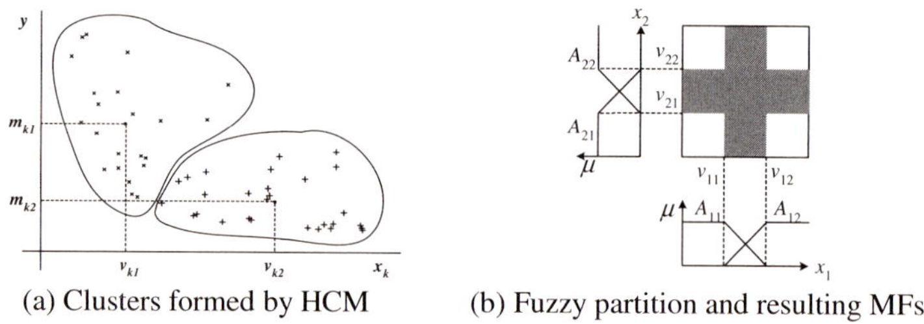

(a) Clusters formed by HCM   (b) Fuzzy partition and resulting MFs

Fig. 2. Identification of the premise part of the rules of the system

The identification of the premise part is completed in the following manner.

Given is a set of data $\mathbf{U}=\{\mathbf{x}_1, \mathbf{x}_2, \ldots, \mathbf{x}_l ; \mathbf{y}\}$, where $\mathbf{x}_k =[\mathrm{x}_{1k}, \ldots, \mathrm{x}_{mk}]^{\mathrm{T}}$, $\mathbf{y} =[\mathrm{y}_1, \ldots, \mathrm{y}_m]^{\mathrm{T}}$, l is the number of variables and , m is the number of data.

[Step 1] Arrange a set of data $\mathbf{U}$ into data set $\mathbf{X}_k$ composed of respective input data and output data.

$$\mathbf{X}_k=[\mathbf{x}_k ; \mathbf{y}] \tag{7}$$

[Step 2] Complete the HCM clustering to determine the centers (prototypes) $\mathbf{v}_{kg}$ with data set $\mathbf{X}_k$.

[Step 2-1] Categorize data set $\mathbf{X}_k$ into c-clusters (in essence this is effectively the granulation of information)

[Step 2-2] Calculate the center vectors $\mathbf{v}_{kg}$ of each cluster.

$$\mathrm{v}_{kg} = \{v_{k1}, \ v_{k2}, \ldots, v_{kc}\} \tag{8}$$

[Step 3] Partition the corresponding input space using the prototypes of the clusters $\mathbf{v}_{kg}$. Associate each cluster with some meaning (semantics), say Small, Big, etc.

[Step 4] Set the initial apexes of the membership functions using the prototypes $\mathbf{v}_{kg}$.

3.2 Consequence Identification

We identify the structure considering the initial values of polynomial functions based upon the information granulation realized for the consequence and antecedents parts.

[Step 1] Find a set of data included in the fuzzy space of the j-th rule.
[Step 2] Compute the prototypes $\mathbf{V}_j$ of the data set by taking the arithmetic mean of each rule.

$$\mathbf{V}_j = \{V_{1j}, V_{2j}, \ldots, V_{kj}; M_j\} \tag{9}$$

[Step 3] Set the initial values of polynomial functions with the center vectors $\mathbf{V}_j$.

The identification of the conclusion parts of the rules deals with a selection of their structure that is followed by the determination of the respective parameters of the local functions occurring there.
The conclusion is expressed as follows.

$$R^j : If\ x_1\ is\ A_{1c}\ and\ \cdots\ and\ x_k\ is\ A_{kc}\ then\ y_j - M_j = f_j(x_1,\cdots,x_k) \tag{10}$$

Type 1 (Simplified Inference): $f_j = a_{j0}$

Type 2 (Linear Inference): $f_j = a_{j0} + a_{j1}(x_1 - V_{j1}) + \cdots + a_{jk}(x_k - V_{jk})$

Type 3 (Quadratic Inference):

$$f_j = a_{j0} + a_{j1}(x_1 - V_{1j}) + \cdots + a_{jk}(x_k - V_{kj}) + a_{j(k+1)}(x_1 - V_{1j})^2 + \cdots + a_{j(2k)}(x_k - V_{kj})^2$$
$$+ a_{j(2k+1)}(x_1 - V_{1j})(x_2 - V_{2j}) + \cdots + a_{j((k+2)(k+1)/2)}(x_{k-1} - V_{(k-1)j})(x_k - V_{kj}) \tag{11}$$

Type 4 (Modified Quadratic Inference):
$$f_j = a_{j0} + a_{j1}(x_1 - V_{1j}) + \cdots + a_{jk}(x_k - V_{kj}) + a_{j(k+1)}(x_1 - V_{1j})(x_2 - V_{2j})$$
$$+ \cdots + a_{j(k(k+1)/2)}(x_{k-1} - V_{(k-1)j})(x_k - V_{kj})$$

The calculations of the numeric output of the model, based on the activation (matching) levels of the rules there, rely on the expression

$$y^* = \frac{\sum_{j=1}^{n} w_{ji} y_i}{\sum_{j=1}^{n} w_{ji}} = \frac{\sum_{j=1}^{n} w_{ji}(f_j(x_1,\cdots,x_k) + M_j)}{\sum_{j=1}^{n} w_{ji}} = \sum_{j=1}^{n} \hat{w}_{ji}(f_j(x_1,\cdots,x_k) + M_j) \tag{12}$$

Here, as the normalized value of w_{ji}, we use an abbreviated notation to describe an activation level of rule R^j to be in the form

$$\hat{w}_{ji} = \frac{w_{ji}}{\sum_{j=1}^{n} w_{ji}} \tag{13}$$

If the input variables of the premise and parameters are given in consequence parameter identification, the optimal consequence parameters that minimize the assumed performance index can be determined. In what follows, we define the performance index as the root mean squared error (RMSE).

$$PI = \frac{1}{m}\sum_{i=1}^{m}(y_i - y_i^*)^2 \tag{14}$$

The minimal value produced by the least-squares method is governed by the following expression:

$$\hat{\mathbf{a}} = (\mathbf{X}^T\mathbf{X})^{-1}\mathbf{X}^T\mathbf{Y} \tag{15}$$

4   Optimization of IG-Based FIS

The need to solve optimization problems arises in many fields and is especially dominant in the engineering environment. There are several analytic and numerical optimization techniques, but there are still large classes of functions that are fully addressed by these techniques. Especially, the standard gradient-based optimization techniques that are being used mostly at the present time are augmented by a differential method of solving search problems for optimization processes. Therefore, the optimization of fuzzy models may not be fully supported by the standard gradient-based optimization techniques, because of the nonlinearity of fuzzy models represented by rules based on linguistic levels. This forces us to explore other optimization techniques such as genetic algorithms. It has been demonstrated that genetic algorithms [13] are useful in a global optimization of such problems given their ability to efficiently use historical information to produce new improved solutions with enhanced performance.

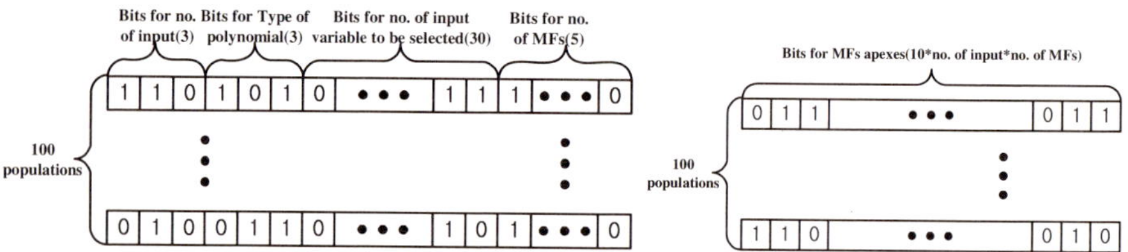

(a) Data structure for structure or parameters identification in respective method

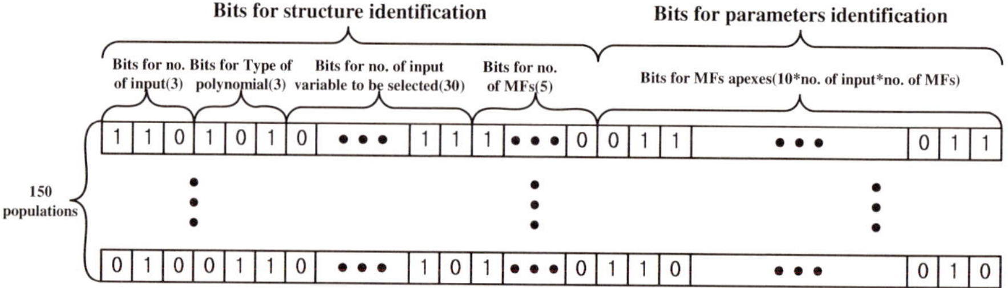

(b) Data structure for structure and parameters identification in consecutive method

Fig. 3. Data structure of genetic algorithms used for the optimization of the fuzzy model

In this study, in order to identify the fuzzy model we determine such a structure as the number of input variables, input variables being selected and the number of the membership functions standing in the premise part and the order of polynomial (Type) in conclusion. The membership parameters of the premise are genetically optimized. For the identification of the system we conduct two methods as a respective and a consecutive method. The former is that the structure of the system is identified first and then the parameters are identified later. And the latter is that the structure and parameters is simultaneously identified in the consecutive chromosomes arrangement. Figure 3 shows an arrangement of the content of the string to be used in genetic optimization. Here, parentheses denote the number of chromosomes allocated to each parameter. For the optimization of the fuzzy model, genetic algorithms use the serial method of binary type, roulette-wheel in the selection operator, one-point crossover in the crossover operator, and invert in the mutation operator. In the case of respective method we use 150 generations and run the GA of a size of 100 individuals for structure identification and GA was run for 300 generations and the population was of size 100. In the other case we use 300 generations and run the GA of a size of 150 individuals. We set up the crossover rate and mutation probability to be equal to 0.6, and 0.1, respectively (the choice of these specific values of the parameters is a result of intensive experimentation; as a matter of fact, those are quite similar to the values reported in the literature).

5 Experimental Studies

This section includes comprehensive numeric study illustrating the design of the proposed fuzzy model. We illustrate the performance of the model and elaborate on its development by experimenting with data coming from the gas furnace process. The time series data (296 input-output pairs) resulting from the gas furnace process has been intensively studied in the previous literatures [9,16,17]. The delayed terms of methane gas flow rate $u(t)$ and carbon dioxide density $y(t)$ are used as six input variables with vector formats such as [$u(t$-3), $u(t$-2), $u(t$-1), $y(t$-3), $y(t$-2), $y(t$-1)]. And as output variable $y(t)$ is used. The first one (consisting of 148 pairs) was used for training. The remaining part of the series serves as a testing set. We consider the MSE (14) being regarded here as a performance index.

We carried out the identification on a basis of the experimental data using GAs to design Max_Min-based and IG-based fuzzy model. The maximal number of input variables was set to be equal to 2 from above the type of vector format. In the case of the fuzzy model by the respective identification, the input variables were picked up to be $y(t$-2), $y(t$-1) for Max_Min-based fuzzy model and $u(t$-3), $y(t$-1) for IG-based fuzzy model. To evaluate the proposed model we designed the Max_Min-based and IG-based fuzzy model for each model. In case of input variables of $y(t$-2), $y(t$-1), the number of membership functions assigned to each input was set up to be 3, 2 and the other was set up to be 3 for each input. At the conclusion part, each model comes with the consequence Type 2 and Type 4, respectively. For each fuzzy model, we conducted the optimization of the parameters of the premise membership functions. In the case of the fuzzy model by the consecutive identification, the input variables were picked up to be $u(t$-3), $y(t$-1) for both of fuzzy models. The number of membership functions assigned to each input was set up to be 3, 2 and 2,3 for each input, respectively. At the conclusion part, each model comes with the consequence Type 3. Table 1 summarizes the performance index for Max_Min-based and IG-based fuzzy model by means of two methodologies. From the Table 1 we know that the performance of IG-based fuzzy model is better than the Max_Min-based fuzzy model.

Table 1. Performance index of Max_Min-based and IG-based fuzzy model

Model	Identification Method	Input variable	No. Of MFs	Type	PI	E_PI
Max/Min_FIS	respective	S^*				0.092	0.212
		P^*	$y(t-2)$	3x2	Type 2	0.090	0.204
IG_FIS		S	$y(t-1)$			0.085	0.218
		P				0.087	0.197
Max/Min_FIS	respective	S				0.017	0.297
		P	$u(t-3)$	3x3	Type 4	0.016	0.270
IG_FIS		S^*	$y(t-1)$			0.015	0.281
		P^*				0.015	0.256
Max/Min_FIS	consecutive	S+P	$u(t-3)$ $y(t-1)$	3x2	Type 3	0.016	0.268
IG_FIS	consecutive	S+P	$u(t-3)$ $y(t-1)$	2x3	Type 3	0.014	0.266

* identified structure by Gas, S: Structure identification, P: Parameters identification respective and consecutive mean respective and consecutive tuning respectively

Figure 4 and 5 depict the values of the performance index produced in successive generation of the GAs. It is obvious that the performance of an IG-based fuzzy model is good from initial generation due to the characteristics of input-output data.

The identification error (performance index) of the proposed model is also compared to the performance of some other models in Table 2. The performance of the proposed model is better in the sense of its approximation and prediction abilities than other works studied in the literatures as shown in Table 2.

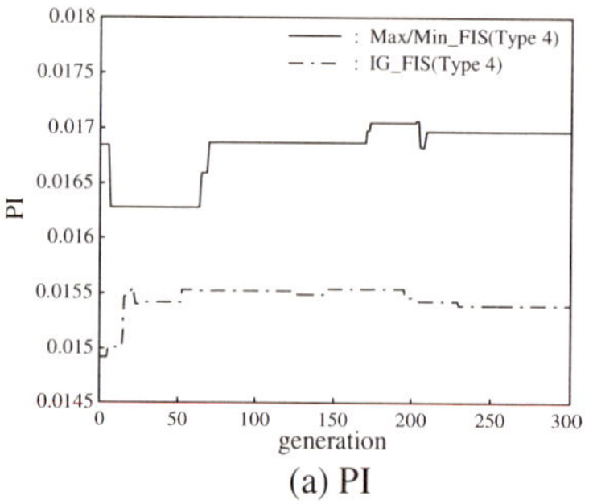

(a) PI

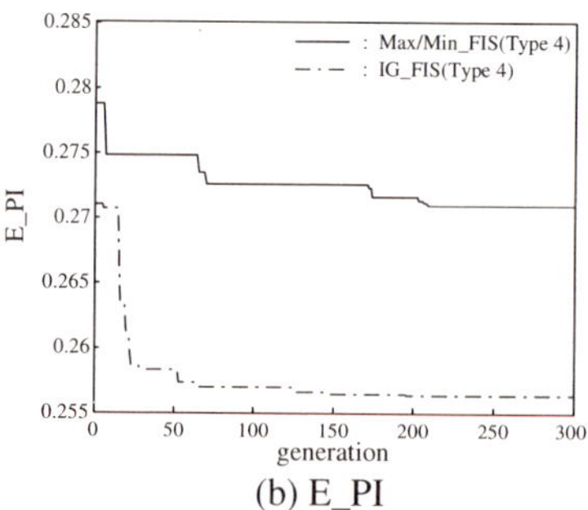

(b) E_PI

Fig. 4. Optimal convergence process of performance index for Max_Min-based and IG-based fuzzy model by means of the respective identification ($u(t-3)$, $y(t-1)$)

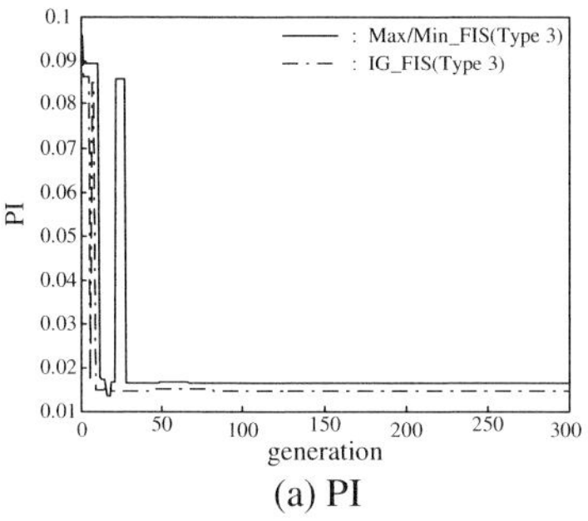

(a) PI

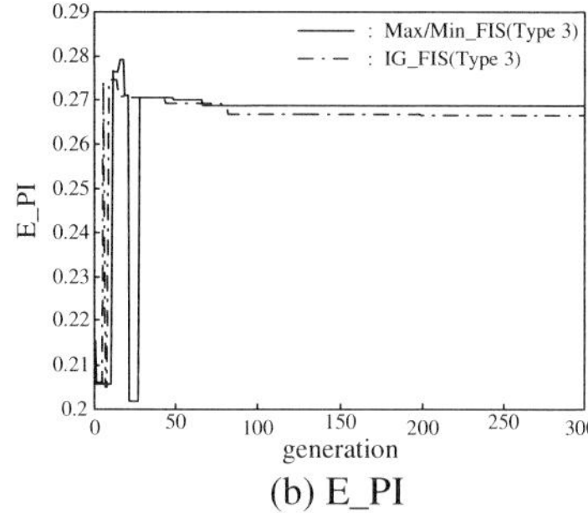

(b) E_PI

Fig. 5. Optimal convergence process of performance index for Max_Min-based and IG-based fuzzy model by means of the consecutive identification ($u(t$-3), $y(t$-1))

Table 2. Comparison of identification error with previous models

Model			PI_t	PI	E_PI	No. of rules
Tong's model[14]			0.469			19
Pedrycz's model[2]			0.776			20
Xu's model[15]			0.328			25
Sugeno's model[7]			0.355			6
Oh et al.'s	Simplified			0.024	0.328	4
Model[9,16]	Linear			0.022	0.326	4
				0.021	0.364	6
HCM+GA[17]	Simplified			0.035	0.289	4
				0.022	0.333	6
	Linear			0.026	0.272	4
				0.020	0.264	6
Our	respective	Type 4		0.015	0.256	9
model	Consecutive	Type 3		0.014	0.266	6

6 Conclusions

In this paper, we have introduced a comprehensive identification framework for information granules-based fuzzy systems and methodologies identification by means of genetic optimization. The underlying idea deals with an optimization of information granules by exploiting techniques of clustering and genetic algorithms. Information granulation realized with HCM clustering help determine the initial parameters of fuzzy model such as the initial apexes of the membership functions and the initial values of polynomial function of the fuzzy rules. The initial parameters are tuned (adjusted) effectively by means of the genetic algorithms and the least square method. And we exploited the methodologies identification by means of genetic algorithms. The experimental studies showed that the model is compact, and its performance is better than some other previous models. The proposed model is effective for nonlinear complex systems, so we can construct a well-organized model.

While the detailed discussion was focused on triangular fuzzy sets, the developed methodology applies equally well to any other class of fuzzy sets as well as a type of nonlinear local model.

Acknowledgements. This work has been supported by KESRI(I-2004-0-074-0-00), which is funded by MOCIE(Ministry of commerce, industry and energy).

References

1. Zadeh, L.A.: Fuzzy sets. Information and Control. **8** (1965) 338-353
2. Tong, R.M.: Synthesis of fuzzy models for industrial processes. Int. J Gen Syst. **4** (1978) 143-162
3. Pedrycz, W.: An identification algorithm in fuzzy relational system. Fuzzy Sets Syst. **13** (1984) 153-167
4. Pedrycz, W.: Numerical and application aspects of fuzzy relational equations. Fuzzy Sets Syst. **11** (1983) 1-18
5. Czogola, E., Pedrycz, W.: On identification in fuzzy systems and its applications in control problems. Fuzzy Sets Syst. **6** (1981) 73-83
6. Takagi, T., Sugeno, M.: Fuzzy identification of systems and its applications to modeling and control. IEEE Trans Syst, Cybern. SMC-**15**(1) (1985) 116-132
7. Sugeno, M., Yasukawa, T.: Linguistic modeling based on numerical data. In: IFSA'91 Brussels, Computer, Management & System Science. (1991) 264-267
8. Ismail, M.A.: Soft Clustering Algorithm and Validity of Solutions. In: Gupta MM, editor. Fuzzy Computing Theory, Hardware and Application. Amsterdam. North Holland. (1988) 445-471
9. Oh, S.K., Pedrycz, W.: Identification of fuzzy systems by means of an auto-tuning algorithm and its application to nonlinear systems. Fuzzy Sets and Syst. **115**(2) (2000) 205-230
10. Zadeh, L.A.: Toward a theory of fuzzy information granulation and its centrality in human reasoning and fuzzy logic. Fuzzy Sets and Syst. **90** (1997) 111-117
11. Pderycz, W., Vukovich, G.: Granular neural networks. Neurocomputing. **36** (2001) 205-224
12. Krishnaiah, P.R., Kanal, L.N., editors.: Classification, pattern recognition, and reduction of dimensionality, volume 2 of Handbook of Statistics. North-Holland Amsterdam (1982)
13. Golderg, D.E.: Genetic Algorithm in search, Optimization & Machine Learning, Addison Wesley (1989)
14. Tong, R. M.: The evaluation of fuzzy models derived from experimental data. Fuzzy Sets Syst. **13** (1980) 1-12
15. Xu, C. W., Zailu, Y.: Fuzzy model identification self-learning for dynamic system. IEEE Trans. on Syst. Man, Cybern. SMC-**17**(4) (1987) 683-689
16. Park, C. S., Oh, S. K., Pedrycz, W.: Fuzzy Identification by means of Auto-Tuning Algorithm and Weighting Factor. The Third Asian Fuzzy Systems Symposium(AFSS). (1998) 701-706
17. Park, B. J., Pedrycz, W., Oh, S.K.: Identification of Fuzzy Models with the Aid of Evolutionary Data Granulation. IEE Proc.-Control Theory and Applications. **148**(05) (2001) 406-418
18. Park, H.S., Oh, S.K.: Fuzzy Relation-based Fuzzy Neural-Networks Using a Hybrid Identification Algorithm. IJCAS. **1**(3) (2003) 289-300

Optimization of Information Granulation-Oriented Fuzzy Set Model Using Hierarchical Fair Competition-Based Parallel Genetic Algorithms

Jeoung-Nae Choi[1], Sung-Kwun Oh[2], and Witold Pedrycz[3]

[1,2] Department of Electrical Engineering, The University of Suwon, San 2-2 Wau-ri, Bongdam-eup, Hwaseong-si, Gyeonggi-do, 445-743, South Korea
ohsk@suwon.ac.kr
[3] Department of Electrical and Computer Engineering, University of Alberta, Edmonton, AB T6G 2G6, Canada and
Systems Research Institute, Polish Academy of Sciences, Warsaw, Poland

Abstract. In this study, we introduce the hybrid optimization of fuzzy inference systems that is based on information granulation and Hierarchical Fair Competition-based Parallel Genetic Algorithms (HFCGA). The granulation is realized with the aid of the Hard C-means clustering and HFCGA is a kind of multi-populations of Parallel Genetic Algorithms (PGA), and it is used for structure optimization and parameter identification of fuzzy set model. It concerns the fuzzy model-related parameters as the number of input variables, a collection of specific subset of input variables, the number of membership functions, and the apexes of the membership function. In the hybrid optimization process, two general optimization mechanisms are explored. The structural optimization is realized via HFCGA and HCM method whereas in case of the parametric optimization we proceed with a standard least square method as well as HFCGA and HCM method as well. A comparative analysis demonstrates that the proposed algorithm is superior to the conventional methods.

Keywords: fuzzy set model, information granulation, genetic algorithms, hierarchical fair competition (HFC), HCM, multi-population.

1 Introduction

In the early 1980s, linguistic modeling [1] and fuzzy relation equation-based approach [2] were proposed as primordial identification methods for fuzzy models. The general class of Sugeno-Takagi models [3] gave rise to more sophisticated rule-based systems where the rules come with conclusions forming local regression models. While appealing with respect to the basic topology (a modular fuzzy model composed of a series of rules) [4], these models still await formal solutions as far as the structure optimization of the model is concerned, say a construction of the underlying fuzzy sets—information granules being viewed as basic building blocks of any fuzzy model.

Some enhancements to the model have been proposed by Oh and Pedrycz [5]. As one of the enhanced fuzzy model, information granulation based fuzzy set fuzzy

S. Greco et al. (Eds.): RSCTC 2006, LNAI 4259, pp. 477–486, 2006.

model was introduced. Over there, binary-coded genetic algorithm was used to optimize structure and premise parameters of fuzzy model, yet the problem of finding "good" initial parameters of the fuzzy sets in the rules remains open.

This study concentrates on optimization of information granulation-oriented fuzzy set model. Also, we propose to use hierarchical fair competition-based parallel genetic algorithm (HFCGA) for optimization of fuzzy model. GAs is well known as an optimization algorithm which can be searched global solution. It has been shown to be very successful in many applications and in very different domains. However it may get trapped in a sub-optimal region of the search space thus becoming unable to find better quality solutions, especially for very large search space. The parallel genetic algorithm (PGA) is developed with the aid of global search and retard premature convergence [8]. In particular, as one of the PGA model, HFCGA has an effect on a problem having very large search space [9].

In the sequel, the design methodology emerges as two phases of structural optimization (based on Hard C-Means (HCM) clustering and HFCGA) and parametric identification (based on least square method (LSM), as well as HCM clustering and HFCGA). Information granulation with the aid of HCM clustering helps determine the initial parameters of fuzzy model such as the initial apexes of the membership functions and the initial values of polynomial function being used in the premise and consequence part of the fuzzy rules. And the initial parameters are adjusted effectively with the aid of the HFCGA and the LSM.

2   Information Granulation (IG)

Roughly speaking, information granules [6] are viewed as related collections of objects (data point, in particular) drawn together by the criteria of proximity, similarity, or functionality. Granulation of information is an inherent and omnipresent activity of human beings carried out with intent of gaining a better insight into a problem under consideration and arriving at its efficient solution. In particular, granulation of information is aimed at transforming the problem at hand into several smaller and therefore manageable tasks. In this way, we partition this problem into a series of well-defined subproblems (modules) of a far lower computational complexity than the original one. The form of information granulation (IG) themselves becomes an important design feature of the fuzzy model, which are geared toward capturing relationships between information granules.

It is worth emphasizing that the HCM clustering has been used extensively not only to organize and categorize data, but it becomes useful in data compression and model identification [7]. For the sake of completeness of the entire discussion, let us briefly recall the essence of the HCM algorithm.

We obtain the matrix representation for hard c-partition, defined as follows.

$$M_C = \left\{ \mathrm{U} \mid u_{gi} \in \{0,1\}, \ \sum_{g=1}^{c} u_{gi} = 1, \ 0 < \sum_{i=1}^{m} u_{gi} < m \right\} \tag{1}$$

[**Step 1**] Fix the number of clusters $c(2 \le c < m)$ and initialize the partition matrix $\mathbf{U}^{(0)} \in M_C$

[Step 2] Calculate the center vectors $\mathbf{v}_g$ of each cluster:

$$\mathbf{v}_g^{(r)} = \{v_{g1},\; v_{g2},\cdots,\; v_{gk},\cdots,\; v_{gl}\} \tag{2}$$

$$v_{gk}^{(r)} = \sum_{i=1}^{m} u_{gi}^{(r)} \cdot x_{ik} \left/ \sum_{i=1}^{m} u_{gi}^{(r)}\right. \tag{3}$$

Where, $[u_{gi}]= \mathbf{U}^{(r)}$, g = 1, 2, …,c, k=1, 2, …,l.

[Step 3] Update the partition matrix $\mathbf{U}^{(r)}$; these modifications are based on the standard Euclidean distance function between the data points and the prototypes,

$$d_{gi} = d(\mathbf{x}_i - \mathbf{v}_g) = \left\| \mathbf{x}_i - \mathbf{v}_g \right\| = \left[\sum_{k=1}^{l} (x_{ik} - v_{gk})^2 \right]^{1/2} \tag{4}$$

$$u_{gi}^{(r+1)} = \begin{cases} 1 & d_{gi}^{(r)} = \min\{d_{ki}^{(r)}\} \;\; \text{for all} \;\; k \in c \\ 0 & \text{otherwise} \end{cases} \tag{5}$$

[Step 4] Check a termination criterion. If

$$\| \mathbf{U}^{(r+1)} - \mathbf{U}^{(r)} \| \leq \varepsilon \;\; (\text{tolerance level}) \tag{6}$$

Stop ; otherwise set $r = r + 1$ and return to **[Step 2]**

3   Design of Fuzzy Set Fuzzy Model with the Aid of IG

The identification procedure for fuzzy models is usually split into the identification activities dealing with the premise and consequence parts of the rules. The identification completed at the premise level consists of two main steps. First, we select the input variables x_1, x_2, …, x_k of the rules. Second, we form fuzzy partitions of the spaces over which these individual variables are defined. The identification of the consequence part of the rules embraces two phases, namely 1) a selection of the consequence variables of the fuzzy rules, and 2) determination of the parameters of the consequence (conclusion part). And the least square error (LSE) method used at the parametric optimization of the consequence parts of the successive rules.

In this study, we use the isolated input space of each input variable and carry out the modeling using characteristics of input-output data set. Therefore, it is important to understand the nature of data. The HCM clustering addresses this issue. Subsequently, we design the fuzzy model by considering the centers (prototypes) of clusters. In this manner the clustering help us determining the initial parameters of fuzzy model such as the initial apexes of the membership functions and the initial values of polynomial function being used in the premise and consequence part of the fuzzy rules.

3.1   Premise Identification

In the premise part of the rules, we confine ourselves to a triangular type of membership functions whose parameters are subject to some optimization. The HCM clustering helps us organize the data into cluster so in this way we capture the characteristics of the experimental data. In the regions where some clusters of data have been identified, we end up with some fuzzy sets that help reflect the specificity of the data set. In the sequel, the modal values of the clusters are refined (optimized) using HFCGA.

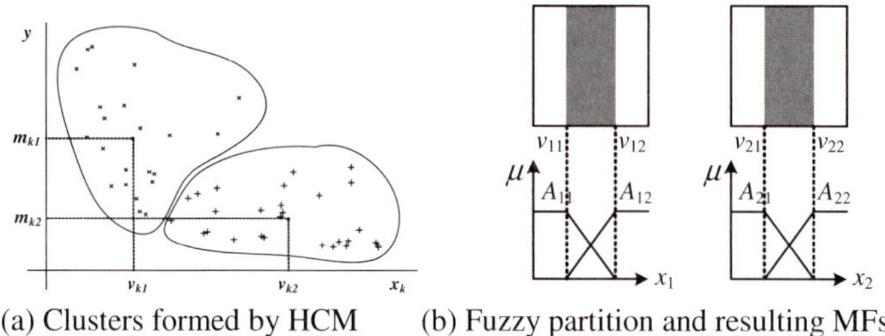

(a) Clusters formed by HCM   (b) Fuzzy partition and resulting MFs

Fig. 1. Identification of the premise part of the rules of the system

The identification of the premise part is completed in the following manner.

Given is a set of data $\mathbf{U}=\{\mathbf{x}_1, \mathbf{x}_2, \ldots, \mathbf{x}_l ; \mathbf{y}\}$, where $\mathbf{x}_k =[x_{1k}, \ldots, x_{mk}]^T$, $\mathbf{y} =[y_1, \ldots, y_m]^T$, l is the number of variables and , m is the number of data.

[Step 1] Arrange a set of data $\mathbf{U}$ into data set $\mathbf{X}_k$ composed of respective input data and output data.

$$\mathbf{X}_k=[\mathbf{x}_k ; \mathbf{y}] \tag{7}$$

$\mathbf{X}_k$ is data set of k-th input data and output data, where, $\mathbf{x}_k =[x_{1k}, \ldots, x_{mk}]^T$, $\mathbf{y} =[y_1, \ldots, y_m]^T$, and $k=1, 2, \ldots, l$.

[Step 2] Complete the HCM clustering to determine the centers (prototypes) $\mathbf{v}_{kg}$ with data set $\mathbf{X}_k$.

[Step 2-1] Classify data set $\mathbf{X}_k$ into c-clusters, which in essence leads to the granulation of information.

We can find the data pairs included in each cluster based on the partition matrix u_{gi} by (5) and use these to identify the structure in conclusion part.

[Step 2-2] Calculate the center vectors $\mathbf{v}_{kg}$ of each cluster.

$$v_{kg} = \{v_{k1}, v_{k2}, \ldots, v_{kc}\} \tag{8}$$

Where, $k=1, 2, \ldots, l, g = 1, 2, \ldots, c$.

[Step 3] Partition the corresponding isolated input space using the prototypes of the clusters $\mathbf{v}_{kg}$. Associate each clusters with some meaning (semantics), say Small, Big, etc.

[Step 4] Set the initial apexes of the membership functions using the prototypes $\mathbf{v}_{kg}$.

3.2 Consequence Identification

We identify the structure considering the initial values of polynomial functions based upon the information granulation realized for the consequence and antecedents parts.

[Step 1] Find a set of data included in the isolated fuzzy space of the j-th rule.

[Step 1-1] Find the input data included in each cluster (information granule) from the partition matrix u_{gi} of each input variable by (5).

[Step 1-2] Find the input data pairs included in the isolated fuzzy space of the j-th rule.

[Step 1-3] Determine the corresponding output data from above input data pairs.

[Step 2] Compute the prototypes $\mathbf{V}_j$ of the data set by taking the arithmetic mean of each rule.

$$\mathbf{V}_j = \{V_{1j}, V_{2j}, \ldots, V_{kj}; M_j\} \tag{9}$$

Where, $k=1, 2, \ldots, l$. $j=1, 2, \ldots, n$. V_{kj} and M_j are prototypes of input and output data, respectively.

[Step 3] Set the initial values of polynomial functions with the center vectors $\mathbf{V}_j$.

The identification of the conclusion parts of the rules deals with a selection of their structure that is followed by the determination of the respective parameters of the local functions occurring there.

In case of Type 2: linear Inference (linear conclusion)

The consequence part of the simplified inference mechanism is a constant. The rules come in the following form

$$R^j : If\ x_k\ is\ A_{kc}\ then\ y_j - M_j = f_j(x_1, \cdots, x_k) \tag{10}$$

The calculations of the numeric output of the model, based on the activation (matching) levels of the rules there, rely on the expression

$$y^* = \frac{\sum_{j=1}^{n} w_{ji} y_i}{\sum_{j=1}^{n} w_{ji}} = \frac{\sum_{j=1}^{n} w_{ji}(f_j(x_1, \cdots, x_k) + M_j)}{\sum_{j=1}^{n} w_{ji}} = \sum_{j=1}^{n} \hat{w}_{ji}(a_{j0} + a_{j1}(x_1 - V_{j1}) + \cdots + a_{jk}(x_k - V_{jk}) + M_j) \tag{11}$$

Here, as the normalized value of w_{ji}, we use an abbreviated notation to describe an activation level of rule R^j to be in the form

$$\hat{w}_{ji} = \frac{w_{ji}}{\sum_{j=1}^{n} w_{ji}} \tag{12}$$

where R^j is the j-th fuzzy rule, x_k represents the input variables, A_{kc} is a membership function of fuzzy sets, a_{j0} is a constant, M_j is a center value of output data, n is the number of fuzzy rules, y^* is the inferred output value, w_{ji} is the premise fitness matching R^j (activation level).

Once the input variables of the premise and parameters have been already specified, the optimal consequence parameters that minimize the assumed performance index can be determined. In what follows, we define the performance index as the mean squared error (MSE).

$$PI = \frac{1}{m} \sum_{i=1}^{m} (y_i - y_i^*)^2 \tag{13}$$

where y^* is the output of the fuzzy model, m is the total number of data, and i is the data number. The minimal value produced by the least-squares method is governed by the following expression:

$$\hat{\mathbf{a}} = (\mathbf{X}^T \mathbf{X})^{-1} \mathbf{X}^T \mathbf{Y} \qquad (14)$$

where

$$\mathbf{x}_i^T = [\, \hat{w}_{1i} \; \cdots \; \hat{w}_{ni} \; (x_{1i} - V_{11})\hat{w}_{1i} \; \cdots \; (x_{1i} - V_{1n})\hat{w}_{ni} \; \cdots \; (x_{ki} - V_{k1})\hat{w}_{1i} \; \cdots \; (x_{ki} - V_{kn})\hat{w}_{ni} \,],$$

$$\hat{\mathbf{a}} = [a_{10} \cdots a_{n0} \, a_{11} \cdots a_{n1} \cdots a_{1k} \cdots a_{nk}]^T,$$

$$\mathbf{Y} = \left[y_1 - \left(\sum_{j=1}^{n} M_j w_{j1} \right) \quad y_2 - \left(\sum_{j=1}^{n} M_j w_{j2} \right) \quad \cdots \quad y_m - \left(\sum_{j=1}^{n} M_j w_{jm} \right) \right]^T$$

$$\mathbf{X} = [\mathbf{x}_1 \quad \mathbf{x}_2 \quad \cdots \quad \mathbf{x}_i \quad \cdots \quad \mathbf{x}_m]^T.$$

4   Optimization by Means of HFCGA

The premature convergence of genetic algorithms is a problem to be overcome. The convergence is desirable, but must be controlled in order that the population does not get trapped in local optima. Even in dynamic-sized populations, the high-fitness individuals supplant the low-fitness or are favorites to be selected, dominating the evolutionary process. Fuzzy model has many parameters to be optimized, and it has very large search space. So HFCGA may find out a solution better than GAs.

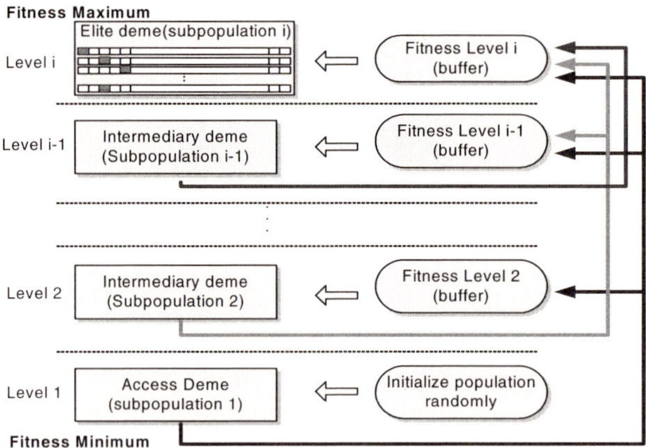

Fig. 2. HFCGA topology

In HFCGA, multiple demes(subpopulation) are organized in a hierarchy, in which each deme can only accommodate individuals within a specified range of fitness. The universe of fitness values must have a deme correspondence. Each deme has an admission threshold that determines the profile of the fitness in each deme.

Individuals are moved from low-fitness to higher-fitness subpopulations if and only if they exceed the fitness-based admission threshold of the receiving subpopulations. Thus, one can note that HFCGA adopts a unidirectional migration operator, where individuals can move to superior levels, but not to inferior ones.

The figure 2 illustrates the topology of HFCGA. The arrows indicate the moving direction possibilities. The access deme (primary level) can send individuals to all other demes and the elite deme only can receive individuals from the others. One can note that, with respect to topology, HFCGA is a specific case of island model, where only some moves are allowed.

HFCGA is implemented as shown in Fig. 2. It is real-coded type, and use five demes (subpopulation), Size of demes is 100, 80, 80, 80, and 60 respectively, where elite deme is given as the least size. And we use linear ranking based selection, modified simple crossover, and dynamic mutation algorithm for each deme.

Identification procedure of fuzzy model consists of two phase, structural identification and parametric identification. HFCGA is used in each phase. At first, in structural identification, we find the number of input variables, input variables being selected and the number of membership functions standing in the premise and the type of polynomial in conclusion. And then, in parametric identification, we adjust apexes of the membership functions of premise part of fuzzy rules. Figure 3 shows an arrangement of chromosomes to be used in HFCGA.

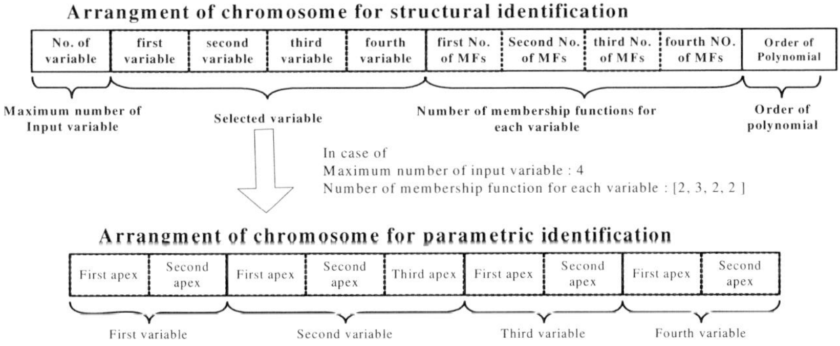

Fig. 3. Arrangement of chromosomes for identification of structure and parameter identification

5 Experimental Studies

In this section we consider comprehensive numeric studies illustrating the design of the fuzzy model. We demonstrate how IG-based FIS can be utilized to predict future values of a chaotic time series. The performance of the proposed model is also contrasted with some other models existing in the literature. The time series is generated by the chaotic Mackey–Glass differential delay equation [10] of the form:

$$\dot{x}(t) = \frac{0.2x(t-\tau)}{1+x^{10}(t-\tau)} - 0.1x(t) \tag{15}$$

The prediction of future values of this series arises is a benchmark problem that has been used and reported by a number of researchers. From the Mackey–Glass time series $x(t)$, we extracted 1000 input–output data pairs for the type from the following the type of vector format such as: $[x(t-30), x(t-24), x(t-18), x(t-12), x(t-6), x(t); x(t+6)]$ where $t = 118$–1117. The first 500 pairs were used as the training data set while the remaining 500 pairs were the testing data set for assessing the predictive performance. We consider the MSE being regarded here as a performance index. We carried out the structure and parameters identification on a basis of the experimental data using HFCGA and real-coded GA (single population) to design IG-based fuzzy model.

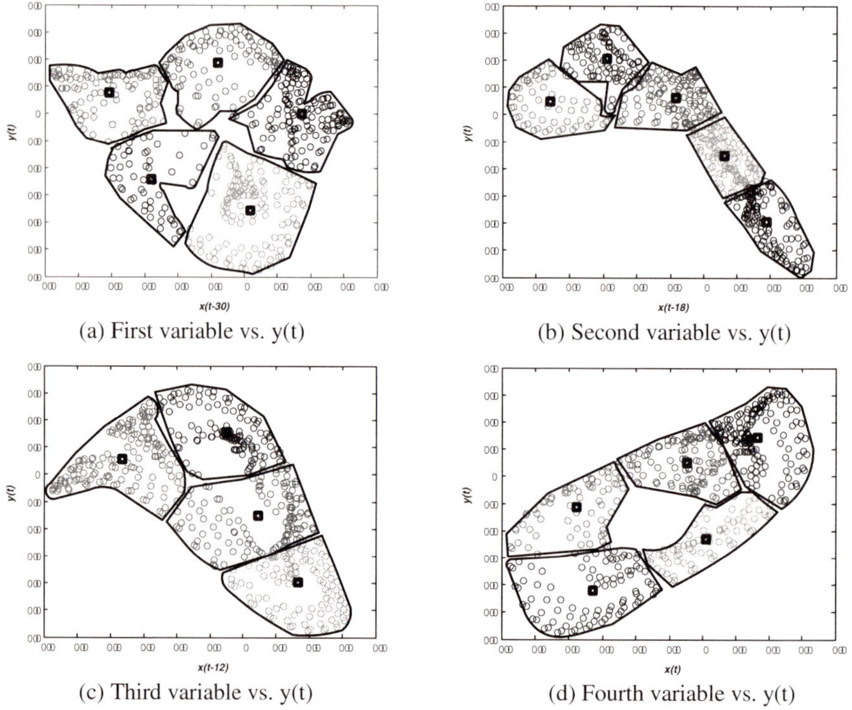

(a) First variable vs. y(t)   (b) Second variable vs. y(t)

(c) Third variable vs. y(t)   (d) Fourth variable vs. y(t)

Fig. 4. Groups and central values through HCM for each input variable

Figure 4 depicts groups and central values through HCM for each input variable. Where, the number of input variables and number of groups (membership function) to be divided are obtained from structural optimization procedure. Clustering results are used for information granulation. Table 1 summarizes the performance index for real-coded GA and HFCGA. It shows that the performance of the HFCGA based fuzzy model is better than real-coded GA based one for premise identification. However, for structure identification, same structure is selected. To compare real-coded GA with HFCGA, show the performance index for the Type 2 (linear inference). Figure 5 show variation of the performance index for real-coded GA and HFCGA in premise identification phase.

Table 1. Performance index of IG-based fuzzy model by means of Real-coded GA and HFCGA

Evolutionary algorithm	Structure					Premise parameter	
	Input variables	No. of MFs	Type	PI	E_PI	PI	E_PI
Real-coded GA	x(t-30)	5	Type 3 (Quadratic)	0.00027	0.00036	0.00019	0.00021
HFCGA	x(t-18)	5				0.00017	0.00017
Real-coded GA	x(t-12)	4	Type 2 (Linear)	0.00266	0.00251	0.00184	0.00159
HFCGA	x(t)	5				0.00135	0.00121

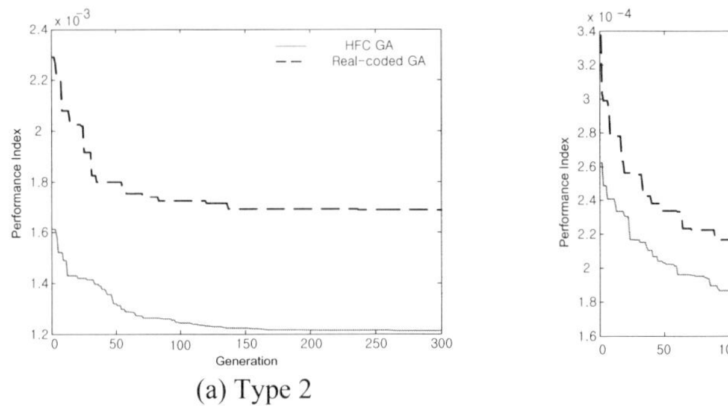

(a) Type 2   (b) Type 3

Fig. 5. Convergence process of performance index for real-coded GA and HFCGA

The identification error (performance index) of the proposed model is also compared with the performance of some other models; refer to Table 2. Here the non-dimensional error index (NDEI) is defined as the root mean square errors divided by the standard deviation of the target series.

Table 2. Comparison of identification error with previous models

Model	No. of rules	PI_t	PI	E_PI	NDEI
	7	0.004			
Wang's model [10]	23	0.013			
	31	0.010			
Cascaded-correlation NN [11]					0.06
Backpropagation MLP [11]					0.02
6th-order polynomial [11]					0.04
ANFIS [12]	16		0.0016	0.0015	0.007
FNN model [13]			0.014	0.009	
Recurrent neural network [14]		0.0138			
Our model	19		0.00019	0.00021	0.00075

6   Conclusions

In this paper, we have developed a comprehensive hybrid identification frame-work for information granulation-oriented fuzzy set model using hierarchical fair competition–based parallel genetic algorithm. The underlying idea deals with an optimization of information granules by exploiting techniques of clustering and genetic algorithms. We used the isolated input space for each input variable and defined the fuzzy space by information granule. Information granulation with the aid of HCM clustering help determine the initial parameters of fuzzy model such as the initial apexes of the membership functions and the initial values of polynomial function being used in the premise and consequence part of the fuzzy rules. The initial parameters are fine-tuned (adjusted) effectively with the aid of HFCGA and the least square method. The experimental studies showed that the model is compact, and its performance is better than some other previous models. The proposed model is effective for nonlinear complex systems, so we can construct a well-organized model.

Acknowledgements. This work was supported by the Korea Research Foundation Grant funded by the Korean Government (MOEHRD)(KRF-2006-311-D00194).

References

1. Tong RM.: Synthesis of fuzzy models for industrial processes. Int. J Gen Syst. 4 (1978) 143-162
2. Pedrycz, W.: An identification algorithm in fuzzy relational system. Fuzzy Sets Syst. 13 (1984) 153-167
3. Takagi, T., Sugeno, M.: Fuzzy identification of systems and its applications to modeling and control. IEEE Trans Syst, Cybern. SMC-15(1) (1985) 116-132
4. Sugeno, M., Yasukawa, T.: Linguistic modeling based on numerical data. In: IFSA'91 Brussels, Computer, Management & System Science. (1991) 264-267
5. Oh, S.K., Pedrycz, W.: Identification of fuzzy systems by means of an auto-tuning algorithm and its application to nonlinear systems. Fuzzy Sets and Syst. 115(2) (2000) 205-230
6. Pderycz, W., Vukovich, G.: Granular neural networks. Neurocomputing. 36 (2001) 205-224
7. Krishnaiah, P.R., Kanal, L.N., editors.: Classification, pattern recognition, and reduction of dimensionality, volume 2 of Handbook of Statistics. North-Holland, Amsterdam. (1982)
8. Lin, S.C., Goodman, E., Punch, W.: Coarse-Grain Parallel Genetic Algorithms: Categorization and New Approach. IEEE Conf. on Parallel and Distrib. Processing. Nov. (1994)
9. Hu, J.J., Goodman, E.: The Hierarchical Fair Competition (HFC) Model for Parallel Evolutionary Algorithms. Proceedings of the 2002 Congress on Evolutionary Computation: CEC2002. IEEE. Honolulu. Hawaii. (2002)
10. Wang, L.X., Mendel, J.M.: Generating fuzzy rules from numerical data with applications. IEEE Trans. Systems, Man, Cybern. **22(6)** (1992) 1414-1427
11. Crowder, R.S. III.: Predicting the Mackey-Glass time series with cascade-correlation learning. In D. Touretzky, G. Hinton, and T. Sejnowski, editors, Proceedings of the 1990 Connectionist Models Summer School. Carnegic Mellon University. (1990) 117-123
12. Jang J.R.: ANFIS: Adaptive-Network-Based Fuzzy Inference System. IEEE Trans. System, Man, and Cybern. **23**(3) (1993) 665-685
13. Maguire, L.P., Roche, B., McGinnity, T.M., McDaid, L.J.: Predicting a chaotic time series using a fuzzy neural network. Information Sciences. **112** (1998) 125-136
14. Li, C.J., Huang, T.Y.: Automatic structure and parameter training methods for modeling of mechanical systems by recurrent neural networks. Applied Mathematical Modeling. **23** (1999) 933-944
15. Park, H.S., Oh, S.K.: Fuzzy Relation-based Fuzzy Neural-Networks Using a Hybrid Identification Algorithm. Int. J. of Control Automation and Systems. **1**(3) (2003) 289-300

A Grey-Based Rough Set Approach to Suppliers Selection Problem

Guo-Dong Li[1], Daisuke Yamaguchi[1], Hui-Shan Lin[2],
Kun-Li Wen[3], and Masatake Nagai[4]

[1] Graduate School of Engineering, Kanagawa University, 221-8686,
Yokohama City, Japan
`guodong_li2004@yahoo.co.jp`
[2] Graduate School of Medical Image,
Yuanpei Institute of Science and Technology, Taiwan
[3] Department of Electrical Engineering, Chienkuo Institute of Technology,
Chunghua City, Taiwan
[4] Faculty of Engineering, Kanagawa University, 221-8686,
Yokohama City, Japan
`masatake4263@oregano.ocn.ne.jp`

Abstract. The suppliers selection problem is one of the most important components in supply chain management. In recent years, rough set theory has emerged as a powerful tool for suppliers selection problem. In this paper, we proposed a grey-based rough set approach to resolve suppliers selection problem. The work is motivated by the following observations: First, in the decision table of rough set theory, attribute values must be known precisely. Generally, decision makers' judgments on attribute often cannot be estimated by the exact numerical value. Second, in rough set theory, the alternatives of ideal suppliers are decided by lower approximation, so the ranks of each ideal supplier is equal. Therefore it is difficult to select the best ideal supplier. The work procedure is shown as follows briefly: First, the attribute values of rough set decision table for all alternatives are decided by linguistic variables that can be expressed in grey number. Second, ideal suppliers are decided by the lower approximation of grey-based rough set theory. Third, the best ideal supplier is decided by grey relational analysis based on grey number. Finally, an example of selection problem of suppliers was used to illustrate the proposed approach.

1   Introduction

With the globalization of economic market and the development of information technology, suppliers selection problem become one of the most important components in supply chain management [1],[2]. The suppliers selection is a multiple attribute decision making (MADM) problem. The decision maker (DM)s always express their preferences on alternatives or on attributes of suppliers, which can be used to help ranking the suppliers or selecting the most desirable one. The preference information on alternatives of suppliers and on attributes belongs to DMs' subjective judgments. Generally, DMs' judgment are often uncertain and

S. Greco et al. (Eds.): RSCTC 2006, LNAI 4259, pp. 487–496, 2006.
© Springer-Verlag Berlin Heidelberg 2006

cannot be estimated by the exact numerical value. Thus the selection problem of suppliers has many uncertainties and becomes more difficult.

Rough set theory [3]-[5] is a widely used tool in data mining and knowledge discovery. Up to present, the rough set approach has been also proposed to deal with the suppliers selection problem under uncertainty [6]. However, in the decision table of rough set theory, attribute values must be known precisely. In addition, the alternatives of ideal suppliers are decided by the lower approximation, so the rank of each ideal supplier is equal. Therefore it is difficult to select the most ideal supplier.

Grey system theory [7],[8] is one of the methods that are used to study uncertainty, it is superior in mathematical analysis of systems with uncertain information. Up to present, fuzzy-based approach has been proposed to deal with the suppliers selection problem under uncertainty [9]. The advantage of grey system theory over fuzzy theory [10], [11] is that grey system theory considers the condition of the fuzziness. That is, grey system theory can flexibly deal with the fuzziness situation [12]. In this paper, we proposed a new grey-based rough set approach to deal with selection problem of suppliers under uncertainty environment. The new approach can overcome above mentioned shortcomings of rough set theory. The work procedure is shown as follows briefly: First, the attribute values of decision table for all alternatives are decided by linguistic variables that can be expressed in grey number. Second, ideal suppliers are decided by the lower approximation of rough set theory. Third, the most ideal supplier is decided by grey relational analysis based on grey number. Finally, an example of selection problem of suppliers was used to illustrate the proposed approach. The experimental result shows that the effectiveness of proposed approach.

This paper is organized as follows: Section 2 describes rough set theory. Section 3 describes grey system theory which include some basic definitions. Section 4 introduces the proposed approach by grey-based rough set. In Section 5, the application and analysis of proposed approach is introduced by an example of suppliers selection. Finally, conclusions are described in Section 6.

2   Rough Set Theory

Rough set theory [3] which is proposed by Pawlak in 1982, is an extension of conventional set theory that supports approximations in decision making. The rough set itself is the approximation of a vague concept set by a pair of precise concepts, called lower and upper approximations, which are a classification of the domain of interest into disjoint categories. The lower approximation is a description of the domain objects which are known with certainty to belong to the subset of interest, whereas the upper approximation is a description of the objects which possibly belong to the subset.

Definition 1. *Let U be the universe and let R be an equivalence relation on U. For any subset $X \subseteq U$, the pair $T = (U, R)$ is called an approximation space. The two subsets*

$$\underline{R}X = \{x \in U | [x]_R \subseteq X\} \tag{1}$$

$$\overline{R}X = \{x \in U \,|\, [x]_R \cap X \neq \phi\} \tag{2}$$

are called the R-lower and R-upper approximation of X, respectively. $R(X) =< \underline{R}X, \overline{R}X >$ is called the rough set of X in T. The rough set $R(X)$ denotes the description of X under the present knowledge, i.e., the classification of U.

We use $POS_R(X) = \underline{R}X$ to denote R-positive region of X, $NEG_R(X) = U - \overline{R}X$ to denote R-negative region of X, and $BN_R(X) = \overline{R}X - \underline{R}X$ to denote the R-borderline region of X. The positive region $POS_R(X)$ or $\underline{R}X$ is the collection of those objects which can be classified with full certainty as members of the set X, using knowledge R. The negative region $NEG_R(X)$ is the collection of objects which can be determined without any ambiguity, employing knowledge R, that they do not belong to the set X.

3   Grey System Theory

Grey system theory [8], originally developed by Deng in 1982, has become a very effective method of solving uncertainty problems under discrete data and incomplete information. The theory includes five major parts, which include grey prediction, grey relation, grey decision, grey programming and grey control. In recent years, grey system theory has now been applied to various areas such as forecasting, system control, decision making and computer graphics.

3.1   Grey System, Grey Set and Grey Number Operation

Definition 2. *A grey system is defined as a system containing uncertain information presented by grey number and grey variables.*

Definition 3. *Let X be the universal set. Then a grey set G of X is defined by its two mappings $\overline{\mu}_G(x)$ and $\underline{\mu}_G(x)$.*

$$\begin{cases} \overline{\mu}_G(x) : x \longrightarrow [0,1] \\ \underline{\mu}_G(x) : x \longrightarrow [0,1] \end{cases} \tag{3}$$

where $\overline{\mu}_G(x) \geq \underline{\mu}_G(x)$, $x \in X, X = R$, (R: Real number set), $\overline{\mu}_G(x)$ and $\underline{\mu}_G(x)$ are the upper and lower membership functions in G respectively. When $\overline{\mu}_G(x) = \underline{\mu}_G(x)$, the grey set G becomes a fuzzy set. It shows that grey theory considers the condition of the fuzziness and can flexibly deal with the fuzziness situation.

Definition 4. *A grey number is one of which the exact value is unknown, while the upper and/or the lower limits can be estimated. Generally grey number is written as $\otimes x, (\otimes x = x|_{\underline{\mu}}^{\overline{\mu}})$.*

Definition 5. *If only the lower limit of x can be possibly estimated and x is defined as lower limit grey number.*

$$\otimes x = [\underline{x}, \infty) \tag{4}$$

Definition 6. *If only the upper limit of x can be possibly estimated and x is defined as lower limit grey number.*

$$\otimes x = (-\infty, \overline{x}] \tag{5}$$

Definition 7. *If the lower and upper limits of x can be estimated and x is defined as interval grey number.*

$$\otimes x = [\underline{x}, \overline{x}] \tag{6}$$

Definition 8. *The basic operation laws of grey numbers $\otimes x_1 = [\underline{x}_1, \overline{x}_1]$ and $\otimes x_2 = [\underline{x}_2, \overline{x}_2]$ can be expressed as follows:*

$$\otimes x_1 + \otimes x_2 = [\underline{x}_1 + \underline{x}_2, \overline{x}_1 + \overline{x}_2] \tag{7}$$

$$\otimes x_1 - \otimes x_2 = [\underline{x}_1 - \overline{x}_2, \overline{x}_1 - \underline{x}_2] \tag{8}$$

$$\otimes x_1 \times \otimes x_2 = [\min(\underline{x}_1\underline{x}_2, \underline{x}_1\overline{x}_2, \overline{x}_1\underline{x}_2, \overline{x}_1\overline{x}_2),$$
$$\max(\underline{x}_1\underline{x}_2, \underline{x}_1\overline{x}_2, \overline{x}_1\underline{x}_2, \overline{x}_1\overline{x}_2)] \tag{9}$$

$$\otimes x_1 \div \otimes x_2 = [\underline{x}_1, \overline{x}_1] \times \left[\frac{1}{\underline{x}_2}, \frac{1}{\overline{x}_2}\right] \tag{10}$$

Definition 9. *The Minkowski space distance of two grey numbers $\otimes x_1$ and $\otimes x_2$ is defined as*

$$L(\otimes x_1, \otimes x_2) = [(\underline{x}_1 - \underline{x}_2)^p + (\overline{x}_1 - \overline{x}_2)^p]^{\frac{1}{p}} \tag{11}$$

In our study, $p = 2$ is used. It represents Euclidean grey space distance.

3.2   Grey Relational Analysis Based on Grey Number

The grey relational analysis (GRA) is an important approach of grey system theory in the application of evaluating a set of alternatives in terms of decision criteria. In GRA, the data that contain same features are regarded as a sequence. As a tool of quantitative analysis, the GRA can be used to measure the relationship between two sequences by calculation their correlative degrees, which is called grey relational grade (GRG). The GRG is expressed by a scalar between 0 and 1. Up to now, the method has been used successfully in many fields. However, in conventional GRA, the data of sequences which are used as real numbers. We use a new GRA based on grey number to more flexibly analyze the uncertain relationship of system factors.

Definition 10. *Considering a reference sequence $\otimes x = \{\otimes x(1), \otimes x(2), \ldots, \otimes x(n)\}$ and m comparative sequences $\otimes x_i = \{\otimes x_i(1), \otimes x_i(2), \ldots, \otimes x_i(n)\}, i = 1, 2, \ldots, m$, where $\otimes x_i(k)$ represents the kth attribute in $\otimes x_i, k = 1, 2, \ldots, n$. The grey relational coefficient (GRC) of $\otimes x_i$ with respect to $\otimes x_0$ at the kth attribute is calculated as [13]*

$$\gamma(\otimes x_0(k), \otimes x_i(k)) = \frac{\Delta_{\max} - \Delta_{0i}(k)}{\Delta_{\max} - \Delta_{\min}} \tag{12}$$

Table 1. The scale of attribute ratings $\otimes v$

Scale	$\otimes v$
Very poor (VP)	[0,1]
Poor (P)	[1,3]
Medium poor (MP)	[3,4]
Fair (F)	[4,5]
Medium good (MG)	[5,6]
Good (G)	[6,9]
Very good (VG)	[9,10]

where

$$\Delta_{\max} = \max_{\forall i, \forall k} L(\otimes x_0(k), \otimes x_i(k)) \tag{13}$$

$$\Delta_{\min} = \min_{\forall i, \forall k} L(\otimes x_0(k), \otimes x_i(k)) \tag{14}$$

$$\Delta_{0i}(k) = L(\otimes x_0(k), \otimes x_i(k)) \tag{15}$$

$L(\otimes x_0(k), \otimes x_i(k))$ is the Euclidean space distance of $\otimes x_0(k)$ and $\otimes x_i(k)$ which is calculated by Eq. (11). The GRG between each comparative sequence $\otimes x_i$ and the reference sequence $\otimes x_0$ can be derived from the average of GRC, which is denoted as

$$\Gamma_{0i} = \sum_{k=1}^{n} \frac{1}{n} \gamma(\otimes x_0(k), \otimes x_i(k)) \tag{16}$$

where Γ_{0i} represents the degree of relation between each comparative sequence and the reference sequence. The higher degree of relation means that the comparative sequence is more similar to the reference sequence than comparative sequences.

4   Proposed Approach by Grey-Based Rough Set

A new grey-based rough set approach is proposed to make the most ideal supplier. This approach is very suitable for solving the group decision-making problem under uncertainty environment.

Assume that an grey information system of selection suppliers is defined by $T = (U, A, V, f_{\otimes})$, where $U = \{S_1, S_2, \ldots, S_m\}$ is a set of m suppliers alternatives called the universe. $A = \{a_1, a_2, \ldots, a_n\}$ is a set of n attributes of suppliers. $f_{\otimes} : U \times A \to V$ is grey description function. $T = (U, A \cup D, f_{\otimes})$ is called grey decision table, where D is a distinguished attribute called decision. The elements of A are called conditions. The attribute ratings $\otimes v$ can be also expressed in grey numbers [14] by 1-7 scale shown in Table 1. The procedures are summarized as follows:

Step 1: Form a committee of decision-maker and identify attribute values of suppliers. Assume that a decision group has K persons, then the values of attribute v_{ij} can be calculated as

$$\otimes v_{ij} = \frac{1}{K}[\otimes v_{ij}^1 + \otimes v_{ij}^2 + \cdots + \otimes v_{ij}^K] \tag{17}$$

Table 2. The grey decision table

Alternatives	Conditional attributes				Decision
	a_1	a_2	$\cdots$	a_n	D
S_1	$\otimes v_{11}$	$\otimes v_{12}$	$\cdots$	$\otimes v_{1n}$	d_1
S_2	$\otimes v_{21}$	$\otimes v_{22}$	$\cdots$	$\otimes v_{2n}$	d_2
$\vdots$	$\vdots$	$\vdots$	$\vdots$	$\vdots$	$\vdots$
S_m	$\otimes v_{m1}$	$\otimes v_{m2}$	$\cdots$	$\otimes v_{mn}$	d_m

Table 3. The normalized grey decision table

Alternatives	Conditional attributes				Decision
	a_1^*	a_2^*	$\cdots$	a_n^*	D
S_1	$\otimes v_{11}^*$	$\otimes v_{12}^*$	$\cdots$	$\otimes v_{1n}^*$	d_1
S_2	$\otimes v_{21}^*$	$\otimes v_{22}^*$	$\cdots$	$\otimes v_{2n}^*$	d_2
$\vdots$	$\vdots$	$\vdots$	$\vdots$	$\vdots$	$\vdots$
S_m	$\otimes v_{m1}^*$	$\otimes v_{m2}^*$	$\cdots$	$\otimes v_{mn}^*$	d_m

where $\otimes v_{ij}^K (i = 1, 2, \cdots, m; j = 1, 2, \cdots, n)$ is the attribute rating value of Kth DM and can be described by grey number $\otimes v_{ij}^K = [\underline{v}_{ij}^K, \overline{v}_{ij}^K]$.

Step 2: Establishment of grey decision table.

The attribute values of $\otimes v_{ij}$ are linguistic variables based on grey number. It is shown in Table 2.

Step 3: Normalization grey decision table.

For benefit attribute, $\otimes v_{ij}^*$ is expressed as

$$\otimes v_{ij}^* = \left[\frac{\underline{v}_{ij}}{v_j^{\max}}, \frac{\overline{v}_{ij}}{v_j^{\max}} \right] \tag{18}$$

$v_j^{\max} = \max_{1 \leq i \leq m} \{\overline{v}_{ij}\}$

For cost attribute, $\otimes v_{ij}^*$ is expressed as

$$\otimes v_{ij}^* = \left[\frac{v_j^{\min}}{\overline{v}_{ij}}, \frac{v_j^{\min}}{\underline{v}_{ij}} \right] \tag{19}$$

$v_j^{\min} = \min_{1 \leq i \leq m} \{\underline{v}_{ij}\}$.

The normalization method mentioned above is to preserve the property that the ranges of normalized grey number belong to $[0, 1]$. It is shown in Table 3.

Step 4: Selection ideal suppliers by grey-based rough set lower approximation [15]. The decision values $d_i, i = 1, 2, \cdots, m$ from MDs are given by {yes, yes or no, no} three types. The final values are decided by most of MDs' judgments. The real numbers of {yes, yes or no, no} are given as {2, 1, 0} by the important degree of suppliers. The lower approximation of ideal suppliers S_* are calculated as

$$\underline{R}S_* = \{S_i \in U | [S_i]_R \subseteq S_*\} \tag{20}$$

where $S_* = \{S_i | d_i = yes\}$.

Table 4. Attribute rating values for suppliers

a_j S_i	D_1	D_2	D_3	D_4	$\otimes v_{ij}$
a_1					
S_1	G	MG	G	G	[5.75, 8.25]
S_2	MG	G	F	MG	[5.00, 6.50]
S_3	F	F	MG	G	[4.75, 6.25]
S_4	F	MG	MG	F	[4.50, 5.50]
S_5	MG	F	F	MG	[4.50, 5.50]
S_6	G	MG	MG	MG	[5.25, 6.75]
S_7	F	MG	MG	F	[4.50, 5.50]
a_2					
S_1	G	G	MG	MG	[5.50, 7.50]
S_2	G	MG	MG	G	[5.50, 7.50]
S_3	F	F	P	F	[3.25, 4.50]
S_4	P	MP	MP	P	[2.00, 3.50]
S_5	MP	MP	M	MP	[2.50, 3.75]
S_6	MP	P	P	MP	[2.00, 3.50]
S_7	P	MP	MP	P	[2.00, 3.50]
a_3					
S_1	G	MG	MG	G	[5.50, 7.50]
S_2	MG	G	G	G	[5.75, 8.25]
S_3	G	G	F	MG	[5.25, 7.25]
S_4	G	MG	MG	G	[5.50, 7.50]
S_5	MG	F	F	MG	[4.50, 5.50]
S_6	F	F	MG	F	[4.25, 5.25]
S_7	G	MG	MG	G	[5.50, 7.50]
a_4					
S_1	F	G	G	G	[5.50, 8.00]
S_2	G	G	F	MG	[5.75, 8.25]
S_3	VG	VG	G	G	[7.50, 9.50]
S_4	G	MG	G	G	[5.75, 8.25]
S_5	MG	MG	G	MG	[5.25, 6.75]
S_6	G	VG	VG	G	[7.50, 9.50]
S_7	G	MG	G	G	[5.75, 8.25]

Step 5: For $\underline{R}S_*$, we used GRA based on grey number to select the most ideal supplier.

– Making most ideal referential supplier S_0 against $\underline{R}S_*$ by

$$S_0 = \left\{ [\max_{\forall i} \underline{v}^*_{i1}, \max_{\forall i} \overline{v}^*_{i1}], [\max_{\forall i} \underline{v}^*_{i2}, \max_{\forall i} \overline{v}^*_{i2}], \ldots, \right.$$
$$\left. [\max_{\forall i} \underline{v}^*_{im}, \max_{\forall i} \overline{v}^*_{im}] \right\} \tag{21}$$

– Calculation of GRG between comparative sequences $\underline{R}S_*$ with reference sequence S_0.

Table 5. The grey decision table

Alternatives	Conditional attributes				Decision
	a_1^*	a_2^*	a_3^*	a_4^*	D
S_1	[0.697, 1.000]	[0.733, 1.000]	[0.667, 0.909]	[0.656, 0.955]	2
S_2	[0.606, 0.788]	[0.733, 1.000]	[0.697, 1.000	[0.724, 1.000]	2
S_3	[0.576, 0.758]	[0.433, 0.600]	[0.636, 0.879]	[0.553 0.700]	1
S_4	[0.545, 0.667]	[0.267, 0.467]	[0.667, 0.909]	[0.636, 0.913]	2
S_5	[0.545, 0.667]	[0.333, 0.500]	[0.545, 0.545]	[0.778, 1.000]	1
S_6	[0.636, 0.818]	[0.267, 0.467]	[0.515, 0.636]	[0.553, 0.700]	0
S_7	[0.545, 0.667]	[0.267, 0.467]	[0.667, 0.909]	[0.636, 0.913]	1

5   Application and Analysis

In this section, we present the case study based on proposed grey-based rough set approach, and the consideration is also discribed.

5.1   Case Study

There is a grey information system $T = (U, A, V, f_\otimes)$ of suppliers selection. The grey decision table is expressed by $T = (U, A \cup D, f_\otimes)$. $U = \{S_i, i = 1, 2, \cdots, 7\}$ are as selected seven suppliers alternatives against four attributes $A = \{a_j, j = 1, 2, 3, 4\}$. The four attributes are product quality, service quality, delivery time and price respectively [6]. a_1, a_2 and a_3 are benefit attributes, the larger values are better. a_4 is cost attributes, the smaller values are better. The calculation procedures are shown as follows:

Step 1: Making attribute rating values for tem suppliers alternatives. A committee of four DMs, D_1, D_2, D_3 and D_4 has been formed to express their preferences and to select the most ideal suppliers. The results of attribute rating values are shown in Table 4.

Step 2: Establishment of grey decision table.

Step 3: Normalization grey decision table. The grey normalized decision table is shown in Table 5.

Step 4: Selection ideal suppliers by grey-based rough set lower approximation. We use R to denote the partition generated by condition attributes A. Here, $[S_i]_R = \{\{S_1\}, \{S_2\}, \{S_3\}, \{S_4, S_7\}, \{S_5\}, \{S_6\}\}$ are obtained.

The subset $S_* \subseteq U = \{S_i | d_i = yes\}$ for ideal suppliers is used. Then $S_* = \{\{S_1\}, \{S_2\}, \{S_4\}\}$ is obtained. The lower approximation of S_* are obtained by $\underline{R}S_* = \{S_i \in U | [S_i]_R \subseteq S_*\}$. Then $\underline{R}S_* = \{\{S_1\}, \{S_2\}\}$ are obtained. Therefore S_1 and S_2 can be viewed as the ideal suppliers.

Step 5: For ideal suppliers S_1 and S_2, we used GRA based on grey number to select the most ideal supplier. The calculation method is shown as follows.

- Making most ideal referential supplier S_0 against S_1 and S_2. According to Eq. (21), S_0 is obtained as

$$S_0 = S^{\max} = \big\{[0.697, 1.000], [0.733, 1.000], [0.697, 1.000], [0.724, 1.000]\big\}$$

– Calculation of GRG between comparative sequences S_1 and S_2 with reference sequence S_0. The values of GRG are $\Gamma_{01}(S_0, S_1) = 0.8077, \Gamma_{02}(S_0, S_2) = 0.7500$.

We can say that the supplier S_1 is the most ideal supplier in seven suppliers. S_1 should be as an important alternative for company.

5.2 Consideration

The selection problem of suppliers is a MADM problem. In conventional MADM methods, the ratings of the attribute must be known precisely. But, DMs' judgment are often uncertain and cannot be estimated by the exact numerical value. Thus, the selection problem of suppliers has many uncertainties and becomes more difficult. Grey system theory is one of new mathematical fields that was born by the concept of grey set. It is one of the methods that are used to study uncertainty of system. The uncertain information can be analyzed by grey set consist of grey number, thus, it become possible for the analysis of uncertain system. Grey system theory over fuzzy theory is that grey system theory considers the condition of the fuzziness. That is, grey system theory can flexibly deal with the fuzziness situation. Grey system theory expand the range of membership function of fuzzy theory to analyze uncertain problem. When the upper membership is same to lower membership, the grey set become fuzzy set. It is obvious that fuzzy set is a special type of grey set. About the analysis method of rough set theory, it is a good tool in data mining and knowledge discovery. However, the attribute values must be known precisely. In addition, the alternatives of ideal suppliers are decided by lower approximation, so the rank of each ideal supplier is equal. Therefore it is difficult to select the most ideal supplier. In this paper, we combine grey system theory with rough set they and proposed grey-based rough set approach to resolve the selection suppliers problem. Furthermore, we introduced grey relational analysis based on grey number to decide the most supplier. Through a verify example, we obtained the effectiveness of proposed approach.

6 Conclusions

In this paper, we proposed a new grey-based rough set approach to deal with selection problem of suppliers under uncertainty environment. An example of selection problem of suppliers was used to illustrate the proposed approach. The experimental result shows that proposed approach is reliable and reasonable. This proposed approach can help in more accurate selection problem, such as management and economic fields etc..

References

1. Hong, W.D., Lyes, B. and Xie, X.L.: A Simulation Optimization Methodology for Supplier Selection Problem. Int. J. Computer Integrated Manufacturing. **18** (2-3) 210–224, 2005

2. Lasch, R. and Janker, C.G.: Supplier Selection and Controlling Using Multivariate Analysis. Int. J. Physical Distribution and Logistics Management. **35** (6) 409–425, 2005.
3. Pawlak, Z.: Rough Sets. Int. J. Computer and Information Sciences. **11** 41–56, 1982
4. Pawlak, Z.: Rough Classification. Int. J. Man-Machine Studies. **20** 469–483, 1984.
5. Polkowski, L. and Skowron, A. (Eds.): Rough Sets in Knowledge Discovery. Physica-Verlag **1**(2) 1998.
6. Wang, S.J. and Hu, H.A.. Application of Rough Set on Supplier's Determination. The Third Annual Conference on Uncertainty. 256–262, Aug. 2005.
7. Deng, J.L.: Control Problems of Grey System. System and Control Letters. **5** 288–294, 1982.
8. Nagai, M. and Yamaguchi, D.: Elements on Grey System Theory and its Applications. Kyoritsu publisher, 2004.
9. Wang, Y.X.: Application of Fuzzy Decision Optimum Model in Selecting Supplier. J. Science Technology and Engineering. **5** (15) 1100–1103, Aug. 2005.
10. Zadeh, L.A.: Fuzzy sets. Information and Control. **8** 338–353, 1965.
11. Bellman, R.E. and Zadeh, L.A.: Decision-Making in a Fuzzy Environment. J. Management Science. **17** (4) 141–164, 1970.
12. Xia, J.: Grey System Theory to Hydrology. Huazhong Univ. of Science and Technology Press, 2000.
13. Nagai, M, Yamaguchi, D. and Li, G.D.: Grey Structural Modeling, J. Grey System. **8** (2) 119-130, Dec. 2005.
14. Li, G.D., Yamaguchi, D., and Nagai, M.: A Grey-Based Approach to Suppliers Selection Problem. In: Proc. Int. Conf. on PDPTA'06, Las Vegas, 818–824, June. 2006.
15. Yamaguchi, D., Li, G.D. and Nagai, M: On the Combination of Rough Set Theory and Grey Theory Based on Grey Lattice Operations, Int. Conf. on RSCTC'06, Kobe, 2006. (Accepted)

A Hybrid Grey-Based Dynamic Model for International Airlines Amount Increase Prediction

Guo-Dong Li[1], Daisuke Yamaguchi[1], Kun-Li Wen[2], and Masatake Nagai[3]

[1] Graduate School of Engineering, Kanagawa University, 221-8686,
Yokohama City, Japan
`guodong_li2006@yahoo.co.jp`
[2] Department of Electrical Engineering, Chienkuo Institute of Technology,
Chunghua City, Taiwan
[3] Faculty of Engineering, Kanagawa University, 221-8686,
Yokohama City, Japan
`masatake4263@oregano.ocn.ne.jp`

Abstract. In this paper, we propose a hybrid grey-based dynamic model, then it is applied to the prediction problem of international airlines amount increase in China. The work is motivated by the following observations: First, a system of international airlines is an uncertain dynamic system, and the effects of other systems on the system being monitored are also unclear. Thus it is difficult for us to predict next annual airlines amount from the system. Second, grey system theory is one of the methods that used to study uncertainty, and it is superior in mathematical analysis of systems with uncertain information. The system of international airlines can be viewed a grey dynamic system, therefore grey dynamic model GM(1,1) which is a single variable first order differential prediction model based on grey system theory can be used to solve the prediction problem. Third, since the development trend of international airlines amount is affected by variant random factors, it is difficult to obtain high predicted accuracy by single grey dynamic model. The work procedure is shown as follows briefly: First, the Markov-chain is integrated into GM(1,1) to enhance the predicted accuracy. Second, we present Taylor approximation method based on grey interval analysis for obtaining high accuracy furthermore. Finally, the statistics data of international airlines amount from 1985 to 2003 in China is used to verify the effectiveness of proposed model.

1 Introduction

The prediction for international airlines amount increase has become one of the most important research topics in airline management system with the economic development in China. A system of international airlines is an uncertain dynamic system, and the effects of other systems on the system being monitored are also unclear. Thus it is difficult for us to predict next annual airlines amount from the system. In 1982, Deng proposed grey system theory [1] to study uncertainty, and it is superior in mathematical analysis of systems with uncertain information.

S. Greco et al. (Eds.): RSCTC 2006, LNAI 4259, pp. 497–506, 2006.

The system of international airlines can be viewed a grey dynamic system. And grey dynamic model GM(1,1), which stands for the first order with one variable based on grey system theory as a prediction model can be used in the prediction problem of international airlines amount increase.

Since the increase trend of international airlines amount is affected by variant random factors, such as economic development, social chance and industrial policy etc., it is not realistic to establish a single grey prediction dynamic model, which can take all the affecting factors into account. As we know, every prediction model is designed with the hope to obtain the characteristics of the system. The more the factors which relate to the system dynamics are considered, the better the prediction will be. Statistics method, on the other hand, becomes a good choice. In this paper, Markov-chain based on statistical method is incorporated with the original grey dynamic model GM(1,1) to further enhance the predicted accuracy. Markov-chain [2] requires the prediction object a stationary process. It was found from the statistics data of international airlines amount of China in past years. Since the change of international airlines amount is a non-stationary process, so it is necessary to combine the two models in prediction. The proposed GM(1,1) model which combines with Markov-chain is defined as MGM(1,1). Furthermore, we present grey interval analysis based on the division state of Markov-chain, then Taylor approximation method is proposed to whiten the grey intervals and obtain the optimal predicted value. The generated model is defined as T-MGM(1,1). The statistics data of international airlines amount from 1985 to 2003 is used to verify the effectiveness of proposed model. The experimental results show that the proposed T-MGM(1,1) dynamic model has proved an effective tool in international airlines amount increase prediction problem.

2   Grey System Theory

In recent years, grey system theory [3] has become a very effective method of solving uncertainty problems under discrete data and incomplete information. The theory includes five major parts, which include grey prediction, grey relation, grey decision, grey programming and grey control. In this section, we describes grey system theory which include basic definitions, 1-AGO, 1-IAGO and GM(1,1) model.

2.1   Basic Definitions

Definition 1. *A grey system is defined as a system containing uncertain information presented by grey intervals and grey variables.*

Definition 2. *In grey system, when a prediction model uses an observed data set, there will be a numerical interval accompanying it. This numerical interval will contain the accuracy and the other sources of uncertainty that are associated with the observed values in the data set. The numerical interval is defined as grey interval.*

Definition 3. *The number of grey interval is defined as grey number. Grey number means that the certain value is unknown, but the rough range is known. The grey interval can be taken as a special grey number $\otimes X_g$, with bound values X_d and X_u:*

$$\otimes X_g = [X_d, X_u] \tag{1}$$

where X_d is the lower limit and X_u is upper limit.

Definition 4. *The whitening method for the grey number is given as*

$$X_g = (1 - \lambda)X_d + \lambda X_u \tag{2}$$

where $\lambda \in [0, 1]$, λ is called whitening coefficient.

2.2   Grey 1-AGO

The most critical feature of GM(1,1) is the use of grey generating approaches to reduce the variation of the original data series by transforming the data series linearly. The most commonly seen and applied grey generating approaches are the accumulative generating operation (AGO) and the inverse accumulative generating operation (IAGO).

Assume that $x^{(0)} = \{x^{(0)}(1), x^{(0)}(2), \ldots, x^{(0)}(n)\}$ is original series of real numbers with irregular distribution.

Then $x^{(1)}$ is viewed as 1-AGO generation series for $x^{(0)}$, if $\forall x^{(1)}(j) \in x^{(1)}$ can satisfy

$$x^{(1)}(j) = \sum_{i=1}^{j} x^{(0)}(i) \tag{3}$$
$$x^{(0)}(i) \in x^{(0)}$$

Then $x^{(1)} = \{\sum_{i-1}^{1} x^{(0)}(i), \sum_{i-1}^{2} x^{(0)}(i), \ldots, \sum_{i-1}^{n} x^{(0)}(i)\}$, which is the first order AGO series obtained from $x^{(0)}$.

2.3   Grey 1-IAGO

From Eq. (3), it is obvious that the original data $x^{(0)}(i)$ can be easily recovered from $x^{(1)}(i)$ as

$$x^{(0)}(i) = x^{(1)}(i) - x^{(1)}(i-1) \tag{4}$$

where $x^{(0)}(1) = x^{(1)}(1), x^{(1)}(i) \in x^{(1)}$. This operation is called first order IAGO.

2.4   Grey Dynamic Model GM(1,1)

If we have $n \geq 4$, $x^{(0)}, x^{(1)} \in R^+$, and can satisfy the precondition:

$$\left.\begin{array}{l} \sigma^{(1)}(i) \in (e^{-\frac{2}{n+1}}, e^{+\frac{2}{n+1}}) \\[2mm] \sigma^{(1)}(i) = \frac{x^{(1)}(i-1)}{x^{(1)}(i)} \end{array}\right\} \tag{5}$$

where $\sigma^{(1)}(i)$ is called class ratio.

The grey dynamic prediction model GM(1,1) can be expressed by one variable, and first order differential equation.

$$\frac{dx^{(1)}}{dt} + ax^{(1)} = b \tag{6}$$

The solution for Eq. (6) is

$$\hat{x}^{(1)}(i+1) = \left(x^{(0)}(1) - \frac{b}{a}\right)e^{-ai} + \frac{b}{a} \tag{7}$$

where the coefficients a and b are called development and grey input coefficient, respectively. Then, by least-square method, the coefficients a and b can be obtained as

$$\begin{bmatrix} a \\ b \end{bmatrix} = (A^T A)^{-1} A^T X_n \tag{8}$$

$$A = \begin{bmatrix} -\frac{1}{2}\left(x^{(1)}(1) + x^{(1)}(2)\right) & 1 \\ -\frac{1}{2}\left(x^{(1)}(2) + x^{(1)}(3)\right) & 1 \\ \vdots & \vdots \\ -\frac{1}{2}\left(x^{(1)}(n-1) + x^{(1)}(n)\right) & 1 \end{bmatrix} \tag{9}$$

$$X_n = \begin{bmatrix} x^{(0)}(2) \\ x^{(0)}(3) \\ \vdots \\ x^{(0)}(n) \end{bmatrix} \tag{10}$$

By 1-IAGO, the predicted equation is,

$$\hat{x}^{(0)}(i+1) = \hat{x}^{(1)}(i+1) - \hat{x}^{(1)}(i)$$
$$= \left(x^{(0)}(1) - \frac{b}{a}\right)(1 - e^a)e^{-ai} \tag{11}$$

where $x^{(0)}(1) = x^{(1)}(1)$.

From Eq. (11), the predicted data series $\hat{x}^{(0)} = \{\hat{x}^{(0)}(1), \hat{x}^{(0)}(2), \ldots, \hat{x}^{(0)}(n+m)\}$, $m \geq 1$ are obtained for original data series $x^{(0)} = \{x^{(0)}(1), x^{(0)}(2), \ldots, x^{(0)}(n)\}$.

3   MGM(1,1) Model

In this paper, we present Markov-chain to enhance predicted accuracy of GM(1,1). The new generated model is defined as MGM(1,1). The original data are first modeled by the GM(1,1), then the residual errors between the predicted values and the actual values for all previous time steps are obtained. The idea of the MGM(1,1) is to establish the transition behavior of those residual errors by Markov transition matrices, then possible correction for the predicted value can be made from those Markov matrices. The detailed procedure is shown as follows.

- **Step 1:** The division of state
  - Establishment of GM(1,1) model
    For original data series $x^{(0)}(i)$, use GM(1,1) model to obtain predicted value $\hat{x}^{(0)}(i)$. Then the residual errors $e(i) = x^{(0)}(i) - \hat{x}^{(0)}(i)$ can be also obtained.
  - Division state by Markov-chain
    Assume that there exists some regular information in the residual errors series of GM(1,1). We can establish Markov state transition matrices, r states are defined for each time step. Thus the dimension of the transition matrix is $r \times r$. The residual errors are partitioned into r equal portions called states. Each state is an interval whose width is equal to a fixed portion of the range between the maximum and the minimum of the whole residual errors. Then, the actual error can be classified into those states.

    Let S_{ij} be the jth state of the ith time step

$$S_{ij} \in \left[L_{ij}, U_{ij} \right], \ j = 1, 2, \ldots, r \tag{12}$$

where L_{ij} and U_{ij} are the lower boundary and upper boundary of the jth state for the ith time step of the residual errors series.

$$L_{ij} = \min e(i) + \frac{j-1}{r} \left(\max e(i) - \min e(i) \right) \tag{13}$$

$$U_{ij} = \min e(i) + \frac{j}{r} \left(\max e(i) - \min e(i) \right) \tag{14}$$

$e(i)$ is residual errors of GM(1,1).

- **Setp 2:** Establishment of transition probability matrix of state
  If the transition probability of state is written as

$$P_{ij}^{(m)} = \frac{M_{ij}^{(m)}}{M_i}, j = 1, 2, \ldots, r \tag{15}$$

where $P_{ij}^{(m)}$ is the probability of transition from state i to j by m steps. $M_{ij}^{(m)}$ is the transition times from state i to j by m steps and M_i is the number of data belonging to the ith state. Because the transition for the last m entries of the series is indefinable, M_i should be counted by the first as $n - m$ entries, n is the quantity of entries of the original series. Then, the transition probability matrix of state can be written as

$$R^{(m)} = \begin{bmatrix} P_{11}^{(m)} & P_{12}^{(m)} & \cdots & P_{1r}^{(m)} \\ P_{21}^{(m)} & P_{22}^{(m)} & \cdots & P_{2r}^{(m)} \\ \vdots & \vdots & \ddots & \vdots \\ P_{r1}^{(m)} & P_{r2}^{(m)} & \cdots & P_{rr}^{(m)} \end{bmatrix} \tag{16}$$

The transition probability matrix of states $R^{(m)}$ reflects the transition rules of the system. The transition probability of states $P_{ij}^{(m)}$ reflects the probability of transition from initial state i to probable state j by m steps. It is the foundation of prediction by the Markov probability matrix. For example, consider $m=1$ and the maximum transition step is 1. Then, $R^{(1)}$ can be obtained. If the predicted original data is located in the ith state, the predicted data of next step is calculated by the row vector of transition probability states $P_{ij}^{(1)}$.

- **Step 3:** Obtaining the predicted value
  The residual error series $e(i)$ is divided into r states, then there is r transition probability vectors. The possibilities of a certain error state for the next step are obtained by the probabilities in r vectors, denoted as $\{a_i(T), i = 1, 2, \ldots, r\}$ at time step T. Define the centers of r states as $\{v_i, i = 1, 2, \ldots, r\}$. Then, the predicted value for the next step is

$$\tilde{x}^{(0)}(T + 1) = \hat{x}^{(0)}(T + 1) + \sum_{i=1}^{r} a_i(T)v_i \tag{17}$$

where

$$a^{(T)} = [a_1(T), a_2(T), \ldots, a_r(T)] = a^{(T-1)} R^{(m)} \tag{18}$$

and

$$\begin{cases} a^{(T+1)} = a^{(T)} R^{(m)} \\ a^{(T+2)} = a^{(T+1)} R^{(m)} \\ \quad\vdots \\ a^{(T+k)} = a^{(T+k-1)} R^{(m)} \end{cases} \tag{19}$$

where $m = 1$.

4   T-MGM(1,1) Model

4.1   Grey Interval Analysis

In Eq. (17), the predicted value $\tilde{x}^{(0)}(T + 1)$ of MGM(1,1) is calculated by the centers of r states as $\{v_i, i = 1, 2, \ldots, r\}$. Actually, these states intervals consist of uncertain grey set which including non-precise information. Only using each center value, thus it will disregard the existences of grey information in the states intervals [4]. According to Definitions 2 and 3, the division states shown in Eq. (12) can be viewed as grey intervals, then jth state of the ith time step can be expressed as

$$\otimes S_{ij} = [L_{ij}, U_{ij}], \quad j = 1, 2, \ldots, r \tag{20}$$

The whitening method for the grey state S_{ij} is given as

$$S_{ij} = (1 - \lambda_j)L_{ij} + \lambda_j U_{ij} \tag{21}$$

where $\lambda_j \in [0, 1]$, λ_j is called whitening coefficient. When $\lambda_j = 0.5$, the value from Eq. (21), become the centers value of r states shown in Eq. (17).

4.2   T-MGM(1,1)

The predicted value of T-MGM(1,1) model based on grey interval analysis can be expressed as

$$\check{x}^{(0)}(T+1) = \hat{x}^{(0)}(T+1) + \sum_{i=1}^{r} a_i(T) \otimes v_i \qquad (22)$$

where

$$\otimes v_i = [L_i, U_i] \qquad (23)$$

The whiten method of $\otimes v_i$ is shown as

$$v_i = (1 - \lambda_i)L_i + \lambda_i U_i \qquad (24)$$

where $\lambda_i \in [0, 1]$, for $i = 1, 2, \ldots, r$.

In this paper, we propose Taylor approximation method to optimize the values of $\{\lambda_i, i = 1, 2, \ldots, r\}$. Taylor approximation method [5] which combines the Taylor development with the least squares method is an approximate calculation method of multi-times to obtain the optimal coefficients values and makes the convergent error reduce to the minimum. Therefore, the whitening coefficients of MGM(1,1) can be optimized by Taylor approximation method [6]. By the optimization process, the coefficients values of $\lambda_i^{(K)}$ are updated for K times, we can obtain the optimal predicted value.

5   Case Study

The three criteria are used for evaluating proposed model. They are the mean square error (MSE), absolute mean error (AME) and absolute error (AE) which are calculated as

$$\text{MSE} = \frac{1}{n} \sum_{i=1}^{n} e^2(i) \qquad (25)$$

$$\text{AME} = \frac{1}{n} \sum_{i=1}^{n} |e(i)| \qquad (26)$$

$$\text{AE} = |e(i)| \qquad (27)$$

where $e(i) = x^{(0)} - \check{x}^{(0)}$.

In this paper, according the statistics data of international airlines amount increase from 1985 to 2003 in China [7], we predict the international airlines amount from 2004 to 2010. The predicted procedures are described below:

- **Step 1:** Input data
  The statistics annual data of international airlines amount from 1985 to 2003 are used to establish model.

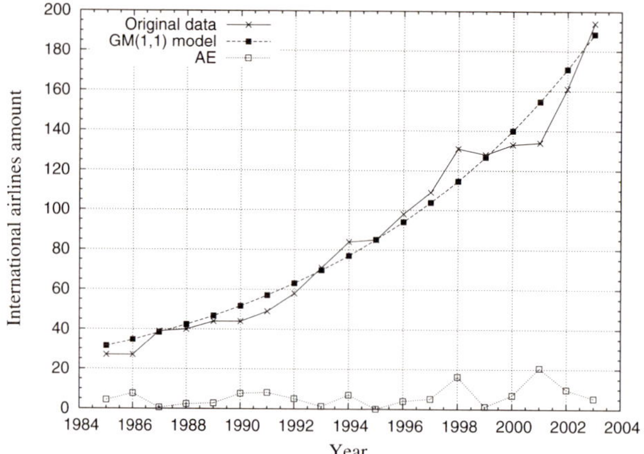

Fig. 1. The predicted values and absolute error AE by GM(1,1) for international airlines amount from 1985 to 2003

– **Setp 2:** Establishment of prediction model GM(1,1)
According to the original data series $\{x^{(0)}(i), i = 1, 2, \ldots, n\}$, we establish the prediction model GM(1,1) by Eq. (7). As the results, the predicted generated data series $\{\hat{x}^{(0)}(i), i = 1, 2, \ldots, n\}$ and original data are plotted in Fig. 1. The absolute error (AE) is also plotted in Fig. 1. We can see that the AE is still very big for GM(1,1) and it cannot exactly match the international airlines system dynamics.

– **Setp 3:** Establishment of prediction model MGM(1,1)
  • The division of state
    According to the predicted data series $\{\hat{x}^{(0)}(i), i = 1, 2, \ldots, n\}$ by GM(1,1), we can obtain its residual error series $e(i)$. From the obtained residual errors, the corresponding intervals are divided into four states for this study. The four states are [-20.58, -11.35], [-11.35, -2.13], [-2.13, 7.10] and [7.10, 16.32]. The four states based on their residual errors are defined.
  • Establishment of transition probability matrix of state
    By the state of each entry, the transition probability matrices of state $R^{(m)}, m = 1$ can be evaluated as

$$R^{(1)} = \begin{bmatrix} 0.000\ 1.000\ 0.000\ 0.000 \\ 0.111\ 0.556\ 0.333\ 0.000 \\ 0.000\ 0.286\ 0.571\ 0.143 \\ 0.000\ 0.000\ 0.000\ 1.000 \end{bmatrix}$$

  • Obtaining predicted values
    According to the four states, we can calculate their centers values. Then $v_1 = -15.97$, $v_2 = -6.74$, $v_3 = 2.48$ and $v_4 = 11.71$ are obtained. The model predicted values by MGM(1,1), and the experimental original data

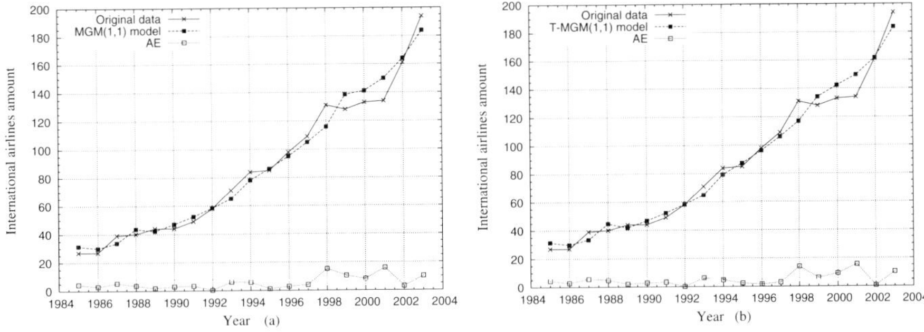

Fig. 2. The predicted values and absolute error AE by (a) MGM(1,1) (b) T-MGM(1,1) for international airlines amount from 1985 to 2003

are plotted in Fig. 2 (a). The AE is also plotted in Fig. 2 (a). It is obvious that the extreme-effect has been somewhat removed and the fitted and predicted curves are on the right track.

– **Setp 4:** Establishment of prediction model T-MGM(1,1)
  - The state division by grey interval analysis
    According to the four states, we can view them as grey interval states. When whitening coefficients λ_i is introduced to whiten the grey intervals, then we use Taylor approximation method to optimize the whiten coefficients and obtain the best high predicted accuracy.
  - Obtaining predicted values
    According to 1 step probability transition matrices $R^{(1)}$ and four grey interval states, for predicted data $\{\check{x}^{(0)}(i), i = 1, 2, \ldots, n\}$ from MGM(1,1), we establish T-MGM(1,1) model to enhance predicted accuracy. We present Taylor approximation method to optimize these whitening coefficients $\{\lambda_i, i = 1, 2, 3, 4\}$. The updated times $K=300$ is set, The evaluation function is convergent. The values $\{\lambda_i, i = 1, 2, 3, 4\}$ are obtained as 0.85, 0.76, 0.04 and 0.96 respectively. The model predicted values by T-MGM(1,1), and the experimental original data are plotted in Fig. 2 (b). The AE is also plotted in Fig. 2 (b). It is obvious that the predicted result is moved a step toward the actual one. The accuracy comparison of three models are listed in Table. 1.
  - Obtaining the predicted value by T-MGM(1,1) model from 2004 to 2010
    By T-MGM(1,1) model, we predict the international airlines amount from 2004 to 2010. The predicted results are listed in Table 2.

Prediction is through obtaining the relation of already-known data to analyze the development tendency of system in the future. We use the already-known airlines data from 1985 to 2003 to establish prediction model GM(1,1). In order to enhance predicted accuracy, the Markov chain and Taylor approximation method based on grey interval analysis are presented to incorporate with GM(1,1). From

Table 1. The accuracy comparison of three models for international airlines amount from 1985 to 2003

Models	MSE	AME	Updated times K	Training Time(sec)	Testing Time(sec)
GM(1,1)	63.32	6.15	0	0	0.5
MGM(1,1)	50.32	5.67	0	0	0.8
T-MGM(1,1)	44.82	5.24	300	1.5	0.8

Table 2. The predicted value of international airlines amount by TMGM(1,1) model from 2004 to 2010

Year	2004	2005	2006	2007	2008	2009	2010
Interational airlines	210.7	231.1	255.0	281.8	311.5	344.4	380.6

the results of accuracy comparison, the T-MGM(1,1) obtained the best accuracy, AME and MSE are 44.82 and 5.24 respectively. We obtained the effectiveness of proposed model. Then by T-MGM(1,1) model, we predicted the airlines amount increase from 2004 to 2010.

6   Conclusions

The major purpose of this paper is to develop the prediction model of international airlines amount increase in China. Through using the statistics data of international airlines amount from 1985 to 2003, we verified the effectiveness of proposed model. The effects are achieved more than conventional GM(1,1) model. And we predicted the international airlines amount from 2004 to 2010 by proposed GM(1,1). For airline management system, the proposed grey-based dynamic model is very useful.

References

1. Deng, J.L.: Control Problems of Grey System. System and Control Letters. **5** 288–294, 1982.
2. Su, S.F., Lin, C.B., and Hsu, Y.T. : A High Precision Global Prediction Approach Based on Local Prediction Approaches. IEEE Trans Syst Man Cybern. **32** (4) 191–94, 2002.
3. Nagai, M. and Yamaguchi, D.: Elements on Grey System Theory and its Applications. Kyoritsu publisher, 2004.
4. Xia, J.: Grey System Theory to Hydrology. Huazhong Univ. of Science and Technology Press, 2000.
5. Aaron, M.R.: The Use of Least Squares in System Design. IRE Trans on Circuit Theory. **3** (4) 224–231, 1956.
6. Li, G.D., Yamaguchi, D. and Nagai, M.: New Methods and Accuracy Improvement of GM According to Laplace Transform. J. Grey Syst. **8** (1) 13–25, 2005.
7. China Statistical Yearbook, National Bureau of Statistics of China, China Statistics Press, 1985-2004.

On the Combination of Rough Set Theory and Grey Theory Based on Grey Lattice Operations

Daisuke Yamaguchi[1], Guo-Dong Li[1], and Masatake Nagai[2]

[1] Graduate School of Kanagawa University, Department of Engineering, 3-27-1
Rokkakubashi, Kanagawa-ku, Yokohama 221-8686, Japan
`daicom0204@yahoo.co.jp`, `guodong_li2004@yahoo.co.jp`
[2] Kanagawa University, Faculty of Engineering, 3-27-1 Rokkakubashi, Kanagawa-ku,
Yokohama 221-8686, Japan
`masatake4263@oregano.ocn.ne.jp`

Abstract. A new rough set named grey-rough set based on the grey
lattice operation in grey system theory is proposed in this paper. Information systems records not only categorical data but also numerical
data including a range of interval. In order to handle interval data in such
information systems, we describe two sorts of new rough approximation
after introduced grey lattice operations: a special grey-rough set based on
the equivalence relation of interval coincidence, and a general grey-rough
set based on the meet operation and the inclusion relation instead of the
equivalence relation. The special grey-rough set is applicable to categorical data and numerical discrete data like the traditional rough set. The
general grey-rough set is applicable to numerical interval data, which
means that the proposal is an advanced method for non-deterministic
information systems. The proposal is illustrated with several examples.

1 Introduction

Rough set theory (rough sets) proposed by Pawlak [1,2,3] is a useful mathematical tool to handle uncertainly. Rough set theory is used in many fields: Data
classification, Feature extraction, Inference, Machine learning and Rule induction
and so on. A lot of methods based on rough set theory are developed and applied.
Pawlak proposed the minimal decision rule induction from the indiscernibly relation, and proposed two rough approximations: the upper approximation which
handles possibility, the lower approximation which handles certainly or necessity. The traditional rough sets deal with categorical data or numerical discrete
data. However, information systems records not only categorical data but also
numerical data including a range of interval.

Grey system theory [4,5,6,7,8] proposed by Deng first handles uncertainly of
grey number. In recent years, a combination of grey system theory and rough set
theory is reported by Zhang [9] and Wu [10], in order to handle uncertainly more
flexibly. Zhang's rough grey set includes new rough approximations based on grey
sets and whitening functions. Wu's grey rough set is that a rough approximation
is defined for the range set.

S. Greco et al. (Eds.): RSCTC 2006, LNAI 4259, pp. 507–516, 2006.

A new combination of rough set theory and grey system theory based on the grey lattice operation [11,12] is proposed in this paper. Two sorts of new rough set named grey-rough set including a rough approximation are proposed: a special grey-rough set is based on the equivalence relation of the interval coincidence, and a general grey-rough set which replaces the equivalence class condition with the grey lattice operation. The grey lattice operation is one of the operations for grey number which modify a range of a given interval of grey number. The proposal does not only deal with categorical data, but also numerical interval data. The proposal expands the treatable value.

2   Grey Lattice Operations

Grey numbers are expanded or contracted their own boundaries of interval by the grey lattice operation. In this section, we summaries these operations, and some of new definitions according to interval analysis [13, 14, 15, 16, 17, 18, 19, 20, 21], interval algebra [22] and lattice theory [23] are added.

Let $\mathbb{U}$ denote an universal set, x an element of $\mathbb{U}(x \in \mathbb{U})$, $\mathbb{R}$ a real number set, and X a set of value range that x may hold respectively.

Definition 1. *Let G be a grey set of $\mathbb{U}$ defined by two mappings of the upper membership function $\overline{\mu}_G(x)$ and the lower membership function $\underline{\mu}_G(x)$ as follows:*

$$\left. \begin{array}{l} \overline{\mu}_G(x) : x \to [0,1] \\ \underline{\mu}_G(x) : x \to [0,1] \end{array} \right\} \tag{1}$$

where $\underline{\mu}_G(x) \leq \overline{\mu}_G(x)$, $x \in \mathbb{U}$. When $\underline{\mu}_G(x) = \overline{\mu}_G(x)$, the grey set G becomes a fuzzy set, which means grey system theory deals with flexibly fuzziness situation.

Definition 2. *When two values $\underline{x}, \overline{x}(\underline{x} = \inf X, \overline{x} = \sup X)$ are given in x, then x is defined using a symbol $\otimes x = x|_{\underline{\mu}}^{\overline{\mu}}$ as follows:*

1. *If $\underline{x} \to -\infty, \overline{x} \to +\infty$, then $\otimes x$ is called black number*
2. *If $\underline{x} = \overline{x}$, $\otimes x$ is called white number or whitened value, and denoted by $\tilde{\otimes}x$*
3. *Otherwise $\otimes x \rightleftarrows [\underline{x}, \overline{x}]$ is called grey number*

Definition 3. *Let '$\rightleftarrows$' denote that two grey numbers $\otimes x$ and $\otimes y$ are coincidence each other, described by*

$$\otimes x \rightleftarrows \otimes y \quad \text{if } \underline{x} = \underline{y} \text{ and } \overline{x} = \overline{y} \tag{2}$$

where $\otimes x \rightleftarrows [\underline{x}, \overline{x}]$ and $\otimes y \rightleftarrows [\underline{y}, \overline{y}]$.

Definition 4. *There are two elements x and y. The notion that x is included by y is denoted by*

$$\otimes x \to \otimes y \quad \text{if } \underline{y} \leq \underline{x} \text{ and } \overline{x} \leq \overline{y} \tag{3}$$

If any real number $a(a \in \mathbb{R})$ or $\tilde{\otimes}x$ are included by $\otimes y$, this notion is described by

$$a \to \otimes y \text{ if } \underline{y} \leq a \text{ and } a \leq \overline{y} \tag{4}$$

$$\tilde{\otimes}x \to \otimes y \text{ if } \underline{y} \leq \tilde{\otimes}x \text{ and } \tilde{\otimes}x \leq \overline{y} \tag{5}$$

Definition 5. *The relation '$\rightarrow$' is consistent with the order relation for three grey numbers $\otimes x, \otimes y$ and $\otimes z$ as follows:*

1. $\otimes x \rightarrow \otimes x$
2. $\otimes x \rightarrow \otimes y, \otimes y \rightarrow \otimes x \Leftrightarrow \otimes x \rightleftarrows \otimes y$
3. $\otimes x \rightarrow \otimes y, \otimes y \rightarrow \otimes z \Rightarrow \otimes x \rightarrow \otimes z$

Definition 6. *The relation '$\rightleftarrows$' is consistent with the equivalence relation for three grey numbers $\otimes x, \otimes y$ and $\otimes z$ as follows:*

1. $\otimes x \rightleftarrows \otimes x$
2. $\otimes x \rightleftarrows \otimes y \Leftrightarrow \otimes y \rightleftarrows \otimes x$
3. $\otimes x \rightleftarrows \otimes y, \otimes y \rightleftarrows \otimes z \Rightarrow \otimes x \rightleftarrows \otimes z$

Definition 7. *The following grey lattice operations are defined for two grey numbers $\otimes x$ of x and $\otimes y$ of y:*

1. Join $(x \cup y)$:

$$\otimes x \vee \otimes y \rightleftarrows [\min(\underline{x}, \underline{y}), \max(\overline{x}, \overline{y})] \tag{6}$$

$$\tilde{\otimes}x \vee \tilde{\otimes}y \rightleftarrows [\min(\tilde{\otimes}x, \tilde{\otimes}y), \max(\tilde{\otimes}x, \tilde{\otimes}y)] \tag{7}$$

2. Meet $(x \cap y)$:

$$\otimes x \wedge \otimes y \rightleftarrows \begin{cases} [\underline{x}, \overline{x}] & \text{if } \otimes x \rightarrow \otimes y \\ [\underline{y}, \overline{y}] & \text{if } \otimes y \rightarrow \otimes x \\ [\underline{x}, \overline{y}] & \text{if } \underline{x} \rightarrow \otimes y \text{ and } \overline{y} \rightarrow \otimes x \\ [\underline{y}, \overline{x}] & \text{if } \underline{y} \rightarrow \otimes x \text{ and } \overline{x} \rightarrow \otimes y \\ \varnothing & \text{otherwise} \end{cases} \tag{8}$$

$$\tilde{\otimes}x \wedge \tilde{\otimes}y \rightleftarrows \begin{cases} \tilde{\otimes}x & \text{if } \tilde{\otimes}x = \tilde{\otimes}y \\ \varnothing & \text{else} \end{cases} \tag{9}$$

3. Complimentary:

$$\otimes x^c = \{x \in X^c | x < \underline{x}, \overline{x} < x\} \tag{10}$$

4. Exclusive Join $(x \oplus y)$:

$$\otimes x \oplus \otimes y = \begin{cases} (\otimes x \vee \otimes y) \wedge (\otimes x^c \vee \otimes y^c) \\ (\otimes x \vee \otimes y) \wedge (\otimes x \wedge \otimes y)^c \end{cases} \tag{11}$$

Theorem 1. *The following laws are satisfied refer to [22, 23]:*

Idempotent: $\otimes x \vee \otimes x \rightleftarrows \otimes x; \; \otimes x \wedge \otimes x \rightleftarrows \otimes x$
Commutative: $\otimes x \vee \otimes y \rightleftarrows \otimes y \vee \otimes x; \; \otimes x \wedge \otimes y \rightleftarrows \otimes y \wedge \otimes x$
Associative: $(\otimes x \vee \otimes y) \vee \otimes z \rightleftarrows \otimes x \vee (\otimes y \vee \otimes z);$
$\quad (\otimes x \wedge \otimes y) \wedge \otimes z \rightleftarrows \otimes x \wedge (\otimes y \wedge \otimes z)$
Distributive: $\otimes x \wedge (\otimes y \vee \otimes z) \rightleftarrows (\otimes x \wedge \otimes y) \vee (\otimes x \wedge \otimes z);$
$\quad \otimes x \vee (\otimes y \wedge \otimes z) \rightleftarrows (\otimes x \vee \otimes y) \wedge (\otimes x \vee \otimes z)$

Absorption: $(\otimes x \vee \otimes y) \wedge \otimes x \rightleftarrows \otimes x$; $(\otimes x \wedge \otimes y) \vee \otimes x \rightleftarrows \otimes x$
Complement: $\otimes x \wedge \otimes x^c \rightleftarrows \varnothing$; $\otimes x \vee \otimes x^c \rightleftarrows \mathbb{R}$
Double Complimentary: $(\otimes x^c)^c \rightleftarrows \otimes x$
De Morgen's law: $(\otimes x \vee \otimes y)^c \rightleftarrows \otimes x^c \wedge \otimes y^c$; $(\otimes x \wedge \otimes y)^c \rightleftarrows \otimes x^c \vee \otimes y^c$

Definition 8. *Some of the whitening functions [11,12] which compute a whitened value from a grey number according to [14,21] are defined as follows:*

Midpoint $\mathrm{mid}(\otimes x) = (\underline{x} + \overline{x})/2$ **Size** $\mathrm{size}(\otimes x) = (|\underline{x}| + |\overline{x}|)/2$
Diameter $\mathrm{dia}(\otimes x) = \overline{x} - \underline{x}$ **Radius** $\mathrm{rad}(\otimes x) = (\overline{x} - \underline{x})/2$
Magnitude $\mathrm{mag}(\otimes x) = \max(|\underline{x}|, |\overline{x}|)$ **Mignitude** $\mathrm{mig}(\otimes x) = \min(|\underline{x}|, |\overline{x}|)$

Sign $\mathrm{sign}(\otimes x) = \begin{cases} 1 & \text{if } 0 < \underline{x} \\ 0 & \text{if } 0 \to \otimes x \\ -1 & \text{if } \overline{x} < 0 \end{cases}$ **Heaviside** $\mathrm{hv}(\otimes x) = \begin{cases} 1 & \text{if } 0 \le \underline{x} \\ 0 & \text{if } \overline{x} < 0 \end{cases}$

Absolute $\mathrm{abs}(\otimes x) = \mathrm{mag}(\otimes x) - \mathrm{mig}(\otimes x)$
Pivot $\mathrm{piv}(\otimes x) = \sqrt{\mathrm{mag}(\otimes x) \cdot \mathrm{mig}(\otimes x)}$
Overlap $\xi(\otimes x, \otimes y) = \frac{\mathrm{dia}(\otimes x \wedge \otimes y)}{\mathrm{dia}(\otimes x \vee \otimes y)}$
where $\otimes x \wedge \otimes y \rightleftarrows \varnothing \Leftrightarrow \xi(\otimes x, \otimes y) = 0$; $\otimes x \rightleftarrows \otimes y \Leftrightarrow \xi(\otimes x, \otimes y) = 1$

3 Special Grey-Rough Sets

3.1 Combination of Rough Set Theory and Grey System Theory

The traditional rough set is based on the equivalence class of given information table. We describe that a rough approximation can be obtained by the equivalence class of the relation '$\rightleftarrows$' in grey system theory.

Definition 9. *Let* $[x]_{GR}$ *denote an equivalence class of the relation '$\rightleftarrows$', which is defined as follows:*

$$[x]_{GR} = \{y \in \mathbb{U} | x \rightleftarrows y\} \tag{12}$$

and $[x]_{GR}$ *holds the following properties:*

1. *$x \in [x]_{GR}$ for any x*
2. *$x \rightleftarrows y$, then $[x]_{GR} = [y]_{GR}$*
3. *$[x]_{GR} \neq [y]_{GR}$, then $[x]_{GR} \cap [y]_{GR} = \varnothing$*

Definition 10. *Let* $A(\mathbb{U}, \rightleftarrows)$ *denote an approximation space and* $\mathbb{U}/ \rightleftarrows$ *be a partition of* $\mathbb{U}$ *in* A.

Definition 11. *Let S be a subset of* $\mathbb{U}$, $GR^*(S)$ *an upper approximation of S, $GR_*(S)$ a lower approximation of S, and $BND(S)$ a boundary respectively, which is defined as follows:*

$$GR^*(S) = \{x \in \mathbb{U} | [x]_{GR} \cap S \neq \varnothing\} \tag{13}$$

$$GR_*(S) = \{x \in \mathbb{U} | [x]_{GR} \subseteq S\} \tag{14}$$

$$BND(S) = GR^*(S) - GR_*(S) \tag{15}$$

We define that a pair $\langle GR^*(S), GR_*(S) \rangle$ *is a special grey-rough set.*

Theorem 2. *A special grey-rough set holds the following properties:*

1. $GR_*(S) \subseteq S \subseteq GR^*(S)$
2. $GR_*(\varnothing) = GR^*(\varnothing) = \varnothing;\ GR_*(\mathbb{U}) = GR^*(\mathbb{U}) = \mathbb{U}$
3. $GR_*(S \cap T) = GR_*(S) \cap GR_*(T);\ GR^*(S \cup T) = GR^*(S) \cup GR^*(T)$
4. $S \subseteq T\ implies\ GR_*(S) \subseteq GR_*(T);\ S \subseteq T\ implies\ GR^*(S) \subseteq GR^*(T)$
5. $GR_*(S \cup T) \supseteq GR_*(S) \cup GR_*(T);\ GR^*(S \cap T) \subseteq GR^*(S) \cap GR^*(T)$
6. $GR_*(\mathbb{U} - S) = \mathbb{U} - GR^*(S);\ GR^*(\mathbb{U} - S) = \mathbb{U} - GR_*(S)$
7. $GR_*(GR_*(S)) = GR^*(GR_*(S)) = GR_*(S);$
   $GR^*(GR^*(S)) = GR_*(GR^*(S)) = GR^*(S)$

Proof. The relation '$\rightleftarrows$' is included by the relation R suggested by Pawlak [1,2], and then every property is consistent. $\qquad\square$

A special grey-rough set is a combination of grey system theory and rough set theory, because this proposal is a new rough approximation for interval data based on the grey lattice operation.

3.2 Illustrative Examples

Example 1 (for categorical data). Table 1 is a sample information table by Pawlak [24] constructed from 6 patients and 4 attributes. The traditional rough set theory deals with such categorical data.

We are able to transfer the given values except Flu from the left-side of Table 1 to the right-side, from {yes, no} to {1, 0}, and from {very high, high, normal} to {2, 1, 0}. A partition by $[p]_{GR}$ on the attributes Headache, Muscle-pain and Temperature is given as follows:

$$\{\{p_1\}, \{p_2, p_5\}, \{p_3\}, \{p_4\}, \{p_6\}\}$$

where $\{p_2, p_5\}$ becomes an equivalence class, because $\otimes p_2 \overrightarrow{\rightharpoonup} \otimes p_5 \leftrightarrow \tilde{\otimes} p_2 - \tilde{\otimes} p_5$ on each attribute. This example is a special case of grey number.

Let $S_1 = \{p | \text{Flu} = \text{yes}\} = \{p_1, p_2, p_3, p_6\}$ be a patient set, and then the upper and the lower approximations of S_1 are given as follows:

$$GR^*(S_1) = \{p_1, p_2, p_3, p_5, p_6\}, GR_*(S_1) = \{p_1, p_3, p_6\}, BND(S_1) = \{p_2, p_5\}$$

Let $S_2 = \{p | \text{Flu} = \text{no}\} = \{p_4, p_5\}$ be another patient set, and then the upper and the lower approximations of S_2 are given as follows:

$$GR^*(S_2) = \{p_2, p_4, p_5\}, GR_*(S_2) = \{p_4\}, BND(S_2) = \{p_2, p_5\}$$

Thus a special grey-rough set is compatible with the traditional rough set, because categorical data equals to the numerical discrete data as a whitened value of grey number in grey system theory.

Table 1. Sample information table by Pawlak [24]

Patient	Headache	Muscle-pain	Temperature	Flu	Headache	Muscle-pain	Temperature	Flu
p_1	no	yes	high	yes	0	1	1	yes
p_2	yes	no	high	yes	1	0	1	yes
p_3	yes	yes	very high	yes	1	1	2	yes
p_4	no	yes	normal	no	0	1	0	no
p_5	yes	no	high	no	1	0	1	no
p_6	no	yes	very high	yes	0	1	2	yes

Table 2. Recomposed AUTO-MPG data set (original data from UCI repository [25])

No.	Manufacturer	M.P.G.	Cylinders	Displacement	Horsepower	Weight	Acceleration	Model-year	Country
1	Audi	[20,36.4]	[4,5]	[97,131]	[67,103]	[2.19,2.95]	[14,19.9]	[70,80]	Germany
2	BMW	[21.5,26]	[4,4]	[121,121]	[110,113]	[2.23,2.60]	[12.5,12.8]	[70,77]	Germany
3	Cadillac	[16.5,23]	[8,8]	[350,350]	[125,180]	[3.90,4.38]	[12.1,17.4]	[76,79]	USA
4	Ford	[15,36.1]	[4,6]	[98,250]	[65,98]	[1.80,3.57]	[13.6,21]	[70,81]	USA
5	Honda	[24,44.6]	[4,4]	[81,120]	[53,97]	[1.76,2.49]	[13.8,18.5]	[74,82]	Japan
6	Mazda	[18,46.6]	[3,4]	[70,120]	[52,110]	[1.97,2.72]	[12.5,19.4]	[72,82]	Japan
7	Subaru	[26,33.8]	[4,4]	[97,108]	[67,93]	[1.99,2.39]	[15.5,18]	[74,81]	Japan
8	Toyota	[19,39.1]	[4,6]	[71,168]	[52,122]	[1.65,2.93]	[12.6,21]	[70,81]	Japan
9	Volkswargen	[25,43.1]	[4,4]	[79,105]	[48,78]	[1.83,2.22]	[12.2,21.5]	[74,82]	Germany
10	Volvo	[17,30.7]	[4,6]	[121,163]	[76,125]	[2.87,3.16]	[13.6,19.6]	[72,81]	Sweden

Example 2 (for interval data). Auto-MPG data set from UCI Repository [25] is used in this example; Table 2 constructed from 8 attributes including Manufacturer is recomposed from the original data by the authors. 108 automobiles of 391 in the original data are classified into 10 manufacturers. In order to evaluate a difference among manufacturers in specifications, maximum and minimum values of those 7 attributes are obtained by the join operation because each automobile model has deferent specifications even the same manufacturer.

Table 3 shows one of the extracted tables on the attributes Cylinders and Model-year. A partition by $[x]_{GR}$ based on the equivalence class of interval is:

$$\{\{1\}, \{2\}, \{3\}, \{4, 8\}, \{5, 9\}, \{6\}, \{7\}, \{10\}\}$$

where each number equals to 'No.' of Table 2. Let $S_1 = \{$No.$|$ Country = Japan$\}$ = $\{5, 6, 7, 8\}$, $S_2 = \{$No.$|$Country = Germany$\}$ = $\{1, 2, 9\}$, $S_3 = \{$No.$|$ Country = USA$\}$ = $\{3, 4\}$ and $S_4 = \{$No.$|$Country = Sweden$\}$ = $\{10\}$ be sample sets respectively, and then the proposal rough approximations are given as follows:

$$GR^*(S_1) = \{4, 5, 6, 7, 8, 9\}, GR_*(S_1) = \{6, 7\}, BND(S_1) = \{4, 5, 8, 9\}$$

$$GR^*(S_2) = \{1, 2, 5, 9\}, GR_*(S_2) = \{1, 2\}, BND(S_2) = \{5, 9\}$$

$$GR^*(S_3) = \{3, 4, 8\}, GR_*(S_3) = \{3\}, BND(S_3) = \{4, 8\}$$

$$GR^*(S_4) = \{10\}, GR_*(S_4) = \{10\}, BND(S_4) = \varnothing$$

Thus the special grey-rough set is possible to apply interval data. The grey-rough set extends a treatable value into interval data.

4   General Grey-Rough Sets

4.1   General Grey-Rough Sets on One Attribute

A general grey-rough set deals with the inclusion and the meet operation of the grey lattice operation instead of the equivalence class, in order to handle uncertainly, possibility and necessity more flexibly for interval data.

Table 3. Extracted AUTO-MPG data set

No.	Manufacturer	Cylinders	Model-year	Country
1	Audi	[4,5]	[70,80]	Germany
2	BMW	[4,4]	[70,77]	Germany
3	Cadillac	[8,8]	[76,79]	USA
4	Ford	[4,6]	[70,81]	USA
5	Honda	[4,4]	[74,82]	Japan
6	Mazda	[3,4]	[72,82]	Japan
7	Subaru	[4,4]	[74,81]	Japan
8	Toyota	[4,6]	[70,81]	Japan
9	Volkswargen	[4,4]	[74,82]	Germany
10	Volvo	[4,6]	[72,81]	Sweden

Definition 12. *Let $IS = (O, A, V, \rho)$ denote an information system in grey system, where*

- *O: set of objects (instances) in IS*
- *A: set of attributes*
- *V: set of values, $V = \mathbb{R}$ in this paper*
- *ρ: information function as $\rho : O \times A \to V$*

Definition 13. *Let x be an object of O, a be an attribute of A, and $\otimes(x, a) \in V$ be a value which x holds on a respectively, where $(x, a) \in O \times A$. Let $\otimes s$ be a value on a, $GL^*(\otimes s)$ be an upper approximation of $\otimes s$, $GL_*(\otimes s)$ be a lower approximation of $\otimes s$, and $BND(\otimes s)$ be a boundary respectively. These approximations are defined as follows:*

$$GL^*(\otimes s) = \{x \in O| \otimes (x, a) \wedge \otimes s \neq \varnothing\} \tag{16}$$

$$GL_*(\otimes s) = \{x \in O| \otimes (x, a) \to \otimes s\} \tag{17}$$

$$BND(\otimes s) = GL^*(\otimes s) - GL_*(\otimes s) \tag{18}$$

$GL(\otimes s)$ is a single-attribute approximation on the attribute a of A.

4.2   General Grey-Rough Sets of Every Attribute

Definition 14. *Let $A = \{a_1, a_2, \cdots, a_n\}$ be a set with n attributes, $S = \{\otimes s_1, \otimes s_2, \cdots, \otimes s_n\}$ be a set containing n values. The object x has n values as $\{\otimes(x, a_1), \otimes(x, a_2), \cdots, \otimes(x, a_n)\}$, then the upper approximation $GW^*(S)$ and the lower approximation $GW_*(S)$ are defined as follows:*

$$GW^*(S) \rightleftarrows [\underline{GW}^*(S), \overline{GW}^*(S)] \tag{19}$$

$$GW_*(S) \rightleftarrows [\underline{GW}_*(S), \overline{GW}_*(S)] \tag{20}$$

$$\underline{GW}^*(S) = \bigcap_{i=1}^{n} GL^*(\otimes s_i) \tag{21}$$

$$\overline{GW}^*(S) = \bigcup_{i=1}^{n} GL^*(\otimes s_i) \tag{22}$$

$$\underline{GW}_*(S) = \bigcap_{i=1}^{n} GL_*(\otimes s_i) \tag{23}$$

$$\overline{GW}_*(S) = \bigcup_{i=1}^{n} GL_*(\otimes s_i) \tag{24}$$

A pair of interval sets $\langle GW^*(S), GW_*(S) \rangle$ is a general grey-rough set of S, where $\underline{GW}_*(S) \subseteq \overline{GW}_*(S)$, $\underline{GW}^*(S) \subseteq \overline{GW}^*(S)$.

$GW(S)$ is a multi-attributes approximation based on $GL(\otimes s)$. Compared with Yao's [26] model and Wu's [10] model, their models of R_* and R^* each have only one solution however the proposal GW_* and GW^* each have two solutions a minimum $\underline{GW}$ and a maximum $\overline{GW}$. $\underline{GW}$ is a set of objects which satisfied with every attribute of A and $\overline{GW}$ is also a set of objects satisfying at least one attribute of A.

Theorem 3. *A general grey-rough set holds the following properties:*

1. $GW_*(S) \subseteq GW^*(S)$
2. $GW_*(\mathbb{R}) = GW^*(\mathbb{R}) = O; \ GW_*(\varnothing) = GW^*(\varnothing) = \varnothing$
3. $GW^*(S \cup T) \supseteq GW^*(S) \cup GW^*(T); \ GW_*(S \cap T) \subseteq GW_*(S) \cap GW_*(T)$
4. $GW_*(S \cup T) \supseteq GW_*(S) \cup GW_*(T); \ GW^*(S \cap T) \subseteq GW^*(S) \cap GW^*(T)$
5. $S \subseteq T \ implies \ GW_*(S) \subseteq GW_*(T); \ S \subseteq T \ implies \ GW^*(S) \subseteq GW^*(T)$
6. $GW_*(S^c) = O - GW^*(S); \ GW^*(S^c) = O - GW_*(S)$

where $S^c = \{\otimes s_1^c, \otimes s_2^c, \cdots, \otimes s_n^c\}$, $S \cup T \rightleftarrows \otimes s_i \vee \otimes t_i$ for all i, $S \cap T \rightleftarrows \otimes s_i \wedge \otimes t_i$ for all i.

Definition 15. *The accuracy of approximation $\alpha(S)$ and the quality of approximation $\gamma(S)$ are defined as follows:*

$$\alpha(S) = \frac{\mathrm{card}\{GW_*(S)\}}{\mathrm{card}\{GW^*(S)\}} \tag{25}$$

$$\gamma(S) = \frac{\mathrm{card}\{GW_*(S)\}}{\mathrm{card}\{O\}} \tag{26}$$

Definition 16. *Let Ξ be a grey relational overlap grade for x of $GW^*(S)$ and $GW_*(S)$ as follows:*

$$\Xi(S, x) = \frac{1}{n} \sum_{i=1}^{n} \xi(\otimes(x, a_i), \otimes s_i) \tag{27}$$

and the order relation of Ξ is consisntent as follows:

1. $\Xi(S, x_j) \le \Xi(S, x_j)$
2. $\Xi(S, x_j) \le \Xi(S, x_k), \Xi(S, x_k) \le \Xi(S, x_j) \Leftrightarrow \Xi(S, x_k) = \Xi(S, x_j), \ j \ne k$
3. $\Xi(S, x_j) \le \Xi(S, x_k), \Xi(S, x_k) \le \Xi(S, x_l) \Rightarrow \Xi(S, x_j) \le \Xi(S, x_l), \ j \ne k \ne l$

4.3 Illastrative Examples

Example 3 (for extracted Auto-MPG data set). A sample information system IS of Table 3 is given as follows:

$$O = \{\text{Audi}, \text{BMW}, \cdots, \text{Volvo}\}, A = \{\text{Cylinder}, \text{Model year}\}, \mathrm{card}\{O\} = 10$$

Assume that a set of Japanese manufacturers and its values are given as follows: Japanese $= \{\text{Honda}, \text{Mazda}, \text{Subaru}, \text{Toyota}\}$

$$\otimes (\text{Japanese}, \text{Cylinder}) \rightleftarrows \bigvee\nolimits_{x \in \text{Japanese}} \otimes(x, \text{Cylinder}) \rightleftarrows [3, 6] \tag{28}$$

$$\otimes (\text{Japanese}, \text{Model year}) \rightleftarrows \bigvee\nolimits_{x \in \text{Japanese}} \otimes(x, \text{Model year}) \rightleftarrows [70, 82] \tag{29}$$

Then the general grey-rough approximation results are shown in Table 4. This table includes the accuracy and the quality of approximations, and also includes

Table 4. Grey-rough approximation result of extracted Auto-MPG data set

S	$\underline{GW}^*(S)$	$\underline{GW}_*(S)$	$\underline{GW}^*(S) - \underline{GW}_*(S)$	$\alpha(S)$	$\gamma(S)$
American	1, 2, 3, 4, 5, 6, 7, 8, 9, 10	1, 2, 3, 4, 7, 8, 10	5, 6, 9	0.7	0.7
German	1, 2, 4, 5, 6, 7, 8, 9, 10	1, 2, 5, 7, 9	4, 6, 8, 10	0.556	0.5
Japanese	1, 2, 4, 5, 6, 7, 8, 9, 10	1, 2, 4, 5, 6, 7, 8, 9, 10	$\varnothing$	1	0.9
Swedish	1, 2, 4, 5, 6, 7, 8, 9, 10	7, 10	1, 2, 4, 5, 6, 8, 9	0.222	0.2

Table 5. Grey-rough approximation result of recomposed Auto-MPG data set

S	$\underline{GW}^*(S)$	$\underline{GW}_*(S)$	$\underline{GW}^*(S) - \underline{GW}_*(S)$	$\alpha(S)$	$\gamma(S)$
American	1, 2, 3, 4, 5, 6, 7, 8, 9, 10	2, 3, 4, 10	1, 5, 6, 7, 8, 9	0.4	0.4
German	1, 2, 4, 5, 6, 7, 8, 9, 10	1, 2, 7, 9	4, 5, 6, 8, 10	0.444	0.4
Japanese	1, 2, 4, 5, 6, 7, 8, 9, 10	2, 5, 6, 7, 8	1, 4, 9, 10	0.556	0.5
Swedish	1, 4, 8, 10	10	1, 4, 8	0.25	0.1

the general grey-rough approximation results of German, American and Swedish manufacturers whose values are obtained through the same way of Japanese.

Example 4 (for recomposed Auto-MPG data set). In the sample information system of Table 2, the all attribute values of Japanse are given as follows:

$$\otimes(\text{Japanese}, \text{MPG}) \rightleftarrows [18, 46.6] \qquad \otimes(\text{Japanese}, \text{Displacement}) \rightleftarrows [70, 168]$$
$$\otimes(\text{Japanese}, \text{Horsepower}) \rightleftarrows [52, 122] \quad \otimes(\text{Japanese}, \text{Weight}) \rightleftarrows [1.65, 2.9]$$
$$\otimes(\text{Japanese}, \text{Acceleration}) \rightleftarrows [12.5, 21]$$

where the values Cylinder and Model-year are the same with Eqs. (28) and (29).

The approximation results are shown in Table 5. The objects of GW^* have relevance to the approximation subject in specifications. According to Table 5, Cadillac (No. 3) is a unique manufacture comes from USA. The objects of GW_* are parts of the approximation subject in specifications: for example BMW (No. 2) is similar to American, Japanese and German automobiles.

5   Conclusion

A new rough set approach based on grey system theory is proposed in this paper. One of the practical applications of the special grey-rough set to decision making is reported by Li [27]. Conclude this paper as follows:

- The special grey-rough set based on the equivalence class of interval is proposed, which is a combination of rough set theory and grey system theory.
- The general grey-rough set based on the inclusion and the meet operation of the grey lattice operation is proposed.
- The special grey-rough set is compatible with the traditional rough set as a special case. The general grey-rough set expands a treatable value into interval data.

Acknowledgement

The authors acknowledge Dr. M. Kitaoka for helpful discussions.

References

1. Pawlak, Z.: Rough Sets. Int. J. Computer and Information Sciences. **11** (1982) 341–356
2. Pawlak, Z.: Rough Classification. Int. J. Man-Machine Studies. **20** (1984) 469–483
3. Polkowski, L. and Skowron, A. (Eds.): Rough Sets in Knowledge Discovery. Physica-Verlag **1, 2** (1998)
4. Deng, J.L.: Grey Systems, China Ocean Press (1988)
5. Xia, J.: Grey System Theory to Hydrology (in Chinese), Huanzhong University of Science and Technology Press (2000)
6. Nagai, M. and Yamaguchi, D.: Elements on Grey System Theory and its Applications (in Japanese), Kyoritsu-Shuppan (2004)
7. Wen, K.L.: Grey Systems: Modeling and Prediction. Yang's Scientific Research Institute (2004)
8. Liu, S.F. and Lin, Y.: Grey Information, Springer (2006)
9. Zhang Q.S. and Chen, G.H.: Rough Grey Sets. Kybernetes **33** (2004) 446–452
10. Wu, S.X., Liu, S.F. and Li, M.Q.: Study of Integrate Models of Rough Sets and Grey Systems. Lecture Notes in Computer Science **3613** (2005) 1313–1323
11. Yamaguchi, D., Li, G.D., Mizutani, K., Nagai, M. and Kitaoka, M.: Rule Extraction and Reduction Algorithm Based on Grey Lattice Classification (in Japanese). In: IPSJ SIG Technical Report **2005**, AL-102-4, (2005) 25–32
12. Yamaguchi, D., Li, G.D., Mizutani, K., Nagai, M. and Kitaoka, M.: Decision Rule Extraction and Reduction Based on Grey Lattice Classification. In: Proc. Fourth Int. Conf. on Machine Learning and Applications (2005) 31–36
13. Young, R.C.: The Algebra of Many-valued Quantities. Mathematische Annalen, 104 (1931) 260–290
14. Ris, F.N.: Tools For the Analysis of Interval Arithmetic. Lecture Notes in Computer Science **29** (1975) 75–98
15. Bierbaum, F. and Schwiertz, K. P.: A Bibliography on Interval-Mathematics. J. of Comput. and App. Math. **4** (1978) 59–86
16. Garloff, J. and Schwiertz, K. P.: A Bibliography on Interval-Mathematics (Continuation). J. Comput. and App. Math. **6** (1980) 67–79
17. Moore, R.E.: Reliability in Coputiong, Academic Press (1988)
18. Oishi, S.: Introduction to Nonlinear Analysis (in Japanese), Corona Publishing (1997)
19. Oishi, S.: Verified Numerical Computation (in Japanese), Corona Publishing (2000)
20. Pedrycz W. (Ed.): Granular Computing, Physica-Verlag (2001)
21. Hansen, E. and Walster, G.W.: Global Optimization Using Interval Analysis Second Edition, Marcel Dekker (2004)
22. Sunaga, T.: Theory of an interval algebra and its application to numerical analysis. In: RAAG Memoirs **2**, Gakujutsu Bunken Fukyu-kai (1958) 29–46
23. Birkhoff, G.: Lattice Theory Third Edition, American Mathematical Society (1967)
24. Pawlak, Z.: Rough Set Elements. In: Rough Sets in Knowledge Discovery **1** Physica-Verlag (1998) 10–30
25. Merz, C.J. and Murphy, P.M.: UCI Repository of machine learning databases: [http://www.ics.uci.edu/~mlearn/MLRepository.html].
26. Yao, Y. Y.: Interval-Set Algebra for Qualitative Knowledge Representation. In: Proc. 5th International Conference on Computing and information (1993) 370–375
27. Li, G.D., Yamaguchi, D., Lin, H.S., Wen, K.L. and Nagai, M.: A grey-based rough set approach to suppliers selection problem, Proc. RSCTC2006 (2006).

An Ontology-Based First-Order Modal Logic

Feng Jiang[1,2], Yuefei Sui[1], and Cungen Cao[1]

[1] Key Laboratory of Intelligent Information Processing, Institute of Computing Technology, Chinese Academy of Sciences, Beijing 100080, P.R. China
[2] Graduate School of Chinese Academy of Sciences, Beijing 100039, P.R. China
jiangkong@163.net, {yfsui, cgcao}@ict.ac.cn

Abstract. First-order modal logic is not just propositional modal logic plus classical quantifier machinery. The situation is much subtler than that. The addition of quantifiers to propositional modal logic may lead to many difficulties. In this paper we aim to solve one of them — the problem of rigidity versus non-rigidity for variables, that is, how to determine the denotations for each variable in different possible worlds or the connections among the denotations of each variable in different possible worlds. Since all the currently proposed semantics for first-order modal logic are not suitable to solve this problem, we proposed an ontology-based first-order modal semantics, in which ontologies are introduced to restrain the modal logic frames and models. An ontology-based counterpart relation S is introduced into each model. By requiring that the assignments of each variable in different possible worlds must accord with the relation S, we can correctly characterize the connections among the denotations of each variable in different worlds.

Keywords: First-order modal logic, rigidity, ontology, counterpart.

1   Introduction

Modal logic is a logic developed firstly in the category of nonclassical logics [1], and has been now widely used as a formalism for knowledge representation in artificial intelligence and an analysis tool in computer science [2],[3]. Along with the study of the modal logic, it has been found that the modal logic has a close relationship with many other knowledge representation theories. The result is the connection of the possible world semantics for the modal epistemic logic S5 with the approximation space in rough set theory [4], where the system S5 has been shown to be useful in the analysis of knowledge in various areas [5].

Propositional modal logic is now a standard tool in many disciplines, but first-order modal logic is not. The addition of quantifiers, however, opens the door to a labyrinth full of twists and problems. For example, the problems with constant domains versus varying domains, the problems with rigidity versus non-rigidity, and the problems with transworld identity [6]. In this paper, we shall mainly discuss the problem of rigidity versus non-rigidity for variables in first-order modal logic.

In Kripke's semantics for first-order modal logic, assignments of variables to individual objects are treated as independent from the possible worlds, that is,

S. Greco et al. (Eds.): RSCTC 2006, LNAI 4259, pp. 517–526, 2006.

assignments do not vary across possible worlds [7]. Variables are interpreted as having the same denotation in all possible worlds, in other words, as rigid designators. While this is natural for many purposes — natural numbers are certainly rigid. Rigid assignment also leads to difficulties in expressing certain things that we may want to say. For instance, in a Kripke's model, the following two wffs are both valid.

$$\mathbf{LI} \quad x = y \rightarrow \Box(x = y). \tag{1}$$

and

$$\mathbf{LNI} \quad x \neq y \rightarrow \Box(x \neq y). \tag{2}$$

Now, the morning star and the evening star are in fact identical objects, so if x and y refer to the object that the phrases 'morning star' and 'evening star' designate (in the real world), certainly $\Box(x = y)$ is the case, since there is only one object involved. But then, how do we express the very natural thought that the morning and evening stars might have been distinct, as the ancient Babylonians believed to be the case? There is simply no way we can do it [8].

Moreover, the authors ([9, 10]) gave three reasons for considering world-dependent assignments to variables. Therefore, Hughes and Cresswell ([10]) proposed Contingent Identity (**CI**) systems, based on the framework of first-order modal logic. In **CI** systems, the above **LI** and **LNI** do not hold. This result is obtained by letting variables range over all individual concepts, where every individual concept is a total function from possible worlds in W to objects in D (the domain of the model). Since individual concepts have different extensions in different worlds, variables also take different values in different worlds. However, it is easy to show that **CI** systems would make the following schema valid:

$$\Box\exists x\alpha \rightarrow \exists x\Box\alpha. \tag{3}$$

But (3) is not intuitively plausible. For example, assume that $\alpha = \varphi(x)$ and $\varphi(x)$ denotes that 'x is the number of the planets'. Then the antecedent is true, for there must be some number which is the number of the planets (even if there were no planets at all there would still be such a number, viz. 0); but the consequent is false, for since it is a contingent matter how many planets there are, there is no number which must be the number of the planets [10]. The counterintuitive characteristic of (3) depends on the extreme liberty of **CI** systems. In **CI** systems we do not put any constraint on individual concepts. This means that any collection of elements from different worlds - 'David Lewis' in w, 'a rock' in w', and 'a blade of grass' in w'' - can be considered as an individual concept [11].

By now, we face adverse conditions. How could we determine the appropriate denotations for each variable in different possible worlds? What are the connections among the denotations of a given variable in different possible worlds? Obviously, both of the two semantics mentioned above are not suitable to do that. Since on the one hand, Kripke's semantics is too stringent, for it requires that variables have the same denotations in all possible worlds. That is, the denotations of a given variable in different possible worlds must be the same object. This kind of connection among the denotations of a given variable in different worlds is obviously unreasonable. For example, assume that W is the set of snapshots of the real world under the temporal relation. Let w_0 be the current snapshot of the real world in which I exist and I am the denotation of variable x in w_0. Then, I exist in any future world by the requirement that x has the same denotation in all possible worlds. On the other hand, **CI** systems are too liberal since they allow arbitrary objects in each possible world to be the denotations of a given variable in that world. That is, there may be no connections among the denotations of a given variable in different possible worlds. This is also unacceptable.

Through careful analysis, we can find that the issue on how to correctly characterize the connections among the denotations of a given variable in different possible worlds is outside of the logic. Modal logic itself can not characterize these connections since they go beyond the scope of the logic. Hence we should appeal to other tools to solve this problem. In [12], Guarino introduced the notion of the *ontological level*, intermediate between the *epistemological level* and the *conceptual level* discussed by Brachman [13], as a way to characterize a knowledge representation formalism taking into account the intended meaning of its primitives. In contrast to the abstract and content-independent *logic level*, the *ontological level* is more close to the knowledge that we want to represent. Therefore, in order to solve the above problem, we should descend from the *logic level* to the *ontological level*. Then ontologies come into our sight. Within the sharing and reuse effort, ontologies have been widely proposed as a means to alleviate model mismatches at the knowledge level. Many definitions of ontologies have been offered in the last decade, but the one that best characterizes the essence of an ontology is based on the related definitions by Gruber [14]: An ontology is a formal, explicit specification of a shared conceptualization. As an attempt to describe all entities within an area of reality and all relationships between those entities, an ontology comprises a set of well-defined terms with well-defined relationships. In general, ontologies provide a shared and common understanding of a domain that can be communicated between people and heterogeneous and distributed application systems [15].

In this paper, we aim to propose an ontology-based first-order modal semantics, which can solve the problem of how to correctly characterize the connections among the denotations of each variable in different possible worlds. The basic idea is as follows. We use a given ontology to restrain the modal logic frames and models since we can represent all concepts and the subsumption relations between concepts in the ontology by a set of first-order logic wffs and these wffs can easily be used in our modal system. In addition, an ontology-based counterpart relation S is introduced into each model, which is similar to the counterpart relation of counterpart theory proposed by David Lewis [16]. Then by requiring that the denotations of a given variable in different worlds must accord with the counterpart relation S, we can correctly characterize the connections among the denotations of a given variable in different possible worlds. The remainder of this paper is organized as follows. In the next section, we introduce some preliminaries. In section 3, we propose an ontology-based first-order modal logic. And section 4 concludes the paper.

2   Preliminaries

In general, first-order modal logic will have its alphabet of symbols: a set of variable symbols, denoted by $VS = \{x_1, x_2, ...\}$; a set of relation symbols, denoted by $PS = \{P_i^n : n, i = 1, 2, ...\}$, where P_i^n is the ith n-place relation symbol; the logical symbols, $\neg$ (negation), $\wedge$ (and), $\vee$ (or), $\supset$ (material implication); quantifier $\forall$ (for all) and $\exists$ (exists); the modal operator symbols $\Box$ (necessity operator) and $\Diamond$ (possibility operator) [17, 18].

Definition 1. *An atomic formula of first-order modal logic is any expression of the form $P(x_1, ..., x_n)$, where P is an n-place relation symbol and $x_1, ..., x_n$ are variables.*

Definition 2. *The set of first-order formulas of first-order modal logic is the smallest set satisfying the following conditions: Every atomic formula is a formula; if φ is a formula, so are $\neg\varphi$, $\Box\varphi$, $\Diamond\varphi$, $\forall x\varphi$ and $\exists x\varphi$; if φ and ψ are formulas and $\circ$ is a binary connective, then $\varphi \circ \psi$ is a formula.*

The modal logic formal system contains the following axioms and inference rules:

- Axioms:

$$A_p1 \quad (\varphi \supset (\psi \supset \varphi));$$
$$A_p2 \quad ((\varphi \supset (\psi \supset \gamma)) \supset ((\varphi \supset \psi) \supset (\varphi \supset \gamma)));$$
$$A_p3 \quad ((\neg\varphi \supset \neg\psi) \supset (\psi \supset \varphi));$$
$$A_p4 \quad (\forall x\varphi(x) \supset \varphi(y)), \text{ where } y \text{ is any variable for } x \text{ in } \varphi(x);$$
$$A_p5 \quad (\forall x(\varphi \supset \psi) \supset (\forall x\varphi \supset \forall x\psi));$$
$$\mathbf{K} \quad (\Box(\varphi \supset \psi) \supset (\Box\varphi \supset \Box\psi));$$
$$\mathbf{T} \quad (\Box\varphi \supset \varphi);$$
$$\mathbf{E} \quad (\neg\Box\neg\varphi \supset \Box\neg\Box\neg\varphi).$$

- Inference rules:

$$\text{N (necessity rule)} \quad \text{if } \vdash \varphi \text{ then } \vdash \Box\varphi;$$
$$\text{UG (universal generalization)} \quad \text{if } \vdash \varphi \text{ then } \vdash \forall x\varphi;$$
$$\text{MP (modus ponens)} \quad \text{if } \vdash \varphi \supset \psi \text{ and } \vdash \varphi \text{ then } \vdash \psi.$$

Since constant domain semantics can be simulated using varying domain semantics and relativized quantifiers [19], in this paper we shall mainly discuss varying domain semantics. *A varying domain semantics (or model)* for first-order modal logic is a structure $M = \langle W, R, D, I \rangle$, where W is a non-empty set of possible worlds; R is a binary relation on W, called the *accessibility relation*; D is a domain function from W to non-empty sets. For $w \in W$, $D(w)$ is the domain of world w and the domain of model M is $D(M) = \bigcup_{w \in W} D(w)$; I is an *interpretation* in the frame $F = \langle W, R, D \rangle$, which assigns to each n-place relation symbol P and to each possible world $w \in W$, some n-place relation on the domain $D(F) = \bigcup_{w \in W} D(w)$ of frame F. Note that here a predicate can be interpreted in a world w as a relation between objects that may not exist in w. In fact, we often refer to something that may not actually exist in real world. For example, George Washington does not exist in the current world, but we can still talk about him. We can say that George Washington is the first president of the United States and George Washington is a man, etc. In addition, I is a *non-rigid interpretation* since I assigns different n-place relati ons to each n-place relation symbol in different possible worlds. This is the case with every semantics proposed for quantified modal logic; after all, if relation symbols behave the same way in all worlds, the semantics essentially collapses since worlds can not be distinguished. Furthermore, notice that in the varying domain semantics, the domains of quantification in different possible worlds are different.

Let $M = \langle W, R, D, I \rangle$ be a model, a rigid assignment to variables in M is defined as follows.

Definition 3. *A valuation in model M is a mapping ν that assigns to each variable x some member $\nu(x)$ of domain $D(M)$.*

Definition 4. *Let $M = \langle W, R, D, I \rangle$ be a model and φ be a formula. For each $w \in W$ and each valuation ν in M, the notion that φ is true at possible world w of M with respect to valuation ν, denoted by $M, w \models_\nu \varphi$, is defined as follows.*
(1) If φ is an atomic formula $P(x_1, ..., x_n)$, then $M, w \models_\nu P(x_1, ..., x_n)$ provided $\langle \nu(x_1), ..., \nu(x_n) \rangle \in I(P, w)$;
(2) $M, w \models_\nu \neg\varphi \Leftrightarrow M, w \not\models_\nu \varphi$;
(3) $M, w \models_\nu \varphi \supset \psi \Leftrightarrow M, w \models_\nu \neg\varphi$ or $M, w \models_\nu \psi$;
(4) $M, w \models_\nu \Box\varphi \Leftrightarrow$ for every $w' \in W$, if wRw' then $M, w' \models_\nu \varphi$;
(5) $M, w \models_\nu \forall x\varphi \Leftrightarrow$ for every x-variant ν' of ν at w in M, $M, w \models_{\nu'} \varphi$, where ν' is an x-variant of ν at w, i.e. ν' and ν agree on all variables except possibly variable x and $\nu'(x) \in D(w)$.

3   Ontology-Based First-Order Modal Semantics

Our first-order modal system will have the same alphabet of symbols and set of formulas as in the first-order modal logic mentioned in section 2. And the semantics of our first-order modal system will be different from that of the system in section 2, in that the assignments to variables are non-rigid. But these assignments are not completely arbitrary since we shall introduce ontologies to restrain them. We may call them restrictedly non-rigid assignments.

Definition 5. *Let L_O be an ontological language, which is based on the first-order logic, e.g. the KIF language [20]. A knowledge frame kf in L_O consists of a set of statements in L_O, and a set of axioms about the basic meta-properties of the symbols in L_O.*

Definition 6. *Given an ontological language L_O, an ontology O is a quadruple $\langle C, \sqsubseteq, f, \tau \rangle$, where*
(1) $C = \{\alpha_1, \alpha_2, ..., \alpha_n\}$ is a set of concepts;
(2) $\sqsubseteq$ is a binary relation on C, called the subsumption relation or is-a relation.
(3) f is a mapping from C to KF, where KF is a set of knowledge frames in L_O.
(4) transformation τ is a mapping from C to 2^C satisfying the following conditions.

- *For any $\alpha, \beta \in C$, if $\alpha \sqsubseteq \beta$ then $\tau(\alpha) \subseteq \tau(\beta)$;*
- *For any $\alpha \in C$, $\alpha \in \tau(\alpha)$;*
- *For any $\alpha \in C$, if $\tau(\alpha) = \{\alpha_1, ..., \alpha_m\}$ then $\tau(\tau(\alpha)) = \bigcup_{i=1}^{m} \tau(\alpha_i)$. And*

there is an n such that $\tau^n(\alpha) = \tau^{n-1}(\alpha)$, where $\tau^0(\alpha) = \alpha, \tau^1(\alpha) = \tau(\alpha)$ and $\tau^n(\alpha) = \tau(\tau^{n-1}(\alpha))$. We shall use $\tau^\star(\alpha)$ to denote $\tau^n(\alpha)$ for the least such n.

The transformation τ in the above definition stipulates the transforming principles between concepts in ontology O. For example, a concept *persons* can transform into two concepts *persons* and *deadpersons*. Furthermore, by virtue of the mapping f in the above definition, we can represent all concepts and the subsumption relations between concepts using a set of knowledge frames in L_O. Since L_O is based on the first order logic, every knowledge frame contains some first-order logic wffs. Therefore, we can use these wffs in our first-order modal logic system since first-order modal logic is an extension of first-order logic.

Definition 7. *Let $O = \langle C, \sqsubseteq, f, \tau \rangle$ be an ontology. Given a first-order modal logic model $M = \langle W, R, D, I \rangle$ and a valuation ν in M. Let $D(M) = \bigcup_{w \in W} D(w)$ denote the domain of model M. For any $w \in W$ and any non-empty concept $\alpha \in C$ (i.e. $f(\alpha) \neq \emptyset$), if there is an object $d \in D(M)$ such that for any $\psi(x) \in f(\alpha)$, $M, w \models_\nu \psi(x)$ and $\nu(x) = d$, where ψ is a formula that contains at least one free variable x, then d is called the instance of concept α in w, denoted by $\alpha_w(d)$. In other words, object d instantiates concept α in w. Let $D_\alpha(w)$ denote the set of all objects in $D(M)$ that instantiate α in w, that is, $D_\alpha(w) = \{d \in D(M) : \alpha_w(d)\}$.*

Notice that in the above definition, an object d that instantiates a concept α in w may not actually exist in w. Since in the current world, we may consider 'George Washington' as an instance of concept *presidents*, even if he died a long time ago. Furthermore, there is no constraint on the model M in the above definition. It may be a model of Kripke's style, or others. Certainly, it may also be a model of our semantics that will be introduced in the following.

Definition 8. *Given an ontology $O = \langle C, \sqsubseteq, f, \tau \rangle$ and a first-order modal logic model $M = \langle W, R, D, I \rangle$. A possible world $w \in W$ is compatible with ontology O if for any object $d \in D(M)$, if d is an instance of concept α in w (i.e. $\alpha_w(d)$), then for any $\beta \in C$ with $\alpha \sqsubseteq \beta$, d is also an instance of concept β in w.*

For example, assume that ontology $O = \langle C, \sqsubseteq, f, \tau \rangle$ and C contains two concepts *students* and *persons* such that *students* $\sqsubseteq$ *persons*. Then, for any possible world w that is compatible with O and any object $d \in D(M)$, if d is a student in w then d must be a person in w.

Definition 9. *Given an ontology $O = \langle C, \sqsubseteq, f, \tau \rangle$, a first-order modal logic frame based on ontology O is a structure $F_O = \langle W, R, D \rangle$, where W is a non-empty set of possible worlds such that each possible world $w \in W$ is compatible with ontology O; R is a binary relation on W, called the accessibility relation; D is a domain function from W to non-empty sets such that for each $w \in W$, $D(w)$ is the domain of world w.*

We use $D(F_O) = \bigcup_{w \in W} D(w)$ to denote the domain of frame F_O which is based on ontology O.

Definition 10. *Given a frame $F_O = \langle W, R, D \rangle$ that is based on an ontology O, we define a distance function $*$ on $W \times W$ such that for any $w, w' \in W$, $*(w, w')$ is the number of the possible worlds between w and w' (including w and w' themselves) if there is a maximal sequence $\langle w_1, ..., w_n \rangle$ such that $w_1 = w$, $w_n = w'$, any two possible worlds in the sequence are different and for every $1 \le i \le n - 1, w_i R w_{i+1}$; otherwise, $*(w, w') = \infty$. We call $*(w, w')$ the distance between w and w' in frame F_O.*

Definition 11. *Given an ontology $O = \langle C, \sqsubseteq, f, \tau \rangle$, a first-order modal logic model based on ontology O is a structure $M_O = \langle W, R, D, I, S \rangle$, where $F_O = \langle W, R, D \rangle$ is a frame based on ontology O; I is an interpretation in the frame F_O such that for any n-place relation symbol P and $w \in W$, $I(P, w) \subseteq D(F_O)^n$ ($D(F_O)$ is the domain of frame F_O); S is a binary relation on $W \times D(F_O)$, such that for any possible worlds $w, w' \in W$ and objects $d, d' \in D(F_O)$,*
> *(1) if $*(w, w') = \infty$ then $\langle \langle w, d \rangle, \langle w', d' \rangle \rangle \notin S$;*
> *(2) if $*(w, w') = n$ and $\langle \langle w, d \rangle, \langle w', d' \rangle \rangle \in S$ then*
>> - *for each concept $\alpha \in C$ such that $d \in D_\alpha(w)$, there is a concept $\beta \in \tau^{n-1}(\alpha)$ such that $d' \in D_\beta(w')$;*
>> - *for each concept $\beta \in C$ such that $d' \in D_\beta(w')$, there is a concept $\alpha \in C$ such that $\beta \in \tau^{n-1}(\alpha)$ and $d \in D_\alpha(w)$.*

The binary relation S in the above definition is similar to the counterpart relations of counterpart theory proposed by David Lewis [16]. Lewis argued against rigid semantics because it requires that objects always have being and be identifiable across possible worlds. He proposed a looser notion: an object in a possible world may have counterparts in other worlds, rather than itself being in other worlds as well. An object of one world could have multiple counterparts in another, or multiple objects of one world could have a single counterpart in another world [8]. This provides much greater flexibility in the semantics than Kripke's system. Therefore, in the above definition, for any $\langle w, d \rangle, \langle w', d' \rangle \in W \times D(F_O)$, $\langle \langle w, d \rangle, \langle w', d' \rangle \rangle \in S$ means that d' in w' is a counterpart of d in w, denoted by $d \overset{ww'}{=} d'$. Since in the above definition, relation S is restricted by ontology O, we may call S an *ontology-based counterpart relation*.

Our ontology-based semantics of first-order modal logic differs from the counterpart theory in the following two points:

(1) In the counterpart theory, there is no restriction on the counterpart relation, except the requirement that the counterpart relation is a kind of similarity

relation, which is reflexive. The counterpart relation is indeterminate because similarity in general is indeterminate. But in our semantics, ontologies are used to restrain the objects and their counterparts in other possible worlds. Therefore, our semantics can avoid the above problem about the counterpart theory.

(2) In the counterpart theory, the domains of different possible worlds are disjoint, therefore, an object can only exist in one world. In our semantics, an object can actually exist in more than one worlds. Therefore, given an object of one world, its counterpart in another world may be itself.

Definition 12. *Given an ontology O and a model $M_O = \langle W, R, D, I, S \rangle$ based on O. A valuation in model M_O is a mapping ν such that for each variable x and $w \in W$, $\nu(x, w) \in D(M_O)$, and for any $w, w' \in W$, if $*(w, w') = n$ then $\langle \langle w, \nu(x, w) \rangle, \langle w', \nu(x, w') \rangle \rangle \in S$, where $D(M_O)$ is the domain of model M_O.*

Since the values assigned to a variable depend on worlds, the above valuation is non-rigid. By now, we can see that although ontologies are used to restrain the counterpart relation S of model M_O, through requiring that the denotations of a given variable in any two worlds whose distance equals n must satisfy the relation S, ontologies are indirectly used to characterize the connections among the denotations of a given variable in different worlds.

Definition 13. *Given an ontology O and a model $M_O = \langle W, R, D, I, S \rangle$ based on O. Let ν and ω be two valuations in model M_O. Given any possible world $w \in W$, we call ω an x-variant of ν at possible world w if ν and ω satisfy the following conditions.*
(1) For all variables y, $y \neq x$ and every $w' \in W$, $\nu(y, w') = \omega(y, w')$;
(2) For every $w' \in W$, $\omega(x, w')$ possibly differs from $\nu(x, w')$ and $\omega(x, w) \in D(w)$.

Definition 14. *Given an ontology O, let $M_O = \langle W, R, D, I, S \rangle$ be a model based on O and φ be a formula. For each $w \in W$ and each valuation ν in M_O, the notion that φ is true at possible world w of model M_O with respect to valuation ν, denoted by $M_O, w \models_\nu \varphi$, is defined as follows.*
(1) If φ is an atomic formula $P(x_1, ..., x_n)$, then $M_O, w \models_\nu P(x_1, ..., x_n)$ provided $\langle \nu(x_1, w), ..., \nu(x_n, w) \rangle \in I(P, w)$;
(2) $M_O, w \models_\nu \neg\varphi \Leftrightarrow M_O, w \not\models_\nu \varphi$;
(3) $M_O, w \models_\nu \varphi \supset \psi \Leftrightarrow M_O, w \models_\nu \neg\varphi$ or $M_O, w \models_\nu \psi$;
(4) $M_O, w \models_\nu \Box\varphi \Leftrightarrow$ for every $w' \in W$, if wRw' then $M_O, w' \models_\nu \varphi$;
(5) $M_O, w \models_\nu \forall x\varphi \Leftrightarrow$ for every x-variant ω of ν at w in M_O, $M_O, w \models_\omega \varphi$.

Definition 15. *Given an ontology O, let $M_O = \langle W, R, D, I, S \rangle$ be a model based on O and φ be a formula. For each $w \in W$, we say that φ is true at possible worlds w of model M_O, denoted by $M_O, w \models \varphi$, if $M_O, w \models_\nu \varphi$ for every valuation ν in M_O; we say that φ is true in model M_O, denoted by $M_O \models \varphi$, if $M_O, w \models \varphi$ for every possible world w of M_O.*

Example 1. Given an ontology $O = \langle C, \sqsubseteq, f, \tau \rangle$, where $C = \{wood, charcoal, persons, deadpersons\}$. We do not assume that $deadpersons \sqsubseteq persons$. A person has some properties of the physical, biological, functional and social aspects, and a dead person has only some properties of the social aspects. In addition, $charcoal \not\sqsubseteq wood$ and $wood \not\sqsubseteq charcoal$. Transformation τ is defined as follows.

$$\tau\,(wood) = \{wood, charcoal\}, \quad \tau(charcoal) = \{charcoal\};$$
$$\tau\,(persons) = \{persons, deadpersons\}, \quad \tau(deadpersons) = \{deadpersons\}.$$

Assume the modal is temporal, and $M_O = \langle W, R, D, I, S \rangle$ is a model based on the ontology O, where $W = \{w, w'\}$, wRw', and $D(w) = \{a, b\}$, $D(w') = \{a', b'\}$. Let

$$D_{wood}(w) = \{a\}, D_{charcoal}(w) = \emptyset, \ D_{persons}(w) = \{b\}, D_{deadpersons}(w) = \emptyset;$$
$$D_{wood}(w') = \emptyset, D_{charcoal}(w') = \{a'\}, \ D_{persons}(w') = \emptyset, D_{deadpersons}(w') = \{b'\}.$$

Since M_O is a model based on the ontology O, from definition 11, there are at most two elements in S, that is, it is possible that $\langle \langle w, a \rangle, \langle w', a' \rangle \rangle \in S$ and $\langle \langle w, b \rangle, \langle w', b' \rangle \rangle \in S$.

Therefore, for any variable x, there are only two possible valuations ν, that is, $\nu(x, w) = a$; $\nu(x, w') = a'$ or $\nu(x, w) = b$; $\nu(x, w') = b'$.

However, in **CI** systems, a valuation ν can be

$$
\begin{array}{c|c|c|c|c|c|c|c|c|c|c|c|c|c|c|c}
\nu(x)(w) = & a & a & a & a & b & b & b & b & a' & a' & a' & a' & b' & b' & b' & b' \\
\hline
\nu(x)(w') = & a & b & a' & b' & a & b & a' & b' & a & b & a' & b' & a & b & a' & b'.
\end{array}
$$

$\square$

4   Conclusion and Further Works

In this paper we discussed the problem of rigidity versus non-rigidity for variables in first-order modal logic, and proposed an ontology-based first-order modal logic, which can effectively solve that problem. Our further work is to analyze the soundness and completeness of our ontology-based first-order modal logic.

Acknowledgements. This work is supported by the Natural Science Foundation (grants no. 60273019, 60496326, 60573063 and 60573064), and the National 973 Programme (grants no. 2003CB317008 and G1999032701).

References

1. Chellas, B. F.: *Modal Logic: An Introduction*, Cambridge University Press (1980)
2. Gabbay, D. M., Hogger, C. J. and Robinson, J. A.: *Handbook of Logic in Artificial Intelligence and Logic Programming*, Vol. 1.4. Clarendon Press, Oxford (1994)
3. Abramsky, S., Gabbay, D. M. and Maibaum, T. S. E., editors: *Handbook of Logic in Computer Science*, Vol. 1.3. Clarendon Press, Oxford (1992)
4. Pawlak, Z.: "Rough sets", *International Journal of Computer and Information Sciences*, **11** (1982) 341–356
5. Fagin, R. F., Halpern, J. Y., Moses, Y. and Vardi, M. Y.: *Reasoning about Knowledge*, MIT press (1996)
6. Fitting, M.: On Quantified Modal Logic. *Fundamenta Informaticae*, 39(1-2) (1999) 105-121

7. Kripke, S.: Semantical considerations on modal logics. In: *Acta Philosophica Fennica, Modal and Many-valued Logics* 16 (1963) 83-94
8. Fitting, M.: First-order intensional logic. *Annals of Pure and Applied Logic,* 127 (1-3) (2004) 171-193
9. Garson, J. W.: Quantification in modal logic. In Gunthner, F. and Gabbay, D., editors: *Handbook of Philosophical Logic.* Kluwer, Dordrecht (2001) 267-323
10. Hughes, G. E. and Cresswell, M. J.: *A new introduction to modal logic.* Routledge, London (1996)
11. Belardinelli, F.: *Quantified Modal Logic and the Ontology of Physical Objects,* Ph. D. thesis, Scuola Normale Superiore in Pisa (2006)
12. Guarino, N.: The Ontological Level. In: Casati, R., et al., Eds., *Philosophy and the Cognitive Science,* Holder-Pichler-Tempsky, Vienna (1994) 443-456
13. Brachman, R. J.: On the Epistemological Status of Semantic Networks. In: Findler, N. V. (Eds.), *Associative Networks: Representation and Use of Knowledge by Computers.* Academic Press (1979)
14. Gruber, T. R.: A Translation Approach to Portable Ontology Specifications. *Knowledge Acquisition,* 5(2) (1993) 199-220
15. Klein, M., Fensel, D., Harmelen, F. and Horrocks, I.: The relation between ontologies and schema-languages: Translating OIL-specifications in XML-Schema. In:*Proc. of the Workshop on Applications of Ontologies and Problem-solving Methods, 14th European Conference on Artificial Intelligence,* Berlin (2000) 20-25
16. Lewis, D.: Counterpart theory and quantified modal logic. *Journal of Philosophy,* 65 (1968) 113-126
17. Zhang, Z. Y., Sui, Y. F. and Cao, C. G.: Fuzzy reasoning based on propositional modal logic, RSCTC, LNCS 3066 (2004) 109-115
18. Zhang, Z. Y., Sui, Y. F. and Cao, C. G.: Description of Fuzzy First-Order Modal Logic Based on Constant Domain Semantics. RSFDGrC (1), LNAI 3642, Regina (2005) 642-650
19. Fitting, M. and Mendelsohn, R.: *First Order Modal Logic,* Kluwer, Dordrecht (1998)
20. Genesereth, M. R.: Knowledge Interchange Format. In: Allen, J., et al., (eds.), *Proc. of the 2nd Int. Conf. on the Principles of Knowledge Representation and Reasoning,* San Francisco, Morgan Kaufman Publishers (1991) 238-249

Enhancing a Biological Concept Ontology to Fuzzy Relational Ontology with Relations Mined from Text

Lipika Dey[1] and Muhammad Abulaish[2]

[1] Department of Mathematics, Indian Institute of Technology Delhi
Hauz Khas, New Delhi – 16, India
lipika@maths.iitd.ernet.in
[2] Department of Mathematics, Jamia Millia Islamia (A central university)
Jamia Nagar, New Delhi – 25, India
abulaish@computer.org

Abstract. In this paper we investigate the problem of enriching an existing biological concept ontology into a fuzzy relational ontology structure using *generic* biological relations and their strengths mined from tagged biological text documents. Though biological relations in a text are defined between a pair of entities, the entities are usually tagged by their concept names in a tagged corpus. Since the tags themselves are related taxonomically, as given in the ontology, the mined relations have to be properly characterized before entering them into the ontology. We have proposed a mechanism to generalize each relation to be defined at the most appropriate level of specificity, before it can be added to the ontology. Since the mined relations have varying degrees of associations with various biological concepts, an appropriate fuzzy membership generation mechanism is proposed to fuzzify the strengths of the relations. Extensive experimentation has been conducted over the entire GENIA corpus and the results of enhancing the GENIA ontology are presented in the paper.

Keywords: Generic biological relation, Biological ontology enhancement, Fuzzy relational ontology.

1 Introduction

The field of Molecular Biology has witnessed a phenomenal growth in research activities in the recent past. Consequently to aid the process of organizing this large repository of knowledge, there has been a considerable effort towards building structured biological ontologies. Gene Ontology (GO) and GENIA ontology are two of the most popular ones. While the GENIA ontology stores only a set of concepts and the structural semantic relations, GO contains a large collection of biological processes along with biological concepts defined manually. Since manually identification of biological relations and their characterization is a labor-intensive task, several approaches have taken place to automate the process.

Generic biological relations can be characterized based on their occurrence patterns within text. The initial approaches focused on identifying a pre-defined set of verbs

S. Greco et al. (Eds.): RSCTC 2006, LNAI 4259, pp. 527–536, 2006.

representing these relations within text. Thomas *et al.* [7] modified a pre-existing parser based on cascaded finite state machines to fill templates with information on protein interactions for three verbs – *interact with, associate with, bind to.* Sekimizu *et al.* [6] have proposed mechanisms for locating a pre-defined collection of seven verbs *activate, bind, interact, regulate, encode, signal* and *function.* However since it is expensive and labour-intensive to pre-define all such relations exhaustively, Rinaldi *et al.* [5] proposed an automated Literature Based Discovery (LBD) method to characterize these seven relations in terms of the participating entities. Ono *et al.* [4] reports a method for extraction of protein-protein interactions using a dictionary look-up approach. After identifying the dictionary-based proteins within the document to analyze, sentences that contain at least two proteins are selected, which are then parsed with Parts-Of-Speech (POS) matching rules. The rules are triggered by a set of keywords, which are frequently used to name protein interactions like *associate, bind* etc. Ciaramita *et al.* [2] have proposed an unsupervised model for learning arbitrary relations between concepts of a molecular biology ontology from the GENIA corpus [3] for the purpose of supporting text-mining and manual ontology building.

In this paper, we present a method for characterizing biological relations mined from a tagged corpus using an ontology-based text-mining approach to extend the underlying ontology into a fuzzy relational ontology. Since biological relations occurring within a text can be directly associated to participating entities, locating only these relations does not provide the true character of the biological relation as an interaction between two biological entities. While it is straightforward to propagate these relations along the ontology tree, consolidating them at the most appropriate level requires significance analysis. For example, analyzing 170 instances out of a total of 219 instances of "expressed in" occurring in the GENIA corpus a break-up reveals that 48 associations are between the concept-pair *<protein_molecule, cell_type>*; 22 instances occur between *<protein_family_or_group, cell_type>*; 21 instances occur between *<protein_molecule, cell_line>*; 10 between *< protein_family_or_group, cell_line>*; 9 between *<DNA_domain_or_region, cell_type>*; 7 between *<RNA_molecule, cell_type>*; 6 between *<DNA_family_or_group, cell_type>*; 5 between *<RNA_molecule, cell_line>*; 4 each between *<RNA_family_or_group, cell_type>* and between *<protein_molecule, tissue>*; 3 each between pairs *<protein_molecule, body_part>* and *<protein_molecule, mono_cell>*; 2 each between pairs *<DNA_domain_or_region, cell_line>*, *<protein_domain_or_region, cell_type>*, *<DNA_domain_or_region, tissue>*, and *<DNA_domain_or_region, body_part>*; 1 instance each between 20 other concept-pairs. While it may not be significant to keep track of the single, dual or triple occurrences, it will also not be appropriate to club all these relations together and state that *"expressed in"* occurs between concepts *substance* and *source*, which is correct but a case of over-generalization. An appropriate characterization should take into account the proportion of instances reaching at a particular concept-pair against the total occurrences at its parent concept-pair. Thus characterized, the relations can be used to enhance the underlying ontology. We have provided experimental validation of the approach over the GENIA corpus [3].

2 Analyzing Frequently Occurring Biological Relations Extracted from GENIA Corpus

The GENIA ontology is a taxonomy of 47 biologically relevant nominal categories in which the top three concepts are *biological source, biological substance* and *other_name*. The *other-name* refers to all biological concepts that are not identified with any other known concept in the ontology. The sub-tree rooted at *source* contains 13 nominal categories and the other rooted at *substance,* contains 34 nominal categories. The GENIA corpus contains 2000 tagged MEDLINE abstracts. Tags are leaf concepts in GENIA ontology. Tags may be nested whereby a tagged Biological entity in conjunction with other entities or processes may be tagged as a different leaf concept. A biological relation is expressed as a binary relation between two biological concepts [4]. Following this definition, while mining for biological relations, we define a relation as an activity co-occurring with a pair of tags within the GENIA corpus. In [1] we had identified a set of 24 root verbs and their 246 variants, which represent biological relations occurring in the GENIA corpus. A complete list of all feasible biological relations and their morphological variants extracted from the GENIA corpus is available on http://www.geocities.com/mdabulaish/BIEQA/. We can enhance the GENIA ontology with these relations.

Since the GENIA corpus is tagged with leaf-level concepts, all relations are defined between entities or between leaf-level concept pairs. However keeping track of all instances may not be useful from the aspect of domain knowledge consolidation. This was illustrated through an example in section 1. Hence our aim is to generalize a relation at an appropriate level of specificity before including it in the ontology. This reduces over-specialization and noise.

All molecular biology concepts in the GENIA ontology are classified into two broad categorirs, *source* and *substance.* Hence the entity pairs occurring with each relation can be broadly classified as belonging to one of the following four categories (i) <source, source> (ii) <source, substance> (iii) <substance, source> and (iv) <substance, substance>. Every instance of a relation belongs to one of these categories and the total number of instances associated to any category can be obtained with appropriate summation. Since a generic concept can represent multiple specific concepts, hence the first step towards characterizing relations is to consolidate the total number of relations belonging to each category, identify the pathways through which they are assigned to a category and then find the most appropriate generalization of the relation in that category.

In order to achieve this, we define a *concept-pair tree* to represent each category. The root node of a concept-pair tree denoted by (L_r, R_r) contains one of the four generic concept-pairs defined earlier. Each node N in a concept-pair tree has two constituent concepts $< C_i, C_j >$ denoted as the LEFT and the RIGHT concepts. The LEFT and RIGHT concepts are specializations of L_r and R_r respectively, as obtained from the underlying ontology. Each *concept-pair tree* stores all possible ordered concept-pairs that match the root concept-pair (L_r, R_r) and is generated using a recursive algorithm, described in the next section.

3   Generating Concept-Pair Trees

The concept-pair tree is represented as an AND-OR tree, where each node has links to two sets of children, denoted by L_1 and L_2. L_1 and L_2 each contain a set of concept-pair nodes. The two sets L_1 and L_2 are themselves connected by the OR operator, while the nodes within each of them are connected with each other through an AND operator. For every node N, the two sets of child nodes L_1 and L_2 are created as follows:

- L_1 consists of concept pairs created by expanding the LEFT concept to consider all its child nodes in the concept ontology, while keeping the RIGHT concept unchanged.
- L_2 is created by keeping the LEFT concept unchanged while considering all children of the RIGHT concept in the concept ontology.
- When any of the concepts LEFT or RIGHT is a leaf-level ontology concept, the corresponding set L_1 or L_2 respectively is NULL.

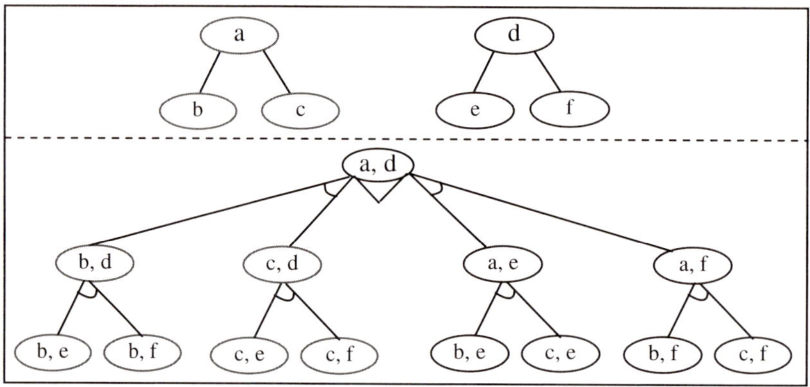

Fig. 1. Sample AND-OR concept-pair tree

Starting from a root concept pair $<L_r, R_r>$, the complete concept-pair tree is created recursively as follows:

$$OR\ [AND\ [<children\ of\ L_r, R_r\ >],\ AND\ [<L_r,\ children\ of\ R_r\ >]]$$

Let us suppose 'a' and 'd' represent two root concepts in a concept ontology, at each of which an ontology sub-tree is rooted, as shown in Fig. 1. The sets L_1 and L_2 for the root node of the concept pair tree, $<a, d>$, are determined as L_1: $<b, d>$, $<c,d>$; L_2: $<a, e>$, $<a, f>$. Fig. 1 shows the resulting AND-OR tree. AND is represented by '$\cup$', OR is represented using the symbol '$\vee$'. It may be noted that leaf-level pairs occur more than once in the tree. Each occurrence defines a path through which relations between that pair may be propagated up for generalization. Two sets of relations converging at a parent node, could be viewed as alternative models for generalization or could be viewed as complementing each other to form the total set at the parent level, depending on whether they are coming via the AND path or the OR path. This is further explained in the next section.

3.1   Mapping the Relation Instances over a Concept-Pair Tree

After creating the four different concept-pair trees for the GENIA ontology, the most feasible representation of a relation for each of these categories is obtained using these. Suppose there are N instances of a relation r_g observed over the corpus. Each of these instances is defined for a pair of leaf-level concepts. Based on the generic category of the leaf-level concepts, each relation instance can be mapped to a leaf node in one of the four concept-pair trees.

For each concept-pair tree T^G, all instances that can be mapped to leaf-level nodes of T^G are mapped at the appropriate nodes. These counts are propagated up in the tree exploiting its AND-OR property. Since each leaf-level node has multiple occurrences in a concept-pair tree, each relation instance is mapped to all such leaf-level nodes. For each non-leaf node in the concept-pair tree, the total number of relations is equal to the number of instances propagated up through all its children in either L_1 or L_2. In order to derive the most appropriate levels for describing a relation, the concept-pair tree is traversed top-down. Starting from the most generic level description at the root level, an information loss function based on set-theoretic approach is applied at each node to determine the appropriateness of defining the relation at that level.

4   Characterizing Relations at Appropriate Levels of Specificity

The process of determining the most specific concept pairs for relations follows a top-down scanning of the AND-OR tree. Starting from the root node, the aim is to determine those branches and thereby those nodes which can account for sufficiently large number of relation instances. When the frequency of a relation drops to an insignificant value at a node the node and all its descendents need not be considered for the relation conceptualization, and may be pruned off without further consideration. The lowest un-pruned node becomes a leaf and is labeled as the most specific concept-pair for defining a relation.

$$Information\ Loss(N) = \frac{\left| IC_P - IC_N \right|}{\left| IC_P + IC_N \right|} \tag{1}$$

where, IC_N = Count of instances of relation r_g at N, IC_P = count of instances of r_g at parent P of N.

Equation 1 defines a loss-function that is applied at every node N to determine the loss of information incurred if this node is pruned off. The loss function is computed as a symmetric difference between the number of instances that reach the node and the number of relation instances that were defined at its parent. Equation 1 states that if the information loss at a node N is above a threshold, it is obvious that the node N accounts for a very small percentage of the relation instances that are defined for its parent. Hence any sub-tree rooted at this node may be pruned off from further consideration while deciding the appropriate level of concept pair association for a relation. For our implementation this threshold has been kept at 10%.

Since a parent node has two alternative paths denoted by the expansion of LEFT and RIGHT respectively, along which a relation may be further specialized, the choice of appropriate level is based on the collective significance of the path composed of retained nodes. For each ANDed set of retained nodes, total information loss for the set is computed as the average information loss for each retained child. The decision to prune off a set of nodes rooted at N is taken as follows: Let information loss for nodes retained at L_1 is E_1 and that for nodes retained at L_2 is E_2.

- If $E_1 = 0$, then L_1 is retained and L_2 is pruned off, otherwise, if $E_2 = 0$ then L_2 is retained and L_1 is pruned off.
- Otherwise, if $E_1 \approx E_2$, i.e., $Min(E_1, E_2)/Max(E_1, E_2) \geq 0.995$ then both the sub-trees are pruned off, and the node N serves as the appropriate level of specification.
- Otherwise, if $E_1 < E_2$, then L_1 is retained and L_2 is pruned off. If $E_2 < E_1$ then L_2 is retained while L_1 is pruned off.

The set of concept-pairs retained are used for conceptualizing the relations.

5   Fuzzification of Relations

Since all relations are not equally frequent in the corpus, hence we associate with each relation a strength S which is computed in terms of relative frequency. Equation 2 computes this strength, where G denotes the category of concept-pairs: *source-substance, source-source, substance-substance* and *substance-source*. $|T^G|$ denotes the total count of all relations that are defined between ordered concept pairs defined in the tree T^G, and $N_{r_g}^G$ denotes the total number of relation instances of type r_g mapped to T^G.

$$\mu_{(C_i, C_j)}^G(r_g) = \frac{1}{2} \left\{ \frac{\left| < C_i, r_g, C_j > \right|}{N_{r_g}^G} + \frac{\left| < C_i, r_g, C_j > \right|}{|T^G|} \right\} \tag{2}$$

Since exact numeric values of strength do not convey much information, hence we choose a fuzzy representation to store the relations. The feasible biological relations are converted into fuzzy relations based on the membership of their strength values to a fuzzy quantifier term set {weak, moderate, strong}. The membership functions for determining the values to each of these categories are derived after analyzing the graphs displaying the distributions of strength. Fig. 2 shows the percentage of feasible relations of each category against the strengths of the relations.

The fuzzy membership functions are derived after analyzing the graphs shown in Fig. 2. Each curve shows only one valley, and this common valley for all trees is observed at strength 0.4. Hence 0.4 is selected for defining the intermediate class "moderate". The membership functions for the categories "weak", and "strong" for each category are obtained through curve-fitting on different sides of the valley, while the membership function for class "moderate" is obtained by using the values surrounding 0.4. The fuzzy membership functions for categories "moderate" and "strong" are always characterized by Gaussian functions, whereas for the category "weak", different types of functions are derived.

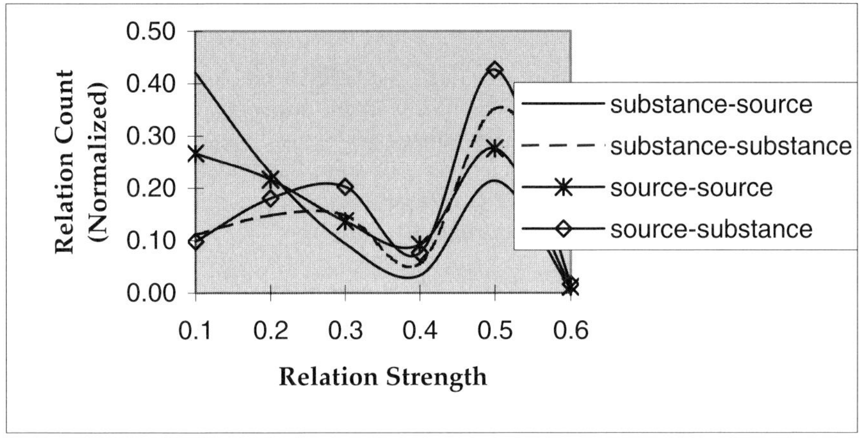

Fig. 2. A plot of relation strengths and their %age counts for all four categories of trees

Table 1. Biological relations and associated generic concept-pairs along with their fuzzy strength

Relation	Generic concept-pairs and their strengths			
	Substance-Source	Substance-Substance	Source-Source	Source-Substance
Induce	(<OC, Nat>, S) (<OC, Art, W>)	(<OC, AA>, S) (<OC, NA>), W)	(<Src, Src>, S)	-------
Inhibits	(<Lip, CT>, W) (<PFG, CT>, W) (<PM, CT>, M) (<DNADR, CT>, W)	(<Sbs, Cmp>, S)	(<CT, Art>, S) (<CT, Nat>, S)	(<Nat, AA>, S) (<Nat, NA>, M)
Activate	(<OC, Nat>, S)	(<Pr, AA>, S) (<Pr, NA>, W)	(<CL, CT>, W) (<CT, CT>, S) (<MC, CT>, W)	(<Src, OC>, S)
Expressed in	(<OC, Src>, S)	(<DNA, OC>, W) (<Pr, AA>, M) (<Pr, NA>, M) (<RNA, OOC >, W)	(<Nat, Org>, W) (<Nat, Tis>, W) (<Nat, CT>, S)	-------

Legend:
OC: Organic compound;   AA: Amino_acid;   NA: Nuclic_acid;   OOC: Other_organic_compound;   Sbs: Substance; Nat: Natural source;   Org: Organism;   CT: Cell_type;   Pr: Protein;   Src: Source;   Tis: Tissue; MC: Mono_cell;   PFG: Protein_family_or_group;   Lip: Lipid;   DNADR: DNA_domain_or_region;   Art: Artificial source;   Cmp: Compound;   PM: Protein_molecule;   S: Strong; M: Moderate; W: Weak

$$\mu_{weak}(x) = a + bx, \text{ where } a = 1.194, b = -2.194 \tag{3}$$

$$\mu_{moderate}(x) = ae^{-\frac{(x-b)^2}{2c^2}}, \text{ where } a = 2.506, b = 0.357, c = 0.032 \tag{4}$$

$$\mu_{strong}(x) = ae^{-\frac{(x-b)^2}{2c^2}}, \text{ where } a = 1.131, b = 0.476, c = 0.049 \tag{5}$$

Sample fuzzy membership functions derived for the category *substance-substance* (shown through dashed line in Fig. 2) is shown below. The membership functions for the fuzzy sets *"weak"*, *"moderate"* and *"strong"* are defined in equations 3, 4 and 5 respectively. Table 1 shows the top 5 relations along with their associated concept pairs and strengths identified for enhancing the GENIA ontology.

6   Enhancing GENIA to a Fuzzy Relational Ontology

We now explain how we propose to extend the GENIA ontology by adding the generic relations to it. Since the relations have variable strengths, hence we propose to maintain a Fuzzy Relational Ontology rather than a crisp ontology structure. In this model there are two categories of relations – *structural* and *generic*. While structural relations are crisp, generic relations have associated fuzzy strengths. We define the Fuzzy Relational Ontology Model as follows:

Definition *(Fuzzy Relational Ontology Model)* – A Fuzzy Relational Ontology Model Θ_f is a 5-tuple of the form

$\Theta_f = (C, P, \Re_s, \Re_g, S)$, where,

- C is a set of concepts

- P is a set of properties. A property $p \in P$ is defined as a unary relation of the form $p(c)$, where $c \in C$ is the concept associated to the property.

- $\Re_s = \{is\text{-}a, kind\text{-}of, part\text{-}of, has\text{-}part\}$ is a set of structural semantic relations between concepts. A structural semantic relation $r_s \in \Re_s$ is defined as a binary relation of the form $r_s(C_i, C_j)$, where $C_i, C_j \in C$ are the concepts related through r_s.

- $\Re_g$ is a set of feasible generic relations between concepts. Like structural semantic relations, a generic relation $r_g \in \Re_g$ can be defined as a binary relation of the form $r_g(C_i, C_j)$, where $C_i, C_j \in C$ are the concepts related through r_g.

- $S = \{weak, moderate, strong\}$, is a term set to represent the strength of the generic biological relations in terms of linguistic qualifiers. A linguistic qualifier $\xi \in S$ is defined as a unary relation of the form $\xi(r_g)$, where $r_g \in \Re_g$ is a feasible generic relation

To accommodate generic relations and their strengths, in addition to existing GENIA ontology classes, the fuzzy GENIA relational ontology structure contains three generic classes - a *"ConcetPair"* class, a *"FuzzyStrength"* class and a *"GenericRelation"* class, where the last one multiply inherits from the earlier two classes. The *ConceptPair* class consists of *HasLeftConcept* and *HasRightConcept* properties whose values are the instances of the GENIA *concept* classes. *FuzzyStrength* class has been defined to store the fuzzy quantifiers that can be associated with the generic relations to represent their strength. This class consists of a single property *TermSet* which is defined as a *symbol* and contains the fuzzy quantifiers "weak", "moderate" and "strong". The *GenericRelation* class has two properties – *LeftRightActors* and *Strength*. The *LeftRightActors* property is a kind of OWL object property which range is bound to the *ConceptPair* class. The *Strength* property is also a kind of OWL object property for which the range is bound to the *FuzzyStrength* class. All mined generic relations are defined as instances of the class *GenericRelation*. Fig. 3. shows a snapshot of a portion of the enhanced Fuzzy GENIA relational ontology structure. A total of 280 strong, 38 moderate and 576 weak relational links were identified for adding to GENIA. It is observed that each instance of relation has a strong or moderate co-occurrence with a maximum of 4 different pairs. However, the maximum number of weak co-occurrences could go up to 17. For example, Table 1 shows 3 strong and 2 weak instances of the relation "induce". In our implementation we have restricted the enhancement to include only strong and moderate relations, to keep the ontology comprehendible.

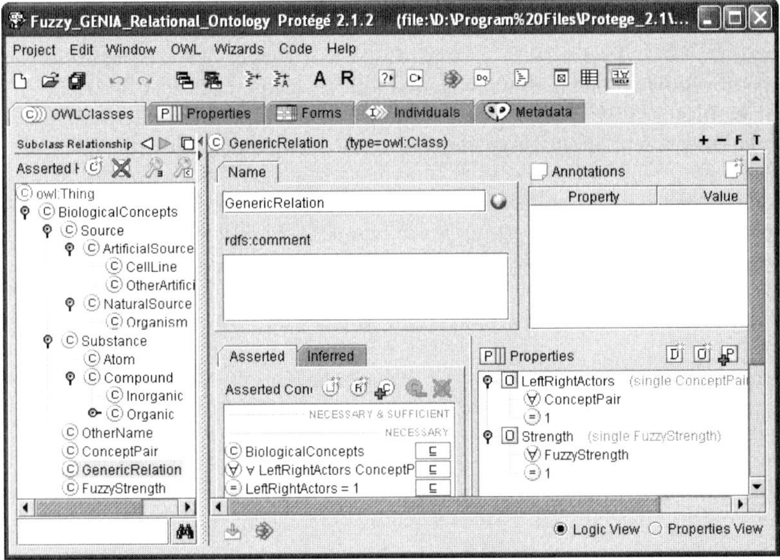

Fig. 3. A snapshot of the Fuzzy Relational GENIA ontology structure

7 Conclusions

In this paper we propose a fuzzy relational ontology model to accommodate generic biological relations into an existing biological ontology. The relations are mined from the GENIA corpus, which contains tagged MEDLINE abstracts. The mined relations which are always defined between a pair of leaf level concepts in the GENIA corpus are generalized using a novel technique. The generalization task is framed as an optimization problem over a AND-OR concept-pair tree. Since the relations occur with varying strengths, the enhanced ontology is modeled as a fuzzy ontology structure. The derivation of the fuzzy membership functions have also been addressed in detail. A glimpse of the experimental results has been provided. Extension of the ontology structure into a rough-fuzzy ontology is being currently studied.

Acknowledgement

The first author is presently on leave from IIT Delhi and has taken up a temporary assignment with Webaroo Technologies Limited. She would like to thank Webaroo Technologies Ltd. for providing the support to attend the conference.

References

1. Abulaish, M., Dey, L.: An Ontology-based Pattern Mining System for Extracting Information from Biological Texts. in: Proceedings of the 10th Int. Conf. on RSFDGrC'05, Canada. LNAI 3642, Part II, Springer (2005) 420-429
2. Ciaramita, M., Gangemi, A., Ratsch, E., Saric, J., Rojas, I.: Unsupervised Learning of Semantic Relations between Concepts of a Molecular Biology Ontology. in: Proceedings of the 19th Int. Joint Conf. on Artificial Intelligence (2005) 659-664
3. Kim, J.-D., Ohta, T., Tateisi, Y., Tsujii, J.: GENIA Corpus – A Semantically Annotated Corpus for Bio-Textmining. Bioinformatics, Vol. 19, Suppl. 1 (2003) i180-i182
4. Ono, T., Hishigaki, H., Tanigami, A., Takagi, T.: Automated Extraction of Information on Protein-Protein Interactions from the Biological Literature. Bioinformatics 17(2) (2001) 155-161
5. Rinaldi, F., Scheider, G., Andronis, C., Persidis, A., Konstani, O.: Mining Relations in the GENIA Corpus. in: Proceedings of the 2nd European Workshop on Data Mining and Text Mining for Bioinformatics, Pisa, Italy (2004)
6. Sekimizu, T., Park, H. S., Tsujii, J.: Identifying the Interaction between Genes and Genes Products Based on Frequently Seen Verbs in Medline Abstract. Genome Informatics 9 (1998) 62–71
7. Thomas, J., Milward, D., Ouzounis, C., Pulman, S., Carroll, M.: Automatic Extraction of Protein Interactions from Scientific Abstracts. in: Pacific Symposium on Biocomputing (2000) 538-549

On a Parthood Specification Method for Component Software

Dai Tri Man Le and Ryszard Janicki

McMaster University, Department of Computing and Software
Hamilton, ON, L8S 4K1 Canada
{ledt, janicki}@mcmaster.ca

Abstract. The Basic Mereology framework of [8] is enriched by adding colimit construction from Category Theory. The new framework is then used to model component-based software architecture.

Keywords: mereology, software components, "part of" relation, software architecture, theory of composition and decomposition.

1   Introduction

Component-based software development focuses on building a large software system by composing pre-existing *parts* such as software components. This paradigm arises in respons to the disadvantages of the object-oriented paradigm which does not have an architectural method to separate the *computational* and *compositional* aspects. However, despite a lot of effort spent on defining *architecture description languages* (ADLs), component based software engineering is still lacking a universally accepted architectural framework. Besides, due to the number of ADLs available in industry, an architectural framework should also be ADL independent so that it can be widely adopted. These reasons led to the development of a simple mathematical framework that is powerful enough to manipulate and (de)compose component parts. We propose *MereoCat*, an architectural framework based on *Basic Mereology* (i.e. theory of "part-whole" relations) of [8] enriched by some simple Category Theory constructions [3,13].

Additional motivation for applying Mereology to Component-based Software (CBS) was provided by the fact that the sense of parthood in CBS is much fuzzier than one might think. While "part-whole" relationships are considered to be one of the most important UML modeling concepts within Object Oriented Modeling (due to the notions of *aggregation, composition* [14,17], as well as within Component Based Modeling through the UML notion of *"structure classifiers"* [6]), o the authors' knowledge, no formal and complete parthood model exists.

Even when a mathematical framework, eg. Set Theory or Category Theory, is used to model software architecture, components and subsystems (as mathematical objects) are treated somewhat *uniformly*, which in our opinion should not be the case due to the nature of parthood within a software system. We argue that preservation of the parthood structures can support different *architectural views*, the improvement of component-based modeling foundations and even practicals aspect like *propagation* of operations [16] on parts.

S. Greco et al. (Eds.): RSCTC 2006, LNAI 4259, pp. 537–546, 2006.

Attempts to formalize the concepts of *"part of"* and *"fusion"* (composition) of parts go back to S. Leśniewski [21], and H. Leonard, N. Goodman [5,12]. Leśniewski invented Mereology (also called Classical Mereology) as an alternative to what is now called "Set Theory", but translation of his ideas into Set Theory is not obvious and often problematic [19,21]. Leonard and Goodman formulated Mereology within Set Theory, which makes the theory more accessible to applications [2,5,19]. Although both models have been substantially extended, applications outside philosophy, cognitive science and pure logic [2,19,21] are rare (*Rough Mereology* [15] is a distinct exception). Only recently, a version of Mereology more suitable for software engineering and motivated by the semantics of Parnas' tabular expressions [9] was proposed by Janicki[1] in [8,7,9] and has been applied to tabular expressions [7,9], and to detect formal discrepancies between two requirement scenarios [11].

In Leśniewski's Mereology, it is assumed that all topological properties like connectedness are implicit. In other words, Leśniewski assumes that when parts are composed, according to their characteristics, they "naturally" connect with one another to produce a whole. This leads to a lot of controversy around the composition of parts and the uniqueness of *mereological sum* in Extensional Mereology [2,4]. For example, the sentences "Jane loves Tom" and "Tom loves Jane" are made of the same parts, but they are obviously not the same. Within the domain of software engineering, more than ever, these controversies need to be settled down, since the same set of components can be used to create different software systems. As a result, the Basic Mereology of [8] and powerful Mereotopology of [2,20,18] do not make such assumptions. In [7] an operational algebraic version of Mereology was created where parts are (de)composed using mereological constructors and destructors instead of the usual mereological sum.

This paper provides a more refined version of Mereology of [7,8] by using a combination of both Mereology and Category Theory to create a more expressive framework for component software. Instead of axiomatizing the connectedness properties like in [2,20,18], we use *morphisms* to describe the connection, and the *colimit* in Category Theory to describe the mereological construction and the part-of relations are built on top of these. We call the resulting framework **MereoCat**, which stands for Mereo-Category.

2 Basic Mereology

In this section we provide some necessary knowledge of *Basic Mereology* [8], the mereology which we argue is the most suitable for Software Components. To make the paper self-sufficient, we start with a survey on the theory of *partial orders*.

Let X be a set. A relation $\preceq \subseteq X \times X$ is called a *partial order* iff it is reflexive $(x \preceq x)$, anti-symmetric $(x \preceq y \wedge y \preceq x \Rightarrow x = y)$, and transitive $(x \preceq y \wedge y \preceq z \Rightarrow x \preceq z)$. If $\preceq$ is a partial order then the pair $(X, \preceq)$ is called a *partially ordered set* or *poset*. A relation $\prec$ defined as $x \prec y \iff x \preceq y \wedge x \neq y$ is called a *strict partial order*. The element $\bot \in X$ satisfying $\forall x \in X. \bot \preceq x$ is called the *bottom* of X. An element $a \in A$ is a *minimal (maximal)* element of A iff $\forall x \in A. \neg(x \prec a)$ $(\forall x \in A. \neg(a \prec x))$. The set of all *minimal*

---

[1] It was the late Zdzisław Pawlak who suggested in 1999 that Leśniewski's ideas might help in solving the problem of defining formally the concept "part-of" for relations and tables.

(maximal) elements of *A* will be denoted by *min(A)* *(max(A))*. The minimal elements of the set $X \setminus \{\bot\}$ are called *atoms* of the poset $(X, \preceq)$, and *Atoms* denotes the set of all atoms of X.

The relation $\widehat{\prec}$ defined as: $x \widehat{\prec} y \Longleftrightarrow x \prec y \wedge \neg(\exists z. x \prec z \prec y)$ is called the *cover* relation for $\preceq$.

Now we will begin with mereological axioms, but to do so we need some definitions. Let $(X, \preceq)$ be a poset (with or without $\bot$). The relation $\preceq$ is now interpreted as *"part of"*; a is a *part of* b iff $a \preceq b$, and a is a *proper part of* b iff $a \prec b$. Notice that "a is a *part of* b" is equivalent to saying that "b is a *whole of* a". The element $\bot$ is interpreted as an empty part. The relation $\circ$, $\dagger$ and $\diamond$ on $X \setminus \{\bot\}$ defined as

$$x \circ y \Longleftrightarrow \exists z \in X \setminus \{\bot\}. z \preceq x \wedge z \preceq y \qquad \text{(overlap)}$$

$$c \dagger y \Longleftrightarrow \neg(x \circ y) \qquad \text{(disjoint)}$$

$$x \diamond y \Longleftrightarrow \exists z \in X \setminus \{\bot\}. x \preceq z \wedge y \preceq z \qquad \text{(underlap)}$$

are called *overlapping, disjointness* and *underlapping* respectively. Two elements *x* and *y overlap* iff they have a common non-empty part, they are disjoint iff they do not have a common non-empty part, and they underlap if they are both parts of another element (see [2,19] for more properties).

We will now introduce the set of axioms which helps us to define Basic Mereology.

$$x \prec y \Rightarrow (\exists z \in X. z \prec y \wedge x \dagger z) \vee x = \bot \qquad \text{(WSP)}$$

$$\forall x \in X \setminus \{\bot\}. \exists y \in Atoms. y \preceq x \qquad \text{(ATM)}$$

$$\bot \in X \qquad \text{(BOT)}$$

$$x \preceq y \Longleftrightarrow x(\widehat{\prec})^* y \qquad \text{(CCL)}$$

$$\forall x \in X. \exists y \in max(X). x \preceq y \qquad \text{(WUB)}$$

where $(\widehat{\prec})^*$ is the reflexive and transitive closure of $\widehat{\prec}$, i.e. $(\widehat{\prec})^* = \bigcup_{i=0}^{\infty} (\widehat{\prec})^i$.

The axiom WSP, called *Weak Supplementation Principle*, is a part of all known mereologies. Among others, it guarantees that if an element has a proper non-empty part, it has more than one. It is widely believed that any reasonable mereology must conform this axiom [19]. The Axiom ATM says that all objects (except the empty part) are built from *elementary elements* called *atoms*. The axiom BOT simply says that the empty part does exist, while CCL states that the part-of relation is the reflexive and transitive closure of the cover relation for $\preceq$. The final axiom WUB (*Weakly Upper Bounded*) in principle means that the set *max(X)* is a roof that cover the whole set. This axiom is crucial when the concept of equivalent parts is introduced (Equivalent parts are not discussed in this paper, but we will keep the axioms consistent with [8]).

Definition 1 ([8]). *A poset* $(X, \preceq)$ *will be called a **Basic Mereology** if it satisfies BOT, WSP, CCL, WUB and ATM.*

Basic Mereology is the mereology that we are going to use in the rest of this paper. For more details on Basic Mereology the reader is referred to [8].

3 Categorical Connector Framework

We assume that the reader is familiar with the basic concepts of elementary Category Theory [3]. In this paper we adopt CommUnity, the architectural design framework invented by Fiadeiro et al. in [13,3] because of its flexibility and generality, which does not restrict us to any specific ADL, and its ability to model different aspects of parallel design and especially its categorical power. To keep the paper as self-sufficient as possible we will give a brief overview of CommUnity's three architectural elements: components, configurations and connectors.

Components, which can be thought in a sense of CBS, are the model entities that perform computations and are able to synchronize with their environments and exchange information through channels. Hence, components are given in terms of their channels and actions in terms of "designs". For example, component design ***print*** consists of input channel i, output channel po and private channel rd. The actions of ***print*** are given in CommUnity as a special form of "guarded commands", except satisfying the guards only means the actions can be executed but does not force them to be executed right away. In ***print***, if $rd=false$ then $print$ is allowed to be executed and changes rd to $true$. Action $prod$ of ***print*** does the "opposite" of action $print$ and also assigns input i to output po. The ***convert*** component does the task of of a conversion module which converts a MSWord document to a PS document.

design print			*design convert*	
in	*i:ps*		*out*	*o:ps*
out	*po:ps*		*prv*	*w:MSWord*
prv	*rd:bool*		*do*	*to_ps[o]: true, false → o:=ps(w)*
do	*print[rd]: ¬rd → po:=i ‖ rd:= true*			
[]	*prod[rd]: rd → rd:= false*			

Configurations are diagrams in a category of designs where objects are designs and morphisms are *superpositions*, also called design morphisms. A design morphism $\sigma : P_1 \to P_2$ identifies that P_2 can be obtained from P_1 by "augmenting" additional behaviors to P_1 while still preserving properties of P_1 in P_2.

From a *meaningful* configuration (e.g. an output channel is not connected to other output channels) [13], a new design can be constructed using the colimit construction. For example, we want to build a new useful design from the previous designs ***print*** and ***convert***, using the configuration in the diagram below where *cable*, ***convert***, and ***print*** are objects and each arrow represents a morphism between them.

Notice that explicit names are not given to the action and channel of *cable* used for interconnection, but • symbols are used instead [13,3]. The reason is the interconnection does not correspond to the global naming but rather to associations (name binding), for examples, we need to explicitly specify that o, to_ps are bound to i and $prod$ respectively.

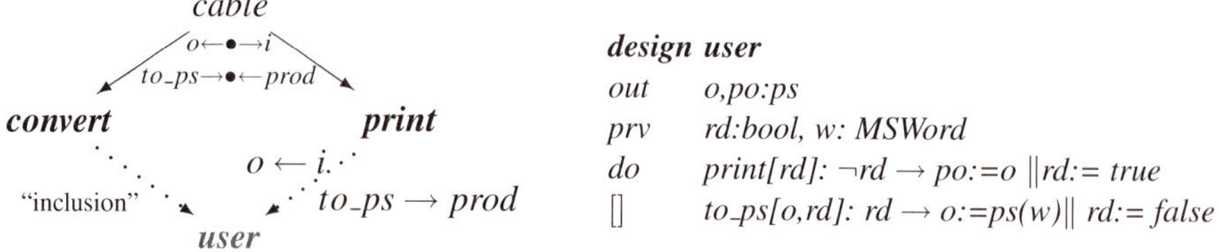

design user	
out	*o,po:ps*
prv	*rd:bool, w: MSWord*
do	*print[rd]: ¬rd → po:=o ‖rd:= true*
[]	*to_ps[o,rd]: rd → o:=ps(w)‖ rd:=false*

Using the colimit construction, the new object **user** and two arrows from **convert** and **print** to **user** are introduced into the diagram. Here the colimit, as the *amalgamated sum* (*"module sum"*), will return the minimal single design representing the whole configuration. *The design objects and design morphisms constitute category **C-DSGN**.*

Connectors are model entities independent from components whose purpose is to coordinate interactions between components as in the spirit of [1]. Connectors are given in CommUnity in terms of a "glue" design and collection of "role" designs. Since the formal concept of connectors is quite lengthy, readers are referred to [13].

4 *MereoCat* for Software Component

4.1 Architectural Views

In the real world, Component Based Software Development for complex systems is more than just composing a system from pre-existing components together using connectors. When a system becomes larger and larger, it helps to understand the architectural structure of the system better by analyzing different architectural views, which are the different abstractions of the same software system. One view is to partition a system vertically into subsystems, which *aggregate* modules implementing related function functionalities. A different view is by looking at the horizontal sections that may have different scope within the system. Layers may belongs to a single subsystem, a part of subsystem or across different subsystems [10].

The categorical framework discussed previously is designed to support composition of subsystems from component designs. However, it is not quite obvious how the framework supports the layer and subsystem views of software architecture. Their approach treats all the designs as categorical objects and strongly emphasizes the properties preserved by morphisms, but also "flattens" down the whole architectural structure. Our goal is to complement their framework by bringing back the depth to the architectural structure using part of relation. We will first start by constructing a suitable part-of relation for software component.

4.2 Construction of Part-of Relation

One of the controversies which is usually discussed within mereology is its transitivity. This can be expressed in term of software component concept as follows. Suppose a component x was used to build a subsystem y and y is again used to build a software system s. Is x is a part of s, since by the rule of encapsulation x is hidden from s by y. Again, such confusion comes from ambiguity in the meaning of "part", because natural language uses the same word "part" for different kinds of part/whole relationships. However, from a more abstract point of view, transitivity does hold [2]. If x is defective, s will not work anymore, since x does contribute to s *indirectly*.

Hence, due to encapsulation, there should exist (at least) two different kinds of parts. The first kind is when a whole can directly access the service provided by a part, and the second kind is when a part *indirectly* contributes the service to the whole by being hidden in another part. We will now characterize the *direct part-of* relation denoted by $\prec_d$, which describe the part-of relation between a whole and its direct parts, as follows:

Definition 2. *Assume that a design S, which can be a software system or subsystem, is constructed using colimit construction from a pair $(C, \textbf{C-DSGN})$ where: (1) C is a set of designs which includes the glue, component and subsystem designs; and (2) \textbf{C-DSGN} is the design category with respect to C. Then we define $\prec_d$ on C as:*

$$\forall P \in C. \ P \prec_d S$$

Definition 2 describes a view of parts and wholes at a single *level* of composition where encapsulation is preserved such that the designs in C will appear to be *"atomic"* with respect to the system (or subsystem). In the previous example, we can now say **convert** $\prec_d$ **user** and **print** $\prec_d$ **user**, but not *cable* $\prec_d$ **user**, since *cable* is precisely used for "name-bindings" but is not really a part which constitutes subsystem **user**.

To have a "multi-level" part-of relation we get the reflexive transitive closure of $\prec_d$:

Definition 3

$$\preceq \ \overset{df}{=} \ (\prec_d)^*$$

Next, let us consider the poset $(X, \preceq)$, where X is the component domain which contains all the designs (components, subsystems, glue and software systems) and the *empty design* $\perp$. Let *Atoms* be the set of all component designs. We have to show that $(X, \preceq)$ is actually a *Basic Mereology*. Hence, $\preceq$ is a correct "part of" relation for CBS.

Proposition 1. *If $(X, \preceq)$ satisfies WUB then $(X, \preceq)$ is a* Basic Mereology.

The proof of Proposition 1 is rather simple. Basically it has to be shown that $(X, \preceq)$ satisfies BOT, WSP, CCL and ATM. We cannot prove that WUB is satisfied in each case here. At this point we are not sure if we always need WUB when equivalent parts are not an issue.

Definition 3 presents the proper definition of the parthood relation in CBS. Besides, the preceding part-of relation construction also shows how closely part-whole relations and encapsulation concept are related. To say some part x is encapsulated, we need the information of what whole hides it, which is equivalent to knowing what whole x is a part of. Therefore, without being able to formalize the part-of relations, it is difficult to formalize the visibility in CBS.

4.3   Naïve *MereoCat*

We are ready to give a formal definition the *MereoCat* System.

Definition 4. *A* **MereoCat** *System is a tuple $MC = (X, Atoms, \perp, \Theta, \preceq, \textbf{C-DSGN})$ where X, Atoms, $\perp$, $\preceq$ C-DSGN as defined previously and*
- $(X, \preceq)$ is a Basic Mereology,
- Θ is the set of constructors, each $\theta \in \Theta$ is a partial function $\theta : X^I \to X$, for some I,
- The semantic of each θ is the colimit construction which constitutes designs from meaningful categorical diagrams of elements in X^I with respect to **C-DSGN**.

As we can see, the **MereoCat** System is the Basic Mereology $(X, \preceq)$ conjuncted with the design morphisms in **C-DSGN**. Connectedness properties are the result of the graph-based semantics of Category Theory, but more than that the connections here embed the abstraction of complex interaction or communication protocols between designs. It can be proven that the **MereoCat** system is a Mereological System in the sense of [7] with the empty set of destructors and a set of constructors defined in categorical style. It can also be proven that **MereoCat** has all the expressive power of Ground Mereotopology [2]. We will not explore these subjects due to lack of space.

We took advantage of the semantics of design morphisms to describe the part-of relationship in Definitions 2, 3 and 4, since according to [13,3], a design morphism $\sigma : P_1 \rightarrow P_2$ identifies a way in which P_1 is "augmented" to become P_2 through the interconnection of *one or more* components (the superposition of additional behavior). Hence, the design of the categorical approach implicitly assumes some of the part-whole relationship in mind, except they have not made it as formal and clear as we do in this paper, since it takes a lot of work to describe a precise definition of a part-of relation.

However, we still call this **MereoCat** System "Naïve **MereoCat**" since it still requires axioms for connectedness and some formal concept of consistency.

5   An Example

Using the previous components **convert** and **print**, we can design a **User-Printer** application where, a user application send a PS document to a "printing server" component **printer** to print the document. All the communication is done through a bounded buffer **buffer**, which prevents **user** from sending a new document when there is no space and prevents **printer** from reading a new message when no new message has been sent. The designs of **buffer** and **printer** are given as follows:

design buffer	*design printer*

design buffer

in   *ci:ps*

out   *co:ps*

prv   *rd: bool; q:queue*

do   *put: ¬full(q) → q:= enqueue (i,q)*

[]prv *next: ¬empty(q) ∧¬ rd*

             → o:=head(q) ∥ q:= tail(q) ∥ rd:=true

[]   *get: rd → rd:= false*

design printer

in   *i:ps*

prv   *busy:bool*

do   *rec: ¬busy → busy:=true*

[]   *end_print:busy → busy:=false*

We can specify the configuration of the situation in two different ways.

The first method is to specify the architectural configuration as in the diagram in the following figure.

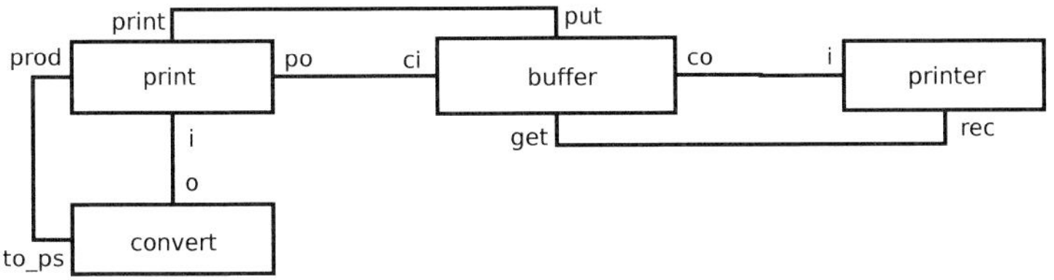

Notice that instead of drawing the categorical diagram as in previous section, we use the "syntactic sugar" of name-binding to associate the correspondent methods and channels of designs. According to the name-binding method of [13], we bind **print** component with the input of **buffer**.

The second method, using MereoCat, is to specify the part-of relation as a way to "modularize" the configuration as in the following figure.

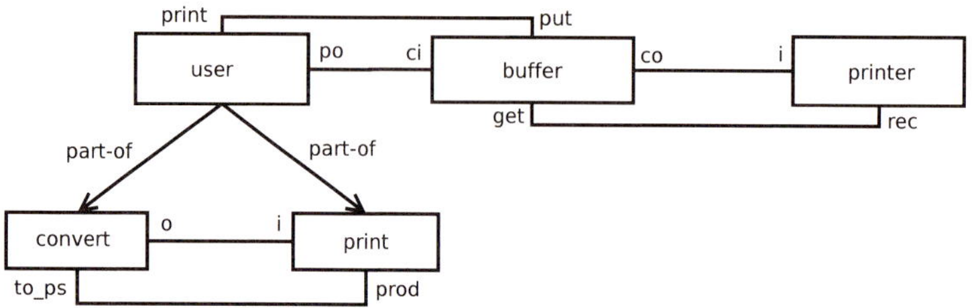

We connect the resulting *subsystem **user*** $= \theta(\boldsymbol{convert}, \boldsymbol{print})$ to **buffer** where θ denotes the constructor that constructs **user** from two components **convert** and **print**. The semantics of θ is the colimit construction (amalgamated sum) as previously discussed in Section 3. As a result, we have a more hierarchical view of the whole **User-Printer** system.

Obviously, we can recursively apply this method to different parts of the system when the system grows larger and larger. Notice that **buffer** (the "glue" design) and its associations (name-bindings) constitute a *connector* according to the connector definition in [13].

6   Other Applications of *MereoCat*

As previously mentioned the first kind of application is to describe different architectural views of a software system. The subsystem view comes straight from the part-whole relation since component aggregation is nothing but a whole that consists of closely related functionalities. Unfortunately, the aggregation concept is usually introduced intuitively rather than formally. However, using the axioms of Basic Mereology in **MereoCat**, one has a means to validate if a relation is aggregation or association. The approach we use in **MereoCat** is to keep the information about the part-of relation when modeling composition and stepwise development of a system as a part of the architectural specification. It saves a lot of effort when recovering the part-of relationship in the resulting product. For example, we can see right away that **user** is a subsystem of **User-Printer**. The process of partitioning a software system into layers will also benefit from the resulting multi-level hierarchy produced by the $\prec_d$ relation restricted to the the system's parts.

The second kind of application is to use **MereoCat** to produce part-whole based modeling method for systems. A part-whole based architecture model of a software system is usually more intuitive and helpful in understanding the architectural structures than that of a non part-whole one. This advantage is concluded in [14] using a case study which analyzes a part-whole and a non part-whole based model of a weather monitoring system within Object Oriented concepts. However, the rational behind that case study does also apply to component-based software as our **User-Printer**. When designing a large software system, in order to reuse as many pre-existing parts as possible, designers are usually more concerned with the detailed interconnection and communication protocols (horizontal relationships) between parts than the hierarchy of design resulting from the grouping of modules into subsystem or layers based on their functionalities. Thus, the resultant designs usually consist of too many vertical dependencies between modules to recover any subsystem or layer architectural view. A good design method should enforce designers to group the system modules into multi-level trees of composition like we did with the ***User-Printer*** application using ***MereoCat***.

Last but not least, ***MereoCat*** can help formalize the *propagation (triggering) of operations*, for which there is a "pervasive" need in both software and database communities as emphasized in Rumbaugh's works [16,17]. Propagation is defined to be the automatic application of an operation to a network of parts. The part-of relations have a great impact on such operations because, for example, the moving/copying/deleting of a whole also moves/copies/deletes all the parts, which are part-of the whole but not the parts *referenced* by the wholes. Hence, without a precise part-of relation, it is very hard to define the formal semantics of propagation. For instance, in the previously discussed example, suppose we need to create a new instance of the client subsystem because a new user is added to the network. In the non part-whole based model of ***User-Printer***, it is not so clear whether it is necessary to create new instances of both ***convert*** and ***print*** or not. However, in the model of ***User-Printer*** using ***MereoCat*** it is rather obvious we need to create the new instances for the parts ***convert*** and ***print*** of ***user*** since we cannot create a new instance of ***user*** without the parts which are used to construct it. We plan to discuss these topics in detail in a journal version of this paper.

7   Conclusion

This paper presents a preliminary formalization of parthood relations in CBS by introducing the ***MereoCat*** System. The lesson learnt is that by considering the part-whole (vertical) relations separately from the interconnection (horizontal) relations, the view of a component system becomes much more transparent. The task of specifying the part-whole relation is more natural than one might think. According to an experiment by Tversky and Hemenway [22], by considering attributes of biological and artificial concepts, they found 58 percent of artificial objects and 42.7 percent of biological objects were parts! This proves how important the part-of relation is as an abstraction underlying the organization of human knowledge.

The paper contributions can be characterized as follows. Firstly, we are able to create ***MereoCat*** to model component software, and by having such a rich philosophical and mathematical foundation from Mereology and Category Theory, we can discuss "parts" and use the phrase "part of" in a more formal and precise manner. Secondly, we were able to explicitly introduce the topological connectedness properties into Mereology using the rich structure of categorical morphism, which according to the authors' knowledge has not ever been done before. Thirdly, we not only use the connector specification framework from [13] to take advantage of its categorical power for the future proofs of our concepts, but also complement it by providing the "depth" into it using our parthood relations.

We are currently working on a mereological refinement notion for ***MereoCat***. With the parthood formalism, we believe the system parts will become much easier to be refined or substituted than a flattened architecture style in [13,3]. For example, we can substitute not just one of components *convert* or *print* but the whole subsystem *user* in the evolution of the system *User-Printer*. It is also important to adopt the mereological equivalence relations from [8] into component software as a way to partition the component domain into classes of equivalent parts, which creates the very theoretical interesting effect of having a "hierarchy of types" in the component domain.

References

1. R. Allen and D. Garlan. A Formal Basis for Architectural Connection. *ACM Transactions on Software Engineering and Methodology*, 6(3):213–249, July 1997.
2. R. Casati and A. Varzi. *Parts and places: the structures of spatial representation*. MIT Press, 1999.
3. J. L. Fiadeiro. *Categories for Software Engineering*. Springer, Berlin, 2004.
4. P. Forrest. Nonclassical mereology and its application to sets. *Notre Dame Journal of Formal Logic*, 43(2):79–94, 2002.
5. N. Goodman. *The structure of appearance*. Dordrecht, Holland, 1977.
6. J. Ivers, P. Clements, D. Garlan, R. Nord, B. Schmerl, and J. Oviedo. Documenting component and connector views with UML 2.0. Technical Report CMU-CS-2004-TR-008, School of Computer Science, Carnegie Mellon University, April 2004.
7. R. Janicki. On a mereological system for relational software specifications. In *Proc. of MFCS '02*, Lecture Notes in Computer Science 2420, pages 375–386. Springer-Verlag, 2002.
8. R. Janicki. Basic mereology with equivalence relations. In *Proc. of MFCS '05*, Lecture Notes in Computer Science 3618, pages 507–519. Springer-Verlag, 2005.
9. R. Janicki and R. Khedri. On a formal semantics of tabular expressions. *Science of Computer Programming*, 39(2–3):189–213, 2001.
10. M. Jazayeri, A. Ran, and F. van der Linden. *Software architecture for product families: principles and practice*. Boston, MA, USA, 2000.
11. R. Khedri, L. Wang, and L. Situ. Requirements specification decomposition: A system testing driven approach. In *Proc. 7th Int'l Seminar On Relational Methods in Computer Science*, pages 97–104, Bad Melente, Germany, 2003.
12. H. S. Leonard and N. Goodman. The calculus of individuals and its uses. *J. Symb. Log.*, 5(2):45–55, 1940.
13. A. Lopes, M. Wermelinger, and J. Luiz Fiadeiro. High-order architectural connectors. *ACM Trans. Softw. Eng. Methodol.*, 12(1):64–104, 2003.
14. R. Motschnig-Pitrik and J. J. Kaasbøll. Part-whole relationship categories and their application in object-oriented analysis. *IEEE Transactions on Knowledge and Data Engineering*, 11(5):779–797, 1999.
15. L. Polkowski and A. Skowron. Rough mereology: A new paradigm for approximate reasoning. *Journal of Approximate Reasoning*, 15:316–333, 1997.
16. J. Rumbaugh. Controlling propagation of operations using attributes on relations. In *OOPSLA '88*, pages 285–296, New York, NY, USA, 1988. ACM Press.
17. J. Rumbaugh and F. Eddy. *Object-Oriented Modeling and Design*. Prentice Hall, 1991.
18. F. Salustri. A formal theory for knowledge-based product model representation. *Knowledge-Intensive CAD II: proceedings of the IFIP WG 5.2 workshop*, 1996.
19. P. Simons. *Parts: A Study in Ontology*. Oxford University Press, Oxford, 1987.
20. B. Smith. Mereotopology: a theory of parts and boundaries. *Data and knowledge engineering*, 20(3):287–303, 1996.
21. J. T. J. Srzednicki and V. F. Rickey (eds.). *Lesniewski's Systems*. Kluwer, 1984.
22. B. Tversky and K. Hemenway. Objects, parts, and categories. *J. Exp. Psychol.: General, vol. 113, no. 2*, pages 169–193, 1984.

Ontology Driven Concept Approximation

Sinh Hoa Nguyen[1], Trung Thanh Nguyen[2], and Hung Son Nguyen[3]

[1] Polish-Japanese Institute of Information Technology
Koszykowa 86, 02-008, Warsaw, Poland
[2] Department of Computer Science, University of Bath
Bath BA2 7AY, United Kingdom
[3] Institute of Mathematics, Warsaw University
Banacha 2, 02-097 Warsaw, Poland
son@mimuw.edu.pl

Abstract. This paper investigates the concept approximation problem using ontology as an domain knowledge representation model and rough set theory. In [7] [8], we have presented a rough set based multi-layered learning framework for approximation of complex concepts assuming the existence of a simple concept hierarchy. The proposed methodology utilizes the ontology structure to learn compound concepts using the rough approximations of the primitive concepts as input attributes. In this paper we consider the extended model for knowledge representation where the concept hierarchies are embedded with additional knowledge in a form of relations or constrains among sub-concepts. We present an extended multi-layered learning scheme that can incorporate the additional knowledge and propose some classes of such relations that assure an improvement of the learning algorithm as well as a convenience of the knowledge modeling process. We illustrate the proposed method and present some results of experiment with data from sunspot recognition problem.

Keywords: ontology, concept hierarchy, rough sets, classification.

1 Introduction

In AI, approximate reasoning is a crucial problem occurring, e.g., during an interaction between two intelligent (human/machine) beings which are using different languages to talk about objects from the same universe. The intelligence skill of those beings (also called agents) is measured by the ability of understanding the other agents. This skill appears in different ways, e.g., as a learning or classification in machine learning and pattern recognition theory, or as an adaptation in evolutionary computation theory. A great effort of researchers in machine learning and data mining has been made to develop efficient methods for approximation of concepts from data [6]. Nevertheless, there exist many problems that are still unsolvable for existing state of the art methods, because of the high complexity of learning algorithms or even unlearnability of hypothesis spaces.

Utilization of domain knowledge into learning process becomes a big challenge for improving and developing more efficient concept approximation methods. In previous papers we have assumed that the domain knowledge was given in form

S. Greco et al. (Eds.): RSCTC 2006, LNAI 4259, pp. 547–556, 2006.
© Springer-Verlag Berlin Heidelberg 2006

of a concept hierarchy [7] [8]. The concept hierarchy, the simplest form of ontology, is a treelike structure with the target concept located at the root, with attributes located at leaves, and with some additional concepts located in internal nodes. We have adopt the layered learning approach [13], and rough set methods to proposed a multi-layered algorithm for induction of "multi-layer rough classifier" (MLRC) from data [7]. We have shown that MLRC has significantly better classification accuracy and shorter classification time comparing with the traditional rough classifiers. Nevertheless, many problems still remain in this research. The problem is related to the choice of the appropriate learning algorithm and the corresponding decision table for approximation of each concept in the hierarchy. Moreover, during experiment execution, we observed a noticeable worsening of accuracy of classifiers in the consecutive layers. This is because, except the own approximation error, the compound classifier can have a mistake even when only one of its component classifiers fails, e.g., it has a misclassification or returns no answer.

The mentioned above problems are probably caused by the simplification of the knowledge representation model, where the only structure of concept ontology was utilized in the learning algorithm. In this paper we consider an extended knowledge representation model, where except the concept hierarchy, we assume that there are some constraints between concepts on the same level. We will present a modified layered learning algorithm that utilizes those constraints as the additional domain knowledge.

The paper is organized as follows. Section 2.2 provides some basic notions of concept ontology, some important classes of concept relations and some basic ideas of rough set theory and the problem of concept approximation. Section 3 presents a multi-layered learning algorithm driven by ontology for the concept approximation problem. Section 4 is devoted to illustration and analyzing the accuracy of the proposed method for the sunspot recognition problem. The paper finishes with summarized conclusions and discussion on possible feature works.

2   Preliminaries

Concepts can be understood as definable sets of objects. Formally, any subset X of a given universe $\mathfrak{U}$ which can be described by a formula of $\mathcal{L}$ is called the concept in $\mathcal{L}$. The *concept approximation problem* can be understood as searching for approximate description – using formulas of a predefined language $\mathcal{L}$ – of concepts that are definable in other language $\mathcal{L}^*$. Inductive learning is the concept approximation method that searches for description of unknown concept using finite set $U \subset \mathfrak{U}$ of training examples.

2.1   The Role of Ontology in Inductive Learning

Ontology is defined in literature as a formal description of concept names and relation types organized in a partial ordering by the concept-subconcept relation [12]. Syntactically, given a logical language $\mathcal{L}$, an ontology is a tuple $\langle V, A \rangle$, where the vocabulary V is a subset of the predicate symbols of $\mathcal{L}$ and the axioms A are a subset of the well-formed formulas of $\mathcal{L}$ [5]. The set V is interpreted as a set of concepts and the set A is a set of relations among concepts present in the set V. A taxonomy is the most commonly used form of ontologies. It is usually a hierarchical classification of concepts in the domain, therefore we would draw it in the form of tree and call it a concept hierarchy.

Nowadays, ontology is used as an alternative knowledge representation model, and it becomes a hot topic in many research areas including (1) ontological specification for software development (2) ontology driven information systems (3) ontology-based semantic search (4) ontology-based knowledge discovery and acquisition [3] [4]. Many applications in data mining make use of taxonomies to describe different levels of generalization of concepts defined within attribute domains [5]. The role of taxonomies is to guide a pattern extraction process to induce patterns in different levels of abstractions.

Ontologies are also useful for concept approximation problems in another context. One can utilized the concept hierarchy describing the relationship between the target concept (defined by decision attribute) and conditional attributes (through additional concepts if necessary) in the induction process. Such hierarchy can be exploited as a guide to decomposition of complex concept approximation problem into simpler ones and to construction of compound classifiers for the target concept from the classifiers for primitive concepts [15].

2.2 Rough Sets and Rough Classifiers

Rough set theory has been introduced by Professor Z. Pawlak [9] as a tool for approximation of concepts under uncertainty. The theory is featured by operating on two definable subsets, i.e., a lower approximation and upper approximation. The first definition, so called the "standard rough sets", was introduced by Pawlak in his pioneering book on rough set theory [9].

Given an information system $\mathbb{S} = (U, A)$, where U is the set of training objects, A is the set of attributes and a concept $X \subset U$. Assuming at the moment that only some attributes from $B \subset A$ are accessible, then this problem can be also described by appropriate decision table $\mathbb{S} = (U, B \cup \{dec_X\})$, where $dec_X(u) = 1$ for $u \in X$, and $dec_X(u) = 0$ for $u \notin X$.

First one can define called the *B-indiscernibility relation* $IND(B) \subset U \times U$ in such a way that $x\ IND(B)\ y$ if and only if x, y are indiscernible by attributes from B, i.e., $inf_B(x) = inf_B(y)$. Let $[x]_{IND(B)} = \{u \in U : (x, u) \in IND(B)\}$ denote the equivalence class of $IND(B)$ defined by x. The lower and upper approximations of X (using attributes from B) are defined by:

$$\mathbf{L}_B(X) = \left\{x : [x]_{IND(B)} \subseteq X\right\}; \quad \mathbf{U}_B(X) = \left\{x : [x]_{IND(B)} \cap X \neq \varnothing\right\}$$

Let us point out that there are many extensions of the standard definition of rough sets, e.g., variable rough set model [14] or tolerance approximation space [11]. In these methods, rough approximations of concepts can be also defined by *rough membership function*, i.e., a mapping $\mu_X : U \to [0, 1]$ such that $\mathbf{L}_{\mu_X} = \{x \in U : \mu_C(x) = 1\}$ and $\mathbf{U}_{\mu_X} = \{x \in U : \mu_X(x) > 0\}$ are lower and upper approximation of a given concept X. In case of the classical rough set theory, the rough membership function is defined by $\mu_X^B(x) = \frac{|X \cap [x]_{IND(B)}|}{|[x]_{IND(B)}|}$.

The inductive learning approach to rough approximations of concepts we assume that U is a finite sample of objects from a universe $\mathfrak{U}$ and $X = \mathcal{C} \cap U$ is the representation of a unknown concept $\mathcal{C} \subset \mathfrak{U}$ in U. The problem can be understood as searching for an extended rough membership function $\mu_\mathcal{C} : \mathfrak{U} \to [0,1]$ for $\mathcal{C} \subset \mathfrak{U}$ such that the corresponding rough approximations defined by $\mu_\mathcal{C}$ are the good approximations of $\mathcal{C}$.

$$
\begin{array}{ccc}
U & \dashrightarrow & \mu_X : U \to [0,1] \\
\cap & & \Downarrow \\
\mathfrak{U} & \dashrightarrow & \mu_\mathcal{C} : \mathfrak{U} \to [0,1]
\end{array}
$$

The algorithm that calculates the value $\mu_\mathcal{C}(x)$ of extended rough membership function for each new unseen object $x \in \mathfrak{U}$ is called *the rough classifier*. In fact, rough classifiers can be constructed by *fuzzification* of other classifiers [1]. The specification of each algorithm for induction of rough classifiers is as follows:

Input: Given a decision table $\mathbb{S}_C = (U, A_C, dec_C)$
Output: Approximation of C in form of a hypothetical classifier $h_C = \{\mu_C, \mu_{\overline{C}}\}$
indicating the membership $\mu_C(x)$ of any object $x \in \mathfrak{U}$ to the concept C or
the membership $\mu_{\overline{C}}(x)$ to its complement $\overline{C}$.

Rule-based, kNN-based and decision tree based rough classifiers are examples of rough classifier types that will be used in next sections. These methods will be used as building blocks for construction of compound classifiers.

3   Ontology Driven Construction of Rough Classifiers

Induction of rough classifiers is the most important step in many applications of rough set theory in the process of knowledge discovery from databases. We have presented a multi-layered learning scheme for approximation of complex concept assuming that a hierarchy of concepts is given. The main idea is to gradually synthesize the target concept from the simpler ones. At the lowest layer, basic concepts are approximated using input features available from the data set. At the next layers, the approximations of compound concepts are synthesized using rough approximations of concepts from the previous layer. This process is repeated for successive layers and it results in the creation of a multi-layer rough classifier (MLRC). The advantages of MLRC have been recognized and confirmed by many experiments over different concept approximation problems [7] [8]. But in case of poor quality (incomplete, noisy) data sets, this learning scheme gives approximations with unsatisfactory accuracy because of the high sensitiveness of compound rough classifiers.

In this paper, except the concept hierarchy, we propose to extend the knowledge representation model by some constraints between concepts on the same level. We show that such constraints can improve the quality of classifiers.

3.1   Knowledge Representation Model with Constraints

Recall that taxonomy, or concept hierarchy, represents a set of concepts and a binary relation which connects a "child" concept with its "parent". The most important relation types are the subsumption relations (written as "is-a" or "is-part-of") defining which objects (or concepts) are members (or parts) of another concepts in the ontology. This model facilitates the user to represent his/her knowledge about relationships between input attributes and target concepts. If no such information available, one can assume the flat hierarchy with the target concept on top and all attributes in the downstairs layer. Besides the "child-parent" relations, we proposed to associate with each parent concept a set of "domain-specific" constraints. We consider two types of constraints: (1) constraints describing relationships between a concept and its sub-concepts; and (2) constraints connecting the "sibling" concepts (having the same parent).

Formally, the extended concept hierarchy is a triple $\mathcal{H} = (\mathbb{C}, \mathbb{R}, Constr)$, where $\mathbb{C} = \{C_1, ..., C_n\}$ is a finite set of concepts including basic concepts (attributes), intermediated concepts and target concept; $\mathbb{R} \subseteq \mathbb{C} \times \mathbb{C}$ is child-parent relation in the hierarchy; and $Constr$ is a set of constraints. In this paper, we consider constraints expressed by association rules of the form $\mathbf{P} \rightarrow_\alpha \mathbf{Q}$, where

- $\mathbf{P}, \mathbf{Q}$ are boolean formulas over the set $\{c_1, ..., c_n, \overline{c_1}, ..., \overline{c_n}\}$ of boolean variables corresponding to concepts from $\mathbb{C}$ and their complements;
- $\alpha \in [0, 1]$ is the confidence of this rule;

In next sections, we will consider only two types of constraints, i.e., the *"children-parent"* type of constraints connecting some "child" concepts with their common parent, and the *"siblings-sibling"* type of constraints connecting some sibling concepts with another sibling.

3.2   Learning Algorithm for Concept Approximation

Let us assume that an extended concept hierarchy $\mathcal{H} = (\mathbb{C}, \mathbb{R}, Constr)$ is given. For compound concepts in the hierarchy, we can use the rough classifiers as a building blocks to develop a multi-layered classifier. More precisely, let $prev(C) = \{C_1, ..., C_m\}$ be the set of concepts, which are connected with C in the hierarchy. The rough approximation of the concept C can be determined by performing two steps: (1) construct a decision table $\mathbb{S}_C = (U, A_C, dec_C)$ relevant for the concept C; and (2) induce a rough classifier for C using decision table $\mathbb{S}_C$. In [7], the training table $\mathbb{S}_C = (U, A_C, dec_C)$ is constructed as follows:

- The set of objects U is common for all concepts in the hierarchy.
- $A_C = h_{C_1} \cup h_{C_2} \cup ... \cup h_{C_m}$, where h_{C_i} is the output of the hypothetical classifier for the concept $C_i \in prev(C)$. If C_i is an input attribute $a \in A$ then $h_{C_i}(x) = \{a(x)\}$, otherwise $h_{C_i}(x) = \{\mu_{C_i}(x), \mu_{\overline{C_i}}(x)\}$.

Repeating those steps for each concept through the bottom to the top layer we obtain a "hybrid classifier" for the target concept, which is a combination of classifiers of various types. In the second step, the learning algorithm should use the decision table $\mathbb{S}_C = (U, A_C, dec_C)$ to "resolve conflicts" between classifiers of its children. One can observe that, if sibling concepts $C_1, ..., C_m$ are independent, the membership function values of these concepts are "sent" to the "parent" C, without any correction. Thus the membership value of weak classifiers may disturb the training table for the parent concept and cause the misclassification when testing new unseen objects. We present two techniques that enable the expert to improve the quality of hybrid classifiers by embedding their domain knowledge into learning process.

1. Using Constraints to Refine Weak Classifiers: Let $R := c_1 \wedge c_2 ... \wedge c_k \rightarrow_\alpha c_0$ be a siblings-sibling constraint connecting concepts $C_1, ..., C_k$ with the concept C_0. We say that the constraint R *fires* for C_0 if

- Classifiers for concepts $C_1, ..., C_k$ are strong (of a high quality).
- Classifier of concepts C_0 is weak (of a low quality).

The refining algorithm always starts with the weakest classifier for which there exist a constraint that fires (see Algorithm 1).

Algorithm 1. Classifier Refining

Input: classifier $h(C_0)$, constraint $R := c_1 \wedge c_2 ... \wedge c_k \rightarrow_\alpha c_0$
Output: Refined classifier $h(C_0)$
  1: **for** each object $x \in U$ **do**
  2:     **if** x are recognized by classifiers of $C_1, ..., C_k$ with high degree **then**
  3:         **if** c_0 is a positive literal **then**
  4:             $\mu_{C_0}(x) := \alpha \cdot \min\{\mu_{C_1}(x), \mu_{C_2}(x), ..., \mu_{C_k}(x)\}$; $\mu_{\overline{C_0}}(x) := 1 - \mu_{C_0}(x)$;
  5:         **else** $\{c_0$ is a negative literal$\}$
  6:             $\mu_{\overline{C_0}}(x) := \alpha \cdot \min\{\mu_{C_1}(x), \mu_{C_2}(x), ..., \mu_{C_k}(x)\}$; $\mu_{C_0}(x) := 1 - \mu_{\overline{C_i}}(x)$
  7:     $h'(C_j) := (\mu_{C_0}, \mu_{\overline{C_0}})$;

---

2. Using Constraints to Select Learning Algorithm: Another problem is how to assign a suitable approximation algorithm for an individual concept in the concept hierarchy? In the previous papers [7] the type of approximation algorithm (knn, decision tree or rule set) for each concept was settled by the user. In this paper we show that the constraints can be treated as a guide to semi-automatic selection of best learning algorithms for concepts in the hierarchy.

Assume that there is a "children-parent" constraints: $\bigwedge_i c_i \rightarrow_\alpha p$ (or $\bigwedge_i c_i \rightarrow_\alpha \overline{p}$) for a concept $P \in \mathbb{C}$. The idea is to choose the learning algorithm that maximizes the confidence of constraints connecting $P's$ children with himself. Let **RS_ALG** be a set of available parameterized learning algorithms, we define an objective function $\Psi_P : \mathbf{RS\_ALG} \rightarrow \Re^+$ to evaluate the quality of algorithms. For each algorithm $\mathbf{L} \in \mathbf{RS\_ALG}$ the value of $\Psi_P(\mathbf{L})$ is depended on two factors:

- Classification quality of $\mathbf{L}(\mathbb{S}_P)$ on a validation set of objects;
- Confidence of the constraints $\bigwedge_i c_i \rightarrow_\alpha p$

The function $\Psi_P(\mathbf{L})$ should be increasing w.r.t. quality of the classifier $\mathbf{L}(\mathbb{S}_P)$ for the concept P (induced by $\mathbf{L}$) and the closeness between the real confidence of the association rule $\bigwedge_i c_i \to p$ and the parameter α. The function Ψ can be used as an objective function to evaluate a quality of approximation algorithm.

Algorithm 2. Induction of multi-layered rough classifier using constraints

---

Input: Decision system $\mathbb{S} = (U, A, d)$, extended concept hierarchy $\mathcal{H} = (\mathbb{C}, \mathbb{R}, Constr)$;
     a set **RS_ALG** of available approximation algorithms
Output: Schema for concept composition
 1: **for** $l := 0$ to max_level **do**
 2:     **for** (any concept C_k at the level l in $\mathcal{H}$) **do**
 3:        **if** $l = 0$ **then**
 4:           $U_k := U$;
 5:           $A_k := B$, where $B \subseteq A$ is a set relevant to define C_k
 6:        **else**
 7:           $U_k := U$
 8:           $A_k = \bigcup O_i$, for all $C_i \in prev(C_k)$, where O_i is the output vector of C_i;
 9:           Choose the best learning algorithm $\mathbf{L} \in \mathbf{RS\_ALG}$ with a maximal objective function $\Psi_{C_k}(\mathbf{L})$
10:           Generate a classifier $H(C_k)$ of concept C_k;
11:           Refine a classifier $H(C_k)$ using a constraint set $Constr$.
12:           Send output signals $O_k = \{\mu_C(x), \mu_{\overline{C}}(x)\}$ to the parent to the next level.

A complete scheme of multi-layered learning algorithm with concept constrains is presented in Algorithm 2.

4   Example and Experimental Results

Sunspots are the subject of interest to many astronomers and solar physicists. Sunspot observation, analysis and classification form an important part of furthering the knowledge about the Sun. Sunspot classification is a manual and very labor intensive process that could be automated if successfully learned by a machine. The main goal of the first attempt to sunspot classification problem is to classify sunspots into one of the seven classes $\{A, B, C, D, E, F, H\}$, which are defined according to the McIntosh/Zurich Sunspot Classification Scheme. More detailed description of this problem can be found in [8].

The data was obtained by processing NASA SOHO/MDI satellite images to extract individual sunspots and their attributes characterizing their visual properties like size, shape, positions. The data set consists of 2589 observations from the period of September 2001 to November 2001. The main difficulty in correctly determining sunspot groups concerns the interpretation of the classification scheme itself. There is a wide allowable margin for each class (see Figure 1). Therefore, classification results may differ between different astronomers doing the classification.

Now, we will present the application of the proposed approach to the problem of sunspot classification. In [8], we have presented a method for automatic

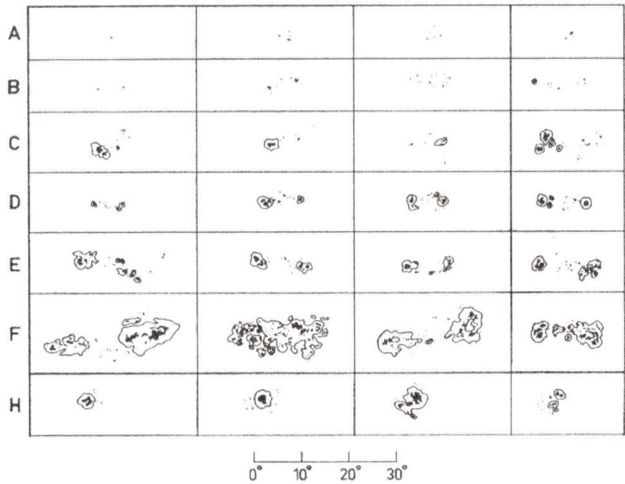

Fig. 1. Possible visual appearances for each class. There is a wide allowable margin in the interpretation of the classification rules making automatic classification difficult.

modeling the domain knowledge about sunspots concept hierarchy. The main part of this ontology is presented in Figure 2.

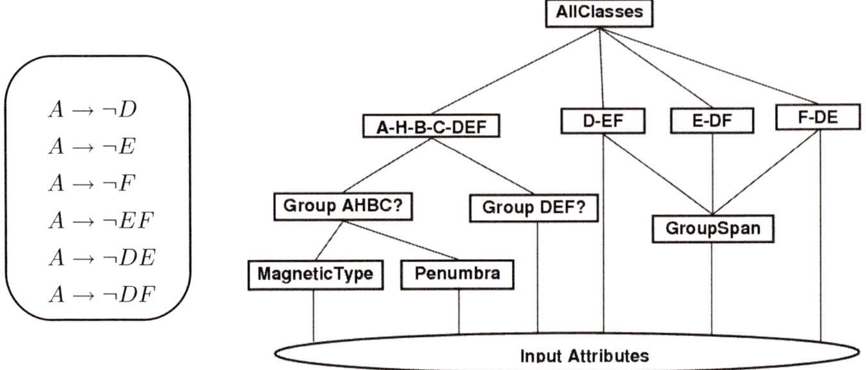

Fig. 2. The concept hierarchy for sunspot recognition problem

We have shown that rough membership function can be induced using different classifiers, e.g., k-NN, decision tree or decision rule set. The problem is to chose the proper type of classifiers for every node of the hierarchy. In experiments with sunspot data, we applied the rule based approach for concepts in the lowest level, decision tree based approach for the concepts in the intermediate levels and the nearest neighbor based approach the target concept.

Figure 3 (left) presents the classification accuracy of "hybrid classifier" obtained by composition of different types of classifiers and "homogenous classifier" obtained by composition of one type of classifiers. The first three bars show qualities of homogenous classifiers obtained by composition of k-NN classifiers, decision tree classifiers and rule based classifiers, respectively. The fourth bar (the gray one) of the histogram displays the accuracy of the hybrid classifier.

The use of constraints also give a profit. In our experiment, these constraints are defined for concepts at the second layer to define the training table for the target concept *AllClasses*. It is because the noticeable breakdown of accuracy have been observed during experiments. We use the strategy proposed in Section 3 to settle the final rough membership values obtained from its children *A-H-B-C-DEF*, *D-EF*, *E-DF*, *F-DE* (see the concept hierarchy). One can observe that using constraints we can promote good classifiers in a composition step. A better classifier has higher priority in a conflict situation. The experiment results are shown in Figure 3. The gray bar of the histogram displays the quality of the classifier induced without concept constraints and the black bar shows the quality of the classifier generated using additional constraints.

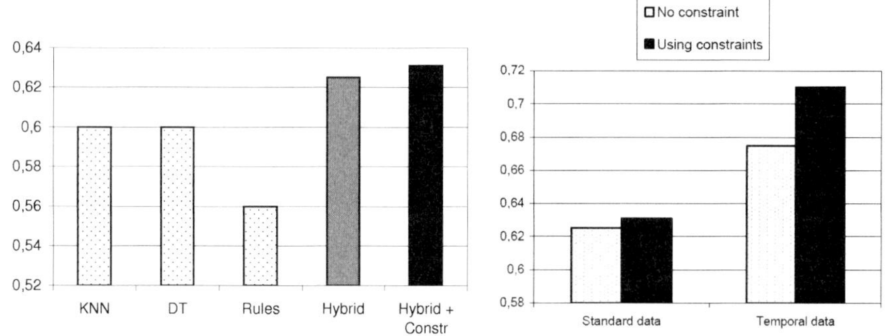

Fig. 3. Accuracy comparison of different layered learning methods

Another approach to manage with sunspot recognition problem is related to temporal features. Comparative results are showed in Figure 3 (right). The first two bars in the graph describe the accuracy of classifiers induced *without* temporal features and the last two bars display the accuracy of classifiers induced *with* temporal features. One can observe a clear advantage of the last classifiers over the first ones. The experimental results also show that the approach for dealing with temporal features and concept constraints considerably improves approximation quality of the complex groups such as B, D, E and F.

5   Conclusions

We presented some extensions of a layered learning approach. Unlike traditional approach, in the layered learning approach the concept approximations are induced not only from available data sets but also from expert's domain knowledge. In the paper, besides a concept dependency hierarchy we have also considered additional domain knowledge in the form of concept constraints. We proposed an approach to deal with some forms of concept constraints. Experimental results with sunspot classification problem have shown advantages of these new approaches in comparison to the standard learning approach.

Acknowledgement. The research has been partially supported by the grant 3T11C00226 from Ministry of Scientific Research and Information Technology of the Republic of Poland and the research grant of Polish-Japanese Institute of Information Technology.

References

1. J. Bazan, H. S. Nguyen, A. Skowron, and M. Szczuka. A view on rough set concept approximation. In G. Wang, Q. Liu, Y. Yao, and A. Skowron, editors, RSFD-GrC'2003, Chongqing, China, volume 2639 of *LNAI*, pages 181–188, Heidelberg, Germany, 2003. Springer-Verlag.
2. J. Bazan, M. Szczuka. RSES and RSESlib - A Collection of Tools for Rough Set Computations, Proc. of RSCTC'2000, LNAI 2005, Springer Verlag, Berlin, 2001
3. J. Davies, D. Fensel and F. van Harmelen (eds), Towards the Semantic Web – Ontology-Driven Knowledge Management. Wiley, London, UK, 2002.
4. A. Gomez-Perez, O. Corcho, M. Fernandez-Lopez. Ontological Engineering, Springer-Verlag, London, Berlin, 2002.
5. J. Han and M. Kamber. Data Mining: Concepts and Techniques. Morgan Kaufmann Publishers, 2000.
6. W. Kloesgen and J. Żytkow, editors. *Handbook of Knowledge Discovery and Data Mining*. Oxford University Press, Oxford, 2002.
7. S.H. Nguyen, J. Bazan, A. Skowron, and H.S. Nguyen. *Layered learning for concept synthesis.* Jim F. Peters, A. Skowron, J.W. Grzymala-Busse, B. Kostek, R.W.Swiniarski, and M. S. Szczuka, editors, Transactions on Rough Sets I, LNCS 3100, pp. 187-208. Springer, 2004.
8. S.H. Nguyen, T.T. Nguyen, and H.S. Nguyen. *Rough Set Approach to Sunspot Classification Problem.* In Proc. of Rough Sets, Fuzzy Sets, Data Mining, and Granular Computing (RSFDGrC 2005), Part II, Regina, Canada, August/September 2005, pp. 263-272. Springer, 2005.
9. Z. Pawlak. Rough sets. *International Journal of Computer and Information Sciences*, 11:341–356, 1982.
10. Z. Pawlak and A. Skowron. A rough set approach for decision rules generation. In *Proc. of IJCAI'93*, pages 114–119, Chambéry, France, 1993. Morgan Kaufmann.
11. A. Skowron. Approximation spaces in rough neurocomputing. In M. Inuiguchi, S. Tsumoto, and S. Hirano, editors, *Rough Set Theory and Granular Computing*, pages 13–22. Springer-Verlag, Heidelberg, Germany, 2003.
12. J. Sowa. *Knowledge Representation: Logical, Philosophical, and Computational Foundations.* Brooks Cole Publishing Co., Pacific Grove, CA (2000)
13. P. Stone. *Layered Learning in Multi-Agent Systems: A Winning Approach to Robotic Soccer.* The MIT Press, Cambridge, MA, 2000.
14. W. Ziarko. Variable precision rough set model. *Journal of Computer and System Sciences*, 46:39–59, 1993.
15. B. Zupan, M. Bohanec, I. Bratko, and J. Demsar, "Machine learning by function decomposition," in Proc. Fourteenth International Conference on Machine Learning, (San Mateo, CA), pp. 421–429, Morgan Kaufmann, 1997

A Statistical Method for Determining Importance of Variables in an Information System

Witold R. Rudnicki[1], Marcin Kierczak[2], Jacek Koronacki[3], and Jan Komorowski[1,2]

[1] ICM, Warsaw University, Pawinskiego 5a, Warsaw Poland
W.Rudnicki@icm.edu.pl
http://www.icm.edu.pl/~rudnicki/
[2] Uppsala University, The Linnaeus Centre for Bioinformatics
Husargatan 3, Uppsala Sweden
[3] Institute of Computer Science, Polish Academy of Sciences, J.K. Ordona 21,
Warsaw, Poland

Abstract. A new method for estimation of attributes' importance for supervised classification, based on the random forest approach, is presented. Essentially, an iterative scheme is applied, with each step consisting of several runs of the random forest program. Each run is performed on a suitably modified data set: values of each attribute found unimportant at earlier steps are randomly permuted between objects. At each step, apparent importance of an attribute is calculated and the attribute is declared unimportant if its importance is not uniformly better than that of the attributes earlier found unimportant. The procedure is repeated until only attributes scoring better than the randomized ones are retained. Statistical significance of the results so obtained is verified. This method has been applied to 12 data sets of biological origin. The method was shown to be more reliable than that based on standard application of a random forest to assess attributes' importance.

1 Introduction

Application of computer programs to decision support or classification of data dates back to the 1970's. Such problems can be formally presented in the form of a decision system which consists of a set of objects O, each of the objects being described by P different attributes, $X_1, X_2, \ldots, X_P$, and a decision attribute Y not equal to any of the attributes whose value may be unknown.

An expert system or, more narrowly, a classifier can be defined as a function $F(X_1, \ldots, X_P) \to Y$.

The first generation of expert systems was designed by human experts whose knowledge was explicitly coded by the *if* **A** *then* **B** rules [1]. The systems could cope with all examples whose decision attribute value could have been predicted by the experts, but were unable to cope with new (unseen) examples with properties not earlier predicted by the experts. Applicability of such systems

S. Greco et al. (Eds.): RSCTC 2006, LNAI 4259, pp. 557–566, 2006.

was limited to simple cases with a small number of attributes. Multi-dimensional problems with complex properties based on uncertain data could not be handled by this rational approach. For a detailed discussion see [1].

Starting in the 1980-ies, machine learning and statistical methods, such as neural networks,decision trees, and many others, were popularized with the aim to address several of the limitations of expert systems [2,3,4,5]. These methods, often collectively called inductive learning, generate models from examples with known Y, which can then be applied to unseen cases. They can successfully cope with high-dimensional problems, albeit the achieved improvement comes with a price.

While the first generation expert systems were hardly tractable for anything but simple and small domains, the newer methods are often even less amenable to human understanding. Some of them are more or less like a black box, where one throws in the description of the object and by a process that is hidden to human inspection the outcome decision comes out automatically. Neural networks are most notorious in this respect, but even several rule-based methods, such as Bayesian networks [6] and in certain circumstances methods based on rough set theory [7,8,9,10], generate decision functions which are not easy to analyse. Such functions may be comprised of thousands, if not hundreds of thousands, of simple rules which are connected by complex, non-linear logical relations. Although the problems that are very complex are often likely to be described by very complex models, we should not give up the possibility of gaining insight into the structure of the generated model. There exist several approaches to obtaining a better legibility of the models. One well-known idea is to make models less exact (cf. Ziarko's approach and approximate attributes in rough sets), which avoids over-fitting and generates simpler models with often higher performance of the model on the unseen examples. A similar idea is to use dynamic reducts that sample the space of examples and allow finding the most important attributes. Another approach to obtaining legible models from large rule sets is rule tuning (see e.g. Ågotnes *et al* [11,12] which often provides a very significant reduction of the cardinality of the rule set and, sometimes, an improvement of the classification quality due to a generalization algorithm used in rule tuning. Yet another approach is the use of templates to discover local models [13,14]. Finally, in the rough set model approach of Kowalczyk, a small subset of attributes is selected using various heuristics and user knowledge to generate simple models.

Unfortunately, for problems with a very high dimension where domain knowledge is not yet available, for instance in functional genomics and other areas of modern molecular biology and medicine, other approaches have to be applied. Interestingly, biomedical researchers are often interested in learning which of the attributes are the important ones. Only later, the researchers investigate classifiers that may be generated using these attributes. Thus, within such a framework, the first task is to identify the most important attributes. This problem is particularly acute for high-dimensional data of biological origin, where the number of attributes X_i can be of order of thousands.

Recently, a new classifier, actually comprised of an ensemble of decision trees, the so-called random forest (RF) has been proposed by Breiman [15]. The RF's classification ability is comparable to, if not better than that of the best methods available, e.g. boosting [16]. In addition, RF offers two features which improve significantly, and in a very natural way, our understanding of a classification problem under scrutiny. These are:

- the assessment of the importance of the contributions of the attributes to the final prediction,
- the assessment of the interactions between the attributes.

In the present study, we show the limits of the importance estimation as originally proposed by Breiman and present a method that aims at discerning the truly most important attributes for classification and in this respect improves significantly upon the original approach of Breiman.

2   The Method

The process of determining whether a given attribute contributes significantly to the final prediction or not, is based on multiple application of RFs, and utilization of the estimate of importance generated by each RF.

Random Forests. Random forest is a classification method that combines results from an ensemble of many, say M, decision trees built on bootstrap samples drawn with replacement from the original training sample. Each bootstrap sample is of the same size, say N, as the original sample. Drawing with replacement guarantees that roughly 1/3 of elements from the original sample are not used in each bootstrap sample (indeed, note that the probability of not drawing a particular element is $(1 - 1/N)^N \approx e^{-1}$). For each tree in the forest, elements of the original sample not used to grow this tree are called out-of-bag or oob elements for the tree.

Assume that each element (object) in the training sample is given as a vector of P attributes. At each stage of tree building, i.e. for each node of any particular tree in the forest, p attributes out of all P attributes are randomly selected, where $p << P$ (say, $p = \sqrt{P}$), and the best split on these p attributes is used to split the data in the node. Each tree is grown to the largest extent possible, i.e. there is no pruning. In this way, RF consisting of M trees is constructed. Classification of each (new) object is made by simple voting of all trees.

Estimation of Attribute Importance. For any k-th attribute, proceed in the following way. In every tree in the forest, put down its oob objects and count the number of votes cast for the correct class. Then randomly permute the values of attribute k in the oob objects, put these objects down the tree and count the number of votes cast for the correct class. Subtract the latter number of votes from that obtained for the original oob data. The average of this difference over all trees in the forest constitutes the raw importance score for attribute k. The normalized score, i.e. the so-called z-score by reference to the standard normal case, is obtained as usual, by dividing the raw score by its standard error.

Apparent Importance of Noisy Attributes. Applying the standard normal theory when calculating p-values corresponding to z-scores obtained is well justified by the observed low correlations between scores for individual trees for a number of data sets (cf. [15]). At the same time, however, we have observed that even if all the attributes are completely random and therefore by design not related to the decision attribute, relatively strong correlations between some attributes and the decision attribute may appear by chance. Such attributes are then singled out by the RF and the classifier effectively based on them is built. As a result, these noisy attributes get z-scores which suggest strong, non-random correlation with the decision attribute. The simulation experiment was performed, that indeed confirmed this hypothesis.

Highest z-score of Permuted Attribute. In order to discern properties which significantly and truly, not by chance, contribute to correct predictions, we propose to find by simulation means how high a z-score of a noisy attribute can get on the average. This can be done by estimating the mean and variance of the distribution of the Highest z-score of Permuted Attribute (HZPA). To this end, we introduce controlled noise into the system by randomly permuting values of the selected attributes, retaining the other attributes untouched and generating bootstrap samples of objects modified in the way described.

The Algorithm. We apply this idea in an iterative 'self-consistent' way into the algorithm which generates statistically validated set of important attributes, with average z-score higher than the average z-score of the HZPA.

Our method is coded as a bash script, which calls RandomForest program and two additonal C programs used to generate permuted data sets and perform statistical computations and selection of the variables. The pseudocode of the algorithm is as follows:

```
RunRandomForests()      // Initial run
SetZlimit()             // Set the z-score which will be
                        // considered provisionally important
BuildNonRandomList()    // build an initial list of provisionally
                        // important attributes
while ( !Glob_Self_Cons )
do                                      // Main Loop
  while ( !Loc_Self_Cons )
  do                                    // Loop for current Zlimit
    for  (i=1;i<=NSTEP;i++)             // NSTEP repetitions
    do
      ShuffleAttributes                 // Create data set with permuted
                                        // unimportant attributes
```

```
    RunRandomForests              // single Random Forest run
  done
  ComputeStatistics               // Computes z-score for all
                                  // important attributes
                                  // and finds AvHZPA
  BuildNewNonRandomList           // Only attributes with
                                  // z-score higher than current
                                  // Zlimit are on the list
  Loc_Self_Cons=CompLists()       // CompLists() returns TRUE
                                  // if old and new list of important
                                  // attributes are identical
 done
 Glob_Self_Cons=ChckGlobCon()     // ChckGlobCon() returns TRUE
                                  // when AvHZPA is lower than current
                                  // Zlimit
 Zlimit=Zlimit+Delta              // Increase current Zlimit
done
```

At the first step, the classifier is used with input vectors consisting of all attributes; z-scores are computed for all attributes, and attributes which have z-score higher than some predefined level are provisionally considered as important, while the remaining ones are considered unimportant. We start with the threshold level equal to 1.0.

The second step consists in running several random forests. Each time the values of the attributes identified in the previous step as unimportant are randomly permuted and values of the important attributes remain unchanged. For each run of RF and all attributes, z-scores are computed, and the average (over all RFs) z-scores for all important attributes are obtained as well. Moreover, for each run of RF, the highest z-score is found among those for the permuted attributes (i.e. HZPA is found), and its average over all RF runs, AvHZPA, is determined for later use. Note that the permuted attribute with the highest z-score can prove different for different RF runs, since they are run on different bootstrap samples.

Attributes which have average scores higher than the current threshold are considered to be temporarily important, and attributes which have average scores lower than the threshold are irreversibly considered to be unimportant. This second step is repeated at each fixed threshold level until all the attributes considered temporarily important have average z-scores higher than the current threshold. After this condition is satisfied, we have a set of temporarily important attributes which we consider "self-consistent at the current threshold level".

Once the self-consistence at a given level has been achieved, in the third step of the procedure, the check is performed if the current threshold level allows one to distinguish the attributes that carry real information from those that do not. If the threshold level is higher than AvHZPA, we conclude that full self-consistence has been reached and the iterative procedure is finished. Otherwise, the threshold is increased and the procedure for reaching self-consistence at this higher threshold level is repeated.

Finally (this step is not included in the pseudocode above), once full self-consistence has been reached, a statistical test of significance is performed for conclusive importance of attributes found important in the third step of the procedure. This test rests on repeating the second step of the procedure, but with a much higher number of iterations (actually, we increase the number of iterations to 1000, while NSTEP was set at 40).

Note that the average score of the non-permuted attributes and the average of the HZPA are obtained from sums of conditionally independent variables, where independence comes from random permutations of the attributes deemed unimportant (the experiment is conditioned on the sample and the fixed values of the attributes deemed important). Therefore, if the number of iterations is sufficiently large, the averages can be assumed to be normally distributed. As the test of significance, a simple one-sided t-test is used, namely the test for equality of two means against the alternative that the mean of z-scores of an attribute tested for importance is higher than the mean of HZPA. We consider the attribute conclusively important if the null hypothesis is rejected at 0.001 significance level. A large number of iterations makes the test sufficiently powerful.

Summarizing, it is indeed a tall order for an attribute to be designated conclusively important. First, full self-consistence requires that the candidates for such designation have average z-scores higher than AvHZPA. And second, an even more stringent requirement is placed in the procedure's final step, namely that the final significance test can be passed by only these attributes whose true average z-score has a chance to be lower than AvHZPA with probability only 0.001, the AvHZPA being obtained on the basis of all attributes conclusively designated unimportant and comprised of the highest scores for each run in the final step.

Additionally, given, say, I attributes designated conlusively important, we generate the distribution of the classification error for the system built on I randomly selected attributes, not including any of the I important attributes determined by the algorithm. We then check if the classification result obtained for the conlusively important attributes is likely to be drawn from the generated distribution.

Computational Complexity. Our algorithm is an overlay superimposed on the original random forest, which calls the original program several times in the iterative fashion. Therefore the computational complexity of the whole algorithm depends both on the computational complexity of the random forest and that of our extension.

Two aspects of the computational complexity should be taken into account - dependence of the number of elementary operations on the number of samples and that on the number of attributes.

Obviously, the complexity of the random forest is of the same order as the complexity of building an individual tree, which is $P^{1/2} N log(N)$.

Regarding our extension, it is easily seen that its complexity is independent of the number of samples. On the other hand, dependence of the number of elementary operations on the number of attributes depends on data under scrutiny. Indeed, the number of iterations depends on the observed importance of attributes. For two limit cases - when an attribute is finally important or is deemed conclusively unimportant in the initial run - the number of iterations of the feature selection algorithm is not affected by the number of attrubutes. However, in the worst case scenario, when an attribute is deemed provisionally important, an additional round of iterations may be necessary to find that it is conclusively unimportant. Therefore, while in the best case the whole algorithm's complexity due to the number of attributes is that of the random forest, i.e., it is of order $P^{1/2}$, in the worst case it is of order $P^{3/2}$. Consequently, the overall complexity of the whole algorithm achieves order $P^{1/2}N \log N$ or $P^{3/2}N \log N$ in the worst case.

3   Data

The algorithm presented in the previous section was applied to twelve data sets of biological origin. The number of objects in the data sets varies between 319 and 820, and the number of attributes for all datasets is 202 including two-valued decision attribute, with the exception of dataset No. 8, where the number of all attributes is 183. Each attribute can take up to twenty categorical values, but usually this number is smaller. For categorical attributes, the device suggested by Theorem 4.5 of [3] was applied to ensure high performance of the classifier. Biologically, each object is a sequence of the HIV protein, and the decision attribute tells, whether virus carrying protein coded with this sequence is, or isn't, resistant to one of the antiviral drugs. Biological implications of our findings will be published elswhere. The data can be accessed at the following URL: http://www.icm.edu.pl/~rudnicki/RoughSets/data/

4   Results and Discussion

The algorithm described is used to find the attributes that contribute significantly to the final prediction. In Table 1, results of the algorithm are compared with those obtained by direct application of the Breiman's approach to finding important attributes. In that approach the random forest is run first with all the attributes, then only the attributes with 'high' z-scores are retained, and finally the forest is run again using only these attributes. In our implementation, z-scores larger than 3 were considered 'high'. Consequently, the attributes with z-scores higher than 3 in the second run are conclusively declared important when using the Breiman's approach.

In the majority of cases classification error is low, and in all cases it is significantly lower than percent error of the random classifier (data not shown).

One may notice that in all cases we found less attributes than suggested by the application of the Breiman algorithm and the assumption that z-score higher than 3 implies importance of an attribute. Interestingly, in all cases, the AvHZPA is significantly higher than 3 and varies considerably between data sets; indeed, it varies between 5.3 and 8.7. Therefore it is impossible to build an *'a priori'*

Table 1. Summary of results for all datasets. The following entries are in the succesive rows: number of objects in each data set (OB), number of important attributes using the method developed in the current study IA (C), number of important attributes obtained using the Breiman approach IA (B), AvHZPA for each data set (AvHZPA) and percent error of the classifier (%ERR).

Data	1	2	3	4	5	6	7	8	9	10	11	12
OB	356	354	353	355	319	354	749	675	820	721	737	767
IA (C)	7	14	20	19	14	15	17	23	30	6	7	7
IA (B)	21	32	39	31	24	23	52	42	59	49	48	58
AvHZPA	8.1	8.3	6.4	5.6	7.0	5.2	6.8	7.3	6.7	8.0	8.7	7.6
%ERR	4.4	11.0	13.9	8.7	24.5	11.6	4.9	18.8	13.9	15.6	26.0	22.6

analytical model of the HZPA distribution and inference has to be based on Monte Carlo-like approach, e.g. as presented in this report.

Accordingly, in Table 2, example results for the final t-test are summarized. Two variables which passed the initial test, have the value of the t-statistic lower than the threshold, set at 3, and consequently they *fail the verification test.*

It is interesting to note that only two variables had z-scores higher than HZPA for all 1000 iterations. Even rather highly scoring attributes had in some iterations scores smaller than HZPA. For example, attribute # 112 had score lower than HZPA in 7 cases out of 1000, despite that its average z-score was almost two times as high as the average of the HZPA.

The results of our study suggest that a single run of the RF classifier, and in particular the attribute importance analysis, may be subject to siginficant random fluctuations generated by spurious correlations between important and unimportant attributes.

Within our approach, this issue has been addressed by multiple application of RFs with randomly permuted values of attributes found unimportant, proper use of the estimates of attributes' importance generated by each RF, and a final test of significance of the results. When looking for important attributes, neither arbitrary selection of the limiting z-score, above which the attribute is considered important, nor (even more artificial) a priori selection of the number of important attributes is needed. Such arbitrary decisions have been replaced by an objective statistical procedure based on comparisons of z-scores for original attributes with the HZPA. Only the attributes which in many bootstrap samples score significantly higher than any attribute which is unimportant by design, can be conjectured to be important.

A related problem has been studied by Gediga and Duentsch within the rough set framework [17,18] several years ago. They have shown limited applicability of statistical methods in assesing the rule importance. Instead, they introduce the notion of casual dependencies in information systems and provide arguments that approximate reducts cannot be applied to measure quality of a model in certain cases.

Their results do not apply to our approach, since the methodology presented here is developed towards minimizing, to any desirable level, the error of the

Table 2. The results for the final step of the algorithm. Sixteen provisionally important attributes were tested using one thousand replications. Subsequent columns represent attribute number (*Attribute*), average z-score (*Z*) over 1000 iterations, standard deviation (*SDev(Z)*) of the mean z-score, average rank (*Rank*) in the importance ranking, standard deviation of the rank (*SDev(R)*), value of t-statistic (t) and the number of instances, when given attribute had higher score than an AvHZPA (*Inst*), respectively.

Attribute	Z	SDev(Z)	Rank	SDev(R)	t	Inst
2	29.11	0.05	2.000	0.000	60.7	1000
4	11.01	0.04	10.20	0.07	8.3	874
28	10.66	0.05	11.04	0.1	6.8	824
35	9.57	0.04	13.42	0.07	3.9	735
36	14.24	0.03	4.58	0.03	18.7	974
38	9.28	0.03	14.16	0.06	3.2	702
67	**8.40**	**0.03**	**15.62**	**0.05**	**0.4**	**578**
77	12.16	0.03	7.71	0.05	12.3	918
79	11.48	0.04	9.22	0.08	9.6	896
112	16.52	0.03	3.05	0.007	25.8	993
145	64.50	0.09	1.000	0.000	141.4	1000
169	13.40	0.03	5.50	0.04	15.8	959
171	11.10	0.04	10.05	0.08	8.4	858
176	13.09	0.05	6.35	0.07	13.8	945
179	**9.03**	**0.04**	**14.48**	**0.07**	**2.2**	**661**
189	11.02	0.04	10.22	0.07	8.4	867
AvHZPA	**8.28**	**0.08**	**14.78**	**0.11**	–	–

second kind (that is to minimize the number of false positives), whereas the approach of Gediga and Duentsch pertains to minimization of the error of the first kind (minimizing the number of false negatives).

Acknowledgments

The authors acknowledge funding from the EU grant HPRI-CT-2001-00153, and Wallenberg Foundation. Computations were performed at ICM, Warsaw University, grant G26-11.

References

1. Cowell, R.G., Dawid, A.P., Lauritzen, S.L., Spiegelharter, D.J. (1999) *Probabilistic networks and expert systems.* Springer-Verlag, New York.
2. Bishop, C.M. (1996) *Neural Networks for Pattern Recognition.* Clarendon Press, Oxford
3. Breiman, L., Friedman, J.H., Olshen, R.A. and Stone, C.J. (1984) *Classification and Regression Trees.* Wadsworth International Group, Monterey, Ca.
4. Ripley, B.D. (1996) *Pattern Recognition and Neural Networks.* Cambridge University Press, Cambridge

5. Hastie, T., Tibshirani, R. and Friedman, J. (2001) *The Elements of Statistical Learning: Data Mining, Inference, and Prediction.* Springer, New York

6. Pearl, J. (1988) *Probabilistic Reasoning in Intelligent Systems: Networks of Plausible Inference.* Morgan Kaufmann Publishers, San Francisco.

7. Pawlak, Z. (1981) Information systems theoretical foundations, *Inf. Syst.* **6**, 205–218. Rough Set Theory

8. Komorowski, J., Oehrn, A, Skowron, A. (2002). ROSETTA Rough Sets. In *Handbook of Data Mining and Knowledge Discovery*, W. Klsgen and J. Zytkow (eds.), pp. 554–559, Oxford University Press.

9. Bazan, J. and Szczuka, M. (2001). RSES and RSESlib A collection of tools for rough set computations. In *Proc. of RSCTC'2000, LNAI 2005*, pp 106–113, Springer-Verlag, Berlin.

10. Pawlak, Z. (1991) *Rough Sets. Theoretical Aspects of Reasoning about Data.* Kluwer Academic Publishers. Rough Set Theory

11. Ågotnes T., Komorowski H. J. and Løken T. Taming Large Rule Models in Rough Set Approaches. In Zytkow J. M. and Rauch J. (Eds.) *Principles of Data Mining and Knowledge Discovery, Third European Conference, PKDD '99, Proceedings.* LNCS **1704**, 193–203

12. Makosa E. Rule Tuning, *MSc Thesis*, The Linnaeus Center for Bioinformatics, Uppsala University, 2005.

13. Nguyen H. S., Nguyen S. H. (1998). Pattern extraction from data. *Fundamenta Informaticae* **34**, 129–144.

14. Nguyen H. S., Skowron A. and Synak P. (1998). Discovery of data patterns with applications to decomposition and classfification problems. In: L. Polkowski and A. Skowron (eds.), *Rough Sets in Knowledge Discovery 2: Applications, Case Studies and Software Systems.* Physica-Verlag, 55–97.

15. Breiman, L. Random Forests, *Machine Learning* **45** (2001), 5–32. Also see the bibliography at: http://www.stat.berkeley.edu/~breiman/RandomForests/cc_papers.htm

16. Freund, Y. and Schapire, R. (1996) Experiments with a new boosting algorithm, *Machine Learning: Proceedings of the Thirteenth International Conference*, Morgan Kauffman, San Francisco, 148–156. Also see the bibliography at: http://www.cs.princeton.edu/~schapire/boost.html

17. Duentsch I. and Gediga G. (1998). Uncertainty Measures of Rough Set Prediction. *Artif. Intell.* **106**, 109–137.

18. Duentsch I. and Gediga G. (1997). Statistical evaluation of rough set dependency analysis. *Int. J. Hum.-Comput. Stud.* **46** 589–604.

Distribution of Determinants of Contingency Matrix

Shusaku Tsumoto and Shoji Hirano

Department of Medical Informatics,
Shimane University, School of Medicine
89-1 Enya-cho, Izumo 693-8501 Japan
`tsumoto@computer.org, hirano@ieee.org`

Abstract. This paper gives a empirical analysis of determinant, which empirically validates the trade-off between sample size and size of matrix. In the former studies, relations between degree of granularity and dependence of contingency tables are given from the viewpoint of determinantal divisors and sample size. The nature of determinantal divisors shows that the increase of the degree of granularity may lead to that of dependence. However, a constraint on the sample size of a contingency table is very strong, which leads to the evaluation formula where the increase of degree of granularity gives the decrease of dependency. This paper gives a further study of the nature of sample size effect on the degree of dependency in a contingency matrix. The results show that sample size will restrict the nature of matrix in a combinatorial way, which suggests that the dependency is closely related with integer programming.

1 Introduction

Although independence is a very important concept, it has not been fully and formally investigated as a relation between two attributes. Tsumoto introduces linear algebra into formal analysis of a contigency table [1]. The results give the following interesting results. First, a contingency table can be viewed as comparison between two attributes with respect to information granularity. Second, algebra is a key point of analysis of this table. A contingency table can be viewed as a matrix and several operations and ideas of matrix theory are introduced into the analysis of the contingency table. Especially, The degree of independence, rank plays a very important role in extracting a probabilistic model from a given contingency table.

Then, thirdly, the results of determinantal divisors show that it seems that the devisors provide information on the degree of dependencies between the matrix of the whole elements and its submatrices and the increase of the degree of granularity may lead to that of dependence [2]. This gives a contradictory view from the intuition that when two attributes has many values, the dependence between these two attributes becomes low.

The key for understanding these conflicts is to consider the constraint on the sample size.

S. Greco et al. (Eds.): RSCTC 2006, LNAI 4259, pp. 567–576, 2006.

In [3] we show that a constraint on the sample size of a contingency table is very strong, which leads to the evaluation formula where the increase of degree of granularity gives the decrease of dependency.

This paper confirms this constraint by using enumerative combinatorics.

The results show that sample size will restrict the nature of matrix in a combinatorial way, which suggests that the dependency is closely related with integer programming.

2   Degree of Dependence

2.1   Contingency Matrix

Definition 1. *Let R_1 and R_2 denote multinominal attributes in an attribute space A which have m and n values. A contingency tables is a table of a set of the meaning of the following formulas: $|[R_1 = A_j]_A|$, $|[R_2 = B_i]_A|$, $|[R_1 = A_j \wedge R_2 = B_i]_A|$, $|U|$ $(i = 1, 2, 3, \cdots, n$ and $j = 1, 2, 3, \cdots, m)$. This table is arranged into the form shown in Table 1, where: $|[R_1 = A_j]_A| = \sum_{i=1}^{m} x_{1i} = x_{\cdot j}$, $|[R_2 = B_i]_A| = \sum_{j=1}^{n} x_{ji} = x_{i\cdot}$, $|[R_1 = A_j \wedge R_2 = B_i]_A| = x_{ij}$, $|U| = N = x_{\cdot\cdot}$ $(i = 1, 2, 3, \cdots, n$ and $j = 1, 2, 3, \cdots, m)$.*

Table 1. Contingency Table $(n \times m)$

	A_1	A_2	$\cdots$	A_n	Sum
B_1	x_{11}	x_{12}	$\cdots$	x_{1n}	$x_{1\cdot}$
B_2	x_{21}	x_{22}	$\cdots$	x_{2n}	$x_{2\cdot}$
$\cdots$	$\cdots$	$\cdots$	$\cdots$	$\cdots$	$\cdots$
B_m	x_{m1}	x_{m2}	$\cdots$	x_{mn}	$x_{m\cdot}$
Sum	$x_{\cdot 1}$	$x_{\cdot 2}$	$\cdots$	$x_{\cdot n}$	$x_{\cdot\cdot} = |U| = N$

Definition 2. *A contigency matrix $M_{R_1,R_2}(m, n, N)$ is defined as a matrix, which is composed of $x_{ij} = |[R_1 = A_j \wedge R_2 = B_i]_A|$, extracted from a contigency table defined in definition 1.*

That is,

$$M_{R_1,R_2}(m, n, N) = \begin{pmatrix} x_{11} & x_{12} & \cdots & x_{1n} & x_{1\cdot} \\ x_{21} & x_{22} & \cdots & x_{2n} & x_{2\cdot} \\ \vdots & \vdots & \vdots & \vdots & \vdots \\ x_{m1} & x_{m2} & \cdots & x_{mn} & x_{m\cdot} \end{pmatrix}.$$

$\square$

For simplicity, if we do not need to specify R_1 and R_2, we use $M(m, n, N)$ as a contingency matrix with m rows, n columns and N samples.

One of the important observations from granular computing is that a contingency table shows the relations between two attributes with respect to intersection of their supporting sets. When two attributes have different number of equivalence classes, the situation may be a little complicated. But, in this case, due to knowledge about linear algebra, we only have to consider the attribute which has a smaller number of equivalence classes. and the surplus number of equivalence classes of the attributes with larger number of equivalnce classes can be projected into other partitions. In other words, a $m \times n$ matrix or contingency table includes a projection from one attributes to the other one.

2.2 Rank of Contingency Matrix ($m \times n$)

In the former paper, Tsumoto obtained the following theorem[1].

Theorem 1. *Let the contingency matrix of a given contingency table be a $m \times n$ matrix. The rank of this matrix is less than $\min(m, n)$. If the rank of the corresponding matrix is 1, then two attributes in a given contingency table are statistically independent. If the rank of the corresponding matrix is n , then two attributes in a given contingency table are dependent. Otherwise, two attributes are contextual dependent, which means that several conditional probabilities can be represented by a linear combination of conditional probabilities. Thus,*

$$
rank = \begin{cases} \min(m, n) & dependent \\ 2, \cdots, \\ \quad \min(m, n) - 1 & contextual\ independent \\ 1 & statistical\ independent \end{cases}
$$

$\square$

2.3 Degree of Granularity and Dependence

Let us assume that the determinant of a give contingency matrix gives the degree of the dependence of the matrix. Then, from the results of linear algebra, we obtain the following theorem.

Theorem 2. *Let A denote a $n \times n$ contingency matrix, which includes N samples. If the rank of A is equal to n, then there exists a matrix B ($n \times n$) which satisfies*

$$
BA = \begin{pmatrix} \rho_1 & & & \\ & \rho_2 & & O \\ & & \ddots & \\ & O & & \rho_n \end{pmatrix} = P,
$$

where $\rho_1 + \rho_2 + \cdots + \rho_n = N$.
It is notable that the value of determinants of P is larger than A:

$$
det A \leq det P
$$

$\square$

Thus, the following theorem is obtained[3].

Theorem 3. *When a contingency matrix A holds $AB = P$, where P is a diagonal matrix, the following inequality holds:*

$$det\, A \leq \left(\frac{N}{n}\right)^n,$$

Proof.

$$det\, A = det(PB^{-1})$$
$$\leq det\, P$$
$$= \rho_1 \rho_2 \cdots \rho_n$$
$$\leq \left(\frac{\rho_1 + \rho_2 + \cdots + \rho_n}{n}\right)^n = \left(\frac{N}{n}\right)^n, \tag{1}$$

where the former equality holdes when $det\, B^{-1} = det\, B = 1$ and the latter equality holds when $\rho_1 = \rho_2 = \cdots = \rho_n = \frac{N}{n}$.

Thus, the maximum value of the determinant of A is at most $\left(\frac{N}{n}\right)^n$. Since N is constant for the given matrix A, the degree of dependence will decrease very rapidly when n becomes very large. That is,

$$det\, A \sim n^{-n}.$$

Thus,

Corollary 1. *The determinant of A will converge into 0 when n increases into infinity.*

$$\lim_{n \to \infty} det\, A = 0.$$

$\square$

This results suggest that when the degree of granularity becomes higher, the degree of dependence will become lower, due to the constraints on the sample size.

However, it is notable that N/n is very important. If N is very large, the rapid decrease will be observed N is close to n.

3   Distribution of Determinant

The next interest is how is the statistical nature of the derminant for $M(m, n, N)$.

First, since a 2×2 matrix is a basic one, let us examine the nature of $det\, M(2, 2, N)$.

3.1   Total Number of $M(2, 2, N)$

Let the four elements of $M(2, 2, N)$ be denoted as a,b,c,d. That is, $x_{11} = a$, $x_{12} = b$, $x_{21} = c$, and $x_{22} = d$. Then, $a + b + c + d = N$.

Let us assume that $a = 0$. Then, $b + c + d = N$. Recursively, we can assume that $b = 0$. Then, for this pair $(a, b) = 0$, we have $(N + 1)$ pairs which satisfies $c + d = N$. In this way, the total number of $M(2, 2, N)$ is obtained as:

$$\sum_{i=0}^{N} \frac{(N + 1 - i) \times (N + 2 - i)}{2}.$$

Simple calculation shows that the above formula is equal to:

$$\frac{1}{6}(N + 1)(N + 2)(N + 3).$$

That is,

Theorem 4. *The total number of a contingency matrix M(2,2,N) is equal to:*

$$\frac{1}{6}(N + 1)(N + 2)(N + 3).$$

(*Proof Sketch*)

The total combination of $M(2, 2, N)$ is given as:

$$\sum_{i=0}^{N} \left(\sum_{k=1}^{(N-i)+1} k \right) = \sum_{i=0}^{N} \frac{(N + 1 - i) \times (N + 2 - i)}{2}$$

$$= \sum_{i=0}^{N} \left\{ \frac{1}{2}(N + 1)(N + 2) \right.$$

$$\left. - \frac{1}{2}(2N + 3)i + \frac{1}{2}i^2 \right\} \tag{2}$$

$$= \frac{1}{6}(N + 1)(N + 2)(N + 3)$$

$\square$

Intuitively, this formula can be interpreted as follows. We have four parameters, a,b,c,d, which will take a value between 0 and N. Thus, the original freedom is 4, and the order of total number can be N^4. However, since a constraint $a + b + c + d = N$ is given, we have only three free parameters, thus the order of total number of $M(2, 2, N)$ is approximately of N^3:

$$\# \; of \; M(2, 2, N) \approx \mathcal{O}(N^3).$$

3.2   Total Number of *det* $= 0$

Enumeration of total number of $det = 0$ is very difficult. However, upper bound can be calculated as follows. When a and d is fixed, we have obtained two constraints:

$$b + c = N - (a + d)$$
$$bc = ad$$

Thus, (b, c) can be obtained as a solution for quadratic equations. If the pair (b, c) is integer, we will have obtained two solutions $(ad - bc = 0)$ for each pair: (b,c) and (c,b).

Therefore, the upper bound of the number of solutions is equal to:

$$\sum_{i=0}^{N}\left(\sum_{k=1}^{(N-i)+1} 2\right) = (N+1)(N+2)$$

Theorem 5. *The upper bound of total number of a contingency matrix M(2,2,N) with determinant being 0 is equal to:*

$$(N+1)(N+2)$$

Thus, the probability that the determinant of a matrix $M(2,2,N)$ is equal to 0 is at most:

$$\frac{(N+1)(N+2)}{\frac{1}{6}(N+1)(N+2)(N+3)} = \frac{6}{N+3}.$$

$\square$

Then, how is the lower bound ? This is the case when (b,c) does not have any integer solution for a given quadratic equations except for trivial solutions. The simple trivial solutions are: $a = 0$ or $d = 0$ with $b = 0$ or $c = 0$. Then, for $a = 0$, $b = 0$, we may have a solution for $c + d = N$, N pairs $(c \neq 0, d \neq 0)$. Totally, 4N pairs. If we consider the cases when three values are equal to 0, such as $a = b = c = 0$, we have 4 pairs. Thus, totally. we have 4(N+1) pairs.

Theorem 6. *The lower bound of total number of a contingency matrix M(2,2,N) with determinant being 0 is equal to:*

$$4(N+1)$$

Thus, the probability that the determinant of a matrix $M(2,2,N)$ is equal to 0 is at least:

$$\frac{4(N+1)}{\frac{1}{6}(N+1)(N+2)(N+3)} = \frac{24}{(N+2)(N+3)}.$$

$\square$

Thus, it is expected that the number of matrices with 0 determinant vibrates between $4(N+1)$ and $(N+1)(N+2)$. The variance will beccome larger when N grows. In other words, the probability of $det = 0$ will vibrate between $\mathcal{O}(1/N^2)$ and $\mathcal{O}(1/N)$. The variance will become larger when N grows.

It is notable that the above discussion can be applied to a general case, such as $ad - bc = k$, or other constraint. For example, if we have a constraint such as $a/(a+b)$ or $a/(a+c)$, then we can analyze a constraint for accuracy or coverage. It will be our future work to investigate such cases.

4   Empirical Validations

For empirical validations, we calculate the whole combination of a 2×2 matrix with fixed sample size $(0 \leq N \leq 100)$ $M(2, 2, N)$.

4.1   Total Number of $M(2, 2, N)$

Figure 1 plots the relation between sample size N and the total number of $M(2, 2, N)$. This figure clearly shows that the relation is polynomial.

On the other hand, Figure 2, which plots the relation between sample size and the total number of matrices with zero determinant, gives an interesting feature. As discussed in Section 3, the total number vibrates and the amplitude of the vibration becomes larger when N grows. Furthermore, the lower bound of

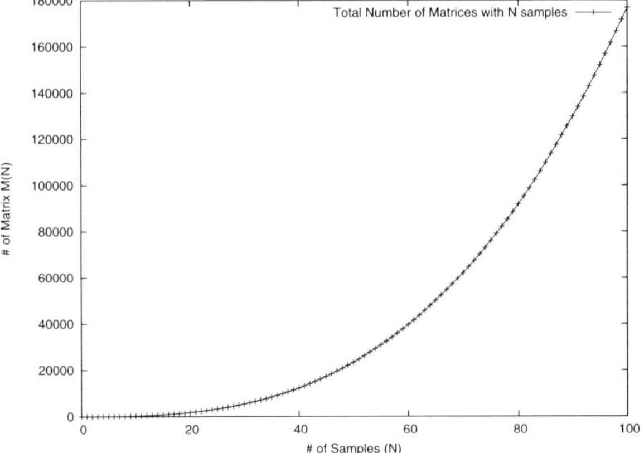

Fig. 1. Total Number of $M(2, 2, N)$

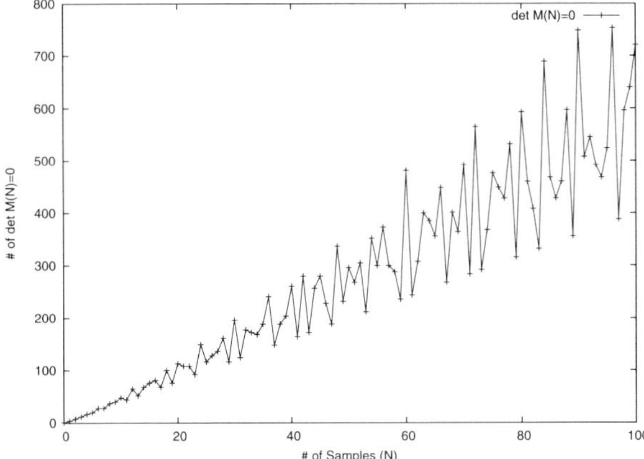

Fig. 2. Number of Matrices with [Det=0] in $M(2, 2, N)$

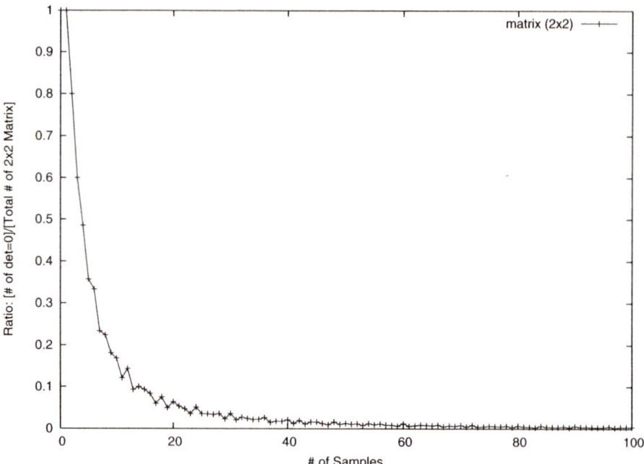

Fig. 3. Ratio of [Det=0] in $M(2,2,N)$

the total number can be approximately equal to a linear function, whereas the upper bound is to a quadratic function.

Finally, the ratio of the number of matrices with zero determinant to the total number of $M(2,2,N)$ is plotted as Figure 3. This figure also confirms the results obtained in Section 3.

4.2   Statistics of Determinant

Figure 4 and 5 show the distributions of the determinant of $M(2,2,10)$ and $M(2,2,50)$. The distribution are symmetric, and the median and average are exactly equal to 0. Furthermore, the number of matrices with 0 determinant is very high, compared with other values.

5   Discussion

In [4], Tsumoto obtained the following theorem.

Theorem 7. *The chi-square test statistics of $M(m,n,N)$ is given as:*

$$X = \sum_{i=1}^{m}\sum_{j=1}^{n} \frac{\left(\sum_{\substack{k\neq i \\ l\neq j}} \Delta_{j,l}^{i,k}\right)^2}{x_{..}x_{i.}x_{.j}}.$$

$\square$

Especially, when $m = n = 2$, this will give us the following equation:

$$X = \sum_{i=1}^{2}\sum_{j=1}^{2} \frac{\Delta^2}{x_{..}x_{i.}x_{.j}},$$

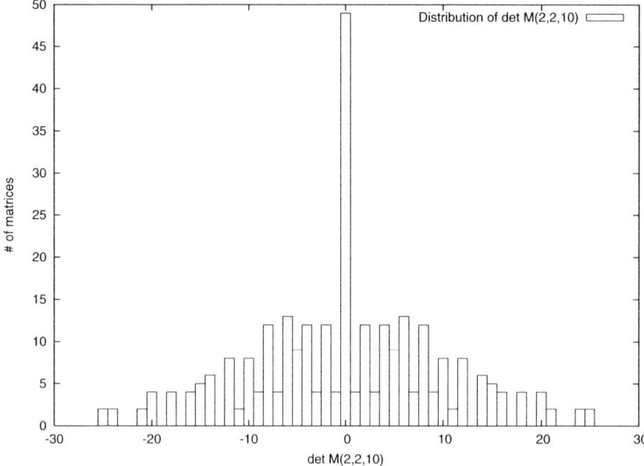

Fig. 4. Distribution of det $M(2,2,10)$

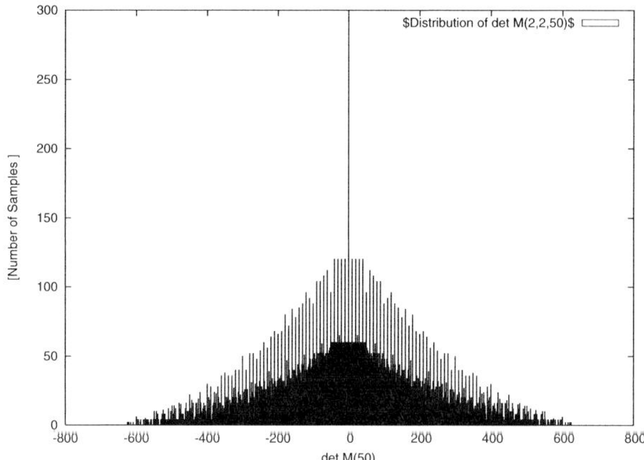

Fig. 5. Distribution of det $M(2,2,50)$

where Δ denotes a determinant of $M(2,2,N)$. Thus, it implies that each residual follows $N(0,1)$ asymptotically:

$$\sigma_{ij} = \frac{\Delta}{\sqrt{x_{..}x_{i.}x_{.j}}}.$$

This fact implies that asymptotically, the distribution of determinants of $M(2,2,N)$ can be approximated by function of $N(0,1)$. It will be our future work to whether this assumption on the residual is reasonable or not.

6 Conclusion

In this paper, the nature of the dependence of a contingency matrix and the statistical nature of the determinant are examined.

Especially, the constraint on the sample size N of a contingency table will determine the number of 2×2 matrices. As N grows, the ratio of matrices with zero determinant rapidly decreases, which shows that the number of matrix with statistical dependence will increase. However, due to the nature of the determinant, the average of absolute value of the determinant also increase with the order of N^2, whereas the increase in the size of total number of matrix is of N^3.

This is a preliminary work on the statistical nature of the determinant, and it will be our future work to investigate the nature of 3×3 or higher dimensional contingency matrices.

References

1. Tsumoto, S.: Statistical independence as linear independence. In Skowron, A., Szczuka, M., eds.: Electronic Notes in Theoretical Computer Science. Volume 82., Elsevier (2003)
2. Tsumoto, S., Hirano, S.: Determinantal divisors for the degree of independence of a contingency matrix. In: Proceedings of NAFIPS 2004, IEEE press (2004)
3. Tsumoto, S., Hirano, S.: Degree of dependence as granularity in contingency table. In Hu, T., Lin, T., eds.: Proceedings of IEEE GrC 2005, IEEE press (2005)
4. Tsumoto, S., Hirano, S.: Interpretation of contingency matrix using marginal distributions. In: Proceedings of RSCTC 2006 (this issue), LNAI, Springer (2006)

Interpretation of Contingency Matrix Using Marginal Distributions

Shusaku Tsumoto and Shoji Hirano

Department of Medical Informatics,
Shimane University, School of Medicine
89-1 Enya-cho, Izumo 693-8501 Japan
`tsumoto@computer.org, hirano@ieee.org`

Abstract. This paper shows formal analysis of a contingency table based on its marginal distributions. The main approach is to make an expected matrix from two given marginal distributions and take the difference between original cell values and expected values to construct a residual matrix. The most important characerics of a residual matrix are following: (1) Its determinant is equal to 0, which implies the rank of this matrix is less than the rank of an original matrix. (2) Each element of a residual matrix can be represented as a linear combination of 2×2 subderminants. These characteristics shows that the residual of a contingency matrix is closely related with 2×2 subderminants, which also shows that the χ^2 test statistic is a function of 2×2 subderminants and marginal sums and suggests that distribution of determinants should have an important meaning for this statistic.

1 Introduction

Statistical independence between two attributes is a very important concept in data mining and statistics. The definition $P(A, B) = P(A)P(B)$ show that the joint probability of A and B is the product of both probabilities. This gives several useful formula, such as $P(A|B) = P(A)$, $P(B|A) = P(B)$. In a data mining context, these formulae show that these two attributes may not be correlated with each other. Thus, when A or B is a classification target, the other attribute may not play an important role in its classification.

Although independence is a very important concept, it has not been fully and formally investigated as a relation between two attributes.

Tsumoto shows formal analysis of statistical independence in a contingency table [1,2]. The first important point is that statistifcal independence in a contingency table is a special form of linear depedence of two attributes. Especially, when the table is viewed as a matrix, the above discussion shows that the rank of the matrix is equal to 1.0[1]. The second important point is that partial statistical independence can be observed between statictical dependence and independence and that this property gives statistical independence when rows or columns are merged[3].

The third important observation is that from the characteristics of the determinants, the larger rank a coreponding matrix has, the higher the two attributes

S. Greco et al. (Eds.): RSCTC 2006, LNAI 4259, pp. 577–586, 2006.

are dependent. This results is shown by a monotonicity of a sequence of determinantal divisors[4]. However, the constraint on the sample size of a contingency table is very strong, which leads to the evaluation formula where the increase of degree of granularity gives the decrease of dependency[2].

In this paper, we focus on decomposition of a contingency matrix by using a matrix of expected values based on marginal distribution (expected matrix). Especially when the rank of a matrix is full, say, r, the difference between a original matrix and the expected matrix will become $r - 1$ at most. Moreover, the sum of rows or columns will become zero, which means that the information of one rank correponds to information on the frequency of a contingency matrix.

The paper is organized as follows: Section 2 shows the results of earlier work. Section 3 gives definitions of marginal distribution, expected matrix and residual matrix. Section 4 shows the definition of difference matrix and its main results. Section 5 provides the meaning of residual matrix. Finally, Section 6 concludes this paper.

2   Definitions and Preliminary Work

2.1   Contingency Matrix

Definition 1. *Let R_1 and R_2 denote multinominal attributes in an attribute space A which have m and n values. A contingency tables $T(R_1, R_2)$ is a table of a set of the meaning of the following formulas: $|[R_1 = A_j]_A|$, $|[R_2 = B_i]_A|$, $|[R_1 = A_j \wedge R_2 = B_i]_A|$, $|U|$ $(i = 1, 2, 3, \cdots, n$ and $j = 1, 2, 3, \cdots, m)$. This table is arranged into the form shown in Table 1, where: $|[R_1 = A_j]_A| = \sum_{i=1}^{m} x_{1i} = x_{\cdot j}$, $|[R_2 = B_i]_A| = \sum_{j=1}^{n} x_{ji} = x_{i \cdot}$, $|[R_1 = A_j \wedge R_2 = B_i]_A| = x_{ij}$, $|U| = N = x_{\cdot \cdot}$ $(i = 1, 2, 3, \cdots, n$ and $j = 1, 2, 3, \cdots, m)$.*

Table 1. Contingency Table $(m \times n)$

	A_1	A_2	$\cdots$	A_n	Sum
B_1	x_{11}	x_{12}	$\cdots$	x_{1n}	$x_{1 \cdot}$
B_2	x_{21}	x_{22}	$\cdots$	x_{2n}	$x_{2 \cdot}$
$\cdots$	$\cdots$	$\cdots$	$\cdots$	$\cdots$	$\cdots$
B_m	x_{m1}	x_{m2}	$\cdots$	x_{mn}	$x_{m \cdot}$
Sum	$x_{\cdot 1}$	$x_{\cdot 2}$	$\cdots$	$x_{\cdot n}$	$x_{\cdot \cdot} = |U| = N$

Definition 2. *A contigency matrix $M_{R_1, R_2}(m, n, N)$ is defined as a matrix, which is composed of $x_{ij} = |[R_1 = A_j \wedge R_2 = B_i]_A|$, extracted from a contigency table defined in definition 1.*

That is,

$$
M_{R_1, R_2}(m, n, N) = \begin{pmatrix} x_{11} & x_{12} & \cdots & x_{1n} \\ x_{21} & x_{22} & \cdots & x_{2n} \\ \vdots & \vdots & \vdots & \vdots \\ x_{m1} & x_{m2} & \cdots & x_{mn} \end{pmatrix}. \qquad \square
$$

For simplicity, if we do not need to specify R_1 and R_2, we use $M(m, n, N)$ as a contingency matrix with m rows, n columns and N samples.

One of the important observations from granular computing is that a contingency table shows the relations between two attributes with respect to intersection of their supporting sets. When two attributes have different number of equivalence classes, the situation may be a little complicated. But, in this case, due to knowledge about linear algebra, we only have to consider the attribute which has a smaller number of equivalence classes. and the surplus number of equivalence classes of the attributes with larger number of equivalnce classes can be projected into other partitions. In other words, a $m \times n$ matrix or contingency table includes a projection from one attributes to the other one.

2.2   Rank of Contingency Matrix ($m \times n$)

In the former paper, Tsumoto obtained the following theorem[1].

Theorem 1. *Let the contingency matrix of a given contingency table be a $m \times n$ matrix. The rank of this matrix is less than $\min(m, n)$. If the rank of the corresponding matrix is 1, then two attributes in a given contingency table are statistically independent. If the rank of the corresponding matrix is n , then two attributes in a given contingency table are dependent. Otherwise, two attributes are contextual dependent, which means that several conditional probabilities can be represented by a linear combination of conditional probabilities. Thus,*

$$rank = \begin{cases} \min(m, n) & dependent \\ 2, \cdots , \\ \qquad \min(m, n) - 1 & contextual\ independent \\ 1 & statistical\ indcpcndcnt \end{cases} \qquad \square$$

In the cases of $m \neq n$, we need a discussion on submatrix and subderminant in the next section.

2.3   Submatrix and Subdeterminant

The next interest is the structure of a corresponding matrix with $1 \leq rank \leq n - 1$. First, let us define a submatrix (a subtable) and subdeterminant.

Definition 3. *Let A denote a corresponding matrix of a given contigency table $(m \times n)$. A corresponding submatrix $A_{j_1 j_2 \cdots j_s}^{i_1 i_2 \cdots i_r}$ is defined as a matrix which is given by an intersection of r rows and s columns of A $(i_1 < i_2 < \cdots < i_r, j_1 < j_2 < \cdots < j_r)$.*

Definition 4. *A subdeterminant of A is defined as a determinant of a submatrix $A_{j_1 j_2 \cdots j_s}^{i_1 i_2 \cdots i_r}$, which is denoted by $det(A_{j_1 j_2 \cdots j_s}^{i_1 i_2 \cdots i_r})$.*

Rank and Subdeterminant. Let Δ_{ij} denote a co-factor of a_{ij} in a square corresponding matrix of A. Then,

$$\Delta_{ij} = (-1)^{i+j} det(A^{1,2,\cdots,i-1,i+1,\cdots,n}_{1,2,\cdots,j-1,j+1,\cdots,n}).$$

It is notable that a co-factor is a special type of submatrix, where only ith-row and j-column are removed from a original matrix. By the use of co-factors, the determinant of A is defined as:

$$det(A) = \sum_{j=1}^{n} a_{ij}\Delta_{ij},$$

which is called *Laplace expansion*.

From this representation, if $det(A)$ is not equal to 0, then $\Delta_{ij} \neq 0$ for $\{a_{i1}, a_{i2}, \cdots, a_{in}\}$ which are not equal to 0. Thus, the following proposition is obtained.

Proposition 1. *If $det(A)$ is not equal to 0 if at least one co-factor of $a_{ij}(\neq 0)$, Δ_{ij} is not equal to 0.*

It is notable that the above definition of a determinant gives the relation between a original matrix A and submatrices (co-factors). Since cofactors gives a square matrix of size $n-1$, the above proposition gives the relation between a matrix of size n and submatrices of size $n-1$. In the same way, we can discuss the relation between a corresponding matrix of size n and submatrices of size $r(1 \leq r < n-1)$.

3   Marginal Distribution and Expected Matrix

In statistical analysis of a contingency table, marginal distribution plays an important role. Especially, marginal distribution is closely related with statistical independence of two attributes.

Let us start first the defintion of marginal distribution (row or column).

Definition 5. *Marginal row distribution of $T(R_1, R_2)$, $\mathbf{mr_{M,R_2}}$ is defined as:*

$$\left(x_{\cdot j}\right) = \left(x_{\cdot 1}\ x_{\cdot 2}\ \cdots\ x_{\cdot m}\right) = \left(1\ 1\ \cdots\ 1\right) \begin{pmatrix} x_{11} & x_{12} & \cdots & x_{1n} \\ x_{21} & x_{22} & \cdots & x_{2n} \\ \vdots & \vdots & \vdots & \vdots \\ x_{m1} & x_{m2} & \cdots & x_{mn} \end{pmatrix}.$$

Marginal column distribution of $T(R_1, R_2)$, $\mathbf{mc_{M,R_1}}$ is defined as:

$$\left(x_{i\cdot}\right) = \begin{pmatrix} x_{1\cdot} \\ x_{2\cdot} \\ \vdots \\ x_{n\cdot} \end{pmatrix} = \begin{pmatrix} x_{11} & x_{12} & \cdots & x_{1n} \\ x_{21} & x_{22} & \cdots & x_{2n} \\ \vdots & \vdots & \vdots & \vdots \\ x_{m1} & x_{m2} & \cdots & x_{mn} \end{pmatrix} \begin{pmatrix} 1 \\ 1 \\ \vdots \\ 1 \end{pmatrix} \qquad \square$$

It is notable that marginal row and column distribution correspond to $P(R_1 = A_i)$ and $P(R_2 = B_j)$.

Then, when statistical independence holds for two attributes, since $P(R_1 = A_i, R_2 = B_j) = P(R_1 = A_i) \times P(R_2 = B_j)$, each cell x_{ij} is obtained from the product of $x_{i\cdot}$ and $x_{\cdot j}$ [3]:

$$\frac{x_{ij}}{x_{\cdot\cdot}} = \frac{x_{i\cdot}}{x_{\cdot\cdot}} \times \frac{x_{\cdot j}}{x_{\cdot\cdot}}.$$

Thus, a expected matrix, whose cell is given by statistical independence of two attributes, is defined as follows.

Definition 6. *A expected matrix* $E_{R_1,R_2}(m, n, N)$ *is defined from* $M_{R_1,R_2}(m, n, N)$ *as follows:*

$$\left(e_{ij} \right),$$

where e_{ij} *is obtained as a product of elements of marginal distribution.*

$$e_{ij} = \frac{x_{i\cdot} \times x_{\cdot j}}{x_{\cdot\cdot}}.$$

$\square$

According to the results in [5], it is notable that this matrix can be decomposed into the product of marginal column and row distributions:

Theorem 2. *A expected matrix* $E_{R_1,R_2}(m, n, N)$ *can be decomposed into:*

$$E_{R_1,R_2}(m, n, N) = \mathbf{mr_{M,R_2}} \otimes \mathbf{mc_{M,R_1}} \tag{1}$$

$\square$

In chi-square test, total sum of the difference between real value and expected value gives the test statistic:

$$X = \sum_{i=1}^{m} \sum_{j=1}^{n} \frac{\left(x_{ij} - \frac{x_{\cdot j} x_{i\cdot}}{x_{\cdot\cdot}} \right)^2}{\frac{x_{\cdot j} x_{i\cdot}}{x_{\cdot\cdot}}}, \tag{2}$$

which approximately follows a χ^2 distribution of $(m-1)(n-1)$ freedom. Thus, the difference between real value and expected value, σ_{ij}:

$$\sigma_{ij} = x_{ij} - \frac{x_{i\cdot} \times x_{\cdot j}}{x_{\cdot\cdot}}.$$

is a very important factor for this test.

From the viewpoint of matrix theory, σ_{ij} is obtained from $M_{R_1,R_2}(m, n, N) - E_{R_1,R_2}(m, n, N)$. We call this matrix *residual matrix*.

Definition 7. *A residual matrix* $S_{R_1,R_2}(m, n, N)$ *is defined as follows:*

$$\left(\sigma_{ij} \right),$$

where σ_{ij} *is obtained as a product of elements of marginal distribution.*

$$\sigma_{ij} = x_{ij} - e_{ij} = x_{ij} - \frac{x_{i\cdot} \times x_{\cdot j}}{x_{\cdot\cdot}}. \tag{3}$$

$\square$

4   Difference Matrix

Let us assume that we have two matrices $A_{R_1,R_2}(m,n,N) = (a_{ij})$ and $B_{R_3,R_4}(m,n,N) = (b_{ij})$ with N samples and the same marginal distributions:

$$a_{..} = b_{..}(=N), \quad \mathbf{mr_{A,R_1}} = \mathbf{mr_{B,R_3}} \quad and \quad \mathbf{mc_{A,R_2}} = \mathbf{mc_{B,R_4}}.$$

We will focus on the difference between $A_{R_1,R_2}(m,n,N)$ and $B_{R_3,R_4}(m,n,N)$, which we call a *difference matrix*:

Definition 8. *The difference matrix $D(m,n,A,B)$ is defined as:*

$$D(m,n,A,B,N) = A_{R_1,R_2}(m,n,N) - B_{R_3,R_4}(m,n,N),$$

where each element d_{ij} is obtained as:

$$d_{ij} = a_{ij} - b_{ij}. \qquad \square$$

Then, several important characteristics are obtained as follows.

Theorem 3. *Let $D_{A,B}(m,n,N)$ denote a difference matrix of $A_{R_1,R_2}(m,n,N) = (a_{ij})$ and $B_{R_3,R_4}(m,n,N) = (b_{ij})$.*
Then,

$$\det\ D_{A,B}(m,n,N) = 0$$

Proof
Since $\mathbf{mr_{A,R_1}} = \mathbf{mr_{B,R_3}}$ and $\mathbf{mc_{A,R_2}} = \mathbf{mc_{B,R_4}}$, for every $i(= 1,2,\cdots,m)$ and $j(= 1,2,\cdots,n)$,

$$a_{i.} = b_{i.} \quad and a_{.j} = b_{.j}.$$

Thus,

$$d_{i.} = 0 \quad and \quad d_{.j} = 0.$$

Since

$$d_{1j} + d_{2j} + \cdots + d_{mj} = 0,$$

at least one row can be described by linear combination of other d_{ij}, which implies the determinant of this matrix is equal to 0. $\qquad \square$

This theorem shows that the rank of $S_{R_1,R_2}(m,n,N)$ is at most $\min(m,n) - 1$, which gives a contextual independence introduced in [3]. When a contingency matrix gives contextual independence, it can be decomposed into a product of three matrices[5]:

$$M(m,n,N) = \mathbf{M_{m\times s}}M(s,s,N')\mathbf{M_{s\times n}}, \tag{4}$$

where where $M(s,s,N')$ denotes the core matrix of $M(m,n,N)$ whose rank is equal to s and $M_{m\times n}$ shows a operator $m \times n$ matrix. Thus, we have obtained a decomposition of a contingency matrix as follows.

Theorem 4

$$A_{R_1,R_2}(m, n, N) = B_{R_3,R_4}(m, n, N) + \mathbf{M_{m \times s}} M'(s, s, N') \mathbf{M_{s \times n}}, \qquad (5)$$

where $M'(s, s, N')$ gives a core matrix of $D_{R_1,R_2}(m, n, N)$ $(s \leq \min(m, n) - 1)$.

$\square$

5   Residual Matrix as Difference Matrix

5.1   Main Results

Let us take the expected matrix of $A_{R_1,R_2}(m, n, N)$ as a special case of $B_{R_3,R_4}(m, n, N)$ in the above section. Then, the difference matrix $D_{A,B}(m, n, N)$ is equivalent to the residual matrix of $A_{R_1,R_2}(m, n, N)$, and we obtain the following corollary, which was reported in [6].

Corollary 1. *Let $S_{R_1,R_2}(m, n, N)$ denote the residual matrix of $A_{R_1,R_2}(m, n, N)$. Then,*

$$\det S_{R_1,R_2}(m, n, N) = 0 \qquad \square$$

Then, we obtained a decomposition of a contingency matrix as follows.

Theorem 5

$$M_{R_1,R_2}(m, n, N) = \mathbf{mr_{M,R_2}} \otimes \mathbf{mc_{M,R_1}} + \mathbf{M_{m \times s}} M'(s, s, N') \mathbf{M_{s \times n}}, \qquad (6)$$

where $M'(s, s, N')$ gives a core matrix of $S_{R_1,R_2}(m, n, N)$ $(s \leq \min(m, n) - 1)$.

$\square$

These features can be charaterized by special cases of difference matrices, as shown in the above section.

Then, what is the original characteristic of residual matrices? The following theorem shows this original feature of residual matrices.

Theorem 6. *The residual of $M_{R_1,R_2}(m, n, N)$ is obtained as:*

$$\sigma_{ij} = \frac{1}{x_{..}} \left\{ x_{ij} \sum_{k \neq i} \sum_{l \neq j} x_{kl} - \left(\sum_{l \neq j} x_{il} \right) \left(\sum_{k \neq i} x_{kj} \right) \right\}$$

$$= \frac{1}{x_{..}} \sum_{\substack{k \neq i \\ l \neq j}} (x_{ij} x_{kl} - x_{kj} x_{il}) = \frac{1}{x_{..}} \sum_{\substack{k \neq i \\ l \neq j}} \Delta_{j,l}^{i,k},$$

where $\Delta_{j,l}^{i,k}$ is the determinant of a 2×2 submatrix of $M_{R_1,R_2}(m, n, N)$ with selection of i and k rows and j and l columns.

Proof.

$$\sigma_{ij} = x_{ij} - \frac{x_{i\cdot} \times x_{\cdot j}}{x_{\cdot\cdot}} = \frac{1}{x_{\cdot\cdot}}\left\{ x_{ij}x_{\cdot\cdot} - \frac{x_{i\cdot} \times x_{\cdot j}}{x_{\cdot\cdot}} \right\}$$

$$= \frac{1}{x_{\cdot\cdot}}\left\{ x_{ij}\left(x_{\cdot j} + \sum_{l \neq j} x_{\cdot l} \right) - \left(x_{ij} + \sum_{l \neq j} x_{il} \right) x_{\cdot j} \right\}$$

$$= \frac{1}{x_{\cdot\cdot}}\left\{ x_{ij}\left(\sum_{k \neq i}\sum_{l \neq j} x_{kl} + \sum_{l \neq j} x_{il} \right) - \left(\sum_{l \neq j} x_{il} \right)\left(x_{ij} + \sum_{k \neq i} x_{kj} \right) \right\}$$

$$= \frac{1}{x_{\cdot\cdot}}\left\{ x_{ij}\sum_{k \neq i}\sum_{l \neq j} x_{kl} - \left(\sum_{l \neq j} x_{il} \right)\left(\sum_{k \neq i} x_{kj} \right) \right\}$$

$$= \frac{1}{x_{\cdot\cdot}}\sum_{\substack{k \neq i \\ l \neq j}}(x_{ij}x_{kl} - x_{kj}x_{il}) \qquad \square$$

5.2 χ^2-Test Statistics and Subdeterminants

This gives another proof of chi-square statistics for 2×2 contingency table. From equation (2), we obtained:

$$X = \left(\frac{\det M(2,2,N)}{x_{\cdot\cdot}} \right)^2 \sum_{i,j=1}^{2}\left\{ \frac{1}{\frac{x_{i\cdot}x_{\cdot j}}{x_{\cdot\cdot}}} \right\}$$

$$= \left(\frac{\det M(2,2,N)}{x_{\cdot\cdot}} \right)^2 \times x_{\cdot\cdot}\frac{\sum_{i,j=1}^{2} x_{i\cdot}x_{\cdot j}}{x_{1\cdot}x_{\cdot 1}x_{2\cdot}x_{\cdot 2}}$$

$$= \frac{\det M(2,2,N)^2 x_{\cdot\cdot}}{x_{1\cdot}x_{\cdot 1}x_{2\cdot}x_{\cdot 2}} = \frac{x_{\cdot\cdot}(x_{11}x_{22} - x_{12}x_{21})^2}{x_{1\cdot}x_{\cdot 1}x_{2\cdot}x_{\cdot 2}}$$

Thus, in case of 2×2 matrices, the chi-square distribution is closely related with the distribution of the determinant. Especially, when the sample size and the marginal distributions are fixed, a chi-square distribution with one freedome gives the asymptotic distribution of $\det M(2,2,N)^2$.

This result can be generalized into $m \times n$ matrix as follows.

$$X = \sum_{i=1}^{m}\sum_{j=1}^{n}\frac{\left(x_{ij} - \frac{x_{\cdot j}x_{i\cdot}}{x_{\cdot\cdot}} \right)^2}{\frac{x_{\cdot j}x_{i\cdot}}{x_{\cdot\cdot}}} = \sum_{i=1}^{m}\sum_{j=1}^{n} x_{\cdot\cdot} \times \frac{(\sigma_{ij})^2}{x_{i\cdot}x_{\cdot j}}$$

$$= \sum_{i=1}^{m}\sum_{j=1}^{n} x_{\cdot\cdot} \times \frac{\left(\frac{1}{x_{\cdot\cdot}}\sum_{\substack{k \neq i \\ l \neq j}} \Delta_{j,l}^{i,k} \right)^2}{x_{i\cdot}x_{\cdot j}} = \sum_{i=1}^{m}\sum_{j=1}^{n}\frac{\left(\sum_{\substack{k \neq i \\ l \neq j}} \Delta_{j,l}^{i,k} \right)^2}{x_{\cdot\cdot}x_{i\cdot}x_{\cdot j}} \qquad (7)$$

Thus, chi-square test statistics is related with square sum of linear combination of 2×2 subdeterminants of an given matrix.

Theorem 7. *The chi-square test statistics of $M(m, n, N)$ is given as:*

$$X = \sum_{i=1}^{m} \sum_{j=1}^{n} \frac{\left(\sum_{\substack{k \neq i \\ l \neq j}} \Delta_{j,l}^{i,k} \right)^2}{x_{..}x_{i.}x_{.j}}$$

$\square$

Therefore, since the above test statistic will approach to χ^2-distribution, whcih can be viewed as a special case of Γ-distribution $(G_A((m-1)(n-1)/2, 2))$, it is expected that the distribution of square sum of 2×2 subdeterminants is closely related with Γ-distribution $G_A(\lambda, \beta)$ whose density function is given as:

$$f(x) = \frac{1}{\Gamma(\lambda)\beta^\lambda} x^{\lambda-1} e^{-\frac{x}{\beta}},$$

where λ and β are a shape parameter and a scale parameter, respectively. In the case of χ^2 distribution, β is equal to 2, and $\lambda = (m-1)(n-1)/2$. Thus, the density function can be derived as:

$$f(x) = \frac{1}{\Gamma(\lambda)2^\lambda} x^{\lambda-1} e^{-\frac{x}{2}}.$$

Furthermore, these results also suggest that

$$\sigma_{ij} = \frac{1}{x_{..}} \sum_{\substack{k \neq i \\ l \neq j}} \Delta_{j,l}^{i,k}$$

follows a normal disitrubtion $N(0, 1)$ in an asymptotic way.

6   Conclusion

In this paper, we focus on the difference between two matrices with the same sample size and the marginal distributions, called difference matrix and we show the following interesting results.

First, the samle sample size and marginal distributions make the determinant of the difference matrix equal to 0. This shows that the information on marginal distributions corresponds to that of one dimension in an given matrix and also show that the residual part of difference matrix gives another information of a contingency table. Secondly, although the number of elements of a matrix grows n^2, the size of marginal distributions is about $2n - 1$. Thus, the finer the granularity generated by two attributes becomes, more the contribution of marginal distributions decreases. This suggests that another type of information should be hidden in a larger size contingency table. Third, although the residual matrix can be viewed as a special case of a difference matrix, the difference between a given and its expected matrix has a distinguished nature: each element of the difference matrix becomes linear combination of determinants of 2×2 submatrices. Thus, this type of difference is closely related with the nature of determinants. Especially, in case of 2×2 matrix, the residual matrix gives a very interesting form:

$$\frac{(-1)^{i+j}}{N} \det\ M(2, 2, N),$$

which gives another proof that chi-square statistic of 2×2 tables is related with the determinant of contingency matrix.

This paper gives preliminary analysis of a contingency matrix and more formal studies will be our future work.

References

1. Tsumoto, S.: Statistical independence as linear independence. In Skowron, A., Szczuka, M., eds.: Electronic Notes in Theoretical Computer Science. Volume 82., Elsevier (2003)
2. Tsumoto, S., Hirano, S.: Degree of dependence as granularity in contingency table. In Hu, T., Lin, T., eds.: Proceedings of IEEE GrC 2005, IEEE press (2005)
3. Tsumoto, S., Hirano, S.: On pseudo statistical independence in a contingency table. In Lin, T., C.J.Liau, eds.: Foundation of Data Mining (Papers from FDM 2004), Springer Verlag (2006)
4. Tsumoto, S., Hirano, S.: Determinantal divisors for the degree of independence of a contingency matrix. In: Proceedings of NAFIPS 2004, IEEE press (2004)
5. Tsumoto, S., Hirano, S.: Characterization of contextual independence of contingency matrix. In: Proceedings of IEEE GrC 2006, IEEE press (2006)
6. Tsumoto, S., Hirano, S.: Decomposition of contingency table as tensor product. In: Proceedings of IEEE WCCI 2006, IEEE press (2006)

A Model of Machine Learning Based on User Preference of Attributes

Yiyu Yao[1], Yan Zhao[1], Jue Wang[2], and Suqing Han[2]

[1] Department of Computer Science, University of Regina,
Regina, Saskatchewan, Canada S4S 0A2
{yyao, yanzhao}@cs.uregina.ca
[2] Laboratory of Complex Systems and Intelligence Science Institute of Automation,
Chinese Academy of Science, Beijing, China 100080
{jue.wang, suqing.han}@mail.ia.ac.cn

Abstract. A formal model of machine learning by considering user preference of attributes is proposed in this paper. The model seamlessly combines internal information and external information. This model can be extended to user preference of attribute sets. By using the user preference of attribute sets, user preferred reducts can be constructed.

1   Introduction

A basic task of machine learning and data mining is to derive knowledge from data. The discovered knowledge in general should be concise, precise, general, easy to understand and practically useful. Typically, knowledge is expressed by using a certain formal language or a representation scheme. It is a crucial issue to select the most suitable features or properties of the objects in a dataset in the machine learning process. This attribute selection problem is studied under many different areas, such as data reduction, feature selection, rule generation, and so on [1,4,5,6].

Many proposals have been made regarding the effectiveness of individual attributes, or subsets of attributes. They can be broadly divided into two classes, the approaches based on internal information and the approaches based on external information. Internal information and external information are so called and distinguished with respect to the dataset. Internal information based approaches typically depend on the syntactic or statistical information of the dataset. For example, an attribute weighting function is designed by using attributes' distribution information or prediction power. The most fit attribute is used firstly in the rule construction process. On the contrary, external information based approaches assign weights to attributes, or rank attributes based on external semantics or constraints. It is important to realize that these two classes are complementary to each other. Together, they may provide a realistic model for machine learning and data mining. That is, it is desirable that one can consider both syntactical and semantical information in a unified framework.

A review of existing research in machine learning observes that the major research efforts have been done on the internal information based approaches, although the external information based approaches may be more meaningful

S. Greco et al. (Eds.): RSCTC 2006, LNAI 4259, pp. 587–596, 2006.

and effective. This may stem from the fact that external information covers a very diverse range, is highly subjective, and usually is not well-defined. Consequently, it may be difficult to build a well-accepted model. In this paper, we only consider very simple cases of external information based on our intuitions. We provide a formal model of machine learning by considering user preference of attributes. The model seamlessly combines internal information and external information.

The rest of the paper is organized as follows. Section 2 discusses the user preference of attributes. Section 3 extends the user preference of attributes to attributes sets. Both qualitative and quantitative representations of these two models are discussed. Section 4 illustrates the usefulness of the proposed model by applying it to reduct construction. The conclusion is made in Section 5.

2   User Preference of Attributes

In many machine learning algorithms, it is implicitly assumed that all attributes are of the same importance from a user's point of view. Consequently, attributes are selected based solely on their characteristics revealed in an information system. This results in a model, which is simple and easy to analyze. At the same time, without considering the semantic information of attributes, the model is perhaps unrealistic. A more applicable model can be built by considering attributes with non-equal importance. This type of external information is normally provided by users in addition to the information system, and is referred to as user judgement or user preference.

User judgement can be expressed in various forms. Quantitative judgement involves the assignment of different weights to different attributes. Qualitative judgement is expressed as an ordering of attributes. In many situations, user judgement is determined by semantic considerations. For example, it may be interpreted in terms of notions that are more intuitive, such as the cost of testing, the easiness of understanding, or the actionability of an attribute. It is virtually impossible to list all practical interpretations of user judgement. In addition, the meaning of a user judgement becomes clear only in a particular context of application. To simplify our discussion, we treat user judgement as a primitive notion. In other words, we only investigate the desirable properties of a user judgement, as well as how to incorporate it into a machine learning process.

A practical issue is how to acquire user preference. One may argue that a user might not be able to precisely and completely express preference on the entire attribute set. For clarity, we simply assume that a user *can* provide such information. This enables us to investigate the real issues without the interference of unnecessary constraints. Practical constraints, although very important, can always be resolved, at least partially, with further understanding of the problem, or the development of additional methods.

2.1   Quantitative User Judgement

A simple and straightforward way to represent user judgement of attributes is to assign them with numerical weights. Formally, it can be described by a mapping:

$$w : At \longrightarrow \Re, \tag{1}$$

where At is a finite non-empty set of attributes, and $\Re$ is the set of real numbers. For an attribute $a \in At$, $w(a)$ is the weight of a. The numerical weight $w(a)$ may be interpreted as the degree of importance of a, the cost of testing a in a rule, or times of occurrence of a in a set (which is also called the frequency of a). This naturally induces an ordering of attributes. For example, if the weights are interpreted as costs, a machine learning algorithm should apply, if possible, attributes with lower costs first. Furthermore, one may also apply arithmetic operations on the weights.

The use of numerical weights for attribute importance has been extensively considered in machine learning. In many learning algorithms, a numerical function is used to compute weights of individual attributes based on their distribution characteristics. According to the computed weights, attributes are selected. For example, entropy-theoretic measures have been studied and used for attribute selection [7].

2.2   Qualitative User Judgement

A difficulty with the quantitative method is the acquisition of the precise and accurate weights of all attributes. On the other hand, a qualitative method only relies on pairwise comparisons of attributes. For any two attributes, we assume that a user is able to state whether one is more important than, or more preferred to, the other. This qualitative user judgement can be formally defined by a binary relation $\succ$ on At. For any two $a, b \in At$:

$$a \succ b \iff \text{ the user prefers } a \text{ to } b. \tag{2}$$

The relation $\succ$ is called a preference relation. If $a \succ b$ holds, we say that the user strictly prefers a to b. In contrast to the quantitative representation, the preference does not say anything regarding the degree of preference, namely, how much a is preferred to b.

In the absence of preference, i.e., if both $\neg(a \succ b)$ and $\neg(b \succ a)$ hold, we say that a and b are indifferent. An indifference relation $\sim$ on At is defined as:

$$a \sim b \iff \neg(a \succ b) \wedge \neg(b \succ a). \tag{3}$$

The indifference of attributes may be interpreted in several ways. A user may consider the two attributes are of the same importance. The indifference may also occur when the comparison of two attributes are not meaningful, as they are incompatible. When both a and b are unimportant, it may not make too much sense to compare them. The indifference represents such an absence of preference. In fact, in many practical situations, one is only interested in expressing preference on a subset of crucial attributes, and considers all unimportant attributes to be the same.

Based on the strict preference and indifference, one can define a preference-indifference relation $\succeq$ on At:

$$a \succeq b \iff a \succ b \vee a \sim b. \tag{4}$$

If $a \succeq b$ holds, we say that b is not preferred to a, or a is at least as good as b. The strict preference can be re-expressed as $a \succ b \iff a \succeq b \wedge \neg(b \succeq a)$.

A user preference relation must satisfy certain axioms in order to represent our intuitive understanding of preference. The following two axioms seem to be reasonable for $\succ$. For any $a, b, c \in At$:

$\quad$ (1). $\quad a \succ b \Longrightarrow \neg(b \succ a)$ (asymmetry);

$\quad$ (2). $\quad (\neg(a \succ b) \wedge \neg(b \succ c)) \Longrightarrow \neg(a \succ c)$ (negative transitivity).

The asymmetry axiom states that a user cannot prefer a to b, and at the same time prefer b to a. The negative transitivity axiom states that if a user does not prefer a to b, nor b to c, then the user should not prefer a to c. If a preference relation $\succ$ on At is asymmetric and negatively transitive, it is called a *weak order*.

A weak order imposes a special structure on the set of attributes. Additional properties of a weak order are summarized in the following lemma [2].

Lemma 1. *Suppose a preference relation $\succ$ on a finite set of attributes At is a weak order. Then,*

- *Exactly one of $a \succ b$, $b \succ a$ and $a \sim b$ relations holds for any two $a, b \in At$;*
- *The indifference relation $\sim$ is an equivalence relation, which induces a partition $At/\sim$ of At;*
- *The relation $\succ'$ on the partition $At/\sim$, defined by $[a]_\sim \succ' [b]_\sim \iff a \succ b$, is a linear order, where $[a]_\sim$ is the equivalence class containing a.*

A linear order is a weak order in which any two distinct elements are comparable. This lemma implies that if $\succ$ is a weak order, the indifference relation $\sim$ divides the set of attributes into disjoint subsets. Furthermore, for any two distinct equivalence classes $[a]_\sim$ and $[b]_\sim$ of $At/\sim$, either $[a]_\sim \succ' [b]_\sim$ or $[b]_\sim \succ' [a]_\sim$ holds. In other words, it is possible to arrange the attributes into several levels so that attributes in a higher level are preferred to attributes in a lower level, and attributes in the same level are indifferent.

When each equivalence class contains exactly one attribute, the preference relation $\succ$ on At is in fact a linear order itself. The ordering has been considered by some authors [3,9]. In general, if we do not care how to order attributes in an equivalence class, we can extend a weak order into a linear order such that a is ranked ahead of b if and only if $a \succeq b$. For a weak order, its linear extension may not be unique [2].

Example 1. The main notions of qualitative user preference can be illustrated by a simple example. Suppose a user preference relation $\succ$ is qualitatively specified on a set of attributes $At = \{a, b, c, d\}$ by the following weak order:

$$c \succ a, c \succ b, d \succ a, d \succ b, d \succ c.$$

This relation $\succ$ satisfies the asymmetry and negative transitivity conditions. Because of the absence of preference relation between attribute a and b, we say

$a \sim b$. Thus, three equivalence classes $\{d\}, \{c\}, \{a, b\}$ can be found. They can also be written as $[d]_\sim, [c]_\sim, [a]_\sim$ (or $[b]_\sim$), respectively. In turn, they can be arranged as three levels in a linear order:

$$\{d\} \succ' \{c\} \succ' \{a, b\}.$$

If one does not care the order of attributes in an equivalence class, we can extend the weak order of attributes into a linear order of attributes. The given weak order can be extended to two linear orders on At:

$$d \succeq c \succeq b \succeq a,$$
$$d \succeq c \succeq a \succeq b.$$

2.3   Connections Between Quantitative and Qualitative Judgements

A quantitative judgement can be easily translated into a qualitative judgement. Given the weights of attributes, we can uniquely determine a preference relation. Suppose $w(a)$ and $w(b)$ represent the importance of $a, b \in At$, a preference relation is defined by:

$$a \succ b \iff w(a) > w(b). \tag{5}$$

When $w(a)$ and $w(b)$ are the costs of testing attributes $a, b \in At$ in a rule, the following preference relation should be used instead,

$$a \succ b \iff w(a) < w(b). \tag{6}$$

In general, two attributes may have the same weights. Therefore, the induced preference relation is indeed a weak order.

The translation to a preference relation only preserves the ordering of attributes implied by the relative weights. The additional information given by the absolute weight values is lost.

In the reverse process, a user preference relation can be represented in terms of the weights of attributes. A rational user's judgement must allow numerical measurement.

The following theorem states that a weak order is both necessary and sufficient for a numerical measurement [2]:

Theorem 1. *Suppose $\succ$ is a preference relation on a finite non-empty set At of attributes. There exists a real-valued function $u : At \to \Re$ satisfying the condition:*

$$a \succ b \iff u(a) > u(b), a, b \in At. \tag{7}$$

if and only if $\succ$ is a weak order. Moreover, u is uniquely defined up to a strictly monotonic increasing transformation.

The function u is referred to as an order-preserving utility function. It provides a quantitative representation of a user preference. That is, the numbers of $u(a), u(b), \ldots$ as ordered by $>$ reflect the order of $a, b, \ldots$ under the preference relation $\succ$.

The utility function also trustfully represents the indifference relation, i.e.,

$$a \sim b \Longleftrightarrow u(a) = u(b), a, b \in At. \tag{8}$$

According to Theorem 1, for a given preference relation, there exist many utility functions. For a utility function, we can only obtain one preference relation. Under the ordinal scale, it is only meaningful to examine the order induced by a utility function. Although numerical values are used, it is not necessarily meaningful to apply them to arithmetic operations.

Example 2. We can easily observe the connections between a preference relation and a set of weights by the running example. Suppose we can define user preference quantitatively on the set $At = \{a, b, c, d\}$. For example, we can define a utility function u_1 as information entropy, therefore, $u_1(a) = 0, u_1(b) = 0, u_1(c) = 0.8, u_1(d) = 1$. We can also define another utility function u_2 as the cost of testing, therefore, $u_2(a) = 2^{10}, u_2(b) = 2^{10}, u_2(c) = 4, u_2(d) = 0$. The two utility functions define two opposite orders for any pair of attributes. They also use different measurement scales. While the utility function u_1 is used, a preference relation is defined by Equation 5; while the utility function u_2 is used, a preference relation is naturally defined by Equation 6. The example identifies that a user preference relations can be induced by more than one utility functions. A utility function can decide a rational user preference.

One can impose addition axioms on user preference. It is then possible to derive quantitative measurements using other scales. Different scales allow more operations [2].

3   User Preference of Attribute Sets

Conceptually, rule learning in an information system can be viewed as two tasks, the selection of a subset of attributes, and the construction of rules using such attributes. The two tasks can in fact be integrated in one algorithm without a clear separation. Ideally, the subset should contain more preferred attributes and avoid including less preferred attributes. In this case, users should be able to express the preference over subsets of attributes. This requires a user preference relation on the power set 2^{At}. In this section, we present the way to derive a preference relation $\succ$ on 2^{At} based on a preference relation $\succ$ on At.

3.1   Basic Properties

For simplicity, we use the same symbol to denote the preference relation on At and the preference relation on 2^{At}. Obviously, the relation $\succ$ on 2^{At} needs to satisfy certain conditions.

By definition, $\succ$ on 2^{At} must be an extension of $\succ$ on At. That is,

$$\text{(E1).} \quad \{a\} \succ \{b\} \Longleftrightarrow a \succ b;$$
$$\text{(E2).} \quad \{a\} \sim \{b\} \Longleftrightarrow a \sim b;$$
$$\text{(E3).} \quad \{a\} \succeq \{b\} \Longleftrightarrow a \succeq b.$$

Suppose $\succ$ on At is a weak order. For a subset of attributes $A \subseteq At$, the cardinality $|A| = k$, we can arrange the attributes of A into a linear order in the form of $a_1 \succeq a_2 \succeq \ldots \succeq a_k$. According to Theorem 1, this requires the following axiom:

$$(\text{T}). \qquad \succ \text{ on } 2^{At} \text{ is a weak order.}$$

The previous axioms may be considered as the basic properties of $\succ$ on 2^{At}. In addition, $\succ$ on 2^{At} must allow quantitative measurements. One may impose on additional conditions, depending on particular applications.

3.2 Qualitative Extensions

For a set of attributes, we can arrange them in a linear order based on the preference-indifference relation $\succeq$. This enables us to derive a possible ordering of subsets by consecutively examining attributes one by one. Based on the directions in which attributes are examined, we define two lexical orders. In the left-to-right lexical order, we compare two sets of attributes from left to right, in order to determine which set of attributes is preferred. In the right-to-left lexical order, we compare attributes in the reverse order.

Definition 1. Left-to-right lexical order: *Given two attribute sets $A : a_1 \succeq a_2 \succeq \ldots \succeq a_m$ and $B : b_1 \succeq b_2 \succeq \ldots \succeq b_n$, let $t = \min\{m, n\}$. We say that A precedes B in the left-to-right lexical order, written $A \succ B$, if and only if*

(a) *there exists a $1 \leq i \leq t$ such that $a_j \sim b_j$ for $1 \leq j < i$ and $a_i \succ b_i$, or*
(b) *$a_i \sim b_i$ for $1 \leq i \leq t$ and $m < n$.*

Definition 2. Right-to-left lexical order: *Given two attribute sets $A : a_1 \succeq a_2 \succeq \ldots \succeq a_m$ and $B : b_1 \succeq b_2 \succeq \ldots \succeq b_n$, let $t = \min\{m, n\}$. We say that A precedes B in the right-to-left lexical order, written $A \succ B$, if and only if*

(a) *there exists a $0 \leq i < t$ such that $a_{m-j} \sim b_{n-j}$ for $0 \leq j < i$ and $a_{m-i} \succ b_{n-i}$, or*
(b) *$a_{m-i} \sim b_{n-i}$ for $0 \leq i < t$ and $m < n$.*

These two lexical orders represent two extreme views and define two different criteria for selecting the winner of attribute sets. Roughly speaking, the meaning of these two can be interpreted as follows. The left-to-right method focuses on the preferred attributes of the two sets. That is, the winner of all attribute sets is determined by comparing the strongest attributes of individual sets. By the left-to-right lexical order, an attribute set A is preferred to another attribute set B if and only if (1) the most preferred attribute of A is preferred to the most preferred attribute of B, or, (2) A is a proper subset consisting of the most preferred attributes of B.

On the other hand, the right-to-left method emphasizes the less preferred attributes of the two sets. The winner of all subsets of attributes is determined by comparing the weakest attributes of individual sets. By the right-to-left lexical order, an attribute set A is preferred to another attribute set B if and only if (1) the least preferred attribute of A is preferred to the least preferred attribute of B, or, (2) A is a proper subset consisting of the least preferred attributes of B.

The left-to-right lexical order encourages an optimistic comparison, and the right-to-left lexical order promotes a pessimistic comparison.

Example 3. The running example can be used to illustrate the differences between two lexical orders. Recall that attributes in Example 1 can be arranged as $\{d\} \succ' \{c\} \succ' \{a, b\}$. For two attribute subsets $A : d \succeq c \succeq a$ and $B : d \succeq a$, since $d \sim d$ and $c \succ a$, then A is the winner according to the left-to-right lexical order. At the same time, since $a \sim a$ and $d \succ c$, thus B is the winner according to the right-to-left lexical order.

For two attribute subsets $C : d \succeq c \succeq a$ and $D : c \succeq b$, since $d \succ c$, then C is the winner according to the left-to-right lexical order. On the other hand, since $a \sim b, c \sim c$ and $|D| < |C|$, then D is the winner according to the right-to-left lexical order.

It is essential to note that both lexical orders satisfy Axioms (E1,2,3) and (T), and should be considered as examples of potential extensions of the preference order from At to 2^{At}. They may provide different preference orders based on their criteria, as we just showed in the example. It may be difficult to argue which one is better based solely on theoretical basis. In real applications, we might also need to consider other extensions.

3.3   Quantitative Extensions

When user preference is given as weights of attributes, one can first define a preference and then use the previously discussed qualitative methods. The numerical weights also offer addition methods. We can extend the weighting function w on At to a weighting function on 2^{At}. For simplicity, we use the same symbol to denote these two functions. Similarly, the extensions are not unique. For example, for $A \subseteq At$, we consider the following possible extensions:

$$
\begin{aligned}
&\text{Additive extension: } w(A) = \textstyle\sum_{a \in A} w(a), \\
&\text{Average extension: } w(A) = \frac{\sum_{a \in A} w(a)}{|A|}, \\
&\text{Maximal extension: } w(A) = \max_{a \in A} w(a), \\
&\text{Minimal extension: } w(A) = \min_{a \in A} w(a).
\end{aligned}
$$

The extensions are not true or false. They are simply useful or not useful for some purposes. One can interpret the meaningful extensions based on the physical meaning of the weighting function on At. It is important to note that only some extensions are meaningful in a particular application.

The values of an extension naturally define an order. For example, if $w(a)$ is a cost measurement function, the above extensions are interpreted as the total cost, average cost, maximal cost and minimal cost, respectively. An attribute set with the minimum cost is normally in favour. If $w(a)$ is an information measurement function, $w(A)$ is the joint information of all attributes in the set.

Normally, an attribute set with the maximal information gain is in favour. Based on the computed weights, we can order subsets of attributes in a similar way as given by Equations 5 and 6.

4   User Preference on Reducts

The usefulness of the proposed model can be illustrated by reduct construction. A reduct is the minimal subset of attributes that preserves the discernible information of an information table. Conceptually, internal information determines a set of reducts, and user preference determines an ordering of reducts. By involving user preference in the reduct construction process, we can observe two directions. First is to choose the user preferred reducts while all reducts are available. Second is to construct a user preferred reduct directly. It is obvious that the second approach is more efficient.

Regarding the two lexical orders, we can define an RLR algorithm for computing the winner reduct of the right-to-left lexical order, and an LRR algorithm for computing the winner reduct of the left-to-right lexical order. We define that an attribute set $R' \subseteq At$ is called a super-reduct of a reduct R if $R' \supseteq R$; and an attribute set $R' \subset At$ is called a partial reduct of a reduct R if $R' \subset R$. Given a reduct, there exist many super-reducts and many partial reducts.

An RLR algorithm uses a deletion strategy, that removes the less preferred attributes one by one from the super-reduct, until a reduct is obtained. An RLR algorithm can start from the largest super-reduct At, or a computed super-reduct $A \subseteq At$. An LRR algorithm uses an addition strategy, that adds the most preferred attributes one by one to an empty set, until a reduct is obtained. It is important to note that as long as an attribute is added, it is hard to remove it. Therefore, the addition strategy should be carried out with caution. The general RLR and LRR algorithms are briefly illustrated below.

A general RLR algorithm:
Input: An information table S with At in a linear preference order.
Output: The winner reduct of the right-to-left lexical order.
(1) $R = At$, $CD = At$.
(2) While $CD \neq \emptyset$:
    (2.1) Consider all attributes in CD from right to left, let $CD = CD - \{a\}$;
    (2.2) If $R - \{a\}$ is a super-reduct, let $R = R - \{a\}$.
(3) Output R.

A general LRR algorithm:
Input: An information table S with At in a linear preference order.
Output: The winner reduct of the left-to-right lexical order.
(1) $R = \emptyset$, $CA = At$.
(2) While R is not a reduct and $CA \neq \emptyset$:
    (2.1) Consider all attributes in CA from left to right;
    (2.2) If $R \cup \{a\}$ is a partial reduct, let $R = R \cup \{a\}$, and $CA = CA - \{a\}$.
(3) Output R.

It is important to note that the deletion strategy and the addition strategy correspond to the RLR algorithm and the LRR algorithm, respectively. The cross effect is not easy to implement, if it is not impossible. The detailed implementation and discussion of these two strategies are presented in our another recent paper [8], and will be addressed more carefully in our following research.

5 Conclusion

We propose a model for machine learning based on user preference of attributes. This model can be extended to user preference of attribute sets. Both qualitative and quantitative representations of user preference on attributes and attribute sets are elaborately explored. With respect to user preference of attribute sets, various of applications, such as the computation of the most preferred reducts, can be intensively studied.

References

1. Blum, A.L. and Langley, P., Selection of relevant features and examples in machine learning, *Artificial Intelligence*, 97, 245-271, 1997.
2. Fishburn, P.C., *Utility Theory for Decision-Making*, John Wiley & Sons, New York, 1970.
3. Han, S.Q. and Wang, J., Reduct and attribute order, *Journal of Computer Science and Technology archive*, 19(4), 429-449, 2004.
4. Jain, A., Duin, P. and Mao, J., Statistical pattern recognition: A review, *IEEE Transactions on Pattern Analysis and Machine Intelligence* 22(1), 4-37, 2000.
5. Kohavi, R. and John, G., Wrappers for feature subset selection, *Artificial Intelligence*, 97(1-2), 273-324, 1997.
6. Swiniarski, R.W. and Skowron, A., Rough set methods in feature selection and recognition, *Pattern Recognition Letters*, 24(6), 833-849, 2003.
7. Yao, Y.Y., Chen, Y.H. and Yang, X.D. A measurement-theoretic foundation for rule interestingness evaluation, *Proceedings of Workshop on Foundations and New Directions in Data Mining in the Third IEEE International Conference on Data Mining (ICDM 2003)*, 221-227, 2003.
8. Yao, Y.Y., Zhao, Y. and Wang, J., On reduct construction algorithms, *Proceedings of the First International Conference on Rough Sets and Knowledge Technology*, 297-304, 2006.
9. Ziarko, W., Rough set approaches for discovering rules and attribute dependencies, in: Klösgen, W. and Żytkow, J.M. (eds.), *Handbook of Data Mining and Knowledge Discovery*, Oxford, 328-339, 2002.

Combining Bi-gram of Character and Word to Classify Two-Class Chinese Texts in Two Steps

Xinghua Fan, Difei Wan, and Guoying Wang

College of Computer Science and Technology, Chongqing University of Posts and
Telecommunications, Chongqing 400065, P.R. China
fanxh@cqupt.edu.cn, wandifei@stu.cqupt.edu.cn,
wanggy@cqupt.edu.cn

Abstract. This paper presents a two-step method of combining two types of
features for two-class Chinese text categorization. First, the bi-gram of
character is regarded as candidate feature, a Naive Bayesian classifier is used to
classify texts. Then, the fuzzy area between two categories is fixed directly
according to the outputs of the classifier. Second, the bi-gram of word with
parts of speech verb or noun is regarded as candidate feature, a Naive Bayesian
classifier same as that in the first step is used to deal with the documents falling
into the fuzzy area, which are thought of classifying unreliable in the previous
step. Our experiment validated the soundness of the proposed method, which
achieved a high performance, with the precision, recall and F_1 being 97.65%,
97.00% and 97.31% respectively on a test set consisting of 12,600 Chinese
texts.

1 Introduction

Text categorization (TC) is a task of assigning one or multiple predefined category
labels to natural language texts. To deal with this sophisticated task, a variety of
statistical classification methods and machine learning techniques have been exploited
intensively [1], including the Naïve Bayesian (NB) classifier [2], the Vector Space
Model (VSM)-based classifier [3], the example-based classifier [4], and the Support
Vector Machine [5].

Text filtering is a basic type of text categorization (two-class TC). There are many
real-life applications [6], a typical one of which is the ill information filtering, such as
erotic information and garbage information filtering on the web, in e-mails and in
short messages of mobile phones. It is obvious that this sort of information should be
carefully controlled. On the other hand, the filtering performance using the existing
methodologies is still not satisfactory in general. The reason lies in that there exist a
number of documents with high degree of ambiguity, from the TC point of view, in a
document collection, that is, there is a fuzzy area across the border of two classes (for
the sake of expression, we call the class consisting of the ill information-related texts,
or, the negative samples, the category of TARGET, and, the class consisting of the ill
information-not-related texts, or, the positive samples, the category of Non-
TARGET). Some documents in one category may have great similarities with some
other documents in the other category, for example, a lot of words concerning love

S. Greco et al. (Eds.): RSCTC 2006, LNAI 4259, pp. 597–606, 2006.

story and sex are likely appear in both negative samples and positive samples if the filtering target is erotic information.

Fan et al observed that most of the classification errors result from the documents of falling into the fuzzy area between two categories, and present a two-step TC method based on Naive Bayesian classifier [6-8], in which the idea is inspired by the fuzzy area between categories: in the first step, the words with parts of speech verb, noun, adjective and adverb are regarded as candidate feature, a Naive Bayesian classifier is used to classify texts and fix the fuzzy area between categories; in the second step, bi-gram of words with parts of speech verb and noun as feature, a Naive Bayesian classifier same as that in the previous step is used to classify documents in the fuzzy area. The two-step categorization framework is very good, but the TC method in [6-8] has a shortcoming: its classification efficiency is not well. The reason lies in that it needs word segmentation to extract the features, and at currently, the speed of segmenting Chinese words is not high.

To overcome the shortcoming, this paper presents a TC method that uses the bi-gram of character as feature at the first step in the two-step framework. Another object of this paper is to explore the biggest puzzled problem in Chinese text categorization: Comparing with a classifier that uses word as feature, why the performance of a classifier that uses the bi-gram of character as feature is better? This is implemented by comparing the experiments in this paper with those in [7]. The rest of this paper is organized as follows. Section 2 describes how to use a Naive Bayesian classifier to fix the fuzzy area between categories, and presents an assumption based on data observation; Section 3 describes experiments; Section 4 describes the related works; Section 5 summaries the whole paper.

2   Fix the Fuzzy Area Between Categories by a Naïve Bayesian Classifier

A Naïve Bayesian classifier is used to fix the fuzzy area in the first step. For a document represented by a binary-valued vector $d = (W_1, W_2, ..., W_{|D|})$, the two-class Naïve Bayesian classifier is given as follows:

$$
\begin{aligned}
f(d) &= \log \frac{\Pr\{c_1|d\}}{\Pr\{c_2|d\}} \\
&= \log \frac{\Pr\{c_1\}}{\Pr\{c_2\}} + \sum_{k=1}^{|D|} \log \frac{1-p_{k1}}{1-p_{k2}} + \sum_{k=1}^{|D|} W_k \log \frac{p_{k1}}{1-p_{k1}} - \sum_{k=1}^{|D|} W_k \log \frac{p_{k2}}{1-p_{k2}}
\end{aligned}
\tag{1}
$$

where $\Pr\{\cdot\}$ is the probability that event $\{\cdot\}$ occurs, c_i is category i, and $p_{ki}=\Pr\{W_k=1|c_i\}$ (i=1,2). If $f(d) \geq 0$, the document d will be assigned the category label c_1, otherwise, c_2. Let:

$$
Con = \log \frac{\Pr\{c_1\}}{\Pr\{c_2\}} + \sum_{k=1}^{|D|} \log \frac{1-p_{k1}}{1-p_{k2}},
\tag{2}
$$

$$X = \sum_{k=1}^{|D|} W_k \log \frac{p_{k1}}{1 - p_{k1}},$$
(3)

$$Y = \sum_{k=1}^{|D|} W_k \log \frac{p_{k2}}{1 - p_{k2}},$$
(4)

where Con is a constant relevant only to the training set, X and Y are the measures that the document d belongs to categories c_1 and c_2 respectively. (1) is rewritten as:

$$f(d) = X - Y + Con$$
(5)

Apparently, $f(d)=0$ is the separate line in a two-dimensional space with X and Y being X-coordinate and Y-coordinate respectively. In this space, a given document d can be viewed as a point (x, y), in which the values of x and y are calculated according to (3) and (4).

As shown in Fig.1, the distance from the point (x, y) to the separate line will be:

$$Dist = \frac{1}{\sqrt{2}}(x - y + Con)$$
(6)

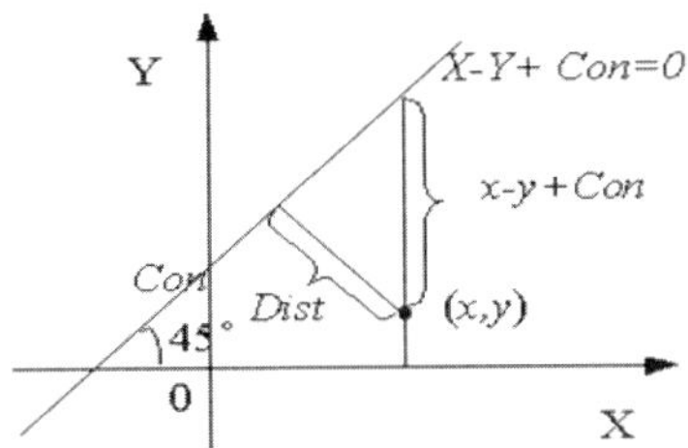

Fig. 1. Distance from point (x, y) to the separate line

An assumption based on data observation
Fig. 2 illustrates the distribution of a training set (refer to Section 3) regarding $Dist$ in the two-dimensional space, with the curve on the left for the negative samples, and the curve on the right for the positive samples. As can be seen in the figure, most of the misclassified documents, which unexpectedly across the separate line, are near the line.

Assumption: the performance of a classifier is relevant to the distance $Dist$ in (6), most of the classifying error gathers in an area near the separate line, and the documents falling into this area only constitute a small portion of the dataset.

Thus, the space can be partitioned into reliable area and unreliable area:

$$\begin{cases} Dist_2 \leq Dist \leq Dist_1, & \text{Decision for } d \text{ is unreliable} \\ Dist > Dist_1, & \text{Assigning the label } c_1 \text{ to } d \text{ is reliable} \\ Dist < Dist_2, & \text{Assigning the label } c_2 \text{ to } d \text{ is reliable} \end{cases}$$
(7)

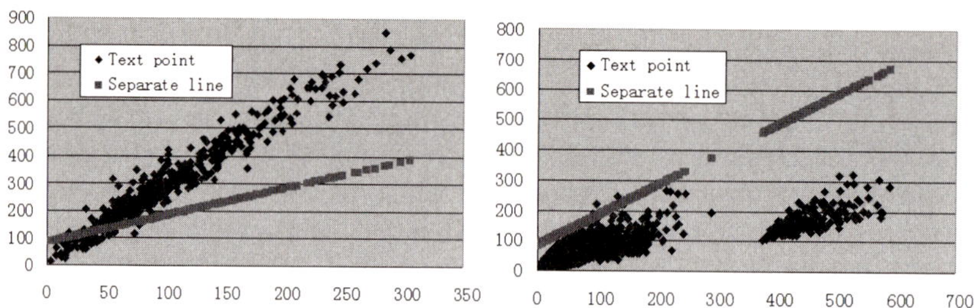

Fig. 2. Distribution of the training set in the two-dimensional space

where $Dist_1$ and $Dist_2$ are constants determined by experiments, $Dist_1$ is positive real number and $Dist_2$ is negative real number.

3   Experiments

The dataset used here is composed of 12,600 documents with 1,800 negative samples of TARGET and 10,800 positive samples of Non-TARGET. It is split into 4 parts randomly, with three parts as training set and one part as testing set. All experiments in this section are performed in 4-fold cross validation.

In the first step, the bi-gram of Chinese character is regarded as feature. The original feature set is further reduced to a much smaller one according to formula (8) or (9). A Naïve Bayesian classifier is then applied to the testing set. In the second step, only the documents that are identified unreliable in terms of (7) in the first step are concerned. This time, the bi-gram of Chinese word with parts-of-speech verb or noun is used as feature, and another Naïve Bayesian classifier same as that in the previous step is trained and applied.

$$MI_1(t_k,c) = \sum_{i=1}^{n} \Pr\{t_k,c_i\} \log \frac{\Pr\{t_k,c_i\}}{\Pr\{t_k\}\Pr\{c_i\}} \tag{8}$$

$$MI_2(t_k,c) = \sum_{i=1}^{n} \log \frac{\Pr\{t_k,c_i\}}{\Pr\{t_k\}\Pr\{c_i\}} \tag{9}$$

where t_k stands for the kth feature, which may be a Chinese character bi-gram or a Chinese word bi-gram, and c_i is the ith predefined category.

The following five methods are tried.

Method-1: Use bi-gram of Chinese character as feature, reduce feature with (8), and classify documents directly without exploiting the two-step strategy.

Method-2: same as Method-1 except feature reduction with (9).

Method-3: same as Method-1 except bi-gram of Chinese word as feature.

Method-4: Use the mixture of bi-gram of Chinese character and bi-gram of Chinese word as feature, reduce features with (8), and classify documents directly.

Method-5: (i.e., the proposed method): Use bi-gram of Chinese character as feature in the first step and then use bi-gram of Chinese word as feature in the second step, reduce feature with (8), and classify the documents in two steps.

To extract the feature in the second step, CSeg&Tag3.0, a Chinese word segmentation and POS tagging system developed by Tsinghua University, is used to perform the morphological analysis for Chinese texts. Note that the proportion of negative samples and positive samples is 1:6. Thus if all the documents in the test set is arbitrarily set to positive, the precision will reach 85.7%. For this reason, only the experimental results for negative samples are considered in evaluation.

Experiment 1: Selecting the feature reduction formula and determining the scale of feature set.

Employing Method-1 and Method-2, the curves that the performance of a classifier changes with the used feature number are drawn and illustrated as Fig.3, in which Fig.3.a and Fig.3.b correspond Method-1 and Method-2 respectively.

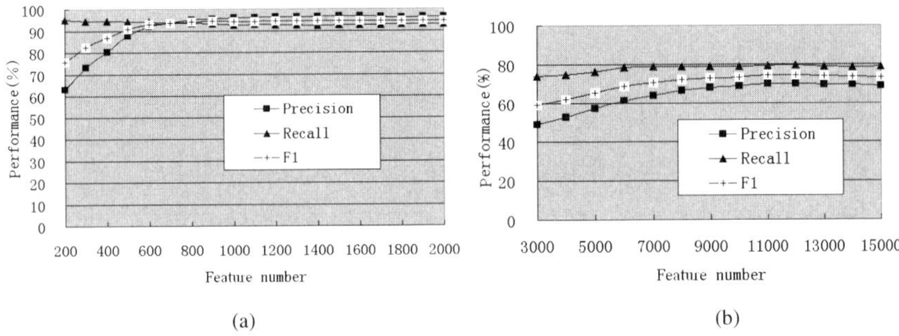

Fig. 3. The curves that the performance of a classifier changes with the used feature number when two kinds of feature reduction method (8) and (9) are exploited

From Fig.3, the scales of feature set for (8) and (9) are determined as 800 and 12000 respectively. In terms of precision, recall and F_1, the corresponding performances are 95.42%, 88.00% and 91.56% in Fig.3.a, and 70.06%, 79.44% and 74.39% in Fig.3.b. Comparing Fig.3.a and Fig.3.b, it shows that formula (8) is superior to formula (9) because not only the performance of Method-1 is higher than that of Method-2 (91.56% vs. 74.39%), but also the used feature number is smaller (800 vs. 12000).

Experiment 2: Validating the *assumption* and determining constant $Dist_1$ and $Dist_2$.
To validate the assumption, the two measures, error rate (**ER**) and region percentage (**RP**), are introduced, which definitions are as follows.

$$ER = \frac{\text{the number of texts misclassed in a given region}}{\text{the number of texts misclassed in a testing set}} \times 100\%$$

$$RP = \frac{\text{the number of texts falling into a give region}}{\text{the number of texts in a testing set}} \times 100\%$$

Employing Method-1, the curves that the performance (including **ER** and **RP**) of a classifier changes with the distance *Dist* are drawn and illustrated as Fig.4. From Fig.4, the constant $Dist_1$ and $Dist_2$ are determined as 32 and –52 respectively, and the corresponding performance of the classifier is given in Table.1.

Fig.4 and Table.1 show that the *assumption* is true because 97.48% classification error occurs in a region ($32 \geq Dist \geq -52$), but all texts in the region is 40.23% of all texts in the testing set.

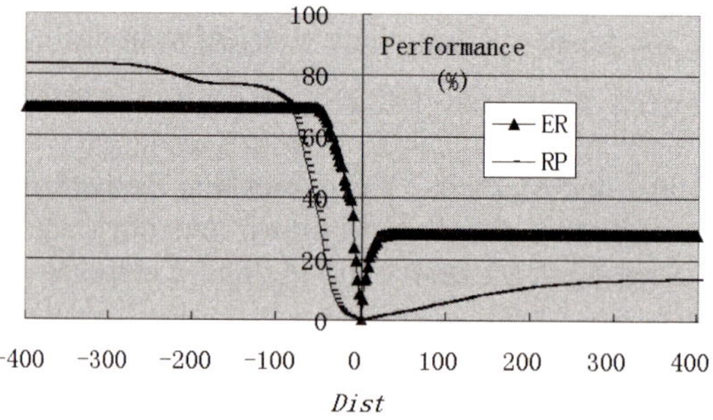

Fig. 4. The curves that error rate and region percentage change with the distance *Dist*

Table 1. The error rate and region percentage in a give region

Region	Error rate	Region percentage
$32 \geq Dist \geq 0$	28.26%	1.88%
$0 \geq Dist \geq -52$	69.22%	38.44%
$32 \geq Dist \geq -52$	97.48%	40.23%

Experiment 3: Comparing the performances of five kinds of methods.

The experimental results of five kinds of methods are given in Table.2. The results of Method-1 and Method-2 result from **Experiment** 1. The results of Method-3 result from reference [7]. Employing Method-4, the curves of the performance of a classifier changing with the used feature number are drawn and illustrated as Fig.5. From Fig.5, the scale of feature set is determined as 2000, and the corresponding performance is illustrated as Table.2. Employing Method-5, the feature number used in the first step is 800, the curves of the performance of a classifier changing with the feature number used in the second step are drawn and illustrated as Fig.6. From Fig.6, the scale of feature set used in the second step is determined as 8500, and the corresponding performance is illustrated as Table 2.

Table 2. The performance of five kinds of methods

Method	Precision	Recall	F_1	Feature number
Method-1	95.42%	88.0%	91.56%	800
Method-2	70.06%	79.44%	74.39%	12000
Method-3	93.15%	94.17%	93.65%	15000
Method-4	97.80%	95.72%	96.71%	2000
Method-5	97.65%	97.0%	97.31%	800+8500

Comparing Method-1, Method-3 and Method-4, it shows that Chinese word bi-gram as feature has better discriminating capability meanwhile with more serious data sparseness: the performances of Method-3 and Method-4 are higher than that of Method-1, but the number of feature used in Method-3 is more than those used in Method-1 and Method-4 (15000 vs. 800 and 2000). Table 2 shows that the proposed method (i.e., Methond-5) has the best performance (F_1 as 97.31%) and good efficiency. It integrates the merit of Chinese character bi-gram and word bi-gram. Using Chinese character bi-gram as feature in the first step aims at its better statistical coverage. For example, the 800 selected features in the first step can treat a majority of documents of constituting 59.77% of the testing set. Especially, Chinese character bi-gram as feature in the first step, it does not need Chinese word segmentation, and achieve a high computational efficiency. On the other hand, using word bi-gram as feature in the second step aims at its better discriminating capability, although the number of feature becomes comparatively large (8500). Comparing Method-5 with Method-1, Method-3 and Method-4, it shows that the two-step approach is superior to either using only one kind of features (Chinese character bi-gram or Chinese word bi-gram) in the classifier, or using the mixture of two kinds of features in one step.

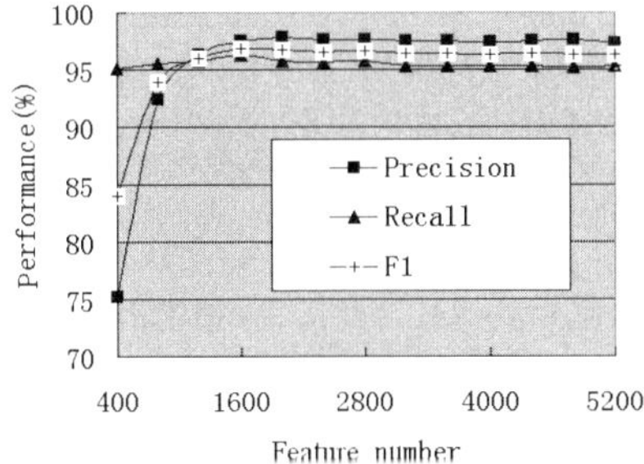

Fig. 5. The curves that the performance changes with the feature number under Method-4

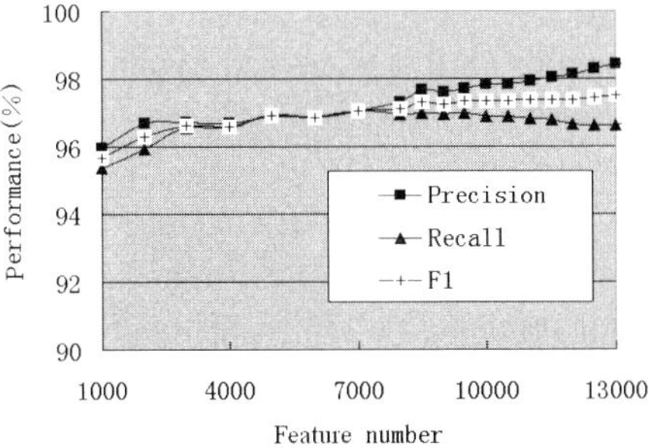

Fig. 6. The curves that the performance changes with the feature number used in the second step when the feature number used in the first step is fixed under Method-5

Comparing bi-gram of character as feature and bi-gram of word as feature
Table 3 gives the experimental results in reference [7]. Method-I, Method-II and
Method-IV in Table 3 are similar to Method-1, Method-2 and Method-4 in this paper
respectively, the differences are that the used feature changes from bi-gram of
Chinese character in this paper to Chinese word with parts-of-speech verb, noun,
adjective or adverb in [7]. Method-III is the same as Method-3. Method-V is similar
to Method-5 except that the feature used in the first step is different, Chinese word
with parts-of-speech verb, noun, adjective or adverb in [7] as feature.

Table 3.

Method	Precision	Recall	F_1	Feature number
Method-I	93.35%	88.78%	91.00%	500
Method-II	78.04%	88.72%	82.67%	4000
Method-III	93.15%	94.17%	93.65%	15000
Method-IV	95.86%	91.11%	93.42%	800
Method-V	97.19%	93.94%	95.54%	500+3000

Comparing Method-1 and Method-I, Method-2 and Method-II, it shows that
Chinese character bi-gram as feature has better performance (91.00% vs. 91.56,
82.67% vs. 74.39% in F_1), and Chinese word as feature need smaller feature number
(500 vs. 800, 4000 vs. 12000), to sum up that the former (Chinese character bi-gram)
has higher efficiency because it does not need Chinese word segmentation.

Comparing Method-4 and Method-IV, Method-5 and Method-V, it shows that the
combination of character and word bi-gram is superior to the combination of word
and word bi-gram because the former has better performance (93.42% vs. 96.71%,
95.54% vs. 97.31% in F_1). Comparing Table 2 and Table 3, it shows that the proposed
method in this paper (i.e., Method-5) has the best performance and efficiency,
although it uses more features (800+8500 vs. 500+3000), but it does not need Chinese
word segmentation in the first step.

Based on experiments and analysis described in above, it shows that bi-gram of
Chinese character as feature has better statistic capability than word as feature, thus the
former has better classification ability in general. But for those documents that have
high degree ambiguity between categories, bi-gram of Chinese word as feature has
better discriminating capability. So, it is easy to obtain high performance if the two
types of features are combined to classify Chinese texts in two steps like this paper.

4   Related Works

Combining multiple methodologies or representations has been studied in several
areas of information retrieval so far, for example, retrieval effectiveness can be
improved by using multiple representations [9]. In the area of text categorization in
particular, many methods of combining different classifiers have been developed. For
example, Yang et al. [10] used simple equal weights for normalized score of each
classifier output so as to integrate multiple classifiers linearly in the domain of Topic
Detection and Tracking; Hull at al. [11] used linear combination for probabilities or

log odds scores of multiple classifier output in the context of document filtering. Larkey et al. [12] used weighted linear combination for system ranks and scores of multiple classifier output in the medical document domain; Li and Jain [13] used voting and classifier selection technique including dynamic classifier selection and adaptive clas sifier. Lam and Lai [14] automatically selected a classifier for each category based on the category-specific statistical characteristics. Bennett et al. [15] used voting, classifier-selection techniques and a hierarchical combination method with reliability indicators.

Comparing with other combination strategy, the two-step method of classifying texts in this paper has a characteristic: the fuzzy area between categories is fixed directly according to the outputs of the classifier.

5   Conclusions

This paper presents a two-step TC method to classify two-class Chinese text, in which bi-gram of character that does not need Chinese word segmentation as candidate feature is used in the first step, and bi-gram of word with parts of speech verb or noun as feature is used in the second step. The proposed method exploits a Naive Bayesian classifier to fix directly the fuzzy area between two categories in the first step. A Naive Bayesian classifier similar to that in the previous is used to deal with the documents of falling into the area in the second step, which are thought of classifying unreliable in the previous step. Experiments show that the method achieves a high performance.

In addition, other conclusions can be drawn from the experiments and analysis: (1) The performance of a classifier is relevant to the distance from text point to separate line in a constructed space, most of the classifying error gathers in an area near the separate line; (2) Formula (8) is superior to (9) in feature reduction in two-class Chinese text categorization; (3) The two-step feature combination is superior to either using only one kind of features (Chinese character bi-gram or Chinese word bi-gram) in the classifier, or using the mixture of two kinds of features in one step; (4) The combination of character bi-gram and word bi-gram is superior to the combination of word and word bi-gram, the former has not only better performance but also better efficiency; (5) Bi-gram of Chinese character as feature has better statistic capability than word as feature, so the former has better classification ability in general; (6) For those documents that have high degree ambiguity between categories, bi-gram of Chinese word as feature has better discriminating capability.

It is worth point out that we believe the proposed method is in principle language independent, though all the experiments are performed on Chinese datasets.

References

1. Sebastiani, F. Machine Learning in Automated Text Categorization. ACM Computing Surveys, 34(1): 1-47, 2002.
2. Lewis, D. Naive Bayes at Forty: The Independence Assumption in Information Retrieval. In Proceedings of ECML-98, 4-15, 1998.

3. Salton, G. Automatic Text Processing: The Transformation, Analysis, and Retrieval of Information by Computer. Addison-Wesley, Reading, MA, 1989.
4. Mitchell, T.M. Machine Learning. McCraw Hill, New York, NY, 1996.
5. Yang, Y., and Liu, X. A Re-examination of Text Categorization Methods. In Proceedings of SIGIR-99, 42-49,1999.
6. Xinghua Fan. Causality Reasoning and Text Categorization, Postdoctoral Research Report of Tsinghua University, P.R. China, April 2004.
7. Xinghua Fan, Maosong Sun, Key-sun Choi, and Qin Zhang. Classifying Chinese texts in two steps. IJCNLP2005, LNAI3651, pp.302-313, 2005.
8. Xinghua Fan, Maosong Sun. A high performance two-class Chinese text categorization method. Chinese Journal of Computers, 29(1), 124-131, 2006.
9. Rajashekar, T. B. and Croft, W. B. Combining Automatic and Manual Index Representations in Probabilistic Retrieval. Journal of the American society for information science, 6(4): 272-283,1995.
10. Yang, Y., Ault, T. and Pierce, T. Combining Multiple Learning Strategies for Effective Cross Validation. In Proceedings of ICML 2000, 1167–1174, 2000.
11. Hull, D. A., Pedersen, J. O. and H. Schutze. Method Combination for Document Filtering. In Proceedings of SIGIR-96, 279–287, 1996.
12. Larkey, L. S. and Croft, W. B. Combining Classifiers in Text Categorization. In Proceedings of SIGIR-96, 289-297, 1996.
13. Li, Y. H., and Jain, A. K. Classification of Text Documents. The Computer Journal, 41(8): 537-546, 1998.
14. Lam, W., and Lai, K.Y. A Meta-learning Approach for Text Categorization. In Proceedings of SIGIR-2001, 303-309, 2001.
15. Bennett, P. N., Dumais, S. T., and Horvitz, E. Probabilistic Combination of Text Classifiers Using Reliability Indicators: Models and Results. In Proceedings of SIGIR-2002, 11-15, 2002.

Combining Monte Carlo Filters with Support Vector Machines for Option Price Forecasting

Shian-Chang Huang[1] and Tung-Kuang Wu[2]

[1] Department of Business Administration, National Changhua University of
Education, Changhua, Taiwan
`shhuang@cc.ncue.edu.tw`
[2] Department of Information Management, National Changhua University of
Education, Changhua, Taiwan
`tkwu@mail.tkwu.net`

Abstract. This study proposes a hybrid model for online forecasting of
option prices. The hybrid predictor combines a Monte Carlo filter with
a support vector machine. The Monte Carlo filter (MCF) is used to infer
the latent volatility and discount rate of the Black-Scholes model, and
makes a subsequent prediction. The support vector machine is employed
to capture the nonlinear residuals between the actual option prices and
the MCF predictions. Taking the option transaction data on the Taiwan
composite stock index, this study examined the forecasting accuracy of
the proposed model. The performance of the hybrid model is superior to
traditional extended Kalman filter models and pure SVM forecasts. The
results can help investors to control and hedge their risks.

1   Introduction

The valuation of financial assets and the pricing of financial derivatives are one
of the most important areas in financial studies in recent years. Evidence of
this importance can be found in the large number of publications. Moreover,
option markets are among the top most popular shares of financial institutions.
To explore the markets well and improve investment yields, the modelling and
online predicting of option prices is very important for practitioners.

Due to the high risk in trading options, an accurate online forecast of option
prices is important for an investor to control and hedge his risk. Traditionally, the
literature of online forecasting of option prices focus on using Kalman filters (KF)
or extended Kalman filters (EKF) as methodologies. However, the KF requires
linearity and Gaussian conditions of the underlying stochastic processes, and the
EKF use a first order linear approximation to simplify the underlying processes,
which are all sub-optimal solutions. These methods are limiting because many
financial time series are stochastic, nonlinear and non-Gaussian. For example,
when one uses the Black-Scholes (BS) model [1] to predict the option price,
there are two latent state variables and the BS formula is nonlinear. Thus the
present article uses the Monte Carlo filter (MCF)[5,7] as a state estimator and
a predictor for the BS model, which does not require the linearity and Gaussian
conditions of the underlying processes.

S. Greco et al. (Eds.): RSCTC 2006, LNAI 4259, pp. 607–616, 2006.

Recently, many nonparametric methods such as neural networks [16] or support vector machines (SVM) [10] are employed to forecast option prices, but these models do not capture important financial characteristics–latent volatility and riskless discount rate of an option, and thus their performances are not satisfactory. Combining MCFs with SVMs is a novel strategy proposed by this article. The nonlinear patterns which can't be predicted by the BS model (or the MCF) is further captured by a SVM in our hybrid model.

Monte Carlo or particle filters (Gordon et al. [5], Kitagawa [7], Pitt and Shephard [11], Merwe et al. [9]) are a sequential learning and inference methods which are important in many applications involving real-time state estimates and on-line forecasting, where data arrival sequentially. For instance, in high-frequency financial analysis, huge transaction data are observed sequentially every minute. Thus we need a fast online forecasting method with the computational simplicity in the form of not having to store all the data, and information from the recent past is given greater weighting than information from the distant past. From a Bayesian perspective, MCFs allow one to compute, recursively in time, a stochastic point-mass approximation of the posterior distribution of the states given the observations. Consequently, MCFs are very suitable for high-frequency online forecasting. For a comprehensive review of Monte Carlo filtering methods see Doucet, Freitas, and Gordon [4].

Support vector machines (SVMs) (Cristianini, N. and J. Shawe-Taylor [3], Schoelkopf, Burges, and Smola [12], Vapnik [14]) are forcefully competing with Neural Networks as tools for solving nonlinear regression and pattern recognition problems. They are based on some beautifully simple ideas and provide a clear intuition of what learning from examples is all about. More importantly they are showing high performances in practical applications. In very simple terms an SVM corresponds to a linear method in a high dimensional feature space that is nonlinearly related to the input space. Even though we think of it as a linear algorithm in the high dimensional feature space, in practice, it does not involve any computations in that high dimensional space. By the use of kernels, all necessary computations are performed directly in input space.

Different forecasting models can complement each other in capturing different patterns of data sets, and both theoretical and empirical studies have concluded that a combination of forecasts outperforms individual forecasting models [2,6,8,13,15,17]. This study presents a hybrid model that combines the MCF and a SVM to forecast an option price. In our hybrid approach, the MCF model serves as a processor to handle the Black-Scholes model predictions (stochastic predictions). Then, the residuals between the actual prices and the Black-Scholes model predictions are fed into the SVM in the hybrid model. The SVM is conducted to further reduce the prediction errors (deterministic nonlinear patterns forecasting). Our empirical results demonstrated that the hybrid model outperforms three individual models, the EKF, MCF, and pure SVM models. These results revealed that neither the MCF model nor the SVM model can capture all of the patterns in the option data. Only the hybrid model can significantly reduce the overall forecasting errors.

The remainder of the paper is organized as follows. Section 2 describes the option price modelling and forecasting methods, including the BS model, the MCF, the SVM and the hybrid models. Section 3 describes the data used in the study, and displays the empirical results with discuss of our empirical findings. Conclusions are given in Section 4.

2   Option Price Modelling and Forecasting

2.1   Black-Scholes Model

Black and Scholes [1] established the price of an European call option through a well known formula, which is the solution to a second order partial differential equation. This closed analytical solution conferred elegance to the proposed formulation and multiplied in extensive and complementary studies. Black and Scholes [1] assumed that the underlying stock price follows a geometric Brownian motion with constant volatility,

$$\frac{dS}{S} = \mu dt + \sigma dW_t, \tag{1}$$

where μ is the expected return and W_t is the Brownian motion. In their paper, Black and Scholes derived the following partial differential equation which governs prices of a call option or a put option,

$$\frac{\partial f}{\partial t} + rS\frac{\partial f}{\partial S} + \frac{1}{2}\sigma^2 S^2 \frac{\partial^2 f}{\partial S^2} = rf, \tag{2}$$

where r is the riskless interest rate or discount rate. The solutions for the call and put option prices are thus

$$C = SN(d_1) - Ke^{-r\tau}N(d_2), \tag{3}$$
$$P = -SN(-d_1) + Ke^{-r\tau}N(-d_2), \tag{4}$$

where C is the call option price, P the put option price, K the strike price, and $\tau = T - t$ the maturity. Parameters d_1 and d_2 are as follows:

$$d_1 = \frac{\ln(S/K) + (r + \sigma^2/2)\tau}{\sigma\sqrt{\tau}}, \tag{5}$$
$$d_2 = d_1 - \sigma\sqrt{\tau}. \tag{6}$$

2.2   Monte Carlo Filters

BS formula in the previous section can be represented as a state-space form:

$$C_t, P_t = F(S_t, K, \tau, r(t), \sigma(t)) + \epsilon_t,$$
$$r(t) = r(t-1) + \varsigma_t,$$
$$\sigma(t) = \sigma(t-1) + \eta_t,$$

where r, σ can be viewed as the hidden states. C_t, P_t the output observations are a nonlinear function of $S_t, K, \tau, r(t), \sigma(t)$. S_t, τ, K are treated as the parameters or the input signals. Consequently, an EKF or MCF can be employed to infer the latent states and makes predictions.

In the following we focus on the estimation of states and predictions of future option prices. The Bayesian state space representation of the nonlinear BS model is given by an initial distribution $p(x_0)$, a measurement density $p(y_t|x_t,\theta)$ and a transition density $p(x_t|x_{t-1},\theta)$,

$$x_t|x_{t-1} \sim p(x_t|x_{t-1},\theta), \tag{7}$$

$$y_t|x_t \sim p(y_t|x_t,\theta), \tag{8}$$

$$x_0 \sim p(x_0), \qquad t = 1, ..., T, \tag{9}$$

where $x_t = (r_t, \sigma_t)$, $\theta = (S_t, \tau, K)$, $y_t = (C_t + \epsilon_t^1, P_t + \epsilon_t^2)$, $\epsilon_t^1, \epsilon_t^2 \sim N(0,1)$, and $\epsilon_t^1, \epsilon_t^2$ are independent measurement noises.

The causality structure of this model can be easily represented through a Directed Acyclic Graph, and under the previous assumptions the filtering and prediction densities can be simplified as follows:

$$p(x_t|y_{1:t},\theta) = \frac{p(y_t|x_t,\theta)p(x_t|y_{1:t-1},\theta)}{p(y_t|y_{1:t-1},\theta)}, \tag{10}$$

$$p(x_t|y_{1:t-1},\theta) = \int_{\mathcal{X}} p(x_t|x_{t-1},\theta)p(x_{t-1}|y_{1:t-1},\theta)dx_{t-1}, \tag{11}$$

where $p(y_t|x_t,\theta)$ is the likelihood, and $p(x_t|x_{t-1},\theta)$ is the predictive distribution of latent states.

At each step $t+1$, as a new observation y_{t+1} becomes available, we are interested in filtering the hidden variables and make a prediction. In particular, we want to approximate the prediction and filtering densities given in equations (11) and (10) by means of sequential Monte Carlo methods. Assume that a weighted sample $\{x_t^i, w_t^i\}_{i=1}^N$ has been drawn from the filtering density at time t. Each simulated value x_t^i is called "particle" and the particles set, $\{x_t^i, w_t^i\}_{i=1}^N$, can be viewed as a random discretization of the state space $\mathcal{X}$, with associated weights w_t^i, and the empirical filtering density can be written as

$$\widehat{p}(x_t|y_{1:t},\theta) = \sum_{i=1}^N w_t^i \delta_{x_t^i}(dx_t). \tag{12}$$

It is possible to approximate, by means of this particle set, the prediction density given in equation (11) as follows:

$$p(x_{t+1}|y_{1:t},\theta) = \int_{\mathcal{X}} p(x_{t+1}|x_t,\theta)p(x_t|y_{1:t},\theta)dx_t \simeq \sum_{i=1}^N w_t^i p(x_{t+1}|x_t^i,\theta), \tag{13}$$

which is called empirical prediction density and is denoted by $\widehat{p}(x_{t+1}|y_{1:t},\theta)$. Assume now that the quantity $E(f(x_{t+1}|y_{1:t+1}))$ is of interest. It can be evaluated numerically by a Monte Carlo sample $\{x_{t+1}^i, w_{t+1}^i\}_{i=1}^N$ drawn from the filtering distribution

$$E(f(x_{t+1})|y_{1:t+1}) \simeq \frac{\frac{1}{N}\sum_{i=1}^N f(x_{t+1}^i)w_{t+1}^i}{\frac{1}{N}\sum_{i=1}^N w_{t+1}^i}.$$

For more details of Monte Carlo filters, we refer to [7,9].

2.3   Support Vector Machines

The support vector machines (SVMs) were proposed by Vapnik [14]. Based on the structured risk minimization (SRM) principle, SVMs seek to minimize an upper bound of the generalization error instead of the empirical error as in other neural networks. Additionally, the SVMs models generate the regress function by applying a set of high dimensional linear functions. The SVM regression function is formulated as follows:

$$y = w\phi(x) + b, \tag{14}$$

where $\phi(x)$ is called the feature, which is nonlinear mapped from the input space x to the future space. The coefficients w and b are estimated by minimizing

$$R(C) = C\frac{1}{N}\sum_{i=1}^N L_\varepsilon(d_i, y_i) + \frac{1}{2}||w||^2, \tag{15}$$

where

$$L_\varepsilon(d, y) = \begin{cases} |d - y| - \varepsilon & |d - y| \geq \varepsilon, \\ 0 & \text{others,} \end{cases} \tag{16}$$

where both C and ε are prescribed parameters. The first term $L_\varepsilon(d, y)$ is called the ε-intensive loss function. The d_i is the actual option price in the ith period. This function indicates that errors below ε are not penalized. The term $\frac{C}{N}\sum_{i=1}^N L_\varepsilon(d_i, y_i)$ is the empirical error. The second term, $\frac{1}{2}||w||^2$, measures the smoothness of the function. C evaluates the trade-off between the empirical risk and the smoothness of the model. Introducing the positive slack variables ξ and ξ^*, which represent the distance from the actual values to the corresponding boundary values of ε-tube. Equation (15) is transformed to the following constrained formation:

$$\min_{w,b,\xi,\xi^*} R(w,\xi,\xi^*) = \frac{1}{2}w^T w + C\left(\sum_{i=1}^N(\xi_i + \xi_i^*).\right) \tag{17}$$

Subject to

$$w\phi(x_i) + b_i - d_i \leq \varepsilon + \xi_i^*, \tag{18}$$

$$d_i - w\phi(x_i) - b_i \leq \varepsilon + \xi_i, \tag{19}$$

$$\xi_i, \xi_i^* \geq 0. \tag{20}$$

After taking the Lagrangian and conditions for optimality, one obtain the dual representation of the model:

$$y = f(x, \alpha, \alpha^*) = \sum_{i=1}^{N} (\alpha_i - \alpha_i^*) K(x, x_i) + b, \tag{21}$$

where $K(x, x_i)$ is called the kernel function. α_i, α_i^* are the solution to the dual problem and b follows from the complementarity Karush-Kuhn-Tucker (KKT) conditions.

2.4 Hybrid Approaches

The hybrid prediction model of call option price C_t can be represented as follows: (similar for put price P_t)

$$\widetilde{C_t} = \widetilde{BS_t} + \widetilde{f_t}, \tag{22}$$

where $\widetilde{BS_t}$ is the MCF prediction based on Black-Scholes, $\widetilde{f_t}$ the nonlinear SVM prediction, and $\widetilde{C_t}$ the overall prediction. Let δ_t represent the residual between the actual option price and the MCF at time t, namely,

$$\delta_t = C_t - \widetilde{BS_t}. \tag{23}$$

The residuals are fed to the SVM, which further reduces the prediction errors, that is,

$$\delta_t = \widetilde{f}(S_t/K, T - t, \delta_{t-1}) + \varepsilon_t, \tag{24}$$

where ε_t is the final residual.

3 Experimental Results and Analysis

The empirical data used in this research are the option transaction data on the Taiwan composite stock index (TWSI) traded in Taiwan Futures Exchange (TWIFEX). We studied the transaction data of call and put option prices from 16 September 2004 to 14 June 2005 with expiration on 15 June 2005. There are 184 observations. This study chooses three types of options. Data with $K = 5800$ represents the in-the-money options for call options in the sample period; data with $K = 6000$ approximates the at-the-money options, while data with $K = 6200$ represents the out-of-money options in the sample period.

In this study, we consider the one-step-ahead forecasting because one-step-ahead forecasting can prevent problems associated with cumulative errors from the previous period for out-of-sample forecasting. The EKF, MCF models are trained in a sequential manner, while the SVM model is trained in a batch manner, that is, 100 data points before the day of prediction are treated as the training data set, and we used daily option closing prices in the remanding eighty days of the data series to evaluate the performances of the various models.

Traditional performance indices such as MSE (mean-squared error), RMSE (root-mean-squared error), MAE (mean absolute error), and MAPE (mean absolute percent error), can be used as measures of forecasting accuracy. In this study, we use RMSE as the performance index, which is shown blow:

$$RMSE = \left(\frac{1}{N} \sum_{t=1}^{N} (d_t - \widehat{d}_t)^2 \right)^{1/2}, \tag{25}$$

where N is the number of forecasting periods, d_i is the actual option price at period t, and $\widehat{d}_t$ is the forecasting option price at period t.

We compare six forecasting model in this paper, the trivial model, EKF, MCF, pure SVM, EKF+SVM, and the new hybrid model. The trivial model takes the current option price as the next day's prediction. The MCF model uses 100 particles for filtering and predictions, and the parameters used in the SVM model are set as follows: $C = 10^4$, $\varepsilon = 0.01$, and $\sigma = 0.1$ for the Gaussian Kernel.

Table 1 shows the forecasting performance of the trivial model, EKF, MCF, pure SVM, EKF+SVM, and the new hybrid model for call option prices with different types of options, while Table 2 provides the performance of these models on predicting put option prices. The actual prices, predicted values and model residuals of various models under the strike price of $K = 6000$ are displayed in Figures 1-3 for reference.

Table 1. Forecasting Performance of Every Model on the Three Call Options

	Out-the-Money $K = 6200$	At-the-Money $K = 6000$	In-the-Money $K = 5800$
Trivial Predictions	0.01600	0.02157	0.02485
EKF Predictions	0.01653	0.01945	0.02049
MCF Predictions	0.01039	0.01085	0.01239
Pure SVM	0.02504	0.03757	0.03309
EKF+SVM	0.01082	0.01708	0.01422
New Hybrid Mode Predictions	0.00289	0.00233	0.00227

The results in Table 1 and 2 indicated that the EKF model does not necessarily yield favorable forecasting results than the trivial prediction model. Sometimes the EKF predictions are even inferior to the trivial prediction method. The performance of the pure SVM is similar, also slightly inferior to the trivial prediction method.

Due to that the BS model is a quite nonlinear model, the linearized version of the EKF model is not a good approximation. As indicated in Table 1 and 2, due to the superior capability to infer two state variables in the nonlinear BS model, the MCF model with just 100 particles systematically outperform the trivial, EKF, and pure SVM models.

Table 2. Forecasting Performance of Every Model on the Three Put Options

	In-the-Money $K = 6200$	At-the-Money $K = 6000$	Out-the-Money $K = 5800$
Trivial Predictions	0.02732	0.02463	0.02059
EKF Predictions	0.02209	0.01965	0.01705
MCF Predictions	0.01102	0.01036	0.00966
Pure SVM	0.04472	0.04382	0.03309
EKF+SVM	0.02719	0.01431	0.00849
New Hybrid Model Predictions	0.00375	0.00246	0.00294

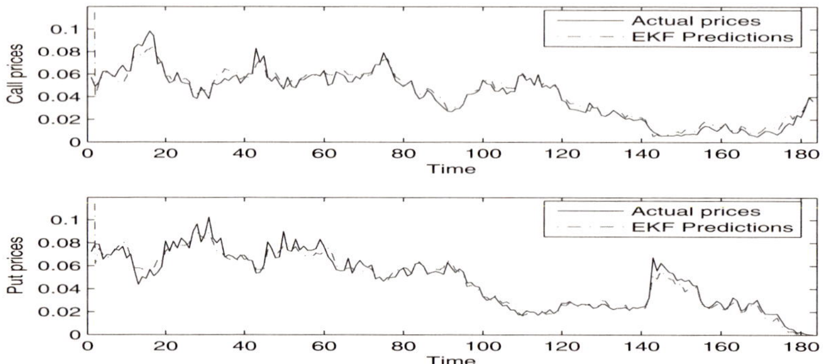

Fig. 1. EKF predictions on the option prices of $K = 6000$: This figure displays predictions of the EKF on the option prices of $K = 6000$ over the sample period

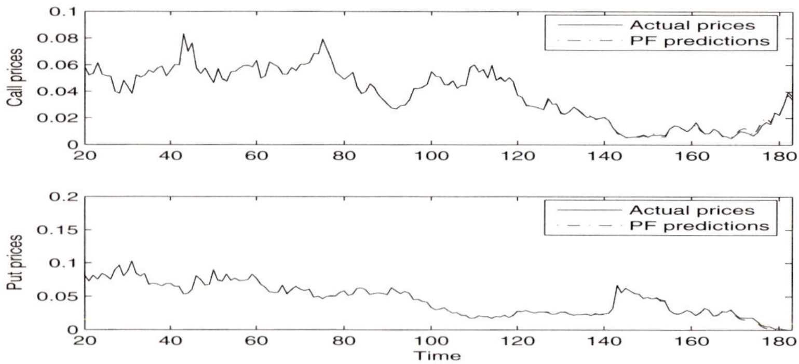

Fig. 2. Monte Carlo filter (Particle filter) predictions on the option prices of $K = 6000$: This figure displays MCF predictions on the option prices of $K = 6000$ over the sample period

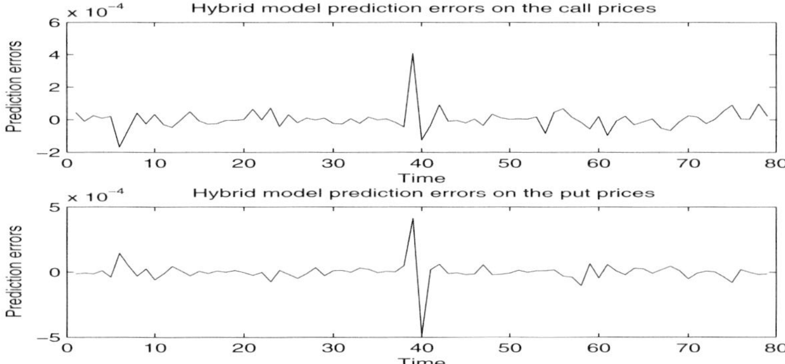

Fig. 3. Final errors of the hybrid model predictions on the option prices of $K = 6000$: This figure displays final errors of the hybrid model predictions on the option prices of $K = 6000$ over the sample period

In two types of hybrid models, EKF+SVM and MCF+SVM, our empirical results indicated that SVM can significantly improve the performance of the original model. The best performance is achieved by combining MCF with SVM. MCF+SVM outperformed the MCF model in terms of all three options. These results revealed that none of the four individual models can capture all of the nonlinear patterns in the option data. Hybrid forecasting is a good strategy.

4   Conclusion

This study proposes to combine a Monte Carlo filter with an support vector machine as an option price predictor. The Monte Carlo filter serves as a state estimator and a predictor for the BS model, and the nonlinear price patterns which can't be captured by the BS model is further captured by the support vector machine.

For more than half a century, the Kalman filter and the extended Kalman filter have dominated many areas of time series forecasting, especially state space models. However, options are nonlinear financial instruments. Their price dynamics are quite nonlinear, and thus linear prediction tools like the Kalman filter and extended Kalman filter are not a good choice for online forecasting. Recently many nonparametric regression methods such as SVM are employed to do the forecasting, but these models do not capture an important financial characteristic–latent volatility of an option, and thus their performances are not satisfactory. Combining Monte Carlo filters with SVMs is a novel strategy proposed by this article. Its performance is promising.

The powerful framework established in this study can also applied to other online forecasting problems. A challenging future task is the Bayesian selection of optimal weighting between the MCF model and the SVM model by data, and to train the SVM by a Bayesian method to adjust its internal parameters.

Acknowledgment

This work was supported in part by the National Science Foundation of Taiwan (NSC 95-2416-H-018-012).

References

1. Black, F. and Scholes, M. S., The pricing of options and corporate liabilities. Journal of Political Economy. **81** (1973), 637–654.
2. Clemen, R., Combining forecasts: a review and annotated bibliography with discussion. International Journal of Forecasting. **5** (1989), 559–608.
3. Cristianini, N. and Shawe-Taylor, J., An Introduction to Support Vector Machines. Cambridge University Press. (2000)
4. Doucet, A., Freitas, N., and Gordon, N. J., editors. Sequential Monte Carlo Methods in Practice. Springer-Verlag. (2001)
5. Gordon, N. J., Salmond, D. J., and Smith, A. F. M., Novel approach to nonlinear/non-Gaussian Bayesian state estimation. IEEE Proceedings. **140(2)** (1993), 107–113.
6. Grace, B. K., Black-Scholes option pricing via genetic algorithms, Applied Economics Letters. **7(2)** (2000), 129–132
7. Kitagawa, G., Monte Carlo filter and smoother for non-Gaussian nonlinear state space models. Journal of Computational and Graphical Statistics. **5** (1996), 1–25.
8. Makridakis, S., Why combining works?. International Journal of Forecasting. **5** (1989), 601–603.
9. Merwe, R., Doucet, A., Freitas, N., and Wan, E., The unscented particle filter. Technical Report CUED/F-INFENG/TR 380, Cambridge University Engineering Department. (2000)
10. Pires, M. M., Marwala, T., American option pricing using multi-layer perceptron and support vector machine, IEEE International Conference on Systems, Man and Cybernetics. **2** (2004), 1279–1285.
11. Pitt, M. K. and Shephard, N., Filtering via simulation: Auxiliary particle filters. Journal of the American Statistical Association. **94(446)** (1999), 590–599.
12. Schoelkopf, B., Burges, C. J. C., and Smola, A. J., Advances in kernel methods–support vector learning. MIT Press, Cambridge, MA. (1999)
13. Terui, N. and Dijk, H. K., Combined forecasts from linear and nonlinear time series models. International Journal of Forecasting. **18** (2002), 421–438.
14. Vapnik, V. N., The Nature of Statistical Learning Theory, New York, Springer-Verlag. (1995)
15. Wu, H. C., Pricing European options based on the fuzzy pattern of Black-Scholes formula, Computers & Operations Research. **31(7)** (2004), 1069–1081.
16. Yao, J. T., Li, Y. L., and Tan, C. L., Option price forecasting using neural networks, Omega-International Journal of Management Science. **28(4)** (2000), 455–466.
17. Zhang, G. P., Times series forecasting using a hybrid ARIMA and neural network model. Neurocomputing. **50** (2003), 159–175.

Domain Knowledge Assimilation by Learning Complex Concepts

Tuan Trung Nguyen

Polish-Japanese Institute of Information Technology
ul. Koszykowa 86, 02-008 Warsaw, Poland
`nttrung@pjwstk.edu.pl`

Abstract. Domain, or background, knowledge has proven to be a key component in the development of high-performance classification systems, especially when the objects of interest exhibit complex internal structures, as in the case of images, time series data or action plans. This knowledge usually comes in extrinsic forms such as human expert advices, often contain complex concepts expressed in quasi-natural descriptive languages and need to be assimilated by the classification system. This paper presents a framework for the assimilation of such knowledge, equivalent to matching different ontologies of complex concepts, using rough mereology theory and rough set methods. We show how this framework allows a learning system to acquire complex, highly structured concepts from an external expert in an intuitive and fully interactive manner. We also argue the need to focus on expert's knowledge elicited from outlier or novel samples, which we deem have a crucial impact on the classification process. Experiments on a large collection of handwritten digits are discussed.

Keywords: Rough mereology, concept approximation, ontology matching, handwritten digit recognition, outlier samples.

1 Introduction

A machine learning problem can be viewed as a search within a space of hypotheses H for a hypothesis h that best fits a set of training samples T. Amongst the most popular approaches to such problems are e.g. statistical learning, decision trees, neural networks or genetic algorithms, commonly referred to as *inductive* learning methods, i.e. methods that generalize from observed training examples by finding features that empirically distinguish positive from negative training examples. Though these methods allow for highly effective learning systems, there often exist proven bounds on the performance of the classifiers they can construct, especially when the samples involved exhibit complex internal structures, such as optical characters, facial images or time series data. It is believed that *analytical* learning methods based on structural analysis of training examples are more suitable in dealing with such samples. In practice, best performances are obtained using a combination of the two learning methods [5].

S. Greco et al. (Eds.): RSCTC 2006, LNAI 4259, pp. 617–626, 2006.

An analytical learning algorithm, in addition to the training set T and a hypothesis space H assume a *domain theory* D which carries prior knowledge about the samples being learned. The search is now for a hypothesis h that best fits T and at the same time conforms to D. In other words, a background or domain knowledge is available to the learning system and may help facilitate the search for the target hypothesis. One of the widely used approach to analytical learning is the *Explanation Based Learning* (EBL) method, which uses specific training examples to analyze, or explain, which features are relevant or irrelevant to the target classification function. The explanations therefore can serve as *search control knowledge* by establishing initial search points or by subsequent altering search directions. In this paper, we investigate an architecture in which the explanation comes from an external, possibly human, expert. Moreover, the explanations will not come as *a priori*, but will be provided by the expert in a two way dialog along with the evolution of the learning system.

One of the first and major challenges of this approach is that the knowledge employed by the external expert is often expressed in a descriptive language, called a *foreign language* L_f, which may contain natural language constructs. This language is usually alien to the learning system, which has its own knowledge encoded in a *domestic language* L_d. This is because the expert and the system have different knowledge *ontologies*, meaning they rely on different *concepts* and *relations* [2]. An *ontology matching*, i.e. a mapping between concepts and, in a further step, relations used by the expert and the learning system is needed.

The expert knowledge ontology, similarly to the samples to which it applies, will be highly structured. More specifically, it has the form of a *lattice*, or acyclic tangled trees of concepts, representing different aspects of the expert's perception about training samples. One can view these concepts as abstract information granules which, together with binding relations amongst them, form the expert's reasoning about the samples. These concepts and, in a further steps, their binding relations have to be translated, or in other words, *approximated* by the learning system by means of its domestic expressions. Examples:

- *SquareFace*(Ed)$\equiv$ (Ed.getFace().Width - Ed.getFace().Height $\leq$ 2.0 cm)
- *IsEclipse*(p)$\equiv$ (s=p.GetSun())$\wedge$(m=p.GetMoon())$\wedge$(s$\cap$m.Area$\geq$ s.Area·0.9)

A key issue is that although the concepts and relations get approximated, their hierarchical structure remains intact in translation. This aims to allow parent concepts be approximated using the approximations of children concepts, essentially building an *approximate reasoning scheme*. We will show how this multi layered approximation can be performed using rough inclusion measures, rough set decision rules and how to ensure the quality of approximation using tools based on rough mereology theory.

The expert's advices are based, in a natural way, on his perception on training samples. Human perception and behavior are subject of extensive research of Cognitive Science and Computational Psychology. We will discuss resemblances and common points of interest between complex concepts' approximation and popular cognitive architectures.

Another important issue is the focus we place on the analysis of atypical, or outlier samples. Recent developments in pattern recognition clearly indicate they are crucial to search refining. They allow to better understand the inter-class dependencies of the sample collection and help to steer the search process through vital points in the search spaces. Together with the explanation based learning approach these outliers, borderline samples often prove to be key in forming effective domain reasoning schemes.

2   Knowledge Elicitation from External Expert

We assume an architecture that allows a learning recognition system to consult a human expert for advices on how to analyze a particular sample or a set of samples. Typically this is done in an iterative process, with the system subsequently incorporating knowledge elicited on samples that could not be properly classified in previous attempts.

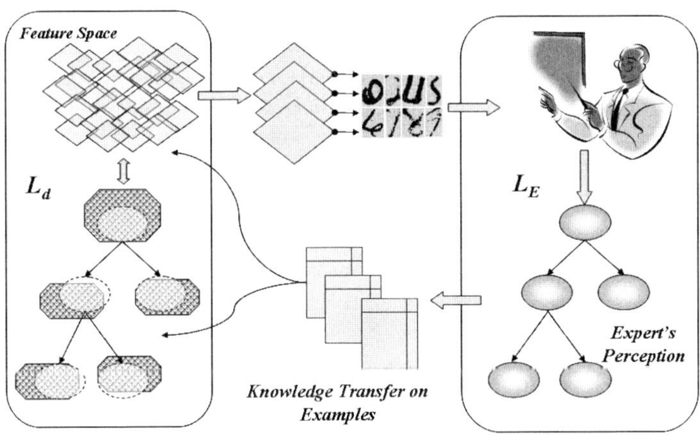

Fig. 1. System's Overview

2.1   Ontology Matching

The knowledge on training samples that comes from a expert obviously reflects his perception about the samples. The language used to describe this knowledge is a component of the expert's ontology which is an integral part of his perception. In a broad view, an ontology consists of a vocabulary, a set of concepts organized in some kind of structures, and a set of binding relations amongst those concepts [2]. We assume that the expert's ontology when reasoning about complex structured samples will have the form of a multi-layered hierarchy, or a lattice, of concepts. A concept on a higher level will be synthesized from its children concepts and their binding relations. The reasoning thus proceeds from the most primitive notions at the lowest levels and work bottom-up towards more complex concepts at higher levels.

As the human perception is inherently tolerant to variation and deviation, the concepts and relations in his ontology are approximate by design. To use the terms of granular computing, they are information granules that encapsulate the autonomous yet interdependent aspects of human perception.

The knowledge elicitation process assumes that samples for which the learning system deems it needs additional explanations are submitted to the expert, which returns not only their correct class identity, but also an explanation on *why*, and perhaps more importantly, *how* he arrived at his decision. This explanation is passed in the form of a rule:

$$[CLASS(u) = k] \equiv \Im(EFeature_1(u), ..., EFeature_n(u))$$

where $EFeature_i$ represents the expert's perception of some characteristics of the sample u, while synthesis operator $\Im$ represents his perception of some relations between these characteristics. In a broader view, $\Im$ constitutes of a *relational structure* that encompasses the hierarchy of experts' concepts expressed by $EFeature_i$.

The ontology matching aims to translate the components of the expert's ontology, such as $EFeature_i$ and binding relations embedded in the $\Im$ structure, expressed in the foreign language L_f, which may have the form of, e.g.

"A six is a digit that has a closed belly below a slanted neck."
$[CLASS(u) = {}^{\prime}6^{\prime}] \equiv a, b$ are parts of u; "Below"(b,a); "SStroke"(a); "CBelly"(b)

into the patterns familiar to the learning system, which involve, e.g. pixels counting or calculations of density or mass center of pixel collections.

The translation must be done so as to preserve the hierarchical structure of the advice, at the same time allow for a flexible matching of a variations of similar domestic patterns to a foreign concept, i.e. the translation result should not be a single patterns, but rather a collection or cluster of patterns.

Single Concept Approximation. A foreign concept C is approximated by a domestic pattern (or a set of patterns) p in term of a rough inclusion measure $Match(p, C) \in [0, 1]$. Such measures take root in the theory of rough mereology [8], and are designed to deal with the notion of inclusion to a degree. An example of concept inclusion measures would be:

$$Match(p, C) = \frac{|\{u \in T : Found(p, u) \wedge Fit(C, u)\}|}{|\{u \in T : Fit(C, u)\}|}$$

where T is a common set of samples used by both the system and the expert to communicate with each other on the nature of expert's concepts, $Found(p, u)$ means a pattern p is present in u and $Fit(C, u)$ means u is regarded by the expert as fit to his concept C.

Our principal goal is, for each expert's explanation, find sets of patterns Pat, $Pat_1,...,Pat_n$ and a relation $\Im_d$ so as to satisfy the following *quality requirement*:

$$\textbf{if } (\forall i : Match(Pat_i, EFeature_i) \geq p_i) \wedge (Pat = \Im_d(Pat_1, ..., Pat_n))$$
$$\textbf{then } Quality(Pat) > \alpha$$

where $p, p_i : i \in \{1, .., n\}$ and α are certain cutoff thresholds, while the *Quality* measure, intended to verify if the target pattern *Pat* fits into the expert's concept of sample class k, can be any, or combination, of popular quality criteria such as *support, coverage,* or *confidence* [9].

In other words, we seek to translate the expert's knowledge into the domestic language so that to generalize the expert's reasoning to the largest possible number of training samples. More refined versions of the inclusion measures would involve additional coefficients attached to e.g. *Found* and *Fit* test function. Adjustment of these coefficients based on feedback from actual data may help optimize the approximation quality.

The use of rough inclusion measures allows for a very flexible approximation of foreign concept. For instance, a stroke at 85 degree to the horizontal in an image can still be regarded as a vertical stroke, though obviously not a 'pure' one. Instead of just answering in a '*Yes/No*' fashion, the expert may express his degrees of belief using such terms as '*Strong*', '*Fair*', or '*Weak*'.

Domestic patterns satisfying the defined quality requirement can be quickly found, taking into account that sample tables submitted to experts are usually not very large. The most effective strategies seem to be genetic algorithms equipped with some greedy heuristics.For example, [7] reported using this kind of tools and methods for a similar problem.

Relations Between Features. Relations between expert's features may include concepts such as '*Above*', '*Below*' or simply '*Near*'. They express not only expert's perceptions about particular concepts, but also the interdependencies among them. Similarly to the stand-alone features, these relations can also be described by the expert with a degree of tolerance.

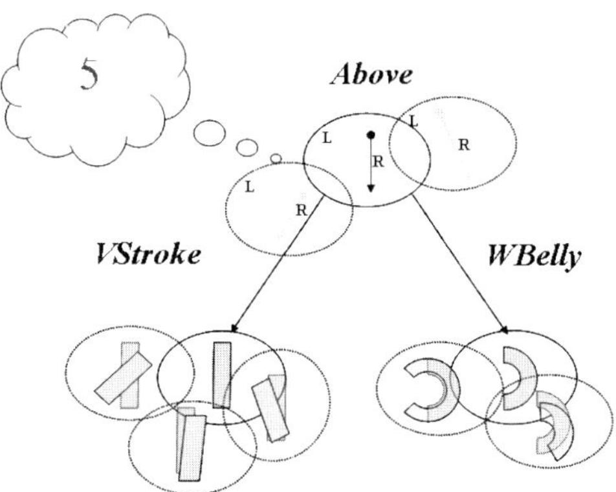

Fig. 2. Tolerant matching by expert

The approximation of these relations has been formalized within the framework of perception structures developed by Skowron [10]. A *perception structure* S, in a simpler form, is defined as:

$$S = (U, M, F, \models, p)$$

where U is a set of samples, F is a family of formulas expressed in domestic language that describe certain features of the samples and M is a family of relational structures in which these formulas can be evaluated, while $p \colon U \to M \times F$ is a *perception function* such that $\forall u \in U : p_1(u) \models p_2(u)$ (p_1 and p_2 are the first and second component projections of p) which means that $p_2(u)$ is satisfied (is true) in the relational structure $p_1(u)$. This may express that some relations among features within samples are observed.

Perception structures, following natural constructs in the expert's foreign language, can involve tolerant matching. Two relational structures might be considered approximately *the same* if they allow for similar formulas to yield similar results in majority of cases when these formulas are applicable.

Layered Approximate Reasoning Paradigm. Let's observe that the approximation quality requirement previously introduced yields a powerful feature of the multi-layered approximation scheme. First, as the target pattern Pat retains its quality regardless of deviations of input patterns, the approximation is *robust* with regards to noisy input data or imperfect performances on lower levels. This also means high reusability of the same framework on changing or evolving data. Second, we have the *global stability*, which guarantees that if only some input patterns Pat'_i are equally "close" or "similar" to $EFeature_i$, then the target pattern $Pat' = \Im_d(Pat'_1, ..., Pat'_n)$ will meet the same quality requirements as Pat to a satisfactory degree. This leads to an approximation of $EFeature_i$ which is *independent* from particular patterns Pat_i. The hierarchy scheme itself therefore becomes a high level search knowledge control mechanism that allow for the classifier system, when conditions are met, to bypass intermediate levels of reasoning without sacrificing too much on approximation quality.

It is noteworthy to observe that our approach, based on approximate reasoning scheme and granular computing, though developed independently, have much in common with theories and methods of Cognitive Science. For example, one of the most fundamental assumption of Unified Theory of Cognition [6] stipulates that human perception are inherently hierarchical and theories on such perception should be deliberately approximate. Most, if not all, cognitive architectures such as SOAR, ACT-R, Prodigy or recently developed ICARUS [4] are based on *knowledge and data chunking*, which follows the hierarchical structure of human perception. Chunking resembles in many ways the layered reasoning paradigm. Many other common issues such as search control, target function learning or external background knowledge assimilation can also be observed.

On the other hand, cognitive architectures seem not to incorporate the approximation of internal predicates or goal seeking strategies to a large extent,

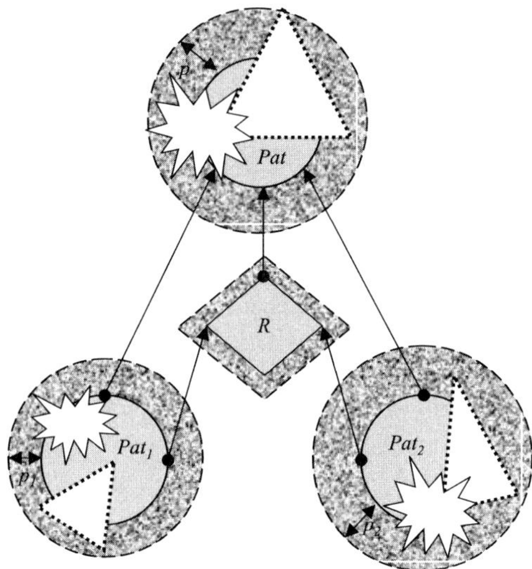

Fig. 3. Quality constraints

while the approximation of concepts and their binding relations is at the core of our approach.

2.2   Analysis of Outlier Cases

Our architecture typically asks for the expert's additional knowledge on samples which escaped previous classification attempts. This eventually results in asking the expert's help on "hard" samples that had defied much of our classification efforts, mainly because they differ to a significant extent from other samples of their class, or belong to a boundary region between several classes.

Outliers are kind of atypical samples that either are markedly different from the rest of their group in terms of some similarity measures, or behave very differently from the norm [1]. These samples previously tended to be treated as bias or noisy input data and were frequently discarded or suppressed in the learning process. However, there is an increasing effort to develop better methods for their analysis, based on the observation that they often carry useful diagnosis on the characteristics of the sample domain and, if properly analyzed, may provide valuable guidance in discovering the causalities underlying the behavior of a learning system. As such, they may prove to be valuable as additional search control knowledge. Most popular measures to detect outliers can be found in [3].

While outlier detection does not pose significant computation problems, their effective use in eliciting additional domain knowledge is believed difficult without support of a human expert.

Having established a mechanism for eliciting expert's knowledge as described above, we can develop outlier detection tests that might be completely independent from the existing similarity measures within the learning system as follows.

For a given training samples u^*, we ask the expert for his explanation on u^* and received a foreign knowledge structure $\Im(u^*)$. Next, we approximate $\Im(u^*)$ under restrictive matching degrees to ensure only the immediate neighborhood of u^* is investigated. Let's say the result of such an approximation is a pattern (or set of pattern) p_u^*. It is now sufficient to check $Coverage(p_u^*)$. If this coverage is high, it signifies that u^* may bear significant information that is also found in many other samples. The sample u^* therefore cannot be regarded as an outlier despite the fact that there may not be many other samples in its vicinity in terms of existing domestic distance measures of the learning system. This test shows that outlier analysis and expert's elicited knowledge are complementary to each other.

In our architecture, outliers may be detected as samples that defied previous classification efforts, or samples that pass the above described outlier test, but may also be selected by the expert himself. In this way, we can benefit from the best of both sources of knowledge.

3   Implementation

The proposed framework and methods have been verified with a OCR system working on the NIST SD 19 handwritten digits. The domestic representational language of digit images involves various simple pixel evaluation functions and the Loci coding scheme, which reflects the local and global topological morphology or strokes in an image.

The expert's advices employ concepts such as *'Circle'*, *'Slanted Strokes'* or *'West Open Belly'*. The expert will explain what he means when he says, e.g. *'Circle'*, by providing a decision table (U, d) with reference samples, where d is the expert decision to which degree he considers that *'Circle'* appears in samples $u \in U$. The samples in U may be provided by the expert, or may be picked up by him among samples explicitly submitted by the system, e.g. those that had been misclassified in previous attempts.

Table 1. Perceived features

	$Circle$
u_1	$Strong$
u_2	$Weak$
...	...
u_n	$Fair$

Table 2. Translated features

	#NESW	Circle
u_1	252	$Strong$
u_2	4	$Weak$
...	...	...
u_n	90	$Fair$

We then attempt to find domestic feature(s) that approximates these degrees of belief using, among other means, genetic algorithms. In this particular example, such feature may be the number of pixels that have black neighbors in all four directions (See Tab. 2).

Having approximated the expert's features $EFeature_i$, we can try to translate his relation $\Im$ into our $\Im_d$ by asking the expert to go through U and provide us with the additional attributes of how strongly he considers the presence of $EFeature_i$ and to what degree he believes the relation $\Im$ holds (See Tab. 3).

Table 3. Perceived relations

	$VStroke$	$WBelly$	$Above$
u_1	$Strong$	$Strong$	$Strong$
u_2	$Fair$	$Weak$	$Weak$
...	...	...	...
u_n	$Fair$	$Fair$	$Weak$

Table 4. Translated relations

	#V_S	#NES	$S_y < B_y$	$Above$
u_1	0.8	0.9	$(Strong, 1.0)$	$(Strong, 0.9)$
u_2	0.9	1.0	$(Weak, 0.1)$	$(Weak, 0.1)$
...	...	...	...	...
u_n	0.9	0.6	$(Fair, 0.3)$	$(Weak, 0.2)$

We then replace the attributes corresponding to $EFeature_i$ with the rough inclusion measures of the domestic feature sets that approximate those concepts (computed in the previous step). In the next stage, we try to add other features, possibly induced from original domestic primitives, in order to approximate the decision d. Such a feature may be expressed by $S_y < B_y$, which tells whether the median center of the stroke is placed closer to the upper edge of the image than the median center of the belly. (See Tab. 4) Again, this task should be resolved by means of adaptive or evolutionary search strategies without too much computing burden, although it is more time-expensive.

The expert's perception *"A '6' is something that has a 'vertical stroke' 'above' a 'belly open to the west'"* is eventually approximated by a classifier in the form of a rule:

if $S(\#BL\_SL > 23)$ **AND** $B(\#NESW > 12\%)$ **AND** $S_y < B_y$ **then** CL='6',

where S and B are designations of pixel collections, #BL_SL and #NESW are numbers of pixels with particular Loci codes, and $S_y < B_y$ reasons about centers of gravity of the two collections.

We compared the performances gained by a standard learning approach with and without the aid of the domain knowledge. The additional knowledge, passed by a human expert on popular classes as well as some atypical samples allowed to reduce the time needed by the learning phase from 205 minutes to 168 minutes, which means an improvement of about 22 percent without loss in classification quality. In case of screening classifiers, i.e. those that decide a sample *does not* belong to given classes, the improvement is around 40 percent. The representational samples found are also slightly simpler than those computed without using the background knowledge.

Table 5. Comparison of performances

	No domain knowledge	With domain knowledge	Gain
Total learning time	205s	168s	22%
Negative classifier learning time	3.7s	2.2s	40%
Positive classifier learning time	28.2s	19.4s	31%
Skeleton graph size	3-5 nodes	2-5 nodes	

4 Conclusion

A formal framework based on multi-layered approximate reasoning schemes for the domain knowledge assimilation problem is proposed. We demonstrated that rough mereology theory and granular computing can be successfully used to transfer domain knowledge expressed in quasi-natural languages into domestic languages of computer learning system. A universal, robust and stable scheme for human-computer ontology matching in a clear, friendly interactive manner is also presented. We also argue that outlier analysis is key to successful domain knowledge elicitation whence elicited domain knowledge can help detect new outlier. Comparison of selected common aspects with cognitive theories and architectures has been outlined. Proposed methods have been verified by an OCR system working on a large handwritten digit dataset.

Acknowledgment. The author would like to express gratitude to Professor Andrzej Skowron for his insightful comments and his invaluable support during the work on this paper. This work has been partly supported by Grant 3 T11C 002 26 funded by the Ministry of Scientific Research and Information Technology of the Republic of Poland.

References

1. Charu C. Aggarwal and Philip S. Yu. Outlier detection for high dimensional data. In *Proceedings of the 2001 ACM SIGMOD International Conference on Management of Data*, pages 37–46, New York, NY, USA, 2001. ACM Press.
2. Dieter Fensel. *Ontologies: A Silver Bullet for Knowledge Management and Electronic Commerce*. Springer-Verlag New York, Inc., Secaucus, NJ, USA, 2003.
3. Victoria Hodge and Jim Austin. A survey of outlier detection methodologies. *Artif. Intell. Rev.*, 22(2):85–126, 2004.
4. P. Langley and J. E. Laird. Cognitive architectures: Research issues and challenges. *(Technical Report)*, 2002.
5. Tom M. Mitchell. *Machine Learning*. McGraw-Hill, New York, 1997.
6. Allen Newell. *Unified theories of cognition*. Harvard University Press, Cambridge, MA, USA, 1994.
7. L.S. Oliveira, R. Sabourin, F. Bortolozzi, and C.Y. Suen. Feature selection using multi-objective genetic algorithms for handwritten digit recognition. In *International Conference on Pattern Recognition (ICPR02)*, pages I: 568–571, 2002.
8. L. Polkowski and A. Skowron. Rough mereology: A new paradigm for approximate reasoning. *Journal of Approximate Reasoning*, 15(4):333–365, 1996.
9. L. Polkowski and A. Skowron. Constructing rough mereological granules of classifying rules and classifying algorithms. In B. Bouchon-Meunier et al, editor, *Technologies for Constructing Intelligent Systems I*, pages 57–70. Physica-Verlag, 2002.
10. A. Skowron. Rough sets in perception-based computing. In *First International Conference on Pattern Recognition and Machine Intelligence (PReMI'05)*. Springer-Verlag, 2005.

Learning Compound Decision Functions for Sequential Data in Dialog with Experts

Wojciech Jaworski

Faculty of Mathematics, Computer Science and Mechanics
Warsaw University, Banacha 2, 02-07 Warsaw, Poland
`wjaworski@mimuw.edu.pl`

Abstract. In this paper, we investigate the problem of learning the decision functions for sequential data describing complex objects that are composed of subobjects. The decision function maps sequence of attribute values into a relational structure, representing properties of the object described by the sequence. This relational structure is constructed in a way that allows us to answer questions from a given language. The decision function is constructed by means of rule system. The rules are learned incrementally in a dialog with an expert. We also present an algorithm that implements the rule system and we apply it to real life problems.

Keywords: Rough sets, Sequential pattern recognition.

Introduction

There are two types of sequential data:

- Data describing changes of objects in some evolving process.
- Data describing structural objects.

The first approach is suitable for physical phenomena, e.g., modeled by differential equations. In this case, surroundings of each point in the sequence is a state of object. The second approach is natural while analysing the data generated as the result of purposeful actions composing objects from simpler objects. Such a property have for example textual data, voice, recorded parameters of car on road.

In this paper, we investigate the problem of the decision function learning for data that belongs to the second mentioned type. The considered decision function maps any sequence of attribute values into a relational structure, representing properties of object described by the sequence. This relational structure is constructed in a way that allows us to answer questions from a given language. The decision function is constructed by means of a rule system. In a consequence, the decision function is compound (consists of vast number of rules), and has compound domain. So it belongs to a huge hypothesis space and according to statistical learning theory [11] cannot be learned only from data.

The function is learned in a dialog with an expert. The expert provides us the domain knowledge: He explains his decisions in natural language. We approximate, in a sense, his language by the rule system. The rule system must be compatible with the expert's way of thinking. Then the rules acquired from

S. Greco et al. (Eds.): RSCTC 2006, LNAI 4259, pp. 627–636, 2006.

the expert are tested on data. Finally, the expert is inquired about the cases than does not match to the rules or are classified improperly. In this way, we extract successive fragments of decision functions which converge to the ideal description of the problem.

Due to the sequential character of data the rule system differs from the one used with data represented by tables. Each object is described by a sequence of attribute values. Complex objects can be decomposed into simple ones, which correspond to the split of the attribute value sequence into smaller parts. However, the distance from the beginning of sequence does not distinguish objects. Decision rules are not applied to the attributes according to their absolute position in sequence. Only the relative position of attributes is important for the rule to recognize the pattern.

Rules are used to recognize objects. Successful rule application means that object described by its construction belongs to the upper approximation of the problem. Information about this object is added to the data as a new attribute. The relational structure that describes the object is assigned to the attribute. The other rules may use such an attribute to recognize more complex objects.

The problem discussed in the paper is relates to the objectives of the Information Extraction (IE) [2,6,10].

IE is a subdiscipline of the Natural Language Processing. Its task is to find information, in text written in a natural language, needed to fill a table with description of some event. The attributes of the event are defined a priori.

The main differences follow the characteristics of the data. IE bases on the fact that in modern languages words are marked out with spaces and meaning of ambiguous parts of document can be determined using heuristic methods [1].

Our aim is to process sequential data in general. This implies that we can't take advantage of any a priori defined partition of the data sequence. We concentrate on solving the problem of ambiguity without the necessity of choosing one out of the contradicting interpretations.

We discover the relational structures during the process of learning instead of using a prori defined table.

We adopted the idea of syntax and semantic parsers well known in computer science [3,4,5,8]. Yet we propose our own approach to representation of rules and parser (rule-applying algorithm).

In Section 1, we formally define objects and attributes. In Section 2, we describe rules system properties. In Section 3 and 4, we define rules. In Section 5, we discuss the representation of data. In Section 6, we propose efficient algorithm for applying rules. In Section 7, we discuss the problem of learning the decision rules. In Section 8, we present applications.

1   Objects, Attributes, Meanings and Relational Structures

We are given a set of *objects* $\mathcal{U}$, a set of *attributes* $\mathcal{A}$, a set of *meanings* $\mathcal{M}$ and a set of *relational structures* $\mathcal{E}$.

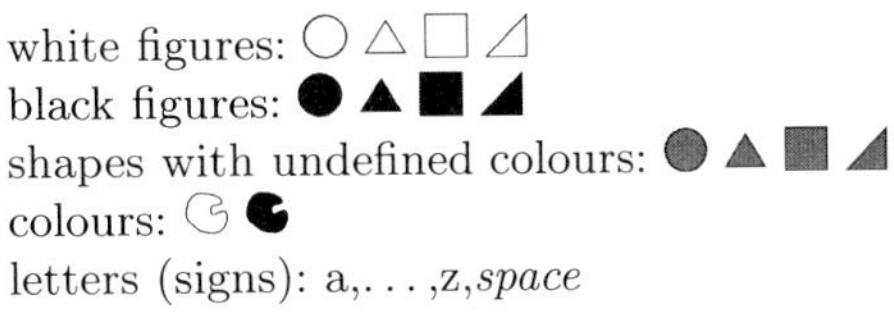

white figures: ○ △ □ ◁
black figures: ● ▲ ■ ◀
shapes with undefined colours: ● ▲ ▨ ◀
colours: ◔ ◖
letters (signs): a,. . .,z,*space*

Fig. 1. Example of the set of objects

The signature of every structure in $\mathcal{E}$ is identical to the signature of the language of questions, which is a set of sentences in some logic. Having a structure from $\mathcal{E}$ we can deduce answers to the questions expressed in the logic.

The example of the set of objects is presented on Fig. 1 and the example of corresponding relational structures is on Fig. 1.

constants: a,. . . , z, space, white, black, circle, triangle, square
unary relations: Shape, Colour
binary relations: Figure

Fig. 2. Signature for the set of relational structures

Each attribute $a \in \mathcal{A}$ is a function $a : \mathcal{U} \to V$, where V is the set of attribute values. Each meaning $e \in \mathcal{M}$ is a function $e : \mathcal{U} \to \mathcal{E}$. Only information defined by attributes from $\mathcal{A}$ is available about objects from $\mathcal{U}$. For each attribute a the function $h : \mathcal{A} \to \mathcal{M}$ returns $h(a)$ — the meaning of a.

We are given an infinite sequence of attributes $\{a_i\}_{i=-\infty}^{\infty}$, where $a_i : \mathcal{U} \to (V \cup \{\#\})$, and a finite set X of attribute value sequences for some elements of $\mathcal{U}$. Each value sequence is finite, i.e., for each $u \in \mathcal{U}$ there exists $n \in \mathbb{N}$ such, that for $0 < i \leq n$ we have $a_i(u) \neq \#$ and for $i > n$ $a_i(u) - \#$ and $a_i(u) - \#$, when $i \leq 0$. In other words, each sequence from X has a finite interval of values from V and every attribute beyond that interval is equal to $\#$.

$$V = \{\mathtt{a}, \ldots, \mathtt{z}, \mathtt{space}, \mathtt{colour}, \mathtt{shape}, \mathtt{figure}\}$$

Fig. 3. Set of attribute values

Objects in $\mathcal{U}$ have a hierarchical structure: $u \in \mathcal{U}$ may be composed of some $u_1, u_2, \ldots, u_k \in \mathcal{U}$. In terms of attributes' sequence it means that the whole sequence describes an object, every $a_i(u)$ describes an object, and every subsequence $\{a_i(u)\}_{i=k}^{n}$ may describe an object.

u_1 in Fig. 1 is composed of two smaller objects

- object ◖ described by sequence $\{a_1(u_1), \ldots, a_5(u_1)\}$ with associated meaning: Colour(black)
- object ● described by sequence $\{a_7(u_1), \ldots, a_{13}(u_1)\}$ with associated meaning: Shape(circle)

objects' ids	attributes													
	a_1	a_2	a_3	a_4	a_5	a_6	a_7	a_8	a_9	a_{10}	a_{11}	a_{12}	a_{13}	a_{14}
u_1	w	h	i	t	e		c	i	r	c	l	e	#	#
u_2	c	i	r	c	l	e	#	#	#	#	#	#	#	#
u_3	b	l	a	c	k		p	o	l	y	g	o	n	#
u_4	w	h	i	t	e		t	r	i	a	n	g	l	e

Fig. 4. Object descriptions in terms of attribute value sequences

We denote the object described by a single a_i as an *atomic object* and we assume that the meaning of atomic objects is a simple function of value of their attributes.

In our example meaning for a_i is equal to its value:

$$h(a_i)(u) = a_i(u).$$

We say that objects u_1, u_2 represented by sequences $\{a_{n+i}(u_1)\}_{i=0}^{k}$ and $\{a_{m+i}(u_2)\}_{i=0}^{k}$ are *indiscernible* if and only if $a_{n+i}(u_1) = a_{m+i}(u_2)$ for each i such that $0 \leq i \leq k$.

- $\{a_1(u_1), \ldots, a_{12}(u_1)\}$ defines $\circ$ in an exact way
- $\{a_1(u_2), \ldots, a_6(u_2)\}$ is incomplete, and thus does not distinguish $\circ$ and $\bullet$
- $\{a_1(u_3), \ldots, a_{13}(u_3)\}$ does not discern $\bullet$, $\blacktriangle$, $\blacksquare$ and $\blacktriangle$ because it is too general
- On the other hand our set of relational structures does not provide distinction between $\triangle$ and $\triangleleft$, so $\{a_1(u_4), \ldots, a_{14}(u_4)\}$ is as exact as possible definition of $\triangle$.

Information about objects from $\mathcal{U}$ is finite but it is not bounded. The number of attributes does not provide itself any useful information. Only the order of attributes is important.

2   Rule System

Our task is to discover the structure of objects from X having their description provided in terms of attributes.

We assume that elements of U are constructed out of some smaller objects. And these objects are represented by subsequences of elements of X. We recognize them by means of rules. The rule application can be interpreted as a process of object recognition. The rule recognizes the sequence of attribute values describing object and returns its meaning.

The rules can be divided into two parts: syntactical and semantic. Each syntactical rule recognizes sequence of attribute values and returns a value of new attribute constructed out from them. Any semantic rule operates on meanings of recognized sequence of attribute values and generates meaning for the newly constructed attribute.

We may derive the following rules for the example presented in previous section:

```
colour ::= w h i t e           _ → {Colour(white)}
colour ::= b l a c k           _ → {Colour(black)}
shape  ::= c i r c l e          _ → {Shape(circle)}
shape  ::= t r i a n g l e      _ → {Shape(triangle)}
shape  ::= p o l y g o n        _ → {Shape(circle), Shape(triangle), Shape(square)}
figure ::= colour space shape
figure ::= shape
```

$$\text{colour} ::= \text{w h i t e} \quad \_ \rightarrow \{\mathrm{Colour(white)}\}$$

figure ::= colour space shape $(C, \_, S) \rightarrow \bigcup_{\mathrm{Colour}(c)\in C} \bigcup_{\mathrm{Shape}(s)\in S} \{\mathrm{Figure}(c,s)\}$

figure ::= shape $\quad S \rightarrow \bigcup_{\mathrm{Shape}(s)\in S} \{\mathrm{Figure(black},s), \mathrm{Figure(white},s)\}$

If we apply the rules to u_4 we obtain the following attributes:

$$a_{1,5}(u_4) = \texttt{colour} \quad h(a_{1,5})(u_4) = \{\mathrm{Colour(white)}\}$$
$$a_{7,14}(u_4) = \texttt{shape} \quad h(a_{7,14})(u_4) = \{\mathrm{Shape(triangle)}\}$$
$$a_{1,14}(u_4) = \texttt{figure} \quad h(a_{1,14})(u_4) = \{\mathrm{Figure(white,triangle)}\}$$
$$a_{7,14}(u_4) = \texttt{figure} \quad h(a_{7,14})(u_4) = \{\mathrm{Figure(white,triangle)}, \mathrm{Figure(black,triangle)}\}.$$

So after the rule application we obtained meaning for the entire sequence.

We construct the upper approximation of the set of meanings in a sense that for each sequence we find all possible meanings. For indiscernible objects we generate rules that recognize the same sequence and return a different attribute value or meaning.

3   Syntactic Rules

Now, we consider the problem of rule representation. Since attribute value sequence may be arbitrary long, there exists infinite number of possible rules. Only a finite subset of them can be learned. We must have decided what class of languages will be recognized by our rule system. We chose regular languages as a trade of between language strength and implementability. Yet for specific tasks another choice could be more appropriate.

We represent syntactic rules using a modification of context-free grammars by adding some special rule, called, a *term accumulation rule*. Formally, let

$$G = (\Sigma, N, X_I, R, +)$$

be such that

- $\Sigma = \bigcup_{u\in\mathcal{U}} \bigcup_i \{a_i(u)\}$ is finite set of atomic objects' names (terminal symbols),
- $N = V \setminus \Sigma$ is a finite set of non-atomic objects' names (non-terminal symbols),
- $X_I \in N$ is the start-symbol of grammar,
- R is a finite set of production rules. Each production has the form $A \rightarrow \alpha$ or $A \rightarrow \beta+$, where A is a non-terminal and α is a sequence of terminals and non-terminals and $\beta \in \Sigma \cup N$; $A \rightarrow \beta+$ is a shortcut for the set of rules: $A \rightarrow \beta, A \rightarrow \beta\beta, A \rightarrow \beta\beta\beta, \ldots$.

- $\prec$ is a binary relation of $\Sigma \cup N$ such that $A \prec B$ if and only if there is a rule $A \to \alpha$ in R such that B belongs to α or there is a rule $A \to B+$,
- $\prec$ is an irreflexive and transitive partial order.

Proposition 1. *A language L can be recognized by a grammar of the defined above type if and only if L is a regular language.*

The purpose of syntactic rules is to parse any sequence from U into X_I.

4   Semantic Rules

In order to obtain the object meaning instead of recognizing its presence we add semantic interpretations to symbols and rules. Let $\mathcal{E}$ be set of relational structures (see Section 1 for a definition and Section 8 for an example). For terminal symbols we define

$$[\![\cdot]\!]_\Sigma : \Sigma \to \mathcal{E}.$$

For each $A \to \alpha_1 \ldots \alpha_n$ rule we define

$$f_{A \to \alpha_1 \ldots \alpha_n} : \mathcal{E}^n \to \mathcal{E}$$

For each $A \to \beta+$ rule we define

$$f_{A \to \beta+} : \mathcal{E}^+ \to \mathcal{E}$$

These semantic functions operates on the relational structures. They compose greater structures out of smaller ones.

Now, we define semantics interpretation of symbols: For each $\sigma \in \Sigma$ let

$$[\![\sigma]\!] = [\![\sigma]\!]_\Sigma.$$

For each $A \in N$ if A was derived using $A \to \alpha_1 \ldots \alpha_n$ rule let

$$[\![A]\!] = f_{A \to \alpha_1 \ldots \alpha_n}([\![\alpha_1]\!], \ldots, [\![\alpha_n]\!]),$$

and if A was derived using $A \to \beta+$ rule as $\beta_1 \ldots \beta_n$ sequence let

$$[\![A]\!] = f_{A \to \beta+}([\![\beta_1]\!], \ldots, [\![\beta_n]\!])$$

Let u be an object, and a an attribute, then

$$[\![a(u)]\!] = h(a)(u)$$

Note that we may add many different semantic actions to each syntactic rule. Obtaining rules that are grammatically identical but differ on semantic level.

5   Data Sequence Representation

Our goal is to find all possible semantic interpretations (the upper approximation) for a given rule set and an attribute value sequence. We represent objects recognized in data sequence as directed acyclic graph whose edges are labelled by attribute values.

Having given attribute value sequence $\{\sigma_i\}_1^n, \sigma_i \in \Sigma$ we create graph with vertexes $V = \{v_0, \ldots, v_n\}$ and set of edges $E = \{v_0 \xrightarrow{\sigma_1} v_1, \ldots, v_{n-1} \xrightarrow{\sigma_n} v_n\}$

Applying the rule $A \to \alpha_1, \ldots, \alpha_k$ consists in finding all paths

$$v_{a_0} \xrightarrow{\alpha_1} v_{a_1} \xrightarrow{\alpha_2} v_{a_2} \ldots v_{a_{k-1}} \xrightarrow{\alpha_k} v_{a_k}$$

and adding for each of them the edge

$$v_{a_0} \xrightarrow{A} v_{a_k}$$

to the graph. Formally, applying the $A \to \beta+$ consisting in finding all paths

$$v_{a_0} \xrightarrow{\beta} v_{a_1} \xrightarrow{\beta} v_{a_2} \ldots v_{a_{k-1}} \xrightarrow{\beta} v_{a_k}$$

and adding for each of them the edge

$$v_{a_0} \xrightarrow{A} v_{a_k}$$

to the graph.

6   Rule-Applying Algorithm

We divide set of symbols into layers: Let $N_0 = \Sigma$ and let

$$N_{n+1} = \{A : \exists_{A \to \alpha_1 \ldots \alpha_k} \forall_i (\alpha_i \in N_n) \vee \exists_{A \to \beta+} (\beta \in N_n)\}$$

Now we divide the rule set R into layers. Let $R_{-1} = \emptyset$ and

$$R_n = (\{A \to \alpha_1 \ldots \alpha_k : \forall_i \alpha_i \in N_n\} \cup \{A \to \beta+ : \beta \in N_n\}) \setminus R_{n-1}.$$

We begin with graph (V, E_0), where $E_0 - E$. We obtain graph (V, E_{n+1}) by applying to (V, E_n) rules from R_n.

In order to do it efficiently we create prefix tree out of every layer: For each rule $A \to \alpha_1 \ldots \alpha_k$ in R_n we create path from the root labelled by symbols α_1 till α_k and we label the leaf tree node by A. For each node we merge path that have identical labels. Using this data structure we can apply all $A \to \alpha$ rules in layer in $\mathcal{O}(|E_n| l \log |\Sigma \cup E| + |E_n||R_n^+|)$ time, where

$$l = \max_{R_n}\{k : A \to \alpha_1 \ldots \alpha_k \in R_n\}$$

Since l, $\log |\Sigma \cup E|$ and number of layers is relatively small $|E_n|$ is crucial for parser performance. The problem is that E_n contains information that we want to obtain as a result of parsing process. If text have exponential number of interpretations $|E_n|$ will increase exponentially. To handle this problem we must reduce the number of interpretations either by throwing away part of them or merging them.

7   Learning

Experiments indicated that the rules can be divided into two kinds:

The rules that describe the structure of sequences. They have complex semantics and, therefore, they must be designed manually in dialog with experts. Fortunately, in typical task there is only a small number of such rules.

The rules that contain the "vocabulary" of the problem. There may be lots of them, but they split into a few groups and all the rules in each group produce the same semantic function. These rules may be learned automatically.

The learning process may be performed analogically as in case of learning decision tables: We create the training sample and using it we generate a classifier. As a classification algorithm we use one of well known classifiers adjusted for sequential data. For example, if we wish to use k-Nearest Neighbour algorithm we introduce a similarity measure on attributes values and use the edit distance to determine similarity of a pair of attribute value sequences.

The other possibility is specific for the sequential data. We learn the context in which the sample is likely to appear instead of learning the sample itself.

One can also combine the above mentioned methods.

In the example presented in the following section we use a semiautomatic way of learning, which takes the advantage of the fact that samples appear in a small number of contexts. We derive rules automatically from the attribute value sequences that are within the context which we manually indicated.

8   Application Example: Semantic Analyser for Sumerian Ur III Economic Text Corpus

The Ur III economic text corpus consists of circa 43500 documents. They describe the process of redistribution of goods in Ancient Sumer during the Ur III period (2100BC-2000BC). The Ur III economic texts were the subject of sumerological research for many years. The tablets were transliterated by many researchers, who didn't have the strict conventions for describing the tablet content. As a result the corpus does not have a uniform format, the description of text arrangement on tablets is not standardized and mixed with Sumerian text. The other problem is that the Sumerian texts itself are often ambiguous on both syntactic and semantic level.

The signature for structures included in $\mathcal{E}$ is composed of following elements:

- constants such as numbers, names, commodities and dates
- unary relations: **Number, Name, Day, Month, Year, Date, Quantity, Commodity Supplier, Receiver**
- 5-tuple relation **Transaction**.

We arranged a rule set into the corpus. Most of the rules (about 3500) recognize Sumerian personal names, names of gods and cities, etc. These rules were generated in semiautomatic way described in Sect. 7. The remaining rules (about 200) describe the structure of the language.

We described contents of the whole tablet as a set of transactions:

```
&P123831 = OIP 121, 101
tablet
obverse
1. 1(disz) sila4 ur-mes ensi2      1 lamb Urmes governor
2. 1(disz)# sila4 da-da dumu lugal  1 lamb Dada son of king
3. 1(disz)# sila4 id-da-a           1 lamb Idda
reverse
1. u4 2(u) 3(asz@t)-kam             Day 23
$ 1 line blank
3. mu-DU                            delivery
4. ab-ba-sa6-ga i3-dab5             Abbasaga received
5. iti sze-KIN-ku5                  month sze-kin-ku5
6. mu en {d}inanna ba-hun           Year when high priest of goddess Innana
left                                          was elevated to office
1. 3(disz)                          3
```

Fig. 5. Example of transliterated cuneiform tablet

Date	Quantity	Commodity	Supplier	Receiver
23-11-AS05	1	sila4	ur-mes ensi2	ab-ba-sa6-ga
23-11-AS05	1	sila4	da-da dumu lugal	ab-ba-sa6-ga
23-11-AS05	1	sila4	id-da-a	ab-ba-sa6-ga

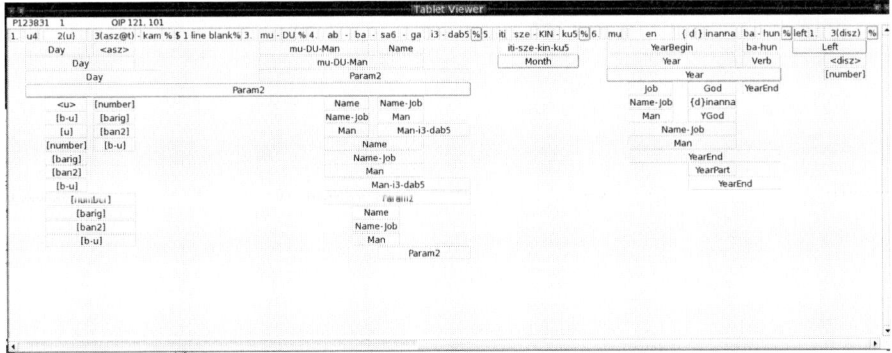

Fig. 6. Rule applying algorithm at work

The system allowed us to transform automatically the data (in this case Sumerian economic document) from the sequential form into a table representing a relational structure. We defined relational structure that represents information contained in texts in a way convenient for further analysis.

9   Conclusions

We investigated the problem of learning the decision functions for sequential data. We proposed a rule system that allows us to map data into a compound decision value.

We introduced a heuristic distinction between rules that may and may not be learned automatically. We outlined the general ideas for the classification algorithms construction.

The question about kinds of rules that may be learned from data and details of construction various classification algorithms require further studies.

In our future work, we plan to define properties of query languages relevant for certain applications and extend the rule system for numerical data. We also plan to combine the process of constructing the relational structure with deductive reasoning, by creating an implicative interpretation for object recognition rules.

We would like also extend the process of learning to the higher level concepts (e.g. soft concepts) that cannot be expressed in an exact way by means of our relational structures.

Acknowledgement. The research has been supported by the grant 3 T11C 002 26 from Ministry of Scientific Research and Information Technology of the Republic of Poland.

References

1. E. Brill "A Simple Rule-Based Part-of-Speech Tagger". *In Proceedings of the Third Conference on Applied Computational Linguistics (ACL)*, Trento Italy.
2. J. Cowie, W. Lehnert. "Information extraction". *Special NLP Issue of the Communications of the ACM*, 1996.
3. Daniel Jurafsky and James H. Martin "Speech and Language Processing: An Introduction to Natural Language Processing, Computational Linguistics, and Speech Recognition", Prentice-Hall, 2000
4. L. Kartunen, J.P. Chanod, G. Grefenstette and A. Schiller "Regular expressions for language engineering", *Natural Language Engineering*, 2:2:305-328,1996
5. D. E. Knuth, *Semantics of context-free languages*. Mathematical Systems Theory, 2(2):127–145, 1968.
6. Ludovic Lebart, Andre Salem, and Lisette Berry, "Exploring Textual Data", Kluwer Academic Publishers, 1997. Review available in Computational Linguistics, 25(1), 1999.
7. Marie-Francine Moens, "Information Extraction: Algorithms and Prospects in a Retrieval Context" *The Information Retrieval Series , Vol. 21*, Springer 2006,
8. G. van Noord , D. Gerdemann "An Extendible Regular Expression Compiter for Finite-State Approaches in Natural Language Processing", *Workshop on Implementing Automata*, Postnam, Germany, 1997
9. S. K. Pal, L. Polkowski, A. Skowron (Eds.), *Rough-Neural Computing: Techniques for Computing with Words*, Cognitive Technologies. Springer-Verlag, 2004.
10. Ed.: Maria Teresa Pazienza. "Information Extraction in the Web Era. Natural Language Communication for Knowledge Acquisition and Intelligent Information Agents". Berlin 2003 Springer-Verlag 8 s. XI, 162. Lecture Notes in Artificial Intelligence, 2700. subser. of Lecture Notes in Computer Science, 2700 ISBN 3540405798
11. V. N. Vapnik, *Statistical Learning Theory*, Wiley, New York, 1998.

Sampling of Virtual Examples to Improve Classification Accuracy for Nominal Attribute Data

Yujung Lee, Jaeho Kang, Byoungho Kang, and Kwang Ryel Ryu

Department of Computer Engineering, Pusan National University,
San 30, Jangjeon-dong, Kumjeong-gu, Busan, Korea
+82-51-{515-9308, 515-9308, 515-9308, 510-2431}
{yjlee, jhkang, bhokang, krryu}@pusan.ac.kr

Abstract. This paper presents a method of using virtual examples to improve the classification accuracy for data with nominal attributes. Most of the previous researches on virtual examples focused on data with numeric attributes, and they used domain-specific knowledge to generate useful virtual examples for a particularly targeted learning algorithm. Instead of using domain-specific knowledge, our method samples virtual examples from a naïve Bayesian network constructed from the given training set. A sampled example is considered useful if it contributes to the increment of the network's conditional likelihood when added to the training set. A set of useful virtual examples can be collected by repeating this process of sampling followed by evaluation. Experiments have shown that the virtual examples collected this way can help various learning algorithms to derive classifiers of improved accuracy.

1 Introduction

Over the past decades, many researchers have been devoted to improving the accuracy of classification in various ways. Several new, improved or combined learning algorithms have been proposed. Ensemble methods, which use multiple classifiers derived from homogeneous or heterogeneous learning algorithms such as bagging [1], boosting [2] and stacking [3], have been developed. In addition, methods of transforming a training set into a more suitable one for learning have been widely investigated. Noisy example elimination [4], numeric attribute discretization [5], new attribute synthesis [6], feature selection [7], and inclusion of unlabeled examples [8] belong to such transformation methods. This paper proposes a method of using virtual examples for learning, which is also a way of transforming the given training set.

A virtual example is an artificial example that does not exist in the original training set. A virtual example is useful when it has a high prior probability and contributes to improving classification accuracy. In order to generate a useful virtual example, we sample a virtual example from a Bayesian network constructed from the original training set, and evaluate it by the increment of the network's conditional likelihood. Once a generated virtual example is found to be useful by this evaluation, it is saved and used to update the network for the next sampling. By repeating the process of sampling a virtual example, we can obtain as many virtual examples as we want. In

S. Greco et al. (Eds.): RSCTC 2006, LNAI 4259, pp. 637 – 646, 2006.

order to determine the appropriate size of the virtual example set to use, we generate candidate virtual example sets of various sizes. The best virtual example set is then selected through cross-validation and statistical significance tests. The selected virtual example set is used for learning, together with the original training set. Experiments with nominal attribute data have shown that our method improves the classification accuracy of various learning algorithms.

The next section digests related research. Section 3 explains in detail our method of generating useful virtual examples from Bayesian networks. Section 4 shows a method of selecting the best virtual example set among candidates. Section 5 evaluates the proposed method and summarizes the experimental results. Finally, Section 6 gives our conclusions and some topics for further research.

2   Related Work

Many previous works have reported promising results improving classification accuracy by using virtual examples. [9] proposed a method that placed a virtual example in the sparse regions of example space and then labeled its class by a neural network generated from the original training set. The method was applied to the robot arm kinematics problem. [10,11] generated virtual examples by using symmetrical image transformation and rotating a two-dimensional prototypical face and weighted-averaging each person's images for face recognition. [12] presented a simple method for a face verification system with a neural network. It generated virtual examples by applying simple geometric transformations to the original images. [13] generated virtual support vectors by using the desired invariance transformations of real support vectors for a digit recognition problem. [14] proposed a simple method that generates virtual examples by applying geometric transformations to images. It improved the performance of a support vector machine for a handwritten Japanese Hiragana character classification. [15] proposed a method of generating a virtual example by combining two text documents of the same category, and improved the accuracy of text classification.

These studies focused on classification problems with numeric attributes only. In their methods, virtual examples were generated by using domain-specific knowledge or by simple heuristics. Their aim of using virtual examples is to improve the accuracy of a particular classifier under investigation. In contrast, our method concentrates on classification problems with nominal attributes. We use Bayesian networks to generate virtual examples without using any domain-specific knowledge. It has been shown that the virtual examples generated by our method can improve the accuracy of classifiers derived by various learning algorithms.

3   Sampling Useful Virtual Examples

A virtual example is considered useful if it has a high prior probability and has positive effects on classification. To obtain virtual examples of a high prior probability, a naïve Bayesian network is constructed from the original training set and then the examples are sampled from this network. To select only those examples that are likely to contribute to the improvement of classification accuracy, each sampled example is evaluated to see whether, if it is included, we could construct the next version of the network with increased conditional likelihood. Although the naïve Bayesian model is used as a means of sampling and evaluation of virtual examples, they can be used not just to improve the performance of naïve Bayes classifier but to improve classifiers derived by other learning algorithms.

3.1 Using Bayesian Network for Sampling

A Bayesian network is defined by a directed acyclic graph $G = \langle W, E \rangle$ and a set of conditional probability tables Θ. Among the nodes in $W = \{x_1, x_2, \ldots, x_{m-1}, x_m\}$, $x_1, x_2, \ldots, x_{m-1}$ represent the random variables corresponding to the attributes and x_m represents the class. A directed edge $\langle x_j, x_i \rangle \in E$ indicates that x_j is a parent of x_i. Note that x_i is conditionally independent of its non-descendents given its parents. Each node i contains a conditional probability table $\theta_i = \{p_{i,j,k} \mid j \in$ the domain of π_i, $k \in$ the domain of $x_i\}$, where π_i is the parents of i and $p_{i,j,k} = P(x_i = k \mid \pi_i = j)$. One popular measure for evaluating the quality of a Bayesian network for a given data is the likelihood. The likelihood of a training set $D = \{X_1, X_2, \ldots, X_n\}$ on a Bayesian network B is

$$L(D|B) = P_B(D) = \Pi_d P_B(X_d) = \Pi_d P_B(x_1 = x_{d,1}, \ldots, x_m = x_{d,m})$$

$$= \Pi_d \Pi_i P_B(x_i = x_{d,i} \mid \pi_i = \pi_{d,i}) \tag{1}$$

where X_d is the d-th example in D, $P_B(D)$ is the posterior probability of D, given B, $x_{d,i}$ is the i-th attribute's value (or class value when $i = m$) of X_d, and $\pi_{d,i}$ is the value of the parent attributes of the i-th attribute of X_d. Having a fixed set of edges E, we can easily determine Θ that maximizes $L(D|B)$ by applying maximum likelihood parameter learning. Let $n_{i,j}$ and $n_{i,j,k}$ be the numbers of examples in D satisfying $\pi_i = j$ and $\pi_i = j \wedge x_i = k$, respectively. Then maximum likelihood parameter learning simply sets $p_{i,j,k}$ to $n_{i,j,k} / n_{i,j}$. It is expected that virtual examples sampled from a Bayesian network of maximum likelihood will have higher prior probabilities than those generated by assigning arbitrary values to the attribute and class variables.

We just saw that it is simple and easy to determine the maximum likelihood value for Θ when E is given, but finding the best structure E is a very difficult problem. Several studies have suggested heuristic methods of searching for a reasonable structure under some constraints [16]. However, these methods usually require considerable time to run. Therefore, in this paper, we adopt a naïve Bayesian network that assumes a strong conditional independence among the attributes, given the class. Naïve Bayes learning algorithm runs very fast and has been successfully applied to many classification problems [17].

After the network structure and the parameters are determined based on the given training set, a virtual example is generated simply as follows. First, a class value is sampled from the class node's probability table. Then, each attribute's value is sampled from the conditional probability table of the corresponding attribute node. Once the class and all the attribute values are determined, a virtual example is obtained.

3.2 Conditional Likelihood as a Measure of Usefulness

We cannot expect to be able to derive a better classifier by using the training set expanded by simply adding the virtual examples sampled from the Bayesian network. Classification accuracy may be bound to the accuracy of the Bayesian network that generates the virtual examples. Therefore, we test each sampled example to see whether it could really improve the classification accuracy. To qualify a virtual example, we introduce a strong but reasonable hypothesis: *If a virtual example is useful, most learning algorithms can generate more accurate classifiers by using it.* Under this hypothesis we expect that a virtual example is probably useful if it potentially increases the accuracy of a certain learned classifier. A proven theorem says that a Bayesian network with a higher conditional likelihood can classify examples more accurately [18]. Some studies also support this theorem by experiments [16, 19, 20, 21]. By adopting the theorem and our hypothesis, a virtual example is regarded as useful if it increases the conditional likelihood of the network from which it is sampled. The conditional likelihood is defined as

$$CL(D|B) = \Pi_d\, P_B(x_{d,m}|\, x_{d,1}, x_{d,2}, \ldots, x_{d,m-1}) \tag{2}$$

where $x_{d,i}$ is the i-th attribute's value (class value when $i = m$) of training example X_d. This conditional likelihood can be easily calculated by applying Bayes rule and the conditional independence assumption as follows:

$$P_B(x_{d,m}|\, x_{d,1}, x_{d,2}, \ldots, x_{d,m-1}) = \alpha\, P_B(x_{d,1}, x_{d,2}, \ldots, x_{d,m-1}\,|\, x_{d,m}) P_B(x_{d,m})$$

$$= \alpha\, P_B(x_{d,m}) \Pi_i\, P_B(x_{d,i}\,|\, x_{d,m}) \tag{3}$$

where α is the normalization constant.

Let B be the Bayesian network constructed from the training set D and B^+ be the same network after incrementally adjusting the conditional probability tables [22] according to $D^+ = D \cup \{v\}$, where v is a virtual example. The virtual example v is considered useful if $CL(D^+|B^+) - CL(D|B) > 0$.

Now, we summarize the procedure for sampling useful virtual examples: (1) a Bayesian network B is built from the original training set D. (2) A virtual example v is sampled from B. (3) B is updated to B^+ by incrementally adjusting the conditional probability tables using $D^+ = D \cup \{v\}$ as a new training set. (4) If $CL(D^+|B^+) - CL(D|B) \leq 0$, go back to step (2). Otherwise, v is qualified and D and B are replaced by D^+ and B^+ and go back to step (2). The procedure continues until a desired number of virtual examples are obtained.

4 Selecting a Virtual Example Set for Learning

Two questions should be answered regarding the generation and use of virtual examples for learning. The first is how many virtual examples we want to generate and use. The second is how we guarantee that the generated virtual examples can really improve the accuracy of learned classifiers. Since we employ naïve Bayesian model to generate virtual examples, we cannot take it for granted to have classifiers other than naïve Bayes be improved by using such virtual examples. One may also be curious if the virtual examples generated and evaluated by naïve Bayesian model could be useful for other type of classifiers when given a problem in which naïve Bayes does not perform well.

To cope with these questions we derive virtual example sets of various sizes and select one from them based on accuracy estimation and a statistical significance test. We first construct b virtual example sets $V_1, V_2, \ldots, V_b$ of increasing sizes from the sequence of useful virtual examples $V = \langle v_1, v_2, \ldots, v_s \rangle$ obtained by the procedure described in the previous section, where $V_i = \{v_j \mid 1 \leq j \leq \lceil i \times (s / b) \rceil \}$. To select a virtual example set of an appropriate size for a particular learning algorithm, we run the learning algorithm to derive $b + 1$ classifiers $h_0, h_1, \ldots, h_b$, where h_0 is the classifier derived by using only the original training set D, and h_i by using $D \cup V_i$. The accuracies of these classifiers are estimated by self cross-validation. When cross-validating, virtual examples are used only for learning but not for testing. If, for every i, h_i shows significantly better accuracy than h_0, then V_i is selected as a candidate. A t-test is applied for this statistical verification. Among all these candidates, the one that shows the best estimated accuracy is selected for final learning without leaving any holdout. The learning algorithm will not choose any virtual example set if none passes the significance test with a certain predetermined confidence level. In that case, we conclude that the virtual examples selectively sampled from naïve Bayesian network are of no help to the learning algorithm at hand for this particular problem. A detailed algorithm of the proposed method is given in Fig. 1.

5   Experimental Results

The proposed method was evaluated by using eleven nominal attribute data sets selected from UCI machine learning repository [23]. Table 1 shows the characteristics of these data sets. The learning algorithms tested include naïve Bayes (*NB*), nearest neighbor (*1-NN*), decision tree (*C4.5*)[24], SVM using sequential minimal optimization (*SMO*) [25], and naïve Bayes tree (*NBtree*), for which the experiments were done with Weka data mining software [26]. In each experiment, the classification accuracy was averaged from the results of ten tenfold cross-validations. Virtual examples were generated up to 500% of the original training set and ten virtual example sets ranging from 50% to 500% were constructed. The confidence level of the t-test for selecting a virtual example set was set at 90%.

Table 2 summarizes the experimental results. The superscript $+V$ indicates that virtual examples were used for learning in addition to the original training examples. If there is a statistically significant difference between the accuracies of classifiers with and without virtual examples, a thick arrow is put at the front of the result. For the significance test, a t-test is used with a confidence level of 90%. NB^{+V} shows significant improvement over *NB* in seven data sets. $1\text{-}NN^{+V}$ and $C4.5^{+V}$ also outperform *1-NN* and *C4.5* in six data sets. *SMO* and *NBtree* outperform their counterparts in five data sets. An interesting result can be found by carefully inspecting Table 2. *NB* showed the worst performance among the five learning algorithms with the audiology data. Although the virtual examples were generated from the naïve Bayesian model, other learning algorithms such as *1-NN*, *C4.5*, and *NBtree* performed significantly

```
procedure Learning-with-Virtual-Examples
   input
       L – learning algorithm to use
       D – training set
       s – maximum number of virtual examples to be generated
       b – number of virtual example sets derived
       c –confidence in t-test for selecting a virtual example set
   output
       h – classifier derived by L with virtual examples

   begin
       V ← ø
       Build a Bayesian network B using D
       Calculate the conditional likelihood cl of D on B
       repeat until |V| < s
           Generate a virtual example v by sampling from B
           Copy B to B⁺ and incrementally update B⁺ with v
           Calculate the conditional likelihood cl⁺ of D on B⁺
           if cl⁺ > cl then
               Add v to V
               B ← B⁺, cl ← cl⁺
       Generate Vˢ = {V₁, V₂, …, V_b}, V_i ← {v_j | 1 ≤ j ≤ ⌈i × s / b⌉}.
       Get accuracy list A₀ by using L with D (ten-ten cross-validations are used)
       a* ← average of A₀, V* ← φ
       for each V_i in Vˢ
           Get accuracy list A_i by using L with D ∪ V_i
           if A_i is significantly higher than A₀ by t-test with confidence c then
               if average of A_i is greater than a* then
                   a* ← average of A_i, V* ← V_i
       Derive a classifier h by using L with D ∪ V*
       return h

   end
```

Fig. 1. The algorithm for generating a classifier with virtual examples

better when they used those virtual examples. These experimental results strongly support our hypothesis introduced in Section 3.

Table 3 shows the effects of different confidence levels used in the procedure of selecting a virtual example set. Confidence levels tried were 0%, 25%, 50%, 60%, 70%, 80%, 90%, and 99%. With each level, we counted the numbers of cases (11 data sets and 5 learning algorithms constitute 55 cases in total.) in which learning with virtual examples showed a significantly higher accuracy than that without (Win), a significantly lower accuracy than that without (Loss), and no difference (Draw). The best result was obtained when the confidence level was set to 90%. However, since the overall results were not that sensitive to various different levels, it seems that our method can reliably generate useful virtual examples even without any t-test.

Table 1. Characteristics of data sets used

Data set	# of examples	# of attributes	# of classes
audiology	226	69	24
breast-c	286	9	2
kr-vs-kp	3,196	36	2
monks-1	556	6	2
monks-2	601	6	2
monks-3	554	6	2
primary	339	17	25
soybean	683	35	19
splice	3,190	62	3
vote	435	16	2
zoo	101	17	7

Table 2. Accuracy of various classifiers with/without virtual examples (unit: percentage)

Data set	NB	NB^{+V}	$1\text{-}NN$	$1\text{-}NN^{+V}$	$C4.5$	$C4.5^{+V}$	SMO	SMO^{+V}	$NBtree$	$NBtree^{+V}$
audiology	73.0	↑ 79.2	75.2	↑ 78.8	77.5	↑ 83.2	81.5	↑ 83.6	78.3	↑ 82.3
breast-c	71.6	72.1	75.5	74.8	75.2	74.2	69.9	↓ 68.5	71.3	↑ 73.8
kr-vs-kp	87.7	↑ 89.7	90.0	90.8	99.4	99.2	95.4	↑ 96.7	97.1	97.8
monks-1	77.4	78.2	72.9	73.3	82.3	81.1	83.9	82.9	90.6	89.4
monks-2	56.7	57.3	55.2	↓ 57.2	56.2	↓ 60.6	58.6	↑ 59.9	60.4	↓ 59.2
monks-3	93.3	93.3	77.1	↑ 83.3	93.4	↑ 94.6	93.3	93.3	93.4	93.4
primary	50.1	↑ 54.8	33.6	↑ 40.0	43.2	↑ 45.9	46.9	46.9	46.0	↑ 47.6
soybean	93.0	↑ 94.1	89.9	↑ 92.9	91.5	↑ 93.8	93.8	↑ 94.9	91.5	↑ 92.5
splice	95.3	↑ 96.1	75.9	↑ 82.4	94.1	↑ 95.8	93.4	↑ 94.5	95.3	95.0
vote	90.1	↑ 92.8	92.6	↑ 93.6	96.3	97.1	96.1	95.0	95.6	↑ 96.8
zoo	93.0	↑ 94.4	96.0	96.0	92.1	↑ 95.0	96.0	96.0	95.1	↓ 94.4
average	80.1	82.0	75.8	78.5	81.8	83.6	82.6	82.9	83.1	83.8

Table 3. Effects of various different confidence levels

Confidence level	0%	25%	50%	60%	70%	80%	90%	95%	99%
Win	24	25	24	26	26	28	29	28	28
Draw	23	23	24	22	22	21	21	21	22
Loss	8	7	7	7	7	3	5	6	5

We select and use a virtual example set of a certain size that is expected to be the best for the targeted learning algorithm, among candidates that passed a statistical significance test. If there is no such candidate, the learning algorithm uses only the original training set. Table 4 shows the frequency of using the virtual example set for

100 experiments. We can see that usage frequencies differ depending on the learning algorithms and data sets. The learning algorithm that showed higher accuracy improvement in a classification problem has a tendency to use virtual example sets more frequently for that problem. In other words, there is a strong correlation between improvement in classification accuracy and usage frequency. For example, *NB*, *SMO*, and *NBtree* showed no significant improvement or even deterioration with the monks-3 data, and their usage frequencies were very low. In contrast, *1-NN* and *C4.5* with the same data showed significant improvement in accuracy and their usage frequencies were relatively high.

Table 4. Usage frequencies of the virtual example set (unit: percentage)

Data set	NB	1-NN	C4.5	SMO	NBtree
audiology	93	96	91	82	74
breast-c	65	45	63	45	65
kr-vs-kp	67	75	46	57	34
monks-1	21	24	25	21	16
monks-2	23	12	42	33	21
monks-3	6	76	78	8	6
primary	75	85	57	56	69
soybean	65	75	65	56	65
splice	68	63	71	74	34
vote	65	43	46	43	54
zoo	21	4	35	2	32

6 Concluding Remarks

We presented a framework for generating and using virtual examples to improve classification accuracy for problems with nominal attributes. A virtual example is sampled from a naïve Bayesian network and its quality is measured by the increment of the network's conditional likelihood after adding it. A statistical significance test is applied to select an appropriate virtual example set, and the selected set is used for learning, together with the original training set. Experimental results have shown that our method can improve the accuracy of classifiers derived from various learning algorithms including naïve Bayes, nearest neighbor, decision tree, support vector machine, and naïve Bayes tree.

We consider two main expansions of our work for future study. First, the proposed method will become much more useful if it can handle data with numeric attributes. We think that it can be achieved by adopting a numeric attribute discretization method or by introducing a Gaussian mixture model to the Bayesian network used for generating virtual examples. Second, we expect that better virtual examples can be obtained more efficiently if we use Bayesian networks with enhanced structures such as TAN [27] rather than just the simple naïve Bayesian networks.

Acknowledgements

This work was supported by National Research Laboratory Program (Contract Number : M10400000279-05J0000-27910) of KISTEP.

References

1. Breiman, L.: Bagging predictors. Machine Learning, Vol. 24. No. 2 (1996) 123-140
2. Freund, Y., R. E. Schapire: Experiments with a new boosting algorithm. Proceedings of the International Conference on Machine Learning (1996) 148-56
3. Wolpert, D. H.: Stacked Generalization Neural Networks. Vol. 5 (1992) 241-259
4. Aha, D. W.: Tolerating Noisy, Irrelevant, and Novel Attributes in Instance-based Learning Algorithms. International Journal of Man-Machine Studies, Vol. 36, No. 2 (1992) 267-287
5. Kohavi, R., Sahami, M.: Error-based and Entropy-based Discretization of Continuous Features. Proc. of the 2nd International Conference on Knowledge Discovery and Data Mining (1996) 114-119
6. Pazzani, M.: Constructive induction of Cartesian product attributes. Information, Statistics and Induction in Science (1996) 66-77
7. Almuallim, H., Dietterich, T. G.: Learning With Many Irrelevant Features. Proc. of the 9th National Conference on Artificial Intelligence (1991) 547-552
8. Nigam, K., McCallum, A., Thrun, S., Mitchell, T.: Text Classification from Labeled and Unlabeled Documents using EM. Machine Learning, Vol. 39, No. 2 (1999) 103-134
9. Cho, S., Cha, K.: Evolution of Neural Network Training Set through Addition of Virtual samples. Proc. of the 1996 IEEE International Conference on Evolutionary Computation (1996) 685-688
10. Marcel, S.: Improving Face Verification using Symmetric Transformation. Proc. of IEICE Transactions on Information and Systems, Vol. E81, No. 1 (1993) 124-135
11. Wen, J., Zhao, J., Luo, S., Huang, H.: Face Recognition Method Based on Virtual Sample. Proc. of the ICII, Vol. 3 (2001) 557-562
12. Thian, N. P. H., Marcel, S., Bengio, S.: Improving Face Authentication Using Virtual Samples. Proc. of the Acoustics, Speech, and Signal International Conference, Vol. 3 (2003) 233-236
13. Burges, C., Scholkopf, B.: Improving the Accuracy and Speed of Support Vector Machines. Proc. of Advances in Neural Information Processing System, Vol. 9, No. 7 (1997)
14. Miyao, H., Maruyama, M., Nakano, Y., Hanamoi, T.: Off-line handwritten character recognition by SVM based on the virtual examples synthesized from on-line characters. Proc. of Eighth International Conference on Document Analysis and Recognition. Vol. 1 (2005) 494-498
15. Lee, K. S., An, D. U.: Performance Improvement by a Virtual Documents Technique in Text Categorization. Korea Information Processing Society, Vol. 11-B, No. 4 (2004) 501-508
16. Friedman, N., Geiger, D., M. Goldszmidt: Bayesian network classifiers. Machine Learning, Vol. 29 (1997) 131-163
17. John, G., Langley, P.: Estimating Continuous Distributions in Bayesian Classifiers. Proc. of the Eleventh Conference on Uncertainty in Artificial Intelligence (1995) 338-345
18. Duda, R. O., Hart, P. E.: Pattern Classification and scene analysis, NewYork, NY: Wiley, (1973)

19. Grossman, D., Domingos, P.: Learning Bayesian Network Classifiers by Maximizing Conditional Likelihood. Proc. of the 21th International Conference on Machine Learning (2004) 361-368
20. Greiner, R., Zhou, W.: Structural Extension to Logistic Regression: Discriminative parameter learning of belief net classifiers. Proc. of the 18th National Conference on Artificial Intelligence (2002) 167-173
21. Burge, J., Lane, T.: Learning Class-Discriminative Dynamic Bayesian Networks. Proc. of the 22th International Conference on Machine Learning (2005) 97-104
22. Roy, N., McCallum, A.: Toward optimal active learning through sampling estimation of error reduction. Proc. of the 18th International Conference on Machine Learning (2004) 441-448
23. Newman, D. J., Hettich, S., Blake, C. L., Merz, C. J.: UCI Repository of machine learning databases [http://www.ics.uci.edu/~mlearn/MLRepository.html]. CA: University of California, Department of Information and Computer Science (1998)
24. Quinlan, J. R.: C4.5 : Programs for Machine Learning, Morgan Kaufmann Publishers (1993)
25. Irvine J. Platt: Fast Training of Support Vector Machines using Sequential Minimal Optimization. Advances in Kernel Methods - Support Vector Learning. B. Schoelkopf, C. Burges, and A. Smola, eds., MIT Press (1998)
26. Witten, I. H., Frank, E.: Data Mining-Practical Machine Learning Tools and Techniques with Java Implementations, Morgan Kaufman Publishers (1999)
27. Friedman, N., Geiger, D., Goldszmidt, M.: Bayesian network Classifiers. Machine Learning, Vol. 29 (1997) 131-163

A Fuzzy-Possibilistic Fuzzy Ruled Clustering Algorithm for RBFNNs Design

A. Guillén, I. Rojas, J. González, H. Pomares, L.J. Herrera, and A. Prieto

Department of Computer Architecture and Technology
Universidad de Granada, Spain

Abstract. This paper presents a new approach to the problem of designing Radial Basis Function Neural Networks (RBFNNs) to approximate a given function. The presented algorithm focuses in the first stage of the design where the centers of the RBFs have to be placed. This task has been commonly solved by applying generic clustering algorithms although in other cases, some specific clustering algorithms were considered. These specific algorithms improved the performance by adding some elements that allow them to use the information provided by the output of the function to be approximated but they did not add problem specific knowledge. The novelty of the new developed algorithm is the combination of a fuzzy-possibilistic approach with a supervising parameter and the addition of a new migration step that, through the generation of RBFNNs, is able to take proper decisions on where to move the centers. The algorithm also introduces a fuzzy logic element by setting a fuzzy rule that determines the input vectors that influence each center position, this fuzzy rule considers the output of the function to be approximated and the fuzzy-possibilistic partition of the data.

1 Introduction

The problem of approximating a given function using an RBFNN $\mathcal{F}$ can be formulated as, given a set of observations $\{(\boldsymbol{x}_k; y_k); k = 1, ..., n\}$ with $y_k = F(\boldsymbol{x}_k) \in \mathbb{R}$ and $\boldsymbol{x}_k \in \mathbb{R}^d$, it is desired to obtain a function $\mathcal{F}$ so $\sum_{k=1}^{n} ||y_k - \mathcal{F}(\boldsymbol{x}_k)||^2$ is minimum. RBFNNs have been widely used to solve this problem because of their capability to approximate any function [6,13].

An RBFNN $\mathcal{F}$ with fixed structure to approximate an unknown function F with d variables and one output is defined as:

$$\mathcal{F}(\boldsymbol{x}_k; C, R, \Omega) = \sum_{i=1}^{m} \phi(\boldsymbol{x}_k; \boldsymbol{c}_i, r_i) \cdot \Omega_i \qquad (1)$$

where $C = \{\boldsymbol{c}_1, ..., \boldsymbol{c}_m\}$ is the set of RBF centers, $R = \{r_1, ..., r_m\}$ is the set of values for each RBF radius, $\Omega = \{\Omega_1, ..., \Omega_m\}$ is the set of weights and $\phi(\boldsymbol{x}_k; \boldsymbol{c}_i, r_i)$ represents an RBF. The activation function most commonly used for classification and regression problems is the Gaussian function because it is

S. Greco et al. (Eds.): RSCTC 2006, LNAI 4259, pp. 647–656, 2006.

continuous, differentiable, it provides a softer output and improves the interpolation capabilities [2,15].

The first step of initialization of the position of the RBF centers has been commonly carried out using clustering algorithms [11,17]. Classical clustering algorithms have been used to solve classification task where the objective is to identify to classify the input data assigning a discrete set of predefined labels, however, in the function approximation problem, the output of the function belongs to a continuous interval. The output of the function is an important element that must be considered when initializing the centers, they should be concentred where the output is more variable since these areas require more RBFs to be modelled.

This paper proposes a new algorithm to solve the task of the initialization of the centers. It is based on a mixed fuzzy-possibilistic supervised approach that, with the use of fuzzy logic and problem specific knowledge, will provide an adequate placement of the centers. The consequence of this is that the final RBFNN obtained after following the rest of the steps dependent from the center initialization, approximates the given function with a smaller error than if other algorithms were applied.

2 Previous Clustering Algorithms

This section describes several clustering algorithms that have been used to determine the centers when designing RBFNNs for function approximation problems.

2.1 Fuzzy C-Means (FCM)

This algorithm presented in [1] uses a fuzzy partition of the data where an input vector belongs to several clusters with a membership value. It defines an objective distortion function to be minimized is:

$$J_h(U, C; X) = \sum_{k=1}^{n} \sum_{i=1}^{m} u_{ik}^h \|\boldsymbol{x}_k - \boldsymbol{c}_i\|^2 \qquad (2)$$

where $X = \{\boldsymbol{x}_1, \boldsymbol{x}_2, ..., \boldsymbol{x}_n\}$ are the input vectors, $C = \{\boldsymbol{c}_1, \boldsymbol{c}_2, ..., \boldsymbol{c}_m\}$ are the centers of the clusters, $U = [u_{ik}]$ is the matrix where the degree of membership is established by the input vector to the cluster, and h is a parameter to control the degree of the partition fuzziness. After applying the least square method to minimize the function in Equation 2, we get the equations to reach the solution trough an iterative process.

2.2 Fuzzy Possibilistic C-Means (FPCM)

In this approach developed in [12], a combination of a fuzzy partition and a possibilistic partition is presented. The point of view of the authors is that the membership value of the fuzzy partition is important to be able to assign a hard label to classify an input vector, but at the same time, it is very useful to use the typicality (possibility) value to move the centers around the input vectors space, avoiding undesirable effects due to the presence of outliers. The distortion function to be minimized is:

$$J_h(U, C, T; X) = \sum_{k=1}^{n} \sum_{i=1}^{m} (u_{ik}^h + t_{ik}^{h_2}) \| \boldsymbol{x}_k - \boldsymbol{c}_i \|^2 \tag{3}$$

with the following constraints: $\sum_{i=1}^{m} u_{ik} = 1 \; \forall k = 1...n$ and $\sum_{k=1}^{n} t_{ik} = 1 \; \forall i = 1...m$.

Let $T = [t_{ik}]$, then, the constraint shown above requires each row of T to sum up to 1 but its columns are free up to the requirement that each column contains at least one non-zero entry, thus, there is a possibility of input vectors not belonging to any cluster. The main improvement in comparison with the FCM algorithm is that, since there are some input vectors that can be outliers, the membership function for them will be small not forcing all clusters to share them.

2.3 Possibilistic Centers Initializer (PCI)

This algorithm [9] adapts the algorithm proposed in [10] using a mixed approach between a possibilistic and a fuzzy partition, combining both approach as it was done in [16]. The objective function to be minimized is defined as:

$$J_h(U^{(p)}, U^{(f)}, C, W; X) = \sum_{k=1}^{n} \sum_{i=1}^{m} (u_{ik}^{(f)})^{h_f} (u_{ik}^{(p)})^{h_p} D_{ikW}^2 + \sum_{i=1}^{m} \eta_i \sum_{k=1}^{n} (u_{ik}^{(f)})^{h_f} (1 - u_{ik}^{(p)})^{h_p}$$

$$\tag{4}$$

where $u_{ik}^{(p)}$ is the possibilistic membership of x_k in the cluster i, $u_{ik}^{(f)}$ is the fuzzy membership of $\boldsymbol{x}_k$ in the cluster i, D_{ikW} is the weighted euclidean distance, η_i is a scale parameter that is calculated by: $\eta_i = \dfrac{\sum_{k=1}^{n} (u_{ik}^{(f)})^{h_f} \| \boldsymbol{x}_k - \boldsymbol{c}_i \|^2}{(u_{ik}^{(f)})^{h_f}}$.

This function is obtained by replacing de distance measure in the FCM algorithm by the objective function of the PCM algorithm, obtaining a mixed approach. The scale parameter determines the relative degree to which the second term in the objective function is compared with the first. This second term forces to make the possibilistic membership degree as big as possible, thus, choosing this value for η_i will keep a balance between the fuzzy and the possibilistic memberships.

The algorithm has a migration step that moves centers allocated in input zones where the target function is stable, to zones where the output variability is higher. The idea of a migration step was introduced in [14] as an extension of Hard C-means.

3   Fuzzy-Possibilistic Centers Initializer (FPCI)

This section introduces the proposed algorithm, describing first the elements that characterize the algorithm: the supervising parameter, the migration process and the distortion function. Then the main body of the algorithm, which integrates the previous components, is introduced.

3.1   Supervising Parameter

Classical clustering techniques do not consider the output of the function that will be approximated by the RBFNN, so there is a need of introducing an element that influences the way in which the centers are placed. This effect can be achieved by changing the similarity criteria that defines the clusters.

In [8], it was presented the concept of expected output of a center which is an hypothetic value for each center that gives a position on the output axis. This element makes possible to compare the output of the centers and the real output of the input vectors. The calculation of the supervising parameter w is performed by:

$$w_{ik} = |F(\boldsymbol{x}_k) - o_i|$$ (5)

where o_i represents the expected output of a center. The parameter w is used in the algorithm in order to modify the similarity criteria during the clustering process, reducing the distance between a center and an input vector if they have similar outputs. Therefore, the distance calculation is performed by:

$$D_{ikW} = d_{ik} \cdot w_{ik}$$ (6)

where d_{ik} is the euclidean distance between the center $\boldsymbol{c}_i$ and the input vector $\boldsymbol{x}_k$.

3.2   Distortion Function

As classical clustering algorithms, the proposed algorithm defines a distortion function that has to be minimized. The distortion function is based in a fuzzy-possibilistic approach as it was presented in [12] although it contains the elements required for a supervised learning. The function is:

$$J_h(U, C, T, W; X) = \sum_{k=1}^{n} \sum_{i=1}^{m} (u_{ik}^{h_f} + t_{ik}^{h_p}) D_{ikW}^2$$ (7)

restricted to the constraints: $\sum_{i=1}^{m} u_{ik} = 1 \; \forall k = 1...n$ and $\sum_{k=1}^{n} t_{ik} = 1 \; \forall i = 1...m$.

The solution is reached by an alternating optimization approach where all the elements defined in the function to be minimized (Equation 7) are actualized iteratively. For the new algorithm proposed in this paper, the equations are:

$$u_{ik} = \cfrac{1}{\displaystyle\sum_{j=1}^{m} \left(\cfrac{t_{ik}^{(h_p-1)/2} D_{ikW}}{t_{jk}^{(h_p-1)/2} D_{jkW}} \right)^{\frac{2}{h_f-1}}} \qquad t_{ik} = \cfrac{1}{1 + \left(\cfrac{D_{ikW}}{\eta_i} \right)^{\frac{1}{h_p-1}}} \tag{8}$$

$$c_i = \cfrac{\displaystyle\sum_{k=1}^{n} t_{ik}^{h_p} u_{ik}^{h_f} x_k w_{ik}^2}{\displaystyle\sum_{k=1}^{n} t_{ik}^{h_p} u_{ik}^{h_f} w_{ik}^2} \qquad o_i = \cfrac{\displaystyle\sum_{k=1}^{n} t_{ik}^{h_p} u_{ik}^{h_f} y_k d_{ik}^2}{\displaystyle\sum_{k=1}^{n} t_{ik}^{h_p} u_{ik}^{h_f} d_{ik}^2} \tag{9}$$

These equations are obtained by differentiating $J_h(U, T, C, W; X)$ (Equation 7) with u_{ik}, t_{ik}, c_i and o_i, therefore the convergence is guaranteed.

3.3   Migration Step

The migration step will allow the algorithm to escape from local minima found during the iterative process, that minimizes the distortion function, and to work with non continuous data sets.

The idea of a migration step was developed in [14], and it was also used in [10], but the migration the new algorithm uses is totally different to the previous ones because it adds problem specific knowledge.

Since the problem is to design an RBFNN to approximate a given function, an RBFNN is generated to decide where to move the centers and if the migration step was correct. The migration is accepted if the distortion function has been decreased or if the error from the output of the RBFNN generated after the migration is smaller than the error from the RBFNN generated before.

To design the RBFNN on each migration step, since the centers are already placed, it is only needed to get the values for each radius, which is calculated using the KNN algorithm with K=1. Once we have these two parameters, the weights for each RBF are computed optimally by solving a linear equation system [7].

$$error_i = \text{Accumulated error between the hypothetic output of the center } c_i$$
$$\text{and the output of the vectors that belong to that center}$$
$$numvec_i = \text{number of vectors that belong to } c_i$$

```
for each center c_i with i = 1...m
    if error_i < mean(error)
        select c_i
    else
        if numvec_i < mean(numvec)
            select c_i
        end
    end
    distortion_i = error_i · numvec_i
end
utility_i = distortion_i / mean(distortion)
```

Each center is assigned an utility value that represents how important is that center in the current partition. The utility of a center is calculated with the following algorithm:

This process excludes the centers that own a big number of input vectors and have a small error from those vectors from the set of centers to be source or destination of the migration. Once the pre-selection of the centers has been done, the center that will be migrated is the one with minimum utility and the center receiving the other center is the one with maximum utility.

Due to the addition of the parameter w both the fuzzy and the possibilistic membership functions loose their interpretability. The combination of them using a fuzzy rule will allow us to decide which input vectors are owned by each cluster. This process is necessary in order to choose which centers will be migrated.

```
for each center c_i
    for each input vector x_k
        distance=||x_k - c_i||
        if (distance< near)
            B_ik = (u_ik · t_ik)/(distance+1 + w_ik)
        else
            B_ik = (u_ik · t_ik)/(distance+1)
        end
    end
end
```

The aim of the rule is that if an input vector is *near* a center, the value of the output of that input vector must influence the position of the center, otherwise, the difference between the expected and the real output is not as important since the center is far. This method alleviates the problem of an input vector being owned by a center just because they have the same output values. In order to set a value for the threshold *near*, the columns of the matrix B must be normalized. An empirical value of 0.05 has been shown to provide a good performance as it will be shown in the experiments.

The complete algorithm for the migration is shown in Figure 1.

3.4   General Scheme

The FPCI algorithm follows the scheme shown in Figure 2. In the new algorithm, centers will be distributed uniformly through the input data space. Proceeding like this, all random elements of the previous algorithm are excluded, obtaining the maximum robustness. The centers expected outputs must be initialized using the same value, thanks to this, all the centers will be in the same conditions so the weighting parameter will influence the centers in the same way in the first iteration of the algorithm. The initialization value is not too important and does not influence in a significant way the final configuration of the centers

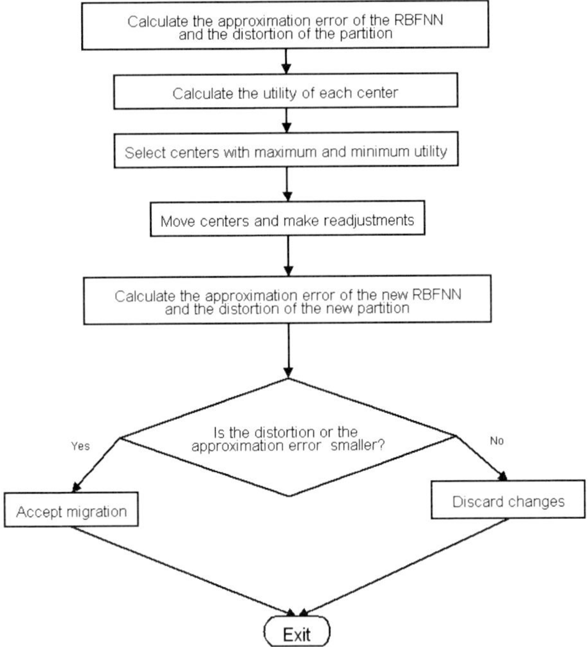

Fig. 1. FPCI migration algorithm

although a fixed value of 1 is assigned in order to avoid any random element in the algorithm. This leads to obtain always the same output for a fixed input, providing a standard deviation of zero when multiple executions are run with the same input.

4   Experimental Results

The target function that will be used in this experiment was presented in [3] and it has been used as a benchmark in [4,5]. The function is defined as:

$$f_1(x_1, x_2) = 1.9 \left(1.35 + e^{x_1} \sin\left(13\left(x_1 - 0.6\right)^2\right) e^{-x_2} \sin\left(7x_2\right)\right), \quad x_1, x_2 \in [0, 1] \tag{10}$$

Figure 3 shows the original function and the training data set that was obtained by selecting randomly 400 points from the original function. The number of test input vectors was 1900, such a big difference between the size of the data sets is to show the generalization abilities of the RBFNN that, learning from a reduced number of examples, are able to generalize and obtain a good approximation of the complete function.

Once the centers were placed by all the algorithms, the radii of the RBFs were calculated using the KNN heuristic with k=1, and then, a local search algorithm

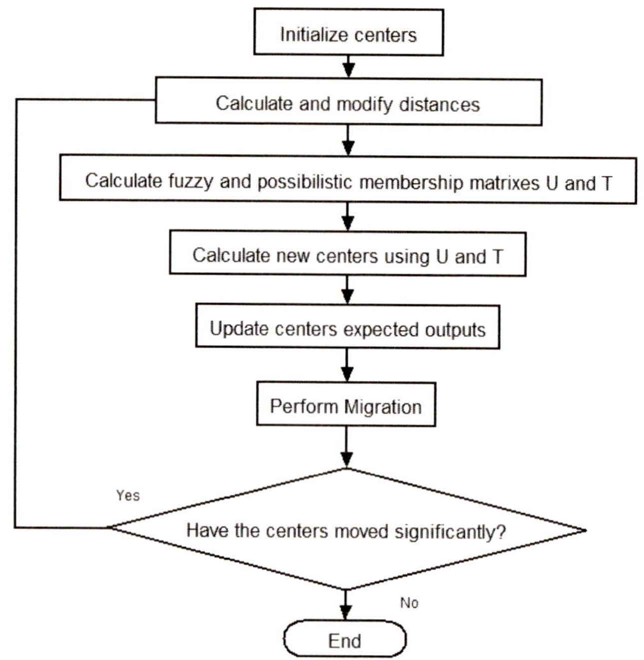

Fig. 2. General scheme of the FPCI algorithm

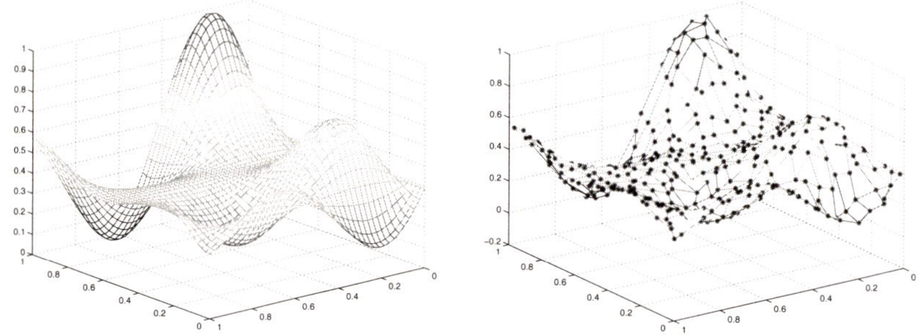

Fig. 3. Target function f_1 and the training set

(Levenberg-Marquardt) was applied to obtain a fine tuning of these parameters. Table 1 shows the approximation errors obtained after designing the RBFNNs using the algorithms described above.

These results show how the best performance is obtained by the proposed algorithm. In general, the other three algorithms have the drawback of lack of robustness. The results obtained using the FPCM show how the combination of a fuzzy partition with a possibilistic one leads to a better performance. The

Table 1. Mean and Standard Deviation of the approximation error (NRMSE) for function f_1 for the training and test set

Clusters	FCM	FPCM	PCI	FPCI
8	0.155(0.039)	0.163(0.037)	0.204(0.042)	0.145(0)
9	0.160(0.019)	0.136(0.035)	0.112(0.023)	0.130(0)
10	0.108(0.030)	0.118(0.035)	0.102(0.011)	0.085(0)
11	0.128(0.073)	0.077(0.012)	0.071(0.015)	0.062(0)
8	0.153(0.040)	0.160(0.036)	0.245(0.119)	0.143(0)
9	0.157(0.017)	0.135(0.034)	0.129(0.061)	0.131(0)
10	0.107(0.027)	0.116(0.032)	0.100(0.011)	0.087(0)
11	0.126(0.050)	0.078(0.012)	0.071(0.015)	0.062(0)

PCI algorithm uses both types of partitions with the addition of an element to consider the output of the function to be approximated, this element makes possible to obtain better results than the other non-supervised algorithms. The new algorithm combines the advantages of using the same type of fuzzy possibilistic partition of the FPCM algorithm with the addition of the supervising parameter and the migration step. These three elements together lead to obtain the smallest approximation errors when is compared with the other algorithms.

Regarding the use of RBFNN to approximate a function, the results the algorithms present show how well they perform when interpolating the modelled function because for all the algorithms, the training and test errors do not differ significantly.

5   Conclusions

Within the different methods to solve the function approximation problem, RBFNNs have shown their good performance although their design still represents a difficult problem. The RBF center initialization is the first stage in the design, and the success of the rest of the stages depends critically in the way the centers are placed. This paper presents a new algorithm that combines several elements of previous algorithms used to place the centers, adding a new element that uses problem specific knowledge. This new element consists in the design of an RBFNN that helps to decide where to move the centers in the migration stage. The migration incorporates also a fuzzy rule that alleviates the problem of loosing interpretability in the supervised method, making more adequate the election of the centers that should be migrated.

References

1. J. C. Bezdek. *Pattern Recognition with Fuzzy Objective Function Algorithms.* Plenum, New York, 1981.
2. A. G. Bors. Introduction of the Radial Basis Function (RBF) networks. *OnLine Symposium for Electronics Engineers*, 1:1–7, February 2001.

3. V. Cherkassky and H.Lari-Najafi. Constrained topological mapping for nonparametric regression analysis. *Neural Networks*, 4(1):27–40, 1991.
4. J. H. Friedman. Multivariate adaptive regression splines (with discussion). *Annals of Statistics*, 19:1–141, 1991.
5. J.H. Friedman. Projection pursuit regression. *Journal of the American Statistical Association*, 76:817–823, 1981.
6. A. Gersho. Asymptotically Optimal Block Quantization. *IEEE Transanctions on Information Theory*, 25(4):373–380, July 1979.
7. J. González, I. Rojas, J. Ortega, H. Pomares, F.J. Fernández, and A. Díaz. Multiobjective evolutionary optimization of the size, shape, and position parameters of radial basis function networks for function approximation. *IEEE Transactions on Neural Networks*, 14(6):1478–1495, November 2003.
8. J. González, I. Rojas, H. Pomares, J. Ortega, and A. Prieto. A new Clustering Technique for Function Aproximation. *IEEE Transactions on Neural Networks*, 13(1):132–142, January 2002.
9. A. Guillén, I. Rojas, J. González, H. Pomares, L.J. Herrera, O. Valenzuela, and A. Prieto. A Possibilistic Approach to RBFN Centers Initialization. *Lecture Notes in Computer Science*, 3642:174–183, 2005.
10. A. Guillén, I. Rojas, J. González, H. Pomares, L.J. Herrera, O. Valenzuela, and A. Prieto. Improving Clustering Technique for Functional Approximation Problem Using Fuzzy Logic: ICFA algorithm. *Lecture Notes in Computer Science*, 3512: 272–280, June 2005.
11. N. B. Karayiannis and G. W. Mi. Growing radial basis neural networks: Merging supervised and unsupervised learning with network growth techniques. *IEEE Transactions on Neural Networks*, 8:1492–1506, November 1997.
12. N. R. Pal, K. Pal, and J. C. Bezdek. A Mixed C–Means Clustering Model. In *Proceedings of the 6th IEEE International Conference on Fuzzy Systems (FUZZ-IEEE'97)*, volume 1, pages 11–21, Barcelona, July 1997.
13. J. Park and J. W. Sandberg. Universal approximation using radial basis functions network. *Neural Computation*, 3:246–257, 1991.
14. G. Patanè and M. Russo. The Enhanced-LBG algorithm. *Neural Networks*, 14(9):1219–1237, 2001.
15. I. Rojas, M. Anguita, A. Prieto, and O. Valenzuela. Analysis of the operators involved in the definition of the implication functions and in the fuzzy inference proccess. *International Journal of Approximate Reasoning*, 19:367–389, 1998.
16. J. Zhang and Y. Leung. Improved possibilistic C–means clustering algorithms. *IEEE Transactions on Fuzzy Systems*, 12:209–217, 2004.
17. Q. Zhu, Y. Cai, and L. Liu. A global learning algorithm for a RBF network. *Neural Networks*, 12:527–540, 1999.

A Partitive Rough Clustering Algorithm

Georg Peters and Martin Lampart

Munich University of Applied Sciences
Faculty of Computer Science/Mathematics
Lothstrasse 34, 80335 Munich, Germany
georg.peters@muas.de, martin_lampart@web.de

Abstract. Since rough sets were introduced by Pawlak about 25 years ago they have become a central part of soft computing. Recently Lingras presented a rough k-means clustering algorithm which assigns the data objects to lower and upper approximations of clusters. In our paper we introduce a rough k-medoids clustering algorithm and apply it to four different data sets (synthetic, colon cancer, forest and control chart data). We compare the results of these experiments to Lingras rough k-means and discuss the strengths and weaknesses of the rough k-medoids.

1 Introduction

Since its introduction rough set theory [8] has gained increasing importance and has become a central concept of soft computing. Recently Lingras et al. [5] suggested a rough set clustering algorithm that assigns data objects to upper and lower approximations with the lower approximation a subset of the upper approximation. Objects in the lower approximation belong to a certain cluster unambiguously while the memberships of objects that do not belong to a lower approximation are not clearly defined due to missing information. These objects belong to the boundary area which is defined as upper approximation without the area covered by the lower approximation.

Consequently an object in a lower approximation of a certain cluster cannot belong to any other cluster - it is a member of one and only one lower approximation. To show that the membership of an objects is unclear it has to be assigned to more than one upper approximation. Nevertheless this object is member of one and only one of the associated clusters only - however its actual membership cannot be determined due to missing information.

Lingras rough k-means clustering algorithms has already been successfully applied to real data such as web-log, forest, vowel and mircoarray data besides others. Mitra [7] extended the rough k-means by an evolutionary component to determine the optimal initial parameters and Peters suggested refinements of the algorithm to improve its performance in the presence of outliers [9], increase its convergence and besides others refinements [10]. Further rough clustering approaches have been suggested by do Prado, Engel and Filho [3] and Voges [11].

In this paper we introduce a rough k-medoids clustering algorithm which belongs to the family of the rough models suggested by Lingras et al. [5] and

S. Greco et al. (Eds.): RSCTC 2006, LNAI 4259, pp. 657–666, 2006.

the classic k-medoids as introduced by Kaufman et al. [4]. The new algorithm is applied to four different data sets and compared to Lingras rough k-means.

The paper is organized as follows. In Section 2 we describe the rough k-means cluster algorithm of Lingras et al. and some of its extensions. Then, in Section 3, we present the new rough k-medoids. In the following Section 4 we evaluate the rough k-medoids by applying it to synthetic and real data. The article concludes with a summary in Section 5.

2   Rough k-Means Cluster Algorithms

2.1   Lingras' k-Means

Lingras et al. rough set clustering algorithm belongs to the branch of rough set theory with a reduced set of properties in comparison to the original ideas of Pawlak [12]. The properties are:

1. A data object belongs to one lower approximation at most.
2. If a data object is no member of any lower approximation it belongs to two or more upper approximations.
3. A lower approximation is a subset of its corresponding upper approximation.

The part of an upper approximation that is not covered by a lower approximation is called boundary area. The means are computed as weighted sums of the data objects $\boldsymbol{X_n}(n = 1, ..., N)$ in the lower approximation (weight w_l) and the boundary area (weight w_b):

$$
\boldsymbol{m_k} =
\begin{cases}
w_l \sum\limits_{\boldsymbol{X_n} \in \underline{C_k}} \dfrac{\boldsymbol{X_n}}{|\underline{C_k}|} + w_b \sum\limits_{\boldsymbol{X_n} \in C_k^B} \dfrac{\boldsymbol{X_n}}{|C_k^B|} & \text{for } C_k^B \neq \emptyset \\[2ex]
w_l \sum\limits_{\boldsymbol{X_n} \in \underline{C_k}} \dfrac{\boldsymbol{X_n}}{|\underline{C_k}|} & \text{otherwise}
\end{cases}
\tag{1}
$$

where $|\underline{C_k}|$ is the number of objects in lower approximation and $|C_k^B| = |\overline{C_k} - \underline{C_k}|$ (with $\overline{C_k}$ the upper approximation) in the boundary area of cluster k ($k = 1, ..., K$). Then Lingras et al. rough set clustering algorithm goes as follows:

1. Define the initial parameters: the weights w_l and w_b, the number of clusters K and a threshold ϵ.
2. Randomly assign the data objects to one lower approximation (and per definitionem to the corresponding upper approximation).
3. Calculate the means according to Eq (1).
4. For each data object, determine its closest mean. If other means are not reasonably farer away as the closest mean (defined by the threshold ϵ) assign the data object to the upper approximations of these close clusters. Otherwise assign the data object to the lower approximation (and per definitionem to the corresponding upper approximation) of the cluster of its closest mean.
5. Check convergence. If converged: STOP otherwise continue with STEP 3.

2.2   Extensions and Variations of the Rough k-Means

Mitra's Evolutionary Rough k-Means. To initialize the rough k-means one has to select the weights of the lower approximation and the boundary area as well as the number of clusters.

Mitra [7] argued that a good initial setting of these parameters is one of the main challenges in rough set clustering. Therefore she suggested an evolutionary version of Lingras rough k-means which automates the selection of the weights and number of clusters. Mitra applied a genetic algorithm to optimize these parameters with respect to the Davies-Bouldin cluster validity criterium [2].

The Davies-Bouldin index is independent of the number of clusters analyzed and does not depend on the partitioning cluster method. So it can be used to compare different partitioning cluster algorithms [2].

Basically the Davies-Bouldin index is the ratio of the sum of the within-cluster scatter to the between cluster separation [1]. Well separated clusters are obtained when the within-cluster scatter is small and the separation between different clusters is large [7]:

$$\frac{1}{K} \sum_{k=1}^{K} \max_{k \neq l} \left\{ \frac{S(U_k) + S(U_l)}{d(U_k, U_l)} \right\} \tag{2}$$

with $S(U_k)+S(U_l)$ the within-cluster distances and $d(U_k, U_l)$ the between-cluster separation. So the Davies-Bouldin index has to be minimized for optimal cluster separation. When analyzing the rough set cluster validation index Mitra took the members of the lower approximations of the clusters [7].

Mitra applied her evolutionary rough clustering method to vowel, forest cover and colon cancer data and compared the results to k-means, PAM, CLARANS, fuzzy k-means and fuzzy k-medoids.

Peters' Refined Rough k-Means Algorithm. Peters presented a refined version of Lingras rough k-means which improves its performance in the presence of outliers [9], its compliance to the classic k-means, its numerical stability and others [10]. He applied the algorithm to a small and a large synthetic data set, forest cover data and microarray gene data from bioinformatics.

3   The New Rough k-Medoids Clustering Algorithm

3.1   Classic k-Medoids Algorithm

Overview. The k-medoids clustering algorithm was introduced by Kaufmann et al. [4]. Instead of calculating a cluster center as mean, in k-medoids clustering the cluster center is represented by a real data object.

Mainly there are the following advantages of the k-medoids in comparison to the k-means. (1) Each cluster has a real data object as its representative rather than an artificial one. (2) The k-medoids delivers better results in the presents of (extreme) outliers since the cluster center is always within the core cluster while applying the k-means could result in cluster centers that are "drawn" out of the core cluster. (3) The k-medoids is less noise sensitive in comparison to the k-means. (4) The objective criterion can be defined freely by the user.

The main drawbacks of the k-medoids are: (1) The algorithm is of combinatoric nature which makes it not as efficient as the k-means. (2) The need for a real data object as cluster center compromises on its quality as representative in comparison to the artificial cluster center in k-means clustering. (3) For small changes in the distribution of the data objects the cluster centers change discontinuously in certain circumstances: they jump from one data object to another.

The Algorithm: Often the compactness of the clustering (CPC) is chosen as objective criterion: $CPC = \sum_{k=1}^{K} CPC(C_k)$ with $CPC(C_k) = \sum_{X_n \in C_k} d(X_n, m_k)$ and C_k the compactness of cluster k. Then the algorithm goes as follows [4]:

1. Define the number of cluster K.
2. Randomly define K data objects as medoids.
3. Assign the remaining data objects (non-medoids) to the cluster of its closest medoid.
4. Swap each medoid with every non-medoid as long as the compactness of the clustering CPC improves.
5. Check convergence. If converged: STOP otherwise continue with STEP 3.

Please note, that the objective criterion of the k-medoids (CPC) is well separated from any other step of the clustering algorithm. Therefore it can be replaced by another objective criterion easily.

3.2   Introducing Rough k-Medoids Clustering

We introduce a new rough cluster algorithm that has its foundations in the rough k-means [6] and the classic k-medoids [4]. It proceeds as follows:

Some Definitions:

- Data set: X_n, $n = 1, ..., N$
- Medoids: m_k of the clusters C_k, $k = 1, ..., K$.
- Distance between the data object X_n and the medoid m_k:
  $d(X_n, m_k) = \|X_n - m_k\|$
- Rough Compactness of the clustering:
  $RCPC = \sum_{k=1}^{K} RCPC(C_k)$
  with $RCPC(C_k) = w_l \sum_{X_n \in \underline{C_k}} d(X_n, m_k) + w_b \sum_{X_n \in (\overline{C_k} - \underline{C_k})} d(X_n, m_k)$.
  The parameters w_l and w_b define the impact of the lower approximation and the boundary area of a cluster on the rough compactness RCPC.

The Algorithm:

1. Select K data objects randomly as medoids: $\boldsymbol{m_k}$, $k = 1, ..., K$. They belong to the lower approximation of the set they are medoids of: $\boldsymbol{m_k} \in \underline{C_k}$.
   The remaining data objects are denoted as $\boldsymbol{X'_m}, m = 1, ..., (N - K)$.
2. Assign the remaining $(N - K)$ data objects $\boldsymbol{X'_m}$ to the K clusters in a two step process. In the first step a data object is assigned to the upper approximation of the cluster to which it is closest. In the second step the data object is assigned to the upper approximation of further reasonably close clusters *or* it is assigned to the lower approximation of the closest cluster. The details are as follows:
   (i) For a given data object $\boldsymbol{X'_m}$ determine its closest medoid $\boldsymbol{m_k}$:
   $$d(\boldsymbol{X'_m}, \boldsymbol{m_k}) = \min_{h=1,...K} d(\boldsymbol{X'_m}, \boldsymbol{m_h}).$$

   Assign $\boldsymbol{X'_m}$ to the upper approximation of the cluster k: $\boldsymbol{X'_m} \in \overline{C_k}$.
   (ii) Determine the clusters C_h that are also close to $\boldsymbol{X'_m}$ - they are not farther away from $\boldsymbol{X'_m}$ than $d(\boldsymbol{X'_n}, \boldsymbol{m_k}) + \epsilon$ where ϵ is a given threshold:
   $$T = \{h : d(\boldsymbol{X'_n}, \boldsymbol{m_h}) - d(\boldsymbol{X'_n}, \boldsymbol{m_k}) \leq \epsilon \wedge h \neq k\}.$$
   - **If** $T \neq \emptyset$ ($\boldsymbol{X'_n}$ is also close to at least one other medoid besides $\boldsymbol{m_k}$)
     Then $\boldsymbol{X'_m} \in \overline{C_h}, \forall h \in T$.
   - **Else** $\boldsymbol{X'_m} \in \underline{C_k}$.
3. Calculate $RCPC_{current}$.
4. Swap every medoid $\boldsymbol{m_k}$ with every data object $\boldsymbol{X'_m}$ and calculate $RCPC_{k \leftrightarrow m}$. Let $RCPC_{k_0 \leftrightarrow m_0} = \min_{\forall k, \forall m} RCPC_{k \leftrightarrow m}$ for $k = 1, ..., K$, $m = 1, ..., (N - K)$.
   - **If** $RCPC_{k_0 \leftrightarrow m_0} < RCPC_{current}$
     Then swap the medoid $\boldsymbol{m_{k_0}}$ and data object $\boldsymbol{X_{m_0}}$ and set $RCPC_{current} = RCPC_{k_0 \leftrightarrow m_0}$. Go back to STEP 2.
   - **Else** STOP.

4   Evaluation of the Rough k-Medoids

The rough k-medoids cluster algorithm will be tested and compared to the rough k-means in four experiments: synthetic, colon cancer, forest and control chart data.

4.1   Synthetic Data

The synthetic data [9] consist of a two dimensional set of ten randomly distributed data objects in an interval of $[0, 1]$. In each of the following experiments the number of clusters is set to two $(K = 2)$.

Rough k-Means. For the rough k-means we obtain a Davies-Bouldin index of $DB_{Means} = 0.403$ for $w_l = 0.95$ and thresholds between $\epsilon \in [0.25, 0.55]$. The assignment of the data objects to the approximations is depicted in Figure 1. The means are located as show in Table 1.

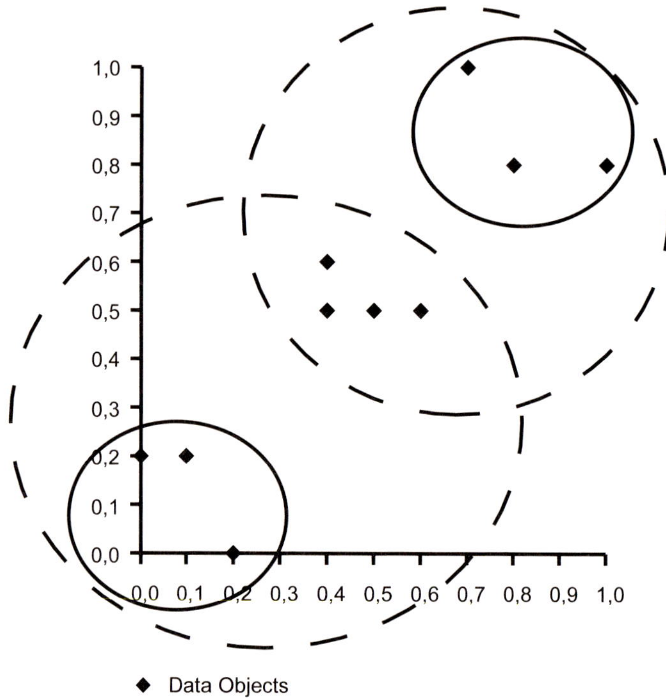

Fig. 1. Clusters for the Synthetic Data Set: Rough k-Means

Rough k-Medoids. Within the range[1] of the initial parameters $w_l \in [0.50, 0.95]$ and thresholds between $\epsilon \in [0.00, 0.30]$ the lowest Davies-Bouldin index that was obtained is $DB_{Medoids,RCPC} = 0.755$. This is significantly worse than the Davies-Bouldin index ($DB_{Means} = 0.403$) obtained by the rough k-means.

In the optimum the upper approximations of the two clusters are empty. The data objects that have been determined as medoids are (see Figure 2): $m_1 = (0.1, 0.2)$ and $m_2 = (0.5, 0.5)$.

However if the objective function, the compactness of the clustering, of the rough k-medoids is replaced by the Davies-Bouldin index the results improve. Now we get a Davies-Bouldin index of $DB_{Medoids,DB} = 0.404$ which is almost equal to the one obtained in rough k-means clustering. The assignment of the data objects to the lower and upper approximations is identical to the results obtained by the rough k-means. The medoids are $m_1 = (0.0, 0.2)$ and $m_2 = (1.0, 0.8)$.

---

[1] Cluster results outside this range lead to lower Davies-Bouldin indexes. However these results were not taken into account since the assignment of the data objects to the approximations seem to be sup-optimal in the sense that the lower approximation of one cluster only has the medoid as member while the lower approximation of the other cluster has four members.

Table 1. Means for Rough k-Means

Mean	x-axis	y-axis
1	0.119	0.153
2	0.815	0.850

4.2   Colon Cancer Data

The colon cancer database (*http://molbio.princeton.edu/colondata*) consists of 62 gene expression data which 2000 features each. In the data set 22 samples are normal and 40 of patients suffering from colon cancer.

Typically the many features of gene expression data are highly correlated. For the following experiment a correlation analysis delivered a reduced set of data with only 21 features.

The number of clusters was set to $K = 2$ reflecting the normal and colon cancer samples. First, in the rough k-medoids algorithm the RCPC is applied as optimization criterion. The optimal results according to the Davies-Bouldin index are depicted in Table 2.

Table 2. Davies-Bouldin Indexes for the Colon Cancer Experiment

Algorithm	Davies-Bouldin Index
Rough k-Means	0.602
Rough k-Medoids	0.530

Second, when the optimization criterion for the rough k-medoids is changed to the Davies-Bouldin index the optimal Davies-Bouldin index remains unchanged ($DB_{Medoids,RCPC} = DB_{Medoids,DBI} = 0.530$). So the cluster validities of both rough k-medoids cluster algorithms do not differ in the colon cancer experiment.

According to the Davies-Bouldin index the obtained results of the rough k-means and the rough k-medoids are in the same range with the rough k-medoids a little bit better.

4.3   Forest Data

The forest data set (*http://kdd.ics.uci.edu*) consist of about 580,000 observations each with 54 features. A data object describes the forest type of an area of $30x30m^2$. Features are, for example, elevation, slope or hillshade in the morning and in the afternoon. Out of the 54 features 44 are qualitative and 10 quantitative. One feature describes 7 different forest types.

To reduced complexity of the data set in the cluster experiment a randomly reduced set of 241 observations with the 10 quantitative features was taken; the number of clusters was set to $K = 3$. The results of the cluster analysis are shown in Table 3.

Again the results for the rough k-means and the rough k-medoids are within the same range. The rough k-means delivered only a little better Davis-Bouldin

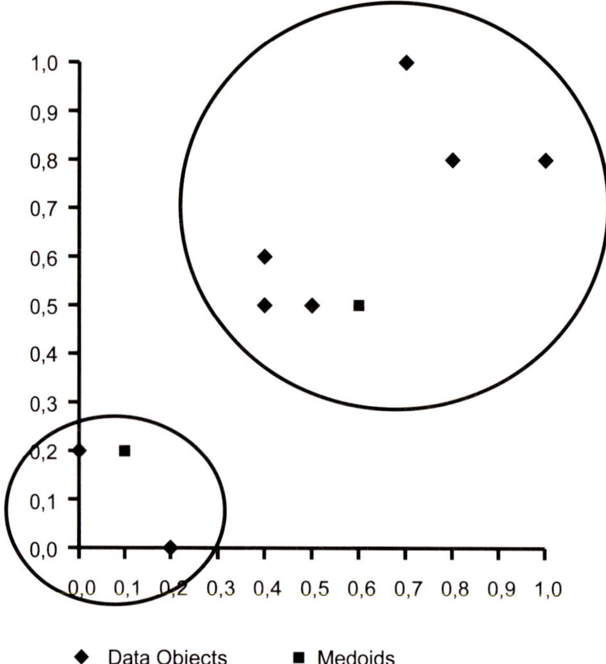

Fig. 2. Clusters for the Synthetic Data Set: Rough k-Medoids

Table 3. Davies-Bouldin Indexes for the Forest Data Experiment

Algorithm	Davies-Bouldin Index
Rough k-Means	0.908
Rough k-Medoids	0.925

index in comparison to the rough k-medoids. However, with the Davies-Bouldin index as objective criterion the rough k-medoids delivers an improved result of $DB_{Medoids,DBI} = 0.484$.

4.4   Control Chart Data

The control data set ($http://kdd.ics.uci.edu$) is synthetically generated and consists of 6 classes each with 100 observations. An object has 60 features. In the experiment 21 randomly selected data objects with all 60 features were clustered into 6 classes ($K = 6$).

The results obtained by the rough k-means and rough k-medoids are comparable again. Both deliver Davies-Bouldin indexes that are in the same range. If one applies the Davies-Bouldin index as objective criterion to the rough k-medoids the index can be improved to $DB_{Medoids,DBI} = 0.462$.

Table 4. Davies-Bouldin Indexes for the Control Chart Experiment

Algorithm	Davies-Bouldin Index
Rough k-Means	0.539
Rough k-Medoids	0.586

5 Conclusion

In the paper we presented a new k-medoids cluster algorithm based on rough set theory and applied it to four data sets. In the experiments we showed that the rough k-medoids delivers comparable results to the rough k-means.

The main advantage of the rough k-medoids cluster algorithm is that the objective criterion is not deeply integrated in the algorithm - in contrast to the rough k-means - but can be easily changed and replaced according to the needs and preferences of the user.

In our case we performed the rough k-medoids with two objective criterions: the rough compactness of the clustering and the Davies-Bouldin index. Obviously we obtained better results, in terms of the Davies-Bouldin index, when we took the second objective criterion. Any other objective criterion can also be implemented easily. This flexibility of the rough k-medoids is its special strength.

The drawback of any k-medoids is its combinatoric algorithm that makes it inefficient for large numbers of data objects and/or high dimensional feature spaces. For a small number of data objects the number of possible medoids is very limited and may lead to stable but coarse clustering results.

However, because of the flexible definition of the objective criterion, the rough k-medoids is a good alternative to the rough k-means for not too small and not too large sets of objects.

References

1. J.C. Bezdek and N.R. Pal. Some new indexes of cluster validity. *IEEE Transactions on Systems, Man, and Cybernetics*, 28:301–315, 1998.
2. D.L. Davies and D.W. Bouldin. A cluster separation measure. *IEEE Transactions on Pattern Analysis and Machine Intelligence*, 1:224–227, 1979.
3. H.A. do Prado, P.M. Engel, and H.C. Filho. Rough clustering: An alternative to find meaningful clusters by using the reducts from a dataset. In *Rough Sets and Current Trends in Computing: Third International Conference, RSCTC 2002*, volume 2475 of *LNCS*, pages 234 – 238, Berlin, 2002. Springer Verlag.
4. J. Kaufman and P.J. Rousseeuw. *Finding Groups in Data: An Introduction to Cluster Analysis*. John Wiley, New York, 1990.
5. P. Lingras and C. West. Interval set clustering of web users with rough k-means. Technical Report 2002-002, Department of Mathematics and Computer Science, St. Mary's University, Halifax, Canada, 2002.
6. P. Lingras and C. West. Interval set clustering of web users with rough k-means. *Journal of Intelligent Information Systems*, 23:5–16, 2004.

7. S. Mitra. An evolutionary rough partitive clustering. *Pattern Recognition Letters*, 25:1439–1449, 2004.

8. Z. Pawlak. Rough sets. *International Journal of Information and Computer Sciences*, 11:145–172, 1982.

9. G. Peters. Outliers in rough k-means clustering. In *Proceed. First International Conference on Pattern Recognition and Machine Intelligence*, volume 3776 of *LNCS*, pages 702–707, Kolkata, 2005. Springer Verlag.

10. G. Peters. Some refinements of rough k-means. *Pattern Recognition*, 39:1481–1491, 2006.

11. K.E. Voges, N.K. Pope, and M.R. Brown. *Heuristics and Optimization for Knowledge Discovery*, chapter Cluster Analysis of Marketing Data Examining On-Line Shopping Orientation: A Comparision of k-Means and Rough Clustering Approaches, pages 207–224. Idea Group Publishing, Hershey PA, 2002.

12. Y.Y. Yao, X. Li, T.Y. Lin, and Q. Liu. Representation and classification of rough set models. In *Proceedings Third International Workshop on Rough Sets and Soft Computing*, pages 630–637, San Jose, CA, 1994.

A Zone-Based Method for Selecting Clusterheads in Wireless Sensor Networks

Kyungmi Kim[1], Hyunsook Kim[2], and Kijun Han[3,*]

Department of Computer Engineering, Kyungpook National University,
1370, Sangyuk-dong, Buk-gu, Daegu, 702-701, Korea
Tel : +82-53-940-8697 Fax : +82-53-957-4846
[1] kmkim@handong.ac.kr, [2] hskim@netopia.knu.ac.kr,
[3] kjhan@knu.ac.kr

Abstract. In this paper, we propose a method for selecting clusterheads, called 'zone-based method for selecting clusterheads', in a wireless sensor network to balance the amount of energy consumption over all nodes without generating any isolated sensor nodes. In our method, the network field is first divided into several zones, and each zone includes clusterheads in proportion to its area, which contributes to distributing clusterheads evenly over the network. Simulation results show that our method outperforms LEACH and PEGASIS in terms of network lifetime.

Keywords: wireless sensor network, clustering, clusterhead selection, multiple hop transmission.

1 Introduction

Due to the development of low cost and low power sensing devices with computational ability, wireless sensing and communication capabilities, wireless sensor networks can be applicable to various environments that monitor a specified parameter in a region. They are especially useful in extremely hostile environments, such as near volcanically active sites, inside a dangerous chemical plant or in disaster area with a nuclear reactor. They also have advantages in inaccessible environments, such as difficult terrains, or on a spaceship [1].

Generally a sensor node consists of sensing elements, microprocessor, limited memory, battery, and low power radio transmitter and receiver. An important feature of wireless sensor networks is that the nodes are unattended, resource-constrained, their energy cannot be recharged. Since the batteries of the sensor nodes are not regularly rechargeable or not replaceable, the lifetime of a system is limited and distributing power consumption to all nodes is a major design factor [2]. Therefore, locating sensor nodes over network fields efficiently is one of the most important topics in sensor networks. Clustering approaches in wireless sensor networks have been proposed in to minimize the energy used to communicate data from nodes to the sink [3-5]. A good clustering scheme should preserve its structure of cluster as much as possible [6].

---

* Corresponding Author.

S. Greco et al. (Eds.): RSCTC 2006, LNAI 4259, pp. 667–676, 2006.
© Springer-Verlag Berlin Heidelberg 2006

In this paper, we propose a method to evenly distribute clusterheads over network field to reduce the energy consumption and the computational overhead. To distribute the clusterheads evenly, the network field is divided into several zones, and the number of clusterheads to be included in each zone is determined in proportion to its area. In our method, the sensed data is transmitted over multiple-hop path through clusterheads. Since reclustering is performed in a single zone independently, the computational overhead will be reduced as compared with the conventional approaches in which reclustering is carried out for all nodes in the network field every round.

This paper is organized as follows. We discuss some related works in section 2 and present an overview and discussion of our method in section 3. In section 4, we compare our method with the existing protocols and show the results. Finally, we conclude the paper in section 5.

2   Related Works

Heinzelman has proposed Low-Energy Adaptive Clustering Hierarchy (LEACH) for efficient routing of data in wireless sensor networks. In LEACH, the sensors elect themselves as clusterheads with some probability and broadcast their decisions. Each sensor node determines to which cluster it wants to belong by choosing the cluster-head that requires the minimum communication energy. The algorithm is run periodically, and the probability of becoming a clusterhead for each period is chosen to ensure that every node becomes a clusterhead at least once within 1/p rounds, where p is 5 percent of the number of all nodes [7]. The positive aspect of LEACH is the fact that the nodes will randomly deplete their power supply, and therefore they should randomly die throughout the network. The randomized clusterheads will make it very difficult to achieve the optimal number of clusterheads [8].

A centralized version of LEACH, called LEACH-C, was proposed in [9]. Unlike LEACH, where nodes self-configure themselves into clusters, LEACH-C uses a centralized algorithm that employs the sink as a cluster formation controller. During the setup phase of LEACH-C, the sink receives information regarding the location and energy level of each node in the network. Using this information, the sink finds a predetermined number of clusterheads and configures the network into clusters. The cluster groupings are chosen to minimize the energy required for non-cluster-head nodes to transmit their data to their respective clusterheads (see Figure 1 (a)) [9].

Power Efficient Gathering in Sensor Information Systems (PEGASIS) [4] enhances network lifetime by increasing local collaboration among sensor nodes. In PEGASIS, sensor nodes are arranged in a chain topology using a greedy algorithm so that each node transmits to and receives from only one of its neighbors. Every rounds, a randomly chosen node from the chain will transmit the aggregated data to the sink, thus reducing the per round energy consumption compared to LEACH [3].

The core ideas of Base station Controlled Dynamic Clustering Protocol (BCDCP) [3] are the formation of balanced clusters where each clusterhead leads an nearly same number of sensor nodes to avoid clusterheads overload, uniform placement of clusterheads throughout the whole sensor fields, and utilization of cluster-head-to-cluster-head routing to transfer the data to the base station as shown in Figure 1 (b).

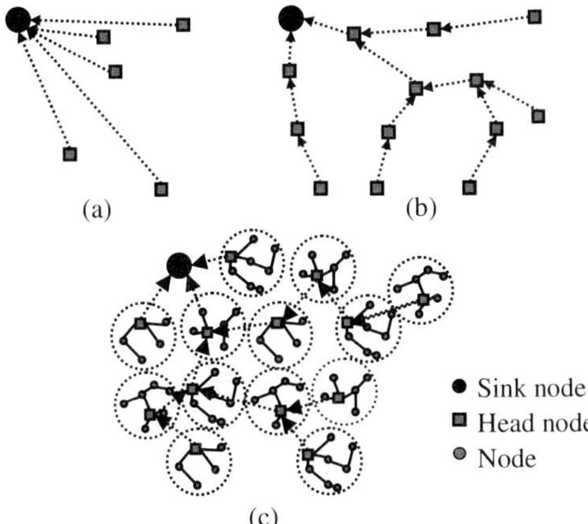

Fig. 1. (a) Single-hop to the sink node, (b) Multi-hop between CH-to-CH (c) Multi-hop between CH-to-CH and node-to-node

3   Proposed Scheme

In this paper, we propose a topology configuring method for wireless sensor networks with an objective of balancing energy consumption over all nodes in the network field without generating any isolated nodes. We call it 'zone-based method for selecting clusterheads'.

Our method starts from dividing a network field into several zones depending on the distance from the origin point. Each sensor node transmits data toward the sink through the nearest neighbor node or clusterhead in each zone. Each clusterhead aggregates data and sends it to the next zone, and continues until all data are transmitted to the sink. The sink node is an essential component which has complex computational abilities, thus making the sensor nodes very simple and cost effective. It has three primary goals:

- prolonging network lifetime by evenly distributing clusterhead over the network,
- balancing energy consumption by selecting clusterhead in proportion to the area of each zone, and
- saving communication energy with multiple-hop transmission.

Several assumptions needed in our method are:

(1) All nodes in the network are uniformly distributed and quasi-stationary, (2) all nodes are homogeneous, energy constrained and location-aware, (3) all nodes are sensing at a fixed rate and always have data to send, (4) the sink is fixed, (5) the sink controls clusterhead selection, and (6) all data sent by the previous nodes are aggregated by a constant bit size.

Our method operates in three phases: (1) zone configuration phase, (2) clustering phase, (3) reclustering and data communication phase as shown in Figure 2. Zone configuration phase is executed just once at the time of network initialization to divide overall network into several zones. Clustering phase is also carried out one time to choose the initial clusterhead in all zones when the network is first deployed. Reclustering and data communication phase is performed for every round in a single zone independently to reduce the computational overhead as much as possible.

(1) ZC: Zone Configuration, (2) CLST: Clustering for all zones
(3) ReCLST$_i$: Reclustering for $ZONE_i$ and Data communication

Fig. 2. Three phases for clusterhead selection

3.1 Zone Configuration Phase

The main activity in this phase is to divide the network field into several zones as shown in Figure 3. The zone is configured based on the zone range (r) which is determined by considering the network size, transmission range, and distribution density of the nodes.

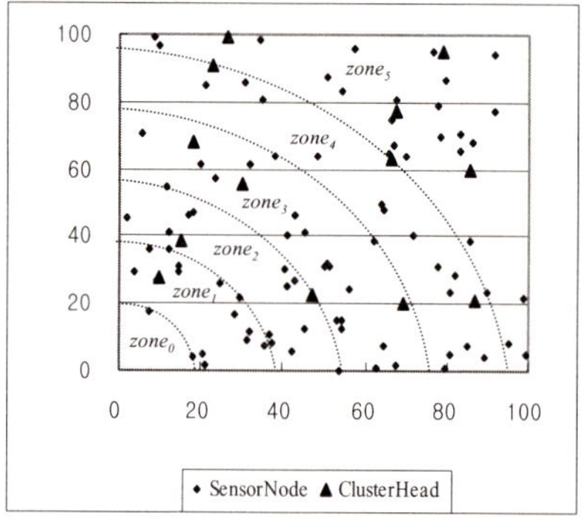

Fig. 3. Zone configuration

The first zone, denoted by $ZONE_0$, contains sensor nodes whose distances to the origin point are less than the zone range (r). The next zone, $ZONE_1$, contains sensor nodes whose distances to the origin point are greater than r but less than $2r$. So, the i-th zone, $ZONE_i$, includes sensor nodes whose distances to the origin point are greater than $i \times r$ but less than $(i+1) \times r$. The last zone covers all remaining sensor nodes beyond the boundary of the previous zone. Thus, the total number of zones configured in the network is given by $(NETWORK\_RANGE)/r + 1$.

After zone configuration, the sink node broadcasts the zone information to have each node know which zone itself is assigned to. The number of clusterheads in each zone is determined in proportion to the area of each zone. In $ZONE_0$, no clusterhead is allowed because this zone has the sink. In $ZONE_1$, we can assign only one clusterhead. The number of clusterheads in $ZONE_2$ is proportional to the area of $ZONE_2$. For example, if the area of $ZONE_2$ is about two times than the area of $ZONE_1$, $ZONE_2$ has two clusterheads. The number of clusterheads in each zone is obtained by

$$N\_CH_i = \frac{Area(ZONE_i)}{Area(ZONE_1)}, \qquad i \geq 2 \tag{1}$$

where N_CH_i is the number of clusterheads elected in $ZONE_i$.

3.2 Clustering Phase

This phase consists of the clusterhead(CH) selection, the cluster setup, and the formation of routing paths. The sink node selects the clusterheads until the desired number of clusterheads in each zone is attained. We select a high density node, which has a good many neighbor nodes, as a clusterhead in each zone. Reclustering is performed for a single zone every round. After the number of rounds equal to a multiple of the number of zones, all clusterheads are replaced once for all zones. Cluster setup operation in this phase means that each node joins in the close clusterhead in the same zone.

Once the clusters and the clusterheads have been identified, the sink node chooses the routing path for any two adjacent clusterheads as illustrated in Figure 1 (b). All sensor nodes transmit data to the close neighbor node until reaching the clusterhead in the cluster as depicted in Figure 1 (c). There is an exception in case that all nodes in $ZONE_0$ where data is transmitted to the sink directly.

3.3 Reclustering and Data Communication Phase

The main functions in this phase are reclustering for a single zone, data gathering, data fusion, and data forwarding. All sensor nodes transmit the sensed information to their clusterhead by multiple-hop paths as shown in Figure 4. Once a clusterhead receives data from any nodes, it performs data fusion on the collected data to reduce the amount of raw data that needs to be sent to the sink.

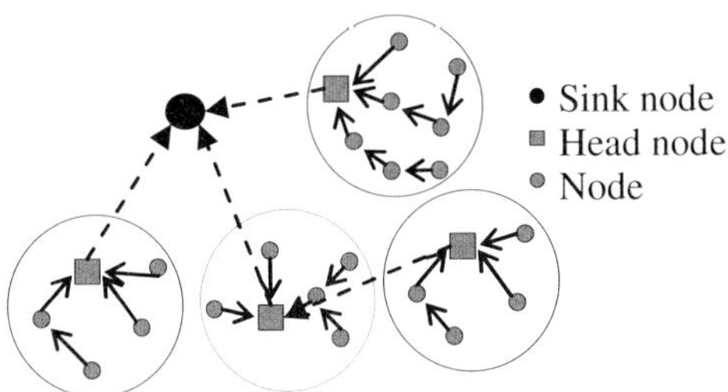

Fig. 4. Multiple-hop data transmissions between nodes and between clusterheads

A sensor node transmits its data to the nearest neighbor node within the cluster that it belongs to. The neighbor node aggregates the data with its own data, and transmits it to the next node until reaching to clusterhead. Similarly, the clusterhead sends its aggregated data to the nearest clusterhead in the next zone until arriving at the sink node.

4 Simulation and Results

To evaluate the performance of our method, we compared its performance with other cluster-based protocols such as LEACH and PEGASIS. We simulated LEACH with a probability of 5% that each node elects itself clusterhead. As a radio model, we use the same one discussed in [8]. The energy costs for the transfer of k-bits data message between two nodes separated by a distance of r meters is given by,

$$E_T(k,r) = E_{Tx} \times k + E_{amp}(r) \times k \tag{2}$$

$$E_R(k) = E_{Rx} \times k \tag{3}$$

where $E_T(k,r)$ indicates the total energy for transmission of the source sensor node, and $E_R(k) = E_{Rx} \times k$ expresses the energy cost incurred in the receiver of the destination sensor node. The parameters E_{Tx}, E_{Rx} are the energy consumption for communication. $E_{amp}(r)$ is the energy required by the transmit amplifier to maintain an acceptable signal-to-noise ratio in order to transfer data messages safely. Also the energy cost for data aggregation is the set as $E_{DA} = 5nJ/bit/message$ [3].

Table 1. Simulation Parameters

Parameter	Value	Parameter	Value
Network size	100 x 100	Transmission energy	50 nJ/bit
Number of nodes	100	Data Aggregation energy	5 nJ/bit/message
Packet size	2000 bits	Transmit amplifier energy	100 pJ/bit/m2
Initial energy of a node	1 J	Zone range (r)	19

Throughout the simulation, we consider a 100 x 100 network configuration with 100 nodes where each node is assigned an initial energy of 1.0 J, the amount of transmission energy is 50 nJ/bit, transmit amplifier energy (E_{amp}) is 100 pJ/bit. The zone range is set by 19 (see Table 1), and the sink node is located at (15, 15) as shown in Figure 5.

In simulations, all nodes are assumed to carry out sensing operation at a fixed rate and always have data to send when they receive query messages from the sink. It is also assumed that all data sent by the previous nodes are aggregated into a data segment with a constant size of 2000 bits. We assume that every node performs data aggregation when forwarding data to the next hop. So, once a node receives data from any sensor nodes, it performs data aggregation on the collected data to reduce the amount of raw data. Table 2 shows the number of clusterheads in each zone in the simulation with the network size of 100 m x 100 m.

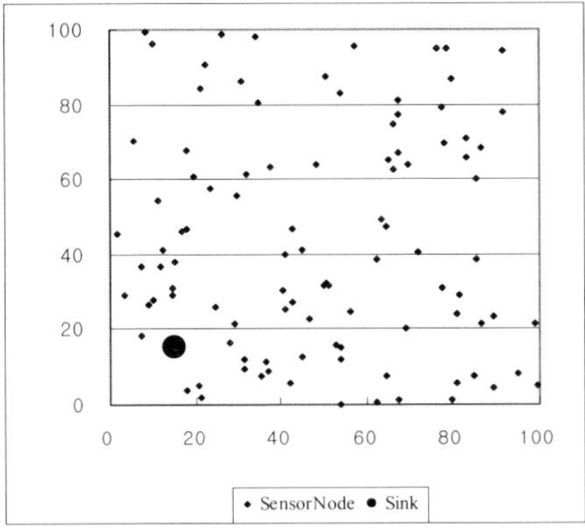

Fig. 5. Network Field Configuration

Table 2. The number of clusterheads in each zone

Zone number	Zone area	Number of clusterheads (N_CH$_i$)	Number of clusterheads used in simulations
ZONE$_0$	283.39	0	0
ZONE$_1$	850.16	1.00	1
ZONE$_2$	1416.93	1.67	2
ZONE$_3$	1983.70	2.33	3
ZONE$_4$	2550.47	3.00	3
ZONE$_5$	2915.28	3.43	4

Figure 6 shows the average transmission distance from all nodes to the sink. From this figure, we can see that our method produces a shorter transmission distance than those of LEACH and PEGASIS. This is because our method offers a multi-hop routing path between any sensor node and the sink. Once the clusters and the clusterheads have been identified, the sink node chooses the routing path for any two adjacent clusterheads as illustrated in Figure 1 (b). All sensor nodes transmit data to the close neighbor node until reaching the clusterhead in the cluster as depicted in Figure 1 (c). There is an exception in case that all nodes in $ZONE_0$ where data is transmitted to the sink directly.

Figure 7 shows the number of rounds when a sensor node is dead for the first time and all sensor nodes are dead. The x-axis represents the number of rounds until the first or the last sensor node dies. This plot clearly shows that our method has more desirable energy expenditure than those of LEACH and PEGASIS. Also, we can see that our method offers a longer number of rounds to the first sensor node death. Also, our method outperforms LEACH and PEGASIS in terms of the system lifetime. As shown in Figure 7, the short transmission distance contributes to extending the number of rounds until the first sensor node and the last sensor node is dead.

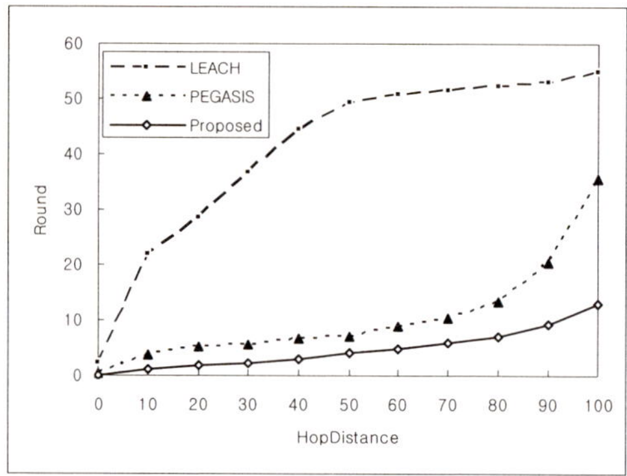

Fig. 6. The average distance to transmit data from nodes to the sink

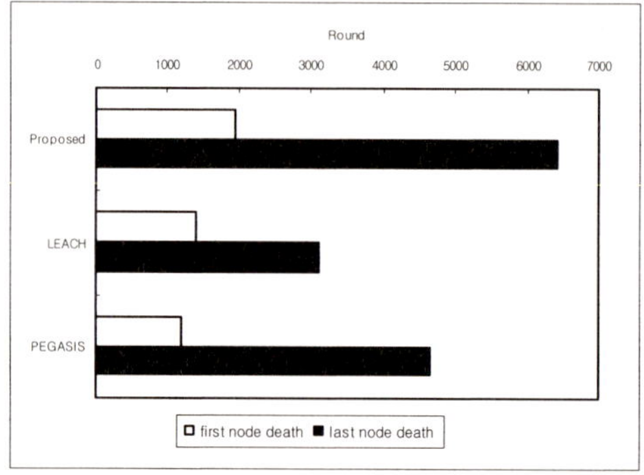

Fig. 7. The number of rounds until the first or the last sensor node dies

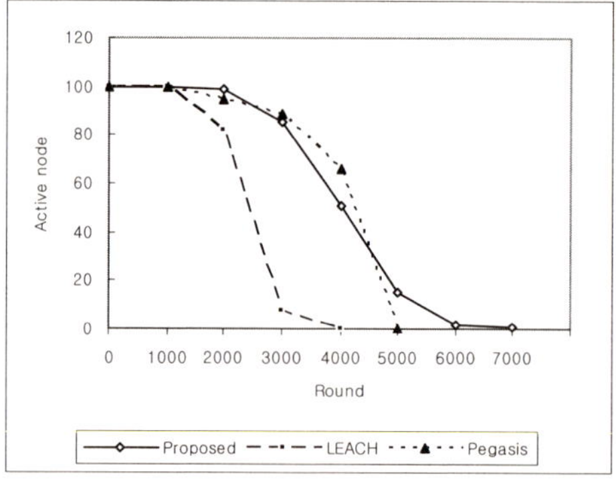

Fig. 8. Number of sensor nodes alive

Figure 8 shows the number of sensor nodes that remain alive in the sensor network. It shows that our method always outperforms LEACH, and roughly competes with PEGASIS. Since we allow a multi-hop routing path for data transmission, the distance required for data transmitting are less than those of LEACH, and a node has sustained more rounds than LEACH.

Figure 9 shows the amount of residual energy at all sensor nodes for each round. This plot shows that our method offers an improvement as compared with LEACH and PEGASIS since the short transmission distance in our method makes a little energy consumption at all nodes.

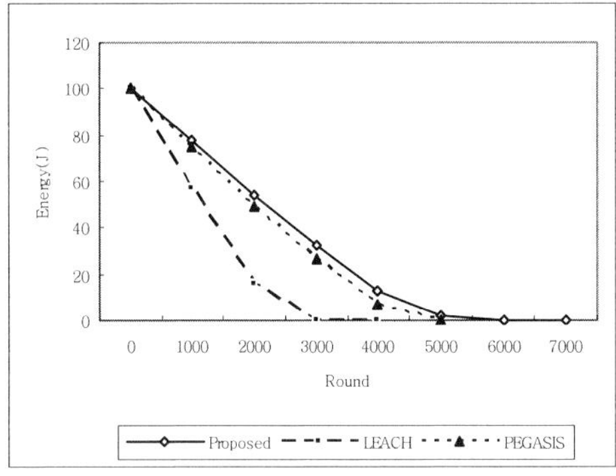

Fig. 9. The amount of residual energy as time goes on

5 Conclusions

In this paper, we propose a topology configuration method for wireless sensor networks with an objective of well balancing energy consumption over all sensor nodes without generating any isolated sensor nodes. Our method has several attractive features:

- a high density node which has a good many neighbor nodes can be selected as clusterhead in a zone,
- reconfiguration of cluster can be carried out in a single zone, not all over network field, to reduce the number of nodes that participate in changing clusterheads, and
- multiple-hop transmissions between nodes or between clusterheads are possible.

Simulation results show that our method outperforms LEACH and PEGASIS in terms of the system lifetime.

References

1. Jamil Ibriq and Imad Mahgoub, "Cluster-Based Routing in Wireless Sensor Networks: Issues and Challenges," in the Proceedings of the 2004 Symposium on Performance Evaluation of Computer Telecommunication Systems, pp. 759-766, March 2004.
2. Pieter Beyens, Ann Nowe and Kris Steenhaut, "High-Density Wireless Sensor Network: a New Clustering Approach for Prediction-based Monitoring," EWSN 2005 - Second European Workshop on Wireless Sensor Networks, Istanbul, Turkey, 2005.

3. Siva D. Muruganathan, Daniel C.F. Ma, Rolly I. Nhasin, and Abraham O. Fapojuwo, "A Centralized Energy-Efficient Routing Protocol for Wireless Sensor Networks," IEEE Communications Magazine, vol. 43, pp. s8-13, March 2005.
4. Stephanic Lindsey and Cauligi S. Raghavendra, "PEGASIS: Power-Efficient Gathering in Sensor Information Systems," Proceedings of the IEEE Aerospace Conference, March 2002.
5. Gayathri Venkataraman, Sabu Emmanuel, Srikanthan Thambipillai, "DASCA : A Degree and Size based Clustering Approach for Wireless Sensor Networks," IASTED International Conference on Networks and Communication Systems (NCS 2005), Thailand, April 2005.
6. Mannak Chatterjee, Sajal K.Das and Damla Turgut, "WCA: A Weighted Clustering Algorithm for Mobile Ad Hoc Networks," Journal of Cluster Computing (Special Issue on Mobile Ad hoc Networks), 5(2): 193-204, April 2002.
7. Wendi Rabiner Heinzelman, Anantha Chandrakasa, and Hari Balakrishnan, "Energy-Efficient Communication Protocol for Wireless Microsensor Networks," Proceedings of the 33rd International Conference on System Sciences (HICSS '00), January 2000.
8. Mohamad Younis, Meenakshi Bangad and Kemal Akkaya, "Base-Station Repositioning for Optimized Performance of Sensor Networks," Vehicular Technology Conference, IEEE 58th Volume 1, Issue , 6-9 October 2003.
9. W. B. Heinzelman, A. P. Chandrakasan, and H. Balakrishnan, "An Application-Specific Protocol Architecture for Wireless Microsensor Networks," IEEE Transactions on Wireless Communication, vol. 1, no. 4, pp. 660-670, October 2002.

An Agglomerative Hierarchical Clustering by Finding Adjacent Hyper-Rectangles

Noboru Takagi

Department of Intelligent Systems Design, Toyama Prefectural University
noboru.takagi@ieee.org

Abstract. This paper proposes a new clustering method based on connecting adjacent hyper-rectangles. Our method searches a set of hyper-rectangles that satisfies the properties that (1) each hyper-rectangle covers some of the samples, and (2) each sample is covered by at least one of the hyper-rectangles. Then, a correction of connected hyper-rectangles is assumed to be a cluster. We apply agglomerative hierarchical clustering method to realize the clustering based on connecting adjacent hyper-rectangles. The effectiveness of the proposed method is shown by applying artificial data sets. This paper also considers on a way for speeding up of the agglomerative hierarchical clustering.

Keywords: agglomerative hierarchical clustering, combinatorial optimization problem, heap sort.

1 Introduction

Clustering (or unsupervised clustering) is a method for grouping samples automatically by referring only similarities or distances between samples. There are many researches on cluster analysis, and many clustering methods have been proposed such as hierarchical clustering and the k-means clustering etc. There are wide application fields on cluster analysis; it applies to pattern classification and multi-variate statistical analysis, for example. On the other hand, if we know classes that samples belong, then this kind of classification problem is called a supervised clustering. There are also many researches on supervised clustering, and recently, supervised clustering based on rough sets theory and two level logic minimization techniques have been studied[1,2,3]. This paper introduces and discusses a new unsupervised clustering.

The k-means clustering is well-known non-hierarchical clustering algorithm. The characteristic feature of k-means clustering is that it classifies samples by referring distances between the centers of clusters. Therefore, the k-means clustering does not work well if it is applied to such samples shown in Figure 1, in which there is a group of samples in the center of the plane and the other samples are distributed on the circle whose center is the first group. For the samples given in Figure 1, it is a natural result if we have two clusters; one is the cluster of the center and the other one is the ring-shaped cluster. Recently, Miyamoto introduced a clustering method based on support vector machine[4],

S. Greco et al. (Eds.): RSCTC 2006, LNAI 4259, pp. 677–686, 2006.

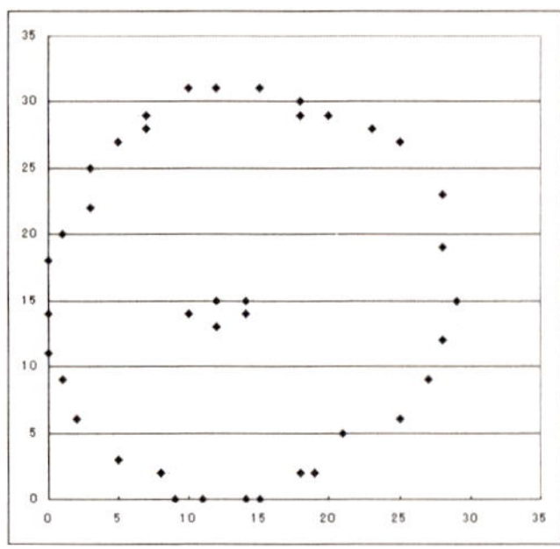

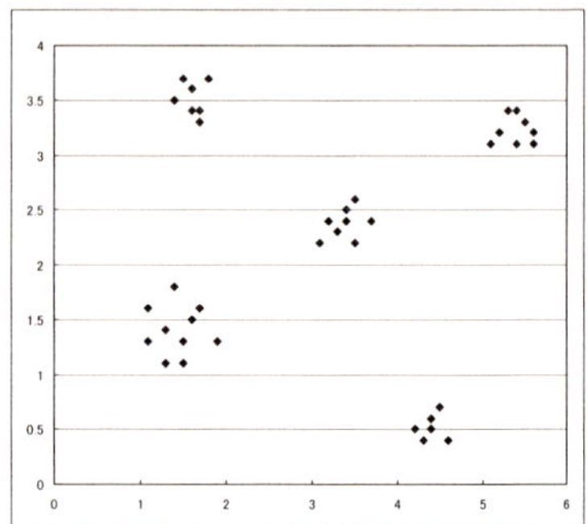

Fig. 1. Artificial Data: The k-means clustering can not find the two clusters; one is the cluster of the center and the other one is the cluster in the ring-shaped

Fig. 2. Samples in Continuous Domain

and this clustering method can find the two clusters when the samples in Figure 1 are applied to his clustering method. But, this clustering method requires the number of clusters as its initial values, and clustering results strongly depend on the initial values.

This paper proposes a new clustering method based on connecting adjacent hyper-rectangles[5]. Each sample is a point in a sample space. This method first considers each sample to be a hyper-rectangle in the sample space. Then, for a pair of two adjacent hyper-rectangles, the method introduces a new hyper-rectangle to make them form a connected component. This process repeats until an evaluation function gives the best. In this method, samples covered by a connected component of hyper-rectangles are assumed to be members of the same cluster. Characteristic features of our method are (1) it does not require none of the initial values, and (2) since clustering results give a set of hyper-rectangles, it is easy to understand how samples distribute in the sample space. This paper also considers on speeding up of hierarchical clustering. A simple realization of hierarchical clustering has $O(n^3)$ time complexity, where n is the number of samples. But, this paper shows an algorithm with $O(n^2 \log n)$ time complexity.

2   Clustering by Connecting Adjacent Hyper-Rectangles

2.1   Outline

Let R be the set of real numbers and $D = \{o_1, o_2, \ldots, o_n\}$ be a finite subset of R^d. In our method, at the first time, the universal set R^d is discretized into a set of finite number of discrete values by referring a given sample data set D. This paper discretizes R^d in the following way. First, every sample o_i $(i = 1, 2, \ldots, n)$ is projected into each of the attribute x_j-coordinate $(j = 1, 2, \ldots, d)$. Then, R^d is discretized into intervals whose width are equal to the minimum distance between two neighboring values. For example, Figure 3 is a discrete space given

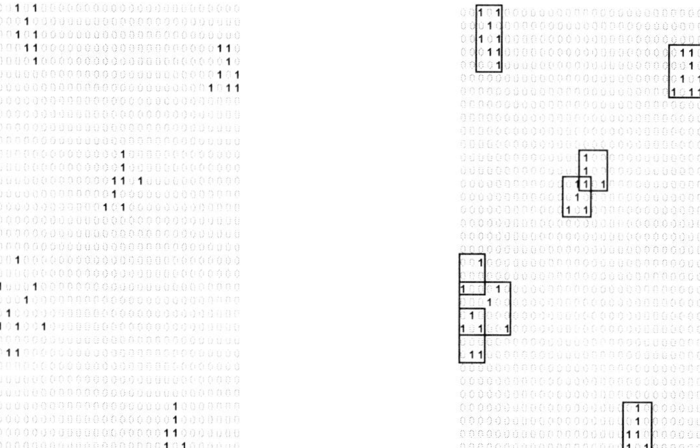

Fig. 3. Samples in Discrete Domain
Fig. 4. Example of Clustering Results: Samples that are covered by a connected component are assumed to be members of the same cluster. So, in this example, there exist the five clusters.

from a continuous sample data set shown in Figure 2. In Figure 3, '1' implies the existence of a sample in the interval corresponding to the discrete value, while '0' implies the absence of samples in the interval. For the discrete sample data set D, our method tries to find an optimum set of clusters by connecting adjacent or neighbor samples into a hyper-rectangle, or introducing a new hyper-rectangle to make them form a connected component. Let us show an abstractive example for our method using the discrete sample data set in Figure 3. In the initial situation, each sample is a hyper-rectangle. Then, after finding a pair of hyper-rectangles that are adjacent to each other, our method may introduce a new hyper-rectangle so that the three hyper-rectangles form a connected component. This process continues in an appropriate number of iterations. Finally, if we meet a result shown in Figure 4, we then consider a set of connected hyper-rectangles as a cluster.

2.2   Evaluation Function

In our method, clustering results are evaluated by the evaluation function f given later in this section. Let REC be a set of t hyper-rectangles $\{r_1, r_2, \ldots, r_t\}$, where r_k $(k = 1, 2, \ldots, t)$ is a hyper-rectangle $r_k = [x_{1k}^L, x_{1k}^R] \times \cdots \times [x_{nk}^L, x_{nk}^R]$. For a discrete sample data set $D = \{o_1, o_2, \ldots, o_n\}$, the minimum and the maximum values $\hat{o}^j$ and $\check{o}^j$ for the attribute x_j are defined below.

$$\hat{o}^j = \min(o_1^j, o_2^j, \ldots, o_n^j) \text{ and } \check{o}^j = \max(o_1^j, o_2^j, \ldots, o_n^j),$$

where $j = 1, 2, \ldots, d$ and $o_i = (o_i^1, o_i^2, \ldots, o_i^d)$ $(i = 1, 2, \ldots, n)$. The universal hyper-rectangle is defined as $[\hat{o}^1, \hat{o}^1] \times \ldots \times [\check{o}^n, \check{o}^n]$. Then, U is the set of discrete

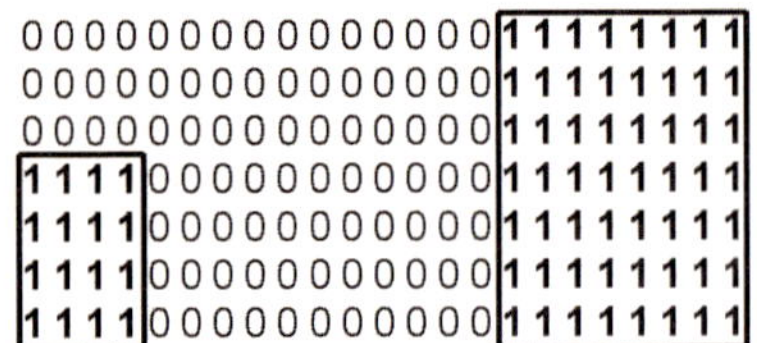

Fig. 5. Non-adjacent Two Rectangles

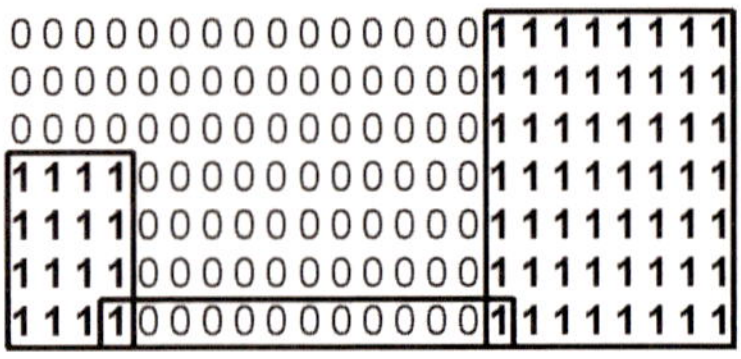

Fig. 6. Example of Undesirable Connected Component: The long thin rectangle connects the non-adjacent two rectangles

points that are included in the universal hyper-rectangle. It is obvious that $D \subseteq U$. Let E be a subset of U whose elements are not members of D, that is, $E = U - D$. $c(\mathrm{REC})$ denotes the number of connected components of REC. So, $c(\mathrm{REC})$ means the number of clusters existing in REC. Then, we give the following function f that can evaluates the clustering quality for the REC.

$$f(\mathrm{REC}) = 2 \cdot \frac{c(\mathrm{REC})}{|D|} + \frac{\left| \bigcup_{k=1}^{t} A_k \right|}{|E|} + \max_{1 \leq k \leq t} \left\{ \max_{1 \leq j \leq d} \frac{d_k^j}{\check{o}^j - \hat{o}^j} \right\}, \qquad (1)$$

where the set A_k is the number of 0-points (which are discrete points with '0') covered by the hyper-rectangle r_k, and d_k^j represents the maximum number of consecutive 0-points of the hyper-rectangle r_k in the x_j-coordinate direction.

The 1st term means that the smaller number of clusters gives the better clustering result. If the number of clusters is small, then the value of the function becomes better. From the view point of the reduction of the number of clusters, the universal hyper-rectangle gives the best result. But, we can not accept this undesirable result. To avoid this undesirable result, we introduce the 2nd term. It counts the 0-points that are covered by hyper-rectangles. A clustering result would be better if hyper-rectangles cover 0-points as small as possible. However, this penalty is not enough to find a desirable clustering result. For example, in Figure 5, there are two rectangles that may not be adjacent to each other. As shown in Figure 6, by adding the long thin rectangle, we can connect the two rectangles with the small number of 0-points. Thus, we introduce the 3rd term into the evaluation function to eliminate such an undesirable situation.

In the evaluation function (1), when the 1st term would be better, then the 2nd and the 3rd terms became worse. Conversely, when the 3rd and the 4th terms would be better, then the 1st term became worse. So, there is a trade-off between the 1st term and the 3rd and the 4th terms.

Let V be the set of all hyper-rectangles such that each of them covers at least one 1-point. Then, our method can be formulated as a combinatorial optimization problem below.

Minimize: $f(A)$
Subject to: $A \subseteq V$

3   Agglomerative Hierarchical Algorithm

In our method, the problem is how to search a set of hyper-rectangles that gives the minimum evaluation value. This paper does not focus on an algorithm how to find the optimum solution. But, the paper focuses on an algorithm that is able to find a near optimum solution with a small amount of the computation time. To achieve this task, we refer the agglomerative hierarchical clustering method. In the agglomerative hierarchical clustering,

1. similarities between any two of clusters is calculated, and then,
2. the two clusters with the best similarity are merged into one cluster,
3. the above two steps repeated until the number of clusters becomes one, that is, until all of the samples belong to one cluster.

3.1   Agglomerative Hierarchical Clustering

For a sample data set D, let $s(o_i, o_j)$ be a similarity between samples o_i and o_j of D, and let $\mathcal{G}$ be a set of clusters. Then, the following is a standard flow of our method.

Step 1: For every sample o_i, set $G_i \leftarrow \{o_i\}$. Then, calculate similarities $s(G_i, G_j)$ between any pair of two clusters G_i and G_j ($i, j = 1, 2, \ldots, n$). Set $\mathcal{G} \leftarrow \{G_1, G_2, \ldots, G_n\}$, $c \leftarrow n$, REC $\leftarrow \emptyset$, and BEST $\leftarrow \mathcal{G}$.

Step 2: Find a pair of clusters (G_p, G_q) whose similarity $s(G_p, G_q)$ is the best among all of the similarities. Let G' be the union $G_p \cup G_q$. Then, remove G_p and G_q from $\mathcal{G}$, add G' into $\mathcal{G}$, and set $c \leftarrow c - 1$. In our method, a set of samples forms a cluster if they are covered by connected component. To make the samples of G' be a cluster, create a new hyper-rectangle in the following way, and add it into REC.

   1 Find a pair of samples $o' \in G_p$ and $o'' \in G_q$ whose similarity $s(\{o'\}, \{o''\})$ is the best among all of the similarities $s(\{x\}, \{y\})$ of $x \in G_p$ and $y \in G_q$.

   2 Create a new hyper-rectangle such that it includes the samples o' and o'', and the size of the new hyper-rectangle is the minimum among all of the hyper-rectangles covering the two samples o' and o''.

Step 3: If $c = 1$, then output BEST, and stop the algorithm.

Step 4: Calculate the evaluation function $f(\text{REC})$. If $c = n$, then BEST $\leftarrow$ REC. If $c < n$ and $f(\text{REC})$ is better than $f(\text{BEST})$, then BEST $\leftarrow$ REC.

Step 5: For every $G_i \in \mathcal{G}$ such that $G_i \neq G'$, calculate the similarity $s(G', G_i)$. Go to Step 2.

3.2   Speeding Up of Hierarchical Clustering

In this section, we discuss the way of speeding up of agglomerative hierarchical clustering. This will be done by introducing the heap data structure. A heap is one of the data structures, and it is first applied to a fast sort algorithm, called the heap sort. A heap H is a one-dimensional array satisfying the following condition.

Heap: $H[1], H[2], \ldots, H[m]$, where m is the number of elements.
Condition: $H[i] \geq H[2i]$ and $H[i] \geq H[2i+1]$ for every $i = 1, 2, \ldots, m/2$.

Therefore, a heap is a one-dimensional array, but it also expresses a partially ordered binary tree. Figure 7 shows an example of a heap H when $m = 10$.

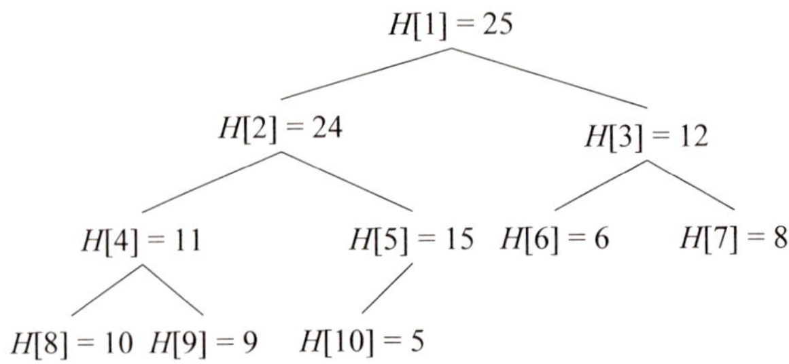

Fig. 7. Example of heap

The following algorithm is a general version of agglomerative hierarchical clustering algorithm (AHC).

Algorithm AHC

Input: A set of samples $\{o_1, o_2, \ldots, o_n\}$
Output: Dendroid diagram

Step 1: Construct n clusters $G_i \leftarrow \{o_i\}$, and let $\mathcal{G} \leftarrow \{G_1, G_2, \ldots, G_n\}$. Calculate the similarity $s(G_i, G_j)$ for every pair of clusters G_i and G_j such that $i \neq j$.
Step 2: Search the pair of clusters G_p and G_q whose similarity is the best. Let $G' \leftarrow G_p \cup G_q$. Then, remove G_p and G_q from $\mathcal{G}$, and add G' to $\mathcal{G}$.
Step 3: If $\mathcal{G}$ includes only one cluster, then output the dendroid diagram, and stop the algorithm.
Step 4: Recalculate the similarity $s(G_i, G_j)$ for every pair of clusters G_i and G_j of $\mathcal{G}$ such that $i \neq j$. Then, go to Step 2.

The time complexity of the algorithm AHC depends on the number of recalculations of similarities. The total number of the recalculations is given below.

$$\frac{1}{2}n(n-1) + \frac{1}{2}(n-1)(n-2) + \cdots + \frac{1}{2} \cdot 2 \cdot 1 = \frac{1}{6}(n^3 - n)$$

Thus, the time complexity of the algorithm AHC is $O(n^3)$.

We use a heap to reduce the number of recalculations of similarities. At the first step, let H be a heap whose size is $m = \frac{1}{2}n(n+1)$, which is the number of all the pairs (o_i, o_j) (where $i \neq j$) of the sample set $\{o_1, o_2, \ldots, o_n\}$. Then, we save all the similarities of the pairs (o_i, o_j) into the heap H. If the heap

H is constructed well, then the pair of clusters G_p and G_q whose similarity is the best exists at the first element $H[1]$ of the heap H. Therefore, the cost for searching the pair G_p and G_q is $O(1)$. Then, the pair G_p and G_q is merged into one cluster G', and we recalculate the similarities $s(G', G_i)$ between G' and the other remaining clusters G_i. After the recalculations, we reconstruct the H in order for it to express a heap. This reconstruction can be done in the cost $O(c \log c)$, where c is the number of clusters.

The following is a sketch of the agglomerative hierarchical clustering with a heap (AHCH).

Algorithm AHCH

Input: A set of samples $\{o_1, o_2, \ldots, o_n\}$
Output: Dendroid diagram

Step 1: Let H be an array whose size is $m = \frac{1}{2}n(n+1)$. Let $G_i \leftarrow \{o_i\}$, and let $\mathcal{G} \leftarrow \{G_1, G_2, \ldots, G_n\}$. Calculate the similarity $s(G_i, G_j)$ for every pair of clusters G_i and G_j such that $i \neq j$. Then, save the similarities in H.

Step 2: Sort the elements of H to satisfy the heap condition.

Step 3: If $\mathcal{G}$ includes only one element, then output the dendroid diagram and stop the algorithm.

Step 4: Let the pair of clusters in $H[1]$ be G_p and G_q (which give the best similarity), and set $G' \leftarrow G_p \cup G_q$. Remove G_p and G_q from $\mathcal{G}$, and then recalculate the similarity $s(G', G_i)$ for every G_i of $\mathcal{G}$, and save the similarity $s(G', G_i)$ in $H[k]$, where k means the place that the similarity $s(G_p, G_i)$ was saved.

Step 5: For every G_i of $\mathcal{G}$, exchange the element $H[k]$ for the last $H[m]$ and remove $H[m]$ (i.e., $m \leftarrow m - 1$), where k is the place that the similarity $s(G_q, G_i)$ is saved. Set $\mathcal{G} \leftarrow \mathcal{G} \cup \{G'\}$.

Step 6: Reconstruct H in order for it to satisfy the heap condition. Go to Step 3.

Suppose a recalculated similarity $s(G', G_i)$ was saved at $H[k]$ of the heap H. If $H[k] < H[2k]$ or $H[k] < H[2k+1]$ hold, then this situation does not satisfy the heap condition. In this case, we exchange $H[k]$ for either one of $H[2k]$ or $H[2k+1]$. This exchanging process will be executed until we meet the heap condition $H[k] \geq H[2k]$ or $H[k] \geq H[2k+1]$. Next, consider the case where $H[k] \geq H[2k]$ and $H[k] \geq H[2k+1]$ hold. In this case, $H[k]$ locally holds the heap condition, but it is possible not to satisfy the heap condition for the ancestors of $H[k]$. So, we have to check if $H[k]$ would not satisfy the heap condition for all the ancestors of $H[k]$.

The cost of the above process is at most the height of the partially ordered binary tree of the heap H. So, the order of this cost is $O(\log m)$ for each $H[k]$ when the number of nodes in the tree is m. The number of the $H[k]$'s that we have to check is equal to the number of clusters $|\mathcal{G}|$. Thus, we can conclude that the reconstruction cost of the heap H in Step 6 is $O(|\mathcal{G}| \log |\mathcal{G}|^2) = O(|\mathcal{G}| \log |\mathcal{G}|)$, since the size of the heap H is equal to the square of the number of clusters $|\mathcal{G}|$.

The time complexity of the algorithm AHCH depends on the number of reconstructions of the heap H in Step 6, whose cost is $O(|\mathcal{G}|\log|\mathcal{G}|)$. Therefore, the overall cost of the algorithm AHCH is given in the following formula.

$$n\log n + (n-1)\log(n-1) + \cdots + 2\log 2,$$

where n is the number of data. Since this summation is approximately equal to $n^2\log n$, we can conclude that the time complexity of the algorithm AHCH is $O(n^2\log n)$. Table 1 shows the CUP times of the algorithms AHC and AHCH, where the CUP is a Pentium4 3.6GHz. We apply the AHCH algorithm to realize our clustering method. The last row of Table 1 shows the CPU time when we add the process for calculating the evaluation function (1) into the AHCH algorithm. The cost for evaluating the function (1) is very fast.

Table 1. Comparison of CPU Times (sec)

# of data	1000	1500	2000	2500	3000
AHC	24	85	212	433	780
AHCH	4	11	25	44	74
Our Method	4	11	26	46	77

4   Experimental Results

This section describes the effectiveness of our method. We employed the Euclidean distance as the similarity of two samples $o_i = (o_i^1, o_i^2, \ldots, o_i^d)$ and $o_j = (o_j^1, o_j^2, \ldots, o_j^d)$ below.

$$s(o_i, o_j) = \sqrt{\sum_{k=1}^{d}(o_i^k - o_j^k)^2}$$

We created three artificial data for estimating the effectiveness of our method. The three sample sets are shown in Figures 8, 9, and 10. There are two clusters in Figure 8 (the two spiral-shaped clusters), also two clusters in Figure 9 (the ring-shaped and the circle clusters), and four clusters in Figure 10 (the two bar-shaped and the two triangular-shaped clusters).

There are many kinds of recalculation methods when we execute the agglomerative hierarchical clustering, such as the nearest neighbor method, the furthest neighbor method, and the group average method, and so on. In this experiment, we applied the nearest neighbor method to the AHCH algorithm. Here, the nearest neighbor method calculates the similarity between two clusters G_i and G_j by the following formula.

$$s(G_i, G_j) = \min_{x \in G_i, y \in G_j} s(x, y)$$

Then, our method can perform well, that is, it can find the two clusters in Figures 8 and 9, respectively, and also can find the four clusters in Figure 10.

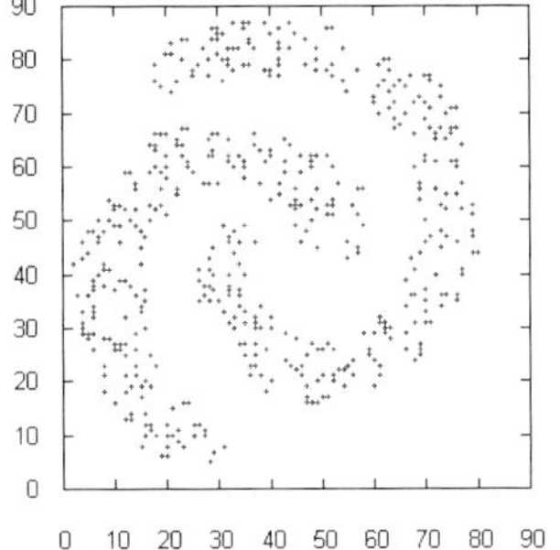

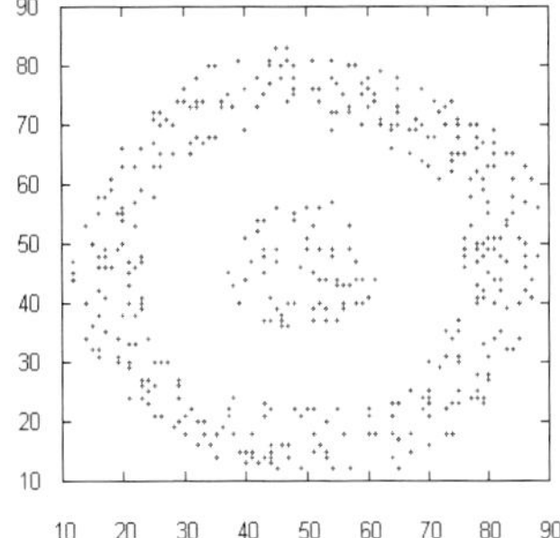

Fig. 8. Artificial Data 1: 438 Samples   **Fig. 9.** Artificial Data 2: 412 Samples

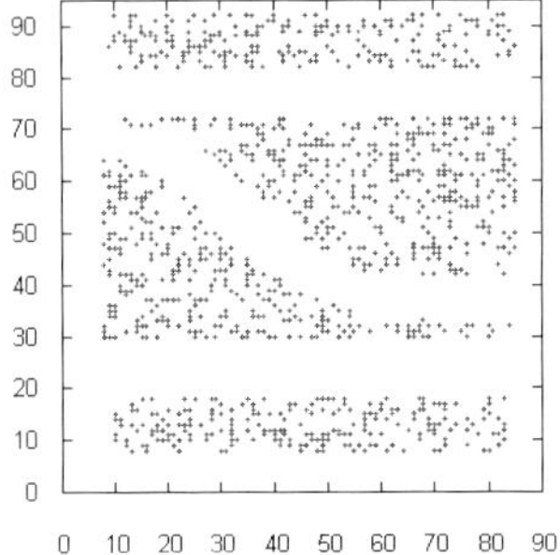

Fig. 10. Artificial Data 3: 1072 Samples

5   Conclusions

This paper introduced a new clustering method based on connecting adjacent
hyper-rectanglesＤThe agglomerative hierarchical clustering method with the
nearest neighbor method is applied to realize an algorithm based on connecting
adjacent hyper-rectangles. The effectiveness of the proposed method is shown
by applying the three artificial data. This paper also considered on the way for
speeding up of agglomerative hierarchical clustering, and this can be done by
introducing a heap memory when we execute the clustering.

There are huge amount of partitions (which mean sets of clusters) on a given
sample data set. Our method can check only a few number of the partitions; it
can check only partitions that are created by the nearest neighbor method. To
find the optimum clustering result, it is necessary to check clusters that are not
created by the hierarchical clustering methods. Overcoming this drawback is one
of the future works. Finally, it is one of characteristic features of our method
that resultant clusters are given in the form of hyper-rectangles. It enables us
to easy understand regions that samples in a cluster are distributed. It suggests
that our method would be applied to pattern classifications.

References

1. J. G. Bazan, M. Szczuka, "RSES and RSESlib – A Collection of Tools for Rough Set Computations", *Rough Set and Current Trends in Computing, Lecture Notes in Artificial Intelligence*, vol. 2005, Springer, pp. 106-113, 2000.
2. J. G. Bazan, M. Szczuka and J. Wroblewski, "A New Version of Rough Set Exploration System", *Rough Set and Current Trends in Computing, Lecture Notes in Artificial Intelligence*, vol. 2475, pp. 397-404, 2002.
3. N. Takagi and J. Han, "A System for Realizing Value Reduction Techenology of Rough Sets", *Proceedings of 4th IEEE International Symposium of Human and Artificial Intelligence Systems*, pp. 247-252, 2004.
4. S. Miyamoto and Y. Nakayama, "Algorithms of Hard c-Means Clustering Using Kernel Function in Support Vector Machines", *J. of Advanced Computational Intelligence*, vol. 7, no. 1, pp. 19-24, 2003.
5. R. Yanagida and N. Takagi, "Consideration on Cluster Analysis Based on Connecting Adjacent Hyper-Rectangles", *Proceedings of IEEE International Conference on Systems, Man, and Cybernetics*, pp. 2795-2800, 2005.

Evaluating Learning Models for a Rule Evaluation Support Method Based on Objective Indices

Hidenao Abe[1], Shusaku Tsumoto[1], Miho Ohsaki[2], and Takahira Yamaguchi[3]

[1] Department of Medical Informatics, Shimane University, School of Medicine
89-1 Enya-cho, Izumo, Shimane 693-8501, Japan
`abe@med.shimane-u.ac.jp, tsumoto@computer.org`
[2] Faculty of Engineering, Doshisha University
1-3 Tataramiyakodani, Kyo-Tanabe, Kyoto 610-0321, Japan
`mohsaki@mail.doshisha.ac.jp`
[3] Faculty of Science and Technology, Keio University
3-14-1 Hiyoshi, Kohoku Yokohama, Kanagawa 223-8522, Japan
`yamaguti@ae.keio.ac.jp`

Abstract. We present an evaluation of a rule evaluation support method for post-processing of mined results with rule evaluation models based on objective indices in this paper. To reduce the costs of rule evaluation task, which is one of the key procedures in data mining post-processing, we have developed the rule evaluation support method with rule evaluation models, which are obtained with objective indices of mined classification rules and evaluations of a human expert for each rule. Then we have evaluated performances of learning algorithms for constructing rule evaluation models on the meningitis data mining as an actual problem, and ten rule sets from the ten kinds of UCI datasets as an article problem. With these results, we show the availability of our rule evaluation support method.

1 Introduction

In recent years, it is required by people to utilize huge data, which are easily stored on information systems, developing information technologies. Besides, data mining techniques have been widely known as a process for utilizing stored data, combining database technologies, statistical methods, and machine learning methods. Although, IF-THEN rules are discussed as one of highly usable and readable output of data mining, to large dataset with hundreds attributes including noises, a rule mining process often obtains many thousands of rules. From such huge rule set, it is difficult for human experts to find out valuable knowledge which are rarely included in the rule set.

To support a rule selection, many efforts have done using objective rule evaluation indices such as recall, precision and interestingness measurements (called 'objective indices' later), which are calculated by the mathematical analysis and do not include any human evaluation criteria. However, it is also difficult to estimate a criterion of a human expert with single objective rule evaluation index

S. Greco et al. (Eds.): RSCTC 2006, LNAI 4259, pp. 687–695, 2006.

[15], because his/her subjective criterion such as interestingness is influenced by the amount of his/her knowledge.

To above issues, we have been developed an adaptive rule evaluation support method for human experts with rule evaluation models, which predict experts' criteria based on objective indices, re-using results of evaluations of human experts. In this paper, we present a performance comparison of learning algorithms for constructing rule evaluation models. Then we discuss about the availability of our rule evaluation model construction approach.

2   Related Work

To avoid the confusion of real human interest, objective index, and subjective index, we clearly define them as follows: **Objective Index:** The feature such as the correctness, uniqueness, and strength of a rule, calculated by the mathematical analysis. It does not include any human evaluation criteria. **Subjective Index:** The similarity or difference between the information on interestingness given beforehand by a human expert and those obtained from a rule. Although it includes some human criterion in its initial state, the similarity or difference are mainly calculated with a mathematical analysis. **Real Human Interest:** The interest felt by a human expert for a rule in his/her mind.

Focusing on interesting rule selection with objective indices, researchers have developed more than forty objective indices based on number of instances, probability, statistics values, information quantity, distance of rules or their attributes, and complexity of a rule [11,21,23]. Most of these indices are used to remove meaningless rules rather than to discover really interesting ones for a human expert, because they can not include domain knowledge. Ohsaki et. al [15] investigated the relation between objective indices and real human interests, taking real data mining results and their human evaluations. In this work, the comparison shows that it is difficult to predict real human interests with a single objective index exactly. However, their work has never shown any concrete method to predict human evaluations with these objective indices.

3   Rule Evaluation Support with Rule Evaluation Model Based on Objective Indices

At practical data mining situations, a human expert repeatedly does costly rule evaluation procedures. In these situations, useful experiences of each evaluation such as focused attributes, interesting their combinations, and valuable facts are not explicitly used by any rule selection system, but tacitly stored in the human expert. To these problems, we suggest a method to construct rule evaluation models based on objective rule evaluation indices as a way to describe criteria of a human expert explicitly, re-using the human evaluations.

We considered the process of modeling rule evaluations of human experts as the process to clear up relationships between the human evaluations and features of input if-then rules. Then, we decided that the process of rule evaluation model

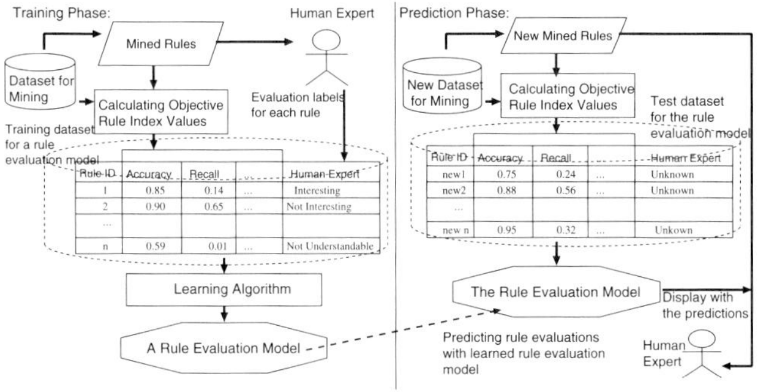

Fig. 1. Overview of the construction method of rule evaluation models

construction can be implemented as a learning task. Fig. 1 shows the process of rule evaluation model construction based on re-use of human evaluations and objective indices.

At the training phase, attributes of a meta-level training data set is obtained by objective indices values. At the same time, a human expert evaluates the whole or part of input rules at least once to join as class of each instance. After obtaining the training data set, its rule evaluation model is constructed by a learning algorithm. At the prediction phase, a human expert receives predictions for new rules based on their values of the objective indices. Since the task of rule evaluation models is a prediction, we need to choose a learning algorithm with higher accuracy as same as current classification problems.

4   Performance Comparisons of Learning Algorithms for Rule Model Construction

In this section, we firstly present the result of an empirical evaluation with the dataset from the result of a meningitis data mining [9]. Then to confirm the performance of our approach, we present the result on the ten kinds of UCI benchmark datasets [10]. In these case studies , we have evaluated rule evaluation construction algorithms from the following three view points: performances of learning algorithms, estimations of minimum training subsets to construct valid rule evaluation models, and contents of learned rule evaluation models.

To construct a dataset to learn a rule evaluation model, 39 objective indices [15] have been calculated for each rule as shown in Table 1.

To these dataset, we applied the following five learning algorithms from Weka [22]: C4.5 decision tree learner [18] called J4.8, neural network learner with back propagation (BPNN) [12], support vector machines (SVM) [1] [17], classification via linear regressions (CLR) [2] [3], and OneR [13].

---

[1] The kernel function was set up polynomial kernel.

[2] We set up the elimination of collinear attributes and the model selection with greedy search based on Akaike Information Metric.

Table 1. Objective rule evaluation indices for classification rules used in this research. **P:** Probability of the antecedent and/or consequent of a rule. **S:** Statistical variable based on P. **I:** Information of the antecedent and/or consequent of a rule. **N:** Number of instances included in the antecedent and/or consequent of a rule. **D:** Distance of a rule from the others based on rule attributes.

Theory	Index Name (**Abbreviation**) [Reference Number of Literature]
P	Coverage (**Coverage**), Prevalence (**Prevalence**) Precision (**Precision**), Recall (**Recall**) Support (**Support**), Specificity (**Specificity**) Accuracy (**Accuracy**), Lift (**Lift**) Leverage (**Leverage**), Added Value (**Added Value**)[21] Klösgen's Interestingness (**KI**)[14], Relative Risk (**RR**)[1] Brin's Interest (**BI**)[2], Brin's Conviction (**BC**)[2] Certainty Factor (**CF**)[21], Jaccard Coefficient (**Jaccard**)[21] F-Measure (**F-M**)[19], Odds Ratio (**OR**)[21] Yule's Q (**YuleQ**)[21], Yule's Y (**YuleY**)[21] Kappa (**Kappa**)[21], Collective Strength (**CST**)[21] Gray and Orlowska's Interestingness weighting Dependency (**GOI**)[7] Gini Gain (**Gini**)[21], Credibility (**Credibility**)[8]
S	χ^2 Measure for One Quadrant (χ^2-**M1**)[6] χ^2 Measure for Four Quadrant (χ^2-**M4**)[6]
I	J-Measure (**J-M**)[20], K-Measure (**K-M**)[15] Mutual Information (**MI**)[21] Yao and Liu's Interestingness 1 based on one-way support (**YLI1**)[23] Yao and Liu's Interestingness 2 based on two-way support (**YLI2**)[23] Yao and Zhong's Interestingness (**YZI**)[23]
N	Cosine Similarity (**CSI**)[21], Laplace Correction (**LC**)[21] ϕ Coefficient (ϕ)[21], Piatetsky-Shapiro's Interestingness (**PSI**)[16]
D	Gago and Bento's Interestingness (**GBI**)[5] Peculiarity (**Peculiarity**)[24]

4.1 Constructing Rule Evaluation Models on an Actual Datamining Result

In this case study, we have taken 244 rules, which are mined from six dataset about six kinds of diagnostic problems as shown in Table 2. These datasets are consisted of appearances of meningitis patients as attributes and diagnoses for each patient as class. Each rule set was mined with each proper rule induction algorithm composed by CAMLET [9]. For each rule, we labeled three evaluations (I:Interesting, NI:Not-Interesting, NU:Not-Understandable), according to evaluation comments from a medical expert.

Table 2. Description of the meningitis datasets and their datamining results

Dataset	#Attributes	#Class	#Mined rules	#'I' rules	#'NI' rules	#'NU' rules
Diag	29	6	53	15	38	0
C_Cource	40	12	22	3	18	1
Culture+diag	31	12	57	7	48	2
Diag2	29	2	35	8	27	0
Course	40	2	53	12	38	3
Cult_find	29	2	24	3	18	3
TOTAL	—	—	244	48	187	9

Comparison on Performances. In this section, we show the result of the comparisons of performances on the whole dataset, recall and precisions of each class label. Since Leave-One-Out holds just one test instance and remains as the training dataset repeatedly for each instance of a given dataset, we can evaluate the performance of a learning algorithm to a new dataset without any ambiguity.

The results of the performances of the five learning algorithms to the whole training dataset and the results of Leave-One-Out are also shown in Table 3. All of the accuracies, Recalls of I and NI, and Precisions of I and NI are higher than predicting default labels.

Table 3. Accuracies(%), Recalls(%) and Precisions(%) of the five learning algorithms

| | On the whole training dataset | | | | | | Leave-One-Out | | | | | | |
| | | Recall of | | | Precision of | | | | Recall of | | | Precision of | | |
	Acc.	I	NI	NU	I	NI	NU	Acc.	I	NI	NU	I	NI	NU
J4.8	85.7	41.7	97.9	66.7	80.0	86.3	85.7	79.1	29.2	95.7	0.0	63.6	82.5	0.0
BPNN	86.9	81.3	89.8	55.6	65.0	94.9	71.4	77.5	39.6	90.9	0.0	50.0	85.9	0.0
SVM	81.6	35.4	97.3	0.0	68.0	83.5	0.0	81.6	35.4	97.3	0.0	68.0	83.5	0.0
CLR	82.8	41.7	97.3	0.0	71.4	84.3	0.0	80.3	35.4	95.7	0.0	60.7	82.9	0.0
OneR	82.0	56.3	92.5	0.0	57.4	87.8	0.0	75.8	27.1	92.0	0.0	37.1	82.3	0.0

These learning algorithms excepting OneR achieve equal or higher performance with combination of multiple objective indices than sorting with single objective index. The accuracies of Leave-One-Out shows robustness of each learningalgorithm. These learning algorithms have achieved from 75.8% to 81.9%.

Estimating Minimum Training Subset to Construct a Valid Rule Evaluation Model. Since the rule evaluation model construction method needs evaluations of mined rules by a human expert, we have estimated minimum training subset to construct a valid rule evaluation model. Table 4 shows accuracies to the whole training dataset with each subset of training dataset. As shown in these results, SVM and CLR, which learn hype-planes, achieves grater than 95% with only less than 10% of training subset. Although decision tree learner and BPNN could learn better classifier to the whole dataset than these hyper-plane learners, they need more training instances to learn accurate classifiers.

Rule Evaluation Models on the Actual Datamining Result Dataset. In this section, we present rule evaluation models to the whole dataset learned with OneR, J4.8 and CLR, because they are represented as explicit models such as a rule set, a decision tree, and a set of linear models.

As shown in Fig. 2, indices used in learned rule evaluation models, they are not only the group of indices increasing with a correctness of a rule, but also they are used some different groups of indices on different models. Almost indices such as YLI1, Laplace Correction, Accuracy, Precision, Recall, and Coverage are the former type of indices on the models. The later indices are GBI and Peculiality,

Table 4. Accuracies(%) on the whole training dataset of the learning algorithms trained by sub-sampled training datasets

%training sample	10	20	30	40	50	60	70	80	90	100
J4.8	73.4	74.7	79.8	78.6	72.8	83.2	83.7	84.5	85.7	85.7
BPNN	74.8	78.1	80.6	81.1	82.7	83.7	85.3	86.1	87.2	86.9
SMO	78.1	78.6	79.8	79.8	79.8	80.0	79.9	80.2	80.4	81.6
CLR	76.6	78.5	80.3	80.2	80.3	80.7	80.9	81.4	81.0	82.8
OneR	75.2	73.4	77.5	78.0	77.7	77.5	79.0	77.8	78.9	82.4

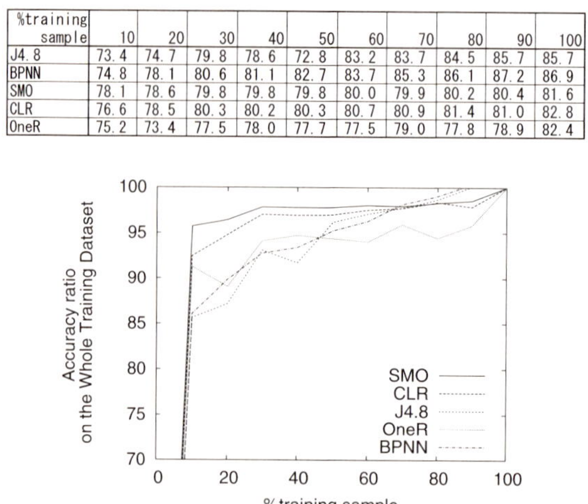

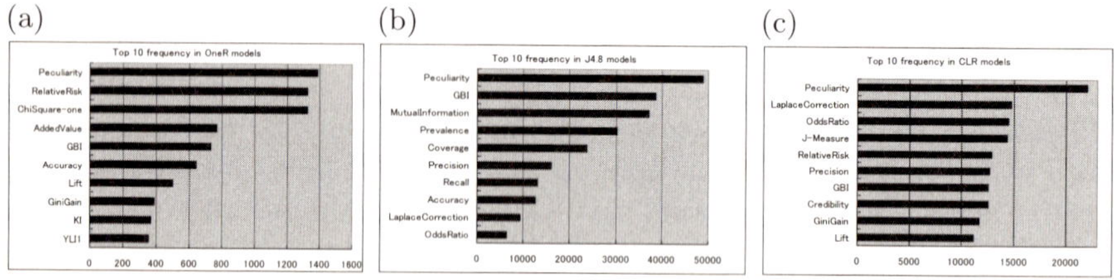

Fig. 2. Top 10 frequencies of indices of learned rule evaluation models by OneR(a), J4.8(b), and CLR(c). Statistics are collected by 10,000 times bootstrap iterations.

which sums up difference of antecedents between one rule and the other rules in the same ruleset. This corresponds to the comment from the human expert.

4.2 Constructing Rule Evaluation Models on Artificial Evaluation Labels

To confirm the performances without any human criteria, we have also evaluated our method with rule sets from the following ten datasets of UCI lachine learning repository: anneal, audiology, autos, balance-scale, breast-cancer, breast-w, colic, credit-a, credit-g, and diabetes. From these datasets, we obtained rule sets with bagged PART, which repeatedly executes PART [4] to bootstrapped training sub-sample datasets. To these rule sets, we calculated the 39 objective indices as attributes of each rule. As for the class of these datasets, we set up three class distributions with multinomial distribution. Table 5 shows us the datasets with three different class distributions. The class distribution for 'Distribution I' is $P = (0.35, 0.3, 0.3)$ where p_i is the probability for class i. Thus

Table 5. The flow to obtain datasets from UCI datasets (on the left flow chart). And the datasets of the rule sets learned from the UCI benchmark (on the right table).

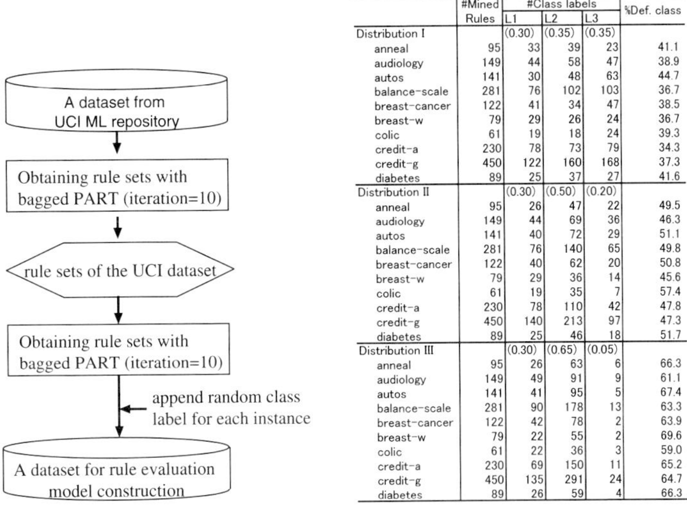

	#Mined Rules	#Class labels			%Def. class
		L1	L2	L3	
Distribution I		(0.30)	(0.35)	(0.35)	
anneal	95	33	39	23	41.1
audiology	149	44	58	47	38.9
autos	141	30	48	63	44.7
balance-scale	281	76	102	103	36.7
breast-cancer	122	41	34	47	38.5
breast-w	79	29	26	24	36.7
colic	61	19	18	24	39.3
credit-a	230	78	73	79	34.3
credit-g	450	122	160	168	37.3
diabetes	89	25	37	27	41.6
Distribution II		(0.30)	(0.50)	(0.20)	
anneal	95	26	47	22	49.5
audiology	149	44	69	36	46.3
autos	141	40	72	29	51.1
balance-scale	281	76	140	65	49.8
breast-cancer	122	40	62	20	50.8
breast-w	79	29	36	14	45.6
colic	61	19	35	7	57.4
credit-a	230	78	110	42	47.8
credit-g	450	140	213	97	47.3
diabetes	89	25	46	18	51.7
Distribution III		(0.30)	(0.65)	(0.05)	
anneal	95	26	63	6	66.3
audiology	149	49	91	9	61.1
autos	141	41	95	5	67.4
balance-scale	281	90	178	13	63.3
breast-cancer	122	42	78	2	63.9
breast-w	79	22	55	2	69.6
colic	61	22	36	3	59.0
credit-a	230	69	150	11	65.2
credit-g	450	135	291	24	64.7
diabetes	89	26	59	4	66.3

Table 6. Accuracies(%) on whole training datasets(left table), and number of minimum training sub-samples to outperform %Def. class(right table).

Left table:

Distribution I	J4.8	BPNN	SVM	CLR	OneR
anneal	74.7	71.6	47.4	56.8	55.8
audiology	47.0	51.7	40.3	45.6	52.3
autos	66.7	63.8	46.8	46.1	56.0
balance-scale	58.0	59.4	39.5	43.4	53.0
breast-cancer	55.7	61.5	40.2	50.8	59.0
breast-w	86.1	91.1	38.0	46.8	54.4
colic	91.8	82.0	42.6	60.7	55.7
credit-a	57.4	48.7	35.7	39.1	54.8
credit-g	49.6	48.2	27.6	39.3	54.9
diabetes	64.0	78.7	41.6	42.7	53.9

Distribution II	J4.8	BPNN	SVM	CLR	OneR
anneal	68.4	66.3	56.8	60.0	56.8
audiology	60.4	61.1	43.6	55.0	56.4
autos	63.1	64.5	52.5	53.2	57.4
balance-scale	61.6	57.7	49.8	55.2	58.0
breast-cancer	68.0	70.5	47.5	58.2	59.8
breast-w	89.9	93.7	49.4	58.2	62.0
colic	77.0	78.7	57.4	62.3	67.2
credit-a	61.3	59.1	41.3	52.6	56.1
credit-g	61.3	59.1	41.3	52.6	56.1
diabetes	79.8	84.3	52.8	53.9	60.7

Distribution III	J4.8	BPNN	SVM	CLR	OneR
anneal	74.7	70.5	67.4	70.5	73.7
audiology	65.8	67.8	63.8	64.4	67.1
autos	85.1	73.8	68.1	70.2	73.8
balance-scale	70.5	69.8	64.8	65.8	69.8
breast-cancer	71.3	77.0	66.4	65.6	77.9
breast-w	74.7	86.1	73.4	68.4	74.7
colic	70.5	77.0	65.6	60.7	73.8
credit-a	70.9	70.0	65.2	65.2	71.3
credit-g	69.6	68.9	64.7	64.9	68.0
diabetes	82.0	88.8	67.4	67.4	73.0

Right table:

Distribution I	J4.8	BPNN	SVM	CLR	OneR
anneal	20	14	17	29	29
audiology	21	18	65	64	41
autos	38	28	76	77	70
balance-scale	12	14	15	15	32
breast-cancer	16	17	22	41	22
breast-w	7	10	10	18	14
colic	8	8	9	22	14
credit-a	9	12	16	30	28
credit-g	40	49	0	87	84
diabetes	14	10	24	33	20

Distribution II	J4.8	BPNN	SVM	CLR	OneR
anneal	29	20	16	42	46
audiology	36	45	–	61	67
autos	49	39	49	123	88
balance-scale	81	84	69	221	168
breast-cancer	31	28	102	40	46
breast-w	14	11	23	30	26
colic	24	20	36	42	36
credit-a	51	74	–	134	109
credit-g	112	245	–	273	275
diabetes	33	25	47	55	54

Distribution III	J4.8	BPNN	SVM	CLR	OneR
anneal	54	58	64	76	–
audiology	64	73	45	76	107
autos	66	102	84	121	98
balance-scale	118	103	133	162	156
breast-cancer	50	31	80	92	80
breast-w	44	36	31	48	71
colic	28	24	46	30	42
credit-a	118	159	–	–	173
credit-g	251	283	353	18	383
diabetes	50	42	60	–	72

the number of class i in each instance D_j become $p_i D_j$. As the same way, the probability vector of 'Distribution II' is $P = (0.3, 0.5, 0.2)$, and 'Distribution III' is $P = (0.3, 0.65, 0.05)$.

Accuracy Comparison on Classification Performances. As shown in the left table of Table 6, J48 and BPNN always work better than just predicting a default class. However, their performances are suffered from probabilistic class distributions to larger datasets such as balance-scale,credit-a and credit-g.

Estimating Minimum Training Subset to Construct a Valid Rule Evaluation Model. As shown in the right table of Table 6, to smaller datasets with balanced class distributions, the five learning algorithms can construct valid models with less than 20% of given training datasets. However, to larger datasets or with unbalanced class distributions, they need more training subsets to construct valid models, because their performances with whole training dataset fall to the percentages of default class.

5   Conclusion

In this paper, we have described rule evaluation support method with rule evaluation models to predict evaluations for an IF-THEN rule based on objective indices.

As the result of the performance comparison with the five learning algorithms, rule evaluation models have achieved higher accuracies than just predicting each default class. Considering the difference between the actual evaluation labeling and the artificial evaluation labeling, it is shown that the medical expert evaluated with certain subjective criterion. In the estimations of minimum training subset for constructing a valid rule evaluation model on the dataset of the actual datamining result, SVM and CLR have achieved more than 95% of achievement ratio compared to the accuracy of the whole training dataset with less than 10% of subset of the training dataset with certain human evaluations. These results indicate the availability of our method to support a human expert.

As future work, we will introduce a selection method of learning algorithms to construct a proper rule evaluation model according to each situation.

References

1. Ali, K., Manganaris,S., Srikant, R.: Partial Classification Using Association Rules. Proc. of Int. Conf. on Knowledge Discovery and Data Mining KDD-1997 (1997) 115–118
2. Brin, S., Motwani, R., Ullman, J., Tsur, S.: Dynamic itemset counting and implication rules for market basket data. Proc. of ACM SIGMOD Int. Conf. on Management of Data (1997) 255–264
3. Frank, E., Wang, Y., Inglis, S., Holmes, G., and Witten, I. H.: Using model trees for classification, Machine Learning, Vol.32, No.1 (1998) 63–76
4. Frank, E, Witten, I. H., Generating accurate rule sets without global optimization, in Proc. of the Fifteenth International Conference on Machine Learning, (1998) 144–151
5. Gago, P., Bento, C.: A Metric for Selection of the Most Promising Rules. Proc. of Euro. Conf. on the Principles of Data Mining and Knowledge Discovery PKDD-1998 (1998) 19–27

6. Goodman, L. A., Kruskal, W. H.: Measures of association for cross classifications. Springer Series in Statistics, 1, Springer-Verlag (1979)

7. Gray, B., Orlowska, M. E.: CCAIIA: Clustering Categorical Attributes into Interesting Association Rules. Proc. of Pacific-Asia Conf. on Knowledge Discovery and Data Mining PAKDD-1998 (1998) 132–143

8. Hamilton, H. J., Shan, N., Ziarko, W.: Machine Learning of Credible Classifications. Proc. of Australian Conf. on Artificial Intelligence AI-1997 (1997) 330–339

9. Hatazawa, H., Negishi, N., Suyama, A., Tsumoto, S., and Yamaguchi, T.: Knowledge Discovery Support from a Meningoencephalitis Database Using an Automatic Composition Tool for Inductive Applications, in Proc. of KDD Challenge 2000 in conjunction with PAKDD2000 (2000) 28–33

10. Hettich, S., Blake, C. L., and Merz, C. J.: UCI Repository of machine learning databases [http://www.ics.uci.edu/~mlearn/MLRepository.html], Irvine, CA: University of California, Department of Information and Computer Science, (1998).

11. Hilderman, R. J. and Hamilton, H. J.: Knowledge Discovery and Measure of Interest, Kluwe Academic Publishers (2001)

12. Hinton, G. E.: "Learning distributed representations of concepts", *Proceedings of 8th Annual Conference of the Cognitive Science Society*, Amherest, MA. REprinted in R.G.M.Morris (ed.) (1986)

13. Holte, R. C.: Very simple classification rules perform well on most commonly used datasets, Machine Learning, Vol. 11 (1993) 63–91

14. Klösgen, W.: Explora: A Multipattern and Multistrategy Discovery Assistant. in Fayyad, U. M., Piatetsky-Shapiro, G., Smyth, P., Uthurusamy R. (Eds.): Advances in Knowledge Discovery and Data Mining. AAAI/MIT Press, California (1996) 249–271

15. Ohsaki, M., Kitaguchi, S., Kume, S., Yokoi, H., and Yamaguchi, T.: Evaluation of Rule Interestingness Measures with a Clinical Dataset on Hepatitis, in Proc. of ECML/PKDD 2004, LNAI3202 (2004) 362–373

16. Piatetsky-Shapiro, G.: Discovery, Analysis and Presentation of Strong Rules. in Piatetsky-Shapiro, G., Frawley, W. J. (eds.): Knowledge Discovery in Databases. AAAI/MIT Press (1991) 229–248

17. Platt, J.: Fast Training of Support Vector Machines using Sequential Minimal Optimization, Advances in Kernel Methods - Support Vector Learning, B. Schölkopf, C. Burges, and A. Smola, eds., MIT Press (1999) 185–208

18. Quinlan, R.: C4.5: Programs for Machine Learning, Morgan Kaufmann Publishers, (1993)

19. Rijsbergen, C.: Information Retrieval, Chapter 7, Butterworths, London, (1979) http://www.dcs.gla.ac.uk/Keith/Chapter.7/Ch.7.html

20. Smyth, P., Goodman, R. M.: Rule Induction using Information Theory. in Piatetsky-Shapiro, G., Frawley, W. J. (eds.): Knowledge Discovery in Databases. AAAI/MIT Press (1991) 159–176

21. Tan, P. N., Kumar V., Srivastava, J.: Selecting the Right Interestingness Measure for Association Patterns. Proc. of Int. Conf. on Knowledge Discovery and Data Mining KDD-2002 (2002) 32–41

22. Witten, I. H and Frank, E.: DataMining: Practical Machine Learning Tools and Techniques with Java Implementations, Morgan Kaufmann, (2000)

23. Yao, Y. Y. Zhong, N.: An Analysis of Quantitative Measures Associated with Rules. Proc. of Pacific-Asia Conf. on Knowledge Discovery and Data Mining PAKDD-1999 (1999) 479–488

24. Zhong, N., Yao, Y. Y., Ohshima, M.: Peculiarity Oriented Multi-Database Mining. IEEE Trans. on Knowledge and Data Engineering, 15, 4, (2003) 952–960

Mining the Most Interesting Patterns from Multiple Phenotypes Medical Data*

Ying Yin, Bin Zhang, Yuhai Zhao, and Guoren Wang

Department of Computer Science and Engineering, Northeastern University
Shengyang 110004, P.R. China
yy_00000000@163.com

Abstract. Mining the most interesting patterns from multiple phenotypes medical data poses a great challenge for previous work, which only focuses on bi-phenotypes (such as abnormal vs. normal) medical data. Association rule mining can be applied to analyze such dataset, whereas most rules generated are either redundancy or no sense. In this paper, we define two interesting patterns, namely VP (an acronym for "Vital Pattern") and PP (an acronym for "Protect Pattern"), based on a statistical metric. We also propose a new algorithm called MVP that is specially designed to discover such two patterns from multiple phenotypes medical data. The algorithm generates useful rules for medical researchers, from which a clearly causal graph can be induced. The experiment results demonstrate that the proposed method enables the user to focus on fewer rules and assures that the survival rules are all interesting from the viewpoint of medical domain. The classifier build on the rules generated by our method outperforms existing classifiers.

1 Introduction

With the recent development of medical science, not only the disease but also many types of the disease can be accurately identified. For example breast cancer can be divided into three different subtypes: BRCA1, BRCA2 and Sporadic. Different subtypes correspond to different patterns. Previous work only focuses on distinguishing several pairs of phenotypes. It is important to medical researcher to mining specific patterns in different phenotypes simultaneously.

Rules are one of the most expressive and human understandable representations of knowledge, which has been widely accepted because of the simplicity of the problem statement and the effectiveness of pruning by support. However, association rule [1] discovery usually produces too many rules and not all of the rules are interesting.

Hence it is important to select the right measure for a given application domain. Utilizing the measure, some uninteresting rule will be prune efficiently. In medical applications, the vital patterns usually exist in every types of the diseases. Optimal rule discovery uncovers rules that maximize an interestingness measure, because it can prune some uninteresting itemsets and hence optimal rule discovery is significantly more efficient than association pation rule discovery. This

---

* The work was supported by the "fifteen" tackle key problem project of National Science and Technology Department under grant no.2004BA721A05.

S. Greco et al. (Eds.): RSCTC 2006, LNAI 4259, pp. 696–705, 2006.

paper aims to find and identify the vital patterns and protect patterns which are important to the medical application.

The main contributions of this work are as follows: (1) explain why mining medical data for VP and PP is an interesting problem, (2) identify useful constraints to make the patterns mined useful for the medical domain, (3) based on the proposed constraints, design an algorithm to discover VP and PP on multiple disease phenotypes, and (4) utilize the VP and PP to perform a causal analysis for a medical data set, which is more clear than association rules and is more suitable to analysis the medical data set.

The remainder of this paper is organized as follows: Section 2 states the definitions of VP and PP. In Section 3, we present the efficient method for identifying VP and PP based on interesting measure, and propose an algorithm to implement it. Experimental results are described in Section 4, where a casual graph is derived, which is understandable results to medical practitioners. Section 5 presents related work for comparison with our approach. We summarize our research and discuss some future work directions in Section 6.

2   Preliminary

In this section, we introduce some basic concepts and give the problem definition.

2.1   The Basics

As shown in Table 1, the medical dataset D consist of a set of rows and a set of columns, where the rows denote patients, $P = \{p_1, p_2..., p_m\}$, and the columns except the last one denote attributes(i.e. symptoms), $L = \{L_1, L_2, ...L_n\}$, while the last one, $T = \{T_1, T_2, ...T_k\}$, is the complete set of class of D. Each patient $p_i \in P$ consists of one or more attributes from L and a class label from T, i.e.$\{A_i, B_i, ..., T_i\}$. Note that every attribute has different expression value, which can evaluate the degree of the symptom. For simplicity, we let the capital letters, such as A, B, C, D, denote attributes and the number, such as 1, 2, 3, 4, denote different values of the symptoms. Table 1 shows a multiple pneumonia medical data with twelve patients and four symptoms with hierarchy. The diseases can be partitioned three types: typeA, typeB, typeC. Bellow are some definitions.

Table 1. An example of a three phenotypes medical data

A	B	C	D	CLASS
A0	B1	C2	D1	T1
A0	B1	C2	D3	T1
A0	B1	C2	D1	T1
A1	B1	C2	D1	T1
A0	B0	C2	D1	T2
A0	B0	C2	D1	T2
A1	B1	C0	D1	T2
A1	B1	C2	D1	T2
A1	B1	C2	D2	T3
A2	B0	C2	D1	T3
A2	B0	C2	D1	T3
A2	B0	C2	D1	T3

Definition 1. *Let D be a dataset with attribute A, $A=\{P_1, P_2, ..., P_n\}$. Let $P = \{P_1 P_2...P_l\} \subseteq A (l=1,2,...,n)$ be an attribute or a subset of attributes. We called an attribute value or a set of attribute-value pairs a* **Pattern***.*

For example, {fever=1(i.e.37^0C), cough=3(i.e.frequency in([40,50]/min))} is a pattern with two attribute-value pairs, denoted by P.

Definition 2. *Let P be a pattern and $T_k \in T$ be a phenotype. The intra-class support of pattern P in phenotype T_k is the ratio of the number of records containing P with the phenotype T_k to the number of phenotype T_k in the data set,* **Intra_Supp** *is an abbreviation of* **Intra_Support***.*

$$Intra\_Supp(P \to T_k) = \frac{Support(P \bigcup T_k)}{Support(T_k)}$$

Definition 3. *Let $I=\{P,Pa,Pab,...,Pabcd\}$ be a pattern set. Pa denotes the superset of pattern P, Pab denotes the superset of pattern P and Pa, Pabcd is the superset of all pattern in I except itself. So all supersets with prefix P are Pa, Pab, Pabc and so on. we say the set I is the* **Prefix Rule Sets** *with common prefix P.*

Definition 4. *The Prefix Rule Sets $I=\{Pa, Pab,..., Pabcde\}$ satisfy $Pa \to T_k$, $Pab \to T_k$,..., $Pabcde \to T_k$, if there not exist pattern $P' \in P$, and $P' \to T_k$, then we called pattern P the* **General pattern** *which induce T_k. If there not exist $Pabcde \in P''$, and $P'' \to T_k$, then we called pattern Pabcde the* **Specific pattern** *which induce T_k.*

Definition 5. Interestingness Measure Odd Ratio *is abbreviated to* **OR***. The Odd Ratio evaluate the relative likelihood of pattern P occurring in different phenotypes. That is say, it estimate the correlation about the pattern with the disease. The OR value lies in the range $[0,\infty]$.*

A pattern'OR for specific T_k is defined as:

$$OR(P \to T_k) = \frac{Supp(P \cup T_k)Supp(\neg P \cup \neg T_k)}{Supp(\neg P \cup T_k)Supp(P \cup \neg T_k)}$$

Supp is abbreviation of Support. $Supp(P \cup T_k)$ denotes the support of pattern P and T_k emerging simultaneously, $Supp(P \cup \neg T_k)=Supp(P)-Supp(P \cup T_k)$, $Supp(\neg P \cup T_k)=Supp(T_k)-Supp(P \cup T_k)$, and $Supp(\neg P \cup \neg T_k)=1-Supp(P)-Supp(T_k)+Supp(P \cup T_k)$.

Definition 6. *Let $P \subseteq A$, $T_k \in T$ denote one of the phenotype disease. We say P is* **Vital Pattern** *if and only if $OR(P \to T_k) \geqslant \delta$ (δ is a given threshold by user).* **VP** *is an abbreviation of Vital Pattern. Some vital pattern combination as* **Vital Pattern Sets***. We say P is* **Protect Pattern** *if and only if $OR(P \to T_k) \leqslant \varepsilon$ (ε is a given threshold by user).* **PP** *is an abbreviation of Protect Pattern. Some protect pattern combination as* **Protect Pattern Sets***.*

Definition 7. *For a given phenotype T_k, an* **optimal rule** *P should satisfy: (1)Pattern P should be frequent in each phenotype; (2)Pattern P should have the highest confidence in the Prefix Rule Set containing it; (3)Pattern P in the Prefix Rule Set containing it should have the maximal interesting in a specific domain. All the optimal rules combination as* **Optimal Rule Sets***.*

2.2   Problem Definition

Given: (1) a multiple phenotype dataset $D = S \times A$ with a set of target diseases, $T=\{T_1, T_2, ..., T_k\}$, (2) γ, the minimum intra-class support($Intra\_Supp$) threshold, (3) δ, a user-specific OR threshold such that a pattern with $OR \geq \delta$ is a vital pattern, and (4) ϵ, a user-specific OR threshold such that a pattern with $OR \leq \epsilon$ is a protect pattern, our task is to mine a pattern set R in which every element satisfies either the definition of vital pattern or the definition of protect pattern.

3   MVP Algorithm

We present our algorithm, called MVP[1], to find all vital patterns and protect patterns satisfying thresholds δ and ϵ respectively in section 3.1 and the effective pruning strategies in section 3.2.

3.1   The Description of MVP Algorithm

We discuss the detail of MVP algorithm below, taking Table 1 as the example, where the minimum intra-class support threshold $\gamma=2$.

The mining process is conducted on a prefix tree as shown in Figure 1, which is build on Table 1. Limited by space, we omit the description of constructing such a prefix tree structure.

From figure 1, we can see 10 candidate 1-patterns at level 1, where the number within brackets denotes the count of patterns. For example, $A_0(4)$ denotes the total count of A_0 is 4. We only use the support-based pruning 1(see the details in section3.2) to generate these candidate patterns(line 2-5). T_k with solid box represents the corresponding rule pruned. For example, T_3 with solid box under $A_0(4)$ means the rule $A_0 \rightarrow T_3$ can be cut by pruning rule 1. Further, if all T_k under some pattern are pruned, then rules containing this pattern will be pruned. For example, the removal of all T_k under C_0 induces 46 rules in the prefix rule set of C_0 pruned, such as $A_0C_0 \rightarrow T_k$, $A_1C_0 \rightarrow T_k$,...,$A_0B_0C_0 \rightarrow T_k$,..., and $A_2B_1C_0D_3 \rightarrow T_k$ will not be generated, and the similar case to D_3. Next, we generate the candidate patterns for the second level. At first, we can pruning some redundancy rules by applying pruning rule 1(line 8~10), such as candidate A_0D_2, A_1B_0, A_1D_2 are remove since Intra_Supp(A_0D_2)=0< γ, Intra_Supp(A_1B_0)=0< γ, Intra_Supp(A_1D_2)=0< γ. It is marked by red ① where the prune rule 1 is applied. Then, we perform the confidence-based pruning rule 2(line 13), which will also be explained in subsection 3.2. For instance, (T$_1$T$_2$) in candidate(A$_0$C$_2$; T$_1$T$_2$) is terminated because of Supp(A$_0$)=Supp(A$_0$C$_2$). It is marked by red ② where the prune rule 2 is applied. At last, OR-based pruning rule 3 is very important but not difficult understand (see subsection 3.2). For example, T$_1$ in candidate (A$_0$D$_1$; T$_1$T$_2$) is removed by line 14 because Supp(A$_0$D$_1 \cup \neg$T$_1$) = Supp(A$_0 \cup \neg$T$_1$) hold. It is marked by red ③ where the prune rule 3 is applied. A complete pseudo-code for mining optimal VP and PP sets is presented in Algorithm 1.

---

[1] MVP stands for Mining Vital and Protect Patterns.

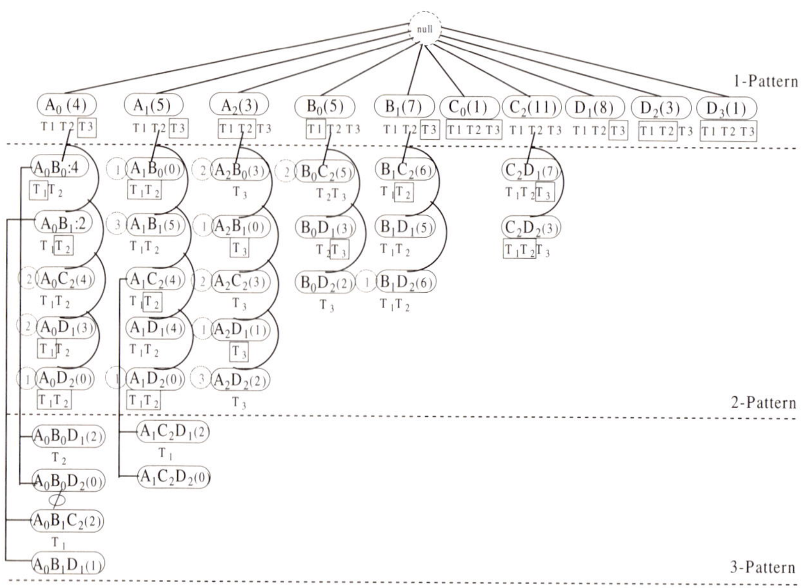

Fig. 1. The MVP algorithm

Algorithm 1. Mining the VP and PP algorithm
Input: data set D, minimum Inter_Class Support θ
Output: Pattern sets R

```
 1: Set R = φ
 2: Count support of 1-patterns in every phenotype
 3: Generate 1-pattern set
 4: Count supports of 1-pattern in different phenotype
 5: Select 1-pattern respectively and add them to R
 6: new pattern set ← Generate(2-pattern set)
 7: while new pattern set is not empty do
 8:     Count Intra_Supp(P,T_k) of candidates in new pattern set
 9:     For each pattern P in (l+1)-pattern set
10:     Applying pruning 1: IF Intra_Supp(P→ T_k)< γ
11:     remove pattern S;
12:     Else if there is a sub pattern P' in l-pattern set
13:     Applying pruning 2: that Supp(P')= Supp(P) or
14:     Applying pruning 2: Supp(P',¬T_k)=Supp(P,¬T_k)
15:     Then remove pattern P;
16:     Count the OR value;
17:     Select VP and PP to R;
18:     ENDIF
19: end while
20: new pattern set ← Generate(next level pattern sets)
21: Return R;
```

The algorithm 1 discuss the support-based pruning, confidence-based pruning, and OR-based pruning. Existing algorithms to find an interesting rule sets are to post-prune an association rule set but this may be very inefficient when the minimum support is low and it will be generate a mount of redundancy rules. Our MVP algorithm makes use of the interestingness measure property to efficiently prune uninteresting rules and save only the maximal interesting rules instead of all ones, and this distinguishes it from an association rule mining algorithm.

Function 1. Generate(l+1)-pattern Set

```
1: Let (l + 1)-pattern set be empty set
2: (Note: Obey by the CI_{k-1} * CI_{k-1} Method to Merge)
3: for  each pair of patterns pP_{l-1} and P_{l-1}q in l-pattern set do
4:     Insert candidate P_{l-1}.pq in (l + 1)-pattern set ;
5:     for  all P_l ⊂ P_{l-1}pq do
6:         if  P_l does not exist in l-pattern set then
7:             Then remove candidate P_{l-1}pq
8:         end if
9:         Return (l+1)-pattern set
10:    end for
11: end for
```

Function 1 as function for generate candidate itemsets. All candidate generation are build on the prefix tree structure. We adopt the $CI_{k-1}*CI_{k-1}$ Merge to obtained the candidate itemset. After rules have been formed, we can prune many redundancy rules, limited by space, we don't explain the function in details.

3.2 Pruning Strategies

We next look at the pruning techniques that are used in MVP, which are essential for the efficiency. Our emphasis here is to show that our pruning steps prevent unnecessary rules generation and only preserve interesting rules, the correctness of our algorithm will be obvious.

Pruning Rule 1. *Given Intra_Supp, Pattern Pa denotes pattern P and all its possible proper supersets, phenotype $T_k \in T$ (k=1,2,3,...) denotes one types of the diseases. If $0 \leqslant Intra\_Supp(P \to T_k) \leqslant \gamma$, then pattern P and its supersets for their' s corresponding phenotype T_k will not be the optimal rule.*

Pruning Rule 2. *If pattern P satisfy Supp(P)= Supp(Pa), Pa denotes its proper superset, then pattern Pa and all its possible proper supersets will not be useful for VP and PP.*

Pruning Rule 3. *If pattern P satisfy $Supp(P \cup T_k) = Supp(Pa \cup T_k)$, Pa denotes its proper superset, then pattern Pa and all its possible proper supersets will not be useful for VP and PP.*

Limited by space, we omit the proof. The above pruning rules are very efficient since it only generates a subset of frequent patterns with maximal interestingness instead of all ones.

Finally, the optimal VP and PP sets are significantly smaller than an association rule set, but is still too big for medical practitioners to review them all. We may only return top-k vital patterns or protect patterns, but they may all come from a section of the data set and lack the representation for all phenotypes. In order to account for all known phenotypes, we aim to retain one vital pattern sets and protect pattern sets for each phenotype T_k. Limited by space, we don't list the top-k algorithm in details.

4 Experiments

The task was support by national nature fund. The pneumonia data come from eight hospitals. The data set contains 20000 cases, where belong to six different pneumonia. Patients are described by 112 attributes, but not all the attributes are useful to mining vital pattern and protect pattern. Some information including age, sex, address, phone number are excluded during the preprocessing. Our goal is to identify VP and PP from multiple pneumonia phenotypes. We set the Intra_Supp as 0.01. It returned 6 phenotypes and corresponding VP and PP. The following are the first four representative patterns with the highest VP and lowest PP. For phenotype T_k, below is the example of VP and PP, the vital pattern is:

Pattern 1: OR=3.06 , Significance Testing : $\chi^2 = 14.08$, P<0.05, it illuminate the pattern is relevant to phenotype T_k.

Fever $= 38^0C \sim 39^0C$

Breath $= 30\sim40$ times/minute

X ray $=$ "thick and weight"

The PP is :

Pattern: OR=1.102

Fever $= 36.5^0C \sim 37^0C$

Moist Rales $=$ "normal"

Limited by space, we don't list all the experiment results. From the experiment results, we can draw a causal graph with respective patterns.

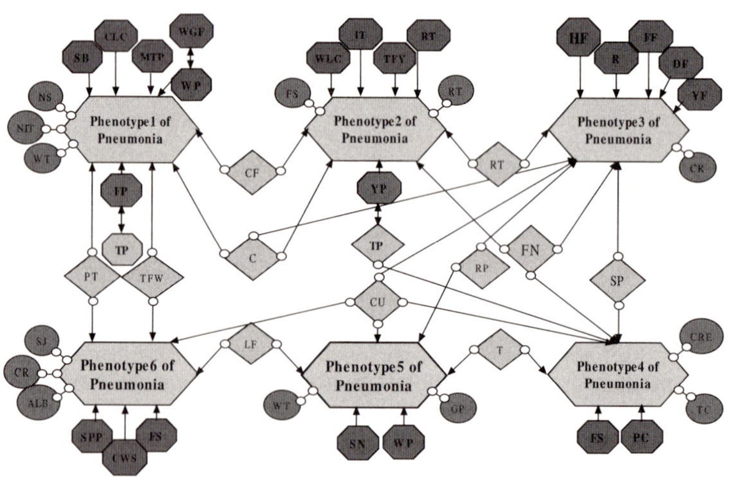

Fig. 2. Causal analysis graph of multiple phenotypes pneumonia

With this causal graph, we can verify that different phenotypes are independent or conditionally independent. The representative edges form a graph with three type of edges:

1. Directed edges ($\rightarrow$) indicating a cause-effect relationship. It means the pattern would be the vital pattern.

2. Bidirected edges ($\leftarrow\rightarrow$) indicating the two patterns are appearance together. It means one pattern's appearance go with another pattern's appearance together.

3. Directed edges with a small circle at its tail (o→) also indicate a cause-effect. It means the pattern are common cause for more than two phenotypes. It will not be the highest vital pattern.

4. Edge with circles at both ends (o–o) indicate that either could be causing the other. It means the pattern would be the protect pattern.

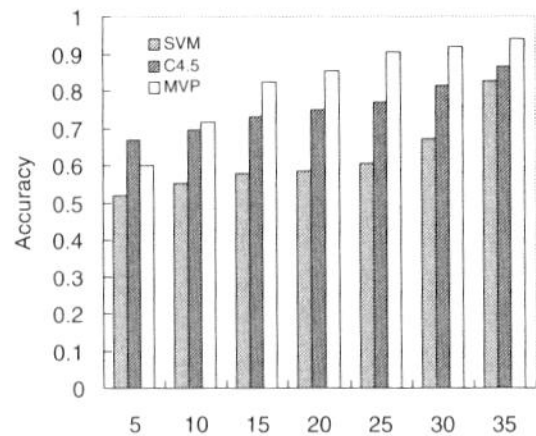

(a) Accuracy vs. algorithms

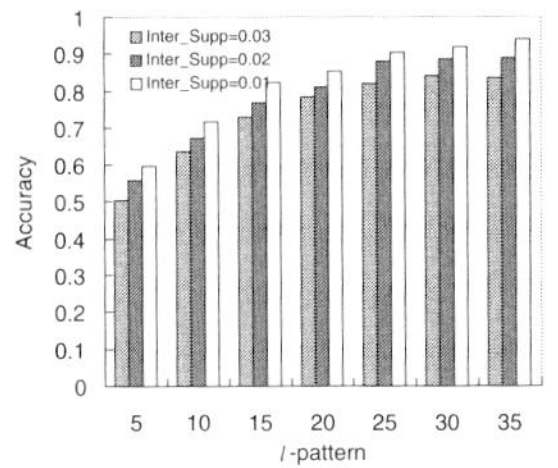

(b) Accuracy vs. support

Fig. 3. Classification accuracy comparison

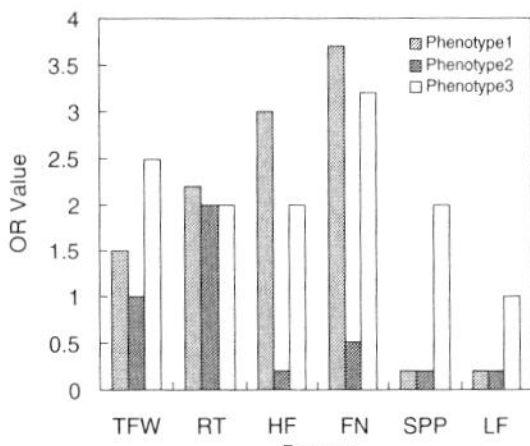

Fig. 4. OR value of pattern vs. phenotypes

We evaluate the performance of MVP algorithm from effectiveness and the classification accuracy. In all experiments, we use Intra_Supp=0.01, unless otherwise specified. Figure 3 presents the comparison of classification accuracies. Figure 3 (a) compare the classification accuracy with the same support by different algorithms(SVM, C4.5, and MVP). Figure 3(b) present the classification accuracy of different pattern selection(range from 5 to 35) with different Intra_Supp. Obviously, the classification accuracy are different with different Intra_Supp.

In figure 4, we compute the pattern′OR value in different phenotypes. We clearly see that each pattern′OR value is different in different phenotypes, which illuminate the different signification of the same pattern in different outcome phenotypes and the importance of interesting measure.

Figure 5 compare the run times of rules with different algorithms(association rules, non-redundant rules and MVP). Figure 5 (a) compare the runtime of rules with the different support(range from 0.01 to 0.07). Figure 5 (b) compare the runtime of rules with the same support by different layer-th. We can see that MVP algorithm always consume the least time, because it prune the redundant rules in each level.

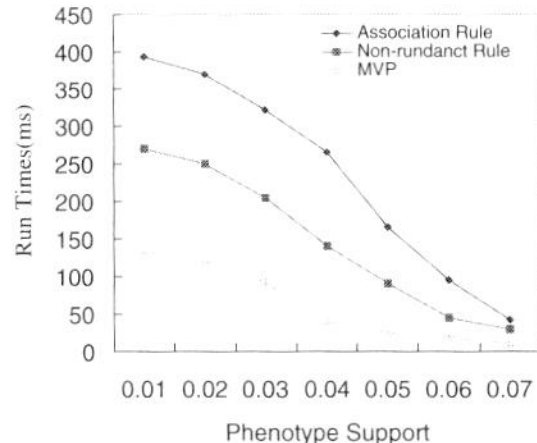

(a) Run times vs. support

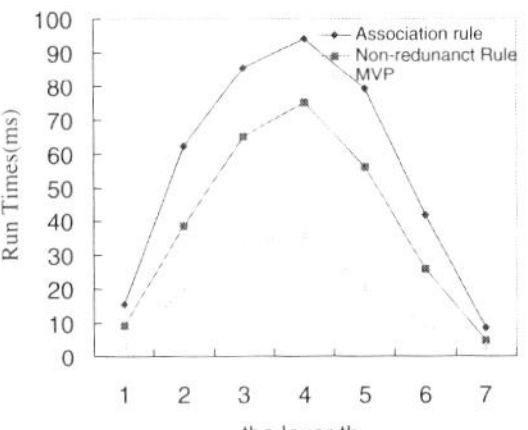

(b) Run times vs. candidate levels

Fig. 5. Comparison of run times of rules

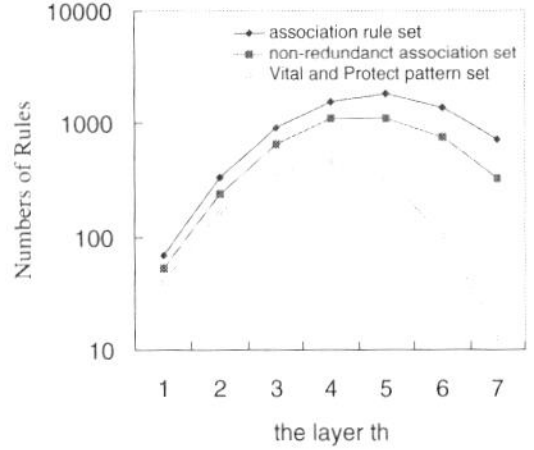

Fig. 6. The numbers of rules vs. algorithms

In comparison with MVP in figure 6, the non-redundant rules and association rules is very inefficient. We can draw a conclusion that MVP only generate the maximal interesting rules which reduce the redundant rules dramatically.

From a series of experiment above, we can prove that our algorithm can discover vital patterns and protect patterns which are important for domain expert and most found patterns are of great interest to domain experts and verified by them and our MVP algorithm is efficient for classification.

5   Related Work

Data Mining is an active research area. One of the most popular approaches to do data mining is discovering association rules [1]. Association rules are generally used with basket, census or financial data [2]. Medical data is generally analyzed with classifier trees [3,4], clustering, or regression. Recent years, association rule mining has been used in medical data analysis. Brossette et al [5] found association rules in hospital infection control and public surveillance data. Sequence patterns have been found in chronic hepatitis data by Ohsaki et al [6], and so on. However, these cases result in too many trivial and similar patterns which is also a problem in the research. It is quite impossible for domain experts to review a huge number of association rules. Liu et al [7] used the standard test to prune insignificant rules and introduced the concept of direction setting rules to summarize the patterns. A crucial aspect of data mining is that the discovered knowledge should be somehow interesting, where the term interestingness arguably has to do with surprisingness (unexpectedness), usefulness and novelty [8]. So fining an interesting measure is very important for a special domain.

6   Conclusions and Future Research Directions

In this paper, we discuss the vital pattern and protect pattern which are important for medical researcher, and propose an interesting measure in order to decide whether the rules are interesting for the biomedical domain. Based on the interesting measure, we propose a new algorithm with efficient pruning rules to mine all optimal VP and PP rules. A causal graph can be deduced using the resulting rules. Our experimental results confirm that our approach is effective and efficient for optimal VP and PP rules generating. Our approach also outperforms the existing approach in performance.

There is an emerging need for mining interesting rules from multiple phenotypes medical data. Interesting rule discovery is efficient and works well by selecting the right measure. Therefore, it is a great alternative for association rule discovery in biomedical domain.

References

1. R. Agrawal, T., Swami, A.: Mining association rules between sets of items in large databases. In: Proc. of ACM SIGMOD 1993 Conference. (1993) 207–216
2. Decker, K.M., Focardi, S.: Technology overview: A report on data mining, technical report cscs tr-95-02. In: Swiss Scientific Computing Center. (1995)

3. J.Li, L.Wong: Using rules to analyse bio-medical data: A comparison between c4.5 and pcl. In: Proc. of Advances in Web-Age Information Management. (2003) 254–265
4. Zhou, Z., Jiang, Y.: Medical diagnosis with c4.5 rule preceded by artificial neural network ensemble. IEEE Transactions on Information Technology in Biomedicine **7** (2003) 37–42
5. JS. E. Brossette, A.P.S., Moser, S.A.: Associarion rules and data mining in hospital infection control and public health surveillance. Journal of American Medical Informatics Association **5** (1998) 373–381
6. M. Ohsaki, Y. Sato, H.Y., Yamaguchi, T.: A rule discovery support system for sequential medical data in the case study of a chronic hepatitis dataset. In: In Proc of the ECML/PKDD-2003 Discovery Challenge Workshop. (2003) 154–165
7. B. Liu, W., Y.Ma: Pruning and summarizing the discovered associations. In: Proc. of 5nd Intl. Conf. on Knowledge Discovery and Data Mining. (1999)
8. M.Kamber, R.Shinghal: Evalusting the interestingness of characteristic rules. In: Proc. of 2nd Intl. Conf. on Knowledge Discovery and Data Mining. (1996) 263–266

Risk Mining: Mining Nurses' Incident Factors and Application of Mining Results to Prevention of Incidents

Shusaku Tsumoto[1], Kimiko Matsuoka[2], and Shigeki Yokoyama[3]

[1] Department of Medical Informatics,
Shimane University, School of Medicine
89-1 Enya-cho, Izumo 693-8501 Japan
[2] Osaka Prefectural General Hospital , Osaka, Japan
[3] Department of Medical Information, Koden Industry,Tokyo, Japan

Abstract. To err is human. How can we avoid near misses and achieve medical safety? From this perspective, we analyzed the nurses' incident data by data mining with the "concept of quality control" that near misses are produced by the system rather than individuals. Nurses' incident data were collected during the 18 months at the emergency room. Significant rules (If-then rules) indicated that the medication errors are likely to occur when mental concentration is disrupted by interruption of work, etc. Based on the results of the analysis, the nurses' medication check system was improved. During the last 6 months, the check system was put into effect. The frequency of the medication errors decreased to about one-twenties or less. It was considered that the data mining analysis contributes the decision support on the improvement of incidents.

1 Introduction

It has passed about twenty years since clinical information are stored electronically as a hospital information system since 1980's. Stored data include from accounting information to laboratory data and even patient records are now started to be accumulated: in other words, a hospital cannot function without the information system, where almost all the pieces of medical information are stored as multimedia databases. Especially, if the implementation of electronic patient records is progressed into the improvement on the efficiency of information retrieval, it may not be a dream for each patient to benefit from the personal database with all the healthcare information, "from cradle to tomb". However, although the studies on electronic patient record has been progressed rapidly, reuse of the stored data has not yet been discussed in details, except for laboratory data and accounting information to which OLAP methodologies are applied. Even in these databases, more intelligent techniques for reuse of the data, such as data mining and classical statistical methods has just started to be applied from 1990's[1,2].

S. Greco et al. (Eds.): RSCTC 2006, LNAI 4259, pp. 706–715, 2006.

Human data analysis is characterized by a deep and short-range investigation based on their experienced "cases", whereas one of the most distinguished features of com-puter-based data analysis is to enable us to understand from the different viewpoints by using "cross-sectional" search. It is expected that the intelligent reuse of data in the hospital information system provides us to grasp the all the characteristics of univer-sity hospital and to acquire objective knowledge about how the hospital management should be and what kind of medical care should be served in the university hospital.

This paper focuses on application of data mining to medical risk management. To err is human. However, medical practice should avoid as many errors as possible to achieve safe medicine. Thus, it is a very critical issue in clinical environment how we can avoid the near misses and achieve the medical safety. Errors can be classified into the following three type of erros. First one is systematic errors, which occur due to problems of system and workflow. Second one is personal errors, which occur due to lack of expertise of medical staff. Finally, the third one is random error. The important point is to detect systematic errors and personal errors, which may be prevented by suitable actions, and data mining is expected as a tool for analysis of those errors.

For this purpose, this paper proposes *risk mining* where data including risk information is analyzed by using data mining methods and mining results are used for risk prevention. We assume that risk mining consists of three major processes: risk detection, risk clarification and risk utilization, as shown in Section 2.

As an illustrative example, we applied risk mining process to analysis of nurses' incident data. First, data collected in 6 months were analyzed by rule induction methods, which detects several important factors for incidents (risk detection). Since data do not include precise information about these factors, we recollect incident data for 6 months to collect precise information about incidents. Then, rule induction is applied to new data. Domain experts discussed all the results obtained and found several important systematic errors in workflow (risk clarification). Finally, nurses changed workflow to prevent incidents and data were recollected for 6 months. Surprisingly, the frequency of medication errors has been reduced to one-tenth (risk utilization).

This paper is organized as follows. Section 2 shows background of our studies. Section 3 proposes three major processes of risk mining. Section 4 gives an illustrative application of risk mining. Finally, Section 5 concludes this paper.

2   Background

A hospital is a very complicated organization where medical staff, including doctors and nurses give a very efficient and specialized service for patients. However, such a complicated organization is not robust to rapid changes. Due to rapid advances in medical technology, such as introduction of complicated chemotherapy, medical workflow has to be changed in a rapid and systematic way. Such rapid changes lead to malpratice of medical staff, sometimes a large-scale accident may occur by chain reaction of small-scale accidents.

Medical accidents include not only careless mistakes of doctors or nurses, but also prescription errors, intrahospital infections or drug side-effects. The cause for such accidents may not be well investigated and it is unknown whether such accidents can be classified into systematic errors or random errors. Since the occurrence of severe accidents is very low, case studies are used for their analysis. However, in such investigations, personal errors tend to be the cause of the accidents. Thus, it is very important to discover knowledge about how such accidents occur in a complicated organization and knowledge about the nature of systematic erors or random errors.

On the other hand, clinical information have been stored electronically as a hospital information system(HIS). The database stores all the data related with medical actions, including accounting information, laboratory examination, treatement and patient records described by medical staffs. Incident or accident reports are not exception: they are also stored in HIS as clinical data. Thus, it is now expected that mining such combined data will give a new insight to medical accidents.

3   Risk Mining

In order to utilize information about risk extracted from information systems, we propose risk mining which integrates the following three important process: risk detection, risk clarification and risk utilization.

3.1   Risk Detection

Patterns or information unexpected to domain experts may be important to detect the possiblity of large scale accidents. So, first, mining patterns or other types of information which are unexpected to domain experts is one of the important processes in risk mining. We call this process *risk detection*, where acquired knowdedge is refered to as *detected risk information*.

3.2   Risk Clarification

Focusing on detected risk information, domain experts and data miners can focus on clarification of modelling the hidden mechanism of risk. If domain experts need more information with finer granularity, we should collect more data with detailed information, and apply data mining to newly collected data. We call this process *risk clarification*, where acquired knowdedge is refered to as *clarified risk information*.

3.3   Risk Utilization

We have to evaluate clarified risk information in a real world environment to prevent risk events. If risk information is not enough to prevention, then more analysis is required. Thus, additional data collection is evoked for a new cycle of risk mining process.

We call this process *risk utilization.* where acquired knowdedge is refered to as *clarified risk information.*

Figure 1 shows the overview of risk mining process.

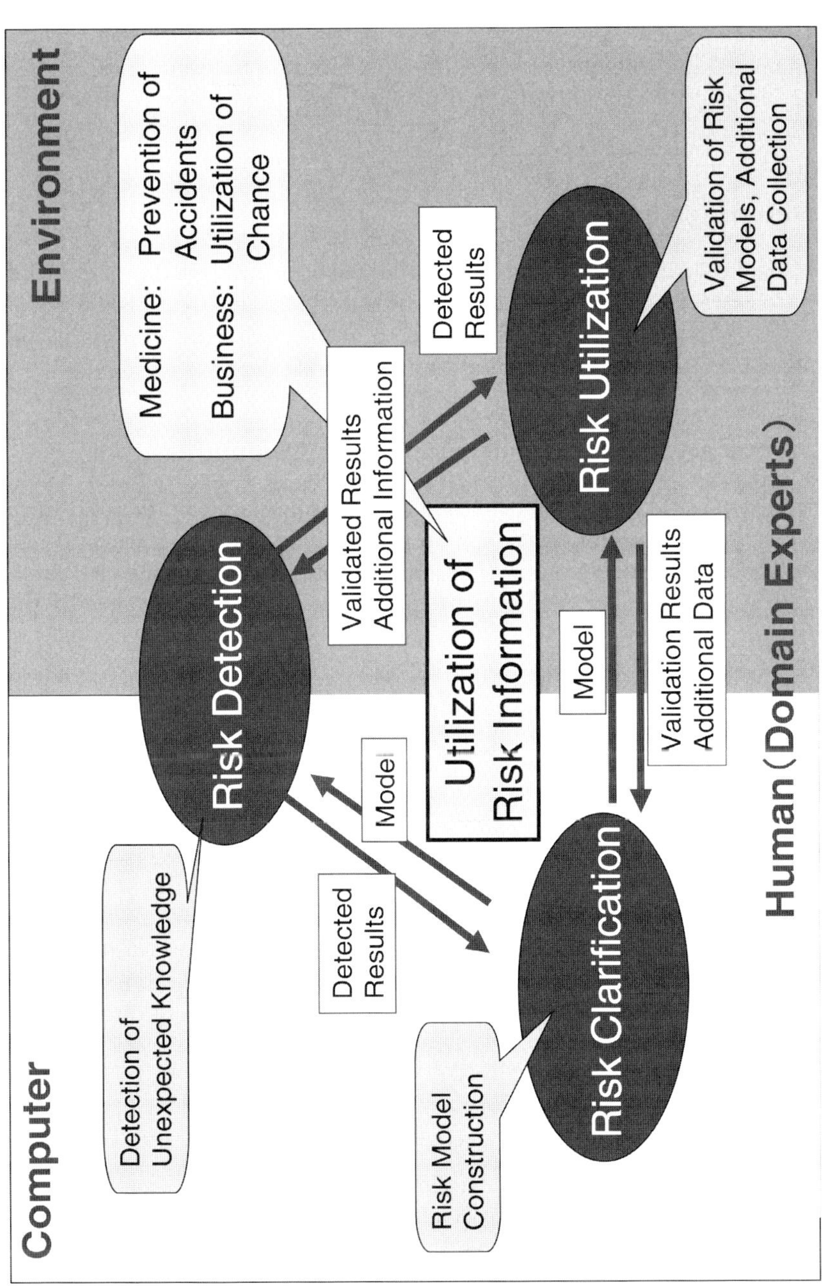

Fig. 1. Risk Mining Proces: Overview

3.4   Elemental Techiques for Risk Mining

Mining Unbalanced Data. A large scale accident rarely occur: usually such it can viewed as a large deviation of small scale accidents, called incidents. Since even the occurence of incidents is very low, the probability of large accidents is nearly equal to 0. On the other hand, most of the data mining methods depend on "frequency" and mining such unbalanced data with small probabilities is one of the difficult problems in data mining research. Thus, for risk mining, techiques for mining unbanced data are very important to detect risk information.

3.5   Interestingness

In convetional data mining, indices for mining patterns are based on frequency. However, to extract unexpected or interesting knowledge, we can introduce measures for unexpectedness or interestingness to extract patterns from data, and such studies have been reported in data mining literature.

3.6   Uncertainty and Granularity: Granular Computing

Since incident reports include information about human actions, these data are described by subjective information with uncertainty, where we need to deal with coarseness and fineness of information (information granularity). Granular computing, including fuzzy sets and rough sets, are closely related with this point.

3.7   Visualization

Visualizing cooccurence events or items may enable domain experts to detect risk information, to clarify the mechanism of risk, or to utilize risk information.

3.8   Structuration: Graph Mining

Risk may be detected or clarified only by relations between several items in a large network structure. Thus, exracting partial structure from network hidden in data is a very important techique, focusing on risk information based on relations between items.

3.9   Clustering

Similarity may find relations between similar objects which seems not to be similar. Or events which seems to occur independently can be grouped into several "similar" events, which enables us to find dependencies between events. For this purpose, clustering is a very important techique.

3.10   Evaluation of Risk Probablity

Since probability is formally defined as a Lebegue measure on a fixed sample space, its performance is very unstable when the definition of sample space is unstable. Especially, when we collect data dynamically, such unstablility frequently occurs. Thus, deep reflection on evaluation of risk probability is very important.

3.11   Human Computer Interaction

This process is very important for risk mining process because of the following reasons. First, risk information may be obtained by deep discussions on mining results among domain experts because mining results may show only small part of the total risk information. Since domain experts have knowledge, which is not described in a datasets, they can compensate for insufficient knowledge to obtain a hypothesis or explanation of mining results. Second, mining results may lead to domain experts' deep understanding of workflow, as shown in Section 4. Interpretation of mining results in risk detection may lead to new data collection for risk clarification. Finally, human computer interaction gives a new aspect for risk utilization. Domain experts can not only performance of risk clarification results, but also look for other possiblities from the rules which seems to be not so important, compared with rules for risk clarification and also evalute the possibility to design a new data collection.

4   Case Study of Risk Mining: Prevention of Medication Errors

4.1   Risk Detection

Dataset. Nurses' incident data were collected by using the conventional sheet of incident reports during 6 months from April, 2001 to September, 2001 at the emergency room in Osaka Prefectural General Hospital.

The dataset includes the types of the near misses, the patients' factors, the medical staff's factors and the shift (early-night, late-night, and daytime) and the number of items of incidents collected was 245.

We applied C4.5[3], decision tree induction and rule induction to this dataset.

Rule Induction. We obtained a decision tree shown in Figure 2 and the following interesting rules.

```
(medication error):
If late-night and lack of checking,
then medication errors occur: probability (53.3%, 8/15).
```

```
(injection error):
If daytime and lack of checking,
then injection incidents occur: probability (53.6%, 15/28).
```

```
(injection error):
If early-night, lack of checking, and error of injection rate,
then injection incidents occur: probability (50%, 2/4)
```

Those rules show that the time shift of nurse and lack of checking were the principal factors for medication and injection errors. Interestingly, lack of expertise (personal errors) was not selected. Thus, time shift and lack of checking could be viewed as risk factor for these errors. Since the conventional format of incident reports did not include furture information about workflow, we had decided to ask nurses' to fill out new report form for each incident. This is the next step in risk clarification.

```
*** Decision tree : First 6 Months ***
┌Injection error—Injection route trouble(an obstruction due to the bending·reflow,
│              the disconnection) = Yes: early-night work (2—>2)
└Injection error—Injection route trouble(an obstruction due to the bending·reflow,
      │         the disconnection) = No
      ├Injection error—Pulled out. (accident and self) = Yes: early-night (2—>2)
      ├Injection error—Pulled out. (accident and self) = No
          ├Injection error— Interrupts for the work = Yes: late-night (5—>3)
          ├Interrupts for the work = No
              ├Injection error—Lack of knowledge for drugs and injection
              │              = Yes: late-night (5—>3)
              ├Injection error—Lack of knowledge for drugs and injection = No
                  ├Injection error—Lack of command on the serious patients
                  │              = Yes: late-night (3—>2)
                  ├Injection error— Lack of command on the serious patients = No
                      ├Injection error—Lack of attention and confirmation
                      │  ( drug to, dosage by, patient at, time in, route ) = No: day-time(6—>4)
                      ├Injection error—Lack of attention and confirmation = Yes
                          ├Injection error—Wrong IV rate of flow = Yes: early-night work (4—>2)
                          ├Injection error—Wrong IV rate of flow = No: day-time (28—>15)
```

Fig. 2. Decision Tree in Risk Detection

4.2   Risk Clarification

Dataset. Just after the first 6 months, we had found that the mental concentration of nurses may be important factors for medical errors. During the next 6 months from October 2001 to March 2002, the detailed interference factors were included in the additional incident report form as the items of "environmental factors".

Figure 3 shows a sheet for additional information. The additional items included the duration of experience at the present ward, the number of nurse, the degree of business, the number of serious patients whether the nursing service was interrupted or not and so on.

We applied C4.5[3], decision tree induction and rule induction to this dataset.

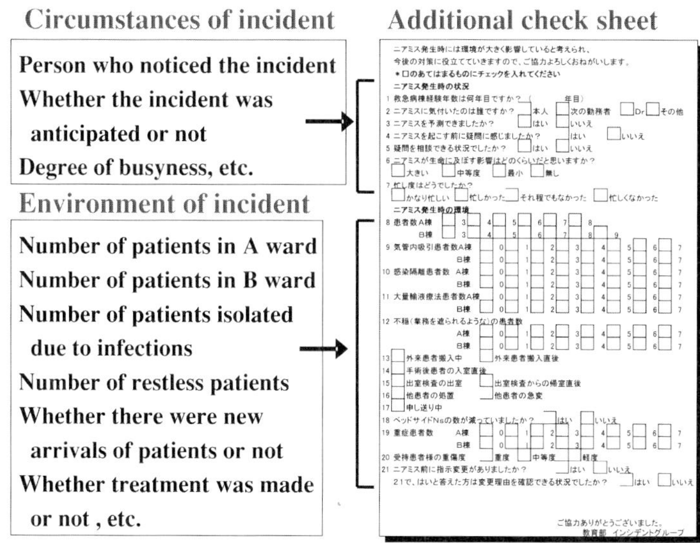

Fig. 3. Sheet for Additional Information

Rule Induction. The following rules were obtained:

```
(medication error):
If the number of disturbing patients is one or more,
    then medi-cation errors occur: probability (90%, 18/20).
```

```
(medication error):
If nurses' work interrupted,
then medication errors occur: probability (80%, 4/5).
```

By addition of "the environmental factors", these high probability rules of medication errors were extracted.

Rule Interpretation. With these results, the nurses discussed their medication check system.

At the emergency room, the nurses in charge of the shift prepared the medication (identification, quantity of medicines, etc.). The time of preparation before the beginning of the shift was occasionally less than 30 minutes when the liaison conference between shifts took time. In such cases, the sorting of medicines could not be made in a advance and must be done during the shift.

If nurses' concentration was disturbed by the restless patients in such situations, double check of the preparation for medicine could not be made, which leads to medication errors.

4.3   Risk Utilization

Therefore, it was decided that two nurses who had finished their shifts would prepare medicines for the next shift, and one nurse in charge of the medication would check the dose and identification of medicines alone (triple check by a total of 3 nurses). (However, heated discussions among domain experts (nurses) needed for this decision, as shown in Section 5.) Improvement was applied to the check system as a result of their discussion. During the last 6 months (April 2002 to October 2002), incident reports were collected.

After introducing the triple check system, the total number of the medication errors during the last 6 months decreased to 24 cases. It was considered that the nurses' medication work was improved by the triple check system during the last 6 months.

5   Discussion for Case Study

5.1   Risk Utilization as Information Sharing

For discussion among domain experts, mining results were presented to medical staffs as objective evidence. Discussion on mining results give a very interactive discussion among the staff of the department of emergency and finally achieve common understanding of the problem on its workflow. Then, it is found that changes in workflow is required for solving the problem: If the staff assigned to the shift cannot prepare medicines, other members who are free should cooperate. However, this idea met a fierce objection in the department at first because of disagreement among nurses about the responsibility of those who prepare medicines. After repeated discussions, it was decided that nurses in charge of medication were responsible for mistakes rather than those who made preparations and nurses in the preceding shift should prepare medicines for the next shift.

During the last 6 months, medication errors were reduced markedly by creating the common perception that liaison (overlapping of shift margins, or paste margins) is important among nurses, and the initial opposition completely subsided. Following this nursing example, we could extend this policy of "paste margins", i.e. mutual support by free staff members, to the entire department.

This process also shows that information granularity is a very important issue for risk clarification.

Items in a conventional report form, such as "lack of checking, lack of attention, etc." are too coarse for risk clarification. Rather, detailed description of environmental factors are much more important to evoke domain experts' discussion and their risk utilizaiton.

6   Conclusion

Since all the clinical information have been stored electronically as a hospital information system(HIS), it is now expected that mining such combined data will give a new insight to medical accidents.

In order to utilize information about risk extracted from information systems, we propose risk mining which integrates the following three important process: risk detection, risk clarification and risk utilization. Risk Detection discovers patterns or information unexpected to domain experts, which can be viewed as a sign of large scale accidents. In risk clarification, domain experts and data miners construct the model of the hidden mechanism of risk, focusing on detected risk information. If domain experts need more information with finer granularity, we should collect more data with detailed information, and apply data mining to newly collected data. Risk utilization evaluated clarified risk information in a real world environment to prevent risk events. If risk information is not enough to prevention, then more analysis is required. Thus, additional data collection is evoked for a new cycle of risk mining process.

As an illustrative example, we applied risk mining process to analysis of nurses' incident data. First, data collected in 6 months were analyzed by rule induction methods, which detects several important factors for incidents (risk detection). Since data do not include precise information about these factors, we recollect incident data for 6 months to collect precise information about incidents. Then, rule induction is applied to new data. Domain experts discussed all the results obtained and found several important systematic errors in workflow (risk clarification). Finally, nurses changed workflow to prevent incidents and data were recollected for 6 months. Surprisingly, the frequency of medication errors has been reduced to one-tenth (risk utilization).

References

1. Tsumoto, S.: Knowledge discovery in clinical databases and evaluation of discovered knowledge in outpatient clinic. Information Sciences (124) (2000) 125–137
2. Tsumoto, S.: G5: Data mining in medicine. In Kloesgen, W., Zytkow, J., eds.: Handbook of Data Mining and Knowledge Discovery. Oxford University Press, Oxford (2001) 798–807
3. Quinlan, J.: C4.5 - Programs for Machine Learning. Morgan Kaufmann, Palo Alto (1993)

Rule Quality Measures in Creation and Reduction of Data Rule Models

Marek Sikora

Silesian University of Technology, Institute of Computer Sciences,
44-100 Gliwice, Poland
Marek.Sikora@polsl.pl

Abstract. Properties of several rule quality measures are characterized in the paper. Possibilities of their application in algorithms of rules induction and reduction are presented. Influence of replacing rules accuracy with the Bayesian confirmation measure has been tested.

1 Introduction

Knowledge discovery in databases is read as a process of extraction of unknown, nontrivial and useful patterns in data. On of the most popular representation of such patterns on its simplicity account is rule form.

$$\text{IF } a_1 \in V_{a_1} \text{ and ... and } a_k \in V_{a_k} \text{ THEN } d=v_d \tag{1}$$

Rules induction is made on the basis of training dataset $DT=(U, A\cup\{d\})$, in which U is the finite set of objects characterized by the set of conditional attributes A and the decision attribute d. Each attribute $a\in A$ is treated as a function $a:U\rightarrow D_a$, where D_a is the range of the attribute a. Consequence of assumed notation is the fact that in the rule of the form (1) we have $\{a_1,..,a_k\}\subseteq A$, $V_{a_i} \subseteq D_{a_i}$ and $v_d\in D_d$. The expression $a\in V$ is called the conditional descriptor, and a set of objects with equal values of decision attributes is the decision class (notation: $X_v=\{x\in U: d(x)=v\}$).

Rule induction can be made, among others, by use of rough sets theory, [12], [17], which is the source of big number of algorithms (and programs) executing rules induction [6],[11],[14],[18]. The algorithms create complete, satisfying or minimal descriptions of decision classes. From among big group of programs that do not come from rough sets theory, family of programs AQ [9] is worthy of notice.

All of the algorithms mentioned above exploit measures that decided either about form of determined rule or about which of already determined rules may be removed or joined. These measures are called the rule quality measures and their main goal is such steering of induction and/or reduction processes that in output rules set there are rules with the best quality. A set composed of rules with good generalization (high classification accuracy) and description (small number of output rules) abilities is the rules set with high quality.

S. Greco et al. (Eds.): RSCTC 2006, LNAI 4259, pp. 716–725, 2006.

In the paper, properties of several rule quality measures are characterized and possibilities of their application in induction and rules number reduction algorithms are presented.

2 Rule Quality Measures

Values of most known rule quality measures [2],[3],[4] can be determined based on analysis of a contingency table, that allow to describe rules behavior with relation to the training set.

An object $x \in U$ recognizes a rule of the form (1) if and only if $\forall i \in \{1,...,k\}$ $a_i(x) \in V_{a_i}$, an object $x \in U$ supports a rule of the form (1), if the rule is recognized by the object and $d(x)=v_d$. A set of objects from the table $\boldsymbol{DT}$ that recognizes the rule r is denoted by $match_{DT}(r)$.

Contingency table for the rule $r \equiv \varphi \rightarrow \psi$ is defined in the following way:

$n_{\varphi\psi}$	$n_{\varphi\neg\psi}$	n_{φ}
$n_{\neg\varphi\psi}$	$n_{\neg\varphi\neg\psi}$	$n_{\neg\varphi}$
n_{ψ}	$n_{\neg\psi}$	

where: $n_{\varphi}= n_{\varphi\psi}+ n_{\varphi\neg\psi}=|U_{\varphi}|$ is the number of objects that recognize the rule $\varphi \rightarrow \psi$; $n_{\neg\varphi}= n_{\neg\varphi\psi}+ n_{\neg\varphi\neg\psi}=|U_{\neg\varphi}|$ is the number of objects that do not recognize the rule $\varphi \rightarrow \psi$; $n_{\psi}= n_{\varphi\psi}+ n_{\neg\varphi\psi}=|U_{\psi}|$ is the number of objects that belong to the decision class described by the rule $\varphi \rightarrow \psi$; $n_{\neg\psi}= n_{\varphi\neg\psi}+ n_{\neg\varphi\neg\psi}=|U_{\neg\psi}|$ is the number of objects that do not belong to the decision class described by the rule $\varphi \rightarrow \psi$; $n_{\varphi\psi}=|U_{\varphi}\cap U_{\psi}|$ is the number of objects that support the rule $\varphi \rightarrow \psi$; $n_{\varphi\neg\psi}=|U_{\varphi}\cap U_{\neg\psi}|$; $n_{\neg\varphi\psi}=|U_{\neg\varphi}\cap U_{\psi}|$; $n_{\neg\varphi\neg\psi}=|U_{\neg\varphi}\cap U_{\neg\psi}|$.

Using information included in the contingency table and the fact that for known decision rule $\varphi \rightarrow \psi$, there are known the values $|U_{\psi}|$ i $|U_{\neg\psi}|$, it is possible to determine values of each measure based on values $n_{\varphi\psi}$ and $n_{\varphi\neg\psi}$. It can be also observed that for any rule $\varphi \rightarrow \psi$, the inequalities $1 \leq n_{\varphi\psi} \leq |U_{\psi}|$, $0 \leq n_{\varphi\neg\psi} \leq |U_{\neg\psi}|$ holds. Hence, the evaluation measure is the function of two variables $q(\varphi \rightarrow \psi): \{1,...,|U_{\psi}|\} \times \{0,...,|U_{\neg\psi}|\} \rightarrow \boldsymbol{R}$.

Two basic evaluation measures are accuracy (designated by $q^{acc}(\varphi \rightarrow \psi)=n_{\varphi\psi}/n_{\varphi}$) and coverage (designated by $q^{cov}(\varphi \rightarrow \psi)=n_{\varphi\psi}/n_{\psi}$) of a rule. Both the measures considered at the same time give the complete view of rule quality, since according to the enumerational induction principle it is known that rules with big accuracy and coverage reflect real dependences. The dependences are true also for objects from outside of the analyzed dataset.

It is easy to prove that along with accuracy increasing, rule coverage decreases. Therefore, attempts at defining quality measures that simultaneously respect accuracy and coverage of a rule are carried on. Numerous papers focused on empirical search of generalization abilities of obtained classifiers depending on rule quality measure used during rules induction [2],[4]. Some of the papers [1],[14],[15] considered influence of applied quality measure on the number of discovered rules. It has special weight in context of knowledge discovery, since a user is usually interested in discovering such model that can be interpreted or is intent on finding several rules that describe the most important dependences.

In quoted researches some evaluation measures reached good results both in classification accuracy and size of classifiers (number of rules). These measures are WS proposed by Michalski, C2 proposed by Bruha [4] and adequately adopted Gain measure used in decision trees induction.

WS measure respect rule accuracy as well as rule coverage:

$$q^{WS}(\varphi \to \psi) = q^{acc}(\varphi \to \psi)\, w_1 + q^{cov}(\varphi \to \psi)\, w_2, \quad w_1, w_2 \in [0,1] \qquad (2)$$

In rules induction system YAILS values of parameters w_1, w_2 for the rule $\varphi \to \psi$ are calculated as follows $w_{1,2} = 0.5 \pm 0.25 * q^{acc}(\varphi \to \psi)$. The measure is monotone with respect to each variable $n_{\varphi\psi}$ and $n_{\varphi\neg\psi}$, and takes values from the interval $[0,1]$.

The measure C2 is described by the formula:

$$q^{C2}(\varphi \to \psi) = \left(\frac{n\, q^{acc}(\varphi \to \psi)}{n - n_\psi} \right)\left(\frac{1 + q^{cov}(\varphi \to \psi)}{2} \right) \qquad (3)$$

The first component of the product in the formula (3) is the separate measure known as the Coleman measure. This measure evaluates dependences between occurrences "the objects u recognizes the rule", and "the objects u belongs to the decision class described by the rule". The modification proposed by Bruha [4] (the second component of the formula (3)) respects the fact that the Coleman measure put too little emphasis on rule coverage. Therefore, application of the Coleman measure in the induction process leads to creation of a big number of rules [1],[15]. The measure C2 is monotone with respect to variables $n_{\varphi\psi}$ and $n_{\varphi\neg\psi}$, its range is the interval $(-\infty, 1)$, for a fixed rule the measure takes minimum if $n_{\varphi\psi}=1$ and $n_{\varphi\neg\psi}=n_{\neg\psi}$.

The Gain measure has origin in the information theory. The measure was adopted to rules evaluation from the decision trees methods (so-called *LimitedGain* criterion):

$$q^{Gain}(\varphi \to \psi) = Info(U) - Info_{\varphi \to \psi}(U) \qquad (4)$$

In the formula (4) *Info(U)* is the entropy of training examples and $Info_{\varphi \to \psi}(U)=(n_\varphi/|U|)Info(\varphi \to \psi)+((|U|-n_\varphi)/|U|)Info(\neg(\varphi \to \psi))$, where $Info(\varphi \to \psi)$, is the entropy of examples covered by the rule $\varphi \to \psi$; $Info(\neg(\varphi \to \psi))$ is the entropy of examples not covered by the rule $\varphi \to \psi$. The measure is not monotone with respect to variables $n_{\varphi\psi}$ and $n_{\varphi\neg\psi}$, and takes values from the interval $[0,1]$. If the accuracy of a rule is less then the accuracy of decision class (accuracy that results form examples distribution in the training set) described by the rule then the measure q^{Gain} is the function decreasing with respect to both variables $n_{\varphi\psi}$ and $n_{\varphi\neg\psi}$, otherwise q^{Gain} is the increasing function.

Recently, so-called "the Bayesian confirmation measure" (denoted by f) was proposed as the alternative for rule accuracy evaluation. Until now there are no published results of applying the measure in rules number generation and/or reduction algorithms. In papers [5],[7],[8] is presented theoretical analysis of the measure f, and is shown, among others, that the measure is monotone with respect to rule accuracy (so, in terminology adopted in our paper, with respect to the variable $n_{\varphi\psi}$).

In standard notation the Bayesian confirmation measure is defined by the formula $q^f(\varphi \rightarrow \psi) = (P(\varphi | \psi) - P(\varphi | \neg \psi))/(P(\varphi | \psi) + P(\varphi | \neg \psi))$, where $P(\varphi | \psi)$ denotes the conditional probability of the fact that objects belonging to the set U and having the property ψ have also the property φ.

It is easy to see that q^f can be also write as follows:

$$q^f(\varphi \rightarrow \psi) = \frac{q^{acc}(\psi \rightarrow \varphi) - q^{acc}(\neg \psi \rightarrow \varphi)}{q^{acc}(\psi \rightarrow \varphi) + q^{acc}(\neg \psi \rightarrow \varphi)} \tag{5}$$

Therefore, by substitution suitable symbols from the contingency table and using the facts that $n_{\psi\varphi} = n_{\varphi\psi}$, $n_{\neg\psi\varphi} = n_{\varphi\neg\psi}$ we obtain the simplified formula:

$$q^f(\varphi \rightarrow \psi) = \frac{n_{\neg\psi}n_{\varphi\psi} - n_{\psi}n_{\varphi\neg\psi}}{n_{\neg\psi}n_{\varphi\psi} + n_{\psi}n_{\varphi\neg\psi}} \tag{6}$$

It can be noticed that the measure q^f does not take into consideration the coverage of evaluated rule, the most clearly it can be observed for two rules with identical accuracy and different coverage. If the rules r_1 and r_2 are accurate then for both of them the equality $n_{\varphi\neg\psi} = 0$ holds. Hence the formula that allow to calculate a value of the measure q^f reduces to $n_{\varphi\psi}/n_{\varphi\psi}$. Then, independently on the number of objects that support rules r_1 and r_2, the value of the measure q^f will be equal to one for both the rules. Interest in the measure q^f is justified by the fact that beside rule accuracy it takes into consideration probability distribution of examples in training set between decision classes. Because of the above argumentation, replacing the accuracy with the measure q^f can be proposed for rule quality measures that use both accuracy and rule coverage simultaneously. Therefore let us consider such modifications of measures WS and C2 in which q^{acc} will be replace with q^f.

3   Rule Quality Measures in Induction and Postprocessing

Rule quality measures fulfill the role of optimality criterion during rules creation or reduction of already existing rule data model.

Process of creation a rule of the form (1) based on a certain data set consists in selection of conditional attributes that will create conditional descriptors and in establishing ranges of the descriptors (i.e. sets V_a). The process is usually iterative and allows to such use of quality measure at each stage that created rule is characterized by big accuracy and coverage.

In experiments described in the next section the modified version of the MODLEM algorithm was used for rules induction. The modification consists in application of the quality measure to evaluate currently created conditional part of a rule. After adding (or modification) the next conditional descriptor, current form of the rule is evaluated. The rule that obtained the best evaluation is remember as the output rule. The carried out tests shown that a value of the evaluation measure increases during rule creation until it achieves some maximum value and then decreases (quality measure has one maximum). This observation allows to define such stop criterion that the algorithm stops rule creation process when the evaluation value begins to decrease [16]. MODLEM can create descriptors of the form *attribute*∈*{attribute_values_set}* and/or *atribute* < (>) *value.* Detailed description of the MODLEM algorithm is published in [18].

Independently on the method of determining the output rules set can be put to reduction using algorithms of joining [13] and/or filtration [1], [15]. Rules set joining and filtration algorithms are shortly presented below.

The aim of rules joining is increasing rules generality (q^{cov}) without needless decreasing of its accuracy (q^{acc}). Joining consists in adding sets of values of corresponding conditional descriptors. If the descriptor $a \in V_a^1$ occurs in the conditional part of the rule $\varphi_1 \rightarrow \psi$ and the descriptor $a \in V_a^2$ occurs in the conditional part of the rule $\varphi_2 \rightarrow \psi$ then after their joining the descriptor $a \in V_a$ with the property: $V_a^1 \subseteq V_a$ and $V_a^2 \subseteq V_a$ will arise. If the attribute a is of the numerical type and descriptors of the form $a \in [v_a^1, v_a^2]$ and $a \in [v_a^3, v_a^4]$ are joined, then the joined descriptor has the form $V_a = [v_{min}, v_{max}]$, where $v_{max} = \max\{v_a^i : i = 2,4\}$ $v_{min} = \min\{v_a^i : i = 1,3\}$.

The algorithm exploits any quality measure q. If for two rules r_1 and r_2, the inequality $q(r_1) > q(r_2)$ holds, then the rule r_2 is stuck on to the rule r_1. Conditional descriptors are joined sequentially, value of the measure evaluating the new rule r decides about the order of joining. To indicate the best descriptor for joining in next iteration the climbing strategy is applied. The joining process is finished while the new rule r recognizes all positive training examples which were recognized by the rules r_1 and r_2.

If r is a new rule and $q(r) \geq \lambda$, then the rule r is substitute in description of the decision class in the place of rules r_1 and r_2, otherwise rules r_1 and r_2 can not be joined. A parameter λ determines the limit value under which rules quality, according to the given quality measure, can not fall down (in particular, for joined rules r_1, r_2, $\lambda = \max\{ q(r_1), q(r_2) \}$). The detailed description of the algorithm can be find in [13].

Filtration consists in removing from the rules set these rules which are unimportant for description readability as well as for classifier's generalization abilities. Simple but effective filtration "Forward" algorithm [15] exploits rules ranking created by rule quality measure.

Initial description of each decision class consists of one – the best rule, then adds one rule to the description of each decision class. If classification accuracy of a class increases, the rule is leaved in the description, if not, the rule is removed and the next rule is considered. Rules ranking established by the quality measure decided about the order of rules consideration. Rules adding to the description of the decision class is finished while classification accuracy is the same as for not filtrated rules set or if the all rules have been considered. During filtration, so-called tuning set of objects is subject to classification (in particular, it can be a part of the training set).

4   Experiments with Data

Experimental researches was carried out on several benchmark data sets (Monks2, Monks3, Breast, Heart [10]) and on data coming from industrial system of monitoring the rock cutting process. Data from the monitoring system describe three decision classes ("low energy", "average energy", "high energy") reflecting the unit cutting energy. Conditional attributes in this set are designed for describing parameters of the cutting process (cutting scale, cutting depth, the geometric blade parameters (blade angle, position angel, revolution angle), the rock type).

Tests were done by the 10-fold cross validation testing method (for monk problems originally prepared training and test sets were used).

Classification process applied rules voting. Each rule recognizing a test object voted for the decision class that it describes (power of a vote is the value of rule quality measure). For each decision class votes were summed up and then the tested object was assigned to the class with the maximum value of the sum.

The first table presents results of application various evaluation measures to modified version of the MODLEM algorithm. Results of joining and filtration for the best scores obtained in the first table (bold-faced type in the first table) are presented in the second and third tables.

The column % contains testing classification accuracy put in percent. The column *Reg.* Denotes the number of determined rules. Results are round to natural numbers.

Table 1. Classification results

Data	Acc.		Gain		C2		WS		C2_f		WS_f	
	%	Reg.	%	Reg.	%	Reg.	%	Reg.	%	Reg.	%	Reg.
Monk2	65	71	64	39	64	71	**68**	**54**	63	58	64	71
Monk3	92	29	96	13	93	23	94	23	**94**	**21**	93	23
Heart	73	62	**78**	**12**	81	37	79	36	79	35	76	21
Breast	67	99	**73**	**37**	66	96	67	84	66	97	66	30
Energy	86	91	63	16	84	50	86	35	**88**	**70**	86	56

Table 2. Joining results

Data	Acc.		Gain		C2		WS		C2_f		WS_f	
	%	Reg.	%	Reg.	%	Reg.	%	Reg.	%	Reg.	%	Reg.
Monk2	68	48	64	45	67	47	68	47	67	47	68	47
Monk3	94	16	97	12	96	14	96	14	97	12	94	14
Heart	79	10	79	9	79	11	79	10	78	12	79	10
Breast	72	35	73	34	72	35	72	34	72	32	72	32
Energy	88	65	80	45	88	58	82	56	88	62	87	63

Table 3. Filtration results

Data	Acc.		Gain		C2		WS		C2_f		WS_f	
	%	Reg.	%	Reg.	%	Reg.	%	Reg.	%	Reg.	%	Reg.
Monk2	69	48	69	44	69	45	69	44	69	44	69	45
Monk3	94	19	93	17	94	19	94	19	94	19	94	19
Heart	79	10	79	10	79	10	79	10	79	10	79	10
Breast	68	28	68	6	68	17	68	16	68	16	68	21
Energy	87	48	87	20	88	41	88	40	87	43	87	45

Tables 2 and 3 show that reduction of the number of determined rules is not big, but this follows from the fact that determining rules algorithm itself generates not many rules.

Results presented in Table 1 illustrate the biggest influence of the given measure on quality of determined rules. As it was reported in many research [1], [2], [4], [13], [14], [15] it is impossible to point at a measure that always gives the best results, but it is possible to show two groups of measures. One of them contains measures that put emphasis on rule coverage (these are, among others, measures used in the our paper), second group includes measures that put the greater emphasis on rule accuracy which leads to determining a lot more rules (these are measures: Accuracy, Brazdil, Coleman, IKIB).

Obviously, application of rule quality measures is sensible only if we admit approximate rules generating. If we determine rules using the local reducts method then the only determined rules quality measure will be rules coverage. (alternatively, rules strength [19], if accuracy and coverage of compared rules will be identical).

It is interested that none of the presented measures generates the same rules rankings, but the rankings are similar. Rules order obtained for the Energy set (20 rules after filtration, classification accuracy 87%) is presented below, rule accuracy is given by the rule number.

In the first column of Table 4 rules ranking established by the measure *accuracy* is shown. In next columns can be seen how the other measures change this order, in particular the measure *Gain* and, in smaller degree, *C2* and *WS* prefer more general rules, and rankings established by the measures *C2_f*, *WS_f* are more similar to the ranking created by the *accuracy*.

Table 4. Rules ranking for the Energy set

	Acc.	Cov.	Gain		C2		WS		C2_f		WS_f	
	1	5	5	0.87	5	0.87	5	0.87	5	0.87	1	1.00
"low	2	4	4	0.88	4	0.88	1	1.00	3	0.96	2	0.98
energy"	3	7	3	0.96	3	0.96	2	0.98	1	1.00	3	0.96
	4	3	2	0.98	2	0.98	3	0.96	2	0.98	5	0.87
	5	2	7	0.76	1	1.00	4	0.88	4	0.88	4	0.88
	6	8	1	1.00	7	0.76	7	0.76	6	0.83	6	0.83
	7	1	8	0.74	6	0.83	6	0.83	7	0.76	7	0.76
	8	6	6	0.83	8	0.74	8	0.74	8	0.74	8	0.74
	1	6	6	0.68	1	1.00	1	1.00	1	1.00	1	1.00
„average	2	5	5	0.83	2	1.00	2	1.00	2	1.00	2	1.00
energy"	3	7	7	0.66	5	0.83	5	0.83	5	0.83	3	0.83
	4	3	1	1.00	3	0.92	3	0.92	3	0.92	4	0.92
	5	1	3	0.92	4	0.92	4	0.92	4	0.92	5	0.92
	6	2	2	1.00	6	0.68	6	0.68	7	0.68	6	0.68
	7	4	4	0.92	7	0.66	7	0.66	6	0.66	7	0.66
	1	1	1	0.95	1	0.95	1	0.95	1	0.95	1	0.95
„high	2	3	3	0.92	3	0.92	3	0.92	3	0.92	3	0.92
energy"	3	5	2	0.92	2	0.92	2	0.92	2	0.92	2	0.92
	4	2	5	0.74	4	0.83	4	0.83	4	0.83	4	0.83
	5	4	4	0.83	5	0.74	5	0.74	5	0.74	5	0.74

However, in every cases rules that are little accurate and little general appear at the end of rankings.

From the realized experiments follows also that replacing accuracy with "the Bayesian confirmation measure" in rules reduction algorithms do not gives any advantages (it is neutral solution). Influence of such replacing can be better seen in algorithms of rules induction, here measures $C2\_f$ and WS_f allowed to reduce a little the number of determined rules keeping similar classification abilities.

5 Summary

The presented rule quality measures applied for decision rules induction allow to generate not big sets of rules which are characterized by good classification abilities. Although the measures do not evaluate rules in the same way, it is possible to indicate groups of measures that evaluate similar rules.

Establishing rules ranking is of great importance for databases exploration tasks, especially for industrial data including noises which leads to approximate rules generation. Selection of several the best, accurate and general to some degree rules that describe bigger part of analysed data set is especially important for domain experts that are recipients of the analysis results. It is obvious that small number of rules can be easy interpreted by a user, while a model composed of tens of patterns becomes very difficult for interpretation. However, it is important for a selected group to be characterized by good generalization abilities.

Until now there are no methodology that enable to indicate for which data set the concrete quality measure may be applied. It depends on the type of analysed data (types of attributes describing decision classes, examples distribution between decision classes, etc) Therefore, at present analysis in realizing rules induction process is done by use of several quality measures.

The presented proposition of determining all rule quality measures as the function of two variables makes possible standardization of notation for all measures and analysis of their monotonicity with respect to each variable. Monotonicity is very important feature that should characterize rule quality measures. The thing is that evaluation measure's value should increase with increasing of accuracy (coverage) under fixed coverage (accuracy). This does not occur in the case of the measure *Gain*. However, it is possible to observe that if accuracy of created or evaluated rule is less than accuracy following from examples distribution in the training set (a priori accuracy) then it is enough to change value's sign of the given measure and then the measure becomes monotone. This change may be of importance during initial process of rule creation when its accuracy can be less than a priori accuracy. Detailed monotony analysis of rule quality measures defined as a function of variables $n_{\varphi\psi}$, $n_{\varphi\neg\psi}$ can be found in [15], analysis for „the Bayesian confirmation measure" is presented, among others, in [5],[7],[8].

Our further works on rule quality measures will proceed in the direction of adaptive application of quality measures in rules induction process. During rules induction with the help of so-called coverage, after induction of the successive rule objects supporting this new generated rule are removed from the training set. This fact influence change of characteristic of remaining part of the training set. In particular, distribution of examples from decision classes changes, probably from this good results are obtained by use of measures WS_f, $C2\_f$, which by replacing q^{acc} with the measure q^f, better respect this irregularity. Hence, during initial stage of rules creation quality measures that put strong emphasis on general rules determining should be applied. Whereas during final stage, when there are already few examples from the given class, rules induction algorithm should produce very accurate rules at the cost of their lower generality.

References

1. Agotnes T., Komorowski J., Loken T.: Taming Large Rule Models in Rough Set Approaches. 3rd European Conference of Principles and Practice of Knowledge Discovery in Databases, Lecture Notes in Artificial Intelligence 1704, 1999, pp. 193-203.
2. An A., Cercone N.: Rule quality measures for rule induction systems: Description and evaluation. Computational Intelligence, Vol. 17, No 3, 2001.
3. Bayardo, R.J., Agrawal, R.: Mining the most interesting rules, in: Proc. of the Fifth ACM-SIGKDD Int'l Conf. on Knowledge Discovery and Data Mining, 1999, p.145-154.
4. Bruha I.: Quality of Decision Rules: Definitions and Classification Schemes for Multiple Rules. Nakhaeizadeh G., Taylor C. C. (ed.) Machine Learning and Statistics, The Interface. John Wiley and Sons, 1997.
5. Brzezińska I., Słowiński R.: Monotonicity of Bayesian confirmation measure in rule support and confidence. Proc. of the AI-METH, Gliwice, November 16-18, 2005.
6. Grzymała-Busse J.: LERS – a system for learning from examples based on rough sets. Słowiński R. (ed.): Intelligent Decision Support. Dordrecht. Kluwer 1992, pp.3-18.
7. Greco, S., Pawlak, Z., Slowinski, R.: Can Bayesian confirmation measures be useful for rough set decision rules. Engineering Applications of Artificial Intelligence, 17, 2004, pp.345-361.
8. Greco S., Matarazzo A., Słowiński R.: Rough membership and Bayesian confirmation measures for parametrized rough sets. Lecture Notes in Artificial Intelligence, Vol. 3641, Springer-Verlag, Berlin Heidelberg, 2005, str.314-325.
9. Kaufman K. A., Michalski R. S.: Learning in Inconsistent World, Rule Selection in STAR/AQ18, Machine Learning and Inference Laboratory Report P99-2, 1999.
10. MLDB http://www.ics.uci.edu/~mlearn/MLRepository.html.
11. Nguyen H. S., Nguyen S. H.: Some Efficient Algorithms for Rough Set Methods. Proceedings of the Sixth International Conference, Information Processing and Management of Uncertainty in Knowledge-Based Systems, vol. 2, Granada, Spain, 1996, 1451-1456.
12. Pawlak Z.: Rough Sets. Theoretical aspects of reasoning about data. Dordrecht: Kluwer, 1991.
13. Sikora M.: An algorithm for generalization of decision rules by joining. Foundation on Computing and Decision Sciences, Vol. 30, No. 3, 2005.
14. Sikora M., Approximate decision rules induction algorithm using rough sets and rule-related quality measures, Archives of Theoretical and Applied Informatics, Nr 4, 2004, pp. xx-xx.
15. Sikora M.: Filtering of decision rules sets using rules quality measures. Studia Informatica Vol. 46, No. 4, Gliwice 2001.

16. Sikora M., Proksa P.: Induction of decision and association rules for knowledge discovery in industrial databases. DM-IEEE, Workshop – Alternative Techniques of Data Mining, Brighton, 01-04, November 2004.
17. Skowron A., Stepaniuk J.: Tolerance approximation spaces. Fundamenta Informaticae 27, 1996, pp. 245-253.
18. Stefanowski J.: Rules induction algorithms in knowledge discovery. Habilitation thesis. Poznan University of Technology, Dissertations No. 361, 2001.
19. Zhong N., Skowron A.: A rough set-based knowledge discovery process. Int. J. Appl. Math. Comput. Sci., Vol. 11, No. 3, 2001, pp. 603-619.

A Distributed Hybrid Heuristics of Mean Field Annealing and Genetic Algorithm for Load Balancing Problem

Chuleui Hong

Software School, Sangmyung University,
Seoul, Korea
`hongch@smu.ac.kr`

Abstract. In this paper, we introduce a novel distributed Mean field Genetic algorithm called MGA for the resource allocation problems in MPI environments, which is an important issue in parallel processing. The proposed MGA is a hybrid algorithm of Mean Field Annealing (MFA) and Simulated annealing-like Genetic Algorithm (SGA). SGA uses the Metropolis criteria for state transition as in simulated annealing to keep the convergence property in MFA. The proposed MGA combines the benefit of rapid convergence property of MFA and the effective genetic operations of SGA. Our experimental results indicate that the composition of heuristic mapping methods improves the performance over the conventional ones in terms of communication cost, load imbalance and maximum execution time.

Keywords: genetic algorithms, mean field annealing, simulated annealing, parallel processing, mapping.

1 Introduction

If tasks are not properly assigned to the processors in distributed memory multiprocessors, processor idle time and the inter-processor communication overhead from load imbalance may lead to poor utilization of parallel processors. This is a load balance mapping problem between tasks and processors [1,2,3,4,5].

The proposed Mean Field Genetic Algorithm (MGA) is a hybrid algorithm based on mean field annealing (MFA) [1,4,6] and genetic algorithm (GA) [7]. MFA has the characteristics of rapid convergence to the equilibrium state while the simulated annealing (SA) [5,8,9] takes long time to reach the equilibrium state[10,11,12].

In the proposed method, the typical genetic algorithm is modified where the evolved new states are accepted by the Metropolis criteria as in simulated annealing. Proposed MGA algorithm takes long time comparing with other mapping algorithm such as MFA and GA, but it must be solved before the execution of a given parallel program in a parallel computer. So the efficient parallel implementation of mapping algorithm is essential for developing parallel programs because the mapping algorithm can be considered as a sequential preprocessing and can be a bottleneck of parallel implementation. We propose two phases of distributed implementation of proposed MGA algorithm. The first phase is for MFA and the second one is for SGA.

S. Greco et al. (Eds.): RSCTC 2006, LNAI 4259, pp. 726–735, 2006.

2 The Mapping Problem in Multiprocessors

The multiprocessor mapping problem is a typical load balancing optimization problem. A mapping problem can be represented with two undirected graphs, called the Task Interaction Graph (TIG) and the Processor Communication Graph (PCG).

TIG is denoted as $G_T(V, E)$. $|V| = N$ vertices are labeled as $(1, 2, ..., i, j, ..., N)$. Vertices of G_T represent the atomic tasks of the parallel program and its weight, w_i, denotes the computational cost of task i for $1 \leq i \leq N$. Edge E represents interaction between two tasks. Edge weight, e_{ij}, denotes the communication cost between tasks i and j that are connected by edge $(i, j) \in E$. The PCG is denoted as $G_P(P, D)$. G_P is a complete graph with $|P| = K$ vertices and $|D| = {}_KC_2$ edges. Vertices of the G_P are labeled as $(1, 2, ..., p, q, ..., K)$, representing the processors of the target multicomputers. Edge weight, d_{pq}, for $1 \leq p,q \leq K$ and $p \neq q$, denotes the unit communication cost between processor p and q.

The problem of allocating tasks to a proper processor is to find a many-to-one mapping function $M: V \rightarrow P$. That is, each vertex of G_T is assigned to a unique node of G_P. Each processor is balanced in computational load (*Load*) while minimizing the total communication cost (*Comm*) between processors.

$$Comm = \sum_{(i,j) \in E, M(i) \neq M(j)} e_{ij} d_{M(i)M(j)}, \quad Load_p = \sum_{i \in V, M(i) = p} w_i, \quad 1 \leq p \leq K \tag{1}$$

$M(i)$ denotes the processor to which task i is mapped, i.e. $M(i) = p$ represents that task i is mapped to the processor p. In Equation (1), if tasks i and j in G_T are allocated to the different processors, i.e. $M(i) \neq M(j)$ in G_P, the communication cost occurs. The contribution of this to *Comm* is the multiplication of the interaction amount of task i and j, e_{ij}, and the unit communication cost of different processors p and q, d_{pq}, where $M(i) = p$ and $M(j) = q$. $Load_p$ in Equation (2) denotes the summation of computational cost of tasks i, w_i, which are allocated processor p, $M(i) = p$.

A spin matrix is used to represent the mapping state of tasks to processors. A spin matrix consists of N task rows and K processor columns representing the allocation state. The value of spin element (i, p), s_{ip}, is the probability of mapping task i to processor p. Therefore, the range of s_{ip} is $0 \leq s_{ip} \leq 1$ and the sum of each row is 1. The initial value of s_{ip} is $1/K$ and s_{ip} converges 0 or 1 as solution state is reached eventually. $s_{ip} = 1$ means that task i is mapped to processor p.

The cost function, $C(s)$, is set to minimize the total communication cost and to equally balance the computational load among processors of Equation (1).

$$C(s) = \sum_{i=1}^{N} \sum_{j \neq i} \sum_{p=1}^{K} \sum_{q \neq p} e_{ij} s_{ip} s_{jq} d_{pq} + r \sum_{i=1}^{N} \sum_{j \neq i} \sum_{p=1}^{K} s_{ip} s_{jp} w_i w_j. \tag{2}$$

e_{ij} : The interaction amount of task i and j in TIG
w_i : The computational cost of task i in TIG
d_{pq} : The unit communication cost of processor p and q in PCG
s_{ip} : The probability of task i mapping to processor p
r : The ratio of communication to computation cost

The first term of cost function, Equation (2), represents inter-processor communication cost (IPC) between two tasks i and j when task i and j are mapped to different processor p and q respectively. Therefore the first IPC term minimizes as two tasks with large interaction amount are mapped to the same processors. The second term of Equation (2) means the multiplication of computational cost of two tasks i and j mapped to the same processor p. The second computation term also minimizes when the computational costs of each processor are almost the same. It is the sum of squares of the amount of tasks in the same processor. The ratio r changes adaptively in the optimization process in order to balance the communication and computation cost. Changing the ratio r adaptively results in better optimal solution than fixing the ratio r. The optimal solution is to find the minimum of the cost function.

3   Distributed Implementation

3.1   Distributed Mean Field Annealing (MFA)

The mean field annealing (MFA) is derived from simulated annealing (SA) based on mean field approximation method in physics [1]. While SA changes the states randomly, MFA makes the system reach the equilibrium state very fast using the mean value estimated by mean field approximation.

The $N \times K$ spin matrix is partitioned column-wise such that each node is assigned an individual or a group of columns in a spin matrix. A node is a computer system that solves mapping algorithm, while the processor is defined in a target parallel computer. Since in our experiment, the number of nodes, P, is generally less than that of processors, K, the group of columns in a spin matrix is assigned to each node. However, in real parallel implementation, the number of nodes and that of processors will be same. When task-i is selected at random in a particular iteration, each node is responsible for updating its spin value, s_{ip}. The pseudo code for the distributed mean field annealing algorithm of each node is as follows.

```
<Distributed Mean Field Annealing>
while cost change is less than ε for
       continuous N annealing process begin
   Select a same task-i at random by using same seed
   Compute the local mean field
```

$$\phi_{ip} = -\sum_{\substack{j \neq i}}^{N}\sum_{\substack{q \neq p}}^{K} e_{ij}\, s_{jq}\, d_{pq} - r\sum_{\substack{j \neq i}}^{N} s_{jp}\, w_i\, w_j \quad \text{for } 1 \leq p \leq K$$

```
   Compute the new spin values at the iᵗʰ row
       by using global sum operation
```

$$s_{ip}^{new} = \frac{e^{\phi_{ip}/T}}{\sum_{p=1}^{K} e^{\phi_{ip}/T}}$$

```
   Compute the cost change due to spin updates
       by using global sum operation
```

$$\Delta C = \sum_{p=1}^{K} \phi_{ip}\left(s_{ip}^{new} - s_{ip}\right)$$

```
Update the spin values at the i^th row
```
$$s_{ip} = s_{ip}^{new} \qquad \text{for} \quad 1 \le p \le K$$
```
Perform global collect
    for a spin value, s_ip, at the i^th row
```
end

In implementing MFA, the cooling schedule has a great effect on the solution quality. Therefore the cooling schedule must be chosen carefully according to the characteristics of problem and cost function. The following parameters must be specified.

Initial temperature (T_0): Initial temperature, T_0, is set such that the probability where the cost change is less than $\varepsilon(=0.5)$ is more than 95% for the number of tasks (N) annealing process

Final temperature (T_f): T_f is set to the temperature where the value of the cost change is in /1,000 for continuous 20 temperature changes.

Length of the Markov chain at a certain temperature T_k (L_k): L_k is the number of state transition to reach the equilibrium state. It is set to the number of state transitions where the cost change is less than for continuous N annealing process.

Decrement strategy of the temperature ($T_{k+1} = \alpha \cdot T_k$): A fixed decrement ratio, α, is set to 0.9 experimentally. This strategy decreases the temperature proportional to the logarithm of the temperature.

3.2 Distributed Simulated Annealing-Like Genetic Algorithm (SGA)

Since GA does not have a concept of temperature comparing with MFA and SA, general GA breaks the convergence property of MFA in the proposed hybrid algorithm. We modified GA such that the new evolved state is accepted with a Metropolis criterion like simulated annealing in order to keep the convergence property of MFA. The modified GA is called SGA. In order to keep the thermal equilibrium of MFA, the new configurations generated by genetic operations are accepted or rejected by the Metropolis Criteria that is used in SA. The followings are parameters for SGA implementation.

Representation of individual: The individual is represented by a string in the order of tasks whose value is allocated processor identification. For example, a string , "1,3,4,1,2", means that tasks are allocated to processors such that task 1 to processor 1, task 2 to processor 3, task 3 to processor 4, task 4 to processor 2, task 5 to processor 2.

Form GA's population from MFA's spin matrix: The individuals are generated randomly with the probability as same as that of spin matrix in MFA. For example, if spin values of an arbitrary i^{th} task, which is the elements of ith row, is 0.2, 0.4, 0.1, 0.1, 0.2, an individual is made such that the ith character in a string can be 1 with a probability of 0.2, 2 with that of 0.4, 3 with that of 0.1, 4 with that of 0.1 and so on.

The size of population: In the experiment, the number of individuals in a population is set to 100.

The cost or objective function: The linear cost function is chosen as same as that of MFA.

Selection: A proportionate selection scheme is used. The individual is chosen randomly with a ratio of individual's cost over sum of population's cost.

Reproduction: The new population is made with individuals chosen by selection operation.

Crossover: After 2 individuals are chosen by turns from population, the part of string is exchanged. So the tasks allocations to processors are exchanged. The size of exchanged part is randomly set less than 1/4 of string length. The probability of crossover is 0.8.

Mutation: An individual is selected with a probability of 0.05. Exchange and displacement operation is implemented on the selected individual. The probability of exchange is 0.1 and displacement is 0.9. The exchange operation selects less than 4 tasks randomly in an individual and then allocations to processors of selected tasks are exchanged. The displacement operation selects 1 or 2 tasks randomly and changes their allocations to processors randomly.

Keeping best individual: The individual with the lowest cost is kept in the next population. This prevents genetic operations from losing the best solution of the previous stage.

Termination condition: The number of genetic operation in a certain temperature is set to the number of tasks. This number is set experimentally.

Simulated annealing-like Genetic Algorithm (SGA): In order to keep the thermal equilibrium of MFA, the new configurations generated by genetic operations are accepted or rejected by the Metropolis Criteria which is used in SA.

$$\Pr[\Delta C \text{ is accepted}] = \min\left(1, \exp\left(\frac{\Delta C}{T}\right)\right) \tag{3}$$

ΔC is the cost change of new state from old state which is made by subtracting the cost of new state from that of old one. T is the current temperature.

Form the MFA's spin matrix from GA's population: This is inverse operation of making GA's population from MFA's spin matrix. After GA finishes, selection and reproduction are applied on the population for the new generation, and then a spin matrix is made on the ratio of task allocations to processors. For example, let the population size be 10 and the problem be as same as fig.1 where there are 6 tasks and 4 processors. The ith character in an individual represents the allocation of task i. If the ith characters in 10 individuals are 1,2,3,4,1,2,3,1,2,1 respectively, the probabilities of task i to processor 1, 2, 3, and 4 are 0.4, 0.3, 0.2, 0.1 respectively also. So, the ith row of a spin matrix is set to 0.4, 0.3, 0.2, 0.1 according to the distribution of task i in GA population.

In the experiment, the subpopulation size in each node is set to the number of tasks, N. Therefore the size of global population is the multiplication of the number of tasks and the number of nodes, $N{\times}P$. The linear cost function is chosen as same as that of MFA. The probabilities of crossover and mutation are 0.8 and 0.05 respectively.

In our synchronous distributed genetic algorithm, each node generates subpopulation randomly from the MFA's spin matrix. And then the subpopulation and its fitness value are broadcast to all other nodes and they form the global population. Next, the individuals are selected as much as the size of subpopulation from the global population randomly. Each node executes the sequential genetic algorithm in parallel. Independent genetic operation are implemented and evaluated to its subpopulation. The duration of isolated evolution is called one *epoch* and the *epoch length* is the number of predefined generations for a node before synchronizing communication among the nodes. The epoch length is set to the *N/P*, where *N* is the number of tasks and *P* is the number of nodes. *max_epoch* is the number of synchronous communications. It is set to *P*.

The pseudo code for the distributed genetic algorithm of each node is as follows.

```
<Distributed SGA>
Initialize subpopulation(P_sub) from MFA spin matrix
for iteration is less than max_epoch begin
   Calculate fitness for P_sub
    for generations = 1 until epoch_length begin
       Select individuals from subpopulation
       Reproduce next population
       for select 2 individuals by turns begin
          Perform crossover with probability of crossover
          Calculate the cost change (ΔC)
          if exp(-ΔC/T)> random[0,1] then
             Accept new individuals
       end
       for all individuals begin
          Perform mutation with probability of mutation
          Calculate the cost change (ΔC)
          if exp(-ΔC/T)> random[0,1] then
             Accept new individuals
       end
    end
    broadcast P_sub to all other nodes;
    select new P_sub randomly;
    Keep the best individual
end
```

3.3 MGA Hybrid Algorithm

A new hybrid algorithm called MGA combines the merits of mean field annealing (MFA) and simulated annealing-like genetic algorithm (SGA). MFA can reach the thermal equilibrium faster than simulated annealing and GA has powerful and various genetic operations such as selection, crossover and mutation.

First, MFA is applied on a spin matrix to reach the thermal equilibrium fast. After the thermal equilibrium is reached, the population for GA is made according to the distribution of task allocation in the spin matrix. Next, GA operations are applied on the population while keeping the thermal equilibrium by transiting the new state with Metropolis criteria. MFA and GA are applied by turns until the system freeze. The followings are the pseudo code for the distributed MGA algorithm of each node.

```
<Distributed MGA Hybrid Algorithm>
Initialize mapping problems /* getting TIG and PCG */
Forms the spin matrix, s=[s_11, …, s_ip, …, s_NK]
```

```
Set the initial ratio r
Get the initial temperature T₀ , and set T= T₀
while T ≥ T_f begin
    Executes MFA
    Forms GA population from a spin matrix of MFA
    Executes SGA
    Forms the spin matrix of MFA from GA population
    Adjusts the ratio r
    T= α×T /*decrease the temperature*/
end
```

Initial temperature, T_0, is set such that the probability where the cost change is less than $\varepsilon(=0.5)$ is more than 95% for the number of tasks (N) annealing process. Final temperature (T_f) is set to the temperature where the value of the cost change is in $\varepsilon/1{,}000$ for continuous N temperature changes. A fixed decrement ratio, α, is set to 0.9 experimentally. This strategy decreases the temperature proportional to the logarithm of the temperature.

4   Simulation Results

The MFA and GA-1(Genetic Algorithm-1) have same linear cost function as that of the proposed MGA. GA-2 has the cost function which minimizes the sum of squares of load in each node. The cost function of GA-2 is generally used and verified as the best one.

In this simulation, the size of tasks is 200 and 400 (only the results of task size of 400 are shown). The multiprocessors are connected with wrap-around mesh topology. The computational costs of each task are distributed uniformly ranging [1..10]. The communication costs between any two tasks ranges [1..5] with uniform distribution. The number of communications is set to 1, 2, or 3 times of the number of tasks. The experiment is performed 20 times varying the seed of random number generator and TIG representing the computational and communication cost.

Table 1 displays total inter-processor communication costs. Comparing with the communication cost of GA-2, those of MFA and GA-1 are much larger than that of GA-2 while that of MGA decreases 9%. Table 1 also displays computational cost imbalance, which is defined as the difference between maximum and minimum computational cost of processors normalized by the maximum cost. The computational cost imbalance of each algorithm displays a little difference, while total communication costs in Table 2 are much more different. This implies that the inter-processor communication cost has a greater effect on the solution quality than the computational cost.

Table 2 shows the maximum completion times of each algorithm. The maximum completion times of MFA and GA-1, which use a linear cost function, are longer than that of GA-2 while the maximum completion time of MGA is averagely 9% shorter than that of GA-2. The performance of MGA decreases as the number of communications, |E|, increases. However, the performance of MGA increases as the problem size increases, so MGA can be applied the large sized problems. Table 2 also shows the execution time of each algorithm. The averaged execution time of MGA is 1.5 and 1.7

times longer than that of GA-2 and MFA respectively. This is a trade-off between the solution quality and execution time.

The proposed MGA takes a long time compared with other heuristic algorithm. So we proposed the efficient distributed implementation of MGA. Fortunately, the both of MFA and GA can be implemented in parallel inherently. The parallel speedup generally increases proportional to the problem size due to reducing synchronization

Table 1. Total inter-processor communication cost and Percent of computational cost imbalance

Problem Size			Total Comm. Time				Comp. Cost. Imbalance			
N	|E|	K	MFA	GA-1	GA-2	MGA	MFA	GA-1	GA-2	MGA
200	200	16	414.6	627.5	523.2	346.8	47%	42%	44%	39%
	400	16	3650.5	3260.9	1907.2	2084.0	68%	49%	70%	61%
	600	16	6525.6	5744.0	3482.1	4215.8	65%	45%	79%	60%
	200	36	539.0	1718.1	858.2	490.5	66%	71%	59%	58%
	400	36	4002.2	4903.4	3096.7	2956.3	85%	73%	81%	77%
	600	36	8608.2	8546.1	5513.0	6231.2	85%	68%	89%	78%
400	400	16	994.3	2370.5	1093.0	629.7	47%	37%	37%	32%
	800	16	8089.1	6714.6	3918.2	4004.2	61%	37%	63%	57%
	1200	16	14677.0	11743.0	7017.9	8348.4	49%	35%	75%	54%
	400	36	1062.7	3539.5	1714.0	852.4	60%	59%	51%	50%
	800	36	10021.0	10360.0	6222.3	5603.0	79%	62%	75%	72%
	1200	36	19937.0	17780.0	11008.0	11868.0	75%	60%	84%	70%

Table 2. Maximum completion time and Running time in seconds

Problem Size			Maximum Completion Time				Running Time(Sec)			
N	|E|	K	MFA	GA-1	GA-2	MGA	MFA	GA-1	GA-2	MGA
200	200	16	138.2	184.6	147.7	120.2	6.2	16.4	19.4	22.4
	400	16	525.9	389.4	326.7	320.1	8.5	19.4	22.2	33.2
	600	16	767.2	579.4	544.7	544.3	11.1	19.8	25.8	42.5
	200	36	84.7	136.6	90.2	72.0	22.1	19.4	30.9	46.9
	400	36	307.3	281.9	222.2	218.5	27.6	22.4	36.7	59.4
	600	36	559.2	454.9	391.0	388.2	33.4	24.5	43.3	74.9
400	400	16	279.1	364.7	284.4	222.8	26.2	61.7	87.4	95.6
	800	16	888.1	709.1	618.8	587.0	40.7	70.3	109.9	150.9
	1200	16	1557.4	1075.2	1041.1	987.5	51.7	63.7	119.1	190.9
	400	36	152.9	244.9	169.6	128.7	94.9	77.6	145.4	212.4
	800	36	617.0	530.7	415.0	385.2	122.9	76.4	138.9	260.6
	1200	36	1065.5	850.5	732.8	693.0	148.1	70.6	154.5	317.5

cost. We can find that the proposed distributed algorithm maintains the solution quality of sequential algorithm. The simulation is implemented in MPI environments that are made up of 600Mhz personal computers running Linux operating system connected via 10Mbps Ethernet.

5 Conclusions

In this paper, we proposed a new hybrid heuristic called MGA. The proposed approach combines the merits of MFA and GA on a load balance problem in distributed memory multiprocessor systems. This new hybrid algorithm is compared and evaluated with MFA and two different GA's (GA-1, GA-2). The solution quality of MGA is superior to that of MFA and GA's while execution time of MGA takes longer than the compared methods. The execution time takes longer in order of MFA, GA-1, GA-2, and MGA. There can be the trade off between the solution quality and execution time by modifying the cooling schedule and genetic operations. MGA was also verified by producing more promising and useful results as the problem size and complexity increases.

The proposed distributed algorithm was easily developed since MFA and GA can be parallelized in a nature. This distributed algorithm also can be applied efficiently to broad ranges of NP-Complete problems.

References

1. Bultan, T., Aykanat, C. : A New Mapping Heuristic Based on Mean Field Annealing. Journal of Parallel & Distributed Computing,16 (1992) 292-305
2. Pinar, A., Hendrickson, B. : Improving Load Balance with Flexibly Assignable Tasks. IEEE Transactions on Parallel & Distributed Systems, Vol. 16, No. 10 (2005) 956-965
3. Park, K., Hong, C.E. : Performance of Heuristic Task Allocation Algorithms. Journal of Natural Science, CUK, Vol. 18 (1998) 145-155
4. Salleh, S., Zomaya, A. Y.: Multiprocessor Scheduling Using Mean-Field Annealing. Proc. of the First Workshop on Biologically Inspired Solutions to Parallel Processing Problems (BioSP3) (1998) 288-296
5. Zomaya, A.Y., Teh, Y.W.: Observations on Using Genetic Algorithms for Dynamic Load-Balancing. IEEE Transactions on Parallel and Distributed Systems, Vol. 12, No. 9 (2001) 899–911
6. Liu, L., Feng, G. : Research on Multi-constrained QoS Routing Scheme Using Mean Field Annealing. Sixth International Conference on Parallel and Distributed Computing Applications and Technologies (PDCAT'05) (2005) 181-185
7. Hong, C.E.: Channel Routing using Asynchronous Distributed Genetic Algorithm. Journal of Computer Software & Media Tech., SMU, Vol. 2. (2003)
8. Soke, A., Bingul, Z. : Hybrid genetic algorithm and simulated annealing for two-dimensional non-guillotine rectangular packing problems. Engineering Applications of Artificial Intelligence, Vol. 19, No. 5 (2006) 557-567
9. Ganesh, K., Punniyamoorthy, M. : Optimization of continuous-time production planning using hybrid genetic algorithms-simulated annealing. International Journal of Advanced Manufacturing Technology, Jul2005, Vol. 26, No. 1. (2005) 148-154

10. Chen, D., Lee, C., Park, C. : Hybrid Genetic Algorithm and Simulated Annealing (HGASA) in Global Function Optimization. 17th IEEE International Conference on Tools with Artificial Intelligence (ICTAI'05) (2005) 126-133
11. Wang, Z., Rahman, M., Wong, Y. : Multi-niche crowding in the development of parallel genetic simulated annealing. Proceedings of the 2005 conference on Genetic and evolutionary computation (GECCO '05) (2005) 1555-1556
12. Tornquist, J., Persson, J. : Train Traffic Deviation Handling Using Tabu Search and Simulated Annealing. Proceedings of the 38th Annual Hawaii International Conference on System Sciences (HICSS'05) (2005)

Enhancing Global Search Ability of Quantum-Behaved Particle Swarm Optimization by Maintaining Diversity of the Swarm

Jun Sun, Wenbo Xu, and Wei Fang

Center of Computational Intelligence and High Performance Computing,
School of Information Technology, Southern Yangtze University,
No. 1800, Lihudadao Road, Wuxi Jiangsu 214122, China
sunjun_wx@hotmail.com,
xwb_sytu@hotmail.com,
wxfangwei@hotmail.com

Abstract. Premature convergence, the major problem that confronts evolutionary algorithms, is also encountered with the Particle Swarm Optimization (PSO) algorithm. Quantum-behaved Particle Swarm (QPSO), a novel variant of PSO, is a global-convergence-guaranteed algorithm and has a better search ability than the original PSO. But like PSO and other evolutionary optimization techniques, premature in QPSO is also inevitable. The reason for premature convergence in PSO or QPSO is that the information flow between particles makes the diversity of the population decline rapidly. In this paper, we propose Diversity-Maintained QPSO (DMQPSO). Before describing the new method, we first introduce the origin and development of PSO and QPSO. DMQPSO, along with the PSO and QPSO, is tested on several benchmark functions for performance comparison. The experiment results show that the DMQPSO outperforms the PSO and QPSO in many cases.

1 Introduction

Over the last decades researchers have been looking for new paradigms in optimization. Swarm intelligence arose as one of the paradigms based on social organisms. The most famous and frequently used meta-heuristics in this class are Ant Colony (AC) algorithm and Particle Swarm Optimization (PSO). PSO, which can be likened to the behavior of a flock of birds or the sociology behavior of a group of people and was first introduced by Kennedy and Eberhart [8], has been used to solve a range of optimization problems, including neural network training [6] and function minimization. The original PSO, however, is not a global convergent optimization algorithm, as has been demonstrated by F. van den Bergh [3]. In the previous work [12], [13], [14], a novel variant of PSO called Quantum-behaved Particle Swarm Optimization (QPSO), which was inspired by quantum mechanics, was proposed. It could be demonstrated mathematically that the QPSO is a global-convergence-guaranteed algorithm and seems to be a promising optimization problem solver.

S. Greco et al. (Eds.): RSCTC 2006, LNAI 4259, pp. 736–745, 2006.
© Springer-Verlag Berlin Heidelberg 2006

Like PSO and other evolutionary algorithm, however, QPSO also encounters the problem of premature convergence, which results in great performance loss and sub-optimal solutions. In QPSO or PSO, the fast information flow between particles seems to be the reason for clustering of particles, which, in turn, makes the diversity of the swarm decline rapidly and leaves QPSO algorithm lead to low diversity with fitness stagnation as an overall result. In this paper, we propose a Diversity-Maintained Quantum-behaved Particle Swarm Optimization (DMQPSO). In DMQPSO, a low bound is set for swarm's diversity measure to prevent premature convergence and therefore enhance the overall performance of QPSO.

The paper is organized as follows. In the next section, PSO is introduced. The origin and development of QPSO is described in Section 3 and DMQPSO is proposed in Section 4. Section 5 is the experiment results and discussion. The paper is concluded in Section 6.

2 PSO Algorithms

Particle Swarm Optimization (PSO), first introduced by J. Kennedy and R. Eberhart [8], is a population-based optimization technique, where a population is called a swarm. A simple explanation of the PSO's operation is as follows. Each particle represents a possible solution to the optimization task at hand. For the remainder of this paper, reference will be made to unconstrained minimization problems. During each iteration each particle accelerates in the direction of its own personal best solution found so far, as well as in the direction of the global best position discovered so far by any of the particles in the swarm. This means that if a particle discovers a promising new solution, all the other particles will move closer to it, exploring the region more thoroughly in the process.

Let M denote the swarm size and n the dimensionality of the search space. Each individual $1 \leq i \leq M$ has the following attributes: A current position in the search space $X_i = (X_{i,1}, X_{i,2}, \cdots, X_{i,n})$, a current velocity $V_i = (V_{i,1}, V_{i,2}, \cdots, V_{i,n})$, and a personal best (**pbest**) position in the search space $P_i = (P_{i,1}, P_{i,2}, \cdots, P_{i,n})$. During each iteration, each particle in the swarm updates its velocity according to (1), assuming that the function f is to be minimized, and that $r_1 \sim U(0,1)$, $r_1 \sim U(0,1)$ are elements from two uniform random sequences in the range $(0,1)$.

$$V_{i,j}(t+1) = w \cdot V_{i,j}(t) + c_1 \cdot r_{1,i}(t) \cdot [P_{i,j}(t) - X_{i,j}(t)] + c_2 \cdot r_{2,i}(t) \cdot [P_{g,j}(t) - X_{i,j}(t)] \quad (1)$$

for all $j \in 1, 2 \cdots, n$, where $V_{i,j}$ is the velocity of the jth dimension of the ith particle, and c_1 and c_2 denote the acceleration coefficients. The new position of a particle is calculated using (2).

$$X_i(t+1) = X_i(t) + V_i(t+1) \quad (2)$$

The personal best (**pbest**) position of each particle is updated using the following formula,

$$P_i(t+1) = \begin{cases} P_i(t), & if \quad f(X_i(t+1)) \geq f(P_i(t)) \\ X_i(t+1), if & f(X_i(t+1)) \leq f(P_i(t)) \end{cases} \tag{3}$$

and the global best (**gbest**) position found by any particle during all previous steps, P_g, is defined as

$$P_g(t+1) = \arg\min_{P_i} f(P_i(t+1)), \quad 1 \leq i \leq M \tag{4}$$

The value of each component in every V_i vector can be clamped to the range $[-V_{max}, V_{max}]$ to reduce the likelihood of particles' leaving the search space. The value of V_{max} is usually chosen to be $k \times X_{max}$, with $0.1 \leq k \leq 1.0$, where X_{max} is the up-limit of the search scope on each dimension [18].

The variable w in (1) is called the inertia weight; this value is typically set up to vary linearly from 0.9 to near 0.4 during the course of training run. Note that this is reminiscent of the temperature adjustment schedule found in Simulated Annealing algorithms. The inertia weight is also similar to the momentum term in a gradient descent neural-network training algorithm.

Acceleration coefficients c_1 and c_2 also control how far a particle will move in a single iteration. Typically, these are both set to a value of 2.0, although assigning different values to c_1 and c_2 sometimes leads to improved performance.

Work by M. Clerc [4], [5] indicated that a constriction factor may help to ensure convergence. Application of the constriction factor results in (5).

$$V_{i,j}(t+1) = \chi[V_{i,j}(t) + c_1 \cdot r_{1,i} \cdot (P_{i,j}(t) - X_{i,j}(t)) + c_2 \cdot r_{2,i} \cdot (P_{g,j}(t) - X_{i,j}(t))] \tag{5}$$

where

$$\chi = \frac{2}{\left| 2 - \varphi - \sqrt{\varphi^2 - 4\varphi} \right|} \tag{6}$$

and $\varphi = c_1 + c_2$, $\varphi > 4$. The constriction factor, as shown in (5) and (6) above, should replace the V_{max} clamping. For other improved version of PSO, one may refer to the literatures such as [1], [2], [9], [10], [11].

3   Quantum-Behaved Particle Swarm Optimization

Trajectory analyses in [5] demonstrated that, to guarantee convergence of PSO algorithm, each particle must converge to its local attractor $p_i = (p_{i,1}, p_{i,2}, \cdots p_{i,n})$, of which the coordinates are defined as:

$$p_{i,j}(t) = (c_1 P_{i,j}(t) + c_2 P_{g,j}(t)) / (c_1 + c_2), \ (j=1,2,\ldots n) \tag{7}$$

or

$$p_{i,j}(t) = \eta \cdot P_{i,j}(t) + (1-\eta) \cdot P_{g,j}(t), \ \eta \sim U(0,1), \ (j=1, 2,\ldots, n) \tag{8}$$

Assume that there is one-dimensional Delta potential well on each dimension at point p_i and each particle has quantum behavior. Solving the *Schrödinger equation* for each dimension, we can get the normalized probability density function Q and distribution function F for each component of the particle's current position.

$$Q\big(X_{i,j}(t+1)\big)=\frac{1}{L_{i,j}(t)}e^{-2\left|p_{i,j}(t)-X_{i,j}(t+1)\right|/L_{i,j}(t)} \tag{9}$$

$$F\big(X_{i,j}(t+1)\big)=e^{-2\left|p_{i,j}(t)-X_{i,j}(t+1)\right|/L_{i,j}(t)} \tag{10}$$

where $L_{i,j}(t)$ is standard deviation of the distribution, which determines search scope of each particle. Employing Monte Carlo method, we can obtain the position of the particle

$$X_{i,j}(t+1)=p_{i,j}(t)\pm\frac{L_{i,j}(t)}{2}\ln(1/u) \qquad u=rand(0,1) \tag{11}$$

where u is a random number uniformly distributed in $(0, 1)$.

In [13], a global point called Mainstream Thought or Mean Best Position of the population is introduced into PSO. The global point, denoted as C, is defined as the average of the *pbest* positions of all particles. That is

$$C(t)=\big(C_1(t),C_2(t),\cdots,C_3(t)\big)=\left(\frac{1}{M}\sum_{i=1}^{M}P_{i,1}(t),\ \ \frac{1}{M}\sum_{i=1}^{M}P_{i,2}(t),\ \ \cdots,\ \ \frac{1}{M}\sum_{i=1}^{M}P_{i,n}(t)\right) \tag{12}$$

where M is the population size and P_i is the **pbest** position of particle i. Then the values of $L_{i,j}(t)$ and the position are evaluated by

$$I_{i,j}(t)=2\beta\cdot\left|C_j(t)-X_{i,j}(t)\right| \tag{13}$$

$$X_{i,j}(t+1)=p_{i,j}\pm\beta\cdot\left|C_j(t)-X_{i,j}(t)\right|\cdot\ln(1/u) \tag{14}$$

where parameter β is called Contraction-Expansion Coefficient, which can be tuned to control the convergence speed of the algorithms. The PSO with equation (14) is called Quantum-behaved Particle Swarm Optimization (QPSO). The QPSO algorithm is described as follows.

```
Initialize population: random X[i]and set P[i]=X[i];
do
    find out mbest using equation (12);
    for i=1 to population size M
        if f(Xi)<f(Pi) then P[i]=X[i];
        g=arg min(f(P[i]));
        for j=1 to dimensionality n
            η=rand(0,1);
            p[i][j]=η*P[i][j]+(1-η)*P[g][j];
            u=rand(0,1)
```

```
    if rand(0,1)>0.5
        X[i][j]=p[i][j]-β*abs(C[j]-X[i][j])*ln(1/u);
    else
        X[i][j]=p[i][j]+β*abs(C[j]-X[i][j])*ln(1/u);
    enif
  endfor
endfor
Until termination criterion is met
```

4 Diversity-Controlled QPSO

A major problem with PSO, QPSO and other evolutionary algorithms in multi-modal optimization is premature convergence, which results in great performance loss and sub-optimal solutions. In a PSO or QPSO system, premature convergence results from the fast information flow between particles due to its collectiveness, which makes diversity of the swarm decline rapidly, leaving PSO or QPSO algorithm with great difficulties of escaping local optima. Therefore, the collectiveness of particles leads to low diversity with fitness stagnation as an overall result. In QPSO, although the search space of an individual particle at each iteration is the whole feasible solution space of the problem, diversity loss of the whole population is also inevitable due to the collectiveness.

In 2002, Ursem has proposed a model called Diversity-Guided Evolutionary Algorithm (DGEA) [16], which applies diversity-decreasing operators (selection, recombination) and diversity-increasing operators (mutation) to alternate between two modes based on a distance-to-average-point measure. The performance of the DGEA clearly shows its potential in multi-modal optimization. Also in 2002, Riget *et al* [16] adopted the idea from Usrem into the basic PSO model with the decreasing and increasing diversity operators used to control the population. This modified model of PSO uses a diversity measure to have the algorithm alternate between exploring and exploiting behavior. They introduced two phases: attraction and repulsion, and the swarm alternate between these phases according to its diversity. The improved PSO algorithm is called Attraction and Repulsion PSO (ARPSO) algorithm. In this paper, we introduce the diversity measure, employed by Uresem and Riget, into Quantum-behaved Particle Swarm Optimization Algorithm, and propose a Diversity-Maintained QPSO (DMQPSO). Instead of measuring diversity of the swarm according to the particles' current position as Riget's work and the previous proposed method in [15], we use as diversity the distance-to-average-point measure of the particles' personal best positions. That is, the diversity of the swarm is measure by

$$diversity\,(S) = \frac{1}{|S| \cdot |A|} \cdot \sum_{i=1}^{|S|} \sqrt{\sum_{j=1}^{n} (P_{i,j} - C_j)^2} \tag{15}$$

where S is the swarm, $|S| = M$ is the population size, $|A|$ is the length of longest the diagonal in the search space, n is the dimensionality of the problem, $P_{i,j}$ is the jth value of the ith particle's personal best (*pbest*) position and C_j is the jth value of the average point of pbest position of particles.

In our proposed DMQPSO, a low bound value d_{low} is set for the diversity measure to prevent the swarm from clustering. That means the diversity will be maintained higher than d_{low}. The procedure of the algorithm is as follows. After the initialization of the swarm, the diversity is high and its declination is absolutely necessary for fitness improvement. After the middle stage of the search, the diversity may decrease to a low level so that the global search ability of the particle swarm is weak and the particles may fail to escape the local optima or sub-optima. Therefore, we can set a low bound for the diversity to keep the swarm possesses global search ability with a certain extent. There are several methods to maintain the diversity. The one used in this paper is that, when the diversity value declines to below d_{low}, mutation operation is exerted on a randomly selected particle's *pbest* position until the diversity value returns to above d_{low}. The mutation operation can be described by the following formula.

$$P_{i,j} = P_{i,j} + \alpha \cdot X_{\max} \cdot \delta, \quad \delta \sim N(0,1), \ (i = 1,2,\cdots M; j = 1,2,\cdots,n) \tag{16}$$

where δ is a random number with standard normal distribution $N(0,1)$ and α is a parameter. With the above specification, we now outline the proposed DMQPSO algorithm below.

```
DMQPSO
Initialize particles' position X[:]and set P[:]=X[:];
for t=1 to Maxiter
   find out the C position of the swarm;
   measure the diversity of the swarm by formula (15);
   if (diversity<dlow)
      Randomly select a particle k;
      for j=1 to n
          P[k][:]=P[k][:]+α*Xmax*δ;  X[k][:]=P[k][:];
          f(Pk)=f(P[k][:]);  f(Xk)=f(Pk);
      endfor
   endif
   for i=1 to population size M;
     if f(Xi)<f(Pi) then P[i]=X[i];
       g=arg min(f(P[i]));
       for j=1 to n
         η=rand(0,1);
         p[i][j]= η*P[i][j]+(1- η)*P[g][j];
         u=rand(0,1)
         if rand(0,1)>0.5
            X[i][j]=p[i][j]-β*abs(C[j]-X[i][j])*ln(1/u);
         else
            X[i][j]=p[i][j]+β*abs(C[j]-X[i][j])*ln(1/u);
         enif
       endfor
     endfor
   endfor
```

In the above algorithm, *Maixter* is the maximum number of iterations the DMQPSO executes for. The value of β is generally linearly on the course of running in most cases.

5   Experiment Results and Discussion

We have tested DMQPSO on four widely known benchmark functions for testing the performance of different evolutionary optimization strategies. These functions are all minimization problems with minimum value zero. The four test functions are:
Rosenbrock, n-dimensional

$$f_1(X) = \sum_{i=1}^{n-1} (100 \cdot (x_{i+1} - x_i^2)^2 + (x_i - 1)^2), \quad (-100 \le x_i \le 100) \tag{17}$$

Rastrigrin, n-dimensional

$$f_2(X) = \sum_{i=1}^{n} (x_i^2 - 10 \cdot \cos(2\pi x_i) - 10), \quad (-10 \le x_i \le 10) \tag{18}$$

Griewank, n-dimensional

$$f_3(X) = \frac{1}{4000} \sum_{i=1}^{n} (x_i - 100)^2 - \prod_{i=1}^{n} \cos\left(\frac{x_i - 100}{\sqrt{i}}\right) + 1, \quad (-600 \le x_i \le 600) \tag{19}$$

Shaffer's f6

$$f_4(X) = 0.5 + \frac{(\sin(\sqrt{x_1^2 + x_2^2})^2}{(1.0 + 0.001(x_1^2 + x_2^2))^2}, \quad (-100 \le x_i \le 100) \tag{20}$$

We tested original PSO with inertia weight (called Standard PSO or SPSO), QPSO and DMQPSO for performance Comparison. In all performance tests, the initial range of the population in all cases listed in Table 1 is asymmetry. Table 1 also lists V_{max} for SPSO. The fitness value is set as function value and the population size is set to be 20, 40 and 80 respectively.

We had 50 trial runs for every instance and recorded mean best fitness and standard deviation of 50 best fitness values. The maximum number of iterations, *Maxiter*, is set as 1000, 1500 and 2000 corresponding to the dimensions 10, 20 and 30

Table 1. The table lists the initial range of the population in the performance tests. The third column is the uplimit of the velocity of the partilce in SPSO.

	Initial Range	V_{max}
f_1	(15, 30)	100
f_2	(2.56, 5.12)	10
f_3	(300, 600)	600
f_4	(30, 100)	100

Table 2. Mean best fitness and standard deviation of all algorithms on Rosenbrock function

M	Dim.	Maxiter	SPSO		QPSO		DMQPSO	
			Mean Best	St. Dev.	Mean Best	St. Dev.	Mean Best	St. Dev.
20	10	1000	94.1276	194.3648	59.4764	153.0842	21.6372	55.7839
	20	1500	204.337	293.4544	110.664	149.5483	31.0208	77.0761
	30	2000	313.734	547.2635	147.609	210.3262	79.8686	127.3118
40	10	1000	71.0239	174.1108	10.4238	14.4799	10.0527	13.1835
	20	1500	179.291	377.4305	46.5957	39.536	48.5732	60.1797
	30	2000	289.593	478.6273	59.0291	63.494	70.3407	65.2116
80	10	1000	37.3747	57.4734	8.63638	16.6746	12.1356	23.2038
	20	1500	83.6931	137.2637	35.8947	36.4702	31.2263	35.0650
	30	2000	202.672	289.9728	51.5479	40.849	46.8169	35.7819

Table 3. Mean best fitness and standard deviation of all algorithms on Rastrigrin function

M	Dim.	Maxiter	SPSO		QPSO		DMQPSO	
			Mean Best	St. Dev.	Mean Best	St. Dev.	Mean Best	St. Dev.
20	10	1000	5.5382	3.0477	5.2543	2.8952	4.4964	2.5785
	20	1500	23.1544	10.4739	16.2673	5.9771	14.7371	4.9460
	30	2000	47.4168	17.1595	31.4576	7.6882	27.5713	7.1196
40	10	1000	3.5778	2.1384	3.5685	2.0678	3.1754	1.7769
	20	1500	16.4337	5.4811	11.1351	3.6046	11.1452	3.2323
	30	2000	37.2796	14.2838	22.9594	7.2455	19.6839	4.6700
80	10	1000	2.5646	1.5728	2.1245	2.2353	2.2351	1.4411
	20	1500	13.3826	8.5137	10.2759	6.6244	7.5875	2.4115
	30	2000	28.6293	10.3431	16.7768	4.4858	17.1367	4.6976

Table 4. Mean best fitness and standard deviation of all algorithms on Griewank function

M	Dim.	Maxiter	SPSO		QPSO		DMQPSO	
			Mean Best	St. Dev.	Mean Best	St. Dev.	Mean Best	St. Dev.
20	10	1000	0.09217	0.0833	0.08331	0.06805	0.0689	0.0762
	20	1500	0.03002	0.03255	0.02033	0.02257	0.0198	0.0168
	30	2000	0.01811	0.02477	0.01119	0.01462	0.0088	0.0083
40	10	1000	0.08496	0.0726	0.06912	0.05093	0.0565	0.0531
	20	1500	0.02719	0.02517	0.01666	0.01755	0.0150	0.0138
	30	2000	0.01267	0.01479	0.01161	0.01246	0.0081	0.0122
80	10	1000	0.07484	0.07107	0.03508	0.02086	0.0352	0.0212
	20	1500	0.02854	0.0268	0.0146	0.01279	0.0156	0.0149
	30	2000	0.01258	0.01396	0.01136	0.01139	0.0076	0.0101

Table 5. Average best fitness and standard deviation of all algorithms on Shaffer's function

M	Dim.	Maxiter	SPSO		QPSO		DMQPSO	
			Mean Best	St. Dev.	Mean Best	St. Dev.	Mean Best	St. Dev.
20	2	2000	2.782E-04	0.001284	0.001361	0.003405	0.0012	0.0032
40	2	2000	4.744E-05	3.593E-05	3.891E-04	0.001923	5.8303e-004	0.0023
80	2	2000	2.568E-10	3.134E-10	1.723E-09	3.303E-09	2.5830e-009	8.729e-009

for first three functions, respectively, The dimension of the last function is 2 and the *Maxiter*, is 2000 for this function. In performance test of the SPSO, the inertia weight w is decreases linearly from 0.9 to 0.4 as in [18]. In performance tests for QPSO and DMQPSO, the Contraction-Expansion Coefficient β is varying from 1.0 to 0.5 linearly when the algorithms are running. For DMQPSO, the low bound value of the diversity, d_{low}, is dynamically decreasing linearly from 5.0×10^{-4} to 1.0×10^{-6}, and the value of α is set to constant 1.0×10^{-5}.

The mean values and standard deviations of best fitness values for 50 runs of each function are recorded in Table 2 to Table 5. On Rosenbrock and Rastrigrin functions, it seems that DMQPSO outperforms QPSO and SPSO when the swarm size is 20. However, when the swarm size is 40 and 80, there are no improvements in terms of statistical significance under the above specified parameter settings. On Griewank function, it is shown that DMQPSO generated better results than QPSO and SPSO when dimension of the problem is 30. However, when the dimension is 10 and 20, there are no remarkable performance differences between QPSO and DMQPSO. On Shaffer's function, the performances of DMQPSO and QPSO are similar, which means that the diversity maintenance method with the specified parameter settings does not work on this function.

6 Conclusion

In this paper, we proposed a diversity maintenance method to enhance the global search ability of QPSO. The improved algorithm is called DMQPSO. The methodology of DMQPSO is setting a low bound for the diversity to prevent the particles from clustering. In our experiments, the value of low bound is dynamically decreasing and mutation operation is implemented on the personal best position of a certain particle once the value of diversity is below the low bound. The experiment results on several benchmark function show that the diversity maintenance method may be a good technique to avoid premature convergence and may result in performance improvement of the QPSO in many cases. Our future works will focus on finding more efficient diversity maintenance methods for QPSO and exploring the applicability of DMQPSO to real world problems.

References

1. Angeline, P. J.: Evolutionary Optimization Versus Particle Swarm Optimization: Philosophy and performance Differences. Evolutionary Programming VII, *Lecture Notes in Computer Science* 1447, Springer (1998) 601-610
2. Van den Bergh, F., Engelbrecht, A. P.: A New Locally Convergent Particle Swarm Optimizer. Proc. 2002 IEEE International Conference on systems, Man and Cybernetics. Piscataway, NJ (2002) 96-101
3. Van den Bergh, F.: An Analysis of Particle Swarm Optimizers. PhD Thesis. University of Pretoria, South Africa (2001)
4. Clerc, M.: The Swarm and Queen: Towards a Deterministic and Adaptive Particle Swarm Optimization. Proc. 1999 Congress on Evolutionary Computation. Piscataway, NJ (1999) 1951-1957

5. Clerc, M., Kennedy, J.: The Particle Swarm: Explosion, Stability, and Convergence in a Multi-dimensional Complex Space. IEEE Transactions on Evolutionary Computation, Vol. 6, No. 1. Piscataway, NJ (2002) 58-73

6. Engelbrecht, A. P., Ismail, A.: Training product unit neural networks. Stability Control: Theory APPL., Vol. 2, No. 1-2, (1999) 59-74

7. Eberhart, R. C., Simpson, P., Dobbins, R.: Computational Intelligence PC Tools: Academic, Ch.6, (1996) 39-43

8. Kennedy, J., Eberhart, R.C.: Particle Swarm Optimization. Proc. IEEE 1995 International Conference on Neural Networks, IV. Piscataway, NJ (1995) 1942-1948

9. Kennedy, J.: Sereotyping: Improving Particle Swarm Performance with Cluster Analysis. Proc. 2000 Congress on Evolutionary Computation, Piscataway, NJ (2000) 1507-1512

10. Kennedy, J.: Small worlds and Mega-minds: Effects of Neighborhood Topology on Particle Swarm Performance. Proc. 1999 Congress on Evolutionary Computation, Piscataway, NJ (1999) 1931-1938

11. Suganthan, P.N.: Particle Swarm Optimizer with Neighborhood Operator. Proc. 1999 Congress on Evolutionary Computation, Piscataway, NJ (1999) 1958-1962

12. Sun, J., Feng, B., Xu, W.-B.: Particle Swarm Optimization with Particles Having Quantum Behavior. Proc. 2004 Congress on Evolutionary Computation, Piscataway, NJ (2004) 325-331

13. Sun, J., Xu, W.-B., Feng, B.: A Global Search Strategy of Quantum-behaved Particle Swarm Optimization. Proc. 2004 IEEE Conference on Cybernetics and Intelligent Systems, Singapore (2004) 111-115

14. Sun, J., Xu, W.-B., Feng, B.: Adaptive Parameter Control for Quantum-behaved Particle Swarm Optimization on Individual Level. Proc. 2005 IEEE International Conference on Systems, Man and Cybernetics. Piscataway, NJ (2005) 3049-3054

15. Sun, J., Xu, W.-B., Fang, W: Quantum-Behaved Particle Swarm Optimization Algorithm with Controlled Diversity. Proc. 2006 International Conference on Computational Science (3), (2006): 847-854

16. Ursem, R. K.: Diversity-Guided Evolutionary Algorithms. Proc. 2002 the Parallel Problem Solving from Nature Conference, LNCS 2439, Granada, Spain. Springer (2001) 462-471

17. Riget, J, Vesterstrøm, J.S.: A Diversity-Guided Particle Swarm Optimizer-the ARPSO, Technical Report, University of Aarhus, Denmark (2002)

18. Shi, Y., Eberhart, R.: Empirical Study of Particle Swarm Optimization. Proc. 1999 Congress on Evolutionary Computation. Piscataway, NJ (1999) 1945-1950

19. Shi, Y., Eberhart, R.C.: A Modified Particle Swarm. Proc. 1998 IEEE International Conference on Evolutionary Computation. Piscataway, NJ (1998) 69-73

Identification and Speed Control of Ultrasonic Motors Based on Modified Immune Algorithm and Elman Neural Networks

Qiao Zhang [1], Xu Xu[2], and Yanchun Liang [1,*]

[1] College of Computer Science and Technology, Jilin University,
Key Laboratory of Symbol Computation and Knowledge Engineering
of Ministry of Education, Changchun 130012, China
[2] College of Mathematics, Jilin University, Changchun 130012, China
ycliang@jlu.edu.cn

Abstract. An improved artificial immune algorithm with a dynamic threshold is presented in this paper. Numerical experiments show that compared with the genetic algorithm and the originally real-valued coding artificial immune algorithm, the improved algorithm possesses high speed of convergence and good performance of preventing the premature convergence. The proposed algorithm is employed to train the network structure, weights, initial inputs of the context units and self-feedback coefficient of the modified Elman network. A novel identifier and controller are constructed successively based on the proposed algorithm. A simulated dynamic system of the ultrasonic motor (USM) is considered as an example of a highly nonlinear system. The novel identifier and controller are applied to perform the speed identification and control of the ultrasonic motors. Numerical results show that both the identifier and controller based on the proposed algorithm possesses not only high convergent precision but also robustness to the external noise.

Keywords: dynamic threshold; artificial immune algorithm; Elman network; ultrasonic motor; system identification; control.

1 Introduction

The immune system is the basic and remarkable defense system against bacteria, viruses and other disease-causing organisms. It can produce millions of antibodies from hundreds antibody genes and can protect animals which are infected by foreign molecules to survive [1-4]. The Artificial Immune System (AIS) or Artificial Immune Algorithm (AIA) was inspired by the immune system. Compared with genetic algorithm (GA), AIA has affinity calculation function, which could explain the relationship not only between the antigen and the antibody but also between antibodies. That makes AIA have the unique characteristic to guarantee the survival of the variant offspring that could match the antigen better. Related papers [5, 6] show that the algorithms based on AIA have much better performance than conventional

---

* Corresponding author.

S. Greco et al. (Eds.): RSCTC 2006, LNAI 4259, pp. 746–756, 2006.
© Springer-Verlag Berlin Heidelberg 2006

probabilistic optimization algorithms. However, it usually takes long time for the binary coding AIA to obtain convergence. Furthermore, it is very difficult for AIA to break away from the local optimal value, which can hold the searching process around this value and can easily lead to the premature during the evolution.

To improve the convergence speed and to prevent the premature convergence, a dynamic threshold artificial immune algorithm (DTAIA) is presented in this paper. The proposed algorithm changes the affinity function of the real-valued coding artificial immune algorithm by considering both the antibody's fitness and the dynamic threshold value.

An ultrasonic motor (USM) is a typical non-linear dynamic system. Due to some excellent performances and useful features, the USM has attracted considerable attention in many practical applications [7-9]. The simulation and control of the USM are important in the applications of the USM. According to the conventional control theory, an accurate mathematical model should be set up. But the USM has strongly nonlinear speed characteristics that vary with the driving conditions [10] and its operational characteristics depend on many factors. Therefore, it is difficult to perform effective identification and control to the USM using traditional methods based on mathematical models of systems.

The dynamic recurrent multilayer network employs dynamic links to memorize feedback information of the history influence. It has great potential development in the fields of system modeling, identification and control [11, 12]. The Elman network is one of the simplest types among the available recurrent networks. In this paper, a modified Elman network is employed to identify and control an USM, and a novel learning algorithm based on an improved artificial immune algorithm is proposed for training the Elman network.

2 Dynamic Threshold Artificial Immune Algorithm (DTAIA)

Toyoo Fukuda proposed an immune algorithm based on the information entropy, which is used to represent the diversity of the population [13]. The information entropy $E(N)$ can be concluded as

$$E(N) = \frac{1}{M} \sum_{j=1}^{M} H_j(N) \tag{1}$$

where N is the number of the antibodies, M is the number of the genes and $H_j(N)$ is the entropy of the jth gene. The entropy $H_j(N)$ is

$$H_j(N) = \sum_{i=1}^{S} P_{ij} \log(\frac{1}{P_{ij}}) \tag{2}$$

where P_{ij} is the probability that the ith allele comes out at the jth gene, and s is the number of the selectable characters in the alphabet.

The affinity between the antibody v and w is defined as follows

$$ay_{v,w} = \frac{1}{1 + H(2)} \tag{3}$$

where $H(2)$ is the information entropy of antibody v and w.

The affinity between antigen and antibody v, αx_v, is defined by

$$\alpha x_v = opt_v \tag{4}$$

where opt_v is the fitness of antibody v.

Considering the model based on the Euclidean distance for affinity calculation [14], the antibody v and antibody w have the affinity if the following inequalities are satisfied

$$d(v, w) < l, \quad \left| \alpha x_v - \alpha x_w \right| < m \tag{5}$$

In Eq. (5), $l>0$ and $m>0$; $d(v, w)$ is the Euclidean distance between the antibody v and antibody w; αx_v is the fitness of antibody v; and αx_w is the fitness of antibody w.

The expectation value e_v of antibody v is calculated as

$$e_v = ax_v / c_v \tag{6}$$

where C_v is the density of antibody v. It can be seen from Eq. (6) that the antibody with both high fitness and low density would have more chance to survive.

In Ref. [14], both l and m of Eq. (5) are constants. Therefore, if two antibodies i and j have the same Euclidean distance with antibody v, but have different fitness values, then the following inequalities hold:

$$d(v, i) = d(v, j) < l \tag{7}$$

$$\mid ax_v - ax_i \mid \neq \mid ax_v - ax_j \mid, \ \mid ax_v - ax_i \mid < m, \ \mid ax_v - ax_j \mid < m \tag{8}$$

It is obvious that the one with less fitness difference is closer to the antibody v.

In order to avoid such problem, we modify the inequalities of (5) and consider that if the following inequality is satisfied

$$f(v, w) = d(v, w) + \mid ax_v - ax_w \mid < L \tag{9}$$

then the antibodies v and w have the affinity. In the improved algorithm, the value of the parameter L is an important factor for determining the density. If L is larger, there will be more antibodies that have affinity with antibody v, which makes higher density of antibody v, and the algorithm will have stronger ability to suppress antibody v to be duplicated. So the diversity will remain relatively high, vice versa.

As well as we know, in the initial period of evolution, the algorithm has little possibility to fall into the local optimum value because of the high diversity. With an increase of the evolution generations, there will be more and more antibodies with high fitness values. If L is a constant, the algorithm can easily become premature and get into the local optimum since the diversity is getting lower and lower. If L is an increasing function of evolution generations, the antibody's diversity and density will be increased efficiently with the increase of the evolution generations and that the suppression will be more powerful to preserve high diversity. So the algorithm would have strong ability to control the reproducing process. In this paper, the dynamic value of L is taken as $L = L_0 \exp(bT)$, here $L_0 > 0$, $b > 0$ and $T > 0$ is the evolution generations.

Just as GA, AIA starts on the initial population that is generated randomly, and uses the reproducing, crossover and mutating operators to produce the filial generation superior to their parents. Through these iterations, the population gradually approaches to the optimum.

We compared the performance of GA, MAIA (model used in Ref. [14]) and the proposed DTAIA by finding the maximum values of F_1, F_3 and the minimum value of F_2.

$$F_1(x_1, x_2, x_3) = 100(x_1^2 - x_2)^2 + (1 - x_1)^2 + x_3, \quad -2.048 \leq x_1, x_2, x_3 \leq 2.048 \tag{10}$$

$$F_2(x_1, x_2, x_3) = \sum_{i=1}^{3} x_i^2, \quad -3.12 \leq x_1, x_2, x_3 \leq 3.12 \tag{11}$$

$$F_3(x_1, x_2, x_3) = \sum_{i=1}^{3} \sin^6(\frac{1}{x_i}), \quad -2.048 \leq x_1, x_2, x_3 \leq 2.048, \quad x_1, x_2, x_3 \neq 0 \tag{12}$$

The colony size is taken as 50 (POPSIZE=50), the max evolvement generation is 500, crossover probability is 0.8 and mutation probability is 0.15. Other parameters are: **MAIA**: m=0.2, l =0.7 at the function F_1 and l=0.05 at the functions F_2 and l=0.1 at the function F_3; **DTAIA**: b =0.0001, l_0 =0.7 at the function F_1 and l_0 =0.042 at the function F_2 and l_0 =0.04 at the function F_3.

The results of the simulated experiments are shown in Table 1. From the table it can be seen that the proposed method is superior to the other two methods in terms of the convergence speed and precision.

Table 1. Comparisons of GA, MAIA and DTAIA

Algorithms	Function F_1		Function F_2		Function F_3	
	Generation of reaching stable stage	Optimum value	Generation of reaching stable stage	Optimum value	Generation of reaching stable stage	Optimum value
GA	440	3907.966	308	0.000	299	3.000
MAIA	263	3907.966	208	0.000	162	3.000
DTAIA	179	3907.970	92	0.000	48	3.000

3   Modified Elman Network and DTAIA-Based Learning Algorithm of Elman Network

Elman neural network (ENN) is a type of recurrent neural network with three layers of neurons. It includes not only input nodes, output nodes and hidden nodes, but also context nodes in this model. The context nodes are used to memorize previous activations of the hidden nodes and can be considered to function as a one-step time delay. The modified Elman network differs from the original Elman network by introducing self-feedback coefficient links to improve its memorization ability. Figure 1 depicts the modified ENN.

Assume that there are r nodes in the input layer, n nodes in the hidden and context layers, respectively, and m nodes in the output layer. Then the input u is an r dimensional vector, the output x of the hidden layer and the output x_c of the context nodes are n dimensional vectors, respectively, the output y of the output layer is m dimensional vector, and the weights W^{I1}, W^{I2} and W^{I3} are $n{\times}n$, $n{\times}r$ and $m{\times}n$ dimensional matrices, respectively. The mathematical model of the modified Elman neural network is

$$x(k) = f(W^{I1}x_c(k) + W^{I2}u(k-1))$$

(13)

$$x_c(k) = \alpha x_c(k-1) + x(k-1)$$

(14)

$$y(k) = W^{I3}x(k)$$

(15)

where $f(x)$ is often taken as the sigmoid function.

$$f(x) = 1/(1 + e^{-x})$$

(16)

and α ($0 \le \alpha < 1$) is the self-feedback coefficient. When the coefficient α is zero, the modified Elman network is identical to the original Elman network.

Let the kth desired output of the system be $y_d(k)$. Define the error as

$$E(k) = (y_d(k) - y(k))^T (y_d(k) - y(k))/2$$

(17)

Differentiating E with respect to W^{I3}, W^{I2} and W^{I1} respectively, according to the gradient descent method, we obtain the learning algorithm for the modified Elman neural network as follows

$$\Delta w_{ij}^{I3} = \eta_3 \delta_i^0 x_j(k) \ (i = 1,2,...,m; j = 1,2,..,n)$$

(18)

$$\Delta w_{jq}^{I2} = \eta_2 \delta_j^h u_q(k-1) \qquad (j = 1,2,...,n; q = 1,2,...,r)$$

(19)

$$\Delta w_{jl}^{I1} = \eta_1 \sum_{i=1}^{m} (\delta_i^0 w_{ij}^{I3}) \partial x_j(k)/\partial w_{jl}^{I1} \qquad (j = 1,2,...,n; l = 1,2,...,n)$$

(20)

where η_1, η_2 and η_3 are learning steps of W^{I1}, W^{I2} and W^{I3} respectively, and

$$\delta_i^0 = (y_{d,i}(k) - y_i(k))g_i'(\cdot)$$

(21)

$$\delta_j^h = \sum_{i=1}^{m} (\delta_i^0 w_{ij}^{I3})f_j'(\cdot)$$

(22)

$$\partial x_j(k)/\partial w_{jl}^{I1} = f_j'(\cdot)x_l(k-1) + \alpha \partial x_j(k-1)/\partial w_{jl}^{I1}$$

(23)

If $g(x)$ is taken as a linear function, then $g_i'(\cdot) = 1$.

The network shown in Figure 1 is considered, where there exist r nodes in the input layer, n nodes in the hidden and context layers, and m nodes in the output layer. The corresponding individual structure can be illustrated in Figure 2, where $\widetilde{X}_C^0 = (x_{C,1}^0,...,x_{C,n}^0)$ is a permutation of the initial inputs of the context unit, $\widetilde{W}^{I1}$, $\widetilde{W}^{I2}$ and $\widetilde{W}^{I3}$ are their respective permutations of the expansion of weight matrices W^{I1}, W^{I2} and W^{I3} by rows. So the number of the elements in the body is $n+n\times n+n\times r+n\times m$. The individuals are trained and evolved by the proposed DTAIA algorithm.

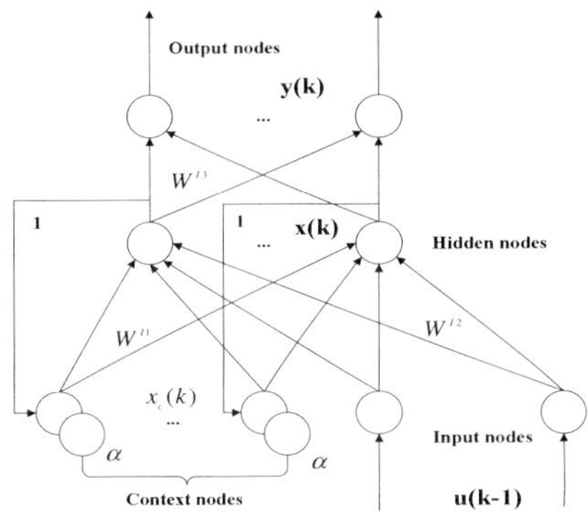

Fig. 1. Architecture of the Elman network

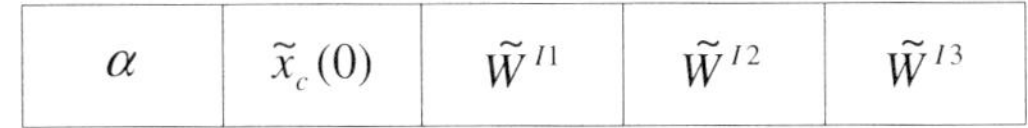

Fig. 2. Architecture of the individual

4   Speed Identification of USM Using the DTAIA-Based Elman Network

A dynamic identifier is constructed to perform the identification of non-linear systems using the DTAIA-based Elman network, which is called DTBEI. The model can be used to identify highly non-linear systems. A simulated dynamic system of the ultrasonic motor is considered as an example of a highly nonlinear system.

The identification model of the motor is shown in Figure 3. Numerical simulations are performed using the model of DTBEI for the speed identification of a longitudinal oscillation USM [15] shown in Figure 4. Some parameters of the USM model are taken as: driving frequency 27.8 kHZ , amplitude of driving voltage 300 V , allowed output moment 2.5 kg·cm, rotation speed 3.8 m/ s .

The curve of the actual motor speed is shown in Figure 5 and Figure 6. A durative external moment of 1 N·m is applied in the time window [0.3999s, 0.7s] as the external disturbances. Figures 7 to 12 show the identification results. The proposed

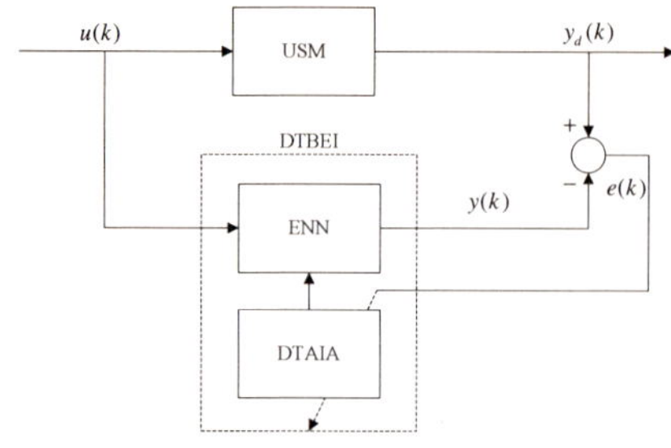

Fig. 3. Identification model of the motor

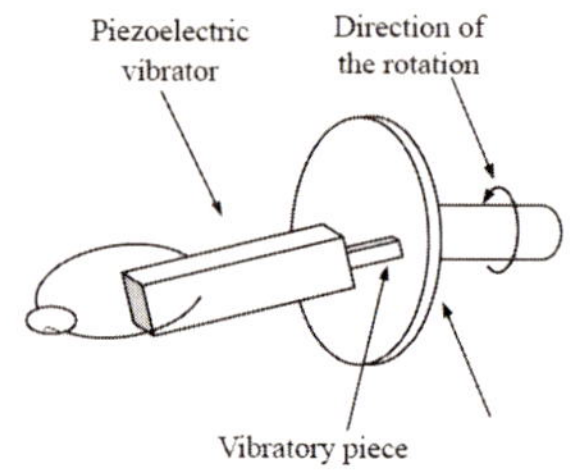

Fig. 4. Schematic diagram of the motor

DTBEI model is compared with the original Elman model using the gradient descent-based learning algorithm. The error is the difference between the identification result and the actual speed. The identification errors using the gradient descent-based learning algorithm are only less than 0.003, while the errors using the proposed method are less than 0.001. The identification error of the DTBEI is about 33.3% that of the Elman model trained by the gradient descent algorithm, and the identification precision is more than 99.9%. These results demonstrate that the proposed method can obtain higher precision and can be used to identify highly non-linear system successfully.

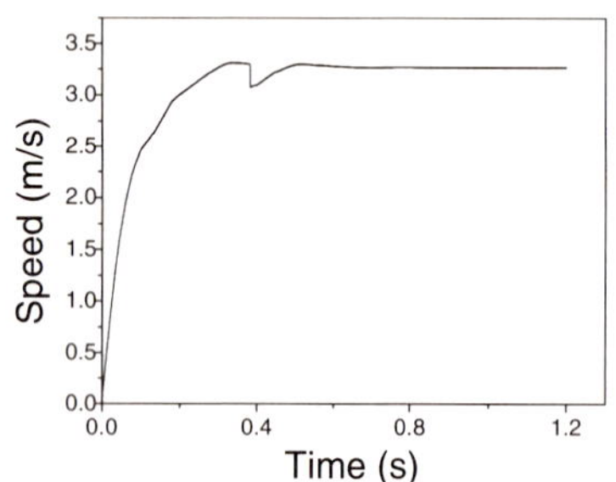

Fig. 5. Actual speed curve of the USM

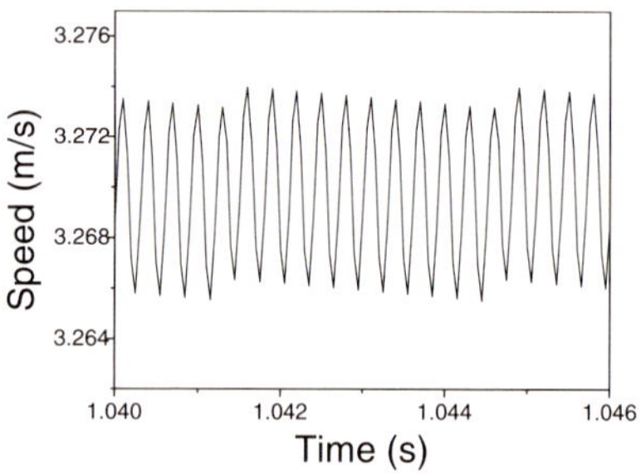

Fig. 6. Amplification of USM speed curve

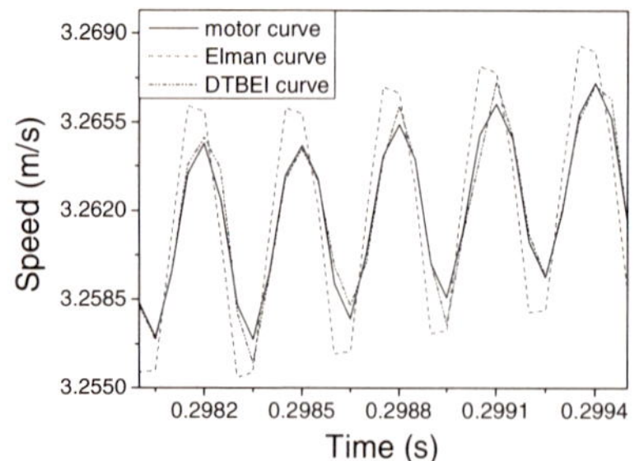

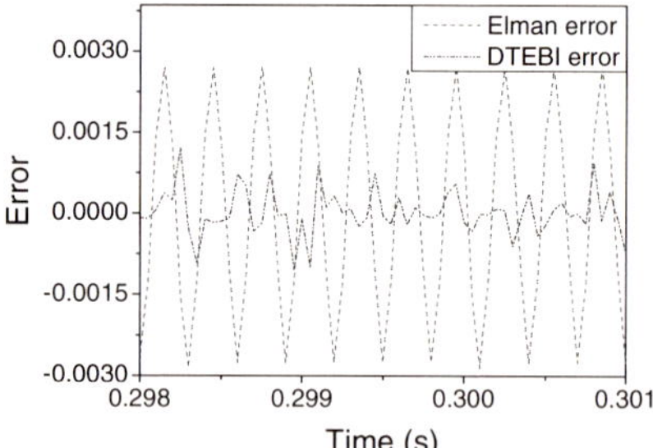

Fig. 7. Speed Identification curves before the disturbance

Fig. 8. Identification error curves before the disturbance

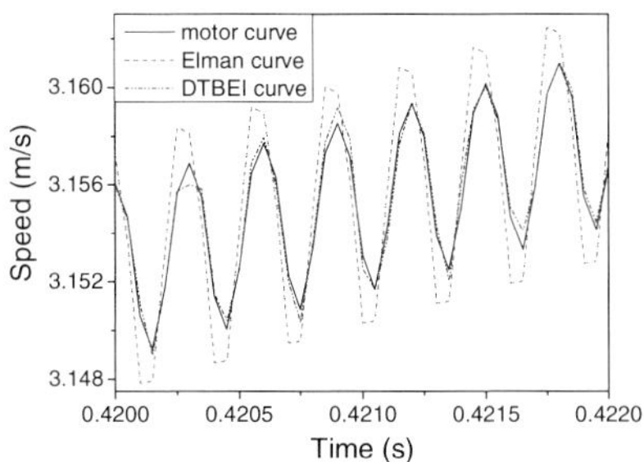

Fig. 9. Speed identification curves during the disturbance

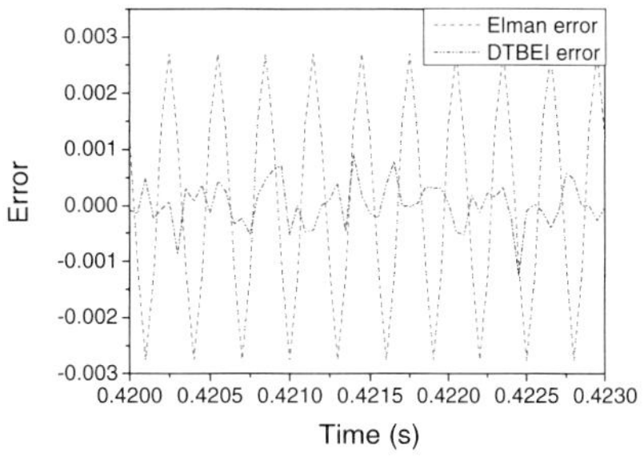

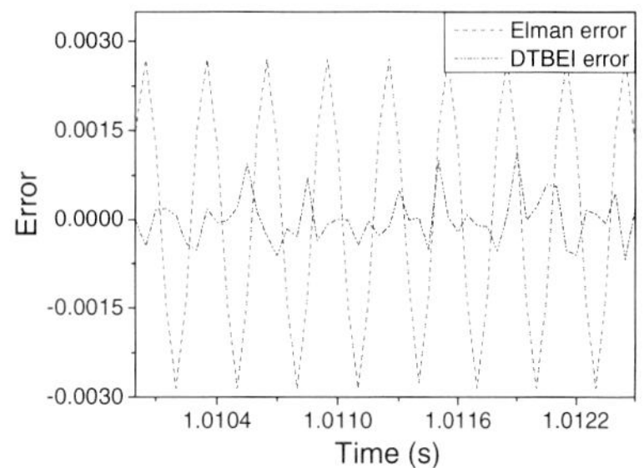

Fig. 10. Identification error curves during the disturbance

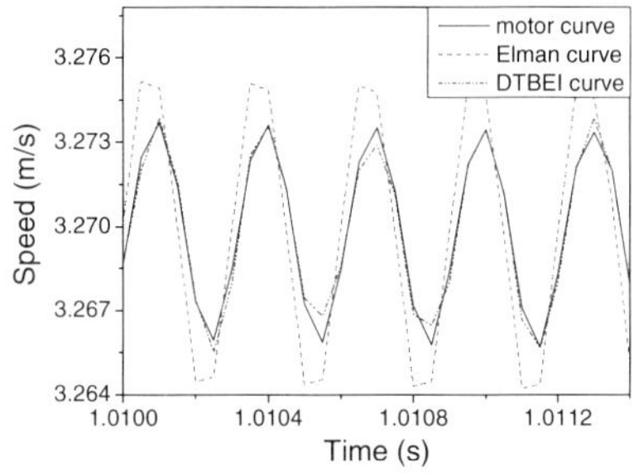

Fig. 11. Speed identification curves of the stable stage

Fig. 12. Identification error curves of the stable stage

5 Speed Control of USM Using the DTAIA-Based Elman Network

A novel controller is specially designed to control non-linear systems using the DTAIA-based Elman network, which is called DTBEC. The USM used in Section 4 is still considered as an example of a highly nonlinear system to examine the performance of the controller DTBEC. In this paper the model is illustrated in Figure 13.

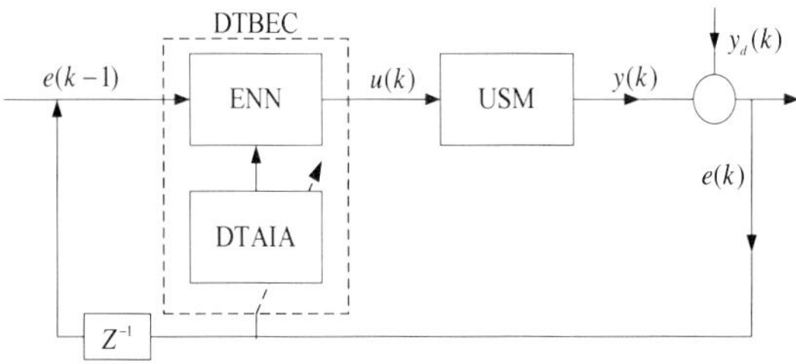

Fig. 13. Speed control model of the motor

In the controller DTBEC, the Elman network is trained by DTAIA on line, and the driving frequency is taken as the control variable. The fitness of an individual is evaluated by

$$f_i(t) = 1/e_i(t)^2 = 1/(y_d(t) - y_i(t))^2 \tag{24}$$

where $f_i(t)$ is the fitness value of the individual i at sampling time t, $y_d(t)$ is the expected output at time t while $y_i(t)$ is the actual output.

Figures 14 to 17 show the USM speed control curves using the DTBEC control strategy when the control speed is changed according to the sin curve and trapezoid curve respectively. From the Figure 14 and Figure 15, which is the amplification of the Figure 14 at the time windows [120s, 130s], it can be seen that the controller performs successfully and the proposed method possesses good control precision. While from the Figure 16 and Figure 17, it also can be seen that the control model possesses rapid adaptability for the sharp change of the control speed. It suggests that the controller presented here exhibits very good robustness and can handle a variety of operating conditions without losing the ability to track a desired course well.

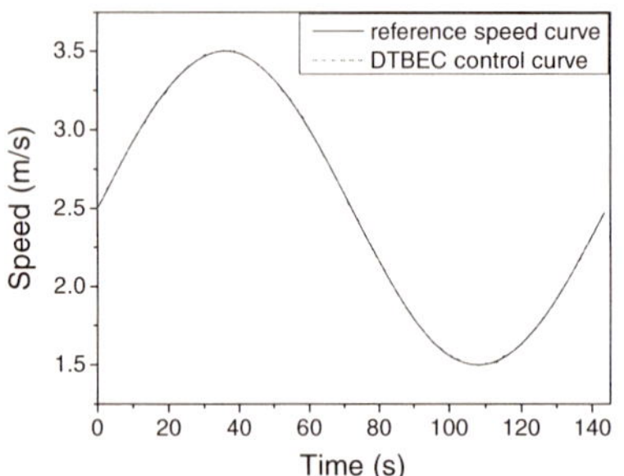

Fig. 14. Speed control curves with sinusoidal type reference speeds

Fig. 15. The amplification of the Fig. 14 at the time windows [120s, 130s]

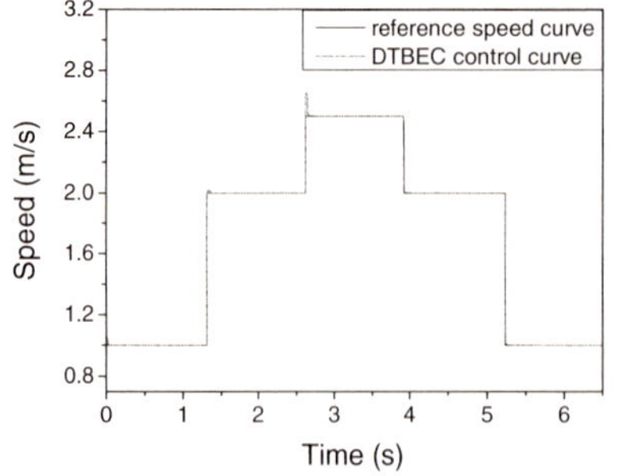
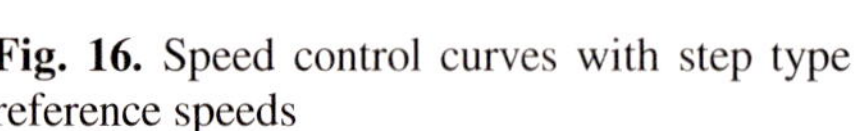
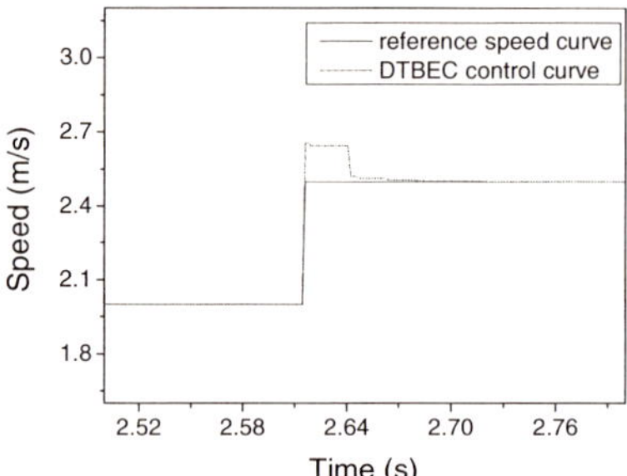

Fig. 16. Speed control curves with step type reference speeds

Fig. 17. The amplification of the Fig. 16 at the time windows [2.5s, 2.8s]

6 Conclusions

By analyzing the principles of artificial immune algorithm and genetic algorithm, we propose an improved immune algorithm DTAIA in order to overcome the shortage of GA and AIA for the tendency towards local optimum value and premature. Simulated experimental results show that the proposed DTAIA is more efficient than the GA algorithm and the real-valued coding AIA.

The proposed algorithm DTAIA can be employed to train the Elman network and to realize effectively the evolution of network construct, weights, initial inputs of the context unit and self-feedback coefficient together. Furthermore, an identifier DTBEI and a controller DTBEC are respectively designed to identify and control non-linear systems on line. Numerical results show that the designed identifier can approximate the nonlinear input-output mapping of the USM quite well, and the controller is tested by using step and sinusoidal types speed. Both of them achieve higher convergence precision and show fairly robust characteristics. Compared with other existing approaches, the proposed methods could be effective alternatives for system identification and control, especially for non-linear dynamic systems.

Acknowledgements. The authors are grateful to the support of the National Natural Science Foundation of China (60433020, 10501017), the science-technology development project of Jilin Province of China (20050705-2), the doctoral funds of the National Education Ministry of China (20030183060), and "985"project of Jilin University.

References

1. Hunt, J. E., Cooke, D.E.: Learning Using an Artificial Immune System. Journal of Network and Computer Applications, 19(1996) 189-212
2. Wen, X., Song, A.: An Immune Evolutionary Algorithm for Sphericity Error Evaluation. International Journal of Machine Tools & Manufacture, 44 (2004) 1077-1084
3. Chun, J. S., Kim, M. K., Jung, H. K., Hong, S. K.: Shape Optimization of Electromagnetic Devices Using Immune Algorithm. IEEE Transactions on Magnetics, 33(1997) 1876-1879
4. Lun, G., Chueh, C.: Multi-objective Optimal Design of Truss Structure with Immune Algorithm. Computers and Structures, 82 (2004) 829-844
5. Kalinli, A., Karaboga, N.: Articificial Immune Algorithm for IIR Filter Design. Engineering Applications of Artificial Intelligence, 18(2005) 919-929
6. Chun, J. S., Jung, H. K., Hahn, S. Y.: A Study on Comparison of Optimization Performances between Immune Algorithm and Other Heuristic Algorithms. IEEE Transactions on Magnetics, 34(1998) 2972-2975
7. Sashida, T., Kenjo, T.: An Introduction to Ultrasonic Motors. Oxford: Clarendon Press(1993)
8. Ueha, S., Tomikawa, T.: Piezoelectric Motors: Theory and Application. Oxford: Science Publications, (1993) 1 – 293
9. Lin, F. J., Wai, R. J., Hong, C. M.: Identification and Control of Rotary Traveling-wave Type Ultrasonic Motor Using Neural Networks. IEEE Transactions on Control Systems Technology, 9(2001) 672-680

10. Senjyu, T., Miyazato, H., Yokoda, S., Uezato, K.: Speed Control of Ultrasonic Motors Using Neural Network. IEEE Transactions on Power Electronics, 13(1998) 381-387
11. Xiong, Z. H., Zhang, J.: A Batch-to-batch Tterative Optimal Control Strategy Based on Recurrent Neural Network Models. Journal of Process Control, 15(2005) 11-21
12. Cong, S., Gao, X. P.: Recurrent Neural Networks and Their Application in System Identification. Systems Engineering and Electronics, 25(2003) 194-197
13. Dasgupta, D.: Artificial Immune Systems and Their Applications. Berlin Heidelberg: Springer – Verlang (1999)
14. Zheng, R. R., Mao, Z. Y.: A Modified Artificial Immune Algorithm. Computer Engineering and Applications, 33(2003) 55-57
15. Xu, X., Liang, Y. C., Lee, H. P., Lin, W. Z., Lim, S. P., Lee, K. H.: Mechanical Modeling of A Longitudinal Oscillation Ultrasonic Motor and Temperature Effect Analysis. Smart Materials and Structures, 12(2003) 514-523

A Hybrid and Intelligent System
for Predicting Lot Output Time
in a Semiconductor Fabrication Factory*

Toly Chen[1] and Yu-Cheng Lin[2]

[1] Department of Industrial Engineering and Systems Management, Feng Chia University,
100, Wenhwa Road, Seatwen, Taichung City, Taiwan
tolychen@ms37.hinet.net
http://www.geocities.com/tinchihchen/
[2] Department of Industrial Engineering and Management,
Overseas Chinese Institute of Technology,
100, Chiaokwang Road, Taichung City, Taiwan
yclin@ocit.edu.tw

Abstract. Predicting the output time of every lot in a semiconductor fabrication factory (wafer fab) is a critical task to the wafer fab. To further enhance the effectiveness of wafer lot output time prediction, a hybrid and intelligent system is constructed in this study. The system is composed of two major parts (a k-means classifier and a back-propagation-network regression) and has three intelligent features: incorporating the future release plan of the fab (look-ahead), example classification, and artificial neural networking. Production simulation is also applied in this study to generate test examples. According to experimental results, the prediction accuracy of the hybrid and intelligent system was significantly better than those of four existing approaches: BPN, case-based reasoning (CBR), FBPN, kM-BPN, by achieving a 9%~44% (and an average of 25%) reduction in the root-mean-squared-error (RMSE) over the comparison basis – BPN.

1 Introduction

Lot output time series is one of the most important time series data in a wafer fab. Predicting the output time for every lot in a wafer fab is a critical task not only to the fab itself, but also to its customers. After the output time of each lot in a wafer fab is accurately predicted, several managerial goals (including internal due-date assignment, output projection, ordering decision support, enhancing customer relationship, and guiding subsequent operations) can be simultaneously achieved [5]. Predicting the output time of a wafer lot is equivalent to estimating the cycle (flow) time of the lot, because the former can be easily derived by adding the release time (a constant) to the latter. There are six major approaches commonly applied to predicting the output/cycle time of a wafer lot: multiple-factor linear combination (MFLC), production

---

* This work was support by the National Science Council, R.O.C.

S. Greco et al. (Eds.): RSCTC 2006, LNAI 4259, pp. 757–766, 2006.

simulation (PS), back propagation networks (BPN), case based reasoning (CBR), fuzzy modeling methods, and hybrid approaches. Among the six approaches, MFLC is the easiest, quickest, and most prevalent in practical applications. The major disadvantage of MFLC is the lack of forecasting accuracy [5]. Conversely, huge amount of data and lengthy simulation time are two shortages of PS. Nevertheless, PS is the most accurate output time prediction approach if the related databases are continuingly updated to maintain enough validity, and often serves as a benchmark for evaluating the effectiveness of another method. PS also tends to be preferred because it allows for computational experiments and subsequent analyses without any actual execution [3]. Considering both effectiveness and efficiency, Chang et al. [4] and Chang and Hsieh [2] both forecasted the output/cycle time of a wafer lot with a BPN having a single hidden layer. Compared with MFLC approaches, the average prediction accuracy measured with the root mean squared error (RMSE) was considerably improved with these BPNs. On the other hand, much less time and fewer data are required to generate an output time forecast with a BPN than with PS. Theoretically, a well-trained BPN (without being stuck to local minima) with a good selected topology can successfully map any complex distribution. However, wafer lot output time prediction is a much more complicated problem, and the results of these studies have shown that BPN remains incapable in solving such a problem. One reason is that there might be multiple complex distributions to model, and these distributions might be quite different (even for the same product type and priority). For example, when the workload level (in the wafer fab or on the processing route or before bottlenecks) is stable, the cycle time of a wafer lot basically follows the well-known Little's law [14], and the output time of the wafer lot can be easily predicted. Conversely, if the workload level fluctuates or keeps going up (or down), predicting the cycle time and output time of a wafer lot becomes much more difficult.

Chang et al. [3] proposed a k-nearest-neighbors based case-based reasoning (CBR) approach which outperformed the BPN approach in forecasting accuracy. Chang et al. [4] modified the first step (i.e. partitioning the range of each input variable into several fuzzy intervals) of the fuzzy modeling method proposed by Wang and Mendel [15], called the WM method, with a simple genetic algorithm (GA) and proposed the evolving fuzzy rule (EFR) approach to predict the cycle time of a wafer lot. Their EFR approach outperformed CBR and BPN in prediction accuracy.

Chen [5] constructed a fuzzy BPN (FBPN) that incorporated expert opinions in forming inputs to the FBPN. Chen's FBPN was a hybrid approach (fuzzy modeling and BPN) and surpassed the crisp BPN especially in the efficiency respect.

To further enhance the effectiveness of wafer lot output time prediction, a hybrid and intelligent system is constructed in this study. The system is composed of two major parts (a k-means (kM) classifier and a BPN regression) and has three intelligent features:

1. Look-ahead: The future release plan of the fab is incorporated.
2. Example classification: Wafer lots are classified before predicting their output times with the BPN.
3. Artificial neural networking: BPN is applied.

The system architecture is shown in Fig. 1. PS is also applied in this study to generate test examples. Using simulated data, the effectiveness of the hybrid and intelligent system is shown and compared with those of four existing approaches, BPN, CBR, FBPN, and kM-BPN.

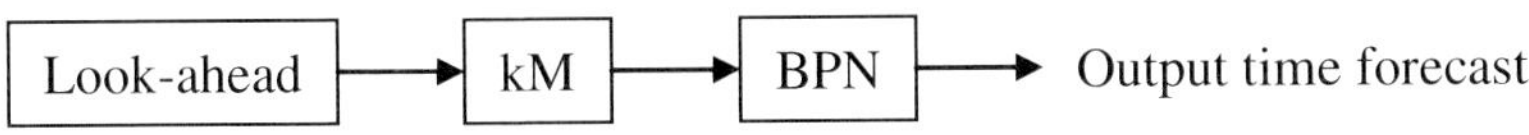

Fig. 1. The system architecture

2 Methodology

Firstly, the look-ahead property of the hybrid and intelligent system is explained.

2.1 Incorporating the Future Release Plan (Look-Ahead)

All aforementioned traditional methods are based on the historical data of the fab. However, a lot of studies have shown that the performance of sequencing and scheduling in a fab relies heavily on the future release plan, which has been neglected in this field. In addition, the characteristic re-entrant production flows of a fab lead to the phenomenon that a lot that will be released in the future might appear in front of another lot that currently exists in the fab. For these reasons, to further improve the accuracy of wafer lot output time prediction, the future release plan of the fab has to be considered (look-ahead). There are many possible ways to incorporate the future release plan in predicting the output time of a wafer lot currently existing in the fab. In this study, the three nearest future discounted workloads on the lot's processing route (according to the future release plan) are proposed for this purpose:

1. *The 1st nearest future discounted workload* ($FDW^{(1)}$): the sum of the (processing time/release time)'s of the operations of the lots that will be released within time [now, now + T_1].
2. *The 2nd nearest future discounted workload* ($FDW^{(2)}$): the sum of the (processing time/release time)'s of the operations of the lots that will be released within time [now + T_1, now + T_1 + T_2].
3. *The 3rd nearest future discounted workload* ($FDW^{(3)}$): the sum of the (processing time/release time)'s of the operations of the lots that will be released within time [now + T_1 + T_2, now + T_1 + T_2 + T_3].

Note that only the operations performed on the machines on the lot's processing route are considered in calculating these future workloads, which then become three additional inputs to the BPN.

2.2 Example Classification with kM – Rationale and Procedure

The rationale for combining kM and BPN for wafer lot output time prediction is explained as follows. As stated previously, wafer lot output time prediction is a complicated problem, in which there might be multiple complex distributions to model, and these distributions might be quite different (even for the same product type and priority).

For this reason, classifying wafer lots under different circumstances seems to be a reasonable treatment. In this respect, kM can serve as a clustering tool for production data in a wafer fab. As a result, the combination of kM and BPN is chosen in this study.

The parameters used in this study are defined:

1. U_n: the average fab utilization at the release time of the n-th example/lot.
2. Q_n: the total queue length on the lot's processing route at the release time.
3. BQ_n: the total queue length before bottlenecks at the release time.
4. FQ_n: the total queue length in the whole fab at the release time. Obviously, $FQ_n \geq Q_n \geq BQ_n$.
5. WIP_n: the fab work-in-process (WIP) at the release time.
6. $D_n^{(i)}$: the latenesses of the i-th recently completed lots.

The procedure of applying kM in forming inputs to the BPN is now detailed. Every lot fed into the BPN is called an example. Examples are pre-classified to m categories before they are fed into the BPN according to their Euclidean distances to the category centers:

$$d(n, j) = \sqrt{\begin{array}{l}(U_n - U_{(j)})^2 + (Q_n - Q_{(j)})^2 + (BQ_n - BQ_{(j)})^2 + (FQ_n - FQ_{(j)})^2 \\ + (WIP_n - WIP_{(j)})^2 + (D_n^{(i)} - D_{(j)}^{(i)})^2 + (FDW_n^{(1)} - FDW_{(j)}^{(1)})^2 \\ + (FDW_n^{(2)} - FDW_{(j)}^{(2)})^2 + (FDW_n^{(3)} - FDW_{(j)}^{(3)})^2\end{array}} \tag{1}$$

$j = 1\sim m,$

where $\{U_{(j)}, Q_{(j)}, BQ_{(j)}, FQ_{(j)}, WIP_{(j)}, D_{(j)}^{(i)}, FDW_{(j)}^{(1)}, FDW_{(j)}^{(2)}, FDW_{(j)}^{(3)}\}$ denotes the parameter set of the j-th category center, which is arbitrarily chosen from those of all examples in the beginning. In this way, lot n is classified to category j with the smallest $d(n, j)$. Each time after all examples are classified, the parameter sets of all category centers are recalculated by averaging those of the examples clustered in the same categories. Example classification is continued until the sum of the average Euclidean distances (SADs) from examples to their category centers in all categories converges to a minimal value:

$$SAD = \sum_{j=1}^{m} \sum_{\text{all lot } n \text{ in category } j} d(n, j) / \text{number of lots in category } j. \tag{2}$$

Examples of different categories are then learned with different BPNs but with the same topology. The procedure for determining the parameters is described in the next section.

2.3 Output Time Prediction with BPN

The configuration of the BPN is established as follows:

1. Inputs: nine parameters associated with the n-th example/lot including U_n, Q_n, BQ_n, FQ_n, WIP_n, $D_n^{(i)}$, $FDW^{(1)}$, $FDW^{(2)}$, and $FDW^{(3)}$. These parameters have to be normalized so that their values fall within [0, 1].

2. Single hidden layer: Generally one or two hidden layers are more beneficial for the convergence property of the network.
3. Number of neurons in the hidden layer: the same as that in the input layer. Such a treatment has been adopted by many studies (e.g. [2, 5]).
4. Output: the (normalized) cycle time forecast of the example.
5. Network learning rule: Delta rule.
6. Transformation function: Sigmoid function,

$$f(x) = 1/(1 + e^{-x}).$$ (3)

7. Learning rate (η): 0.01~1.0.
8. Batch learning.

The procedure for determining the parameter values is now described. A portion of the examples is fed as "training examples" into the BPN to determine the parameter values. Two phases are involved at the training stage. At first, in the forward phase, inputs are multiplied with weights, summated, and transferred to the hidden layer. Then activated signals are outputted from the hidden layer as:

$$h_l = 1/(1 + e^{-n_l^h}),$$ (4)

where

$$n_l^h = I_l^h - \theta_l^h,$$ (5)

$$I_l^h = \sum_{i=1}^{9} w_{il}^h x_i.$$ (6)

h_l's are also transferred to the output layer with the same procedure. Finally, the output of the BPN is generated as:

$$o = 1/(1 + e^{n^o}),$$ (7)

where

$$n^o = I^o - \theta^o,$$ (8)

$$I^o = \sum_{l=1}^{9} w_l^o h_l.$$ (9)

Then the output o is compared with the normalized actual cycle time a, for which the RMSE is calculated:

$$RMSE = \sqrt{\sum_{\text{all examples}} (o - a)^2 / \text{number of examples}}.$$ (10)

Subsequently in the backward phase, the deviation between o and a is propagated backward, and the error terms of neurons in the output and hidden layers can be calculated respectively as:

$$\delta^o = o(1-o)(a-o),\tag{11}$$

$$\delta_l^h = h_l(1-h_l)w_l^o\delta^o.\tag{12}$$

Based on them, adjustments that should be made to the connection weights and thresholds can be obtained as

$$\Delta w_l^o = \eta\delta^o h_l,\tag{13}$$

$$\Delta w_{il}^h = \eta\delta_l^h x_i,\tag{14}$$

$$\Delta\theta^o = -\eta\delta^o,\tag{15}$$

$$\Delta\theta_l^h = -\eta\delta_l^h.\tag{16}$$

To accelerate convergence, a momentum can be added to the learning expressions. For example,

$$\Delta w_l^o = \eta\delta^o h_l + \alpha(w_l^o(t) - w_l^o(t-1)).\tag{17}$$

Theoretically, network-learning stops when the RMSE falls below a pre-specified level, or the improvement in the RMSE becomes negligible with more epochs, or a large number of epochs have already been run. Then the remaining portion of the adopted examples in each category is used as "test examples" and fed into the BPN to evaluate the accuracy of the network that is also measured with the RMSE. Finally, the BPN can be applied to predicting the cycle time of a new lot. When a new lot is released into the fab, the nine parameters associated with the new lot are recorded and compared with those of each category center. Then the BPN with the parameters of the nearest category center is applied to forecasting the cycle time of the new lot. The data acquisition and transformation processes are shown in Fig. 2. In this study, BPN was implemented on the software "NeuroSolutions 4.0".

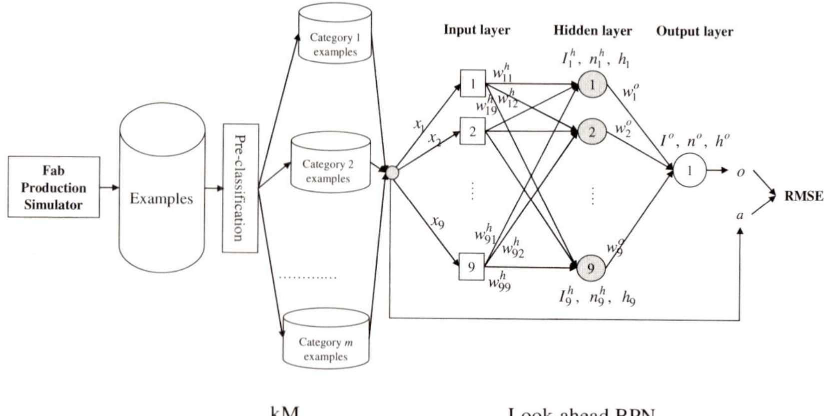

Fig. 2. The data acquisition and transformation processes

3   A Demonstrative Example from a Simulated Wafer Fab

In practical situations, the history time series data of each lot is only partially available in the factory. Further, some information of the previous lots such as Q_n, BQ_n, and FQ_n is not easy to collect on the shop floor. Therefore, a simulation model is often built to simulate the manufacturing process of a real wafer fabrication factory [1-5, 8, 11]. Then, such information can be derived from the shop floor status collected from the simulation model [3]. To generate test data, a simulation program coded using Microsoft Visual Basic .NET is constructed to simulate a wafer fabrication environment with assumptions as follows.

1. The distributions of the interarrival times of orders are exponential.
2. The distributions of the interarrival times of machine downs are exponential.
3. The distribution of the time required to repair a machine is deterministic.
4. The percentages of lots with different product types in the fab are predetermined. As a result, this study is only focused on fixed-product-mix cases. However, the product mix in the simulated fab does fluctuate and is only approximately fixed in the long term.
5. The percentages of lots with different priorities released into the fab are controlled.
6. The priority of a lot cannot be changed during fabrication.
7. Lots are sequenced on each machine first by their priorities, then by the first-in-first-out (FIFO) policy. Such a sequencing policy is a common practice in many foundry fabs.
8. A lot has equal chances to be processed on each alternative machine/head available at a step.
9. A lot cannot proceed to the next step until the fabrication on its every wafer has been finished. No preemption is allowed.

The basic configuration of the simulated wafer fab is the same as a real-world wafer fabrication factory which is located in the Science Park of Hsin-Chu, Taiwan, R.O.C. A trace report was generated every simulation run for verifying the simulation model. The simulated average cycle times have also been compared with the actual values to validate the simulation model. Assumptions 1~3, and 7~9 are commonly adopted in related studies (e.g. [2-5]), while assumptions 4~6 are made to simplify the situation. There are five products (labeled as A~E) in the simulated fab. A fixed product mix is assumed. The percentages of these products in the fab's product mix are assumed to be 35%, 24%, 17%, 15%, and 9%, respectively. The simulated fab has a monthly capacity of 20,000 pieces of wafers and is expected to be fully utilized (utilization = 100%). Purchase orders (POs) with normally distributed sizes (mean = 300 wafers; standard deviation = 50 wafers) arrive according to a Poisson process, and then the corresponding manufacturing orders (MOs) are released for these POs a fixed time after. Based on these assumptions, the mean inter-release time of MOs into the fab can be obtained as (30.5 days/month * 24 hours/day) / (20000 wafers/month / 300 wafers) = 11 hours. An MO is split into lots of a standard size of 24 wafers per lot. Lots of the same MO are released one by one every 11 / (300/24) = 0.85 hours. Three types of priorities (normal lot, hot lot, and super hot lot) are randomly assigned to lots. The percentages of lots with these priorities released into the fab are restricted to be approximately 60%, 30%, and 10%, respectively. Each product has 150~200 steps and 6~9 reentrances to the most bottleneck machine. The singular production characteristic "reentry" of the semiconductor industry is clearly reflected in the example. It also shows the difficulty for the production planning and scheduling people to provide an accurate due-date for the product with such a complicated routing. Totally 102 machines (including alternative machines) are provided to process single-wafer or batch operations in the fab. Thirty replicates of the simulation are successively run. The time required for each simulation replicate is about 12 minute on a PC with 512MB RAM and Athlon™ 64 Processor 3000+ CPU. A horizon of twenty-four months is simulated. The maximal cycle time is less than three months. Therefore, four months and an initial WIP status (obtained from a pilot simulation run) seemed to be sufficient to drive the simulation into a steady state. The statistical data were collected starting at the end of the fourth month. For each replicate, data of 30 lots are collected and classified by their product types and priorities. Totally, data of 900 lots can be collected as training and testing examples. Among them, 2/3 (600 lots, including all product types and priorities) are used to train the network, and the other 1/3 (300 lots) are reserved for testing. The three parameters in calculating the future discounted workloads are specified as: T_1 = one week; T_2 = 1.5 weeks; T_3 = 2 weeks.

3.1 Results and Discussions

To evaluate the effectiveness of the hybrid and intelligent system and to make some comparisons with four approaches – BPN, CBR, FBPN, and kM-BPN, all the five methods were applied to five test cases containing the data of full-size (24 wafers per lot) lots with different product types and priorities. The convergence condition was established as either the improvement in the RMSE becomes less than 0.001 with one more epoch, or 1000 epochs have already been run. The minimal RMSEs achieved by applying the four approaches to different cases were recorded and compared in Table 1 (the proposed system is indicated with look-ahead kM-BPN). As noted in Chang and Liao [5], the k-nearest-neighbors based CBR approach should be fairly compared with a BPN trained with only randomly chosen k cases. The latter (BPN) was also adopted as the comparison basis, and the percentage of improvement on the minimal RMSE (a negative value indicates a reduction was achieved) by applying another approach is enclosed in parentheses following the performance measure. The optimal value of parameter k in the CBR approach was equal to the value that minimized the RMSE [5]. According to experimental results, the following discussions are made:

1. From the effectiveness viewpoint, the prediction accuracy (measured with the RMSE) of the hybrid and intelligent system was significantly better than those of the other approaches by achieving a 9%~44% (and an average of 25%) reduction in the RMSE over the comparison basis – BPN. The average advantages over CBR and FBPN were 22% and 21%, respectively.
2. As the lot priority increases, the superiority of the hybrid and intelligent system over BPN and CBR becomes more evident.
3. The effect of look-ahead is revealed with the fact that look-ahead kM-BPN outperformed kM-BPN with an average advantage of 2%.
4. The effect of classification is obvious because kM-BPN considerably outperformed BPN in all cases.

Table 1. Comparisons of the RMSEs of various approaches

RMSE \ Product (priority)	A (normal)	A (hot)	A (super hot)	B (normal)	B (hot)
BPN	177.1	102.27	12.23	286.93	75.98
FBPN	171.82 (-3%)	89.5 (-12%)	11.34 (-7%)	286.14 (-0%)	76.14 (+0%)
CBR	172.44 (-3%)	86.66 (-15%)	11.59 (-5%)	295.51 (+3%)	78.85 (+4%)
kM-BPN	161.95 (-9%)	78.25 (-23%)	11.61 (-5%)	190.79 (-34%)	43.06 (-43%)
Look-ahead kM-BPN	154.42 (-13%)	77.15 (-25%)	11.14 (-9%)	188.3 (-34%)	42.72 (-44%)

4 Conclusions and Directions for Future Research

To further enhance the effectiveness of wafer lot output time prediction, a hybrid and intelligent system is constructed in this study. The system is composed of two major parts (a kM classifier and a BPN regression) and has three intelligent features: look-ahead, example classification, and artificial neural networking. For evaluating the effectiveness of the proposed hybrid and intelligent system and to make some comparisons with four approaches – BPN, CBR, FBPN, and kM-BPN. PS is applied in this study to generate test data. Then all the five methods are applied to five cases elicited from the test data. According to experimental results, the prediction accuracy of the hybrid and intelligent system was significantly better than those of the other approaches by achieving a 9%~44% (and an average of 25%) reduction in the RMSE over the comparison basis – BPN. The average advantages over CBR and FBPN were 22% and 21%, respectively.

However, to further evaluate the effectiveness of the proposed hybrid and intelligent system, it has to be applied to fab models of different scales, especially a full-scale actual wafer fab. In addition, the proposed hybrid and intelligent system can also be applied to cases with changing product mixes or loosely controlled priority combinations, under which the cycle time variation is often very large. These constitute some directions for future research.

References

1. Barman, S.: The Impact of Priority Rule Combinations on Lateness and Tardiness. IIE Transactions 30 (1998) 495-504
2. Chang, P.-C., Hsieh, J.-C.: A Neural Networks Approach for Due-date Assignment in a Wafer Fabrication Factory. International Journal of Industrial Engineering 10(1) (2003) 55-61
3. Chang, P.-C., Hsieh, J.-C., Liao, T. W.: A Case-based Reasoning Approach for Due Date Assignment in a Wafer Fabrication Factory. In: Proceedings of the International Conference on Case-Based Reasoning (ICCBR 2001), Vancouver, British Columbia, Canada (2001)

4. Chang, P.-C., Hsieh, J.-C., Liao, T. W.: Evolving Fuzzy Rules for Due-date Assignment Problem in Semiconductor Manufacturing Factory. Journal of Intelligent Manufacturing 16 (2005) 549-557
5. Chen, T.: A Fuzzy Back Propagation Network for Output Time Prediction in a Wafer Fab. Journal of Applied Soft Computing 2/3F (2003) 211-222
6. Goldberg, D. E.: Genetic Algorithms in Search, Optimization, and Machine Learning. Addison-Wesley, Reading, MA (1989)
7. Lin, C.-Y.: Shop Floor Scheduling of Semiconductor Wafer Fabrication Using Real-time Feedback Control and Prediction. Ph.D. Dissertation, Engineering-Industrial Engineering and Operations Research, University of California at Berkeley (1996)
8. Vig, M. M., Dooley, K. J.: Dynamic Rules for Due-date Assignment. International Journal of Production Research 29(7) (1991) 1361-1377
9. Wang, L.-X., Mendel, J. M.: Generating Fuzzy Rules by Learning from Examples. IEEE Transactions on Systems, Man, and Cybernetics 22(6) (1992) 1414-1427

Combining SOM and GA-CBR for Flow Time Prediction in Semiconductor Manufacturing Factory

Pei-Chann Chang[1,2], Yen-Wen Wang[3], and Chen-Hao Liu[2]

[1] Department of Information Management, Yuan-Ze University
[2] Department of Industrial Engineering and Management, Yuan-Ze University,
135 Yuan-Dong Rd., Taoyuan 32026, Taiwan, R.O.C.
[3] Department of Industrial Engineering and Management, Ching-Yun University, 229
Chien-Hsin Rd., Taoyuan 320, Taiwan, R.O.C.
iepchang@saturn.yzu.edu.tw

Abstract. Flow time of semiconductor manufacturing factory is highly related to the shop floor status; however, the processes are highly complicated and involve more than hundred of production steps. Therefore, a simulation model with the production process of a real wafer fab located in Hsin-Chu Science-based Park of Taiwan is built. In this research, a hybrid approach by combining Self-Organizing Map (SOM) and Case-Based Reasoning (CBR) for flow time prediction in semiconductor manufacturing factory is proposed. And Genetic Algorithm (GA) is applied to fine-tune the weights of features in the CBR model. The flow time and related shop floor status are collected and fed into the SOM for classification. Then, corresponding GA-CBR is selected and applied for flow time prediction. Finally, using the simulated data, the effectiveness of the proposed method (SGA-CBR) is shown by comparing with other approaches.

Keywords: Flow time prediction, Case-Based Reasoning, Genetic Algorithms, Self-Organizing Map.

1 Introduction

Flow time prediction is an important feature of a semiconductor manufacturing problem, which is the basis used to estimate the due date of a new order under current shop floor status. Traditionally, assigning due date for each order is accomplished by the production planning and control staffs based on their knowledge of the manufacturing processes and shop floor status. The production planning and scheduling staffs usually estimate the flow time of each order based on products manufactured before and schedule its release to the shop floor for production. Even if the product specification is exactly the same, the status of the shop floor such as jobs in the system, shop loading and jobs in the bottleneck machine may not be identical to the previous production. As a result, due date estimated by the production planning and scheduling staffs might subject to errors.

As the advance in artificial intelligence (AI), tools in soft computing have been widely applied in manufacturing planning and scheduling problems. Ref. [2] reported

S. Greco et al. (Eds.): RSCTC 2006, LNAI 4259, pp. 767–775, 2006.

that back-propagation neural networks (BPN) could be more effective than some traditional direct procedures for due date assignment since neural network can obtain a probable result even if the input data are incomplete or noisy. Using a k-nearest-neighbors (KNN) based case-based reasoning (CBR) approach with dynamic feature weights and non-linear similarity functions; ref. [6] found that further performance improvement could be made. This paper constructs a case-based prediction system with the aid of a Self-Organizing Map (SOM), Genetic Algorithm (GA) and CBR, and we call it SGA-CBR in the rest of the article. The SOM is first used to classify the data, and after the classification GA is used to construct the CBR prediction method by searching the best weights combination.

The rest of the paper is organized as follows: Section 2 reviews some related literatures. Section 3 briefly describes the case that will be discussed in this research. Section 4 presents the framework of the methodology applied in the flow time prediction method. Section 5 presents some experimental results of various models including other compared methods. Section 6 discusses the simulated results from these different models and then the conclusion is made.

2 Literature Review

CBR is a general problem solving method with a simple and appealing definition [10] that emphasizes finding appropriate past experience to the solution of new problems. It solves problems using or adapting solutions from previous experiences. CBR is a problem-solving approach that takes advantage of the knowledge gained from previous attempts to solve a particular problem. Ref. [7] applied the CBR technique to the software estimation problem and found that CBR performs somewhat superior to regression modeling based on the same data. The successful applications of the CBR system in the prediction problem can refer to ref. [8], [12], [17], and [18].

For a CBR system, the retrieval of appropriate cases relies on a similarity metric which takes into account the distance between pairs of cases in their state space of variables, also commonly called "features". Similarity measurements between pairs of features play a central role in CBR [11]. Many CBR systems represent cases using features and employ a similarity function to measure the similarities between new and prior cases [15]. A CBR system may perform ineffectively in retrieving cases when the features are irrelevant for cases matching. Therefore, to minimize the bias associated with the features, it is crucial to identify the most salient features leading to effective case retrieval. Generally, the performance of the similarity metric and the weighting of features are keys to this reasoning process [10].

In general, feature weights are used to denote the relevance of features. They allow similarity functions to emphasize features according to their relevance. Several research works attempted to determine feature weight settings with the aid of GA. Ref. [16] proposed methods for feature subset selection using genetic algorithms. Ref. [1] developed a GA-based, weighted K-NN approach to construct CBR. They suggested that the types of similarity functions, feature weights, and the indexing method could affect the retrieval performance of CBR. To the best of our knowledge, none of the above studies considered the non-linear feature value distance between an old case and a new case. Therefore, this paper aims to investigate the effect of GA-based feature weighting together with a number of non-linear similarity functions.

3 Problem Description

The basic configuration of the wafer fabrication factory is same as a real-world one located in the Science-Based Park in Hsin-Chu, Taiwan, R.O.C. There are 66 single-server or multiple-server workstations in the shop floor. The major wafer manufacturing processes are divided into two sections, i.e., the front-end process and the back-end process. A flowchart of the basic front-end processes is described in Figure 1. The production steps are just a step-by-step process. Real floor shop manufacturing processes are more complicated with many detailed processing procedures.

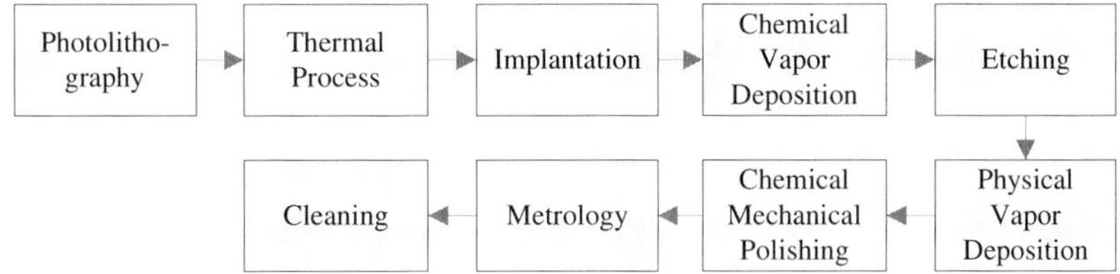

Fig. 1. Basic Front-End Processes

After the front-end processes, wafers are fed into the back-end processes. A simple flowchart of the back-end processes is also shown in Figure 2.

Fig. 2. Basic Back-End Processes

The time series plot of 300 flow time data is depicted in Figure 3. The pattern of the flow time is not stable in this plot. The traditional approach by human decision is very inaccurate and very prone to fail when the shop status is totally different even for

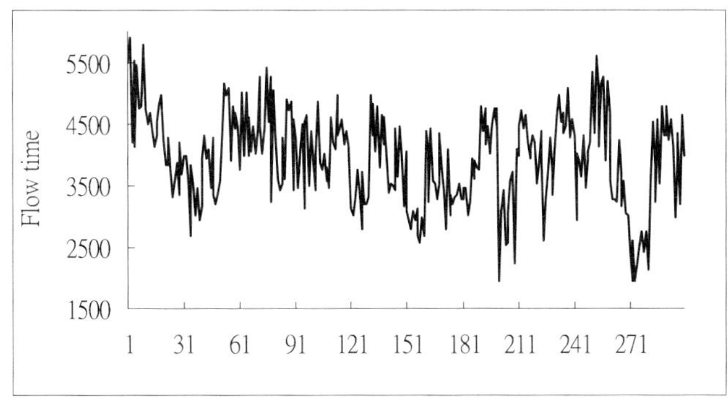

Fig. 3. Time Series Plot of Flow Time

the same product. This is the motive for this research to develop an approach to cut down the forecasting error based on such non-stationary situation.

4   A Hybrid System Combining SOM and GA-CBR

This research first uses SOM to cluster past cases to the different groups, and the training cases in each sub-group are used to train the best weights between features by GA. In the testing process, the most similar sub-group to the new case then could be retrieved by CBR from past case. New case is compared to each case within the selected group in order to find the most similar case to get the forecasting flow time of the new case. Hopefully, the hybrid model could improve the effect of flow time forecasting. The framework of SGA-CBR can be described as figure 4. Totally 300 records of data are randomly divided into 240 records of training data and 60 records of testing data. Following briefly describes the operation process for the SGA-CBR:

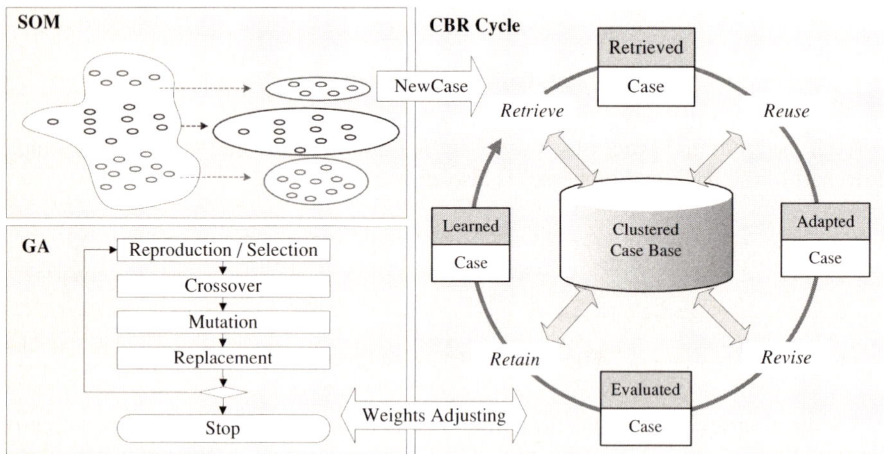

Fig. 4. The Framework of the research

Step 1. Classify the training data by SOM

From the data collected, each new case is composed of six features: order quantities (X_1), existing order qualities when the order arrived (X_2), average shop workload when the order arrived (X_3), average queuing length when the order arrived (X_4), workstation queue when the order arrived (X_5), and utilization rate of work station when the order arrived (X_6). Uses these six features to be the input variables of SOM, and SOM will produce output-processing elements similar to neighboring elements, which means that the cases in the same group would have similar connection weight.

Training Process

Step 2. Initial weights generation

Randomly generate the initial weights W_j^i of the $j-th$ feature in sub-group i.

Step 3. Case retrieving

This step would find out the most matching case from case base using similarity rule in order to predict the flow time for the new case. The similarity rule as follows:

$$S_{mn} = Dis\left(C_m^i, C_n^i\right), \ \forall n \neq m \tag{1}$$

S_{mn} is the similarity degree between case m (C_m^i) and n (C_n^i) in group i. And $Dis(\ )$ is the distance between two cases, $Dis(\ )$ is compute as:

$$Dis\left(C_m^i, C_n^i\right) = \sqrt{\sum_f W_j^i \left(F_f^m - F_f^n\right)^2} \tag{2}$$

where F_f^m means the value of the $f-th$ feature of case m. Thus, $Dis(C_m^i, C_n^i)$ computes the summarized weighted distance between case m and n.

Step 4. Case reusing

After the steps above, KNN is added to gain more matching cases to forecast the flow time of case. For example, when $k = 5$ in the sub-group, the forecast flow time of new case is determined by the 5 best matching cases. And the parameter k of each sub-group is generated by trail-and-error separately.

Step 5. Error computing

Root of mean square error (RMSE) is adopted to be the performance measure in this research.

$$RMSE = \sqrt{\frac{\sum_{l=1}^{N}\left(forecasted\ value - real\ value\right)^2}{N}} \tag{3}$$

where, N is the total number of case in the sub-group.

Table 1. Parameters settings in GA

Parameters	Setting
Selection	Binary tournament
Crossover	Single point crossover
Crossover rate	0.85
Mutation	Swap mutation
Mutation rate	0.1
Reproduction	Elitism strategy
Population size	30
Stopping criteria	1000

Step 6. Weights revising by GA

Uses GA approach to find the optimal weight for each feature in the sub-group. Some parameters setting of GA are list in following:

Step 7. Cases and weights retaining

The best weight combination of each sub-group is retained for the further testing process.

Testing Process

Step 8. New testing case retrieving

The same as process above, similarity rule is used to compute the similarity of cases.

Step 9. New testing case reusing

Find the most k similar cases of new case.

Step 10. Forecasted flow time generating

Forecast the flow time of new case from k similar cases.

5 Experimental Results

5.1 Data Clustered by SOM

The main purpose of data clustering is to reduce the effect of data noise. As mentioned previously, SOM is applied to cluster the data in this study. The cluster results diagram can be found in figure 5, which shows the results of two and three clusters for 240 data. The number of clusters might influence the forecasting result; therefore, the number of clusters will be discussed in the next sub-section.

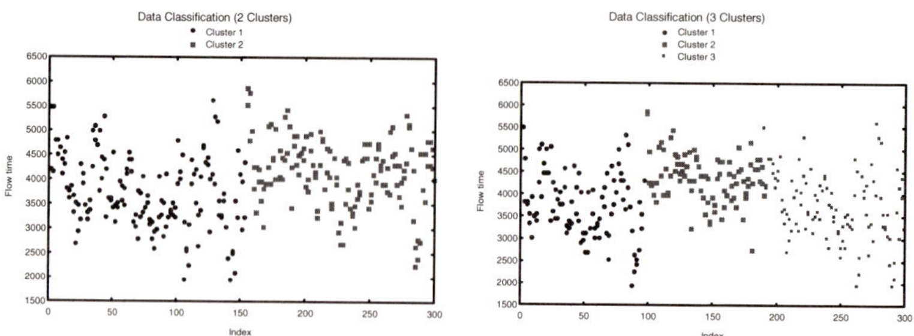

Fig. 5. The two and three clustered results by using SOM

5.2 SGA-CBR with Different Clusters

Forecast results under different number of cluster are shown in figure 6. By observing the figure 6, when the cluster number is increasing, the forecasting and real data will be more matched. Furthermore, according to the Mean Absolute Percentage Error (MAPE) and RMSE, figure 7 shows the performance of different number of clusters.

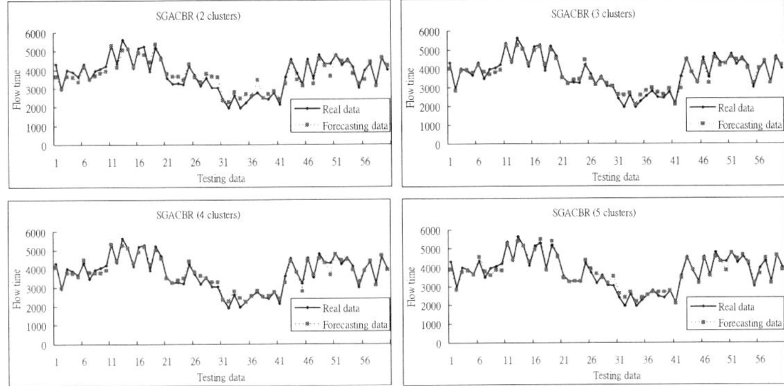

Fig. 6. SGACBR with different number of cluster

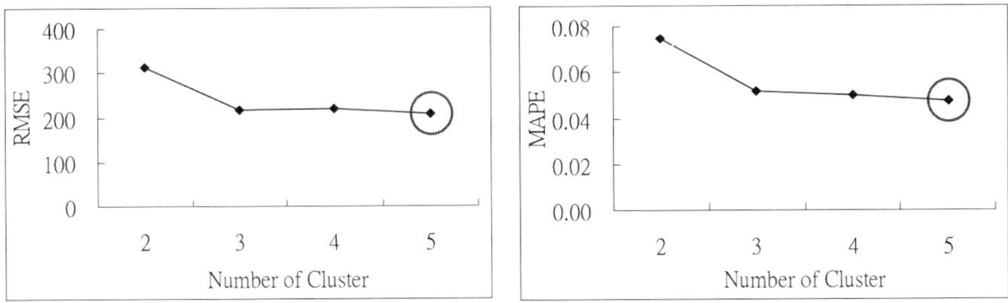

Fig. 7. The convergence chart of MAPE and RMSE from different number of cluster

Table 2. Parameters settings in GA

Number of Cluster	2	3	4	5
MAPE	7.44 %	5.18 %	5.01 %	4.73 %
RMSE	312.5231	218.3532	218.6860	208.2776

We chose 5 clusters as the number of sub-groups in the research. As shown in Table 2, we can find that when the number of clusters is large than 3, the accuracy of forecasting will converge, and it has no obviously improvement when using large number of clusters. Therefore, further cluster number will stop to test.

5.3 Comparison with Other Methodology

Other forecasting methodologies are compared with SGA-CBR in this research, such as general CBR, Back-propagation neural network (BPN), GA and fuzzy rule based method (GA&WM), GA and CBR hybrid method (GA-CBR), and Fuzzy rule based

SOM method (SOM&WM). The detail of these methods can refer to the previous research [3], [4], and [6].

By observing table 3, SGA-CBR proposed in this research performs superior to other methods that performed well in the previous research. The reason why SGA-CBR of this research outperforms others is because GA can fine-tune the weights. CBR is one of the famous forecasting methods while resolving this kind of forecasting problem with multiple features considering. By adopting the Euclidean distance to retrieve the similar cases, CBR is an effective and efficient method. Otherwise, in the real world, each feature may play a different important role. It means we should take different importance of each feature into consideration; thus, we use GA to search the best weights combination of features in our CBR process.

Table 3. Parameters settings in GA

Methodology	RMSE	Improving rate
CBR	538	-
BPN	480	10.78%
GA&WM	479	10.97%
GA-CBR	391	27.32%
SOM&WM	320	40.52%
SGA-CBR	208	61.34%

In the comparative study, the overall average RMSE of SGA-CBR is 208, the overall average RMSE of other methods can be found in table 3. Hence the results of our limited comparative studies show that the proposed SGA-CBR method produces the lowest RMSE value.

6 Conclusion

The experimental results in section 5 demonstrate the effectiveness of the SGA-CBR that is superior to other effective approaches. In summary, this research has the following important contribution in the flow time prediction area and these contributions might be interested to other academic researchers and industrial engineers and managers:

No matter what kind of data, some noise may influence the forecasting result a lot. In the recent research, data preprocessing seems to be more and more important. After the numerical testing of this study, data pre-clustering is a better way to increase the forecasting accuracy. As shown in table 3, the methods with SOM clustering (SOM&WM, and SGA-CBR) perform better than other method without data classifier.

This research compared some well forecasting methods; RMSE was the performance measure index. SGA-CBR proposed in this research was the best one with the minimum RMSE.

This research discussed how to integrate the SOM and GA-CBR approaches to construct a hybrid system of flow time prediction. It can help industrial managers to make a better project scheduling or some other forecasting matters.

References

1. Brill, F.Z., Brown, D.E., Martin, W.N.: Fast Genetic Selection of Features for Neural Network Classifiers. IEEE Transactions on Neural Networks, Vol. 32. (1992) 324-328
2. Chang, P.C., Hsieh, J.C.: A Neural Networks Approach for Due Date Assignment in A Wafer Fabrication Factory. Int. J. Ind. Eng., Vol. 10. (2003) 55-61
3. Chang, P.C., Hsieh, J.C., Liao T.W.: Evolving Fuzzy Rules for Due-Date Assignment Problem in Semiconductor Manufacturing Factory. Journal of Intelligent Manufacturing, Vol. 16. 5 (2005) 549-557
4. Chang, P.C., Liao, T.W.: Combing SOM and Fuzzy Rule Base for Flow Time Prediction in Semiconductor Manufacturing Factory. Applied Soft Computing, Vol. 6. (2006) 198-206
5. Chiu C.C.: A Case-based Customer Classification Approach for Direct Marketing. Expert Systems with Applications, Vol. 22. (2002) 163-168
6. Chiu, C.C., Chang, P.C., Chiu, N.H.: A Case-based Expert Support System for Due Date Assignment in A Wafer Fabrication Factory. J. Intell. Manuf., Vol. 14. (2003) 287-296
7. Finnie, G.R., Witting, G.E.: Estimating Software Development Effort with Case-Based Reasoning. Lecture Notes in Computer Science, Vol. 1266. Springer-Verlag, Berlin Heidelberg New York (1995) 13-22
8. Jo, H., Han, I., Lee, H.: Bankruptcy Prediction Using Case-Based Reasoning, Neural Networks and Discriminant Analysis. Expert Systems and Applications, Vol. 13. (1997) 97-108.
9. Kim, K., Han, I.: Maintaining Case-based Reasoning Systems Using A Genetic Algorithms Approach. Expert Systems with Applications, Vol. 21. (2001) 139-145
10. Kim, S.H., Shin, S.W.: Identifying the Impact of Decision Variables for Nonlinear Classification Tasks. Expert Systems with Applications, Vol. 18. (2000) 201-214
11. Kolodner, J.L.: An Introduction to Case-Based Reasoning. Artificial Intelligence Review, Vol. 6. (1992) 3-34
12. Liao, T.W., Zhang, Z.M., Mount, C.R.: A Case-Based Reasoning System for Identifying Failure Mechanisms. Engineering Applications of Artificial Intelligence, Vol. 13. (2000) 199-213
13. Louis, S.J., Xu, Z.: Genetic Algorithms for Open Shop Scheduling and Re-Scheduling. In Proceedings of the ISCA 11th International Conference on Computers and Their Applications. (1996) 99-102
14. Ramsey, C., Grefensttete, J.: Case-based Initialization of Genetic Algorithms. Proceeding of the Fifth International Conference on Genetic Algorithms, San Mateo, California (1993)
15. Shin, K., Han, I.: Case-Based Reasoning Supported by Genetic Algorithms for Corporate Bond Rating. Expert Systems with Applications, Vol. 16. (1999) 85-95
16. Siedlecki, W., Sklansky, J.: A Note on Genetic Algorithms for Large-Scale Feature Selection. Pattern Recognition Letters, Vol. 10. (1989) 335-347
17. Watson, I., Gardingen, D.: A Distributed Cased-Based Reasoning Application for Engineering Sales Support. In Proc. 16th Int. Joint Conf. on Artificial Intelligence, Vol. 1. (1999) 600-605
18. Watson, I., Watson, H.: CAIRN: A Case-Based Document Retrieval System. In Proc. of the 3rd United Kingdom Case-Based Reasoning Wrokshop, University of Manchester, Filer, N & Watson, I (Eds). (1997)

Developing Intelligent Applications in Social E-Mail Networks

Wenbin Li[1,5], Ning Zhong[1,2], Y.Y. Yao[1,3], Jiming Liu[1,4], and Chunnian Liu[1]

[1] The International WIC Institute, Beijing University of Technology
Beijing 100022, China
[2] Dept. of Information Engineering, Maebashi Institute of Technology
460-1 Kamisadori-Cho, Maebashi-City 371-0816, Japan
[3] Department of Computer Science, University of Regina
Regina, Saskatchewan, Canada S4S 0A2
[4] School of Computer Science, University of Windsor
Windsor, Ontario, Canada N9B 3P4
[5] Shijiazhuang University of Economics, Shijiazhuang 050031, China

Abstract. Both complex network and Web Intelligence (WI) are novel and promising research fields. This paper primarily discusses how to develop intelligent applications in social e-mail networks (SENs) with WI-related techniques. It gives a common architecture and discusses some important issues such as creating SENs automatically and SEN analysis for developing such applications. Also, this paper describes a full process of implementing an application via studying an illustrative example.

1 Introduction

E-mail has become a pervasive communication means in the information society. As an asynchronous and efficient way of communication between human and human, human and machine, or machine and machine, it now pervades business, social and technical exchanges. In a group, an enterprise, or the whole world, e-mail communication relationship results in a social network. Hence, e-mail is a highly relevant area for research on communities and social networks [5].

Just as a computer network consists of computers and their connections, a social e-mail network (SEN) consists of e-mail users and e-mails which logically connect users. In our view, although a SEN is a logical network, if we design each node in the SEN as an agent and view e-mails as the soft communication media between them, we can implement similar intelligent applications with that on the computer networks. Our perspective motivates us to study how to develop such applications and the infrastructure.

This paper gives a systematic investigation about SEN by surveying related work. And, it describes the mechanism of implementing intelligent applications in SENs, and provides an illustrative example. Especially, how e-mail social networks meets WI (Web Intelligence) [8,9] is the keystone in this work, because developing social intelligence is one of ultimate goals of WI research [8].

S. Greco et al. (Eds.): RSCTC 2006, LNAI 4259, pp. 776–785, 2006.

The rest of this paper is organized as follows. In Section 2, some related work is surveyed. Section 3 proposes the architecture for developing applications in SENs. Section 4 discusses the all-important task in our architecture, i.e., creating SENs automatically. In Section 5, we briefly introduce SEN analysis techniques that are important for many applications in SENs. Also, we describe the potential applications in SENs and provide an illustrative example in Section 6. Finally, Section 7 gives concluding remarks and future directions.

2   Related Work

The study of SEN has attracted much attention from communities of sociologists, computer scientists, physicists and so on. In our opinion, the existing research work can be categorized into four types: (1) mining in SENs, (2) anti-virus and anti-spam using SENs, (3) searching in SENs, and (4) studying the statistical properties of SENs. Below, we survey some of the related work.

P. Oscar, et al. show how to use an e-mail social network which is constructed solely *from sender and recipient information available in the e-mail headers* to distinguish "spam" and "legitimate" e-mails associated with his/her own circles of friends [10]. J. Golbeck, et al. present an e-mail scoring mechanism based on a social network augmented with reputation ratings [4]. Furthermore, they describe how to use this method to score and filter e-mails. In their work, the social network is built *from the user's own e-mail folders.* H. Ebel, et al. construct an e-mail social network *from server log files*, and show that the network exhibits a scale-free link distribution and pronounce small-world behavior [3]. A. Culotta, et al. design an end-to-end system extracting a user's social network. This system builds the social network *from the user's e-mail inbox*, and finds sender's information from the Web automatically [1]. M.E.J. Newman, et al. discuss e-mail networks and the spread of computer viruses [7]. They construct an e-mail network *according to address books gathered from a large university computer system* serving 27841 users. J.R. Tyler, et al. describe a methodology to identify the communities practice *from e-mail logs within an organization* [5]. This method is also available for identifying the leadership roles within the communities.

The main differences between the above work and this paper are that firstly, our work constructs dynamic SENs with automated techniques; Secondly, we focus on developing applications in SENs, just as on physical networks, and the infrastructure.

3   The Architecture of Applications in SENs

As mentioned above, SENs can be used for the tasks of anti-virus and anti-spam. In our view, the possible applications in SENs are not limited to such two tasks. On the one hand, SENs are a knowledge base which records users' name, relationship between users, even other background knowledge about users. And, in many occasions, knowledge is a necessary condition for implementing intelligent applications. The knowledge base denoted by the whole network facilitates the implementing process for automated applications in SENs. On the other hand, although SENs are logical networks, while when we provide the same infrastructure with physical networks such as media, protocols and so on, we can implement similar applications in SENs as on those physical networks.

Figure 1 gives a common architecture for the applications implemented in SENs. In this figure, **Operable E-mail** is a type of XML-based e-mail with maneuverability, which is defined by us. So-called maneuverability means that the Operable E-mail allows users enclose predefined commands that can be parsed and executed by agents in e-mail. We do not describe how to design Operable E-mail here because of the space limitation of this paper. Comparison with traditional e-mail, Operable E-mail is designed to take scripts of our language similar to KQML [6]. Agents distinguish such e-mails from the traditional ones by judging whether a specified field appears in an e-mail's header or not. When an agent receives an Operable E-mail from another agent, it will parse and execute the enclosed commands predefined by us. For example, if user A wants to download a file from B automatically. A should enclose the "download" command with the filename in an Operable E-mail and send it to B. When B's agent receives such a message, it will respond A automatically. In this way, B is released from some time-consuming work such as responding manually.

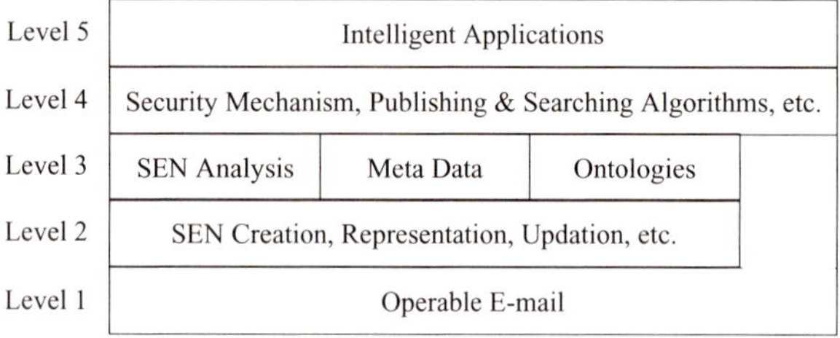

Fig. 1. The architecture of the applications in SENs

The second level in the architecture is to build, represent and update SENs. We will discuss these issues, respectively, in the next section in detail. In our solutions, both the processes of building and updating depend on exchanging information enclosed in Operable E-mails by agents. Thus, the Operable E-mail can be viewed as the soft communication media connecting all agents in a SEN. And the syntax and semantic transferred on such a media can be viewed as the communication protocols.

Media and protocols are other necessary conditions for implementing communication and applications in SENs, but they are not enough. As shown in Figure 1, in the level 3, Meta Data, Ontologies, SEN analysis are other conditions for our work. Meta Data denotes the description data for each node in a SEN. Ontologies provide the semantic support for the automated communication between agents. SEN analysis is the essential for many applications in SENs, as shown in Section 5. In the level 4, the security mechanism aims at providing a safe communication channel. The publishing/searching algorithms are used to push or pull information in SENs. With the support of the levels 1~4, we can implement intelligent applications in the level 5.

4 Constructing Dynamic SENs

For any research work in a SEN, the all-important task is to construct the SEN. Below, we discuss algorithms for building SENs.

4.1 Traditional Methods

For different research aims, researchers adopt different methods to build SENs. In general, the following methods can be used to construct SENs. They are (1) the method based on personal inboxes, (2) the method based on contact books, and (3) the method based on log files of one or multiple e-mail servers. The methods (1) and (2) are used to build personal SENs. While, the third one is used to construct larger SENs for a school, an enterprise or an office via tracking communication history of all users in their e-mail servers.

The main idea of the first method is as follows. Suppose that A is a user, he/she sends an e-mail to the user B, also "cc" (or "bcc") this message to the user C. Then, a network with three nodes (i.e. A, B, and C) can be built. And this network has two edges: $A \rightarrow C$ and $A \rightarrow B$. It is obvious that the scale of the network constructed by this method is limited.

The second method builds SENs based on the contact books stored in e-mail servers, whose process is briefly described as follows. Suppose that the user A records B in his/her book, furthermore, B records C in his/her book. Then, we can get a network with three nodes and two edges. These two edges are $A \rightarrow B$ and $B \rightarrow C$, respectively. However, the SENs cannot completely reflect the real relationship between users since many users do not use contact books.

The third method does not have the disadvantages as the above methods. Although different e-mail servers have the different style of log files, any kind of log files has the necessary information for the building task. Table 1 shows the style of Exchange 2003 log files. And Algorithm 1 gives the building algorithm based on such log files.

The aim of this work is to develop intelligent applications in SENs of one or multiple enterprises (even the whole world). However, from the above description, we can see that the traditional methods are not fit for our need. Thus, we will discuss the automated method for creating dynamic SENs in any range.

4.2 The Automated Method

In the range of one or multiple enterprises (even the whole world), the communication relationship between e-mail users denotes a social network which changes continually. In this network, new nodes and edges are added oftentimes. At the same time, some nodes disappear from the network because they did not

Table 1. The style of Exchange 2003 log files

No.	Field	No.	Field	No.	Field
1	Date	2	Time	3	client-ip
4	Client-hostname	5	Partner-Name	6	Server-hostname
7	server-IP	8	**Recipient-Address**	9	Event-ID
10	MSGID	11	Priority	12	Recipient-Report-Status
13	total-bytes	14	Number-Recipients	15	Origination-Time
16	Encryption	17	service-Version	18	Linked-MSGID
19	Message-Subject	20	**Sender-Address**		

Data: *log.* //*log* is a log file
Result: *matrix.* //for storing the SEN
initialize a hash table *ht*;
$matrix[][3] = 0$; $index = 0$;
while *NOT EOF(log)* **do**
    to read a line from *log*;
    x = Recipient-address; y = Sender-Address;
    if *str_contract(y, x) is not in ht* **then**
        $matrix[index][1] = y$; $matrix[index][2] = x$; $matrix[index][3] = 1$;
        ht.add(str_contact(y, x), $index$); $index$++;
    end
    else
        $temp = ht$.get(str_contact(y, x));
        $matrix[temp][3] + = 1$;
    end
end

Algorithm 1. Pseudocode for creating SENs from log files

contact other nodes for a long time. How to build such a dynamic SEN is the all-important task for our work, as shown in Figure 1. Below, we give a method for automatically creating SENs.

The main idea of our method is as follows. We design each e-mail client as an agent. It can monitor its owner's inbox and construct the personal SEN with the first traditional method described in Section 4.1. Then the enterprise SEN constituted by all users can be formed by that each agent exchanges its personal SEN under the support of a specified mechanism. Before describing the method in detail, we give some definitions at first.

Definition 1. *(**Single/Double Relationship**) Suppose that $send(x, y)$ is true if and only if the user x once sent e-mails to y, and $x \neq y$. Then, if $send(x, y) \wedge \sim send(y, x)$ is true, we call that the user x has a **single relationship** with y. If $send(x, y) \wedge send(y, x)$ is true, then the user x has a double relationship with y.*

Definition 2. *(**Stranger**) If the user x has a **single relationship** with another user y, we call that x is a **stranger** of y, denoted by $stranger(y, x)$.*

Definition 3. *(Direct Friend) If the user x has a **double relationship** with another user y, we call that x is a **direct friend** of y, denoted by $friend_1(x, y)$.*

Based on the above definitions, a SEN can be represented by some Prolog [2] facts and rules. For example, the SEN shown in Figure 2(a) can be denoted by the following facts: $user(A)$; $user(B)$; $user(C)$; $user(D)$; $stranger(B, A)$; $stranger(D, A)$; $stranger(B, C)$; $friend_1(B, D)$; $friend_1(C, D)$; $friend_1(x, y)$: $-friend_1(y, x)$.

Below, we describe the creating process of the SEN shown in Figure 2(a) to illustrate our automated method. At the beginning, the Prolog fact databases respectively maintained by the agents of users A, B, C and D are null. Some days later, the agent of A will know that A has a **single relationship** with B as well as D. That is, this agent has the following facts: $user(A)$; $user(B)$; $user(D)$; $stranger(D, A)$, $stranger(B, A)$. Similarly, the agent of B will know below Prolog facts: $user(A)$; $user(B)$; $user(C)$; $user(D)$; $stranger(B, A)$; $stranger(B, C)$; $friend_1(B, D)$. At the same time, the agents of C and D will create their fact databases.

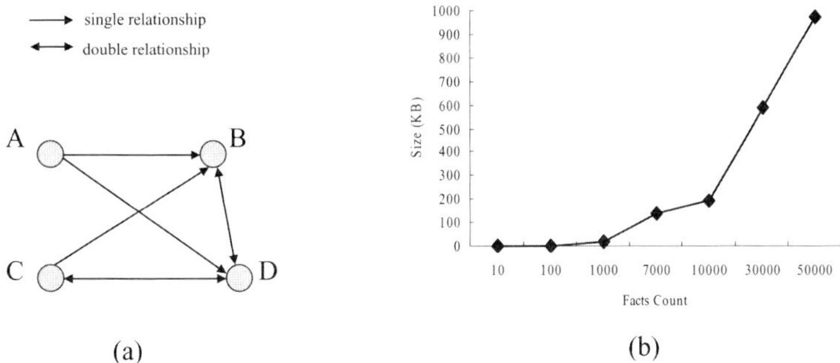

Fig. 2. A SEN and the space complexity for storing SENs

Here, the count of facts added in the database of A's agent is 5. The agents of B, C and D get 7, 5, 7 new facts, respectively. When the count of the changed facts of an agent is larger than a pre-given threshold, the agent will enclosed these facts into an Operable E-mail, and then sent this e-mail to its **direct friends** to update their local SENs. In the above example, suppose that the threshold is 6. Then, the agents of B and D will send their new facts to other agents. Concretely, B's agent will send an Operable E-mail to D's, and the agent of D will send a message with the new facts to B's and C's. After that, the agents of B, C and D will create the full SEN as shown in Figure 2(a). Furthermore, all agents continue to track users' inboxes to catch the new changes. When the changes are accumulated to the exchanging degree, the new facts will be promulgated in the SEN. In this way, all agents maintain a dynamic SEN.

However, we still do not answer some important questions with respect to our method, such as how to control the updating frequency and network flux, as well as the space complexity for storing SENs.

As mentioned above, the updating process is implemented via sending Operable E-mails. It is obvious that too many messages will affect the bandwidth of the networks, also will overload the e-mail servers. Thus, we should control the updating frequency as possible as we can to reduce the times of sending Operable E-mails. In order to do that, we suggest some measures below. Firstly, we should set an appropriate updating threshold. Secondly, we can adopt the selective broadcast method. That is, an agent selects some **direct friends** while not the all to send the updating information. The received nodes can be selected randomly. Or, we can select the nodes with a higher out-degree (see Definition 4) as the received nodes. Thirdly, we should adopt an accumulative method to update. For example, in the SEN shown in Figure 2(a), when C's agent received an updating information from the agent of B, it will inform its **direct friends** this information with that changed in its side. Fourthly, each fact waited to be updated has the information of *hops* and *source node*. When the hops of the fact is greater than a threshold, the fact will be not sent anymore. In addition, any fact will not be sent back to the source node.

Besides the updating frequency, the space complexity is another factor affecting the bandwidth of the networks. Figure 2(b) shows us the relationship between the count of facts and the needed disk space. From that figure, we can see that the space complexity is in our acceptable range even the changed records are very large.

5   SEN Analysis

SEN analysis is an important component for supporting intelligent applications, as shown in Figure 1. Many applications are based on the analysis techniques. So-called SEN analysis is to analyze the statistical properties of a SEN, such as in/out-degree, degree distribution, clustering coefficient and so on.

H. Ebel, et al. use the third traditional method (see Section 4.1) to build a SEN. They report that networks composed of persons connected by exchanged e-mails show both the characteristics of small-world networks and scale-free networks [3]. Scale-free networks are characterized by a power-law distribution of a node's degree (see Definition 5) and dynamics of the network are strongly affected by nodes with a great number of connections. The characteristics of the small-world property are as follows: (1) a high probability that two neighbors of one node are connected themselves, and (2) a small average length of the shortest path between two nodes. Furthermore, H. Ebel et al. claim that the scale-free nature of the e-mail network strongly eases persistence and propagation of e-mail viruses but also points to effective countermeasures. P. Oscar, et al. provide an anti-spam method based on clustering coefficient analysis (see Definition 6) [10]. Also, there are open research issues based on SENs analysis.

Definition 4. *(In/Out-Degree), $D_{in}(x)$ The in-degree of a node x is defined as $|\ \{\ y\ |\ send(y,x)\ \}|$. The out-degree of the node x is $|\ \{\ x\ |\ send(x,y)\ \}|$. Here, y is another node.*

Definition 5. *(In-Degree Distribution)* *The degree distribution is the rule that the probability $p(k)$ of the node with k in-degree changes with k. Here, $k >= 0$. Similarly, we can define out-degree distribution.*

Definition 6. *(The "Clustering Coefficient" of an node x, $C(x)$)* *For simplification, we discuss it on undirected SENs. $C(x) = \frac{2E_x}{D(x)(D(x)-1)}$, where E_x is the sum of degree of all nodes which have single or double relationship with x, and $D(x)$ the degree of x.*

6   Developing Applications in SENs

6.1   The Potential Applications in SENs

Although a SEN is a *logical network*, just as we can implement many applications on a *physical network*, we can develop many functions on the SEN. However, the SEN should possess the similar conditions (see Figure 1) with the physical network. This subsection enumerates some potential (but not limited to) intelligent applications in SENs.

Auction/Giveaway: Suppose that user A wants to sell his saloon car that he does not use, and other strangers B, C and D want to buy such a car. A, B, C and D tell their agents what they want via writing an operable e-mail. Then, A's agent will promulgate his owner's information on its SEN, at the same time, agents of B, C and D will search in the SEN. After they "meet" in this virtual network, they will transparently negotiate with the protocols of the SEN. At last, A, B, C, and D will receive the round-table result respectively reported by their agents.

Information Dissemination/Subscription: In the simplest case, suppose that you subscribe your interested information in a SEN via Operable E-mail. With suitable supporting semantic, your agent will automatically (1) find all corresponding nodes which publish information, (2) match subscription in the SEN, and (3) track changes and find new dissemination nodes in the SEN, and so on.

Asynchronous Sharing: Suppose that A, B, C, D, ... are members of a task group. A is the manager, and he/she is often asked to send attachments relative to a task by the group members. He/She is tired of the frequent interruption. Hence, A wants to share a folder in which all files concerned about the task are stored, then B, C, D, ... can fetch files they need. However, B, C, D, ... can only communicate with A by e-mails, that is to say, they cannot access the sharing folder in the current network environment with a traditional way. It is fortunate that A can share those files in his/her SEN. The imaginary process of sharing files in the SEN consists of (1) A tells his/her agent what files are shared, who can access them in the SEN, and permissions for those users, (2) B, C, D ... write an operable e-mail to ask A's agent what they can download or upload, (3) A's agent returns information about what B, C, D can download, (4) B, C, D ... write another Operable E-mail to A's agent to download the needed files, (5) A's agent responds B, C, D ... automatically.

Anti-Spam and Anti-Virus: Nodes of spam makers in a SEN always have distinct characteristics, e.g., they have lower clustering coefficient [10,3]. Hence, we believe that the global SEN is very promising for anti-spam and anti-virus tasks.

6.2   An Illustrative Example

This section illustrates the process of implementing intelligent applications on the SEN created in the whole world by depicting a case in details.

Definition 7. (The ith level friend, $friend_i$) *Suppose that the user A has a node x in a SEN, and B has y, where $B \neq A$. If the length of the shortest path between x and y is i ($i>1$), then we call that A is B's i^{th} level friend (or B is A's). We use $friend_i(A, B)$ to denote that.*

Suppose that A is a user whose agent is a. The user A wants to publish a piece of information to sell a car on the global SEN, and he only wants to sell it to the users from the set $S_1 = \{x \mid friend_i(x, A), 1=<i<=3\}$. Another user B wants to buy a car, and he/she only wants to buy it from the users from the set $S_2 = \{y \mid friend_i(y, B), 1=<i<=2\}$. In tradition, A registers his/her information in some sites δ. B searches selling data in sites γ. This way has following disadvantages: (1) if $\delta \cap \gamma = \emptyset$, A cannot sell his/her car to a potential buyer B. (2) the traditional way cannot contain A and B's demands. (3) A and B should deal with everything by hand, for example, register, find, and negotiate with each other etc. However, all these problems can be solved on the global SEN.

For simplicity, we suppose that $S_1=\{B, C, D\}$, and the agents of B, C and D are b, c, and d, respectively. We can adopt "push" or "pull" way to implement such an application.

When the first way is used. a encloses the selling information input by A into an Operable E-mail, and obtains the set S_1 according to its global SEN. Then, a sends this e-mail to the inboxes of the users in S_1. When b, c and d receive that e-mail, they will parse the content in it automatically. As mentioned above, only B wants to buy a car. Hence, b will negotiate with a automatically, and return the round-table result to A and B.

When we adopt the "pull" solution. b will enclose the buying information input by b into an Operable E-mail with "Query" command at first. Secondly, b obtains the S_2 from its global SEN. Then, b sends the e-mail to the inbox of each user in S_2. When any agent of a user in S_2 receives that e-mail, it will parse the Operable E-mail automatically. In S_2, only A wants to sell a car. Hence, in the next step, b will negotiate with a without the intervention of their users. In the end, a and b will report the result to their owner respectively.

Both the "pull" and "push" solutions generate some Operable E-mails. As a result, the e-mail servers may suffer from these e-mails. To solve this problem, we can let agents delete these e-mails after dealing with them.

7   Concluding Remarks

In the paper, we mainly describe the mechanism of implementing intelligent applications in SENs. We attempt to provide a more complete picture of what SENs can do and how to do, as well as to show that developing automated and novel applications in SENs is an important issue in WI research. Still, many issues are not discussed in this paper, such as how to protect the privacy for users, how the agents negotiate automatically, how to store the publishing information and so on. All these problems will be studied in our future work.

Acknowledgments

This work is partially supported by the NSFC major research program: "Basic Theory and Core Techniques of Non-Canonical Knowledge" (60496322), the Open Foundation of Beijing Municipal Key Laboratory of Multimedia and Intelligent Software Technology, the Project (06213558) of Dept. of Science and Technology of Hebei Province, and the Project (Y200606) of Shijiazhuang University of Economics.

References

1. A. Culotta, R. Bekkerman, A. McCallum.: Extracting Social Networks and Contact Information from Email and the Web. In: Proceedings of the First Conference on Email and Anti-Spam, (2004).
2. C.N. Liu, D.H. Chao.: *Prolog: Its Applications and Implementation.* Science Press, Beijing, China, (1990).
3. H. Ebel, L.I. Mielsch, S. Bornholdt.: Scale-free Topology of E-mail Networks. *Phys. Rev. E* 66 (2002) 035103(R).
4. J. Golbeck, J. Hendler.: Reputation Network Analysis for Email Filtering. In: Proceedings of the First Conference on Email and Anti-Spam, (2004).
5. J.R. Tyler, D.M. Wilkinson, B.A. Huberman.: Email as Spectroscopy: Automated Discovery of Community Structure within Organizations. *Communities and Technologies* (2003) 81-96.
6. KQML. *http://www.cs.umbc.edu/kqml/*
7. M.E.J. Newman, S. Forrest, J. Balthrop.: Email Networks and the Spread of Computer Viruses. *Phys. Rev. E*, (2002), 66(035101).
8. N. Zhong, J.M. Liu, Y.Y. Yao (eds.).: *Web Intelligence.* Springer, (2003).
9. N. Zhong, J.M. Liu, Y.Y. Yao.: Envisioning Intelligent Information Technologies (iIT) from the Stand-Point of Web Intelligence (WI). *Communications of the ACM* (in press), (2006).
10. P.O. Boykin, V. Roychowdhury.: Personal Email Networks: An Effective Anti-Spam Tool. *IEEE Computer*, (2005) 38(4): 61-68.

Functional Extension of the RSDS System

Zbigniew Suraj[1,2] and Piotr Grochowalski[3]

[1] Chair of Computer Science, Rzeszow University, Poland
[2] Institute of Computer Science,
State School of Higher Education in Jaroslaw, Poland
[3] Institute of Mathematics, Rzeszow University, Poland
{zsuraj, piotrg}@univ.rzeszow.pl

Abstract. The aim of this work is to describe a way of using of the bibliographical database system and to present new functional possibilities regarding its research aspect as well. The system has been designed and created in order to facilitate the access to descriptions of publications and applications related to the rough set theory and its use. This system has been fitted up with basic possibilities of database use. There are also special extensions of basic possibilities in the system, in particular:

- new versions of an advanced searching,
- information about co-authors for every author in the system,
- a module of a graph – statistical analysis of the content of the system,
- a module of a classification of scientific publications according to a projected classifier,
- an interactive map of the world showing who and where in the world works on the development of the rough set theory and its applications.

Keywords: rough sets, data mining, knowledge discovery, pattern recognition, database systems.

1 Introduction

The system of bibliographical database called Rough Set Database System (the *RSDS* system, or in short: the system) has been designed and created in order to facilitate the access to descriptions of publications concerning the rough set theory and its applications. The access to the system is free and possible via http://www.rsds.wsiz.rzeszow.pl. According to the present version of the system, new bibliographical descriptions of publications have been added to the database, and the database has been verified regarding accuracy and excessiveness of the stored data. As a result of conducted operations the data stored in the system is reliable and in most cases they have abstracts and keywords added. At the moment there are over 3000 publications in the system that have been written by over 1600 authors. Descriptions of publications in the system are classed in accordance with 12 publication types (specified in the specification BibTeX), i.e., article, book, booklet, inbook, incollection, inproceedings, manual, mastersthesis, phdthesis, proceedings, techreport, unpublished. Functionality of

S. Greco et al. (Eds.): RSCTC 2006, LNAI 4259, pp. 786–795, 2006.

the created system is based on possibilities: adding, modifying, searching and data transforming (descriptions of publications) in the system. To simplify the maintenance of the system by users there were created separate sections (group of menu) that make possible to move around the whole system.

System user is able to login to it through *Login* section. For registered users there are given possibilities such as: inserting new data in the system using a special form, modifying inserted data, classifying publications in accordance with a designed classifier. All system users are able to gain information (bibliographical descriptions publications).

In the section called *Search* there are two kinds of searching possible: alphabetical and advanced. An advanced search allows to find bibliographic data according to criteria. After finding the searched data, the system is able to generate and download the text file including these data (in the format of plain text or BibTeX).

In the section called *Statistics* there are dynamically generated statistics, that describe system usage, data and their analysis.

In the system there are present information concerning the software connected with the rough sets and biographies of outstanding people working actively into the rough set domain.

The actual version of the system has been given new extensions which make it more functional. The basic possibilities of the system have been exactly described in publications [1,2,3].

This paper is organized as follows. Section 2 presents the way in which one can use new extensions added into the system. Section 3 is devoted to open questions and directions for future work. Conclusions are given in section 4.

2   Functional Extension of the System

2.1   Searching Data

In order to find descriptions of publications on a given subject one has to use the section *Search*. There are three versions of searching available in this section: alphabetical, advanced version 1, advanced version 2. The alphabetical searching contains the following options of searching: searching according to titles, authors, editors, conferences, journals and years of publishing. The option of searching according to authors has been extended and given new possibilities, i.e., information related to co-authors for a given author as well as the number of their common publications. If one wants to use this information he has to choose the alphabetical searching according to authors and then display the list of chosen authors whose names start with a particular letter of the alphabet. When the author is chosen from the list a user will see the list of the author's publications and above the publications one will see the list of all coauthors for that author together with the number of their common publications. After clicking the coauthor's name the list of his publications will be displayed.

The option of advanced searching version 1 has been extended on the list that contains particular authors, editors, journals, conferences and editors present in

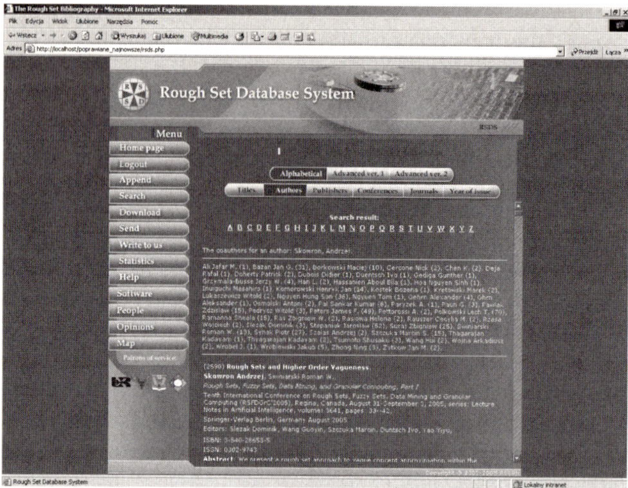

Fig. 1. The result of searching for publications (an alphabetical searching according to authors) with the list of co-authors for a given author

the system. These lists make it easier to search for data necessary to prepare conditions of searching. The lists have been equipped with the mechanism of "self-organizing", i.e., writing in the letters in the text field over the list will cause narrowing the data in the list to the data compatible with an introduced pattern. The option of advanced version 2 is a new option which at the moment finds information in the system and puts the results of searching into categories according to a designed classifier described in a section 2.4.

2.2   Statistics

This section which contains statistical information about the system has been rebuilt and given new possibilities:

- *Page 4* - includes information about what percent of all authors have written particular number of publications.
- *Page 5* - contains the analysis of data in the system with a division into defined time periods. We have assumed that such a period will be 5 years and therefore the periods are defined as follows: 1981-85, 1986-90,.... The designated factors allow to answer different questions concerning the development of the rough set theory and its applications. These factors are: the average number of authors for one piece of work, the average number of publications for one author, the number of publications with particular number of co-authors, the number of authors having a common publication etc.
- *Page 6* - contains the same analysis as page 5 with the only difference that we have used different time periods here, i.e., 1981-85, 1981-90,....

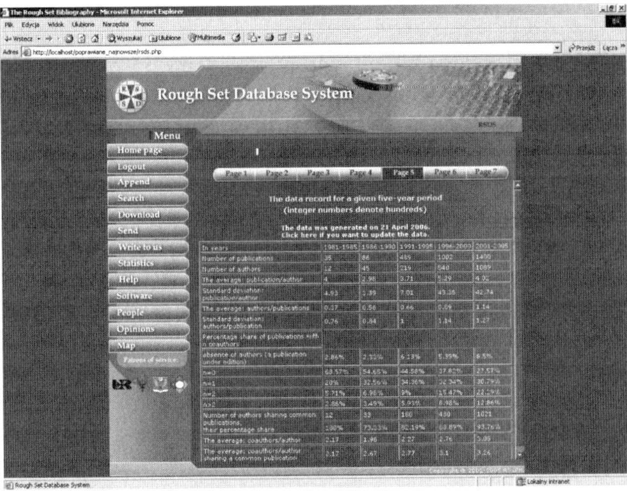

Fig. 2. The analysis of data in the system with a division into particular five-years (Page 5)

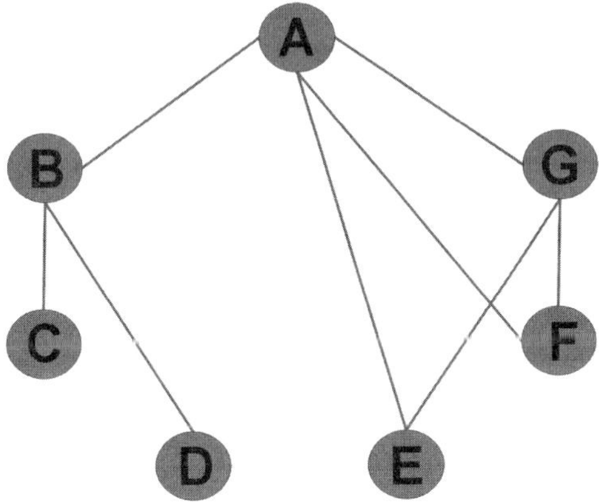

Fig. 3. An exemplary structure of a collaboration graph

- *Page 7* contains the analysis of the so-called *collaboration graph.* (The vertices of the graph are the authors in our database, and two vertices are joined by an edge if the two authors have published a joint paper.)

  An exemplary structure of the collaboration graph is presented in the Fig. 3, where the vertices at the graph were marked with the letters A,..., G.

The above statistics (except the analysis of the graph of collaboration) are generated dynamically, i.e., every change in the system carries the change of the attributed factors. A detailed analysis of the obtained results in generated statistics has been presented in the paper [4].

2.3   Interactive Map of the World

The possibilities of the system have been augmented about an interactive map of the world illustrating where in the world the rough set theory is being developed and used, as well as allowing for different kind of searching for information in the system.

The realized map has been divided into 4 main parts:

- the map of the world,
- maps of the continents,
- maps of the countries,
- information about chosen rough set research groups (people).

After the map has been started (a map section in the main menu of the system) the map of the world is displayed with a division into continents. In this part one can obtain information about: how many rough set research groups are there on a given continent and how many authors come from a given continent.

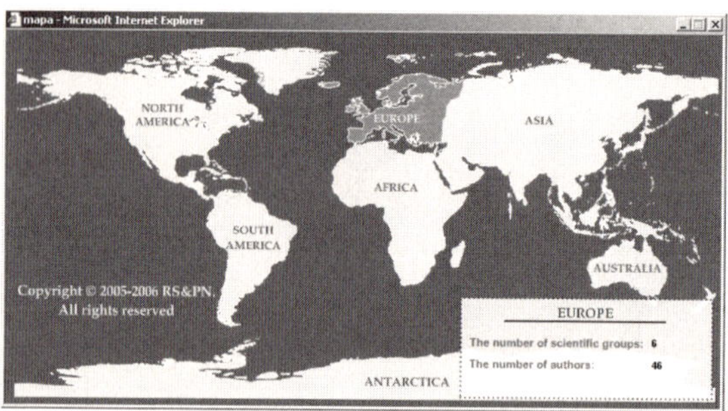

Fig. 4. An interactive map of the world - a map of the world (part 1)

After choosing the continent we go to a detailed map of the continent with the countries marked on it. In this part we can also obtain information about the number of rough set research groups and the number of authors depending on the country. In the top right-hand corner of the window there is a list of the countries where we can find people who deal with the rough sets. This is to facilitate navigation.

When we choose a particular country we can move to the map with the cities (research centers), where we can find research groups (people) working on the rough set theory and its applications.

After choosing the city we obtain information about the research groups in a given city and information who is the leader of the group. When we choose a particular group we will move to the part with information about this group:

- The name of the research group (if the group has WWW web site the name is a reference to this site).

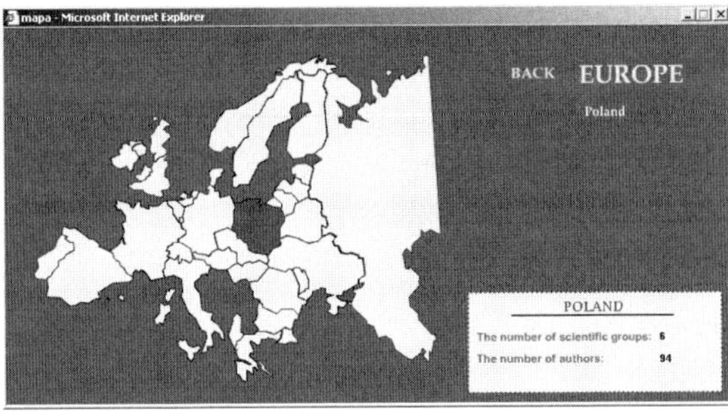

Fig. 5. An interactive map of the world - a map of particular continent (part 2)

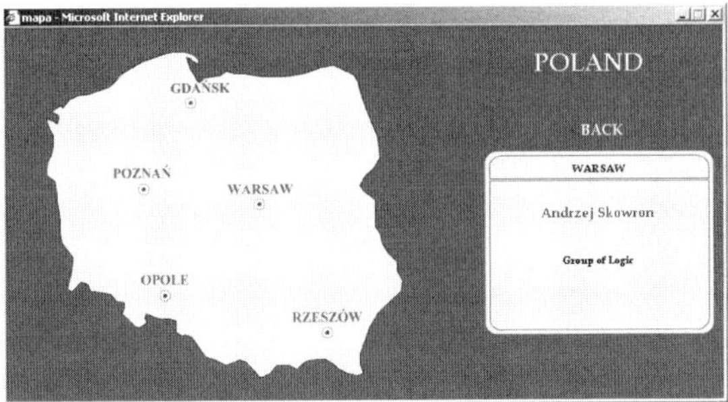

Fig. 6. An interactive map of the world - a map of a chosen country (part 3)

- The leader and members of the group (each name is a reference to the publication of a particular person in the system).
- E-mail address of a given person - an icon of an envelop (from this level, if we have the mail program configured in the system we can send an e-mail message to a given person).
- WWW web site of a person - an icon of a house (this icon symbolizes the WWW web site of a person and is a reference to this site).

The created map of the world can be also used to find descriptions of publications when we only have information about the origin of the author.

2.4 Classifier

In the system there has been defined a classifier according to which we can classify publications in the system. At present, in the system according to the option *Advanced version 2* when searching for information we use information about classification of publications in the system.

The classifier had been divided into 8 main groups which include subgroups describing the parent groups.

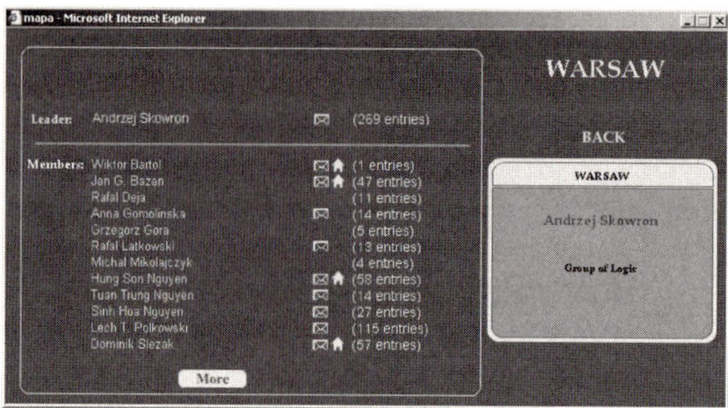

Fig. 7. An interactive map of the world - detailed information for a chosen scientific group (part 4)

Generally, the structure of the classifier looks as follows: In the classifier the main groups were marked with the letters A,..., H, while the subgroups with successive numbers 1,..., 48. The main groups have been prepared in order to describe all directions of the research over the rough sets and these are:

A. Foundations
B. Applications in
C. Methods
D. Methodology
E. Software systems
F. History
G. Didactics
H. Others

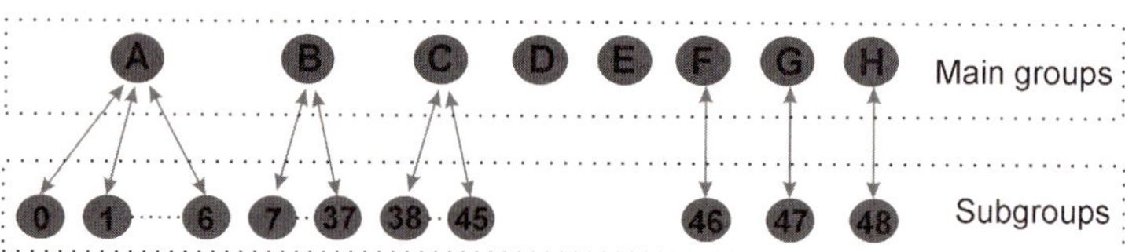

Fig. 8. A structure of a classifier

In order to start the option of classifying publications one has to log into the system. After logging in, the option of classifying is started and will be possible to use if a bibliographical description of a given publication will be displayed. After clicking on the link *Classify* again the description of publications will be displayed with the classifier below. In this classifier we can define to which group a given publication will be classified by means of marking particular groups. In order to avoid mistakes when marking sub-groups, automatically a parent group will be marked. If one wants to send a defined classification into the system, one has to press the button *Submit*. Before sending the classifier to the system it will be displayed in order to verify it in a simple form consisting of the name of the main group, designation of a sub-group or main group itself (if a given publication has been attributed to all sub-groups of the parent group), e.g. B, A.1, A.2–5. After pressing the button *Submit* the classifier will be sent into the system which will allow to use this information in the system, and it will also displayed with the description of a given publication. In case of an incorrect classification of a publication one will be able to classify it again and sending a new classification into the system will cause deleting the old one.

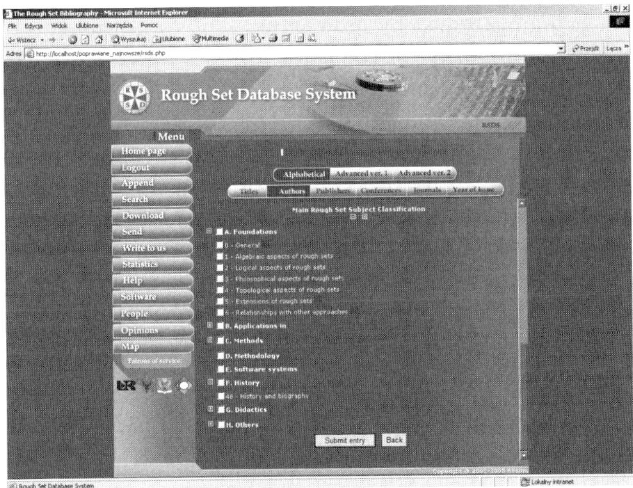

Fig. 9. The screenshot displaying the classification of a given publication

3   Open Questions and Directions for Future Work

Research problems connected with the system and considered by us can be divided into two groups:

1. studies related to the system functioning,
2. studies related to data analysis.

The first group contains research concerning "information search", search engine optimization service and search results grouping. Our studies over "information search" are based on constructing an intelligent searching information mechanism for our system, to generalize it later for other systems that store data. We want the mechanism to be based on semantic data analysis and defined ontology of concepts, to gain the most appropriate results in the process of searching. The studies described above can also be helpful in creating an intelligent searching facilitator for users.

In the system we have defined classifier used for publication classifying on account of contents included in them. Relying on it, it is possible to undertake studies connected with dividing the information thematic groups created on the basis of search results content analysis.

In the group of studies concerning data analysis we have undertaken research connected with statistical and graphical analysis of data included in the system. We conducted the statistical analysis in various time periods determining different statistical parameters which enabled us to detect some abnormalities that characterize the development of rough sets theory.

The graphical analysis is based on the defined graph C of cooperation analysis which enabled us to determine some of the social phenomenons that exist in environment being examined by us. Further studies in this group can be conducted relying on continuation of the same graph C of cooperation analysis by appointing some sub-graphs that describe cooperation of authors among various research directions over the defined sets methodology. During the next step of graph C analysis searching for answers for the following items appears: searching for the differences between groups of the rough sets researchers, the extend of works of a particular person in the first period of his/her research work (taken into consideration a defined initial period) constitutes ground for his/her further research, what are the differences between defined cooperation patterns among scientists depending on the type of academy (institution) or their different decent. Another graph type that can be constructed and analyzed is bipartite graph B, which means that the vertices of the first type are papers and the vertices of the second type are the names of their authors, and the edge joins particular paper with its author. During such graph analysis many questions can be raised such as: the number of papers written by particular authors, etc.

4   Conclusions

The extensions added into the system cause that it turns from an ordinary bibliographical data base into a complex system which can not only store information about scientific publications but also it can analyze stored information - which may be recognized as the origin of an "intelligent system of processing information". On the basis of these extensions we will be trying to develop an intelligent part of the system.

On the basis of a graph-statistical analysis of the content of the system one can come to interesting conclusions about the development of the rough sets methodology as well as a co-operation between the authors of scientific publications in this field. An interactive map of the world in an innovative element in processing information in data base systems and it allows to search for information (which has been described in the work). A module of a classification of publications is the beginning of an intelligent mechanism of adding and finding information in the system.

Acknowledgment. We would like to thank the anonymous referees for critical remarks and useful suggestions to improve the presentation of the paper. We wish also to thank our colleagues from the Research Group on Rough Sets and Petri

Nets for their helpful comments as well as for help in creating the *RSDS* system. The research has been partially supported by the grant 3 T11C 005 28 from the Ministry of Scientific Research and Information Technology of the Republic of Poland.

References

1. Suraj, Z., Grochowalski, P. : The Rough Sets Database System: An Overview, *Bulletin of International Rough Set Society*, Vol. 7, No. 1, 2003, Shimane, Japan, pp. 75-81.
2. Suraj, Z., Grochowalski, P.: The Rough Sets Database System: An Overview, in: *Proc. 4th International Conference on Rough Sets and Current Trends in Computing 2004*, Uppsala, Sweden, Lecture Notes in Artifical Intelligent, Springer-Verlag, Heidelberg 2004, pp. 841-849.
3. Suraj, Z., Grochowalski, P.: The Rough Set Database System: An Overview, in: Peters, J.F., Skowron, A., *Transactions on Rough Sets III*, Lecture Notes in Computer Science 3400, Springer-Verlag, Berlin 2005, pp. 190-201.
4. Suraj, Z., Grochowalski, P.: Patterns of Collaborations in Rough Set Research (submitted to International Symposium on Fuzzy and Rough Sets, ISFUROS 2006, Santa Clara, Cuba, 2006).

Hybrid Music Filtering for Recommendation Based Ubiquitous Computing Environment

Jong-Hun Kim[1], Kyung-Yong Jung[2], and Jung-Hyun Lee [1]

[1] Department of Computer Science & Engineering Inha University
Yonghyun-Dong, Nam-Gu, Incheon, Korea
`jhkim@hci.inha.ac.kr, jhlee@inha.ac.kr`
[2] School of Computer Information Engineering, Sangji University, Korea
`kyjung@sangji.ac.kr`

Abstract. Existing studies on music recommendation systems pose the problem of being incapable of proposing proper recommendations according to user conditions due to limited metadata obtained from users using a content-based filtering method. Although some studies have been conducted in recent years on recommendation systems employing a great amount of environmental information, they have been unable to satisfy information requested by the user. Thus, this study defines context information required to select music and proposes a hybrid filtering method that exploits a content-based filtering and collaborative filtering method in ubiquitous environments. In addition, this study developed a music recommendation system based on these filtering methods which significantly improved user satisfaction for music selection.

Keywords: Content-based Filtering, Collaborative Filtering, Ubiquitous Computing, Recommendation System.

1 Introduction

A ubiquitous computing environment is a world that obtains required information without restrictions to time and location by connecting a large number of intelligent computers to various wire and wireless networks. Within this ubiquitous environment, it is easy to listen to music regardless of location using a variety of devices. Furthermore, the necessity for a service that recommends appropriate music requested by users has increased because users cannot afford to investigate every file among such a vast number of music files.

A music search system that only provides the results of queries by rank using music information in a web environment. Although a music search system has the advantage of being easily implemented, it may produce unwanted worthless information due to the exclusion of a user's interests and becomes a reason for a decrease in user satisfaction. In recent years, a recommendation system has been actively studied that predicts and recommends only information requested by a user. Music recommendation systems currently exist on the Web in which users can share and recommend music using their own ID despite possessing no music data. Professional music portal sites in Korea, such as Bugs Music, provide various recommendation services according to the period, age, and theme. Moreover, a large

S. Greco et al. (Eds.): RSCTC 2006, LNAI 4259, pp. 796–805, 2006.

number of overseas users have joined last.fm and have enjoyed the personalized music-broadcasting program using profiles collected by an audioscrobbler. These systems allow users to recommend music from a vast amount of music data.

In this recommendation system, the similarity between the content of an item and user information was measured to recommend information desired by the user, and a content-based filtering method that based the rank on this measurement was also used. However, the recommendation of multimedia data is still limited[1] and is not highly reliable due to filtering only being based on static information. In particular, with a music recommendation system in the present web service environment, it is difficult to exactly recommend music that is desired by users because real-time context information like weather significantly affects a user's music selection.

Thus, this paper proposes a hybrid music filtering method that applies a statistics-based content-based filtering and collaborative filtering method in order to recommend music in a ubiquitous environment. In order to apply context information to a content-based filtering, data regarded as a factor in music selection was configured as context information and was based on ontology. In addition, data obtained using various sensors and an Radio Frequency Identification (RFID) Tag based on Open Service Gateway Initiative (OSGi) could be recognized as exact context information through an ontology database and inference engine. Recognized context information will be used in a hybrid music filtering process and service a recommendation according to high user preference. Collaborative filtering can be used to rate music lists recommended by a content-based filtering method according to user preferences.

A Hybrid Music Recommendation System (HMRS) was developed to evaluate this filtering method. The system used in this study consisted of three large sections; a Context Manager section, Service Manager section, and Music Recommendation Manager section.

2 Hybrid Music Filtering Using Context Information

This system defines contexts to recommend music by considering surrounding contexts and user information and configures a music list using a content-based filtering and collaborative filtering. The initial profile of content-based filtering can be updated using the music title selected by users and the context information recognized in an OSGi environment in a music service. This profile is statistically analyzed and recommends a music list that corresponds to the context information from the Music Content Information Database (MCIDB) when a user inquires about a music service. The collaborative filtering method used for recommendation employed a Music Content Information Database and Rating DB. Based on the preference for a neighbored item with similar preferences, the priority of recommended music was altered to employ a content-based filtering method by estimating the preference of the item by new users.

2.1 Configuration and Definition of Context Information

Brown's definition[2] is an accurate method to develop application services, used to configure and determine proper context for a music recommendation service in this system.

This system determines the following factors which affect music selection: user sex, age, temperature, and weather before the configuration and determination of context.

The configuration of context information for HMRS consists of user information (sex, age), weather, and outdoor temperature. In addition, user location information in the home is configured as context information. This allows a music recommendation service to employ certain applications regardless of the user's location in the home.

Table 1 presents the definition of context information as different spaces, such as class 5 for age, class 4 for temperature, class 7 for weather, and class 6 for location information. The service area is limited to homes, and the users' location is limited to the Balcony, Bathroom, Bedroom, Guestroom, Kitchen, and Living-room.

Table 1. Configuration and Definition of Context Information

Sex	Age		Weather	Temperature		Location
class	num.	class	class	F°	class	class
MA-LE	0~7	Infant	Clear, Sunny, Cloudy, Shower, Rain, Snow, Storm	-4~30.2	Cold	Balcony, Bathroom, Bedroom, Guestroom, Kitchen, Living-room
	8~19	Child		32~68	Cool	
	20~35	Young Adult		69.8~86	Warm	
FEM-ALE	36~50	Adult		87.8~	Hot	
	51~	Old Adult				

This system was implemented the ubiquitous network based on an OSGi framework in order to acquire automatic sensing datas. User information, temperature, and location information can be input from sensors based on OSGi framwork. User sex, age, and location information can be traced using an RFID Tag which is attached to a user's watch, and temperature information can be obtained from a temperature sensor through real-time Zigbee communication. However, although weather information is predefined as ontology, its data can be established as a database retrieved from the Internet.

The context of HMRS based on the context information used in this study is defined as Web Ontology Language (OWL) that is used on a Semantic Web in order to configure and express exact contexts and various relationships.

2.2   Items Based Collaborative Filtering

Collaborative filtering technique selects items (music) for a user based in the opinions of other users. Generally, collaborative filtering techniques do not rely on content-based information about items, considering only human judgments on the value of items. Collaborative filtering technique consider every user as an expert for his taste, so that personalized recommendations can be provided based on the expertise of taste-related users. Collaborative filtering has been applied to several domains of information. For example, MovieCritic, Music, Ringo[3,4], GroupLens[5]. Most collaborative filtering systems collect the user opinions as ratings on a numerical scale, leading to a sparse matrix rating (*user*, *item*) in short $r_{u,i}$. Collaborative filtering technique then uses this rating matrix in order to derive predictions. Several algorithms have been proposed on how to use the rating matrix to predict rating[3,4,6]. In our HMRS, we apply a commonly used algorithm, proposed in the GroupLens project and also applied in Ringo, which is based on vector correlation using the Pearson correlation coefficient.

Usually the task of a collaborative filtering technique is to predict the rating of a particular user u for an item i. The system compares the user u's rating with the rating of all other users, who have rated the considered item i. Then a weighted average of the other users rating is used as a prediction. If I_u is set of items that a user u has rated then we can define the mean rating of user u by Equation (1).

$$\overline{r_u} = \frac{1}{|I_u|} \sum_{i \in I_u} r_{u,i} \tag{1}$$

Collaborative filtering algorithms predict the rating based on the rating of similar users. When Pearson correlation coefficient is used, similarity is determined from the correlation of the rating vectors of user u and the other users a by Equation (2).

$$w(u,a) = \frac{\sum_{i \in I_u \cap I_a}(r_{u,i} - \overline{r_u})(r_{a,i} - \overline{r_a})}{\sqrt{\sum_{i \in I_u \cap I_a}(r_{u,i} - \overline{r_u})^2 \bullet \sum_{i \in I_u \cap I_a}(r_{a,i} - \overline{r_a})^2}} \tag{2}$$

It can be noted that $w(u,a) \in [-1,+1]$. The value of $w(u,a)$ measures the similarity between the two users' rating vectors. A high absolute value signifies high similarity and low absolute value dissimilarity. The general predict formula is based in the assumption that the prediction is a weighted average of the other users rating. The weights refer to the amount of similarity between the user u and the other users by Equation (3). The factor k normalizes the weights.

$$p^{collab}(u,i) = \overline{r_u} + k \sum_{a \in U_i} w(u,a)(r_{a,i} - \overline{r_a}) \qquad k = \frac{1}{\sum_{a \in U_i} w(u,a)} \tag{3}$$

Sometimes the correlation coefficient between two users is undefined because they not rated common objects ($I_u \cap I_a = \emptyset$). In such cased the correlation coefficient is estimated by a default voting ($w_{\text{default}} = 2$), which is the measured mean of typically occurring correlation coefficient.

2.3   Content-Based Filtering Based Statistical Method

This system remembers and creates a profile based on a selected item and context information when users are faced with specific context. In addition, when a user requires a recommended service, this system recommends a similar item to the user's former selection based on this profile. Thus, a content-based filtering method can be used to rank a recommendation list.

A content-based filtering method keeps the information related to items and recommends these items to the user who inputs a keyword, which is related to the property of the information. This method has been largely used in the field of information search[7].

To establish a Music Content Information Database (MCIDB), an automatic establishing method in web documents and user input methods were used. In an automatic establishing method, web documents can be extracted by a web robot agent. In addition, a database can be built using the analysis of morphology.

Table 2 shows the recorded value of the 'Angel in the Snow' in the MCIDB in which the key word was obtained by analyzing the song title using a morphological analysis.

Table 2. Example of a Music Content Information Database

Music Information	Extracted Nouns
Title	Angel In The Snow
Singer	A-Ha
Genre	Pop
Age	Young Adult
Weather	Snow
Temperature	Cold
Keyword	Angel, Snow

The earlier profile was configured as a title selected by the user according to the weather, temperature, location, and recommended ages from a music content information database. This means that context data, such as weather, temperature, location and age profiles, could be obtained. Furthermore, a type of query profile is an additional profile configured using a music list which is selected from specific context. The query profile used in this profile becomes a selected music list according to the specific context of a user. For example, the profile can be automatically configured with the selected music list when context is presented as male-young_adult-snow-cold-bedroom. A profile can be produced according to a user's selected item for each context data set.

The recommendation method used in this system is as follows:

First, the frequency of words reappearing can be calculated using a morphological analysis method for a profile that corresponds to context information when a user requires a recommended service. For instance, if the context information is assumed to be male-young_adult-snow-cold-bedroom when a user requires a recommended service, the frequency of words reappearing can be calculated by analyzing the morphology of snow, cold, bedroom, young adult, and the query profiles (male-young_adult-snow-cold-bedroom). The frequency of a specific word reappearing can be expressed as $P(W_i)$ represented in Equation. (4).

$$P(W_i) = Freq_{max}(W_i) / \sum_{i=1}^{N} Freq_{max}(W_i) \times 100, \qquad 1 \le i \le N \qquad (4)$$

where W_i is the ith word in a specific profile, $Freq_{max}(W_i)$ is the total appearance number of W_i in the profile, and N is the total word in the profile except for the duplicated word.

Second, this method searches for the word that appears most frequently with each profile and song title, which coincides with the key word in the MCIDB and configures a list based on the results of these searches. Third, it combines these results into a single list excluding duplicate song titles. Fourth, it configures the priority of the list. In this process, the list was produced using a content-based filtering method and reconfigured as a high preference based music recommendation list utilizing collaborative filtering.

3 System Design and Implementation

This chapter designed and implemented the HMRS that was able to recommend proper music by estimating context information in a Java-based OSGi framework using the context definition and filtering method proposed in Chapter 2.

The OSGi is a type of industrial standard proposed by an OSGi organization in order to establish a standard connection method for Internet devices, such as household information devices and security systems. It is JES-based gateway software, which is an open architecture Java embedded server able to provide high quality multimedia services with a high security level regardless of platform application software. In particular, it is an open architecture network technology that can support various network techniques[8].

Fig. 1 presents the diagram of the overall system. The HMRS designed in this paper analyzed and suggested various data transferred from context recognition sensors and established it as information to recommend proper music through a filtering process for user profiles and MCIDB. In order to perform this process, the HMRS consisted of a Context Manager, Service Manager, and Music Recommendation Manager.

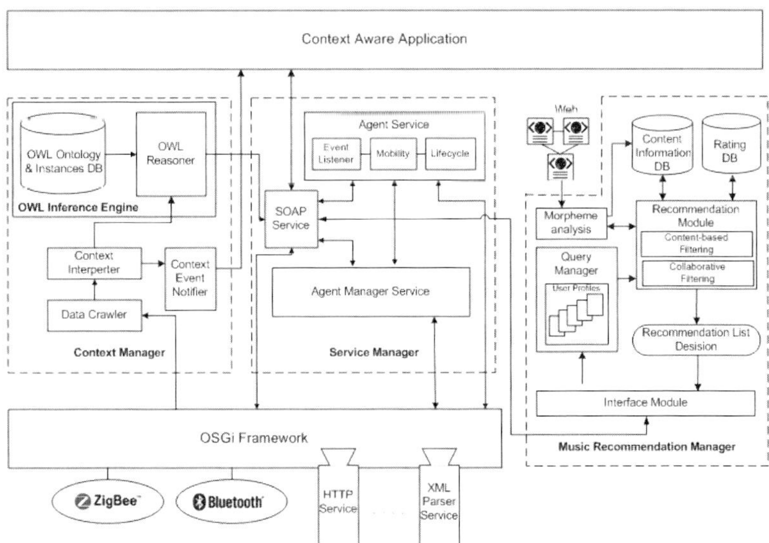

Fig. 1. The Hybrid Music Recommendation System Using Content-based Filtering and Collaborative Filtering

The Context Manager transfered data generated by events to a context analyzer and that data was transfered to an OWL inference engine. The OWL inference engine transferred data received from the context manager to the Service Manager in which data was transformed as information using an OWL inferencer including OWL ontology object database. The Service Manager consisted of a Bundle Service that provided music recommendation service as a bundle in a Simple Object Access Protocol (SOAP) Service, OSGi framework installed device in order to transfer information received from the OWL inference engine to the HMRS, and an Application and Bundle Manager Service that supported the management of the mobility of bundles. The Music Recommendation Manager played a role in the decision of an optimal music recommendation list in a recommendation module by applying the recommendation list that corresponded to certain context information received from the Service Manager with the user profiles, the MCIDB and the rating DB to a filtering process in a recommendation module.

The system proposed in this study used an ontology inferencer Jena 2.0 and developed an OSGi gateway using the Knopflerfish 1.3.3, an open architecture source project which implemented a service framework.

4 Evaluation

Experiments were carried out to observe the recommendation system performance of our proposed method, especially in comparison with other method. The test environment consisted of the Context Manager and Service Manager as a bundle in an OSGi gateway on a home network in which the Music Recommendation Manager was implemented on a Desktop Personal Computer (PC). In addition, the MCIDB consisted of 300 pop songs.

In this paper, Rank Score Measure (RSM) and Mean Absolute Error (MAE), both suggested by paper[9] are used to gauge performance. MAE is used, in order to evaluate single item recommendation systems. RSM is used to evaluate the performance of systems that recommend items from ranked lists.

The RSM of an item in a ranked list is determined by user evaluation or user visits. The RSM is measured under the premise that the probability of choosing an item lower in the list decreases exponentially. Suppose that each item is put in a decreasing order of value j, based on the weight of the preference. Equation (5) calculates the expected utility of user u_a's RSM using the ranked item list.

$$R_a = \sum_j \frac{\max(V_{a,j} - d, 0)}{2^{(j-1)/(\alpha-1)}} \tag{5}$$

In Equation (5), d is the mid-average value of the item, and α is the half-life. The half-life is the number of items in a list that have a 50/50 chance of either review or visit. In the evaluation phase of this paper a half-life value of 5 is used. In Equation (6), the RSM is used to measure the accuracy of the predictions regarding the user.

$$R = 100 \times \frac{\sum_a R_a}{\sum_a R_a(\max)} \tag{6}$$

In Equation (6), if the user has evaluated or visited an item ranking highly in a ranked list, $R_u(\max)$ is the maximum expected utility of the RSM.

The accuracy of the MAE, expressed as Equation (7), is determined by the absolute value of the difference between the predicted value and real value of user evaluation.

$$s_a = \frac{1}{m_a} \sum_{j \in p_a} | p_{a,j} - v_{a,j} | \tag{7}$$

In Equation (7), $P_{a,j}$ is the predicted preference, $v_{a,j}$ the real preference, and m_a the number of items that have been evaluated by the new user.

To verify this hypothesis the following experiments were conducted. Data used in the test applied in this study was collected using a web-based questionnaire answered by 500 users. 100 of these users were treated as test users. This experiment uses the following methods: The proposed Hybrid Music Recommendation System using content-based filtering and collaborative filtering (HMRS_CC), the former memory based methods used a Pearson correlation coefficient (P_Corr), the recommendation method only used content-based filtering (Content). Predictions were computed for the items using each of the different predictors. The quality of the various prediction algorithms was measured by comparing the predicted values for the ratings to the actual ratings. Various methods were used to compare performance by changing the number of clustering users. Fig. 2 and Fig. 3 demonstrate the RSM and MAE of the number of users based on Equation (6) and Equation (7).

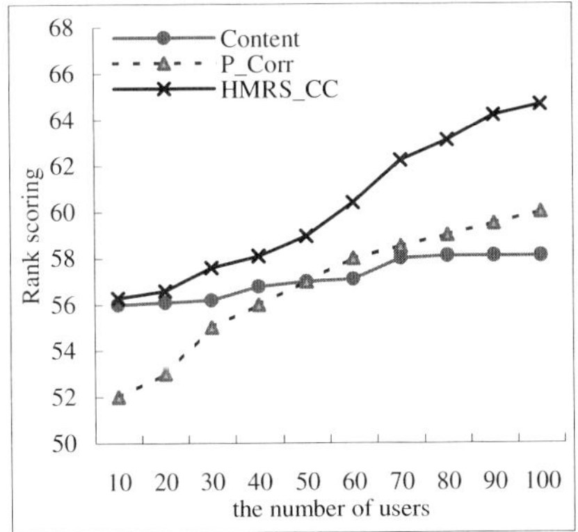
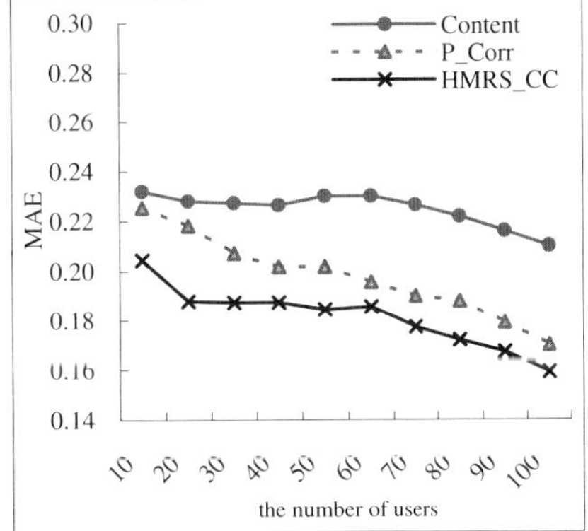

Fig. 2. RSM at varying the number of users   **Fig. 3.** MAE at varying the number of users

In Fig. 2 and Fig. 3, as the number of users increases, the performance of the HMRS_CC, and the P_Corr also increases, whereas the method using Content shows no notable change in performance. In terms of prediction accuracy, it is evident that method HMRS_CC, which uses the recommendation system using context information, is superior to the P_Corr method.

The proposed hybrid music recommendation system using content-based filtering and collaborative filtering (HMRS_CC) and hypothesized that it would outperform only the content-based filtering approach. However, it is also important to compare the proposed approach with that obtained using a combination of content-based filtering and collaborative filtering. In comparing the proposed method and those

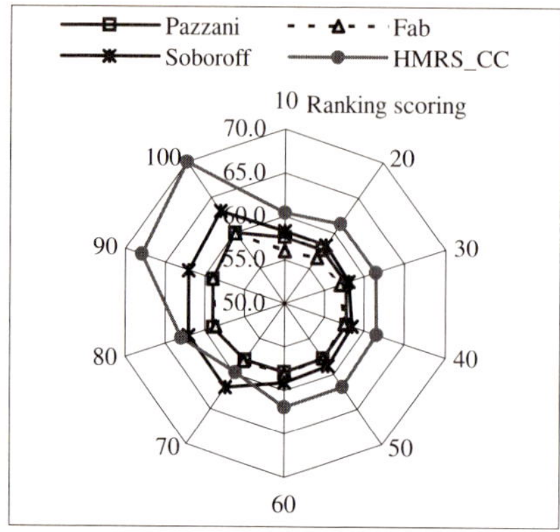

Fig. 4. Rank scoring of nth rating

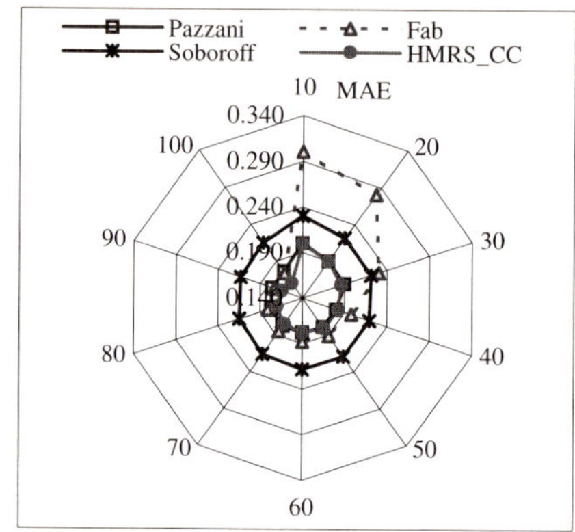

Fig. 5. MAE of nth rating

proposed by Soboroff[11], Pazzani[10] and, Fab[7], analysis of the predictive accuracy values, such as the RSM and MAE, can be achieved. Fig. 4 and Fig. 5 demonstrate the RSM and MAE as the frequency with which the user evaluates the nth rating number is increased. Fig. 4 and Fig. 5 demonstrate a system proposed by Soboroff exhibiting lower performance when the number of evaluations is lower. The other methods demonstrate higher performance than that of Soboroff. As a result, the method developed by Pazzani and the HMRS_CC method present the highest accuracy rates.

5   Conclusions and Future Work

Existing music recommendation systems recommend music by passively receiving user information. This system cannot sustain appropriate search results due to the diversity of user conditions and is limited to data obtained from questionnaires.

Thus, this paper aggressively obtained and recognized user context data from an OSGi frame and processed the data through content-based filtering. In addition, this paper developed a content-based filtering method based on data from a ubiquitous environment and increased the level of precision in recommendations compared to other recommendation systems using a collaborative filtering method simultaneously.

Future studies resolve to develop a module that automatically updates the rating DB established by a questionnaire utilizing user context recognition. In addition, studies will be conducted to reduce delays in recommendation speeds due to the high use of multiple profiles in the HMRS.

Acknowledgement

This research was supported by the Brain Korea 21 Project in 2006.

References

1. H. –C. Chen, and A. L. P. Chen, "A music recommendation system based on music data grouping and user interests," Proc. of the CIKM'01 (2001) 231-238
2. P. J. Brown, J. D. Bovey, and X. Chen, "Context-Aware Application: From the Laboratory to the Marketplace," IEEE Personal Communication (1997) 58-64
3. J. S. Breese, D. Heckerman, C. Kadie, "Empirical Analysis of Predictive Algorithms for Collaborative Filtering," Proc. of the 14th Conference on Uncertainty in AI (1998)
4. J. Herlocker, et al., "An Algorithm Framework for Performing Collaborative Filtering," In Proc. of ACM SIGIR'99 (1999)
5. P. Resnick, et. al., "GroupLens: An Open Architecture for Collaborative Filtering of Netnews," Proc. of ACM CSCW'94 (1994) 175-186
6. K. Y. Jung, J. H. Lee, "Prediction of User Preference in Recommendation System using Association User Clustering and Bayesian Estimated Value," LNAI 2557, 15th Australian Joint Conference on Artificial Intelligence (2002) 284-296
7. M. Balabanovic, and Y. Shoham, "Fab: Content-based, Collaborative Recommendation," Communication of the Association of Computing Machinery, Vol. 40, No. 3 (1997) 66-72
8. P. Dobrev, D. Famolari, C. Kurzke, and B. A. Miller, "Device and Service Discovery in Home Networks with OSGi," IEEE Communications Magazine, Vol. 40, Issue 8, August (2002) 86-92
9. J. L. Herlocker, J. A. Konstan, L. G. Terveen, and J. T. Riedl, "Evaluating Collaborative Filtering Recommender Systems," ACM Transactions on Information Systems (TOIS) archive, Vol. 22, No. 1 (2004) 5-53
10. K. Miyahara, M. J. Pazzani, "Collaborative Filtering with the Simple Bayesian Classifier," In Proc. of the 6th Pacific Rim International Conference on Artificial Intelligence (2000) 679-689
11. I. Soboroff, C. K. Nicholas, "Related, but not Relevant: Content-Based Collaborative Filtering in TREC-8," Information Retrieval, Vol. 5, No. 2-3 (2002) 189-208
12. F. Bagci, H. Schick, J. Petzold, W. Trumler, and T. Ungerer, "Support of Reflective Mobile Agents in a Smart Office Environment," Proceedings of the 18th International Conference on Architecture of Computing Systems (2005) 79-92
13. K. Romer, T. Schoch, F. Mattern and T. Dubendorfer, "Smart Identification Frameworks for Ubiquitous Computing Application," IEEE International Conference on Pervasive Computing and Communication (2003)
14. L. Gong, "A Software Architecture for Open Service Gateways," IEEE Internet Computing, Vol. 5, No. 1 (2001) 64-70
15. S. Lee, S. Lee, K. Lim, and J. Lee, "The Design of Webservices Framework Support Ontology Based Dynamic Service Composition," Proceedings of the Second Asia Information Retrieval Symposium, LNCS 3689 (2005) 721-726

A Novel Color Image Watermarking Method Based on Genetic Algorithm and Hybrid Neural Networks*

Yinghua Lu[1], Jialing Han[1,2], Jun Kong[1,2,**], Yulong Yang[1], and Gang Hou[1,3]

[1] Computer School, Northeast Normal University, Changchun, Jilin Province, China
[2] Key Laboratory for Applied Statistics of MOE, China
[3] College of Humanities and Science, Northeast Normal University, Changchun, China
{luyh, hanjl147, kongjun}@nenu.edu.cn

Abstract. In this paper, a novel intensity adaptive color image watermarking algorithm based on genetic algorithm is presented. The adaptive embedding scheme in color image's three component sub-images' wavelet coefficients, which belong to texture-active regions, not only improves image quality, but also furthest enhances security and robustness of the watermarked image. Then a novel watermark recovering method is proposed based on hybrid neural networks, which enhance the performance of watermark system successfully. The experimental results show that our method is more flexible than traditional methods and successfully fulfills the compromise between robustness and image quality.

1 Introduction

With the widespread use of digital multimedia and the development in computer industry, digital multimedia contents suffer from infringing upon the copyrights with the digital nature of unlimited duplication, easy modification and quick transfer over the Internet [1]. As a result, copyright protection has become a serious issue. Hence, in order to solve this problem, digital watermarking technique has become an active research area [2] [4].

In the past a few years, most of the watermarking schemes employ gray-level images to embed the watermarks, whereas their application to color images is scarce and usually works on the luminous or individual color channel. Fleet [3] embedded watermarks into the yellow-blue channel's frequency domain. Kutter et al. [5] proposed another color image watermarking scheme that embedded the watermark into the blue-channel of each pixel by modifying its pixel value. But they didn't notice that the capacity of hiding information in different color channel is varied with the image changing. In this paper, a novel watermarking embedding method based on genetic algorithm (GA) is proposed. GA is applied to analyze the influence on original image when embedding and the capacity of resisting attacks in every channel. Then the optimized intensity is selected for every color channel. Using GA can improve image

* This work is supported by science foundation for young teachers of Northeast Normal University, No. 20061002, China.
** Corresponding author.

S. Greco et al. (Eds.): RSCTC 2006, LNAI 4259, pp. 806–814, 2006.

quality and furthest enhance security and robustness of the watermarked image simultaneously. This algorithm fulfills an optimal compromise between the robustness and image quality. Then a watermarking recovering method is proposed based on hybrid neural networks. Neural networks can distinguish the prototype of extracting watermark even when it is not clear under sharp attacking.

This paper is organized as follows: the watermark embedding algorithm and extraction algorithm are described in Section 2 and Section 3, respectively. Experimental results are presented in Section 4. Section 5 depicts the watermark recovering method. Finally, conclusions are given in Section 6.

2   The Embedding Algorithm

Let the original color image be I with size $M \times N \times 3$. Our goal is to embed a watermark W with size $H \times L$ into the DWT special frequency bands of I, and have a watermarked reconstruction I' after optimization.

Before the embedding procedure, the host image needs to be analyzed to obtain the embedding position.

2.1   The Host Image Analyzing

Based on human visual system's characteristic, the human eyes have different sensitivity to noise in areas with different luminance and texture. So we consider analyzing the host image before watermark embedding to ensure the imperceptibility of the proposed watermarking scheme [4].

In our study, three gray-scale images are separated from the host RGB image. For the purpose of getting active regions in host image and taking less time, the block-variance analyzing is employed, which divides the host image into sub-blocks and computes each sub-block's variance for detecting texture active regions. For example, the process of analyzing Red component image is presented as follows:

Step 1: Divide the Red component image into un-overlapped 8×8 sub-blocks in spatial domain.

Step 2: Compute each image sub-block's variance, which can measure the relative smoothness and contrast of the intensity in a region.

Step 3: Compute image's average variance. Compare each block's variance with the average variance. If block's variance is greater than the average value, the block is classified as the texture active blocks (TAB).

Step 4: All the pieces of the TAB are divided into three parts, according their variance in decreasing order, to compose the texture-most-active sub-blocks, the texture-median-active sub-blocks and the texture-low-active sub-blocks, respectively.

The blocks' visual mask effect varied with texture features, so we embed watermark based on their own intensity to ensure the robustness and the imperceptibility of watermarking scheme simultaneously.

The other two blue and green component images are analyzed in the same manner.

2.2 Intensity Optimizing Using GA

For the selected sub-blocks, the discrete wavelet decomposition is adopted in frequency domain to embed watermarks. The multi-resolution feature and compatibility to JPEG-2000 compression standard [7] of wavelet transform make the embedded watermark robust to compression operation. Intensity optimal selecting algorithm is described as follows:

1. Transform the selected sub-blocks using discrete wavelet transform. Select coefficients to embed watermark W.
2. Insert watermark signal at coefficients called w_co using additive modulation. Every texture sub-block of the component sub-image has its own embedding intensity as $\alpha(i)$. w_co^w denotes the wavelet coefficients after embedding.

$$w\_co^w = w\_co + \alpha(i) \times W \quad i = 1,2,3,\cdots 9. \tag{1}$$

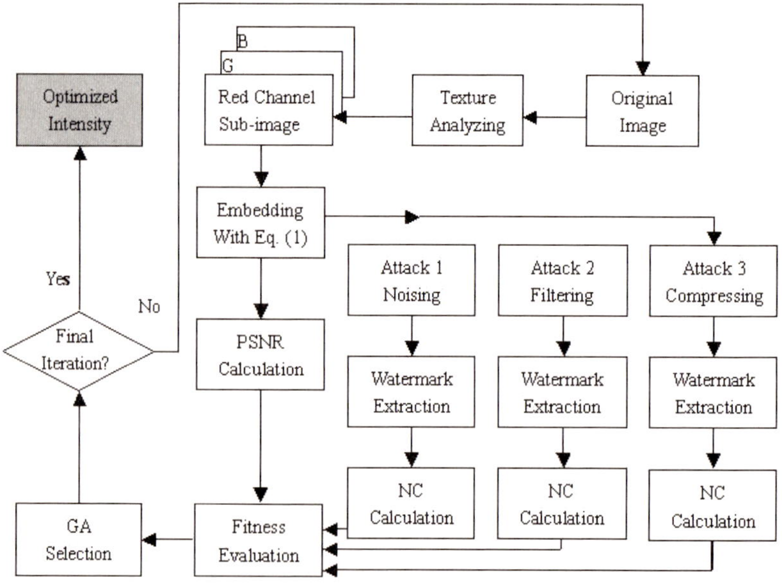

Fig. 1. The flowchart of intensity optimizing algorithm

3. Perform the inverse discrete wavelet transform on w_co^w.
4. Embed the watermarked sub-images back into the original host image to get the watermarked color image I'.
5. Apply the attacking schemes on I', and then adopt the GA training process to search for the optimal intensity for each channel.

The flowchart for illustrating intensity optimal selecting algorithm using GA is shown in Fig. 1.

Not all watermarking applications require robustness to all possible signal processing operations. In addition, the watermarked image after attacking needs to be worthy of using or transmitting. Therefore, some attacks like image-cropping is not employed in our GA training procedure [8]. In this paper, three major attacking schemes are employed, namely, additive noise attack, median filtering attack, and JPEG attack with quality factor of 50%. The quality of watermark extracted from embedded image I' is measured by the normalized correlation (NC). The NC between the embedded watermark $W(i, j)$ and the extracted watermark $W'(i, j)$ is defined as,

$$NC = \frac{\sum_{i=1}^{H} \sum_{j=1}^{L} W(i, j) \times W'(i, j)}{\sum_{i=1}^{H} \sum_{j=1}^{L} [W(i, j)]^2} . \tag{2}$$

The watermarked image's quality is represented by the peak signal-to-noise ratio (PSNR) between the original color image I and watermarked image I', as follows,

$$PSNR = 10 \times \log_{10} (\frac{M \times N \times \max(I^2(i, j))}{\sum_{i=1}^{M} \sum_{j=1}^{N} [I(i, j) - I'(i, j)]^2}) . \tag{3}$$

After obtaining the PSNR of the watermarked image and the three NC values after attacking, we are ready to adopt the GA training process. The fitness function in the mth iteration is defined as:

$$f_m = -(PSNR_m + \lambda \sum_{i=1}^{3} NC_{m,i}) , \tag{4}$$

where f_m is fitness value, λ is the weighting factor for the NC values. Because the PSNR values are dozens of times larger than the NC values in the GA fitness function, the NC values are magnified with the weighting factors λ in the fitness function to balance the influences caused by both the imperceptibility and robustness requirements.

2.3 Watermark Embedding

The first five steps of watermark embedding algorithm are the same as intensity optimal selecting algorithm, and then the obtained optimal intensity is used to form watermarked image. Fig. 2 is the block-diagram of the embedding algorithm.

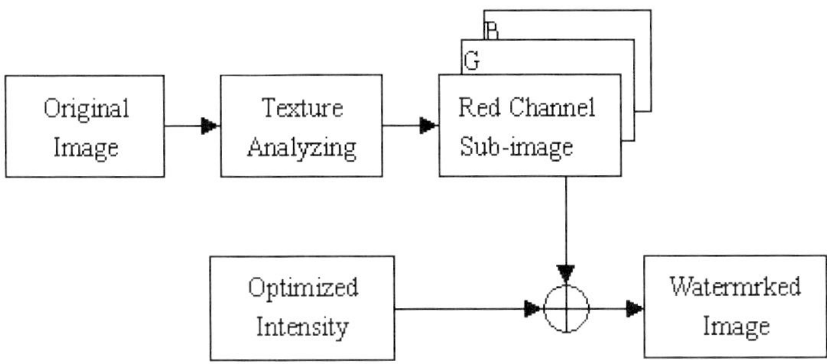

Fig. 2. The block-diagram of embedding algorithm

3 Watermark Extracting

Watermark extraction algorithm is the exact inverse process of embedding algorithm. The watermark can be extracted just when we get the optimal intensity as the secret keys.

4 Experimental Results

The performance of digital watermarking system can be characterized by the following aspects: imperceptibility, security and robustness. All these aspects are evaluated by experimental results respectively in our study. In our simulation, 'Lena' image and 'Baboon' image with the size of 256×256 are taken as test images and watermark with size of 64×64 is shown in Fig. 4(d). The result images of test image 'Lena' and 'Baboon' are shown in Fig. 3(b) and Fig. 3(d).

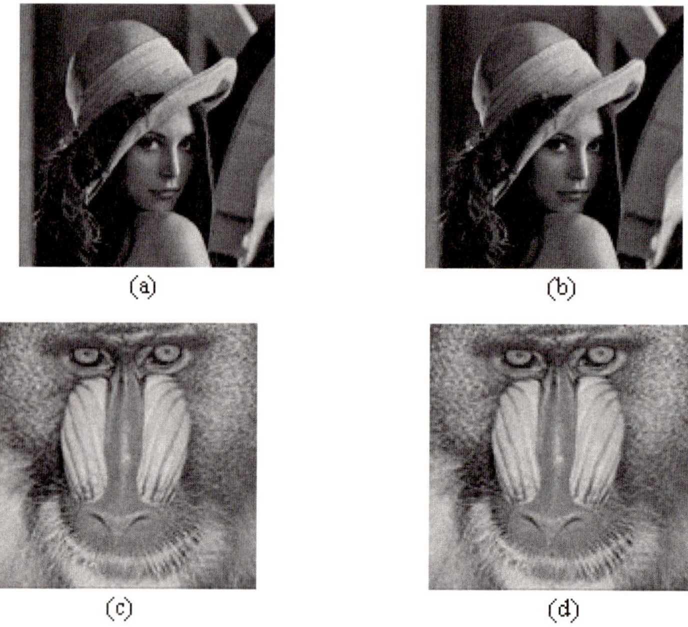

Fig. 3. (a) (c) Original host image 'Lena' and 'Baboon', (b) (d) Result image watermarked

When free of any attacks, the PSNR of the watermarked image 'Lena' is 35.8487, NC is 1 and the PSNR of the watermarked image 'Baboon' is 36.3028 and NC is 1.

In the GA training process, ten individuals are chosen for every iteration. The crossover operation is selected as scattered function in the MATLAB Genetic Algorithm Toolbox. The selection operation is selected as stochastic uniform function and the mutation operation is Gaussian function with the scale value 1.0 and the shrink value 1.0. The training iterations are set to 200. The fitness values converge after 200 iterations, and the optimized intensity with the optimal fitness value is 31, 27, 24, 18, 17, 16, 14, 14, and 13 respectively.

The result images under different attacks and the watermarks exacted are depicted in Fig. 4. Seen from Table 1, the conclusion can be drawn that our algorithm is robust to attacks encountered always in image processing and transmission.

Table 1. Experimental results under different attacks of our scheme (measured by NC)

Attack Type	Baboon	Lena	Airplane
Attack-free	1	1	1
Additive noising	0.9137	0.9139	0.9479
Filtering	0.9320	0.9536	0.9139
JPEG QF=80	0.9957	0.9830	0.9957
JPEG QF=50	0.9801	0.9547	0.9861
JPEG QF=30	0.9639	0.9390	0.9752

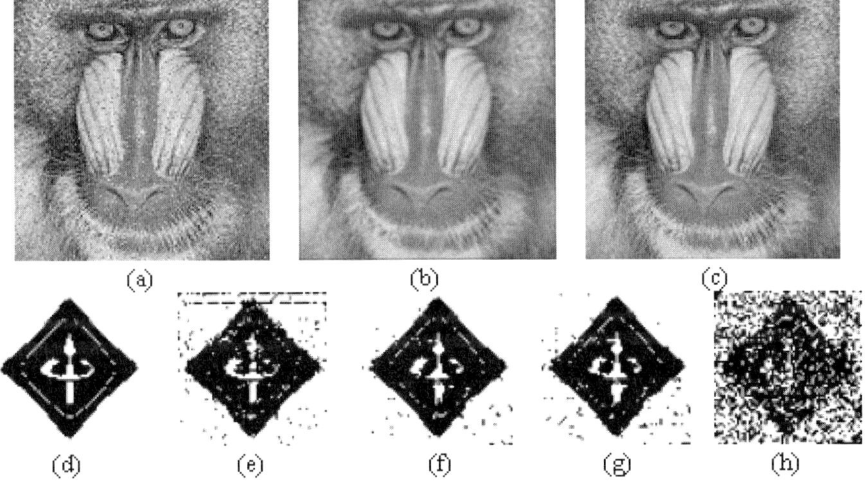

Fig. 4. (a) Result image of watermarked 'Baboon' under additive noising attack, (b) Watermarked image under filtering attack, (c) Watermarked image under compressing attack, (d) Original watermark, (e-g) Extracted watermarks from (a-c) using our method, respectively. (g) Extracted watermark from (c) using Kutter's method.

To evaluate the robustness of the proposed watermarking scheme, Kutter's algorithm is simulated as comparison. The results under several attacks of Kutter's algorithm are shown in Table 2.

Compared with Table 1, it can be concluded that our algorithm is more robust than Kutter's, especially in resisting additive nosing and JPEG compressing.

Table 2. Experimental results under different attacks of Kutter's scheme (measured by NC)

Attack-free	Noising	Filtering	JPEG QF=80	JPEG QF=50	JPEG QF=30
0.9684	0.9546	0.9362	0.6386	0.5925	0.5071

5 Watermark Recovering

From the experimental results above, the conclusion can be drawn that our algorithm is robust to many kinds of attacks. In order to get better capability, a watermarking recovering method is proposed based on hybrid neural networks. Neural networks can distinguish the prototype of extracting watermark even when it is not clear under sharp attacking. Hybrid back-propagation (BP) neural networks are employed to identify the characteristics of extracting watermark, which are extracted using principal components analysis (PCA).

5.1 Hybrid Neural Network Training

Attacking original watermark with different kinds of attacks to get a set as the training set of the neural networks. Then PCA is employed to analyze watermarks, and the above ten eigenvalues are chosen as the input in training pattern. The structure of the neural networks is depicted in Fig. 5. Every type of attack has its own neural

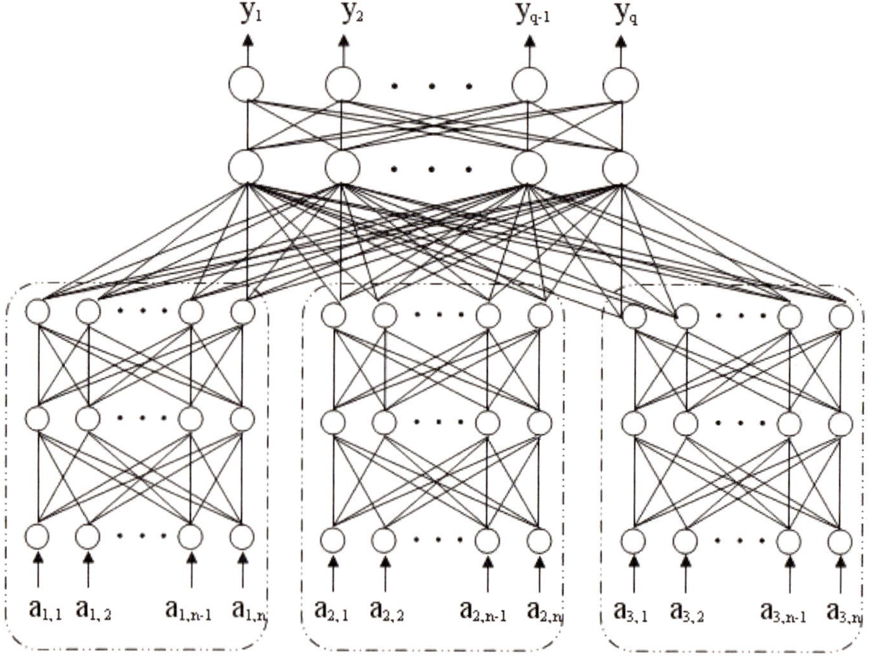

Fig. 5. The structure of the neural networks used in our watermark techniques

networks, and their outputs are chosen as input of the final neural networks. These attacks include noising, filtering and JPEG compressing. The neural networks for specific attack are able to recover watermarks which are under such attack too effectively. Then a final neural network is employed. This method can distinguish the prototype of extracting watermarks even when they were under multiple attacks simultaneously.

Every node in final output layer represents different watermarks. The eigenvalue as input vector is defined by $P_k = (a_{t,1}, a_{t,2}, \cdots, a_{t,n})$, and the desired output for the neural networks corresponding to the input is defined by $T_k = (y_1, y_2, \cdots, y_q)$, where n and q stand for the number of input and output nodes respectively, k is the number of training patterns, and t is the number of attack type. The sub-neural networks include an input layer with ten nodes, a hidden layer with twenty hidden nodes, and an output layer with q nodes, which can be varied with the number of watermarks' type. The final neural network include an input layer with $3 \times q$ nodes, which are the output of the sub-networks, a hidden layer with twenty hidden nodes, and an output layer with q nodes as above.

5.2   Watermark Recovering Based on the Trained Neural Networks

The trained neural networks perform a highly adaptive capacity in identifying watermarks. Taking an extracted watermark from an embedding image after attacking as a test image, the above ten eigenvalues are chosen as the input, the prototype of attacked watermark can be recognized clearly using neural networks. In the experiments, even NC of the test watermark is 0.1628, which is shown in Fig. 6(a), the trained neural networks also can associate its corresponding original watermark, as shown in Fig. 6(b). So it can conclude that the proposed watermark recovering method is an important complementation in watermark system.

(a)   (b)

Fig. 6. (a) Test watermark, (b) Corresponding watermark of (a)

6   Conclusion

A novel embedding intensity adaptive color image watermarking method is proposed in this paper. A color image is divided into three channels firstly. Then genetic algorithm is applied to analyze the influence on the original image when embedding and the capacity of resisting attacks in every channel. At last, the watermark is embedded in R, G and B channels respectively. Using genetic algorithm is not only able to improve image quality, but also furthest enhance security and robustness of the watermarked image. Using hybrid neural networks, the proposed watermark recovering method enhances the performance of watermarking technique successfully. This algorithm fulfills an optimal compromise between the robustness and image quality.

References

1. W. N. Cheung: Digital Image Watermarking in the Spatial and Transform Domains. Proceedings of TENCON'2000, Sept. 24-27,2000,3
2. Xu-Dong Zhang, Jian Feng, Kwok-Tung Lo: Image Watermarking using Tree-based Spatial-frequency Feature of Wavelet Transform. Journal of Visual Communication and Image Representation 14(2003) 474-491
3. D. Fleet, D. Heeger: Embedding invisible information in color images. Proc. 4th IEEE International conference on Image Processing, Santa Barbara, USA, 1(1997) 532-535
4. Jun Kong, Wei Wang, Yinghua Lu, Jialing Han, Gang Hou: Joint spatial and frequency domains watermarking algorithm based on wavelet packets transform. Lecture Notes in Computer Science, Volume 3809 (2005), 934-937
5. M. Kutter, F. Jordan, F. Bossen: Digital watermarking of color images using amplitude modulation. J. Electron. Imaging 7(2) (1998) 1064-1087
6. M. Gen, R. Cheng: Genetic Algorithms and Engineering Design. Wiley, New York, NY, 1997
7. M. A. Suhail, M. S. Obaidat, S. S. Ipson, B. Sadoun: A Comparative Study of Digital Watermarking in JPEG and JPEG 2000 Environments. Information Sciences 151(2003) 93-105
8. Chin-Shiuh Shieh, Hsiang-Cheh Huang, Feng-Hsing Wang, Jeng-Shyang Pan: Genetic watermarking based on transform-domain techniques. Pattern Recognition 37(2004) 555-565
9. Pao-Ta Yu, Hung-Hsu Ysai, Jyh-Shyan Lin: Digital watermarking based on neural networks for color images. Signal Processing 81(2001) 663-671
10. I. J. Cox, J. Kilian, F.T. Leighton, T. Shamoon: Secure spread spectrum watermaking for multimedia. IEEE Trans. Image Process 6(12) (1997) 1673-1687
11. E. Ganic, A.M. Eskicioglu: Robust DWT-SVD domain image watermarking: embedding data in all frequencies. Proceedings of 2004 Multimedia and Security Workshop on Multimedia and Security, (2004) 166-174
12. Piyu Tsai, Yu-Chen Hu, Chin-Chen Chang: A color image watermarking scheme based on color quantization. Signal Processing 84(2004) 95-106
13. Joong-Jae Lee, Won Kim, Na-Yong Lee: A new incremental watermarking based on dual-tree complex wavelet transform. The journal of supercomputing, 33, 133-140, 2005
14. Chin-Chen Chang, Piyu Tsai, Chia-Chen Lin: SVD-based digital image watermarking scheme. Pattern Recognition Letters 26(2005) 1577-1586
15. Frank Y. Shih, Scott Y.T. Wu: Combinational image watermarking in the spatial and frequency domains. Pattern Recognition 36(2003) 969-975

Calibration of Omnidirectional Camera by Considering Inlier Distribution

Yongho Hwang and Hyunki Hong

Dept. of Image Eng., Graduate School of Advanced Imaging Science, Multimedia and Film,
Chung-Ang Univ.
hwangyh@wm.cau.ac.kr, honghk@cau.ac.kr

Abstract. This paper presents a new self-calibration algorithm of omnidirectional camera from uncalibrated images by considering the inlier distribution. First, one parametric non-linear projection model of omnidirectional camera is estimated with the known rotation and translation parameters. After deriving projection model, we can compute an essential matrix of the camera with unknown motions, and then determine the camera positions. The standard deviations are used as a quantitative measure to select a proper inlier set. The experimental results showed that we can achieve a precise estimation of the omnidirectional camera model and extrinsic parameters including rotation and translation.

1 Introduction

The seamless integration of synthetic objects with real photographs or video images has long been one of the central topics in computer vision and computer graphics [1,2]. Generating a high quality synthesized image requires first matching the geometric characteristics of both the synthetic and real cameras, and then shading the synthetic objects so that they appear to be illuminated by the same lights as the other objects in the background image. In general, the integration of synthetic objects in a realistic and believable way is labor intensive process and not always successful due to the enormous complexities of real-world. Therefore, an automatic tool to reconstruct 3D structure and illumination environment of the scene allows users to alleviate much effort for realistic composition.

Since the fisheye lens has a wide field of view, it is widely used to capture the scene and illumination from all directions from far less number of omnidirectional images. This paper presents a new self-calibration algorithm for estimating the omnidirectional camera model from uncalibrated images. First, we derive one parametric non-linear projection model of the omnidirectional camera, and estimate the model by considering a distribution of the inlier set. In order to estimate the camera model, our method uses the standard deviation which represents the degree of the point distribution in each sub-region relative to the entire image. After deriving projection model of the camera, we can compute an essential matrix of the camera with unknown camera motions, and then determine the relative rotation and translation.

S. Greco et al. (Eds.): RSCTC 2006, LNAI 4259, pp. 815 – 823, 2006.

2 Previous Studies

Many researches for self-calibration and 3D reconstruction from omnidirectional images have been proposed up to now. In addition, these approaches are combined widely with IBL (Image-Based Lighting) [2, 5] due to their merits.

Xiong et al register four fisheye lens images to create the spherical panorama, while self-calibrating its distortion and field of view [3]. However, camera setting is required, and the calibration results may be incorrect according to lens because it is based on equi-distance camera model. Sato et al simplify user's direct specification of a geometric model of the scene by using an omnidirectional stereo algorithm, and measure the radiance distribution. However, because of using the omnidirectional stereo, it is required in advance a strong camera calibration for capturing positions and internal parameters, which is complex and difficult process [5].

Previous studies	Image Acquisition	Methods
UC Berkeley / Y. Xiong [3]	self-calibration of fisheye lens and capturing the spherical panorama with 3~4 images	- restricted camera parameters: by rotating the camera 90 degrees - based on equi-distance camera model
Columbia Univ. / S. K. Nayar [4]	using planar, ellipsoidal, hyperboloidal and paraboloidal mirrors for stereo	- modeling catadioptric system by pre-calibrated camera
Univ. of Tokyo / K. Ikeuchi [5]	using omnidirectional pairs for scene modeling & scene radiance computing	- 3D reconstruction and lighting - strong pre-calibration and scene constraints
Univ. of Amsterdam / B. Krose [6]	using omnidirectional sensor on the mobile robot for scene reconstruction	- using robot odometry for camera poses estimation and tracking - calibrated catadioptric sensors
Czech Tech. Univ. / T. Pajdla [7, 8]	automatic estimation of projection model of dioptric lens without calibration objects and scene constraints	- no optimal method to estimate projection model - no consideration of image sequence
Czech Tech. Univ. / T. Pajdla [7, 8]	automatic reconstruction of uncalibrated omnidirectional images	- applications problems in image sequence: correspondence, frame grouping

Although previous studies on calibration of omnidirectional images have been widely presented, there were few methods about estimation of one parametric model and extrinsic parameters of the camera [6~8]. Pajdla et al metntioned one parametric non-linear projection model has smaller possibility to fit outliers, and explanied that simultaneous estimation of a camera model and epipolar geometry may be affected by sampling corresponding points between a pair of the omindirectional images [9]. However, it requires further consideration about various inlier sampling methods: 8-points algorithm, RANSAC (RANdom Sampling Consensus), LMS (Least-Median-Squares) [10]. This paper presents a robust calibration algorithm for one parametric model by considering inlier distribution.

3 One-Parametric Projection Model

The camera projection model describes how 3D scene is transformed into 2D image. The light rays are emanated from the camera center, which is the camera position, and determined by a rotationally symmetric mapping function f as follows:

$$f(u,v) = f(\mathbf{u}) = r / \tan\theta \tag{1}$$

where, $r = \sqrt{u^2 + v^2}$ is the radius of a point (u, v) with respect to the camera center and θ is the angle between a ray and the optical axis.

The mapping function f has various forms determined by lens construction [7,11]. The precise two-parametric non-linear model for Nikon FC-E8 fisheye converter as follows:

$$\theta = \frac{ar}{1+br^2}, \quad r = \frac{a - \sqrt{a^2 - 4b\theta^2}}{2b\theta}, \tag{2}$$

where a, b are parameters of the model. On the assumption that the maximal view angle θ_{max} is known, the maximal radius r_{max} corresponding to θ_{max} can be easily

(a)   (b)

Fig. 1. Input images were taken by Nikon FC-E8 fisheye converter mounted on Nikon Coolpix995 with 1530 x 1530 pixels and 20 correspondences marked by red circles. (a) omnidirectional image captured at the reference position, (b) at relatively rotated and translated position (rotation **R**: -30° around y-axis, unit translation vector **T**: (t_x,t_y,t_z)=(0.9701, 0, 0.2425)).

Fig. 2. Corresponding epipolar curves superimposed on Fig. 1(b)

obtained from the normalized view field image. It allows to obtain the one-parametric non-linear model as follows:

$$\theta = \frac{ar}{1 + \dfrac{r^2}{r_{max}}\left(a/\theta_{max} - 1/r_{max}\right)} \quad , \tag{3}$$

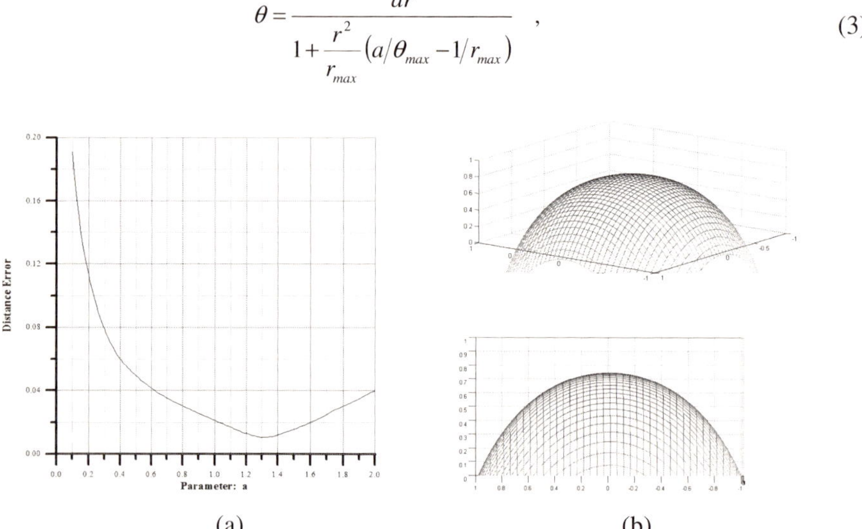

(a)   (b)

Fig. 3. (a) Sum of distance between epipolar curves and correspondence points by change of parameter a, (b) estimated projection model, parameter $a = 1.3$

In order to estimate one parametric non-linear projection model, we use two omnidirectional images with known relative camera direction and translation. 20 corresponding points between images are established by the commercial program MatchMover pro3.0 [12]. Since the relative rotation and translation parameters are known in estimation of the camera model, we can draw an epipolar curve as shown in Fig. 2. In addition, we obtain the parameter a minimizing a distance of the epipolar curves and the projected points as follows:

$$\arg\min_{a} \frac{1}{N}\sum_{i=1}^{N} d(curve_i, pt_i), \tag{4}$$

where, N and $d(,)$ are the number of correspondences and Euclidean distance between a curve and a point, respectively. $curve_i$ is the i-th epipolar curve, and pt_i is the i-th corresponding point. The distance error graph for the parameter a is shown in Fig. 3 (a). We obtained the minimum error when a is 1.3, and then the estimated projection model is represented in Fig. 3 (b).

4 Essential Matrix and Camera Pose Estimation

We expand Eq. 1 to Taylor series with respect to a and b at a_0 and b_0 [7]. By omitting the nonlinear part of the Taylor series, we obtain function $\tilde{f}$, which is linear in a and b as follows:

$$\tilde{f}(r,a,b) = f(r,a,b) + f_a(r,a_0,b_0)(a-a_0) + f_b(r,a_0,b_0)(b-b_0), \qquad (5)$$

where,

$$f_a(r,a_0,b_0) = -\frac{r^2\left(1+\left(\tan\dfrac{a_0 r}{1+b_0 r^2}\right)^2\right)}{\left(\tan\dfrac{a_0 r}{1+b_0 r^2}\right)^2 (1+b_0 r^2)}, \; f_b(r,a_0,b_0) = -\frac{a_0 r^2}{(1+b_0 r^2)} f_a(r,a_0,b_0), \; a_0 = {\theta_{max}}\Big/{r_{max}}, b_0 = 0.$$

The vector $\mathbf{p}$ can be written by using Eq. 1 and 5 as follows:

$$\mathbf{p} = \left[\left(\begin{array}{c} u \\ v \\ f\,() - a_0 s - b_0 t + a\left(s + \dfrac{t}{\theta_m}\right) - t \end{array}\right)\right] = \left[\left(\begin{array}{c} u \\ v \\ w \end{array}\right) + a\left(\begin{array}{c} 0 \\ 0 \\ \gamma \end{array}\right)\right] \qquad (6)$$

$$= \mathbf{x} + a\boldsymbol{\gamma}$$

where, $s = f_a()$, $t = f_b()$, $w = f - a_0 s - (b_0 + 1)t$, $\gamma = s + \dfrac{t}{\theta_m}$.

The epipolar constraint [10] for vector $\mathbf{p_1}$ in the left and $\mathbf{p_2}$ in the right image that corresponds to the same scene point reads as:

$$\mathbf{p}_2^T \mathbf{F}\mathbf{p}_1 = 0, \quad (\mathbf{x}_2 + a\boldsymbol{\gamma}_2)^T \mathbf{F}(\mathbf{x}_1 + a\boldsymbol{\gamma}_1) = 0. \qquad (7)$$

After arranging of unknown parameters into the vector $\mathbf{f}$, we obtain the following equation:

$$(\mathbf{D}_1 + a\mathbf{D}_2 + a^2\mathbf{D}_3)\mathbf{f} = 0, \qquad (8)$$

where matrices $\mathbf{D}_i$ and vector $\mathbf{f}$ are as follows:

$$\mathbf{D}_1 = \begin{bmatrix} u_1 u_2 & v_1 u_2 & w_1 u_2 & u_1 v_2 & v_1 v_2 & w_1 v_2 & u_1 w_2 & v w_2 & w w_2 \end{bmatrix},$$
$$\mathbf{D}_2 = \begin{bmatrix} 0 & 0 & \gamma_1 u_2 & 0 & 0 & \gamma_1 v_2 & u_1 \gamma_2 & v_1 \gamma_2 & \gamma_1 w_2 + w_1 \gamma_2 \end{bmatrix},$$
$$\mathbf{D}_3 = \begin{bmatrix} 0 & 0 & 0 & 0 & 0 & 0 & 0 & 0 & \gamma_1 \gamma_2 \end{bmatrix},$$
$$\mathbf{f} = \begin{bmatrix} f_1 & f_2 & f_3 & f_4 & f_5 & f_6 & f_7 & f_8 & f_9 \end{bmatrix}^T.$$

An initial set of correspondences is obtained by tracking salient image features. After the correspondences are obtained, the essential matrix relating each image to the reference image is estimated by the normalized 8-point algorithm. The rotation $\mathbf{R}$ and translation $\mathbf{T}$ can be determined from the singular value decomposition. There are 4 possible combinations of rotation and translation which result in the same essential matrix. The correct combination can be found by recovering the depths to each tracked point according to the relative poses implied by each combination. The correct combination is the one for which most recovered depths are positive. The angle between a ray and an epipolar plane is used as the error function, instead of the distance of a point from its epipolar curve [13].

5 Quantitative Measure for Inlier Distribution

One of the main problems on the estimation of omnidirectional camera is the fact that the essential matrix can be very sensitive to errors on the point locations. The essential matrix contains relative orientation and position between both cameras. Therefore, when estimating the essential matrix, we have to choose the inliers, which represent sufficiently the depths of the scene points and change of the image due to camera motion, among several feature points. In order to cope with the unavoidable outliers inherent in the given correspondence matches, we use 9-points RANSAC that calculates the point distribution for each essential matrix.

In general, the evenly distributed corresponding points can thoroughly represent the image variation by the camera motion. In this paper, the standard deviation of the point density in the sub-region and that in an entire image is used to evaluate whether the points are evenly distributed. First, 3D patches of the hemi-spherical camera model are segmented by the same solid angle, and then they are projected into 2D image plane. Fig. 4 shows the segmented sub-regions by the proposed method.

$$\Delta\theta = 0.5\pi / int\left(\sqrt{N}\right), \quad \Delta\phi = 2\pi / int\left(\sqrt{N}\right), \tag{9}$$

where N is the number of the inliers, and $int(\cdot)$ means conversion to integer. The proposed method computes the standard deviation of two densities that represents a degree of the point distribution in each sub-region relative to the entire. The obtained information is used as a quantitative measure to choose the evenly distributed point sets. The standard deviation of the point density is defined as:

$$\sigma_p = \sqrt{\frac{1}{N_S}\sum_{i=1}^{N_S}\left(P_{S_i} - \frac{N}{N_S}\right)^2}, \tag{10}$$

where N_S is the number of sub-regions, N and P_{Si} are the number of inliers and that in the i-th sub-region, respectively.

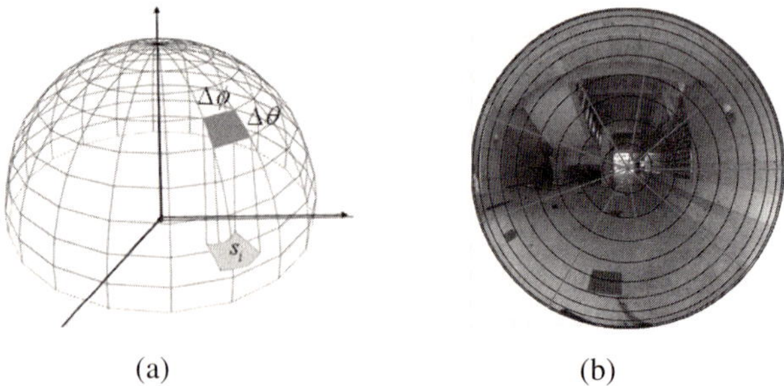

(a)   (b)

Fig. 4. Segmented sub-regions by proposed method. (a) Segmented 3D patch by uniform solid angle in hemi-spherical model, (b) 2D projected sub-regions and inlier set (red dots).

The proposed method chooses the inlier set by using the standard deviation of distribution of corresponding points by Eq. 10. Then we find the inlier set with the least standard deviation. In the final step, we estimate the essential matrix from the selected inlier set by minimizing a cost function that is the sum of the distance error of the inliers [7].

6   Experimental Results

We have compared the experimental results of previous method such as 9-poins RANSAC without considering inliers distribution [9] and the proposed method. Fig. 5 shows the regions for selecting inlier sets. Since points near the center have no special contribution to the final fitting, the center region is omitted [9].

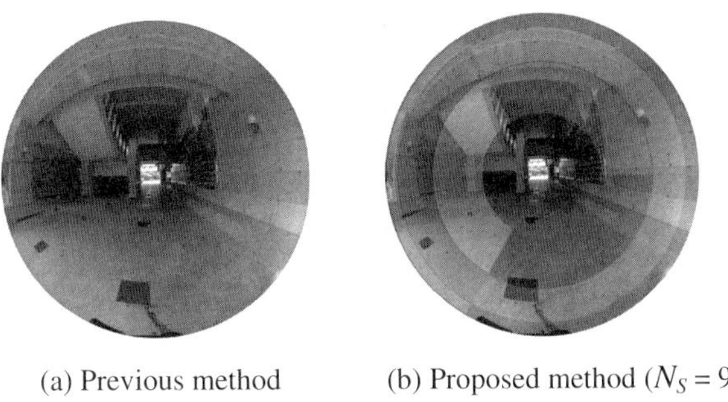

(a) Previous method   (b) Proposed method ($N_S = 9$)

Fig. 5. Interest regions for selecting inlier sets

The input images (1530×1530) and corresponding points between two consecutive images are showed in Fig. 6. The correspondences between two images were established by MatchMover pro 3.0 automatically [12].

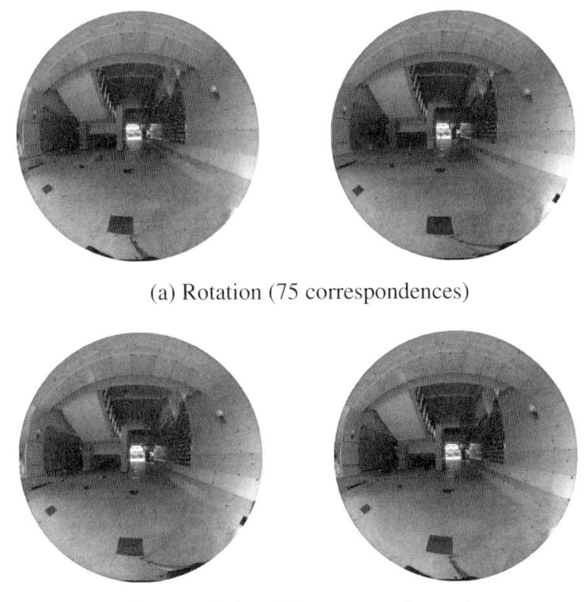

(a) Rotation (75 correspondences)

(b) Translation (90 correspondences)

Fig. 6. Input images and corresponding points between two views

Fig. 7 shows the computed epipole distance error. In these results, the proposed method obtains more precise results over the previous method according to an iteration number. In general, when the camera is translated, many feature points may be occluded according to the scene complexity. Therefore, more epipole distance error is obtained in the case of the camera translation than the rotation.

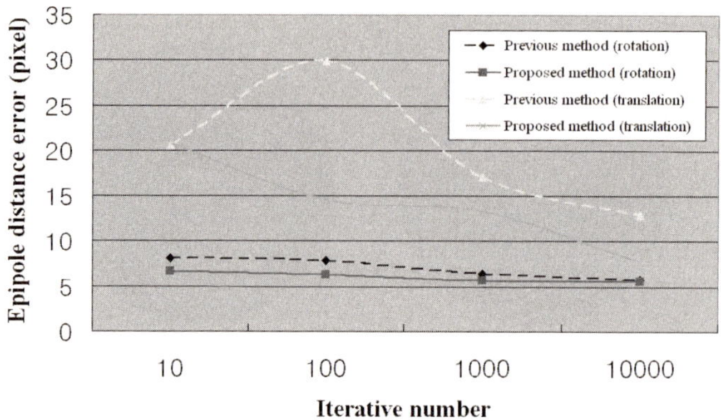

Fig. 7. Experimental results on the omnidirectional image pair

Fig. 8 shows the estimated one-parametric projection model. In the results, we have ascertained that the proposed method is converged to more stable shape than the previous at the same iteration number.

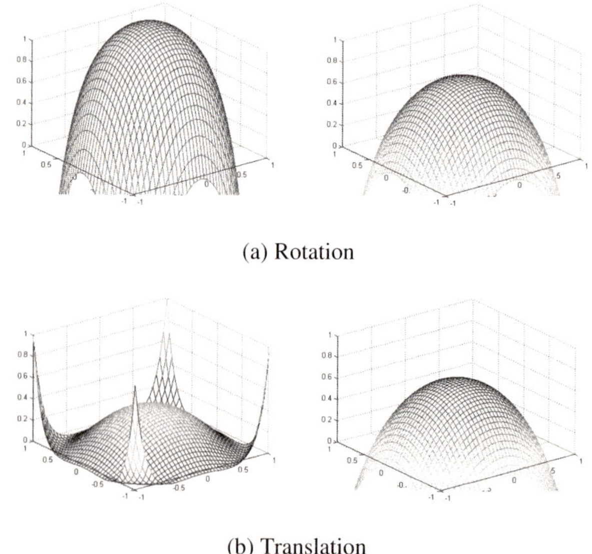

(a) Rotation

(b) Translation

Fig. 8. Estimated one-parametric projection model after 10000 iterations. Left: previous method. Right: proposed method.

7 Conclusions

This paper presents a novel approach to estimate one parametric model of the omnidirectional camera by considering the inlier distribution. The proposed method divides the entire image into the sub-regions, and then examines the number of the inliers in each sub-region and the area of each region. By considering the point distribution, we can choose the inlier set reflecting the scene structure and camera movement, so achieve more precise estimation of the essential matrix. In addition to using both hemispherical coordinates of two cameras, we identify 3D position of the light sources with respect to the camera positions. And then photo-realistic scenes can be generated in the reconstructed illumination environment. Further study will include an integration of scene and illumination reconstruction for photo-realistic image synthesis.

Acknowledgments. This work was supported by the Korea Research Foundation Grant funded by the Korean Government (MOEHRD) (KRF-2005-041-D00700).

References

1. A. Fournier, A. Gunawan, and C. Romanzin, "Common illumination between real and computer generated scenes," *Proc. of Graphics Interface*, pp.254-262, 1993.
2. P. Debevec, "Rendering synthetic objects into real scenes: bridging traditional and image-based graphics with global illumination and high dynamic range photography," *Proc. of Siggraph*, pp.189-198, 1998.
3. Y. Xiong and K. Turkowski, "Creating image based VR using a self-calibrating fisheye lens," *Proc. of Computer Vision and Pattern Recognition*, pp.237-243, 1997.
4. S. A. Nene and S. K. Nayar, "Stereo with mirrors," *Proc. of Int. Conf. on Computer Vision*, pp.1087-1094, 1998.
5. I. Sato, Y. Sato, and K. Ikeuchi, "Acquiring a radiance distribution to superimpose virtual objects onto a real scene," *IEEE Trans. on Visualization and Computer Graphics*, vol.5, no.1, pp.1-12. 1999.
6. R. Bunschoen and B. Krose, "Robust scene reconstruction from an omnidirectional vision system," *IEEE Trans. on Robotics and Automation*, vol.19, no.2, pp.358-362, 2003.
7. B. Micusik and T. Pajdla, "Estimation of omnidiretional camera model from epipolar geometry," *Proc. of Computer Vision and Pattern Recognition*, pp.485-490, 2003.
8. B. Micusik, D. Martinec, and T. Pajdla, "3D Metric reconstruction from uncalibrated omnidirectional Images," *Proc. of Asian Conf. on Computer Vision*, pp.545-550, 2004.
9. B. Micusik and T. Pajdla, "Omnidirectional camera model and epipolar estimateion by RANSAC with bucketing," *IEEE Scandinavian Conf. Image Analysis*, pp. 83-90, 2003.
10. R. Hartley and A. Zisserman: Multiple View Geometry in Computer Vision, Cambridge Univ., 2000.
11. J.Kumler and M.Bauer. "Fisheye lens designs and their relative performance," http://www.coastalopt.com/fisheyep.pdf.
12. http://www.realviz.com
13. J. Oliensis, "Extract two-image structure from motion," *IEEE Transactions on Pattern Analysis and Machine Intelligence*, vol.24, no.12, pp.1618-1633, 2002.

Modified Hough Transform for Images Containing Many Textured Regions*

Yun-Seok Lee, Seung-Hun Yoo, and Chang-Sung Jeong**

Department of Electronics Engineering, Korea University,
Anam-Dong, Seongbuk-Gu, Seoul, Korea
{ruhmreich, capstoney}@korea.ac.kr,
csjeong@charlie.korea.ac.kr

Abstract. Images which have a lot of textured regions make the result of Hough transform (HT) very poor. This paper presents an improved HT that deals with such a textured image by diminishing the effect of noise edges and using weighted voting score. The method first eliminates the noise edges resulted from textured regions; then, the method casts votes for edges upon the accumulator array with weight score in accordance with the number of sequential votes. Our modified HT is efficient in that it produces important lines first such as verge of building, avoiding improper lines taken from the noise edges.

1   Introduction

Hough Transform (HT) is a voting process for detecting discontinuous patterns in images. An accumulator array is used for the votes, where the bin of the accumulator array which has the maximum votes is recognized as a desired pattern. The first introduced HT was a method for detecting straight lines [10]. Hough used the slope-intercept equation ($y = ax + b$), but it has a critical disadvantage in that it gives infinity value as a line approaches the vertical.

Alternatively, straight lines can be parameterized by length and angle as ($r = x \cos\theta + y \sin\theta$) [11], which is called standard HT (SHT). However, SHT has some disadvantages in memory consumption, computation time and peak detection. Thus, there have been many improved versions of SHT, e.g. fast HT [4], adaptive HT [6], combinatorial HT [2] and hierarchical HT [7]. Those algorithms reduced the complexity of the detection of local peaks, but those still have to consider all the orientations for the scanning of HT.

A new method of HT, probabilistic HT [9], and its modified version, randomized HT [8] were proposed. The randomized HT is based on the fact that a parameter point can be determined uniquely by using n features in the image. However, any version of probabilistic HT should carefully select the number of points for the vote; otherwise it produces improper result.

* This work was supported by KIPA Information Technology Research Center, University Research Program by Ministry of Information & Communication, Seoul Metropolitan and Brain Korea 21 projects.

** Corresponding author.

S. Greco et al. (Eds.): RSCTC 2006, LNAI 4259, pp. 824–833, 2006.
© Springer-Verlag Berlin Heidelberg 2006

Despite various versions of HT for the improvement of its performance, it has still a "blind" characteristic. The fact that HT cannot discern lines in the same parameter space is the worst weakness. Besides, the previous versions of HT have paid little attention to the application to which they are applied, so that such weaknesses give the result of HT incorrect information, especially in real world images such as building image. Real world images have many objects and various textured regions which have a mass of short edges. Thus, it is very possible for a group of parallel edges to be detected as a line when the HT line parameter pierces those edges.

Recently, Furukawa et al. presented a robust peak detection algorithm in Hough space [13]. The algorithm analyzes the butterfly shape in the accumulator space to extract accurate peak that matches a line segment. This algorithm focuses on peak detection, but it did not consider the voting process.

Our algorithm is useful for 3-dimensional building reconstruction where frame lines of a building are extracted using a line extractor such as HT, so as to match the lines between related images [1]. On the other hand, the common HT gives many improper lines consisting of noise edges, so that it additionally requires a procedure for selecting important lines from the result. We first eliminate some edge points that may prevent important lines from being detected; then we use a weighted voting process.

2   Improved HT

The purpose of our algorithm is to detect straight lines which are perceptually important in an image. The proposed algorithm consists of two steps. The first step is to eliminate unimportant edge points. Then, HT with weight score is performed.

2.1   The First Step: Eliminating Unimportant Edges

Most HT algorithms start with an edge image. Our algorithm also uses Canny edge detector [5]. However, Canny edge detector has an uncertainty about the scale parameter and the edge location. As the scale value of the detector grows larger, the detector gives strong edges; but the locations of the edges are incorrect. Even though the small scale parameter contributes to the location of edge, it gives a lot of shabby edges.

We propose an edge elimination step as a preprocessing of HT (see Fig 1). It does not matter whether edge detector has a small scale parameter value, because disturbing parts of the edge image will be eliminated. For the scale value of the edge detector, we use 1.0. Then, the covariance of the edge distribution is estimated.

Textured regions in image have a lot of noise edges after the image gets through the edge detector, and the edge distribution within that region is large.

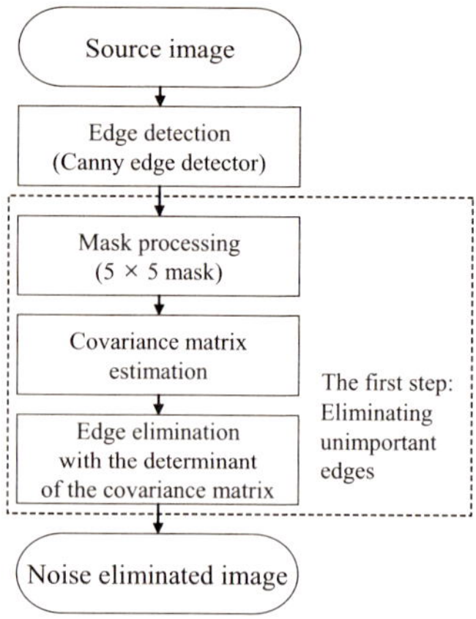

Fig. 1. The first step of proposed HT algorithm

On the contrary, clear parts around a strong edge have a small distribution. Therefore, the covariance matrix is used to see which part of an edge image may ill-affect the result. We used 2×2 covariance matrix because the image is 2 dimension in which two variables, x and y for each coordinate, exist. To estimate the covariance of the edge pixels within a mask area, we restricted the size of the mask to 5×5, since wide mask processing has a large variation. The mask moves from an edge point to the next one in the edge image to get the covariance around each edge point. Given n edge points in a mask area, the covariance matrix is

$$C = \begin{pmatrix} c_{11} & c_{12} \\ c_{21} & c_{22} \end{pmatrix}, \tag{1}$$

where

$$c_{11} = \frac{1}{n}\Sigma_{i=1,\dots,n}(x_i - x_m)^2, \tag{2}$$

$$c_{12} = c_{21} = \frac{1}{n}\Sigma_{i=1,\dots,n}(x_i - x_m)(y_i - y_m), \tag{3}$$

$$c_{22} = \frac{1}{n}\Sigma_{i=1,\dots,n}(y_i - y_m)^2 \tag{4}$$

and

$$x_m = \frac{1}{n}\Sigma_{i=1,\dots,n}x_i, \quad y_m = \frac{1}{n}\Sigma_{i=1,\dots,n}y_i. \tag{5}$$

The distributions of x and y are dependent on each other, so that the covariance value can be easily deduced from the determinant of the covariance matrix, i.e. $det = c_{11}c_{22} - c_{12}c_{21}$. If the determinant is larger than a certain threshold, the edge point at the origin of the mask will be erased, because a large determinant of a matrix means that the elements are not oriented. On the contrary, a straight line gets zero determinant of the covariance matrix in its distribution because it is oriented. However, considering the stepwise shape of edge in pixel coordinates, even the covariance determinant of a straight line may have a small value. If the determinant is zero, the small eigenvalue of the covariance matrix, which means the second principal axis of dispersed data, is also zero. Guru et al. used the small eigenvalue to detect a line [3]; in our case, however, it is sufficient to use the determinant of the covariance instead of the eigenvalue, because it simplifies the processing.

The proper threshold for the determinant is needed to eliminate unsuitable edge points. Empirically, we found that the threshold value of 10.0 produces good results for 1.0 scale factor of Canny edge detector. If the threshold is larger than 10.0, there are still lots of noisy parts; if it is less than 10.0, many parts of strong lines are eliminated. The edge point in the edge image will remain if its determinant of the covariance in the mask area is less than the threshold as follows:

$$p(x, y) = \begin{cases} 1, & \text{if } det(x, y) \leq t \\ 0, & \text{otherwise} \end{cases}, \tag{6}$$

where $det(x, y)$ is determined by edge points within the mask area of which the center is $p(x, y)$. In this equation, t is the threshold, and 1 indicates remaining and 0 indicates being erased.

2.2 The Second Step: Accumulation with Weight Score

Fig. 2(a) is a synthetic edge image that contains a group of short lines and an ordinary line. If a common HT is applied to the image, the result will first give incorrect information as Fig. 2(b) shows. On the other side, our algorithm overcomes such a problem (Fig. 2(c)). Although the total number of votes for the detected line in Fig. 2(b) and that for the detected line in Fig. 2(c) are the same, our accumulation processing makes a difference between real line and noise group, because we use the following function:

$$a(r, \theta) = \sum_i n_i(r, \theta)^k \quad \text{if } n_i(r, \theta) \geq t_n, \tag{7}$$

(a)	(b)	(c)

Fig. 2. (a) Synthetic edge image. Gray lines indicate the maximum votes in accumulator array. (b) The result of a common HT; (c) the result of our modified voting system.

where $a(r, \theta)$ is the accumulator bin for r and θ (refer to Introduction), $n_i(r, \theta)$ is the length of the i-th line overlapping with the HT line of r and θ. The length of a line is simply the number of sequential votes for the current r and θ. Thus, when the line meets the best matching parameter values, it has high score; and the long line can have higher score because it is accumulated with the power sum. The length of a line should be longer than t_n; otherwise, the score will be zero. The threshold t_n was 3 in our experiments because we simply considered an edge of 1 or 2 length as a noise edge.

Since HT is iteratively performed whenever r and/or θ is changed, the direction of the scanning of image follows the current r and θ. Therefore, without any need of additional process for the estimation of the length of each edge line, our algorithm just needs one buffer that is used for temporary accumulation, and it receives sequential votes instead of the current accumulation bin until there is no vote. The cumulated value in the buffer itself becomes the length of a line lying over the current parameters of HT, and the value with the power sum will be added to the current accumulation bin. Then, the buffer is initialized and used for the next line to vote.

In Eq. (7), the problem is how to determine the value k of the power sum. If k is large, very short lines also have great voting scores irrespective of their lengths. If k is around 1.0, it will be meaningless. We have found that the results are good when k is a number between 1.5 and 2.0; so we used nearly mid value, 1.8. The below algorithm describes this second step.

1. Start HT with Yuen's quantization (refer to [12]).
2. Increase r and/or θ (refer to the equation in Introduction).
   (a) Follow the HT line of the current parameters in the image space and vote the pixel overlapping with the HT line upon a temporary buffer.
   (b) Repeat (a) until there is no vote.
   (c) If the votes of the buffer is less than t_n, then go to (a); otherwise, go to the next.
   (d) Accumulate the votes of the buffer with Eq. (7) into the current bin of the accumulator array.
   (e) Initialize the buffer and go back to (a) until the HT line meets the end.
3. Repeat 2 until the end of r and θ.
4. Search the peak from the accumulator array and draw the line corresponding to the peak.

3   Experimental Results

In our experiments, we selected only one maximum peak from the accumulator array per iteration; then, the edges corresponding to the peak are deleted from the edge image. This processing is repeated several times, so that it produces the lines matching the maximum peaks in order of their magnitude. The reason is that the purpose of this paper is not to address efficient peak detection and that the lines should be carefully extracted for other applications such as 3-dimensional building modeling. All the source images were obtained from Visual Geometry Group at Oxford University (see Fig. 3).

We also have used Yuen's quantization [12], since it is simple and deals with the memory economically. In these experiments, all the scale factors of Canny detector were 1.0, which gave a lot of edges with correct positions. The value k of the power sum was 1.8, and the threshold for the determinant of the covariance matrix was 10. The common HT we have used for the comparison was the SHT. Also, we manually selected some lines referring to the edge image because the output can be obtained only from explicit edges, aside from human perception.

3.1   House Image

As shown in Fig. 4(f), one can consider that important edges lie on the roof and the bottom of the house. The edge image shows that the image has a lot of textured regions, especially in the wall of the house (Fig. 4(a)). Through the first step, relative noisy parts of the edge image were erased as seen in Fig. 4(b). We detected 9 lines in this image with the maximum value of the votes per iteration, but the SHT gave improper lines (Fig. 4(c)), comparing to our algorithm. In this result, the SHT with the first step has not remarkable differences with the SHT without it (Fig. 4(d)). However, our algorithm shows better performance than the SHT (Fig. 4(e)).

3.2   College Image

This image has also textured features in the wall (Fig. 3(c)), and the lines likely to be detected is shown in Fig. 5(f). Figs. 5(a) and 5(b) show the results of edge

(a)   (b)   (c)

Fig. 3. Source images: (a) House image; (b) Church image; (c) College image

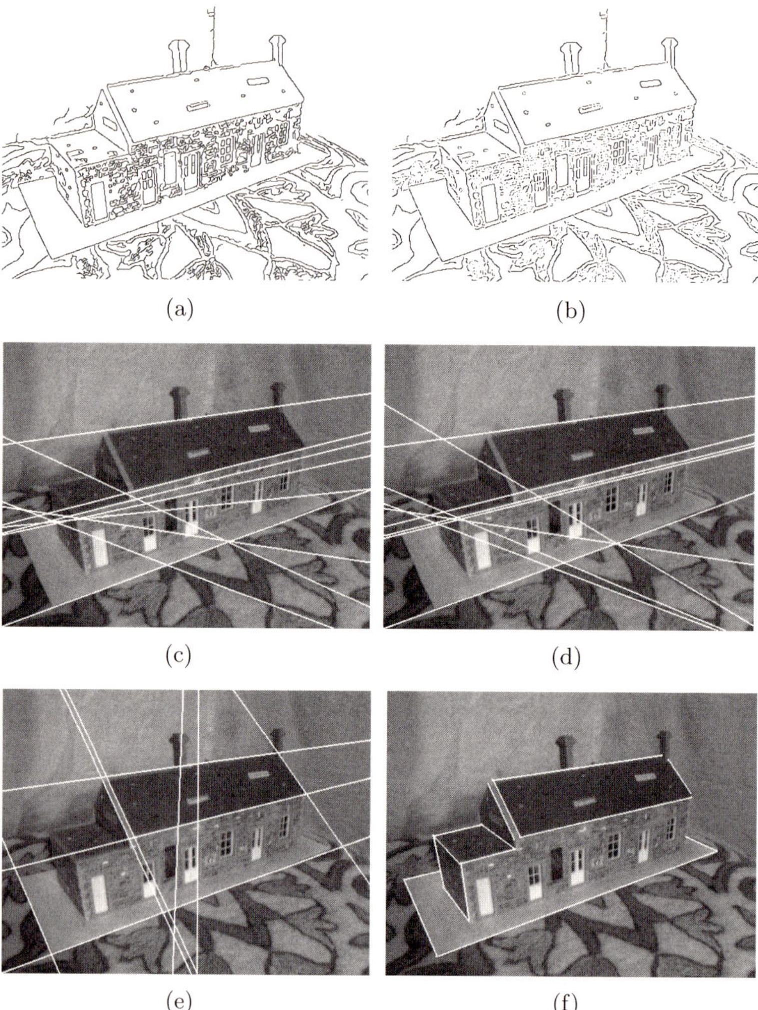

Fig. 4. House image: (a) edge image; (b) the result of the first step; (c) the result of SHT; (d) the result of SHT after the first step; (e) the result of our algorithm; (f) manually selected lines (superimposed white lines)

detection and noise edge elimination. We detected 8 lines, but the SHT did not give a good result for this image (Fig. 5(c)). However, our first step improves the performance of the result as seen in Fig. 5(d). Our voting system gives the best performance as the lines on the verges of the wall indicate (Fig. 5(e)). Nevertheless, there is some unsatisfying information. For example, a missing line is found in the bottom verge of the front roof. Besides, the line through a bench in the middle of the image is not important line. The result might be affected by the quantization scheme for the accumulator, and it seems that there is still a blind characteristic.

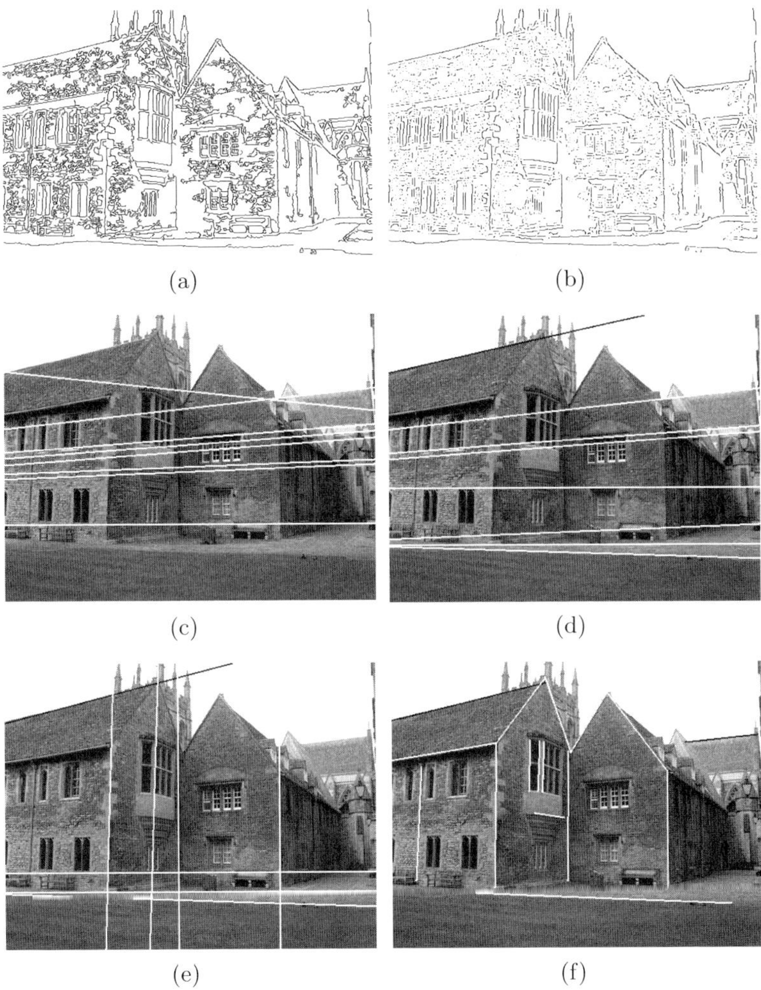

Fig. 5. College image: (a) edge image; (b) the result of the first step; (c) the result of SHT; (d) the result of SHT after the first step; (e) the result of our algorithm; (f) manually selected lines (superimposed white and black lines)

3.3   Church Image

As shown in Fig. 6(a), there are many noise edges. After noise edge elimination (Fig. 6(b)), there are still some noise that may affect the final result. Church image shows great differences between algorithms. We extracted 11 lines, but the SHT gave too inappropriate result. Many lines have got together into the tower (Fig. 6(c)). However, with our first step, the performance of the SHT is slightly improved (Fig. 6(d)). The best performance is shown in Fig. 6(e), where the

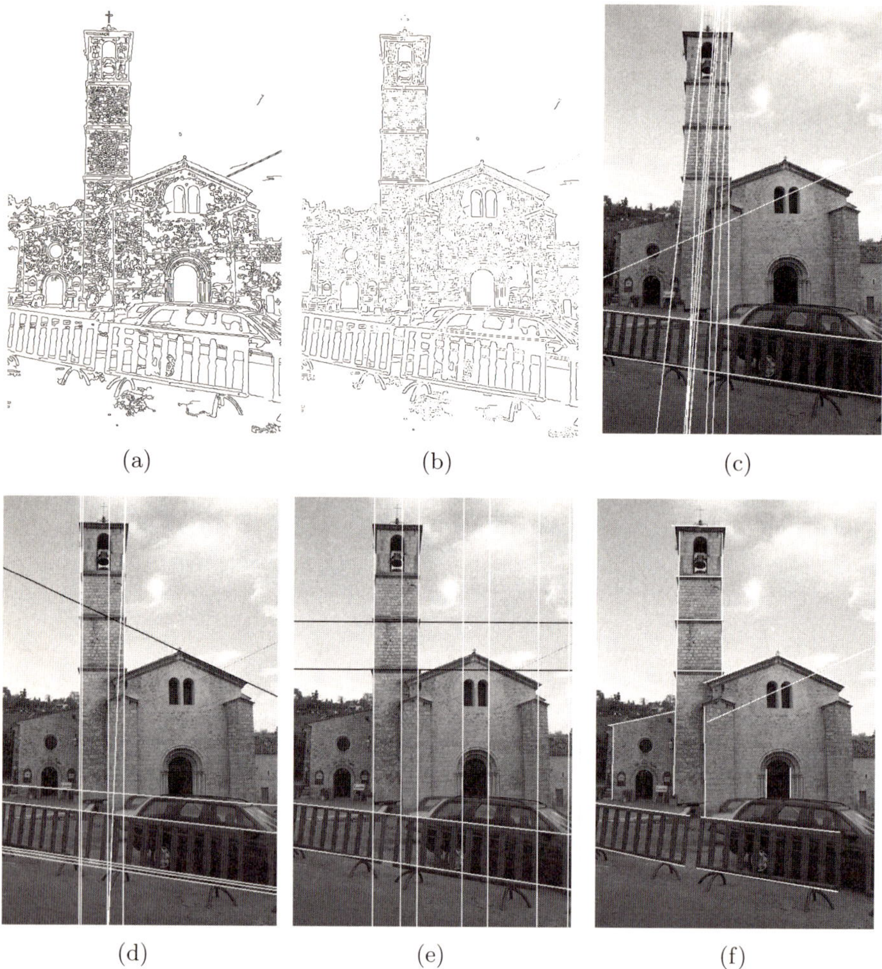

Fig. 6. Church image: (a) edge image; (b) the result of the first step; (c) the result of SHT; (d) the result of SHT after the first step; (e) the result of our algorithm; (f) manually selected lines (superimposed white lines)

verges of the tower and the lines of the front fence are detected, but the lines are slightly deviated to the vertical and horizontal direction, compared to Fig. 6(f).

4   Conclusions

This paper has addressed a simple and efficient method for the enhancement of HT. In summary, our algorithm consists of two steps: The first step is the elimination of noisy parts of the edge image, and the second is the accumulation with weight score. Noisy parts of the image have large determinant of the covariance matrix, while straight lines have almost zero determinant. A long edge has a great weight for its vote into the corresponding accumulator bin. Our algorithm uses the proper rate of the weight score according to the length of a line which means the number of sequential votes.

The algorithm is suitable for architectural images which have a lot of textured regions. The purpose of our algorithm differs from previous versions of HT. Commonly, the previous HTs have paid little attention to the application to which they are applied. In fact, the performance, speed and memory management are important for HT; however, if HT is used as a preprocessing for other vision applications, a robust HT that is able to be used for any kind of image is needed. On the other hand, our algorithm detects important lines first, so that other applications such as 3-dimensional building modeling can use this algorithm for a feature extraction.

The line detection is a difficult field in computer vision, but it is necessary for high level image processing and computer vision. HT is a good algorithm for the line detection, even though it has a blind characteristic. Therefore, the HT that is able to overcome those disadvantages is being demanded.

References

1. C. Schmid, A. Zisserman: Automatic line matching across views, Proc. IEEE Conf. on Computer Vision and Pattern Recognition, 1997, pp. 666-671.
2. D. Ben-Tzvi, M.B. Sandler: A combinatorial Hough transform, Pattern Recognition Lett. 11 (3), 1990, pp. 167-174.
3. D.S. Guru, B.H. Shekar, P. Nagabhushan: A simple and robust line detection algorithm based on small eigenvalue analysis, Pattern Recognitin Letters 25 (2004), pp. 1-13.
4. H. Li, M.A. Lavin, R.J. Le Master: Fast Hough transform: A hierarchical approach, Comput. Vision Graphics Image Process. 36, 1986, pp. 139-161.
5. J.F. Canny: A computational approach to edge detection, IEEE Trans. Pattern Anal. Machine Intell. 8 (6), 1986, pp. 679-698.
6. J. Illingworth, J. Kittler: The adaptive Hough transform, IEEE Trans. Pattern Anal. Machine Intell. 9 (5), 1987, pp. 690-698.
7. J. Princen, J. Illingworth, J. Kittler: A hierarchical approach to line extraction based on the Hough transform, Comput. Vision Graphics Image Process. 52 (1), 1990, pp. 57-77.
8. L. Xu, E. Oja, P. Kultanen: A new curve detection method: Randomized Hough transform (RHT), Pattern Recognition Lett. 11 (5), 1990, pp. 331-338.
9. N. Kiryati, Y. Eldar, A.M. Bruckstein: A probabilistic Hough transform, Pattern Recognition 24 (4), 1991, pp. 303-316.
10. P.V.C. Hough: Method and means for recognizing complex patterns, U.S. Patent No. 3069654, 1962.
11. R.O. Duda, P.E. Hart: Use of Hough transformation to detect lines and curves in pictures, Commun. ACM 15 (1), 1972, pp. 11-15.
12. S.Y.K. Yuen: An approach to quantization of Hough space, Proc. 7th Scandinavian Conf. Image Analysis (1991), pp. 733-740.
13. Y. Furukawa and Y. Shinagawa: Accurate and robust line segment extraction by analyzing distribution around peaks in Hough space, Computer Vision and Image Understanding 92 (2003), pp. 1-25.

Relative Color Polygons for Object Detection and Recognition

Thi Thi Zin, Sung Shik Koh, and Hiromitsu Hama

Graduate School of Engineering, Osaka City University, 3-3-138, Sugimoto,
Sumiyoshi-ku, Osaka-shi, 558-8585 Japan
{thithi, koh}@sys.info.eng.osaka-cu.ac.jp,
hama@info.eng.osaka-cu.ac.jp

Abstract. This paper proposes a new framework of the color model for outdoor scene image detection and recognition. This model enables us to manipulate easily the color of an image. Here, the concept of 'relative color polygon' for an object composed of uniform color regions is introduced on a 2D color space (XY space). Then the color similarity is defined using three kinds of parameters of the polygon: length and slope of every side and angle of adjacent sides. This paper addresses how to decide the color similarity by using the facts about color shifting on the XY space. The feasibility of the proposed framework has been confirmed through the experimental results using outdoor scene images taken under a great variety of various illumination conditions.

1 Introduction

Color has been widely used in various tasks such as image segmentation, pattern recognition and classification, and so on. Clearly, for such tasks to be successful, the color must be stable across illumination change [1]. A color image is a function of many parameters, for example, light source color, scene and object geometry, object shape and albedo, and camera parameters. Existing works in relevant aspects of color vision can be divided into two categories: computational color constancy and physics-based modeling. In addition, there are many researches who related to color vision in the areas of parametric classification [2][3], machine learning techniques [4], color-based segmentation [5], color-contrast landmark detection [6], illumination estimation [7], and color indexing [1][8][9].

Moreover, the problem of color representation affects almost every field in computer vision. Many methods have been suggested for modeling and representing colors. The *RGB* color space is widely used for image capture and display, however it is not always considered the appropriate representation for color. Other color spaces have been suggested to create more intuitive color representation. There are many such spaces (*HLS*, *HSV*, *L*a*b** and so on), but they are not enough to overcome the difficulties under illumination changes. So, we introduce Relative Color (RC) polygons defined on a 2D color space (XY space) that is well suited to image processing in outdoor scenes. One application of the proposed system is shown in Fig.1.

S. Greco et al. (Eds.): RSCTC 2006, LNAI 4259, pp. 834–843, 2006.
© Springer-Verlag Berlin Heidelberg 2006

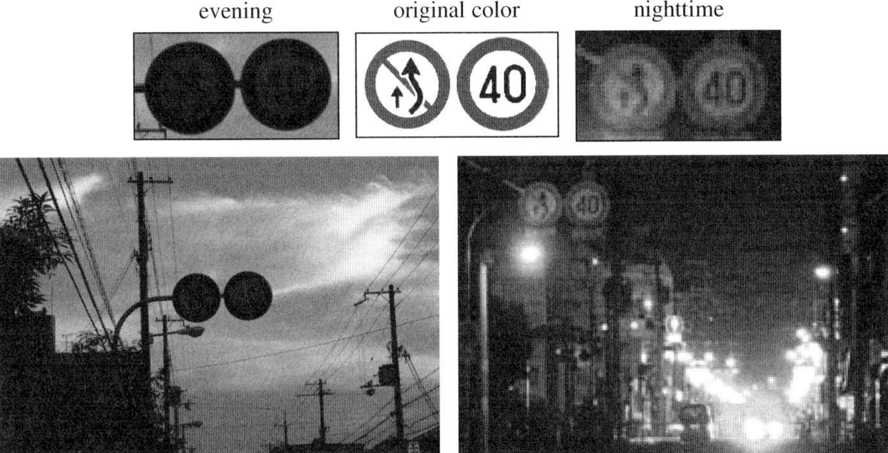

Is it possible to judge that the above road signs' colors are similar with the original colors?

Fig. 1. Scenes to decide the color similarity for road sign recognition

This paper is organized as follows. In Section II, we define the *XY* color space with chromatic and achromatic regions. Section III introduces RC polygons, some parameters for color similarity, and explains the advantages of RC polygons. The evaluation and discussions are included in Section IV. Finally, Section V concludes this paper.

2   Color Space

Color is very important for image processing and computer vision. In 1931, CIE defined the virtual primary colors *XYZ* as the standard [10]. The representation of the *RGB* color space in 3D-polar coordinates (hue, saturation and brightness) can sometimes simplify this task by revealing characteristics not visible in the rectangular coordinate representation. The *rgb* space (Eq.(1)) is a normalized form of the *RGB* space and is used to eliminate the effect of brightness. Here, we define the *XY* space using the *rgb* space. This space is suitable for image processing especially in outdoor scene images. The aspect of the *XY* space is described in Fig.2. In this paper, we mainly focus on the chromatic region. In Fig.2(c-d), the ellipse region painted by black color represents the achromatic region which is predefined by using the pixel values of white color from various types of signboards under different illumination conditions. Here, the *XY* space is defined as follows.

$$r = \frac{R}{R+G+B}, \; g = \frac{G}{R+G+B}, \; b = \frac{B}{R+G+B}. \tag{1}$$

$$\vec{E}_x = \left(\frac{\sqrt{2}}{2}, -\frac{\sqrt{2}}{2}, 0 \right), \tag{2}$$

$$\vec{E}_y = \left(-\frac{\sqrt{6}}{6}, -\frac{\sqrt{6}}{6}, \frac{\sqrt{6}}{3} \right), \tag{3}$$

where $\vec{E}_x$ and $\vec{E}_y$ are perpendicular to each other and unit vectors.

$$\vec{E}_x \perp \vec{E}_y \,,\; \left| \vec{E}_x \right| = \left| \vec{E}_y \right| = 1 \text{ (unit vector)}. \tag{4}$$

Each pixel value of an input image is transformed from the RGB space to the point (X,Y) on the XY space as follows.

$$\vec{a} = (r,g,b) - \left(\frac{1}{3}, \frac{1}{3}, \frac{1}{3} \right), \tag{5}$$

$$X = \vec{a} \cdot \vec{E}_x, \; Y = \vec{a} \cdot \vec{E}_y. \tag{6}$$

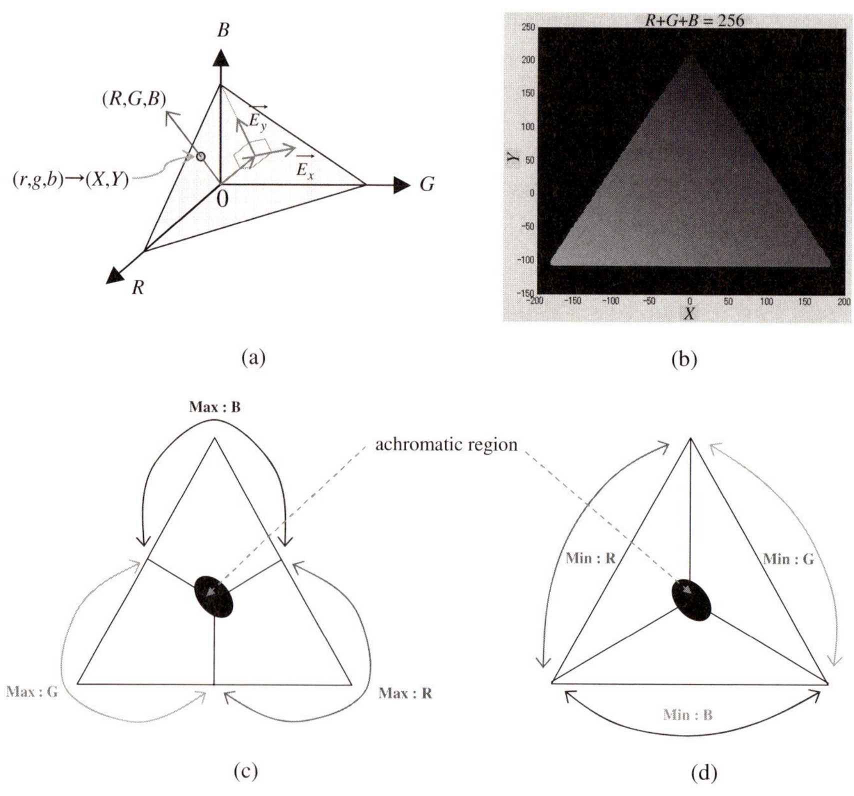

Fig. 2. XY space: (a) relation between RGB and XY space, (b) XY space with colors, (c) and (d) analysis of XY space

3 RC Polygons

Color representation is a crucial factor for color image segmentation and recognition. Many attempts have been made to find the best color space for the task, yet no one model has proven to be always superior to others [11]. Here, we introduce RC polygons defined on the XY space. In order to explain the reason for using RC polygons, we take examples of road signs. Most road signs consist of two or more uniform color regions. Ones considered here are composed of three colors: red, white, and blue. The outdoor scene colors always vary due to illumination changes and weather conditions. For example, Fig.3(a) shows the road sign images taken at different times in the same day. Although their respective pixel values are significantly different from those of the other time on the conventional RGB space (Fig.3(b)), they change slightly on the XY space (Fig.3(c)). In Fig.3(c), the triangles of red, white, and blue colors on the XY space are very similar and look homothetic one another even though their illumination conditions are quite different.

In the case of more than three uniform color regions, the triangle becomes the polygon called the RC polygon as shown in Fig.4. Although the place and the lighting always changing in outdoor scene images, the RC polygons keep their shapes. According to this investigation, we can decide robust color similarity between objects with uniform color regions in different images. For the sake of checking similarity, three parameters are introduced:

- length of every side,
- slope of every side,
- angle of adjacent sides.

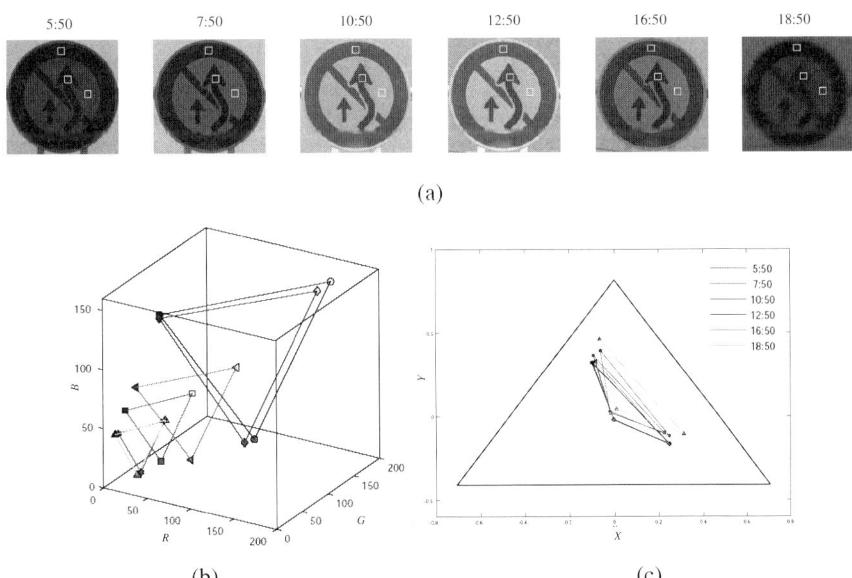

Fig. 3. Color changing of road signs within one day: (a) images of the same road sign taken at the different times, (b) their cropped colors on RGB space, (c) RC polygons on XY space

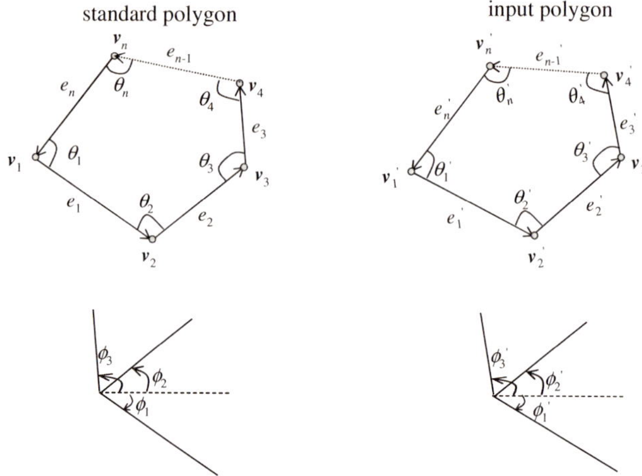

Fig. 4. RC polygons and criterions for similarities

If the following conditions are satisfied for every $k=1,...,n$, then we can conclude that the two polygons are homothetic, in other words, the colors of the input object are similar with those of the standard one. Then the color similarity between two RC polygons is formulized as follows (Fig.4):

$$Th_{d1} \le \frac{d'_k}{d_k} \le Th_{d2}, \tag{7}$$

$$\left| \theta'_k - \theta_k \right| \le Th_\theta, \tag{8}$$

$$\left| \phi'_k - \phi_k \right| \le Th_\phi, \tag{9}$$

where, |.| is the absolute value and angles are expressed by the inferior angles,

$$d'_k = e'_k \bigg/ \sum_{i=1}^{n} e'_i, \quad d_k = e_k \bigg/ \sum_{i=1}^{n} e_i, \, (k=1,...,n), \tag{10}$$

and n is the number of sides of the polygon, and the parameters θ_k, ϕ_k, v_k, and e_k are the angle of adjacent sides, the slope of the sides, the vertex, and the length of the sides for the standard RC polygon, respectively. Then $\theta_k{'}$, $\phi_k{'}$, $v_k{'}$, and e' are the corresponding parameters of the input RC polygon. Eq.(7) and (8) are deeply linked, but not the same. According to our experiences, Th_θ and Th_ϕ are approximately $22°$ in their maximums in outdoor scene images. In order to be applicable to outdoor and indoor scene images with various color temperatures at the same time, it is enough to decide the threshold values by pre-experimental results as follows:

$$Th_\theta = Th_\phi = 38°, \tag{11}$$

$$Th_{d1} = 0.7, \, Th_{d2} = 1.5. \tag{12}$$

To put it briefly, we use only four kinds of thresholds. Unlike as other approaches, the proposed algorithm does not need many images to decide the standard values of these parameters (the standard RC polygon). That is, it is enough to use only one good condition (daytime) image for a standard. This point is the big advantage over many other methods.

To check the stability of the RC polygons, some experiments are conducted under six fluorescent lamps with color temperatures (3000K, 3200K, 5000K, 5500K, 6700K, and 7200K) using six chromatic color regions (cyan, yellow, magenta, red, green, and blue). Fig.5 shows the color board images taken under single directional lighting (Geometrical condition: 45-n (45-0) by CIE) and RC polygons when the color temperature changes. According to this figure, it is seen that the RC polygons are homothetic. Moreover, to confirm the effectiveness of the proposed method, we extend the color board images to visual information signboard images at different times under outdoor scenes. In this paper, all chromatic colors and white color (achromatic) are mainly treated, but black color is not considered in this system. Because the color value of a black pixel is so small that the movement of this color is too much sensitive and not stable. Almost all signboards are composed of not so many color regions, but the similarity of RC polygons can be kept when using many.

In Fig.6(a), the component colors of the visual signboard are orange, red, white, and green. The RGB ratios of these colors at each hour (from 9AM to 4PM) are expressed in Fig.6(c). Due to various illumination changes, the red and orange colors are very difficult to distinguish from each other on the RGB space. If we use absolute color values like as color bounding boxes (BBs), we will face with mis-classifying. Even though the illumination effect is strongly influenced on an image, all colors move to the same direction. This fact agrees with our RC polygons and the criterions for similarities. Therefore, the RC polygon on the XY space can easily solve such a problem as shown in Fig.6(b).

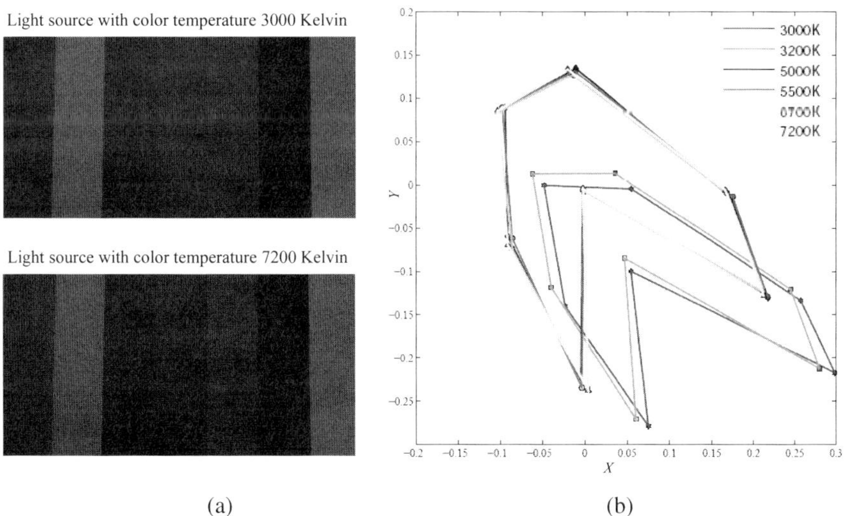

(a)   (b)

Fig. 5. Color movements against with color temperature: (a) input images, and (b) RC polygons on XY space

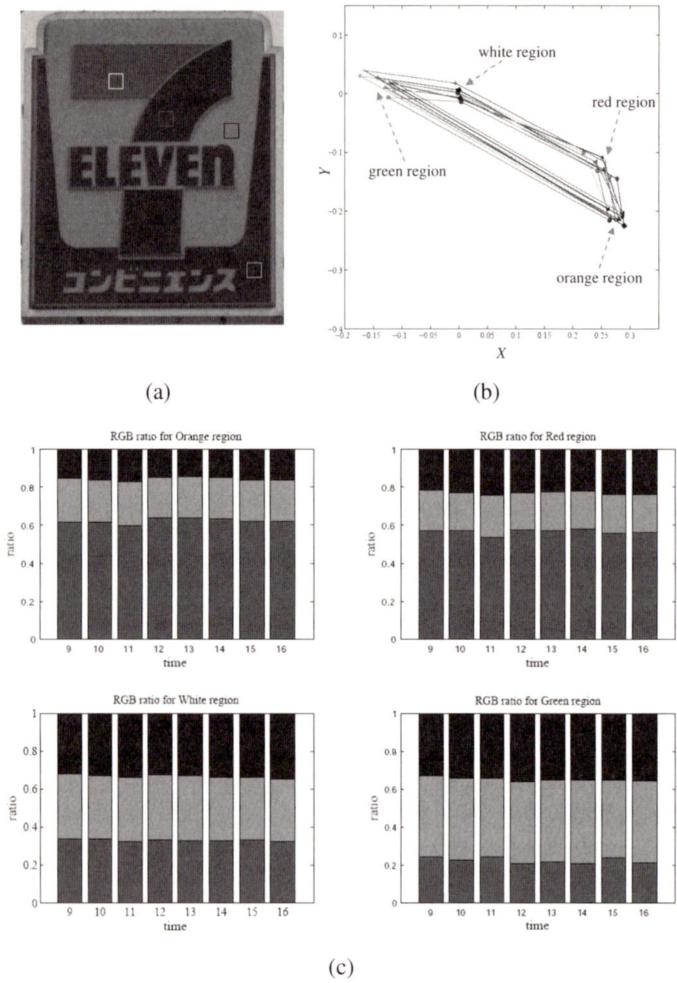

(a)

(b)

(c)

Fig. 6. Example of a commercial signboard: (a) cropped uniform color regions (orange, red, white and green), (b) RC polygons on *XY* space, and (c) *RGB* color ratios for orange, red, white, and green, respectively

4   Evaluation and Discussions

The proposed framework has been evaluated through experiments with a large and diverse set of road sign images acquired from different weather conditions (sunny, cloudy, and rainy) and different illumination conditions (day, dusk, and night). The system was implemented in Matlab 7.0.4 and executed on a personal computer with AMD Athlon™ XP 2800+ Processor. There are many difficult situations for segmentation and recognition of outdoor scenes images taken by various kinds of digital cameras from outdoor scenes under a great variety of illumination changes. That is why we choose road sign for testing. Some of these difficulties are:

- changing illumination due to outdoor lighting conditions varying from day to night,
- reflection and specular highlights due to electric bulbs, headlights of cars,
- decreasing visibility due to weather conditions, for example, rain and fog,
- color fading away after long exposure due to sunlight and so on.

The recognition of road signs is more difficult than other commercial signboards which are always well maintained.

One of the most significant characteristics of all road signs is the combination of distinctive colors. Many color segmentation methods have been implemented on the *RGB* color space [3][12], *HSV* [2][13][14] and *YUV* [15]. Many researchers used BB methods on the *RGB* color space, for example, BB1 in Example 1. According to BB1, the road sign segmentation under good illumination conditions may be well done, but it faces immediately big problems under bad illumination conditions as shown in Fig.1 and Fig.7. In Table1, the *B* components are larger than other components even though in a red color region in Fig.7. So BB1 can't solve such a problem. Most of papers suggested that the *HSV* color space might be more flexible to the disturbance caused by lighting problems, but it didn't significantly improve any performance in our experiments. Vitabile et al. [2] used dynamic pixel aggregation techniques in the *HSV* color space using BB2 in Example 2. The system performance decreased when the processed images are characterized by predominant sets of pixels whose attributes fall into the *HSV* achromatic and/or unstable areas. From these results, it can be seen that the road sign colors can't be detected only by color BBs under such bad illumination conditions.

Example 1: BB1 (*in RGB color space*)

> *RED*   : if (R>80) AND (R-G>20) AND (R-B>20),
> *WHITE* : if(R>150) AND (G>150) AND (B>150).

Example 2: BB2 (*in HSV color space*)

> *Chromatic:* $S \geq 0.5$ *and* $0.2 < V \leq 0.9$,
> *Unstable chromatic:* $0.25 < S < 0.5$ *and* $0.2 < V \leq 0.9$,
> *Achromatic:* $S \leq 0.25$ *or* $V \leq 0.2$ *or* $V \geq 0.9$.

In fact, we have already tried the road sign color separation by a linear learning method [16][17], and looked into the color nature of road signs. The road sign colors, such as red, blue and white, were successfully separated in the three dimensional *RGB* color space by a hyper-plane at daytime but couldn't do at night-time. Therefore, we have found out it is impossible to solve simultaneously under all illumination conditions even though many color BBs are prepared. To handle this kind of problems, we proposed the relative color method for road sign colors in our past studies [18]. In order to address the above difficulties, we apply the RC polygons that can successfully achieve the recognition of outdoor scene images. Thus, almost all of road sign colors are detected and recognized under all illumination conditions even though at night-time. Thus the RC polygons, that is, the 'relative color' is very powerful and effective not only for bad illumination conditions, but also for removing noises. We will have the chance to present the outcome at the next time. In Fig.7(b), the blue dotted line triangle is the standard RC polygon from Fig.3 (10:50AM). Although the images of Fig.7(a) are strongly blue color influenced images, their color vertices keeps their relative shape of RC polygon. Therefore, the proposed RC polygon is very suitable for outdoor scene segmentation and recognition.

To evaluate the proposed system performance, 300 images under a great variety of illumination changes were processed. By using this method, about 95% of images matched correctly to the standard images. There are 5% failure cases left. The reasons are: (i) deteriorated uniform color regions by occlusion or partial highlight due to leaves, street lamps, headlights and so on, and (ii) very dark images, for example, RGB values less than 10 in chromatic color.

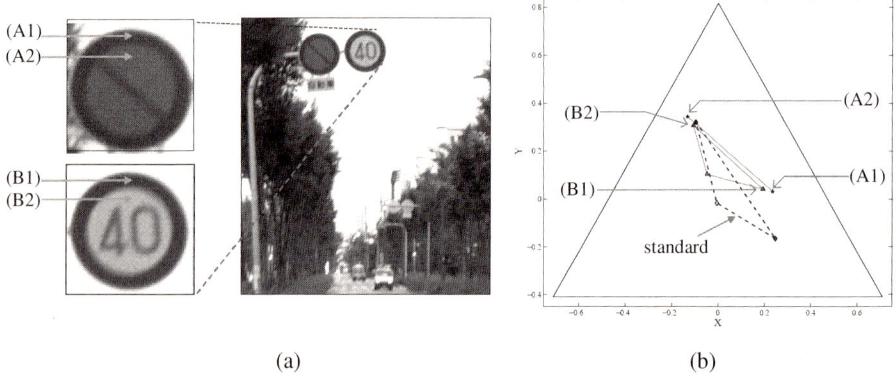

(a)   (b)

Fig. 7. Color composition in a road sign: (a) strongly blue color influenced images, (b) on *XY* space

Table 1. Color components in *RGB* and *HSV* space

pixels	R	G	B	H	S	V	Colors
(A1)	100	41	105	0.82	0.61	0.41	*Red*
(A2)	63	88	188	0.63	0.67	0.74	*Blue*
(B1)	105	52	106	0.83	0.51	0.42	*Red*
(B2)	134	155	202	0.62	0.34	0.79	*White*

5 Conclusions

Large amounts of information are embedded in the natural scene. We have introduced the RC polygons on the *XY* space and discussed several illumination problems in outdoor scenes. Experiments have shown the robustness and efficiency of the proposed methods. For experiments, we used 300 images including road signs and other visual information signboards under a great variety of illumination changes including nighttime, foggy day and rainy day. Road signs and visual information signboards are good examples of objects composed of uniform color regions. The proposed method can potentially be applicable to various tasks such as image retrieval, image indexing, image reproduction, image enhancement, segmentation and recognition of objects with uniform color regions, and so on. Furthermore, it may be also possible to estimate the color temperature of the light source based on the RC polygons.

Acknowledgement

The second author's work was supported by the Korea Research Foundation Grant funded by Korea Government (MOEHRD, Basic Research Promotion Fund) (M01-2004-000-20052-0).

References

1. M.J. Swain and D.H. Ballard: Color Indexing. International Journal of Computer Vision, vol. 7, no. 1, (1991) 11-32
2. S. Vitabile, G. Pollaccia, G. Pilato, and E. Sorbello: Road Signs Recognition Using a Dynamic pixel aggregation Technique in the HSV Color Space. In Proc. of 11th International Conference on Image Analysis and Processing, Palermo, Italy, (2001) 572-577
3. Lukas Sekanina and Jim Torresen: Detection of Norwegian Speed Limit Signs. In proc. of 16th European Simulation Multi-conference. Darmstadt, Germany, (2002) 337-340
4. S. Buluswar and B. Draper: Color Recognition in Outdoor Images. In proc. of the International Conference on Computer Vision, (1998) 171-177
5. Dmitry P. Nikolaev and Petr P. Nikolayev: Linear Color Segmentation and its Implementation. Computer Vision and Image Understanding. vol.94, (2004) 115-139
6. Eduardo Todt and Carme Torras: Color-contrast Landmark Detection and Encoding in Outdoor Images. LNCS, vol. 3691, (2005) 612-619
7. S.Tominaga: Natural image database and its use for scene illuminant estimation. Journal of Electronic Imaging, vol. 11, no. 5, (2002) 434-444
8. B.V. Funt and G.D. Finlayson : Color Constant Color Indexing. IEEE Trans. on PAMI, vol. 17, no. 5, (1995) 522-529
9. T. Syeda-Mahmood and Y. Q. Cheng: Indexing Colored surfaces in images. In Proc. of International Conference on Pattern Recognition, Vienna, Austria, vol.3, (1996) 8-12
10. Colorimetric Observers, ISO/CIE Std. 10 527, (1986)
11. Y. S. H.D. Cheng, X.H. Jiang, and J. Wang: Color image segmentation: advances and prospects. Pattern Recognition, vol. 34, (2001) 2259–2281
12. A. de la Escalera, L. Moreno, M. A. Salichs, and J.M. Armingol: Road Traffic Sign Detection and Classification. IEEE Trans. on Industrial Electronics, vol. 44, no. 6, (1997) 848-859
13. G.Piccioli, E.De Micheli, P. Parodi, and M.Campani: Robust method for road sign detection and recognition. Image and Vision Computing, vol.14, no.3,(1996) 209-223
14. Thi Thi Zin, C. Liao, T. Kaneko, Y. Yanagihara, and H. Hama: Recognition of Road Environment by Using Color Information from Moving Video Images. In Proc. of the 7th Image Media Processing Symposium, (2002) 109-110
15. W.G. Shadeed, D.I. Abu-Al-Nadi, and M.J. Mismar: Road traffic Sign Detection in Color Images. In Proc. of the 10th IEEE International Conference on Electronic, Circuits and Systems, vol.2, (2003) 890-893
16. Marvin Minsky and Seymour Papert: Perceptrons. MIT Press, (1969)
17. Masamichi Shimura: Pattern Recognition and Learning Machines. Syokodo Press, (1970)
18. Thi Thi Zin and H.Hama: A Robust Road Sign Recognition Using Segmentation with Morphology and Relative Color. The Journal of the Institute of Image Information and Television Engineers, vol. 59, no. 9 (2005)1333(81)-1342(90)

Rough Set Based Image Segmentation
of Video Sequences

Young Sub Song and Hang Joon Kim

Department of Computer Engineering, Kyungpook National Univ., 1370, Sangyuk-dong,
Puk-gu, Daegu, 702-701, Republic of Korea
{yssong, hjkim}@ailab.knu.ac.kr

Abstract. We describe a rough set based segmentation method of video
sequences. In a frame, there are many objects and a background. We represent
theses objects and a background by regions. We consider that each object or
background is a region. This region is represented by a rough set. Rough set is
approximately representation of a crisp set. Our method consists of two phases.
First phase is updating regions phase that consist three steps. First step is setting
initial parameters. We use previous regions' parameters to initial parameters.
Second step is updating object regions. Updating is by hill climbing method
with our evaluation function. Third step is updating a background region. The
background region is updated by using other regions. In second phase, we make
a segmentation map of frame using the regions. An ambiguous pixel's label is
decided using distance with regions.

Keywords: image segmentation, rough set, video sequences, region.

1 Introduction

Segmentation is making several non-overlapping partitions from an image. Image
segmentation is necessary in many image processing fields such as image
understanding, object recognition and etc. There are many researches for image
segmentation. The current work focuses on spatiotemporal methods of segmentation
on video sequences. There are many segmentation approaches such as context based
approach, motion based approach, and so on. Context based segmentation determine a
pixel included a partition using the pixel's location of total data's distribution [1].
Motion based segmentation is considering that partitions or pixels have a velocity or
acceleration, so we know where is the partition previously [2]. There are some
researches of image segmentation using a rough set [3] [4] [5]. But, these researches
are not based on video sequences.

We describe a rough set based segmentation method of video sequences. We
consider that an image is composed many objects and a background. And an object
has close spatial location and similar color. Each object or background is represented
by a region, and a region is presented by a rough set. A pixel in a frame is an element
of these rough sets. A rough set is approximately representation of a crisp set [6] [7].
A rough set is represented by a pair of crisp sets. The pair of crisp sets is a lower
approximation and an upper approximation. In rough set theory, we know that a pixel

S. Greco et al. (Eds.): RSCTC 2006, LNAI 4259, pp. 844–851, 2006.

is belonging to a rough set approximately. So each region has minimum area and maximum area. These two areas are presented by two concentric ellipsoids in five-dimension. Our method consists of next two phases. First phase is updating regions phase that consist three steps. First step is setting initial parameters. We use previous regions' parameters to initial parameters. Second step is updating object regions. Updating is by hill climbing method with our evaluation function. Third step is updating a background region. The background region is updated by using other regions. Next phase is making segmentation map using current regions and a current frame. In second phases, we have to verifying that a pixel's label. A pixel of a region's lower approximation has a label of the region. But a pixel of regions' upper approximation has a label of a region that has minimum distance with the pixel.

The paper proceeds as follows: In section 2, we introduce the concept of rough sets. Section 3 describes about our image modeling with rough sets. In section 4, we describe our rough set based segmentation method. In section 5, our experiment and the result are showing.

2 Concept of Rough Sets

A rough set is an approximately representation of a crisp set. On the rough set theory, we know that a rough set includes an element approximately. So an element is included a rough set, or is not included a rough set, or is included a rough set approximately. A rough set is represented by a pair of crisp sets. The pair of crisp sets are a lower approximation and an upper approximation. In case of an information system (U, A), the U is a non-empty set of finite objects and the V is a non-empty finite set of attributes such that $a : U \rightarrow V_a$ for $\forall a \in A$. Then the U is the universe set. In this case, a rough set RX is representing a crisp set X, then the rough set is defined as following:

$$RX = \left\langle \underline{R}X,\ \overline{R}X \right\rangle, \tag{1}$$

where the $\underline{R}X$ is the lower approximation of the rough set and the $\overline{R}X$ is the upper approximation of the rough set. A lower approximation of a rough set $\underline{R}X$ is composed of all the elementary sets included in X, and a upper approximation of a rough set $\overline{R}X$ is composed of all the elementary sets which have non-empty set intersection with X. A lower approximation is defined as following:

$$\underline{R}X = \{x \in U \mid [x]_P \subseteq X\}\ or$$
$$\underline{R}X = \bigcup\{E \mid E \in U \mid IND(R),\ E \subseteq X\} \tag{2}$$

And an upper approximation is defined as following:

$$\overline{R}X = \{x \in U \mid [x]_P \cap X \neq \phi\}\ or$$
$$\overline{R}X = \bigcup\{E \mid E \in U \mid IND(R),\ E \cap X \neq \phi\} \tag{3}$$

In above definitions, the $IND(R)$ is an equivalence relation. The equivalence relation is defined as following:

$$IND(R) = \{(x, y) \in U \times U \mid \forall a \in R, f(x,a) = f(y,a)\}. \tag{4}$$

And there is a boundary of a rough set. The boundary is a set of elements which is not know exactly that the X includes the elements. The boundary is defined as following:

$$BN(R) = \overline{R}X - \underline{R}X . \tag{5}$$

Fig. 1 shows an example of representing a rough set. There is an object X, and two ellipses. An ellipse which include the object is upper approximation, and an ellipse which included the object is lower approximation.

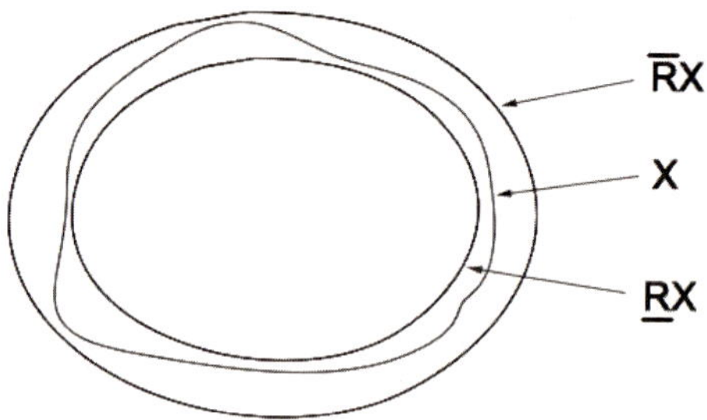

Fig. 1. An Example of representing a rough set

3   Image Modeling with Rough Sets

A frame is made up of constant number pixels. And a pixel has a location and a color. We consider a pixel as a five-dimensional vector. So, a pixel **p** is represent to $\begin{bmatrix} p_x & p_y & p_r & p_g & p_b \end{bmatrix}^T$. There are many objects and a background in a frame. We consider that each objects and background consist of a region. A region consists of pixels that have close spatial locations and similar colors. Each region is represented by a rough set. All of these rough set's lower approximations and upper approximations are a subset of a frame. So we consider a frame as a set of rough set. A region's lower approximation is a set of pixels which is must be included in the region. And a region's upper approximation is a set of pixels which is may be included in the region.

We make the shape of region's rough set as two concentric ellipsoids in five-dimension. The two ellipsoids are a lower ellipsoid and an upper ellipsoid. A lower ellipsoid is representing a region's lower approximation, and an upper ellipsoid is representing a region's upper approximation. So we represent a region R_i by a central five-dimension point $\mathbf{p}^i_{center}$, five axes lengths $l^i_{(axe\,index)}$, a rotation angle d_i and a marginal value m_i. The central point is two ellipsoids' center. The five axes are a lower ellipsoid's axes. The rotation angle is a rotation angle for axes of a lower ellipsoid's location. The marginal value is a number that shows how much bigger an upper ellipsoid then a lower ellipsoid.

A region of an object's rough set is defined as follows:

$$Object = \left\langle \underline{Object}, \overline{Object} \right\rangle \qquad (6)$$

$$\underline{Object} = \left\{ \mathbf{p} \mid Distance(\mathbf{p}, Object) \le 1 \right\}$$

$$\overline{Object} = \left\{ \mathbf{p} \mid Distance(\mathbf{p}, Object) \le m \right\}$$

where,

$$Distance(\mathbf{p}, Object) = \left(\frac{\bar{x} \cos d + \bar{y} \sin d}{l_x} \right)^2 + \left(\frac{\bar{x} \sin d - \bar{y} \cos d}{l_y} \right)^2 \qquad (7)$$

$$+ \left(\frac{r - r_c}{l_r} \right)^2 + \left(\frac{g - g_c}{l_g} \right)^2 + \left(\frac{b - b_c}{l_b} \right)^2$$

$$(x, y, r, g, b) = \mathbf{p}$$

$$(x_c, y_c, r_c, g_c, b_c) = \mathbf{p}_{center}$$

$$\bar{x} = x - x_c$$

$$\bar{y} = y - y_c$$

$$Distance(\mathbf{p}, Background) = C$$

The rough set representing a background is made using all rough sets of objects. A background's lower approximation is a set of pixels which is not included in any object. And a background's upper approximation is a set of pixels which is may not included in any object. A background's rough set is defined as follows:

$$Background = \left\langle \underline{Background}, \overline{Background} \right\rangle \qquad (8)$$

$$\underline{Background} = U - \bigcup \overline{Object}$$

$$\overline{Background} = U - \bigcup \underline{Object}$$

where U is a universal set. The universal set is the set of all pixels in the current frame. So $\underline{Background} \cup \left(\bigcup \overline{Object} \right)$ and $\overline{Background} \cup \left(\bigcup \underline{Object} \right)$ are always equals to universal set.

Fig. 2 shows an example of above image modeling with rough sets. Fig. 2a is an original image. And Fig. 2b is the rough sets of original image. In this figure, a pair of concentric ellipses means a rough set. The inside ellipse is lower approximation, and outside ellipse is upper approximation. The color of ellipse is a center color of the rough set. The white space is lower approximation of background. Fig. 2c shows a segmentation map using rough sets and the current frame.

(a)   (b)   (c)

Fig. 2. An example of image modeling. (a) original image. (b) image modeling via a rough sets. (c) image segmentation using our method.

4 Segmentation Method

The segmentation method for a frame of video sequences consists of two phases. First phase is updating regions. In this phase, we update the previous regions to make current regions using the current frame. Next phase is a making segmentation map. In second phase, we make a segmentation map using the current frame and the current regions. Following sections 4.1 and 4.2 are detailed methods for an each phase.

4.1 Updating Regions

Method for an updating current rough sets is consist of three steps. First step is setting initial parameters of regions. Second step is updating regions of object. Third step is updating region of background. Followings are each step's detailed methods:

Step 1: For initial parameters of current regions, we use the parameters of previous frame's regions. Because variations of object between frames are slightly, we know the current region is similar to the previous region. But region of background is set to an empty set, initially. We calculate the region of background in step 3.

Step 2: This step is a updating current regions of object. We use hill climbing method for this step. So for the updating, we need an evaluation function for an evaluating a fitness between regions and a frame. The fitness between regions and a frame is higher in proportion to a summation of fitness which between each region and the frame. And there are no collisions between rough set's lower approximations. So, the evaluation function is defined as following:

$$f_{evaluation}(\{R_i\}, frame) = \sum f_{fitness}(R_i, frame) - Penalty(\{R_i\}, frame) \qquad (9)$$

In above definition 9, we need a fitness function for a region and a frame. The fitness function is calculated by using pixels in the region. The pixels in a same region have similar parameters, so a smaller variation of the pixels' parameter gets higher fitness. And the region's size is also important. The fitness function is defined as following:

$$f_{fitness}(R, frame) = Score_{variation}(R, frame) \cdot Score_{size}(R) \qquad (10)$$

In above definition 10, we need two score functions. The score of variation is calculated by using the region and the pixels in the frame. Each pixel has weight of proportion to a region. The score of variation is weighted summation using the weight. And the score of size is calculated by using the region's size in five dimensions. So, these score functions are defined as following:

$$Score_{variation}(R, frame) = \sum_{\forall \mathbf{p} \in frame} \frac{Weight(\mathbf{p}, R)}{Distance(\mathbf{p}, R)} \tag{11}$$

$$Weight(\mathbf{p}, R) = \begin{cases} 1 & , Distance(\mathbf{p}, R) \leq 1 \\ w_{boundary} & , 1 < Distance(\mathbf{p}, R) \leq m \\ 0 & , others \end{cases}$$

$$Score_{size}(R) = \sqrt{\pi \cdot l_x \cdot l_y \cdot l_r \cdot l_g \cdot l_b}$$

And we introduce the penalty function. The penalty is for collisions of rough set's lower approximations. The collision means that some pixel is an element of two or more rough set's lower approximations. So we want that there is no collision. The penalty function is summation of all penalties of pixel. So, the total penalty function is defined as following:

$$Penalty(\{R_i\}, frame) = \sum_{\forall \mathbf{p} \in frame} Penalty(\mathbf{p}, \{R_i\}) \tag{12}$$

$$Penalty(\mathbf{p}, \{R_i\}) = \begin{cases} k \cdot S_P, & k > 1 \\ 0, & others \end{cases}$$

In above definition 12, the k is the number of lower approximations which have the pixel as a element. And the S_P is a constant number of a unit penalty score.

Step 3: Updating the region of background is the current step working. All regions of object are calculated already. So we can calculate the region of background by using formula 7.

4.2 Making a Segmentation Map

In this phase, we introduce the method for a making segmentation map. For a making segmentation map, we use a frame and regions. The frame is already segmented to regions. The segmentation's result is non-overlapping partitions. But a pixel is a element of many regions, possibly. So, we need to verify which region a pixel is belonging.

For a making segmentation map, we verify each pixel in the frame is belonging to which region. A pixel which is an element of a region's lower approximation is belonging to the region. And a pixel which is not an element of any region's lower approximation is belonging to a region that the region has the pixel as upper approximation's element and the region have minimum distance to the pixel. The function which verifies a pixel's label is defined as following:

$$f_{verify}\left(\mathbf{p}, \{RS_i \mid 1 \leq i \leq k\}\right) \tag{13}$$

$$= \begin{cases} j & , \mathbf{p} \in \underline{RS_j}\,, 1 \leq j \leq k \\ \arg\min_i Distance(\mathbf{p}, R_i) & , j \in \{l \mid \mathbf{p} \in \overline{RS_l}\}\,, others \end{cases}$$

In above function, we use the Eq. 7 function for the distance function.

5 Experimental Results

We have an experiment by our method. The input video sequences are video chatting images of a man. There is an object and a background. An object is the man's face,

(a)   (b)   (c)

Fig. 3. Segmentation result. (a) original image. (t=1, 16, 31, 46) (b) image modeling via a rough sets. (c) image segmentation using our method.

and other area in image is the background. In the experiment images, the face's movement is faster then normal video chatting images. The video sequences' frame rate is 15 frames in a second.

Fig. 3 is result images of the experiment. Fig. 3a is the original images. Their frame numbers are 1, 16, 31 and 46. So a time interval between images is a second. Fig. 3b is images of represented modeling by rough sets. The object's lower approximation area covers in part of man's face. And the man's face is in the upper approximation area. Fig. 3c is result segmentation of our method. There is some noise, but the results follow the man's face.

6 Conclusion

In this study, we describe a rough set based method for segmenting video sequences. There area many objects and a background in a frame. Each objects and a background consist of a region. We represent these regions to rough sets. So each region has minimum area and maximum area. These two areas are presented by two concentric ellipsoids in five-dimension. Our method consists of next two phases. First phase is updating regions phase that consist three steps. First step is setting initial parameters. We use previous regions' parameters to initial parameters. Second step is updating object regions. Updating is by hill climbing method with our evaluation function. Third step is updating a background region. The background region is updated by using other regions. Second phase is making segmentation map phase. A lower approximation of an object is the object's area. And a pixel in upper approximation of regions is decided by distance between the pixel and the regions. The experiments result shows that the object's movement is detected, but there is some noise. We need to more experiments in variable situation, and more images with many objects.

References

1. Jacob Goldberger, Hayit Greenspan: Context-Based Segmentation of Image Sequences. IEEE Transactions on Pattern Analysis and Machine Intelligence, Vol. 28, No. 3, pp. 463-468, March 2006.
2. Abdol-Reza Mansouri and Janusz Konrad,: Multiple motion segmentation with level sets. IEEE Transaction on Image Processing, Vol. 12, No. 2, pp 201-220, February 2003.
3. Zdzislaw Pawlak: Rough classification. Int. J. Human-Computer Studies, Vol. 51, Issue 2, pp 369-383, August 1999.
4. Jiye Liang, Zhongzhi Shi, Deyu Li: Applications of Inclusion Degree in Rough set theory. Int. J. Computational Cognition, Vol. 1, No. 2, pp 67-78, June 2003.
5. Du Wei-feng, Li Hai-ming, Gao Yan, Meng Dan: Another Kind of Fuzzy Rough Sets. Granular Computing, 2005 IEEE Int. conference, Vol. 1, pp 145-148, July 2005
6. Akash Mohabey, A. K. Ray : Rough Set Theory based Segmentation of Color Images. Fuzzy Information Processing Society, 2000. NAFIPS. 19th Int. conference of the North American, pp 338-342, July 2000.
7. Sankar K. Pal, Pabitra Mitra: Multispectral Image Segmentation Using the Rough-Set-Initialized EM Algorithm. IEEE Transaction on Geoscience and Remote Sensing, Vol. 40, No. 11, November 2002.

Two Dimensional Laplacianfaces Method for Face Recognition

Niu Ben[1], Simon Chi Keung Shiu[1], and Sankar Kumar Pal[2]

[1] Department of Computing, Hong Kong Polytechnic University, Hong Kong, China
`{csckshiu, csniuben}@comp.polyu.edu.hk`
[2] Machine Intelligence Unit, Indian Statistical Institute, Kolkata, India
`sankar@isical.ac.in`

Abstract. In this paper we propose the two dimensional Laplacianfaces method for face recognition. The new algorithm is developed based on the two techniques, i.e., locality preserved embedding and image based projection. The two dimensional Laplacianfaces method is not only computationally more efficient but also more accurate than the one dimensional Laplacianfaces method in extracting the facial features for human face authentication. Extensive experiments are performed to test and evaluate the new algorithm using the Yale and the AR face databases. The experimental results indicate that the two dimensional Laplacianfaces method significantly outperforms the existing two dimensional Eigenfaces, the two dimensional Fisherfaces and the one dimensional Laplacianfaces methods under the various settings of experiment conditions.

1 Introduction

The Laplacianfaces is a recently developed method for face recognition [1]. It is a natural generalization of the locally linear embedding (LLE) [2] algorithm that can effectively handle the nonlinearity of the image space for dimensionality reduction. It was observed to outperform significantly the popular Eigenfaces and the Fisherfaces methods on the Yale, the MSRA and the PIE face databases [1]. However, like the Eigenfaces and the Fisherfaces, the Laplacianfaces method involves handling the eigen problem whose computation and memory complexity scales up quickly with the dimensionlity of the training image vectors. In order to address this problem, Liu et al. [3], Yang et al. [4]-[6], Xiong et al. [7], and Jing et al. [8] applied the image based projection technique to develop the two dimensional Eigenfaces and Fisherfaces methods, respectively. The complexity of the algorithms is reduced dramatically from $m^2 \times n^2$ to m^2 (or n^2). In addition, as the size of the matrices in the eigen equations is reduced they can be more accurately evaluated. So, the objective function in the algorithm can be fully optimized to achieve the best result of classification [4]. The two dimensional Eigenfaces and the Fisherfaces methods are successful for face recognition. But it is unclear whether or not the image based projection technique can also be applied effectively to improve the performance of the Laplacianfaces method. In this paper, we develop the two dimensional Laplacianfaces method utilizing this

S. Greco et al. (Eds.): RSCTC 2006, LNAI 4259, pp. 852–861, 2006.

technique. Extensive experiments have been performed to investigate the performance of the new algorithm for face recognition.

2 Two Dimensional Laplacianfaces

2.1 Idea and Algorithm

Let X denote an n-dimensional unitary column vector, A represents an image of m rows and n columns. In the one dimensional Laplacianfaces method, the sample image, A, has to be transformed to form a vector of $m \times n$ dimensions prior to training. Instead, in the new algorithm, two dimensional Laplacianfaces method, we project the image matrice directly onto the vector X,

$$Y = AX . \tag{1}$$

The obtained m-dimensional vector Y is called the projection feature vector. Given a set of training images $T = \{A_1, \ldots, A_i, \ldots, A_j, \ldots, A_N\}$ the objective function of the two dimensional Laplacianfaces method is defined as,

$$\min \sum_{ij} \left\| Y_i - Y_j \right\|^2 S_{ij} \tag{2}$$

where Y_i is the projection feature vector corresponding to the image A_i, $\|\cdot\|$ is the L_2 norm and S_{ij} is the similarity between the image A_i and A_j in the observation space and is defined as,

$$S_{ij} = \begin{cases} \exp(-\left\| A_i - A_j \right\|^2 / t), & \text{if } x_i \text{ is among the k nearest neighbors of } x_j, \\ & \quad \text{or } x_j \text{ is among the k nearest neighbors of } x_i, \\ 0, & \text{otherwise,} \end{cases} \tag{3}$$

where k is the size of the local neighborhood, t is the window width determining the rate of decay of the similarity function. As shown in Equation (3) the objective function imposes a heavy penalty if two arbitrary neighboring samples A_i and A_j in the original space are mapped far apart. By minimizing this criterion it is ensured that if A_i and A_j are near to each other then their projection feature vectors Y_i and Y_j are close as well. By taking several algebraic steps the objective function of the two dimensional Laplacianfaces method is converted to,

$$
\sum_{ij}\left\|Y_i - Y_j\right\|^2 S_{ij}
$$

$$
= \sum_{ij}\left\|A_i X - A_j X\right\|^2 S_{ij}
$$

$$
= \sum_{ij}[X^T(A_i - A_j)^T(A_i - A_j)X]S_{ij} \tag{4}
$$

$$
= X^T[\sum_i A_i^T A_i \sum_j S_{ij} - \sum_{ij} A_i^T S_{ij} A_j]X
$$

$$
= X^T A^T(D-S)AX
$$

$$
= X^T A^T LAX
$$

where $A^T = [A_1^T, \ldots, A_N^T]$, D is the diagonal matrice with $d_{ii} = \sum_j S_{ij}$, S is the similarity matrice, and L is called the Laplacian matrice. Since the entry of the matrice D indicates how important each point is a constraint is imposed as follows,

$$
X^T A^T DAX = 1. \tag{5}
$$

Finally, the two dimensional Laplacianfaces method is formulated as,

$$
\arg\min \quad X^T A^T LAX \tag{6}
$$

$$
\text{s.t. } X^T A^T DAX = 1.
$$

The optimal projection vector X that minimizes the objective function can be obtained by solving the following generalized eigen problem,

$$
A^T LAX = \lambda A^T DAX \tag{7}
$$

where both L and D are symmetric and positive semidefinite. The eigenvectors corresponding to the first d smallest eigenvalues are used for feature extraction.

2.2 Feature Extraction

Let us denote the optimal projection vectors as $X_1, \ldots, X_d$. For a given input image A, let $Y_i = AX_i$, $i = 1, \cdots, d$. A set of projection feature vectors, $Y_1, \ldots, Y_d$, can then be obtained. Note that the features extracted in the two dimensional Laplacianfaces method are vectors while in the original algorithm they are scalars. The projection vectors are used to form an $m \times d$ matrice $B = [Y_1, \ldots, Y_d]$ which is called the feature matrice of the sample image A.

2.3 Classification

After obtaining the feature matrices of all the training images the nearest neighbor classifier is used for classification. The distance between any two feature matrices $B_i = [Y_{i1}, \ldots, Y_{id}]$ and $B_j = [Y_{j1}, \ldots, Y_{jd}]$ is defined as,

$$
d(B_i, B_j) = \sum_{p=1}^{d}\left\|Y_{ip} - Y_{jp}\right\|. \tag{8}
$$

Suppose that the feature matrices are $B_1, ..., B_N$ and each of these samples is assigned a class identity C. Given an input testing image B, if $d(B, B_1) = \min d(B, B_j)$ and B_1 belongs to class C, then B is classified as belonging to C.

3 Experimental Results

In this section, we experimentally evaluate the proposed two dimensional Laplacianfaces method on two well known face databases, Yale and AR. While the Yale database is used to test the performance of the face recognition algorithms under the condition of the varied training sample size, the AR database is used to examine the performance of the algorithms under various conditions of the illumination, the facial expression and the time sessions. The experiments are performed on a Pentium 4 2.6GHz PC with 512MB RAM memory under Matlab 7.1 platform.

3.1 Results on Yale Database

The Yale face database [9] contains 165 images of 15 individuals, each subject has 11 images of the size 100×80, manually cropped and resized to 50×40. The images are captured under various facial expressions and illumination conditions. Here, seven tests are performed using different number of samples for training. More specifically, in the k-th test, we used the first k image samples per class for training and the remaining samples for testing. To determine the proper parameters of the neighborhood size and the window width of the Gaussian functions we use the global-to-local strategy [10]. The top recognition rate for each testing and the number of the projection vectors used for feature extraction are listed in Table 1.

Table 1. Top recognition rate (%) and number of components used

Method	Number of training samples of each class						
	2	3	4	5	6	7	8
Eigenfaces	87.4	89.2	89.5	87.8	84.0	91.7	88.9
	(28)	(14)	(39)	(25)	(48)	(25)	(30)
Fisherfaces	90.4	88.3	87.6	86.7	84.0	91.7	88.9
	(10)	(10)	(14)	(11)	(9)	(9)	(6)
Laplacianfaces	90.9	90.8	89.7	89.4	87.7	93.3	95.6
	(15)	(23)	(18)	(20)	(20)	(23)	(24)
2D Eigenfaces	87.4	87.5	89.5	87.8	84.0	91.7	91.1
	(12)	(3)	(10)	(6)	(14)	(14)	(3)
2D Fisherfaces	86.7	87.5	90.5	87.8	86.7	91.7	95.6
	(9)	(9)	(12)	(4)	(3)	(2)	(1)
2D Laplacianfaces	**94.1**	**95.0**	**95.2**	**96.7**	**97.3**	**96.7**	**97.8**
	(8)	**(2)**	**(3)**	**(3)**	**(2)**	**(3)**	**(1)**

It can be observed that the proposed two dimensional Laplacianfaces method outperforms the other five methods significantly and consistently (also indicated in Fig. 1), while the one dimensional Laplacianfaces method shows slightly better performance than the other four algorithms. Also, compared with the 2D Eigenfaces and the 2D Fisherfaces, the 2D Laplacianfaces method requires fewer components to achieve the top accuracy of classification in six of the seven tests, as highlighted with bold font.

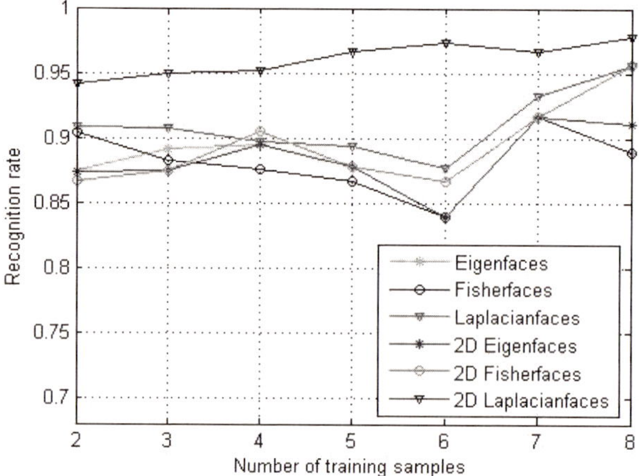

Fig. 1. Top recognition rate with varying number of training samples

Fig. 2 shows the average recognition rate changing over the number of the projection vectors. For each number of dimensions we average the recognition accuracies obtained using different number of samples for training. Note that for the Fisherfaces and the 2D Fisherfaces methods the maximum number of the available projection vectors is 14 because there are 15 classes of data in the database and the rank of the between class

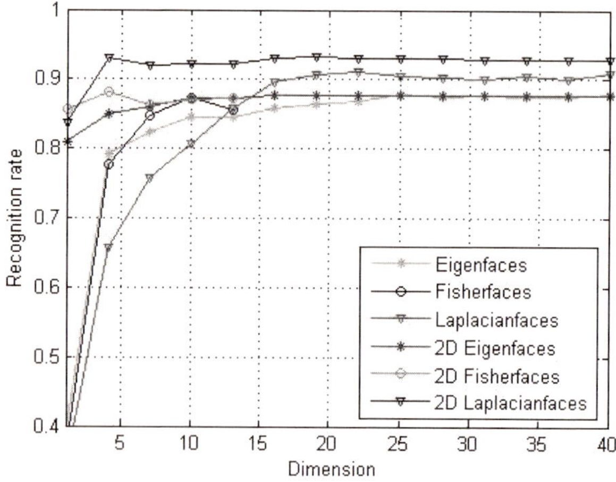

Fig. 2. Average recognition rate with varying dimension of projection vectors

scatter matrice is at most 14. The result in Fig. 2 indicates that the proposed 2D Laplacianfaces algorithm is not only more accurate but also very stable in outperforming the other algorithms.

In Table 2 and 3 we list and compare the computation and the memory complexities of the two types of Laplacianfaces methods. Here, m and n is the number of the rows and the columns of the image matrices. L, M and N is the number of the projection vectors, the testing samples and the training samples, respectively.

Table 2. Time and memory complexities

Method	Complexity		
	Time (training)	Time (testing)	Memory
Laplacianfaces	$O(m^2n^2L + mnN^2)$	$O(MNL)$	$O(m^2n^2)$
2D Laplacianfaces	$O(n^2L + mnN^2)$	$O(mMNL)$	$O(n^2)$

In Table 2 we can see that when $MN \leq (m^2 - 1)n$ the 2D Laplacianfaces requires not only fewer memory space but also less time than the 1D Laplacianfaces method in training and testing. In Table 3 we list the average time and the memory space that are used to achieve the top recognition rate under the configurations shown in Table 1.

Table 3. Time and memory space used for training and testing

Method	Average time (sec.) and memory cost			
	Time (training)	Time (testing)	Total Time	Size of matrix
Laplacianfaces	1,540	0.56	1540.56	2000×2000
2D Laplacianfaces	4.55	4.68	9.21	40×40

As can be seen in Table 3 while the one dimensional Laplacianfaces method requires averagely 1,540 seconds for training the proposed two dimensional Laplacianfaces needs only 4.55 seconds. Also, the size of the matrix drops from 2000×2000 to 40×40, which improves significantly the memory efficiency of the algorithm.

3.2 Results on AR Database

The AR face database [11] contains over 4,000 face images of 126 individuals taken in two time sessions under the variations of illumination, facial expression and occlusion conditions. Each person has 26 images. In our experiment we consider using a subset of 14 images of each person for training and testing. Fig. 3 shows the selected sample images of one subject. The global-to-local strategy is used for parameter selection.

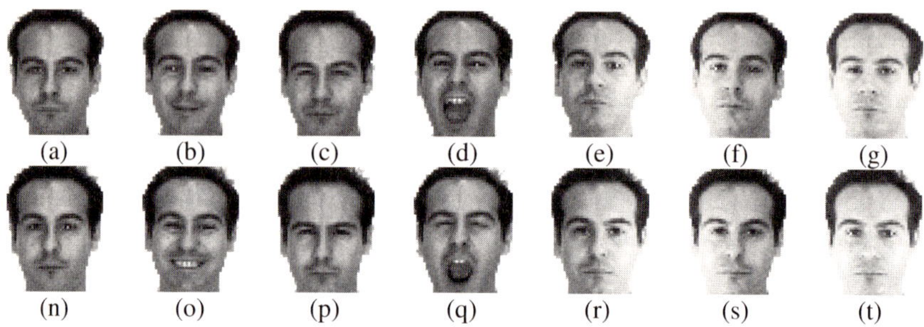

Fig. 3. Sample images for one subject of the AR database

In Fig. 3, the images (a)-(g) and (n)-(t) are drawn from the first and the second time sessions respectively. For each session the first four images (a)-(d) and (n)-(q) involve the variation of facial expressions (neutral, smile, anger, scream) while the images (e)-(g) and (r)-(t) are taken under different lighting conditions (left light on, right light on, all sides light on). The images are manually cropped and normalized to 50×40 pixels. We design and perform three experiments to investigate the performance of the 2D Eigefaces, the 2D Fisherfaces and the 2D Laplacianfaces methods under the variations of facial expressions, time sessions, and illuminations. The indices of the images of each person used in the three tests are listed in Table 4.

Table 4. Indices of training and testing images

Data set	Experiment conditions		
	Illumination	Expression	Time
Training set	{e, s}	{a, n}	{a, b, c, d, e, f, g}
Testing set	{f, g, r, t}	{b, c, d, o, p, q}	{n, o, p, q, r, s, t}

Table 5 shows the top recognition rate, the number of the dimensions of feature vectors used for classification, and the testing time of the three algorithms.

Table 5. Performance of three algorithms using image based projection technique

	Experiment	Top recognition rate (%)	Dimension	Classification time (sec.)
Expression	2D Eigenfaces	95.4	10	5.547
	2D Fisherfaces	95.6	10	5.281
	2D Laplacianfaces	**97.8**	**4**	**4.765**
Time	2D Eigenfaces	65.2	22	42.42
	2D Fisherfaces	68.6	14	28.75
	2D Laplacianfaces	**71.5**	**4**	**17.66**
Illumination	2D Eigenfaces	80.2	27	12.375
	2D Fisherfaces	91.4	9	3.765
	2D Laplacianfaces	**93.7**	**3**	**1.975**

As we can see in Table 5 the proposed 2D Laplacianfaces method outperforms the 2D Fisherfaces and the 2D Eigenfaces methods in all the three tests. It improves the recognition rate by 2.4%, 6.3%, 3.5% over the 2D Eigenfaces, and 2.2%, 2.9%, 2.3% over the 2D Fisherfaces, respectively. It requires also fewer dimensions of projection vectors and time to achieve the top recognition rate as shown in the column 5 of Table 5. Fig. 4 to Fig. 6 show the relationship between the accuracy of the three algorithms and the dimension of the feature vectors used for recognition.

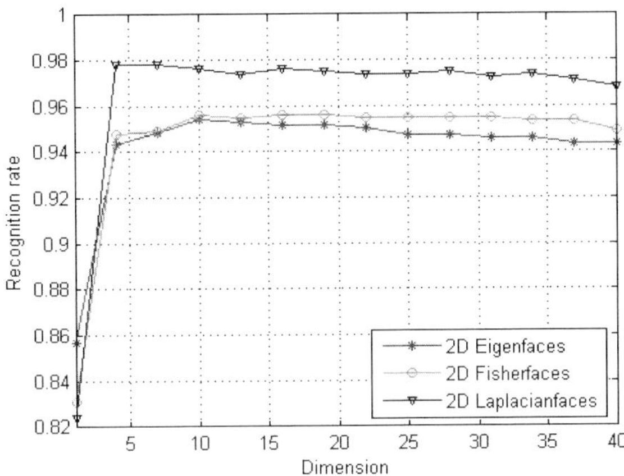

Fig. 4. Recognition rate over dimensions of feature vectors (Expressions)

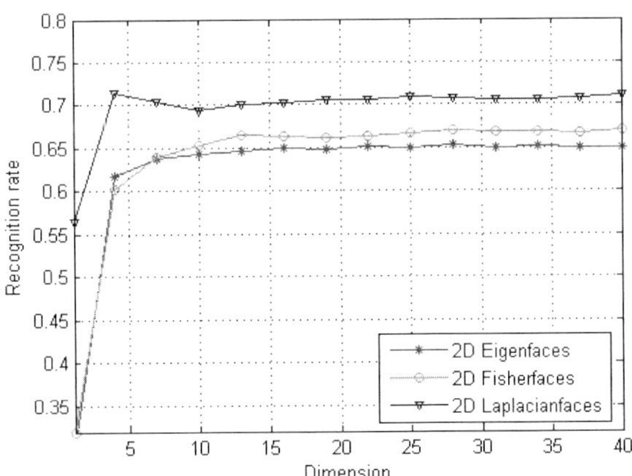

Fig. 5. Recognition rate over dimensions of feature vectors (Time)

In the figures we can see that for the 2D Laplacianfaces method most of the effective discriminant information can be characterized by using only a small number of components as opposed to the other two methods where more components have to

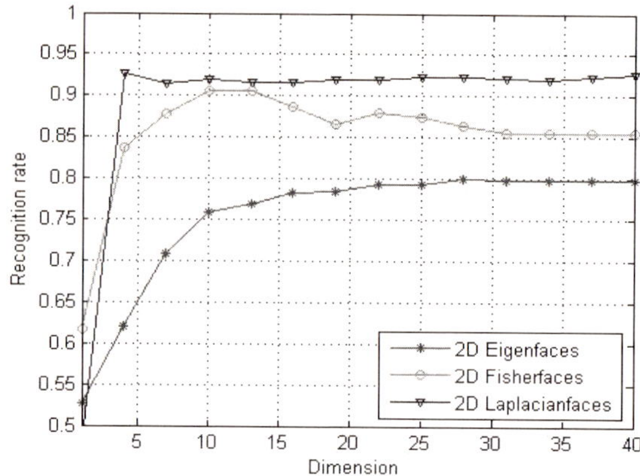

Fig. 6. Recognition rate over dimensions of feature vectors (Illumination)

be employed to achieve the top recognition rate. The new method is also stable in outperforming the 2D Fisherfaces and the 2D Laplacianfaces methods with various number of feature vectors as shown in Fig. 4 to Fig 6.

4   Conclusions

In this paper we developed the two dimensional Laplacianfaces method and applied it to solve the face recognition problem. The new method has the following properties, a) It is locality preserving, which enables the Laplacianfacaes method to handle the nonlinearity of the data set more effectively for feature extraction. b) It is more efficient than the one dimensional Laplacianfaces by taking advantage of the image based projection technique. c) The new algorithm requires fewer feature vectors to achieve the highest accuracy rate of classification. Experimental results on the Yale and the AR face image databases show that the new algorithm is not only more efficient but also more accurate than the 1D Laplacianfaces, the 2D Fisherfaces, and the 2D Eigenfaces methods for face recognition.

Acknowledgement

This research work is supported by the Hong Kong Polytechnic University Research Grants A-PD55 and G-T643.

References

1. X. He, S. Y, P. Niyogi, and H.J. Zhang, "Face Recognition Using Laplacianfaces," IEEE Trans. Pattern Analysis and Machine Intelligence, vol. 27, no. 3, pp. 328- 340, Mar. 2005.
2. S.T. Roweis and L.K. Saul, "Nonlinear Dimensionality Reduction by Locally Linear Embedding," Science, 290, pp. 2323-2326, 2000.
3. K. Liu, Y. Q. Cheng, and J. Y. Yang, "Algebraic Feature Extraction for Image Recognition based on an Optimal Discrimination Criterion," Pattern Recognition, vol. 26, no. 6, pp. 903-911, 1993.

4. J. Yang, D. Zhang, A.F. Frangi, and J.Y. Yang, " Two Dimensional PCA: A New Approach to Appearance Based Face Representation and Recongition," IEEE Trans. Pattern Analysis and Machine Intelligence, vol. 26, no. 1, Jan. 2004.
5. J. Yang and J. Y. Yang, "From Image Vector to Matrix: a Straightforward Image Projection Technique – IMPCA vs. PCA," Pattern Recognition, vol. 35, no. 9, pp. 1997-1999, 2002.
6. J. Yang, D. Zhang, Y. Xu, and J.Y. Yang, "Two Dimensional Discriminant Transform for Face Recognition," Pattern Recognition, vol. 38, no. 7, pp. 1125-1129, 2005.
7. H. Xiong, M.N.S. Swamy, M.O. Ahmad, "Two Dimensional FLD for Face Recognition," Pattern Recognition, vol. 38, no. 7, pp. 1121-1124, 2005.
8. X. Jing, H.S. Wong, and D. Zhang, "Face Recognition based on 2D Fisherface Approach," Pattern Recognition, vol. 39, no. 4, pp. 707-710, 2006.
9. Yale Univ. Face Database, http://cvc.yale.edu/projects/yalefaces/yalefaces.html, 2002.
10. K.-R. Müller, S.Mika, G. Rätsch, K.Tsuda, and B. Schölkopf, "An Introduction to Kernel-Based Learning Algorithms," IEEE Trans. Neural Networks, vol. 12, no. 2, pp. 181-201, 2001.
11. A.M. Martinez and R. Benavente, "The AR Face Database," CVC Technical Report, no. 24, June 1998.

Unsupervised Learning of Image Recognition with Neural Society for Clustering

Marcin Wojnarski

Warsaw University, Faculty of Mathematics, Informatics and Mechanics
ul. Banacha 2, 02-097 Warszawa, Poland
`mwojnars@ns.onet.pl`

Abstract. New algorithm for partitional data clustering is presented, *Neural Society for Clustering* (NSC). Its creation was inspired by hierarchical image understanding, which requires unsupervised training to build the hierarchy of visual features. Existing clustering algorithms are not well-suited for this task, since they usually split natural groups of patterns into several parts (like k-means) or give crisp clustering. Neurons comprising NSC may be viewed as a society of autonomous individuals, proceeding along the same simple algorithm, based on four principles: of locality, greediness, balance and competition. The same principles govern large groups of entities in economy, sociology, biology and physics. Advantages of NSC are demonstrated in experiment with visual data. The paper presents also a new method for objective and quantitative comparison of clustering algorithms, based on the notions of entropy and mutual information.

1 Introduction

To understand and reliably recognize complex images we need a multi-layer hierarchical system of visual features – small and simple in the bottom, more and more complex in higher layers. This is how visual perception in the brain is organized. Several methods for creation of such hierarchy were already proposed: LeNet convolutional neural network developed by LeCun et al. [1]; HMAX model of object recognition in cortex by Riesenhuber and Poggio [2]; recent extension of HMAX by Serre et al. [3]; Neural Abstraction Pyramid by Behnke [4].

However, their performance is still very far from performance of the brain. One of the reasons for this is underestimation of unsupervised training and neglecting the possibility of information extraction from patterns themselves, while the fact that unsupervised training does not require class labels is a big advantage, especially when creation of a hierarchical system is considered.

Generally, there are three ways to build a hierarchy of visual features: (1) manually, by giving a mathematical description of every feature; (2) with supervised training, by providing examples of input patterns together with their class labels; (3) with unsupervised training, when class labels are not available.

The main weakness of the first approach is that we do not know what features should be represented in each layer. We know only roughly what features are recognized at first stages of visual perception. Moreover, the features represented by biological neurons are fuzzy so it is difficult to define them mathematically.

Supervised training for large, multi-layer systems is intractable, as target classification is known only in the last layer and it is difficult to back-propagate this information through many layers, composed of thousands of units. We might try to use supervised training for each layer separately, starting with the first one and going up the hierarchy when the previous layer is trained. However, with this method we must know what features are needed in each layer and we have to (manually) label all occurrences of all the features in training data.

With unsupervised training, we can build the hierarchy in the most natural order: from the bottom to the top, layer by layer, without need to label manually huge amount of data. The reason why unsupervised algorithm could create useful features is that visual stimuli are *not* random combinations of pixels. The stimuli are composed of structures characteristic for the domain of the problem being solved. These structures occur much more frequently in training images than they would in purely random data, where pixels are picked independently of each other. Examples of such frequent structures in the task of face recognition would be the shapes of mouth, nose or chin. Thus, an unsupervised algorithm which discovers unusually frequent patterns could produce features that are useful for image understanding.

To give even stronger evidence that unsupervised training is essential for hierarchical image recognition, we might wonder how the brain learns to recognize images. Can it be supervised learning? If so, who or what is the supervisor? There are two possibilities: parents (environment) or genes. The first possibility is unlikely, since supervision from environment requires well-developed perception to communicate information between learner and supervisor – and perception is just what has to be learned. Genes certainly hold large amount of information about organization of visual perception, since they must describe algorithms which drive development of perception, but they surely do not describe precisely every single connection between neurons. Firstly because this is huge amount of information, too big to be stored in genome. Secondly, this would be extremely inflexible, making adaptation to environment almost impossible.

The above argument shows that unsupervised training must form the basis of visual perception development in the brain, so perhaps it could be applied to computer vision, as well. Moreover, we know that biological perception can develop properly only in the presence of stimuli, which is yet another argument for the use of stimuli-driven training in computer vision.

2   Clustering Algorithms

To build the hierarchy in unsupervised manner, we need a *clustering* algorithm to train a single layer. More precisely, this should be a *partitional* algorithm [5], and it must define a partition of the whole input space, not only of the training set. It would be also desirable to obtain fuzzy partition, instead of crisp. Only few existing methods satisfy these requirements. The most popular approaches

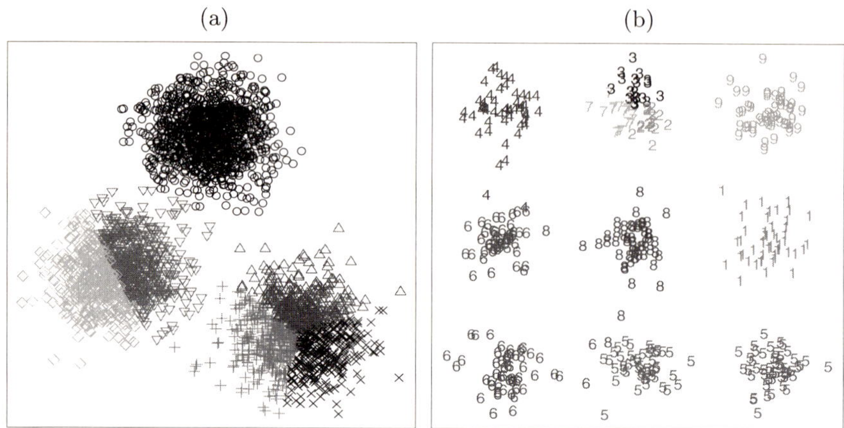

Fig. 1. Partitions obtained by k-means when k is larger (a) or the same (b) as the number of natural groups in data. In both cases some groups are split into 2 or 3 parts.

are k-means and gaussian mixture model (GMM) [5,6] trained with Expectation Maximization algorithm. However, both of them have serious disadvantages, which are overcome by the new algorithm introduced in this paper.

2.1   K-Means

The k-means algorithm finds cluster centers $\mathbf{c}_1, \ldots, \mathbf{c}_k$ by minimizing:

$$\mathcal{E}(\mathbf{c}_1, \ldots, \mathbf{c}_k) = \sum_{i=1}^{n} \min_{j=1,\ldots,k} \|\mathbf{x}_i - \mathbf{c}_j\|^2 \,, \tag{1}$$

where n is the number of training patterns [5,6].

One of the weaknesses of k-means is that it partitions natural groups in the data into several separate clusters, even if k is exactly equal to the number of groups. This fact is illustrated in Figure 1. Two data sets composed of gaussian groups of points in the plane are clustered by k-means. For the first one, $k = 6$, which is more than the number of groups (3) – like in most of applications, where the exact number of groups is unknown and larger k should be chosen. For the second data set, k is equal to the number of groups (9). In both cases some groups are split into 2 or 3 parts, like a pie. Moreover, several groups from the second data set fall into the same cluster.

The above-mentioned characteristic of k-means is a weakness if the algorithm is used to build a hierarchy of visual features, as information propagated to the next layer incorrectly discriminates between patterns representing the same distorted prototype, thus biasing feature learning in the next layer.

Another disadvantage of k-means for hierarchical image understanding is that it assigns every pattern to exactly one cluster, in a crisp way, while some patterns may lie on the border between two or more features (then several clusters should activate), and some others may lie far away from all cluster centers (then all clusters should be inactivated).

2.2   Gaussian Mixture Models

In gaussian mixture modelling we want to estimate the probability density function of data using a combination of parameterized normal densities [6]:

$$f(\mathbf{x}; \Theta) = \sum_{i=1}^{k} w_i \phi(\mathbf{x}; \theta_i) \, , \tag{2}$$

such that $\sum w_i = 1$, $\Theta = (\theta_1, \ldots, \theta_k, w_1, \ldots, w_k)$. The mixture is interpreted as a fuzzy partition of the input space, with cluster membership functions defined by posterior probabilities that pattern x belongs to component i. Parameters Θ of the mixture are found by maximization of the *log-likelihood* L of the data $\mathbf{X} = (\mathbf{x}_1, \ldots, \mathbf{x}_n)$, as a function of Θ, which is usually done with Expectation Maximization (EM) algorithm [6]:

$$L(\Theta; \mathbf{X}) = \log f(\mathbf{X}; \Theta) = \sum_i \log f(\mathbf{x}_i; \Theta) \, . \tag{3}$$

Clustering with gaussian mixtures seems to be much more sophisticated than k-means, thus perhaps it could give better results. E.g. if the number of components is bigger than the number of natural groups in the data, the mixture model may (sometimes) converge to a solution where several gaussians share the same parameters – this situation is easy to detect and fix. Moreover, GMM clustering is fuzzy, which is better for hierarchical image understanding.

However, despite the sophistication and complexity of GMM+EM algorithm, for multi-attribute data, e.g. images, it behaves exactly like k-means (!) – this is what "curse of dimensionality" means for GMM. It comes out that the boundaries between fuzzy clusters defined by GMM get so small in multidimensional space that in fact they disappear. The clustering becomes crisp and then the EM update rule becomes the same as in k-means.

3   Neural Society for Clustering

This section introduces a new clustering algorithm, *Neural Society for Clustering* (NSC), which may be seen as a type of a single-layer artificial neural network. However, the most important part of the system – its training algorithm – is devised in a completely different way than for standard neural networks. The algorithm is not a result of applying an optimization method to some error function, but instead it is designed to satisfy several simple principles formulated in natural language. These principles govern real societies in sociology, economy, biology or even physics – that is why the presented system is called "society" instead of "network".

Similar methodology, like the use of *locality* or *greediness* rules, can be found in *Local Transfer Function Classifier* (LTF-C) – a neural network for classification problems introduced by Wojnarski [7]. LTF-C-based systems are double winners of the EUNITE[1] world-wide machine-learning competitions, on "Modelling the Bank's Client behaviour using Intelligent Technologies" (2002) and "Prediction of product quality in glass manufacturing process" (2003).

3.1 General Assumptions

NSC is composed of some number of neurons, which generate activations in the range of $[0; 1]$. Every neuron corresponds to one cluster – the neuron activation defines cluster membership function – thus clusters are fuzzy and may overlap, or some regions of the input space may belong to no cluster (or have very low value of membership function).

Further in this paper, we will also use the notion of a neural *receptive field*, i.e. the subset of the input space on which the activation of a given neuron is high. Receptive field is a fuzzy set and in fact it is exactly the cluster represented by the neuron. Moreover, to find proper values of adaptive parameters of a neuron means to find a proper receptive field for that neuron, so a neuron is in fact the receptive field. Thus, in the following sections we will use the notions of cluster, neuron and receptive field interchangeably.

Training process is composed, as usually, of some number of cycles. Each cycle consists of: drawing randomly a training pattern, computing responses of all neurons and adjusting adaptive parameters.

3.2 The Principles

Creation of the training algorithm is a two-stage process. First, general principles of the training are formulated. Then, specific mathematical formulas are devised, which should satisfy the general rules. The principles of NSC are the following:

- *Locality*: the neuron must be activated to undergo training.
- *Greediness*: the neuron wants to be activated as often as possible, so it gets positive feedback after (moderate) activation.
- *Balance*: total activation of the network should be moderate, so neurons get negative feedback when total activation is too large and positive otherwise.
- **Competition**: if several neurons activate simultaneously, only the winner gets positive feedback, others – negative.

The greediness principle does not affect fully activated neurons, because they do not need a feedback – full activation cannot be even larger. The competition principle is the most important one, as it drives the process of setting *decision borders* (the borders between clusters) in appropriate positions. Let us

---

[1] European Network of Excellence on Intelligent Technologies for Smart Adaptive Systems, http://www.eunite.org/.

consider a simple situation depicted in Figure 2. There are two groups of one-dimensional training patterns (dashes), distributed according to the presented density function. There are also two neurons, represented by their activation functions. However, the decision border (point where both activations are equal) lies far away from the minimum of the density. Will it get closer in next cycles?

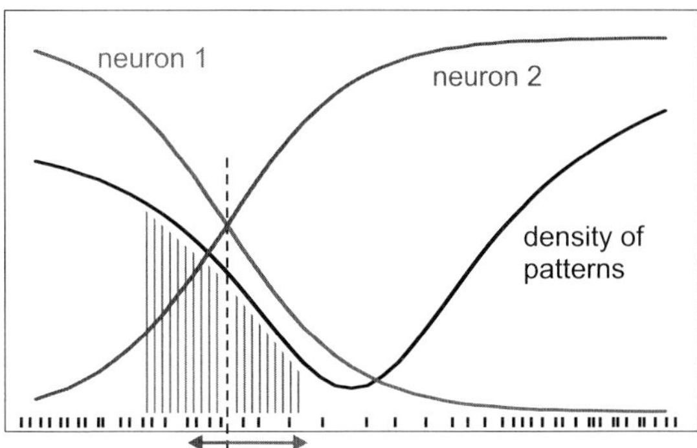

Fig. 2. Illustration of the competition principle. Two neurons (activation functions are shown) with overlapping reception fields compete, which leads to repositioning of decision border (*dashed line*). There is unequal distribution (*dashed regions*) of training patterns (*dashes* in the bottom) on both sides of the border, so their influence (*arrows*) is unbalanced and the border moves towards the minimum of density function.

The training process has stochastic nature (patterns are picked randomly), so we cannot say with certainty what will happen, but we can estimate an expected modification of neuron positions in the next cycle. Let us consider possible choices of the next training pattern x:

1. x lies far away from the decision border, where one of the neurons is fully activated and another one is quiet. In this case modification of adaptive parameters will be very small, due to the principles of locality (non-activated neuron does not undergo training) and greediness (fully activated neuron does not undergo training because its activation cannot be greater any more).
2. x lies to the left from the border, in its vicinity. Then, both neurons activate moderately, but the first one is the winner, so due to the competition principle it gets positive feedback and moves the reception field towards x – that is to the right. The second neuron is the loser, so it gets negative feedback and moves the reception field further from x – which also means to the right. Thus, the decision border gets moved to the right, as well, which is denoted by the right arrow in Figure 2.
3. x lies to the right from the border, in its vicinity. This situation is opposite to the previous one: now the second neuron is the winner, so it moves towards x, that is to the left. Similarly, the loser moves further from x, which also means to the left. In this way, the decision border moves to the left, as well.

The crucial point to observe is that the distribution of patterns on both sides of the border is unequal – the dashed area in Figure 2 is larger on the left side of the border than on the right. Hence, the right arrow is longer than the left one and the resultant force affecting the border is directed towards a minimum of density function. Thus, the competition rule drives repositioning of decision borders, forcing them to move towards decreasing density.

Note that similar principles as given above lie in the basis of many processes in sociology, economy, biology or physics. For example, the greediness and competition rules govern free-market economy – and this similarity with NSC is not a surprise, as one of major problems which an economic system must solve is how to cluster possible business activities and allocate them to firms. Moreover, the free-market economy achieves this goal by self-organization, as NSC.

3.3   The Training Algorithm

Till now, we have not specified the form of the neural activation function, because the principles are so general that they can be applied to very different types of activation functions. In this paper, we will assume sigmoidal form of activations:

$$f_i(\mathbf{x}) = \sigma \left(\mathbf{w}_i^{\mathrm{T}} \mathbf{x} - \alpha_i \right), \tag{4}$$

where $\mathbf{x}$ denotes a presented pattern (vector), $\mathbf{w}_i$ is a vector of weights, α_i is a threshold, i is the index of a neuron and σ denotes logistic function:

$$\sigma(t) = \frac{1}{1 + \exp(-t)} . \tag{5}$$

After every cycle, weights and thresholds are adjusted according to the formulas:

$$\mathbf{w}_i \leftarrow \mathbf{w}_i + \eta^{\mathrm{w}} F_i \, \mathbf{x} , \tag{6}$$

$$\alpha_i \leftarrow \alpha_i - \eta^{\alpha} F_i , \tag{7}$$

where η^{w} and η^{α} are predefined positive constants and F_i is the *total force* affecting the neuron with index i. The total force indicates whether the presented pattern would have positive or negative influence on the neuron. Namely, if the force is positive, the weights and the threshold are modified in such a way that the neuron activation would be stronger if the same pattern x is presented again. The total force is a combination of *balance force*, B_i, and *competition force*, C_i:

$$F_i = \gamma B_i + (1 - \gamma) C_i , \tag{8}$$

where γ is a constant in $(0, 1)$. Force B_i realizes the balance principle – it keeps total activation of neurons around one, while force C_i realizes the competition and greediness principles – it shifts receptive fields and decision boundaries:

$$B_i = y_i \left(1 - \sum_j y_j \right) , \tag{9}$$

$$C_i = y_i(1 - y_i)s_i \ .$$

$$(10)$$

In the above formulas, y_i denotes activation of neuron i in the last cycle, the sum runs over all neurons, and s_i is the winner indicator after the last presentation:

$$s_i = \begin{cases} +1, & \text{if neuron } i \text{ is the winner} \\ -1, & \text{if neuron } i \text{ is a loser} \end{cases} \ .$$

$$(11)$$

Factors y_i in the above formulas guarantee that locality principle is satisfied.

4   The Conformity Index

To perform a quantitative comparison of clustering algorithms, we devised the *conformity index*, κ, which measures similarity between two partitions of a data set. In our experiment, the first partition was the one obtained by NSC or k-means, and the second was true classification of the data (for NSC the clustering had to be made crisp by taking the most activated neuron for every pattern).

The difficulty in comparing partitions is that we do not know which clusters in the first partition correspond to which clusters in the second and it is usually impossible to draw exact correspondence. To solve this problem, an information-theoretic approach is used. Given two partitions P_1 and P_2 of a data set D, they are treated as random variables defined on D as a discrete stochastic space, with values in sets of cluster labels. Uniform distribution on D is assumed. Then, the conformity index is calculated as mutual information of P_1 and P_2 normalized by their joint entropy [8]:

$$\kappa(P_1, P_2) = \frac{\mathrm{I}(P_1; P_2)}{\mathrm{H}(P_1, P_2)} \ .$$

$$(12)$$

Intuitively, this index says what part of the whole information carried by P_1 *or* P_2 is contained in *both* of them. Such an index catches the intuition of similar partitions very well. It takes values between 0 (iff the partitions are stochastically independent) and 1 (iff the partitions are identical).

5   Experiment

Experiment with a set of artificially generated images was carried out. The data contained 20x20-pixel gray-scale images of four types: three groups of horizontal segments in different positions (top, middle, bottom) and a group of vertical segments. Each group contained 100 patterns of diverse length, orientation and exact position, as shown in Figure 3. Note the proximity of neighboring horizontal groups and the fact that vertical segments intersected with horizontal ones from all groups. The groups were also very wide in terms of Euclidean distance between extreme patterns. Pixel values were between 0 (black) and 1 (white).

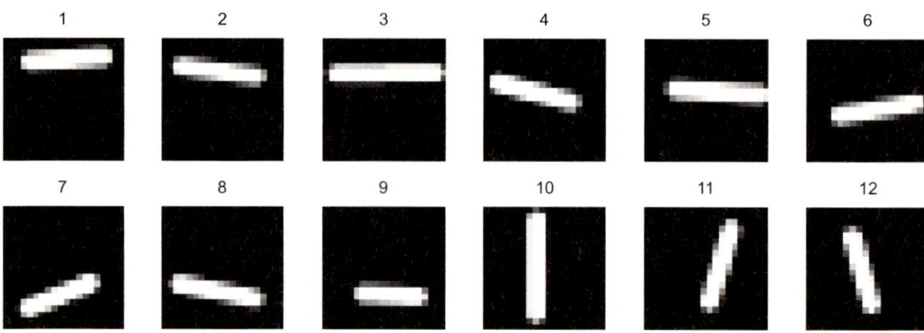

Fig. 3. Examples of training patterns. There are four groups of images: top horizontal segments (1-3), middle horizontal (4-6), bottom horizontal (7-9) and vertical (10-12).

(a)   (b)

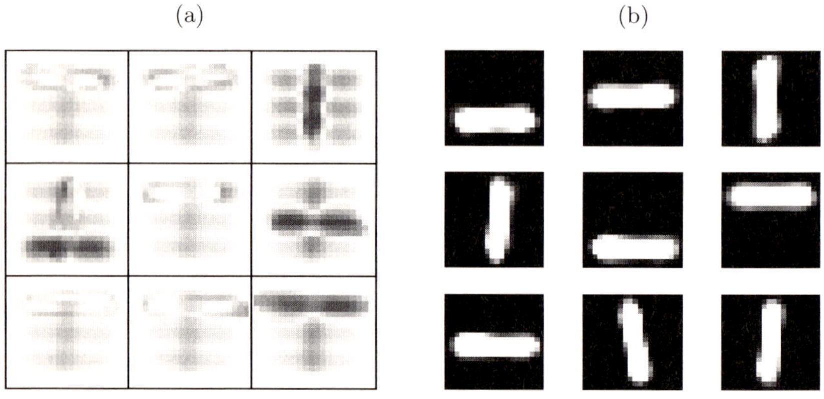

Fig. 4. (a) Weights of neurons of NSC (absolute values are depicted). Note the exact correspondence between meaningful neurons and genuine groups in the data. Unnecessary neurons atrophied and do not activate; (b) Cluster centers generated by k-means. Note that each group but the top horizontal was split into several clusters.

The data were clustered by NSC and k-means with 9 neurons or centers. Obtained neural weights and cluster centers are presented in Figure 4. Conformity index of the partitions was: 0.96 for NSC and 0.67 for k-means.

We may observe in Figure 4 that k-means splits natural groups into several clusters. Moreover, the cluster centers represent images that are asymmetric, distorted and far from prototypes of the groups. Such images are inappropriate as features in hierarchical image understanding. On the other hand, NSC can properly recognize the whole groups – unnecessary neurons are simply not used, their receptive fields are pushed away from the training patterns by competition and finally atrophy. As conformity index shows, the obtained partition corresponds almost perfectly to true classification.

The number of training cycles of NSC was 800. Values of parameters: $\eta^{w} = \eta^{\alpha} = 0.1$, $\gamma = 0.3$. Neuron thresholds were initialized with 3 and weights with randomly picked training patterns scaled by 0.1.

6   Discussion

New clustering algorithm, *Neural Society for Clustering*, was presented in this paper. Development of this algorithm was motivated by the desire to build in unsupervised manner a hierarchical system for image understanding and recognition, although NSC is a general-purpose method. Existing clustering algorithms – k-means and Expectation Maximization for gaussian mixture model – are not well-suited for this task due to their tendency to split groups of similar patterns into several parts and because of crisp nature of the partition they produce when applied to multi-variable data. NSC gives fuzzy clustering and do not split natural groups of patterns – it can recognize if some neurons are unnecessary. NSC is based on four principles: of locality, greediness, balance and competition. The same principles govern real societies in economy, sociology and biology.

The paper presented results obtained by NSC and k-means in clustering of a data set of images. The results showed that NSC gives indeed a clustering which is very close to real partition into classes – contrary to k-means, which produces very fragmented partition. In order to quantitatively compare the algorithms, a measure of quality of partition, conformity index, was devised, based on the notions of entropy and mutual information. This index is intuitive and its boundary values are easy to interpret.

In the future, we plan to carry out experiments with real-world data sets, containing visual as well as non-visual data. We also plan to extend the presented algorithm to build a hierarchy of visual features.

Acknowledgements

The research has been supported by the grant 3T11C00226 from Ministry of Scientific Research and Information Technology of the Republic of Poland.

References

1. LeCun, Y., Bottou, L., Bengio, Y., Haffner, P.: Gradient-based learning applied to document recognition. Proceedings of the IEEE **86**(11) (1998) 2278–2324
2. Riesenhuber, M., Poggio, T.: Hierarchical models of object recognition in cortex. Nature Neuroscience **2**(11) (1999) 1019–1025
3. Serre, T., Wolf, L., Poggio, T.: Object recognition with features inspired by visual cortex. In: IEEE CVPR. Volume 2. (2005) 994–1000
4. Behnke, S.: Hierarchical Neural Networks for Image Interpretation. Volume 2766 of Lecture Notes in Computer Science. Springer (2003)
5. Jain, A.K., Murty, M.N., Flynn, P.J.: Data clustering: a review. ACM Computing Surveys **31**(3) (1999) 264–323
6. Ripley, B.D.: Pattern recognition and neural networks. Cambridge University Press, Cambridge (1996)
7. Wojnarski, M.: LTF-C: Architecture, training algorithm and applications of new neural classifier. Fundamenta Informaticae **54**(1) (2003) 89–105
8. Cover, T.M., Thomas, J.A.: Elements of Information Theory. Wiley (1991)
9. Jain, A.K., Law, M.H.C.: Data clustering: A user's dilemma. In: PReMI. (2005) 1–10

A Framework for Unsupervised Selection of Indiscernibility Threshold in Rough Clustering

Shoji Hirano and Shusaku Tsumoto

Department of Medical Informatics, Shimane University, School of Medicine
89-1 Enya-cho, Izumo, Shimane 693-8501, Japan
hirano@ieee.org, tsumoto@computer.org

Abstract. Indiscernibility threshold is a parameter in rough clustering that controls the global ability of equivalence relations for discriminating objects. During its second step, rough clustering iteratively refines equivalence relations so that the coarseness of classification of objects meets the given level of indiscernibility. However, as the relationships between this parameter and resultant clusters have not been studied yet, users should determine its value by trial and error. In this paper, we discuss the relationships between the threshold value of indiscernibility degree and clustering results, as a framework for automatic determination of indiscernibility threshold. The results showed that the relationships between indiscernibility degree and the number of clusters draw a globally convex but multi-modal curve, and the range of indiscernibility degree that yields best cluster validity may exist on a local minimum around the global one which generates single cluster.

Keywords: Indiscernibility, Clustering, Rough Sets.

1 Introduction

Clustering is characterized as a task of forming groups of similar objects based on the predefined (dis-)similarity measure and grouping criteria. A lot of approaches, for example, agglomerative/divisive hierarchical clustering, k-means and EM algorithms, have been proposed in the literature [1][2] and widely used for exploratory analysis of real-world data. In order to find the best partition of objects that maximizes both inter-cluster homogeneity and between-clusters isolation, clustering methods usually employ geometric measures such as the variance of distances. However, it becomes difficult to form appropriate clusters if only a dissimilarity matrix is available as intrinsic information for analysis and the raw attribute values of data are unavailable or inaccessible. This is because the lack of attribute-value information may bring a difficulty in computing the global properties of groups such as centroids. Additionally, the choice of global coherence/isolation measures is limited if the dissimilarity is defined as a subjective or relative measure, because such a measure may not satisfy the triangular inequality for any triplets of objects. Although conventional hierarchical clusterings are known to be able to deal with relative or subjective measures, they

S. Greco et al. (Eds.): RSCTC 2006, LNAI 4259, pp. 872–881, 2006.

involve other problems such as erosion or expansion of data space by intermediate objects between large clusters and the results are dependent on the orders of object handling [2].

In order to deal with this problem, we have proposed an indiscernibility-based clustering method called rough clustering [3]. Rough clustering groups objects according to the classification induced by a set of N equivalence relations where N denotes the number of objects. First, an equivalence relation that performs binary classification according to the local information is independently assigned to each object. Next, global assessment of classifications is done according to a parameter called indiscernibility degree. The equivalence relations are iteratively refined so that the classification of objects meets the given level of indiscernibility. Consequently, adequately coarse clusters are obtained.

In rough clustering, two factors affect the resultant clusters: (1) initial equivalence relations that form the basic partition of objects, (2) threshold value of indiscernibility degrees. In previous work, we have shown that (1) minor disturbance in the initial equivalence relations would be absorbed in refinement steps [4], and (2) there might be a range of indiscernibility degree that yield high cluster validity. However, these findings were dependent on the determination method of initial equivalence relations used in the experiments; in that case density-based determination method. Thus the intrinsic property of the indiscernibility degree should be analyzed in more systematic way.

In this paper, we discuss the relationships between the threshold value of indiscernibility degree and clustering results as a framework for automatic determination of indiscernibility threshold. For the purpose of sccluding the effect of the determination method of initial equivalence relations, we employ the perfect initial equivalence relations that are derived from class labels of objects. Based on the perfect equivalence relations, we first examine the relationship between the threshold value of indiscernibility degree and resultant clusters. After that, we apply random disturbance to the perfect relations, and examine how the result changes.

The remainder of this paper is organized as follows. Section 2 gives a brief explanation of rough clustering. Section 3 describes experimental results on artificial datasets, and Section 4 concludes the technical results.

2   Rough Clustering

This section gives a brief overview of rough clustering, which is also referred to as indiscernibility-based clustering. This method is based on iterative refinement of N binary classifications, where N denotes the number of objects. First, an equivalence relation, that classifies all objects into two classes according to the local relative proximity, is assigned to each of N objects. Next, for each pair of objects, the number of binary classifications in which the pair is included in the same class is counted. This number is termed the indiscernibility degree. If the indiscernibility degree of a pair is larger than a user-defined threshold value, the equivalence relations may be modified so that all of the equivalence relations commonly classify the pair into the same class. This process is repeated until class assignment becomes stable. Consequently, we may obtain the clustering result that follows a given level of granularity. The main benefits of this method is that (1) it can handle relative proximity, where no geometric measure such as centroids can not be defined, (2) it can take dissimilarity matrix as input and does not require any direct reference to the original data value.

There are two parameters that control the behavior of this clustering method: the threshold value T_h for refinement of equivalence relations and the number N_r of iteration of refinement. As shown in the experiments, N_r can be determined automatically, because the equivalence relations will be stable after several cycles of refinement. The refinement process can be terminated when no candidates for refinement appear.

2.1   Assignment of Initial Equivalence Relations

Let $U = \{x_1, x_2, ..., x_N\}$ be the set of objects we are interested in. An equivalence relation R_i for object x_i is defined by

$$U/R_i = \{P_i, \ U - P_i\}, \tag{1}$$

where

$$P_i = \{x_j | \ d(x_i, x_j) \leq Th_{di}\}, \quad \forall x_j \in U. \tag{2}$$

$d(x_i, x_j)$ denotes dissimilarity between objects x_i and x_j, and Th_{di} denotes an upper threshold value of dissimilarity for object x_i. The equivalence relation, R_i classifies U into two categories: P_i, which contains objects similar to x_i and $U - P_i$, which contains objects dissimilar to x_i. When $d(x_i, x_j)$ is smaller than Th_{di}, object x_j is considered to be indiscernible to x_i. U/R_i can be alternatively written as $U/R_i = \{\{[x_i]_{R_i}\}, \{\overline{[x_i]_{R_i}}\}\}$, where $[x_i]_{R_i} \cap \overline{[x_i]_{R_i}} = \phi$ and $[x_i]_{R_i} \cup \overline{[x_i]_{R_i}} = U$ hold.

Methods for constructing initial equivalence relations, including the choice of dissimilarity measure, is arbitrary under the condition that it has the ability of performing binary classification of U. For example, one can simply use Euclidean distance and k-means with cluster number 2, if it is appropriate based on the property of the data. We have introduced a method for constructing initial equivalence relations based on the denseness of the objects in [3]; however, one may use another approach for this purpose.

2.2   Refinement of Initial Equivalence Relations

In the second stage, we perform global optimization of initial equivalence relations so that they produce adequately coarse classification to the objects. The global similarity of objects is represented by a newly introduced measure, the *indiscernibility degree*. Rough clustering takes a threshold value of the indiscernibility degree as an input and associates it with the user-defined granularity of the categories. Given the threshold value, we iteratively refine the initial equivalence relations in order to produce categories that meet the given level of granularity.

Now let us assume $U = \{x_1, x_2, x_3, x_4, x_5\}$ and classifications of U by $\mathbf{R} = \{R_1, R_2, R_3, R_4, R_5\}$ is given as follows.

$$\begin{aligned}
U/R_1 &= \{\{x_1, x_2, x_3\}, \{x_4, x_5\}\}, \\
U/R_2 &= \{\{x_1, x_2, x_3\}, \{x_4, x_5\}\}, \\
U/R_3 &= \{\{x_2, x_3, x_4\}, \{x_1, x_5\}\}, \\
U/R_4 &= \{\{x_1, x_2, x_3, x_4\}, \{x_5\}\}, \\
U/R_5 &= \{\{x_4, x_5\}, \{x_1, x_2, x_3\}\}.
\end{aligned} \tag{3}$$

This example contains three types of equivalence relations: $R_1\ (= R_2 = R_5)$, R_3 and R_4. Since each of them classifies U slightly differently, classification of U by the family of equivalence relations $\mathbf{R}$, $U/\mathbf{R}$, contains four very small, almost independent categories.

$$U/\mathbf{R} = \{\{x_1\}, \{x_2, x_3\}, \{x_4\}, \{x_5\}\}. \tag{4}$$

In the following we present a method to reduce the variety of equivalence relations and to obtain coarser categories.

First, we define an *indiscernibility degree*, $\gamma(x_i, x_j)$, for two objects x_i and x_j as follows.

$$\gamma(x_i, x_j) = \frac{\sum_{k=1}^{|U|} \delta_k^{indis}(x_i, x_j)}{\sum_{k=1}^{|U|} \delta_k^{indis}(x_i, x_j) + \sum_{k=1}^{|U|} \delta_k^{dis}(x_i, x_j)}, \tag{5}$$

where

$$\delta_k^{indis}(x_i, x_j) = \begin{cases} 1, \text{if } (x_i \in [x_k]_{R_k} \wedge x_j \in [x_k]_{R_k}) \\ 0, \text{otherwise.} \end{cases} \tag{6}$$

and

$$\delta_k^{dis}(x_i, x_j) = \begin{cases} 1, \text{ if } (x_i \in [x_k]_{R_k} \wedge x_j \notin [x_k]_{R_k}) \\ \text{or if } (x_i \notin [x_k]_{R_k} \wedge x_j \in [x_k]_{R_k}) \\ 0, \text{ otherwise.} \end{cases} \tag{7}$$

Equation (6) shows that $\delta_k^{indis}(x_i, x_j)$ takes 1 only when the equivalence relation R_k regards both x_i and x_j as indiscernible objects, under the condition that both of them are in the same equivalence class as x_k. Equation (7) shows that $\delta_k^{dis}(x_i, x_j)$ takes 1 only when R_k regards x_i and x_j as discernible objects, under the condition that either of them is in the same class as x_k. By summing $\delta_k^{indis}(x_i, x_j)$ and $\delta_k^{dis}(x_i, x_j)$ for all $k(1 \le k \le |U|)$ as in Equation (5), we obtain the percentage of equivalence relations that regard x_i and x_j as indiscernible objects. Note that in Equation (6), we excluded the case when x_i and x_j are indiscernible but not in the same class as x_k. This is to exclude the case where R_k does not significantly put weight on discerning x_i and x_j. As mentioned in Section 2.1, P_k for R_k is determined by focusing on similar objects rather than dissimilar objects. This means that when both of x_i and x_j are highly dissimilar to x_k, their dissimilarity is not significant for x_k, when determining the dissimilarity threshold Th_{dk}. Thus we only count the number of equivalence relations that certainly evaluate the dissimilarity of x_i and x_j.

From its definition, a large $\gamma(x_i, x_j)$ represents that x_i and x_j are commonly regarded as indiscernible objects by the large number of the equivalence relations. Therefore, if an equivalence relation R_l discerns the objects that have high γ value, we consider that it represents excessively fine classification knowledge and refine it according to the following procedure (note that R_l is rewritten as R_i below for the purpose of generalization).

Let $R_i \in \mathbf{R}$ be an initial equivalence relation on U. A refined equivalence relation $R_i' \in \mathbf{R}'$ of R_i is defined as

$$U/R_i' = \{P_i', \ U - P_i'\}, \tag{8}$$

where P_i' denotes a set of objects represented by

$$P_i' = \{x_j | \gamma(x_i, x_j) \geq T_h\}, \quad \forall x_j \in U. \tag{9}$$

and T_h denotes the lower threshold value of the indiscernibility degree above, in which x_i and x_j are regarded as indiscernible objects. It represents that when $\gamma(x_i, x_j)$ is larger than T_h, R_i is modified to include x_j into the class of x_i.

2.3   Iterative Refinement of Equivalence Relations

It should be noted that the state of the indiscernibility degrees could also be changed after refinement of the equivalence relations, since the degrees are re-calculated using the refined family of equivalence relations $\mathbf{R}'$. Thus we iterate the refinement process using the same T_h until the categories become stable. Note that each refinement process is performed using the previously 'refined' set of equivalence relations.

3   Experimental Results

3.1   Perfect Equivalence Relations

Our aim is to analyze the relationships between the threshold value T_h of indiscernibility degree γ and cluster numbers, while minimizing the influence of methods for determining initial equivalence relations in step 1. We prepared equivalence relations called perfect equivalence relations, which can classify the data into correct groups. Taking them as initial equivalence relations, we performed step 2 of the rough clustering several times by changing T_h and observed the change of resultant clusters. We also performed clustering experiments on randomly disturbed perfect equivalence relations.

A perfect equivalence relation R_i for object x_i is denoted as follows.

$$U/R_i = \{P_i, \ U - P_i\}, \tag{10}$$

where

$$P_i = \{x_j | \ c[x_i] = c[x_j]\}, \quad \forall x_j \in U. \tag{11}$$

where $c[x_i]$ denotes the class label of x_i assigned when creating the dataset. Obviously, the types of perfect equivalence relations in $\mathbf{R}$ are equal to the number

Table 1. Number of data points in datasets

Dataset	CBS 1	CBS 2	CBS 3	CBS 4	CBS 5	total
c3-1	52	40	93	–	–	185
c3-2	224	31	177	–	–	432
c5-1	52	171	148	215	55	641
c5-2	64	164	126	58	155	567

of classes in the dataset, because if objects x_i and x_j belong to the same class, R_i and R_j become identical.

3.2 Datasets

We artificially created a total of four numerical datasets named c3-1, c3-2, c5-1, and c5-2 shown in Table 1. Datasets c3-1 and c3-2 contain three clusters, and c5-1 and c5-2 contain five clusters respectively. The number of data points in each cluster was controlled to be substantially different and in balanced, because the balanced data may induce special effect of T_h on a specific range. The data points were generated based on a two-dimensional normal distribution for easy visualization; however, note that the geometric distribution of data points is not significant in this experiment because we used only their class labels for creating the perfect equivalence relations.

3.3 Procedures

The following procedure was applied to each dataset.

1. Form perfect initial equivalence relations: according to E's. (10) and (11), assign a perfect initial equivalence relation for each $x_i \in U$.
2. Disturb the initial relations: Select one of the following disturbance operation randomly at each time and apply it to initial relations. This process is repeated $card(P_i) \times \rho$ times, where ρ denotes disturbance ratio (from 0.0 to 1.0, interval 0.2).

   Delete: Randomly select one element in P_i and remove it from P_i.

   Add: Randomly select one element from U and add it to P_i.

   Replace: Randomly select one element from P_i and replace it with randomly selected element in U.
3. Clustering: Apply the iterative refinement process of rough clustering to the disturbed initial equivalence relations and obtain clusters. This process is repeated by changing T_h (from 0 to 1.0, interval 0.05) . For each T_h, calculate the validity of clustering result according to the following measure.

$$v_{\mathbf{R}}(C) = \min \left(\frac{|X_{\mathbf{R}} \cap C|}{|X_{\mathbf{R}}|}, \frac{|X_{\mathbf{R}} \cap C|}{|C|} \right),$$

where $X_{\mathbf{R}}$ and C denote the obtained clusters and original classes, respectively.

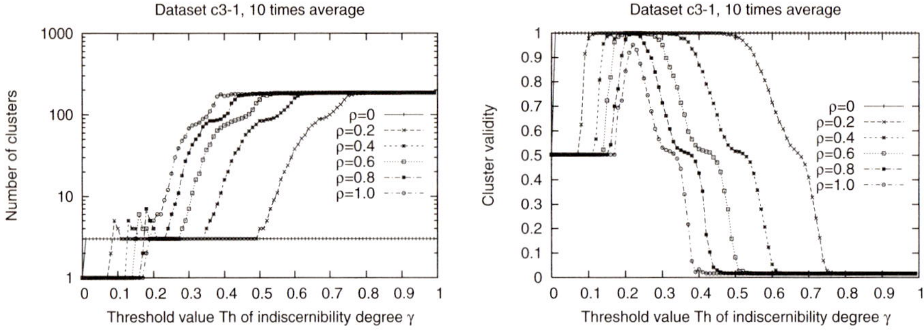

Fig. 1. Results for Dataset c3-1. Left: Number of clusters. Right: Cluster Validity.

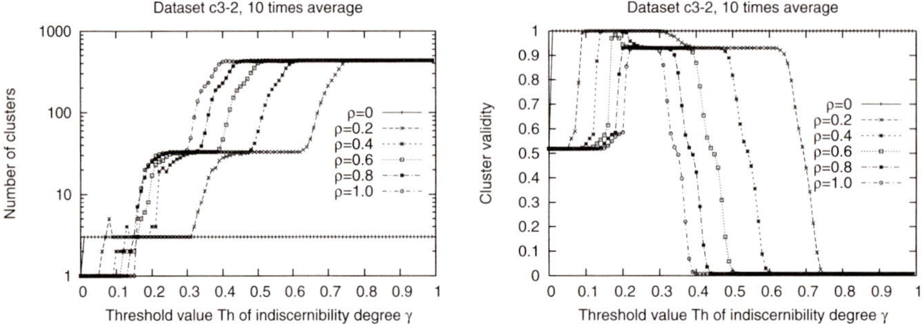

Fig. 2. Results for Dataset c3-2. Left: Number of clusters. Right: Cluster Validity.

3.4   Results and Discussions

Figures 1-4 show the results on the four datasets respectively. Each of the figures consists of two sub-figures: Th-Number of clusters curves (left) and Th-Cluster Validity curves (right). The horizontal axis corresponds to the threshold value T_h of indiscernibility degree γ. The vertical axis corresponds to the number of clusters or cluster validity for the left or right figure, respectively. Each figure contains six curves indexed by "$\rho = x$", which corresponds to the ratio of disturbance of the perfect initial equivalence relations described previously.

Let us first see the global characteristics the curves. At $T_h = 0$, every equivalence relation was modified to include all objects. This means that, regardless of the characteristics of initial equivalence relations, all objects would be grouped into the same cluster. Therefore the number of clusters was always 1 at $T_h = 0$. The cluster validity took a constant value which was dependent only to the class distribution of the dataset (around 0.5 or 0.3 for the datasets used here).

When $\rho = 0$, initial equivalence relations were identical to the perfect relations since no disturbance was applied. In this case the indiscernibility degrees were 0 for all pairs of objects belonging to different clusters, and 1 for those belonging to the same cluster. Therefore, correct clusters of validity=1 were formed for all values of $T_h > 0$ without any refinement.

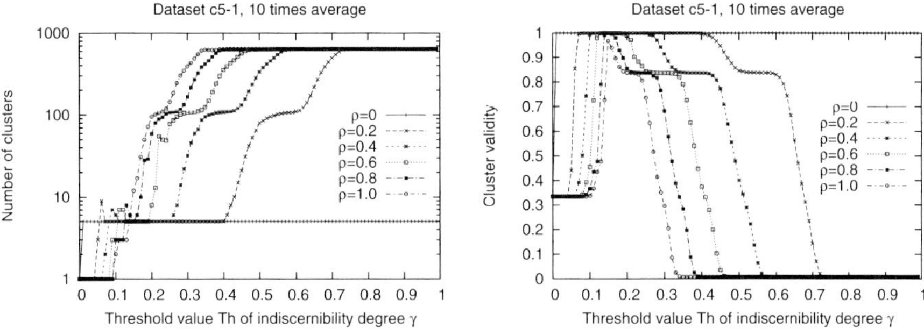

Fig. 3. Results for Dataset c5-1. Left: Number of clusters. Right: Cluster Validity.

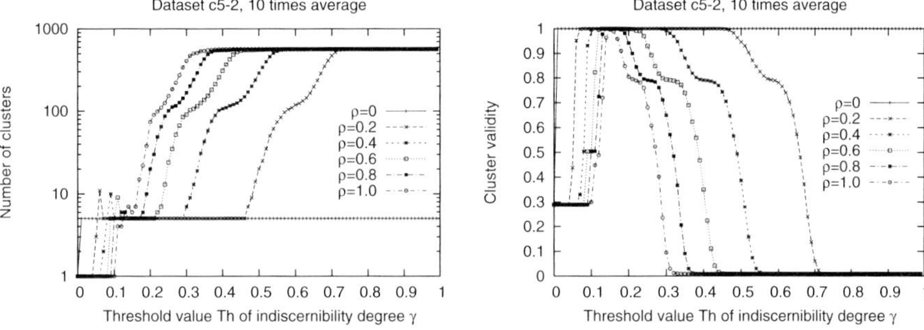

Fig. 4. Results for Dataset c5-2. Left: Number of clusters. Right: Cluster Validity.

If $\rho > 0$, situations become close to those of real-world datasets. The variety of initial equivalence relations drastically increase because of disturbance. Even a small difference of equivalence relations results in producing fine clusters due to the increase of total discrimination ability. Hence, without refinement of the relations, excessively large number of fine clusters would be produced. Let us first see the case of dataset c3-1 in Figure 1. For large values of $T_h > 0.8$, only a few equivalence relations satisfied the condition for refinement in CEQ. (9). As most of the relations remained unchanged, the number of induced clusters kept high value - almost equal to the number of objects in the dataset. When T_h became smaller, the number of equivalence relations to be refined increased. The refinement made classification coarser and made the number of clusters smaller, inducing the increase of cluster validity. The level of T_h for starting this improvement was higher if ρ was smaller, because at smaller ρ initial equivalence relations were only slightly and locally modified from the perfect equivalence. Therefore, the indiscernibility degree of each object pairs kept high value, while the types of equivalence relations are quite large. As ρ becomes larger, more severe and global disturbance could occur. Since it induced the decrease of average level of the indiscernibility, the values of T_h should be smaller to do the necessary refinement.

For $0.5 > T_h > 0.1$, the number of clusters kept 3 with the highest validity of 1. In this range, the method could produce the correct cluster assignment with the help of iterative refinement of the disturbed initial equivalence relations. The range became narrow as ρ became small. For example, when $\rho = 0.6$ the range was about $2.7 > T_h > 1.8$ and when $\rho = 1.0$, there was no range of T_h that could generate the correct cluster assignment. If there exists too much disturbance, the level of indiscernibility degrees for objects that should belong to the same cluster would be close to those of objects that belong to different clusters. Hence it would be difficult to form correct clusters, especially for small clusters.

For small values of $T_h < 0.1$, the number of clusters decreased to 1, followed by the decrease of cluster validity. In this range, too coarse cluster was obtained due to too much refinement of equivalence relations. Let us denote by min_γ the minimum value of indiscernibility degrees. Actually, for $Th < min_\gamma$, the results are identical with the case of $T_h = 0$, due to the discrete property of indiscernibility degree.

The above characteristics were commonly observed for all the other datasets used in this experiment. It demonstrated that, by changing the threshold value of indiscernibility degree, we could control the roughness of classification knowledge, namely, granularity of the data.

Furthermore, an interesting feature about the number of clusters was observed on all datasets. Around $T_h = 0.1 - 0.2$, there existed a short spike at the left end of the range for yielding the correct number of clusters. Although it could disappears on extremely disturbed cases, the convex features of the curve may be used for determining the best range of T_h semi-automatically.

4   Conclusions

In this work, we have empirically investigated the characteristics of indiscernibility degree in rough clustering. By the use of perfect equivalence relations, we could observe more basic relationships between the threshold value of indiscernibility degree and resultant clusters, without the effect of methods for determining initial equivalence relations. The result demonstrated that the threshold parameter might be associated with roughness of knowledge, which also controls the granularity of dataset. Additionally, although it still requires exploratory approach, the convex shape of th-AC curve suggested the possibility of guiding appropriate range of the thresholds. It remains as a future work to investigate the reason why these spikes occur. The future work also include comparison with other methods, e.g, classical hierarchical and partitional clustering methods [2] and rough set-based clustering methods [5].

References

1. Berkhin, P.: Survey of clustering data mining techniques. Accrue Software Research Paper. URL: http://www.accrue.com/products/researchpapers.html (2002)
2. Everitt B. S., Landau S., Leese M. (2001): Cluster Analysis Fourth Edition. Arnold Publishers.

3. Hirano, S., Tsumoto, S.: An indiscernibility-based clustering method with iterative refinement of equivalence relations - rough clustering -. Journal of Advanced Computational Intelligence and Intelligent Informatics **7** (2003) 169–177
4. Hirano, S., Tsumoto, S.: On Constructing Clusters from Non-Euclidean Dissimilarity Matrix by Using Rough Clustering. Lecture Notes in Artificial Intelligence, **4012** (2006) 5-16, Springer.
5. Lingras P., Rough set clustering for web mining. Proceedings of the 2002 IEEE International Conference on Fuzzy Systems (2002) 1039–1044.

A Fuzzy Neighborhood Model for Clustering, Classification, and Approximations

Sadaaki Miyamoto[1] and Satoshi Hayakawa[2]

[1] Department of Risk Engineering
School of Systems and Information Engineering
University of Tsukuba, Ibaraki 305-8573, Japan
miyamoto@risk.tsukuba.ac.jp
[2] Graduate School of Systems and Information Engineering
University of Tsukuba, Ibaraki 305-8573, Japan
satossu@soft.risk.tsukuba.ac.jp

Abstract. A fuzzy neighborhood model for analyzing information systems having topological structures on occurrences of keywords is proposed and algorithms of clustering, classification and approximations similar to generalized rough sets are developed. Real applications include text mining and clustering of keywords on the web. An illustrative example is given.

1   Introduction

Motivations for a new theory of text mining and web information analysis are becoming stronger. From the viewpoint of rough sets [9,10], the classical framework of classifications of the universal set is frequently insufficient, and more general structure of the topology should be considered, as texts and web information have natural topologies.

Topologies in general applications can be of different types. First, topologies in the sense of mathematics in applications should actually be metrics or distances, and it is true that texts and web information have natural distances. However, the distances in these applications are difficult to compute, or require huge computation, as the distances should be calculated even between very far elements.

What we propose in this paper is fuzzy neighborhoods that are calculated from the distances. The fuzzy neighborhoods have finite supports, in other words, they are zero outside of finite sets whereby calculation becomes easier. It should also be noted that the fuzzy neighborhoods are different from the mathematical neighborhood. Instead, the former is simply fuzzy sets naturally induced from distances.

We study methods of clustering, classification, and approximation using this model of fuzzy neighborhood. The approximation is similar to that used in generalized rough set [12].

S. Greco et al. (Eds.): RSCTC 2006, LNAI 4259, pp. 882–890, 2006.

2   Term Space and Fuzzy Neighborhood Space

Throughout this paper, we assume $A(x)$ means the membership value of fuzzy set A at x instead of the classical symbol $\mu_A(x)$. Moreover supp(A) means the crisp set on which $A(x) > 0$.

The fuzzy neighborhood model basically consists of the quadruple

$$< T, O, R, N > \tag{1}$$

in which T is called a term set in which generic elements are denoted by $t, t', t_i, \ldots \in T$; O is called an occurrence space in which generic elements are denoted by $o, o', o_i, \ldots \in O$. T is generally a finite set, while O can be either finite or infinite, and we need not observe all elements of O in general. R is a fuzzy relation on $T \times O$, while N is a fuzzy relation on $O \times O$. We moreover define a family of fuzzy sets $N[o]$ of the same symbol:

$$N(o, o') = N[o](o'), \quad \forall o' \in O. \tag{2}$$

That is, $N[o]$ is a fuzzy set that is dependent on o, which is defined by the above equation. The fuzzy set $N[o]$ is called a *fuzzy neighborhood* of $o \in O$.

The above is a very simple and general model but when we add more structures and give adequate interpretations, this model becomes an useful framework in applications.

Let $\mathcal{P}_T$ be the projection of a fuzzy set of $T \times O$ onto T:

$$\mathcal{P}_T(R)(t) = \sup_{o \in O} R(t, o).$$

while

$$\mathcal{P}_O(R)(t) = \sup_{t \in T} R(t, o).$$

We assume

$$\text{supp}(P_T(R)) = T, \tag{3}$$

but generally

$$\text{supp}(P_O(R)) \neq O. \tag{4}$$

In applications, the set T is a set of keywords which we wish to classify or make approximations. In real worlds, the keywords may occur many times in a text, or distributed on web pages. Hence keyword occurrences are represented by $o, o' \ldots \in O$. When o means a keyword t, $R(t, o) = 1$. However, there are similar keywords and hence generally $0 \leq R(t, o) \leq 1$. When an occurrence o does not correspond to any keyword t, $R(t, o) = 0$. Hence (3) implies that all keywords occur at least once in O including fuzzy correspondence, and (4) means there are nonsense or uninteresting occurrences in O. We hereafter use the word of a *term* instead of a *keyword*.

$N[o]$ shows a neighborhood of occurrence o. When a distance $d(o, o')$ is defined on O, we can define $N[o]$ by the next procedure.

(i) Let $f\colon \mathbf{R} \cup \{0\} \to [0,1]$ be a strictly monotonically decreasing function such that $f(0) = 1$ and there exists a positive number M satisfying

$$f(x) = 0, \quad M \le x < +\infty. \tag{5}$$

(ii) Define $N[o]$ by

$$N[o](o') = f((d(o,o'))). \tag{6}$$

Notice that the relation $N(o,o')$ defined by (6) satisfies the symmetry

$$N(o,o') = N(o',o).$$

There are, however, other ways to define directly the neighborhoods and hence generally the relation is not always symmetric.

We moreover state additional assumptions.

(I) Reflexivity: $N(o,o) = 1$ for all $o \in O$.
(II) Finiteness: For an arbitrary $o \in O$, $|\mathrm{supp}(N[o])| < +\infty$, i.e., the number of elements which have nonzero membership values are finite.

The interpretation of $N[o]$ is straightforward, If $N[o](o') > N[o](o'')$, then o' is nearer to o than o''. If $N[o](o') = 0$, then the relation of o to o' is neglected by the model.

2.1   Text Mining: Term Relations in Text Sets

Let the set of documents be $\mathcal{D} = \{d_1, d_2, \ldots, d_n\}$. A document d consists of a sequence of occurrences. For simplicity suppose an occurrence corresponds to a unique term. We handle a sequence of occurrences, and accordingly we define $Sqnc(d)$ is the sequence of occurrences. For example assume $Sqnc(d) = abcde$ and term of a, b, d is t; term of c and e is t'. Then $Sqnc(d) = ttt'tt'$ using the term symbols.

From technical reason we define concatenation of two document sequences by $Sqnc(d)|Sqnc(d')$. Thus if

$$Sqnc(d) = abcd, \qquad Sqnc(d') = vwxyz,$$

then

$$Sqnc(d)|Sqnc(d') = abcdvwxyz.$$

The whole sequence X of the document set $\mathcal{D}$ is

$$X = Sqnc(d_1)|Sqnc(d_2)|\cdots|Sqnc(d_n).$$

A natural distance D is defined:

$$D(a,b) = \{\text{ number of term occurrences between } a \text{ and } b\ \} + 1$$

For the above d and d', $D(v,w) = 1$ and $D(v,z) = 4$. Thus for this distance the fuzzy neighborhood is naturally defined. The next two are typical examples.

Crisp and fuzzy neighborhoods $N_{C_K}[a]$ and $N_{F_K}[a]$:

$$N_{C_K}[a](x) = \begin{cases} 1 & (D(a,x) \leq K), \\ 0 & (D(a,x) > K). \end{cases}$$

$$N_{F_K}[a](x) = \begin{cases} 1 - D(a,x)/K & (D(a,x) \leq K), \\ 0 & (D(a,x) > K). \end{cases}$$

The meanings of these neighborhoods are clear.

2.2   Information on Web

Although information on web has complicated structures, the simplest formulation is to assume the set of occurrences to be a network. Thus, the distance on the network is defined by the shortest path and then the present framework should be employed. It should be noted that fast algorithms of shortest path can be employed. The above notations are directly applicable and we omit the details.

3   Methods of Classification and Clustering

Relatively simple methods as well as advanced algorithms can be developed based on this framework. We describe simple classification methods and algorithms of clustering.

3.1   Nearest Neighbor and k-Nearest Neighbor Classifications

Since the present model is nonprobabilistic, parametric methods cannot be applied, and hence the well-known approaches of nearest neighbor and k-nearest neighbor [2] should be used. Clearly the objective of classification is to obtain classification rules defined on the term set T based on partial information based on previous observations.

Partial information is assumed to be on occurrences. Thus we assume crisp subsets C_1 and C_2 of O such that $C_1 \cap C_2 = \emptyset$. These sets represents class 1 and 2, respectively.

Our objective is to classify a term t into one of the two classes. Note

$$R^{-1}(t) = R(t, \cdot), \quad i = 1, 2. \tag{7}$$

is a fuzzy set of O

To define a generalized k-nearest neighbor method, let us review the OWA operator with weight $w = (w_1, \ldots, w_k)$:

$$OWA(A, w) = \sum_{i=1}^{k} w_i \cdot Ord(A; i) \tag{8}$$

in which $Ord(A; i)$ is the i-th largest element when $A(o_1), \ldots, A(o_n)$ are arranged into decreasing order. Hence $Ord(A, 1)$ is the largest, $Ord(A, 2)$ is the second largest, and $Ord(A, n)$ is the smallest among $A(o_1), \ldots, A(o_n)$.

Using the OWA operator, the following rule can be applied when t should be classified:

$$t \rightarrow \text{class 1} \iff OWA(C_1 \wedge R^{-1}(t), w) > OWA(C_2 \wedge R^{-1}(t), w),$$
$$t \rightarrow \text{class 2} \iff OWA(C_1 \wedge R^{-1}(t), w) < OWA(C_2 \wedge R^{-1}(t), w),$$

and note that the class of t cannot be decided when $OWA(C_1 \wedge R^{-1}(t)) = OWA(C_2 \wedge R^{-1}(t))$.

This method is rather simple and does not use the topology defined by N. A natural method using N is to extend C_i into $N \circ C_i$. Thus the extended rule is:

$$t \rightarrow \text{class 1} \iff OWA(C_1 \wedge (N \circ R^{-1})(t), w) > OWA(C_2 \wedge (N \circ R^{-1})(t), w),$$
$$t \rightarrow \text{class 2} \iff OWA(C_1 \wedge (N \circ R^{-1})(t), w) < OWA(C_2 \wedge (N \circ R^{-1})(t), w).$$

Moreover we can use $N^j \circ R^{-1}$ $(j = 2, 3, \ldots)$ or $N^* \circ R^{-1}$ instead of $N \circ R^{-1}$, where N^* is the transitive closure of N.

3.2 Agglomerative Hierarchical Clustering

Different methods of agglomerative hierarchical clustering [3,5] of terms can be considered. We begin with the simplest method of the transitive closure.

The Method of Transitive Closure

Let us suppose that N is a symmetric relation. A reflexive and symmetric relation S on $T \times T$ which represents similarity between two terms can be derived using R and N:

$$S = R \circ N \circ R^{-1}. \tag{9}$$

It has been well-known that the transitive closure

$$S^* = S \circ S^2 \circ \cdots \tag{10}$$

is a fuzzy equivalence relation that generates the same hierarchical classification as the single link method in agglomerative clustering [5,7,4].

Similarity Measures and General Procedure

While the above method employs the sup-min composition, other natural idea to use the sum is also adequate.

$$p_1(t, t') = \sum_{a \in O} \sum_{b \in O} R(t, a) \otimes N(a, b) \otimes R(t', b) \tag{11}$$

$$s_1(t, t') = \frac{p_1(t, t')}{\sqrt{p_1(t, t) p_1(t', t')}}. \tag{12}$$

The operation $\otimes$ is a t-norm type of operation including the minimum and algebraic product. Note moreover that the similarity measure s_1 is normalized.

We next show the general procedure **AHC** of agglomerative clustering in which $\mathcal{G} = \{G_1, \ldots, G_C\}$ is a family of clusters $G_1, \ldots, G_C$ which forms a partition of T.

Algorithm AHC (Agglomerative Hierarchical Clustering).
AHC0.   Put the number of clusters $C = |T|$; initialize clusters:
$$G_i = \{t_i\}, \ i = 1, \ldots, C; \ \ s(G_i, G_j) = s(t_i, t_j), \ \ \text{all } i, j.$$
AHC1.   Calculate $(G, G') = \arg \max_{1 \leq i,j \leq C, i \neq j} s(G_i, G_j)$.

Put $\hat{G} = G \cup G'$. Remove G, G' from $\mathcal{G}$ and add $\hat{G}$ to $\mathcal{G}$.
AHC2.   Let $C = C - 1$. If $C = 1$, output the dendrogram and stop.
Else update $s(\hat{G}, G'')$, $\forall G'' \in \mathcal{G}$, and go back to **AHC1**.
End of AHC.

Note 1. Gnenerally the maximizing pair (G, G') is not unique in which case one of them should be selected. In the case of SL, this selection has no effect in the output, whereas other methods may have different outputs according to the selection [5,7].

Calculation of $s_1(G, G')$ uses natural idea of *regarding terms in a cluster to be identical.* Hence we have

$$p_1(G, G') = \sum_{t \in G} \sum_{t' \in G'} p_1(t, t') \tag{13}$$

$$s_1(G, G') = \frac{p_1(G, G')}{\sqrt{p_1(G, G)p_1(G', G')}}. \tag{14}$$

Crisp and Fuzzy c-Means Clustering
Crisp and fuzzy c-means algorithms [1,2] are most well-known methods of non-hierarchical clustering. These methods use cluster centers and hence similarity between a term or cluster and the center should be defined.

We describe fuzzy c-means algorithm based on an entropy [6,7,4], but the standard algorithm [1] is derived likewise.

Let G_i be a fuzzy cluster

$$G_i = \sum_{t_k \in T} u_{ik} | t_k$$

Put also

$$\|G_i\|^2 = \sum_k u_{ik}^2 \|t_k\|^2,$$

Note 2. u_{ik} is the membership of t_k to the cluster i [1,7], and $\sum_{t_k \in T} u_{ik} | t_k$ is an abbreviated notation of the fuzzy set G_i where the membership is $\mu_{G_i}(t_k) = u_{ik}$, $t_k \in T$.

A cluster center, denoted by z_i, is assumed to be a fuzzy set of terms

$$z_i = \sum_{t_k \in T} w_{ik} | t_k \tag{15}$$

We should determine w_{ik} that satisfies

$$\max_z s_1(G_i, z_i).$$

We also put

$$p_1(G_i, z) = \sum_{t_k \in T} u_{ik} p_1(t_k, z),$$

$$s_1(G_i, z) = \frac{p_1(G_i, z)}{\|G_i\| \sqrt{\sum_{t_k \in T} w_{ik}^2 \|t_k\|^2}}.$$

The detailed calculation of z_i is omitted here; the solution of w_{ik} is given by

$$w_{ik} = \left(\sum_{t_r \in T} \frac{\|t_k\|^4 (\sum_{t_s \in T} u_{is} X_r)^2}{\|t_r\|^2 (\sum_{t_s \in T} u_{is} X_k)^2} \right)^{-\frac{1}{2}},$$

where $X_i = \sum_{a \in O} \sum_{t' \in T} \sum_{b \in O} R(t_i, a) \otimes N(a, b) \otimes R(t', b)$. The membership u_{ik} for clusters is given by the ordinary formula:

$$u_{ik} = \frac{\exp(\lambda s(G_i, z_i))}{\sum_k \exp(\lambda s(G_k, z_k))} \tag{16}$$

Hence iterative calculation of the last equation and the cluster center until convergence leads to the solution of fuzzy c-means clustering.

For crisp c-means, the membership employs the following nearest center allocation rule instead of (16), while the cluster centers are using the same formula as the entropy-based fuzzy c-means.

$$u_{ik} = \begin{cases} 1 & (i = \arg \min_{1 \le j \le c} \|x_k - v_i\|), \\ 0 & (\text{otherwise}). \end{cases}$$

4   Upper and Lower Approximations

Given a fuzzy set A of T, we can define upper approximation $U(A)$ and lower approximation $L(A)$ using the fuzzy neighborhood.

For this purpose we consider two families of subsets of T:

$$\mathcal{U}(A) = \{C \in 2^T : A \circ R \circ N \subseteq C \circ R\},$$
$$\mathcal{L}(A) = \{D \in 2^T : D \circ R \circ N \subseteq A \circ R\}.$$

The minimum subset in $\mathcal{U}(A)$ is defined to be the upper approximation and the maximum element in $\mathcal{L}(A)$ is the lower approximation.

$$U(A) = \bigcap_{C \in \mathcal{U}(A)} C, \qquad L(A) = \bigcup_{D \in \mathcal{L}(A)} D.$$

5   An Illustrative Example

To save space, a simple illustrative example and results from the crisp and fuzzy c-means are described, as they are most advanced methods among those described above. Consider the text mining model in section 2.1. Three classes of $\{A, B, C, D, C\}$, $\{i, j, k, l\}$, and $\{X, Y, Z\}$ should be clustered. Five data sets one of which is shown next have been prepared. In the next example, a colon shows separation of documents and hence a neighborhood does not intersect between two sequences with a comma.

```
E,C,A:i,j,l:X,Y:j,i,k:D,E,B:X,Z,Y:i,l,j:E,C,B:
X,Z,Z:j,l:B,D:k,i:X,Z:B,A:i,l:B,A,A,C,D:X,Y,Y
```

The neighborhoods are given by

$$N(x, y) = \begin{cases} F(D(x, y)) & (D(x, y) \leq K), \\ 0 & (K < D(x, y)). \end{cases}$$

where either $F(D(x, y)) = 1$ or $F(D(x, y)) = 1/D^2(x, y)$ is used. The data sets are basically well-separated for the three classes, the objective is to check whether or not the algorithms correctly work. As a result, fuzzy c-means always provide the correct result when the algorithm is convergent, while crisp c-means mostly produce the correct result with a few exceptions. However, the ratio of convergence is not high, as shown in the next tables that show convergence ratios in percentages with different values of K and the two choices of $F(D(x, y))$.

Crisp neighborhood $F = 1$:

K	2	3	4	5	6	7
Data1	4	0	0	0	0	0
Data2	32.5	71.5	79	87	53.5	0
Data3	52.5	57	89.5	84	94.5	99.5
Data4	0	0	0	0	0	0
Data5	51.5	16	0	0	0	0

Fuzzy neighborhood $F = \frac{1}{D^2}$:

K	2	3	4	5	6	7
Data1	3.5	2	1.5	2	3.5	1.5
Data2	57.5	61.5	79	70	65.5	60.5
Data3	16	19.5	26	18.5	31.5	32.5
Data4	2.5	1	3	2.5	1	1
Data5	61.5	58.5	51.5	50	52	57.5

In short, these results show that the methods of c-means correctly work, but there are much rooms for further improvement.

6   Conclusion

We have described a model of fuzzy neighborhood space in which methods of classification, clustering, and approximations of terms have been proposed. In applications, clustering of information on the web such as vivisimo [11] and Lingo [8] is promising. Moreover text mining techniques using this framework are more advanced than current algorithms, since the fuzzy neighborhood space can handle refined structures of various texts.

Since the present framework is new, there are many possibilities for further research in both theory and applications.

Acknowledgment

This study has partly been supported by the Grant-in-Aid for Scientific Research,No.16650044, Japan Ministry of Education, Culture, Sports, Science and Technology.

References

1. J.C. Bezdek, *Pattern Recognition with Fuzzy Objective Function Algorithms*, Plenum, New York, 1981.
2. R.O. Duda, P.E. Hart, D.G. Stork, *Pattern Classification, 2nd Ed.*, Wiley, New York, 2001.
3. B.S. Everitt, *Cluster Analysis, 3rd Ed.*, Arnold, London, 1993.
4. Z.Q. Liu, S. Miyamoto, eds., *Soft Computing and Human-Centered Machines* Springer, Tokyo, 2000.
5. S. Miyamoto, *Fuzzy Sets in Information Retrieval and Cluster Analysis*, Kluwer, Dordrecht, 1990.
6. S. Miyamoto, M. Mukaidono, Fuzzy c-means as a regularization and maximum entropy approach, *Proc. of the 7th International Fuzzy Systems Association World Congress (IFSA'97)*, June 25-30, 1997, Prague, Czech, Vol.II, pp.86–92, 1997.
7. S. Miyamoto, *Introduction to Cluster Analysis: Theory and Applications of Fuzzy Clustering*, Morikita-Shuppan, Tokyo, 1990 (in Japanese).
8. S. Osiński, J. Stefanowski, D. Weiss, Lingo: Search Results Clustering Algorithm Based on Singular Value Decomposition. In: *Advances in Soft Computing, Intelligent Information Processing and Web Mining, Proceedings of the International IIS: IIPWM'04 Conference*, Zakopane, Poland, 2004, pp. 359–368.
9. Z. Pawlak, Rough sets, *International Journal of Computer and Information Sciences*, **11**, pp. 341–356, 1982.
10. Z. Pawlak, *Rough Sets: Theoretical Aspects of Reasoning about Data*, Kluwer, Dordrecht, 1991.
11. http://vivisimo.com/
12. Y.Y. Yao, S.K.M. Wong, T.Y. Lin, A review of rough set models, in T.Y.Lin, N.Cercone, eds., *Rough Sets and Data Mining: Analysis of Imprecise Data*, Kluwer, Boston, 1997, 47–75.

A Proposal for Comparison of Impression Evaluation Data Among Individuals by Using Clustering Method Based on Distributed Structure of Data

Shou Kuroda, Tomohiro Yoshikawa, and Takeshi Furuhashi

Dept. of Computational Science and Engineering, Nagoya University
Furo-cho, Chikusa-ku, Nagoya 464-8603, Japan
kuroda@cmplx.cse.nagoya-u.ac.jp

Abstract. In the field of marketing, companies often carry out a questionnaire to consumers for grasping their impressions of products. Analyzing the evaluation data obtained from consumers enables us to grasp the tendency of the market and to find problems and/or to make hypotheses that are useful for the development of products. Semantic Differential (SD) method is one of the most useful methods for quantifying human-impressions to the objects. The purpose of this study is to develop a method for visualization of individual features in data. This paper proposes the clustering method based on Orthogonal Procrustes Analysis (OPA). The proposed method can cluster subjects among whom the distributed structures of the SD evaluation data are similar. The analysis by this method leads to discovery of majority/minority groups and/or groups which have unique features. In addition, it enables us to analyze the similarity/difference of objects and impression words among clusters and/or subjects by comparing the cluster centers and/or transformation matrices. This paper applies the proposed method to an actual SD evaluation data. It shows that this method can investigate the similar relationships among the objects in each group and compare the similarity/difference of impression words used for the evaluation of objects among subjects in the same cluster.

1 Introduction

In the field of marketing, companies often carry out a questionnaire to consumers for grasping their impressions of products. Analyzing the evaluation data obtained from consumers enables us to grasp the tendency of the market and to find problems and/or to make hypotheses that are useful for the development of products. Semantic Differential (SD) method is one of the most useful methods for quantifying humans' impressions to the objects. The SD method uses some pairs of adjectives (impression words) having antithetical meanings with five/seven discrete levels, and subjects (consumers) evaluate the objects with these adjectives.

There are two types of principal approaches to analyze SD evaluation data. The first approach is to analyze the averaged data by using statistical methods. The second one is to analyze the individual data based on individual differences. The first approach transforms the structure of data from "Subjects" × "Objects" × "Impression Words" into "Objects" × "Impression Words" by averaging the SD evaluation data to apply statistical methods. This approach is useful to discover the common factors for whole subjects.

S. Greco et al. (Eds.): RSCTC 2006, LNAI 4259, pp. 891–898, 2006.

However, this approach loses the information of individual features which the evaluation data originally has. The second approach can cover this shortcoming. Murakami et al. [1] examined the modeling and the evaluation of the individual differences included in the SD evaluation data employing three-mode factor analysis, and they described the rotation of factors and the decision method for the number of factors. Nakamori et al. [2] proposed the method to recognize the impression words as fuzzy objects in the factor space by mapping individual SD evaluation data onto the factor space composed of the average data. Toyoda [3] proposed an exploratory positioning analysis method based on a three-mode multivariate statistical model to analyze SD evaluation data. Yamamoto et al. [4] proposed useful method to analyze the differences of impression among subjects by the application of the Procrustes analysis (Orthogonal Procrustes Analysis: OPA) to SD evaluation data with an assumption that the information of the objects is equal to the subjects. The OPA identifies an orthogonal transformation matrix to minimize the sum of squares of the residual between two data distributions [5].

It is general that SD evaluation data obtained from many subjects are classified by stratified criterion based on the purpose of the analysis such as age, living area, occupation and so on. In addition, Yamamoto et al. [6] proposed a clustering method based on the individuality that is different from the conventional stratified analysis. The method defines the difference of the data structure and distribution between the averaged SD evaluation data and the individual one as the individuality of scale and that of impression words, and it classifies the subjects into four groups based on these individualities.

The purpose of this study is to develop a method for visualization of individual features in SD evaluation data. The authors focuse on the distributed structure of data. The distributed structure represents the relationships among the objects, which depend on each subject's sensibility. Then this paper defines the distributed structure as one of the individual features, and tries to cluster the subjects based on it. This paper also uses Cluster Analysis (CA) and Principal Component Analysis (PCA) for the visualization of the clustering results.

This paper proposes the clustering method based on OPA. The proposed method can cluster subjects among whom the distributed structures of the SD evaluation data are similar. The analysis by this method leads to discovery of majority/minority groups and/or groups which have unique features. In addition, it enables us to analyze the similarity/difference of objects and impression words among clusters/subjects by comparing the cluster centers/transformation matrices.

This paper applies the proposed method to an actual SD evaluation data, which is the evaluation of laptop photo images by SD method, and it analyzes the data through the visualized results. It describes some features of discovered majority and minority groups, and it shows that this method can investigate the similar relationships among the objects in each group and compare the similarity/difference of impression words used for the evaluation of objects among subjects in the same cluster.

2   Proposed Method

This paper uses the OPA [5] for comparing distributed structures. The proposed method defines the value of objective function of the OPA as the dissimilarity measure between individuals. Matrix $\boldsymbol{A}_i$ represents the i-th SD evaluation data, in which the number of data points (objects) is n, and the number of dimensions (impressin words) is p. Matrix $\boldsymbol{B}_k$ represents the k-th cluster center matrix, which has the same size with $\boldsymbol{A}_i$.

The residual matrix $\boldsymbol{E}_{ik}$ is defined as Eq. (1) using the orthogonalization transformation matrix $\boldsymbol{T}_i$ identified by OPA for transforming the matrix $\boldsymbol{A}_i$ into the matrix $\boldsymbol{B}_k$.

$$\boldsymbol{E}_{ik} = \boldsymbol{A}_i \boldsymbol{T}_i - \boldsymbol{B}_k \tag{1}$$

Therefore, the dissimilarity measure between the matrix $\boldsymbol{A}_i$ and the matrix $\boldsymbol{B}_k$ is defined as

$$\mathrm{tr}\left\{ \boldsymbol{E}_{ik}^T \boldsymbol{E}_{ik} \right\} = \mathrm{tr}\left\{ (\boldsymbol{A}_i \boldsymbol{T}_i - \boldsymbol{B}_k)^T (\boldsymbol{A}_i \boldsymbol{T}_i - \boldsymbol{B}_k) \right\}. \tag{2}$$

The objective function of the proposed method is expressed as

$$\sum_{k=1}^{C} \sum_{i \in G_k} \mathrm{tr}\left\{ \boldsymbol{E}_{ik}^T \boldsymbol{E}_{ik} \right\} = \sum_{k=1}^{C} \sum_{i \in G_k} \mathrm{tr}\left\{ (\boldsymbol{A}_i \boldsymbol{T}_i - \boldsymbol{B}_k)^T (\boldsymbol{A}_i \boldsymbol{T}_i - \boldsymbol{B}_k) \right\}, \tag{3}$$

where C is the number of clusters, and G_k is the set of individual indexes that belong to the k-th cluster.

The matrix $\boldsymbol{T}_i$ must satisfy the condition of orthogonal transformation matrix.

$$\boldsymbol{T}_i^T \boldsymbol{T}_i = \boldsymbol{T}_i \boldsymbol{T}_i^T = I \tag{4}$$

Lagrange function for optimizing the objective function in the proposed method is described as Eq. (5) by combining Eq. (3) and Eq. (4).

$$\begin{aligned} F(\boldsymbol{T}, \boldsymbol{B}, \boldsymbol{L}) = & \sum_{k=1}^{C} \sum_{i \in G_k} \mathrm{tr}\left\{ (\boldsymbol{A}_i \boldsymbol{T}_i - \boldsymbol{B}_k)^T (\boldsymbol{A}_i \boldsymbol{T}_i - \boldsymbol{B}_k) \right\} \\ & + \sum_{j=1}^{N} \mathrm{tr}\left\{ \boldsymbol{L}_j \left(\boldsymbol{T}_j^T \boldsymbol{T}_j - \boldsymbol{I} \right) \right\} \end{aligned} \tag{5}$$

The symbols used in Eq. (5) are shown in Table 1. In the proposed method, $\boldsymbol{B}_k$ and $\boldsymbol{T}_i$ to optimize Eq. (5) are determined by iterative optimization.

Eq. (6) must be set to $\boldsymbol{0}$ for the derivation of optimal $\boldsymbol{B}_k$.

$$\frac{\partial F}{\partial \boldsymbol{B}_k} = \sum_{i \in G_k} (-\boldsymbol{A}_i \boldsymbol{T}_i - \boldsymbol{A}_i \boldsymbol{T}_i + 2\boldsymbol{B}_k) = \boldsymbol{0} \tag{6}$$

From Eq. (6), the optimal $\boldsymbol{B}_k$ (cluster center matrix) is derived as

$$\boldsymbol{B}_k = \frac{1}{|G_k|} \sum_{i \in G_k} \boldsymbol{A}_i \boldsymbol{T}_i. \tag{7}$$

Then Eq. (8) must be set to $\boldsymbol{0}$ for the derivation of optimal $\boldsymbol{T}_i$.

$$\frac{\partial F}{\partial \boldsymbol{T}_i} = \sum_{k=1}^{C} \left(2\boldsymbol{A}_i^T \boldsymbol{A}_i \boldsymbol{T}_i - 2\boldsymbol{A}_i^T \boldsymbol{B}_k \right) + \boldsymbol{T}_i \left(\boldsymbol{L}_i + \boldsymbol{L}_i^T \right) = \boldsymbol{0} \tag{8}$$

Table 1. List of symbols used in Eq. (5)

C	Number of clusters
G_k	Set of individual indexes that belong to k-th cluster
N	Number of individuals (matrices A)
k	Subscript that shows index of cluster
i, j	Subscripts that show index of individual (matrix A)
A_i	Individual that is clustering object (Size is $[n \times p]$)
T_i	Orthogonalization transformation matrix (Size is $[p \times p]$)
B_k	k-th cluster center matrix (Size is $[n \times p]$)
L	Lagrange coefficient matrix (Size is $[p \times p]$)
I	Identity matrix (Size is $[p \times p]$)

$$\left(\frac{L_i + L_i^T}{2} \right) = T_i^T A_i^T \sum_{k=1}^{C} B_k - C T_i^T A_i^T A_i T_i \tag{9}$$

Since $\left(L_i + L_i^T \right)$ is symmetric matrix, it has the following relationship.

$$\frac{L_i + L_i^T}{2} = \left(\frac{L_i + L_i^T}{2} \right)^T \tag{10}$$

Eq. (11) is derived from Eq. (9) and Eq. (10).

$$T_i^T M_i = M_i^T T_i \text{, where } M_i = A_i^T \sum_{k=1}^{C} B_k . \tag{11}$$

Eq. (12) is derived by multiplying the left side of Eq. (11) by T_i and the right side by T_i^T.

$$\left. \begin{array}{l} M_i = T_i M_i^T T_i \\ T_i^T M_i T_i^T = M_i^T \end{array} \right\} \tag{12}$$

Eq. (13) is derived from Eq. (12).

$$M_i M_i^T = T_i M_i^T M_i T_i^T \tag{13}$$

Then Singular Value Decomposition (SVD) is applied to $M_i M_i^T$ and $M_i^T M_i$, respectively.

$$V_i D_{i\lambda} V_i^T = T_i W_i D_{i\lambda} W_i^T T_i^T , \tag{14}$$

where V_i and W_i are orthogonal $[p \times p]$ matrices consisting of the singular vectors of $M_i M_i^T$ and $M_i^T M_i$, respectively. $D_{i\lambda}$ is a diagonal matrix whose elements are expressed by singular values.

Therefore, the optimal T_i(transformation matrix) is solved by

$$T_i = V_i W_i^T . \tag{15}$$

The algorithm of the proposed method is as follows:

Step 1. Each distribution matrix A_i is preprocessed for conforming the distribution center and the scale, when it is necessary.

Step 2. Initial cluster k $(k \in \{1, ..., C\})$ for each A_i is randomly assigned.
Step 3. Initialization of $T_i = I$
Step 4. Each cluster center matrix B_k is calculated by Eq. (7).
Step 5. Each distribution matrix A_i is assigned to the cluster that has the smallest evaluation value to Eq. (2).
Step 6. All B are fixed, and each optimal T_i is calculated by Eq. (15).
Step 7. All T are fixed, and each optimal B_k is calculated by Eq. (7).
Step 8. If each B_k and T_i is converged, iteration is end. Otherwise, go to **Step 5**.

In **Step 6**, each row vector of V_i and W_i composing Eq. (15) has the degree of freedom of sign inversion. Consequently, the sign of each row vector is serially reversed and the combination minimizing the objective function is calculated. The matrix T_i is updated by using V_i and W_i consisted of the row vectors of these combinations.

3   Experiment

30 laptop photo images were employed as the objects for the SD evaluation. This experiment requested 22 subjects to evaluate the objects by SD method including 21 impression words. Table 2 shows the impression words used in the experiment. IW-xx will be employed in this paper instead of each impression word for simplicity.

3.1   Result and Discussion

This section discusses the result by the proposed method when the number of cluster was five. Table 3 shows the result of clustering.

The number of subjects belonging to each cluster was $\{2, 4, 4, 8, 4\}$, respectively. A majority (cluster 4) and a minority (cluster 1) group were found in the SD evaluation data. This paper applied the cluster analysis by Ward's method to the distance matrix (similarity matrix) among objects calculated by each cluster center distribution for the cluster 1 and cluster 4. Fig. 1 and Fig. 2 represent impression relationships among the objects in each group. The acquired dendrogram showed that they had some characteristic differences among objects. For example, though the distance in the dendrogram between object 6 and 14 was less than 0.5 in cluster 4 (majority), those in cluster 1 (minority) was approximately 1.5. In addition, though object $\{20,23,18,29\}$ were same cluster (0.5) in cluster 4, object$\{20,23\}$ and object$\{18,29\}$ were the farthest distance (3.0) in cluster 1. It is thought that these two groups have different individuality for similarities among the objects.

3.2   Comparison of Impression Evaluation

Eq. (16) represents the relationship among the SD evaluation data A_i, the orthogonal transformation matrix T_i of subject i and the cluster center matrix B_k of cluster k that subject i belongs.

$$B_k \simeq A_i T_i \tag{16}$$

Table 2. Impression words

IW-01	Ugly	Beautiful
IW-02	Thick	Thin
IW-03	Cheerful	Gloomy
IW-04	Interesting	Boring
IW-05	Cold	Warm
IW-06	Unrefined	Neat
IW-07	Humorous	Serious
IW-08	Popular	Unpopular
IW-09	Rectilinear	Rounded
IW-10	Individual	Uniformed
IW-11	Hard	Soft
IW-12	Simple	Complicated
IW-13	Unseemly	Noble
IW-14	Expensive	Cheap
IW-15	New	Old
IW-16	Cool	Clumsy
IW-17	Formal	Casual
IW-18	Heavy	Light
IW-19	Weak	Strong
IW-20	Loose	Tight
IW-21	Clean	Dirty

Table 3. Result of clustering

Subject	Index of clustering	Subject	Index of clustering
sub-11	1	sub-03	4
sub-13	1	sub-06	4
sub-01	2	sub-09	4
sub-04	2	sub-10	4
sub-15	2	sub-16	4
sub-21	2	sub-19	4
sub-07	3	sub-20	4
sub-12	3	sub-05	5
sub-17	3	sub-08	5
sub-18	3	sub-14	5
sub-02	4	sub-22	5

Principal Component Analysis (PCA) is applied to B_k.

$$P_k = B_k C_k \simeq A_i T_i C_k, \tag{17}$$

where P_k is the matrix of Principal Component (PC) score, and C_k is that of PC coefficient. When we consider $T_i C_k$ as the matrix of PC coefficient of A_i, we can

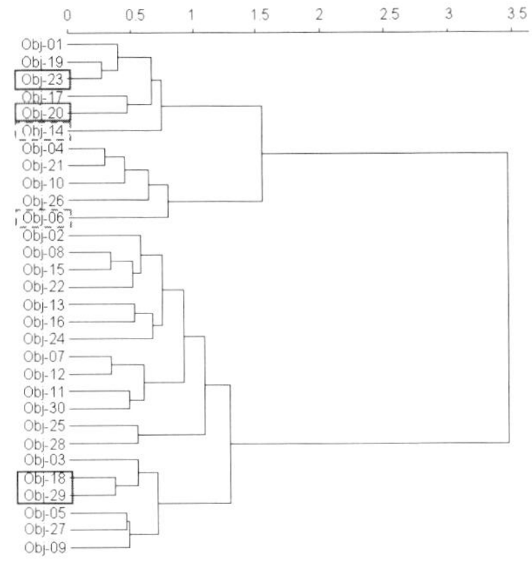

Fig. 1. Minority group (cluster 1)

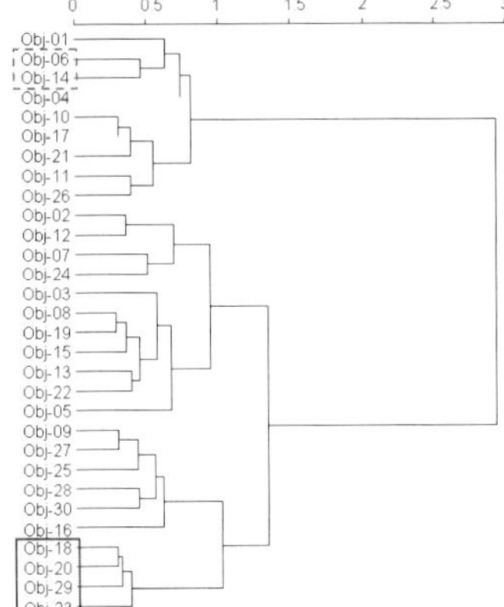

Fig. 2. Majority group (cluster 4)

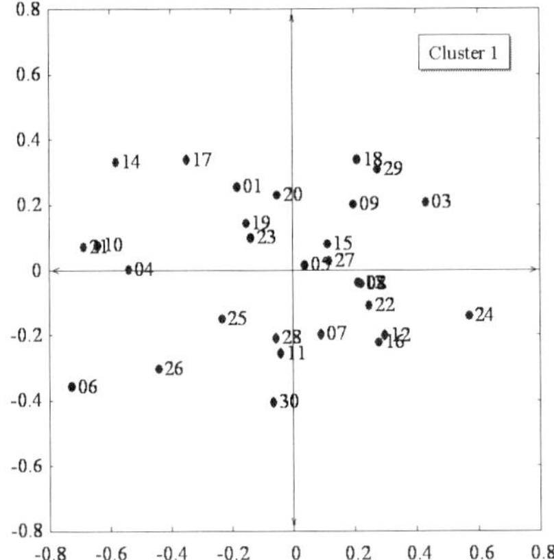

Fig. 3. PC score of objects

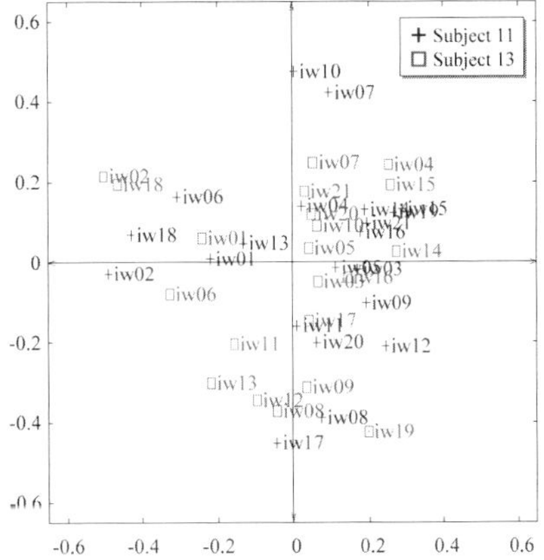

Fig. 4. Impression words of subjects

relate the SD evaluation data to the objects, and we can also relate impression words of subjects in the same group on the same PC space of objects.

Fig. 3 and Fig. 4 show the result of applying Eq. (17) to the cluster 1 (subject 11 and 13). Fig. 3 shows the distribution of the objects in cluster 1. Fig. 4 shows the relationship of impression words between subject 11 and subject 13 corresponding to Fig. 3. The numbers plotted in Fig. 3 represent the indexes of objects. Cumulative contributing rate by these two principal components was 60.2%. In Fig. 4, impression words represented by principal component coefficients of each subject are plotted on principal components of Fig. 3. In subject 11, IW-02 (Thick - Thin), IW-06 (Unrefined - Neat) and IW-18 (Heavy - Light) have a strong influence to PC1 (horizontal axis). Subject 13 also has a similar tendency. They evaluated Obj-{04,06,10,14,21, etc} by using structure impression words of laptop products whose meaning can be easily shared. It is inferred that these objects have stronger structural feature than other objects. In addition, Fig. 4 shows they were impressed "Beautiful" (IW-01) to the objects having "Neat", "Thin" and "Light" structure. Moreover, the bottom-left area in Fig. 4 shows that subject 13 evaluated object 06 using some impression words such as "Neat", "Soft", "Noble" and so on while subject 11 used "Thin" and "Casual". It suggests that the evaluation of subject 13 for these objects in this area was more meticulous than subject 11. In addition, "Thin" for subject 11 was close to "Neat" for subject 13.

4   Conclusion

This paper defined the distributed structure of objects in the space of impression words as individual feature, and it proposed the clustering method based on the OPA for clustering of the individual feature. This paper applied the proposed method to the actual SD evaluation data obtained from subjects, and it showed that this method enabled us to discover majority/minority groups. It also showed that the analysis by the proposed method could investigate the similar relationships among the objects in each group and compare the similarity/difference of impression words used for the evaluation of objects among subjects in the same cluster. For the future works, we will examine the validity of the result acquired by the proposed method.

Acknowledgment

A part of this study was supported by The 21st century COE program "Frontiers of Computational Science", Grant-in-Aid for Scientific Research from the Ministry of Education, Culture, Sports, Science and Technology (base research©(2) No.16500126).

References

[1] Takashi, M., Pieter, M.K.: Three-mode models and individual differences in semantic differential data. Multivariate Behavioral Research **38**(2) (2003) 247–283
[2] NAKAMORI, Y., KAWANAKA, A.: Expression of vagueness in factor space. Japan Society for Fuzzy Theory and Intelligent Informatics (in Japanese) **11**(5) (1999) 797–807
[3] Toyoda, H.: An exploratory positioning analysis: Three-mode multivariate analysis for semantic differential data. The Japanese Journal of Psychology **72**(3) (2001) 213–218
[4] Yamamoto, K., Kojima, T., Yoshikawa, T., Furuhashi, T.: A basic study on discovering relationships of impression words among individuals using visualization method. IEEE Workshop on Advanced Robotics and its Social Impacts(ARSO) (2005)
[5] Akca, M.D.: Generalized procrustes analysis and its applications in photogrammetry. Institute of Geodesy and Photogrammetry, Swiss Federal Institute of Technology Zurich (ETHZ) (2003)
[6] YAMAMOTO, K., YOSHIKAWA, T., FURUHASHI, T.: A proposal on stratification method for SD evaluation data considering individuality. In: FAN Symposium 2005 in Kyoto, Society of Instrument and Control Enginners (in Japanese). (2005) 495–500

Extending Microaggregation Procedures for Time Series Protection

Jordi Nin and Vicenç Torra

IIIA-CSIC
Campus UAB s/n
08193 Bellaterra (Catalonia, Spain)
jnin@iiia.csic.es
vtorra@iiia.csic.es

Abstract. Privacy is becoming a pervasive issue, as nowadays information is gathered by all kind of information systems.

In this paper we introduce a method for database protection in the case that the data under consideration is expressed in terms of time series. We propose the use of microaggregation for this purpose and extend standard microaggregation so that it works for this kind of data.

Keywords: privacy, masking methods, time series, microaggregation, clustering, time series distances.

1   Introduction

In the last years, the need for tools to ensure data privacy is increasing as people is more and more concerned with privacy issues. At the same time, there is an increasing demand of data by researchers and decision makers. Privacy preserving data mining and inference control [13] are to develop tools for data protection with the aim that protected data can be released for further study without compromising the privacy of data respondents.

Masking methods [13] are the specific tools that are used for data protection. Among all masking methods, perturbative ones are those that modify the original data so that the perturbed data avoids disclosure. Nevertheless, data perturbation might cause data to lose their utility. This is so because a *maximum* perturbation makes disclosure impossible but at the same time data is useless for any analysis. Instead, when no perturbation is applied, we have maximum data utility (only original data is published) but data permit disclosure. To measure all these aspects, some measures have been defined. They are the so-called measures for information loss (to evaluate in what extent data has lost its utility), and measures for disclosure risk. Besides, there are scores and other functions to combine or visualize these measures to evaluate the tradeoff between data utility and disclosure risk.

Most masking methods have been developed for standard databases. That is, databases in which records take values on a set of variables. Information loss and disclosure risk measures have been defined for such kind of records.

S. Greco et al. (Eds.): RSCTC 2006, LNAI 4259, pp. 899–908, 2006.

Due to the increasing amount of information currently available, and due to the increasing rate on data storage, data is no longer a static object but it has a temporal component. Therefore, it is of interest the study of masking methods for temporal data protection. That is, the protection of time series. Some research has been done in this line. See *e.g.* [1].

In this paper we develop a new method for time series protection. The method is based on microaggregation [2], a tool for data protection that has a good performance in standard numerical data with respect to information loss and disclosure risk measures as shown in [4]. Microaggregation is one of the standard tools for database protection commonly in use in National Statistical Offices (see *e.g.* [6]).

Microaggregation requires the definition of a distance on the data. In microaggregation for standard data such distance is usually the Euclidean distance. In the case of time series, several distance on time series can be considered. In this paper we propose and use two different distances: the short time series distance and Euclidean distance. We can see in section 2.3 the formal definition of these distances and in section 3 we will study how the choice of the distance affects microaggregation results.

The structure of the paper is as follows. In Section 2 we describe some preliminaries required in the rest of the paper. In particular, this section describes standard microaggregation and some distance functions for time series. Then, in Section 3, we propose our method for time series protection. In Section 4 we describe the experiments done. The paper finishes with some conclusions and some research lines for future work.

2   Preliminaries

This section presents standard microaggregation and some results on time series that are needed in the rest of this work.

2.1   Microaggregation

Microaggregation is a masking method for database protection. From the procedural point of view, it works as follows:

1. Clusters are built from the original data. Each cluster should contain at least k records.
2. A representative is built for each cluster.
3. Original records are replaced by the corresponding representatives.

The fact of having clusters containing at least k records is to ensure data privacy. Note that after microaggregation is applied, we will have at least k records indistinguishable for each cluster (with respect to the variables clustered).

This method was originally defined on numerical data. Then, it was extended to categorical data [11]. The method can be formally defined in terms of an optimization problem. Nevertheless, it was proven that finding the optimal solution of such optimization problem is an NP-problem [9]. Therefore, some research has been done to find heuristic approaches. One of the methods is the so-called MDAV (Maximum Distance Average Vector)-generic algorithm [5]. This method is described in the next section.

2.2   MDAV-Generic Algorithm

The MDAV-generic algorithm is an heuristic algorithm for clustering records in a dataset R. Each cluster is constrained to have at least k records. The algorithm is as follows:

<u>Algorithm</u> (MDAV-generic) (R: dataset, k: integer) <u>is</u>
    1. <u>while</u> $(|R| > k)$ <u>do</u>
        (1.a) Compute the average record $\tilde{x}$ of all records in R
        (1.b) Consider the most distant record x_r to the average record $\tilde{x}$ using
             and appropriate distance
        (1.c) Form a cluster around x_r. The cluster contains x_r together with
             the $k - 1$ closest records to x_r
        (1.d) Remove these records from dataset R
    2. <u>if</u> $(|R| > k)$ <u>then</u>
        (2.a) Find the most distant record x_s from record x_r (from step 1.b)
        (2.b) Form a cluster around x_s. The cluster contains x_s together with
             the $k - 1$ closest records to x_s
        (2.c) Remove these records from dataset R
    3. <u>end if</u>
    4. <u>end while</u>
    5. form a cluster with the remaining records

This algorithm is generic and it can be applied to different kind of data using appropriate definitions of distance and average. That is, we need to formulate what the *most distant record* means, and which are the *closest records* of a given record. Additionally, we need to define *the average record* of a set of records. This average record is needed in step (1.a) and later to mask the original data. Recall that we need to build a representative for each cluster and then replace each original record by the corresponding representative.

In [2] this method is applied to numerical data, using the Euclidean distance for computing the distance between records and the arithmetic mean to compute the average. In [5] this method was extended to categorical data using appropriate functions.

2.3   Time Series

Now we turn into the problem of defining distances for time series. We focus on numerical time series. Formally speaking, a time series is defined by pairs $\{(v_k, t_k)\}$ for $k = 1, \ldots, N$ where t_k corresponds to the temporal variable and v_k is the variable that depends on time (dependent variable). Naturally, $t_{k+1} > t_k$. Stock prices are examples of time series, as they depend on time.

There are different methods to compute the distances between time series. We can use distance based on raw values of equal or unequal length, cross-correlation matrix, vectors of feature-value pairs, probability-based functions and so on. See [12] for more details.

For our experiments we have implemented two different distance functions, Euclidean distance and the Short Time Series distance proposed by Möller-Levet et al. in [7].

Let x and v be two N-dimensional time series. Let x be defined by the pairs $\{(x_k, t_k)\}$ for $k = 1, \ldots, N$ and let v defined by the pairs $\{(x_k, t_k)\}$ for $k = 1, \ldots, N$. Note that we assume that the two time series under consideration have exactly the same length and that they are aligned. That is, the temporal component in both series is exactly the same. Also, note that we use x and v for both denoting the time serie and the dependent variable.

Then, the Euclidean distance is defined by:

$$d_{EU}(x, v) = \sqrt[2]{\sum_{k=1}^{N} (x_k - v_k)^2}$$

The short time series distance, STS distance in short, is defined as

$$d_{STS}(x, v) = \sqrt[2]{\sum_{k=1}^{N} \left(\frac{v_{k+1} - v_k}{t_{k+1} - t_k} - \frac{x_{k+1} - x_k}{t_{k+1} - t_k} \right)^2}$$

3   Time Series Microaggregation

To specialize the MDAV-generic algorithm for time series we need to make the distances concrete, and then consider the particular average functions. We have implemented the algorithm described in Section 2.2 with the following parameterizations:

Distance functions: We have used Euclidean and STS distances: d_{EU} and d_{STS} as defined in Section 2.3.

Average: We have used a kind of arithmetic mean. The mean has been defined component-wise. That is, given the set $V = \{v^j\}_{j=1,\ldots,J}$ with time series v^j for $j = 1, \ldots, J$, each one with v_k^j, we define $\tilde{v}_k = (1/J) \sum_{j=1,\ldots,J} v_k^j$.

Therefore, we have applied the MDAV-generic algorithm where $\tilde{x}$ is the average of all records (time series) in R. These distance functions have been used to determine the most distant records as well as the closest records to a given record r.

Different distance functions cause the microaggregation algorithm to compute different clusters. While Euclidean distance makes clusters based on the distance between data components, the STS distance makes clusters based on the shape of the time series. This is illustrated in the following example.

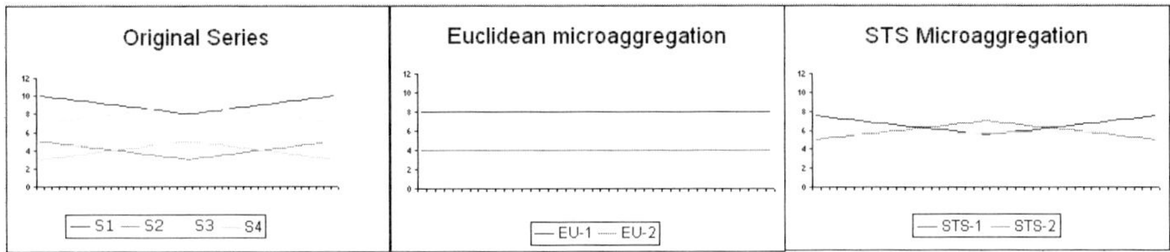

Fig. 1. Graphical representation of distance function selection

Example 1. Figure 1 (left) illustrates this problem: 4 series are to be microaggregated. The results of microaggregating these 4 series into 2 clusters using Euclidean and STS distances are given, respectively, in middle and right figures of Figure 1. It can be seen that the Euclidean distance gathers together the most near series although they have different shapes (and, thus, the outcomes are just lines but that mainly keep the original values). Instead, the STS distance gathers series according to shapes (and, thus, the outcomes keep such shapes but not the original position of the series).

In this example, we have used point-wise average for computing the representative of each cluster.

According to this, in the step of selecting the distance function, we have the opportunity to model how the microaggregation procedure makes the clusters and decide which information is the most important to be kept in the final protected model.

4   Experiments

We have applied our method to a data set consisting on several time series. We describe below the data considered. We have applied our algorithm to these data, testing different values of k. In particular, we have used: $k \in \{2, 3, 6, 9, 12\}$.

4.1   Data

The data under consideration correspond to the Stock Exchange information of the thirty five most important Spanish companies. These companies are ranked in the so-called Ibex35 stock market. We have got historical information about company prices in the Ibex35 stock market for about a year from [10]. This information is publicly available.

We have obtained thirty five files, one for each company ranked in the Ibex35 stock market. These files have been processed to obtain a new file with the opening prices of the companies. In this way, we have 35 time series. Tables 1 and 2 give details on the 35 series considered for applying microaggregation.

The selection of economic data was done for two main reasons. First, data can be obtained easily and free in electronic markets. Second, economic information clearly corresponds to a time series structure, so it is a good example for our method.

Table 1. Original data for one company (Abertis) in Ibex35. Thirty five files with this structure were downloaded.

Abertis	opening value	maximum value	minimum value	closing value	volume
06-21-2005	19.94	19.94	19.81	19.89	841
06-22-2005	19.95	20.10	19.88	19.99	799
06-23-2005	19.90	20.05	19.90	19.95	708
...	...	...	...	...	...
04-27-2006	20.93	20.97	20.67	20.95	2507
04-28-2006	21.00	21.00	20.65	20.92	2442

Table 2. 35 time series corresponding to the opening prices of all companies in the Ibex35 stock market

Company name	business	05-03-2005	05-04-2005	05-05-2005	...	04-27-2006	04-28-2006
Abertis	Building firm	19,94	19,95	19,90	...	20,93	21,00
Acciona	Building firm	76,85	79,00	81,40	...	139,65	134,65
Acerinox	Steel firm	11,75	11,58	11,55	...	13,72	13,29
ACS	Building firm	22,05	22,38	22,41	...	33,14	32,87
Altadis	Tobacco firm	33,85	34,28	34,68	...	37,75	37,25
Antena3 TV	Private television	17,25	17,11	16,92	...	21,84	21,67
Arcelor	Steel firm	16,64	16,47	16,22	...	34,03	33,13
Banco Popular	Bank	10,00	9,98	9,94	...	12,12	12,06
Banco Sabadell	Bank	21,12	21,14	21,29	...	28,47	28,87
Bankinter	Bank	42,63	42,65	42,70	...	55,80	54,90
BBVA	Bank	12,87	12,77	12,79	...	17,44	17,32
Cintra	Building firm	8,97	9,00	9,05	...	10,88	10,85
ENAGAS	Energy firm	13,63	13,73	13,90	...	17,93	17,57
Endesa	Energy firm	18,18	18,37	18,45	...	26,51	26,35
F.C. Contratas	Building firm	46,67	46,32	45,93	...	64,10	64,25
Ferrovial	Building firm	50,60	52,00	51,95	...	65,15	65,00
Gamesa	Aeronautics industry	11,27	11,35	11,42	...	17,41	16,93
Gas Natural	Energy firm	23,30	23,57	23,45	...	24,40	24,31
Iberdrola	Energy firm	21,40	21,63	21,59	...	25,89	25,80
Iberia	AirLine	2,47	2,49	2,50	...	2,24	2,22
Inditex	Textile firm	21,97	21,94	21,70	...	32,85	32,41
Indra	New Technology firm	15,60	15,65	15,85	...	16,73	16,41
Metrovacesa	Building firm	49,57	50,75	52,65	...	72,95	71,90
NH Hoteles	Hotel firm	10,89	11,06	11,03	...	14,28	14,35
Prisa	Press firm	16,06	16,19	16,12	...	14,65	14,69
R. E. Española	Energy firm	20,90	21,24	21,15	...	27,92	27,87
Repsol YPF	Energy firm	21,35	21,26	21,28	...	24,02	23,77
SCH	Bank	9,52	9,58	9,59	...	12,15	12,19
Sogecable	Private television	30,23	30,24	30,55	...	30,78	30,20
Telecinco	Private television	19,42	19,48	19,30	...	20,70	20,63
Telefónica	Telecom firm	13,54	13,51	13,51	...	12,77	12,74
Telefónica Móvil	Telecom firm	8,76	8,75	8,80	...	10,52	10,46
TPI	Telecom firm	6,90	7,09	7,05	...	8,90	8,82
Unión Fenosa	Energy firm	24,04	24,40	24,59	...	31,00	30,70
Vallehermoso	Building firm	19,50	19,93	19,37	...	27,51	27,44

Before applying microaggregation, time series were standardized to avoid any scale problems. This standardization step consists in normalizing the data values using the mean and the standard deviation. We have calculated the mean and the standard deviation for all values in all time series.

4.2   Microaggregation and Results

In Figure 2 we can see all time serials of the Ibex35 stock market and in Figures 3 and 4 we can see the cluster centroids when we use, respectively, Euclidean and STS distances. In these figures the cluster size is fixed to six series per cluster.

The clusters obtained with the Euclidean distance and cluster size fixed to six are as follows:

Cluster 1: Abertis, Antena 3 TV, Enagas, Endesa, Indra and Telecinco

Cluster 2: Acciona, Altadis, Bankinter, F.C. Contratas, Ferrovial and Metrovacesa

Cluster 3: ACS, Inditex, Red Eléctrica Española, Repsol YPF, Sogecable and Unión Fenosa

Cluster 4: Arcelor, Banco Sabadell, Gas Natural, Iberdrola and Vallehermoso

Cluster 5: Banco Popular, Cintra, Iberia, SCH, Telefónica Móvil and TPI

Cluster 6: BBVA, Gamesa, NH Hoteles, Prisa and Telefónica

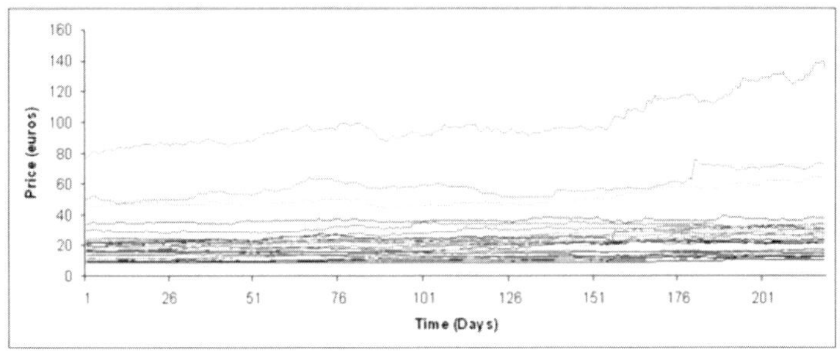

Fig. 2. Graphical representation of Ibex35 time series

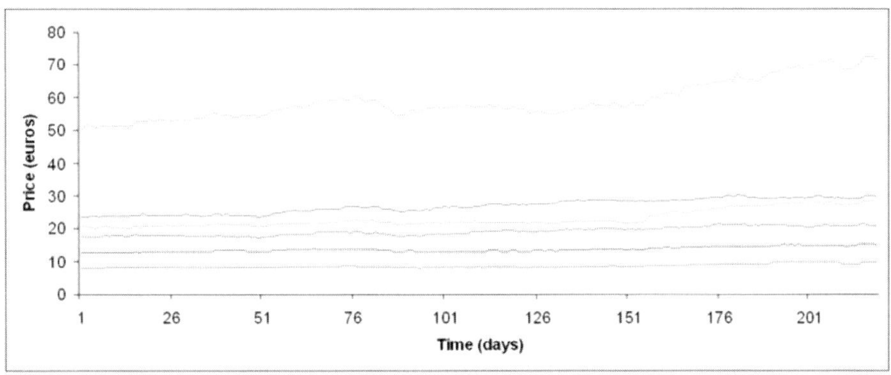

Fig. 3. Graphical representation of Euclidean distance clustering

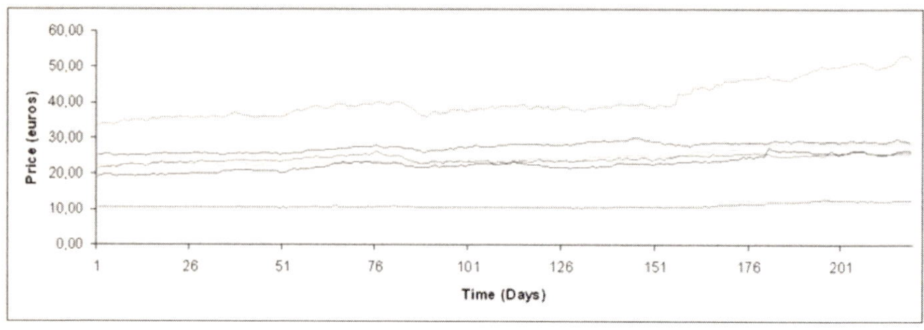

Fig. 4. Graphical representation of STS distance clustering

If we compare these results with Table 2, we can see that the companies in the first cluster have the lowest opening prices, the prices of these companies are around seventeen during June 2005 and around twenty-one during April 2006. In the second cluster, on the other side, we have companies with the highest opening prices, around fifty three during June 2005 and seventy-one during April 2006. The remaining clusters are between these opening values.

The clusters obtained using the STS distance and cluster size fixed to six are as follows:

Cluster 1: Abertis, ACS, Arcelor, F.C. Contratas and Vallehermoso
Cluster 2: Acerinox, Enagas, Ferrovial, Indra, Prisa and Red Eléctrica Española
Cluster 3: Altadis, Inditex, Repsol YPF, Sogecable and Telecinco
Cluster 4: Antena 3 TV, Bankinter, Endesa, Gamesa, Gas Natural and Iberdrola
Cluster 5: Banco Popular, Banco Sabadell, Iberia, Telefónica, Telefónica Móvil and TPI
Cluster 6: BBVA, Cintra, Metrovacesa, NH Hoteles, SCH and Unión Fenosa

In this case (see Table 2), clusters are not based on the opening prices but on the business type. If we observe the first cluster we notice that five of the six companies in the cluster are construction firms and if we check the fourth cluster we take into account that three companies are energy firms or in the fifth cluster three companies are telecommunications firms. On the remaining clusters we can find the same effect with two or more companies.

This effect in STS distance is possible because stock markets have been affected for social or external conditions like the price of money or fuel and all companies with a similar business have similar trends during a certain time.

From these results we can say that Euclidean distance measures differences between time serial values, and this distance benefits time series with closer sample values. Meanwhile STS distance measures difference between trends, this measure clusters time series with respect to their closer *shape*.

5   Conclusions and Future Work

In this paper, we have introduced a new method for protection of time series based on microaggregation. We have applied our approach using two different distances for time series. In particular, a distance based on the Euclidean distance and the STS distance. We have applied our approach to a data set defined in terms of time series.

The comparison of the two distances shows that the Euclidean distance gathers time series with similar values, while the STS one focuses on the *shape* of the series instead of the values themselves. This corresponds to the effect illustrated in Figure 1 and described in Example 1.

As future work we include the analysis of the method with respect to information loss and disclosure risk measures (some preliminary results can be found in [8]). These measures are required to properly evaluate the performance of the new methods and compare different approaches.

Although not analysed in this paper, the procedure for computing the representative of a cluster is also a relevant point. Further work is also needed in this direction.

Acknowledgements

This work was partly funded by the Spanish Ministry of Education and Science under project SEG2004-04352-C04-02 "PROPRIETAS".

References

1. Abowd, J. M., Woodcock, S. D., (2001), Disclosure Limitation in Longitudinal Linked Data, in P. Doyle, J. I. Lane, J. J. M. Theeuwes, L. V. Zayatz (Eds), Confidentiality, Disclosure and Data Access: Theory and Practical Applications for Statistical Agencies, North-Holland, 215-277.
2. Domingo-Ferrer, J., Mateo-Sanz, J. M., (2002), Practical data-oriented microaggregation for statistical disclosure control, IEEE Trans. on Knowledge and Data Engineering, 14 189-201.
3. Domingo-Ferrer, J., Torra, V., (2001), Disclosure methods and information loss for microdata, in P. Doyle, J. I. Lane, J. J. M. Theeuwes, L. V. Zayatz (Eds), Confidentiality, Disclosure and Data Access: Theory and Practical Applications for Statistical Agencies, North-Holland, 91-110.
4. Domingo-Ferrer, J., Torra, V., (2001), A quantitative comparison of disclosure methods for microdata, in P. Doyle, J. I. Lane, J. J. M. Theeuwes, L. V. Zayatz (Eds), Confidentiality, Disclosure and Data Access: Theory and Practical Applications for Statistical Agencies, North-Holland, 111-133.
5. Domingo-Ferrer, J., Torra, V., (2005), Ordinal, Continuous and Heterogeneous k-Anonymity Through Microaggregation, Data Mining and Knowledge Discovery, 11 195-212
6. Felso, F., Theeuwes, J., Wagner, G. G., (2001), Disclosure Limitation Methods in Use: Results of a Survey, in P. Doyle, J. I. Lane, J. J. M. Theeuwes, L. V. Zayatz (Eds), Confidentiality, Disclosure and Data Access: Theory and Practical Applications for Statistical Agencies, North-Holland, 17-42.

7. Möller-Levet, C. S., Klawonn, F., Cho, K.-H., Wolkenhauer, O., (2003), Fuzzy clustering of short time series and unevenly distributed sampling points, Proceedings of the 5th International Symposium on Intelligent Data Analysis, Berlin, Germany, August 28-30, 2003.

8. Nin, J., Torra, V.,(2006), Distance based re-identication for time series, Analysis of distances, Proc. Privacy in Statistical Databases (PSD 2006), in press

9. Oganian, A., Domingo-Ferrer, J., (2001), On the complexity of microaggregation, in Second Eurostat-UN/ECE Joint Work Session on Statistical Data Confidentiality, Skopje, Macedonia, March.

10. Stock Exchange web, Sabadell Bank, http://www.bsmarkets.com/

11. Torra, V., (2004), Microaggregation for categorical variables: a median based approach, Proc. Privacy in Statistical Databases (PSD 2004), Lecture Notes in Computer Science, 3050 162-174.

12. Warren Liao, T., (2005), Clustering of time series data - a survey, Pattern Recognition, 38 1857-1874.

13. Willenborg, L., de Waal, T., (2001), Elements of Statistical Disclosure Control, Lecture Notes in Statistics, Springer-Verlag.

Lattice-Valued Hierarchical Clustering for Analyzing Information Systems

Sadaaki Miyamoto

Department of Risk Engineering
Faculty of Systems and Information Engineering
University of Tsukuba, Ibaraki 305-8573, Japan
miyamoto@risk.tsukuba.ac.jp

Abstract. A generalization of hierarchical clustering is proposed in which the dendrogram is replaced by clusters attached to a lattice diagram. Hence the method is called lattice-valued hierarchical clustering. Different algorithms of lattice-valued clustering are described with application to information systems in the form of tables studied in rough sets. A simple example is given whereby how the concept of the lattice-valued hierarchical clustering is related to classifications in rough sets is shown.

1   Introduction

Data clustering is one of main tools for data mining in various fields of sciences and engineering. Among various techniques, the methods of agglomerative hierarchical clustering [2,4,3] are old and still known to be most useful. A reason for the usefulness is much information is provided from the output of the dendrogram of the agglomerative clustering process.

In this paper we consider a generalization of hierarchical clustering in which the dendrogram is replaced by clusters attached to a lattice diagram [1]. Hence we can call the method herein that of lattice-valued hierarchical clustering.

The information system in the form of a table should be considered as a typical application of the lattice-valued hierarchical clustering, where the collection of all subsets of the attribute set forms the lattice.

After reviewing the standard agglomerative clustering procedure, a formal definition of hierarchical classification is given. A simple method of lattice-valued clustering which is related to studies in rough set studies is described, and its generalizations are proposed using measures of dissimilarity. Finally, two problems for further studies are mentioned.

2   Agglomerative Hierarchical Clustering

Let the objects for clustering be $o_1, \ldots, o_n$ and the set of objects be $\mathcal{O} = \{o_1, \ldots, o_n\}$. Generally a cluster which is denoted by G_i is a subset of $\mathcal{O}$ and the family of clusters is denoted by $\mathcal{G} = \{G_1, G_2, \ldots, G_K\}$ where the clusters form a partition of $\mathcal{O}$:

S. Greco et al. (Eds.): RSCTC 2006, LNAI 4259, pp. 909–917, 2006.
© Springer-Verlag Berlin Heidelberg 2006

$$\bigcup_{i=1}^{K} G_i = \mathcal{O}, \qquad G_i \cap G_j = \emptyset \quad (i \neq j). \tag{1}$$

Agglomerative clustering uses a dissimilarity measure (also called a distance) between two clusters $d(G, G')$ $(G, G' \in \mathcal{G})$ which is called inter-cluster dissimilarity. Sometimes a similarity measure $s(G, G')$ is used. The difference between a dissimilarity measure and a similarity measure is that a smaller $d(G, G')$ means G and G' are more similar, whereas a smaller $s(G, G')$ implies G and G' are less similar. In the following we discuss mainly $d(G, G')$; discussion of $s(G, G')$ is found in [4,5].

2.1   General Procedure of Agglomerative Clustering

We first describe a general procedure of agglomerative clustering [4,5].

Algorithm AHC (Agglomerative Hierarchical Clustering):
AHC1.   Assume that initial clusters are given by
   $\mathcal{G} = \{\hat{G}_1, \hat{G}_2, \ldots, \hat{G}_N\}$,
   Set $K = N$ (K is the number of clusters) and
   $G_i = \hat{G}_i$ $(i = 1, \ldots, K)$.
   Calculate $d(G, G')$ for all pairs $G, G' \in \mathcal{G}$.
AHC2.   Search the pair of miminum dissimilarity:

$$(G_p, G_q) = \arg \min_{G,G' \in \mathcal{G}} d(G, G'). \tag{2}$$

and let

$$m_K = d(G_p, G_q) = \min_{G,G' \in \mathcal{G}} d(G, G'). \tag{3}$$

   Merge: $G_r = G_p \cup G_q$.
   Add G_r to $\mathcal{G}$ and delete G_p, G_q from $\mathcal{G}$.
   $K = K - 1$. If $K = 1$ then stop and output the dendrogram.
AHC3.   Update dissimilarity $d(G_r, G'')$ for all $G'' \in \mathcal{G}$.
   Go to AHC2.
End AHC.

In AHC, the detail of constructing a dendrogram is omitted (see e.g., [4,5]). Notice that the above algorithm is a generalization of an ordinary agglomerative clustering. That is, the initial clusters are objects in an ordinary algorithm: $G_j = \{o_j\}$ $(N = n)$ while the present algorithm does not use this assumption.

   Two well-known methods are the single link and the complete link. In these methods we do not care about how the initial dissimilarity measure is defined; we simply assume $d(o_i, o_j)$ is given in some way. Note that inter-cluster dissimilarity is given as follows.

   – the single link (SL): $d(G, G') = \min\limits_{o \in G, o' \in G'} d(o, o')$.
   – the complete link (CL): $d(G, G') = \max\limits_{o \in G, o' \in G'} d(o, o')$.

The basic definition of $d(G_r, G'')$ in AHC3 uses one of the above definitions of the inter-cluster dissimilarity for SL and CL.

An important issue in agglomerative clustering is efficient updating of a dissimilarity measure. Ordinary methods such as the single link, complete link, *etc.* [2] have respective updating formulas using the dissimilarity matrix $[d_{ij}]$ in which $d_{ij} = d(G_i, G_j)$ and after merging, $d_{rj} = d(G_r, G_j)$ can be calculated solely from $d(G_p, G_j)$ and $d(G_q, G_j)$ instead of the above basic definitions. Namely, the single link and the complete link respectively use

$$d(G_r, G'') = \min\{d(G_p, G''), d(G_q, G'')\}$$

and

$$d(G_r, G'') = \max\{d(G_p, G''), d(G_q, G'')\}.$$

2.2 Formalization of Agglomerative Clustering

For later use, let us define a *refinement* between two partitions. Assume that $\mathcal{G} = \{G_1, G_2, \ldots, G_K\}$ and $\mathcal{G}' = \{G'_1, G'_2, \ldots, G'_L\}$ are two partitions of $\mathcal{O}$. We say $\mathcal{G}'$ is a refinement of $\mathcal{G}$ iff

$$\forall G \in \mathcal{G}, \ \exists G' \in \mathcal{G}' \text{ such that } G' \subseteq G. \tag{4}$$

We write $\mathcal{G}' \triangleright \mathcal{G}$ iff $\mathcal{G}'$ is a refinement of $\mathcal{G}$.

For the single link and the complete link, the levels of the merging m_j satisfy the next monotonicity property.

$$m_N \leq m_{N-1} \leq \cdots \leq m_2 \tag{5}$$

Denote the clusters formed at the level $\alpha = m_i$ by

$$\mathcal{G}(\alpha) = \{G_1(\alpha), G_2(\alpha), \ldots, G_K(\alpha)\}. \tag{6}$$

It then is easy to see

$$\mathcal{G}(\alpha') \triangleright \mathcal{G}(\alpha) \tag{7}$$

when $\alpha' \leq \alpha$ in case when a dissimilarity measure is used. Notice that $\alpha' \leq \alpha$ should be replaced by $\alpha' \geq \alpha$ and $m_N \geq m_{N-1} \geq \cdots \geq m_2$ should be employed instead of (5) when a similarity measure is used.

A hierarchical classification is formally defined by such $\mathcal{G}(\alpha)$. That is, suppose that a monotone sequence of real numbers (5) is given and $\mathcal{G}(\alpha)$ ($\alpha \in \{m_N, m_{N-1}, \ldots, m_2\}$) satisfies (7). Then we have a hierarchical classification. If such a hierarchical classification is generated from a dissimilarity or similarity measure, or by some other computational methods, we have an algorithm of the hierarchical clustering.

3   Lattice-Valued Clustering and Information Table

The last observation leads us to a generalization to a method of lattice-valued hierarchical clustering. Let P be a poset (partially ordered set) in which the partial order is denoted by $\alpha \succ \beta$ $(\alpha, \beta \in P)$.

Let us consider a family of classifications $\mathcal{G}(\alpha)$ $(\alpha \in P)$. Instead of the real value, the parameter value is in poset P.

We say $\mathcal{G}(\alpha)$ is a poset-valued hierarchical classification iff

$$\alpha \succ \beta \;\Rightarrow\; \mathcal{G}(\alpha) \rhd \mathcal{G}(\beta). \tag{8}$$

Among poset-valued classifications we are particularly interested in case when P is a lattice. In order to make our motivation clear, we describe a typical example which is not very new and related to studies in rough sets. Information systems which are also called information tables or decision tables are studied in rough sets [6,7]. Since what we consider is not rough approximations but clustering, we use notations in relational databases [8] that seem more convenient than usual symbols used in rough sets. Let

$$\mathcal{A} = \{a_1, a_2, \ldots, a_m\}$$

be a relational schema in which $a_1, a_2, \ldots, a_m$ are attributes. For each attribute a_i, we have the corresponding domain D_i. An information table $\mathcal{T}$ is a finite subset of the product $D_1 \times \cdots \times D_m$, or in other words, $\mathcal{T}$ is a relation. An element $t \in \mathcal{T}$ is called a tuple using the term in relational database. Let us assume $\mathcal{T} = \{t_1, \ldots, t_n\}$ and an attribute value of t with respect to a_i is denoted by $t(a_i)$. Thus,

$$t = (t(a_1), \ldots, t(a_m)).$$

For a given subset $A = (a_{i_1}, \ldots, a_{i_r})$ of the attribute set $\mathcal{A}$, define

$$t(A) = (t(a_{i_1}), \ldots, t(a_{i_r})).$$

For a given set $T(\subset \mathcal{T})$ of tuples, we define

$$T(A) = \{\, t(A) : t \in T \,\}.$$

We hence have

$$t \in T \;\Rightarrow\; t(A) \in T(A),$$

while the converse $\Leftarrow$ is not true in general.

For a given subset $A(\subseteq \mathcal{A})$ of attributes, we define a relation R_A:

$$t R_A t' \;\Longleftrightarrow\; t(A) = t'(A).$$

It is easy to see that R_A is an equivalence relation.

Note that $\mathcal{A}$ is a lattice in which the natural inclusion of subsets is the pre-ordering and the union and the intersection are respectively sup and inf operation of the lattice: $\sup(A, A') = A \cup A'$ and $\inf(A, A') = A \cap A'$.

We have the quotient set, in other words, a classification

$$\mathcal{G}(A) = \mathcal{T}/R_A = \{\,[t]_{R_A} : t \in T\,\}$$

where

$$[t]_{R_A} = \{t' \in \mathcal{T} : tR_A t'\} = \{t' \in \mathcal{T} : t(A) = t'(A)\}.$$

We thus have the next proposition.

Proposition 1. *The above defined equivalence relation R_A generates a hierarchical classification. That is, we have*

$$B \supseteq A \Rightarrow \mathcal{G}(B) \rhd \mathcal{G}(A).$$

We thus have a lattice-valued hierarchical classification or a simple method of lattice-valued hierarchical clustering.

Example 1. Consider seven tuples shown in Table 1 with the schema $\mathcal{A} = (D, E, F)$. Here these three letters are attributes. The lattice is $\Lambda = 2^{\mathcal{A}} = \{\emptyset, D, E, F, DE, DF, FE, DEF\}$ where the abbreviated symbol DE implies $\{D, E\}$, and so on. We have

$$\mathcal{G}(DEF) = \mathcal{T}/R_{DEF} = \{t_1, \ldots, t_7\},$$
$$\mathcal{G}(DE) = \mathcal{T}/R_{DE} = \{t_1 t_2, t_3 t_4, t_5 t_6, t_7\}$$

etc. where $t_i t_j$ is an abbreviated symbol for $\{t_i, t_j\}$.

Figure 1 shows the Hasse diagram of $\Lambda = 2^{\mathcal{A}}$ together with the partitions attached to each element of the lattice.

3.1   Dissimilarity Measures Between Tuples

When each $t(a_i)$ is a numerical value, we can easily define a dissimilarity measure between two tuples. For example, the followings are natural measures:

$$d_2(t, t'; B) = \sum_{a_i \in B} |t(a_i) - t'(a_i)|^2 \tag{9}$$

$$d_E(t, t'; B) = \sqrt{\sum_{a_i B} |t(a_i) - t'(a_i)|^2}, \tag{10}$$

$$d_1(t, t'; B) = \sum_{a_i \in B} |t(a_i) - t'(a_i)|. \tag{11}$$

Table 1. An example of an information table

T	D	E	F
t_1	a_1	b_1	c_1
t_2	a_1	b_1	c_2
t_3	a_1	b_2	c_1
t_4	a_1	b_2	c_2
t_5	a_2	b_1	c_1
t_6	a_2	b_1	c_2
t_7	a_2	b_2	c_1

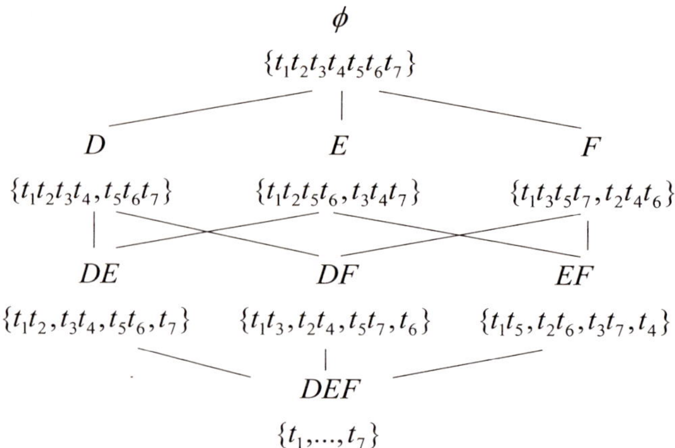

Fig. 1. An example of the lattice-valued clustering

Usually, B is taken to be the all attributes: $B = \mathcal{A}$, later we take B to be all subsets of $\mathcal{A}$, as expected. Notice also that a dissimilarity measure is dependent on B and hence the symbol $d(t, t'; B)$ shows the dependence explicitly.

In contrast to the above three measures, normalized measures using the number of attributes in B (denoted by $|B|$) can also be used:

$$d'_2(t, t'; B) = d_2(t, t')/|B|, \tag{12}$$

$$d'_E(t, t'; B) = d_E(t, t')/|B|, \tag{13}$$

$$d'_1(t, t'; B) = d_1(t, t')/|B|. \tag{14}$$

Let $d(t, t')$ be a dissimilarity measure, e.g., one of the above six measures. Our question is how we can generalize the last method to generate lattice-valued clusters with $\Lambda = 2^{\mathcal{A}}$.

Let us fix the set B to be a subset: $B \in 2^{\mathcal{A}}$. A simple method is to use connected components generated from the network on the vertices $\mathcal{T}$ with $d(t, t'; B)$ and the threshold ϵ, which is defined as follows.

1. Consider first the complete graph whose vertices are all tuples of $\mathcal{T}$. Put the value $d(t, t'; B)$ on the edge $\{t, t'\}$.
2. Delete all those edges $\{t, t'\}$ which satisfy $d(t, t'; B) > \epsilon$.
3. Let the obtained connected components be $G_1^\epsilon(B), \ldots, G_K^\epsilon(B)$ of which the set of vertices are $V(G_1^\epsilon(B)), \ldots, V(G_K^\epsilon(B))$, respectively.

We define the equivalence relation:

$$t R_B^\epsilon t' \iff t, t' \in V(G_j^\epsilon).$$

It is obvious that equivalence classes are generated from this definition [4], in other words, we are considering

$$\mathcal{G}(B) = \{V(G_1^\epsilon(B)), \ldots, V(G_K^\epsilon(B))\}.$$

We proceed to consider how the lattice-valued hierarchical clusters are generated by changing subset B.

Let us take $d(t, t'; B)$ to be one of (9), (10), and (11). We easily observe

$$C \supseteq B \;\Rightarrow\; d(t, t'; C) \geq d(t, t'; B). \tag{15}$$

Accordingly,

$$d(t, t'; B) > \epsilon \;\Rightarrow\; d(t, t'; C) > \epsilon,$$

and hence the connected components given C is finer than those with B. In other words, we have the following.

Proposition 2. *Assume that the connected components above described are used for the classifications. If*

$$C \supseteq B \;\Rightarrow\; d(t, t'; C) \geq d(t, t'; B) \tag{16}$$

holds, we have

$$C \supseteq B \;\Rightarrow\; \mathcal{G}(C) \triangleright \mathcal{G}(B).$$

This proposition implies that while the measures (9), (10), and (11) are useful for the present purpose, the other three normalized measures (12), (13), and (14) do not always generate hierarchical classifications.

Symbolic and nonnumerical values of $t(a_i)$ can be handled likewise. There are ways to define dissimilarity or similarity measures between the two symbolic values. A simple method is as follows.

1. Let

$$d(t(a_i), t'(a_i)) = \begin{cases} 0 & (t(a_i) = t'(a_i)), \\ 1 & (t(a_i) \neq t'(a_i)). \end{cases} \tag{17}$$

2. Define

$$d(t, t'; B) = \sum_{a_i \in B} w_i d(t(a_i), t'(a_i)). \tag{18}$$

where w_i is a positive weight constant attached to a_i. The method in Proposition 1 is a special case when $0 < \epsilon < 1$ and $w_i = 1$ using the last dissimilarity.

Example 2. Let us consider Table 1 again in which we assume $d(t(E), t'(E)) = 1$ for $t(E) \neq t'(E)$ and $d(t(F), t'(F)) = 1$ for $t(F) \neq t'(F)$, but $d(t(D), t'(D)) = 0.4$ for $t(D) \neq t'(D)$. Put $w_D = w_E = w_F = 1$ and $\epsilon = 0.5$. We now have the hierarchical clusters shown in Fig. 2 instead of Fig. 1.

3.2   Various Generalizations

Since the present method is in its initial stage of consideration, we have many future research possibilities. In this section we briefly mention two of them.

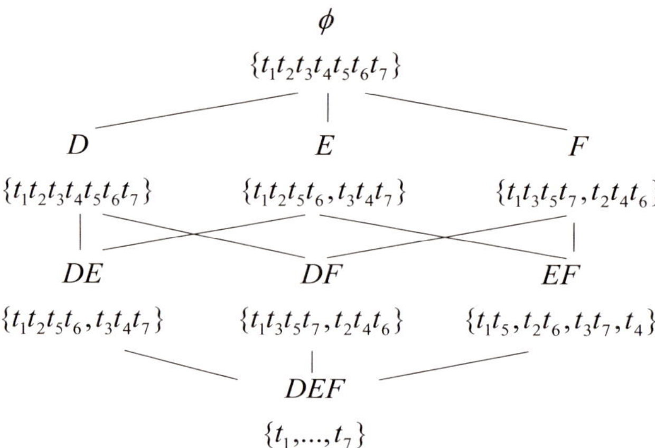

Fig. 2. Example of the lattice-valued clustering where a dissimilarity measure is used

Many Attributes: Generally we have many attributes where the Hasse diagram is very large, and hence to show the whole Hasse diagram would be impossible. In such a case hierarchical clusters along a path from $\emptyset$ to the universe should be shown instead of all the Hasse diagram.

For example, we can show clusters along the path $\emptyset - D - DE - DEF$ in Example 1:

$$\emptyset - \{t_1 t_2 \cdots t_7\}$$
$$D - \{t_1 t_2 t_3 t_4, t_5 t_6 t_7\}$$
$$DE - \{t_1 t_2, t_3 t_4, t_5 t_6, t_7\}$$
$$DEF - \{t_1, \ldots, t_7\}.$$

For such a path, the hierarchical clusters can be represented like a dendrogram.

Single Link and Other Methods: The above stated method of the connected components is equivalent to a classification derived from the single link with the threshold ϵ (cf. [4]). A natural question is whether the complete link or other methods of agglomerative clustering can be used instead of the single link. It seems that the other methods, e.g., the complete link, do not work correctly from the theoretical viewpoint. More precisely, the condition (8) does not hold in general even for the dissimilarities satisfying (16).

4   Conclusion

We have proposed the method of lattice-valued clustering in order to analyze information systems in the form of tables. As we have seen above, there are many problems for future study in both theoretical and practical senses. In practice, software development for the lattice-valued hierarchical clustering algorithms with an adequate display of the output will be necessary.

Acknowledgment. This study has partly been supported by the Grant-in-Aid for Scientific Research, 16650044, Japan Ministry of Education, Culture, Sports, Science and Technology.

References

1. G. Birkhoff, *Lattice Theory*, Amer. Math. Soc., 1967.
2. B.S. Everitt, *Cluster Analysis, 3rd Ed.*, Arnold, London, 1993.
3. Z.Q. Liu, S. Miyamoto, eds., *Soft Computing and Human-Centered Machines* Springer, Tokyo, 2000.
4. S. Miyamoto, *Fuzzy Sets in Information Retrieval and Cluster Analysis*, Kluwer, Dordrecht, 1990.
5. S. Miyamoto, *Introduction to Cluster Analysis: Theory and Applications of Fuzzy Clustering*, Morikita-Shuppan, Tokyo, 1990 (in Japanese).
6. Z. Pawlak, Rough sets, *International Journal of Computer and Information Sciences*, **11**, pp. 341–356, 1982.
7. Z. Pawlak, *Rough Sets*, Kluwer Academic Publishers, Dordrecht, 1991.
8. J.D. Ullman, *Database and Knowledge-base Systems: Volume I*, Computer Science Press, Rockville, Maryland, 1988.

Postsupervised Hard c-Means Classifier

Hidetomo Ichihashi, Katsuhiro Honda, and Akira Notsu

Graduate School of Engineering, Osaka Prefecture University
1-1 Gakuen-cho, Naka-ku, Sakai, Osaka 599-8531 Japan
{ichi, honda, notsu}@cs.osakafu-u.ac.jp

Abstract. Miyamoto *et al.* derived a hard clustering algorithms by defuzzifying a generalized entropy-based fuzzy c-means in which covariance matrices are introduced as decision variables. We apply the hard c-means (HCM) clustering algorithms to a postsupervised classifier to improve resubstitution error rate by choosing best clustering results from local minima of an objective function. Due to the nature of the prototype based classifier, the error rates can easily be improved by increasing the number of clusters with the cost of computer memory and CPU speed. But, with the HCM classifier, the resubstitution error rate along with the data set compression ratio is improved on several benchmark data sets by using a small number of clusters for each class.

1 Introduction

There are four types of basic ideas representing clusters, i.e., crisp, probabilistic, fuzzy, and possibilistic. Examples of alternating optimization algorithms of clustering that can generate memberships to clusters as well as a set of cluster centers from unlabeled object data are hard c-means (HCM) [2], Gaussian mixture models (GMM), fuzzy c-means (FCM) [1], and possibilistic c-means [10]. Miyamoto *et al.* [12] proposed a generalized hard c-means clustering (HCM-g) by introducing Mahalanobis distances. The approach is originated from the FCM clustering with regularization by KL-information (FCM-K). FCM-K is a special case of the entropy regularized FCM (FCM-e) [11], which has a close relationship to GMM or deterministic annealing by Rose [16]. Though the FCM-K is similar to these statistical clustering methods, its representation of the objective function is rather simple and does not strictly follow the EM algorithm and Bayes' rule. This reinterpretation of statistical clustering approaches leads to a general FCM objective function, but it is still limited to a few models of fuzzy clustering.

Various membership functions different from those in the standard FCM clustering (FCM-s) [1] and FCM-e can be used in an FCM clustering algorithm with the iteratively reweighted least square (IRLS) technique [4]. Cluster memberships are defined by a function of Mahalanobis distances or Euclidean distances between data vectors and cluster centers. The algorithms of GMM, FCM-e and FCM-K are the special cases of IRLS fuzzy c-means clustering (IRLS-FCM). The algorithm is applied to a postsupervised classifier design and is called IRLS-FCM classifier [7,9]. One of the classifiers with Cauchy membership function improved

S. Greco et al. (Eds.): RSCTC 2006, LNAI 4259, pp. 918–927, 2006.
© Springer-Verlag Berlin Heidelberg 2006

the classification performance in terms of the generalization ability and the receiver operating characteristics [7,9] for some benchmark data sets.

By replacing the clustering phase of the classifier with HCM-g, we propose a new fuzzy classifier in which the cluster centers and the covariance matrices are determined by the HCM-g. In this postsupervised design, the clustering is implemented by using the data from one class at a time. When working with the data class by class, the prototypes (cluster centers) that are found for each labeled class already have the assigned physical labels. Therefore the hard clustering algorithm can be implemented in the unsupervised phase, and then, the parameters in the membership function are chosen so that the resubstitution error rate attains minimum in the supervised phase. The clustering is also known as a combinatorial optimization problem and the algorithm produces many local minima, from which we can choose to improve classification accuracy. The strategy for classification is not just based on the hard clustering results but also on fuzzy memberships to the hard clusters.

The classification algorithms using Mahalanobis distances should include steps to check that the covariance matrices are nonsingular and hence invertible. The way of handling singular covariance matrices in the mixture of probabilistic principal component analysis (MPCA) [17] is employed to prevent unexpected termination of HCM-g and improve the convergence of the algorithm.

In supervised classifier design, a data set is usually crisply partitioned into a training set and a test set. Testing a classifier designed with the training set means finding its misclassification rate. The standard method for doing this is to submit the test set to the classifier and count errors. This yields the performance index by which the classifier is judged because it measures the extent to which the classifier generalizes to the test data. When the test set is equal to the training set, the error rate is called the resubstitution error rate. This error rate is not reliable for assessing the generalization ability of the classifier, but this is not an impediment to using as a basis for comparison of different designs. If training set is large enough and its substructure is well delineated, we expect classifiers trained with it to yield good generalization ability. It is not very easy to choose the classifier or its parameters when applying to real classification problems, because the best classifier for the test set is not necessarily the best for the training set. Since the FCM classifier proposed in [7,8] is designed to maximize the accuracy for test set, HCM-g classifier, which is also one of the FCM classifiers, is designed to maximize the accuracy for training set. In this paper we confine our discussion to the resubstitution classification error rate and the data set compression ratio as performance criteria. Please refer to [7,8] for the generalization ability (classification accuracy on test sets) of the IRLS-FCM classifier.

The trained classifiers are tested on the benchmark data sets from the UCI ML repository (http://www.ics.uci.edu/˜ mlearn/). The proposed HCM-g classifier with small number of clusters shows relatively low error rates on several data sets. Also concerning storage requirements and classification speed, the HCM-g classifier gives a good performance and efficiency.

2   Postsupervised Classifier with Fuzzy and Hard c-Means Clustering

FCM clustering partitions data set by introducing memberships to fuzzy clusters. The clustering criterion used to define good clusters for fuzzy c-means partitions is the FCM objective function.

2.1   Entropy Regularized FCM

In [11], an entropy term and a positive parameter λ are introduced in the FCM objective function. This approach is referred to as entropy regularization. By replacing the entropy term with K-L information term, we can consider the minimization of the following objective function under the constraints that both the sum of u_{ik} and the sum of π_i with respect to i equal one respectively [6].

$$J_e = \sum_{i=1}^{c}\sum_{k=1}^{n} u_{ik}d_{ik}^2 + \lambda \sum_{i=1}^{c}\sum_{k=1}^{n} u_{ik} \log \frac{u_{ik}}{\pi_i}$$

$$+ \sum_{i=1}^{c}\sum_{k=1}^{n} u_{ik} \log |A_i| \tag{1}$$

d_{ik} is the Mahalanobis distance between datum $\boldsymbol{x}_k$ and the i-th cluster center. (1) is defined as an FCM objective function, though, it is a reinterpretation of GMM. If $u_{ik} \simeq \pi_i$ for all k and i, the partition becomes very fuzzy, but when λ is 0 the optimization problem with respect to u_{ik} reduces to a linear one and the solution u_{ik} are obtained at extremal point, i.e., u_{ik} equals 0 or 1. Fuzziness of the clusters can be controlled by λ whereas it is usually fixed to 2 in the GMM.

Equations for variable update in the iterative algorithm are as follows. Let r dimensional vector $\boldsymbol{v}_i$ denote prototype parameter (i.e., cluster center). u_{ik} denotes the membership of k-th object datum to i-th cluster.

$$d_{ik}^2 = (\boldsymbol{x}_k - \boldsymbol{v}_i)^\top A_i^{-1}(\boldsymbol{x}_k - \boldsymbol{v}_i) \tag{2}$$

is the squared Mahalanobis distance from $\boldsymbol{x}_k$ to i-th cluster prototype, where A_i is a covariance matrix of data samples of the i-th cluster.

$$A_i = \frac{\sum_{k=1}^{n} u_{ik}(\boldsymbol{x}_k - \boldsymbol{v}_i)(\boldsymbol{x}_k - \boldsymbol{v}_i)^\top}{\sum_{k=1}^{n} u_{ik}}. \tag{3}$$

$$\boldsymbol{v}_i = \frac{\sum_{k=1}^{n} u_{ik}\boldsymbol{x}_k}{\sum_{k=1}^{n} u_{ik}}. \tag{4}$$

$$\pi_i = \frac{\sum_{k=1}^{n} u_{ik}}{\sum_{j=1}^{c}\sum_{k=1}^{n} u_{jk}} = \frac{1}{n}\sum_{k=1}^{n} u_{ik}. \tag{5}$$

From objective function (1), Miyamoto $et\ al.$ [12] derived the generalized hard clustering HCM-g by setting $\lambda = 0$. The HCM-g is a defuzzified clustering algorithm of FCM-K.

2.2   IRLS-FCM Classifier

When each covariance matrix A_i is a unit matrix, a general form of the FCM objective function can be written as :

$$J_g = \sum_{i=1}^{c} \sum_{k=1}^{n} u_{ik}^m d_{ik}^2 + \lambda \sum_{i=1}^{c} \sum_{k=1}^{n} R(u), \tag{6}$$

where m and λ are fuzzifiers.

When $m=1$ and $R(u) = u_{ik}\mathrm{log}u_{ik}$, (6) is the objective function of entropy regularized FCM, whose algorithm is the same as the EM algorithm for GMM with a unit covariance matrix and equal cluster volume.

When $m > 1$ and $\lambda = 0$, (6) is the standard FCM objective function.

When $m = 1$ and $R(u) = u_{ik}^2$, (6) is the FCM objective function with quadratic regularization [13,14].

When $m > 1$ and $R(u) = u_{ik}^m$, (6) is an FCM objective function from which (8) with unit covariance matrix is derived.

The objective function (1) includes the entropy term and is the only case where covariance matrices (A_i) are taken into account. Although Gustafson and Kessel's modified FCM [3] is derived from an objective function with fuzzifier m, we need to specify the value of determinant $|A_i|$ for all i.

A simplification of the FCM clustering is to discard objective function method and use the iteratively reweighted least square (IRLS) technique, which is known as a solution technique in robust M-estimation [4,5]. The M-estimators try to reduce the effect of outliers by replacing the squared residuals with ρ-function, which is chosen to be less increasing than square. Instead of solving directly this problem, we can implement it as the IRLS. While the IRLS approach does not guarantee the convergence to a global minimum, experimental results have shown reasonable convergence points. If one is concerned about local minima, the algorithm can be run multiple times with different initial conditions

We implicitly define ρ-function through the weight function [9] and try to minimize only the first and third terms of (1). The weight u should be recomputed after each iteration in order to be used in the next iteration. In robust M-estimation, the function $u_{ik} = w(d_{ik})$ provides adaptive weighting. The influence from $\boldsymbol{x}_k$ is decreased when $|\boldsymbol{x}_k - \boldsymbol{v}_i|$ is very large and suppressed when it is infinitely large.

To facilitate competitive movements of cluster centers, we need to define the weight function to be normalized as:

$$u_{ik} = \frac{u_{ik}^*}{\sum_{l=1}^{c} u_{lk}^*}. \tag{7}$$

Examples of membership functions used in [8] are of the forms of

$$u_{ik}^{*(1)} = \pi_i / (\lambda + d_{ik}^2/0.1)^{1/(m-1)} |A_i|^{-1/\gamma}, \tag{8}$$

$$u_{ik}^{*(2)} = \pi_i \mathrm{exp}(-d_{ik}^2/\lambda) |A_i|^{-1/\gamma}. \tag{9}$$

$u^{*(1)}$ is a modified and parameterized multivariational version of Cauchy's weight function in M-estimator or of the PDF of Cauchy distribution. The classifier with Cauchy membership function improved the classification performance in terms of generalization ability [8] and receiver operating characteristics [9] for some benchmark data sets. $u^{*(2)}$ is a modified Welsch's weight function in M-estimator. Both the functions take into account covariance matrices in an analogous manner with Gaussian PDF. It should be noted that if we choose $u^{*(2)}$ in (9) with $\lambda = 2, \gamma = 2$, then the IRLS-FCM is the same as GMM. This paper focuses on the classifier with $u^{*(2)}$. Although the classification accuracy by using (8) in terms of 10-CV is slightly better than that by (9), we use (9) in this paper, because HCM-g is originated from (6). The clustering algorithm is the repetition of (4), (5) and (7). After completing the clustering for each class, the classification is performed by computing class memberships. Let α_q denote the mixing proportion of class q, i.e., the *a priori* probability of class q. When we adopt (9), the class membership of k-th datum $\boldsymbol{x}_k$ to class q is computed as:

$$u_{qjk}^{*(1)} = \pi_{qj}\exp(-d_{qjk}^2/\lambda)|A_{qj}|^{-1/\gamma}, \tag{10}$$

$$\tilde{u}_{qk}^{(1)} = \alpha_q \sum_{j=1}^{c} u_{qjk}^{*(1)} \Big/ \sum_{s=1}^{Q} \alpha_s \sum_{j=1}^{c} u_{sjk}^{*(1)}. \tag{11}$$

The modification of covariance matrices in the mixture of probabilistic principal component analysis (MPCA) [17] is applied in the IRLS-FCM classifier for preventing singular matrices.

Let A'_i denotes an approximation of covariance matrix A_i in (8)-(9) as:

$$A'_i = P_i^p(\Delta_i^p - \sigma_i I_p)P_i^{p\top} + P_i(\sigma_i I_r)P_i^\top, \tag{12}$$

where P_i is an $r \times r$ matrix of eigenvectors of A_i. $\Delta_i =\mathrm{diag}(\delta_{i1}, ..., \delta_{ir})$ is an $r \times r$ diagonal matrix of eigenvalues. r equals the dimensionality of input samples. P_i^p is an $r \times p$ matrix of eigenvectors corresponding to the p largest eigenvalues, where $p < r - 1$. P_i^p is an $r \times p$ matrix and Δ_i^p is a $p \times p$ diagonal matrix. p is chosen so that all A'_is are nonsingular and the classifier maximizes its classification performance. $\sigma_i = (\mathrm{trace}(A_i) - \Sigma_{l=1}^p \delta_{il})/(r - p)$ and $P_i(\sigma_i I_r)P_i^\top = \sigma_i I_r$.

When $p=0$, A_i is reduced to a unit matrix and d_{ik} in (2) is reduced to Euclidean distance. This modification can be used for both the fuzzy and hard classifiers to compute distances in (2).

The IRLS-FCM classifier stated above is of a fuzzy approach and postsupervised, and the IRLS clustering phase can be replaced by a hard clustering algorithm. Although the main thesis of Miyamoto *et al.* [12] is the sequential hard clustering algorithm, we confine our discussion to its simple batch algorithm of hard clustering. The objective function of the HCM-g is (1) with $\lambda = 0$. We only use (9) for HCM-g classifier. The simple HCM classifier uses A_i of unit matrix, and thus, d_{ik} in (2) is reduced to Euclidean distance.

An alternating optimization algorithm of HCM-g is the repetition of (3) through (5) and

$$u_{ik} = \begin{cases} 1 & ; \ i = \arg\min_{1 \le j \le c} \ d_{jk}^2 + \log|A_j| \\ 0 & ; \ \text{otherwise} \end{cases} \tag{13}$$

The modification of covariance matrices by (12) is not always enough for preventing singular matrices, thus we modify (13) as:

$$u_{ik} = \begin{cases} M & ; \ i = \arg\min_{1 \le j \le c} \ d_{jk}^2 + \log|A_j| \\ \frac{1-M}{c-1} & ; \ \text{otherwise} \end{cases} \tag{14}$$

where M is a positive constant little smaller than 1.

As we will show in the numerical comparisons, HCM-g produces many local minima than FCM-K or GMM. Our proposed classifier is of postsupervised and, thus, the optimum clustering result with respect to the objective function does not guarantee the minimum classification error. Our strategy is to select the best one in terms of classification error from many local minima of the clustering criterion of HCM-g. Parameter values used for HCM-g classifier are chosen by the golden section search method [15].

3   Numerical Comparisons

Figs.1-2 show clustering results of artificial 2-D data. HCM-g produces many different results for a nonseparate data set as shown in Fig.1. Five different clustering results are obtained by 10 trials of HCM-g, while the results similar to the one shown in Fig.2 are obtained 9 times out of 10 trials of GMM. As we apply the classifier to data with more than two classes, we usually have many more local minima of the clustering criterion. Convergence speed by HCM-g is much faster than GMM. HCM-g needs only around 10 iterations, while GMM needs more than 50.

We used 8 data sets of Iris, Wisconsin breast cancer, Ionosphere, Glass, Liver disorder, Pima Indian Diabetes, Sonar and Wine as shown in Table 1. These data sets are available from the UCI ML repository (http://www.ics.uci.edu/~mlearn/) and were used to compare the generalization ability of various prototype-based classifiers such as k-nearest neighbor (k-NN), k-means (hard clustering), and learning vector quantization (LVQ) in [18]. Iris-V represents a 2-class problem discriminating between the iris versicolor and the other two iris subspecies. Incomplete samples in the breast cancer data set were eliminated. All attribute values of each data set were normalized to zero mean and unit variance. Classification error rates $\pm$ standard deviation (s.d.) by IRLS-FCM classifier using $u^{*(2)}$ and 10-fold cross validation (10-CV) with a default partition are shown in Table 2. The chosen parameters are shown in Table 3. Since $u^{*(2)}$ is an exponential function, when $\lambda = 2, \gamma = 2, c = 1$, IRLS-FCM is the same as the discriminant analysis based on normal population, which is also

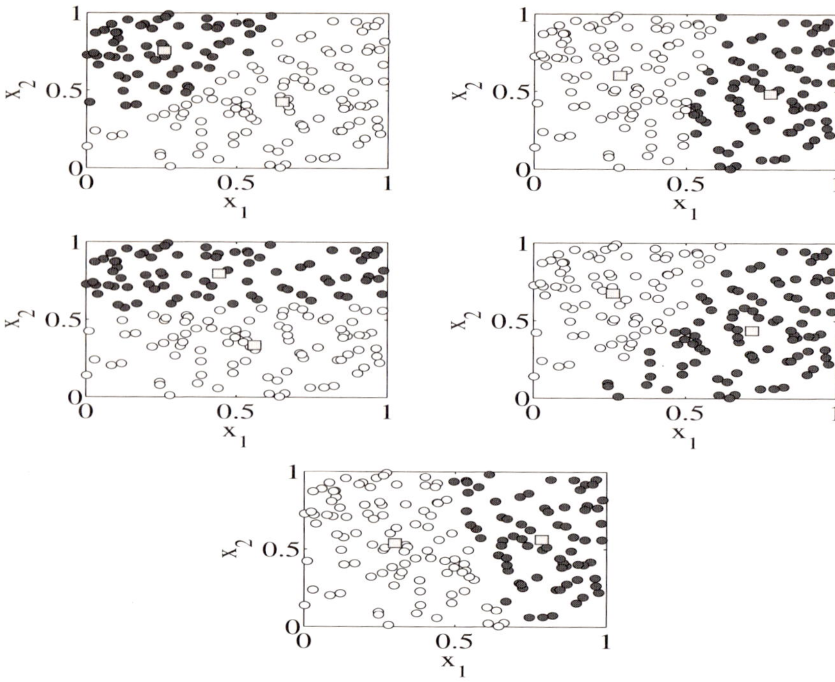

Fig. 1. Five different clustering results observed by 10 trials of HCM-g

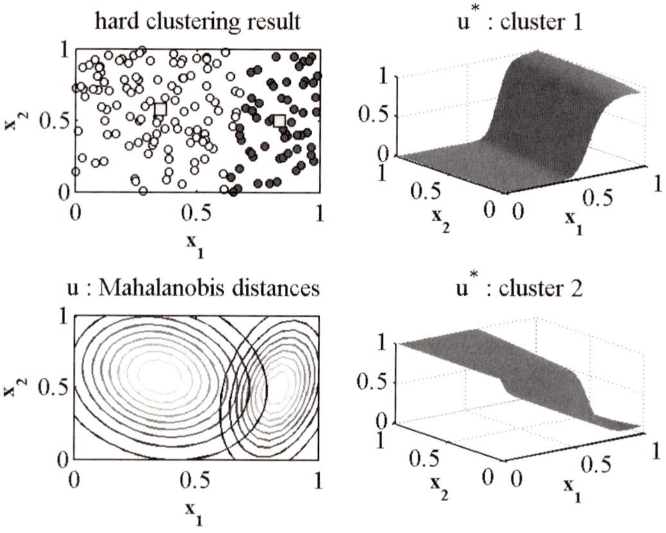

Fig. 2. Result observed 9 times out of 10 trials by GMM

Table 1. Data sets used in the experiments

	features	objects	classes
Iris	4	150	3
Iris-V	4	150	2
Breast	9	683	2
Iono	33	351	2
Glass	9	214	6
Liver	6	345	2
Pima	8	768	2
Sonar	60	208	2
Wine	13	178	3

Table 2. Classification error rates $\pm$ s.d.: Results by IRLS-FCM and Gaussian (quadratic) classifier using $u^{*(2)}$ and 10-fold CV with a default partition

	IRLS-FCM $u^{*(2)}$	Gaussian $u^{*(2)}, \lambda = 2, \gamma = 2, c = 1$
Iris	1.33	2.0 $p{=}3$
Iris-Vc	2.0	3.33 $p{=}2$
Breast	2.79 ± 0	4.41 $p{=}3$
Iono	4.86	5.71 $p{=}3$
Glass	31.90	42.38 $p{=}5$
Liver	30.59	40.29 $p{=}3$
Pima	24.74	25.13 $p{=}2$
Sonar	11.95 ± 1.57	19.0 $p{=}7$
Wine	0	0.59 $p{=}9$

Table 3. Parameters used in IRLS-FCM $(u^{*(2)})$

	parameters
Iris	$\lambda = 2.5, \gamma = 1, p = 3, c = 1$
Iris-V	$\lambda = 1.8, \gamma = 1.8, p = 2, c = 1$
Breast	$\lambda = 1.5, A_{qj} = I, \pi_{qj} = \alpha_q = 1, c = 3$
Iono	$\lambda = 2.0, \gamma = 2.6, p = 3, c = 1$
Glass	$\lambda = 0.3, \gamma = 2, p = 5, c = 1$
Liver	$\lambda = 0.5, \gamma = 11, p = 5, c = 1$
Pima	$\lambda = 3, \gamma = 3, p = 3, c = 1$
Sonar	$\lambda = 2.2, A_{qj} = I, \pi_{qj} = \alpha_q = 1, c = 30$
Wine	$\lambda = 1.5, \gamma = 2, p = 9, c = 1$

known as Gaussian classifier or quadratic classifier. Table 2 shows how generalization ability is improved by parameterizing p, λ and γ. The parameters used in IRLS-FCM $(u^{*(2)})$ are shown in Table 3.

Best resubstitution error rates from a 500 trials for each data set by HCM-g classifier and LVQ are shown in Table 4. Initial value of LVQ learning rate β was set as 0.3 and was changed as in [18], i.e., $\beta(t+1) = \beta(t) \times 0.8$ where t ($=1, ...,$ 100) denotes iteration number. For $c > 2$, we set $p = 0$ for HCM-g. When $p = 0$, HCM-g is a simple hard clustering with Euclidean distances. Naturally, as the number c is increased, the error rate decreases and for example when $c = 50$ the rate is 1.17% for the breast cancer data. For the glass data, when $c{=}2$ and (13) was used, all trials unexpectedly terminated due to singular covariance matrices, though, by using (14) the algorithm successfully converged.

Despite the continuous increase in computer memory capacity and CPU speed, especially in data mining, storage and efficiency issues become even more and more prevalent. For this reason we also measured the compression ratios of the

Table 4. Best resubstitution error rates from a 500 trials by HCM-g and LVQ classifiers

	$c=2$	$c=5$	$c=10$	LVQ $c=5$	LVQ $c=10$
Iris	**0**	1.33	0.67	2.0	1.33
Iris-V	**0**	1.33	2.0	2.0	0.67
Breast	2.2	3.07	2.20	2.34	**1.61**
Iono	**1.99**	5.13	3.99	7.41	5.70
Glass	**7.94**	17.76	13.08	20.56	18.22
Liver	**20.29**	25.51	23.77	27.54	21.45
Pima	19.53	20.57	19.79	20.18	**18.88**
Sonar	**0**	5.77	0.48	4.81	1.92
Wine	**0**	**0**	**0**	**0**	**0**

Table 5. Parameter values used for HCM-g classifier

	$c=2$ p, λ, γ	$c=5, p=0$ λ	$c=10, p=0$ λ
Iris	$2, 1.6, 1.3$	0.18	0.16
Iris-V	$2, 1.4, 1.2$	0.08	0.01
Breast	$1, 2.2, 2.1$	1.6	1.02
Iono	$2, 3.8, 2.1$	3.1	3.3
Glass	$5, 1.1, 2.0$	0.50	0.12
Liver	$4, 3.1, 2.1$	1.7	0.63
Pima	$7, 2.0, 2.0$	1.9	1.4
Sonar	$10, 1.9, 2.6$	4.3	2.1
Wine	$1, 1.0, 1.9$	1.9	2.2

Table 6. Compression ratio (%)

	$c=2$	$c=5$	$c=10$
Iris	6.0	10	20
Iris-V	4.0	6.7	13.3
Breast	0.6	1.5	2.9
Iono	1.7	2.8	5.7
Glass	16.8	14.0	28.0
Liver	3.0	2.9	5.8
Pima	2.1	1.3	2.6
Sonar	10.6	4.8	9.6
Wine	3.4	8.42	16.9

trained classifiers in Table 6. The ratio is defined as $Ratio = (p+1) \times c \times$ number of classes $\div$ number of data samples. The ratios for HCM-g ($c > 2$) and LVQ are the same. The prototype based HCM-g classifier demonstrates relatively low compression ratios. Parameter values used for HCM-g classifier are chosen by the golden section search method [15] and are shown in Table 5.

HCM-g with $c=2$ attains the lowest error rate for 7 data sets as indicated by boldface letters in Table 4.

4   Concluding Remarks

We have applied the generalized hard clustering algorithm with covariance structure to a postsupervised classifier to improve resubstitution error rate by choosing best clustering results from local minima of the clustering criterion. The resubstitution error rates and the data set compression ratios are improved on several benchmark data sets by introducing HCM-g with $c=2$. Although the approximation method of covariance matrices is effective, it does not always guarantee the stable convergence of HCM-g clustering. Further modification is to be developed for preventing unexpected termination of the algorithm.

References

1. Bezdek, J.C.: *Pattern Recognition with Fuzzy Objective Function Algorithms*, Plenum Press (1981)
2. Duda, R.O., Hart, P.E.: *Pattern Classification and Scene Analysis*, Wiley, New York, (1973).
3. Gustafson, E.E., and Kessel, W.C.: Fuzzy clustering with a fuzzy covariance matrix, *IEEE CDC*, San Diego, California, (1979) 761-766
4. Holland, P.W., Welsch, R.E.: Robust Regression Using Iteratively Reweighted Least-squares, *Communications in Statistics* **A6** (9) (1977) 813-827
5. Huber, P.J.,: *Robust Statistics*. New York:Wiley, first edition (1981)
6. Ichihashi, H., Miyagishi, K.: Honda, K.: Fuzzy c-Means Clustering with Regularization by K-L Information. *Proc. of 10th IEEE International Conference on Fuzzy Systems*, **3**, Melboroune, Australia (2001) 924-927
7. Ichihashi, H., Honda, K.: Fuzzy c-Means Classifier for Incomplete Data Sets with Outliers and Missing Values. *Proc. of the International Conference on Computational Intelligence for Modelling, Control and Automation*, Vienna, Austria (2005) 457-564
8. Ichihashi, H., Honda, K., Hattori, T.: Regularized Discriminant in the Setting of Fuzzy c-Means Classifier. *Proc. of the IEEE World Congress on Computational Intelligence*, Vancouver, Canada (2006)
9. Ichihashi, H., Honda, K., Matsuura, F.: ROC Analysis of FCM Classifier With Cauchy Weight. *Proc. of the 3rd International Conference on Soft Computing and Intelligent Systems*, Tokyo, Japan (2006)
10. Krishnapuram, R., Keller, J.: A Possibilistic Approach to Clustering, *IEEE Transactions on Fuzzy Systems* **1** (1993) 98-110
11. Liu, Z.Q., Miyamoto, S. (Eds.): *Softcomputing and Human-Centered Machines*, Springer-Verlag (2000)
12. Miyamoto, S., Yasukochi, T., Inokuchi, R.: A Family of Fuzzy and Defuzzified c-Means Algorithms. *Proc. of the International Conference on Computational Intelligence for Modelling, Control and Automation*, Vienna, Austria (2005) 170-176
13. Miyamoto, S., Umayahara, K.: Fuzzy Clustering by Quadratic Regularization. *Proc. of FUZZ-IEEE'98*, Anchorage, Alaska, (1998) 1394-1399
14. Miyamoto, S., Suizu, D., Takata, O.: Methods of Fuzzy c-Means and Possibilistic Clustering Using a Quadratic Term, *Scientiae Mathematicae Japonicae* **60**, (2) (2004) 217-233
15. Press, W.H., Teukolsky, S.A., Vetterling, W. T., Flannery, B.P.: *Numerical Recipes in C, The Art of Scientific Computing, second edition*, Cambridge University Press, Cambridge, (1999)
16. Rose, K.: Deterministic Annealing for Clustering, Compression, Classification, Regression, and Related Optimization Problems. *Proc. of the IEEE* **86** (11) (1998) 2210-2239
17. Tipping, M.E., Bishop, C.M.: Mixtures of Probabilistic Principal Component Analysers. *Neural Computation* **11** (1999) 443-482
18. Veenman, C.J., Reinders, M.J.T.: The Nearest Sub-class Classifier: A Compromise Between the Nearest Mean and Nearest Neighbor Classifier. *IEEE Transactions on PAMI* **27** (9) (2005) 1417-1429

Rule Induction Via Clustering Decision Classes

Yoshifumi Kusunoki and Masahiro Inuiguchi

Department of Systems Innovation
Graduate School of Engineering Science, Osaka University
1-3, Machikaneyama, Toyonaka, Osaka 560-8531, Japan
kusunoki@inulab.sys.es.osaka-u.ac.jp, inuiguti@sys.es.osaka-u.ac.jp

Abstract. In this paper, we examine the effects of the application of LEM2 to a hierarchical structure of decision classes. We consider classification problems with multiple decision classes by nominal condition attributes. To such a problem, we first apply an agglomerative hierarchical clustering method to obtain a dendrogram of decision classes, i.e., a hierarchical structure of decision classes. At each branch of the dendrogram, we then apply LEM2 to induce rules inferring a cluster to which an object belongs. A classification system suitable for the proposed rule induction method is designed. By a numerical experiment, we compare the proposed methods with different similarity measure calculations, the standard application of LEM2 and a method with randomly generated dendrogram. As the result, we generally demonstrate the advantages of the proposed method.

1 Introduction

Rough set analysis [9] provides useful tools for data analysis. For example, based on rough set, we can induce minimal rules from a given decision table. Many algorithms for rule induction have been proposed [1,2,3]. Those algorithms are usually applied to induce rules inferring the membership to single decision classes. Under the induced rules, a new object can be classified by evaluations of rules in view of strength, specificity and matching factor.

However, for the classification of a new object, induction of rules inferring the membership to single decision classes is not compulsory. We may induce rules inferring the membership to one of decision classes for classifying a new object. For example, if rules inferring the membership to 'D_1 or D_2' and 'D_2 or D_3' are obtained as a part of all induced rules and if a new object satisfies conditions of those rules but not others, then the object can be classified into D_2. Even when no conditions of rules are satisfied or the conclusions of applicable rules are conflict, we may classify a new object by evaluations of rules in view of strength, specificity, matching factor and so on in the same way as in the standard approaches.

From this point of view, we propose grouping decision classes and applying a rule induction method to groups of decision classes. The conditions to be a member of a large class are often simpler than those of a small class. Therefore,

S. Greco et al. (Eds.): RSCTC 2006, LNAI 4259, pp. 928–938, 2006.

by grouping decision classes before rule induction, we may obtain simpler rules. Moreover simpler rules can be induced with less computation effort. Then this approach may be computationally efficient.

The problem is how to group decision classes. The overlaps among groups is allowed so that a set of groups build a cover of decision classes. A desired cover is such that, for each decision class, there exist groups whose intersection include the class only. However, to obtain such a desired cover is not an easy task. Then we consider to apply an agglomerative hierarchical clustering algorithm [7,11] for grouping decision classes.

An agglomerative hierarchical clustering algorithm was already applied to group decision classes and hierarchical classifier was proposed in Kim and Landgrebe [5]. Moreover, instead of an agglomerate hierarchical clustering algorithm, a newly proposed divisive hierarchical clustering algorithm was applied to grouping decision classes in Kumar et al. [6]. Those methods are very similar to the method proposed in this paper. However, their aim is to treat high-dimensional numerical condition attribute data and a large number of decision classes and they did not treat nominal condition attribute data.

Turning on rough set literature, Tsumoto [13] proposed a rule induction method with grouping target concepts based on rough sets. The methods for grouping as well as for rule induction are both based on the coverage. However, in some cases, the rules seem to be passive. Jelonek and Stefanowski [4] proposed the n^2-classifier and showed its advantages in classification accuracy. In the approach, they did not obtain a hierarchical structure of decision classes but a cover of decision classes composed of all pairs of decision classes. Stefanowski [12] showed the advantages of the n^2-classifier with MODLEM in classification accuracy and in computation time over the standard MODLEM classifier.

In this paper, we focus on classification problems with multiple decision classes by nominal condition attributes. We use LEM2 [2] as a rule induction method. We examine the performance of the application of LEM2 to a dendrogram of decision classes obtained by an agglomerative hierarchical clustering algorithm. At each branch of the dendrogram, we then apply LEM2 to induce rules inferring a cluster to which an object belongs. A classification system suitable for the proposed rule induction method is designed. By numerical experiments, we compare the proposed methods with different similarity measure calculations, the standard application of LEM2 and a method with randomly generated dendrogram. As the result, we demonstrate the advantages of the proposed method.

This paper is organized as follows. In Section 2, we briefly review rough sets and a rule induction method. The proposed method is described in Section 3. The similarity between groups of decision classes is defined for the application of the agglomerative hierarchy clustering algorithm and a classification method suitable for the hierarchical structure are explained. In Section 4, the proposed methods with different settings are compared with the standard application of LEM2 by numerical experiments. Concluding remarks are given in Section 5.

2 Rough Sets and Rule Induction

2.1 A Decision Table and Rough Sets

Rough sets are often applied to analysis of decision tables. A decision table is defined by a 4-tuple $\mathcal{T} = \langle U, C \cup \{d\}, V, \rho \rangle$, where U is a finite set of objects, C is a finite set of condition attributes and d is a decision attribute, $V = \bigcup_{a \in C \cup \{d\}} V_a$ and V_a is a set of all values of attribute $a \in C \cup \{d\}$ and $\rho : U \times C \cup \{d\} \to V$ is called an information function which is a total function.

Given a decision table, we can define an indiscernibility relation with regard to an attribute set $A \subseteq C \cup \{d\}$ by $R_A = \{(x, y) \in U \times U : \rho(x, a) = \rho(y, a), \forall a \in A\}$. R_A is reflexive, symmetric and transitive. Namely, R_A is an equivalence relation. An equivalence class $[x]_A$ can be defined as $[x]_A = \{y \in U : (y, x) \in R_A\}$. The set of all equivalence classes $\{[x]_A : x \in U\}$ becomes a partition of U. When $A = \{d\}$, an equivalence class D_i in $\{[x]_{\{d\}} : x \in U\} = \{D_i, i = 1, 2, ..., p\}$ is called a decision class, where p is the cardinality of $\{\rho(x, d) : x \in U\}$ and thus we have $D_i \neq D_j$ for $i \neq j$.

Lower and upper approximations of a set of objects $X \subseteq U$ by means of an attribute set $A \subseteq C$ are defined by

$$A_*(X) = \{x \in U : [x]_A \subseteq X\}, \quad A^*(X) = \{x \in U : [x]_A \cap X \neq \emptyset\}. \qquad (1)$$

$A_*(X)$ is a set of objects surely classified as members of X by using all attributes in A while $A^*(X)$ is a set of objects possibly classified as members of X by using all attributes in A.

2.2 Rule Induction

Based on rough sets, rules inferring the membership to a class X are induced from a decision table. Induced decision rules are represented by 'if $\rho(u, a_1) = v_{a_1}$ and $\ldots$ and $\rho(u, a_m) = v_{a_m}$ then $u \in X$', where $a_k \in C$, $v_{a_k} \in V_{a_k}$ and u is an unknown object whose condition attribute values are known. Here the information function ρ is extensively used for $u \notin U$ and $\rho(u, a_j)$ takes the known value of condition attribute a_j.

In this paper, we use LEM2 [2] as the rule induction algorithm. LEM2 produces a minimal set of minimal decision rules that covers all objects in $B = C_*(X)$ or $C^*(X)$ as an input data. We can obtain a minimal set of rules surely inferring D_i by setting $B = C_*(D_i)$, and a minimal set of rules possibly inferring D_i by setting $B = C^*(D_i)$. The algorithm of LEM2 is omitted in this paper but found in Grzymala-Busse [2].

3 Rule Induction Via Clustering Decision Classes

3.1 Grouping Decision Classes

In this paper, we group decision classes before the application of LEM2. To grouping decision classes, we apply an agglomerative hierarchical clustering (AHC) algorithm [7,11].

In the AHC algorithm, the initial clusters are singletons of decision classes. Then similarities/distances between clusters are calculated. The most similar/ least distant two clusters are merged into one cluster and similarities/distances between clusters are updated. The merging and similarity/distance updating processes are iterated until all clusters are merged into one cluster. The description of AHC algorithm is omitted since it is well-known in the literature [7,11].

3.2   Similarity

Now we define the similarity between groups of decision classes we use in the AHC algorithm. The similarity is defined by the following steps:

(a) we define a similarity between two objects,
(b) we define a similarity between an object and a set of objects using the similarity defined in (a),
(c) we define a similarity between two sets of objects using the similarity defined in (b).
(d) we define a similarity between two groups of decision classes in the same spirit of (c).

Given a decision table $\mathcal{T} = \langle U, C \cup \{d\}, V, \rho \rangle$, the similarity between two objects x, $y \in U$ is defined by

$$s(x, y) = \frac{|\{a \in C : \rho(x, a) = \rho(y, a)\}|}{|C|}. \tag{2}$$

This similarity represents the ratio of common condition attribute values between objects x and y, and is in the same idea as the distance based on simple matching [11]. Moreover, it is related to an Archimedean rough inclusion discussed by Polkowski [10].

Using the similarity between two objects, we define the similarity between an object $y \in U$ and a set $X \subseteq U$ by

$$s(y, X) = \varphi(\langle s(y, x) : x \in B(X) \rangle), \tag{3}$$

where $B(X)$ is $C_*(X)$ or $C^*(X)$ and $\langle s(y, x) : x \in B(X) \rangle$ is a multiset of similarities. $\varphi : \mathcal{M} \to [0, 1]$ is a function such as a mean, a median, a maximum, or an OWA operation and $\mathcal{M}$ is a set of finite multisets whose elements are real numbers in $[0, 1]$.

Using the similarity between an object and a decision class, we further define the similarity between two sets X and $Y \subseteq U$ by

$$s(X, Y) = \max(\psi(\langle s(y, X) : y \in B(Y) \rangle), \ \psi(\langle s(x, Y) : x \in B(X) \rangle)), \tag{4}$$

where $\psi : \mathcal{M} \to [0, 1]$ is also a function such as a mean, a median, a maximum, or an OWA operation.

Since decision classes are sets of objects, the similarity between decision classes D_i and D_j is defined by $S(D_i, D_j)$. In the same way, we can define the similarity between groups G_i and G_j of decision classes by

$$s(G_i, G_j) = s\left(\bigcup_{D_k \in G_i} D_k, \bigcup_{D_l \in G_j} D_l \right). \tag{5}$$

The adoption of the similarity defined above is based on an idea that we may induce simple rules from a set of objects having similar condition attribute patterns.

When $C_*(D_i) = C^*(D_i) = D_i$, $i = 1, 2, \ldots, p$, the adoption of the maximum operation for both of φ and ψ, the similarity is same as single-linkage [7,11]. The adoptions of the minimum operation and the arithmetic mean for both of functions φ and ψ are same as complete-linkage [7,11] and average-linkage between groups [7,11]. Those adoptions are advantageous in the computational efficiency than many other adoptions since the updating of similarity by merging clusters is performed easily from similarities between clusters before the mergence.

Moreover, the adoption of the arithmetic mean for both functions φ and ψ is advantageous in computation of the similarities between initial clusters. The reason is as follows. We have

$$s(D_i, D_j) = \frac{1}{|D_i| \times |D_j|} \sum_{u \in D_i} \sum_{v \in D_j} \sum_{a \in C} ||\rho(u, a) = \rho(v, a)||$$

$$= \frac{1}{|D_i| \times |D_j|} \sum_{a \in C} \sum_{u \in D_i} \sum_{v \in D_j} ||\rho(u, a) = \rho(v, a)||,$$

where $||statement||$ is a truth value of $statement$, i.e., if $statement$ is true then $||statement|| = 1$, and otherwise $||statement|| = 0$. $|D|$ shows the number of objects in D. Let the domain of attribute a be $V_a = \{v_a^1, \ldots, v_a^t\}$ and let $n_k(v_a^s)$ be the number of objects u in D_k such that $\rho(u, a) = v_a^s \in V_a$. Namely, $n_i(v_a^s) = |\{u \in D_i : \rho(u, a) = v_a^s\}|$ and $n_j(v_a^s) = |\{u \in D_j : \rho(u, a) = v_a^s\}|$ for $s = 1, 2, \ldots, t$. Then, we obtain the following equality:

$$\sum_{u \in D_i} \sum_{v \in D_j} ||\rho(u, a) = \rho(v, a)|| = \sum_{s=1}^{t} n_i(v_a^s) \times n_j(v_a^s).$$

Utilization of this property makes the calculations of $s(D_i, D_j)$ faster.

3.3   Rule Induction and Classification Through the Dendrogram

Applying the AHC algorithm, we obtain a dendrogram as a result. At each branch of a dendrogram, we apply LEM2 twice. One application is for inducing rules inferring the inclusion in the left cluster and the other is for inducing rules inferring the inclusion in the right cluster. Therefore, if we have p decision classes, we apply LEM2 $2(p-1)$ times. Note that the number of objects we use in LEM2 decreases as the depth of the dendrogram increases. This is because we need to consider only objects satisfying conditions of rules obtained at a pass from the wth branch to the root when we induce rules at the wth branch. Therefore, the computation effort for one execution of LEM2 decreases as the depth of the dendrogram increases. This implies that the proposed approach do not always require more computational effort than the standard approach.

After we induce all rules, we should built a classification system applicable for any new objects. In the classification system of LERS including LEM2 as a module of rule induction, given condition attribute values of a new object, a decision class to which the object could belong is selected based on *strength*, *specificity* and *matching factor*. $Strength(r)$ is the total number of objects in given decision table correctly classified by rule r. $Specificity(r)$ is the total number of attribute-value pairs in the condition of rule r. $Matching\_factor(r)$ is the ratio of the number of matched attribute-value pairs of rule r to the total number of attribute-value pairs of rule r.

When conditions of some rules obtained by LEM2 are satisfied with the object, the following measure $Supp(D_i)$ called *support* is used:

$$Supp(D_i) = \sum_{matching\ rules\ r\ inferring\ D_i} Strength(r) \times Specificity(r), \qquad (6)$$

where r is called a *matching rule* if condition of r is satisfied. For convenience, when $Supp(D_i)$ is not defined, we treat $Supp(D_i) = 0$. When no conditions of rules obtained by LEM2 are satisfied with the object, the following measure $M(D_i)$ is used:

$$M(D_i) = \sum_{\substack{partially\ matching \\ rules\ r\ inferring\ D_i}} Matching\_factor(r) \times Strength(r) \times Specificity(r),$$

$$\qquad (7)$$

where r is called a *partially matching rule* if at least one attribute-value pair in condition of r is satisfied.

The classification can be performed as follows: if $Supp(D_i) > 0$ for a decision class D_i, the decision class D_{i*} with the largest $Supp(D_{i*})$ is selected. Otherwise, the decision class D_{i*} with the largest $M(D_{i*})$ is selected.

We may apply this idea to build a classification system based on the proposed approach. Namely, we decide a cluster including a given new object at each branch of dendrogram. Let G_1 and G_2 be left and right clusters at a branch. We can define measures $Supp(G_j)$ and $M(G_j)$ by replacing D_i with G_j in (6) and (7). Following the idea described above, when one of $Supp(G_1)$ and $Supp(G_2)$ is positive, we select G_j with larger $Supp(G_j)$. Otherwise, we select G_j with larger $M(G_j)$.

However, this classification method will not be always advantageous. If a cluster G_1 includes much more objects in a given decision table than the other cluster G_2, $Supp(G_1)$ and $M(G_1)$ can often take a larger value than $Supp(G_2)$ and $M(G_2)$ because $Strength$ with respect to G_1 is larger than that with respect to G_2. Even in this case, in average, we may have a case when rules inferring the inclusion in G_2 are more matching than rules inferring the inclusion in G_1.

Taking this into consideration, we propose the following measures to classify a new object. When conditions of some induced rules inferring the inclusion in G_i are satisfied with the object, the following measure $\overline{Supp}(G_i)$ called *average support* is used:

$$\overline{Supp}(G_i) = \sum_{matching\ rules\ r\ inferring\ G_i} \frac{Strength(r) \times Specificity(r)}{|G_i|}, \qquad (8)$$

where $|G_i|$ is the number of objects included in cluster G_i. For convenience, when $\overline{Supp}(G_i)$ is not defined, we treat $\overline{Supp}(G_i) = 0$. When no conditions of rules inferring the inclusion in G_i are satisfied with the object, the following measure $\overline{M}(G_i)$ is used:

$$\overline{M}(G_i) = \sum_{\substack{partially\ matching \\ rules\ r\ inferring\ G_i}} \frac{Matching\_factor(r) \times Strength(r) \times Specificity(r)}{|G_i|}.$$

$$(9)$$

The classification can be performed as follows at each branch of the dendrogram: when one of $\overline{Supp}(G_1)$ and $\overline{Supp}(G_2)$ is positive, we select G_j with larger $\overline{Supp}(G_j)$. Otherwise, we select G_j with larger $\overline{M}(G_j)$.

4   Numerical Experiments

In order to examine the performance of the proposed approach, we did numerical experiments. We compare several specifications of the proposed approaches and the standard application of LEM2. Moreover, in order to examine the advantages of the AHC algorithm with the similarity described in Section 3, we compare the proposed approaches with the method using a randomly generated dedrogram instead of the dedrogram generated by the AHC algorithm.

We used seven data sets obtained from UCI Machine Learning Repository [8]. Due to the paper size we skip the details of data sets. All condition attributes are treated as nominal attributes. No inconsistency is not included in all data sets, i.e., we have $C_*(D_i) = D_i = C^*(D_i)$ for all decision classes D_i.

The evaluation is made by the 10-fold cross-validation technique. We executed 10-fold cross-validation technique 10 times. The evaluation is made by the average and standard deviation of the 10 time execution of 10-fold cross-validation technique. We evaluate the simplicity of the obtained rules, the classification accuracy (ACC) and the computation time (TIME) to obtain rules. The evaluation of the simplicity is done by the number of rules (NUM), the average number (LEN) of attribute-value pairs in the condition of a rule and the total number of attribute-value pairs (SIZE) in whole rules composing a classification system.

We examined many specifications of the proposed approach, the standard LEM2 approach (LEM2) and the approach with randomly generated dendrograms (RANDOM) on the same PC machine. Among many specifications of the proposed approach, we show the results of the proposed approaches using four pairs of functions φ and ψ shown in the first column of Tables 1. and 2. For the proposed approaches and RANDOM, we used $\overline{Supp}$ and $\overline{M}$ to classify a new object while for LEM2, we used $Supp$ and M. The adoption of $Supp$ and M for LEM2 is because it is used the standard applications of LEM2. On the other hand, the adoption of $\overline{Supp}$ and $\overline{M}$ for others is because its performances were in general better than that in the adoption of $Supp$ and M.

The results of the numerical experiments are shown in Tables 1 and 2. In Tables 1 and 2 'mean' stands for the arithmetic mean. An entry in the form of $ave \pm dev$ in those tables show the average ave and the standard deviation dev. In those tables, asterisk $*$ shows the non-rejection of the null hypothesis

Table 1. The result of numerical experiments (part 1)

(a) Data set 'car'

Method	NUM	LEN	SIZE	ACC(%)	TIME(ms)
(mean,mean)	145.31 ± 0.63	4.00 ± 0.00	581.31 ± 3.10	98.77 ± 0.19	59.00 ± 1.84
(max,max)	145.31 ± 0.63	4.00 ± 0.00	581.31 ± 3.10	98.77 ± 0.19	$88.60^* \pm 2.15$
(min,min)	145.31 ± 0.63	4.00 ± 0.00	581.31 ± 3.10	98.77 ± 0.19	$87.50^* \pm 2.16$
(max,mean)	150.90 ± 0.66	4.07 ± 0.01	614.17 ± 3.30	98.59 ± 0.18	238.40 ± 2.42
LEM2	212.42 ± 0.99	5.19 ± 0.00	1102.86 ± 5.90	95.14 ± 0.40	123.10 ± 0.70
Random	$197.23^* \pm 21.32$	4.46 ± 0.18	882.79 ± 124.40	97.39 ± 0.81	104.40 ± 24.29

(b) Data set 'dermatology'

Method	NUM	LEN	SIZE	ACC(%)	TIME(ms)
(mean,mean)	25.70 ± 0.22	2.08 ± 0.03	53.39 ± 0.74	95.15 ± 0.67	$20.40^{**} \pm 1.85$
(max,max)	25.16 ± 0.39	2.02 ± 0.03	50.84 ± 0.92	96.69 ± 0.50	$23.00^* \pm 2.53$
(min,min)	27.15 ± 0.30	2.06 ± 0.03	55.90 ± 0.90	$93.75^* \pm 0.63$	23.80 ± 1.17
(max,mean)	25.70 ± 0.22	2.08 ± 0.03	53.39 ± 0.74	95.15 ± 0.67	60.30 ± 2.69
LEM2	19.45 ± 0.16	3.50 ± 0.03	67.91 ± 0.75	90.24 ± 0.91	20.40 ± 0.66
Random	30.65 ± 2.18	2.26 ± 0.06	$69.35^* \pm 6.33$	$91.96^* \pm 2.74$	$20.80^* \pm 3.31$

(c) Data set 'letter-recognition'

Method	NUM	LEN	SIZE	ACC(%)	TIME(s)
(mean,mean)	6877.24 ± 13.28	3.25 ± 0.00	22385.45 ± 59.28	79.78 ± 0.13	97.23 ± 0.62
(max,max)	6834.33 ± 13.93	3.36 ± 0.00	22932.57 ± 76.85	78.44 ± 0.23	125.10 ± 2.97
(min,min)	7502.20 ± 27.03	3.53 ± 0.01	26500.23 ± 132.09	74.87 ± 0.25	216.89 ± 4.46
(max,mean)	6899.65 ± 11.92	3.10 ± 0.00	21402.25 ± 50.16	80.19 ± 0.15	433.70 ± 2.20
LEM2	3136.24 ± 8.59	4.22 ± 0.00	13246.08 ± 31.50	77.33 ± 0.20	68.08 ± 0.37
Random	7427.40 ± 90.72	3.46 ± 0.03	25676.99 ± 494.09	75.80 ± 0.63	171.95 ± 13.05

(d) Data set 'nursery'

Method	NUM	LEN	SIZE	ACC(%)	TIME(s)
(mean,mean)	405.49 ± 0.94	4.49 ± 0.00	1818.71 ± 4.05	99.85 ± 0.02	1.60 ± 0.02
(max,max)	$448.27^* \pm 1.89$	$4.63^* \pm 0.01$	$2073.69^* \pm 10.09$	$99.65^* \pm 0.03$	5.31 ± 0.05
(min,min)	522.34 ± 2.18	4.96 ± 0.01	2591.88 ± 13.34	$99.24^* \pm 0.13$	7.14 ± 0.07
(max,mean)	$433.61^* \pm 3.78$	$4.69^* \pm 0.01$	$2031.01^* \pm 12.84$	$99.73^* \pm 0.05$	17.95 ± 0.07
LEM2	532.38 ± 0.94	5.37 ± 0.00	2858.91 ± 6.04	98.83 ± 0.07	3.38 ± 0.04
Random	470.06 ± 54.11	4.74 ± 0.17	2234.64 ± 312.77	99.48 ± 0.37	$2.70^* \pm 0.90$

Table 2. The result of numerical experiments (part 2)

(e) Data set 'optdigits'

Method	NUM	LEN	SIZE	ACC(%)	TIME(s)
(mean,mean)	$938.01\pm_{3.43}$	$3.59\pm_{0.01}$	$3363.77\pm_{17.79}$	$86.54\pm_{0.37}$	$39.79\pm_{0.33}$
(max,max)	$982.90\pm_{3.85}$	$3.40\pm_{0.01}$	$3339.68\pm_{17.95}$	$85.72\pm_{0.37}$	$46.14^{\star}\pm_{0.36}$
(min,min)	$984.50\pm_{7.36}$	$3.56\pm_{0.02}$	$3502.52^{\star}\pm_{28.69}$	$85.22^{\star}\pm_{0.30}$	$48.58\pm_{0.64}$
(max,mean)	$966.51^{\star}\pm_{3.79}$	$3.39\pm_{0.01}$	$3273.86\pm_{14.92}$	$85.99\pm_{0.36}$	$79.91\pm_{0.26}$
LEM2	$601.53\pm_{1.86}$	$4.63\pm_{0.01}$	$2784.48\pm_{12.01}$	$82.35\pm_{0.53}$	$37.56\pm_{0.48}$
Random	$964.67\pm_{22.07}$	$3.64\pm_{0.05}$	$3512.88\pm_{85.46}$	$84.64\pm_{0.96}$	$45.47\pm_{3.78}$

(f) Data set 'pendigits'

Method	NUM	LEN	SIZE	ACC(%)	TIME(s)
(mean,mean)	$2566.79\pm_{6.24}$	$2.24\pm_{0.00}$	$5749.70^{\star}\pm_{13.77}$	$86.40\pm_{0.26}$	$22.89\pm_{0.23}$
(max,max)	$2582.76\pm_{7.12}$	$2.25\pm_{0.00}$	$5822.05\pm_{18.45}$	$86.36\pm_{0.22}$	$23.67\pm_{0.61}$
(min,min)	$2665.59^{\star}\pm_{7.41}$	$2.40^{\star}\pm_{0.01}$	$6407.75\pm_{32.48}$	$85.52^{\star}\pm_{0.24}$	$51.44\pm_{1.87}$
(max,mean)	$2616.17^{\star}\pm_{7.02}$	$2.22\pm_{0.00}$	$5804.90\pm_{19.31}$	$86.26\pm_{0.14}$	$50.76\pm_{0.34}$
LEM2	$1976.70\pm_{2.76}$	$2.91\pm_{0.00}$	$5744.92\pm_{8.27}$	$81.76\pm_{0.22}$	$20.67\pm_{0.67}$
Random	$2637.39\pm_{54.81}$	$2.38\pm_{0.03}$	$6270.21\pm_{144.05}$	$85.79\pm_{0.55}$	$40.49\pm_{7.31}$

(g) Data set 'zoo'

Method	NUM	LEN	SIZE	ACC(%)	TIME(ms)
(mean,mean)	$15.65\pm_{0.22}$	$1.20\pm_{0.01}$	$18.85\pm_{0.30}$	$94.73^{\star}\pm_{1.27}$	$3.40^{\star\star}\pm_{0.80}$
(max,max)	$14.45\pm_{0.14}$	$1.14\pm_{0.01}$	$16.44\pm_{0.20}$	$95.02^{\star}\pm_{1.49}$	$3.70^{\star\star}\pm_{1.27}$
(min,min)	$15.72\pm_{0.24}$	$1.21\pm_{0.01}$	$19.08\pm_{0.31}$	$94.95^{\star}\pm_{2.19}$	$3.30^{\star\star}\pm_{1.00}$
(max,mean)	$14.44\pm_{0.13}$	$1.14\pm_{0.01}$	$16.39\pm_{0.13}$	$95.53\pm_{1.62}$	$5.70\pm_{0.78}$
LEM2	$9.62\pm_{0.10}$	$2.12\pm_{0.01}$	$20.32\pm_{0.14}$	$94.24\pm_{1.18}$	$3.90\pm_{1.51}$
Random	$18.77\pm_{1.64}$	$1.39\pm_{0.10}$	$26.14\pm_{3.98}$	$93.48^{\star}\pm_{1.57}$	$4.10^{\star}\pm_{1.76}$

'the averages of the method and LEM2 are same' in t-test, star $\star$ shows the non-rejection of the null hypothesis 'the average of the method and RANDOM are same' in t-test.

From Tables 1 and 2, we observe that, generally speaking, the hierarchical structure may improve the classification accuracy. Even in RANDOM, the classification accuracy ACC is improved or comparable with LEM2 in data sets except 'letter-recognition' and 'zoo'. This is surprising since the results can be improved no matter how adequate the hierarchical structure is. However the hierarchical structures obtained by the AHC algorithms improve more in many data sets. The proposed approach with the adoption of the arithmetic mean for functions φ and ψ is most advantageous in the classification accuracy than other methods.

The number (NUM) of rules are increased in the approaches using the hierarchical structure but the average number (LEN) of attribute-value pairs in a rule decreases. The total number of attribute-value pairs (SIZE) in whole rules is comparable or depends on a given data set.

The advantages using the AHC algorithms over RANDOM except case (min, min), i.e., complete-linkage method appear especially in the simplicity of the obtained classification system. Taking the standard deviation into consideration, the results of RANDOM are not stable and then we recognize the significance of the AHC algorithms.

The computation time (TIME) of the proposed approaches are comparable to LEM2. Especially, we observe that the adoption of the arithmetic mean for functions φ and ψ, i.e., (mean,mean) is more advantageous in computation time than the other adoptions.

To sum up, the proposed approach with the adoption of the arithmetic mean for functions φ and ψ seems to be better than the standard application of LEM2 in the classification accuracy and it is comparable with LEM2 in computation time.

5   Concluding Remarks

In this paper, we have proposed to group decision classes by an AHC algorithm before the application of LEM2. We have demonstrated by numerical experiments that the proposed approach using the AHC algorithm with the arithmetic mean is advantageous than the standard application of LEM2.

Many further investigations on the proposed method remain. Among them, comparison with n^2-classification method [4,12] and examinations in numerical data sets are the next steps of this research.

The authors express our appreciation to Professor J. Stefanowski for his valuable and constructive suggestions. The second author acknowledges that this work has been partially supported by the Grant-in-Aid for Scientific Research (B) No. 17310098.

References

1. Bazan, J. G., Nguyen, H. S., Nguyen, S. H., Synak, P. and Wróblewski, J.: Rough Set Algorithm in Classification Problem, in: *Rough Set Methods and Applications*, L. Polkowski, S. Tsumoto and T. Y. Lin (eds.), Physica-Verlag, Heidelberg, (2000), 49–88.
2. Grzymala-Busse, J. W.: LERS – A system for learning from examples based on rough sets, in: *Intelligent Decision Support: Handbook of Applications and Advances of the Rough Sets Theory*, R. Słowiński (ed.), Kluwer Academic Publishers, Dordrecht, (1992), 3–18.
3. Grzymala-Busse, J. W. and Stefanowski, J.: Three Discretization Methods for Rule Induction, International Journal of Intelligent Systems, **16**, (2001), 29–38.
4. Jelonek, J. and Stefanowski, J.: Experiments on solving multiclass learning problems by n^2-classifier, in: Proc. AI-METH 2002, Gliwice, (2002) 297–301.
5. Kim, B. and Landgrebe, D.A.: Hierarchical classifier design in high-dimensional numerous class cases, *IEEE Trans. Geoscience and Remote Sensing*, **29**(4) (1991) 518–528.
6. Kumar, S., Ghosh, J. and Crawford, M.M.: Hierarchical fusion of multiple classifiers for hyperspectral data analysis, *Pattern Analysis & Applications*, **5** (2002) 210–220.
7. Miyamoto, S.: *Introduction to Cluster Analysis* (in Japanese), Morikita, Tokyo, (1999).

8. Newman, D. J., Hettich, S., Blake, C. L., Merz, C. J.: UCI Repository of machine learning databases [http://www.ics.uci.edu/~mlearn/MLRepository.html], (1998).
9. Pawlak, Z.: Rough sets, *Int. J. Inform. Comp. Sci.* **11**(5), (1982), 341–356.
10. Polkowski, L.: Concerning granular computing based on Archimedean rough inclusion, *Proc. IPMU 2004*, CD-ROM, July, (2004).
11. Rokach, L. and Maimon, O.: Clustering methods, in O. Maimon and L. Rokach (eds.), *Data Mining and Knowledge Discovery Handbook*, Springer-Verlag, New York, (2005) 321–352.
12. Stefanowski, J.: The bagging and n^2-classifiers based on rules induced by MOD-LEM, in S. Tsumoto et al. (eds.), *RSCTC 2004*, LNAI 3066, Springer-Verlag, Berlin, (2004) 488–497.
13. Tsumoto, S.: Automated extraction of hierarchical decision rules from clinical databases using rough set model, *Expert Systems with Applications*, **24**, (2003), 189–197.

Several Formulations for Graded Possibilistic Approach to Fuzzy Clustering

Katsuhiro Honda[1], Hidetomo Ichihashi[1], Akira Notsu[1],
Francesco Masulli[2], and Stefano Rovetta[2]

[1] Graduate School of Engineering, Osaka Prefecture University,
1-1 Gakuen-cho, Sakai, Osaka, 599-8531, Japan
{honda, ichi, notsu}@cs.osakafu-u.ac.jp
http://www.cs.osakafu-u.ac.jp/hi/index.html
[2] Department of Computer and Information Sciences, University of Genova and
CNISM, Via Dodecaneso 35 - 16146 Genova, Italy
{masulli, rovetta}@disi.unige.it

Abstract. Fuzzy clustering is a useful tool for capturing intrinsic structure of data sets. This paper proposes several formulations for soft transition of fuzzy memberships from probabilistic partition to possibilistic one. In the proposed techniques, the free memberships are given by introducing additional penalty term used in Possibilistic c-Means. The new features of the proposed techniques are demonstrated in several numerical experiments.

1 Introduction

Fuzzy c-Means (FCM) [1] is a well known fuzzy clustering algorithm whose goal is to partition objects (data points, individuals) into several clusters by estimating fuzzy memberships of objects to each cluster. In the FCM clustering, an additional weighting parameter called "fuzzifier" is introduced into the objective function of (hard) k-Means clustering [2] in order to fuzzify the degree of memberships, i.e., the constraints on the membership parameters are generalized so that they can take arbitrary values from the interval of $[0, 1]$ instead of $\{0, 1\}$. Because the sum of memberships of objects with respect to clusters are constrained to be 1, the fuzzy memberships are often said to be "probabilistic".

Recently, several other techniques for fuzzifying membership assignment have been proposed based on regularization approaches. Miyamoto and Mukaidono [3] considered the singularity in the hard clustering which implies the case where proper partition is not obtained by the Lagrangian multiplier method, and introduced an entropy term as the regularization term with a positive parameter into the objective function of k-Means clustering. Because the fuzzification technique derives the similar algorithm to that of entropy-constrained fuzzy clustering by Deterministic Annealing (DA) [4], the clustering model is often compared with probabilistic mixture models [5]. Then, Ichihashi *et al.* [6] proposed a clustering algorithm, which is similar to the EM algorithm for Gaussian Mixture

S. Greco et al. (Eds.): RSCTC 2006, LNAI 4259, pp. 939–948, 2006.

Models (GMMs), by using the regularization technique with Kullback-Leibler divergences (K L information).

In spite of its usefulness, the "probabilistic" partition has a problem of noise sensitivity because the probabilistic constraint forces noise samples to belong to one or several clusters with some degree. Then, Krishnapuram and Keller proposed the Possibilistic c-Means (PCM) algorithm [7] by giving up the constraint of sum to 1. This mode seeking algorithm is useful for outlier rejection in fuzzy membership assignment, and the memberships can be regarded as the probability that an experimental outcome coincides with one of mutually independent events. However, it is possible that sets of events are neither mutually independent nor completely mutually exclusive. Then, Masulli and Rovetta [8,9] proposed the graded possibilistic approach to clustering with regularization by entropy. In the approach, soft transition from probabilistic to possibilistic partition is performed by using the graded possibilistic constraint.

This paper proposes two other formulations for soft transition of fuzzy memberships from probabilistic partition to possibilistic one. One is a modified version of the original FCM algorithm, in which the updating rule for memberships is a hybrid of FCM and PCM. The other is an enhanced version of the FCM algorithm with regularization by K-L information. In the proposed techniques, the free memberships drawn from the interval of $[0, 1]$ are given by introducing an additional penalty term used in PCM. The new features of the proposed techniques are demonstrated in several numerical experiments.

2   Fuzzy c-Means and Possibilistic c-Means

2.1   Fuzzy c-Means and Several Fuzzification Techniques

Fuzzy c-Means (FCM) [1] is an unsupervised classification technique that is a fuzzified version of k-Means clustering [2]. In the k-Means (hard c-Means) clustering, objects to be classified are assigned to one of C clusters where each cluster has its prototypical mean vector. The membership assignment is based on minimization of within-group-sum-of-errors, i.e., nearest prototype classification. Then, the two step iterative algorithm is composed of calculation of mean vectors and assignment of objects.

The FCM algorithm proposed by Bezdek *et al.* [1] uses the objective function of generalized within-group-sum-of-errors

$$L^s_{fcm} = \sum_{c=1}^{C} \sum_{i=1}^{n} u^{\theta}_{ci} d^2_{ci}. \tag{1}$$

d^2_{ci} is the clustering criterion of the distance between the ith object $\boldsymbol{x}_i$ and the cth prototypical mean vector (cluster center) $\boldsymbol{b}_c$, and $u_{ci} \in [0, 1]$ represents the membership of the ith object to the cth cluster. θ is an additional weighting exponent. If $\theta = 1$, the clustering model is reduced to the (hard) k-Means model. The larger the θ, the fuzzier the memberships. So, the weighting exponent is usually set to be $\theta > 1$ and is called the "fuzzifier". The memberships are often calculated under the constraint of

$$\sum_{c=1}^{C} u_{ci} = 1, \qquad i = 1, \cdots, n. \tag{2}$$

Because the memberships are obtained by a formula similar to the updating rule for posterior probabilities in the EM algorithm with probabilistic mixture models, the constraint is called the "probabilistic constraint" [10].

In the original FCM algorithm, called the "standard FCM algorithm", the updating rules for parameters are given as

$$\boldsymbol{b}_c = \frac{\sum_{i=1}^{n} u_{ci}^{\theta} \boldsymbol{x}_i}{\sum_{i=1}^{n} u_{ci}^{\theta}}, \tag{3}$$

$$u_{ci} = \left[\sum_{l=1}^{C} \left(\frac{d_{ci}^2}{d_{li}^2} \right)^{\frac{1}{\theta-1}} \right]^{-1}. \tag{4}$$

Another approach to fuzzification of the hard c-Means clustering is the regularization of the objective function. Miyamoto and Mukaidono [3] introduced a regularization term with a positive parameter λ into the objective function. Using the entropy term, the objective function of the FCM clustering based on the regularization technique is defined as

$$L^e_{fcm} = \sum_{c=1}^{C} \sum_{i=1}^{n} u_{ci} d_{ci}^2 + \lambda \sum_{c=1}^{C} \sum_{i=1}^{n} u_{ci} \log u_{ci}, \tag{5}$$

where the entropy term works like the weighting exponent in the standard FCM algorithm, and transforms the linear programming problem into the nonlinear optimization problem with respect to memberships u_{ci}. The parameter λ plays a role for tuning the degree of fuzziness of membership values. The larger the λ, the fuzzier the memberships. This fuzzification technique is called the "regularization by entropy." The updating rules for cluster centers and memberships are derived as follows:

$$\boldsymbol{b}_c = \frac{\sum_{i=1}^{n} u_{ci} \boldsymbol{x}_i}{\sum_{i=1}^{n} u_{ci}}. \tag{6}$$

$$u_{ci} = \frac{\exp(-\frac{1}{\lambda} d_{ci}^2)}{\sum_{l=1}^{c} \exp(-\frac{1}{\lambda} d_{li}^2)}, \tag{7}$$

The regularization approach can also be performed by using other regularization terms. Ichihashi $et\ al.$ [6] generalized the regularized objective function replacing the entropy term with K-L information term and proposed an FCM-type counterpart of the GMMs with full unknown parameters. The clustering technique is called the FCM clustering with regularization by K-L information (KLFCM) and the objective function is defined as follows:

$$L_{klfcm} = \sum_{c=1}^{C} \sum_{i=1}^{n} u_{ci} d_{ci}^2 + \lambda \sum_{c=1}^{C} \sum_{i=1}^{n} u_{ci} \log \frac{u_{ci}}{\pi_c} + \sum_{c=1}^{C} \sum_{i=1}^{n} u_{ci} \log |\Sigma_c|, \qquad (8)$$

where d_{ci}^2 is the (squared) Mahalanobis distance $d_{ci}^2 = (\boldsymbol{x}_i - \boldsymbol{b}_c)^\top \Sigma_c^{-1} (\boldsymbol{x}_i - \boldsymbol{b}_c)$, and all the elements of Σ_c are also decision variables. Eq.(8) is minimized under the condition that both the sum of u_{ci} and the sum of π_c with respect to c equal 1, respectively. If $u_{ci} \simeq \pi_c$ for all i and c, the K-L information term becomes 0 and the membership assignment is very fuzzy; but when λ is 0 the solution u_{ci}'s are obtained at the extremal point (0 or 1). Fuzziness of the partition can be controlled by λ. From the necessary conditions, the updating rules for u_{ci}, π_c, Σ_c are given as follows:

$$u_{ci} = \frac{\pi_c \exp\left(-\frac{1}{\lambda} d_{ci}\right) |\Sigma_c|^{-\frac{1}{\lambda}}}{\sum_{l=1}^{C} \pi_l \exp\left(-\frac{1}{\lambda} d_{li}\right) |\Sigma_l|^{-\frac{1}{\lambda}}}, \qquad (9)$$

$$\pi_c = \frac{1}{n} \sum_{i=1}^{n} u_{ci}, \qquad (10)$$

$$\Sigma_c = \frac{\sum_{i=1}^{n} u_{ci} (\boldsymbol{x}_i - \boldsymbol{b}_c)(\boldsymbol{x}_i - \boldsymbol{b}_c)^\top}{\sum_{i=1}^{n} u_{ci}}, \qquad (11)$$

and the cluster center $\boldsymbol{b}_c$ is given by Eq.(6). Because π_c represents the proportion of objects belonging to the cth cluster, it is regarded as the capacity of the cluster. The algorithm is equivalent to the EM algorithm with GMMs if and only if the fuzzification coefficient $\lambda = 2$. When $\lambda \neq 2$, there is no corresponding mixture density. In the KLFCM clustering, K-L information term is used for both optimization of cluster capacities and fuzzification of memberships while Hathaway [5] interpreted the clustering criterion as the sum of K-L information for updating memberships [11].

2.2   Possibilistic c-Means

Krishnapuram and Keller [7] proposed the possibilistic clustering by giving up the probabilistic constraint. The objective function is formulated as

$$L_{pcm}^s = \sum_{c=1}^{C} \sum_{i=1}^{n} u_{ci}^\theta d_{ci}^2 + \sum_{c=1}^{C} \eta_c \sum_{i=1}^{n} (1 - u_{ci})^\theta, \qquad (12)$$

where $\eta_c, c = 1, \cdots, C$ are suitable positive numbers. The first term demands that the distances from the objects to the prototypes be as low as possible, whereas the second term forces the u_{ci} to be as large as possible avoiding the trivial solution. Then, the updating rule for memberships is given as

$$u_{ci} = \frac{1}{1 + \left(\frac{d_{ci}^2}{\eta_c}\right)^{\frac{1}{\theta-1}}}. \tag{13}$$

The value of η_c controls the bandwidth of the possibility (membership) distribution for each cluster and determines the distance at which the membership value of an object in a cluster becomes 0.5. In [7], η_c was calculated by using the fuzzy intra-cluster distance as

$$\eta_c = K \frac{\sum_{i=1}^n u_{ci}^\theta d_{ci}^2}{\sum_{i=1}^n u_{ci}^\theta}, \tag{14}$$

and K is typically chosen to be 1.

Another formulation for Possibilistic c-Means can be derived by modifying the FCM clustering with regularization by entropy [12,13],

$$L_{pcm}^e = \sum_{c=1}^C \sum_{i=1}^n u_{ci} d_{ci}^2 + \lambda \sum_{c=1}^C \sum_{i=1}^n (u_{ci} \log u_{ci} - u_{ci}) \tag{15}$$

The updating rule for memberships is given as $u_{ci} = \exp(-\frac{1}{\lambda} d_{ci}^2)$.

3   Soft Transition to Possibilistic Partition

3.1   DA-Based Soft Transition

Masulli and Rovetta [8,9] proposed the graded possibilistic approach to clustering, in which soft transition from probabilistic to possibilistic constraint is performed by using the graded possibilistic constraint. Assume that a class of constraints is expressed by a unified formulation: $\Psi = \sum_{c=1}^C u_{ci}^{[\xi]} - 1$, where $[\xi]$ is an interval variable representing an arbitrary real number included in the range $[\underline{\xi}, \overline{\xi}]$, i.e., there must exist a scalar exponent $\xi^* \in [\underline{\xi}, \overline{\xi}]$ such that the equality $\Psi = 0$ holds. The constraint can be implemented by using a running parameter α. The extrema of the interval are written as a function of α, where $\underline{\xi} = \alpha, \overline{\xi} = \frac{1}{\alpha}$ and $\alpha \in [0,1]$. Then, the constraint with an interval is represented as a set of two inequalities: $\sum_{c=1}^C u_{ci}^\alpha \geq 1$ and $\sum_{i=1}^C u_{ci}^{\frac{1}{\alpha}} \leq 1$.

For implementation of the graded possibilistic clustering, the following algorithm can be used. When we use the entropy regularization (or DA approach), the memberships are updated as

$$u_{ci} = \frac{\phi_{ci}}{\kappa_i}, \tag{16}$$

where ϕ_{ci} is a free membership of x_i to the cth cluster drawn from the interval of $[0,1]$ and is given as

$$\phi_{ci} = \exp\left\{-\frac{d_{ci}^2}{\lambda}\right\}. \tag{17}$$

κ_i takes one of the following three values.

$$\kappa_i = \left(\sum_{l=1}^{C} \phi_{li}^{\frac{1}{\alpha}} \right)^{\alpha} \qquad \text{if } \sum_{l=1}^{C} \phi_{li}^{\frac{1}{\alpha}} > 1, \tag{18}$$

$$\kappa_i = \left(\sum_{l=1}^{C} \phi_{li}^{\alpha} \right)^{\frac{1}{\alpha}} \qquad \text{if } \sum_{l=1}^{C} \phi_{li}^{\alpha} < 1, \tag{19}$$

$$\kappa_i = 1 \qquad\qquad\qquad \text{else.} \tag{20}$$

Eq.(18) transforms memberships that are above the upper boundary onto the boundary ($\sum_{l=1}^{C} u_{li}^{\frac{1}{\alpha}} = 1$) while Eq.(19) transforms memberships under the lower boundary onto the boundary ($\sum_{l=1}^{C} u_{li}^{\alpha} = 1$). When $\alpha = 1$, Eqs.(18) and (19) derive $\kappa_i = \sum_{l=1}^{C} \phi_{li}$, and memberships u_{ci}'s are reduced to the probabilistic ones ($\sum_{c=1}^{C} u_{ci} = 1$). On the other hand, $\alpha = 0$ provides the possibilistic membership assignment because all of κ_i's are given by Eq.(20). Then, the value of α should be gradually decreased from 1 to 0.

3.2 Soft Transition with Standard Fuzzification Technique

The key in generalizing the graded possibilistic approach to other fuzzification techniques is how to define the free memberships of Eq.(17). In this subsection, a free membership drawn from the interval of $[0, 1]$ is formulated in the frame of the standard fuzzification technique. In order to generalize the updating rule for memberships, the additional penalty term used in PCM is introduced into the objective function of FCM as follows:

$$L_{fcm}^{gs} = \sum_{c=1}^{C} \sum_{i=1}^{n} u_{ci}^{\theta} d_{ci}^{2} + \sum_{c=1}^{C} \eta_c \sum_{i=1}^{n} (1 - u_{ci})^{\theta}. \tag{21}$$

Then, Eq.(16) is calculated with the following free membership ϕ_{ci}:

$$\phi_{ci} = \frac{1}{1 + \left(\dfrac{d_{ci}^{2}}{\eta_c} \right)^{\frac{1}{\theta - 1}}}, \tag{22}$$

where η_c is a predefined constant. We can see that $d_{ci}^{2} = 0$ derives $\phi_{ci} = 1$, and ϕ_{ci} moves toward 0 as $d_{ci}^{2} \to \infty$.

Here, it is obvious that the free membership of Eq.(22) derives the possibilistic partition of PCM when $\alpha = 0$. Then, the parameter η_c plays a similar role with that of PCM and can be given in the same way with PCM. On the other hand, when $\alpha = 1$, the updating rule has some connection with that of FCM. Substituting Eq.(22), Eq. (16) with $\alpha = 1$ is written as

$$u_{ci} = \frac{\phi_{ci}}{\sum_{l=1}^{C} \phi_{li}} = \frac{\dfrac{(d_{ci}^{2})^{-\frac{1}{\theta-1}}}{(d_{ci}^{2})^{-\frac{1}{\theta-1}} + (\eta_c)^{-\frac{1}{\theta-1}}}}{\sum_{l=1}^{C} \dfrac{(d_{li}^{2})^{-\frac{1}{\theta-1}}}{(d_{li}^{2})^{-\frac{1}{\theta-1}} + (\eta_l)^{-\frac{1}{\theta-1}}}}. \tag{23}$$

By the way, the updating rule of Eq.(4) can be written as

$$u_{ci} = \frac{(d_{ci}^2)^{-\frac{1}{\theta-1}}}{\sum_{l=1}^{C}(d_{li}^2)^{-\frac{1}{\theta-1}}} = \frac{\frac{(d_{ci}^2)^{-\frac{1}{\theta-1}}}{\sum_{l=1}^{C}(d_{li}^2)^{-\frac{1}{\theta-1}}}}{\sum_{l=1}^{C}\frac{(d_{li}^2)^{-\frac{1}{\theta-1}}}{\sum_{k=1}^{C}(d_{ki}^2)^{-\frac{1}{\theta-1}}}}. \tag{24}$$

Then, the proposed model is equivalent to the standard FCM if $(\eta_c)^{-\frac{1}{\theta-1}} = \sum_{l=1}^{C}(d_{li}^2)^{-\frac{1}{\theta-1}} - (d_{ci}^2)^{-\frac{1}{\theta-1}}$ for all c.

Assume that η_c is fixed for all i and c. When η_c is large, all u_{ci}'s tend to take the same value of $1/C$, i.e., the membership assignment becomes very fuzzy. On the other hand, when η_c is enough close to 0, the value of Eq.(23) becomes similar to that of Eq.(24) because

$$\frac{(d_{ci}^2)^{-\frac{1}{\theta-1}}}{(d_{ci}^2)^{-\frac{1}{\theta-1}} + (\eta_c)^{-\frac{1}{\theta-1}}} \simeq \frac{(d_{ci}^2)^{-\frac{1}{\theta-1}}}{(\eta_c)^{-\frac{1}{\theta-1}}}, \tag{25}$$

and

$$\sum_{l=1}^{C} \frac{(d_{li}^2)^{-\frac{1}{\theta-1}}}{(d_{li}^2)^{-\frac{1}{\theta-1}} + (\eta_c)^{-\frac{1}{\theta-1}}} \simeq \frac{1}{(\eta_c)^{-\frac{1}{\theta-1}}} \sum_{l=1}^{C}(d_{li}^2)^{-\frac{1}{\theta-1}}. \tag{26}$$

Therefore, the value of η_c should be gradually increased from a positive small value to Eq.(14).

3.3   Soft Transition with Regularization by K-L Information

In the same manner, the graded possibilistic approach to the FCM clustering with regularization by K-L information can be formulated as follows:

$$L_{klfcm}^{g} = \sum_{c=1}^{C}\sum_{i=1}^{n} u_{ci}d_{ci}^2 + \lambda\sum_{c=1}^{C}\sum_{i=1}^{n} u_{ci}\log\frac{u_{ci}}{\pi_c} + \sum_{c=1}^{C}\sum_{i=1}^{n} u_{ci}\log|\Sigma_c|$$
$$+ \sum_{c=1}^{C}\lambda\log\eta_c\sum_{i=1}^{n}(1-u_{ci}) + \lambda\sum_{c=1}^{C}\sum_{i=1}^{n}(1-u_{ci})\log(1-u_{ci}), \tag{27}$$

where d_{ci}^2 is the (squared) Mahalanobis distance. Then, Eq.(16) is calculated with the following free membership ϕ_{ci}:

$$\phi_{ci} = \frac{\pi_c\exp\left(-\frac{1}{\lambda}d_{ci}\right)|\Sigma_c|^{-\frac{1}{\lambda}}}{\pi_c\exp\left(-\frac{1}{\lambda}d_{ci}\right)|\Sigma_c|^{-\frac{1}{\lambda}} + \frac{1}{\eta_c}}, \tag{28}$$

where η_c is a predefined constant.

Here, the free membership of Eq.(28) derives a possibilistic partition when $\alpha = 0$, and the parameter η_c plays a similar role with that of PCM. Considering the similarity between KLFCM and GMMs, it is a natural choice that

$\frac{1}{\eta_c} = K\pi_c \exp\left(-\frac{1}{\lambda}\right)|\Sigma_c|^{-\frac{1}{\lambda}}$ because the within-group variance is 1 in the Mahalanobis distance. Then K can be chosen to be 1. On the other hand, when $\alpha - 1$, the updating rule becomes more similar to that of KLFCM as η_c moves toward 0. Therefore, the value of η_c should be gradually increased from a positive small value to $\left[K\pi_c \exp\left(-\frac{1}{\lambda}\right)|\Sigma_c|^{-\frac{1}{\lambda}}\right]^{-1}$ in the graded possibilistic clustering.

By the way, other parameters can be updated in the same manner with KLFCM so long as we use the same constraint except for the probabilistic constraint of Eq.(2).

4   Numerical Experiments

This section shows the results of numerical experiments that were performed by using an artificial data set consisting of 100 samples with 2-D observation. The data set was partitioned into 2 clusters using the proposed formulations.

First, the standard FCM and its generalized model were applied to the data set. The derived fuzzy classification functions are shown in Figs. 1 and 2, in which the objects to be classified are represented by "o" and the gray scale shows the maximum membership value, i.e., the membership degree belonging

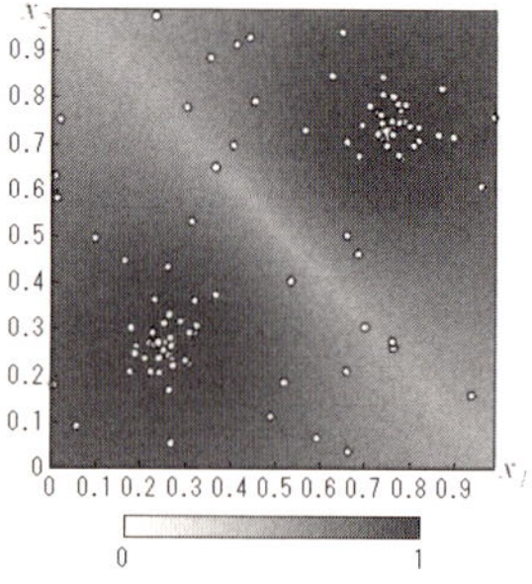

Fig. 1. Fuzzy classification function by standard FCM with $\theta = 2.0$

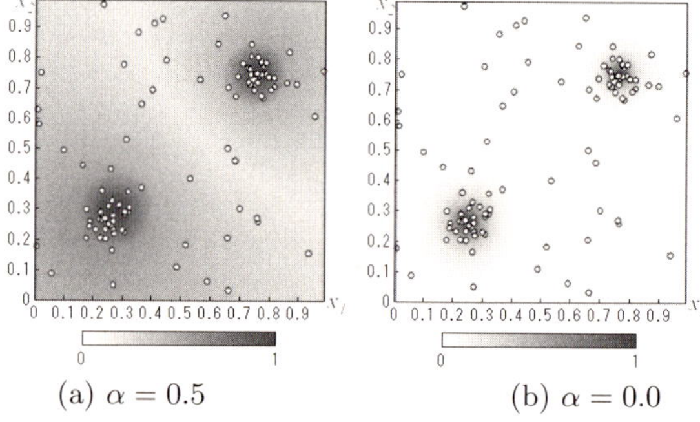

(a) $\alpha = 0.5$ (b) $\alpha = 0.0$

Fig. 2. Fuzzy classification function by graded possibilistic approach with standard fuzzification with $\theta = 2.0$

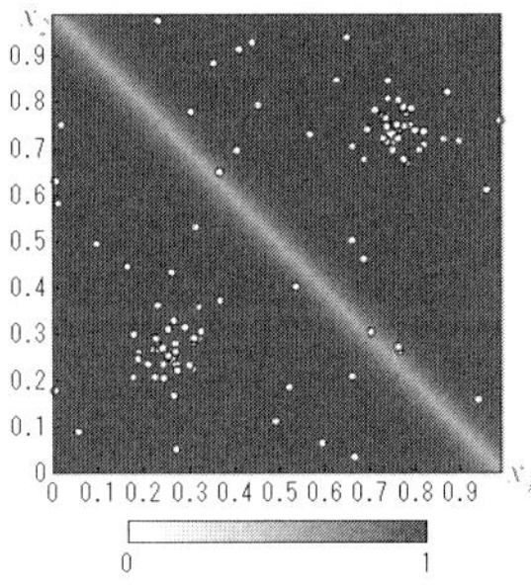

Fig. 3. Fuzzy classification function by KLFCM with $\lambda = 2.0$

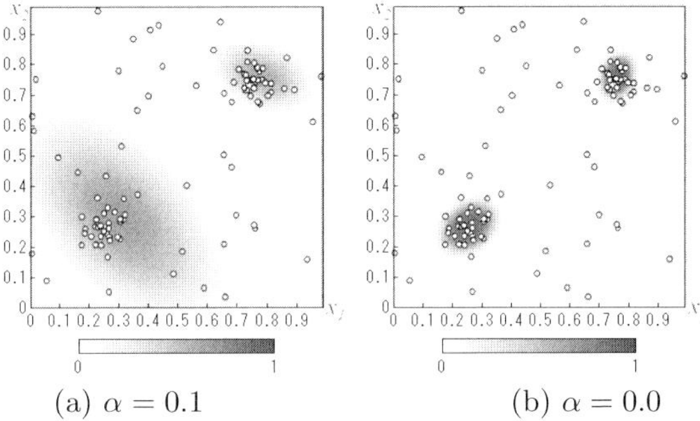

(a) $\alpha = 0.1$ (b) $\alpha = 0.0$

Fig. 4. Fuzzy classification function by graded possibilistic approach with regularization by K-L information with $\lambda = 2.0$

to the nearest cluster center. In the graded possibilistic approach, η_c was given as $\eta_c = 0.0001\alpha + (1-\alpha)\frac{\sum_{i=1}^{n} u_{ci}^{\theta} d_{ci}^{2}}{\sum_{i=1}^{n} u_{ci}^{\theta}}$. The figures show that the possibilistic partition is a good property of the mode seeking algorithm and the graded possibilistic approach performs the soft transition well. Furthermore, the intermediate model ($\alpha = 0.5$) reflects the features of both of probabilistic and possibilistic partition.

Next, the graded possibilistic approach is performed using the regularization by K-L information. Here, it has been shown that the KLFCM algorithm is sensitive to initial partition and often falls into local minima where we have a very large cluster (global cluster) and several very small clusters with a few objects. In this experiment, the initial partition was given by the standard FCM algorithm and the lower limit of variance (covariance) was set as 0.02 in order to avoid a global cluster. The derived fuzzy classification functions are shown in Figs. 3 and 4. η_c was given as $\eta_c = 0.0001\alpha + (1-\alpha)\left[\pi_c \exp\left(-\frac{1}{\lambda}\right)|\Sigma_c|^{-\frac{1}{\lambda}}\right]^{-1}$. The figures show that the KLFCM-based model could capture not only the cluster centers but also the capacities and the shapes of clusters.

In this way, the proposed approach is useful for performing the soft transition from probabilistic to possibilistic partition.

5   Conclusion

This paper proposed several formulations for graded possibilistic approach in the FCM clustering. In the proposed techniques, the free memberships drawn from the interval of $[0, 1]$ are given by introducing an additional penalty term used in PCM. The probabilistic partition of the conventional clustering algorithm can be derived by using a small penalty weight while the weight plays a role for tuning the bandwidth of the possibility (membership) distribution for each cluster in the possibilistic partition. Application to real world data sets is remained in future work.

References

1. Bezdek, J.C.: Pattern Recognition with Fuzzy Objective Function Algorithms. Plenum Press (1981)
2. MacQueen, J.B.: Some Methods of Classification and Analysis of Multivariate Observations. Proc. 5th Berkeley Symposium on Math. Stat. and Prob. (1967) 281–297
3. Miyamoto, S., Mukaidono, M.: Fuzzy c-Means as a Regularization and Maximum Entropy Approach. Proc. 7th Int. Fuzzy Syst. Assoc. World Cong. **2** (1997) 86–92
4. Rose, K., Gurewitz, E., Fox, G.: A Deterministic Annealing Approach to Clustering. Pattern Recognition Letters **11** (1990) 589–594
5. Hathaway, R.J.: Another Interpretation of the EM Algorithm for Mixture Distributions. Statistics & Probability Letters **4** (1986) 53–56
6. Ichihashi, H., Miyagishi, K., Honda, K.: Fuzzy c-Means Clustering with Regularization by K-L Information. Proc. of 10th IEEE Int. Conf. Fuzzy Systems **3** (2001) 924–927
7. Krishnapuram, R., Keller, J.M.: A Possibilistic Approach to Clustering. IEEE Trans. Fuzzy Systems **1** (1993) 98–110
8. Masulli, F., Rovetta, S.: The Graded Possibilistic Clustering Model. IJCNN 2003 Conference Proceedings (2003) 791–796
9. Masulli, F., Rovetta, S.: Soft Transition from Probabilistic to Possibilistic Fuzzy Clustering. IEEE Trans. Fuzzy Systems **14** (2006) 516–527
10. Höppner, F., Klawonn, F., Kruse, R., Runkler, T.: Fuzzy Cluster Analysis, Jhon Wiley & Sons (1999)
11. Honda, K., Ichihashi, H.: Regularized Linear Fuzzy Clustering and Probabilistic PCA Mixture Models. IEEE Trans. Fuzzy Systems, **13** (2005) 508–516
12. Davé, R.N., Krishnapuram, R.: Robust Clustering Methods: A Unified View. IEEE Trans. Fuzzy Systems, **5** (1997) 270–293
13. Shibuya, K., Miyamoto, S., Takata, O., Umayahara, K.: Regularization and Constraints in Fuzzy c-Means and Possibilistic Clustering. J. Japan Society for Fuzzy Theory and Systems, **13** (2001) 707–715 (in Japanese)

Author Index

Printing: Mercedes-Druck, Berlin
Binding: Stein+Lehmann, Berlin

Lecture Notes in Artificial Intelligence (LNAI)

Vol. 4093: X. Li, O.R. Zaïane, Z. Li (Eds.), Advanced Data Mining and Applications. XXI, 1110 pages. 2006.

Vol. 4092: J. Lang, F. Lin, J. Wang (Eds.), Knowledge Science, Engineering and Management. XV, 664 pages. 2006.

Vol. 4088: Z.-Z. Shi, R. Sadananda (Eds.), Agent Computing and Multi-Agent Systems. XVII, 827 pages. 2006.

Vol. 4087: F. Schwenker, S. Marinai (Eds.), Artificial Neural Networks in Pattern Recognition. IX, 299 pages. 2006.

Vol. 4068: H. Schärfe, P. Hitzler, P. Øhrstrøm (Eds.), Conceptual Structures: Inspiration and Application. XI, 455 pages. 2006.

Vol. 4065: P. Perner (Ed.), Advances in Data Mining. XI, 592 pages. 2006.

Vol. 4062: G. Wang, J.F. Peters, A. Skowron, Y. Yao (Eds.), Rough Sets and Knowledge Technology. XX, 810 pages. 2006.

Vol. 4049: S. Parsons, N. Maudet, P. Moraitis, I. Rahwan (Eds.), Argumentation in Multi-Agent Systems. XIV, 313 pages. 2006.

Vol. 4048: L. Goble, J.-J.C.. Meyer (Eds.), Deontic Logic and Artificial Normative Systems. X, 273 pages. 2006.

Vol. 4045: D. Barker-Plummer, R. Cox, N. Swoboda (Eds.), Diagrammatic Representation and Inference. XII, 301 pages. 2006.

Vol. 4031: M. Ali, R. Dapoigny (Eds.), Advances in Applied Artificial Intelligence. XXIII, 1353 pages. 2006.

Vol. 4029: L. Rutkowski, R. Tadeusiewicz, L.A. Zadeh, J.M. Zurada (Eds.), Artificial Intelligence and Soft Computing – ICAISC 2006. XXI, 1235 pages. 2006.

Vol. 4027: H.L. Larsen, G. Pasi, D. Ortiz-Arroyo, T. Andreasen, H. Christiansen (Eds.), Flexible Query Answering Systems. XVIII, 714 pages. 2006.

Vol. 4021: E. André, L. Dybkjær, W. Minker, H. Neumann, M. Weber (Eds.), Perception and Interactive Technologies. XI, 217 pages. 2006.

Vol. 4020: A. Bredenfeld, A. Jacoff, I. Noda, Y. Takahashi (Eds.), RoboCup 2005: Robot Soccer World Cup IX. XVII, 727 pages. 2006.

Vol. 4013: L. Lamontagne, M. Marchand (Eds.), Advances in Artificial Intelligence. XIII, 564 pages. 2006.

Vol. 4012: T. Washio, A. Sakurai, K. Nakajima, H. Takeda, S. Tojo, M. Yokoo (Eds.), New Frontiers in Artificial Intelligence. XIII, 484 pages. 2006.

Vol. 4008: J.C. Augusto, C.D. Nugent (Eds.), Designing Smart Homes. XI, 183 pages. 2006.

Vol. 4005: G. Lugosi, H.U. Simon (Eds.), Learning Theory. XI, 656 pages. 2006.

Vol. 3978: B. Hnich, M. Carlsson, F. Fages, F. Rossi (Eds.), Recent Advances in Constraints. VIII, 179 pages. 2006.

Vol. 3963: O. Dikenelli, M.-P. Gleizes, A. Ricci (Eds.), Engineering Societies in the Agents World VI. XII, 303 pages. 2006.

Vol. 3960: R. Vieira, P. Quaresma, M.d.G.V. Nunes, N.J. Mamede, C. Oliveira, M.C. Dias (Eds.), Computational Processing of the Portuguese Language. XII, 274 pages. 2006.

Vol. 3955: G. Antoniou, G. Potamias, C. Spyropoulos, D. Plexousakis (Eds.), Advances in Artificial Intelligence. XVII, 611 pages. 2006.

Vol. 3949: F.A. Savacı (Ed.), Artificial Intelligence and Neural Networks. IX, 227 pages. 2006.

Vol. 3946: T.R. Roth-Berghofer, S. Schulz, D.B. Leake (Eds.), Modeling and Retrieval of Context. XI, 149 pages. 2006.

Vol. 3944: J. Quiñonero-Candela, I. Dagan, B. Magnini, F. d'Alché-Buc (Eds.), Machine Learning Challenges. XIII, 462 pages. 2006.

Vol. 3937: H. La Poutré, N.M. Sadeh, S. Janson (Eds.), Agent-Mediated Electronic Commerce. X, 227 pages. 2006.

Vol. 3932: B. Mobasher, O. Nasraoui, B. Liu, B. Masand (Eds.), Advances in Web Mining and Web Usage Analysis. X, 189 pages. 2006.

Vol. 3930: D.S. Yeung, Z.-Q. Liu, X.-Z. Wang, H. Yan (Eds.), Advances in Machine Learning and Cybernetics. XXI, 1110 pages. 2006.

Vol. 3918: W.-K. Ng, M. Kitsuregawa, J. Li, K. Chang (Eds.), Advances in Knowledge Discovery and Data Mining. XXIV, 879 pages. 2006.

Vol. 3913: O. Boissier, J. Padget, V. Dignum, G. Lindemann, E. Matson, S. Ossowski, J.S. Sichman, J. Vázquez-Salceda (Eds.), Coordination, Organizations, Institutions, and Norms in Multi-Agent Systems. XII, 259 pages. 2006.

Vol. 3910: S.A. Brueckner, G.D.M. Serugendo, D. Hales, F. Zambonelli (Eds.), Engineering Self-Organising Systems. XII, 245 pages. 2006.

Vol. 3904: M. Baldoni, U. Endriss, A. Omicini, P. Torroni (Eds.), Declarative Agent Languages and Technologies III. XII, 245 pages. 2006.

Vol. 3900: F. Toni, P. Torroni (Eds.), Computational Logic in Multi-Agent Systems. XVII, 427 pages. 2006.

Vol. 3899: S. Frintrop, VOCUS: A Visual Attention System for Object Detection and Goal-Directed Search. XIV, 216 pages. 2006.

Vol. 3898: K. Tuyls, P.J. 't Hoen, K. Verbeeck, S. Sen (Eds.), Learning and Adaption in Multi-Agent Systems. X, 217 pages. 2006.

Vol. 3891: J.S. Sichman, L. Antunes (Eds.), Multi-Agent-Based Simulation VI. X, 191 pages. 2006.

Vol. 3890: S.G. Thompson, R. Ghanea-Hercock (Eds.), Defence Applications of Multi-Agent Systems. XII, 141 pages. 2006.

Vol. 3885: V. Torra, Y. Narukawa, A. Valls, J. Domingo-Ferrer (Eds.), Modeling Decisions for Artificial Intelligence. XII, 374 pages. 2006.

Vol. 3881: S. Gibet, N. Courty, J.-F. Kamp (Eds.), Gesture in Human-Computer Interaction and Simulation. XIII, 344 pages. 2006.

Vol. 3874: R. Missaoui, J. Schmidt (Eds.), Formal Concept Analysis. X, 309 pages. 2006.